THE LAW OF EU EXTERNAL RELATIONS

The Law of EU External Relations

Cases, Materials, and Commentary on the EU as an International Legal Actor

PIETER JAN KUIJPER

JAN WOUTERS

FRANK HOFFMEISTER

GEERT DE BAERE

AND

THOMAS RAMOPOULOS

OXFORD

UNIVERSITY PRESS

OXFORD
UNIVERSITY PRESS

Great Clarendon Street, Oxford, OX2 6DP,
United Kingdom

Oxford University Press is a department of the University of Oxford.
It furthers the University's objective of excellence in research, scholarship,
and education by publishing worldwide. Oxford is a registered trade mark of
Oxford University Press in the UK and in certain other countries

Published in the United States of America by Oxford University Press
198 Madison Avenue, New York, NY 10016, United States of America

British Library Cataloguing in Publication Data

Data available

Library of Congress Control Number: 2013937551

ISBN 978-0-19-968247-8 (Hbk)
978-0-19-968248-5 (Pbk)

Printed in Great Britain by
CPI Group (UK) Ltd, Croydon, CR0 4YY

Foreword

This volume of annotated documents and judgments relating to the foreign relations powers of the European Union (EU) and the practice of the Union in the field of international law and organizations has a double purpose.

First, it can serve as a teaching tool for a course or a seminar on the foreign relations powers of the EU and on how these powers are used in practice. Especially in this field, where so much of the law is determined by judgments and opinions of the Court of Justice of the EU and by documents that lay down the interpretation or application of that law by one or more institutions of the Union, there is hardly a better way to study the subject than directly from the documents and the cases themselves. There are already several good monographs and introductory manuals on the subject matter that have appeared on the market in the past few years. We hope that this book can serve as a suitable companion volume to them.

Second, the book also offers to diplomats and other practitioners in the field of the external relations of the EU an indispensable first initiation in the legal foundations of what after the Treaty of Lisbon is called the external action of the Union. Without having some understanding of that legal foundation, it is impossible to operate effectively in the field of EU external action.

We have sought to combine chapters on the general basis of the Union's external action and its relationship to international law (Chapters 1–5 and 12–13) with chapters which further explore the law and practice of the EU in the specialized fields of external action, such as common commercial policy, development cooperation, cooperation with third countries, humanitarian aid, enlargement and neighbourhood policies, external environmental policy, and common foreign and security policy, as well as a chapter specifically dedicated to EU sanctions and countermeasures (Chapters 6–11). In addition, the chapters contain numerous cross-references with a view to facilitating the establishment of connections between different issues and fields of law. This structure will enable lecturers to make their own choice from these specialized policy areas to complement the general chapters and to orient their courses as they wish. It will also allow the practitioner to target the specific policy area that he or she has to become familiar with in a short space of time and, if necessary, to refer back to the general chapters for additional background material.

In choosing the primary materials, the authors have been careful to select, also in the chapters on the general legal foundations of EU external action, extracts that can be seen as representative of a larger category of documents. Thus, in the chapter on mixed agreements, for example, both bilateral and multilateral mixed agreements have been picked so as to be representative of the larger group of these two variants of mixed agreements.

The authors have made an effort to limit the annotations of the cases and materials to what was strictly necessary to place them in their context and to clarify links to documents presented elsewhere in the book. If we have truncated cases and documents, it has been with a view to omitting what was superfluous or repetitive in the light of the place and function of the extract in the overall collection.

The original idea for this collection of cases and materials came from Pieter Jan Kuijper and Frank Hoffmeister, shortly after the former's departure from the External Relations and Trade team of the Commission Legal Service for the University of Amsterdam. They involved Professor Jan Wouters in the project right from the beginning. A first selection of documents took shape during 2009–10. For her help during this first phase of the project, the authors owe many thanks to Ms Serena Egidi, at the time student assistant at the Faculty of Law of the University of Amsterdam.

When a second effort had to be made to revise and expand this first draft, precious assistance in manpower was forthcoming from Jan Wouters and his Leuven Centre for Global Governance Studies. Geert De Baere joined the team and Thomas Ramopoulos proved himself so valuable as an editorial assistant that in the end he became an author in his own right. His energy and staying power have been crucial to the final completion of the project. Finally, the authors wish to thank Oxford University Press and the editorial staff for International and European Law under John Louth for encouragement and support throughout the process of preparing the book. With their help, we will endeavour to keep the book up to date through a companion website.

We hope that this book will find its way into the hands of all who are interested in the external action of the EU and its practice in the fields of international law and international organizations. We would be happy to receive any corrections, remarks, and suggestions that our readers may care to provide. The book represents the state of the law up to 1 January 2013.

The authors

Contents

Contents

Table of Cases

Court of Justice of the European Union

Permanent Court of International Justice

Appellate Body of the World Trade Organization

Arbitral Awards

National Cases

Canada

Switzerland

United Kingdom

Table of Legal Instruments

EU Documents

Treaties, Protocols, and Declarations

Treaty establishing the European Steel and
Coal Community of (ECSC) (Paris Treaty)
(1951)... 63, 64, 232, 380, 393, 415, 426,
854, 1027, 1028, 1029
Art 71... 380, 381
Art 87... 63

Treaty establishing the European Economic
Community (Treaty of Rome) (EEC)
(1957)... 1, 8, 9, 10, 15, 23, 62, 63, 64, 69, 81,
108, 113, 156, 174, 232, 260, 377, 378, 380, 381,
390, 391, 657, 814, 854, 935, 949, 1000, 1001,
1002, 1016, 1027, 1031, 1042, 1043, 1060,
1064, 1069
Pt III, Title I... 111
Title III, Chap I... 814
Art 3... 5, 9, 12, 395
Art 3(e)... 5
Art 4(1)... 81
Art 5... 5, 8, 1064
Art 6... 383
Art 7... 110
Art 30... 930
Art 38(3)... 110
Arts 48... 110, 940
Art 48 *et seq*... 939
Art 48(2)... 948
Art 49... 110, 940
Art 50... 110, 125, 940
Arts 52–56... 110
Art 55... 110
Art 56... 110
Art 58... 110
Arts 58–65... 110
Art 74... 5, 10
Art 75... 3, 4, 5, 6, 7, 8, 9, 10
Art 75(1)... 5, 6, 7, 10
Art 84(2)... 126
Art 85... 81, 82, 126, 148, 149
Art 86... 81, 82, 126, 148, 149
Art 89... 81

Art 90... 126, 149
Art 92... 126, 148, 149
Art 92(3)(a)... 126
Art 93... 148
Art 95... 930, 931, 932, 935, 936
Art 100... 815
Art 100a... 834
Arts 103–116... 383
Art 110... 1069
Art 111... 1069
Arts 111–114... 373
Art 112... 378, 379
Art 113... 4, 69, 374, 377, 378, 379, 380, 381,
382, 383, 384, 385, 386, 817, 818, 819, 1069,
1070
Art 113(1)... 129
Art 113(2)... 379, 817
Art 113(3)... 382
Art 113(4)... 817
Art 114... 4, 379, 380, 381, 389, 396, 1069
Art 115... 1030
Art 116... 6, 7, 23, 24, 383, 385
Art 118a... 814
Art 118a(3)... 814, 815
Art 130r... 818
Art 130r(1)... 818
Art 130r(2)... 818
Art 130s... 813, 817, 818, 834
Art 145... 383
Art 164... 63, 64
Art 169... 378
Art 173... 3, 378, 967, 971
Art 177... 14, 929, 930, 931, 962, 963, 1042,
1070, 1071
Art 177(1)(b)... 939
Art 184... 971
Art 210... 1, 4, 19
Art 219... 63
Art 224... 85, 1000, 1001
Art 227(2)... 113
Art 228... 6, 7, 8, 69, 80, 81, 82, 377, 378, 383,
389, 930, 939, 961, 962, 963, 1071
Art 228(1)... 6, 7, 9, 14, 377, 378, 380
Art 228(2)... 11, 933

Regulations

Directives

Decisions

Joint Actions

Common Positions

Interinstitutional Agreements

Presidency Conclusions

Declarations and Statements

Other EU Documents

International Documents

Treaties

Conventions

International Statutes and Constitutions

Declarations

National Documents

Constitutions

List of Abbreviations

AA	American Airlines
ACP	African, Caribbean, and Pacific
ADA	Anti-Dumping Agreement
AP	Accession Partnership
ATAA	Air Transport Association of America
CFI	Court of First Instance
CFSP	Common Foreign and Security Policy
CITES	Convention on International Trade in Endangered Species of Wild Fauna and Flora
CJEU	Court of Justice of the EU
COREPER	Committee of Permanent Representatives
DRAMs	Dynamic Random Access Memories
EC	European Community
ECHO	European Community Humanitarian Assistance Office
ECHR	European Convention on Human Rights
ECJ	European Court of Justice
ECOSOC	Economic and Social Council
EDA	European Defence Agency
EEAS	European External Action Service
EEC	European Economic Community
ENI	European Neighbourhood Instrument
ENP	European Neighbourhood Policy
ENPI	European Neighbourhood and Partnership Instrument
EPC	European Political Cooperation
ERTA/AETR	European Road Transport Agreement/Accord européen relatif au travail des équipages des véhicules effectuant des transports internationaux par route
ESS	European Security Strategy
ETS	Emissions Trading Scheme
EU	European Union
EUMC	EU Military Committee
EUMS	EU Military Staff
FAO	Food and Agriculture Organization of the United Nations
FICF	Federation of French Mustard Producers
GATS	General Agreement on Trade in Services

GATT	General Agreement on Tariffs and Trade
IAEA	International Atomic Energy Agency
ICJ	International Court of Justice
IGC	Intergovernmental Conference
ILO	International Labour Organization
INC	Intergovernmental Negotiating Committee
IWC	International Whaling Commission
MTCR	Missile Technology Control Regime
NATO	North Atlantic Treaty Organization
OECD	Organisation for Economic Co-operation and Development
PFOS	Perfluoroctane Sulfonate
PLO	Palestine Liberation Organization
PNR	Passenger Name Records
PSC	Political and Security Committee
REIO	Regional Economic Integration Organization
RIO	Regional Integration Organizations
SC	Security Council
SOFAs	Status of Forces Agreements
SOMAs	Status of Mission Agreements
TAIEX	Technical Assistance and Information Exchange Instrument
TEC	Treaty establishing the European Community
TEU	Treaty on European Union
TFEU	Treaty on the Functioning of the European Union
TRIPs	Trade-Related Aspects of Intellectual Property Rights
UAL	United Airlines
UK	United Kingdom
UN	United Nations
UNCLOS	UN Convention on the Law of the Sea
UNCTAD	UN Conference on Trade and Development
UNEP	United Nations Environment Programme
UNFCCC	UN Framework Convention on Climate Change
UNGA	UN General Assembly
US	United States
VCDR	Vienna Convention on Diplomatic Relations
WCO	World Customs Organization
WTO	World Trade Organization
WWII	World War II

1

Personality and Powers of the EU

1.1 The classical cases before the Treaty of Lisbon: ERTA and Laying-up Fund

International legal personality is an important requirement for international organizations in order to be able to act on the international plane. Treaty provisions concerning the legal personality of what was initially the European Economic Community (EEC), then the European Community (EC), and finally the European Union (EU) have always been ambiguous (see Article 210 EEC and then Article 281 Treaty establishing the European Community (TEC)). It was never clear whether the provision in question was restricted to legal personality under the national law of the Member States or also included international legal personality. In the Treaty on European Union (TEU) before Lisbon a provision on personality was entirely absent, even though the relevant treaty provided for a treaty-making power for the Council (Article 24 TEU). In spite of these textual ambiguities and the doctrinal arguments that they caused,[1] in practice both the EC and the old EU enjoyed rather uncontested international legal personality in that they concluded numerous international agreements.[2] Moreover, as to the more contested question of the legal personality of the old EU, it has been observed that the Union anyway fulfilled the criteria for an international organization to enjoy international legal personality, set out by the International Court of Justice (ICJ) in 1949.[3]

[1] For further analysis of the theoretical debate surrounding the question of international legal personality of the EU before Lisbon, see G. Maganza, Réflexions sur le traité d'Amsterdam, contexte général et quelques aspects particuliers, *Annuaire Français de Droit International*, vol. 43, 1997, 668–9; J. Klabbers, Presumptive Personality: The European Union in International Law, *International Law Aspects of the European Union* (M. Koskenniemi (ed.), The Hague: Kluwer Law International, 1998), 231–53; A. Dashwood, External Relations Provisions of the Amsterdam Treaty, *Common Market Law Review*, vol. 35, 1998, 1038–41; N.A.E.M. Neuwahl, Legal Personality of the European Union—International and Institutional Aspects, *The European Union and the International Legal Order: Discord or Harmony?* (V. Kronenberger (ed.), The Hague: T.M.C. Asser Press, 2001), 3–22; P. Eeckhout, *External Relations of the European Union: Legal and Constitutional Foundations* (Oxford: Oxford University Press, 2004), 154–60; P. de Schoutheete and S. Andoura, The Legal Personality of the European Union, *Studia Diplomatica*, vol. LX: 2007, no. 1; D. McGoldrick, The International Legal Personality of the European Community and the European Union, *50 Years of the European Treaties: Looking Back and Thinking Forward* (M. Dougan and S. Currie (eds), Oxford and Portland, OR: Hart Publishing, 2009), 18–217.

[2] J.C. Piris, *The Lisbon Treaty: A Legal and Political Analysis* (Cambridge: Cambridge University Press, 2010), 86–7.

[3] Reparation for Injuries Suffered in the Services of the United Nations, *ICJ Reports* (1949) 173, at 178–9. See further ibid. 87, fn. 26; F. Hoffmeister, The Contribution of EU Practice to International Law in *Developments in EU External Relations Law* (M. Cremona (ed.), Oxford: Oxford University Press, 2008), 42, fn. 29. Also, for an analysis of the question of the international legal personality of the EU before Lisbon on the basis of the test followed by the ICJ in the Reparation Case, see P. Gautier, The Reparation for Injuries Case Revisited: The Personality of the European Union, *Max Planck Yearbook of United Nations Law*, vol. 4, 2000, 331–61.

Directly linked to the question of international legal personality is the question of its scope. Is its scope limited to those cases in which the Treaty has foreseen explicit treaty-making powers, or does it extend, at least potentially, to all domains covered by the Treaty? If the latter is the case, is the treaty-making power exclusive to the Union in all these domains or is it limited in some way? Furthermore, what is the legal situation, when the Union finds itself in a position, where for formal reasons it cannot act on the international plane in a field where it has already enacted internal legislation? This happens quite frequently when international agreements do not accept international organizations as parties and other international organizations restrict membership to states. What is, in such a situation, the freedom of action, and what are the obligations of EU Member States?[4] All these questions are posed and answered, at least in principle, in a long line of Court cases that started with the so-called European Road Transport Agreement (ERTA) case.

Below, the *ERTA* case is included, as well as the essence of one other old case: Opinion 1/76. These two cases have produced a whole progeny of cases in which they were interpreted and applied to different situations. In Section 1.2, we include Opinion 1/03, a rather recent one in this line of cases which, just like the *ERTA* case, begins with a general statement about the external relations powers of the EU, while referring to the most important of the intermediate cases—which can be looked up by anyone in need of further detail about the external relations powers of the EU.

The Lisbon Treaty has made a rather awkward attempt to codify the principles of the *ERTA* case, Opinion 1/76 and the case law summarized in Opinion 1/03.[5] The quality and the consequences of this codification will be briefly discussed in Section 1.3 as well. It remains, however, indispensable to know and understand the case law included below to have a complete view of what is behind Article 47 TEU and Articles 3 and 216 Treaty on the Functioning of the European Union (TFEU).

Judgment of the Court of 31 March 1971, Commission of the European Communities v. Council of the European Communities, Case 22/70, European Court Reports 1971, p. 263 (ERTA case), paras. 1–32, 68–92, 100.

This is *the* classical case on the external powers of what is now the EU and the echo of the core point of this judgment can still be found in Articles 3(2) and 216(1) TFEU. The case concerned an arrangement arrived at, not by the Council, but by the Member States meeting in the margin of the Council, to the effect that they all would

---

[4] In this regard, see also Chapter 5.

[5] See also M. Cremona, Defining Competence in EU External Relations: Lessons from the Treaty Reform Process, *Law and Practice of External Relations: Salient Features of a Changing Landscape* (A. Dashwood and M. Maresceau (eds), Cambridge: Cambridge University Press, 2008), 36, where she argues that '[t]he definition and delimitation of competence is an aspect of external relations in which the Treaty of Lisbon has made significant attempt to rationalize and codify existing law, including case law'.

conclude the European Road Transport Agreement (ERTA). The Commission appealed this 'decision' to the European Court of Justice (ECJ), now the Court of Justice of the European Union (CJEU), arguing that the Community should have concluded this agreement and not the Member States. The judgment consists of three parts: (1) a generous interpretation of what constitutes an 'act' that can be subject to an action for annulment before the Court (here left out); (2) a general explanation of the Court about the implications of the EC Treaty interpreted as a whole for the treaty-making power of the Community, both as to its scope in general and as to where this power should be considered to be exclusive to the Community; and (3) an application of the Court's general approach to the particular case at hand—which, contrary to the expectations elicited by (2) does not lead to the annulment of the Member States' arrangement providing their collective, but individual conclusion of ERTA, taking into account the difficult position in which the Member States found themselves. Having acted as they did, the Member States had not breached their duty of loyalty in respect of the Community as laid down in Article 5 TEC (now Article 4(3) TEU). Note also that the judgment does not leave unmentioned that the relevant internal legislation actually contained a provision to the effect that the Community could negotiate and conclude agreements in the field covered by that legislation. In spite of this explicit authorization, the Court went ahead with writing a judgment of principle on the Community's foreign relations powers.

Grounds

1. By an application lodged on 19 may 1970 the Commission of the European Communities has requested the annulment of the Council's proceedings of 20 March 1970 regarding the negotiation and conclusion by the Member States of the Community, under the auspices of the United Nations Economic Commission for Europe, of the European agreement concerning the work of crews of vehicles engaged in international road transport (AETR).
2. As a preliminary objection, the Council has submitted that the application is inadmissible on the ground that the proceedings in question are not an act the legality of which is open to review under the first paragraph of Article 173 of the Treaty.
3. To decide this point, it is first necessary to determine which authority was, at the relevant date, empowered to negotiate and conclude the AETR.
4. The legal effect of the proceedings differs according to whether they are regarded as constituting the exercise of powers conferred on the Community, or as acknowledging a coordination by the Member States of the exercise of powers which remained vested in them.
5. To decide on the objection of inadmissibility, therefore, it is necessary to determine first of all whether, at the date of the proceedings in question, power to negotiate and conclude the AETR was vested in the Community or in the Member States.

1 – The initial question

6. The Commission takes the view that Article 75 of the Treaty, which conferred on the Community powers defined in wide terms with a view to implementing

the common transport policy, must apply to external relations just as much as to domestic measures in the sphere envisaged.

7. It believes that the full effect of this provision would be jeopardized if the powers which it confers, particularly that of laying down 'any appropriate provisions', within the meaning of subparagraph (1)(c) of the article cited, did not extend to the conclusion of agreements with third countries.

8. Even if, it is argued, this power did not originally embrace the whole sphere of transport, it would tend to become general and exclusive as and where the common policy in this field came to be implemented.

9. The Council, on the other hand, contends that since the Community only has such powers as have been conferred on it, authority to enter into agreements with third countries cannot be assumed in the absence of an express provision in the Treaty.

10. More particularly, Article 75 relates only to measures internal to the Community, and cannot be interpreted as authorizing the conclusion of international agreements.

11. Even if it were otherwise, such authority could not be general and exclusive, but at the most concurrent with that of the Member States.

12. In the absence of specific provisions of the Treaty relating to the negotiation and conclusion of international agreements in the sphere of transport policy—a category into which, essentially, the AETR falls—one must turn to the general system of Community law in the sphere of relations with third countries.

13. Article 210 provides that 'the Community shall have legal personality'.

14. This provision, placed at the head of part six of the Treaty, devoted to 'general and final provisions', means that in its external relations the Community enjoys the capacity to establish contractual links with third countries over the whole field of objectives defined in part one of the Treaty, which part six supplements.

15. To determine in a particular case the Community's authority to enter into international agreements, regard must be had to the whole scheme of the Treaty no less than to its substantive provisions.

16. Such authority arises not only from an express conferment by the Treaty—as is the case with Articles 113 and 114 for tariff and trade agreements and with Article 238 for association agreements—but may equally flow from other provisions of the Treaty and from measures adopted, within the framework of those provisions, by the Community institutions.

17. In particular, each time the Community, with a view to implementing a common policy envisaged by the Treaty, adopts provisions laying down common rules, whatever form these may take, the member states no longer have the right, acting individually or even collectively, to undertake obligations with third countries which affect those rules.

18. As and when such common rules come into being, the Community alone is in a position to assume and carry out contractual obligations towards third countries affecting the whole sphere of application of the Community legal system.

19. With regard to the implementation of the provisions of the Treaty the system of internal Community measures may not therefore be separated from that of external relations.

20. Under Article 3(e), the adoption of a common policy in the sphere of transport is specially mentioned amongst the objectives of the Community.

21. Under Article 5, the Member States are required on the one hand to take all appropriate measures to ensure fulfilment of the obligations arising out of the Treaty or resulting from action taken by the institutions and, on the other hand, to abstain from any measure which might jeopardize the attainment of the objectives of the Treaty.

22. If these two provisions are read in conjunction, it follows that to the extent to which Community rules are promulgated for the attainment of the objectives of the Treaty, the Member States cannot, outside the framework of the Community institutions, assume obligations which might affect those rules or alter their scope.

23. According to Article 74, the objectives of the Treaty in matters of transport are to be pursued within the framework of a common policy.

24. With this in view, Article 75(1) directs the Council to lay down common rules and, in addition, 'any other appropriate provisions'.

25. By the terms of subparagraph (a) of the same provision, those common rules are applicable 'to international transport to or from the territory of a Member State or passing across the territory of one or more Member States'.

26. This provision is equally concerned with transport from or to third countries, as regards that part of the journey which takes place on Community territory.

27. It thus assumes that the powers of the Community extend to relationships arising from international law, and hence involve the need in the sphere in question for agreements with the third countries concerned.

28. Although it is true that Articles 74 and 75 do not expressly confer on the Community authority to enter into international agreements, nevertheless the bringing into force, on 25 March 1969, of Regulation no 543/69 of the Council on the harmonization of certain social legislation relating to road transport (OJ L 77, p. 49) necessarily vested in the Community power to enter into any agreements with third countries relating to the subject-matter governed by that regulation.

29. This grant of power is moreover expressly recognized by Article 3 of the said regulation which prescribes that: 'the Community shall enter into any negotiations with third countries which may prove necessary for the purpose of implementing this regulation'.

30. Since the subject-matter of the AETR falls within the scope of Regulation no 543/69, the Community has been empowered to negotiate and conclude the agreement in question since the entry into force of the said regulation.

31. These Community powers exclude the possibility of concurrent powers on the part of member states, since any steps taken outside the framework of the Community institutions would be incompatible with the unity of the common market and the uniform application of Community law.

32. This is the legal position in the light of which the question of admissibility has to be resolved.

[...]

3 – Substance

68. Essentially, the Commission disputes the validity of the proceedings of 20 March 1970 on the ground that they involved infringements of provisions of the Treaty, more particularly of Articles 75, 228 and 235 concerning the distribution of powers between the Council and the Commission, and consequently the rights which it was the Commission's duty to exercise in the negotiations on the AETR.

(a) Submission relating to infringement of Articles 75 and 228.

69. The Commission claims that in view of the powers vested in the Community under Article 75, the AETR should have been negotiated and concluded by the Community in accordance with the Community procedure defined by Article 228(1).

70. Although the Council may, by virtue of these provisions, decide in each case whether it is expedient to enter into an agreement with third countries, it does not enjoy a discretion to decide whether to proceed through inter-governmental or Community channels.

71. By deciding to proceed through inter-governmental channels it made it impossible for the Commission to perform the task which the Treaty entrusted to it in the sphere of negotiations with third countries.

72. In the absence of specific provisions in the Treaty applicable to the negotiation and implementation of the agreement under discussion, the appropriate rules must be inferred from the general tenor of those articles of the Treaty which relate to the negotiations undertaken on the AETR.

73. The distribution of powers between the Community institutions to negotiate and implement the AETR must be determined with due regard both to the provisions relating to the common transport policy and to those governing the conclusion of agreements by the Community.

74. By the terms of Article 75(1), it is a matter for the Council, acting on a proposal from the Commission and after consulting the Economic and Social Committee and the Assembly, to lay down the appropriate provisions, whether by regulation or otherwise, for the purpose of implementing the common transport policy.

75. According to Article 228(1), where agreements have to be concluded with one or more third countries or an international organization, such agreements are to be negotiated by the Commission and concluded by the Council, subject to any more extensive powers which may have been vested in the Commission.

76. As a subsidiary point, since the negotiations took place under the auspices of the United Nations Economic Commission for Europe, the first paragraph of Article 116 has also to be taken into account. By the terms of that paragraph, from the end of the transitional period onwards, member states shall 'proceed within the framework of international organizations of an economic character only by common action', the implementation of such common action being within the powers of the Council, basing its decisions on proposals submitted by the Commission.

77. If these various provisions are read in conjunction, it is clear that wherever a matter forms the subject of a common policy, the member states are bound in every case to act jointly in defence of the interests of the Community.

78. This requirement of joint action was in fact respected by the proceedings of 20 March 1970, which cannot give rise to any criticism in this respect.

79. Moreover, it follows from these provisions taken as a whole, and particularly from Article 228(1), that the right to conclude the agreement was vested in the Council.

80. The Commission for its part was required to act in two ways, first by exercising its right to make proposals, which arises from article 75(1) and the first paragraph of Article 116, and, secondly, in its capacity as negotiator by the terms of the first subparagraph of Article 228(1).

81. However, this distribution of powers between institutions would only have been required where negotiations were undertaken at a time when the vesting of powers in the Community had taken effect, either by virtue of the Treaty itself or by virtue of measures taken by the institutions.

82. In this connexion it must be borne in mind that an earlier version of the AETR had been drawn up in 1962, at a period when, because the common transport policy was not yet sufficiently developed, power to conclude this agreement was vested in the Member States.

83. The stage of negotiations of which the proceedings in question formed part was not aimed at working out a new agreement, but simply at introducing into the version drawn up in 1962 such modifications as were necessary to enable all the contracting parties to ratify it.

84. The negotiations on the AETR are thus characterized by the fact that their origin and a considerable part of the work carried out under the auspices of the Economic Commission for Europe took place before powers were conferred on the Community as a result of Regulation no 543/69.

85. It appears therefore that on 20 March 1970 the Council acted in a situation where it no longer enjoyed complete freedom of action in its relations with the third countries taking part in the same negotiations.

86. At that stage of the negotiations, to have suggested to the third countries concerned that there was now a new distribution of powers within the Community might well have jeopardized the successful outcome of the negotiations, as was indeed recognized by the Commission's representative in the course of the Council's deliberations.

87. In such a situation it was for the two institutions whose powers were directly concerned, namely, the Council and the Commission, to reach agreement, in accordance with Article 15 of the Treaty of April 1965 establishing a single Council and a single Commission of the European Communities, on the appropriate methods of cooperation with a view to ensuring most effectively the defence of the interests of the Community.

88. It is clear from the minutes of the meeting of 20 March 1970 that the Commission made no formal use of the right to submit proposals open to it under Articles 75 and 116.

89. Nor did it demand the simple application of Article 228(1) in regard to its right of negotiation.

90. It may therefore be accepted that, in carrying on the negotiations and concluding the agreement simultaneously in the manner decided on by the Council, the member states acted, and continue to act, in the interest and on behalf of the Community in accordance with their obligations under Article 5 of the Treaty.

91. Hence, in deciding in these circumstances on joint action by the Member States, the Council has not failed in its obligations arising from Articles 75 and 228.

92. For these reasons, the submission must be rejected.

[...]

100. The application must therefore be dismissed.

Thus, the Court for the first time recognizes implied external competences of the EC based on 'the whole scheme of the Treaty no less than to its substantive provisions' (paragraph 15) and even on 'measures adopted [...] by the Community institutions' (paragraph 16). Once such measures have been adopted by the Union, Member States can no longer enter into international binding agreements in the same field. Thus, the so-called 'ERTA rule' or 'ERTA principle' consists in upholding exclusive external EC (by now EU) competence when the conclusion of an international agreement by one or even all Member States would 'affect' internal legislation (or would 'alter its scope', as later case law added). However, it is pertinent to note here that given the broad scope of most of the international agreements that the Union aspires to conclude and the complexities of applying the ERTA doctrine in practice to such broad agreements, most of these agreements, in a spirit of compromise inside the Council of Ministers, are concluded as so-called mixed agreements. That is to say that they are concluded by the Union and the Member States together forming one party to the agreement.[6]

Opinion of the Court of 26 April 1977, Draft Agreement establishing a European laying-up fund for inland waterway vessels, Opinion 1/76, European Court Reports 1977, p. 741.

Together with Opinion 1/75 on the scope and exclusive character of the common commercial policy of the Community discussed in Chapter 7 (see p. 377), this is one of the first Opinions based on Article 218(11) TFEU (at the time Article 228(6) TEC). Unlike in the *ERTA* case, here internal legislation on the laying-up of Rhine barges was not yet in place at the moment the EC needed to conclude an agreement with Switzerland. That agreement was indispensable to the success of the internal legislation aiming to reduce the capacity of the Rhine fleet and had to be concluded together with it. The Court has followed this logic and in the process made clear that in principle it was possible to regard the first exercise of external relations power, even without pre-existing internal legislation on the same subject matter, as exclusive to the Community, if it was

[6] P. Eeckhout, Bold Constitutionalism and Beyond, The Past and Future of EU Law: The Classics of EU Law Revisited on the 50th Anniversary of the Rome Treaty (M.P. Maduro and L. Azoulai (eds), Oxford and Portland, OR: Hart Publishing, 2010), 220. See also Chapter 4.

necessary to realize one of the objectives of the EC Treaty. In later cases, the CJEU has been rather restrictive in the application of its own doctrine. However, just as with the ERTA doctrine, this doctrine has found its way into Articles 3 and 216 TFEU.

The question of principle about the treaty-making power is covered in only seven paragraphs at the beginning of the Opinion. The rest of the Opinion is dedicated to the critical discussion of issues of principle relating to the decision-making procedure and the institutions created by the Agreement establishment of the Laying-up Fund, and in particular to questions whether or not these procedures and institutions are sufficiently respectful of the Union and its institutions. This is an aspect of its case law, to which the Court would later return several times, notably in the Opinions on the EEA (see Chapter 2, p. 62).

Grounds

On 15 September 1976 the Court of Justice received a request for an opinion submitted by the Commission of the European Communities pursuant to the second paragraph of Article 228(1) of the Treaty establishing the European Economic Community, according to which:

'the Council, the Commission or a Member State may obtain beforehand the opinion of the Court of Justice as to whether an agreement envisaged is compatible with the provisions of this Treaty. Where the opinion of the Court of Justice is adverse, the Agreement may enter into force only in accordance with Article 236.'

The reasoning of the Court

I

1. The object of the system laid down by the Draft Agreement and expressed in the Statute annexed thereto is to rationalize the economic situation of the inland waterway transport industry in a geographical region in which transport by inland waterway is of special importance within the whole network of international transport. Such a system is doubtless an important factor in the common transport policy, the establishment of which is included in the activities of the Community laid down in Article 3 of the EEC Treaty. In order to implement this policy, Article 75 of the Treaty instructs the Council to lay down according to the prescribed procedure common rules applicable to international transport to or from the territory of one or more Member States. This article also supplies, as regards the Community, the necessary legal basis to establish the system concerned.

2. In this case, however, it is impossible fully to attain the objective pursued by means of the establishment of common rules pursuant to Article 75 of the Treaty, because of the traditional participation of vessels from a third state, Switzerland, in navigation by the principal waterways in question, which are subject to the system of freedom of navigation established by international agreements of long standing. It has thus been necessary to bring Switzerland into the scheme in question by means of an international agreement with this third state.

3. The power of the Community to conclude such an agreement is not expressly laid down in the Treaty. However, the Court has already had occasion to state, most

recently in its judgment of 14 July 1976 in joined cases 3, 4 and 6/76, Cornelis Kramer and others, (1976) ECR 1279, that authority to enter into international commitments may not only arise from an express attribution by the Treaty, but equally may flow implicitly from its provisions. The Court has concluded inter alia that whenever Community law has created for the institutions of the Community powers within its internal system for the purpose of attaining a specific objective, the Community has authority to enter into the international commitments necessary for the attainment of that objective even in the absence of an express provision in that connexion.

4. This is particularly so in all cases in which internal power has already been used in order to adopt measures which come within the attainment of common policies. It is, however, not limited to that eventuality. Although the internal Community measures are only adopted when the international agreement is concluded and made enforceable, as is envisaged in the present case by the proposal for a regulation to be submitted to the Council by the Commission, the power to bind the Community vis-à-vis third countries nevertheless flows by implication from the provisions of the Treaty creating the internal power and in so far as the participation of the Community in the international agreement is, as here, necessary for the attainment of one of the objectives of the Community.

5. In order to attain the common transport policy, the contents of which are defined in Articles 74 and 75 of the Treaty, the Council is empowered to lay down 'any other appropriate provisions', as expressly provided in Article 75(1) I. The Community is therefore not only entitled to enter into contractual relations with a third country in this connexion but also has the power, while observing the provisions of the Treaty, to cooperate with that country in setting up an appropriate organism such as the public international institution which it is proposed to establish under the name of the 'European laying-up fund for inland waterway vessels'. The Community may also, in this connexion, cooperate with a third country for the purpose of giving the organs of such an institution appropriate powers of decision and for the purpose of defining, in a manner appropriate to the objectives pursued, the nature, elaboration, implementation and effects of the provisions to be adopted within such a framework.

6. A special problem arises because the Draft Agreement provides for the participation as contracting parties not only of the Community and Switzerland but also of certain of the Member States. These are the six states which are party either to the revised Convention of Mannheim for the navigation of the Rhine of 17 October 1868 or the Convention of Luxembourg of 27 October 1956 on the canalization of the Moselle, having regard to the relationship of the latter to the Rhine Convention. Under Article 3 of the Agreement, these states undertake to make the amendments of the two abovementioned conventions necessitated by the implementation of the Statute annexed to the Agreement.

7. This particular undertaking, given in view of the second paragraph of Article 234 of the Treaty, explains and justifies the participation in the Agreement, together with the Community, of the six abovementioned states. Precisely because of that undertaking the obstacle presented by the existence of certain provisions of the

Mannheim and Luxembourg Conventions to the attainment of the scheme laid down by the Agreement will be removed. The participation of these states in the Agreement must be considered as being solely for this purpose and not as necessary for the attainment of other features of the system. In fact, under Article 4 of the Agreement, the enforceability of this measure and of the Statute extends to the territories of all the Member States including those who are not party to the agreement; it may therefore be said that, except for the special undertaking mentioned above, the legal effects of the Agreement with regard to the Member States result, in accordance with Article 228(2) of the Treaty, exclusively from the conclusion of the latter by the Community. In these circumstances, the participation of the six Member States as contracting parties to the Agreement is not such as to encroach on the external power of the Community. There is therefore no occasion to conclude that this aspect of the Draft Agreement is incompatible with the Treaty.

II

8. The participation of these Member States in the negotiations, though justified for the abovementioned purpose, has however produced results extending beyond that objective which are incompatible with the requirements implied by the very concepts of the Community and its common policy. In fact, this situation seems to be at the root of an ambiguity concerning the field of application of the Agreement and the Statute. Thus, under Article 4, the Agreement and the Statute are enforceable on the territory of the nine Member States and Switzerland whilst the general obligations laid down in Article 6 concern the 'contracting parties', that is, the Community as such and the seven contracting states.

9. In the Statute itself there are various groupings of those who are either given rights or placed under duties; sometimes all the Member States of the Community and Switzerland (as in Articles 39, 43, 45 and 46), sometimes the Member States, with one exception, and Switzerland (which is the scheme of the provision laid down in Article 27 on the composition of the Supervisory Board), sometimes the Community as such and Switzerland (in Article 40, concerning the publication of the measures adopted by the Fund) and sometimes five states to which a special function is reserved in the decision-making process (Article 27(5) of the Statute). On the whole, the part played by the institutions of the Community is extremely limited: the Commission provides the chairman and the secretarial services for the Supervisory Board but without exercising a right to vote therein. The determinative functions in the operation of the Fund are performed by the states. In fact, under Article 27(1) the Supervisory Board consists of 'representatives' who receive their 'powers' and 'authority' from the states concerned.

10. The Court considers that these provisions, and more particularly those on the organization and the deliberations of the Supervisory Board, the controlling organ of the Fund, call in question the power of the institutions of the Community and, moreover, alter in a manner inconsistent with the Treaty the relationships between Member States within the context of the Community as it was in the beginning and when the Community was enlarged.

11. More particularly, it is necessary to point out two factors in this connexion:

(a) the substitution in the structure of the organs of the Funds, of several Member States in place of the Community and its institutions in a field which comes within a common policy which Article 3 of the Treaty has expressly reserved to 'the activities of the Community';

(b) the alteration, as a result of this substitution, of the relationships between Member States, contrary to a requirement laid down right from the second paragraph of the recitals of the preamble to the Treaty, according to which the objectives of the Community must be attained by 'common action', given that under Article 4 that action must be carried out by the institutions of the Community each one acting within the limits of its powers. More precisely, the following appear to be incompatible with the concept of such common action:

– the complete exclusion, even voluntary, of a specific Member State from any participation in the activity of the Fund,

– the power reserved to certain Member States under the third subparagraph of Article 27(1) of the Statute to take no part in a matter which comes within a common policy, and finally,

– the fact that, in the decision-making procedure of the Fund, special prerogatives are reserved to certain states by derogation from the concepts which, within the Community, obtain with regard to the adoption of decisions within the field of the common policy involved in this case.

12. Thus it appears that the Statute, far from restricting itself to the solution of problems resulting from requirements inherent in the external relations of the Community, constitutes both a surrender of the independence of action of the Community in its external relations and a change in the internal constitution of the Community by the alteration of essential elements of the community structure as regards both the prerogatives of the institutions and the position of the Member States vis-a-vis one another. The Court is of the opinion that the structure thereby given to the Supervisory Board and the arrangement of the decision-making procedure within that organ are not compatible with the requirements of unity and solidarity which it has already had occasion to emphasize in its judgment of 31 March 1971 in case 22/70, Commission v Council (AETR), (1971) ECR 263 and, at greater length, in its Opinion 1/75 of 11 November 1975, (1975) ECR 1355 and OJ C 268, p. 18.

13. The attempt belatedly to introduce into the functioning of the Supervisory Board by means of Article 5 of the Draft Regulation concepts which are closer to the requirements of the Treaty is no proper way to correct faults which are inherent in the structure of the Fund as set out in the text negotiated by the Commission.

14. The Court has examined all aspects of this question and it has duly considered the difficulties which may arise in the search for a practical solution to the problems posed by the organization of a public international institution managed by the Community and a single third country while maintaining the mutual independence of the two partners. Doubtless the specific nature of the interests involved may explain the desire, within the context of organs of management, to have recourse to administrative bodies more directly concerned with the problems of inland navigation. Does this objective justify the creation of a mixed organization in which the presence of national representatives on the Supervisory Board

together with the chairman and the Swiss representative would ensure the defence of the interests of the Community? After considering the arguments for and against, the Court has reached the conclusion that it is no doubt possible to attain an appropriate balance in the composition of the organs of the Fund but that this must not result in weakening the institutions of the Community and surrendering the bases of a common policy even for a specific and limited objective. The possibility that the Agreement and the Statute, according to the statements of the Commission, might constitute the model for future arrangements in other fields has confirmed the Court in its critical attitude: the repetition of such procedures is in fact likely progressively to undo the work of the Community irreversibly, in view of the fact that each time the undertakings involved will be entered into with third countries. It was for these reasons that an adverse decision finally prevailed within the Court as regards this aspect of the proposal.

III

15. As regards the powers of decision given to the organs of the Fund, Article 39 of the Statute provides that decisions of the organs of the Fund having general application shall be binding in their entirety and directly applicable in all Member States of the Community and in Switzerland. The question has been raised whether the grant of such powers extending to all the territory of the Community to a public international organ separate from the Community comes within the powers of the institutions. More particularly, there arises the problem whether the institutions may freely transfer to non-Community organisms powers or part of the powers granted by the Treaty and thus create for the Member States the obligation to apply directly in their legal systems rules of law which are not of Community origin adopted in forms and under conditions which are not subject to the provisions and guarantees contained in the Treaty.

16. However, it is unnecessary in this opinion to solve the problem thus posed. In fact the provisions of the Statute define and limit the powers which the latter grants to the organs of the Fund so clearly and precisely that in this case they are only executive powers. Thus the field in which the organs may take action is limited to the sphere of the voluntary laying-up of the excess carrying capacity subject to the condition that financial compensation is paid by a fund financed by contributions levied on the vessels using the inland waterways covered by the Fund. Here a further point arises out of the third paragraph of Article 1 of the Agreement according to which the Fund may not be used with the aim of fixing a permanent minimum level for freight rates during all periods of slack demand or of remedying structural imbalance. More particularly, the rate of contributions, that is, the basic rate and the adjustment coefficients, for the first year of the operation of the system is laid down in the actual terms of the Statute and subsequent amendments by decision of the Supervisory Board must either remain within certain limits or result from a unanimous decision.

IV

17. The legal system contained in the Draft Agreement provides for the grant of certain powers to an organ, the Fund Tribunal, which, in particular by its composition, differs

from the Court of Justice established by the Treaty. The Tribunal is to be invested with power to give judgments relating to the activities of the Fund on applications lodged against the organs of the Fund or the states in conditions laid down in Article 43 of the Statute and on applications for a declaration that there has been a failure to fulfil an obligation brought against one of the states on the territory of which the Statute has binding force (but not the Community as such), in the conditions laid down in Article 45. Moreover, the Tribunal is to have power to give preliminary rulings on applications referred to it by the national courts in the conditions laid down in Article 44. With regard to the latter applications it is necessary to note that they may concern not only the validity and interpretation of decisions adopted by the organs of the Fund but also the interpretation of the Agreement and the Statute.

18. However, as the Court has had occasion to state, in particular in its judgment of 30 April 1974 in case 181/73, Haegemann v Belgian State, (1974) ECR 449, an agreement concluded by the Community with a third state is, as far as concerns the Community, an act of one of the institutions within the meaning of subparagraph (b) of the first paragraph of Article 177 of the Treaty. It follows that the Court, within the context of the Community legal order, has jurisdiction to give a preliminary ruling on the interpretation of such an agreement. Thus the question arises whether the provisions relating to the jurisdiction of the Fund Tribunal are compatible with those of the Treaty relating to the jurisdiction of the Court of Justice.

19. According to the observations submitted to the Court, the rules on jurisdiction contained in the Statute may be interpreted in different ways. According to one interpretation, the jurisdiction of the Tribunal would replace that of the Court as regards the interpretation of the Agreement and Statute. According to another interpretation, the jurisdiction of the Tribunal and that of the Court would be parallel so that it would be for the national court of a Member State to refer the matter to one or other of the two legal organs.

20. It is not for the Court within the context of a request for an opinion pursuant to the second paragraph of Article 228(1) to give a final judgment on the interpretation of texts which are the subject of a request for an opinion. In the present case, it is sufficient to state that it will be for the legal organs in question to make such an interpretation. It is to be hoped that there is only the smallest possibility of interpretations giving rise to conflicts of jurisdiction; nevertheless no one can rule out a priori the possibility that the legal organs in question might arrive at divergent interpretations with consequential effect on legal certainty.

21. It is not feasible to establish a legal system such as that provided for in the Statute, which on the whole gives individuals effective legal protection, and at the same time to escape the consequences which inevitably follow from the participation of a third state. The need to establish judicial remedies and legal procedures which will guarantee the observance of the law in the activities of the Fund to an equal extent for all individuals may justify the principle underlying the system adopted. While approving the concern reflected by the provisions of the Statute to organize within the context of the Fund legal protection adapted to meet the difficulties of the situation, the Court is however obliged to express certain reservations as regards the compatibility of the structure of the 'Fund Tribunal' with the Treaty.

22. In the case of the second interpretation set out in paragraph 19 above, the Court considers that a difficulty would arise from the implementation of Article 6 of the Draft Regulation because the six members of the Court required to sit on the Fund Tribunal might be prejudicing their position as regards questions which might come before the Court of Justice of the Community after being brought before the Fund Tribunal and vice versa. The arrangement suggested might conflict with the obligation on the judges to give a completely impartial ruling on contentious questions when they come before the Court. In extreme cases the Court might find it impossible to assemble a quorum of judges able to give a ruling on contentious questions which had already been before the Fund Tribunal. For these reasons, the Court considers that the Fund Tribunal could only be established within the terms of Article 42 of the Statute on condition that judges belonging to The Court of Justice were not called upon to serve on it.

Operative part
In conclusion,
the Court
gives the following opinion:
the Draft Agreement on the establishment of a European laying-up fund for inland waterway vessels is incompatible with the EEC Treaty.

1.2 Further jurisprudential development

Opinion of the Court of 7 February 2006, Competence of the Community to conclude the new Lugano Convention on jurisdiction and the recognition and enforcement of judgments in civil and commercial matters, Opinion 1/03, European Court Reports 2006, p. I-1145, paras. 114–132.

The Council of Ministers requested this Opinion. A sizeable minority of Member States within the Council had argued that the Convention of Lugano, which extended the regime of EC Regulation No. 44/2001 on jurisdiction and the recognition and enforcement of judgments in civil and commercial matters to certain third countries, was not covered by the ERTA doctrine. This was the case, it was argued, although the Convention was largely identical to Regulation No. 44/2001. Thus, it did not come under the exclusive treaty-making power of the Community. The Court, as in the ERTA case, began its Opinion with a broad statement of its views and a summary of its case law on the exclusive external relations powers of the EC. It is this part of the Opinion that is included here, since it draws together all the strands of the Court's case law developing ERTA and Opinion 1/76 of over thirty years and attempts to weave them into a coherent whole. Later in the Opinion, and which is not included here, the Court came to the conclusion that the Convention of Lugano was covered by the ERTA doctrine.

Substance

Competence of the Community to conclude international agreements

114. The competence of the Community to conclude international agreements may arise not only from an express conferment by the Treaty but may equally flow implicitly from other provisions of the Treaty and from measures adopted, within the framework of those provisions, by the Community institutions (see *ERTA*, paragraph 16). The Court has also held that whenever Community law created for those institutions powers within its internal system for the purpose of attaining a specific objective, the Community had authority to undertake international commitments necessary for the attainment of that objective even in the absence of an express provision to that effect (Opinion 1/76, paragraph 3, and Opinion 2/91, paragraph 7).

115. That competence of the Community may be exclusive or shared with the Member States. As regards exclusive competence, the Court has held that the situation envisaged in Opinion 1/76 is that in which internal competence may be effectively exercised only at the same time as external competence (see Opinion 1/76, paragraphs 4 and 7, and Opinion 1/94, paragraph 85), the conclusion of the international agreement being thus necessary in order to attain objectives of the Treaty that cannot be attained by establishing autonomous rules (see, in particular, *Commission* v *Denmark*, paragraph 57).

116. In paragraph 17 of the *ERTA* judgment, the Court established the principle that, where common rules have been adopted, the Member States no longer have the right, acting individually or even collectively, to undertake obligations with non-member countries which affect those rules. In such a case, the Community also has exclusive competence to conclude international agreements.

117. In the situation addressed by the present opinion, that principle is relevant in assessing whether or not the Community's external competence is exclusive.

118. In paragraph 11 of Opinion 2/91, the Court stated that that principle also applies where rules have been adopted in areas falling outside common policies and, in particular, in areas where there are harmonising measures.

119. The Court noted in that regard that, in all the areas corresponding to the objectives of the Treaty, Article 10 EC requires Member States to facilitate the achievement of the Community's tasks and to abstain from any measure which could jeopardise the attainment of the objectives of the Treaty (Opinion 2/91, paragraph 10).

120. Giving its opinion on Part III of Convention No 170 of the International Labour Organisation concerning safety in the use of chemicals at work, which is an area already largely covered by Community rules, the Court took account of the fact that those rules had been progressively adopted for more than 25 years with a view to achieving an ever greater degree of harmonisation designed, on the one hand, to remove barriers to trade resulting from differences in legislation from one Member State to another and, on the other hand, to provide, at the same time, protection for human health and the environment. It concluded that that part of that Convention was such as to affect those Community rules and that consequently Member States could not undertake

such commitments outside the framework of the Community (Opinion 2/91, paragraphs 25 and 26).

121. In Opinion 1/94, and in the *Open Skies* judgments, the Court set out three situations in which it recognised exclusive Community competence. Those three situations, which have been the subject of much debate in the course of the present request for an opinion and which are set out in paragraph 45 hereof are, however, only examples, formulated in the light of the particular contexts with which the Court was concerned.

122. Ruling in much more general terms, the Court has found there to be exclusive Community competence in particular where the conclusion of an agreement by the Member States is incompatible with the unity of the common market and the uniform application of Community law (*ERTA*, paragraph 31), or where, given the nature of the existing Community provisions, such as legislative measures containing clauses relating to the treatment of nationals of non-member countries or to the complete harmonisation of a particular issue, any agreement in that area would necessarily affect the Community rules within the meaning of the *ERTA* judgment (see, to that effect, Opinion 1/94, paragraphs 95 and 96, and *Commission* v *Denmark*, paragraphs 83 and 84).

123. On the other hand, the Court did not find that the Community had exclusive competence where, because both the Community provisions and those of an international convention laid down minimum standards, there was nothing to prevent the full application of Community law by the Member States (Opinion 2/91, paragraph 18). Similarly, the Court did not recognise the need for exclusive Community competence where there was a chance that bilateral agreements would lead to distortions in the flow of services in the internal market, noting that there was nothing in the Treaty to prevent the institutions from arranging, in the common rules laid down by them, concerted action in relation to non-member countries or from prescribing the approach to be taken by the Member States in their external dealings (Opinion 1/94, paragraphs 78 and 79, and *Commission* v *Denmark*, paragraphs 85 and 86).

124. It should be noted in that context that the Community enjoys only conferred powers and that, accordingly, any competence, especially where it is exclusive and not expressly conferred by the Treaty, must have its basis in conclusions drawn from a specific analysis of the relationship between the agreement envisaged and the Community law in force and from which it is clear that the conclusion of such an agreement is capable of affecting the Community rules.

125. In certain cases, analysis and comparison of the areas covered both by the Community rules and by the agreement envisaged suffice to rule out any effect on the former (see Opinion 1/94, paragraph 103; Opinion 2/92, paragraph 34, and Opinion 2/00, paragraph 46).

126. However, it is not necessary for the areas covered by the international agreement and the Community legislation to coincide fully. Where the test of 'an area which is already covered to a large extent by Community rules' (Opinion 2/91, paragraphs 25 and 26) is to be applied, the assessment must be based not only on the scope of the rules in question but also on their nature and content. It is also

necessary to take into account not only the current state of Community law in the area in question but also its future development, insofar as that is foreseeable at the time of that analysis (see, to that effect, Opinion 2/91, paragraph 25).

127. That that assessment must include not only the extent of the area covered but also the nature and content of the Community rules is also clear from the Court's case-law referred to in paragraph 123 of the present opinion, stating that the fact that both the Community rules and the international agreement lay down minimum standards may justify the conclusion that the Community rules are not affected, even if the Community rules and the provisions of the agreement cover the same area.

128. In short, it is essential to ensure a uniform and consistent application of the Community rules and the proper functioning of the system which they establish in order to preserve the full effectiveness of Community law.

129. Furthermore, any initiative seeking to avoid contradictions between Community law and the agreement envisaged does not remove the obligation to determine, prior to the conclusion of the agreement, whether it is capable of affecting the Community rules (see in particular, to that effect, Opinion 2/91, paragraph 25, and *Commission* v *Denmark*, paragraphs 101 and 105).

130. In that regard, the existence in an agreement of a so-called 'disconnection clause' providing that the agreement does not affect the application by the Member States of the relevant provisions of Community law does not constitute a guarantee that the Community rules are not affected by the provisions of the agreement because their respective scopes are properly defined but, on the contrary, may provide an indication that those rules are affected. Such a mechanism seeking to prevent any conflict in the enforcement of the agreement is not in itself a decisive factor in resolving the question whether the Community has exclusive competence to conclude that agreement or whether competence belongs to the Member States; the answer to that question must be established before the agreement is concluded (see, to that effect, *Commission* v *Denmark*, paragraph 101).

131. Lastly, the legal basis for the Community rules and more particularly the condition relating to the proper functioning of the internal market laid down in Article 65 EC are, in themselves, irrelevant in determining whether an international agreement affects Community rules: the legal basis of internal legislation is determined by its principal component, whereas the rule which may possibly be affected may be merely an ancillary component of that legislation. The purpose of the exclusive competence of the Community is primarily to preserve the effectiveness of Community law and the proper functioning of the systems established by its rules, independently of any limits laid down by the provision of the Treaty on which the institutions base the adoption of such rules.

132. If an international agreement contains provisions which presume a harmonisation of legislative or regulatory measures of the Member States in an area for which the Treaty excludes such harmonisation, the Community does not have the necessary competence to conclude that agreement. Those limits of the external competence of the Community concern the very existence of that competence and not whether or not it is exclusive.

133. It follows from all the foregoing that a comprehensive and detailed analysis must be carried out to determine whether the Community has the competence to conclude an international agreement and whether that competence is exclusive. In doing so, account must be taken not only of the area covered by the Community rules and by the provisions of the agreement envisaged, insofar as the latter are known, but also of the nature and content of those rules and those provisions, to ensure that the agreement is not capable of undermining the uniform and consistent application of the Community rules and the proper functioning of the system which they establish.

1.3 Codification

Articles 1 and 47 TEU as amended by the Treaty of Lisbon, Articles 3 and 216 TFEU.

The Treaty articles included below contain the provisions that are directly linked to the case law of the Court as it had developed over the years. Article 47 TEU is identical to Article 210 EEC as interpreted in the *ERTA* case. However, it should be noted that Article 47—read in light of the last sentence of Article 1 TEU—introduces a single international legal personality for the EU, thereby doing away with the pre-existing duality of legal personalities of the EC and the old EU. This development has allowed for the streamlining of the process of negotiation and conclusion of international agreements as explained in Chapter 3. Therefore, it seems well founded to expect, as has been suggested, that the Court will interpret this provision in line with its *ERTA* jurisprudence, 'remov[ing] the current uncertainties over the extent of the Union's international capacity'.[7] Articles 3 and 216 TFEU include implicit references to the *ERTA* case and Opinion 1/76 as developed by the Court. The results of this codification are unfortunate. First, Article 216 now is formulated in such a way that it may be read so as to negate the idea, expressed in the *ERTA* case, that the potential treaty-making power of the Union covers all areas of Union competence, since it refers only to the clauses where the Treaty explicitly provides for treaty-making powers. These are undoubtedly more numerous now than at the time of the *ERTA* case in 1970. Yet there are still, as then, areas of Union competence where there is no reference to treaty-making power, but which are covered by the general character of the Union's international personality. Furthermore, the exclusive treaty-making power is slightly differently defined in Article 3(2) compared with its definition in Article 216. What the consequences will be of these modifications and whether the Court will interpret this as a new constitutional restriction which overturns part of its case law or rather as a codification of it remains to be seen.

---

[7] M. Cremona, Defining Competence in EU External Relations: Lessons from the Treaty Reform Process, *Law and Practice of External Relations: Salient Features of a Changing Landscape* (A. Dashwood and M. Maresceau (eds), Cambridge: Cambridge University Press, 2008), 38.

Treaty on European Union

Article 1 (last sentence)

The Union shall replace and succeed the European Community

Article 47

The Union shall have legal personality.[8]

Treaty on the Functioning of the European Union

Article 3

1. The Union shall have exclusive competence in the following areas:

(a) customs union;

(b) the establishing of the competition rules necessary for the functioning of the internal market;

(c) monetary policy for the Member States whose currency is the euro;

(d) the conservation of marine biological resources under the common fisheries policy;

(e) common commercial policy.

2. The Union shall also have exclusive competence for the conclusion of an international agreement when its conclusion is provided for in a legislative act of the Union or is necessary to enable the Union to exercise its internal competence, or in so far as its conclusion may affect common rules or alter their scope.

Article 216

1. The Union may conclude an agreement with one or more third countries or international organisations where the Treaties so provide or where the conclusion of an agreement is necessary in order to achieve, within the framework of the Union's policies, one of the objectives referred to in the Treaties, or is provided for in a legally binding Union act or is likely to affect common rules or alter their scope.

2. Agreements concluded by the Union are binding upon the institutions of the Union and on its Member States.

Select Bibliography

Cremona, M., Extending the Reach of the AETR Principle: Comment on Commission v Greece (C-45/07), *European Law Review*, vol. 34(5), 2009, 754–68.

Eeckhout, P., Bold Constitutionalism and Beyond, *The Past and Future of EU Law: The Classics of EU Law Revisited on the 50th Anniversary of the Rome Treaty* (M.P. Maduro and L. Azoulai (eds), Oxford and Portland, OR: Hart Publishing, 2010), 218–23.

Hillion, C., A Look Back at the *Open Skies* Judgments, *Views of European Law from the Mountain: Liber Amicorum Piet Jan Slot* (M. Bulterman, L. Hancher, A. McDonnell, and H. Sevenster (eds), The Netherlands: Kluwer Law International, 2009), 257–65.

---

[8] The Treaty of Lisbon is accompanied by the following Declaration 24: 'The Conference confirms that the fact that the European Union has a legal personality will not in any way authorise the Union to legislate or to act beyond the competences conferred upon it by the Member States in the Treaties.'

——, *ERTA, ECHR and Open Skies*: Laying the Grounds of the EU System of External Relations, *The Past and Future of EU Law: The Classics of EU Law Revisited on the 50th Anniversary of the Rome Treaty* (M.P. Maduro and L. Azoulai (eds), Oxford and Portland, OR: Hart Publishing, 2010), 224–33.

Hoffmeister, F., The Contribution of EU Practice to International Law, *Developments in EU External Relations Law* (M. Cremona (ed.), Oxford: Oxford University Press, 2008), 38–42.

Kuijper, P.J., Fifty Years of EC/EU External Relations: Continuity and the Dialogue Between Judges and Member States as Constitutional Legislators, *Fordham International Law Journal*, vol. 31, 2007–08, 1578–602.

Kuijper, P.J. The Opinion on the Lugano Convention and the Implied External Relations Powers of the European Union, *Justice, Liberty, Security: New Challenges for EU External Relations* (B. Martenczuk and S. van Thiel (eds), Brussels: Brussels University Press, 2008), 187–210.

——, Re-reading External Relations Cases in the Field of Transport: The Function of Community Loyalty, *Views of European Law from the Mountain: Liber Amicorum Piet Jan Slot* (M. Bulterman, L. Hancher, A. McDonnell, and H. Sevenster (eds), The Netherlands: Kluwer Law International, 2009), 291–300.

Mengozzi, P., The EC External Competencies: From ERTA Case to the Opinion in the Lugano Convention, *The Past and Future of EU Law: The Classics of EU Law Revisited on the 50th Anniversary of the Rome Treaty* (M.P. Maduro and L. Azoulai (eds), Oxford and Portland, OR: Hart Publishing, 2010), 213–17.

Post, R., Constructing the European Polity: *ERTA* and the *Open Skies* Judgments, *The Past and Future of EU Law: The Classics of EU Law Revisited on the 50th Anniversary of the Rome Treaty* (M.P. Maduro and L. Azoulai (eds), Oxford and Portland, OR: Hart Publishing, 2010), 234–47.

2

International Representation of the EU

2.1 Introduction

The succession of the EC by the EU, as well as the clear affirmation of the single international legal personality of the Union, discussed in Chapter 1, are significant for the international representation of the Union. Together with the abolition of the pillar structure, these changes allow for a more simplified representation of the EU abroad, as a prerequisite to achieve one of the goals of the Lisbon Treaty, which was to instil more coherence, effectiveness, stability, and visibility in the external relations of the Union. That said, as discussed below and as further elaborated in Chapter 11, the Common Foreign and Security Policy (CFSP) has maintained its particularity in the EU framework. In addition, issues pertaining to the remaining difficulties in achieving a more unified international representation of the Union in the case of mixed agreements or in the face of rules of international organizations or instruments not allowing for EU participation are discussed in Chapter 5.

This chapter delves into the specific provisions of the Treaties, secondary law, and practice that determine which actors are tasked to *externally* represent the Union in third states, international organizations and international fora, as well as international dispute settlement mechanisms and diplomatic exchanges. The *internal* decision-making processes for the adoption of EU positions prior to the negotiation, signing, and conclusion of legally binding or non-binding international agreements, is dealt with in Chapter 3. The issue of competences and how their allocation affects the international representation of the Union is only incidentally touched upon here.

2.2 Historical evolution

The international representation of the EU was historically fragmented, mirroring the pillar structure of the Treaties. The EEC and then the EC had no explicit reference to the external representation of the Community. However, Article 116 of the Treaty of Rome (EEC) already provided for an obligation of the Member States to 'proceed within the framework of international organisations of an economic character only by common action'. The Treaty establishing the European Community (TEC) made clear in Article 211 TEC that the Commission is the guardian of Community law, whereas

Article 282 TEC empowered the Commission to represent the Community in its Member States. As late as 2006, the Court of Justice found, based on these two provisions together with Article 281 TEC on the legal personality of the Community (see Chapter 1), that the Commission was to represent the Community abroad. On this basis, the Commission had developed in the course of time its network of Commission Delegations abroad representing it in third countries and in international organizations—a network which the Lisbon Treaty turned into Union delegations (see Section 2.4).

Treaty establishing the European Economic Community (Treaty of Rome)
Article 116

From the end of the transitional period onwards, Member States shall, in respect of all matters of particular interest to the common market, proceed within the framework of international organisations of an economic character only by common action. To this end, the Commission shall submit to the Council, which shall act by a qualified majority, proposals concerning the scope and implementation of such common action.

During the transitional period, Member States shall consult each other for the purpose of concerting the action they take and adopting as far as possible a uniform attitude.

Treaty establishing the European Community (Treaty of Amsterdam)
Article 211

In order to ensure the proper functioning and development of the common market, the Commission shall:

— ensure that the provisions of this Treaty and the measures taken by the institutions pursuant thereto are applied,

[...]

Article 282

In each of the Member States, the Community shall enjoy the most extensive legal capacity accorded to legal persons under their laws; it may, in particular, acquire or dispose of movable and immovable property and may be a party to legal proceedings. To this end, the Community shall be represented by the Commission.

Judgment of the Court (Grand Chamber) of 12 September 2006, R.J. Reynolds Tobacco Holdings, Inc. and Others v. Commission of the European Communities, Case C-131/03 P, European Court Reports 2006, p. I-7795, para. 94.

94. It is sufficient to point out in that regard that Article 211 EC provides that the Commission is to ensure that the provisions of the Treaty and the measures taken pursuant thereto are applied, that under Article 281 EC the Community has legal personality and that Article 282 EC, although restricted to Member States on its wording, is the expression of a general principle and states that

the Community has legal capacity and is, to that end, to be represented by the Commission.

Prior to the Lisbon Treaty, in CFSP matters the rotating Presidency was responsible for representing the Union. This had already been the case with European Political Cooperation (EPC), which originated in the early 1970s and preceded the creation of CFSP under the Maastricht Treaty. As is known, the Single European Act of 1986 constituted the first effort to integrate the EPC in the framework of the Treaties and emphasized that a unified projection and cohesiveness of Europe implied that it 'speaks with a single voice' on the international scene (see fifth recital of its preamble). In introducing the CFSP as the Union's second pillar, the Maastricht Treaty did not only articulated the role of the rotating Presidency but also gave a supplementary role to the former and next Presidencies, whereas it foresaw that the Commission was also 'fully associated' with the international representation of the EU in CFSP. The Treaty of Amsterdam eliminated the role of the former Presidency but introduced the office of the High Representative for CFSP who, among others, was to assist the Presidency in its external representation obligations. With regard to the former third pillar (police and judicial cooperation in criminal matters) suffice it to say here that although Article 37 TEC provided that the same arrangements for the international representation in matters falling under the second pillar applied, in practice the Commission took the lead in this field.

Single European Act
Article 30
[...]
10.(a) The Presidency of European Political Co-operation shall be held by the High Contracting Party which holds the Presidency of the Council of the European Communities.

   (b) The Presidency shall be responsible for initiating action and co-ordinating and representing the positions of the Member States in relations with third countries in respect of European Political Co-operation activities. It shall also be responsible for the management of Political Co-operation and in particular for drawing up the timetable of meetings and for convening and organizing meetings.

[...]

Treaty on European Union (Treaty of Maastricht)
Article J.5

1. The Presidency shall represent the Union in matters coming within the common foreign and security policy.
2. The Presidency shall be responsible for the implementation of common measures; in that capacity it shall in principle express the position of the Union in international organizations and international conferences.

3. In the tasks referred to in paragraphs 1 and 2, the Presidency shall be assisted if need be by the previous and next Member States to hold the Presidency. The Commission shall be fully associated in these tasks.

[...]

Treaty on European Union (Treaty of Amsterdam)

Article 18

(ex Article J.8)

1. The Presidency shall represent the Union in matters coming within the common foreign and security policy.
2. The Presidency shall be responsible for the implementation of decisions taken under this Title; in that capacity it shall in principle express the position of the Union in international organisations and international conferences.
3. The Presidency shall be assisted by the Secretary-General of the Council who shall exercise the function of High Representative for the common foreign and security policy.
4. The Commission shall be fully associated in the tasks referred to in paragraphs 1 and 2. The Presidency shall be assisted in those tasks if need be by the next Member State to hold the Presidency.
5. The Council may, whenever it deems it necessary, appoint a special representative with a mandate in relation to particular policy issues.

Treaty establishing the European Community (Treaty of Amsterdam)

Article 37

(ex Article K.9)

Within international organisations and at international conferences in which they take part, Member States shall defend the common positions adopted under the provisions of this title.

Articles 18 and 19 shall apply as appropriate to matters falling under this title.

2.3 International representation after Lisbon

2.3.1 Constitutional principles applying to the international representation of the EU

The principles of sincere cooperation (Article 4(3) TEU), conferral (Article 5(2) TEU), consistency (Article 21(3) TEU), and unity govern the external representation of the EU. As the Court of Justice reiterated recently in *Commission v. Sweden* (Case C-246/07), the principle of sincere cooperation is 'of general application' in the external actions of the Union, irrespective of the nature of the competences of the EU. In addition, it applies mutually to the institutions of the Union as well as to its Member States. The legal consequences of the principle of sincere cooperation as developed by the Court of Justice, are examined in some detail in Chapter 5 (see p. 226). In the same judgment, the Court recalled its well-established case law with regard to the requirement of unity in the external representation of the Union regardless of the nature of the competences. As for the principle of consistency, after Lisbon it falls within the jurisdiction of the Court of Justice, giving the Court the opportunity to elaborate further on the exact content of consistency in the international representation of the EU as well as on its relationship to the principle of sincere cooperation. Such an exercise may prove challenging in light of the lack of specific guidance within the Treaties as to what exactly this duty entails, especially in the external representation of the Union.

Treaty on European Union

Article 4

[...]

3. Pursuant to the principle of sincere cooperation, the Union and the Member States shall, in full mutual respect, assist each other in carrying out tasks which flow from the Treaties. The Member States shall take any appropriate measure, general or particular, to ensure fulfilment of the obligations arising out of the Treaties or resulting from the acts of the institutions of the Union.

The Member States shall facilitate the achievement of the Union's tasks and refrain from any measure which could jeopardise the attainment of the Union's objectives.

Article 5

(ex Article 5 TEC)

[...]

2. Under the principle of conferral, the Union shall act only within the limits of the competences conferred upon it by the Member States in the Treaties to attain the objectives set out therein. Competences not conferred upon the Union in the Treaties remain with the Member States.

[...]

Article 21

[...]

3. [...]

The Union shall ensure consistency between the different areas of its external action and between these and its other policies. The Council and the Commission, assisted by the High Representative of the Union for Foreign Affairs and Security Policy, shall ensure that consistency and shall cooperate to that effect.

Judgment of the Court (Grand Chamber) of 20 April 2010, European Commission v. Kingdom of Sweden, Case C-246/07, European Court Reports 2010, p. I-3317, paras. 71–73.

71. In that regard, the Court has already held that this duty of genuine cooperation is of general application and does not depend either on whether the Community competence concerned is exclusive or on any right of the Member States to enter into obligations towards non-member countries (Case C-266/03 *Commission v*

Luxembourg [2005] ECR I-4805, paragraph 58, and Case C-433/03 *Commission* v *Germany* [2005] ECR I-6985, paragraph 64).

72. In the present case, the Commission has pointed out that it was not claiming that the Community had exclusive competence to submit a proposal for the listing of PFOS in Annex A to the Stockholm Convention. It must therefore be assumed that competence is shared. In that sense the present case can be distinguished from the situation at issue in Case C-45/07 *Commission* v *Greece* [2009] ECR I-701, which concerned exclusive competence.

73. Where it is apparent that the subject-matter of an agreement or convention falls partly within the competence of the Community and partly within that of its Member States, it is essential to ensure close cooperation between the Member States and the Community institutions, both in the process of negotiation and conclusion and in the fulfilment of the commitments entered into. That obligation to cooperate flows from the requirement of unity in the international representation of the Community (Ruling 1/78 [1978] ECR 2151, paragraphs 34 to 36 (by analogy with the EAEC Treaty); Opinion 2/91 [1993] ECR I-1061, paragraph 36; Opinion 1/94 [1994] ECR I-5267, paragraph 108; and Case C-25/94 *Commission* v *Council* [1996] ECR I-1469, paragraph 48).

2.3.2 Institutional framework for the international representation of the EU

The Treaty of Lisbon simplified considerably the legal framework governing the international representation of the EU and further introduced a number of innovations to it. However, the divide between the CFSP and the non-CFSP fields of external relations still persists after Lisbon. Thus, according to Article 17(1) TEU the Commission 'shall ensure the Union's external representation' except for CFSP. This article reproduces in the text of the Treaties the findings of the Court in the aforementioned Case C-131/03 P of the Court of Justice as well as long-standing practice.

In CFSP, which has maintained its intergovernmental character and still follows 'specific rules and procedures' (Article 24(1) TEU), it is the President of the European Council and the High Representative for Foreign Affairs and Security Policy who represent the Union. The President of the European Council is responsible for representing the Union abroad on CFSP matters 'at his or her level and in that capacity' (Article 15(6) TEU). In other words, he represents the Union at the level of heads of state or government, leaving all other aspects of EU representation in CFSP, such as the day-to-day representation and the meetings at ministerial level, to the High Representative (Article 27(2) TEU).

The High Representative is one of the major innovations of the Lisbon Treaty, merging the previous position of the High Representative for CFSP with that of the Commissioner for External Relations. The High Representative is also responsible for the overall coordination of EU external relations (Article 18(4) TEU). In addition, according to Article 220 TFEU, which replaced previous Articles 302–4 TEC, the High Representative together with the Commission are tasked to handle the relations of the EU with international organizations. The High Representative can also propose to the Council to appoint Special Representatives to represent the Union on specific issues, always under the authority of the High Representative (Article 33 TEU). Furthermore, with respect to

CFSP and the representation of the EU at the United Nations (UN) Security Council in particular, the Treaties contain Article 34(2) TEU. This article obliges EU Member States occupying a seat at the UN Security Council to ask that the High Representative is heard by the Security Council as long as there is a common EU position on a topic that is on the latter's agenda.

Treaty on European Union

Article 15

[...]

6. The President of the European Council:

[...]

The President of the European Council shall, at his level and in that capacity, ensure the external representation of the Union on issues concerning its common foreign and security policy, without prejudice to the powers of the High Representative of the Union for Foreign Affairs and Security Policy.

[...]

Article 17

1. The Commission shall promote the general interest of the Union and take appropriate initiatives to that end. [...] With the exception of the common foreign and security policy, and other cases provided for in the Treaties, [the Commission] shall ensure the Union's external representation. [...]

[...]

Article 18

[...]

4. The High Representative shall be one of the Vice-Presidents of the Commission. He shall ensure the consistency of the Union's external action. He shall be responsible within the Commission for responsibilities incumbent on it in external relations and for coordinating other aspects of the Union's external action. In exercising these responsibilities within the Commission, and only for these responsibilities, the High Representative shall be bound by Commission procedures to the extent that this is consistent with paragraphs 2 and 3.

[...]

Article 24

(ex Article 11 TEU)

1. [...]

The common foreign and security policy is subject to specific rules and procedures. It shall be defined and implemented by the European Council and the Council acting unanimously, except where the Treaties provide otherwise. The adoption of legislative acts shall be excluded. The common foreign and security policy shall be put into effect by the High Representative of the Union for Foreign Affairs and Security Policy and by Member States, in accordance with the Treaties. The specific role of the European Parliament and of the Commission in this area is defined by the Treaties. The Court of

Justice of the European Union shall not have jurisdiction with respect to these provisions, with the exception of its jurisdiction to monitor compliance with Article 40 of this Treaty and to review the legality of certain decisions as provided for by the second paragraph of Article 275 of the Treaty on the Functioning of the European Union.

[…]

Article 27
[…]

2. The High Representative shall represent the Union for matters relating to the common foreign and security policy. He shall conduct political dialogue with third parties on the Union's behalf and shall express the Union's position in international organisations and at international conferences.

[…]

Article 33
(ex Article 18 TEU)

The Council may, on a proposal from the High Representative of the Union for Foreign Affairs and Security Policy, appoint a special representative with a mandate in relation to particular policy issues. The special representative shall carry out his mandate under the authority of the High Representative.

Article 34
(ex Article 19 TEU)

[…]

2. In accordance with Article 24(3), Member States represented in international organisations or international conferences where not all the Member States participate shall keep the other Member States and the High Representative informed of any matter of common interest.

Member States which are also members of the United Nations Security Council will concert and keep the other Member States and the High Representative fully informed. Member States which are members of the Security Council will, in the execution of their functions, defend the positions and the interests of the Union, without prejudice to their responsibilities under the provisions of the United Nations Charter.

When the Union has defined a position on a subject which is on the United Nations Security Council agenda, those Member States which sit on the Security Council shall request that the High Representative be invited to present the Union's position.

Treaty on the Functioning of the European Union
TITLE VI

THE UNION'S RELATIONS WITH INTERNATIONAL ORGANISATIONS AND THIRD COUNTRIES AND UNION DELEGATIONS

Article 220
(ex Articles 302 to 304 TEC)

1. The Union shall establish all appropriate forms of cooperation with the organs of the United Nations and its specialised agencies, the Council of Europe, the Organisation for

Security and Cooperation in Europe and the Organisation for Economic Cooperation and Development.

The Union shall also maintain such relations as are appropriate with other international organisations.

2. The High Representative of the Union for Foreign Affairs and Security Policy and the Commission shall implement this Article.

The High Representative is assisted by the European External Action Service (EEAS) established by Council Decision 2010/427/EU of 26 July 2010 (EEAS Decision) (Article 27(3) TEU, Article 1(3) EEAS Decision). The EEAS is a 'functionally autonomous body of the Union under the authority of the High Representative'. In addition to supporting the High Representative/Vice-President, it is also expected to 'assist the President of the European Council, the President of the Commission, and the Commission in the exercise of their respective functions in the area of external relations' (Article 2(2) EEAS Decision). The EEAS draws its personnel from the Commission, the Council Secretariat, and the Diplomatic Services of the Member States (Article 27(3) TEU). The Service has taken over the former Commission Delegations that have now become Union Delegations (Article 1(4) EEAS Decision). Union Delegations are 'under the authority of the High Representative' (Article 221(2) TFEU) and represent the Union abroad in its entirety and not just the Commission, as used to be the case (Article 221(1) TFEU; Article 5 EEAS Decision). It is for this reason that they receive instructions from either the High Representative for matters touching on CFSP or the Commission on non-CFSP policies (Article 5(3) EEAS Decision).

Treaty on European Union

Article 27

[...]

3. In fulfilling his mandate, the High Representative shall be assisted by a European External Action Service. This service shall work in cooperation with the diplomatic services of the Member States and shall comprise officials from relevant departments of the General Secretariat of the Council and of the Commission as well as staff seconded from national diplomatic services of the Member States. The organisation and functioning of the European External Action Service shall be established by a decision of the Council. The Council shall act on a proposal from the High Representative after consulting the European Parliament and after obtaining the consent of the Commission.

Treaty on the Functioning of the European Union

Article 221

1. Union delegations in third countries and at international organisations shall represent the Union.

2. Union delegations shall be placed under the authority of the High Representative of the Union for Foreign Affairs and Security Policy. They shall act in close cooperation with Member States' diplomatic and consular missions.

Council Decision 2010/427/EU of 26 July 2010 establishing the organisation and functioning of the European External Action Service, 3.8.2010, Official Journal of the European Union L 201/30.

THE COUNCIL OF THE EUROPEAN UNION,
Having regard to the Treaty on European Union, and in particular Article 27(3) thereof,
Having regard to the proposal from the High Representative of the Union for Foreign Affairs and Security Policy ('the High Representative'),
Having regard to the Opinion of the European Parliament,
Having regard to the consent of the European Commission,

Whereas:
(1) The purpose of this Decision is to establish the organisation and functioning of the European External Action Service ('EEAS'), a functionally autonomous body of the Union under the authority of the High Representative, set up by Article 27(3) of the Treaty on European Union ('TEU'), as amended by the Treaty of Lisbon. This Decision and, in particular, the reference to the term 'High Representative' will be interpreted in accordance with his/her different functions under Article 18 TEU.
(2) In accordance with the second subparagraph of Article 21(3) TEU, the Union will ensure consistency between the different areas of its external action and between those areas and its other policies. The Council and the Commission, assisted by the High Representative, will ensure that consistency and will cooperate to that effect.
(3) The EEAS will support the High Representative, who is also a Vice-President of the Commission and the President of the Foreign Affairs Council, in fulfilling his/her mandate to conduct the Common Foreign and Security Policy ('CFSP') of the Union and to ensure the consistency of the Union's external action as outlined, notably, in Articles 18 and 27 TEU. The EEAS will support the High Representative in his/her capacity as President of the Foreign Affairs Council, without prejudice to the normal tasks of the General Secretariat of the Council. The EEAS will also support the High Representative in his/her capacity as Vice-President of the Commission, in respect of his/her responsibilities within the Commission for responsibilities incumbent on it in external relations, and in coordinating other aspects of the Union's external action, without prejudice to the normal tasks of the Commission services.
(4) In its contribution to the Union's external cooperation programmes, the EEAS should seek to ensure that the programmes fulfil the objectives for external action as set out in Article 21 TUE, in particular in paragraph (2)(d) thereof, and that they respect the objectives of the Union's development policy in line with Article 208 of the Treaty on the Functioning of the European Union ('TFEU'). In this context, the EEAS should also promote the fulfilment of the objectives of the European Consensus on Development and the European Consensus on Humanitarian Aid.
(5) It results from the Treaty of Lisbon that, in order to implement its provisions, the EEAS must be operational as soon as possible after the entry into force of that Treaty.

(6) The European Parliament will fully play its role in the external action of the Union, including its functions of political control as provided for in Article 14(1) TEU, as well as in legislative and budgetary matters as laid down in the Treaties. Furthermore, in accordance with Article 36 TEU, the High Representative will regularly consult the European Parliament on the main aspects and the basic choices of the CFSP and will ensure that the views of the European Parliament are duly taken into consideration. The EEAS will assist the High Representative in this regard. Specific arrangements should be made with regard to access for Members of the European Parliament to classified documents and information in the area of CFSP. Until the adoption of such arrangements, existing provisions under the Inter-institutional Agreement of 20 November 2002 between the European Parliament and the Council concerning access by the European Parliament to sensitive information of the Council in the field of security and defence policy will apply.

(7) The High Representative, or his/her representative, should exercise the responsibilities provided for by the respective acts founding the European Defence Agency, the European Union Satellite Centre, the European Union Institute for Security Studies, and the European Security and Defence College. The EEAS should provide those entities with the support currently provided by the General Secretariat of the Council.

(8) Provisions should be adopted relating to the staff of the EEAS and their recruitment where such provisions are necessary to establish the organisation and functioning of the EEAS. In parallel, necessary amendments should be made, in accordance with Article 336 TFEU, to the Staff Regulations of Officials of the European Communities ('Staff Regulations') and the Conditions of Employment of Other Servants of those Communities ('CEOS') without prejudice to Article 298 TFEU. For matters relating to its staff, the EEAS should be treated as an institution within the meaning of the Staff Regulations and the CEOS. The High Representative will be the Appointing Authority, in relation both to officials subject to the Staff Regulations and agents subject to the CEOS. The number of officials and servants of the EEAS will be decided each year as part of the budgetary procedure and will be reflected in the establishment plan.

(9) The staff of the EEAS should carry out their duties and conduct themselves solely with the interest of the Union in mind.

(10) Recruitment should be based on merit whilst ensuring adequate geographical and gender balance. The staff of the EEAS should comprise a meaningful presence of nationals from all the Member States. The review foreseen for 2013 should also cover this issue, including, as appropriate, suggestions for additional specific measures to correct possible imbalances.

(11) In accordance with Article 27(3) TEU, the EEAS will comprise officials from the General Secretariat of the Council and from the Commission, as well as personnel coming from the diplomatic services of the Member States. For that purpose, the relevant departments and functions in the General Secretariat of the Council and in the Commission will be transferred to the EEAS, together with officials and temporary agents occupying a post in such departments or functions. Before 1 July 2013, the EEAS will recruit exclusively officials originating from the General Secretariat of the

Council and the Commission, as well as staff coming from the diplomatic services of the Member States. After that date, all officials and other servants of the European Union should be able to apply for vacant posts in the EEAS.

(12) The EEAS may, in specific cases, have recourse to specialised seconded national experts ('SNEs'), over whom the High Representative will have authority. SNEs in posts in the EEAS will not be counted in the one third of all EEAS staff at Administrator ('AD') level which staff from Member States should represent when the EEAS will have reached its full capacity. Their transfer in the phase of setting up of the EEAS will not be automatic and will be made with the consent of the authorities of the originating Member States. By the date of expiry of the contract of an SNE transferred to the EEAS under Article 7, the relevant function will be converted into a temporary agent post in cases where the function performed by the SNE corresponds to a function normally carried out by staff at AD level, provided that the necessary post is available under the establishment plan.

(13) The Commission and the EEAS will agree on detailed arrangements relating to the issuing of instructions from the Commission to delegations. These should provide in particular that when the Commission will issue instructions to delegations, it will simultaneously provide a copy thereof to the Head of Delegation and to the EEAS central administration.

(14) Council Regulation (EC, Euratom) No 1605/2002 of 25 June 2002 on the Financial Regulation applicable to the general budget of the European Communities (the 'Financial Regulation') should be amended in order to include the EEAS in Article 1 thereof, with a specific section in the Union budget. In accordance with the applicable rules, and as is the case for other institutions, a part of the annual report of the Court of Auditors will also be dedicated to the EEAS, and the EEAS will respond to such reports. The EEAS will be subject to the procedures regarding the discharge as provided for in Article 319 TFEU and in Articles 145 to 147 of the Financial Regulation. The High Representative will provide the European Parliament with all necessary support for the exercise of the European Parliament's right as discharge authority. The implementation of the operational budget will be the Commission's responsibility in accordance with Article 317 TFEU. Decisions having a financial impact will, in particular, comply with the responsibilities laid down in Title IV of the Financial Regulation, especially Articles 64 to 68 thereof regarding liability of financial actors, and Article 75 thereof regarding expenditure operations.

(15) The establishment of the EEAS should be guided by the principle of cost-efficiency aiming towards budget neutrality. To this end, transitional arrangements and a gradual build-up of capacity will have to be used. Unnecessary duplication of tasks, functions and resources with other structures should be avoided. All opportunities for rationalisation should be availed of.

In addition, a number of additional posts for Member States' temporary agents will be necessary, which will have to be financed within the framework of the current multiannual financial framework.

(16) Rules should be laid down covering the activities of the EEAS and its staff as regards security, the protection of classified information, and transparency.

(17) It is recalled that the Protocol on the Privileges and Immunities of the European Union will apply to the EEAS, its officials and other agents, who will be subject either to the Staff Regulations or the CEOS.

(18) The European Union and the European Atomic Energy Community continue to be served by a single institutional framework. It is therefore essential to ensure consistency between the external relations of both, and to allow the Union Delegations to undertake the representation of the European Atomic Energy Community in third countries and at international organisations.

(19) The High Representative should, by mid-2013, provide a review of the organisation and functioning of the EEAS, accompanied, if necessary, by proposals for a revision of this Decision. Such a revision should be adopted no later than the beginning of 2014,

HAS ADOPTED THIS DECISION:

Article 1

Nature and scope

1. This Decision establishes the organisation and functioning of the European External Action Service ('EEAS').

2. The EEAS, which has its headquarters in Brussels, shall be a functionally autonomous body of the European Union, separate from the General Secretariat of the Council and from the Commission with the legal capacity necessary to perform its tasks and attain its objectives.

3. The EEAS shall be placed under the authority of the High Representative of the Union for Foreign Affairs and Security Policy ('High Representative').

4. The EEAS shall be made up of a central administration and of the Union Delegations to third countries and to international organisations.

Article 2

Tasks

1. The EEAS shall support the High Representative in fulfilling his/her mandates as outlined, notably, in Articles 18 and 27 TEU:

— in fulfilling his/her mandate to conduct the Common Foreign and Security Policy ('CFSP') of the European Union, including the Common Security and Defence Policy ('CSDP'), to contribute by his/her proposals to the development of that policy, which he/she shall carry out as mandated by the Council and to ensure the consistency of the Union's external action,

— in his/her capacity as President of the Foreign Affairs Council, without prejudice to the normal tasks of the General Secretariat of the Council,

— in his/her capacity as Vice-President of the Commission for fulfilling within the Commission the responsibilities incumbent on it in external relations, and in coordinating other aspects of the Union's external action, without prejudice to the normal tasks of the services of the Commission.

2. The EEAS shall assist the President of the European Council, the President of the Commission, and the Commission in the exercise of their respective functions in the area of external relations.

Article 3

Cooperation

1. The EEAS shall support, and work in cooperation with, the diplomatic services of the Member States, as well as with the General Secretariat of the Council and the services of the Commission, in order to ensure consistency between the different areas of the Union's external action and between those areas and its other policies.

2. The EEAS and the services of the Commission shall consult each other on all matters relating to the external action of the Union in the exercise of their respective functions, except on matters covered by the CSDP. The EEAS shall take part in the preparatory work and procedures relating to acts to be prepared by the Commission in this area.

This paragraph shall be implemented in accordance with Chapter 1 of Title V of the TEU, and with Article 205 TFEU.

3. The EEAS may enter into service-level arrangements with relevant services of the General Secretariat of the Council, the Commission, or other offices or interinstitutional bodies of the Union.

4. The EEAS shall extend appropriate support and cooperation to the other institutions and bodies of the Union, in particular to the European Parliament. The EEAS may also benefit from the support and cooperation of those institutions and bodies, including agencies, as appropriate. The EEAS internal auditor will cooperate with the internal auditor of the Commission to ensure a consistent audit policy, with particular reference to the Commission's responsibility for operational expenditure. In addition, the EEAS shall cooperate with the European Anti-Fraud Office ('OLAF') in accordance with Regulation (EC) No 1073/1999. It shall, in particular, adopt without delay the decision required by that Regulation on the terms and conditions for internal investigations. As provided in that Regulation, both Member States, in accordance with national provisions, and the institutions shall give the necessary support to enable OLAF's agents to fulfil their tasks.

Article 4

Central administration of the EEAS

1. The EEAS shall be managed by an Executive Secretary-General who will operate under the authority of the High Representative. The Executive Secretary-General shall take all measures necessary to ensure the smooth functioning of the EEAS, including its administrative and budgetary management. The Executive Secretary-General shall ensure effective coordination between all departments in the central administration as well as with the Union Delegations.

2. The Executive Secretary-General shall be assisted by two Deputy Secretaries-General.

3. The central administration of the EEAS shall be organized in directorates-general.

(a) It shall, in particular, include:

— a number of directorates-general comprising geographic desks covering all countries and regions of the world, as well as multilateral and thematic desks. These departments shall coordinate as necessary with the General Secretariat of the Council and with the relevant services of the Commission,

— a directorate-general for administrative, staffing, budgetary, security and communication and information system matters, working in the EEAS framework managed by the Executive Secretary-General. The High Representative shall appoint, in accordance with the normal rules of recruitment, a Director-General for budget and administration who shall work under the authority of the High Representative. He/she shall be responsible to the High Representative for the administrative and internal budgetary management of the EEAS. He/she shall follow the same budget lines and administrative rules as are applicable in the part of Section III of the Union's budget which falls under Heading 5 of the Multiannual Financial Framework,

— the crisis management and planning directorate, the civilian planning and conduct capability, the European Union Military Staff and the European Union Situation Centre, placed under the direct authority and responsibility of the High Representative, and which shall assist him/her in the task of conducting the Union's CFSP in accordance with the provisions of the Treaty while respecting, in accordance with Article 40 TEU, the other competences of the Union.

The specificities of these structures, as well as the particularities of their functions, recruitment and the status of the staff shall be respected.

Full coordination between all the structures of the EEAS shall be ensured.

(b) The central administration of the EEAS shall also include:

— a strategic policy planning department,

— a legal department under the administrative authority of the Executive Secretary-General which shall work closely with the Legal Services of the Council and of the Commission,

— departments for interinstitutional relations, information and public diplomacy, internal audit and inspections, and personal data protection.

4. The High Representative shall designate the chairpersons of Council preparatory bodies that are chaired by a representative of the High Representative, including the chair of the Political and Security Committee, in accordance with the detailed arrangements set out in Annex II to Council Decision 2009/908/EU of 1 December 2009 laying down measures for the implementation of the European Council Decision on the exercise of the Presidency of the Council, and on the chairmanship of preparatory bodies of the Council.

5. The High Representative and the EEAS shall be assisted where necessary by the General Secretariat of the Council and the relevant departments of the Commission. Service-level arrangements may be drawn up to that effect by the EEAS, the General Secretariat of the Council and the relevant Commission departments.

Article 5

Union delegations

1. The decision to open or close a delegation shall be adopted by the High Representative, in agreement with the Council and the Commission.

2. Each Union Delegation shall be placed under the authority of a Head of Delegation. The Head of Delegation shall have authority over all staff in the delegation, whatever their status, and for all its activities. He/she shall be accountable to the High Representative for the overall management of the work of the delegation and for ensuring the coordination of all actions of the Union.

Staff in delegations shall comprise EEAS staff and, where appropriate for the implementation of the Union budget and Union policies other than those under the remit of the EEAS, Commission staff.

3. The Head of Delegation shall receive instructions from the High Representative and the EEAS, and shall be responsible for their execution.

In areas where the Commission exercises the powers conferred upon it by the Treaties, the Commission may, in accordance with Article 221(2) TFEU, also issue instructions to delegations, which shall be executed under the overall responsibility of the Head of Delegation.

4. The Head of Delegation shall implement operational credits in relation to the Union's projects in the corresponding third country, where sub-delegated by the Commission, in accordance with the Financial Regulation.

5. The operation of each delegation shall be periodically evaluated by the Executive Secretary-General of the EEAS; evaluation shall include financial and administrative audits. For this purpose, the Executive Secretary-General of the EEAS may request assistance from the relevant Commission departments. In addition to internal measures by the EEAS, OLAF shall exercise its powers, notably by conducting anti-fraud measures, in accordance with Regulation (EC) No 1073/1999.

6. The High Representative shall enter into the necessary arrangements with the host country, the international organisation, or the third country concerned. In particular, the High Representative shall take the necessary measures to ensure that host States grant the Union delegations, their staff and their property, privileges and immunities equivalent to those referred to in the Vienna Convention on Diplomatic Relations of 18 April 1961.

7. Union delegations shall have the capacity to respond to the needs of other institutions of the Union, in particular the European Parliament, in their contacts with the international organisations or third countries to which the delegations are accredited.

8. The Head of Delegation shall have the power to represent the Union in the country where the delegation is accredited, in particular for the conclusion of contracts, and as a party to legal proceedings.

9. The Union delegations shall work in close cooperation and share information with the diplomatic services of the Member States.

10. The Union delegations shall, acting in accordance with the third paragraph of Article 35 TEU, and upon request by Member States, support the Member States in their diplomatic relations and in their role of providing consular protection to citizens of the Union in third countries on a resource-neutral basis.

Article 6

Staff

1. This Article, except paragraph 3, shall apply without prejudice to the Staff Regulations of Officials of the European Communities ('Staff Regulations') and the Conditions of Employment of Other Servants of those Communities ('CEOS'), including the amendments made to those rules, in accordance with Article 336 TFEU, in order to adapt them to the needs of the EEAS.

2. The EEAS shall comprise officials and other servants of the European Union, including personnel from the diplomatic services of the Member States appointed as temporary agents.

The Staff Regulations and the CEOS shall apply to this staff.

3. If necessary, the EEAS may, in specific cases, have recourse to a limited number of specialised seconded national experts (SNEs).

The High Representative shall adopt rules, equivalent to those laid down in Council Decision 2003/479/EC of 16 June 2003 concerning the rules applicable to national experts and military staff on secondment to the General Secretariat of the Council, under which SNEs are put at the disposal of the EEAS in order to provide specialised expertise.

4. The staff of the EEAS shall carry out their duties and conduct themselves solely with the interests of the Union in mind. Without prejudice to the third indent of Article 2(1) and Articles 2(2) and 5(3), they shall neither seek nor take instructions from any government, authority, organisation or person outside the EEAS or from any body or person other than the High Representative. In accordance with the second paragraph of Article 11 of the Staff Regulations, EEAS staff shall not accept any payments of any kind whatever from any other source outside the EEAS.

5. The powers conferred on the appointing authority by the Staff Regulations and on the authority authorised to conclude contracts by the CEOS shall be vested in the High Representative, who may delegate those powers inside the EEAS.

6. Recruitment to the EEAS shall be based on merit whilst ensuring adequate geographical and gender balance. The staff of the EEAS shall comprise a meaningful presence of nationals from all the Member States. The review provided for in Article 13(3) shall also cover this issue, including, as appropriate, suggestions for additional specific measures to correct possible imbalances.

7. Officials of the Union and temporary agents coming from the diplomatic services of the Member States shall have the same rights and obligations and be treated equally, in particular as concerns their eligibility to assume all positions under equivalent conditions. No distinction shall be made between temporary agents coming from national diplomatic services and officials of the Union as regards the assignment of duties to perform in all areas of activities and policies implemented by the EEAS. In accordance with the provisions of the Financial Regulation, the Member States shall support the Union in the enforcement of financial liabilities of EEAS temporary agents coming from the Member States' diplomatic services which result from a liability under Article 66 of the Financial Regulation.

8. The High Representative shall establish the selection procedures for EEAS staff, which shall be undertaken through a transparent procedure based on merit with the objective of securing the services of staff of the highest standard of ability, efficiency and integrity, while ensuring adequate geographical and gender balance, and a meaningful presence of nationals from all Member States in the EEAS. Representatives of the Member States, the General Secretariat of the Council and of the Commission shall be involved in the recruitment procedure for vacant posts in the EEAS.

9. When the EEAS has reached its full capacity, staff from Member States, as referred to in the first subparagraph of paragraph 2, should represent at least one third of all EEAS

staff at AD level. Likewise, permanent officials of the Union should represent at least 60 % of all EEAS staff at AD level, including staff coming from the diplomatic services of the Member States who have become permanent officials of the Union in accordance with the provisions of the Staff Regulations. Each year, the High Representative shall present a report to the European Parliament and the Council on the occupation of posts in the EEAS.

10. The High Representative shall lay down the rules on mobility so as to ensure that the members of the staff of the EEAS are subject to a high degree of mobility. Specific and detailed arrangements shall apply to the personnel referred to in the third indent of Article 4(3)(a). In principle, all EEAS staff shall periodically serve in Union delegations. The High Representative shall establish rules to that effect.

11. In accordance with the applicable provisions of its national law, each Member State shall provide its officials who have become temporary agents in the EEAS with a guarantee of immediate reinstatement at the end of their period of service to the EEAS. This period of service, in accordance with the provisions of Article 50b of the CEOS, shall not exceed eight years, unless, it is extended for a maximum period of two years in exceptional circumstances and in the interest of the service.

Officials of the Union serving in the EEAS shall have the right to apply for posts in their institution of origin on the same terms as internal applicants.

12. Steps shall be taken in order to provide EEAS staff with adequate common training, building in particular on existing practices and structures at national and Union level. The High Representative shall take appropriate measures to that effect within the year following the entry into force of this Decision.

[...]

Article 8

Budget

1. The duties of authorising officer for the EEAS section of the general budget of the European Union shall be delegated in accordance with Article 59 of the Financial Regulation. The High Representative shall adopt the internal rules for the management of the administrative budget lines. Operational expenditure shall remain within the Commission section of the budget.

2. The EEAS shall exercise its powers in accordance with the Financial Regulation applicable to the general budget of the European Union within the limits of the appropriations allocated to it.

3. When drawing up estimates of administrative expenditure for the EEAS, the High Representative will hold consultations with, respectively, the Commissioner responsible for Development Policy and the Commissioner responsible for Neighbourhood Policy regarding their respective responsibilities.

4. In accordance with Article 314(1) TFEU, the EEAS shall draw up estimates of its expenditure for the following financial year. The Commission shall consolidate those estimates in a draft budget, which may contain different estimates. The Commission may amend the draft budget as provided for in Article 314(2) TFEU.

5. In order to ensure budgetary transparency in the area of external action of the Union, the Commission will transmit to the budgetary authority, together with the

draft general budget of the European Union, a working document presenting, in a comprehensive way, all expenditure related to the external action of the Union.

6. The EEAS shall be subject to the procedures regarding the discharge provided for in Article 319 TFEU and in Articles 145 to 147 of the Financial Regulation. The EEAS will, in this context, fully cooperate with the institutions involved in the discharge procedure and provide, as appropriate, the additional necessary information, including through attendance at meetings of the relevant bodies.

Article 9

External action instruments and programming

1. The management of the Union's external cooperation programmes is under the responsibility of the Commission without prejudice to the respective roles of the Commission and of the EEAS in programming as set out in the following paragraphs.

2. The High Representative shall ensure overall political coordination of the Union's external action, ensuring the unity, consistency and effectiveness of the Union's external action, in particular through the following external assistance instruments:
— the Development Cooperation Instrument,
— the European Development Fund,
— the European Instrument for Democracy and Human Rights,
— the European Neighbourhood and Partnership Instrument,
— the Instrument for Cooperation with Industrialised Countries,
— the Instrument for Nuclear Safety Cooperation,
— the Instrument for Stability, regarding the assistance provided for in Article 4 of Regulation (EC) No 1717/2006.

3. In particular, the EEAS shall contribute to the programming and management cycle for the instruments referred to in paragraph 2, on the basis of the policy objectives set out in those instruments. It shall have responsibility for preparing the following decisions of the Commission regarding the strategic, multiannual steps within the programming cycle:

(i) country allocations to determine the global financial envelope for each region, subject to the indicative breakdown of the multiannual financial framework. Within each region, a proportion of funding will be reserved for regional programmes;

(ii) country and regional strategic papers;

(iii) national and regional indicative programmes.

In accordance with Article 3, throughout the whole cycle of programming, planning and implementation of the instruments referred to in paragraph 2, the High Representative and the EEAS shall work with the relevant members and services of the Commission without prejudice to Article 1(3). All proposals for decisions will be prepared by following the Commission's procedures and will be submitted to the Commission for adoption.

4. With regard to the European Development Fund and the Development Cooperation Instrument, any proposals, including those for changes in the basic regulations and the programming documents referred to in paragraph 3, shall be prepared jointly by the relevant services in the EEAS and in the Commission under the responsibility of the

Commissioner responsible for Development Policy and shall be submitted jointly with the High Representative for adoption by the Commission.

Thematic programmes, other than the European Instrument for Democracy and Human Rights, the Instrument for Nuclear Safety Cooperation and that part of the Instrument for Stability referred to in the seventh indent of paragraph 2, shall be prepared by the appropriate Commission service under the guidance of the Commissioner responsible for Development Policy and presented to the College of Commissioners in agreement with the High Representative and the other relevant Commissioners.

5. With regard to the European Neighbourhood and Partnership Instrument, any proposals, including those for changes in the basic regulations and the programming documents referred to in paragraph 3, shall be prepared jointly by the relevant services in the EEAS and in the Commission under the responsibility of the Commissioner responsible for Neighbourhood Policy and shall be submitted jointly with the High Representative for adoption by the Commission.

6. Actions undertaken under: the CFSP budget; the Instrument for Stability other than the part referred to in the seventh indent of paragraph 2; the Instrument for Cooperation with Industrialised Countries; communication and public Diplomacy actions, and election observation missions, shall be under the responsibility of the High Representative/the EEAS. The Commission shall be responsible for their financial implementation under the authority of the High Representative in his/her capacity as Vice-President of the Commission. The Commission department responsible for this implementation shall be co-located with the EEAS.

Article 10

Security

1. The High Representative shall, after consulting the Committee referred to in point 3 of Section I of Part II of the Annex to Council Decision 2001/264/EC of 19 March 2001 adopting the Council's security regulations, decide on the security rules for the EEAS and take all appropriate measures in order to ensure that the EEAS manages effectively the risks to its staff, physical assets and information, and that it fulfils its duty of care and responsibilities in this regard. Such rules shall apply to all EEAS staff, and all staff in Union Delegations, regardless of their administrative status or origin.

2. Pending the Decision referred to in paragraph 1:

— with regard to the protection of classified information, the EEAS shall apply the security measures set out in the Annex to Decision 2001/264/EC,

— with regard to other aspects of security, the EEAS shall apply the Commission's Provisions on Security, as set out in the relevant Annex to the Rules of Procedure of the Commission.

3. The EEAS shall have a department responsible for security matters, which shall be assisted by the relevant services of the Member States.

4. The High Representative shall take any measure necessary in order to implement security rules in the EEAS, in particular as regards the protection of classified information and the measures to be taken in the event of a failure by EEAS staff to comply with the security rules. For that purpose, the EEAS shall seek advice from the Security Office

of the General Secretariat of the Council, from the relevant services of the Commission and from the relevant services of the Member States.

Article 11

Access to documents, archives and data protection

1. The EEAS shall apply the rules laid down in Regulation (EC) 1049/2001 of the European Parliament and of the Council of 30 May 2001 regarding public access to European Parliament, Council and Commission documents. The High Representative shall decide on the implementing rules for the EEAS.

2. The Executive Secretary-General of the EEAS shall organise the archives of the service. The relevant archives of the departments transferred from the General Secretariat of the Council and the Commission shall be transferred to the EEAS.

3. The EEAS shall protect individuals with regard to the processing of their personal data in accordance with the rules laid down in Regulation (EC) No 45/2001 of the European Parliament and of the Council of 18 December 2000 on the protection of individuals with regard to the processing of personal data by the Community institutions and bodies and on the free movement of such data. The High Representative shall decide on the implementing rules for the EEAS.

Article 12

Immovable property

1. The General Secretariat of the Council and the relevant Commission services shall take all necessary measures so that the transfers referred to in Article 7 can be accompanied by the transfers of the Council and Commission buildings necessary for the functioning of the EEAS.

2. The terms on which immovable property is made available to the EEAS central administration and to the Union Delegations shall be decided on jointly by the High Representative and the General Secretariat of the Council and the Commission, as appropriate.

Article 13

Final and general provisions

1. The High Representative, the Council, the Commission and the Member States shall be responsible for implementing this Decision and shall take all measures necessary in furtherance thereof.

2. The High Representative shall submit a report to the European Parliament, the Council and the Commission on the functioning of the EEAS by the end of 2011. That report shall, in particular, cover the implementation of Article 5(3) and (10) and Article 9.

3. By mid-2013, the High Representative shall provide a review of the organisation and functioning of the EEAS, which will cover inter alia the implementation of Article 6(6), (8) and (11). The review shall, if necessary, be accompanied by appropriate proposals for the revision of this Decision. In that case, the Council shall, in accordance with Article 27(3) TEU, revise this Decision in the light of the review by the beginning of 2014.

4. This Decision shall enter into force on the date of its adoption. The provisions on financial management and recruitment shall take effect once the necessary

amendments to the Staff Regulations, the CEOS and the Financial Regulation, as well as the amending budget, have been adopted. To ensure a smooth transition, the High Representative, the General Secretariat of the Council and the Commission shall enter into the necessary arrangements, and they shall undertake consultations with the Member States.

5. Within one month after the entry into force of this Decision, the High Representative shall submit to the Commission an estimate of the revenue and expenditure of the EEAS, including an establishment plan, in order for the Commission to present a draft amending budget.

6. This Decision shall be published in the Official Journal of the European Union.

ANNEX
DEPARTMENTS AND FUNCTIONS TO BE TRANSFERRED TO THE EEAS

The following is a list of all the administrative entities to be transferred en bloc to the EEAS. This prejudges neither the additional needs and the allocation of resources to be determined in the overall budget negotiations establishing the EEAS, nor decisions on the provision of adequate staff responsible for support functions, nor the linked need for service-level arrangements between the General Secretariat of the Council and the Commission and the EEAS.

1. GENERAL SECRETARIAT OF THE COUNCIL

All staff in the departments and functions listed below shall be transferred en bloc to the EEAS, except for a very limited number of staff to perform the normal tasks of the General Secretariat of the Council in line with the second indent of Article 2(1), and except for certain specific functions which are indicated below:

Policy Unit

CSDP and crisis management structures

— Crisis Management and Planning Directorate (CMPD)
— Civilian Planning and Conduct Capability (CPCC)
— European Union Military Staff (EUMS)
— Departments under the direct authority of DGEUMS
— Concepts and Capability Directorate
— Intelligence Directorate
— Operations Directorate
— Logistics Directorate
— Communications and Information Systems Directorate
— EU Situation Centre (SITCEN)

Exception:

— Staff in the SITCEN supporting the Security Accreditation Authority

Directorate-General E

— Entities placed under the direct authority of the Director-General
— Directorate for the Americas and the United Nations
— Directorate for the Western Balkans, Eastern Europe and Central Asia
— Directorate for Non-Proliferation of Weapons of Mass Destruction
— Directorate for Parliamentary Affairs in the area of CFSP

— New York Liaison Office
— Geneva Liaison Office
Officials of the General Secretariat of the Council on secondment to European Union Special Representatives and CSDP missions

2. COMMISSION (INCLUDING DELEGATIONS)

All staff in the departments and functions listed below shall be transferred en bloc to the EEAS, except for a limited number of staff mentioned below as exceptions.
Directorate-General for External Relations
— All hierarchy posts and support staff directly attached to them
— Directorate A (Crisis Platform and Policy Coordination in CFSP)
— Directorate B (Multilateral Relations and Human Rights)
— Directorate C (North America, East Asia, Australia, New Zealand, EEA, EFTA, San Marino, Andorra, Monaco)
— Directorate D (European Neighbourhood Policy Coordination)
— Directorate E (Eastern Europe, Southern Caucasus, Central Asia Republics)
— Directorate F (Middle East, South Mediterranean)
— Directorate G (Latin America)
— Directorate H (Asia, except Japan and Korea)
— Directorate I (Headquarters resources, information, interinstitutional relations)
— Directorate K (External Service)
— Directorate L (Strategy, Coordination and Analysis)
— Task Force on the Eastern Partnership
— Unit Relex-01 (Audit)
Exceptions:
— Staff responsible for the management of financial instruments
— Staff responsible for the payment of salaries and allowances to staff in delegations
External Service
— All Heads of Delegation and Deputy Heads of Delegation and support staff directly attached to them
— All political sections or cells and staff
— All information and public diplomacy sections and staff
— All administration sections
Exceptions
— Staff responsible for the implementation of financial instruments
Directorate-General for Development
— Directorate D (ACP II – West and Central Africa, Caribbean and OCT) except OCT task force
— Directorate E (Horn of Africa, East and Southern Africa, Indian Ocean and Pacific)
— Unit CI (ACP I: Aid programming and management): Staff responsible for programming
— Unit C2 (Pan-African issues and institutions, governance and migration): Staff responsible for Pan-African relations
— Applicable hierarchy posts and support staff directly attached to them.

The combined effect of the aforementioned changes is, among others, that the Treaties after Lisbon do not recognize any formal role for the rotating Presidency in the international representation of the EU. It should be noted, though, that the arrangements with regard to the representation of the EU abroad, agreed upon before the coming into force of the Lisbon Treaty, continue to apply in third countries where there is no Union Delegation.[1] According to these arrangements, the Member State holding the rotating Presidency will represent the Union there. If the Member State holding the Presidency does not have an accredited resident representative in the third country, the onus of representation will fall on the Member State that will have the following EU Presidency. If that Member State does not have a representative there either, the Union will be represented in rotation for a period of six months by another Member State which has a representation in the third country in accordance with the order in which the Member States are to hold the EU Presidency. Obviously, such cases are few and their number will continue to decrease as the network of Union Delegations grows.

Table 2.1 Depiction of the actors representing the EU internationally[2]

	CFSP	Non-CFSP	
		External action—international agreements (TFEU, Title V)	External aspects of sectoral policies
Heads of state or government level	President of the EU Council	President of the European Commission	
Ministerial level	High Representative	Commissioners (including the High Representative acting as Vice-President)	
Administrative level	European External Action Service (EEAS)	Commission services EEAS HQ services	
In third countries/ at international organizations		EU Delegations	

The post-Lisbon legal framework of the international representation of the Union has given rise to divergent interpretations as to the question on whose behalf the Union actors speak. This problem proved to be particularly acute in international organizations and fora which deal with issues touching on both EU and Member States' competences. In particular, some Member States have maintained that Union actors should make it clear in their statements when they speak on behalf of the EU or on behalf of the EU and its Member States, mirroring the internal allocation of competences.

---

[1] See European External Action Service, EU Diplomatic Representation in Third Countries—Second half of 2012, 14.6.2012, Ares(2012)715024.
[2] Table taken from European Commission, Vademecum on the External Action of the European Union, SEC(2011)881/3, at 17.

This internal debacle led to the blocking of numerous EU statements in multilateral fora.[3] An agreement was reached in October 2011 on internal general arrangements on EU statements in multilateral organizations. However, the European Commission expressed its concerns in this regard in a Declaration issued immediately afterwards. These two documents are to be found below.

Indeed, these arrangements pose a number of practical and legal issues. Not only do they not clarify the situation with respect to the delivery of statements in multilateral fora, but they arguably constitute a backward movement toward the era before Lisbon. The text of the arrangements states that 'Member States agree on a case by case basis whether and how to co-ordinate and be represented externally. The Member States may request EU actors or a Member State, notably the Member State holding the rotating Presidency of the Council, to do so on their behalf.' This passage defies directly the requirement for unity in the external actions of the Union, whereas the reference to a role for the rotating Presidency in the external representation of the Union seems to ignore the letter and spirit of Lisbon. Finally, the 'disclaimer' clarifying that the presentation of statements does not affect the internal division of competences adds little, since according to settled case law of the Court of Justice the Treaties cannot be modified by subsequent practice. Nonetheless, it constitutes another clear indication of the mistrust of EU Member States toward the institutional framework of the Union governing its international representation. It is to be expected that sooner or later these differences will end up before the Court of Justice.

In a number of multilateral fora, Member State delegations are actively involved in a practice of 'burden sharing' with the EU Delegation. This is, for instance, the case in the UN Human Rights Council. This is, though, an 'internal' practice, the delivery of statements being made by the EU representative. On the contrary, in some other multilateral fora, such as the International Atomic Energy Agency (IAEA) in Vienna and the UN Conference on Disarmament in Geneva, the role of the EU representative is limited, with EU Member States often preferring that the rotating Presidency delivers agreed statements.

Council of the European Union, 'EU Statements in multilateral organisations— General Arrangements', 24.10.2011, 15901/11.

At its meeting on 22 October 2011, the Council endorsed the General Arrangements for EU Statements in multilateral organizations as set out in the Annex.

EU Statements in multilateral organisations
General Arrangements
1. This document offers a number of general arrangements with regard to the delivery of EU Statements in multilateral organisations.

---

[3] European External Action Service, Report by the High Representative to the European Parliament, the Council and the Commission, 22/12/2011, para. 17.

2. The Treaty of Lisbon enables the EU to achieve coherent, comprehensive and unified external representation. The EU Treaties provide for close and sincere cooperation between the Member States and the Union. Given the sensitivity of representation and potential expectations of third parties, it is essential that, in conformity with current practice, the preparation of statements relating to the sensitive area of competences of the EU and its Member States should remain internal and consensual.

3. The following arrangements apply

• The EU can only make a statement in those cases where it is competent and there is a position which has been agreed in accordance with the relevant Treaty provisions.

• External representation and internal coordination does not affect the distribution of competences under the Treaties nor can it be invoked to claim new forms of competences.

• Member States and EU actors will coordinate their action in international organisations to the fullest extent possible as set out in the Treaties.

• The EU actors and the Member States will ensure the fullest possible transparency by ensuring that there is adequate and timely prior consultation on statements reflecting EU positions to be made in multilateral organisations.

• Member States agree on a case by case basis whether and how to co-ordinate and be represented externally. The Member States may request EU actors or a Member State, notably the Member State holding the rotating Presidency of the Council, to do so on their behalf.

• Member States will seek to ensure and promote possibilities for the EU actors to deliver statements on behalf of the EU.

• Member States may complement statements made on behalf of the EU whilst respecting the principle of sincere cooperation.

• EU representation will be exercised from behind an EU nameplate unless prevented by the rules of procedure of the forum in question.

• EU actors will conduct local coordination and deliver statements on behalf of the EU unless prevented by the rules of procedure of the forum concerned (default setting). Where practical arrangements such as those at the World Trade Organisation, at the Food and Agricultural Organisation and in burden sharing exist for coordination and/or representation, such arrangements will be implemented for the preparation and delivery of the statement on behalf of the EU from behind the EU nameplate.

4. Practical guidelines:

Statements will reflect EU positions agreed in conformity with the decision making procedures as foreseen in the Treaties.

• Should the statement refer exclusively to actions undertaken by or responsibilities of the EU in the subject matter concerned including in the CFSP, it will be prefaced by 'on behalf of the European Union'.

• Should the statement express a position common to the European Union and its Member States, pursuant to the principle of unity of representation, it will be prefaced by 'on behalf some of the EU and its Member States'. The introduction 'on behalf of the EU and its Member States' does not preclude references to 'the EU' or to 'the Member States of the EU' later in the text, where such reference accurately reflects the factual situation.

Should the Member States agree to collective representation by an EU actor of issues relating to the exercise of national competences, the statement will be prefaced by 'on behalf of the Member States'. The introduction 'on behalf of the Member States' does not preclude references to the 'EU' later in the text, where such reference accurately reflects the factual situation.

5. Disclaimer

The Member States and the Council, the Commission and the EEAS accept the following disclaimer:

'The adoption and presentation of statements does not affect the distribution of competences or the allocation of powers between the institutions under the Treaties. Moreover, it does not affect the decision-making procedures for the adoption of EU positions by the Council as provided in the Treaties'.

6. Should a problem arise in the application of these arrangements that cannot be solved through local coordination, the Head of the EU delegation will refer the matter to the EEAS which will, in close consultation with the Commission, submit when appropriate the matter to Coreper for decision.

7. These arrangements, agreed at Coreper level, are forwarded to the Council for its endorsement. The EEAS and the Commission services will present a report on their implementation at the latest by the end of 2012. In light of this Report, the arrangements could, if so decided by Coreper, be reviewed.

Statement by the Commission to be entered into the minutes of the Council session endorsing the General Arrangements.

The Commission takes note of the Council endorsement on general arrangements for the delivery of EU Statements in multilateral organisations (document 15855/11). These arrangements bring clarity on a number of principles regarding the coordination and external representation of the European Union.

The Commission recalls that the relevant provisions of the treaties provide that the President of the European Council, the Commission, the High Representative for Foreign Affairs and Security Policy and the EU Delegations ensure the external representation of the European Union, regardless of the categories and areas of competence conferred upon the European Union.

The Commission confirms its interpretation of references to 'national competence' as competence not conferred to the European Union.

The Commission also recalls that the practical arrangements currently in place at the World Trade Organisation are not affected by these General Arrangements and that hence the latter do not imply any change in the scope for Member States to make statements on the common commercial policy.

The Commission confirms its intention to review the practical arrangements for the World Trade Organisation and the Food and Agricultural Organisation in due course in order to align them with the Lisbon Treaty.

The Commission reserves the right to use of all legal means at its disposal to ensure the respect of the provisions of the Treaties.

2.4 Diplomatic relations of the EU

Union Delegations and Offices constitute the diplomatic network of the EU abroad. However, questions have arisen regarding their legal status since the EU is not (and cannot be) a party to the Vienna Convention on Diplomatic Relations (VCDR) of 1961,[4] which regulates diplomatic relations, as the VCDR is only open to states (Articles 48 and 50 VCDR). Still, the Union has been successful in securing the protection of this international legal framework and establishing diplomatic relations by mutual consent (Article 2 VCDR).[5]

With regard to the establishment of diplomatic relations, the EEAS Decision determines that the High Representative in agreement with the Council and the European Commission decides on the opening or closing of a Union Delegation (Article 5(1) EEAS Decision). It further tasks the High Representative to negotiate an 'Establishment Agreement' with the third country or international organization that will grant the Union Delegation equivalent diplomatic privileges and immunities as those referred to in the VCDR (Article 5(6) EEAS Decision). As to the diplomatic missions of third countries to the EU, the Union not being legally empowered to accord them diplomatic privileges and immunities. Article 16 of Protocol No. 7 on the privileges and immunities of the EU tasks Belgium, where the EU has its seat, to grant them. It is worth noting here that agreements of the EU with third countries on the activities of CFSP missions in these countries also contain provisions granting these missions diplomatic privileges and immunities. Below we include the relevant articles from the EU–Albania Agreement of 2003 and the EU–Georgia Agreement of 2008 on the activities of the EU Monitoring Missions in these countries. These two examples also illustrate the changes in the language used in such provisions.

In addition, the accreditation procedure of the Head of Delegation follows the practice of states. A 'letter of credence' signed post-Lisbon by both the President of the European Council and the President of the Commission, is submitted to the receiving state or international organization. However, the 'EU Ambassador' does not follow the *ordre protocollaire* of the national heads of missions stipulated in Article 16 VCDR. Rather, his seniority is always after every head of a national mission holding the rank of ambassador. What is more, members of the staff of Union Delegations do not have diplomatic passports but a *laissez-passer* document (Article 6 of Protocol No. 7).

Vienna Convention on Diplomatic Relations 1961

Article 2

The establishment of diplomatic relations between States, and of permanent diplomatic missions, takes place by mutual consent.

[...]

---

[4] Vienna Convention on Diplomatic Relations, signed at Vienna on 18 April 1961, entry into force 24 April 1964, UNTS, vol. 500, p. 95.

[5] See J. Wouters and S. Duquet, The EU and International Diplomatic Law: New Horizons?, *The Hague Journal of Diplomacy*, vol. 7, 2012, 45.

Article 16

1. Heads of mission shall take precedence in their respective classes in the order of the date and time of taking up their functions in accordance with article 13.

2. Alterations in the credentials of a head of mission not involving any change of class shall not affect his precedence.

3. This article is without prejudice to any practice accepted by the receiving State regarding the precedence of the representative of the Holy See.

[...]

Article 48

The present Convention shall be open for signature by all States Members of the United Nations or of any of the specialized agencies Parties to the Statute of the International Court of Justice, and by any other State invited by the General Assembly of the United Nations to become a Party to the Convention, as follows: until 31 October 1961 at the Federal Ministry for Foreign Affairs of Austria and subsequently, until 31 March 1962, at the United Nations Headquarters in New York.

[...]

Article 50

The present Convention shall remain open for accession by any State belonging to any of the four categories mentioned in article 48. The instruments of accession shall be deposited with the Secretary General of the United Nations.

Template of Establishment Agreement

Agreement between the Government
of [the Kingdom/Republic of] XXX and the European
Union on the Establishment and the Privileges and Immunities
of the Delegation of the European Union in [idem] XXX

The Government of [*idem*] XXX and the European Union,
Desirous of further strengthening and developing the friendly relations and co-operation between [*idem*] XXX and the European Union,
Wishing to lay down terms concerning the establishment on the territory of [*idem*] XXX of a Delegation of the European Union and concerning the privileges and immunities of that Delegation, have agreed as follows:

Article 1

The Government of [*idem*] XXX hereby agrees to the establishment on its territory of a Delegation of the European Union.

Article 2

1. The European Union and the European Atomic Energy Community shall each have legal personality on the territory of [*idem*] XXX.

2. The European Union and the EAEC shall have the capacity to conclude contracts, to acquire and dispose of immovable and movable property as necessary

for the effective fulfilment of their duties, in accordance with the procedural and administrative requirements imposed by the law of [*idem*] XXX, and to conduct legal proceedings, and shall be represented for that purpose by the European Commission.

Article 3

1. The Delegation of the European Union, its Head and its members, as well as the members of their families forming part of their respective households, shall, on the territory of [*idem*] XXX, enjoy such rights, privileges and immunities and be subject to such obligations as correspond to those laid down in the Vienna Convention on Diplomatic Relations of 18 April 1961 and respectively accorded to and assumed by Diplomatic Missions accredited to [*idem*] XXX, the heads and members of those Missions, as well as the members of their families forming part of their respective households.
2. The other provisions of the Vienna Convention on Diplomatic Relations of 18 April 1961 shall be applicable *mutatis mutandis*.
3. Those rights and privileges and immunities shall be accorded on condition that, in conformity with the provisions of article 16 of the Protocol 7 on the privileges and immunities of the European Union annexed to the Treaty on the European Union and the Treaty on the Functioning of the European Union, the Member States of the European Union accord the same rights and privileges and immunities to the Mission of [*idem*] XXX, to its Head and to its members, as well as to the members of their families forming part of their respective households.

Article 4

The Government of [*idem*] XXX hereby recognises the *laissez-passer* issued by the European Union to officials and other servants of its institutions as valid travel documents.

Article 5

Any dispute concerning the interpretation of this Agreement shall be settled by consultations between the two Contracting Parties with the aim of arriving at a conciliation.

Article 6

Each Contracting Party shall notify the other of the completion of the respective procedures necessary for the approval of the present Agreement, which will enter into force on the date of reception of the second notification.

IN WITNESS WHEREOF, the undersigned, duly authorised to this effect, have signed this Agreement.

Done at   on   2010.

....
For the Government of   For the European Union
[*idem*] XXX   The HR/VP

Protocol (No 7) on the Privileges and Immunities of the European Union annexed to the Treaty on European Union and the Treaty on the Functioning of the European Union, 26.10.2012, Official Journal of the European Union C 326/266.

Article 6

(ex Article 7)

Laissez-passer in a form to be prescribed by the Council, acting by a simple majority, which shall be recognised as valid travel documents by the authorities of the Member States, may be issued to members and servants of the institutions of the Union by the Presidents of these institutions. These laissez-passer shall be issued to officials and other servants under conditions laid down in the Staff Regulations of Officials and the Conditions of Employment of other servants of the Union.

The Commission may conclude agreements for these laissez-passer to be recognised as valid travel documents within the territory of third countries.

CHAPTER VI

PRIVILEGES AND IMMUNITIES OF MISSIONS OF THIRD COUNTRIES ACCREDITED TO THE EUROPEAN UNION

Article 16

(ex Article 17)

The Member State in whose territory the Union has its seat shall accord the customary diplomatic immunities and privileges to missions of third countries accredited to the Union.

AGREEMENT

between the European Union and Albania on the status of the European Union Monitoring Mission in Albania[6]

[…]

Article 8

Privileges and immunities

1. The EUMM shall be granted the status of a diplomatic mission.
2. Monitors shall be granted, during their mission, the privileges and immunities of Diplomatic Agents, in accordance with the Vienna Convention on Diplomatic Relations.
3. The Mission Office in Tirana, other Offices, and all means of transport of the EUMM shall be inviolable.
4. The privileges and immunities provided for in this article shall be granted to Monitors during their mission, and thereafter, with respect to acts previously performed during their mission.

[6] 10.4.2003, OJ L 93/50.

5. The Host Party shall facilitate all movements of the Head of Mission and personnel of the EUMM. The EUMM shall provide the Host Party with a list of members of the EUMM and inform the Host Party in advance of the arrival and departure of personnel belonging to the EUMM. Personnel belonging to the EUMM shall carry their national passport, as well as an EUMM identity card.

6. The Host Party recognises the right of the Sending Parties and of the EUMM to import, free of duty or other restrictions, equipment, provisions, supplies and other goods required for the exclusive and official use of the EUMM. The Host Party also recognises their right to purchase such items on the territory of the Host Party as well as to export or otherwise dispose of such equipment, provisions, supplies and other goods so purchased or imported. The Host Party also recognises the right of the Monitors to purchase and/or import free of duty or other restrictions items required for their own personal use, and to export such items.

AGREEMENT

between the European Union and Georgia on the status of the European Union Monitoring Mission in Georgia[7]

[...]

Article 6

Privileges and immunities of EUMM Georgia personnel granted by the Host State

1. EUMM Georgia personnel shall not be liable to any form of arrest or detention, in accordance with international law.

2. Papers, correspondence and property of EUMM Georgia personnel shall enjoy inviolability, except in case of measures of execution which are permitted pursuant to paragraph 6 of this Article.

3. EUMM Georgia personnel shall enjoy immunity from the criminal jurisdiction of the Host State under all circumstances. The immunity from criminal jurisdiction of EUMM Georgia personnel may be waived by the Sending State or EU institution concerned, as the case may be. Such waiver must always be express.

4. EUMM Georgia personnel shall enjoy immunity from the civil and administrative jurisdiction of the Host State in respect of words spoken or written and all acts performed by them in the exercise of their official functions. If any civil proceeding is instituted against EUMM Georgia personnel before any Host State court, the Head of Mission and the competent authority of the Sending State or EU institution shall be notified immediately. Prior to initiation of the proceeding before the court, the Head of Mission and the competent authority of the Sending State or EU institution shall certify to the court whether the act in question was

---

[7] 21.11.2008, OJ L 310/31.

committed by EUMM Georgia personnel in the exercise of their official functions. If the act was committed in the exercise of official functions, the proceeding shall not be initiated and the provisions of Article 17 shall apply. If the act was not committed in the exercise of official functions, the proceeding may continue. The certification by the Head of Mission and the competent authority of the Sending State or EU institution is binding upon the jurisdiction of the Host State who may not contest it.

The initiation of proceedings by EUMM Georgia personnel shall preclude them from invoking immunity from jurisdiction in respect of any counter-claim directly connected with the principal claim.

5. EUMM Georgia personnel are not obliged to give evidence as witnesses.

6. No measures of execution may be taken in respect of EUMM Georgia personnel, except in the case where a civil proceeding not related to their official functions is instituted against them. Property of EUMM Georgia personnel, which is certified by the Head of Mission to be necessary for the fulfilment of their official functions, shall be free from seizure for the satisfaction of a judgement, decision or order. In civil proceedings EUMM Georgia personnel shall not be subject to any restrictions on their personal liberty or to any other measures of constraint.

7. The immunity of EUMM Georgia personnel from the jurisdiction of the Host State does not exempt them from the jurisdictions of the respective Sending States.

8. EUMM Georgia personnel shall with respect to services rendered for EUMM Georgia be exempt from social security provisions which may be in force in the Host State.

9. EUMM Georgia personnel shall be exempt from any form of taxation in the Host State on the salary and emoluments paid to them by EUMM Georgia or the Sending States, as well as on any income received from outside the Host State.

10. The Host State shall, in accordance with such laws and regulations as it may adopt, permit entry of and grant exemption from all customs duties, taxes, and related charges other than charges for storage, cartage and similar services, on articles for the personal use of EUMM Georgia personnel. The Host State shall also allow the export of such articles. For goods and services purchased on the domestic market EUMM Georgia personnel shall be exempt from VAT (the price shall not include VAT) and taxes according to the laws of the Host Party.

11. The personal baggage of EUMM Georgia personnel shall be exempt from inspection, unless there are serious grounds for presuming that it contains articles that are not for the personal use of EUMM Georgia personnel, or articles the import or export of which is prohibited by the law or controlled by the quarantine regulations of the Host State. Such inspection shall be conducted only in the presence of the concerned EUMM Georgia personnel or of an authorised representative of EUMM Georgia.

Accreditation Letter

The President of the European Council		The President of the European Commission

to

His Majesty King xxxx
King of xxxx

Your Majesty,

The European Union, desirous of maintaining and strengthening the harmonious relations which exist between the Kingdom of xxxx and the European Union, has decided to accredit to Your Majesty Mr. xxxx YYYY in the quality of Head of the Delegation of the European Union to the Kingdom of xxxx, with residence in the Kingdom of xxxx.

Mr. xxxx YYYY will have the rank and courtesy title of Ambassador.

The personal qualities of Mr. xxxx YYYY, and the zeal and devotion which he has constantly displayed in the discharge of the duties entrusted to him, have convinced us that he will fully merit Your Majesty's approbation and esteem.

In this confidence, we request that Your Majesty will receive Mr. xxx YYYY favourably and will give entire credence to all that he will communicate to Your Majesty in accordance with the instructions of the European Union and especially when he will convey to Your Majesty the assurances of our highest consideration.

Brussels,

Herman VAN ROMPUY   José Manuel BARROSO

The diplomatic functions of Union Delegations resemble those of national diplomatic missions as described in Article 3(1) VCDR. Naturally, though, Union Delegations have to respect the internal allocation of competences and are, therefore, more restricted in their actions in comparison with national missions. Further, Union Delegations and Member States' diplomatic missions abroad have to cooperate (Article 35 TEU), whereas according to Article 5(10) of the EEAS Decision the former have to support the latter 'in their diplomatic relations and in their role of providing consular protection to citizens of the Union in third countries on a resource-neutral basis'.

Vienna Convention on Diplomatic Relations 1961

Article 3

1. The functions of a diplomatic mission consist, inter alia, in:
(a) Representing the sending State in the receiving State;

(b) Protecting in the receiving State the interests of the sending State and of its nationals, within the limits permitted by international law;

(c) Negotiating with the Government of the receiving State;

(d) Ascertaining by all lawful means conditions and developments in the receiving State, and reporting thereon to the Government of the sending State;

(e) Promoting friendly relations between the sending State and the receiving State, and developing their economic, cultural and scientific relations.

Treaty on European Union

Article 35

(ex Article 20 TEU)

The diplomatic and consular missions of the Member States and the Union delegations in third countries and international conferences, and their representations to international organisations, shall cooperate in ensuring that decisions defining Union positions and actions adopted pursuant to this Chapter are complied with and implemented.

They shall step up cooperation by exchanging information and carrying out joint assessments.

They shall contribute to the implementation of the right of citizens of the Union to protection in the territory of third countries as referred to in Article 20(2)(c) of the Treaty on the Functioning of the European Union and of the measures adopted pursuant to Article 23 of that Treaty.

As for the diplomatic correspondence of the EU, this takes place most often through demarches and notes verbales. EU Delegations conduct demarches and transmit notes verbales to the authorities of a third country or to an international organization under the instructions of the Commission for non-CFSP matters and the High Representative for CFSP matters. Thus, as is to be expected, the institutional framework governing the international representation of the Union applies to diplomatic correspondence too. However, if it is in the interest of the Union, the Commission may on an exceptional basis extend an invitation to a number of Member States to join the Union Delegation in making the demarches. Further, the Union Delegation in any event has to debrief the Member States' delegations on the ground in the third country or international organization where the demarche was conducted. As for notes verbales, these may also be transmitted by the Commission or the High Representative, when they are directed to diplomatic missions accredited to the EU. Below are the templates for demarches and notes verbales on non-CFSP matters. In addition to these, a note verbale by the then Directorate-General for External Relations of the Commission—now integrated in the EEAS—to the Republic of South Africa, as well as one by the Ministry of State of Palau to the Commission, are included.

Template for demarche instructions

EU TERMS OF REFERENCE

Instruction to EU Delegation(s)

Request to carry out demarche on [Insert short title]

Scene setter: [A very short explanation of the purpose of the demarche max. 100 words.]

Delivery: [Any appropriate official on the diplomatic list of an EU Delegation, under the authority of the Head of Delegation, can carry out a demarche. Unless there is a specific instruction (e.g. the Head of Delegation should call on the Minister of Foreign Affairs) the Head of Delegation has the discretion to determine who should carry out the demarche and which official(s) in the third country should receive it. **The timeframe** for carrying out the demarche should also be indicated. The participation of MS in carrying out the demarche may be considered in exceptional circumstances. If **MS participation** is envisaged, this should be indicated.]

Key points: [These are the talking points to be delivered. Whenever possible these should be tailored to the country receiving them. The Delegation—or MS Embassy]—carrying out the demarche can leave these points with the third country government official (in the form of a nonpaper, note verbale or aide-memoire etc.—as per local custom) to provide a written record. If MS participation is envisaged, the talking points should include a specific reference to the reason for their presence.]

Defensive points (as needed): [To be provided if counter-arguments are expected.]

Background: [A substantial background briefing is needed, in particular when the main expertise lies in Brussels and not with the Delegation—or MS Embassy representing the EU—]

Template for report on demarche

Report on demarche on [Insert short title]

Summary: [A very short summary on the demarche max. 100 words.]

Details: [The name and level of the official who received the demarche and record of any response. The report should also indicate if MS participated in the demarche.]

Comments: [Analysis of the third country's response by the EU Delegation—or the MS locally representing the EU—]

MS Participation: [Details of any MS participation]

Template I: Note Verbale from Commission service to a third country/international organisation's diplomatic representation accredited to the EU
[for more details, one should refer to the related paragraph of the Vademecum on the external action of the EU]

(header) COM logo

The European Commission presents its compliments to the Embassy / Permanent Mission of [...] and has the honour to [inform / advise / request etc.]

...

The European Commission avails itself of this opportunity to renew to the Embassy / Permanent Mission of [...] the assurances of its highest consideration.

Initial

Stamp

Place, date

(left-hand bottom corner)
Address of the recipient of the Note Verbale

(footer) Contact details of the Commission

Template II: Note Verbale from the Commission transmitted by the EUDEL to the authorities of a host third country or international organisation
[*for more details, one should refer to the related paragraph of the Vademecum on the external action of the EU*]

(header) EU DELEGATION logo

The EU Delegation to [...] presents its compliments to the Ministry of Foreign Affairs / [...] and has the honour to [inform / advise / request etc.]

...

The EU Delegation to [...] avails itself of this opportunity to renew to the Ministry of Foreign Affairs of / [...] the assurances of its highest consideration.

Initial

Stamp

Place, date

(left-hand bottom corner)
Address of the recipient of the Note Verbale

(footer) Contact details of the EU Delegation

COMMISSION OF THE EUROPEAN COMMUNITIES
DIRECTORATE GENERAL I A
EXTERNAL POLITICAL RELATIONS

NOTE VERBALE

The Directorate-General for External Political Relations of the Commission of the European Communities presents its compliments to the Mission of the Republic of South Africa to the European Communities and has the honour to inform the Mission that certain terms contained in the text of the 'Agreement between the Commission of the European Communities and the Government of the Republic of South Africa on the Establishment and the Privileges and Immunities of the Delegation of the European Communities in the Republic of South Africa' (the Agreement) be modified as follows:

'The term "European Union" should be replaced by "European Communities" in Article 2, 3 and 4 of the Agreement';

This modification is necessary to ensure full conformity with Article A of the Treaty on the European Union (Treaty of Maastricht) which provides that the European Union is founded on the <u>European Communities</u>, supplemented by the policies and forms of cooperation established by the Treaty.

The Directorate-General for External Political Relations suggests that these modifications, if acceptable to the Government of the Republic of South Africa, be an integral part of the Agreement and that this be confirmed in writing.

The Directorate-General for External Political Relations has the honour to avail itself of this opportunity to renew to the Mission of the Republic of South Africa the assurance of its highest consideration.

Brussels,

To the Mission of the Republic of South Africa to the European Communities
Rue de la Loi, 26
1040 Bruxelles

MINISTRY OF STATE REPUBLIC OF PALAU

Note 053/MS/99

The Ministry of State of the Republic of Palau presents its compliments to the Commission of the European Communities—Protocol—and has the honor to inform the latter that the Government of the Republic of Palau expresses its wish to establish diplomatic relations between the Republic of Palau and the European Communities.

The Ministry of State of the Republic of Palau avails itself of this opportunity to renew to the Commission of the European Communities—Protocol—the assurance of its highest consideration.

..., REPUBLIC OF PALAU
18 October 1999

2.5 Representation of the EU in judicial proceedings

There is no explicit reference in the EU Treaties regarding the capacity of the EU to subject itself to binding international dispute settlements, nor to who is responsible to represent the Union there. In spite of this, agreements concluded by the Community with third states provided from very early on for the settlement of disputes between the parties by a court, tribunal or through third-party arbitration. Such provisions are to be found among others in the 1963 Association Agreement with Turkey in Article 25(2), the 1994 Agreement establishing the World Trade Organization (WTO) in Annex 2, the United Nations Convention on the Law of the Sea of 10 December 1982 (UNCLOS), to which the EU became party in 1998, as well as in the Euro-Mediterranean Agreement between the European Communities and Morocco of 2000 in Article 86 and the Convention on the Protection and Promotion of the Diversity of Cultural Expressions in Article 25 and the Annex to the Convention, included in Chapter 4.[8] The Court of Justice pronounced itself in this regard in Opinion 1/91, included below.

Opinion of the Court of 14 December 1991, Draft agreement between the Community, on the one hand, and the countries of the European Free Trade Association, on the other, relating to the creation of the European Economic Area, Opinion 1/91, European Court Reports 1991, p. I-6079, paras. 31–35, 40–46.

The Court was asked to give an Opinion on the compatibility of the EEC Treaty with the judicial system that was to be established by the European Economic Area Agreement. The Court found that the Union has the power to submit itself to the jurisdiction of a court created by an agreement to which it is a party. However, the Court insisted on safeguarding the autonomy of the EU legal order in maintaining that it remained the only competent judicial organ to interpret EU law.[9] The Court had the opportunity to restate this in Case C-459/03 in paragraph 123 reproduced in Chapter 5 (see p. 238). The effects of this Opinion are prevalent in Article 111(3) and (4) of the EEA Agreement—included immediately after the excerpts of this Opinion—which the Court subsequently found in its Opinion 1/92 not to infringe on the autonomy of the EU legal order. Extracts of Opinion 1/92 are also included below.

31. The interpretation of the expression 'Contracting Party' which the EEA Court will have to give in the exercise of its jurisdiction will be considered first, followed by the effect of the case-law of that court on the interpretation of Community law.
32. As far as the first point is concerned, it must be observed that the EEA Court has jurisdiction under Article 96(1)(a) of the agreement with regard to the settlement of disputes between the Contracting Parties and that, according to Article 117(1)

---

[8] However, it should be noted that in the latter Convention Art. 25(4) allows parties at the time of ratification, acceptance, approval, or accession to the Convention, to make a declaration that they do not recognize the Conciliation procedure provided for in Art. 5 and the Annex.

[9] See Opinion 1/00 [2002] ECR I-3493, paras. 12–13.

of the agreement, the EEA Joint Committee or a Contracting Party may bring such a dispute before the EEA Court.

33. The expression 'Contracting Parties' is defined in Article 2(c) of the agreement. As far as the Community and its Member States are concerned, it covers the Community and the Member States, or the Community, or the Member States, depending on the case. Which of the three possibilities is to be chosen is to be deduced in each case from the relevant provisions of the agreement and from the respective competences of the Community and the Member States as they follow from the EEC Treaty and the ECSC Treaty.

34. This means that, when a dispute relating to the interpretation or application of one or more provisions of the agreement is brought before it, the EEA Court may be called upon to interpret the expression 'Contracting Party', within the meaning of Article 2(c) of the agreement, in order to determine whether, for the purposes of the provision at issue, the expression 'Contracting Party' means the Community, the Community and the Member States, or simply the Member States. Consequently, the EEA Court will have to rule on the respective competences of the Community and the Member States as regards the matters governed by the provisions of the agreement.

35. It follows that the jurisdiction conferred on the EEA Court under Article 2(c), Article 96(1)(a) and Article 117(1) of the agreement is likely adversely to affect the allocation of responsibilities defined in the Treaties and, hence, the autonomy of the Community legal order, respect for which must be assured by the Court of Justice pursuant to Article 164 of the EEC Treaty. This exclusive jurisdiction of the Court of Justice is confirmed by Article 219 of the EEC Treaty, under which Member States undertake not to submit a dispute concerning the interpretation or application of that treaty to any method of settlement other than those provided for in the Treaty. Article 87 of the ECSC Treaty embodies a provision to the same effect.

[...]

40. An international agreement providing for such a system of courts is in principle compatible with Community law. The Community's competence in the field of international relations and its capacity to conclude international agreements necessarily entails the power to submit to the decisions of a court which is created or designated by such an agreement as regards the interpretation and application of its provisions.

41. However, the agreement at issue takes over an essential part of the rules—including the rules of secondary legislation—which govern economic and trading relations within the Community and which constitute, for the most part, fundamental provisions of the Community legal order.

42. Consequently, the agreement has the effect of introducing into the Community legal order a large body of legal rules which is juxtaposed to a corpus of identically-worded Community rules.

43. Furthermore, in the preamble to the agreement and in Article 1, the Contracting Parties express the intention of securing the uniform application of the provisions of the agreement throughout their territory. However, the objective of uniform application and equality of conditions of competition which is pursued in this way

and reflected in Article 6 and Article 104(1) of the agreement necessarily covers the interpretation both of the provisions of the agreement and of the corresponding provisions of the Community legal order.

44. Although, under Article 6 of the agreement, the EEA Court is under a duty to interpret the provisions of the agreement in the light of the relevant rulings of the Court of Justice given prior to the date of signature of the agreement, the EEA Court will no longer be subject to any such obligation in the case of decisions given by the Court of Justice after that date.

45. Consequently, the agreement's objective of ensuring homogeneity of the law throughout the EEA will determine not only the interpretation of the rules of the agreement itself but also the interpretation of the corresponding rules of Community law.

46. It follows that in so far as it conditions the future interpretation of the Community rules on free movement and competition the machinery of courts provided for in the agreement conflicts with Article 164 of the EEC Treaty and, more generally, with the very foundations of the Community.

Agreement on the European Economic Area, Official Journal L 1, 3.1.1994, p. 3.

Section 3
Settlement of disputes
Article 111

1. The Community or an EFTA State may bring a matter under dispute which concerns the interpretation or application of this Agreement before the EEA Joint Committee in accordance with the following provisions.

2. The EEA Joint Committee may settle the dispute. It shall be provided with all information which might be of use in making possible an in-depth examination of the situation, with a view to finding an acceptable solution. To this end, the EEA Joint Committee shall examine all possibilities to maintain the good functioning of the Agreement.

3. If a dispute concerns the interpretation of provisions of this Agreement, which are identical in substance to corresponding rules of the Treaty establishing the European Economic Community and the Treaty establishing the European Coal and Steel Community and to acts adopted in application of these two Treaties and if the dispute has not been settled within three months after it has been brought before the EEA Joint Committee, the Contracting Parties to the dispute may agree to request the Court of Justice of the European Communities to give a ruling on the interpretation of the relevant rules.

   If the EEA Joint Committee in such a dispute has not reached an agreement on a solution within six months from the date on which this procedure was initiated or if, by then, the Contracting Parties to the dispute have not decided to ask for a ruling by the Court of Justice of the European Communities, a Contracting Party may, in order to remedy possible imbalances,

– either take a safeguard measure in accordance with Article 112(2) and following the procedure of Article 113;

– or apply Article 102 mutatis mutandis.

4. If a dispute concerns the scope or duration of safeguard measures taken in accordance with Article 111(3) or Article 112, or the proportionality of rebalancing measures taken in accordance with Article 114, and if the EEA Joint Committee after three months from the date when the matter has been brought before it has not succeeded to resolve the dispute, any Contracting Party may refer the dispute to arbitration under the procedures laid down in Protocol 33. No question of interpretation of the provisions of this Agreement referred to in paragraph 3 may be dealt with in such procedures. The arbitration award shall be binding on the parties to the dispute.

Opinion of the Court of 10 April 1992, Draft agreement between the Community, on the one hand, and the countries of the European Free Trade Association, on the other, relating to the creation of the European Economic Area, Opinion 1/92, European Court Reports 1992, p. I-2821, para. 36.

36. As for the arbitration procedures, it is sufficient to observe that, according to Article 111(4) of the agreement, no question of interpretation of provisions of the agreement which are identical to provisions of Community law may be dealt with by such procedures. It follows that the settlement of disputes by arbitration is not liable adversely to affect the autonomy of the Community legal order.

As for the representation of the EU in international dispute settlement mechanisms, this has become the prerogative of the Commission through practice and has at times been affirmed in secondary legislation of the Union.[10] Still, in light of the fact that the EU is more often than not party to mixed bilateral or multilateral agreements, the Commission has to coordinate with EU Member States in order to determine the appropriate defendant in each case before a third-party dispute settlement. In practice, the Legal Service of the European Commission represents the Union in international litigations, whereas it coordinates with Member States and further provides them with expertise on the few occasions that the latter find themselves to be defendants alone or together with the EU.

  With regard to the particular case of the ICJ, the EU has no formal standing before it. According to Article 34(1) of the ICJ Statute only States have standing before the Court. However, since 2005 Article 43(2) of the Rules of Court allows the EU under specific conditions to intervene in a contentious case after an invitation by the ICJ. The Union can, of course, like any other international organization present its views to the Court

---

[10] See F. Hoffmeister, The European Union and the Peaceful Settlement of International Disputes, *Chinese Journal of International Law*, vol. 11(1), 2012, 80–1.

in advisory proceedings pursuant to Article 66(2) of the Statute of the Court. Immediately below are the aforementioned articles from the Statute and the Rules of the Court, as well as from a passage in the judgment of the ICJ in the *Romania v. Ukraine* case that refers to the new avenue opened to the EU pursuant to Article 43(2) of the Rules of Court.[11]

STATUTE OF THE INTERNATIONAL COURT OF JUSTICE

[...]

CHAPTER II—COMPETENCE OF THE COURT

Article 34

1. Only states may be parties in cases before the Court.

[...]

CHAPTER IV—ADVISORY OPINIONS

[...]

Article 66

[...]

2. The Registrar shall also, by means of a special and direct communication, notify any state entitled to appear before the Court or international organization considered by the Court, or, should it not be sitting, by the President, as likely to be able to furnish information on the question, that the Court will be prepared to receive, within a time-limit to be fixed by the President, written statements, or to hear, at a public sitting to be held for the purpose, oral statements relating to the question.

[...]

RULES OF COURT

Article 43

[...]

2. Whenever the construction of a convention to which a public international organization is a party may be in question in a case before the Court, the Court shall consider whether the Registrar shall so notify the public international organization concerned. Every public international organization notified by the Registrar may submit its observations on the particular provisions of the convention the construction of which is in question in the case.

[...]

---

[11] The Court had already referred to this novelty in para. 4 of its judgment of 8 October 2007 in the Case concerning Territorial and Maritime Dispute Between Nicaragua and Honduras in the Caribbean Sea (*Nicaragua v. Honduras*). However, in that judgment it inaccurately referred to the EU instead of the then EC. This mistake is illuminating of the difficulty facing international organizations and third states when trying to understand the complex structure and allocation of competences of the Union. In the case included here, the ICJ corrected its prior mistake.

International Court of Justice, Case concerning delimitation in the Black Sea (Romania v. Ukraine), Judgment of 3 February 2009, para. 3.

3. Pursuant to the instructions of the Court under Article 43 of the Rules of Court, the Registrar addressed to States parties to the United Nations Convention on the Law of the Sea of 10 December 1982 the notifications provided for in Article 63, paragraph 1, of the Statute of the Court. In addition, the Registrar addressed to the European Community, which is also party to that Convention, the notification provided for in Article 43, paragraph 2, of the Rules of Court, as adopted on 29 September 2005, and asked that organization whether or not it intended to furnish observations under that provision. In response, the Registrar was informed that the European Community did not intend to submit observations in the case.

Select Bibliography

Hoffmeister, F., The European Union and the Peaceful Settlement of International Disputes, *Chinese Journal of International Law*, vol. 11(1), 2012, 77–105.

—— and Ondrusek, P., The European Community in International Litigation, *Revue Héllenique de Droit International*, vol. 61, 2008, 205–24.

Lieb, J., von Ondarza, N., and Schwarzer, D. (eds), *The European Union in International Fora: Lessons for the Union's External Representation after Lisbon*, (Baden-Baden: Nomos, 2011).

Martenczuk, B., The External Representation of the European Union: From Fragmentation to a Single European Voice? *Frieden in Freiheit: Festschrift für Michael Bothe zum 70. Geburtstag* (A. Fischer-Lescano, H.-P. Gasser, T. Marauhn, and N. Ronzitti (eds), Baden-Baden: Nomos, 2008) 941–56.

Wouters, J. and Duquet, S., The EU and International Diplomatic Law: New Horizons?, *The Hague Journal of Diplomacy*, vol. 7, 2012, 31–49.

3

Treaty-making Procedures

3.1 Historical evolution

In this chapter, we discuss the provisions governing the internal procedure for the negotiation, signing, and conclusion of international agreements by the Union. We also make reference to non-legally binding agreements, which are prevalent in the external relations of the EU. The Rome Treaty endowed the European Economic Community (EEC) with the power to conclude trade agreements (Article 113 EEC) or association agreements (Article 238 EEC), but also contained a general treaty-making clause (Article 228 EEC). Whereas the former two provisions remained largely unchanged over the years, the general clause was updated several times. With the Treaty of Amsterdam (1997), the renumbered Article 300 EC had thus become the central norm. It laid down the procedures for the negotiation, signing, and conclusion of international agreements between the Community and one or more states or international organizations.

In parallel, under the three-pillar structure of the EU since the Treaty of Maastricht (1992), new provisions on agreements falling under the Common Foreign and Security Policy (CFSP) (Article 24 TEU) or under Justice and Home Affairs (Article 38 TEU) were added. Also, Article 24 TEU was modified with the Treaties of Amsterdam (1997) and Nice (2000), making it clear that such treaties are negotiated by the Member State holding the rotating Presidency of the Council and concluded by the Council itself (as an institution and not as a meeting of representatives of the Member States) on behalf of the EU. In 2000–09, treaty-making had therefore different legal bases for the first pillar, on the one hand, and for the second and third pillars, on the other hand.

The Treaty of Lisbon did away with this distinction. Nowadays, Article 218 TFEU is the sole provision on treaty-making of the Union. However, the subject matter of the envisaged agreement will still play a role, in order to ascertain the legal basis for the Union to conclude it and to identify the respective powers of the institutions in this process. Thus, Article 207 TFEU (ex-Article 133 TEC) on common commercial policy and Article 209 (ex-Article 179 TEC) on development cooperation introduce special provisions to the single negotiation procedure. Further, Article 219 TFEU (ex-Article 111 TEC) expressly maintains the derogation to the 218 TFEU procedure when it comes to agreements on monetary policies.[1]

---

[1] Other Treaty provisions allowing for the Union to conclude international agreements are: Art. 8(2) TEU (general provision on agreements with neighbouring countries, aiming to establish an area of prosperity and good neighbourliness), Art. 37 TEU (CFSP), Art. 79(3) TFEU (readmission), Art. 186 2nd para. TFEU (research and technological development and space), Art. 191(4) 1st subpara. TFEU (environment), Art. 212(3) 1st subpara. TFEU (economic, financial, and technical cooperation with third countries), and Art. 214(4) 1st subpara. TFEU (humanitarian aid).

The old Article 310 EC (ex-Article 238 EEC) became Article 217 TFEU, and Article 216 TFEU provides for the different scenarios of the Union's treaty-making power.[2]

Treaty on the Functioning of the European Union
Article 218

1. Without prejudice to the specific provisions laid down in Article 207, agreements between the Union and third countries or international organisations shall be negotiated and concluded in accordance with the following procedure.

2. The Council shall authorise the opening of negotiations, adopt negotiating directives, authorize the signing of agreements and conclude them.

3. The Commission, or the High Representative of the Union for Foreign Affairs and Security Policy where the agreement envisaged relates exclusively or principally to the common foreign and security policy, shall submit recommendations to the Council, which shall adopt a decision authorizing the opening of negotiations and, depending on the subject of the agreement envisaged, nominating the Union negotiator or the head of the Union's negotiating team.

4. The Council may address directives to the negotiator and designate a special committee in consultation with which the negotiations must be conducted.

5. The Council, on a proposal by the negotiator, shall adopt a decision authorising the signing of the agreement and, if necessary, its provisional application before entry into force.

6. The Council, on a proposal by the negotiator, shall adopt a decision concluding the agreement. Except where agreements relate exclusively to the common foreign and security policy, the Council shall adopt the decision concluding the agreement:

(a) after obtaining the consent of the European Parliament in the following cases:

(i) association agreements;

(ii) agreement on Union accession to the European Convention for the Protection of Human Rights and Fundamental Freedoms;

(iii) agreements establishing a specific institutional framework by organising cooperation procedures;

(iv) agreements with important budgetary implications for the Union;

(v) agreements covering fields to which either the ordinary legislative procedure applies, or the special legislative procedure where consent by the European Parliament is required.

The European Parliament and the Council may, in an urgent situation, agree upon a time-limit for consent.

(b) After consulting the European Parliament in other cases. The European Parliament shall deliver its opinion within a time-limit which the Council may set depending on the urgency of the matter. In the absence of an opinion within that time-limit, the Council may act.

7. When concluding an agreement, the Council may, by way of derogation from paragraphs 5, 6 and 9, authorise the negotiator to approve on the Union's behalf

---

[2] See Chapter 1.

modifications to the agreement where it provides for them to be adopted by a simplified procedure or by a body set up by the agreement. The Council may attach specific conditions to such authorisation.

8. The Council shall act by a qualified majority throughout the procedure. However, it shall act unanimously when the agreement covers a field for which unanimity is required for the adoption of a Union act as well as for association agreements and the agreements referred to in Article 212 with the States which are candidates for accession. The Council shall also act unanimously for the agreement on accession of the Union to the European Convention for the Protection of Human Rights and Fundamental Freedoms; the decision concluding this agreement shall enter into force after it has been approved by the Member States in accordance with their respective constitutional requirements.

9. The Council, on a proposal from the Commission or the High Representative of the Union for Foreign Affairs and Security Policy, shall adopt a decision suspending application of an agreement and establishing the positions to be adopted on the Union's behalf in a body set up by an agreement, when that body is called upon to adopt acts having legal effects, with the exception of acts supplementing or amending the institutional framework of the agreement.

10. The European Parliament shall be immediately and fully informed at all stages of the procedure.

11. A Member State, the European Parliament, the Council or the Commission may obtain the opinion of the Court of Justice as to whether an agreement envisaged is compatible with the Treaties. Where the opinion of the Court is adverse, the agreement envisaged may not enter into force unless it is amended or the Treaties are revised.

3.2 Negotiations

Under Article 218(3) TFEU, the first step is a recommendation from the Commission (or the High Representative of the Union for Foreign Affairs and Security Policy when the envisaged agreement relates exclusively or principally to CFSP) to the Council. The latter shall authorize the Commission (or the High Representative for CFSP agreements) to open the necessary negotiations (Article 218(2) TFEU). The negotiator shall conduct these negotiations in consultation with special committees appointed by the Council to assist him in this task and within the framework of such directives as the Council may issue to him (Article 218(4) TFEU). The recommendation is a confidential document (EU-restricted) in which the negotiator explains to the Council the background and Union interests for the negotiations.

Once the Council has adopted the negotiation directives to the negotiator (by a non-published decision), the latter negotiates on behalf of the Union with the third state in question.[3] The negotiations are usually finalized when the chief negotiators initial a common text. Initialling by a representative of the Commission or the High Representative for the Union is covered by the negotiating directives.

---

[3] For negotiations with and accession to international organizations, see Chapter 5.

Recommendation from the Commission to the Council to authorise the Commission to open negotiations of a plurilateral anti-counterfeiting trade agreement, 27.2.2008, SEC(2008) 255 final.

A. EXPLANATORY MEMORANDUM

1. The protection of intellectual property rights (IPR) is important not only for promoting innovation and creativity, but also for developing employment and improving competitiveness. It should allow the inventor or creator to derive a legitimate profit from his/her invention or creation while maintaining an appropriate balance between protection and access to intellectual property, exclusive rights and competition. It should also allow the widest possible dissemination of works, ideas and new know-how. At the same time, it should not hamper freedom of expression, the free movement of information, or the protection of personal data.

2. However, without effective means of enforcing intellectual property rights, innovation and creativity are discouraged and investment diminished. It is therefore necessary to ensure that the substantive law on intellectual property, which is nowadays largely part of the *acquis communautaire*, is applied and enforced effectively internationally.

3. The proliferation of infringements of intellectual property rights poses an ever increasing threat to the sustainable development of the world economy. The consequences of such infringements include (1) depriving legitimate businesses and their workers of income; (2) discouraging innovation and creativity; (3) threatening consumer health and safety; (4) providing an easy source of revenue for organized crime; and (5) loss of tax revenue.

4. At international level, all Member States, as well as the Community itself as regards matters within its competence, are bound by the Agreement on Trade-Related Aspects of Intellectual Property (the TRIPS Agreement), approved, as part of the multilateral negotiations of the Uruguay Round, by Council Decision 94/800/EC(3) and concluded in the framework of the World Trade Organisation (WTO).

5. The TRIPs Agreement contains, in particular, provisions on the means of enforcing intellectual property rights, which are minimum common standards applicable at international level and implemented in all Member States.

6. There are also international conventions to which all Member States are parties and which also contain provisions on the means of enforcing intellectual property rights. These include, in particular, the Paris Convention for the Protection of Industrial Property, the Berne Convention for the Protection of Literary and Artistic Works, and the Rome Convention for the Protection of Performers, Producers of Phonograms and Broadcasting Organisations.

7. Having identified IPR as one of their key competitive assets, there is a growing concern in the European Union, as well as in several other countries, about the increasing misappropriation of the intellectual property of their most competitive industries around the world. This led to a number of initiatives on the multilateral (WTO, G8, Organisation for Economic Co-operation and Development (OECD), World Health Organisation (WHO)), bilateral (Free Trade Agreements with high IPR standards, IPR dialogues, technical assistance) and even unilateral (US 301

Special, EU Priority countries' list) fields. In the last few months, there have been new calls for a strengthening of the international IPR framework, namely in the framework of the G8 and the OECD.

8. The main proposal for the strengthening of IPR enforcement practices and rules is an initiative presented by the United States of America and Japan for a new Anti-Counterfeiting Trade Agreement (ACTA).

9. ACTA will establish, among nations committed to strong IPR protection, a common standard for IPR enforcement to combat global infringements of intellectual property rights by increasing international cooperation and coordination among enforcement authorities, promoting technical assistance and partnerships with industry, defining the framework of practices that contribute to effective enforcement of IPRs, and strengthening relevant IPR enforcement measures themselves. This last chapter should include provisions on civil, criminal and customs measures, as well as procedural rules. It also includes provisions on dispute settlement. ACTA's enforcement measures will apply, at least to those IP rights covered by Part III (Enforcement of IPR) of the TRIPs Agreement. However, it is not foreseen to include in the scope of ACTA any rules regarding the substantive protection of intellectual property rights.

10. It is important for the European Union to be at the forefront of efforts to improve IPR enforcement and to work with other partners to make them as effective as possible. It would be politically damaging to do otherwise. Joining the ACTA negotiating process will send a strong message of our concern for the key competitiveness tool that is IPR. But, more importantly, it will have positive effects on the situation in the field, resulting from the increased level of cooperation between enforcement authorities and from the harmonised high standards of IPR enforcement.

B. RECOMMENDATION

In the light of the above, the Commission hereby recommends:

- that the Council authorise the Commission to negotiate a plurilateral Anti-Counterfeiting Trade Agreement.
- that the Presidency of the Council of the European Union, on behalf of the Member States, be associated to the negotiations as specified in the attached negotiating directives.
- that the Council appoint a special committee to assist in this task, and;
- that the Council issue the appended negotiating directives.

ANNEX

DIRECTIVES FOR THE NEGOTIATION BY THE COMMISSION OF A PLURILATERAL ANTI-COUNTERFEITING TRADE AGREEMENT

Vehicle

1. A plurilateral Anti-Counterfeiting Trade Agreement.

Parties

2. In the initial phase, ACTA will be negotiated among a number of interested trading partners in setting out the parameters for an enforcement system that will fight

IPR infringements effectively. Preliminary contacts have taken place between the United States of America, Japan, Canada, Switzerland and the European Union.

3. At a second phase, but still before the launch of the negotiations, it is intended to outreach to other developed and developing countries sharing the concerns of the above mentioned partners. ACTA will be negotiated among this enlarged group of countries. Mexico, South Korea, Australia, New Zealand, Uruguay, Morocco and Singapore have participated in preparatory meetings.

4. At a third phase, i.e. once ACTA is concluded, other countries would have the option to join the agreement as part of an emerging consensus in favour of a strong IPR enforcement standard.

Provisions

5. Provisions will be organised into three main categories:

5.1 *International Cooperation*: Cooperation among the parties to the agreement is a key component of the agreement—including sharing of information and cooperation between national law enforcement authorities, capacity building and technical assistance and cooperation with the private sector.

5.2. *Enforcement Practices*: It is necessary to establish enforcement practices that promote strong intellectual property protection in coordination with right holders and trading partners. Such 'best practices' would support the respective application of the relevant legal tools by both authorities and right-holders, as outlined by the Legal Framework. Examples: public/private advisory groups; raising of consumer public awareness; fostering of IPR expertise within law enforcement structures; publication information on enforcement procedures and actions; promotion of domestic coordination between enforcement agencies; destruction of IP infringing goods and seizure of implementing materials.

5.3. *Legal Framework*: It is essential to have a strong and modern legal framework so that law enforcement agencies, the judiciary, and private citizens have the most up-to-date tools necessary to effectively bring counterfeiters and pirates to justice. Parties will agree on provisions designed to ensure that authorities and right holders have appropriate tools for strong IPR enforcement, particularly in the following areas:

– Customs enforcement
– Civil and administrative enforcement
– Criminal enforcement
– Specific measures regarding optical disc piracy, Internet distribution and information technology and other means used for the infringement of IPR (including those regarding pharmaceutical products, designs and geographical indications)
– Dispute settlement
– Special measures for developing countries

Structure and organisation of the negotiations

6. The European Commission—on behalf of the European Community and its Member States—will be in charge of the overall negotiations of ACTA. The Commission shall conduct the negotiations in consultation with the Article 133 Committee and other relevant committees, such as the Working Party on Intellectual Property and shall report regularly to these committees on the progress of the negotiations.

7. On matters relating to the determination of:
   - the type and level of criminal penalties to be applied by ACTA parties for infringements of intellectual property rights;
   - dispositions on penal procedural law;
   - dispositions on cooperation between national enforcement authorities extending beyond those foreseen in Community legislation;
   the Presidency of the Council of the European Union, on behalf of the Member States, will be fully associated to the negotiation. On these matters, the negotiating documents shall be established through the Article 133 Committee and other relevant committees, such as the Working Party on Intellectual Property.

Start and conclusion of negotiations

8. It is foreseen to start the formal negotiating process, including all the countries that may have decided to join ACTA after the outreach process in February 2008.
9. The European Commission and Member States will not put deadline constraints ahead of their goal to reach an agreement allowing for the effective improvement of the fight against IPR infringements internationally.

Council Decision of 6 March 2012 authorising the opening of negotiations for an international agreement on the creation of the EU–LAC foundation as an international organisation, 6851/12.

THE COUNCIL OF THE EUROPEAN UNION,
Having regard to the Treaty on the Functioning of the European Union, and in particular Article 218(3) and (4),
Having regard to the recommendation from the European Commission,
Whereas negotiations should be opened with a view to concluding an international agreement on the creation of the EU–LAC Foundation as an international organisation between the European Union and its Member States and the Latin American and Caribbean countries,

HAS ADOPTED THIS DECISION:

Article 1

1 The Commission is hereby authorised to open negotiations for an international agreement on the creation of the EU–LAC Foundation as an international organisation between the European Union and its Member States and the Latin American and Caribbean countries.
2. The negotiations shall be conducted on the basis of the negotiating directives set out in the addendum to this Decision.

Article 2

The Commission is nominated as the Union's negotiator.

Article 3

The negotiations shall be conducted in consultation with the Latin America Working Group (COLAT/AMLAT).

Article 4

This Decision is addressed to the Commission.

3.3 Signature

As any other subject of international law, the Union can choose how to express consent to be bound (compare Articles 11–14 of the 1969 Vienna Convention on the Law of Treaties). The first option is to express consent to be bound by signing the agreement. This was most often done in commercial policy, where the European Parliament did not have to be previously consulted according to Article 300(3) 1st subparagraph EC. In such cases, the Council, acting under Article 300(2) EC, immediately took a decision on the 'conclusion' of the Treaty and empowered a person to sign the Treaty in order to bind the Community internationally.

Council Decision 2007/451/EC of 30 May 2007 approving the conclusion of the Agreement between the European Community and the Government of Ukraine on trade in certain steel products, Official Journal L 178, 6.7.2007, pp. 22–3.

THE COUNCIL OF THE EUROPEAN UNION,
Having regard to the Treaty establishing the European Community, and in particular Article 133, in conjunction with Article 300(2) thereof,
Having regard to the proposal from the Commission,

Whereas:
(1) The Partnership and Cooperation Agreement between the European Communities and their Member States and Ukraine, entered into force on 1 March 1998.
(2) Trade in certain steel products is governed by Title III of that Agreement, with the exception of Article 14 thereof, and by the provisions of an agreement on quantitative arrangements.
(3) For the years 1995 to 2001, trade in certain steel products was the subject of agreements between the Parties, and in 2002, 2003 and up to 19 November 2004 of specific arrangements. A further Agreement was concluded on 19 November 2004 covering the period up to 31 December 2004. Thereafter, an Agreement was concluded covering the period 2005 and 2006.
(4) Council Decision of 13 November 2006 authorised the Commission to open negotiations with a view to renewing the agreements on trade in certain steel products concluded between the European Community, of the one part, and Ukraine, of the other part.
(5) Following that Decision, a new Agreement, covering the period up to 31 December 2007 and the following years, has been negotiated between the Parties.
(6) The Agreement should be approved,

HAS DECIDED AS FOLLOWS:

Article 1

1. The Agreement between the European Community and the Government of Ukraine on trade in certain steel products is hereby approved.

2. The text of the Agreement is attached to this Decision.

Article 2

The President of the Council is hereby authorised to designate the person(s) empowered to sign the Agreement in order to bind the Community.

3.4 Conclusion

Nowadays, under Article 218(6) TFEU, the one-step procedure can only be applied for CFSP agreements (see Council Decision 2011/318/CFSP below). In all other cases, the European Parliament must be either asked for consent or consulted, therefore triggering a two-step procedure on the international level (see Council Decision 2011/118/EU further below). Hence, the Council will first take a decision on signature under Article 218(5), thereby empowering a representative (not necessarily a Commission representative) to sign the authentic text. This act triggers the good faith obligation reflected in Article 18(a) of the Vienna Convention to refrain from acts which would defeat the object and purpose of the agreement.[4] The Union's consent to be bound is, however, only expressed in a second step through an act of approval. As a general rule, the Council takes such decisions on 'conclusion' after consulting the European Parliament according to Article 218(6)(b) TFEU. In five cases, the European Parliament must give its consent (Article 218(6)(a) TFEU). This is true for association agreements, the accession agreement to the European Convention on Human Rights (ECHR), agreements establishing a specific institutional framework by organizing cooperation procedures, agreements having important budgetary implications for the Union,[5] and agreements covering fields to which either the ordinary legislative procedure or the special legislative procedure with consent by the European Parliament applies.

Council Decision 2011/318/CFSP of 31 March 2011 on the signing and conclusion of the Framework Agreement between the United States of America and the European Union on the participation of the United States of America in European Union crisis management operations, Official Journal L 143, 31.5.2011, p. 1.

THE COUNCIL OF THE EUROPEAN UNION,

Having regard to the Treaty on European Union, and in particular Article 37 thereof, and the Treaty on the Functioning of the European Union, and in particular Article 218(5) and (6) thereof,

Having regard to the proposal from the High Representative of the Union for Foreign Affairs and Security Policy (HR),

---

[4] See also Case T-115/94 *Opel Austria GmbH v. Council of the European Union* [1997] ECR II-00039, paras 90–4.

[5] See Case C-189/97 *European Parliament v. Council* [1999] ECR I-4741, paras 29–33.

Whereas:

(1) Conditions regarding the participation of third States in Union crisis management operations should be laid down in an agreement establishing a framework for such possible future participation, rather than defining those conditions on a case-by-case basis for each operation concerned.

(2) Following the adoption of a Decision by the Council on 26 April 2010 authorising the opening of negotiations, the HR negotiated a framework agreement between the United States of America and the European Union on the participation of the United States of America in European Union crisis management operations (the Agreement).

(3) The Agreement should be approved,

HAS ADOPTED THIS DECISION:

Article 1

The Framework Agreement between the United States of America and the European Union on the participation of the United States of America in European Union crisis management operations (the Agreement) is hereby approved on behalf of the Union. The text of the Agreement is attached to this Decision.

Article 2

The President of the Council is hereby authorised to designate the person(s) empowered to sign the Agreement in order to bind the Union.

Article 3

The Agreement shall be applied on a provisional basis as from the date of signature thereof, pending the completion of the procedures for its conclusion.

Article 4

The President of the Council shall, on behalf of the Union, give the notification provided for in Article 10(1) of the Agreement.

Article 5

This Decision shall enter into force on the date of its adoption.

Council Decision 2011/118/EU of 18 January 2011 on the conclusion of the Agreement between the European Union and Georgia on the readmission of persons residing without authorization, Official Journal L 52, 25.2.2011, pp. 45–65.

THE COUNCIL OF THE EUROPEAN UNION,

Having regard to the Treaty on the Functioning of the European Union, and in particular Article 79(3), in conjunction with Article 218(6)(a)(v), thereof,

Having regard to the proposal from the Commission,

Having regard to the consent of the European Parliament,

Whereas:

(1) In accordance with Council Decision 2010/687/EU, the Agreement between the European Union and Georgia on the readmission of persons residing without

authorisation (hereinafter 'the Agreement') was signed, on behalf of the European Union, on 17 June 2010, subject to its conclusion at a later date.

(2) The Agreement should be approved.

(3) The Agreement establishes a Joint Readmission Committee which may adopt its rules of procedure. It is appropriate to provide for a simplified procedure for the establishment of the Union position in this case.

(4) In accordance with Article 3 of Protocol (No 21) on the position of the United Kingdom and Ireland in respect of the Area of Freedom, Security and Justice, annexed to the Treaty on European Union and to the Treaty on the Functioning of the European Union, the United Kingdom has notified its wish to take part in the adoption and application of this Decision.

(5) In accordance with Articles 1 and 2 of Protocol (No 21) on the position of the United Kingdom and Ireland in respect of the Area of Freedom, Security and Justice, annexed to the Treaty on European Union and to the Treaty on the Functioning of the European Union, and without prejudice to Article 4 of that Protocol, Ireland is not taking part in the adoption of this Decision and is not bound by it or subject to its application.

(6) In accordance with Articles 1 and 2 of Protocol (No 22) on the position of Denmark, annexed to the Treaty on European Union and to the Treaty on the Functioning of the European Union, Denmark is not taking part in the adoption of this Decision and is not bound by it or subject to its application,

HAS ADOPTED THIS DECISION:

Article 1

The Agreement between the European Union and Georgia on the readmission of persons residing without authorisation (hereinafter 'the Agreement') is hereby approved on behalf of the Union.

The text of the Agreement is attached to this Decision.

Article 2

The President of the Council shall designate the person empowered to proceed, on behalf of the Union, to the notification provided for in Article 23(2) of the Agreement, in order to express the consent of the Union to be bound by the Agreement.

Article 3

The Commission, assisted by experts from Member States, shall represent the Union in the Joint Readmission Committee established by Article 18 of the Agreement.

Article 4

The position of the Union within the Joint Readmission Committee with regard to the adoption of its rules of procedure as required pursuant to Article 18(5) of the Agreement shall be taken by the Commission after consultation with a special committee designated by the Council.

Article 5

This Decision shall enter into force on the day of its adoption.

In the past, the opening phrase of Article 300(2) EC contained the proviso that the power of the Council to decide on signing, provisional application, and conclusion of Community agreements is 'subject to the powers vested in the Commission'. Such powers were derived from Articles 302 or 303 EC when cooperation with other international organizations takes the form of an international agreement. The Commission's authority to implement the budget under Article 274 EC also allowed it to conclude financial agreements with third states. Further, the Commission powers contained in the Protocol on Privileges and Immunities (1965) were relevant when concluding seat agreements for Commission delegations with third states.

In contrast, the European Court of Justice (ECJ) did not accept that the European Commission would be competent to conclude administrative agreements with third states which produce legal effects for the Community. When France brought an action against the Commission because it had reached an agreement with the US Administration on anti-trust cooperation without implicating the Council, the Court held as follows:

Judgment of the Court of 9 August 1994, French Republic v. Commission of the European Communities, Case C-327/91, European Court Reports 1994, p. I-03641, paras. 26–43.

26. [...] the question is whether the Commission was competent under Community law to conclude such an agreement.

27. As the Court explained in Opinion 1/75 of 11 November 1975 ([1975] ECR 1355), Article 228 uses the expression 'agreement' in a general sense to indicate any undertaking entered into by entities subject to international law which has binding force, whatever its formal designation.

28. Furthermore, as the Advocate General has pointed out in paragraph 37 of his Opinion, Article 228 constitutes, as regards the conclusion of treaties, an autonomous general provision, in that it confers specific powers on the Community institutions. With a view to establishing a balance between those institutions, it provides that agreements between the Community and one or more States are to be negotiated by the Commission and then concluded by the Council, after consulting the European Parliament where required by the Treaty. However, the power to conclude agreements is conferred on the Council 'subject to the powers vested in the Commission in this field'.

29. According to the French Government, those powers vested in the Commission are limited to agreements to be concluded by the Commission for the recognition of Community laissez-passer (Article 7 of the Protocol on the Privileges and Immunities of the European Communities). The French Government acknowledges that those powers may also extend to the conclusion of agreements which it describes as administrative or working agreements and which include, by way of example, the establishment of relations with the organs of the United Nations and the other international organizations referred to in Article 229 of the EEC Treaty.

30. The Commission, relying on what it describes as international administrative agreements, maintains, first, that the exception provided for in Article 228 should

not be interpreted in the restrictive manner suggested by the French Government. It points out that, if those who drafted the Treaty had really sought to limit its power to conclude treaties, the French version of Article 228 would have conferred power on the Council 'sous réserve des compétences attribuées à la Commission' and not 'reconnues à la Commission'.

31. Instead, the use of the term 'reconnues' in the French version shows, according to the Commission, that it may derive its powers from sources other than the Treaty, such as the practices followed by the institutions. Moreover, reasoning by analogy from the third paragraph of Article 101 of the Euratom Treaty, the Commission considers that it can itself negotiate and conclude agreements or contracts whose implementation does not require action by the Council and can be effected within the limits of the relevant budget without giving rise to any new financial obligations on the part of the Community, provided that it keeps the Council informed.

32. That argument cannot be accepted.

33. First, the expression 'sous réserve des compétences reconnues à la Commission' derogates from the rule empowering the Council to conclude international agreements.

34. Second, according to the second subparagraph of Article 4(1) of the EEC Treaty, 'each institution shall act within the limits of the powers conferred upon it by this Treaty'. Consequently, the term 'reconnues' in the French version of Article 228 of the Treaty cannot have any meaning other than 'attribuées'.

35. Third, other language versions of Article 228 use terms suggesting that the powers in question are 'attribuées' rather than 'reconnues'. That is the case in particular as regards the versions in Danish ('som paa dette omraade er tillagt Kommissionen'), German ('der Zustaendigkeit, welche die Kommission auf diesem Gebiet besitzt'), Dutch ('van de aan de Commissie te dezer zake toegekende bevoegheden') and English ('the powers vested in the Commission in this field').

36. Fourth, and in any event, a mere practice cannot override the provisions of the Treaty.

37. It follows from the foregoing that the Commission cannot claim to derive from Article 228 of the Treaty powers analogous to those which it enjoys by virtue of the third paragraph of Article 101 of the Euratom Treaty.

38. First, as the Advocate General has pointed out in paragraph 26 of his Opinion, Article 101 provides for a procedure which is quite different from that referred to in Article 228 of the EEC Treaty.

39. Second, the EEC and the Euratom Treaties were negotiated simultaneously and signed on the same day; accordingly, if those negotiating the two treaties had intended to grant the Commission the same powers, they would have done so expressly.

40. The Commission's final argument against the French Government's plea is that its power to conclude international agreements is all the more clear-cut in the present case, since the EEC Treaty has conferred on it specific powers in the field of competition. Under Article 89 of the Treaty and Regulation No 17 of the Council of 6 February 1962, the first regulation implementing Articles 85 and 86 of the EEC Treaty (OJ, English Special Edition 1959–1962, p. 87), the Commission is entrusted with the task of ensuring the application of the principles laid down in

Articles 85 and 86 of the EEC Treaty and the application of Council Regulation (EEC) No 4064/89 of 21 December 1989 on the control of concentrations between undertakings (OJ 1990 L 257, p. 14).

41. That argument cannot be accepted either. Even though the Commission has the power, internally, to take individual decisions applying the rules of competition, a field covered by the Agreement, that internal power is not such as to alter the allocation of powers between the Community institutions with regard to the conclusion of international agreements, which is determined by Article 228 of the Treaty.

42. The plea alleging lack of competence on the part of the Commission to conclude the Agreement at issue must therefore be upheld.

43. It follows, without there being any need to examine the other pleas relied on by the French Republic, that the act whereby the Commission sought to conclude the Agreement with the United States regarding the application of the competition laws of the European Communities and the United States must be declared void.

Under Article 218(6) TFEU, the general reserve power for the Commission to conclude treaties itself is not maintained. It hence appears that the Council must take conclusion decisions itself, unless it authorizes the Commission to do so, for example under Article 218(7) TFEU relating to modifications of agreements. In contrast, the Treaty of Lisbon did not abolish the Euratom Treaty, which continues to exist as a separate legal entity. Here, it is noteworthy that Article 101(2) of the Euratom Treaty entrusts the Commission with the conclusion of agreements in the nuclear energy field on behalf of the European Atomic Energy Community.

Commission Decision 2006/890/Euratom of 4 December 2006 concerning the conclusion on behalf of the European Atomic Energy Community of a Framework Agreement on a Multilateral Nuclear Environmental Programme in the Russian Federation and of the Protocol on Claims, Legal Proceedings and Indemnification to the Framework Agreement on a Multilateral Nuclear Environmental Programme in the Russian Federation (notified under document number C(2006) 5219), Official Journal L 343, 8.12.2006, pp. 85–6.

THE COMMISSION OF THE EUROPEAN COMMUNITIES,
Having regard to the Treaty establishing the European Atomic Energy Community, and in particular Article 101(2) thereof,

Whereas:
(1) In accordance with the directives adopted by the Council Decision of 10 April 2000, the Commission participated in the negotiations with the Russian Federation on an Agreement on a Multilateral Nuclear Environmental Programme in the Russian Federation and a Protocol on Claims, Legal Proceedings and Indemnification.
(2) A Framework Agreement on a Multilateral Nuclear Environmental Programme in the Russian Federation (MNEPR) and the Protocol on Claims, Legal Proceedings and

Indemnification to the Framework Agreement on a MNEPR were signed in Stockholm on 21 May 2003.

(3) The Framework Agreement was signed by the European Community, the European Atomic Energy Community, Norway, Sweden, Denmark, Finland, Belgium, France, Germany, the United Kingdom, the Netherlands and Russia.

(4) The MNEPR Framework Agreement establishes a multilateral legal framework for nuclear-related projects carried out by western countries in north-west Russia, and the Protocol on Claims, Legal Proceedings and Indemnification aims to settle issues of liability arising from activities undertaken in this context.

(5) The MNEPR is designed to facilitate projects addressing problems regarding radio-active waste and spent nuclear fuel and decommissioning of nuclear submarines and icebreakers in the Russian Federation. It is focusing initially on the north-west region, but the Framework Agreement states that the MNEPR may also apply to projects or any other form of cooperation in other areas of nuclear activities, including nuclear safety, if so agreed by the Parties concerned.

(6) The present bilateral Memorandum of Understanding signed between the European Commission on behalf of the Communities and the Russian Federation in 1995, cover-ing the implementation of the Technical Assistance Programmes in the Field of Nuclear Safety and which address nuclear liability issues will not be applicable to projects under the new Instrument for Nuclear Safety Cooperation.

(7) All the EU Member States which have signed the Framework Agreement have deposited their ratification instruments with the Depositories, the last one being the United Kingdom which ratified the Framework Agreement in April 2006.

(8) The European Atomic Energy Community is now in a position to conclude the MNEPR Framework Agreement,

HAS ADOPTED THIS DECISION:

Sole Article

1. The Framework Agreement on a Multilateral Nuclear Environmental Programme in the Russian Federation and the Protocol on Claims, Legal Proceedings and Indemnification to the Framework Agreement on a Multilateral Nuclear Environmental Programme in the Russian Federation are hereby concluded on behalf of the European Atomic Energy Community.

2. The texts of the Framework Agreement and of the Protocol are attached to this decision. This Decision is addressed to the Member States.

3.5 Provisional application

One drawback of the two-step procedure is that considerable time may lapse between signature and conclusion. In order to bridge this time gap, it is possible to declare pro-visional application of the Agreement in line with Article 25 of the Vienna Convention. In the Union, this decision is solely vested in the Council when taking the decision on signature (Article 218(5) TFEU), whereas the European Parliament is to be subsequently informed about it (Article 218(10) TFEU).

Council Decision 2010/397/EU of 3 June 2010 on the signing, on behalf of the European Union, and on provisional application of the Fisheries Partnership Agreement between the European Union and Solomon Islands, Official Journal L 190, 22.7.2010, pp. 1–2.

THE COUNCIL OF THE EUROPEAN UNION,

Having regard to the Treaty on the Functioning of the European Union, and in particular Article 43(2) in conjunction with Article 218(5) thereof,

Having regard to the proposal from the European Commission,

Whereas:

(1) The Union has negotiated with Solomon Islands a Fisheries Partnership Agreement providing Union vessels with fishing opportunities in the waters over which Solomon Islands has sovereignty or jurisdiction in respect of fisheries.

(2) As a result of those negotiations, a new Fisheries Partnership Agreement was initialled on 26 September 2009.

(3) The Partnership Agreement between the European Community and Solomon Islands on fishing off Solomon Islands is to be repealed and replaced by the new Fisheries Partnership Agreement.

(4) The new Fisheries Partnership Agreement should be signed on behalf of the Union.

(5) In order to guarantee the continuation of fishing activities by Union vessels, it is essential that the new Fisheries Partnership Agreement be applied as quickly as possible. Both parties have therefore initialled an Agreement in the form of an Exchange of Letters providing for the provisional application of the Fisheries Partnership Agreement as from 9 October 2009 pending its entry into force.

(6) It is in the Union's interest to approve the Agreement in the form of an Exchange of Letters on the provisional application of the Fisheries Partnership Agreement,

HAS ADOPTED THIS DECISION:

Article 1

The signing of the Fisheries Partnership Agreement between the European Union and Solomon Islands is hereby approved on behalf of the Union, subject to its conclusion. The text of the Agreement is attached to this Decision.

Article 2

The President of the Council is hereby authorised to designate the person(s) empowered to sign the Agreement on behalf of the Union, subject to its conclusion.

Article 3

The Agreement in the form of an Exchange of Letters on the provisional application of the Fisheries Partnership Agreement between the European Union and Solomon Islands is hereby approved on behalf of the Union.

The text of the said Agreement in the form of an Exchange of Letters is attached to this Decision.

Article 4

The President of the Council is hereby authorised to designate the person(s) empowered to sign the Agreement in the form of an Exchange of Letters on the provisional application of the Fisheries Partnership Agreement in order to bind the Union.

Article 5

This Decision shall enter into force on the day of its adoption.

3.6 Suspension

A decision on the suspension of an agreement, dating back to the time that the relevant Treaty article (Article 224 EEC Treaty) did not yet contain an explicit reference to the possibility of suspension, was taken when the Yugoslav civil war broke out. It intended to have immediate effect on the application of the Cooperation Agreement with Yugoslavia and its associated agreements and Protocols, while the EC started the necessary procedures to denounce these agreements. This decision was taken by the Council alone on the recommendation of the Commission. Under the explicit provision of Article 218(9) of the Lisbon text the procedure remains the same.[6]

Decision of the Council and the Representatives of the Governments of the Member States, meeting within the Council of 11 November 1991 suspending the application of the Agreements between the European Community, its Member States and the Socialist Federal Republic of Yugoslavia, 91/586/ECSC, EEC, OJ L 315, 15.11.1991, p. 47.

Whereas the European Community and its Member States have concluded with the Socialist Federal Republic of Yugoslavia a Cooperation Agreement and related Protocols and Instruments, as well as an Agreement on ECSC products;

Whereas, in their declarations of 5 and 28 October 1991, the European Community and its Member States, meeting within the framework of European Political Cooperation, took note of the crisis in Yugoslavia; whereas the United Nations Security Council expressed, in resolution 713 (1991), the concern that the prolongation of this situation constituted a threat to international peace and security;

Whereas the pursuit of hostilities and their consequences on economic and trade relations, both between the Republics of Yugoslavia and with the Community, constitute a radical change in the conditions under which the Cooperation Agreement between the European Economic Community and the Socialist Federal Republic of Yugoslavia (1) and its Protocols, as well as the Agreement concerning the European Coal and Steel

---

[6] See in this regard Council Decision (2011/523/EU) of 2 September 2011 partially suspending the application of the Cooperation Agreement between the European Economic Community and the Syrian Arab Republic, OJ L 228, 3.9.2011, p. 19 and Council Decision 2012/123/CFSP of 27 February 2012 amending Decision 2011/523/EU partially suspending the application of the Cooperation Agreement between the European Economic Community and the Syrian Arab Republic, OJ L54, 28.2.2012, p. 18.

Community, were concluded; whereas they call into question the application of such Agreements and Protocols;

Whereas the appeal launched by the European Community and its Member States, meeting within the framework of European Political Cooperation on 6 October 1991 at Haarzuilens, calling for compliance with the cease-fire agreement reached in The Hague on 4 October 1991, has not been heeded;

Whereas, in the declaration of 6 October 1991, the European Community and its Member States, meeting within the framework of European Political Cooperation, announced their decision to terminate the Agreements between the Community and Yugoslavia should the agreement reached in the Hague on 4 October 1991 between the parties to the conflict, in the presence of the President of the Council of the European Communities and the President of the Conference on Yugoslavia, not be observed;

Whereas the Community has started the necessary procedures to denounce the above-mentioned Agreements;

On the recommendation of the Commission,

HAVE DECIDED AS FOLLOWS:

1. The application of the abovementioned Agreements is hereby suspended with imme-diate effect.

2. This Decision shall be published in the Official Journal of the European Communities.

As can be deduced from the recitals of the decision, it was based on the customary rule of changed circumstances (*rebus sic stantibus*) in international law. In a case before the European Court of Justice, this basis was tested and not found wanting.

Judgment of the Court of 16 June 1998, A. Racke GmbH & Co. v. Hauptzollamt Mainz, Case C-162/96, European Court Reports 1998, p. I-3655, paras. 23–61.

23. In the light of those considerations, the Bundesfinanzhof decided to stay the pro-ceedings and refer the following questions to the Court of Justice for a preliminary ruling:

'1. Is Council Regulation (EEC) No 3300/91 of 11 November 1991 suspending the trade concessions provided for by the Cooperation Agreement between the European Economic Community and the Socialist Federal Republic of Yugoslavia (OJ 1991 L 315, p. 1) valid?

2. If not, what are the consequences of invalidity as regards customs duty charged in early May 1992 on wines originating in Serbia which were imported between mid-November 1991 and April 1992 and cleared for warehousing in a customs warehouse?

Are the quota-related preferential customs duties granted in 1992 for wines from the territory of the former Yugoslavia other than Serbia applicable in that respect?'

Question 1

24. By way of a preliminary observation, it should be noted that even though the Vienna Convention does not bind either the Community or all its Member States,

a series of its provisions, including Article 62, reflect the rules of international law which lay down, subject to certain conditions, the principle that a change of circumstances may entail the lapse or suspension of a treaty. Thus the International Court of Justice held that '[t]his principle, and the conditions and exceptions to which it is subject, have been embodied in Article 62 of the Vienna Convention on the Law of Treaties, which may in many respects be considered as a codification of existing customary law on the subject of the termination of a treaty relationship on account of change of circumstances' (judgment of 2 February 1973, Fisheries Jurisdiction (United Kingdom v Iceland), ICJ Reports 1973, p. 3, paragraph 36).

The jurisdiction of the Court

25. The Commission has expressed doubts as to the jurisdiction of the Court to rule on the first question because it relates to the validity of the disputed regulation under rules of customary international law. Even though the regulation constitutes an act of the Community within the meaning of subparagraph (b) of the first paragraph of Article 177 of the Treaty, the preliminary rulings procedure does not permit the development of an argument based on international law alone, and in particular on the principles governing the termination of treaties and the suspension of their operation.

26. As the Court has already held in Joined Cases 21/72 to 24/72 International Fruit Company v Produktschap voor Groenten en Fruit [1972] ECR 1219, paragraph 5, the jurisdiction of the Court to give preliminary rulings under Article 177 of the Treaty concerning the validity of acts of the Community institutions cannot be limited by the grounds on which the validity of those measures may be contested.

27. Since such jurisdiction extends to all grounds capable of invalidating those measures, the Court is obliged to examine whether their validity may be affected by reason of the fact that they are contrary to a rule of international law (International Fruit Company, paragraph 6).

28. The Court therefore has jurisdiction to rule on the first question.

The validity of the disputed regulation

29. It should be noted that the question whether the disputed regulation is valid having regard to customary international law has arisen incidentally in a dispute in which Racke claims that the preferential rates of customs duty provided for in Article 22 of the Cooperation Agreement should be applied.

30. It therefore needs to be examined first whether Article 22(4), which, as the purpose of the quota regulations cited in the order for reference demonstrates, applies to the main proceedings in this case, is capable of conferring rights to preferential customs treatment directly upon individuals.

31. The Court has consistently held that a provision of an agreement concluded by the Community with non-member countries must be regarded as being directly applicable when, regard being had to its wording and the purpose and nature of the agreement itself, the provision contains a clear and precise obligation which is not subject, in its implementation or effects, to the adoption of any subsequent measure (see, in particular, Case 12/86 Demirel v Stadt Schwäbisch Gmünd [1987] ECR 3719, paragraph 14).

32. In order to determine whether the provision contained in Article 22(4) of the Cooperation Agreement meets those criteria, it is necessary first to examine its wording.

33. By its very wording, that provision requires Community measures to implement it in order to enable the annual Community tariff quota to be opened in accordance with the detailed rules laid down by Article 2(1) and (2) of the Additional Protocol, the Community having no discretion as to the adoption of those measures. The Community is obliged to carry out, within a certain period, an exact calculation of customs duties in accordance with those provisions.

34. It follows that, as regards the preferential customs treatment for which it makes provision, Article 22(4) of the Cooperation Agreement is capable of conferring rights upon which individuals may rely before national courts.

35. That finding is, moreover, borne out by examination of the purpose and nature of the agreement of which Article 22(4) forms part.

36. The aim of the Cooperation Agreement is to promote the development of trade between the contracting parties and progressively to remove barriers affecting the bulk of their trade. After the end of the first stage of that liberalisation, on 30 June 1985, the Additional Protocol established the further trade arrangements. It is in that context that Article 22(4), as amended by Article 4 of the Additional Protocol, lays down in respect of certain wines a Community tariff quota within which dismantling of customs duties on importation into the Community is to take place.

37. It next needs to be examined whether, when invoking in legal proceedings the preferential customs treatment granted to him by Article 22(4) of the Cooperation Agreement, an individual may challenge the validity under customary international law rules of the disputed regulation, suspending the trade concessions granted under that Agreement as from 15 November 1991.

38. In that respect, the Council maintains that the adoption of the disputed regulation was preceded, logically and legally, by the adoption of Decision 91/586, suspending the application of the Cooperation Agreement on the international level. Adoption of the disputed regulation became necessary in its turn, since the trade concessions provided for in the Agreement had been implemented in the past by an internal Community regulation.

39. The Council submits that, since international law does not prescribe the remedies for breach of its rules, the possible breach of those rules by Decision 91/586 does not necessarily lead to the restoration in force of the Cooperation Agreement and hence, at the Community level, to the invalidity of the disputed regulation by reason of its being contrary to the restored Agreement. Breach of international law might for instance also be penalised by means of damages, leaving the Cooperation Agreement suspended. The Council therefore argues that, in assessing the validity of the disputed regulation, the Court does not need to examine whether suspension of the Cooperation Agreement by Decision 91/586 infringed rules of international law.

40. It is important to note at the outset that the question referred by the national court concerns only the validity of the disputed regulation under rules of customary international law.

41. As far as the Community is concerned, an agreement concluded by the Council with a non-member country in accordance with the provisions of the EC Treaty is an act of a Community institution, and the provisions of such an agreement form an integral part of Community law (see Demirel, cited above, paragraph 7).

42. If, therefore, the disputed regulation had to be declared invalid, the trade concessions granted by the Cooperation Agreement would remain applicable in Community law until the Community brought that Agreement to an end in accordance with the relevant rules of international law.

43. It follows that a declaration of the invalidity of the disputed regulation by reason of its being contrary to rules of customary international law would allow individuals to rely directly on the rights to preferential treatment granted to them by the Cooperation Agreement.

44. For its part, the Commission doubts whether, in the absence of an express clause in the EC Treaty, the international law rules referred to in the order for reference may be regarded as forming part of the Community legal order. Thus, in order to challenge the validity of a regulation, an individual might rely on grounds based on the relationship between him and the Community, but does not, the Commission argues, have the right to rely on grounds deriving from the legal relationship between the Community and a non-member country, which fall within the scope of international law.

45. It should be noted in that respect that, as is demonstrated by the Court's judgment in Case C-286/90 Poulsen and Diva Navigation [1992] ECR I-6019, paragraph 9, the European Community must respect international law in the exercise of its powers. It is therefore required to comply with the rules of customary international law when adopting a regulation suspending the trade concessions granted by, or by virtue of, an agreement which it has concluded with a non-member country.

46. It follows that the rules of customary international law concerning the termination and the suspension of treaty relations by reason of a fundamental change of circumstances are binding upon the Community institutions and form part of the Community legal order.

47. In this case, however, the plaintiff is incidentally challenging the validity of a Community regulation under those rules in order to rely upon rights which it derives directly from an agreement of the Community with a non-member country. This case does not therefore concern the direct effect of those rules.

48. Racke is invoking fundamental rules of customary international law against the disputed regulation, which was taken pursuant to those rules and deprives Racke of the rights to preferential treatment granted to it by the Cooperation Agreement (for a comparable situation in relation to basic rules of a contractual nature, see Case C-69/89 Nakajima v Council [1991] I-2069, paragraph 31).

49. The rules invoked by Racke form an exception to the pacta sunt servanda principle, which constitutes a fundamental principle of any legal order and, in particular, the international legal order. Applied to international law, that principle requires that every treaty be binding upon the parties to it and be performed by them in good faith (see Article 26 of the Vienna Convention).

50. The importance of that principle has been further underlined by the International Court of Justice, which has held that 'the stability of treaty relations requires that the plea of fundamental change of circumstances be applied only in exceptional cases' (judgment of 25 September 1997, Gabcíkovo-Nagymaros Project (Hungary v Slovakia), at paragraph 104, not yet published in the ICJ Reports).

51. In those circumstances, an individual relying in legal proceedings on rights which he derives directly from an agreement with a non-member country may not be denied the possibility of challenging the validity of a regulation which, by suspending the trade concessions granted by that agreement, prevents him from relying on it, and of invoking, in order to challenge the validity of the suspending regulation, obligations deriving from rules of customary international law which govern the termination and suspension of treaty relations.

52. However, because of the complexity of the rules in question and the imprecision of some of the concepts to which they refer, judicial review must necessarily, and in particular in the context of a preliminary reference for an assessment of validity, be limited to the question whether, by adopting the suspending regulation, the Council made manifest errors of assessment concerning the conditions for applying those rules.

53. For it to be possible to contemplate the termination or suspension of an agreement by reason of a fundamental change of circumstances, customary international law, as codified in Article 62(1) of the Vienna Convention, lays down two conditions. First, the existence of those circumstances must have constituted an essential basis of the consent of the parties to be bound by the treaty; secondly, that change must have had the effect of radically transforming the extent of the obligations still to be performed under the treaty.

54. Concerning the first condition, the preamble to the Cooperation Agreement states that the contracting parties are resolved 'to promote the development and diversification of economic, financial and trade cooperation in order to foster a better balance and an improvement in the structure of their trade and expand its volume and to improve the welfare of their populations' and that they are conscious 'of the need to take into account the significance of the new situation created by the enlargement of the Community for the organisation of more harmonious economic and trade relations between the Community and the Socialist Federal Republic of Yugoslavia'. Pursuant to those considerations, Article 1 of the Agreement provides that its object 'is to promote overall cooperation between the contracting parties with a view to contributing to the economic and social development of the Socialist Federal Republic of Yugoslavia and helping to strengthen relations between the parties'.

55. In view of such a wide-ranging objective, the maintenance of a situation of peace in Yugoslavia, indispensable for neighbourly relations, and the existence of institutions capable of ensuring implementation of the cooperation envisaged by the Agreement throughout the territory of Yugoslavia constituted an essential condition for initiating and pursuing that cooperation.

56. Regarding the second condition, it does not appear that, by holding in the second recital in the preamble to the disputed regulation that 'the pursuit of hostilities and their consequences on economic and trade relations, both between the Republics of Yugoslavia and with the Community, constitute a radical change in the conditions under which the Cooperation Agreement between the European Economic Community and the Socialist Federal Republic of Yugoslavia and its Protocols ... were concluded' and that 'they call into question the application of such Agreements and Protocols', the Council made a manifest error of assessment.

57. Whilst it is true, as Racke argues, that a certain volume of trade had to continue with Yugoslavia and that the Community could have continued to grant tariff

concessions, the fact remains, as the Advocate General has pointed out in para-graph 93 of his Opinion, that application of the customary international law rules in question does not require an impossibility to perform obligations, and that there was no point in continuing to grant preferences, with a view to stimulating trade, in circumstances where Yugoslavia was breaking up.

58. As for the question raised in the order for reference whether, having regard to Article 65 of the Vienna Convention, it was permissible to proceed with the suspen-sion of the Cooperation Agreement with no prior notification or waiting period, this Court observes that, in the joint statements of 5, 6 and 28 October 1991, the Community and the Member States announced that they would adopt restrictive measures against those parties which did not observe the ceasefire agreement of 4 October 1991 which they had signed in the presence of the President of the Council and the President of the Conference on Yugoslavia; moreover, the Community had made known during the conclusion of that agreement that it would bring the Cooperation Agreement to an end in the event of the ceasefire not being observed (Bull. EC 10-1991, paragraphs 1.4.6, 1.4.7 and 1.4.16).

59. Even if such declarations do not satisfy the formal requirements laid down by Article 65 of the Vienna Convention, it should be noted that the specific procedural requirements there laid down do not form part of customary international law.

60. Examination of the first question has thus disclosed no factor of such a kind as to affect the validity of the suspending regulation.

61. Given the reply to the first question referred, there is no need to adjudicate on the second.

3.7 Position of the EU in respect of a draft decision having legal effects to be taken by treaty body or an organ of an international organization

The possibility that the Council decides on such positions has been included in the Treaty since Amsterdam. This part of Article 218(9) has so far not been applied very consistently. The Commission was not always inclined to make proposals, especially in the field of commercial policy, where its use might upset the established ways of proceeding both inside the Union and inside the World Trade Organization (WTO). In other cases it was the Council that was not enthusiastic to avail itself of the pos-sibilities of this provision, especially in the environmental field, where the Council preferred a policy of muddling through without clarifying Union competence and hence normally adopted vague and broad Council conclusions to prepare negotia-tions in the treaty bodies of the various Multilateral Environmental Agreements. In one instance this has led to a Court case (see Chapter 10, pp. 815-16). After the entry into force of the Lisbon Treaty, the provision has become more important though. For example, regarding EU positions on the acceptance of new members in the WTO, the Council nowadays adopts formal decisions under Article 218(9) TFEU on the basis of Commission proposals.

Council Decision 2012/17/EU of 14 December 2011 establishing the position to be taken by the European Union within the relevant instances of the World Trade Organization on the accession of the Russian Federation to the WTO, Official Journal L 6, 10.1.2012, p. 6.

THE COUNCIL OF THE EUROPEAN UNION,
Having regard to the Treaty on the Functioning of the European Union, and in particular Articles 91, 100(2) and 207, in conjunction with Article 218(9) thereof,
Having regard to the proposal from the European Commission,

Whereas:
(1) In June 1993 the Government of the Russian Federation applied for accession to the Marrakesh Agreement establishing the World Trade Organization (WTO), pursuant to Article XII of that Agreement.
(2) A Working Party on the accession of the Russian Federation was established on 16 June 1993 in order to reach agreement on terms of accession acceptable to the Russian Federation and all WTO Members.
(3) The Commission, on behalf of the Union, has negotiated a comprehensive series of market opening and other regulatory commitments on the part of the Russian Federation which satisfy the Union's requests, are consistent with its objectives and in line with the development level of the Russian Federation.
(4) These commitments are now embodied in the Protocol of Accession of the Russian Federation to the WTO.
(5) Accession to the WTO is expected to make a positive and lasting contribution to the process of economic reform and sustainable development in the Russian Federation.
(6) The Protocol of Accession should therefore be approved.
(7) Article XII of the Agreement establishing the WTO provides that the terms of accession are to be agreed between the acceding Member and the WTO, and that the WTO Ministerial Conference approves the terms of accession on the WTO side. Paragraph 2 of Article IV of the Agreement establishing the WTO provides that in the intervals between meetings of the Ministerial Conference, its functions shall be conducted by the General Council.
(8) Accordingly, it is necessary to establish the position to be taken by the Union within the relevant instances of the WTO, be it the Ministerial Conference or the General Council, on the accession of the Russian Federation to the WTO,

HAS ADOPTED THIS DECISION:

Article 1

The position to be taken by the European Union within the relevant instances of the World Trade Organization on the accession of the Russian Federation to the WTO is to approve the accession.

Article 2

This Decision shall enter into force on the day of its adoption.

3.8 Termination of agreements

While Article 218 TFEU EC contains detailed provisions on treaty-making and suspension, it is silent on termination. To identify the applicable procedure, recourse can be had to constitutional principles common to the Member States, EU practice, and the general institutional balance established by the Treaty in external relations. In particular, it needs to be resolved which role is reserved for the European Parliament when the EU is to denounce an international agreement to which it is a party.

3.8.1 Constitutional principles in the Member States

Nine Member States regulate the termination procedure in their constitutions. **The Netherlands**[7] require parliamentary approval of termination decisions of all agreements by the executive unless an Act of Parliament specifies otherwise. The other eight Member States (**Bulgaria**,[8] **Denmark**,[9] **Estonia**,[10] **Spain**,[11] **Finland**,[12] **Lithuania**,[13] **Poland**,[14] and **Sweden**[15]) involve the Parliament for such subject matters for which the Parliament has a corresponding right of approval in the treaty-making stage. This approach can be understood as applying a sort of 'actus contrarius' principle related to international agreements.

The constitutions of the other eighteen Member States do not address the termination procedure. Distilling from information contained in an academic survey of

---

[7] Art. 91(1) of the Dutch Constitution: 'The Kingdom shall not be bound by treaties, nor shall such treaties be denounced without the prior approval of the Parliament. The cases in which approval is not required shall be specified by Act of Parliament.'

[8] Art. 85(1) of the Bulgarian Constitution: 'The National Assembly shall ratify or denounce by law all international instruments which (... (1)–(8)).'

[9] Art. 19(1), second sentence of the Danish Constitution: 'Provided that without the consent of the Parliament the King shall not undertake any act whereby the territory of the Realm will be increased or decrease, nor shall he enter into any obligation which for fulfilment requires the concurrence of the Parliament, or which otherwise is of major importance; nor shall the King, except with the consent of the Parliament, terminate any international treaty entered into with the consent of the Parliament.'

[10] Art. 65(4) of the Estonian Constitution: 'The Parliament shall ratify and denounce foreign treaties in accordance with Article 121.' The latter article contains the list of subject matters on which Parliament is involved.

[11] Art. 96(2) of the Spanish Constitution: 'To denounce international treaties and agreements, the same procedure established for their approval in Article 94 shall be used.' Art. 94 lists the subject matters which require prior authorization of the Spanish Parliament for the ratification of treaties.

[12] Art. 94(1) of the Finnish Constitution: 'The acceptance of the Parliament is required for such treaties and other international obligations that contain provisions of a legislative nature, are otherwise significant, or otherwise require approval by the Parliament under this Constitution. The acceptance of the Parliament is required also for the denouncement of such obligations.'

[13] Art. 67(16) of the Lithuanian Constitution: 'The Parliament shall (...) (16) ratify or denounce international treaties whereto the Republic of Lithuania is a party, and consider other issues of foreign policy.' Art. 138 of the Constitution contains the list of subject matters on which the Parliament is involved in ratification or termination.

[14] Art. 89(1) of the Polish Constitution: 'Ratification of an international agreement by the Republic of Poland, as well as denunciation thereof, shall require prior consent granted by statute—if such agreement concerns: ... (1)–(5).'

[15] Ch. 10, Art. 4 of the Swedish Constitution: 'The provisions of Articles 1 to 3 shall apply, mutatis mutandis, to the commitment of the Realm to any international obligation in any form other than an agreement and to any denunciation of an international agreement or obligation.' The referred articles specify that the government concludes international treaties after prior consent by the Parliament in a number of listed cases.

1996[16] and in a report from the Venice Commission of 1998,[17] it appears that this silence leans generally in favour of an executive prerogative to denounce international agreements. This is the current situation in **Belgium**,[18] **Czech Republic**,[19] **Cyprus**,[20] **Germany**,[21] **France**,[22] **Greece**,[23] **Italy**,[24] **Luxemburg**,[25] **Malta**,[26] and the **United Kingdom**.[27]

In **Austria**,[28] **Ireland**,[29] **Slovakia**,[30] and **Latvia**[31] there is no indication that national parliaments have to give prior consent to the termination of treaties by the executive.

[16] P.M. Eisemann (ed.), *The Integration of International and European Community Law into the National Legal Order—A Study of the Practice in Europe*, (The Hague: Kluwer Law International, 1996); here referred to as *Eisemann*.

[17] Venice Commission, Report on the Legal Foundation for Foreign Policy, Addendum, 3rd June 1998, available at the website of the Venice Commission (<http://www.venice.coe.int/webforms/documents/CDL-DI(1998)003add-e.aspx>).

[18] The Belgian Constitution is generally silent on the termination of federal treaties. However, it contains a specific rule on how to terminate them, when the subject matter falls into the competence of the regions and the communities after the constitutional reform in 1993. According to Art. 167(5.1) of the Belgian Constitution: 'The King may denounce treaties concluded before 18 May 1993 and covering matters described in Paragraph (3) of common accord with those Community or Regional Governments concerned.' This can be seen as an indicator that the power of termination treaties is generally vested in the King.

[19] Art. 49 of the Czech Constitution requires the consent of Parliament for concluding certain categories of treaties. Government Resolution No. 328/1993 points to a right of the government to denounce treaties.

[20] There is no precise information available on this point. However, given that the constitutional system of Cyprus is largely inspired by the UK system, it can be assumed that termination of treaties is vested in the powers of the executive, as Arts 50 and 169(1) and (2) restricted parliamentary involvement in the treaty-making stage.

[21] Art. 59(2) of the Basic Law involves the German Parliament in the ratification of treaties in certain cases. The provision is not applied by analogy to termination in practice (J.A. Frowein and K. Oellers-Frahm, Allemagne, *Eisemann* (note 16), p. 80: 'Il est vrai que le Gouvernement fédéral a dénoncé des traités internationaux sans l'approbation parlementaire. Ceci paraît d'ailleurs être conforme au système de répartition des compétences établi par la Loi Fondamentale.'

[22] According to Presidential Decree no. 53-192 of 14 March 1953, confirmed by Decree no. 86-707 of 11 April 1986, the Minister of Foreign Affairs ratifies, renews, and denounces all international agreements.

[23] Venice Commission report (note 17), p. 27, saying that the Minister of Foreign Affairs denounces treaties without requiring Parliament's approval even where its consent was needed for the conclusion of the treaty concerned.

[24] Practice in Italy seems to be inconsistent. Academic commentators are split as well. T. Treves and M. Frigessi die Rattalma, *Eisemann* (note 16), p. 377 note: 'L'opinion qui prévaut est que la compétence pour la dénonciation appartient au Gouvernement sans que soit nécessaire une intervention du Parlement.'

[25] R. Biever, N. Edon, and L. Weitzel, Luxemburg, *Eisemann* (note 16), p. 414: 'Il apparaît que, dans la pratique, la dénonciation est opérée, dans les formes prescrites par le traité en cause, par le ministre des Affaires étrangères, sans que cette dénonciation soit préc´dée d'une demande d'autorisation de la Chambre des députés.'

[26] According to Art. 4 of the Ratification of Treaties Act V of 9 March 1983, the minister informs the Parliament after the termination of the treaty.

[27] Venice Commission report (note 17), p. 28, stressing that the executive power denounces international agreements without needing the authorization of Parliament.

[28] Under Art. 50(1) of the Austrian constitution, the federal Parliament ratifies political treaties. It is unknown whether the provision is applied by analogy to the termination of treaties.

[29] According to Art. 29.4.1 of the Irish Constitution, the government's power to act in external relations is wide and may be presumed to cover termination. The national report on Ireland (C.R. Symmons, Ireland, *Eisemann* (note 16), p. 330, mentions that there are no domestic rules governing the denunciation or suspension of a treaty.

[30] Pursuant to Art. 86 of the Slovak Constitution, the Parliament gives consent to the ratification of certain categories of treaties. It is unknown whether this provision is applied by analogy to the termination process.

[31] According to Art. 68 of the Latvian Constitution, all international agreements which settle matters that may be decided by the legislative process require the approval of Parliament. It is unknown whether this provision is applied by analogy to the termination process.

In contrast, parliamentary involvement in the termination procedure is supported by law in **Hungary**,[32] by practice in **Slovenia**[33] and **Romania**,[34] and by doctrine in **Portugal**.[35]

In sum, there are mainly two competing constitutional traditions in the Member States. The Parliament-friendly *actus contrarius* shared by many Nordic and Southern Member States is opposed to the executive-friendly approach of, *inter alia*, Germany, France, and the UK. The new Member States are also split between these two categories. Thus, there is no constitutional principle *common* to the Member States. Accordingly, while both the *actus contrarius* and the executive prerogative theory can be linked to certain constitutional traditions, neither of them can be simply transposed to the European level.

3.8.2 **EU practice**

EU practice on termination differs according to policy areas.

In the *trade field*, the EU decided to terminate treaties without involvement of the Parliament. The Council terminated a Community agreement about public procurement in the telecommunications sector upon proposal of the Commission.[36] The Council also terminated the ACP sugar protocol, again without consulting the Parliament.[37]

In contrast, in the *fisheries field*, the Parliament was consulted in the two decisions on denunciation taken so far (Sweden,[38] Angola[39]). A Commission proposal for a Council decision to terminate the fisheries cooperation agreement with Mauritania without consultation of the Parliament[40] was not taken up by the Council.

---

[32] According to Art. 19(3)(f) of the Hungarian Constitution, the Parliament concludes international agreements of outstanding importance to the foreign relations of Hungary. The procedure for all the international treaties of Hungary is laid down in Act 50 of 2005, Art. 12 of which specifies that the same procedural rules apply for the conclusion, modification, or termination of treaties. According to Art. 7 of the same Act (on empowerment for the recognition of the binding force of the treaties), the Parliament gives empowerment for the recognition of the binding force of the treaty if the treaty is of significant importance for foreign policy (there is a list of these, e.g. relating to a subject regulated by Acts which require qualified majority or if it goes against existing Acts in Hungary, etc.); in all other cases, the government grants empowerment.

[33] Venice Commission report (note 17), p. 51, according to which the Slovenian Parliament initiates the procedure for amendment or denouncement of an international treaty.

[34] Venice Commission report (note 17), p. 44, according to which the Romanian Parliament also denounces treaties in practice, although Arts 11 and 91 of the Romanian Constitution only contain provisions on parliamentary ratification.

[35] R.M. Moura Ramos, Portugal, *Eisemann* (note 16), pp. 472-3.

[36] Council Decision 2004/589/EC, of 19 July 2004 concerning the notification to the Republic of Korea of the withdrawal of the European Community from the Agreement on telecommunications procurement between the European Community and the Republic of Korea, OJ L 260, 6.8.2004, p. 8.

[37] Council Decision of 2007/627/EC 28 September 2007, denouncing on behalf of the Community Protocol 3 on ACP sugar, OJ, L 255, 29.9.2007, p. 38.

[38] Council Decision 92/530/EEC of 12 November 1992 denouncing the Fisheries Agreement between the former German Democratic Republic and Sweden, OJ L 334, 19.11.1992, p. 33.

[39] Council Regulation 1185/2006 of 24 July 2006 denouncing the Agreement between the European Economic Community and the Government of the People's Republic of Angola on fishing off Angola and derogating from Regulation (EC) No 2792/1999, OJ L 214, 4.8.2006, p. 10.

[40] Proposal for a Council Decision on the termination of the Protocol setting out the fishing opportunities and financial contribution under the Fisheries Partnership Agreement between the European Community and Mauritania, 13.12.2007, COM(2007) 782 final.

The denunciation of a cooperation agreement with the Former Yugoslavia was done by the Council on a proposal by the Commission after having obtained consent of the Parliament.[41]

Finally, one can refer to the Passenger Name Records (PNR) case, where after annulment of the decision to conclude the PNR Agreement by the ECJ following the action of the European Parliament,[42] the Council and the Commission terminated the PNR Agreement with the US in July 2006 without prior involvement of the Parliament.[43]

All this occurred, however, prior to the Lisbon Treaty, where the Parliament was only consulted on the conclusion of many agreements (and did not have the right to give consent, as nowadays under Article 218(6)(a)(v)).

3.8.3 Institutional balance between EU institutions

As both the constitutional practices of the Member States and of the EU itself do not provide clear guidance, the correct procedure for terminating EU agreements should be found by analysing the institutional balance between EU institutions in the external relations field more broadly. One approach could be to apply the *actus contrarius* theory, according to which the identical procedure should be followed for concluding and terminating an agreement. However, a number of considerations militate against such a mechanical transposition.

First, in the conclusion stage, Parliament is often called upon to exercise a typical legislative function. Since certain agreements have a legal impact on the EU citizens when being implemented, Parliament has a legitimate role to play in order to prevent legislation by the executive organs 'through the backdoor' of concluding international agreements. Moreover, where an international agreement has consequences for EU legislation on which Parliament co-legislated, it is natural that it is involved. By contrast, at the termination stage, the stakes are usually not that high. Terminating an agreement would often 'free' the Union and its citizens from obligations otherwise due. For doing so, it is less imperative to involve the Parliament. Arguably, where the termination of an agreement would also 'give up' certain directly applicable rights conferred on EU citizens vis-à-vis the treaty partner, the case for parliamentary involvement would become stronger from a democratic point of view?

Second, Parliament is consulted or asked to give its assent in the conclusion stage in order to exercise a political assessment of the agreement for the Union's external relations. While the same reason applies for involving the Parliament in the termination

---

[41] Council Decision 91/602/EEC of November 1991, denouncing the Cooperation Agreement between the European Economic Community and the Socialist Federal Republic of Yugoslavia, OJ 1991 L 325, 27.11.1991, p. 23.

[42] ECJ, Joined Cases C-317/04 and C-318/04 *Parliament v. Council and Commission* [2006] ECR I-4721.

[43] Notice concerning the denunciation of the Agreement between the European Community and the United States of America on the processing and transfer of PNR data by air carriers to the United States Department of Homeland Security, Bureau of Customs and Border Protection, OJ C 219, 12.9.2006, p. 1.

stage for politically important agreements, that is less evident for agreements of a more technical character. It would not make much sense to consult the Parliament on subject matters which would belong to the ordinary management of external relations by the executive.

Third, there is no trace of the *actus contrarius* doctrine in the EC Treaty. In contrast, the Treaty explicitly regulates the case of suspension of treaties. One could argue that termination is much closer to suspension of a treaty in certain situations. According to Article 218(9) TFEU, a decision to suspend a Union agreement is taken by the Council on a proposal from the Commission, while the Parliament is subsequently informed. Indeed, in particular in situations where termination of an agreement seems essential as an immediate foreign policy reaction (e.g. to sanction severe human rights abuses in a third country), the procedural requirements for suspension and termination should be identical.

In the absence of an express provision in the EC Treaty on how to terminate EU agreements, there is thus a certain discretion vested in the institutions. Rather than mechanically importing the *actus contrarius* theory into Union law, which reflects the constitutional tradition of only a certain number of Member States, the institutional balance in external relations has to be observed as a general legal yardstick, taking due account of the specific content of the agreement and the circumstances surrounding its termination. Hence, the procedure to terminate an EU agreement may differ on a case-by-case basis: all three modes of the Parliament's involvement (subsequent information, prior consultation, or assent) seem to be defendable.

3.9 Non-legally binding agreements (Memoranda of Understanding)

It must be stressed that Article 218 TFEU only applies to the conclusion of legally binding agreements. When a negotiated text remains in the realm of political commitments only, the Commission, as the main Union representative, may well sign it in its own name. The Court confirmed this position with respect to the EC–US Transatlantic Guidelines on regulatory dialogue. Below there is also a Memorandum of Understanding (MoU) signed on 30 November 2009 between Directorate-General Enterprise and its Chinese counterpart, the Ministry of Industry and Information Technology. However, it is interesting to note that in another very recent example of non-legally binding agreements in the field of industry and entrepreneurship not included here, that of the letters of intent with Mexico, the responsible Commissioner was authorized to sign on behalf of the Union as a whole, with his counterparts signing on behalf of Mexico. Fianlly, a most recent MoU signed on 8 October 2012 between the EU this time, not just a Directorate-General, and UNESCO is also included here. It is also noteworthy that this MoU was signed on the EU side by both the Director-General for Development and the High Representative of the Union for CFSP/Vice-President of the Commission.

Judgment of the Court (Full Court) of 23 March 2004, French Republic v. Commission of the European Communities, Case C-233/02, European Court Reports 2002, p. I-2759, paras. 38–46.

38. By its first plea, the French Government merely submits that the Guidelines should have been concluded by the Council rather than by the Commission, in accordance with Article 300 EC, since they constitute a legally binding agreement.

39. On the other hand, the French Government in no way claims that a measure exhibiting the characteristics of the Guidelines must, even if it has no binding force, come under the sole competence of the Council. There is therefore no need for the Court to extend the subject-matter of the action of which it is seized.

40. Nevertheless, this judgment cannot be construed as upholding the Commission's argument that the fact that a measure such as the Guidelines is not binding is sufficient to confer on that institution the competence to adopt it. Determining the conditions under which such a measure may be adopted requires that the division of powers and the institutional balance established by the Treaty in the field of the common commercial policy be duly taken into account, since in this case the measure seeks to reduce the risk of conflict related to the existence of technical barriers to trade in goods.

41. Moreover, both the Transatlantic Economic Partnership and the Action Plan were approved by the Council, as is made clear in the memorandum of 9 April 2002 sent by the Commission to the committee set up pursuant to Article 133(3) EC, and the committee was regularly informed of the progress of the negotiations relating to the drafting of the Guidelines by the Commission's services.

42. In the light of that clarification, the intention of the parties must in principle be the decisive criterion for the purpose of determining whether or not the Guidelines are binding, as the Commission rightly contends.

43. In the present case, that intention is clearly expressed, as the Advocate General observed in paragraphs 56 and 57 of his Opinion, in the text of the Guidelines itself, paragraph 7 of which specifies that the purpose of the document is to establish guidelines which regulators of the United States Federal Government and the services of the Commission 'intend to apply on a voluntary basis'. In those circumstances, and without its being necessary to consider the specific importance which the use of the terms 'should' or 'will' rather than 'shall' could assume in an international agreement concluded by the Community, it need only be stated that on the basis of that information, the parties had no intention of entering into legally binding commitments when they concluded the Guidelines.

44. As pointed out by the Commission, without contradiction by the French Government, the history of the negotiations confirms that the intention of the parties not to enter into binding commitments was expressly reiterated throughout the negotiations on the Guidelines.

45. It follows that the Guidelines do not constitute a binding agreement and therefore do not fall within the scope of Article 300 EC.

46. Accordingly, the first plea in law is unfounded.

Memorandum of Understanding on a Dialogue and Consultation Mechanism on Industrial sectors

between

The Enterprise and Industry Directorate-General of the European Commission

and

The Ministry of Industry and Information Technology of the People's Republic of China

The Enterprise and Industry Directorate-General of the European Commission and the Ministry of Industry and Information Technology of the People's Republic of China (hereinafter referred to as 'the two sides'), guided by the principles of trust and mutual benefit, and within their respective sphere of competences, have reached the following understanding on promoting the cooperation in the industrial sectors of the European Union and China.

Article 1

The two sides establish a long-term dialogue and consultation mechanism on industrial sector related issues.

The two sides intend to, share information and experience concerning their respective industrial development, contribute to improving conditions for the development of enterprises, promote the sustainable development and prosperity of the industrial sectors in the European Union and China, and make active contributions to the developments of the European Union–China trade relationship.

Article 2

While complying with their laws and policies, both sides decide to conduct a constructive dialogue on their present policies, legislations and measures related to industrial sectors, as well as on standardization and future strategies; to discuss issues of mutual concern, and to promote cooperation and exchanges in the industrial sectors of the European Union and China.

In reference to the 'Memorandum of Understanding on Establishing Dialogue in the Shipbuilding Industry' between the Enterprise and Industry Directorate-General and the Trade Directorate-General of the European Commission and the former Commission of Science, Technology and Industry for National Defense of China agreed in May 2007, and the 'Cooperation Agreement of the Small and Medium-sized Enterprises' between the Enterprise and Industry Directorate-General of the European Commission and the National Development and Reform Commission of China agreed in July 2006, both sides acknowledge that they are now of the competence of the Ministry of Industry and Information Technology on the Chinese side and that the two Memorandum of Understanding remain unchanged as to the participants on the European Commission's side.

Article 3

According to the actual needs of industrial development, the two sides will conduct a constructive dialogue through mutual consultation on an annual basis. The level and composition of representation will be equivalent, while taking into account the differences in the organizational structure of the respective administrations. If mutually agreed, representatives from the related industries can be invited to participate according to the needs of the agenda for the dialogue and subjects.

The two sides will bear their own costs needed for the meeting, including international and domestic travel fees and accommodation fees. The host will actively provide appropriate support and assistance to the visiting delegations.

The official languages used in the dialogue are English and Chinese. After each meeting, meeting minutes will be written in both English and Chinese.

Article 4

The two sides will appoint liaison bodies for better implementation of the Memorandum of Understanding. The Unit of International Affairs of Directorate of Coordination, Planning and International Affairs of the Enterprise and Industry Directorate General will be appointed as the liaison body for the European Commission side, the Department of International Cooperation of the Ministry of Industry and Information Technology for the Chinese side. The two bodies will identify relevant matters, including, among others, coordination and liaison, meeting arrangements and dialogue topics.

Article 5

This Memorandum of Understanding may be amended and supplemented or terminated by mutual consent.

Article 6

This Memorandum of Understanding will start from the date of signature.

This Memorandum of Understanding is reflecting official intent only and the two sides do not intend it to create any legal obligations.

Done in two equal originals in Nanjing on 30th November, 2009 in English and Chinese languages.

For the Directorate General for Enterprise and Industry of the European Commission	For the Ministry of Industry and Information Technology of the People's Republic of China

---

MEMORANDUM OF UNDERSTANDING

Concerning the establishment of a partnership between the United Nations Educational, Scientific and Cultural Organisation Secretariat and its subsidiary bodies (hereinafter referred to as 'UNESCO') and the European Union, jointly referred to hereinafter as 'the two Sides'.

The two Sides acknowledge the longstanding cooperation between the European Union and UNESCO, in particular in light of the Commission's Communications to the European Council and Parliament 'Building and Effective partnership with the United Nations in the fields of Development and Humanitarian Affairs' and 'The European Union and the United Nations: the choice of multilateralism';

The longstanding cooperation also builds on the previous exchanges of letters dated 2 and 15 September 1964, 12 December 1972 and 14 February 1973 between UNESCO (René Maheu) and Commission (Jean Rey and François-Xavier Ortoli); and the Provisions applicable to Cooperation between the European Commission and UNESCO (1995); as well as the Financial and Administrative Framework Agreement (FAFA) between the European Community and the United Nations signed on 29 April 2003, to which UNESCO acceded on 23 February 2004;

The two Sides recognise the respective responsibilities of the two Sides in their areas of competence;

The two Sides hereby confirm a partnership (hereinafter referred to as 'the partnership') with the aim of enhancing and increasing their dialogue on policy issues, cooperation and exchange of data and information in their efforts to achieve their common goals and objectives in the areas identified in detail under section C of this Memorandum.

A. PRINCIPLES AND OBJECTIVES

 (1) Through this partnership, the two Sides express their wish to develop and struc-
     ture their dialogue on policy issues, cooperation and exchange of data and infor-
     mation in areas of common interest.
 (2) The partnership will aim at an increased coherence and efficiency, as well as at an
     enhanced quality and impact, of the activities of the two Sides in the areas cov-
     ered by the partnership.
 (3) The two Sides share fundamental values such as respect for human dignity, free-
     dom, democracy, equality, the rule of law and respect for human rights, and in
     particular freedom of expression.
 (4) The two Sides share the objectives of development through the promotion of the
     Millennium Development Goals (MDGs) and other internationally agreed devel-
     opment targets, including the Education for All (EFA) goals.
 (5) The two Sides share the objective of promoting cultural diversity and intercul-
     tural dialogue, as well as that of making culture a vector for human, social and
     economic development.
 (6) The two Sides share the objective of raising awareness about the importance of
     education as an essential pillar for human, social and economic development,
     and they cooperate to that effect, including by co-ordinating efforts in the field of
     quality, relevance and content of education in partner countries.
 (7) The two Sides acknowledge the importance of media, in particular audio-visual
     media, as levers for education and social betterment, as well as their contribution
     to cultural, economic and political development.
 (8) The two Sides share the objective of promoting science, technology and innova-
     tion, as well as recognize their role in addressing global challenges and driving

economic and social progress, and share the objective of promoting them for the sake of inclusive and sustainable development.

(9) The two Sides promote fundamental values in the areas of research and innovation and cooperate in bioethics and ethics of science and new technologies.

(10) The two Sides promote the integrated management of oceans.

(11) The present partnership complements and further develops the ongoing overall cooperation between the European Union and UNESCO.

(12) The partnership will be based on the respect and mutual understanding of the respective strengths, organizational structures, mandates and institutional capacities of the two organisations.

(13) The objectives of this partnership will be achieved through:
   – fostering collaboration on approaches, including evidence based approaches, to policy development and recommendations;
   – improving dialogue and knowledge sharing;
   – promoting best practices;
   – creating synergies where appropriate.

(14) A particular effort will be made to enhance cooperation between the European Union Delegations and UNESCO Field Offices and Category 1 Institutes at the country level, also involving as appropriate other UNESCO Centres.

(15) This Memorandum of Understanding does not create rights or obligations under international law nor commit either partner financially.

B. PRIORITIES

(16) In the area of development the partnership will apply to those countries classified as 'developing' according to the OECD-DAC list of recipients.

(17) UNESCO and the European Union will work together closely at the global, regional and country levels in the areas of cooperation identified in section C of this Memorandum.

(18) UNESCO's global priorities will be mainstreamed, within the areas identified for cooperation in section C of this Memorandum.

(19) Civil society involvement will be encouraged within the areas identified for cooperation in section C of this Memorandum.

C. AREAS FOR DIALOGUE AND COOPERATION

(20) The two Sides will increase dialogue on policy issues, cooperation and exchange of data and information in their efforts to achieve their common objectives, notably in the following areas:
   – education and culture, including their potential as vectors for development;
   – media, in particular audio-visual media, and their regulatory framework;
   – science, technology and innovation, including their potential for capacity building;
   – integrated maritime policy;
   – human rights, in particular freedom of expression;
   – bioethics and ethics of science and new technologies.

D. ARRANGEMENTS

(21) The following arrangements in the paragraphs below will apply for the partnership:

(22) Dialogue on policy issues will be pursued through working meetings focused on thematic areas.

(23) Review meetings will be held as appropriate.

(24) The focal points for the partnership will be the Directorate General responsible for development cooperation and the European External Action Service (Global and Multilateral Affairs Directorate) on the one hand, and the Bureau for Strategic Planning of UNESCO on the other. The focal points will ensure coordination with and involvement of other services, as necessary.

(25) The two Sides may invite each other to meetings and working groups relevant to this partnership on the basis of reciprocity subject to the due observance of existing rules and regulations of the respective organisations.

(26) The two Sides will inform and consult each other, as appropriate, on issues of mutual interest in the areas identified in detail under section C of this Memorandum.

(27) The two Sides will take all necessary communication measures to maximise the visibility of this partnership and, more specifically, of their shared objectives and principles, with the aim of increasing awareness and understanding within the general public and specialised audiences.

E. REVIEW

(28) This Memorandum may be reviewed, in writing, by mutual arrangement of the two Sides at any time.

Done in 2 originals in the English language, in Paris, on 8 October 2012.

FOR UNESCO	FOR THE EUROPEAN UNION	
Irina BOKOVA Director-General	Andris PIEBALGS European Commissioner for Development	Catherine ASHTON High Representative of the Union for Foreign Affairs and Security Policy/Vice-President of the European Commission

Select Bibliography

Cremona, M., Who Can Make Treaties? The European Union, *The Oxford Guide to Treaties* (D.B. Hollis (ed.), Oxford: Oxford University Press, 2012), 93–124.

Dörr, O. and Schmalenbach, K. (eds), *Vienna Convention on the Law of Treaties: A Commentary* (Berlin Heidelberg: Springer, 2012).

Eeckhout, P., *The External Relations of the European Union*, 2nd edn (Oxford: Oxford University Press, 2011).

Gatti, M. and Manzini, P., External Representation of the European Union in the Conclusion of International Agreements, *Common Market Law Review* 49, 2012, 1703-34.

Koutrakos, P., *EU International Relations Law* (Oxford: Hart Publishing, 2006), 137-50.

Kuijper, P.J., The Court and the Tribunal of the EC and the Vienna Convention on the Law of Treaties 1969, *Legal Issues of European Integration*, 1-23, 1999, 11-16.

——, The European Courts and the Law of Treaties: The Continuing Story, *The Law of Treaties Beyond the Vienna Convention* (E. Cannizzaro (ed.), Oxford: Oxford University Press, 2011), 256-78.

4

Mixed Agreements

4.1 Introduction

Agreements that are concluded simultaneously by the EU and all of the Member States are commonly called mixed agreements. This technique of concluding international agreements has been followed, except in the domain of trade policy, from the very beginning of the existence of the European Communities. Normally, mixed agreements have been concluded for the simple reason that the matters covered by an international agreement are often not limited to the domains covered by the powers granted by the Community treaties to the Communities, or nowadays to the EU. Thus, Member States have to complement Union powers with their own. This is often the case, when multilateral treaties are concluded by the Union where the scope of such treaties is not determined by the Union. Even if it concerns a bilateral treaty, however, the ambitions of both parties often make it impossible to restrict the scope of the international agreement strictly to the powers devolved by the founding Treaty to the Union.

In addition, there are situations in which EU Member States insist on the mixed character of the agreement for political reasons, even if from a pure legal point of view there is no need to make the agreement mixed. This is perfectly illustrated by the Association Agreement with Turkey, included below. This is a so-called pre-accession association agreement comparable to other early pre-accession associations concluded in the 1960s and 1970s with Greece and with Cyprus and Malta. The latter two were pure Community agreements, whereas the one with Greece was, as the one with Turkey, a mixed agreement. It is obvious that the size and political importance of the partner country made a difference when opting for a mixed agreement or not.

The only limitation on Member State manipulation of agreements with a view to making them mixed, even when no serious reason for doing so can be detected, is the economy of legal bases preached by the Court of Justice in connection with all Union acts, but in several instances also with respect to the conclusion of international agreements. Thus, in Case C-268/94 *Portugal v. Council* concerning the EU cooperation agreement with India, the Court stated that this agreement had to be analysed as to its essential object and not with respect to individual clauses in order to determine its legal basis. Clauses that were merely ancillary to or did not modify the essential object of the agreement (development cooperation) should not be taken into account for the determination of the legal basis of the decision approving and concluding the agreement, including in cases where such clauses referred to subjects that fell wholly or in part under Member State competence.[1] However, in the meantime the Court has perhaps restricted the possibilities of the approach discounting ancillary provisions, especially when it concerns questions of competence in its *Opinion 1/08* (see Chapter 7, p. 402, at para. 166). These questions are likely to be clarified in a pending case where the Commission has challenged a Decision of the Council and of the Representatives of the Governments of the Member States of the EU, meeting within the Council, to sign an Air Transport Agreement between the US, the EU, Norway, and Iceland. The Commission argues that the decision should have been solely taken by the Council as an EU institution. Moreover, by joining the two decisions into one act, the Council has divested the qualified majority rule set out in the first subparagraph of Article 218(8) TFEU of its very nature.[2]

The selection below demonstrates that mixed agreements are not only multilateral or bilateral, but may further be concluded in many different domains: not just in the almost all-encompassing scope of association agreements, but also in specialized areas, like non-discrimination of people with disabilities and the protection of cultural diversity. It also demonstrates that one can have mixed agreements that start out as framework agreements and develop largely through additional protocols and binding decisions of the Association Council, such as the Association Agreement with Turkey; or agreements that are very broad and detailed from the beginning, though also equipped with an Association Council that may take binding decisions, such as the Association Agreement with Egypt (see Chapter 9, p. 730).

4.2 A bilateral mixed agreement

Agreement establishing an Association between the European Economic Community and Turkey, Official Journal L 361, 31.12.1977, pp. 29–44.

As already mentioned, this Association Agreement was mixed mainly for political reasons and was supposed to develop gradually over the years by decisions of the Association Council. Originally, however, an Additional Protocol, adopted through the treaty procedure, was necessary for the first step on this road. It contained further objectives and initial steps towards inegrating Turkey gradually into the Community internal

---

[1] Case C-268/94 *Portugal v. Council* [1996] ECR I-6207, paras. 24–9 (human rights), 56–68 (drug abuse), and 69–77 (intellectual property).

[2] Action brought on 18 January 2012—*European Commission v. Council of the European Union* (Case C-28/12), OJ C 73, 10.3.2012, p. 73. See also Action brought on 1 March 2012—*European Commission v. Council of the European Union* (Case C-114/12), where the same issues are raised by the Commission. See further Action brought on 6 August 2012—*European Commission v. Council of the European Union* (Case C-377/12) OJ C 319, 20.10.2012, p. 3. With this last application the Commission asks for the annulment of the Council Decision on the signing, on behalf of the Union, of the Framework Agreement on Partnership and Cooperation between the European Union and its Member States, of the one part, and the Republic of the Philippines, of the other part of 14 May 2012 (2012/272/EU) insofar as the Council has added the legal bases relating to transport (Arts 91 and 100 TFEU), readmission (Art. 79(3) TFEU), and environment (Art. 191(4) TFEU).

market. Later on, the objective of a certain freedom of movement of Turkish workers who had migrated to the Community, laid down in Article 12 of the Association Agreement, was sought through two decisions of the Association Council, namely Decisions 1/80 and 3/80. Decision 1/80 contained the first steps on the road to free movement for Turkish workers inside the Community, not yet between the Community and Turkey. Decision 3/80 laid down certain provisions on the migration of social security so as to minimize the disadvantages of such labour mobility of Turks inside the EC. Together with the non-discrimination principle of Article 37 of the Protocol of 1970, these two Decisions have meant a lot for the position of Turkish workers and their families, as appears clearly from a large number of judgments of the CJEU on the interpretation of these Decisions.[3] Finally, the envisaged Customs Union between the EU and Turkey was brought about by Decision 1/95 of the Association Council; this decision is also increasingly at the root of important CJEU cases[4] and even WTO Panel and Appellate Body reports.[5]

Sections of all these instruments that together form the most important parts of the Customs Union between the EU and Turkey are here reproduced in their chronological order so as to enable the reader to obtain an overview of the law of this customs union.

It is noteworthy that in such a 'bilateral' mixed agreement, it is clear from the construction of the agreement itself that the Community (presently the Union) and the Member States together operate as one party to the agreement.

AGREEMENT
establishing an Association between the European Economic Community and Turkey
(signed at Ankara, 12 September 1963)

PREAMBLE
HIS MAJESTY THE KING OF THE BELGIANS,
THE PRESIDENT OF THE FEDERAL REPUBLIC OF GERMANY,
THE PRESIDENT OF THE FRENCH REPUBLIC,
THE PRESIDENT OF THE ITALIAN REPUBLIC,
HER ROYAL HIGHNESS THE GRAND DUCHESS OF LUXEMBOURG,
HER MAJESTY THE QUEEN OF THE NETHERLANDS,
and
THE COUNCIL OF THE EUROPEAN ECONOMIC COMMUNITY,
of the one part, and

---

[3] See: Joined Cases C-7/10 and C-9/10 *Kahveci and Inan*, not yet reported; Case C-187/10 *Unal*, not yet reported; Joined Cases C-300/09 and C-301/09 *Toprak and Oguz*, not yet reported, para. 55; Case C-303/08 *Bozkurt*, not yet reported, para. 41; Case C-230/03 *Sedef* [2006] ECR I-157; Case C-1/97 *Birden* [1998] ECR I-7747; Case C-237/91 *Kus* [1992] ECR I-6781; Case C-192/89 *Sevince* [1990] ECR I-3461; Case C-262/96 *Sürül* [1999] ECR I-2685; Joined Cases C-102/98 and C-211/98 *Kocak and Örs* [2000] ECR I-1287; Case C-373/02 *Sakir Öztürk* [2004] ECR I-03605.

[4] See: Case C-372/06 *Asda Stores* [2007] ECR I-11223; Case C-204/07 P—*C.A.S. v. Commission* [2008] ECR I-06135.

[5] WTO DS/34, Turkey—Textiles.

THE PRESIDENT OF THE REPUBLIC OF TURKEY,
of the other part,

DETERMINED to establish ever closer bonds between the Turkish people and the
peoples brought together in the European Economic Community;
RESOLVED to ensure a continuous improvement in living conditions in Turkey and
in the European Economic Community through accelerated economic progress and
the harmonious expansion of trade, and to reduce the disparity between the Turkish
economy and the economies of the Member States of the Community;
MINDFUL both of the special problems presented by the development of the Turkish
economy and of the need to grant economic aid to Turkey during a given period;
RECOGNIZING that the support given by the European Economic Community to the
efforts of the Turkish people to improve their standard of living will facilitate the accession of Turkey to the Community at a later date;
RESOLVED to preserve and strengthen peace and liberty by joint pursuit of the ideals
underlying the Treaty establishing the European Economic Community;
HAVE DECIDED to conclude an Agreement establishing an Association between the
European Economic Community and Turkey in accordance with Article 238 of the
Treaty establishing the European Economic Community, and to this end have desig-
nated as their Plenipotentiaries:

[…]

TITLE I
PRINCIPLES
Article 1

By this Agreement an Association is established between the European Economic
Community and Turkey.

Article 2

1. The aim of this Agreement is to promote the continuous and balanced strengthening
of trade and economic relations between the Parties, while taking full account of the
need to ensure an accelerated development of the Turkish economy and to improve the
level of employment and the living conditions of the Turkish people.
2. In order to attain the objectives set out in paragraph 1, a customs union shall be
progressively established in accordance with Article 3, 4 and 5.
3. Association shall comprise:
(a) a preparatory stage;
(b) a transitional stage;
(c) a final stage.

Article 3

1. During the preparatory stage Turkey shall, with aid from the Community, strengthen
its economy so as to enable it to fulfil the obligations which will devolve upon it during
the transitional and final stages.
The detailed rules for this preparatory stage, in particular those for aid from the Community,
are set out in the Provisional Protocol and in the Financial Protocol to this Agreement.

2. The preparatory stage shall last five years, unless it should be extended in accordance with the conditions laid down in the Provisional Protocol.

The change-over to the transitional stage shall be effected in accordance with Article 1 of the Provisional Protocol.

Article 4

1. During the transitional stage the Contracting Parties shall, on the basis of mutual and balanced obligations:

- establish progressively a customs union between Turkey and the Community;
- align the economic policies of Turkey and the Community more closely in order to ensure the proper functioning of the Association and the progress of the joint measures which this requires.

2. This stage shall last not more than twelve years, subject to such exceptions as may be made by mutual agreement. The exceptions must not impede the final establishment of the customs union within a reasonable period.

Article 5

The final stage shall be based on the customs union and shall entail closer coordination of the economic policies of the Contracting Parties.

Article 6

To ensure the implementation and the progressive development of the Association, the Contracting Parties shall meet in a Council of Association which shall act within the powers conferred upon it by this Agreement.

Article 7

The Contracting Parties shall take all appropriate measures, whether general or particular, to ensure the fulfilment of the obligations arising from this Agreement.

They shall refrain from any measures liable to jeopardize the attainment of the objectives of this Agreement.

TITLE II

IMPLEMENTATION OF THE TRANSITIONAL STAGE

Article 8

In order to attain the objectives set out in Article 4, the Council of Association shall, before the beginning of the transitional stage and in accordance with the procedure laid down in Article 1 of the Provisional Protocol, determine the conditions, rules and timetables for the implementation of the provisions relating to the fields covered by the Treaty establishing the Community which must be considered; this shall apply in particular to such of those fields as are mentioned under this Title and to any protective clause which may prove appropriate.

Article 9

The Contracting Parties recognize that within the scope of this Agreement and without prejudice to any special provisions which may be laid down pursuant to Article 8, any discrimination on grounds of nationality shall be prohibited in accordance with the principle laid down in Article 7 of the Treaty establishing the Community.

Chapter 1

The customs union

Article 10

1. The customs union provided for in Article 2(2) of this Agreement shall cover all trade in goods.

2. The customs union shall involve:

- the prohibition between Member States of the Community and Turkey, of customs duties on imports and exports and of all charges having equivalent effect, quantitative restrictions and all other measures having equivalent effect which are designed to protect national production in a manner contrary to the objectives of this Agreement;
- the adoption by Turkey of the Common Customs Tariff of the Community in its trade with third countries, and an approximation to the other Community rules on external trade.

Chapter 2

Agriculture

Article 11

1. The Association shall likewise extend to agriculture and trade in agricultural products, in accordance with special rules which shall take into account the common agricultural policy of the Community.

2. 'Agricultural products' means the products listed in Annex II to the Treaty establishing the Community, as at present supplemented in accordance with Article 38(3) of that Treaty.

Chapter 3

Other economic provisions

Article 12

The Contracting Parties agree to be guided by Articles 48, 49 and 50 of the Treaty establishing the Community for the purpose of progressively securing freedom of movement for workers between them.

Article 13

The Contracting Parties agree to be guided by Articles 52 to 56 and Article 58 of the Treaty establishing the Community for the purpose of abolishing restrictions on freedom of establishment between them.

Article 14

The Contracting Parties agree to be guided by Articles 55, 56 and 58 to 65 of the Treaty establishing the Community for the purpose of abolishing restrictions on freedom to provide services between them.

Article 15

The rules and conditions for extension to Turkey of the transport provisions contained in the Treaty establishing the Community, and measures adopted in implementation of those provisions shall be laid down with due regard to the geographical situation of Turkey.

Article 16

The Contracting Parties recognize that the principles laid down in the provisions on competition, taxation and the approximation of laws contained in Title I of Part III of the Treaty establishing the Community must be made applicable in their relations within the Association.

Article 17

Each State party to this Agreement shall pursue the economic policy needed to ensure the equilibrium of its overall balance of payments and to maintain confidence in its currency, while taking care to ensure a continuous, balanced growth of its economy in conjunction with stable prices. Each State party to this Agreement shall pursue a conjunctural policy, in particular a financial and monetary policy, which furthers these objectives.

Article 18

Each State party to this Agreement shall pursue a policy with regard to rates of exchange which ensures that the objectives of the Association can be attained.

Article 19

The Member States of the Community and Turkey undertake to authorize, in the currency of the country in which the creditor or the beneficiary resides, any payments or transfers connected with the movement of goods, services or capital, and any transfers of capital or earnings, to the extent that the movement of goods, services, capital and persons between them has been liberalized pursuant to this Agreement.

Article 20

The Contracting Parties shall consult each other with a view to facilitating movements of capital between Member States of the Community and Turkey which will further the objectives of this Agreement.
They shall actively seek all means of promoting the investment in Turkey of capital from countries of the Community which can contribute to Turkish economic development. With respect to arrangements for foreign capital residents of all Member States shall be entitled to all the advantages, in particular as regards currency and taxation, which Turkey accords to any other Member State or to a third country.

Article 21

The Contracting Parties hereby agree to work out a consultation procedure in order to ensure coordination of their commercial policies towards third countries and mutual respect for their interests in this field, *inter alia* in the event of subsequent accession to or association with the Community by third countries.

TITLE III

GENERAL AND FINAL PROVISIONS

Article 22

1. In order to attain the objectives of this Agreement the Council of Association shall have the power to take decisions in the cases provided for therein. Each of the Parties shall take the measures necessary to implement the decisions taken. The Council of Association may also make appropriate recommendations.

2. The Council of Association shall periodically review the functioning of the Association in the light of the objectives of this Agreement. During the preparatory stage, however, such reviews shall be limited to an exchange of views.

3. Once the transitional stage has been embarked on, the Council of Association shall adopt appropriate decisions where, in the course of implementation of the Association arrangements, attainment of an objective of this Agreement calls for joint action by the Contracting Parties but the requisite powers are not granted in this Agreement.

Article 23

The Council of Association shall consist of members of the Governments of the Member States and members of the Council and of the Commission of the Community on the one hand and of members of the Turkish Government on the other.

The members of the Council of Association may arrange to be represented in accordance with its rules of procedure.

The Council of Association shall act unanimously.

Article 24

The office of President of the Council of Association shall be held for a term of six months by a representative of the Community and a representative of Turkey alternately. The term of office of the first President may be shortened by a decision of the Council of Association.

The Council of Association shall adopt its rules of procedure.

The Council of Association may decide to set up committees to assist in the performance of its tasks, and in particular a committee to ensure the continuing cooperation necessary for the proper functioning of this Agreement.

The Council of Association shall lay down the terms of reference of these committees.

Article 25

1. The Contracting Parties may submit to the Council of Association any dispute relating to the application or interpretation of this Agreement which concerns the Community, a Member State of the Community, or Turkey.

2. The Council of Association may settle the dispute by decision; it may also decide to submit the dispute to the Court of Justice of the European Communities or to any other existing court or tribunal.

3. Each Party shall be required to take the measures necessary to comply with such decisions.

4. Where the dispute cannot be settled in accordance with paragraphs 2 of this Article, the Council of Association shall determine, in accordance with Article 8 of this

Agreement, the detailed rules for arbitration or for any other judicial procedure to which the Contracting Parties may resort during the transitional and final stages of this Agreement.

Article 26

This Agreement shall not apply to products within the province of the European Coal and Steel Community.

Article 27

The Council of Association shall take all appropriate steps to promote the necessary cooperation and contacts between the European Parliament, the Economic and Social Committee and other organs of the Community on the one hand and the Turkish Parliament and the corresponding organs in Turkey on the other.

During the preparatory state, however, such contacts shall be limited to relations between the European Parliament and the Turkish Parliament.

Article 28

As soon as the operation of this Agreement has advanced far enough to justify envisaging full acceptance by Turkey of the obligations arising out of the Treaty establishing the Community, the Contracting Parties shall examine the possibility of the accession of Turkey to the Community.

Article 29

1. This Agreement shall apply to the European territories of the Kingdom of Belgium, of the Federal Republic of Germany, of the French Republic, of the Italian Republic, of the Grand Duchy of Luxembourg and of the Kingdom of the Netherlands on the one hand and to the territory of the Turkish Republic on the other.

2. The Agreement shall also apply to the French overseas departments so far as concerns those of the fields covered by it which are listed in the first subparagraph of Article 227(2) of the Treaty establishing the Community.

The conditions for applying to those territories the provisions of this Agreement relating to other fields shall be decided at a later date by agreement between the Contracting Parties.

Article 30

The Protocols annexed to this Agreement by common accord of the Contracting Parties shall form an integral part thereof.

Article 31

This Agreement shall be ratified by the Signatory States in accordance with their respective constitutional requirements, and shall become binding on the Community by a decision of the Council taken in accordance with the Treaty establishing the Community and notified to the Parties to this Agreement.

The instruments of ratification and the notifications of conclusion shall be exchanged at Brussels.

Article 32

This Agreement shall enter into force on the first day of the second month following the date of exchange of the instruments of ratification and the notification referred to in Article 31.

Article 33

This Agreement is drawn up in two copies in the Dutch, French, German, Italian and Turkish languages, each of these texts being equally authentic.

Additional Protocol [...] signed on 23 November 1970, annexed to the Agreement establishing the Association between the European Economic Community and Turkey and on measures to be taken for their entry into force—Final Act—Declarations, Unofficial translation, Official Journal L 293, 29.12.1972, pp. 4–56.

[...]

Article 1

This Protocol lays down the conditions, arrangements and timetables for implementing the transitional stage referred to in Article 4 of the Agreement establishing an Association between the European Economic Community and Turkey.

TITLE I

FREE MOVEMENT OF GOODS

Article 2

1. Chapter I, Section I, and Chapter II of this Title shall apply:
(a) to goods produced in the Community or in Turkey, including those wholly or partially obtained or produced from products coming from third countries which are in free circulation in the Community or in Turkey;
(b) to goods coming from third countries and in free circulation in the Community or in Turkey.
2. Products coming from third countries shall be considered to be in free circulation in the Community or in Turkey if the import formalities have been complied with and any customs duties or charges having equivalent effect which are payable have been levied in the Community or in Turkey, and if they have not benefited from a total or partial drawback of such duties or charges.
3. Goods imported from third countries into the Community or into Turkey and accorded special customs treatment by reason of their country of origin or of exportation, shall not be considered to be in free circulation in the territory of one Contracting Party if they are re-exported to the other Contracting Party. The Council of Association may, however, make exceptions to this rule under conditions which it shall lay down.
4. Paragraphs 1 and 2 shall apply only to goods exported from the Community on or after the date of signature of this Protocol.

Article 3

1. Chapter I, Section I, and Chapter II of this Title shall likewise apply to goods obtained or produced in the Community or in Turkey, in the manufacture of which were used products coming from third countries and not in free circulation either in the Community or in Turkey. These provisions shall, however, apply to those goods only if the exporting State charges a countervailing levy, the rate of which is a percentage of the duties laid down in the Common Customs Tariff for third country products used in their manufacture. This percentage, fixed by the Council of Association for each of such periods as it may determine, shall be based on the tariff reduction granted on those goods in the importing State. The Council of Association shall also lay down the rules for the countervailing levy, taking into account the relevant rules in force before 1 July 1968 in trade between Member States.

2. The countervailing levy shall not, however, be charged on exports from the Community or from Turkey of goods obtained or produced under the conditions mentioned in this Article while the reduction of customs duties on the majority of goods imported into the territory of the other Contracting Party does not exceed 20%, taking into account the various timetables for tariff reductions fixed by this Protocol.

Article 4

The Council of Association shall determine the methods of administrative cooperation to be used in implementing Articles 2 and 3, taking into account the methods laid down by the Community with regard to trade between Member States.

Article 5

1. If either Contracting Party considers that differences arising from the application to imports of customs duties, quantitative restrictions or any measures having equivalent effect, or from any other measure of commercial policy, threaten to deflect trade or to cause economic difficulties in its territory, it may bring the matter before the Council of Association, which shall, if necessary, recommend appropriate methods for avoiding any harm liable to result therefrom.

2. Where deflections occur or economic difficulties arise and the Party concerned considers that they call for immediate action, that Party may itself take the necessary protective measures, and shall notify the Council of Association thereof without delay; the Council of Association may decide whether the Party concerned shall amend or abolish those measures.

3. In the choice of such measures preference shall be given to those which least disturb the operation of the Association and, in particular, the normal development of trade.

Article 6

During the transitional stage the Contracting Parties shall, in so far as may be necessary for the proper functioning of the Association, take steps to approximate their law, regulation or administrative action in respect of customs matters, taking into account the approximations already effected by the Member States of the Community.

CHAPTER I

THE CUSTOMS UNION

Section I

Elimination of customs duties between the Community and Turkey

Article 7

1. The Contracting Parties shall refrain from introducing between themselves any new customs duties on imports or exports or charges having equivalent effect, and from increasing those already applied, in their trade with each other at the date of entry into force of this Protocol.

2. The Council of Association may, however, authorize the Contracting Parties to introduce new customs duties on exports or charges having equivalent effect if they are necessary for the attainment of the objectives of the Agreement.

Article 8

Customs duties on imports and charges having equivalent effect, in force between the Community and Turkey, shall be progressively abolished in accordance with Articles 9 to 11.

Article 9

On the entry into force of this Protocol, the Community shall abolish customs duties and charges having equivalent effect on imports from Turkey.

Article 10

1. For each product, the basic duty on which Turkey is to apply the successive reductions shall be the duty actually applied in respect of the Community at the date of signature of this Protocol.

2. The timetable for the reductions to be effected by Turkey shall be as follows: the first reduction shall be made on the entry into force of this Protocol. The second and third shall be applied three years and five years later. The fourth and subsequent reductions shall be made each year in such a way that the final reduction is made at the end of the transitional stage.

3. Each reduction shall be made by lowering the basic duty on each product by 10%.

Article 11

Notwithstanding Article 10(2) and (3), Turkey shall progressively abolish, over a period of twenty-two years, in accordance with the following timetable, the basic duties in respect of the Community on the products listed in Annex 3: a reduction of 5% on each duty shall be made on the entry into force of this Protocol. Three further reductions, each of 5%, shall be made three, six and ten years later.

Eight further reductions, each of 10%, shall be made twelve, thirteen, fifteen, seventeen, eighteen, twenty, twenty-one and twenty-two years respectively after the entry into force of this Protocol.

Article 12

1. Turkey may, during the first eight years of the transitional stage, make the amendments to Annex 3 which are needed to protect the development of a processing

industry which did not exist in Turkey at the time of entry into force of this Protocol, or to ensure the expansion in accordance with the Turkish development plan in force at the time, of an existing processing industry. Such amendments may, however, only be made on condition that:
– in aggregate they relate to not more than 10% by value of imports from the Community in 1967, calculated at 1967 prices;
– the value of imports from the Community of all products listed in Annex 3, calculated at 1967 prices, is not increased.
Products added to Annex 3 may immediately be made liable to duties calculated in accordance with Article 11; those products which are removed from that list shall immediately be made liable to duties calculated in accordance with the provisions of Article 10.

2. Turkey shall notify the Council of Association of the measures which it proposes to take pursuant to the above provisions.

3. To the same end as that mentioned in paragraph 1 above, and within the limit of 10% of imports from the Community in 1967, the Council of Association may authorize Turkey, during the transitional stage, to reintroduce, increase or impose customs duties on imports of products subject to the arrangements set out in Article 10.
These tariff measures shall not, for any of the tariff headings which they affect, raise the duty on imports from the Community to more than 25% ad valorem.

4. The Council of Association may derogate from paragraphs 1 and 3.

Article 13

1. Irrespective of the provisions of Articles 9 to 11, each Contracting Party may suspend in whole or in part the collection of duties applied by it to products imported from the other Party, in particular, as regards Turkey, for the purpose of stimulating imports of certain products necessary for its economic development; the other Contracting Party shall be informed of such measures.

2. The Contracting Parties declare their readiness to reduce their duties in trade with the other Party more rapidly than is provided for in Article 9 to 11 if its general economic situation and the situation of the economic sector concerned so permit. The Council of Association shall make recommendations to this end.

Article 14

Where, in respect of a country outside the Association, Turkey applies a shorter timetable than is provided for in Articles 10 and 11 to the elimination of a charge having effect equivalent to a customs duty, the same timetable shall be applied to the elimination of that charge in respect of the Community.

Article 15

Without prejudice to Article 7(2), the Contracting Parties shall, at the latest four years after the entry into force of this Protocol, abolish between themselves, customs duties on exports and charges having equivalent effect.

Article 16

1. Article 7(1) and Articles 8 to 15 shall also apply to customs duties of a fiscal nature.

2. On the entry into force of this Protocol the Community and Turkey shall inform the Council of Association of their customs duties of a fiscal nature.

3. Turkey shall retain the right to substitute for these customs duties of a fiscal nature an internal tax which complies with the provisions of Article 44.

4. If the Council of Association finds that substitution for any customs duty of a fiscal nature meets with serious difficulties in Turkey, it shall authorize that country to retain the duty on condition that it shall abolish it not later than the end of the transitional stage. Such authorization must be requested within twelve months of the entry into force of this Protocol.

Turkey may provisionally continue to apply such a duty until a decision has been taken by the Council of Association.

Section II

Adoption by Turkey of the Common Customs Tariff

Article 17

The Turkish Customs Tariff shall be aligned on the Common Customs Tariff during the transitional stage on the basis of the duties actually applied by Turkey in respect of third countries at the date of signature of this Protocol, and in accordance with the following rules:

1. In the case of products on which the duties actually applied by Turkey at the date indicated above do not differ by more than 15% either way from the duties in the Common Customs Tariff, the latter duties shall be applied one year after the second reduction of duties provided for in Article 10.

2. In any other case Turkey shall, one year after the second reduction of duties provided for in Article 10, apply duties reducing by 20% the difference between the duty actually applied at the date of signature of this Protocol and the duty in the Common Customs Tariff.

3. When the fifth and seventh reductions of customs duties provided for in Article 10 are applied, this difference shall be further reduced by 20%.

4. The Common Customs Tariff shall be applied in its entirety when the tenth reduction of customs duties provided for in Article 10 is applied.

Article 18

Notwithstanding Article 17 Turkey shall, for the products listed in Annex 3, align its customs tariff over a period of twenty-two years in accordance with the following rules:

1. In the case of products for which the duties actually applied by Turkey on the date of signature of this Protocol do not differ from the Common Customs Tariff duties by more than 15% either way, the latter duties shall be applied from the date of the fourth reduction of duties provided for in Article 11.

2. In any other case Turkey shall, from the date of the fourth reduction of duties provided for in Article 11, apply duties reducing by 20% the difference between the duty actually applied at the date of signature of this Protocol and the duty in the Common Customs Tariff.

3. When the seventh and ninth reductions provided for in Article 11 are applied, this difference shall be further reduced by 30% and 20%, respectively.

4. The Common Customs Tariff shall be applied in its entirety at the end of the twenty-second year.

Article 19

1. In the case of particular products making up not more than 10% of the total value of its imports in 1967, Turkey may, after consultation in the Council of Association, defer until the end of the twenty-second year after the entry into force of this Protocol the reductions of duties in respect of third countries which it should otherwise make under Articles 17 and 18.

2. In the case of particular products making up not more than 5% of the total value of its imports in 1967, Turkey may, after consultation in the Council of Association, retain after a period of twenty-two years customs duties in respect of third countries which are higher than those in the Common Customs Tariff.

3. However, the application of the preceding paragraphs must not prejudice the free movement of goods within the Association and shall not entitle Turkey to invoke the provisions of Article 5.

4. Where alignment of the Turkish Customs Tariff with the Common Customs Tariff has been accelerated, Turkey shall maintain in favour of the Community a preference equivalent to that resulting from the arrangements provided for in this Chapter.

As regards the products listed in Annex 3, no such acceleration may take place before the end of the transitional stage, unless prior authorization has been given by the Council of Association.

5. As regards customs duties which have been authorized pursuant to the first subparagraph of Article 16(4) or which Turkey may provisionally maintain in accordance with the second subparagraph of Article 16(4), Articles 17 and 18 need not be applied. On expiry of the authorization, Turkey shall apply the duties provided for in Articles 17 and 18.

Article 20

1. To facilitate the importation of particular goods from countries with which Turkey has concluded bilateral trade agreements, Turkey may, with the prior authorization of the Council of Association, grant tariff quotas at reduced or zero rates of duty, if the functioning of those agreements is appreciably affected by the application of this Protocol or by measures taken in pursuance thereof.

2. Such authorization shall be deemed to have been given when the tariff quotas mentioned in the preceding paragraph comply with the following conditions:

(a) the total annual value of such quotas does not exceed 10% of the average value of Turkish imports from third countries during the past three years for which statistics are available, excluding from such imports those which were made with the help of the means referred to in Annex 4. Imports from third countries admitted free of duty within the framework of Annex 4 shall be deducted from this 10%;

(b) in the case of each product, the value of imports provided for within the framework of the tariff quotas shall not exceed one third of the average value of Turkish imports of that product from third countries in the past three years for which statistics are available.

3. Turkey shall notify the Council of Association of measures which it envisages taking in pursuance of paragraph 2.

At the end of the transitional stage the Council of Association may decide whether the provisions of paragraph 2 should be repealed or amended.

4. In no case may the duty under a tariff quota be lower than that actually applied by Turkey to imports from the Community.

CHAPTER II

ELIMINATION OF QUANTITATIVE RESTRICTIONS BETWEEN THE CONTRACTING PARTIES

Article 21

Quantitative restrictions on imports and all measures having equivalent effect shall, without prejudice to the following provisions, be prohibited between the Contracting Parties.

Article 22

1. The Contracting Parties shall refrain from introducing any new quantitative restrictions on imports or measures having equivalent effect.

2. However, as regards Turkey, this obligation shall, at the date of the entry into force of this Protocol, apply only to 35% of Turkish imports on private account from the Community in 1967. This percentage shall be increased to 40%, 45%, 60% and 80%, three, eight, thirteen and eighteen years after the entry into force of this Protocol.

3. Six months before each of the dates of the last three increases the Council of Association shall review the consequences for the economic development of Turkey of increasing the degree of liberalization and shall, if this is necessary for achievement of an accelerated development of the Turkish economy, decide to postpone the increase for a period which it shall determine.

In the absence of a decision, the increase shall be postponed for one year. The review procedure shall be repeated six months before expiry of that period. A further postponement of a year shall take place if the Council of Association again takes no decision.

At the end of this second period, Turkey shall implement the increase in the degree of liberalization unless a decision to the contrary has been taken by the Council of Association.

4. A list of products whose importation from the Community has been liberalized shall be supplied to the Community at the time of signature of this Protocol. The list shall be consolidated in respect of the Community. The lists of products liberalized at the deadlines mentioned in paragraph 2 shall also be supplied to the Community and consolidated in its respect.

5. Turkey may reintroduce quantitative restrictions on imports of products which have been liberalized but not consolidated pursuant to this Article, on condition that it opens quotas in favour of the Community equal to at least 75% of the average imports from the Community during the three years preceding that reintroduction. These quotas shall be subject to the provisions of Article 25(4).

6. In no case may Turkey apply to the Community a treatment less favourable than that accorded to third countries.

Article 23

Without prejudice to Article 22(5) the Contracting Parties shall, in their trade with one another, refrain from making more restrictive the quantitative restrictions on imports and measures having equivalent effect existing at the date of entry into force of this Protocol.

Article 24

The Community shall, on the entry into force of this Protocol, abolish all quantitative restrictions on imports from Turkey. This liberalization shall be consolidated in respect of Turkey.

Article 25

1. Turkey shall progressively abolish quantitative restrictions on imports from the Community in accordance with the provisions of the following paragraphs.
2. One year after the entry into force of this Protocol quotas in favour of the Community shall be opened for imports of each product which has not been liberalized in Turkey. These quotas shall be fixed so as to correspond to the average imports from the Community in the last three years for which statistics are available, excluding imports financed:
(a) by special aid resources connected with specific investment projects;
(b) without allocation of foreign currency;
(c) under the law on the promotion of foreign capital investment.
3. Where, in respect of a product which has not been liberalized, imports from the Community in the first year after the entry into force of this Protocol amount to less than 7% of total imports of that product, a quota equal to 7% of those imports shall be opened one year after the entry into force of this Protocol.
4. Three years after the entry into force of this Protocol Turkey shall increase the aggregate of the quotas so opened by not less than 10% over the amount thereof for the preceding year and by not less than 5% by value of the quota for each product. These amounts shall be increased every two years in the same proportion in relation to the preceding period.
5. From the thirteenth year after the entry into force of this Protocol each quota shall be increased every two years by at least 20% in relation to the preceding period.
6. Where, in respect of a product which has not been liberalized, there have been no imports into Turkey in the first year after the entry into force of this Protocol, the rules for opening and increasing quotas shall be laid down by the Council of Association.
7. If the Council of Association finds that during two successive years the imports of any product which has not been liberalized have been appreciably below the level of the quota opened, that quota shall not be taken into account in calculating the total value of the quotas. In such case Turkey shall abolish quota restrictions on that product in respect of the Community.

8. All quantitative restrictions on imports into Turkey shall be abolished not later than twenty-two years after the entry into force of this Protocol.

Article 26

1. The Contracting Parties shall, within twenty-two years, abolish all measures having an effect equivalent to quantitative restrictions on imports from each other. The Council of Association shall recommend the progressive adjustments to be made during this period, taking into account provisions adopted within the Community.

2. In particular, Turkey shall, in accordance with the timetables laid down in Articles 10 and 11, progressively abolish the deposits required from importers for imports of goods from the Community.

Moreover, deposits amounting to more than 140% of the dutiable value for customs purposes of goods imported from the Community, in the case of motor vehicle spare parts and accessories falling within heading No 87.06 of the Turkish Customs Tariff, and to more than 120% of that value in the case of other products, shall be reduced to these levels on the entry into force of this Protocol.

Article 27

1. Quantitative restrictions on exports, and all measures having equivalent effect, shall be prohibited between the Contracting Parties.

The Community and Turkey shall, by the end of the transitional stage at the latest, abolish between themselves all quantitative restrictions on exports and any measures having equivalent effect.

2. Notwithstanding the preceding paragraph, the Community and Turkey may, after consultation in the Council of Association, retain or introduce restrictions on exports of basic products to the extent necessary to promote the development of specific sectors of their economies or to meet any shortage of those products.

In that event, the Party concerned shall open in favour of the other Party a quota which takes into account the average exports for the last three years for which statistics are available and the normal development of trade resulting from the progressive achievement of the customs union.

Article 28

Turkey declares its readiness to abolish quantitative restrictions on imports from and exports to the Community more rapidly than is provided for in the preceding Articles, if its general economic situation and the situation of the economic sector concerned so permit. To this end the Council of Association shall make recommendations to Turkey.

Article 29

The provisions of Articles 21 to 27 shall not preclude prohibitions or restrictions on imports, exports or goods in transit justified on grounds of public morality, public policy or public security; the protection of health and life of humans, animals or plants; the protection of national treasures possessing artistic, historic or archeological value; or the protection of industrial and commercial property. Such prohibitions or restrictions shall not, however, constitute a means of arbitrary discrimination or a disguised restriction on trade between the Contracting Parties.

Article 30

1. The Contracting Parties shall progressively adjust any State monopolies of a commercial character so as to ensure that when the period of twenty-two years has ended no discrimination regarding the conditions under which goods are procured and marketed exists between nationals of Member States of the Community and nationals of Turkey.

The provisions of this Article shall apply to any body through which a Member State or Turkey, in law or in fact, either directly or indirectly supervises, determines or appreciably influences imports or exports between the Community and Turkey. These provisions shall also apply to monopolies delegated by the State to others.

2. The Contracting Parties shall refrain from introducing any new measure which is contrary to the principles laid down in paragraph 1 or which restricts the scope of the Articles dealing with the abolition of customs duties and quantitative restrictions between the Contracting Parties.

3. The procedure and the timetable in accordance with which the Turkish monopolies mentioned in this Article are to be adjusted and the barriers to trade between the Community and Turkey are to be lowered, shall be laid down by the Council of Association not later than six years after the entry into force of this Protocol.

Until the Council of Association takes the decision provided for in the preceding subparagraph, each Contracting Party shall apply to products subject to a monopoly in the territory of the other Contracting Party treatment at least as favourable as that applied to like products of the most-favoured third country.

4. The obligations on the Contracting Parties shall be binding only in so far as they are compatible with existing international agreements.

CHAPTER III
PRODUCTS SUBJECT TO SPECIFIC RULES ON IMPORTATION INTO THE COMMUNITY AS A RESULT OF THE IMPLEMENTATION OF THE COMMON AGRICULTURAL POLICY

Article 31

The arrangements for agricultural products set out in Chapter IV shall apply to products which are subject, on importation into the Community, to specific rules as a result of the implementation of the common agricultural policy.

CHAPTER IV
AGRICULTURE

Article 32

This Protocol shall extend to agricultural products, save as otherwise provided in Article 33 to 35.

Article 33

1. Over a period of twenty-two years Turkey shall adjust its agricultural policy with a view to adopting, at the end of that period, those measures of the common agricultural policy which must be applied in Turkey if free movement of agricultural products between it and the Community is to be achieved.

2. During the period mentioned in paragraph 1, the Community shall, in establishing and subsequently developing its agricultural policy, take into account the interests of Turkish agriculture. Turkey shall furnish the Community with all information which is relevant in this connection.

3. The Community shall inform Turkey of proposals from the Commission regarding the establishment and development of the common agricultural policy, and of the opinions issued and decisions taken regard to such proposals.

4. The Council of Association shall decide what information on agriculture shall be supplied by Turkey to the Community.

5. The proposals from the Commission mentioned in paragraph 3, and the measures in respect of agriculture which Turkey envisages taking in accordance with paragraph 1, may be the subject of consultation in the Council of Association.

Article 34

1. At the end of the period of twenty-two years the Council of Association, having established that Turkey has adopted the measures of the common agricultural policy which are referred to in Article 33(1), shall adopt the provisions necessary for achieving the free movement of agricultural products between the Community and Turkey.

2. The provisions referred to in paragraph 1 may include any necessary derogations from the rules laid down in this Protocol.

3. The Council of Association may alter the date referred to in paragraph 1.

Article 35

1. Pending the adoption of provisions under Article 34 and by way of derogation from Articles 7 to 11, 15 to 18, 19(1) and (5), 21 to 27, and 30, the Community and Turkey shall grant each other preferential treatment in their trade in agricultural products. The scope of such preferential treatment and the arrangements therefor shall be decided by the Council of Association.

2. The treatment to be accorded from the beginning of the transitional stage is, however, laid down in Annex 6.

3. One year after the entry into force of this Protocol and every two years thereafter, the Council of Association shall, at the request of either Contracting Party, review the results of the preferential treatment for agricultural products. It may decide upon improvements which prove to be necessary for progressive attainment of the objectives of the Agreement of Association.

4. Article 34(2) shall apply.

TITLE II

MOVEMENT OF PERSONS AND SERVICES

CHAPTER I

WORKERS

Article 36

Freedom of movement for workers between Member States of the Community and Turkey shall be secured by progressive stages in accordance with the principles set out in Article 12 of the Agreement of Association between the end of the twelfth and the twenty-second year after the entry into force of that Agreement.

The Council of Association shall decide on the rules necessary to that end.

Article 37

As regards conditions of work and remuneration, the rules which each Member State applies to workers of Turkish nationality employed in the Community shall not discriminate on grounds of nationality between such workers and workers who are nationals of other Member States of the Community.

Article 38

While freedom of movement for workers between Member States of the Community and Turkey is being brought about by progressive stages, the Council of Association may review all questions arising in connection with the geographical and occupational mobility of workers of Turkish nationality, in particular the extension of work and residence permits, in order to facilitate the employment of those workers in each Member State.

To that end, the Council of Association may make recommendations to Member States.

Article 39

1. Before the end of the first year after the entry into force of this Protocol the Council of Association shall adopt social security measures for workers of Turkish nationality moving within the Community and for their families residing in the Community.

2. These provisions must enable workers of Turkish nationality, in accordance with arrangements to be laid down, to aggregate periods of insurance or employment completed in individual Member States in respect of old-age pensions, death benefits and invalidity pensions, and also as regards the provision of health services for workers and their families residing in the Community. These measures shall create no obligation on Member States to take into account periods completed in Turkey.

3. The abovementioned measures must ensure that family allowances are paid if a worker's family resides in the Community.

4. It must be possible to transfer to Turkey old-age pensions, death benefits and invalidity pensions obtained under the measures adopted pursuant to paragraph 2.

5. The measures provided for in this Article shall not affect the rights and obligations arising from bilateral agreements between Turkey and Member States of the Community, in so far as these agreements provide more favourable arrangements for Turkish nationals.

Article 40

The Council of Association may make recommendations to Member States and Turkey for encouraging the exchange of young workers; the Council of Association shall be guided in the matter by the measures adopted by Member States in implementation of Article 50 of the Treaty establishing the Community.

CHAPTER II
RIGHT OF ESTABLISHMENT, SERVICES AND TRANSPORT
Article 41

1. The Contracting Parties shall refrain from introducing between themselves any new restrictions on the freedom of establishment and the freedom to provide services.

2. The Council of Association shall, in accordance with the principles set out in Articles 13 and 14 of the Agreement of Association, determine the timetable and rules for the progressive abolition by the Contracting Parties, between themselves, of restrictions on freedom of establishment and on freedom to provide services.

The Council of Association shall, when determining such timetable and rules for the various classes of activity, take into account corresponding measures already adopted by the Community in these fields and also the special economic and social circumstances of Turkey. Priority shall be given to activities making a particular contribution to the development of production and trade.

Article 42

1. The Council of Association shall extend to Turkey, in accordance with the rules which it shall determine, the transport provisions of the Treaty establishing the Community with due regard to the geographical situation of Turkey. In the same way it may extend to Turkey measures taken by the Community in applying those provisions in respect of transport by rail, road and inland waterway.

2. If provisions for sea and air transport are laid down by the Community, pursuant to Article 84(2) of the Treaty establishing the Community, the Council of Association shall decide whether, to what extent and by what procedure provisions may be laid down for Turkish sea and air transport.

TITLE III
CLOSER ALIGNMENT OF ECONOMIC POLICIES

CHAPTER I
COMPETITION, TAXATION AND APPROXIMATION OF LAWS
Article 43

1. The Council of Association shall, within six years of the entry into force of this Protocol, adopt the conditions and rules for the application of the principles laid down in Articles 85, 86, 90 and 92 of the Treaty establishing the Community.

2. During the transitional stage Turkey may be considered as being in the situation specified in Article 92(3)(a) of the Treaty establishing the Community. Accordingly, aid to promote Turkish economic development shall be considered to be compatible with the proper functioning of the Association if such aid does not alter the conditions of trade to an extent inconsistent with the mutual interests of the Contracting Parties.

At the end of the transitional stage, the Council of Association shall, taking into account the economic situation of Turkey at the time, decide whether it is necessary to extend the period during which the preceding subparagraph shall apply.

Article 44

1. Neither Contracting Party shall impose, directly or indirectly, on the products of the other Party any internal taxation of any kind in excess of that imposed directly or indirectly on similar domestic products.

Neither Contracting Party shall impose on the products of the other Party any internal taxation of such a nature as to afford indirect protection to other products.

The Contracting Parties shall, not later than the beginning of the third year after the entry into force of this Protocol, repeal any provisions existing at the date of its signature which conflict with the above rules.

2. In trade between the Community and Turkey, repayment of internal in respect of exported products shall not exceed the internal taxation imposed on those products, whether directly or indirectly.

3. Where a turnover tax calculated on a cumulative multi-stage tax system is levied, average rates for products or groups of products may be established, in the case of internal taxation imposed on imported products or of repayments allowed on exported products, provided that there is no infringement of the principles laid down in the preceding paragraphs.

4. The Council of Association shall ensure that the above provisions are applied, taking into account the experience of the Community in the field covered by this Article.

Article 45

As regards trade between the Community and Turkey, and in the case of charges other than turnover taxes, excise duties and other forms of indirect taxation, remissions and repayments in respect of exports may not be granted, and countervailing charges in respect of imports may not be imposed, unless the measures contemplated have been approved in advance by the Council of Association and for a limited period.

Article 46

The Contracting Parties may adopt any protective measures which they consider to be needed to overcome difficulties due to the absence of a decision by the Council of Association on the rules and conditions of application provided for in Article 43(1), or to the non-application of those decisions or of Articles 44 or 45.

Article 47

1. If, during the period of twenty-two years, the Council of Association, on application by a Contracting Party, finds that dumping is being practised in trade between the Community and Turkey, it shall address recommendations to the person or persons with whom such practices originate for the purpose of putting an end to them.

2. The injured Party may, after notifying the Council of Association, take suitable protective measures where:

(a) the Council of Association has taken no decision pursuant to paragraph 1 within three months from the making of the application;

(b) despite the issue of recommendations under paragraph 1, the dumping practices continue.

Moreover, where the interests of the injured Party call for immediate action, that Party may, after informing the Council of Association, introduce interim protective measures which may include anti-dumping duties. Such measures shall not remain in force more than three months from the date of the application, or from the date on which the injured Party takes protective measures under (b) of the preceding subparagraph.

3. Where protective measures have been taken under (a) of the first subparagraph of paragraph 2, or under the second subparagraph of that paragraph, the Council of Association may, at any time, decide that such protective measures shall be suspended pending the issue of recommendations under paragraph 1.

The Council of Association may recommend the abolition or amendment of protective measures taken under (b) of the first subparagraph of paragraph 2.

4. Products which originated in or were in free circulation in one of the Contracting Parties and which have been exported to the other Contracting Party shall, on reimportation, be admitted into the territory of the former Contracting Party free of all customs duties, quantitative restrictions or measures having equivalent effect.

The Council of Association may make any appropriate recommendations for the application of this paragraph; it shall be guided by Community experience in this field.

Article 48

The Council of Association may recommend the Contracting Parties to take measures to approximate the laws, regulations or administrative provisions in respect of fields which are not covered by this Protocol but have a direct bearing on the functioning of the Association, and of fields covered by this Protocol but for which no specific procedure is laid down therein.

CHAPTER II
ECONOMIC POLICY
Article 49

In order to facilitate attainment of the objectives set out in Article 17 of the Agreement of Association, the Contracting Parties shall regularly consult each other in the Council of Association to coordinate their economic policies.

The Council of Association shall, where necessary, recommend appropriate measures.

Article 50

1. The Contracting Parties declare their readiness to undertake the liberalization of payments beyond the extent provided for in Article 19 of the Agreement of Association, in so far as their economic situation in general and the state of their balance of payments in particular so permit.

2. In so far as movements of goods, services and capital are limited only by restrictions on payments connected therewith, these restrictions shall be progressively abolished by applying, mutatis mutandis, the provisions relating to the abolition of quantitative restrictions, the provision of services and to capital movements.

3. The Contracting Parties undertake not to make more restrictive the arrangements which they apply to transfers connected with the invisible transactions listed in Annex

III to the Treaty establishing the Community, without the prior agreement of the Council of Association.

4. If need be, the Contracting Parties shall consult each other on measures to be taken to enable the payments and transfers mentioned in Article 19 of the Agreement of Association and in this Article to be effected.

Article 51

In order to further the objectives set out in Article 20 of the Agreement of Association, Turkey shall, on the entry into force of this Protocol, endeavour to improve the treatment accorded to private capital from the Community which can contribute to the development of the Turkish economy.

Article 52

The Contracting Parties shall endeavour to avoid introducing any new foreign exchange restrictions on the movement of capital and current payments connected therewith between themselves, and shall endeavour not to make the existing arrangements more restrictive.

The Contracting Parties shall simplify to the maximum extent possible authorization and control formalities applicable to the conclusion and carrying out of capital transactions and transfers, and shall, in so far as is necessary, consult each other for the purpose of achieving such simplification.

CHAPTER III
COMMERCIAL POLICY

Article 53

1. The Contracting Parties shall consult each other in the Council of Association in order to achieve, during the transitional stage, the coordination of their commercial policies in relation to third countries, in particular in the fields mentioned in Article 113(1) of the Treaty establishing the Community.

For this purpose, each Contracting Party shall, at the request of the other Party, furnish all relevant information on agreements which it concludes and which contain tariff or commercial provisions, as well as on changes which it makes in its external trade arrangements.

Where such agreements or changes might have a direct and particular effect on the functioning of the Association, there shall be appropriate consultation in the Council of Association in order to take into account the interests of the Contracting Parties.

2. At the end of the transitional stage, the Contracting Parties, meeting in the Council of Association, shall coordinate their commercial policies more closely with the aim of achieving a commercial policy based on uniform principles.

Article 54

1. If the Community concludes an agreement of association or a preferential agreement having a direct and particular effect on the functioning of the Association, appropriate consultation shall take place in the Council of Association in order to enable

the Community to take into account the mutual interests stated in the Agreement of Association between the Community and Turkey.

2. Turkey shall, where necessary to prevent barriers to the movement of goods within the Community, endeavour to take all appropriate measures for the solution of any practical problem which may arise in connection with trade between Turkey and countries linked to the Community by an association agreement or a preferential agreement.

Where such measures have not been taken, the Council of Association may adopt the necessary provisions for ensuring the proper functioning of the Association.

Article 55

Consultations shall take place in the Council of Association on the implementation of 'Regional Cooperation for Development' (RCD).

The Council of Association may adopt any necessary provisions. These must not impede the proper functioning of the Association.

Article 56

In the event of a third State acceding to the Community, appropriate consultations shall take place in the Council of Association so as to ensure that account can be taken of the mutual interests of the Community and Turkey stated in the Agreement of Association.

TITLE IV

GENERAL AND FINAL PROVISIONS

Article 57

The Contracting Parties shall progressively adjust the conditions for participation in contracts awarded by public authorities and public undertakings, and by private undertakings which have been granted special or exclusive rights, so that by the end of the period of twenty-two years there is no discrimination between nationals of Member States and nationals of Turkey established in the territory of the Contracting Parties.

The Council of Association shall determine the timetable and rules for this adjustment; when doing so it shall be guided by the solutions adopted by the Community in this field.

Article 58

In the fields covered by this Protocol:

– the arrangements applied by Turkey in respect of the Community shall not give rise to any discrimination between Member States, their nationals or their companies or firms;

– the arrangements applied by the Community in respect of Turkey shall not give rise to any discrimination between Turkish nationals or Turkish companies or firms.

Article 59

In the fields covered by this Protocol Turkey shall not receive more favourable treatment than that which Member States grant to one another pursuant to the Treaty establishing the Community.

Article 60

1. If serious disturbances occur in a sector of the Turkish economy or prejudice its external financial stability, or if difficulties arise which adversely affect the economic situation in a region of Turkey, Turkey may take the necessary protective measures.
The Council of Association shall be notified immediately of those measures and of the rules for their application.

2. If serious disturbances occur in a sector of the economy of the Community or of one of more Member States, or prejudice the external financial stability of one or more Member States, or if difficulties arise which adversely affect the economic situation in a region of the Community, the Community may take, or authorize the Member State or States concerned to take, the necessary protective measures.
The Council of Association shall be notified immediately of such measures and of the rules for their application.

3. In the choice of measures to be taken in pursuance of paragraphs 1 and 2, preference shall be given to those which will least disturb the functioning of the Association. These measures shall not exceed what is strictly necessary to remedy the difficulties that have arisen.

4. Consultations may take place in the Council of Association on the measures taken in pursuance of paragraphs 1 and 2.

Article 61

Without prejudice to the special provisions of this Protocol, the transitional stage shall be twelve years.

Article 62

This Protocol and the Annexes thereto shall form an integral part of the Agreement establishing an Association between the European Economic Community and Turkey.

Article 63

1. This Protocol shall be ratified by the Signatory States in accordance with their respective constitutional requirements and shall be validly concluded on behalf of the Community by a decision of the Council, taken in accordance with the provisions of the Treaty establishing the Community; the decision shall be notified to the Contracting Parties to the Agreement establishing an Association between the European Economic Community and Turkey.
The instruments of ratification and the notification of conclusion shall be exchanged at Brussels.

2. This Protocol shall enter into force on the first day of the month following the date of the exchange of the instruments of ratification and of the notification mentioned in paragraph 1.

3. If this Protocol does not enter into force at the beginning of a calendar year, the Council of Association may shorten or lengthen the periods laid down in this Protocol, in particular those in which free movement of goods is to be achieved, so that they may terminate at the end of a calendar year.

[...]

Decision no. 1/80 of the EC-Turkey Association Council of 19 September 1980 on the development of the Association (96/142/EC).

[...]

CHAPTER II: Social Provisions

SECTION 1: Questions relating to employment and the free movement of workers

Article 6

1. Subject to Article 7 on free access to employment for members of his family, a Turkish worker duly registered as belonging to the labour force of a Member State:
• shall be entitled in that Member State, after one year's legal employment, to the renewal of his permit to work for the same employer, if a job is available;
• shall be entitled in that Member State, after one year's legal employment, to the renewal of his permit to work for the same employer, if a job is available;
• shall be entitled in that Member State, after three years of legal employment and subject to the priority to be given to workers of Member States of the Community, to respond to another offer of employment, with an employer of his choice, made under normal conditions and registered with the employment services of that State, for the same occupation;
• shall enjoy free access in that Member State to any paid employment of his choice, after four years of legal employment.
1. Annual holidays and absences for reasons of maternity or an accident at work or short periods of sickness shall be treated as periods of legal employment. Periods of involuntary unemployment duly certified by the relevant authorities and long absences on account of sickness shall not be treated as periods of legal employment, but shall not affect rights acquired as the result of the preceding period of employment.
2. The procedures for applying paragraphs 1 and 2 shall be those established under national rules.

Article 7

The members of the family of a Turkish worker duly registered as belonging to the labour force of a Member State, who have been authorized to join him:
– shall be entitled—subject to the priority to be given to workers of Member States of the Community—to respond to any offer of employment after they have been legally resident for at least three years in that Member State;
– shall enjoy free access to any paid employment of their choice provided they have been legally resident there for at least five years.
Children of Turkish workers who have completed a course of vocational training in the host country may respond to any offer of employment there, irrespective of the length of time they have been resident in that Member State, provided one of their parents has been legally employed in the Member State concerned for at least three years.

Article 8

1. Should it not be possible in the Community to meet an offer of employment by calling on the labour available on the employment market of the Member States

and should the Member States, within the framework of their provisions laid down by law, regulation or administrative action, decide to authorize a call on workers who are not nationals of a Member State of the Community in order to meet the offer of employment, they shall endeavour in so doing to accord priority to Turkish workers.

2. The employment services of the Member State shall endeavour to fill vacant positions which they have registered and which the duly registered Community labour force has not been able to fill with Turkish workers who are registered as unemployed and legally resident in the territory of that Member State.

Article 9

Turkish children residing legally in a Member State of the Community with their parents who are or have been legally employed in that Member State, shall be admitted to courses of general education, apprenticeship and vocational training under the same educational entry qualifications as the children of nationals of that Member State. They may in that Member State be eligible to benefit from the advantages provided for under the national legislation in this area.

Article 10

1. The Member States of the Community shall as regards remuneration and other conditions of work grant Turkish workers duly registered as belonging to their labour forces treatment involving no discrimination on the basis of nationality between them and Community workers.

2. Subject to the application of Articles 6 and 7, the Turkish workers referred to in paragraph 1 and members of their families shall be entitled, on the same footing as Community workers, to assistance from the employment services in their search for employment.

Article 11

Nationals of the Member States duly registered as belonging to the labour force in Turkey, and members of their families who have been authorized to join them, shall enjoy in that country the rights and advantages referred to in Articles 6, 7, 9 and 10 if they meet the conditions laid down in those Articles.

Article 12

Where a Member State of the Community of Turkey experiences or is threatened with disturbances on its employment market which might seriously jeopardize the standard of living or level of employment in a particular region, branch of activity or occupation, the State concerned may refrain from automatically applying Articles 6 and 7. The State concerned shall inform the Association Council of any such temporary restriction.

Article 13

The Member States of the Community and Turkey may not introduce new restrictions on the conditions of access to employment applicable to workers and members of their families legally resident and employed in their respective territories.

Article 14

1. The provisions of this section shall be applied subject to limitations justified on grounds of public policy, public security or public health.

2. They shall not prejudice the rights and obligations arising from national legislation or bilateral agreements between Turkey and the Member States of the Community where such legislation or agreements provide for more favourable treatment for their nationals.

Article 15

1. So as to be in a position to ensure the harmonious application of the provisions of this section and determine that they are applied in such a way as to exclude the danger of disturbance of the employment markets, the Association Committee shall periodically exchange information in order to improve mutual knowledge of the economic and social situation, including the state of and outlook for the labour market in the Community and in Turkey. It shall each year present a report on its activities to the Association Council.

2. The Association Committee shall be authorized to enlist the assistance of an ad hoc Working Party in order to implement paragraph 1.

Article 16

1. The provisions of this section shall apply from 1 December 1980.

2. From 1 June 1983, the Association Council shall, particularly in the light of the reports on activities referred to in Article 15 examine the results of application of the provisions of this section with a view to preparing solutions which might apply as from 1 December 1983.

SECTION 2: Social and cultural advancement and the exchange of young workers

Article 17

The Member States and Turkey shall co-operate, in accordance with their domestic situations and their legal systems, in appropriate schemes to promote the social and cultural advancement of Turkish workers and the members of their family, in particular literacy campaigns and courses in the language of the host country, activities to maintain links with Turkish culture and access to vocational training.

Article 18

The Association Committee shall prepare a recommendation to be forwarded by the Association Council to the Member States of the Community and Turkey with a view to the implementation of any action that may enable young workers who have received their basic training in their own country to complement their vocational training by participating in in-service training, under the conditions set out in Article 40 of the Additional Protocol. It shall monitor the actual implementation of this provision.

[...]

Decision no. 3/80 of the Association Council of 19 September 1980 on the application of the social security schemes of the Member States of the European Communities to Turkish workers and members of their families, Official Journal C 110, 25.4.1983, p. 60.

[...]

Article 2

Persons covered

This Decision shall apply:

– to workers who are or have been subject to the legislation of one more Member States and who are Turkish nationals,

– to the members of the families of these workers, resident in the territory of one of he Member States,

– to the survivors of these workers.

Article 3

Equality of treatment

1. Subject to the special provisions of this Decision, persons resident in the territory of one of the Member States to whom this Decision applies shall be subject to the same obligations and enjoy the same benefits under the legislation of any Member State as the nationals of that State.

2. The provisions of paragraph 1 shall apply to the right to elect members of the organs of social security institutions or to participate in their nomination, but shall not affect the legislative provisions of any Member State relating to eligibility or methods of nomination of persons concerned to those organs.

Article 4

Matters covered

1. This Decision shall apply to all legislation concerning the following branches of social security:

(a) sickness and maternity benefits;

(b) invalidity benefits, including those intended for the maintenance or improvement of earning capacity;

(c) old-age benefits;

(d) survivors' benefits;

(e) benefits in respect of accidents at work and occupational diseases;

(f) death grants;

(g) unemployment benefits;

(h) family benefits.

2. This Decision shall apply to all general and special social security schemes, whether contributory or non-contributory, and to schemes concerning the liability of an employer or shipowner in respect of the benefits referred to in paragraph 1.

3. The provisions of Title III shall not, however, affect the legislative provisions of any Member State concerning a shipowner's liability.

4. This Decision shall not apply to social and medical assistance or to benefit schemes for victims of war and its consequences.

[...]

Decision no. 1/95 of the EC-Turkey Association Council of 22 December 1995 on implementing the final phase of the Customs Union (96/142/EC), Official Journal L 35, 13.2.1996, pp. 1–46.

[...]

Article 1

Without prejudice to the provisions of the Ankara Agreement, its Additional and Supplementary Protocols, the Association Council hereby lays down the rules for implementing the final phase of the Customs Union, laid down in Articles 2 and 5 of the abovementioned Agreement.

CHAPTER I

FREE MOVEMENT OF GOODS AND COMMERCIAL POLICY

Article 2

This Chapter shall apply to products other than agricultural products as defined in Article 11 of the Association Agreement. The special provisions relating to agricultural products are set out in Chapter II of this Decision.

Article 3

1. This Chapter shall apply to goods:
– produced in the Community or Turkey, including those wholly or partially obtained or produced from products coming from third countries which are in free circulation in the Community or in Turkey,
– coming from third countries and in free circulation in the Community or in Turkey.
2. Products from third countries shall be considered to be in free circulation in the Community or in Turkey if the import formalities have been complied with and any customs duties or charges having equivalent effect which are payable have been levied in the Community or in Turkey, and if they have not benefited from a total or partial reimbursement of such duties or charges.
3. The customs territory of the Customs Union shall comprise:
– the customs territory of the Community as defined in Article 3 of Council Regulation (EEC) No 2913/92 of 12 October 1992 establishing the Community Customs Code,
– the customs territory of Turkey.
4. This Chapter shall also apply to goods obtained or produced in the Community or in Turkey, in the manufacture of which products coming from third countries and not in free circulation either in the Community or in Turkey were used.
These provisions shall, however, apply to those goods only if the import formalities have been complied with and any customs duties or charges having equivalent effect

payable on third-country products used in their manufacture have been levied in the exporting State.

5. If the exporting State does not apply the provisions of the second subparagraph of paragraph 4, the goods referred to in the first subparagraph of paragraph 4 shall not be considered to be in free circulation and the importing State shall therefore apply the customs legislation applying to goods from third countries.

6. The Customs Cooperation Committee set up by Decision No 2/69 of the Association Council shall determine the methods of administrative cooperation to be used in implementing paragraphs 1, 2 and 4.

SECTION I
Elimination of customs duties and charges having equivalent effect
Article 4

Import or export customs duties and charges having equivalent effect shall be wholly abolished between the Community and Turkey on the date of entry into force of this Decision. The Community and Turkey shall refrain from introducing any new customs duties on imports or exports or any charges having equivalent effect from that date. These provisions shall also apply to customs duties of a fiscal nature.

SECTION II
Elimination of quantitative restrictions or measures having equivalent effect
Article 5

Quantitative restrictions on imports and all measures having equivalent effect shall be prohibited between the Parties.

Article 6

Quantitative restrictions on exports and all measures having equivalent effect shall be prohibited between the Parties.

Article 7

The provisions of Articles 5 and 6 shall not preclude prohibitions or restrictions on imports, exports or goods in transit justified on grounds of public morality, public policy or public security; the protection of health and life of humans, animals or plants; the protection of national treasures possessing artistic, historic or archaeological value; or the protection of industrial and commercial property. Such prohibitions or restrictions shall not, however, constitute a means of arbitrary discrimination or a disguised restriction on trade between the Parties.

Article 8

1. Within five years from the date of entry into force of this Decision, Turkey shall incorporate into its internal legal order the Community instruments relating to the removal of technical barriers to trade.

2. The list of these instruments and the conditions and detailed arrangements governing their implementation by Turkey shall be laid down by decision of the Association Council within a period of one year from the date of entry into force of this Decision.

3. This provision shall not preclude the application by Turkey, with effect from the date of entry into force of this Decision, of Community instruments deemed to be of particular importance.

4. The Parties stress the importance of effective cooperation between them in the fields of standardization, metrology and calibration, quality, accreditation, testing and certification.

Article 9

When Turkey has put into force the provisions of the Community instrument or instruments necessary for the elimination of technical barriers to trade in a particular product, trade in that product between the Parties shall take place in accordance with the conditions laid down by those instruments, without prejudice to the application of the provisions of this Decision.

Article 10

1. With effect from the date of entry into force of this Decision, and during the period required for the application by Turkey of the instruments referred to in Article 9, Turkey shall refrain from impeding the placing on the market or taking into service on its territory of products from the Community the conformity of which with the Community Directives defining the requirements to be met by such products has been attested to, in accordance with the conditions and the procedures laid down in those Directives.

2. By way of derogation from paragraph 1, if Turkey finds that a product, the conformity of which with the Community Directives has been attested to in accordance with paragraph 1, and which is used in accordance with its intended purpose, fails to satisfy one of the requirements referred to in Article 7, it may take all appropriate measures, in accordance with the conditions and procedures provided for in paragraph 3, to withdraw the product in question from the market, or to prohibit or restrict its being placed on the market or taken into service.

3. (a) If Turkey is considering taking a measure under paragraph 2, it shall, forthwith, notify the Community through the Customs Union Joint Committee and shall provide all relevant information.

(b) The Parties shall immediately enter into consultations within the Customs Union Joint Committee to find a mutually acceptable solution.

(c) Turkey may not take a measure mentioned in paragraph 2 until one month has elapsed after the date of notification provided for in paragraph 3 (a) unless the consultation procedure under paragraph 3 (b) has been concluded before the expiry of the time limit. When exceptional circumstances requiring immediate action render prior examination impossible, Turkey may apply forthwith the measure strictly necessary to remedy the situation.

(d) Turkey shall forthwith inform the Customs Union Joint Committee of the measure it has taken and shall provide all relevant information.

(e) The Community may at any time request the Customs Union Joint Committee to review such measure.

4. The provisions of paragraphs 1 and 2 shall apply, mutatis mutandis, to foodstuffs.

Article 11

During the period required for the application by Turkey of the instruments referred to in Article 9, the Community will accept the results of the procedures applied in Turkey for assessing the conformity of industrial products with the requirements of Community law, provided that those procedures are in conformity with the requirements in force in the Community, and on the understanding that, in the motor vehicles sector, Council Directive 70/156/EEC of 6 February 1970 on the approximation of the laws of the Member States relating to the type-approval of motor vehicles and their trailers shall apply in Turkey.

SECTION III
Commercial policy
Article 12

1. From the date of entry into force of this Decision, Turkey shall, in relation to countries which are not members of the Community, apply provisions and implementing measures which are substantially similar to those of the Community's commercial policy set out in the following Regulations:
– Council Regulation (EC) No 3285/94 common rules for imports),
– Council Regulation (EC) No 519/94 (common rules for imports from certain third countries),
– Council Regulation (EC) No 520/94 (Community procedure for administering quantitative quotas (implementing provisions: Commission Regulation (EC) No 738/94,
– Council Regulations (EC) No 3283/94 and (EC) No 3284/94 (protection against dumped and subsidized imports),
– Council Regulation (EC) No 3286/94 (Community procedures in the field of the common commercial policy),
– Council Regulation (EEC) No 2603/69 (establishing common rules for exports),
– Council Decision 93/112/EEC (officially supported export credits),
– Council Regulation (EC) No 3036/94 (outward processing arrangements for textiles and clothing),
– Council Regulation (EC) No 3030/93 (textile imports under common rules),
– Council Regulation (EC) No 517/94 (textile imports under autonomous arrangements),
– Council Regulation (EC) No 3951/92 (textile imports from Taiwan).
2. In conformity with the requirements of Article XXIV of the GATT Turkey will apply as from the entry into force of this Decision, substantially the same commercial policy as the Community in the textile sector including the agreements or arrangements on trade in textile and clothing. The Community will make available to Turkey the cooperation necessary for this objective to be reached.
3. Until Turkey has concluded these arrangements, the present system of certificates of origin for the exports of textile and clothing from Turkey into the Community will remain in force and such products not originating from Turkey will remain subject to

the application of the Communities commercial policy in relation to the third countries in question.

4. The provisions of this Decision shall not constitute a hindrance to the implementation by the Community and Japan of their Arrangement relating to trade in motor vehicles, mentioned in the Annex to the Agreement on safeguards attached to the Agreement setting up the World Trade Organization.

Before the entry into force of this Decision, Turkey and the Community will define the modalities of cooperation in order to prevent the circumvention of the said Arrangement.

In the absence of such modalities, the Community reserves the right to take, in respect of imports into its territory, any measure rendered necessary by the application of the said Arrangement.

SECTION IV

Common Customs Tariff and preferential tariff policies

Article 13

1. Upon the date of entry into force of this Decision, Turkey shall, in relation to countries which are not members of the Community, align itself on the Common Customs Tariff.

2. Turkey shall adjust its customs tariff whenever necessary to take account of changes in the Common Customs Tariff.

3. The Customs Cooperation Committee shall determine what measures are appropriate to implement paragraphs 1 and 2.

Article 14

1. Turkey shall be informed of any decisions taken by the Community to amend the Common Customs Tariff, to suspend or reintroduce duties and any decision concerning tariff quotas or ceilings in sufficient time for it simultaneously to align the Turkish customs tariff on the Common Customs Tariff. Prior consultations shall be held within the Customs Union Joint Committee for this purpose.

2. Where the Turkish customs tariff cannot be aligned simultaneously on the Common Customs Tariff, the Customs Union Joint Committee may decide to grant a period of time for this to be undertaken. Under no circumstances may the Customs Union Joint Committee authorize Turkey to apply a customs tariff which is lower than the Common Customs Tariff for any product.

3. If Turkey wishes to suspend on temporary basis or resume duties other than as envisaged in paragraph 1, Turkey will make a prompt notification to the Community. Consultations on the abovementioned decisions will be held in the Joint Customs Union Committee.

Article 15

By way of derogation from Article 13 and in accordance with Article 19 of the Additional Protocol, Turkey may retain until 1 January 2001 customs duties higher than the Common Customs Tariff in respect of third countries for products agreed by the Association Council.

Article 16

1. With a view to harmonizing its commercial policy with that of the Community, Turkey shall align itself progressively with the preferential customs regime of the Community within five years as from the date of entry into force of this Decision. This alignment will concern both the autonomous regimes and preferential agreements with third countries. To this end, Turkey will take the necessary measures and negotiate agreements on mutually advantageous basis with the countries concerned. The Association Council shall periodically review the progress made.

2. In each of the cases referred to in paragraph 1 the granting of these tariff preferences shall be conditional on compliance with provisions relating to the origin of products identical to those governing the granting of such preferences by the Community.

3. (a) Where, during the period referred to in paragraph 1, Turkey maintains a tariff policy different from that of the Community, goods imported from third countries into the Community and released for free circulation with preferential treatment by reason of their country of origin or of exportation shall be subject to the payment of a compensatory levy if they are imported into Turkey, in the following circumstances:

– they have been imported from countries to which the same preferential tariff treatment is not granted by Turkey, and

– they can be identified as imported from these countries, and

– the duty to be paid in Turkey is at least five percentage points higher than that applicable in the Community, and

– an important distortion of traffic related to these goods has been observed.

(b) The Customs Union Joint Committee shall establish the list of the goods to which the compensatory levy applies, as well as the amount of this levy.

SECTION V

Processed agricultural products not covered by Annex II to the Treaty establishing the European Community

Article 17

The provisions of this Section apply to goods listed in Annex 1.

Article 18

Notwithstanding Article 13, Turkey may apply on imports from third countries of goods listed in Annex 1 an agricultural component. The agricultural component shall be established in accordance with Article 19.

Article 19

1. The agricultural component applicable to goods imported into Turkey shall be obtained by adding together the quantities of basic agricultural products considered to have been used for the manufacture of the goods in question multiplied by the basic amount corresponding to each of these basic agricultural products as defined in paragraph 3.

2. (a) The basic agricultural products to be taken into account are listed in Annex 2.

(b) The quantities of basic agricultural products to be taken into account are set out in Annex 3.

(c) In the case of goods classified under the nomenclature codes for which reference is made in Annex 3 to Annex 4, the amounts of the agricultural component to be taken into account are set out in Annex 4.

3. The basic amount corresponding to each basic agricultural product is the amount of the charge applicable on import into Turkey of the agricultural product originating in a non-preferential third country during the reference period applicable to agricultural products. The basic amounts are set out in Annex 5.

Article 20

1. Notwithstanding Article 4, Turkey and the Community may apply agricultural components established in accordance with the provisions below in trade with each other.

2. Such agricultural components, reduced in accordance with Article 22 where applicable, shall only apply to goods listed in Annex 1.

3. The Community shall apply to Turkey the same specific duties that represent the agricultural component applicable to third countries.

4. Turkey shall apply to imports from the Community the agricultural component applied in accordance with Article 19.

Article 21

Notwithstanding the modalities set out in this Decision a derogation regime is foreseen for the goods listed in the Annex 6/Table 1 and Annex 6/Table 2 in which the import charges in Turkey will be reduced in three steps over a period of three years for the former and one year for the latter. The level of those import charges is set in Annex 6/Table 1 and Annex 6/Table 2.

At the end of the relevant periods the provisions of this Section shall apply fully.

Article 22

1. Where, in trade between the Community and Turkey, the duty applicable to a basic agricultural product is reduced, the agricultural component determined in accordance with Article 20(4) for imports into Turkey or that referred to in Article 20(3), for imports into the Community, shall be reduced proportionately.

2. Where the reductions referred to in paragraph 1 are effected within the limits of a quota, a list of goods and quantities to which the reduced agricultural component is applicable shall be drawn up by the Association Council.

3. The provisions of paragraphs 1 and 2 above apply to the import charges referred to in Article 21.

Article 23

If imports of one or more of the products covered by the derogation regime cause or threaten to cause in Turkey serious disturbances which may endanger the objectives of the Customs Union for processed agricultural products, consultations between the Parties shall be held within the Customs Union Joint Committee, with a view to finding a mutually acceptable solution.

If such a solution cannot be found, the Customs Union Joint Committee may recommend appropriate ways of maintaining the proper functioning of the Customs Union without prejudice to the provisions of Article 63.

CHAPTER II
AGRICULTURAL PRODUCTS
Article 24

1. The Association Council hereby reaffirms the Parties' common objective to move towards the free movement of agricultural products between themselves as provided for in Articles 32 to 35 of the Additional Protocol.

2. The Association Council notes that an additional period is required to put in place the conditions necessary to achieve free movement of these products.

Article 25

1. Turkey shall adjust its policy in such a way as to adopt the common agricultural policy measures required to establish freedom of movement of agricultural products. It shall communicate to the Community the decisions taken in that respect.

2. The Community shall take account as far as possible of Turkish agriculture's interests when developing its agricultural policy and shall notify Turkey of the relevant Commission proposals and the decisions taken on the basis of these proposals.

3. Consultations may be held within the Association Council on the proposals and decisions referred to in paragraph 2 and on the measures which Turkey intends to take in the agricultural field pursuant to paragraph 1.

Article 26

The Community and Turkey shall progressively improve, on a mutually advantageous basis, the preferential arrangements which they grant each other for their trade in agricultural products. The Association Council shall regularly examine the improvements made to these preferential arrangements.

Article 27

The Association Council shall adopt the provisions necessary to achieve the free movement of agricultural products between the Community and Turkey once it has established that Turkey has adopted the common agricultural policy measures referred to in Article 25(1).

CHAPTER III
CUSTOMS PROVISIONS
Article 28

1. On the date of entry into force of this Decision, Turkey shall adopt provisions in the following fields, based on Council Regulation (EEC) No 2913/92 of 12 October 1992 establishing the Community Customs Code and Commission Regulation (EEC) No 2454/93 of 2 July 1993 (16) laying down the implementing provisions thereof:
(a) origin of goods;
(b) customs value of goods;
(c) introduction of goods into the territory of the Customs Union;
(d) customs declaration;

(e) release for free circulation;

(f) suspensive arrangements and customs procedures with economic impact;

(g) movement of goods;

(h) customs debt;

(i) right of appeal.

2. Turkey shall take the measures necessary to implement, on the date of entry into force of this Decision, provisions based on:

(a) Council Regulation (EEC) No 3842/86 of 1 December 1986 laying down measures to prohibit the release for free circulation of counterfeit goods (17) and Commission Regulation (EEC) No 3077/87 of 14 October 1987 laying down the implementing measures thereof (18);

(b) Council Regulation (EEC) No 918/83 of 28 March 1983 setting up a Community system of reliefs from customs duties (19) and Commission Regulations (EEC) No 2287/83, (EEC) No 2288/83, (EEC) No 2289/83 and (EEC) No 2290/83 of 29 July 1983 laying down the implementing measures thereof (20);

(c) Council Regulation (EEC) No 616/78 on proof of origin for certain textile products falling within Chapter 51 or Chapters 53 to 62 of the Common Customs Tariff and imported into the Community, and on conditions for the acceptance of such proof (21).

3. The Customs Cooperation Committee shall lay down the appropriate measures to implement paragraphs 1 and 2.

Article 29

Mutual assistance on customs matters between the administrative authorities of the Parties shall be governed by the provisions of Annex 7, which on the Community side, covers those matters falling under the Community competence.

Article 30

The Customs Cooperation Committee shall elaborate the appropriate provisions on mutual assistance on the recovery of debts, before the entry into force of this Decision.

CHAPTER IV
APPROXIMATION OF LAWS
SECTION I
Protection of intellectual, industrial and commercial property
Article 31

1. The Parties confirm the importance they attach to ensuring adequate and effective protection and enforcement of intellectual, industrial and commercial property rights.

2. The Parties recognize that the Customs Union can function properly only if equivalent levels of effective protection of intellectual property rights are provided in both constituent parts of the Customs Union. Accordingly, they undertake to meet the obligations set out in Annex 8.

SECTION II

Competition

A. Competition rules of the Customs Union

Article 32

1. The following shall be prohibited as incompatible with the proper functioning of the Customs Union, in so far as they may affect trade between the Community and Turkey: all agreements between undertakings, decisions by associations of undertakings and concerted practices which have as their object or effect the prevention, restriction or distortion of competition, and in particular those which:

(a) directly or indirectly fix purchase or selling prices or any other trading conditions;

(b) limit or control production, markets, technical development or investment;

(c) share markets or sources of supply;

(d) apply dissimilar conditions to equivalent transactions with other trading parties, thereby placing them at a competitive disadvantage;

(e) make the conclusion of contracts subject to acceptance by the other parties of supplementary obligations which, by their nature or according to commercial usage, have no connection with the subject of such contracts.

2. Any agreements or decisions prohibited pursuant to this Article shall automatically be void.

3. The provisions of paragraph 1 may, however, be declared inapplicable in the case of:

– any agreement or category of agreements between undertakings,

– any decision or category of decisions by associations of undertakings,

– any concerted practice or category of concerted practices

which contributes to improving the production or distribution of goods or to promoting technical or economic progress, which allowing consumers a fair share of the resulting benefit, and which does not:

(a) impose on the undertakings concerned restrictions which are not indispensable to the attainment to these objectives;

(b) afford such undertakings the possibility of eliminating competition in respect of a substantial part of the products in question.

Article 33

1. Any abuse by one or more undertakings of a dominant position in the territories of the Community and/or of Turkey as a whole or in a substantial part thereof shall be prohibited as incompatible with the proper functioning of the Customs Union, in so far as it may affect trade between the Community and Turkey.

2. Such abuse may, in particular, consist in:

(a) directly or indirectly imposing unfair purchase or selling prices or other unfair trading conditions;

(b) limiting production, markets or technical development to the prejudice of consumers;

(c) applying dissimilar conditions to equivalent transactions with other trading parties, thereby placing them at a competitive disadvantage;

(d) making the conclusion of contracts subject to acceptance by the other parties of supplementary obligations which, by their nature or according to commercial usage, have no connection with the subject of such contracts.

Article 34

1. Any aid granted by Member States of the Community or by Turkey through State resources in any form whatsoever which distorts or threatens to distort competition by favouring certain undertakings or the production of certain goods shall, in so far as it affects trade between the Community and Turkey, be incompatible with the proper functioning of the Customs Union.

2. The following shall be compatible with the functioning of the Customs Union:

(a) aid having a social character, granted to individual consumers, provided that such aid is granted without discrimination related to the origin of the products concerned;

(b) aid to make good the damage caused by natural disasters or exceptional occurrences;

(c) aid granted to the economy of certain areas of the Federal Republic of Germany affected by the division of Germany, in so far as such aid is required in order to compensate for the economic disadvantages caused by that division;

(d) for a period of five years from the entry into force of this Decision, aid to promote economic development of Turkey's less developed regions, provided that such aid does not adversely affect trading conditions between the Community and Turkey to an extent contrary to the common interest.

3. The following may be considered to be compatible with the functioning of the Customs Union:

(a) in conformity with Article 43(2) of the Additional Protocol, aid to promote the economic development of areas where the standard of living is abnormally low or where there is serious underemployment;

(b) aid to promote the execution of an important project of common European interest or to remedy a serious disturbance in the economy of a Member State of the Community or of Turkey;

(c) for a period of five years after the entry into force of this Decision, in conformity with Article 43(2) of the Additional Protocol, aids aiming at accomplishing structural adjustment necessitated by the establishment of the Customs Union. The Association Council shall review the application of that clause after the aforesaid period.

(d) aid to facilitate the development of certain economic activities or of certain economic areas, where such aid does not adversely affect trading conditions between the Community and Turkey to an extent contrary to the common interest;

(e) aid to promote culture and heritage conservation where such aid does not adversely affect trading conditions between the Community and Turkey to an extent contrary to the common interest;

(f) such other categories of aid as may be specified by the Association Council.

Article 35

Any practices contrary to Articles 32, 33 and 34 shall be assessed on the basis of criteria arising from the application of the rules of Articles 85, 86 and 92 of the Treaty establishing the European Community and its secondary legislation.

Article 36

The Parties shall exchange information, taking into account the limitations imposed by the requirements of professional and business secrecy.

Article 37

1. The Association Council shall, within two years following the entry into force of the Customs Union, adopt by Decision the necessary rules for the implementation of Articles 32, 33 and 34 and related parts of Article 35. These rules shall be based upon those already existing in the Community and shall inter alia specify the role of each competition authority.

2. Until these rules are adopted,

(a) the authorities of the Community or Turkey shall rule on the admissibility of agreements, decisions and concerted practices and on abuse of a dominant position in accordance with Articles 32 and 33;

(b) the provisions of the GATT Subsidies Code shall be applied as the rules for the implementation of Article 34.

Article 38

1. If the Community or Turkey considers that a particular practice is incompatible with the terms of Articles 32, 33 or 34, and

– is not adequately dealt with under the implementing rules referred to in Article 37, or

– in the absence of such rules, and if such practice causes or threatens to cause serious prejudice to the interest of the other Party or material injury to its domestic industry, it may take appropriate measures after consultation within the Joint Customs Union Committee or after 45 working days following referral for such consultation. Priority shall be given to such measures that will least disturb the functioning of the Customs Union.

2. In the case of practices incompatible with Article 34, such appropriate measures may, where the General Agreement on Tariffs and Trade applies thereto, only be adopted in conformity with the procedures and under the conditions laid down by the General Agreement on Tariffs and Trade and any other relevant instrument negotiated under its auspices which are applicable between the Parties.

B. Approximation of legislation

Article 39

1. With a view to achieving the economic integration sought by the Customs Union, Turkey shall ensure that its legislation in the field of competition rules is made compatible with that of the European Community, and is applied effectively.

2. To comply with the obligations of paragraph 1, Turkey shall

(a) before the entry into force of the Customs Union, adopt a law which shall prohibit behaviours of undertakings under the conditions laid down in Articles 85 and 86 of the EC Treaty. It shall also ensure that, within one year after the entry into force of the Customs Union, the principles contained in block exemption Regulations in force in the Community, as well as in the case-law developed by EC authorities, shall be applied in Turkey. The Community shall inform Turkey as soon as possible of any procedure related to the adoption, abolition, or modification of block exemption Regulations by the EC after the entry into force of the Customs Union. After such information has been given, Turkey shall have one year to adapt its legislation, if necessary;

(b) before the entry into force of the Customs Union, establish a competition authority which shall apply these rules and principles effectively;

(c) before the entry into force of this Decision, adapt all its aids granted to the textile and clothing sector to the rules laid down in the relevant Community frameworks and guidelines under Articles 92 and 93 of the EC Treaty. Turkey shall inform the Community of all its aid schemes to this sector as adapted in accordance with these frameworks and guidelines. The Community shall inform Turkey as soon as possible of any procedure related to the adoption, abolition or modification of such frameworks and guidelines by the Community after the entry into force of the Customs Union. After such information as been given, Turkey shall have one year to adapt its legislation;

(d) within two years after the entry into force of this Decision, adapt all aid schemes other than those granted to the textile and clothing sector to the rules laid down in Community frameworks and guidelines under Articles 92 and 93 of the EC Treaty. The Community shall inform Turkey as soon as possible of any procedure related to the adoption, abolition or modification of such frameworks and guidelines by the Community. After such information has been given, Turkey shall have one year to adapt its legislation;

(e) within two years after the entry into force of the Customs Union, inform the Community of all aid schemes in force in Turkey as adapted in accordance with point (d). If a new scheme is to be adopted, Turkey shall inform the Community as soon as possible of the content of such scheme;

(f) notify the Community in advance of any individual aid to be granted to an enterprise or a group of enterprises that would be notifiable under Community frameworks or guidelines had it been granted by a Member State, or of individual aid awards outside of Community frameworks or guidelines above an amount of ECU 12 million and which would have been notified under EC law had it been granted by a Member State.

Regarding individual aids granted by Member States and subject to the analysis by the Commission, on the basis of Article 93 of the EC Treaty, Turkey will be informed on the same basis as the Member States.

3. The Community and Turkey shall communicate to each other all amendments to their laws concerning restrictive practices by undertakings. They shall also inform each other of the cases when these laws have been applied.

4. In relation to information supplied under paragraph 2, points (c), (e) and (f), the Community shall have the right to raise objections against an aid granted by Turkey which it would have deemed unlawful under EC law had it been granted by a Member State. If Turkey does not agree with the Community's opinion, and if the case is not resolved within 30 days, the Community and Turkey shall each have the right to refer the case to arbitration.

5. Turkey shall have the right to raise objections and seize the Association Council against an aid granted by a Member State which it deems to be unlawful under EC law. If the case is not resolved by the Association Council within three months, the Association Council may decide to refer the case to the Court of Justice of the European Communities.

Article 40

1. The Community shall inform Turkey as soon as possible of the adoption of any Decision under Articles 85, 86 and 92 of the EC Treaty which might affect Turkey's interests.

2. Turkey shall be entitled to ask information about any specific case decided by the Community under Articles 85, 86 and 92 of the EC Treaty.

Article 41

With regard to public undertakings and undertakings to which special or exclusive rights have been granted, Turkey shall ensure that, by the end of the first year following the entry into force of the Customs Union, the principles of the Treaty establishing the European Economic Community, notably Article 90, as well as the principles contained in the secondary legislation and the case-law developed on this basis, are upheld.

Article 42

Turkey shall progressively adjust, in accordance with the conditions and the time-table laid down by the Association Council any State monopolies of a commercial character so as to ensure that, by the end of the second year following the entry into force of this Decision, no discrimination regarding the conditions under which goods are procured and marketed exists between nationals of the Member States and of Turkey.

Article 43

1. If the Community or Turkey believes that anti-competitive activities carried out on the territory of the other Party are adversely affecting its interests or the interests of its undertakings, the first Party may notify the other Party and may request that the other Party's competition authority initiate appropriate enforcement action. The notification shall be as specific as possible about the nature of the anti-competitive activities and their effects on the interests of the notifying Party, and shall include an offer for such further information and other cooperation as the notifying Party is able to provide.

2. Upon receipt of a notification under paragraph 1 and after such other discussion between the Parties as may be appropriate and useful in the circumstances, the competition authority of the notified Party will consider whether or not to initiate enforcement

action, with respect to the anti-competitive activities identified in the notification. The notified Party will advise the notifying Party of its decision. If enforcement action is initiated, the notified Party will advise the notifying Party of its outcome and, to the extent possible, of significant interim developments.

3. Nothing in this Article limits the discretion of the notified Party under its competition laws and enforcement policies as to whether or not to undertake enforcement action with respect to the notified anti-competitive activities, or precludes the notifying Party from undertaking enforcement action with respect to such anti-competitive activities.

SECTION III

Trade defence instruments

Article 44

1. The Association Council shall review upon the request of either Party the principle of application of trade defence instruments other than safeguard by one Party in its relations with the other. During any such review, the Association Council may decide to suspend the application of these instruments provided that Turkey has implemented competition, State aid control and other relevant parts of the acquis communautaire which are related to the internal market and ensured their effective enforcement, so providing a guarantee against unfair competition comparable to that existing inside the internal market.

2. The modalities of implementation of anti-dumping measures set out in Article 47 of the Additional Protocol remain in force.

Article 45

By derogation from the provisions of Section II of Chapter V, the consultation and decision-making procedures referred to in that section shall not apply to trade defence measures taken by either Party.

In the framework of the application of trade policy measures towards third countries, the Parties shall endeavour, through exchange of information and consultation, to seek possibilities for coordinating their action when the circumstances and international obligations of both Parties allow.

Article 46

By derogation from the principle of the free movement of goods laid down in Chapter I where one Party has taken or is taking anti-dumping measures or other measures pursuant to trade policy instruments as referred to in Article 44 in its relations with the other Party or with third countries, that Party may make imports of the products concerned from the territory of the other Party subject to the application of those measures. In such cases it shall inform the Customs Union Joint Committee accordingly.

Article 47

When completing the formalities involved in importing products of a type covered by trade policy measures, provided for in the preceding Articles, the authorities of the importing State shall ask the importer to indicate the origin of the products concerned on the customs declaration.

Additional supporting evidence may be requested where absolutely necessary because of serious and well-founded doubts in order to verify the true origin of the product in question.

SECTION IV

Government procurement

Article 48

As soon as possible after the date of entry into force of this Decision, the Association Council will set a date for the initiation of negotiations aiming at the mutual opening of the Parties' respective government procurement markets.

The Association Council will review progress in this area annually.

SECTION V

Direct taxation

Article 49

No provision of this Decision shall have the effect:

– of extending the fiscal advantages granted by either Party in any international agreement or arrangement by which it is bound,

– of preventing the adoption or application by either Party of any measure aimed at preventing the avoidance or evasion of taxes,

– of opposing the right or either Party to apply the relevant provisions of its tax legislation to taxpayers whose position as regards place of residence is not identical.

Indirect taxation

Article 50

1. Neither Party shall, directly or indirectly, impose on the products of the other Party any internal taxation of any kind in excess of that imposed directly or indirectly on similar domestic products.

Neither Party shall impose on the products of the other Party any internal taxation of such a nature as to afford indirect protection to other products.

2. Products exported to the territory of either of the parties shall not qualify for refunds of internal indirect taxation which exceed the indirect taxation directly or indirectly imposed on those products.

3. The Parties shall repeal any provisions existing at the date of the entry into force of this Decision which conflict with the above rules.

Article 51

The Association Council may recommend the Parties to take measures to approximate laws, regulations or administrative provisions in respect of fields which are not covered by this Decision but have a direct bearing on the functioning of the Association, and of fields covered by this Decision but for which no specific procedure is laid down therein.

CHAPTER V
INSTITUTIONAL PROVISIONS
SECTION I
The EC-Turkey Customs Union Joint Committee
Article 52

1. In accordance with Article 24 of the Association Agreement, an EC-Turkey Customs Union Joint Committee is hereby established. The Committee shall carry out exchange of views and information, formulate recommendations to the Association Council and deliver opinions with a view to ensuring the proper functioning of the Customs Union.

2. The Parties shall consult within the Committee on any point relating to the implementation of this Decision which gives rise to a difficulty for either of them.

3. The Customs Union Joint Committee shall adopt its rules of procedure.

Article 53

1. The Customs Union Joint Committee shall consist of representatives of the Parties.

2. The office of Chairman of the Customs Union Joint Committee shall be held alternately, for a period of six months, by the representative of the Community, i.e. the European Commission, and the representative of Turkey.

3. In order to carry out its duties, the Customs Union Joint Committee shall meet, as a general rule, at least once a month. It shall also meet on the initiative of its Chairman or at the request of one of the Parties in accordance with its rules of procedure.

4. The Customs Union Joint Committee may decide to establish any subcommittee or working party to assist it in carrying out its duties. The Customs Union Joint Committee shall lay down the composition and rules of operation of such subcommittees or working parties in its rules of procedure. Their duties shall be determined by the Customs Union Joint Committee in each individual case.

SECTION II
Consultation and decision procedures
Article 54

1. In areas of direct relevance to the operations of the Customs Union, and without prejudice to the other obligations deriving from Chapters I to IV Turkish legislation shall be harmonized as far as possible with Community legislation.

2. Areas of direct relevance to the operation of the Customs Union shall be commercial policy and agreements with third countries comprising a commercial dimension for industrial products, legislation on the abolition of technical barriers to trade in industrial products, competition and industrial and intellectual property law and customs legislation.

The Association Council may decide to extend the list of areas where harmonization is to be achieved in the light of the Association's progress.

3. The procedural rules provided for the Articles 55 to 60 shall apply for the purposes of this Article.

Article 55

1. Wherever new legislation is drawn up by the Commission of the European Communities in an area of direct relevance to the operation of the Customs Union and the Commission of the European Communities consults experts from Member States of the Community, it shall also informally consult Turkish experts.

2. When transmitting its proposal to the Council of the European Union, the Commission of the European Communities shall send copies thereof to Turkey.

3. During the phase preceding the decision of the Council of the European Union, the Parties shall, at the request of either of them, consult each other again within the Customs Union Joint Committee.

4. The Parties shall cooperate in good faith during the information and consultation phase with a view to facilitating, at the end of the process, the decision most appropriate for the proper functioning of the Customs Union.

Article 56

1. Where it adopts legislation in an area of direct relevance to the functioning of the Customs Union as defined in Article 54(2), the Community shall immediately inform Turkey thereof within the Customs Union Joint Committee to allow Turkey to adopt corresponding legislation which will ensure the proper functioning of the Customs Union.

2. Where there is a problem for Turkey in adopting the corresponding legislation, the Customs Union Joint Committee shall make every effort to find a mutually acceptable solution maintaining the proper functioning of the Customs Union.

Article 57

1. The principle of harmonization defined in Article 54 shall not affect Turkey's right, without prejudice to its obligations deriving from Chapters I to IV to amend legislation in areas of direct relevance to the functioning of the Customs Union provided the Customs Union Joint Committee has concluded that the amended legislation does not affect the proper functioning of the Customs Union or that the procedures referred to in the paragraphs 2 to 4 of this Article have been accomplished.

2. Where Turkey is contemplating new legislation in an area of direct relevance to the functioning of the Customs Union, it shall informally seek the views of the Commission of the European Communities on the proposed legislation in question so that the Turkish legislator may take his decision in full knowledge of the consequences for the functioning of the Customs Union.

The Parties shall cooperate in good faith with a view to facilitating, at the end of the process, the decision most appropriate for the proper functioning of the Customs Union.

3. Once the proposed legislation has reached a sufficiently advanced stage of drafting, consultations shall be held within the Customs Union Joint Committee.

4. Where Turkey adopts legislation in an area of direct relevance to the functioning of the Customs Union, it shall forthwith inform the Community within the Customs Union Joint Committee.

If Turkey's adoption of such legislation is likely to disrupt the proper functioning of the Customs Union, the Customs Union Joint Committee shall endeavour to find a mutually acceptable solution.

Article 58

1. If, at the end of the consultations undertaken under the procedure provided for in Article 56(2) or Article 57(4), a mutually acceptable solution cannot be found by the Customs Union Joint Committee and if either Party considers that discrepancies in the legislation in question may affect the free movement of goods, deflect trade or create economic problems on its territory, it may refer the matter to the Customs Union Joint Committee which, if necessary, shall recommend appropriate ways of avoiding any injury which may result.

The same procedure will be followed if differences in the implementation of legislations in an area of direct relevance to the functioning of the Customs Union, cause or threaten to cause impairment of the free movement of goods, deflections of trade or economic problems.

2. If discrepancies between Community and Turkish legislation or differences in their implementation in an area of direct relevance to the functioning of the Customs Union, cause or threaten to cause impairment of the free movement of goods or deflections of trade and the affected Party considers that immediate action is required, it may itself take the necessary protection measures and notify the Customs Union Joint Committee thereof; the latter may decide whether to amend or abolish these measures. Priority should be given to measures which least disturb the functioning of the Customs Union.

Article 59

In areas of direct relevance to the proper functioning of the Customs Union, the Commission of the European Communities shall ensure Turkish experts are involved as far as possible in the preparation of draft measures to be submitted subsequently to the committees which assist the Commission of the European Communities in the exercise of its executive powers. In this regard, when drafting proposals, the Commission of the European Communities shall consult experts from Turkey on the same basis as it consults experts from the Member States of the Community. Where the matter referred to the Council of the European Union is in accordance with the procedure applying to the type of committee concerned, the Commission of the European Communities shall transmit to the Council of the European Union the views of the Turkish experts.

Article 60

Turkish experts shall be involved in the work of a number of technical committees which assist the Commission of the European Communities in the exercise of its executive powers in areas of direct relevance to the functioning of the Customs Union where this is required to ensure the proper functioning of the Customs Union. The procedure for such participation shall be decided by the Association Council before the entry into force of this Decision. The list of Committees is contained in Annex 9. If it appears to the Parties that such an involvement should be extended to other Committees, the Customs Union Joint Committee may address the necessary recommendations to the Association Council for decisions.

SECTION III
Settlement of disputes
Article 61

Without prejudice to paragraphs 1 to 3 of Article 25 of the Ankara Agreement, if the Association Council fails to settle a dispute relating to the scope or duration of protection measures taken in accordance with Article 58(2), safeguard measures taken in accordance with Article 63 or rebalancing measures taken in accordance with Article 64, within six months of the date on which this procedure was initiated, either Party may refer the dispute to arbitration under the procedures laid down in Article 62. The arbitration award shall be binding on the Parties to the dispute.

Article 62

1. If a dispute has been referred to arbitration there shall be three arbitrators.
2. The two parties to the dispute shall each appoint one arbitrator within 30 days.
3. The two arbitrators so designated shall nominate by common agreement one umpire who shall not be a national of either Party. If they cannot agree within two months of their appointment, the umpire shall be chosen by them from seven persons on a list established by the Association Council. The Association Council shall establish and review this list in accordance with its rules of procedure.
4. The arbitration tribunal shall sit in Brussels. Unless the Parties decide otherwise, it shall adopt its rules of procedure. It shall take its decisions by majority.

SECTION IV
Safeguard measures
Article 63

The Parties confirm that the mechanism and modalities of safeguard measures provided for in Article 60 of the Additional Protocol remain valid.

Article 64

1. If a safeguard or protection measure taken by a Party creates an imbalance between the rights and obligations under this Decision, the other Party may take rebalancing measures in respect of that Party. Priority shall be given to such measures as will least disturb the functioning of the Customs Union.
2. The procedures provided for in Article 63 shall apply.

CHAPTER VI
GENERAL AND FINAL PROVISIONS
Entry into force
Article 65

1. This Decision shall enter into force on 31 December 1995.

2. During the year 1995, progress in the implementation of this Decision shall be examined regularly within the Association Committee, which will report to the Association Council.

3. Before the end of October 1995 the two Parties shall consider within the Association Council whether the provisions of this Decision for the proper functioning of the Customs Union are fulfilled.

4. On the basis of the report(s) of the Association Committee, if Turkey on one side or the Community and its Member States on the other side considers that the provisions referred to in paragraph 3 have not been met, this Party can notify to the Association Council its decision to ask for a postponement of the date referred to in paragraph 1. In such a case this date is deferred to 1 July 1996.

5. In this case paragraphs 2 to 4 shall apply mutatis mutandis.

6. The Association Council may take other appropriate decisions.

Interpretation

Article 66

The provisions of this Decision, in so far as they are identical in substance to the corresponding provisions of the Treaty establishing the European Community shall be interpreted for the purposes of their implementation and application to products covered by the Customs Union, in conformity with the relevant decisions of the Court of Justice of the European Communities.

[...]

4.3 Multilateral mixed agreements

4.3.1 Convention on the Rights of Persons with Disabilities

Council Decision on the signing, on behalf of the European Community, of the United Nations' Convention on the Rights of Persons with Disabilities; Council Decision concerning the conclusion, by the European Community, of the United Nations Convention on the Rights of Persons with Disabilities; Optional Protocol to the United Nations Convention on the Rights of Persons with Disabilities.

These three documents concerning the signing and the conclusion by the EC of the UN Convention on the Rights of Persons with Disabilities (including below in Annex I of the Council Decision on the conclusion of the Convention by the EC) serve to demonstrate a number of things. First, the structure of a classical multilateral convention negotiated and opened for ratification within the framework of the UN does not permit in the same way as a bilateral agreement to make it clear to the treaty partners that the Union and the Member States adhere to the convention as a bloc. This can lead to all kinds of misunderstandings with treaty partners about the way in which the convention is going to be applied by the Union and its Member States (see commentary on the Cultural

Diversity Convention, pp. 170–2). Second, the wish of the EC(EU) to become a party to this Convention shows how the successive amendments to the Community Treaty since the Maastricht Treaty of 1992 have influenced the external powers of the Union. These powers have been extended in scope inter alia by the broad non-discrimination clause of Article 13 EC (now Article 10 TFEU), on which the participation of the Union in this Convention is based as a matter of substance. The powers of the Union have also grown in technicality; the rule that gives the Union the possibility to sign an international agreement separate from its conclusion is a recent addition to what is now Article 218 TFEU (formerly Article 300 EC). Third, the decision of the Council by which the Union finally concluded the Convention, also included here, was taken some two years after the signature, presumably after all the Member States had also ratified. It should be noted that considerably longer delays are not exceptional in the case of mixed agreements. Finally, attention should be drawn to the reservation made by the Council in Annex III of the Decision, with respect to discrimination on the grounds of disability in the armed forces of the Member States. This reservation has been proposed by the Commission, albeit with a slightly different wording, concerning the conclusion of the Convention.[6]

Council Decision on the signing, on behalf of the European Community, of the United Nations' Convention on the Rights of Persons with Disabilities, Brussels, 20.3.2007, 7404/07.

THE COUNCIL OF THE EUROPEAN UNION,
Having regard to the Treaty establishing the European Community, and in particular Articles 13
and 95, read in conjunction with the second sentence of the first subparagraph of Article 300(2)
thereof,
Having regard to the proposal from the Commission,

Whereas:
(1) The Commission has negotiated, on behalf of the Community, the accession of the Community to the United Nations' Convention on the Rights of Persons with Disabilities and to the Optional Protocol thereto.
(2) Negotiations were successfully concluded and the Convention will be open for signature by the States and, within their areas of competence, by regional integration organisations at the United Nations' headquarters in New York as of 30 March 2007.
(3) The Member States have stated that they consider signing the relevant instruments as soon as possible and that the European Community should also be empowered to sign.
(4) Subject to its possible conclusion at a later date, the Convention should be signed on behalf of the Community,

---

[6] See Proposal for a Council Decision concerning the conclusion by the European Community of the United Nations Convention on the Rights of Persons with Disabilities, 2.9.2008, COM(2008) 530 final/2.

HAS DECIDED AS FOLLOWS:

Sole Article

1. Subject to its possible conclusion at a later date, the President of the Council is authorised to designate the persons who are empowered, on behalf of the Community, to sign the Convention on the Rights of Persons with Disabilities.

2. The text of the Convention is attached to this Decision.

3. A declaration on the Optional Protocol is attached to this Decision.

COUNCIL DECLARATION
on the signing on behalf of the European Community
of the Optional Protocol to the United Nations' Convention
on the Rights of Persons with Disabilities

The Council of the European Union shall reconsider the question of signing the Optional Protocol to the United Nations' Convention on the Rights of Persons with Disabilities by the European Community as soon as possible.

Council Decision 2010/48/EC of 26 November 2009 concerning the conclusion, by the European Community, of the United Nations Convention on the Rights of Persons with Disabilities, Official Journal L 23, 27.1.2010, pp. 35–61.

THE COUNCIL OF THE EUROPEAN UNION,

Having regard to the Treaty establishing the European Community, and in particular Articles 13 and 95 in conjunction with the second sentence of the first paragraph of Article 300(2) and the first subparagraph of Article 300(3) thereof,

Having regard to the proposal from the Commission,

Having regard to the opinion of the European Parliament,

Whereas:

(1) In May 2004, the Council authorised the Commission to conduct negotiations on behalf of the European Community concerning the United Nations Convention on the Protection and Promotion of the Rights and Dignity of Persons with Disabilities (hereinafter referred to as the UN Convention).

(2) The UN Convention was adopted by the United Nations General Assembly on 13 December 2006 and entered into force on 3 May 2008.

(3) The UN Convention was signed on behalf of the Community on 30 March 2007 subject to its possible conclusion at a later date.

(4) The UN Convention constitutes a relevant and effective pillar for promoting and protecting the rights of persons with disabilities within the European Union, to which both the Community and its Member States attach the greatest importance.

(5) The UN Convention should be thus approved, on behalf of the Community, as soon as possible.

(6) Such approval should, however, be accompanied by a reservation, to be entered by the European Community, with regard to Article 27(1) of the UN Convention, in order to state that the Community concludes the UN Convention without prejudice to the Community law-based right, as provided under Article 3(4) of Council Directive 2000/78/EC, of its Member States not to apply to armed forces the principle of equal treatment on the grounds of disability.

(7) Both the Community and its Member States have competence in the fields covered by the UN Convention. The Community and the Member States should therefore become Contracting Parties to it, so that together they can fulfil the obligations laid down by the UN Convention and exercise the rights invested in them, in situations of mixed competence in a coherent manner.

(8) The Community should, when depositing the instrument of formal confirmation, also deposit a declaration under Article 44(1) of the Convention specifying the matters governed by the Convention in respect of which competence has been transferred to it by its Member States;

HAS DECIDED AS FOLLOWS:

Article 1

1. The UN Convention on the Rights of Persons with Disabilities is hereby approved on behalf of the Community, subject to a reservation in respect of Article 27(1) thereof.

2. The text of the UN Convention is set out in Annex I to this Decision. The text of the reservation is contained in Annex III to this Decision.

Article 2

1. The President of the Council is hereby authorised to designate the person(s) empowered to deposit, on behalf of the European Community, the instrument of formal confirmation of the Convention with the Secretary-General of the United Nations, in accordance with Articles 41 and 43 of the UN Convention.

2. When depositing the instrument of formal confirmation, the designated person(s) shall, in accordance with Article 44.1 of the Convention, deposit the Declaration of Competence, set out in Annex II to this Decision, as well as the Reservation, set out in Annex III to this Decision.

Article 3

With respect to matters falling within the Community's competence and without prejudice to the respective competences of the Member States, the Commission shall be a focal point for matters relating to the implementation of the UN Convention in accordance with Article 33(1) of the UN Convention. The details of the function of focal point in this regard shall be laid down in a Code of Conduct before the deposition of the instrument of formal confirmation on behalf of the Community.

Article 4

1. With respect to matters falling within the Community's exclusive competence, the Commission shall represent the Community at meetings of the bodies created by

the UN Convention, in particular the Conference of Parties referred to in Article 40 thereof, and shall act on its behalf as concerns questions falling within the remit of those bodies.

2. With respect to matters falling within the shared competences of the Community and the Member States, the Commission and the Member States shall determine in advance the appropriate arrangements for representation of the Community's position at meetings of the bodies created by the UN Convention. The details of this representation shall be laid down in a Code of Conduct to be agreed before the deposition of the instrument of formal confirmation on behalf of the Community.

3. At the meetings referred to in paragraphs 1 and 2 the Commission and the Member States, when necessary in prior consultation with other institutions of the Community concerned, shall closely cooperate, in particular as far as the questions of monitoring, reporting and voting arrangements are concerned. The arrangements for ensuring close cooperation shall also be addressed in the Code of Conduct referred to in paragraph 2.

Article 5

This Decision shall be published in the Official Journal of the European Union.

ANNEX I
CONVENTION ON THE RIGHTS OF PERSONS WITH DISABILITIES
[...]

Article 27
Work and employment

1. States Parties recognize the right of persons with disabilities to work, on an equal basis with others; this includes the right to the opportunity to gain a living by work freely chosen or accepted in a labour market and work environment that is open, inclusive and accessible to persons with disabilities. States Parties shall safeguard and promote the realization of the right to work, including for those who acquire a disability during the course of employment, by taking appropriate steps, including through legislation, to, inter alia:

(a) prohibit discrimination on the basis of disability with regard to all matters concerning all forms of employment, including conditions of recruitment, hiring and employment, continuance of employment, career advancement and safe and healthy working conditions;

(b) protect the rights of persons with disabilities, on an equal basis with others, to just and favourable conditions of work, including equal opportunities and equal remuneration for work of equal value, safe and healthy working conditions, including protection from harassment, and the redress of grievances;

(c) ensure that persons with disabilities are able to exercise their labour and trade union rights on an equal basis with others;

(d) enable persons with disabilities to have effective access to general technical and vocational guidance programmes, placement services and vocational and continuing training;

(e) promote employment opportunities and career advancement for persons with disabilities in the labour market, as well as assistance in finding, obtaining, maintaining and returning to employment;

(f) promote opportunities for self-employment, entrepreneurship, the development of cooperatives and starting one's own business;

(g) employ persons with disabilities in the public sector;

(h) promote the employment of persons with disabilities in the private sector through appropriate policies and measures, which may include affirmative action programmes, incentives and other measures;

(i) ensure that reasonable accommodation is provided to persons with disabilities in the workplace;

(j) promote the acquisition by persons with disabilities of work experience in the open labour market;

(k) promote vocational and professional rehabilitation, job retention and return-to-work programmes for persons with disabilities.

[...]

Article 33
National implementation and monitoring

1. States Parties, in accordance with their system of organization, shall designate one or more focal points within government for matters relating to the implementation of the present Convention, and shall give due consideration to the establishment or designation of a coordination mechanism within government to facilitate related action in different sectors and at different levels.

2. States Parties shall, in accordance with their legal and administrative systems, maintain, strengthen, designate or establish within the State Party, a framework, including one or more independent mechanisms, as appropriate, to promote, protect and monitor implementation of the present Convention. When designating or establishing such a mechanism, States Parties shall take into account the principles relating to the status and functioning of national institutions for protection and promotion of human rights.

Article 34
Committee on the Rights of Persons with Disabilities

1. There shall be established a Committee on the Rights of Persons with Disabilities (hereafter referred to as 'the Committee'), which shall carry out the functions hereinafter provided.

2. The Committee shall consist, at the time of entry into force of the present Convention, of twelve experts. After an additional sixty ratifications or accessions to the Convention, the membership of the Committee shall increase by six members, attaining a maximum number of eighteen members.

3. The members of the Committee shall serve in their personal capacity and shall be of high moral standing and recognized competence and experience in the field covered by the present Convention. When nominating their candidates, States Parties are

invited to give due consideration to the provision set out in article 4, paragraph 3, of the present Convention.

4. The members of the Committee shall be elected by States Parties, consideration being given to equitable geographical distribution, representation of the different forms of civilization and of the principal legal systems, balanced gender representation and participation of experts with disabilities.

5. The members of the Committee shall be elected by secret ballot from a list of persons nominated by the States Parties from among their nationals at meetings of the Conference of States Parties. At those meetings, for which two thirds of States Parties shall constitute a quorum, the persons elected to the Committee shall be those who obtain the largest number of votes and an absolute majority of the votes of the representatives of States Parties present and voting.

6. The initial election shall be held no later than six months after the date of entry into force of the present Convention. At least four months before the date of each election, the Secretary General of the United Nations shall address a letter to the States Parties inviting them to submit the nominations within two months. The Secretary-General shall subsequently prepare a list in alphabetical order of all persons thus nominated, indicating the State Parties which have nominated them, and shall submit it to the States Parties to the present Convention.

7. The members of the Committee shall be elected for a term of four years. They shall be eligible for re-election once. However, the term of six of the members elected at the first election shall expire at the end of two years; immediately after the first election, the names of these six members shall be chosen by lot by the chairperson of the meeting referred to in paragraph 5 of this article.

8. The election of the six additional members of the Committee shall be held on the occasion of regular elections, in accordance with the relevant provisions of this article.

9. If a member of the Committee dies or resigns or declares that for any other cause she or he can no longer perform her or his duties, the State Party which nominated the member shall appoint another expert possessing the qualifications and meeting the requirements set out in the relevant provisions of this article, to serve for the remainder of the term.

10. The Committee shall establish its own rules of procedure.

11. The Secretary-General of the United Nations shall provide the necessary staff and facilities for the effective performance of the functions of the Committee under the present Convention, and shall convene its initial meeting.

12. With the approval of the General Assembly of the United Nations, the members of the Committee established under the present Convention shall receive emoluments from United Nations resources on such terms and conditions as the Assembly may decide, having regard to the importance of the Committee's responsibilities.

13. The members of the Committee shall be entitled to the facilities, privileges and immunities of experts on mission for the United Nations as laid down in the elevant sections of the Convention on the Privileges and Immunities of the United Nations.

Article 35

Reports by States Parties

1. Each State Party shall submit to the Committee, through the Secretary-General of the United Nations, a comprehensive report on measures taken to give effect to its obligations under the present Convention and on the progress made in that regard, within two years after the entry into force of the present Convention for the State Party concerned.

2. Thereafter, States Parties shall submit subsequent reports at least every four years and further whenever the Committee so requests.

[...]

Article 40

Conference of States Parties

1. The States Parties shall meet regularly in a Conference of States Parties in order to consider any matter with regard to the implementation of the present Convention.

2. No later than six months after the entry into force of the present Convention, the Conference of States Parties shall be convened by the Secretary-General of the United Nations. The subsequent meetings shall be convened by the Secretary-General biennially or upon the decision of the Conference of States Parties.

Article 41

Depositary

The Secretary-General of the United Nations shall be the depositary of the present Convention.

[...]

Article 44

Regional integration organizations

1. 'Regional integration organization' shall mean an organization constituted by sovereign States of a given region, to which its member States have transferred competence in respect of matters governed by the present Convention. Such organizations shall declare, in their instruments of formal confirmation or accession, the extent of their competence with respect to matters governed by the present Convention. Subsequently, they shall inform the depositary of any substantial modification in the extent of their competence.

[...]

Article 46

Reservations

1. Reservations incompatible with the object and purpose of the present Convention shall not be permitted.

[...]

Article 47

Amendments

1. Any State Party may propose an amendment to the present Convention and submit it to the Secretary-General of the United Nations. The Secretary-General shall communicate any proposed amendments to States Parties, with a request to be notified whether they favour a conference of States Parties for the purpose of considering and deciding upon the proposals. In the event that, within four months from the date of such communication, at least one third of the States Parties favour such a conference, the Secretary-General shall convene the conference under the auspices of the United Nations. Any amendment adopted by a majority of two thirds of the States Parties present and voting shall be submitted by the Secretary General to the General Assembly of the United Nations for approval and thereafter to all States Parties for acceptance.

[…]

Article 48

Denunciation

A State Party may denounce the present Convention by written notification to the Secretary General of the United Nations. The denunciation shall become effective one year after the date of receipt of the notification by the Secretary-General.

[…]

ANNEX II

DECLARATION CONCERNING THE COMPETENCE OF THE EUROPEAN COMMUNITY WITH REGARD TO MATTERS GOVERNED BY THE UNITED NATIONS CONVENTION ON THE RIGHTS OF PERSONS WITH DISABILITIES

(Declaration made pursuant to Article 44(1) of the Convention)

Article 44(1) of the United Nations Convention on the Rights of Persons with Disabilities (hereinafter referred to as the Convention) provides that a regional integration organisation in its instrument of formal confirmation or accession is to declare the extent of its competence with respect to matters governed by the Convention.

The current members of the European Community are the Kingdom of Belgium, the Republic of Bulgaria, the Czech Republic, the Kingdom of Denmark, the Federal Republic of Germany, the Republic of Estonia, Ireland, the Hellenic Republic, the Kingdom of Spain, the French Republic, the Italian Republic, the Republic of Cyprus, the Republic of Latvia, the Republic of Lithuania, the Grand Duchy of Luxembourg, the Republic of Hungary, the Republic of Malta, the Kingdom of the Netherlands, the Republic of Austria, the Republic of Poland, the Portuguese Republic, Romania, the Republic of Slovenia, the Slovak Republic, the Republic of Finland, the Kingdom of Sweden and the United Kingdom of Great Britain and Northern Ireland.

The European Community notes that for the purpose of the Convention, the term 'State Parties' applies to regional integration organisations within the limits of their competence.

The United Nations Convention on the Rights of Persons with Disabilities shall apply, with regard to the competence of the European Community, to the territories in which the Treaty establishing the European Community is applied and under the conditions laid down in that Treaty, in particular Article 299 thereof.

Pursuant to Article 299, this Declaration is not applicable to the territories of the Member States in which the said Treaty does not apply and is without prejudice to such act or positions as may be adopted under the Convention by Member States concerned on behalf and in the interests of those territories.

In accordance with Article 44(1) of the Convention, this Declaration indicates the competences transferred to the Community by the Member States under the Treaty establishing the European Community, in the areas covered by the Convention.

The scope and the exercise of Community competence are, by their nature, subject to continuous development and the Community will complete or amend this Declaration, if necessary, in accordance with Article 44(1) of the Convention.

In some matters the European Community has exclusive competence and in other matters competence is shared between the European Community and the Member States. The Member States remain competent for all matters in respect of which no competence has been transferred to the European Community.

At present:

1. The Community has exclusive competence as regards the compatibility of State aid with the common market and the Common Custom Tariff.

To the extent that provisions of Community law are affected by the provision of the Convention, the European Community has an exclusive competence to accept such obligations with respect to its own public administration. In this regard, the Community declares that it has power to deal with regulating the recruitment, conditions of service, remuneration, training etc. of non-elected officials under the Staff Regulations and the implementing rules to those Regulations.

2. The Community shares competence with Member States as regards action to combat discrimination on the ground of disability, free movement of goods, persons, services and capital agriculture, transport by rail, road, sea and air transport, taxation, internal market, equal pay for male and female workers, trans-European network policy and statistics.

The European Community has exclusive competence to enter into this Convention in respect of those matters only to the extent that provisions of the Convention or legal instruments adopted in implementation thereof affect common rules previously established by the European Community. When Community rules exist but are not affected, in particular in cases of Community provisions establishing only minimum standards, the Member States have competence, without prejudice to the competence of the European Community to act in this field. Otherwise competence rests with the Member States. A list of relevant acts adopted by the European Community appears in the Appendix hereto. The extent of the European Community's competence ensuing from these acts must be assessed by reference to the precise provisions of each measure, and in particular, the extent to which these provisions establish common rules.

3. The following EC policies may also be relevant to the UN Convention: Member States and the Community shall work towards developing a coordinated strategy for employment. The Community shall contribute to the development of quality of education by encouraging cooperation between Member States and, if necessary, by supporting and supplementing their action. The Community shall implement a vocational training policy which shall support and supplement the action of the Member States. In order to promote its overall harmonious development, the Community shall develop and pursue its actions leading to the strengthening of its economic and social cohesion. The Community conducts a development cooperation policy and economic, financial and technical cooperation with third countries without prejudice to the respective competences of the Member States.

Appendix

COMMUNITY ACTS WHICH REFER TO MATTERS GOVERNED
BY THE CONVENTION

The Community acts listed below illustrate the extent of the area of competence of the Community in accordance with the Treaty establishing the European Community. In particular the European Community has exclusive competence in relation to some matters and in some other matters competence is shared between the Community and the Member States. The extent of the Community's competence ensuing from these acts must be assessed by reference to the precise provisions of each measure, and in particular, the extent to which these provisions establish common rules that are affected by the provisions of the Convention.

[...]

ANNEX III

RESERVATION BY THE EUROPEAN COMMUNITY TO ARTICLE 27(1)
OF THE UN CONVENTION ON THE RIGHTS OF PERSONS WITH
DISABILITIES

The European Community states that pursuant to Community law (notably Council Directive 2000/78/EC of 27 November 2000 establishing a general framework for equal treatment in employment and occupation), the Member States may, if appropriate, enter their own reservations to Article 27(1) of the Disabilities Convention to the extent that Article 3(4) of the said Council Directive provides them with the right to exclude non-discrimination on the grounds of disability with respect to employment in the armed forces from the scope of the Directive. Therefore, the Community states that it concludes the Convention without prejudice to the above right, conferred on its Member States by virtue of Community law.

Optional Protocol to the United Nations Convention on the Rights of Persons with Disabilities, 13 December 2006, Doc.A/61/611.

The States Parties to the present Protocol have agreed as follows:

Article 1

1. A State Party to the present Protocol ('State Party') recognizes the competence of the Committee on the Rights of Persons with Disabilities ('the Committee') to receive and consider communications from or on behalf of individuals or groups of individuals subject to its jurisdiction who claim to be victims of a violation by that State Party of the provisions of the Convention.

2. No communication shall be received by the Committee if it concerns a State Party to the Convention that is not a party to the present Protocol.

Article 2

The Committee shall consider a communication inadmissible when:

(a) The communication is anonymous;

(b) The communication constitutes an abuse of the right of submission of such communications or is incompatible with the provisions of the Convention;

(c) The same matter has already been examined by the Committee or has been or is being examined under another procedure of international investigation or settlement;

(d) All available domestic remedies have not been exhausted. This shall not be the rule where the application of the remedies is unreasonably prolonged or unlikely to bring effective relief;

(e) It is manifestly ill-founded or not sufficiently substantiated; or when

(f) The facts that are the subject of the communication occurred prior to the entry into force of the present Protocol for the State Party concerned unless those facts continued after that date.

Article 3

Subject to the provisions of article 2 of the present Protocol, the Committee shall bring any communications submitted to it confidentially to the attention of the State Party. Within six months, the receiving State shall submit to the Committee written explanations or statements clarifying the matter and the remedy, if any, that may have been taken by that State.

Article 4

1. At any time after the receipt of a communication and before a determination on the merits has been reached, the Committee may transmit to the State Party concerned for its urgent consideration a request that the State Party take such interim measures as may be necessary to avoid possible irreparable damage to the victim or victims of the alleged violation.

2. Where the Committee exercises its discretion under paragraph 1 of this article, this does not imply a determination on admissibility or on the merits of the communication.

Article 5

The Committee shall hold closed meetings when examining communications under the present Protocol. After examining a communication, the Committee shall forward its suggestions and recommendations, if any, to the State Party concerned and to the petitioner.

Article 6

1. If the Committee receives reliable information indicating grave or systematic violations by a State Party of rights set forth in the Convention, the Committee shall invite that State Party to cooperate in the examination of the information and to this end submit observations with regard to the information concerned.

2. Taking into account any observations that may have been submitted by the State Party concerned as well as any other reliable information available to it, the Committee may designate one or more of its members to conduct an inquiry and to report urgently to the Committee. Where warranted and with the consent of the State Party, the inquiry may include a visit to its territory.

3. After examining the findings of such an inquiry, the Committee shall transmit these findings to the State Party concerned together with any comments and recommendations.

4. The State Party concerned shall, within six months of receiving the findings, comments and recommendations transmitted by the Committee, submit its observations to the Committee.

5. Such an inquiry shall be conducted confidentially and the cooperation of the State Party shall be sought at all stages of the proceedings.

Article 7

1. The Committee may invite the State Party concerned to include in its report under article 35 of the Convention details of any measures taken in response to an inquiry conducted under article 6 of the present Protocol.

2. The Committee may, if necessary, after the end of the period of six months referred to in article 6.4, invite the State Party concerned to inform it of the measures taken in response to such an inquiry.

Article 8

Each State Party may, at the time of signature or ratification of the present Protocol or accession thereto, declare that it does not recognize the competence of the Committee provided for in articles 6 and 7.

Article 9

The Secretary-General of the United Nations shall be the depositary of the present Protocol.

Article 10

The present Protocol shall be open for signature by signatory States and regional integration organizations of the Convention at United Nations Headquarters in New York as of 30 March 2007.

Article 11

The present Protocol shall be subject to ratification by signatory States of this Protocol which have ratified or acceded to the Convention. It shall be subject to formal confirmation by signatory regional integration organizations of this Protocol which have formally confirmed or acceded to the Convention. It shall be open for accession by any

State or regional integration organization which has ratified, formally confirmed or acceded to the Convention and which has not signed the Protocol.

Article 12

1. 'Regional integration organization' shall mean an organization constituted by sovereign States of a given region, to which its member States have transferred competence in respect of matters governed by the Convention and this Protocol. Such organizations shall declare, in their instruments of formal confirmation or accession, the extent of their competence with respect to matters governed by the Convention and this Protocol. Subsequently, they shall inform the depositary of any substantial modification in the extent of their competence.

2. References to 'States Parties' in the present Protocol shall apply to such organizations within the limits of their competence.

3. For the purposes of article 13, paragraph 1, and article 15, paragraph 2, any instrument deposited by a regional integration organization shall not be counted.

4. Regional integration organizations, in matters within their competence, may exercise their right to vote in the meeting of States Parties, with a number of votes equal to the number of their member States that are Parties to this Protocol. Such an organization shall not exercise its right to vote if any of its member States exercises its right, and vice versa.

Article 13

1. Subject to the entry into force of the Convention, the present Protocol shall enter into force on the thirtieth day after the deposit of the tenth instrument of ratification or accession.

2. For each State or regional integration organization ratifying, formally confirming or acceding to the Protocol after the deposit of the tenth such instrument, the Protocol shall enter into force on the thirtieth day after the deposit of its own such instrument.

Article 14

1. Reservations incompatible with the object and purpose of the present Protocol shall not be permitted.

2. Reservations may be withdrawn at any time.

Article 15

1. Any State Party may propose an amendment to the present Protocol and submit it to the Secretary-General of the United Nations. The Secretary-General shall communicate any proposed amendments to States Parties, with a request to be notified whether they favour a meeting of States Parties for the purpose of considering and deciding upon the proposals. In the event that, within four months from the date of such communication, at least one third of the States Parties favour such a meeting, the Secretary-General shall convene the meeting under the auspices of the United Nations. Any amendment adopted by a majority of two thirds of the States Parties present and voting shall be submitted by the Secretary-General to the General Assembly for approval and thereafter to all States Parties for acceptance.

2. An amendment adopted and approved in accordance with paragraph 1 of this article shall enter into force on the thirtieth day after the number of instruments of acceptance deposited reaches two thirds of the number of States Parties at the date of adoption of the amendment. Thereafter, the amendment shall enter into force for any State Party on the thirtieth day following the deposit of its own instrument of acceptance. An amendment shall be binding only on those States Parties which have accepted it.

Article 16

A State Party may denounce the present Protocol by written notification to the Secretary-General of the United Nations. The denunciation shall become effective one year after the date of receipt of the notification by the Secretary-General.

Article 17

The text of the present Protocol shall be made available in accessible formats.

Article 18

The Arabic, Chinese, English, French, Russian and Spanish texts of the present Protocol shall be equally authentic.

4.3.2 Convention on Cultural Diversity

Recommendation from the Commission to the Council to authorize the Commission to participate, on behalf of the Community, in the negotiations within UNESCO on the Convention on the Protection of the Diversity of Cultural Contents and Artistic Expressions; Council Decision of 18 May 2006 on the conclusion of the Convention on the Protection and Promotion of the Diversity of Cultural Expressions; Code of conduct between the Council, the Member States and the Commission for the participation of the Community and its Member States in meetings regarding the implementation of the Convention on the Protection and Promotion of the Diversity of Cultural Expressions.

The three documents included here, concerning the UNESCO Convention on the Protection of the Diversity of Cultural Contents and Artistic Expressions ('Cultural Diversity Convention') serve to illustrate primarily three important issues.

First, the Community, in practice represented by the Commission, cannot always remain content with its status as observer in the UN system of international organizations and other organizations in the same mould. This is particularly so, when core aspects of the Union, such as the internal market, are touched by important subjects of a negotiation and drafting of a Convention or the taking of a binding decision in the framework of such an international organization, as was the case with the present Convention. The Commission has negotiated forcefully in such situations to obtain all the rights that its Member States have in such negotiations. In that way it was not handicapped by the minimal rights an observer has: an observer has to speak last after all the Members have spoken, may raise no points of order, may make no text proposals or advance amendments, and may not vote. This last prohibition, of course, remained: the Member States can vote and do so jointly if Community coordination is effective. But in many instances, of which this is only one, the Commission has obtained the other rights that are normally reserved to the Member States of the organization so as to enable it to participate effectively in the negotiations in organs of international organizations. In that respect there was a special feature to the UNESCO Convention: the drafting and negotiation was done in the UNESCO Executive Council, the non-plenary organ. Hence, this was the first time that the Commission obtained the right to speak, propose, and amend in an executive organ of an international organization of the UN type.[7]

Second, multilateral mixed agreements pose a special problem to the Non-Member States parties (or hoping to become parties) to such agreements, as they cannot see on the face of the treaty (as was possible with the bilateral mixed association agreement between the EEC, the Member States, and Turkey) that the Community (now the Union) and the Member States constitute one bloc for the purpose of the agreement or convention concerned. This implies, for example, that insofar as the Community implements the agreement concerned, the Member States do not obtain rights and duties under the international agreement in respect of each other and that third states will be confronted with the fact that the Union has subrogated the rights and duties of the Member States under the Agreement. In some instances, the EU has negotiated so-called disconnection clauses in order to clarify this situation. It is not useful to go into a far-ranging analysis of these disconnection clauses, the name of which has become a misnomer over the years.[8] Suffice it to say here that in the particular case of the Cultural Diversity Convention the Community did not negotiate a disconnection case, but reduced it to a disconnection declaration. The text of this declaration follows the second document.

Third, another perennial problem of mixed agreements comes after their conclusion: how to handle the cooperation between the Member States and the Commission inside the relevant international organization or the relevant treaty bodies in such a way that the unity of representation of the Union, so much prized by the CJEU, especially in Opinion 1/94, can be maintained. This has given rise to so-called Codes of Conduct between the Council and/or the Member States and the Commission. A prominent case of success in bringing about such a Code of Conduct was that designed for the Food and Agriculture Organization of the United Nations (FAO), to the point that it has been enforced by the Court of Justice in spite of its rather murky status (see Case 25/94 *Commission v. Council* [1996] ECR I-1469); a prominent case of failure to agree on such a code has been the case of the WTO after Opinion 1/94 (although a partial code was agreed in the field of services negotiations). The example of the Code of Conduct in the case of the UNESCO Cultural Diversity Convention demonstrates, once again, the very informal status of such codes; they are mostly laid down in documents of the Committee of Permanent Representatives (COREPER), as in the case at hand, that have in no way been confirmed or adopted by the Council. However, after

---

[7] On the topic of the EU in the UN, see also Chapter 5.

[8] See further M. Cremona, Disconnection Clauses in EU Law and Practice, *Mixed Agreements Revisited* (C. Hillion and P. Koutrakos (eds), Oxford and Portland, OR: Hart Publishing, 2010), 160–86.

the precedent of the FAO Code of Conduct, there is little doubt that also this document without formal status would be enforced by the Court, unless the Court were to find that the Code went against the principle of loyal cooperation as laid down in Article 4(3) TEU (formerly Article 10 EC).

Some of these and other issues return, in a more comparative perspective in Chapter 5, but in the case of the UNESCO Cultural Diversity Convention several of them come together in a way that is often characteristic for multilateral mixed agreements of the EU.

Recommendation from the Commission to the Council to authorize the Commission to participate, on behalf of the Community, in the negotiations within UNESCO on the Convention on the Protection of the Diversity of Cultural Contents and Artistic Expressions, 1.9.2004, SEC (2004) 1062 final.

1. INTRODUCTION

The October 2003 General Conference of UNESCO unanimously called on the Director General of UNESCO to submit to the 33rd session of the General Conference, in October 2005, a preliminary draft convention on the protection of the diversity of cultural contents and artistic expressions.

Following this decision, the UNESCO Secretariat organised the work in two phases. The first phase involved the Secretariat convening around fifteen independent experts, chosen by the Director-General, in order to prepare a framework for a draft convention. This group of experts met three times between December 2003 and May 2004 and, at the end of its work, produced a text constituting a basis for the preliminary draft convention (hereinafter referred to as the 'PDC'). This was transmitted by the Secretariat to the members of UNESCO on 16 July 2004. The transmission of the PDC, accompanied by the Director-General's preliminary report, marked the start of the second phase of work on the convention, i.e. the intergovernmental negotiation phase proper.

The PDC defines a series of complementary objectives concerning the preservation and promotion of cultural diversity, the development of cultural policies and the encouragement of intercultural dialogue and international cooperation. To this end, it defines 'culture', 'cultural diversity' and 'cultural expressions' in a relatively broad way and provides a list of cultural goods and services whose distinctive nature it recognises, and a list of cultural policies.

The PDC defines fundamental principles: for example respect for human rights and fundamental freedoms, complementarity of economic and cultural aspects of development, sustainable cultural development, transparency, and balance, openness and proportionality of cultural policies.

In relation to these principles, the core section of the PDC deals with the rights and obligations of the States Parties both at national level (development of cultural policies, promoting creation and access to culture, respect for intellectual property, protection of vulnerable cultural expressions, information and transparency, education and public awareness-raising, participation of civil society) and at international level (promotion of the principles and objectives of the convention in other international arenas, aid for co-production, establishment of a 'Cultural Diversity Observatory', cooperation for development, and preferential treatment for developing countries).

The PDC also sets up three follow-up bodies (General Assembly, Intergovernmental Committee and Advisory Group).

A procedure for the settlement of disputes is envisaged, in order to settle questions of interpretation or application of the convention. Three stages are foreseen: (1) negotiation, (2) mediation or good offices, (3) a choice of arbitration by an ad hoc UNESCO tribunal or by the International Court of Justice, or an ad hoc conciliation procedure as defined by the convention.

The only article which at this stage presents two options covers the relationship between the UNESCO convention and other international instruments. Option B gives systematic primacy to existing international instruments. Option A gives primacy to existing international instruments, in absolute terms as regards instruments relating to intellectual property rights to which members are parties and, for all other instruments, 'except where the exercise of those rights and obligations would cause serious damage or threat to the diversity of cultural expressions'.

The intergovernmental negotiations will begin on 20 September 2004, with the convening of the first negotiating session at UNESCO headquarters. A second session is envisaged around February 2005, and a third session will probably have to be scheduled around spring 2005, before the September 2005 Executive Council. The Executive Council is the body which will have to decide to place the preliminary draft convention on the agenda of the September–October 2005 General Conference for adoption.

2. COMMUNITY COMPETENCE

The preliminary draft convention affects internal and external policies at both Member State and Community levels.

2.1. The scope and logic of the PDC affect fields of Community jurisdiction.

The scope of the PDC—and in particular of the principles, rights and obligations enshrined in it—refers in particular to a broadly defined concept of 'cultural policies'.

The PDC is thus likely to affect the acquis communautaire and Community policies specifically in the cultural field, for example cultural policy (Culture 2000), audiovisual policy ('Television without Frontiers' Directive, MEDIA Programme), freedom of movement for cultural goods and services intellectual property, and cultural aspects of our development policies.

It also follows from the definition of cultural policies that the scope of the affected policies and measures includes those which have an influence on the cultural sector. Thus, in addition to Community measures designed to achieve a specific cultural objective, those taken under other policies which affect cultural expressions and in particular cultural goods and services (e.g. tax policies relating to the internal market, competition, international trade, etc.) are also covered.

Moreover, the PDC affects not only existing instruments, but also the Community's capacity to develop new instruments.

It should be noted in this context that some of the principles which would be applicable to all cultural policy measures as defined by the PDC have an extremely broad scope, in particular the principles of openness and proportionality.

Under the terms of the consistent case law of the Court of Justice, and in particular the EART case law, 'each time the Community, with a view to implementing a common policy envisaged by the Treaty, adopts provisions laying down common rules, whatever form they may take, the Member States no longer have the right, acting individually or even collectively, to undertake obligations with third countries which affect those rules or alter their scope'. This rule has even been widened by case law after the EART judgment to include nonexclusive competences.

2.2. Certain provisions of the PDC urge the Parties to take specific measures which fall within the scope of areas of Community competence.

By way of example, the following provisions can in particular affect Community competences:

• Free circulation and mobility of artists and creators

Obligations in this field are likely to affect various aspects of policies in a broader context than the cultural context alone. This question can indeed affect free movement of persons, and in particular workers within the meaning of the internal market in the EU (Title III, Chapter 1 of the Treaty, and in particular Article 39), immigration issues (Title IV of the Treaty), or negotiations within the World Trade Organisation (WTO) on the opening of European markets to the entry of temporary cultural workers performing specific cultural services (Article 133 of the Treaty). These fields fall within the Community competence, often exclusively.

• Facilitation of access to global markets for works from developing countries

Here, customs policy instruments, such as reduction of the duties on certain cultural products imported into the European Union, as well as the treatment of trade in services and movement of persons, could be involved. The exclusive competence of the Community for trade matters would then in particular be affected (Article 133 of the Treaty).

• Relationship to other international instruments

The existence in the PDC of two alternatives as regards relations with other international instruments will entail negotiations likely to affect the Community's exclusive competence in trade matters (Article 133 of the Treaty), particularly concerning the commitments entered into by the European Community and its Member States with regard to the WTO. Option A is also likely to affect Community competences as regards intellectual property.

• International consultation and coordination

Consultation and/or coordination obligations in other international fora are likely to affect Community competences and procedures, in particular as regards external trade.

• Intellectual property

The provisions concerning intellectual property in the PDC are likely to affect the acquis communautaire in the field, as well as the existing international framework (cf. international treaties under the auspices of the World Intellectual Property Organisation, WIPO).

2.3. Moreover, the international cooperation dimension present in numerous provisions of the PDC could create obligations at Community level or affect the development of forthcoming generations of cooperation programmes and projects, particularly within the framework of development cooperation policy. The aspect relating to international cooperation in general has therefore implications on the Community policies and instruments in that field.

The legal impact of the PDC at Community level will depend on the evolution of the text during the negotiations—a matter to which the Community will have to pay particular attention.

2.4. The absence of a disconnection clause to preserve the specific relations between the Parties in a single regional integration area would require the PDC to regulate the relationships between Member States of the European Union as regards cultural diversity matters. That would open the way to violations of the acquis communautaire, including fundamental principles guaranteed by the EC Treaty such as non-discrimination, freedom of establishment and freedom of movement of goods, services, capital and persons within the Community, and Community competition rules.

A specific clause must therefore aim at guaranteeing the primacy of Community law over the provisions of the convention regarding relationships between Member States.

Moreover, the Community will have to make sure that the provisions concerning the signature and the ratification of the convention enable it to become Party to the convention.

3. CONCLUSION

In conclusion, it ensues from the above that Community policies and instruments are affected by the convention and that it is for the Community to negotiate its participation in the convention, to preserve its acquis and competences, and to assert its interests in the context of these negotiations.

The Commission considers that it is important for the Community and its Member States to confirm at international level their commitment to cultural diversity. It considers that a common European Union approach is necessary in order to contribute effectively to the development of a world-wide strategy for the safeguarding and the promotion of cultural diversity.

The Treaty and the consistent case law of the Court of Justice make it compulsory for the European Community to ensure the unity of its representation in international organisations, even where shared competences are involved.

In addition, in view of the above, and in line with its Communication to the Council and the European Parliament of 27 August 2003, the Commission considers necessary that the Council decides that the European Community participates in the negotiations in UNESCO on the preliminary draft convention, in order to preserve the Community acquis and competences and to assert the interests of the Community in these negotiations.

* * *

In view of the above, the Commission recommends that the Council decide:

that the European Community should take part in the negotiations in UNESCO on the convention on the protection of the diversity of cultural contents and artistic expressions, in order to preserve the Community acquis and competences and to assert the interests of the Community;

that the Commission should negotiate on behalf of the European Community on the basis of the attached negotiating directives, in consultation with a special committee appointed by the Council to assist the Commission in this task;

that, insofar as the agreement comes partly under the Member States competence and, partly, under Community competence, the Commission and the Member States should closely cooperate during the negotiations, with a view to achieving unity in the international representation of the Community.

ANNEX

NEGOTIATING DIRECTIVES

(1) The Commission shall ensure that the provisions of the future UNESCO convention on the protection of the diversity of cultural contents and artistic expressions are consistent with the acquis communautaire and with the objectives, procedures and measures of the relevant Community policies, in particular as regards culture, audio-visual, internal market, competition, intellectual property, international trade and cooperation for development. It shall also ensure the safeguarding of the Community's capacity to develop its policies in accordance with the Treaties.

(2) The Commission shall ensure that the future convention contains appropriate provisions guaranteeing the primacy of Community law over the provisions of the convention with regard to the relationships between Member States of the European Union.

(3) The Commission shall ensure that the future convention contains appropriate provisions enabling the European Community to become a contracting party to it.

(4) The Commission shall report regularly to the special committee appointed by the Council on the progress of negotiations and, if necessary, refer to it any difficulty which would appear during the negotiations.

Council Decision 2006/515/EC of 18 May 2006 on the conclusion of the Convention on the Protection and Promotion of the Diversity of Cultural Expressions, Official Journal L 201, 25.7.2006, pp. 15–30.

THE COUNCIL OF THE EUROPEAN UNION,

Having regard to the Treaty establishing the European Community, and in particular Articles 133, 151, 181 and 181a in conjunction with the second sentence of the first subparagraph of Article 300(2), and the first subparagraph of Article 300(3), thereof,

Having regard to the proposal from the Commission,

Having regard to the Opinion of the European Parliament,

Whereas:

(1) In November 2004, the Council authorised the Commission to participate, on behalf of the Community, in negotiations at the United Nations Educational, Scientific and Cultural Organisation (UNESCO) concerning a Convention on the Protection and Promotion of the Diversity of Cultural Expressions, hereinafter referred to as the 'UNESCO Convention'. The Commission participated in these negotiations, together with the Member States.

(2) The UNESCO Convention was adopted at the General Conference of UNESCO in Paris on 20 October 2005.

(3) The UNESCO Convention constitutes a relevant and effective pillar for promoting cultural diversity and cultural exchanges, to which both the Community, as reflected in Article 151(4) of the Treaty, and its Member States, attach the greatest importance. It contributes towards ensuring mutual respect and understanding between cultures at world level.

(4) The UNESCO Convention should be approved as soon as possible.

(5) Both the Community and its Member States have competence in the fields covered by the UNESCO Convention. The Community and the Member States should therefore become Contracting Parties to it, so that together they can fulfil the obligations laid down by the UNESCO Convention and exercise the rights invested in them by it, in situations of mixed competence in a coherent manner,

HAS DECIDED AS FOLLOWS:

Article 1

1. The UNESCO Convention on the Protection and Promotion of the Diversity of Cultural Expressions is hereby approved on behalf of the Community.

2. The text of the UNESCO Convention is contained in Annex 1(a) to this Decision.

Article 2

1. The President of the Council is hereby authorised to designate the person(s) empowered to deposit the instrument of accession, on behalf of the Community, with the Director-General of UNESCO, in accordance with Article 27(4) of the UNESCO Convention.

2. The President of the Council is hereby authorised to designate the person(s) empowered to deposit, on behalf of the Community, the declaration of competence contained in Annex 1(b) to this Decision, in accordance with Article 27(3)(c) of the UNESCO Convention.

3. The President of the Council is hereby authorised to designate the person(s) empowered to issue the Unilateral Declaration reproduced in Annex 2 to this Decision at the time of the deposition of the instrument of accession.

Article 3

In respect of matters falling within the Community's competence, the Commission shall represent the Community at meetings of the bodies created by the UNESCO Convention, in particular the Conference of the Parties referred to in Article 22 thereof, and shall negotiate on its behalf concerning questions falling within the remit of those bodies.

Article 4

This Decision shall be published in the Official Journal of the European Union.

ANNEX 1(a)

CONVENTION

on the protection and promotion of the diversity of cultural expressions

The General Conference of the United Nations Educational, Scientific and Cultural Organization, meeting in Paris from 3 to 21 October 2005 at its 33rd session,

AFFIRMING that cultural diversity is a defining characteristic of humanity,

CONSCIOUS that cultural diversity forms a common heritage of humanity and should be cherished and preserved for the benefit of all,

BEING AWARE that cultural diversity creates a rich and varied world, which increases the range of choices and nurtures human capacities and values, and therefore is a mainspring for sustainable development for communities, peoples and nations,

RECALLING that cultural diversity, flourishing within a framework of democracy, tolerance, social justice and mutual respect between peoples and cultures, is indispensable for peace and security at the local, national and international levels,

CELEBRATING the importance of cultural diversity for the full realization of human rights and fundamental freedoms proclaimed in the Universal Declaration of Human Rights and other universally recognized instruments,

EMPHASIZING the need to incorporate culture as a strategic element in national and international development policies, as well as in international development cooperation, taking into account also the United Nations Millennium Declaration (2000) with its special emphasis on poverty eradication,

TAKING INTO ACCOUNT that culture takes diverse forms across time and space and that this diversity is embodied in the uniqueness and plurality of the identities and cultural expressions of the peoples and societies making up humanity,

RECOGNIZING the importance of traditional knowledge as a source of intangible and material wealth, and in particular the knowledge systems of indigenous peoples, and its positive contribution to sustainable development, as well as the need for its adequate protection and promotion,

RECOGNIZING the need to take measures to protect the diversity of cultural expressions, including their contents, especially in situations where cultural expressions may be threatened by the possibility of extinction or serious impairment,

EMPHASIZING the importance of culture for social cohesion in general, and in particular its potential for the enhancement of the status and role of women in society,

BEING AWARE that cultural diversity is strengthened by the free flow of ideas, and that it is nurtured by constant exchanges and interaction between cultures,

REAFFIRMING that freedom of thought, expression and information, as well as diversity of the media, enable cultural expressions to flourish within societies,

RECOGNIZING that the diversity of cultural expressions, including traditional cultural expressions, is an important factor that allows individuals and peoples to express and to share with others their ideas and values,

RECALLING that linguistic diversity is a fundamental element of cultural diversity, and REAFFIRMING the fundamental role that education plays in the protection and promotion of cultural expressions,

TAKING INTO ACCOUNT the importance of the vitality of cultures, including for persons belonging to minorities and indigenous peoples, as manifested in their freedom to create, disseminate and distribute their traditional cultural expressions and to have access thereto, so as to benefit them for their own development,

EMPHASIZING the vital role of cultural interaction and creativity, which nurture and renew cultural expressions and enhance the role played by those involved in the development of culture for the progress of society at large,

RECOGNIZING the importance of intellectual property rights in sustaining those involved in cultural creativity,

BEING CONVINCED that cultural activities, goods and services have both an economic and a cultural nature, because they convey identities, values and meanings, and must therefore not be treated as solely having commercial value,

NOTING that while the processes of globalization, which have been facilitated by the rapid development of information and communication technologies, afford unprecedented conditions for enhanced interaction between cultures, they also represent a challenge for cultural diversity, namely in view of risks of imbalances between rich and poor countries,

BEING AWARE of Unesco's specific mandate to ensure respect for the diversity of cultures and to recommend such international agreements as may be necessary to promote the free flow of ideas by word and image,

REFERRING to the provisions of the international instruments adopted by Unesco relating to cultural diversity and the exercise of cultural rights, and in particular the Universal Declaration on Cultural Diversity of 2001,

ADOPTS THIS CONVENTION ON 20 OCTOBER 2005.

I. OBJECTIVES AND GUIDING PRINCIPLES
Article 1

Objectives
The objectives of this Convention are:
(a) to protect and promote the diversity of cultural expressions;
(b) to create the conditions for cultures to flourish and to freely interact in a mutually beneficial manner;
(c) to encourage dialogue among cultures with a view to ensuring wider and balanced cultural exchanges in the world in favour of intercultural respect and a culture of peace;
(d) to foster interculturality in order to develop cultural interaction in the spirit of building bridges among peoples;
(e) to promote respect for the diversity of cultural expressions and raise awareness of its value at the local, national and international levels;
(f) to reaffirm the importance of the link between culture and development for all countries, particularly for developing countries, and to support actions undertaken nationally and internationally to secure recognition of the true value of this link;

(g) to give recognition to the distinctive nature of cultural activities, goods and services as vehicles of identity, values and meaning;

(h) to reaffirm the sovereign rights of States to maintain, adopt and implement policies and measures that they deem appropriate for the protection and promotion of the diversity of cultural expressions on their territory;

(i) to strengthen international cooperation and solidarity in a spirit of partnership with a view, in particular, to enhancing the capacities of developing countries in order to protect and promote the diversity of cultural expressions.

Article 2

Guiding principles

1. Principle of respect for human rights and fundamental freedoms
2. Principle of sovereignty
3. Principle of equal dignity of and respect for all cultures
4. Principle of international solidarity and cooperation
5. Principle of the complementarity of economic and cultural aspects of development
6. Principle of sustainable development
7. Principle of equitable access
8. Principle of openness and balance

II. SCOPE OF APPLICATION

Article 3

Scope of application

This Convention shall apply to the policies and measures adopted by the Parties related to the protection and promotion of the diversity of cultural expressions.

III. DEFINITIONS

Article 4

Definitions

For the purposes of this Convention, it is understood that:

1. Cultural diversity

'Cultural diversity' refers to the manifold ways in which the cultures of groups and societies find expression. These expressions are passed on within and among groups and societies.

Cultural diversity is made manifest not only through the varied ways in which the cultural heritage of humanity is expressed, augmented and transmitted through the variety of cultural expressions, but also through diverse modes of artistic creation, production, dissemination, distribution and enjoyment, whatever the means and technologies used.

2. Cultural content

'Cultural content' refers to the symbolic meaning, artistic dimension and cultural values that originate from or express cultural identities.

3. Cultural expressions

'Cultural expressions' are those expressions that result from the creativity of individuals, groups and societies, and that have cultural content.

4. Cultural activities, goods and services

'Cultural activities, goods and services' refers to those activities, goods and services, which at the time they are considered as a specific attribute, use or purpose, embody or convey cultural expressions, irrespective of the commercial value they may have. Cultural activities may be an end in themselves, or they may contribute to the production of cultural goods and services.

5. Cultural industries

'Cultural industries' refers to industries producing and distributing cultural goods or services as defined in paragraph 4 above.

6. Cultural policies and measures

'Cultural policies and measures' refers to those policies and measures relating to culture, whether at the local, national, regional or international level that are either focused on culture as such or are designed to have a direct effect on cultural expressions of individuals, groups or societies, including on the creation, production, dissemination, distribution of and access to cultural activities, goods and services.

7. Protection

'Protection' means the adoption of measures aimed at the preservation, safeguarding and enhancement of the diversity of cultural expressions.

'Protect' means to adopt such measures.

8. Interculturality

'Interculturality' refers to the existence and equitable interaction of diverse cultures and the possibility of generating shared cultural expressions through dialogue and mutual respect.

IV. RIGHTS AND OBLIGATIONS OF PARTIES

Article 5

General rule regarding rights and obligations

1. The Parties, in conformity with the Charter of the United Nations, the principles of international law and universally recognized human rights instruments, reaffirm their sovereign right to formulate and implement their cultural policies and to adopt measures to protect and promote the diversity of cultural expressions and to strengthen international cooperation to achieve the purposes of this Convention.

2. When a Party implements policies and takes measures to protect and promote the diversity of cultural expressions within its territory, its policies and measures shall be consistent with the provisions of this Convention.

Article 6

Rights of parties at the national level

1. Within the framework of its cultural policies and measures as defined in Article 4.6 and taking into account its own particular circumstances and needs, each Party may adopt measures aimed at protecting and promoting the diversity of cultural expressions within its territory.

2. Such measures may include the following:

(i) regulatory measures aimed at protecting and promoting diversity of cultural expressions;

(ii) measures that, in an appropriate manner, provide opportunities for domestic cultural activities, goods and services among all those available within the national territory for the creation, production, dissemination, distribution and enjoyment of such domestic cultural activities, goods and services, including provisions relating to the language used for such activities, goods and services;

(iii) measures aimed at providing domestic independent cultural industries and activities in the informal sector effective access to the means of production, dissemination and distribution of cultural activities, goods and services;

(iv) measures aimed at providing public financial assistance;

(v) measures aimed at encouraging non-profit organizations, as well as public and private institutions and artists and other cultural professionals, to develop and promote the free exchange and circulation of ideas, cultural expressions and cultural activities, goods and services, and to stimulate both the creative and entrepreneurial spirit in their activities;

(vi) measures aimed at establishing and supporting public institutions, as appropriate;

(vii) measures aimed at nurturing and supporting artists and others involved in the creation of cultural expressions;

(viii) measures aimed at enhancing diversity of the media, including through public service broadcasting.

Article 7

Measures to promote cultural expressions

1. Parties shall endeavour to create in their territory an environment which encourages individuals and social groups:

(a) to create, produce, disseminate, distribute and have access to their own cultural expressions, paying due attention to the special circumstances and needs of women as well as various social groups, including persons belonging to minorities and indigenous peoples;

(b) to have access to diverse cultural expressions from within their territory as well as from other countries of the world.

2. Parties shall also endeavour to recognize the important contribution of artists, others involved in the creative process, cultural communities, and organizations that support their work, and their central role in nurturing the diversity of cultural expressions.

Article 8

Measures to protect cultural expressions

1. Without prejudice to the provisions of Articles 5 and 6, a Party may determine the existence of special situations where cultural expressions on its territory are at risk of extinction, under serious threat, or otherwise in need of urgent safeguarding.

2. Parties may take all appropriate measures to protect and preserve cultural expressions in situations referred to in paragraph 1 in a manner consistent with the provisions of this Convention.

3. Parties shall report to the Intergovernmental Committee referred to in Article 23 all measures taken to meet the exigencies of the situation, and the Committee may make appropriate recommendations.

Article 9

Information sharing and transparency
Parties shall:
(a) provide appropriate information in their reports to Unesco every four years on measures taken to protect and promote the diversity of cultural expressions within their territory and at the international level;
(b) designate a point of contact responsible for information sharing in relation to this Convention;
(c) share and exchange information relating to the protection and promotion of the diversity of cultural expressions.

Article 10

Education and public awareness
Parties shall:
(a) encourage and promote understanding of the importance of the protection and promotion of the diversity of cultural expressions, inter alia, through educational and greater public awareness programmes;
(b) cooperate with other Parties and international and regional organizations in achieving the purpose of this article;
(c) endeavour to encourage creativity and strengthen production capacities by setting up educational, training and exchange programmes in the field of cultural industries. These measures should be implemented in a manner which does not have a negative impact on traditional forms of production.

Article 11

Participation of civil society
Parties acknowledge the fundamental role of civil society in protecting and promoting the diversity of cultural expressions. Parties shall encourage the active participation of civil society in their efforts to achieve the objectives of this Convention.

Article 12

Promotion of international cooperation
Parties shall endeavour to strengthen their bilateral, regional and international cooperation for the creation of conditions conducive to the promotion of the diversity of cultural expressions, taking particular account of the situations referred to in Articles 8 and 17, notably in order to:
(a) facilitate dialogue among Parties on cultural policy;
(b) enhance public sector strategic and management capacities in cultural public sector institutions, through professional and international cultural exchanges and sharing of best practices;
(c) reinforce partnerships with and among civil society, non-governmental organizations and the private sector in fostering and promoting the diversity of cultural expressions;
(d) promote the use of new technologies, encourage partnerships to enhance information sharing and cultural understanding, and foster the diversity of cultural expressions;
(e) encourage the conclusion of co-production and co-distribution agreements.

Article 13

Integration of culture in sustainable development
Parties shall endeavour to integrate culture in their development policies at all levels for the creation of conditions conducive to sustainable development and, within this framework, foster aspects relating to the protection and promotion of the diversity of cultural expressions.

Article 14

Cooperation for development
Parties shall endeavour to support cooperation for sustainable development and poverty reduction, especially in relation to the specific needs of developing countries, in order to foster the emergence of a dynamic cultural sector by, inter alia, the following means:
(a) the strengthening of the cultural industries in developing countries through:
(i) creating and strengthening cultural production and distribution capacities in developing countries;
(ii) facilitating wider access to the global market and international distribution networks for their cultural activities, goods and services;
(iii) enabling the emergence of viable local and regional markets;
(iv) adopting, where possible, appropriate measures in developed countries with a view to facilitating access to their territory for the cultural activities, goods and services of developing countries;
(v) providing support for creative work and facilitating the mobility, to the extent possible, of artists from the developing world;
(vi) encouraging appropriate collaboration between developed and developing countries in the areas, inter alia, of music and film;
(b) capacity-building through the exchange of information, experience and expertise, as well as the training of human resources in developing countries, in the public and private sector relating to, inter alia, strategic and management capacities, policy development and implementation, promotion and distribution of cultural expressions, small-, medium- and micro-enterprise development, the use of technology, and skills development and transfer;
(c) technology transfer through the introduction of appropriate incentive measures for the transfer of technology and know-how, especially in the areas of cultural industries and enterprises;
(d) financial support through:
(i) the establishment of an International Fund for Cultural Diversity as provided in Article 18;
(ii) the provision of official development assistance, as appropriate, including technical assistance, to stimulate and support creativity;
(iii) other forms of financial assistance such as low interest loans, grants and other funding mechanisms.

Article 15

Collaborative arrangements
Parties shall encourage the development of partnerships, between and within the public and private sectors and non-profit organizations, in order to cooperate with developing

countries in the enhancement of their capacities in the protection and promotion of the diversity of cultural expressions. These innovative partnerships shall, according to the practical needs of developing countries, emphasize the further development of infrastructure, human resources and policies, as well as the exchange of cultural activities, goods and services.

Article 16

Preferential treatment for developing countries
Developed countries shall facilitate cultural exchanges with developing countries by granting, through the appropriate institutional and legal frameworks, preferential treatment to artists and other cultural professionals and practitioners, as well as cultural goods and services from developing countries.

Article 17

International cooperation in situations of serious threat to cultural expressions
Parties shall cooperate in providing assistance to each other, and, in particular to developing countries, in situations referred to under Article 8.

Article 18

International Fund for Cultural Diversity
1. An International Fund for Cultural Diversity, hereinafter referred to as 'the Fund', is hereby established.
2. The Fund shall consist of funds-in-trust established in accordance with the Financial Regulations of Unesco.
3. The resources of the Fund shall consist of:
(a) voluntary contributions made by Parties;
(b) funds appropriated for this purpose by the General Conference of Unesco;
(c) contributions, gifts or bequests by other States; organizations and programmes of the United Nations system, other regional or international organizations; and public or private bodies or individuals;
(d) any interest due on resources of the Fund;
(e) funds raised through collections and receipts from events organized for the benefit of the Fund;
(f) any other resources authorized by the Fund's regulations.
4. The use of resources of the Fund shall be decided by the Intergovernmental Committee on the basis of guidelines determined by the Conference of Parties referred to in Article 22.
5. The Intergovernmental Committee may accept contributions and other forms of assistance for general and specific purposes relating to specific projects, provided that those projects have been approved by it.
6. No political, economic or other conditions that are incompatible with the objectives of this Convention may be attached to contributions made to the Fund.
7. Parties shall endeavour to provide voluntary contributions on a regular basis towards the implementation of this Convention.

Article 19

Exchange, analysis and dissemination of information

1. Parties agree to exchange information and share expertise concerning data collection and statistics on the diversity of cultural expressions as well as on best practices for its protection and promotion.

2. Unesco shall facilitate, through the use of existing mechanisms within the Secretariat, the collection, analysis and dissemination of all relevant information, statistics and best practices.

3. Unesco shall also establish and update a data bank on different sectors and governmental, private and non-profit organizations involved in the area of cultural expressions.

4. To facilitate the collection of data, Unesco shall pay particular attention to capacity-building and the strengthening of expertise for Parties that submit a request for such assistance.

5. The collection of information identified in this article shall complement the information collected under the provisions of Article 9.

V. RELATIONSHIP TO OTHER INSTRUMENTS

Article 20

Relationship to other treaties: mutual supportiveness, complementarity and non-subordination

1. Parties recognize that they shall perform in good faith their obligations under this Convention and all other treaties to which they are parties. Accordingly, without subordinating this Convention to any other treaty,

(a) they shall foster mutual supportiveness between this Convention and the other treaties to which they are parties; and

(b) when interpreting and applying the other treaties to which they are parties or when entering into other international obligations, Parties shall take into account the relevant provisions of this Convention.

2. Nothing in this Convention shall be interpreted as modifying rights and obligations of the Parties under any other treaties to which they are parties.

Article 21

International consultation and coordination

Parties undertake to promote the objectives and principles of this Convention in other international forums. For this purpose, Parties shall consult each other, as appropriate, bearing in mind these objectives and principles.

VI. ORGANS OF THE CONVENTION

Article 22

Conference of Parties

1. A Conference of Parties shall be established. The Conference of Parties shall be the plenary and supreme body of this Convention.

2. The Conference of Parties shall meet in ordinary session every two years, as far as possible, in conjunction with the General Conference of Unesco. It may meet in

extraordinary session if it so decides or if the Intergovernmental Committee receives a request to that effect from at least one-third of the Parties.

3. The Conference of Parties shall adopt its own rules of procedure.

4. The functions of the Conference of Parties shall be, inter alia:

(a) to elect the Members of the Intergovernmental Committee;

(b) to receive and examine reports of the Parties to this Convention transmitted by the Intergovernmental Committee;

(c) to approve the operational guidelines prepared upon its request by the Intergovernmental Committee;

(d) to take whatever other measures it may consider necessary to further the objectives of this Convention.

Article 23

Intergovernmental Committee

1. An Intergovernmental Committee for the Protection and Promotion of the Diversity of Cultural Expressions, hereinafter referred to as 'the Intergovernmental Committee', shall be established within Unesco. It shall be composed of representatives of 18 States Parties to the Convention, elected for a term of four years by the Conference of Parties upon entry into force of this Convention pursuant to Article 29.

2. The Intergovernmental Committee shall meet annually.

3. The Intergovernmental Committee shall function under the authority and guidance of and be accountable to the Conference of Parties.

4. The Members of the Intergovernmental Committee shall be increased to 24 once the number of Parties to the Convention reaches 50.

5. The election of Members of the Intergovernmental Committee shall be based on the principles of equitable geographical representation as well as rotation.

6. Without prejudice to the other responsibilities conferred upon it by this Convention, the functions of the Intergovernmental Committee shall be:

(a) to promote the objectives of this Convention and to encourage and monitor the implementation thereof;

(b) to prepare and submit for approval by the Conference of Parties, upon its request, the operational guidelines for the implementation and application of the provisions of the Convention;

(c) to transmit to the Conference of Parties reports from Parties to the Convention, together with its comments and a summary of their contents;

(d) to make appropriate recommendations to be taken in situations brought to its attention by Parties to the Convention in accordance with relevant provisions of the Convention, in particular Article 8;

(e) to establish procedures and other mechanisms for consultation aimed at promoting the objectives and principles of this Convention in other international forums;

(f) to perform any other tasks as may be requested by the Conference of Parties.

7. The Intergovernmental Committee, in accordance with its Rules of Procedure, may invite at any time public or private organizations or individuals to participate in its meetings for consultation on specific issues.

8. The Intergovernmental Committee shall prepare and submit to the Conference of Parties, for approval, its own Rules of Procedure.

Article 24

Unesco Secretariat

1. The organs of the Convention shall be assisted by the Unesco Secretariat.

2. The Secretariat shall prepare the documentation of the Conference of Parties and the Intergovernmental Committee as well as the agenda of their meetings and shall assist in and report on the implementation of their decisions.

VII. FINAL CLAUSES

Article 25

Settlement of disputes

1. In the event of a dispute between Parties to this Convention concerning the interpretation or the application of the Convention, the Parties shall seek a solution by negotiation.

2. If the Parties concerned cannot reach agreement by negotiation, they may jointly seek the good offices of, or request mediation by, a third party.

3. If good offices or mediation are not undertaken or if there is no settlement by negotiation, good offices or mediation, a Party may have recourse to conciliation in accordance with the procedure laid down in the Annex of this Convention. The Parties shall consider in good faith the proposal made by the Conciliation Commission for the resolution of the dispute.

4. Each Party may, at the time of ratification, acceptance, approval or accession, declare that it does not recognize the conciliation procedure provided for above. Any Party having made such a declaration may, at any time, withdraw this declaration by notification to the Director-General of Unesco.

Article 26

Ratification, acceptance, approval or accession by Member States

1. This Convention shall be subject to ratification, acceptance, approval or accession by Member States of Unesco in accordance with their respective constitutional procedures.

2. The instruments of ratification, acceptance, approval or accession shall be deposited with the Director-General of Unesco.

Article 27

Accession

1. This Convention shall be open to accession by all States not Members of Unesco but members of the United Nations, or of any of its specialized agencies, that are invited by the General Conference of Unesco to accede to it.

2. This Convention shall also be open to accession by territories which enjoy full internal self-government recognized as such by the United Nations, but which have not attained full independence in accordance with General Assembly resolution 1514 (XV),

and which have competence over the matters governed by this Convention, including the competence to enter into treaties in respect of such matters.

3. The following provisions apply to regional economic integration organizations:

(a) This Convention shall also be open to accession by any regional economic integration organization, which shall, except as provided below, be fully bound by the provisions of the Convention in the same manner as States Parties;

(b) In the event that one or more Member States of such an organization is also Party to this Convention, the organization and such Member State or States shall decide on their responsibility for the performance of their obligations under this Convention. Such distribution of responsibility shall take effect following completion of the notification procedure described in subparagraph (c). The organization and the Member States shall not be entitled to exercise rights under this Convention concurrently. In addition, regional economic integration organizations, in matters within their competence, shall exercise their rights to vote with a number of votes equal to the number of their Member States that are Parties to this Convention. Such an organization shall not exercise its right to vote if any of its Member States exercises its right, and vice-versa;

(c) A regional economic integration organization and its Member State or States which have agreed on a distribution of responsibilities as provided in subparagraph (b) shall inform the Parties of any such proposed distribution of responsibilities in the following manner:

(i) in their instrument of accession, such organization shall declare with specificity, the distribution of their responsibilities with respect to matters governed by the Convention;

(ii) in the event of any later modification of their respective responsibilities, the regional economic integration organization shall inform the depositary of any such proposed modification of their respective responsibilities; the depositary shall in turn inform the Parties of such modification;

(d) Member States of a regional economic integration organization which become Parties to this Convention shall be presumed to retain competence over all matters in respect of which transfers of competence to the organization have not been specifically declared or informed to the depositary;

(e) 'Regional economic integration organization' means an organization constituted by sovereign States, members of the United Nations or of any of its specialized agencies, to which those States have transferred competence in respect of matters governed by this Convention and which has been duly authorized, in accordance with its internal procedures, to become a Party to it.

4. The instrument of accession shall be deposited with the Director-General of Unesco.

Article 28

Point of contact

Upon becoming Parties to this Convention, each Party shall designate a point of contact as referred to in Article 9.

Article 29

Entry into force

1. This Convention shall enter into force three months after the date of deposit of the thirtieth instrument of ratification, acceptance, approval or accession, but only with respect to those States or regional economic integration organizations that have deposited their respective instruments of ratification, acceptance, approval, or accession on or before that date. It shall enter into force with respect to any other Party three months after the deposit of its instrument of ratification, acceptance, approval or accession.

2. For the purposes of this Article, any instrument deposited by a regional economic integration organization shall not be counted as additional to those deposited by Member States of the organization.

Article 30

Federal or non-unitary constitutional systems

Recognizing that international agreements are equally binding on Parties regardless of their constitutional systems, the following provisions shall apply to Parties which have a federal or non-unitary constitutional system:

(a) with regard to the provisions of this Convention, the implementation of which comes under the legal jurisdiction of the federal or central legislative power, the obligations of the federal or central government shall be the same as for those Parties which are not federal States;

(b) with regard to the provisions of the Convention, the implementation of which comes under the jurisdiction of individual constituent units such as States, counties, provinces, or cantons which are not obliged by the constitutional system of the federation to take legislative measures, the federal government shall inform, as necessary, the competent authorities of constituent units such as States, counties, provinces or cantons of the said provisions, with its recommendation for their adoption.

Article 31

Denunciation

1. Any Party to this Convention may denounce this Convention.

2. The denunciation shall be notified by an instrument in writing deposited with the Director-General of Unesco.

3. The denunciation shall take effect 12 months after the receipt of the instrument of denunciation. It shall in no way affect the financial obligations of the Party denouncing the Convention until the date on which the withdrawal takes effect.

Article 32

Depositary functions

The Director-General of Unesco, as the depositary of this Convention, shall inform the Member States of the Organization, the States not members of the Organization and regional economic integration organizations referred to in Article 27, as well as the United Nations, of the deposit of all the instruments of ratification, acceptance, approval or accession provided for in Articles 26 and 27, and of the denunciations provided for in Article 31.

Article 33

Amendments

1. A Party to this Convention may, by written communication addressed to the Director-General, propose amendments to this Convention. The Director-General shall circulate such communication to all Parties. If, within six months from the date of dispatch of the communication, no less than one half of the Parties reply favourably to the request, the Director-General shall present such proposal to the next session of the Conference of Parties for discussion and possible adoption.

2. Amendments shall be adopted by a two-thirds majority of Parties present and voting.

3. Once adopted, amendments to this Convention shall be submitted to the Parties for ratification, acceptance, approval or accession.

4. For Parties which have ratified, accepted, approved or acceded to them, amendments to this Convention shall enter into force three months after the deposit of the instruments referred to in paragraph 3 of this Article by two-thirds of the Parties. Thereafter, for each Party that ratifies, accepts, approves or accedes to an amendment, the said amendment shall enter into force three months after the date of deposit by that Party of its instrument of ratification, acceptance, approval or accession.

5. The procedure set out in paragraphs 3 and 4 shall not apply to amendments to Article 23 concerning the number of Members of the Intergovernmental Committee. These amendments shall enter into force at the time they are adopted.

6. A State or a regional economic integration organization referred to in Article 27 which becomes a Party to this Convention after the entry into force of amendments in conformity with paragraph 4 of this Article shall, failing an expression of different intention, be considered to be:

(a) Party to this Convention as so amended; and

(b) a Party to the unamended Convention in relation to any Party not bound by the amendments.

Article 34

Authoritative texts

This Convention has been drawn up in Arabic, Chinese, English, French, Russian and Spanish, all six texts being equally authoritative.

Article 35

Registration

In conformity with Article 102 of the Charter of the United Nations, this Convention shall be registered with the Secretariat of the United Nations at the request of the Director-General of Unesco.

ANNEX
CONCILIATION PROCEDURE

Article 1

Conciliation Commission

A Conciliation Commission shall be created upon the request of one of the Parties to the dispute. The Commission shall, unless the Parties otherwise agree, be composed of five members, two appointed by each Party concerned and a President chosen jointly by those members.

Article 2
Members of the Commission

In disputes between more than two Parties, Parties in the same interest shall appoint their members of the Commission jointly by agreement. Where two or more Parties have separate interests or there is a disagreement as to whether they are of the same interest, they shall appoint their members separately.

Article 3
Appointments

If any appointments by the Parties are not made within two months of the date of the request to create a Conciliation Commission, the Director-General of Unesco shall, if asked to do so by the Party that made the request, make those appointments within a further two-month period.

Article 4
President of the Commission

If a President of the Conciliation Commission has not been chosen within two months of the last of the members of the Commission being appointed, the Director-General of Unesco shall, if asked to do so by a Party, designate a President within a further two-month period.

Article 5
Decisions

The Conciliation Commission shall take its decisions by majority vote of its members. It shall, unless the Parties to the dispute otherwise agree, determine its own procedure. It shall render a proposal for resolution of the dispute, which the Parties shall consider in good faith.

Article 6
Disagreement

A disagreement as to whether the Conciliation Commission has competence shall be decided by the Commission.

ANNEX 1(b)

Declaration of the European Community in application of Article 27(3)(c) of the Convention on the Protection and Promotion of the Diversity of Cultural Expressions

The current members of the European Community are the Kingdom of Belgium, the Czech Republic, the Kingdom of Denmark, the Federal Republic of Germany, the Republic of Estonia, the Hellenic Republic, the Kingdom of Spain, the French Republic, Ireland, the Italian Republic, the Republic of Cyprus, the Republic of Latvia, the

Republic of Lithuania, the Grand Duchy of Luxembourg, the Republic of Hungary, the Republic of Malta, the Kingdom of the Netherlands, the Republic of Austria, the Republic of Poland, the Portuguese Republic, the Republic of Slovenia, the Slovak Republic, the Republic of Finland, the Kingdom of Sweden and the United Kingdom of Great Britain and Northern Ireland.

This Declaration indicates the competences transferred to the Community by the Member States under the Treaties, in the areas covered by the Convention.

The Community has exclusive competence for the common commercial policy (Articles 131–134 of the Treaty), except for the commercial aspects of intellectual property and trade in services in those areas set out in Article 133(5) and (6) of the Treaty (in particular, in this context, trade in cultural and audiovisual services) where responsibility is shared between the Community and the Member States. It conducts a development cooperation policy (Articles 177–181 of the Treaty) and a policy of cooperation with industrialised countries (Article 181a of the Treaty) without prejudice to the respective competences of the Member States. It has shared competence as regards the free movement of goods, persons, services and capital (Articles 23–31 and 39–60 of the Treaty), competition (Articles 81–89 of the Treaty) and the internal market, including intellectual property (Articles 94–97 of the Treaty). Pursuant to Article 151 of the Treaty, in particular paragraph 4 thereof, the Community takes cultural aspects into account in its action under other provisions of the Treaty, in particular in order to respect and to promote the diversity of its cultures.

The Community Acts listed below illustrate the extent of the area of competence of the Community in accordance with the provisions establishing the European Community.

Council Decision 94/800/EC of 22 December 1994 concerning the conclusion on behalf of the European Community, as regards matters within its competence, of the Agreements reached in the Uruguay Round multilateral negotiations (1986 to 1994) (OJ L 336, 23.12.1994, p. 1).

Council Regulation (EC) No 2501/2001 of 10 December 2001 applying a scheme of generalised tariff preferences for the period from 1 January 2002 to 31 December 2004 — Statements on a Council Regulation applying a scheme of generalised tariff preferences for the period from 1 January 2002 to 31 December 2004 (OJ L 346, 31.12.2001, p. 1).

Council Decision 2005/599/EC of 21 June 2005 concerning the signing, on behalf of the European Community, of the Agreement amending the Partnership Agreement between the members of the African, Caribbean and Pacific Group of States, of the one part, and the European Community and its Member States, of the other part, signed in Cotonou on 23 June 2000 (OJ L 209, 11.8.2005, p. 26).

Council Regulation (EC) No 2698/2000 of 27 November 2000 amending Regulation (EC) No 1488/96 on financial and technical measures to accompany the reform of economic and social structures in the framework of the Euro-Mediterranean Partnership (MEDA) (OJ L 311, 12.12.2000, p. 1).

Council Regulation (EEC) No 3906/89 of 18 December 1989 on economic aid to the Republic of Hungary and the Polish People's Republic, and subsequent amendments, still applicable to Bulgaria and Romania (OJ L 375, 23.12.1989, p. 11).

Council Regulation (EC) No 2666/2000 of 5 December 2000 on assistance for Albania, Bosnia and Herzegovina, Croatia, the Federal Republic of Yugoslavia and the Former Yugoslav Republic of Macedonia and repealing Regulation (EC) No 1628/96 and amending Regulations (EEC) No 3906/89 and (EEC) No 1360/90 and Decisions 97/256/EC and 1999/311/EC (OJ L 306, 7.12.2000, p. 1).

Council Regulation (EEC) No 443/92 of 25 February 1992 on financial and technical assistance to, and economic cooperation with, the developing countries in Asia and Latin America (OJ L 52, 27.2.1992, p. 1).

Council Regulation (EC, Euratom) No 99/2000 of 29 December 1999 concerning the provision of assistance to the partner States in Eastern Europe and Central Asia (OJ L 12, 18.1.2000, p. 1).

Decision No 792/2004/EC of the European Parliament and of the Council of 21 April 2004 establishing a Community action programme to promote bodies active at European level in the field of culture (OJ L 138, 30.4.2004, p. 40).

Decision No 508/2000/EC of the European Parliament and the Council of 14 February 2000 establishing the Culture 2000 programme (OJ L 63, 10.3.2000, p. 1).

Decision No 1419/1999/EC of the European Parliament and of the Council of 25 May 1999 establishing a Community action for the European Capital of Culture event for the years 2005 to 2019 (OJ L 166, 1.7.1999, p. 1).

Council Decision of 22 September 1997 regarding the future of European cultural action OJ C 305, 7.10.1997, p. 1.

Council Decision of 22 September 1997 on cross-border fixed book prices in European linguistic areas (OJ C 305, 7.10.1997, p. 2).

Council Directive 89/552/EEC of 3 October 1989 on the coordination of certain provisions laid down by Law, Regulation or Administrative Action in Member States concerning the pursuit of television broadcasting activities (OJ L 298, 17.10.1989, p. 23). Directive amended by Directive 97/36/EC of the European Parliament and of the Council (OJ L 202, 30.7.1997, p. 60).

Council Decision 2000/821/EC of 20 December 2000 on the implementation of a programme to encourage the development, distribution and promotion of European audiovisual works (MEDIA Plus—Development, Distribution and Promotion) (2001–2005) (OJ L 336, 30.12.2000, p. 82).

Decision No 163/2001/EC of the European Parliament and of the Council of 19 January 2001 on the implementation of a training programme for professionals in the European audiovisual programme industry (MEDIA-Training) (2001–2005) (OJ L 26, 27.1.2001, p. 1).

Council Regulation (EC) No 659/1999 of 22 March 1999 laying down detailed rules for the application of Article 93 of the EC Treaty (OJ L 83, 27.3.1999, p. 1), relating to State aid.

Directive 2004/48/EC of the European Parliament and the Council of 29 April 2004 on the enforcement of intellectual property rights (OJ L 157, 30.4.2004, p. 45).

Directive 2001/29/EC of the European Parliament and of the Council of 22 May 2001 on the harmonisation of certain aspects of copyright and related rights in the information society (OJ L 167, 22.6.2001, p. 10).

Directive 2001/84/EC of the European Parliament and of the Council of 27 September 2001 on the resale right for the benefit of the author of an original work of art (OJ L 272, 13.10.2001, p. 32).

Council Directive 93/83/EEC of 27 September 1993 on the coordination of certain rules concerning copyright and rights related to copyright applicable to satellite broadcasting and cable retransmission OJ L 248, 6.10.1993, p. 15).

Council Directive 93/98/EEC of 29 October 1993 harmonising the term of protection of copyright and certain related rights (OJ L 290, 24.11.1993, p. 9).

Council Directive 92/100/EEC of 19 November 1992 on rental right and lending right and on certain rights related to copyright in the field of intellectual property (OJ L 346, 27.11.1992, p. 61)

The exercise of Community competence is, by its nature, subject to continuous development. In this respect, therefore, the Community reserves the right to notify other future declarations regarding the distribution of competences between the European Community and the Member States.

ANNEX 2

Unilateral declaration on behalf of the community in connection with deposition of the instrument of accession

'As regards the Community competences described in the Declaration pursuant to Article 27(3)(c) of the Convention, the Community is bound by the Convention and will ensure its due implementation. It follows that the Member States of the Community which are party to the Convention in their mutual relations apply the provisions of the Convention in accordance with the Community's internal rules and without prejudice to appropriate amendments being made to these rules.'

Code of conduct between the Council, the Member States and the Commission for the participation of the Community and its Member States in meetings regarding the implementation of the Convention on the Protection and Promotion of the Diversity of Cultural Expressions, 1.2.2007, 5914/07.

1. The UNESCO Convention on the implementation of the Convention on the Protection and Promotion of the Diversity of Cultural Expressions will come into force on 18 March 2007.

2. So as to ensure good cooperation between the Council, the Commission and the Member States in the preparation of meetings regarding the implementation of the Convention, the Cultural Affairs Committee has developed a Code of Conduct, the text of which is reproduced in Annex.

3. Coreper is invited to take note of the Code, which is supported by all delegations and the Commission.

ANNEX
Code of Conduct
between the Council, the Member States and the Commission
for the participation of the Community and its Member States
in meetings regarding the implementation of the Convention on the Protection and
Promotion of the Diversity of Cultural Expressions

Bearing in mind the requirement of unity of the international representation of the European Community and its Member States in accordance with the EC Treaty and the case law of the European Court of Justice also at the stage of implementation of international obligations;

The Council, the Member States and the Commission agree on the following code of conduct:

NATURE AND SCOPE OF THE CODE

1. a) This Code of Conduct sets out the informal arrangements between the Council, the Member States and the Commission in preparation for the meetings regarding the implementation of the Convention on the Protection and Promotion of the Diversity of Cultural Expressions (hereinafter 'the Convention'), adopted by the General Conference of UNESCO in Paris, on 20 October 2005.

b) The code will apply to all meetings organized within the framework of UNESCO which are relevant for the implementation of the Convention, in particular to meetings of the Conference of Parties and the Intergovernmental Committee. The code also applies mutatis mutandis to Article 33 of the Convention on amendments.

DIVISION OF TASKS BASED ON COMPETENCE

2. On matters falling within the competence of Member States, in particular:
– Aspects of cultural policies within the competence of the Member States;
– Public awareness and education;
– Issues concerning international cooperation in the field of culture, in particular with developing countries (except for trade related issues);
– Issues related to human rights;
– Follow-up bodies and mechanisms;
– Any other matters falling exclusively or primarily within the competence of the Member States;

The Presidency will convene on its own initiative or at the request of the Commission or a Member State coordination meetings of EU Member States' delegations before, during and after each meeting referred to in paragraph 1, aiming at elaborating coordinated positions. The Presidency will express these coordinated positions.

3. The Commission will:
Express, on behalf of the Community, Community positions on matters falling within Community competence, in particular in relation to:
– Free movement of goods, persons, services and capital (Art. 23–31 and 39–60 EC);
– Common rules on competition, in particular concerning aids granted by states (Art. 81–89 EC);

– Internal market (Art. 94–97 EC);
– Community measures taken within the sphere of intellectual property (Art. 95 and 308);
– Common commercial policy, including the commitments taken by the Community in other international organisations, in particular as a member of the WTO (Art. 131 to 134 EC);
– Legislative Acts taken under title IV on Visas, Asylum, Immigration (Art. 61–69 EC), subject to the special position of the United Kingdom, Ireland and Denmark under that Title;
– Community measures taken in the sphere of development cooperation (Art. 177 to 181 EC) as well as cooperation with industrialised countries (Art. 181a EC), without prejudice to Member States' capacity to express positions on measures taken under their national competence.
– Any other matters falling exclusively or primarily within Community competence.
4. The Presidency and the Commission will agree on which of them will be delivering any statement to be made on behalf of the Community and its Member States in cases where the respective competencies are inextricably linked. The Commission will present the common position when the preponderance of the matter concerned lies within the competence of the Community, and the Presidency will present the common position when the preponderance of the matter concerned lies within the competence of the Member States.

SPEAKING

5. a) In the case the Presidency is not represented in meetings referred to in paragraph 1, the position of the Community and its Member States reached in the coordination process on matters covered by paragraph 2 and, as appropriate, in paragraph 4, is presented by the delegate of the Member State represented which comes first in the list of rotation for the EU Presidency.
b) In the case that the European Community is not represented in the meetings referred to in paragraph 1 and, in particular the Intergovernmental Committee, the Presidency or the delegate of the Member State which comes first in the list of rotation for the EU Presidency will pass the floor to the Commission, for matters which are covered by paragraph 3 or, as appropriate, the statement on matters covered by paragraph 4.
6. Without prejudice to paragraph 8, a Member State other than the one holding the Presidency or representing it may take the floor, after due coordination, to support and/or develop the Community or the common position. In addition, after having informed the Presidency, Member States may take the floor on issues related to the information and reporting on national measures of implementation, notably as far as implementation of Articles 9 and 19 of the Convention is concerned, and to support and/or develop the coordinated position.

VOTING

7. a) Subject to paragraph 8, and in accordance with Article 27.3.b and d of the Convention, the Commission, on behalf of the European Community, will exercise the Community's voting rights on the basis of Community or common positions reached

in the coordination process on matters referred to in paragraph 3, and, as appropriate, in paragraph 4.

It may be agreed that in cases where the Community is not represented, the Member States will exercise their voting rights on those matters, on the basis of common positions.

b) Subject to paragraph 8, and in accordance with Article 27.3.b and d of the Convention, the Member States will exercise their voting rights on matters referred to in paragraph 2, and, as appropriate, in paragraph 4 on the basis of coordinated or common positions reached in the coordination process.

ESTABLISHING OF POSITIONS

8. a) All positions of the Community and its Member States referred to in paragraphs 3 and 4 will be duly coordinated. In matters referred to in paragraph 2, Member States will aim at elaborating coordinated positions. Draft statements on positions will be circulated among Member States beforehand.

b) The Commission and the Member States will use best endeavours in coordination meetings on the spot to establish an agreed position.

c) If no agreement can be reached on the repartition of competences or on matters covered by paragraphs 3 and 4, then the matter will be referred without undue delay to the Cultural Affairs Committee, and, when applicable, other Council bodies. If no agreement can be reached in these bodies, the matter will be referred to the Permanent Representatives Committee. However, in cases where meetings of the Cultural Affairs Committee and, when applicable, of the relevant other Council bodies cannot be convened in time, the matter will be directly referred to the Permanent Representatives Committee.

SPEAKING AND VOTING IN CASES OF DISAGREEMENT

9. Where no agreement between the Commission and the Member States is reached in accordance with paragraph 8 c), Member States may speak and vote on matters falling clearly within their competence on condition that the position will be coherent with Community policies and in conformity with Community law. The Commission may speak and vote on matters falling clearly within Community competence to the extent necessary to defend the Community acquis.

ANNEX to ANNEX

Policy objectives

for the Community and its Member States

for meetings relating to the implementation of the Convention

The Community and its Member States will pursue, inter alia, the following objectives:

a) When the members of the Intergovernmental Committee are appointed, the Community and its Member States will endeavour to maximise its representation.

b) When the rules of procedure of the Intergovernmental Committee are laid down, the Community and its Member States shall seek to ensure that the Commission, as the representative of the European Community, will be admitted as an observer, and that there is a rule governing the observers' right to speak in the Committee.

Select Bibliography

Hillion, C. and Koutrakos, P., *Mixed Agreements Revisited: The EU Member States in the World* (Oxford and Portland, OR: Hart Publishing, 2010).

O'Keeffe, D. and Schermers, H.G. (eds), *Mixed Agreements* (Deventer: Kluwer Law and Taxation Publishers, 1983).

5

The EU in International Organizations

5.1 The right to accession of the EU under Union law

Article 216(1) TFEU empowers the Union to conclude agreements with 'one or more third countries *or international organisations*'.[1] Furthermore, the Court of Justice established in the fifth paragraph of Opinion 1/76 that the Union, in principle, has the power to cooperate with third countries in establishing an international organization.[2] However, these matters are only sparsely regulated in the TFEU. The general provision on the EU's relationship with other international organizations is Article 220 TFEU. Apart from that, a number of provisions on cooperation with international organizations exist with respect to specific areas of competence, such as the environment (Article 191 TFEU),[3] development cooperation (Article 211 TFEU), or cooperation with third countries (Article 212 TFEU).[4]

Treaty on the Functioning of the European Union

Article 220

1. The Union shall establish all appropriate forms of cooperation with the organs of the United Nations and its specialised agencies, the Council of Europe, the Organisation for Security and Cooperation in Europe and the Organisation for Economic Cooperation and Development.

The Union shall also maintain such relations as are appropriate with other international organisations.

2. The High Representative of the Union for Foreign Affairs and Security Policy and the Commission shall implement this Article.

5.2 The right to accession of the EU under international law

The situation is less straightforward from an international law point of view. In particular, Article 15 of the Vienna Convention on the Law of Treaties does not embody a right

---

[1] Emphasis added. See also Chapter 1.
[2] See Chapter 1.
[3] See Chapter 10.
[4] See Chapter 8.

to accession for every subject of international law to every treaty to which it wishes to become a party. The conditions under which newcomers are allowed to join the multilateral convention or organization in question depend on the will of the original parties.

Against that background, third countries have accepted the Union as a valuable treaty partner over time. However, in particular where Member States continue to be parties to such conventions or international organizations (mixed membership), the third states or the international organization in question have a legitimate interest to fix certain conditions under which the Union and its Member States will function within the multilateral setting. They would, *inter alia*, like to make sure that either the Union or the Member States exercise certain rights (avoiding over-representation of the EU) and to have legal certainty with respect to liability. An important precedent was laid down in the UN Convention on the Law of the Sea (UNCLOS) of 1982. While Article 305(1)(f) allowed 'international organizations' to become a party to the Convention, Annex IX thereof (included below) further specified the entry conditions.

In later UN practice, the essentials of this precedent were laid down in a somewhat shortened clause. Nowadays, two points mark the entry conditions for the Union. There must be a demonstration during the negotiations that the Member States have (wholly or partially) transferred competences to the Union in the subject area of the international agreement, and a declaration of competence must be deposited with the instrument of acceptance. Because these clauses refer to 'regional economic integration organizations', they are often referred to as 'REIO' clauses; for example Article 22 of the 1992 UN Framework Convention on Climate Change (UNFCCC) included here. More recently, such clauses tend to refer simply to 'regional integration organizations' (RIO clauses), such as Article 44 of the UN Convention on the Rights of Persons with Disabilities, included above (see Chapter 4, p. 163).

In the alternative, the international organization acceding to an international instrument can also be named as such. That has been the practice in the Council of Europe vis-à-vis the EU. Early Council of Europe Conventions, which had not been open for accession by the EU, have been made accessible through the adoption of additional Protocols, such as most notably Protocol No. 14, which allows for EU accession to the European Convention on Human Rights (ECHR). Most newer Conventions already contain a clause that allows the Union to become a party straight away, for example the Convention on the counterfeiting of medical products and similar crimes involving threats to public health. Both examples are included below. Occasionally, the EU has also been directly named in certain international commodity agreements as a Party. Such is the case with Article 4 of the International Coffee Agreement of 2007 to be found below.

Annex IX (Participation by International Organizations) of the UN Convention on the Law of the Sea of 10 December 1982.

Article 1

Use of terms

For the purposes of article 305 and of this Annex, 'international organization' means an intergovernmental organization constituted by States to which its member States have transferred competence over matters governed by this Convention, including the competence to enter into treaties in respect of those matters.

Article 2

Signature

An international organization may sign this Convention if a majority of its member States are signatories of this Convention. At the time of signature an international organization shall make a declaration specifying the matters governed by this Convention in respect of which competence has been transferred to that organization by its member States which are signatories, and the nature and extent of that competence.

Article 3

Formal confirmation and accession

1. An international organization may deposit its instrument of formal confirmation or of accession if a majority of its member States deposit or have deposited their instruments of ratification or accession.

2. The instruments deposited by the international organization shall contain the undertakings and declarations required by articles 4 and 5 of this Annex.

Article 4

Extent of participation and rights and obligations

1. The instrument of formal confirmation or of accession of an international organization shall contain an undertaking to accept the rights and obligations of States under this Convention in respect of matters relating to which competence has been transferred to it by its member States which are Parties to this Convention.

2. An international organization shall be a Party to this Convention to the extent that it has competence in accordance with the declarations, communications of information or notifications referred to in article 5 of this Annex.

3. Such an international organization shall exercise the rights and perform the obligations which its member States which are Parties would otherwise have under this Convention, on matters relating to which competence has been transferred to it by those member States. The member States of that international organization shall not exercise competence which they have transferred to it.

4. Participation of such an international organization shall in no case entail an increase of the representation to which its member States which are States Parties would otherwise be entitled, including rights in decision-making.

5. Participation of such an international organization shall in no case confer any rights under this Convention on member States of the organization which are not States Parties to this Convention.

6. In the event of a conflict between the obligations of an international organization under this Convention and its obligations under the agreement establishing the organization or any acts relating to it, the obligations under this Convention shall prevail.

Article 5

Declarations, notifications and communications

1. The instrument of formal confirmation or of accession of an international organization shall contain a declaration specifying the matters governed by this Convention in

respect of which competence has been transferred to the organization by its member States which are Parties to this Convention.

2. A member State of an international organization shall, at the time it ratifies or accedes to this Convention or at the time when the organization deposits its instrument of formal confirmation or of accession, whichever is later, make a declaration specifying the matters governed by this Convention in respect of which it has transferred competence to the organization.

3. States Parties which are member States of an international organization which is a Party to this Convention shall be presumed to have competence over all matters governed by this Convention in respect of which transfers of competence to the organization have not been specifically declared, notified or communicated by those States under this article.

4. The international organization and its member States which are States Parties shall promptly notify the depositary of this Convention of any changes to the distribution of competence, including new transfers of competence, specified in the declarations under paragraphs 1 and 2.

5. Any State Party may request an international organization and its member States which are States Parties to provide information as to which, as between the organization and its member States, has competence in respect of any specific question which has arisen. The organization and the member States concerned shall provide this information within a reasonable time. The international organization and the member States may also, on their own initiative, provide this information.

6. Declarations, notifications and communications of information under this article shall specify the nature and extent of the competence transferred.

Article 6

Responsibility and liability

1. Parties which have competence under article 5 of this Annex shall have responsibility for failure to comply with obligations or for any other violation of this Convention.

2. Any State Party may request an international organization or its member States which are States Parties for information as to who has responsibility in respect of any specific matter. The organization and the member States concerned shall provide this information. Failure to provide this information within a reasonable time or the provision of contradictory information shall result in joint and several liability.

Article 7

Settlement of disputes

1. At the time of deposit of its instrument of formal confirmation or of accession, or at any time thereafter, an international organization shall be free to choose, by means of a written declaration, one or more of the means for the settlement of disputes concerning the interpretation or application of this Convention, referred to in article 287, paragraph 1(a), (c) or (d).

2. Part XV applies mutatis mutandis to any dispute between Parties to this Convention, one or more of which are international organizations.

3. When an international organization and one or more of its member States are joint parties to a dispute, or parties in the same interest, the organization shall be deemed to have accepted the same procedures for the settlement of disputes as the member States; when, however, a member State has chosen only the International Court of Justice under article 287, the organization and the member State concerned shall be deemed to have accepted arbitration in accordance with Annex VII, unless the parties to the dispute otherwise agree.

Article 8

Applicability of Part XVII
Part XVII applies mutatis mutandis to an international organization, except in respect of the following:
(a) the instrument of formal confirmation or of accession of an international organization shall not be taken into account in the application of article 308, paragraph l;
(b)(i) an international organization shall have exclusive capacity with respect to the application of articles 312 to 315, to the extent that it has competence under article 5 of this Annex over the entire subject-matter of the amendment;
(ii) the instrument of formal confirmation or of accession of an international organization to an amendment, the entire subject-matter over which the international organization has competence under article 5 of this Annex, shall be considered to be the instrument of ratification or accession of each of the member States which are States Parties, for the purposes of applying article 316, paragraphs 1, 2 and 3;
(iii) the instrument of formal confirmation or of accession of the international organization shall not be taken into account in the application of article 316, paragraphs 1 and 2, with regard to all other amendments;
(c) (i) an international organization may not denounce this Convention in accordance with article 317 if any of its member States is a State Party and if it continues to fulfil the qualifications specified in article 1 of this Annex;
(ii) an international organization shall denounce this Convention when none of its member States is a State Party or if the international organization no longer fulfils the qualifications specified in article 1 of this Annex. Such denunciation shall take effect immediately.

1992 United Nations Framework Convention on Climate Change.

[...]

Article 22

1. The Convention shall be subject to ratification, acceptance, approval or accession by States and by regional economic integration organizations. It shall be open for accession from the day after the date on which the Convention is closed for signature. Instruments of ratification, acceptance, approval or accession shall be deposited with the Depositary.
2. Any regional economic integration organization which becomes a Party to the Convention without any of its Member States being a party shall be bound by all the obligations under the Convention. In the case of such organizations, one or more

of whose members is a Party to the Convention, the organization and its member States shall decide on their respective responsibilities for the performance of their obligations under the Convention. In such cases, the organization and the member States shall not be entitled to exercise rights under the Convention concurrently.

3. In their instrument of ratification, acceptance, approval or accession regional economic integration organizations shall declare the extent of their competence with respect to the matters governed by the Convention. These organizations shall also inform the Depository, who shall in turn inform the Parties, of any substantial modification in the extent of their competence.'

[...]

Protocol No. 14 to the Convention for the Protection of Human Rights and Fundamental Freedoms, amending the control system of the Convention.

[...]

Article 17

Article 59 of the Convention shall be amended as follows:

1. A new paragraph 2 shall be inserted which shall read as follows:
   '2. The European Union may accede to this Convention.'
2. Paragraphs 2, 3 and 4 shall become paragraphs 3, 4 and 5 respectively.

[...]

Council of Europe Convention on the counterfeiting of medical products and similar crimes involving threats to public health.

[...]

Article 28

Signature and entry into force

1. This Convention shall be open for signature by the member States of the Council of Europe, the European Union and the non-member States which have participated in its elaboration or enjoy observer status with the Council of Europe. It shall also be open for signature by any other non-member State of the Council of Europe upon invitation by the Committee of Ministers. The decision to invite a non-member State to sign the Convention shall be taken by the majority provided for in Article 20.d of the Statute of the Council of Europe, and by unanimous vote of the representatives of the Contracting States entitled to sit on the Committee of Ministers. This decision shall be taken after having obtained the unanimous agreement of the other States/ European Union having expressed their consent to be bound by this Convention.

[...]

4. In respect of any State or the European Union, which subsequently expresses its consent to be bound by the Convention, it shall enter into force on the first day of the month following the expiration of a period of three months after the date of the deposit of its instrument of ratification, acceptance or approval.

[...]

International Coffee Agreement (2007).

[...]

Article 4

Membership of the Organisation

1. Each Contracting Party shall constitute a single Member of the Organisation.
2. A Member may change its category of membership on such conditions as the Council may agree.
3. Any reference in this Agreement to a Government shall be construed as including the European Community and any intergovernmental organisation having exclusive competence in respect of the negotiation, conclusion and application of this Agreement.

[...]

Finally, a further distinction should also be made between two different situations: first, the Union can at times become a founding member of an international organization; and second, the Union may seek to join an already existing international organization. Both situations raise somewhat different issues under international law.

With respect to the first situation, the Community famously became a founding member of the WTO. Article XIV of the Agreement establishing the WTO is included here.

However, as regards the second situation, many international organizations dating from before the establishment of the European Communities have no provision in their constitutions to accommodate other international organizations wishing to become members. The UN is perhaps the paradigmatic example of that genus. The only way for the Union to join such an international organization would be to persuade the existing members to amend the constitution of the organization (in the case of the UN, in accordance with the onerous procedure of Article 108 of the UN Charter) in order to enable other international organizations to become members. Should that be successful, the Union and the Member States can become members of the relevant international organizations alongside each other.

A well-known example of such a construction is the Food and Agricultural Organization of the United Nations (FAO). The FAO admitted the then EEC as a member, alongside its Member States, by a decision of 26 November 1991, taken under Article II(3) and (5) FAO Constitution. As with the FAO, any international organization of which both the Union and the Member States are parties will have to determine whether both the Union and the Member States get voting rights and, if so, how these are to be exercised.[5]

By contrast, as things currently stand, the EU cannot become a member of the UN itself. Nevertheless, the Commission established an information office in New York in 1964 in order to foster relations with third states within the UN framework. On 11 October 1974, the General Assembly of the United Nations (UNGA) requested the UN Secretary-General 'to invite the European Economic Community to participate in the

---

[5] See, for example, as regards the Stockholm Convention on Persistent Organic Pollutants: Case C-246/07, *Commission v. Sweden*, [2010] ECR I-3317, on which see G. De Baere, "O, Where is Faith? O, Where is Loyalty?" Some Thoughts on the Duty of Loyal Co-operation and the Union's External Environmental Competences in the Light of the *PFOS* Case, *European Law Review*, vol. 36, 2011, 405–19.

sessions and work of the General Assembly in the capacity of observer',[6] making it the first non-state actor to enjoy permanent observer status at the UN. That status applies as much to the UNGA's committees and sub-committees as it does to the plenary. Likewise, the EC/EU has an observer status at the Economic and Social Council (ECOSOC),[7] including in most of its functional commissions, as well as in UN subsidiary organs. It is also a full participant at the Commission on Sustainable Development,[8] and has been invited to participate in the Peacebuilding Commission as an 'institutional donor'[9] and a 'relevant international organization'.[10]

The most recent development in the status of the EU in the UN has been the adoption on 3 May 2011 by the UNGA at its 88th plenary meeting of Resolution 65/276 *Participation of the European Union in the work of the United Nations*, granting the Union a form of enhanced observer status. This came as a result of concerted efforts by the EU and its Member States in the face of significant objections by a number of UN members. The considerable difficulties this effort faced indicate that the possibility for the EU to become a full member of the UN soon is rather marginal.[11]

Agreement establishing the World Trade Organization

[...]

Article XIV

Acceptance, Entry into Force and Deposit

1. This Agreement shall be open for acceptance, by signature or otherwise, by contracting parties to GATT 1947, and the European Communities, which are eligible to become original Members of the WTO in accordance with Article XI of this Agreement. Such acceptance shall apply to this Agreement and the Multilateral Trade Agreements annexed hereto. This Agreement and the Multilateral Trade Agreements annexed hereto shall enter into force on the date determined by Ministers in accordance with paragraph 3 of the Final Act Embodying the Results of the Uruguay Round

---

[6] Status of the European Economic Community in the General Assembly, UN Doc. A/RES/3208(XXIX). Compare Art. 12(2) Constitution of the International Labour Organization (ILO): 'The International Labour Organization may make appropriate arrangements for the representatives of public international organizations to participate without vote in its deliberations.' Further on the Union's position in the ILO: Rudi Delarue, ILO-EU Cooperation on Employment and Social Affairs, *The United Nations and the European Union: An Ever Stronger Partnership* (Jan Woutres, Frank Hoffmeister, and Tom Ruys (eds), The Hague: TMC Asser Press 2006), 93–114.

[7] By virtue of Rule 79 of the Rules of Procedure of the Economic and Social Council, UN Doc. E/5715/Rev.2: 'Representatives of intergovernmental organizations accorded permanent observer status by the General Assembly and of other intergovernmental organizations designated on an ad hoc or continuing basis by the Council on the recommendation of the Bureau, may participate, without the right to vote, in the deliberation of the Council on questions within the scope of the activities of the organization.'

[8] ECOSOC Decision 1995/201, *Full Participation of the European Community in the Commission on Sustainable Development*.

[9] *The Peacebuilding Commission*, UN Doc. A/RES/60/180, point 9.

[10] A/RES/60/180, point 7(b).

[11] See further: P.A. Serrano de Haro, *Participation of the EU in the Work of the UN: General Assembly Resolution 65/276*, The Hague: CLEER Working Papers 2012/4; and G. De Baere and E. Paasivirta, Identity and Difference: The EU and the UN as Part of Each Other, *The Emergence of the European Union's International Identity—Views from the Global Arena* (H.C.F.J.A. de Waele and J.J. Kuipers (eds), The Hague/Boston/London: Martinus Nijhoff Publishers, forthcoming 2013).

of Multilateral Trade Negotiations and shall remain open for acceptance for a period of two years following that date unless the Ministers decide otherwise. An acceptance following the entry into force of this Agreement shall enter into force on the 30th day following the date of such acceptance.

[...]

FAO Constitution

[...]

Article II

Membership and Associate Membership

[...]

3. The Conference may by a two-thirds majority of the votes cast, provided that a majority of the Member Nations of the Organization is present, decide to admit as a Member of the Organization any regional economic integration organization meeting the criteria set out in paragraph 4 of this Article, which has submitted an application for membership and a declaration made in a formal instrument that it will accept the obligations of the Constitution as in force at the time of admission. Subject to paragraph 8 of this Article, references to Member Nations under this Constitution shall include Member Organizations, except as otherwise expressly provided.

4. To be eligible to apply for membership of the Organization under paragraph 3 of this Article, a regional economic integration organization must be one constituted by sovereign States, a majority of which are Member Nations of the Organization, and to which its Member States have transferred competence over a range of matters within the purview of the Organization, including the authority to make decisions binding on its Member States in respect of those matters.

5. Each regional economic integration organization applying for membership in the Organization shall, at the time of such application, submit a declaration of competence specifying the matters in respect of which competence has been transferred to it by its Member States.

6. Member States of a Member Organization shall be presumed to retain competence over all matters in respect of which transfers of competence have not been specifically declared or notified to the Organization.

7. Any change regarding the distribution of competence between the Member Organization and its Member States shall be notified by the Member Organization or its Member States to the Director-General, who shall circulate such information to the other Member Nations of the Organization.

8. A Member Organization shall exercise membership rights on an alternative basis with its Member States that are Member Nations of the Organization in the areas of their respective competences and in accordance with rules set down by the Conference.

9. Except as otherwise provided in this Article, a Member Organization shall have the right to participate in matters within its competence in any meeting of the Organization, including any meeting of the Council or other body, other than bodies of restricted membership referred to below, in which any of its Member States are entitled to participate. A Member Organization shall not be eligible for election or designation to any such body, nor shall it be eligible for election or designation to any body established

jointly with other organizations. A Member Organization shall not have the right to participate in bodies of restricted membership specified in the rules adopted by the Conference.

10. Except as otherwise provided in this Constitution or in rules set down by the Conference, and Article III paragraph 4 notwithstanding, a Member Organization may exercise on matters within its competence, in any meeting of the Organization in which it is entitled to participate, a number of votes equal to the number of its Member States which are entitled to vote in such meeting. Whenever a Member Organization exercises its right to vote, its Member States shall not exercise theirs, and conversely.

[...]

United Nations General Assembly Resolution A/65/PV.88 of 3 May 2011 on Participation of the European Union in the work of the United Nations, UN Doc. A/RES/65/276.

The General Assembly,

Bearing in mind the role and authority of the General Assembly as a principal organ of the United Nations and the importance of its effectiveness and efficiency in fulfilling its functions under the Charter of the United Nations,

Recognizing that the current interdependent international environment requires the strengthening of the multilateral system in accordance with the purposes and principles of the United Nations and the principles of international law,

Recognizing also the importance of cooperation between the United Nations and regional organizations, as well as the benefits to the United Nations of such cooperation,

Acknowledging that it is for each regional organization to define the modalities of its external representation,

Recalling its resolution 3208 (XXIX) of 11 October 1974, by which it granted observer status to the European Economic Community,

Recalling also that, consistent with the relevant legal provisions, the European Union has replaced the European Community and is a party to many instruments concluded under the auspices of the United Nations and an observer or participant in the work of several specialized agencies and bodies of the United Nations,

Noting that the States members of the European Union have entrusted the external representation of the European Union, previously performed by the representatives of the member State holding the rotating Presidency of the Council of the European Union, to the following institutional representatives: the President of the European Council, the High Representative of the Union for Foreign Affairs and Security Policy, the European Commission, and European Union delegations, which have assumed the role of acting on behalf of the European Union in the exercise of the competences conferred by its member States,

Mindful of the modalities for the participation of observer States and entities, and other observers in the work of the United Nations, as set out in the respective resolutions,

1. *Reaffirms* that the General Assembly is an intergovernmental body whose membership is limited to States that are Members of the United Nations;

2. *Decides* to adopt the modalities set out in the annex to the present resolution for the participation of the representatives of the European Union, in its capacity as observer, in the sessions and work of the General Assembly and its committees and working groups, in international meetings and conferences convened under the auspices of the Assembly and in United Nations conferences;

3. *Recognizes* that, following a request on behalf of a regional organization that has observer status in the General Assembly and whose member States have agreed arrangements that allow that organization's representatives to speak on behalf of the organization and its member States, the Assembly may adopt modalities for the participation of that regional organization's representatives, such as those set out in the annex to the present resolution;

4. *Requests* the Secretary-General to inform the General Assembly during its sixty-fifth session on the implementation of the modalities set out in the annex to the present resolution.

88th plenary meeting
3 May 2011

ANNEX

PARTICIPATION OF THE EUROPEAN UNION IN THE WORK OF THE UNITED NATIONS

1. In accordance with the present resolution, the representatives of the European Union, in order to present positions of the European Union and its member States as agreed by them, shall be:

(a) Allowed to be inscribed on the list of speakers among representatives of major groups, in order to make interventions; (b) Invited to participate in the general debate of the General Assembly, in accordance with the order of precedence as established in the practice for participating observers and the level of participation; (c) Permitted to have its communications relating to the sessions and work of the General Assembly and to the sessions and work of all international meetings and conferences convened under the auspices of the Assembly and of United Nations conferences, circulated directly, and without intermediary, as documents of the Assembly, meeting or conference; (d) Also permitted to present proposals and amendments orally as agreed by the States members of the European Union; such proposals and amendments shall be put to a vote only at the request of a Member State; (e) Allowed to exercise the right of reply regarding positions of the European Union as decided by the presiding officer; such right of reply shall be restricted to one intervention per item.

2. The representatives of the European Union shall be ensured seating among the observers.

3. The representatives of the European Union shall not have the right to vote, to co-sponsor draft resolutions or decisions, or to put forward candidates.

4. A precursory explanation or recall of the present resolution shall be made only once by the President of the General Assembly at the start of each session.

5.3 The procedure of accession under Union law

Inside the Union legal order, the treaty-making procedure under Article 218 TFEU also applies to concluding multilateral conventions and becoming a member of another international organization.[12] Accordingly, a recommendation from the Commission to the Council invites the Council to issue negotiating guidelines. Once they are adopted, the Commission will negotiate the multilateral convention in question on behalf of the Union. For mixed conventions, most often the Commission will speak for the subject matters which wholly or predominantly fall within Union competence, whereas the Presidency will speak for the Member States for the remaining subjects. Upon a Commission proposal, the Council decides upon the signature and conclusion of the international agreement or the accession to the international organization. As the international organization will often qualify as 'an agreement establishing a specific institutional framework by organising cooperation procedures'[13] within the meaning of Article 218(6)(a)(iii) TFEU, the European Parliament will have to give its prior consent to accession. A textbook example of the intra-EU procedure was the accession of the Union (then Community) to the Hague Conference on International Private law, an important law-making international organization. Here we include the Proposal made by the Commission and the Council decision on the accession to the Hague Conference that duly followed it. On that basis, the EC became a Member of the Hague Conference on 3 April 2007. With the entry into force of the Treaty of Lisbon on 1 December 2009, the EU replaced and succeeded to the EC.

Council Decision 2006/719/EC of 5 October 2006 on the accession of the Community to the Hague Conference on Private International Law, Official Journal L 297, 26.10.2006, pp. 1–2.

THE COUNCIL OF THE EUROPEAN UNION,

Having regard to the Treaty establishing the European Community, and in particular Article 61(c), in conjunction with the first subparagraph of Article 300(2) and the second subparagraph of Article 300(3) thereof,

---

[12] See Chapter 3.

[13] Given that most agreements involving a cooperation procedure establish some sort of institutional framework, the latter can hardly be the distinguishing feature of this type of agreement. The Court would have had the chance to resolve the issue in *Parliament v. Council* (C-566/08), removed from the register on 25 February 2010 [2010] OJ C234/30. In that case, the Parliament sought the annulment of Council Decision 2008/780/EC of 29 September 2008 on the conclusion, on behalf of the EC, of the Southern Indian Ocean Fisheries Agreement [2008] OJ L268/27. The European Parliament argued that the agreement fell within the category of 'agreements establishing a specific institutional framework by organising cooperation procedures'. Consequently, the contested decision required the assent of the European Parliament, rather than merely its consultation. The Court referred the case to the Grand Chamber and was therefore presumably going to deal with the issue as a matter of principle. However, the Parliament withdrew the case after the entry into force of the Treaty of Lisbon, presumably because of its significantly enlarged powers with regard to international agreements. Nonetheless, the category still exists under Art. 218(6)(a)(iii) TFEU, and a clarification by the Court would have been welcome.

Having regard to the proposal from the Commission,
Having regard to the assent of the European Parliament,

Whereas:

[...]

(3) It is essential that the Community be granted a status that corresponds to its new role as a major international player in the field of civil judicial cooperation and that it be able to exercise its external competence by participating as a full member in the negotiations of conventions by the HCCH in areas of its competence.

(4) By decision of 28 November 2002, the Council authorised the Commission to negotiate the conditions and modalities of Community accession to the HCCH.

(5) By a joint letter from the Commission and the Presidency to the HCCH of 19 December 2002, the Community applied to become a member of the HCCH, and requested the opening of negotiations.

(6) In April 2004, a Special Commission on General Affairs and Policy of the HCCH expressed the unanimous view that, as a matter of principle, the Community should become a Member of the HCCH and determined certain criteria and procedures for the modalities of its membership.

(7) In June 2005, the Diplomatic Conference of the HCCH adopted by consensus the amendments to the Statute of the HCCH (Statute) necessary to allow the accession of a Regional Economic Integration Organisation and the Members of the HCCH were subsequently invited to cast their votes on the amendments, if possible within a period of nine months.

(8) The amendments to the Statute will enter into force three months after the Secretary General of the HCCH has informed the Members that the required two-thirds majority for amending the Statute has been reached. Shortly after the entry into force, an extraordinary meeting of the Council on General Affairs and Policy will formally decide upon the Community's accession to the HCCH.

(9) The outcome of the negotiations on the revision of the Statute is satisfactory, taking into account the interests of the Community.

(10) Article 2A of the revised Statute entitles the Community, as a Regional Economic Integration Organisation, to become a Member of the HCCH.

(11) The Community should accede to the HCCH.

[...]

HAS DECIDED AS FOLLOWS:

Sole Article

1. The Community shall accede to the Hague Conference on Private International Law (HCCH) by means of the declaration of acceptance of the Statute of the HCCH (Statute), as set out in Annex I to this Decision, as soon as the HCCH has taken the formal decision to admit the Community as a Member.

2. The Community shall also deposit a declaration of competence specifying the matters in respect of which competence has been transferred to it by its Member States, as set out in Annex II to this Decision, and a declaration on certain matters concerning the HCCH, as set out in Annex III to this Decision.

3. The President of the Council is hereby authorised to carry out such procedures as may be necessary to give effect to paragraphs 1 and 2.

4. The text of the Statute is attached to this Decision as Annex IV.

5. For the purpose of this Decision the term 'Member State' shall mean Member States with the exception of Denmark.

Sometimes, the international legal act allowing accession of the Union to the multilateral convention or international organization in question will have entered into force before the Union actually accedes. However, at other times, the relevant amendment will be pending, for example with respect to the Convention on International Trade in Endangered Species of Wild Fauna and Flora (CITES).[14] In such a situation, the question arises whether it is possible to apply the amendment provisionally, thereby granting the Union an interim status in the organization. Recent practice of the World Customs Organization (WCO) points in that direction: the then Community was invited to exercise rights and obligations akin to membership ad interim, pending the entry into force of an amendment of the 1950 Brussels Convention establishing the WCO. Inside the EU, the Council accepted this invitation upon a proposal of the Commission under Article 218(5) TFEU (then Article 300(2) TEC).

Council Decision 2007/668/EC of 25 June 2007 on the exercise of rights and obligations akin to membership ad interim by the European Community in the World Customs Organisation, Official Journal L 274, 18.10.2007, pp. 11–12.

THE COUNCIL OF THE EUROPEAN UNION,

Having regard to the Treaty establishing the European Community, and in particular Article 133 thereof, in conjunction with the second subparagraph of Article 300(2) thereof,

Whereas:

(1) The Council decided on 19 March 2001 to authorise the Commission to negotiate on behalf of the European Community, the accession of the European Community to the World Customs Organisation.

(2) The Convention establishing a Customs Cooperation Council is expected to be amended by the Council of the World Customs Organisation at its 109th/110th session in June 2007 to allow customs or economic unions, including the European Community to acquire membership of the World Customs Organisation.

[…]

---

[14] See CITES, Notification No. 2010/039 to the Parties: Bonn and Gaborone Amendments to the text of the Convention (Geneva, 1 December 2010) (<http://www.cites.org/eng/notif/2010/E039.pdf>), para. 4: 'On 30 April 1983, at the second extraordinary meeting of the Conference of the Parties (Gaborone, Botswana), Article XXI was amended to make the Convention open to accession by organizations of regional economic integration composed of sovereign States, such as the European Community. However this amendment has not yet entered into force because, to date, only 47 States that were party to the Convention on 30 April 1983 have accepted it. The amendment will enter into effect for Parties that have deposited an instrument of acceptance once it is accepted by 54 (i.e. two-thirds) of the 80 States that were party to the Convention on 30 April 1983. For any other State that is a Party at the time of entry into force of the amendment, it will come into effect 60 days after that Party has deposited its instrument of acceptance of the amendment. States that become party after the amendment has entered into force will accede to the Convention as amended.'

(9) In view of the above the Council should provide for the exercise of rights and obligations akin to membership ad interim by the European Community in the World Customs Organisation, including the payment of an annual contribution,

HAS DECIDED AS FOLLOWS:

Sole Article

1. The Member States of the European Community shall vote in favour of the Council of the World Customs Organisation decision according to which the European Community shall, as an interim measure, be granted rights akin to those enjoyed by World Customs Organisation Members, subject to the conditions contained therein.

2. The European Community accepts the rights and obligations akin to those of World Customs Organisation members as laid down in the World Customs Organisation Council decision pending the entry into force of the amendment of the Convention establishing a Customs Cooperation Council.

3. The European Commission is authorised to communicate to the World Customs Organisation that the European Community accepts the rights and obligations akin to those of World Customs Organisation members and to submit to the World Customs Organisation the required declaration of competence as specified in the Annex.

4. The European Community shall pay an annual contribution to the World Customs Organisation to strengthen the work of the World Customs Organisation and to cover additional administrative expenses as of 1 July 2007.

5.4 The functioning of the EU and its Member States as parties to a multilateral convention or members of an international organization

In most cases where the Union has become a party to a multilateral convention or member of an international organization, it has joined next to its Member States. To manage mixed membership, the Court has derived in Opinion 1/94 (WTO) a duty to ensure close cooperation between the Member States and the EU institutions, which flows from the requirement of unity in the international representation of the Union (which in turn is based on the duty of loyalty under what is now Article 4(3) TEU).

Opinion of the Court of 15 November 1994, Competence of the Community to conclude international agreements concerning services and the protection of intellectual property (WTO Agreement), Opinion 1/94, European Court Reports 1994, p. I-5267, paras. 106–9.

IX. The duty of cooperation between the Member States and the Community institutions

106. At the hearing, the Commission drew the Court's attention to the problems which would arise, as regards the administration of the agreements, if the Community and the Member States were recognized as sharing competence to participate in

the conclusion of the GATS and TRIPs agreements. While it is true that, in the negotiation of the agreements, the procedure under Article 113 of the Treaty prevailed subject to certain very minor adjustments, the Member States will, in the context of the WTO, undoubtedly seek to express their views individually on matters falling within their competence whenever no consensus has been found. Furthermore, interminable discussions will ensue to determine whether a given matter falls within the competence of the Community, so that the Community mechanisms laid down by the relevant provisions of the Treaty will apply, or whether it is within the competence of the Member States, in which case the consensus rule will operate. The Community's unity of action vis-à-vis the rest of the world will thus be undermined and its negotiating power greatly weakened.

107. In response to that concern, which is quite legitimate, it must be stressed, first, that any problems which may arise in implementation of the WTO Agreement and its annexes as regards the coordination necessary to ensure unity of action where the Community and the Member States participate jointly cannot modify the answer to the question of competence, that being a prior issue. As the Council has pointed out, resolution of the issue of the allocation of competence cannot depend on problems which may possibly arise in administration of the agreements.

108. Next, where it is apparent that the subject-matter of an agreement or convention falls in part within the competence of the Community and in part within that of the Member States, it is essential to ensure close cooperation between the Member States and the Community institutions, both in the process of negotiation and conclusion and in the fulfilment of the commitments entered into. That obligation to cooperate flows from the requirement of unity in the international representation of the Community (Ruling 1/78 [1978] ECR 2151, paragraphs 34 to 36, and Opinion 2/91, cited above, paragraph 36).

109. The duty to cooperate is all the more imperative in the case of agreements such as those annexed to the WTO Agreement, which are inextricably interlinked, and in view of the cross-retaliation measures established by the Dispute Settlement Understanding. Thus, in the absence of close cooperation, where a Member State, duly authorized within its sphere of competence to take cross-retaliation measures, considered that they would be ineffective if taken in the fields covered by GATS or TRIPs, it would not, under Community law, be empowered to retaliate in the area of trade in goods, since that is an area which on any view falls within the exclusive competence of the Community under Article 113 of the Treaty. Conversely, if the Community were given the right to retaliate in the sector of goods but found itself incapable of exercising that right, it would, in the absence of close cooperation, find itself unable, in law, to retaliate in the areas covered by GATS or TRIPs, those being within the competence of the Member States.

In order to organize this coordination, sometimes so-called 'codes of conduct' or 'arrangements' are agreed upon.

Arrangement between the Council and the Commission regarding preparation for Codex Alimentarius (Annex III to Council Decision 2003/822/EC of 17 November 2003 on the accession of the European Community to the Codex Alimentarius Commission, Official Journal L 309, 26.11.2003, pp. 14–21).

Meetings and statements and exercise of voting rights

1. Scope of application of the coordination procedure

These coordination procedures will apply to any meeting of the Codex Alimentarius Commission or any of its subsidiary bodies, including working groups and to replies to Circular Letters.

2. Codex Alimentarius Circular Letters

2.1. With the aim of respecting the deadline for replying to the Codex Circular Letters, the Commission shall send, at regular intervals not exceeding two months, to the Member States a table listing, separately, all outstanding, announced and anticipated Circular Letters, identifying those Circular Letters for which it intends to prepare a draft common reply on behalf of the Community and the time frame in which this will be done and giving as far as possible its opinion on the competence status for each of them.

2.2. When the Commission indicates that a common reply is to be prepared, the Member States will refrain from answering directly the identified Codex Circular Letters but can point out to the Commission the specific issues or points that pose them a problem and the orientation they suggest to adopt in the reply.

2.3. The Commission will prepare a draft common reply taking into account the indication of the Member States and will communicate the draft rapidly to the Member States for further comments through the national Codex Points of Contact or any specific point designated by Member States. The Commission, on the basis of the received comments, will prepare a revision of the common reply, indicating the received comments and explaining where applicable why some of them were not taken into consideration.

2.4. A Member State may also indicate to the Commission that a particular Circular Letter needs a common reply. In such a case the Commission will prepare a draft reply with the technical assistance of this Member State.

2.5. When the Commission considers that it is not necessary to prepare a common reply, the Member States are entitled to answer directly the Codex Circular Letters for which no common reply is foreseen. However, in this case, the Member States which intend to send comments directly will circulate a draft among the other Member States and the Commission before sending it to Codex in order to verify that there is no opposition from the Commission or any other Member State.

2.6. The Commission and the Member States will make a serious effort to reach a common position as soon as possible. If the draft common reply is acceptable to the Member States, it will be sent to the secretariat of the Codex Alimentarius. But if there is still a substantial amount of divergence of opinion, the Commission will send the draft to the Council Secretariat for the purpose of organising a coordinating meeting to resolve the remaining differences, and the relevant procedure set out in section 3 below will apply.

3. Coordination procedure in the Council

3.1. To prepare for any Codex Alimentarius meeting, coordination meetings will be held:

— in Brussels, within the competent Council Working Party (usually Codex Alimentarius Working Party), as early as possible and as many times as necessary ahead of the Codex Alimentarius meeting, and, in addition,

— on-the-spot, particularly at the beginning and, if necessary, during and at the end of the Codex Alimentarius meeting, with further coordination meetings being called whenever necessary throughout the series of meetings.

3.2. The coordination meetings will agree on statements to be made on behalf of only the Community or on behalf of the Community and its Member States. Statements to be made on behalf of the Member States only do not form part of the Community coordination as such, but may of course also be subject to coordination at these meetings if so agreed by the Member States. The Community or common positions are usually agreed upon in the form of a negotiating position, a statement or an outline of a statement. When reference is made in this arrangement to a 'statement', it should be considered to refer also to other forms in which the Community or common position is agreed.

3.3. The Commission will on receipt send any Codex Alimentarius meeting agenda to the Council Secretariat for circulation to Member States together with an indication of the agenda items on which it is intended that a statement be made and whether this statement will be made on behalf of the Community or the Community and its Member States. In the case of agenda items which may necessitate taking a decision by consensus or by a vote in a Codex Alimentarius meeting, the Commission will give an indication on whether it is the Community or its Member States who should vote.

3.4. The Commission will send draft statements and position papers to the Council Secretariat for circulation to Member States as soon as possible but at least one week before the coordination meeting. For the preparation of draft statements or position papers, the Commission will rely on the technical expertise of the Member States. The Council Secretariat will ensure that the draft statements are transmitted promptly through the national Codex Points of Contact or any specific point designated by Member States.

3.5. The coordination meetings will decide on the exercise of responsibilities with respect to statements and voting in relation to each item of the Codex Alimentarius meeting agenda, on which a statement may be made or a vote is expected.

3.6. The Commission will inform Member States in advance of coordination meetings, through the Council Secretariat, of:

(a) its proposals regarding the exercise of responsibilities on a particular topic;

(b) its proposals in regard to statements on a particular topic.

3.7. If the Commission and the Member States in coordination meetings within the competent Council Working Party or on the spot cannot agree a common position, including for reasons of disagreement on the repartition of competence, with regard to questions referred to in points 3.6(a) and (b), the matter will be referred to the Permanent Representatives Committee which shall decide on the basis of the majority laid down in the relevant Community law dealing with the subject matter under consideration.

3.8. Decisions referred to in paragraph 3.7 are without prejudice to the respective competence of the Community and its Member States in the areas under consideration.

3.9. Should it prove impossible on the part of the Commission to prepare statements in time for the coordination meeting (due to the non-availability of the Codex Alimentarius documentation), the Commission will outline to the Member States, at least one week before the Codex Alimentarius meeting, the main elements of a Community or common position and the statement to be made accordingly. When necessary in exceptional circumstances, an on-the-spot coordination meeting will examine again these elements and the statement with the representatives of the Commission and of the Member States present in the meeting.

3.10. When during Codex Alimentarius meetings the need arises for a statement to be made, in order to respond to the evolution or the dynamics of the negotiations, by the Community representative on behalf of the Community or on behalf of the Community and its Member States, a draft statement will be coordinated on the spot and the relevant part of paragraph 3.9 will apply.

3.11. During Codex discussions, in order to react to proposals not covered by the agreed Community position, Member States and the Commission after due coordination where possible shall be able to propose an initial response and explore alternative options without giving a formal commitment. The Commission and Member States shall pay full regard to the established Community position and its underlying rationale, and will coordinate on the spot as soon as possible to confirm or change the provisional positions.

4. Statements and voting in the Codex Alimentarius meetings

4.1. Where an agenda item deals with matters of exclusive Community competence, the Commission shall speak and vote for the Community. After due coordination, the Member States may also speak in order to support and/or develop the Community position.

4.2. Where an agenda item deals with matters of exclusive national competence, Member States shall speak and vote.

4.3. Where an agenda item deals with matters containing elements of both national and Community competence, the Presidency and the Commission shall express the common position. After due coordination, Members States may speak to support and/or develop the common position. The Member States or the Commission, as appropriate, will vote on behalf of the Community and its Member States in accordance with the common position. The decision on who will be voting is made in the light of where the preponderance of the competence lies (e.g. mainly Member State or mainly Community competence).

4.4. Where an agenda item deals with matters containing elements both of national and of Community competence and the Commission and the Member States have not been able to agree a common position as referred to in point paragraph 3.7, Member States may speak and vote on matters falling clearly within their competence. In accordance with the Codex Alimentarius rules of procedure, the Commission may speak and vote on matters falling clearly within Community competence and for which a Community position has been adopted.

4.5. On matters for which there is no agreement between the Commission and the Member States on repartition of competence, or where it has not been possible to obtain the majority needed for a Community position, a maximum effort will be made to clarify the situation or achieve a Community position. Pending this, and after due coordination, the Member States and/or the Commission, as appropriate, would be entitled to speak on condition that the position expressed will be coherent with Community policies and previous Community positions, and in conformity with Community law.

4.6. During the first two years from the Community's accession to the Codex Alimentarius Commission, the results of the coordination meetings in the competent Council Working Party on the exercise of responsibilities with respect to statements and voting in relation to each item of the Codex Alimentarius meeting agenda will be communicated to the Codex Alimentarius Secretariat. After the initial period of two years, the single, general Declaration made will be considered applicable, unless there is a specific request for clarification from another Codex Alimentarius member or it is decided otherwise in the competent Council Working Party.

4.7. Within the framework of paragraph 4.1 or 4.3, where a Member State has particular important concerns in respect of a dependent territory, and this concern cannot be accommodated in a common or Community position, that Member State shall retain the right to vote and speak in respect of its dependent territory, bearing in mind the interests of the Community.

5. Drafting and working groups

5.1. The Member States and the Commission are entitled to participate voluntarily and speak in the drafting and working groups of the Codex Alimentarius which are technical informal meetings attended only by some members of the Codex Alimentarius and where no formal decisions are taken. The representatives of the Member States and the Commission will make a serious effort to reach an agreed position and to defend this during the discussions in drafting and working groups.

5.2. The Commission and the Member State representatives participating in Codex drafting and working groups, without prejudice to the question of the competence, notify the other Member States promptly of draft reports drawn up by the group's rapporteur and coordinate with Member States regarding the position to be taken. In the absence of specific coordination on the draft reports, the Commission or Member State representatives on the drafting and working groups will use as orientation the coordinated statements and the coordination meeting discussions, as indicated in section 4.

6. Review of the arrangement

At the request of a Member State or the Commission, the arrangement will be reviewed, taking account of experience gained from its operation.

Such arrangements work on the assumption that the Commission and the Council can agree which agenda topic to be dealt with in the international organization, falls within either Union or Member States' competence. Exceptionally, disagreements may persist even if the matter is brought before COREPER, and ultimately the Council. In such situations, the Court of Justice may be called upon to verify whether the choices made are properly based on Union law, as in the *FAO* case partly included here.

Judgment of the Court of 19 March 1996, Commission of the European Communities v. Council of the European Union, Case C-25/94, European Court Reports 1996, p. I-1469, paras. 40–51.

The Commission brought a case against the Council because the latter had decided to give the Member States the right to vote in the FAO for the adoption of an agreement to promote compliance with management and conservation measures by fishing vessels on the high seas. The Court accepted the admissibility of the action and found as follows on substance:

40. The parties do not dispute that there is shared competence and an agreement on a common position but disagree as to whether the Agreement submitted for adoption by the FAO Conference concerns an issue whose main thrust lies in an area within the exclusive competence of the Community.

41. The Community has the internal power to take any measure for the conservation of the biological resources of the sea (Joined Cases 3/76, 4/76 and 6/76 Kramer and Others [1976] ECR 1279).

42. It is settled law that it follows from the very duties and powers which Community law has established and assigned to the institutions of the Community on the internal level that the Community has authority to enter into international commitments for the conservation of the resources of the sea (Kramer and Others, paragraph 33).

43. In the declaration of competence which it sent to the FAO on acquiring membership, the Community therefore stated that it had exclusive competence in all matters concerning fisheries which are aimed at protecting fishing grounds and conserving the biological resources of the sea.

44. It has also been consistently held that, as regards the high seas, the Community has the same regulatory powers, in areas falling within its authority, as are recognized under international law to the State whose flag the vessel flies or in which it is registered (Case C-405/92 Mondiet v Islais [1993] ECR I-6133, paragraph 12).

45. In the present case, when the Council adopted the contested decision, the essential object of the draft Agreement submitted for adoption by the Conference of the FAO was compliance with international conservation and management measures by fishing vessels on the high seas; it no longer contained the provisions on flagging on which the Council based its conclusion that the thrust of the Agreement did not lie in an area within the exclusive competence of the Community.

46. The Council is wrong in maintaining that the functions of licences to fish on the high seas, issued by Member States subject to compliance with conservation and management measures, are comparable to those of authorizations to fly a particular flag. As the Commission has stressed, fishing licences are a traditional means of managing fishing resources which, inter alia, give fishing vessels access to waters and resources and thus differ fundamentally from the general conditions which the Member States may lay down, under international law, in allowing ships of all categories to fly their flags.

47. As for the provisions relating to the imposition of possibly penal sanctions or to assistance for developing countries which, according to the Council, fall within the competence of the Member States, these do not, in any event, appear to occupy a prominent position in the draft Agreement.

48. It must be remembered that where it is apparent that the subject-matter of an agreement or convention falls partly within the competence of the Community and partly within that of its Member States, it is essential to ensure close cooperation between the Member States and the Community institutions, both in the process of negotiation and conclusion and in the fulfilment of the commitments entered into. That obligation to cooperate flows from the requirement of unity in the international representation of the Community (Ruling 1/78 [1978] ECR 2151, paragraphs 34 to 36, Opinion 2/91 [1993] ECR I-1061, paragraph 36, and Opinion 1/94 [1994] ECR I-5267, paragraph 108). The Community institutions and the Member States must take all necessary steps to ensure the best possible cooperation in that regard (Opinion 2/91, paragraph 38).

49. In the present case, section 2.3 of the Arrangement between the Council and the Commission represents fulfilment of that duty of cooperation between the Community and its Member States within the FAO. It is clear, moreover, from the terms of the Arrangement, that the two institutions intended to enter into a binding commitment towards each other. Nor has the Council contested its effect at any moment in the proceedings.

50. Consequently, by concluding that the draft Agreement concerned an issue whose thrust did not lie in an area within the exclusive competence of the Community and accordingly giving the Member States the right to vote for the adoption of that draft, the Council acted in breach of section 2.3 of the Arrangement which it was required to observe.

51. The Council's decision of 22 November 1993 must therefore be annulled.

[...]

Judgment of the Court (Second Chamber) of 12 February 2009, Commission of the European Communities v. Hellenic Republic, Case C-45/07, European Court Reports 2009, p. I-701, paras. 14–38.

Accordingly, when an agenda item in an international organization relates to a subject matter falling within Union competence, a Union position must be submitted. This is evident where the Union itself has managed to become a member to the organization and can be represented by the Commission. However, the division of competences must also be complied with where the Union has not been granted membership. In such situations, the EU Member States together with the Commission as an observer, may put forward the Union position. Consequently, Member States are not to make unilateral proposals, even for non-binding acts, as the Court underlined with respect to the International Maritime Organization (IMO).

[...]

14. The Commission argues that, since the adoption of the Regulation, integrating both Chapter XI-2 of the Annex to the SOLAS Convention and the ISPS Code into Community law, the Community has enjoyed exclusive competence to assume international obligations in the area covered by that regulation. It follows, in its submission, that the Community alone is competent to ensure that the standards on the subject are properly applied at Community level and to discuss with other IMO Contracting States the correct implementation of or subsequent developments in those standards, in accordance with the two measures referred to. The Member States therefore no longer have competence to submit to the IMO national positions on matters falling within the exclusive competence of the Community, unless expressly authorised to do so by the Community.

15. In that connection, it must first be observed that, under Article 3(1)(f) EC, the setting of a common policy in the sphere of transport is specifically mentioned as one of the objectives of the Community (see also Case 22/70 Commission v Council [1971] ECR 263, paragraph 20, 'AETR').

16. Second, under Article 10 EC, the Member States must both take all appropriate measures to ensure fulfilment of the obligations arising out of the EC Treaty or resulting from action taken by the institutions and also abstain from any measure which might jeopardise the attainment of the objectives of the Treaty (AETR, paragraph 21).

17. If those two provisions are read in conjunction, it follows that to the extent to which Community rules are promulgated for the attainment of the objectives of the Treaty, the Member States cannot, outside the framework of the Community institutions, assume obligations which might affect those rules or alter their scope (AETR, paragraph 22).

18. It is common ground that the provisions of the Regulation, which has as its legal basis Article 80(2) EC, the second subparagraph of which refers to Article 71 EC, are Community rules promulgated for the attainment of the objectives of the Treaty.

19. It is thus necessary to examine whether, by submitting to the IMO Maritime Safety Committee the contested proposal, which the Hellenic Republic does not dispute is a national proposal, that Member State may be regarded as having assumed obligations which might affect the provisions of the Regulation.

20. The Commission argues that the case-law arising from AETR applies to non-binding measures such as the contested proposal, whereas the Hellenic Republic submits that, by making such a proposal in the context of its active participation in an international organisation, it did not assume an obligation within the meaning of that case-law. That Member State adds that, in any event, the fact that it submitted the contested proposal to the IMO did not lead to the adoption of new rules within that international organisation.

21. However, as the Advocate General noted at point 36 of his Opinion, in asking the IMO Maritime Safety Committee to examine the creation of check lists or other appropriate tools for assisting the Contracting States of the SOLAS Convention in monitoring whether ships and port facilities complied with the requirements of Chapter XI-2 of the Annex to that convention and the ISPS Code, the Hellenic Republic submitted to that committee a proposal which initiates a procedure

which could lead to the adoption by the IMO of new rules in respect of Chapter XI-2 and or/the ISPS code.

22. The adoption of such new rules would as a consequence have an effect on the Regulation, the Community legislature having decided, as is apparent from both Article 3 of that regulation and Annexes I and II thereto, to incorporate in substance both of those international instruments into Community law.

23. In those circumstances, since it set in motion such a procedure with the contested proposal, the Hellenic Republic took an initiative likely to affect the provisions of the Regulation, which is an infringement of the obligations under Articles 10 EC, 71 EC and 80(2) EC.

24. That interpretation cannot be undermined by the Hellenic Republic's argument that the Commission infringed Article 10 EC by refusing to include the contested proposal on the agenda for the meeting on 14 March 2005 of the Maritime Safety Committee (Marsec committee), which is provided for in Article 11(1) of the Regulation and chaired by the Commission's representative.

25. It is true that, in order to fulfil its duty of genuine cooperation under Article 10 EC, the Commission could have endeavoured to submit that proposal to the Maritime Safety Committee and allowed a debate on the subject. As is apparent from Article 2(2)(b) of the Standard rules of procedure, such a committee is also a forum enabling exchanges of views between the Commission and the Member States. The Commission, in chairing that committee, may not prevent such an exchange of views on the sole ground that a proposal is of a national nature.

26. None the less, any breach by the Commission of Article 10 EC cannot entitle a Member State to take initiatives likely to affect Community rules promulgated for the attainment of the objectives of the Treaty, in breach of that State's obligations, which, in a case such as the present, arise under Articles 10 EC, 71 EC and 80(2) EC. Indeed, a Member State may not unilaterally adopt, on its own authority, corrective or protective measures designed to obviate any breach by an institution of rules of Community law (see, by analogy, Case C-5/94 Hedley Lomas [1996] ECR I-2553, paragraph 20 and case-law cited).

27. In support of its argument, the Hellenic Republic also invokes a gentleman's agreement allegedly adopted by the Council of the European Union in 1993 under which Member States are permitted to submit proposals to the IMO, not only collectively but also individually, where no common position has been established beforehand.

28. However, the documents comprising that alleged gentleman's agreement do not bear out the Hellenic Republic's argument. As the Advocate General noted in point 46 of his Opinion, it is apparent in essence from those documents that the exclusive competence of the Community does not preclude the Member States from actively participating in the IMO, provided that the positions adopted by those States within that international organisation are coordinated at Community level beforehand. It is common ground, in the present case, that no such coordination occurred.

29. Moreover, a gentleman's agreement, even if it had the scope ascribed to it by the Hellenic Republic, could not, in any event, affect the division of powers between the Member States and the Community, such as it results from the provisions of

the Treaty; it cannot permit a Member State, acting individually in the context of its participation in an international organisation, to assume obligations likely to affect Community rules promulgated for the attainment of the objectives of the Treaty (see, to that effect, Case 204/86 Greece v Council [1988] ECR 5323, paragraph 17).

30. Similarly, the Hellenic Republic's argument that an obligation to abstain from active participation in the IMO will not ensure that the Community interest is protected, since the Community is not a member of that international organisation, cannot be accepted. The mere fact that the Community is not a member of an international organisation in no way authorises a Member State, acting individually in the context of its participation in an international organisation, to assume obligations likely to affect Community rules promulgated for the attainment of the objectives of the Treaty.

31. Moreover, the fact that the Community is not a member of an international organisation does not prevent its external competence from being in fact exercised, in particular through the Member States acting jointly in the Community's interest (see, to that effect, Opinion 2/91 [1993] ECR I-1061, paragraph 5).

32. The Hellenic Republic also relies on Article 9(1) of the Regulation, which in its submission confers exclusive competence on the Member States for implementing the safety requirements laid down by that regulation, which are based on the amendments to the SOLAS Convention and the ISPS Code.

33. In that connection, it is sufficient to note that the competence of the Member States, which stems from that provision, does not imply that they have an external competence to take initiatives likely to affect the provisions of the regulation.

34. At the hearing, the Hellenic Republic also invoked Article 307(1) EC, arguing that, since it became an IMO member before it joined the Community, its obligations towards the IMO and, more specifically, its obligation to participate actively in that international organisation as a member of it are not affected by the provisions of the Treaty.

35. However, it must be borne in mind that Article 307(1) EC is designed to apply only if there is an incompatibility between, on the one hand, an obligation arising under the international convention, concluded by the Hellenic Republic before its accession to the Community and by which that State became an IMO member, and, on the other, an obligation arising under Community law (see, to that effect, Case C-62/98, *Commission v Portugal* [2000] ECR I-5171, paragraphs 46 and 47).

36. First, the whole thrust of the Hellenic Republic's argument is that its submission of the contested proposal to the IMO Maritime Safety Committee is not at variance with that Member State's obligations under Community law, which rules out precisely the possibility of relying on Article 307(1) EC.

37. Second, the Hellenic Republic does not establish that it was required to submit the contested proposal to that committee by virtue of the IMO's founding documents and/or legal instruments drawn up by that international organisation.

38. Consequently, it must be declared that, by submitting the contested proposal to the IMO, the Hellenic Republic has failed to fulfil its obligations under Articles 10 EC, 71 EC and 80(2) EC.

Judgment of the Court (Grand Chamber) of 20 April 2010, European Commission v. Kingdom of Sweden, Case C-246/07, European Court Reports 2010, p. I-3317, paras. 69–105.

However, it must be kept in mind that the scope of the duty of sincere cooperation as laid down in Article 4(3) TEU does not necessarily coincide with the scope of Union competences, and may in fact impose certain duties on the Member States even if they are acting wholly or partly within the scope of their own competences. That insight is of crucial importance within the framework of mixed action within international organizations, as Sweden found out when it proposed that perfluorooctane sulfonate (PFOS) be added to Annex A to the Stockholm Convention on Persistent Organic Pollutants, despite an apparent Union strategy not to propose such addition for the time being. In its judgment in the *PFOS* case, the Court clarified that loyalty may include a duty for the Member States to abstain from acting under certain circumstances.

69. In all the areas corresponding to the objectives of the Treaty, Article 10 EC requires Member States to facilitate the achievement of the Community's tasks and to abstain from any measure which could jeopardise the attainment of the objectives of the Treaty (Opinion 1/03 [2006] ECR I-1145, paragraph 119, and Case C-459/03 *Commission v Ireland* [2006] ECR I-4635, paragraph 174).

70. The Kingdom of Sweden considers that the duty of cooperation in good faith provided for in Article 10 EC is limited in scope when what are involved are areas in which competence is shared between the Community and the Member States.

71. In that regard, the Court has already held that this duty of genuine cooperation is of general application and does not depend either on whether the Community competence concerned is exclusive or on any right of the Member States to enter into obligations towards non-member countries (Case C-266/03 *Commission v Luxembourg* [2005] ECR I-4805, paragraph 58, and Case C-433/03 *Commission v Germany* [2005] ECR I-6985, paragraph 64).

72. In the present case, the Commission has pointed out that it was not claiming that the Community had exclusive competence to submit a proposal for the listing of PFOS in Annex A to the Stockholm Convention. It must therefore be assumed that competence is shared. In that sense the present case can be distinguished from the situation at issue in Case C-45/07 *Commission v Greece* [2009] ECR I-701, which concerned exclusive competence.

73. Where it is apparent that the subject-matter of an agreement or convention falls partly within the competence of the Community and partly within that of its Member States, it is essential to ensure close cooperation between the Member States and the Community institutions, both in the process of negotiation and conclusion and in the fulfilment of the commitments entered into. That obligation to cooperate flows from the requirement of unity in the international representation of the Community (Ruling 1/78 [1978] ECR 2151, paragraphs 34 to 36 (by analogy with the EAEC Treaty); Opinion 2/91 [1993] ECR I-1061, paragraph 36;

Opinion 1/94 [1994] ECR I-5267, paragraph 108; and Case C-25/94 *Commission* v *Council* [1996] ECR I-1469, paragraph 48).

74. The Court has held that Member States are subject to special duties of action and abstention in a situation in which the Commission has submitted to the Council proposals which, although they have not been adopted by the Council, represent the point of departure for concerted Community action (Case 804/79 *Commission* v *United Kingdom* [1981] ECR I-1045, paragraph 28; *Commission* v *Luxembourg*, paragraph 59; and *Commission* v *Germany*, paragraph 65).

75. Likewise, the Court has held that the adoption of a decision authorising the Commission to negotiate a multilateral agreement on behalf of the Community marks the start of a concerted Community action at international level and requires for that purpose, if not a duty of abstention on the part of the Member States, at the very least a duty of close cooperation between the latter and the Community institutions in order to facilitate the achievement of the Community tasks and to ensure the coherence and consistency of the action and its international representation (*Commission* v *Luxembourg*, paragraph 60, and *Commission* v *Germany*, paragraph 66).

76. In the present case, it is settled ground that, at the time when the Kingdom of Sweden submitted the proposal for the listing of PFOS in Annex A to the Stockholm Convention on 14 July 2005, the Council had not adopted any formal decision as regards a proposal to list substances in that annex. However, the Court must examine whether, as the Commission maintains, there was at the time a Community strategy in that regard which was not to propose the listing of PFOS immediately in the context of that convention, inter alia for economic reasons.

77. In that regard, it does not appear to be indispensable that a common position take a specific form for it to exist and to be taken into consideration in an action for failure to fulfil the obligation of cooperation in good faith, provided that the content of that position can be established to the requisite legal standard (see, to that effect, *Commission* v *Council*, paragraph 49).

78. As regards PFOS, it must be borne in mind, as a preliminary point, that, as at March 2005, that substance had not been included in the Aarhus Protocol or the Stockholm Convention.

79. In the conclusions which it adopted in March 2005 with a view to the first Conference of the Parties to the Stockholm Convention, the Council recommended that the Community and the Member States consider a proposal for the inclusion of 'up to three additional substances' in the relevant Annexes to that convention. The experts of the Community and Member States were asked, as a first priority, to explore the list of substances under the Aarhus Protocol 'as the source for these substances since these are already controlled as POPs in the [European Union]'.

80. Since PFOS had not, at that time, been included in the Aarhus Protocol and was not yet regulated as a POP within the Union, it did not, according to those conclusions of the Council, have to be taken into consideration in the first proposals to be submitted, whether in respect of that protocol or the Stockholm Convention.

81. Furthermore, the restriction on the number of substances to be proposed ('up to three'), read in the light of point 5(h) of those conclusions, reinforces the argument that economic considerations were part of the Community strategy as regards the Stockholm Convention, which it must be recalled is intended to apply worldwide and Article 13 of which provides for financial aid to developing countries or countries with economies in transition. In point 5(h) the Council recommends that 'financial rules and a budget are adopted to allow the effective implementation of the decisions of the [Conference of the Parties to the Stockholm Convention] by the Secretariat'.

82. In accordance with those conclusions of the Council, and as was pointed out in paragraph 37 of this judgment, two substances, of which PFOS was not one, were proposed by the Community and the Member States during the first meeting of the Conference of the Parties to the Stockholm Convention, which was held in May 2005.

83. It is apparent from the minutes of the meeting of the Council's Working Party on International Environmental Issues of 6 July 2006, the content of which is summarised in paragraphs 38 and 39 of this judgment, that the discussion related to the nomination of substances both under the Aarhus Protocol and the Stockholm Convention. Although those minutes do not expressly mention the economic considerations which were discussed, that fact is not disputed by the Kingdom of Sweden and is admitted inter alia by the Kingdom of the Netherlands.

84. It is apparent from those minutes that the immediate objective was the nomination under the Aarhus protocol of the substances mentioned in paragraphs 30 and 38 of this judgment, which were already covered by Community legislation.

85. It was at that time envisaged that PFOS would be nominated under that protocol as soon as the Commission had submitted a proposal for Community legislation on control measures in respect of that substance. All the subsequent events (the adoption of the Council's decision on 8 September 2005, the submission of a proposed amendment to Directive 76/769 on 5 December 2005, the proposal, of the same date, to list PFOS in the relevant Annexes to that protocol) show that that was in fact the case.

86. Furthermore, as regards the proposals under the Stockholm Convention, the minutes of the meeting of the Council's Working Party on International Environmental Issues of 6 July 2005 state that 'Agreement was reached by the [Working Party for International Environmental Issues]' that some substances should be nominated at the Second Conference of the Parties. However, there was no agreement on the substances to be proposed and discussion of that issue was postponed.

87. Contrary to what the Kingdom of Sweden and the interveners maintain, it appears that there was no 'decision-making vacuum' or even a waiting period equivalent to the absence of a decision. A number of factors lend support to the argument that the Council's Working Party on International Environmental Issues did not intend to reach a decision on 6 July 2005—but certainly thereafter—on the substances to be proposed under the Stockholm Convention in addition to those already proposed in May 2005. The urgency of deciding first on the substances to be proposed under the Aarhus Protocol and the economic considerations

connected with proposals under that convention may be mentioned in that regard.

88. Subsequent events have borne out that intention to act and to make proposals under the Stockholm Convention, namely the Council's recommendation of 9 March 2006 and the decision adopted by the Council in April 2006, which is mentioned in paragraph 43 of this judgment, authorising the Commission to present such proposals as regards pentachlorobenzene, octabromodiphenyl ether and short-chained chlorinated paraffins.

89. In any event, it may be regarded as established that, in 2005, there was a common strategy not to propose, at that time, to list PFOS in Annex A to the Stockholm Convention, since, as is apparent from the Council's conclusions of March 2005, the experts of the Member States and of the Community were to choose the substances to be proposed from among those already covered by the Aarhus Protocol and that, as is apparent from the minutes of the meeting of the Council's Working Party on International Environmental Issues of 6 July 2005, PFOS was not one of those substances.

90. Furthermore, in connection with the Stockholm Convention, the institutions of the Union considered it preferable to take into account all the relevant factors, including economic factors, when deciding on the strategy to be adopted by the Union and its Member States in relation to that substance. That led them not to propose immediately that PFOS be prohibited under that agreement, but to propose it, as a first priority, under another agreement, that is, the Aarhus Protocol.

91. It follows that, in unilaterally proposing the addition of PFOS to Annex A to the Stockholm Convention, the Kingdom of Sweden dissociated itself from a concerted common strategy within the Council.

92. Moreover, as is apparent from examination of the decision-making process provided for by that convention, the Kingdom of Sweden's unilateral proposal has consequences for the Union. It must be pointed out, in that regard, that the Convention establishes an institutional and procedural framework containing a body of specific rules for the adoption of amendments, including the listing of new substances in Annexes A, B or C.

93. Under Article 8(9) of the Stockholm Convention, a proposal to list a substance in Annex A to that convention is to be the subject of a positive or negative recommendation on the part of the Persistent Organic Pollutants Review Committee. As Article 23(2) of the Convention states, a regional economic integration organisation, such as the Union, is not to exercise its right to vote if any of its Member States exercises its right to vote, and vice versa. Article 25(2) of the Stockholm Convention also provides that in the case of such an organisation, one or more of whose member States is, like that organisation, a Party to that Convention, the organisation and the member States are not to be entitled to exercise rights under the Convention concurrently.

94. The submission of a proposal for the listing of a substance under the Convention of Stockholm by a Member State could therefore give rise to a situation where either the Union voted against that proposal, thus depriving the Member State making the proposal of the possibility of defending its own proposal at the level

of the Conference of the Parties, or that Member State exercised its right to vote in favour of its own proposal, thus depriving the Union of the possibility of exercising its right to vote with a number of votes equal to the number of its Member States and leaving the other Member States free to vote for or against the proposal.

95. In that regard, it must be pointed out that the declaration deposited by the Community in accordance with Article 25(3) of the Stockholm Convention does not contain specific rules as regards the allocation of competence between itself and the Member States. That declaration states that '[t]he Community is responsible for the performance of those obligations resulting from the Convention which are covered by Community law in force' and that '[t]he exercise of Community competence is, by its nature, subject to continuous development'.

96. In any event, it must be pointed out that the Union does not represent a sufficient number of votes to oppose the adoption of an amendment to an Annex to the Stockholm Convention. It should be added that, with regard to a party which, like the Union, has not made use of the possibility of making a declaration under Article 25(4) of that convention, an amendment to an Annex which has been decided on by the Conference of the Parties enters into force, subject to the method known as 'opting out', on the expiry of a period of one year from the date on which the depositary communicated the amended Annex.

97. The Kingdom of Sweden and the interveners maintain that, in such a case, the Union could, in any event, make use of that possibility of 'opting out' and notify a declaration under Article 22(3)(b) and (4) of the Stockholm Convention that it is unable to accept the amendment of an Annex.

98. That argument is, however, based on the assumption that the Union would be in a position to make a declaration of non-acceptance of an amendment proposed and voted for by one or more Member States. Under Article 25(2) of the Stockholm Convention, the Union and its Member States are not entitled to exercise rights under the Convention concurrently. At the hearing the parties set out different interpretations of Article 25(2) of the Stockholm Convention.

99. However, even supposing, despite Article 25(2) of the Stockholm Convention, that the Union could still notify a declaration of non-acceptance of an amendment proposed and voted for by several Member States, such a situation could give rise to legal uncertainty for the Member States, the Secretariat of the Stockholm Convention and non-member countries which are parties to that convention.

100. Irrespective of that aspect, it is common ground that the objective sought by depositing a proposal for the listing of a substance in Annex A to the Stockholm Convention is the adoption of an international legal rule which will be binding on the parties to that convention. Since the Union is a party to that convention, it could be bound by the resulting amendment to that annex, provided it has not previously, in compliance with the internal procedures set out in Article 14(1) of the POPs regulation, notified a declaration of non-acceptance within a period of one year from the date on which the depositary communicated that annex, as amended.

101. Examination of the decision-making process provided for by the Stockholm Convention thus shows that a proposal to list a substance in Annex A to that convention has consequences for the Union.

102. In that regard, the assertion by the Kingdom of Sweden and the interveners that a proposal to list a substance in the Annex to an international convention which is binding on the Union is equivalent to a national measure that is more stringent than a minimum Union measure and is permitted by Article 176 EC cannot be accepted. The Union could be bound by an amendment to an Annex to the Stockholm Convention whereas it is not bound by such a national measure.

103. As was pointed out in paragraph 74 of this judgment, the Court has held that Member States are subject to special duties of action and abstention in a situation in which the Commission has submitted to the Council proposals which, although they have not been adopted by the Council, represent the point of departure for concerted Community action (*Commission v Germany*, paragraph 65). That is especially true in a situation such as that in the present case which is characterised, as established in paragraph 91 of this judgment, by a unilateral proposal which dissociates the Member State in question from a concerted common strategy within the Council and was submitted within an institutional and procedural framework such as that of the Stockholm Convention.

104. Such a situation is likely to compromise the principle of unity in the international representation of the Union and its Member States and weaken their negotiating power with regard to the other parties to the Convention concerned.

105. Consequently, the Commission's first complaint, alleging breach of Article 10 EC, is well founded.

5.5 Legal effects of mixed membership in the EU legal order

Another consequence of mixed membership to a multilateral convention or an international organization is the 'Unionization' of those parts of the international convention, for which the Union has declared competence. It not only follows that Member States are under a duty to implement those parts under Article 216(2) TFEU (a duty which can be sanctioned by an infringement procedure under Article 258 TFEU in case of non-compliance), but also to refrain from bringing international disputes against each other relating to those parts. Otherwise, they would violate the monopoly of the Court of Justice of the EU to interpret and apply Union law under Article 344 TFEU (ex-Article 292 TEC). This point was at the heart of the so-called *Mox Plant* case, where the Commission brought a case against Ireland for having brought a case against the UK before the International Tribunal for the Law of the Sea under UNCLOS, although the subject matter had been covered by the Community declaration of competence upon accession to UNCLOS:

Declaration Concerning the Competence of the European Community with Regard to Matters Governed by the United Nations Convention on the Law of the Sea of 10 December 1982 and the Agreement of 28 July 1994 Concerning the Application of Part XI of that Convention.

[...]

(Declaration made pursuant to Article 5(1) of Annex IX to the Convention and to Article 4(4) of the Agreement)

Article 5(1) of Annex IX to the United Nations Convention on the Law of the Sea provides that the instrument of formal confirmation of an international organisation shall contain a declaration specifying the matters governed by the Convention in respect of which competence has been transferred to the organisation by its Member States which are Parties to the Convention.

[...]

The European Communities were established by the Treaties of Paris (ECSC) and of Rome (EEC and Euratom), signed on 18 April 1951 and 25 March 1957 respectively.... [Those Treaties] were amended by the Treaty on European Union, signed in Maastricht on 7 February 1992

[...]

In accordance with the provisions referred to above, this declaration indicates the competence that the Member States have transferred to the Community under the Treaties in matters governed by the Convention.

[...]

The Community has exclusive competence for certain matters and shares competence with its Member States for certain other matters.

1. Matters for which the Community has exclusive competence

– The Community points out that its Member States have transferred competence to it with regard to the conservation and management of sea fishing resources. Hence in this field it is for the Community to adopt the relevant rules and regulations (which are enforced by the Member States) and, within its competence, to enter into external undertakings with third States or competent international organisations.

[...]

– By virtue of its commercial and customs policy, the Community has competence in respect of those provisions of Parts X and XI of the Convention and of the Agreement of 28 July 1994 which are related to international trade.

2. Matters for which the Community shares competence with its Member States

– With regard to fisheries, for a certain number of matters that are not directly related to the conservation and management of sea fishing resources, for example research and technological development and development cooperation, there is shared competence.

– With regard to the provisions on maritime transport, safety of shipping and the prevention of marine pollution contained, inter alia in Parts II, III, V, VII and XII of the Convention, the Community has exclusive competence only to the extent that such provisions of the Convention or legal instruments adopted in implementation thereof affect common rules established by the Community. When Community rules exist but are not affected, in particular in cases of Community provisions establishing only minimum standards, the Member States have competence, without prejudice to the competence of the Community to act in this field. Otherwise competence rests with the Members States.

A list of relevant Community acts appears in the Appendix. The extent of Community competence ensuing from these acts must be assessed by reference to the precise provisions of each measure, and in particular, the extent to which these provisions establish common rules.

[...]

APPENDIX

COMMUNITY ACTS WHICH REFER TO MATTERS GOVERNED BY THE CONVENTION AND THE AGREEMENT

– In the maritime safety and prevention of marine pollution sectors

[...]

Council Directive 93/75/EEC of 13 September 1993 concerning minimum requirements for vessels bound for or leaving Community ports and carrying dangerous or polluting goods (OJ L 247, 5.10.1993, p. 19)

[...]

– In the field of protection and preservation of the marine environment (Part XII of the Convention)

[...]

Council Directive 85/337/EEC of 27 June 1985 on the assessment of the effects of certain public and private projects on the environment (OJ L 175, 5.7.1985, p. 40)

[...]

– Conventions to which the Community is a party

Convention for the prevention of marine pollution from land-based sources, Paris, 4 June 1974 (Council Decision75/437/EEC of 3 March 1975, published in OJ L 194, 25.7.1975, p. 5)

Protocol amending the Convention for the prevention of marine pollution from land-based sources, Paris, 26 March 1986 (Council Decision 87/57/EEC of 22 December 1986, published in OJ L 24, 27.1.1987, p. 46)

[...]

The Court responded to the Commission's application by emphasizing that an international agreement, such as UNCLOS, cannot affect the autonomy of the then Community legal system and that the system for the resolution of disputes set out in the Treaty must in principle take precedence over that contained in UNCLOS. Ireland could therefore not bring a case against the UK before the UNCLOS Tribunal concerning the interpretation or application of provisions of the Convention coming within the scope of the competence of the then Community which the latter exercised by acceding to UNCLOS.

Judgment of the Court (Grand Chamber) of 30 May 2006, Commission of the European Communities v. Ireland, Case C-459/03, European Court Reports 2006, p. I-4635, paras. 80–139.

80. It is necessary to specify at the outset that, by its first head of complaint, the Commission is criticising Ireland for failing to respect the exclusive jurisdiction of

the Court by bringing before the Arbitral Tribunal a dispute between it and another Member State concerning the interpretation and application of provisions of the Convention involving obligations assumed by the Community in the exercise of its external competence in regard to protection of the environment, and for thereby breaching Article 292 EC. The articles of the EAEC Treaty to which the Commission refers in its submissions relate to the second and third heads of complaint.

81. Under Article 300(7) EC, '[a]greements concluded under the conditions set out in [that] article shall be binding on the institutions of the Community and on Member States'.

82. The Convention was signed by the Community and subsequently approved by Decision 98/392. It follows that, according to settled case-law, the provisions of that convention now form an integral part of the Community legal order (see, inter alia, Case C-344/04 IATA and ELFAA [2006] ECR I-0000, paragraph 36).

83. The Convention was concluded by the Community and all of its Member States on the basis of shared competence.

84. The Court has already ruled that mixed agreements have the same status in the Community legal order as purely Community agreements, as these are provisions coming within the scope of Community competence (Case C-13/00 Commission v Ireland, paragraph 14).

85. From this the Court has concluded that, in ensuring respect for commitments arising from an agreement concluded by the Community institutions, the Member States fulfil, within the Community system, an obligation in relation to the Community, which has assumed responsibility for the due performance of that agreement (Case C-13/00 Commission v Ireland, paragraph 15).

86. As the Convention is a mixed agreement, it is for that reason necessary to examine whether the provisions of that agreement relied on by Ireland before the Arbitral Tribunal in connection with the dispute concerning the MOX plant come within the scope of Community competence.

87. It follows from the wording of Ireland's statement of claim (set out in paragraph 35 of the present judgment) that that Member State is essentially criticising the United Kingdom for granting authorisation to operate the MOX plant without having met a number of obligations arising under the Convention.

88. With the exception of Article 123 of the Convention, all of the provisions relied on in that regard feature in Part XII of that Convention, entitled 'Protection and preservation of the marine environment'.

89. Ireland criticises the United Kingdom in particular for having breached, in the first place, Article 206 of the Convention by failing in its obligation to carry out a proper assessment of the environmental impact of all activities associated with the MOX plant on the marine environment of the Irish Sea, secondly, Articles 123 and 197 of the Convention by failing in its obligation to cooperate with Ireland in order to protect the marine environment of the Irish Sea, a sea which is semi-enclosed, and, finally, Articles 192, 193 and/or 194 and/or 207, 211 and 213 of the Convention by failing to take the measures necessary to prevent, reduce and control pollution of the marine environment of the Irish Sea.

90. The Court has already interpreted Article 175(1) EC as being the appropriate legal basis for conclusion, on behalf of the Community, of international agreements on protection of the environment (see, in this regard, Opinion 2/00 [2001] ECR I-9713, paragraph 44).

91. That conclusion is reinforced by the reading of Article 175(1) EC in conjunction with the fourth indent in Article 174(1) EC, which expressly includes 'promoting measures at international level to deal with regional or worldwide environmental problems' among the objectives to be pursued within the framework of policy on the environment.

92. Admittedly, as indicated in Article 176 EC, that external competence of the Community in regard to the protection of the environment, in this case the marine environment, is not exclusive but rather, in principle, shared between the Community and the Member States (see, to that effect, Opinion 2/00, paragraph 47).

93. However, the question as to whether a provision of a mixed agreement comes within the competence of the Community is one which relates to the attribution and, thus, the very existence of that competence, and not to its exclusive or shared nature.

94. It follows that the existence of the Community's external competence in regard to protection of the marine environment is not, in principle, contingent on the adoption of measures of secondary law covering the area in question and liable to be affected if Member States were to take part in the procedure for concluding the agreement in question, within the terms of the principle formulated by the Court in paragraph 17 of the AETR judgment.

95. The Community can enter into agreements in the area of environmental protection even if the specific matters covered by those agreements are not yet, or are only very partially, the subject of rules at Community level, which, by reason of that fact, are not likely to be affected (see, in that regard, Opinion 2/00, paragraphs 44 to 47, and Case C-239/03 Commission v France [2004] ECR I-9325, paragraph 30).

96. That being so, it is necessary to establish whether and to what extent the Community, by becoming a party to the Convention, elected to exercise its external competence in matters of environmental protection.

97. In this regard, the reference, in the first citation in the preamble to Decision 98/392, to Article 130s(1) of the EC Treaty (now, after amendment, Article 175(1) EC) as one of the provisions constituting the legal basis of the decision approving the Convention indicates that this was indeed the case.

98. Furthermore, the fifth recital in the preamble to that decision states that approval of the Convention by the Community is designed to enable it to become a party to it within the limits of its competence.

99. The Declaration of Community competence referred to in Article 1(3) of that decision, which forms part of the Community's instrument of formal confirmation constituting Annex II to the Decision, specifies the extent and the nature of the areas of competence transferred by the Member States to the Community in

the matters dealt with by the Convention in respect of which the Community accepts the rights and obligations provided for by that convention.

100. Ireland submits that Article 4(3) of Annex IX to the Convention, in particular the notion of 'transfer of competence' which features there, and the Declaration of Community competence must be construed as meaning that, in regard to shared competence, the only areas of competence transferred and exercised by the Community when it became a party to the Convention are those which have become exclusive as a result of having been affected, within the meaning of the principle set out in paragraph 17 of the AETR judgment.

101. This, it claims, is a particular feature of the Convention, which allows only the transfer of exclusive competence of the Community, the other areas of competence and the relevant responsibilities remaining within the purview of the Member States.

102. According to Ireland, as the Community provisions in issue are only minimum rules, they are not in principle affected; consequently, the related areas of shared competence have not been transferred within the framework of the Convention.

103. By contrast, the Commission avers that the Declaration of Community competence must be understood as meaning that the areas of shared competence in question are transferred and exercised by the Community even if they relate to matters in respect of which there are at present no Community rules.

104. It is necessary to point out in this regard that the second sentence of the first paragraph of the second indent of point 2 of the Declaration of Community competence states, with regard to, inter alia, the provisions of the Convention relating to the prevention of marine pollution, that '[w]hen Community rules exist but are not affected, in particular in cases of Community provisions establishing only minimum standards, the Member States have competence, without prejudice to the competence of the Community to act in this field'.

105. Consequently, that declaration confirms that a transfer of areas of shared competence, in particular in regard to the prevention of marine pollution, took place within the framework of the Convention, and without any of the Community rules concerned being affected, within the terms of the principle set out in the AETR judgment.

106. However, that passage of the Declaration of Community competence makes the transfer of areas of shared competence subject to the existence of Community rules, even though it is not necessary that those rules be affected.

107. In the other cases, that is to say, those in which there are no Community rules, competence rests with the Member States, in accordance with the third sentence of the first paragraph of the second indent of point 2 of the Declaration of Community competence.

108. It follows that, within the specific context of the Convention, a finding that there has been a transfer to the Community of areas of shared competence is contingent on the existence of Community rules within the areas covered by the Convention provisions in issue, irrespective of what may otherwise be the scope and nature of those rules.

109. In this regard, the appendix to the Declaration of Community competence, while not exhaustive, constitutes a useful reference base.

110. It appears that the matters covered by the provisions of the Convention relied on by Ireland before the Arbitral Tribunal are very largely regulated by Community measures, several of which are mentioned expressly in the appendix to that declaration.

111. Thus, with regard to the head of complaint alleging failure to meet the obligation to carry out a proper assessment of the environmental impact of all of the activities associated with the MOX plant on the marine environment of the Irish Sea, based on Article 206 of the Convention, it must be stated that this matter is the subject of Directive 85/337, which is mentioned in the appendix to the Declaration of Community competence.

112. Ireland also cannot question the relevance of Directive 85/337 since it itself referred to that directive in its statement of claim before the Arbitral Tribunal as a measure which could serve as a reference for the interpretation of the relevant provisions of the Convention.

113. In addition, Ireland derived a number of arguments from that directive in support of its complaint in its pleadings before the Arbitral Tribunal.

114. The same observation also holds true for the complaint which Ireland bases on Articles 192, 193, 194, 207, 211 and 213 of the Convention, in so far as that complaint relates to the obligation to take the measures necessary to prevent, reduce and control pollution in the Irish Sea.

115. In its pleadings before the Arbitral Tribunal, Ireland derived several arguments from Directive 85/337 with a view to supporting that complaint in regard to the obligation to prevent pollution. The relevance of Directive 85/337 to the matter under consideration is therefore manifest.

116. Furthermore, that complaint, in so far as it concerns international transfers of radioactive substances connected to the activity of the MOX plant, is closely linked to Directive 93/75, which is also mentioned in the appendix to the Declaration of Community competence and regulates the minimum requirements for vessels bound for or leaving Community ports and carrying dangerous or polluting goods.

117. Furthermore, with regard to the complaint derived from Articles 123 and 197 of the Convention concerning the lack of cooperation on the part of the United Kingdom and, in particular, its refusal to provide Ireland with certain information, such as the full version of the PA report, it must be held that the provision of information of this kind comes within the scope of Council Directive 90/313/EEC of 7 June 1990 on the freedom of access to information on the environment (OJ 1990 L 158, p. 56).

118. In addition, as has been stated in paragraph 31 of the present judgment, Ireland set out that same head of complaint before the arbitral tribunal established pursuant to the Convention for the Protection of the Marine Environment of the North-East Atlantic on the basis of Article 9 of that convention, a convention which it once again invoked in its application initiating proceedings before the Arbitral Tribunal as a reference base for the interpretation of the Convention provisions in issue.

The Convention for the Protection of the Marine Environment of the North-East Atlantic was concluded by the Community and, moreover, replaced the Paris conventions for the prevention of marine pollution from land-based sources, themselves mentioned in the appendix to the Declaration of Community competence.

119. It is also common ground that, in its pleadings before the Arbitral Tribunal, Ireland based its arguments in support of the head of claim in issue simultaneously on Directive 85/337, Directive 90/313 and the Convention for the Protection of the Marine Environment of the North-East Atlantic.

120. Those matters suffice to establish that the Convention provisions on the prevention of marine pollution relied on by Ireland, which clearly cover a significant part of the dispute relating to the MOX plant, come within the scope of Community competence which the Community has elected to exercise by becoming a party to the Convention.

121. It follows that the provisions of the Convention relied on by Ireland in the dispute relating to the MOX plant and submitted to the Arbitral Tribunal are rules which form part of the Community legal order. The Court therefore has jurisdiction to deal with disputes relating to the interpretation and application of those provisions and to assess a Member State's compliance with them (see, in that connection, Case C-13/00 Commission v Ireland, paragraph 20, and Case C-239/03 Commission v France, paragraph 31).

122. It is, however, necessary to determine whether this jurisdiction of the Court is exclusive, such as to preclude a dispute like that relating to the MOX plant being brought by a Member State before an arbitral tribunal established pursuant to Annex VII to the Convention.

123. The Court has already pointed out that an international agreement cannot affect the allocation of responsibilities defined in the Treaties and, consequently, the autonomy of the Community legal system, compliance with which the Court ensures under Article 220 EC. That exclusive jurisdiction of the Court is confirmed by Article 292 EC, by which Member States undertake not to submit a dispute concerning the interpretation or application of the EC Treaty to any method of settlement other than those provided for therein (see, to that effect, Opinion 1/91 [1991] ECR I-6079, paragraph 35, and Opinion 1/00 [2002] ECR I-3493, paragraphs 11 and 12).

124. It should be stated at the outset that the Convention precisely makes it possible to avoid such a breach of the Court's exclusive jurisdiction in such a way as to preserve the autonomy of the Community legal system.

125. It follows from Article 282 of the Convention that, as it provides for procedures resulting in binding decisions in respect of the resolution of disputes between Member States, the system for the resolution of disputes set out in the EC Treaty must in principle take precedence over that contained in Part XV of the Convention.

126. It has been established that the provisions of the Convention in issue in the dispute concerning the MOX plant come within the scope of Community competence which the Community exercised by acceding to the Convention, with the result that those provisions form an integral part of the Community legal order.

127. Consequently, the dispute in this case is indeed a dispute concerning the interpretation or application of the EC Treaty, within the terms of Article 292 EC.

128. Furthermore, as it is between two Member States in regard to an alleged failure to comply with Community-law obligations resulting from those provisions of the Convention, this dispute is clearly covered by one of the methods of dispute settlement established by the EC Treaty within the terms of Article 292 EC, namely the procedure set out in Article 227 EC.

129. In addition, it is not open to dispute that proceedings such as those brought by Ireland before the Arbitral Tribunal fall to be described as a method of settlement of a dispute within the terms of Article 292 EC inasmuch as, under Article 296 of the Convention, the decisions delivered by such a tribunal are final and binding on the parties to the dispute.

130. Ireland contends, however, by way of alternative submission, that, if the Court were to conclude that the provisions of the Convention invoked before the Arbitral Tribunal form an integral part of Community law, that conclusion would also be unavoidable with regard to the provisions of the Convention dealing with dispute settlement. Consequently, it submits, the initiation of proceedings before an arbitral tribunal referred to in Article 287(1)(c) of the Convention constitutes a method of dispute settlement provided for in the EC Treaty, within the terms of Article 292 EC.

131. That argument must be rejected.

132. As has been pointed out in paragraph 123 of the present judgment, an international agreement such as the Convention cannot affect the exclusive jurisdiction of the Court in regard to the resolution of disputes between Member States concerning the interpretation and application of Community law. Furthermore, as indicated in paragraphs 124 and 125 of the present judgment, Article 282 of the Convention precisely makes it possible to avoid such a breach occurring, in such a way as to preserve the autonomy of the Community legal system.

133. It follows from all of the foregoing that Articles 220 EC and 292 EC precluded Ireland from initiating proceedings before the Arbitral Tribunal with a view to resolving the dispute concerning the MOX plant.

134. This finding cannot be brought into question by the fact that the application by Ireland instituting proceedings before the Arbitral Tribunal also relates to certain obligations of the United Kingdom concerning the risks connected with terrorism.

135. Without it being necessary to rule on the question as to whether that part of the dispute comes within the scope of Community law, suffice it to hold that, as follows from paragraph 120 of the present judgment, a significant part of the dispute in this case between Ireland and the United Kingdom relates to the interpretation or application of Community law. It is for the Court, should the need arise, to identify the elements of the dispute which relate to provisions of the international agreement in question which fall outside its jurisdiction.

136. As the jurisdiction of the Court is exclusive and binding on the Member States, the arguments put forward by Ireland concerning the advantages which arbitration proceedings under Annex VII to the Convention would present in

comparison with an action brought before the Court under Article 227 EC cannot be accepted.

137. Even if they were assumed to have been demonstrated, such advantages could not in any event justify a Member State in avoiding its Treaty obligations with regard to judicial proceedings intended to rectify an alleged breach of Community law by another Member State (see, to that effect, Case 232/78 Commission v France [1979] ECR 2729, paragraph 9).

138. Finally, with regard to the arguments put forward by Ireland concerning urgency and the possibility of obtaining interim measures under Article 290 of the Convention, suffice it to point out that, under Article 243 EC, the Court may prescribe any necessary interim measures in cases before it. It is evident that such measures may therefore be ordered in the context of proceedings brought under Article 227 EC.

139. In the light of all of the foregoing, the first head of complaint must be upheld.

Select Bibliography

Cremona, M., *Member States as Trustees of the Community Interest: Participating in International Agreements on Behalf of the European Community* (Florence: EUI Working Paper, Department of Law, Law 2009/17).

De Baere, G., "O, Where is Faith? O, Where is Loyalty?" Some Thoughts on the Duty of Loyal Co-operation and the Union's External Environmental Competences in the Light of the *PFOS* Case, *European Law Review*, vol. 36, 2011, 405–19.

—— and Paasivirta, E., Identity and Difference: The EU and the UN as Part of Each Other, *The Emergence of the European Union's International Identity—Views from the Global Arena* (H.C.F.J.A. de Waele and J.J. Kuipers (eds), The Hague/Boston/London: Martinus Nijhoff Publishers, forthcoming 2013).

Heliskoski, J., Internal Struggle for International Presence: The Exercise of Voting Rights Within the FAO, *The General Law of EC External Relations* (A. Dashwood and C. Hillion (eds), London: Sweet & Maxwell, 2000), 79–99.

Hoffmeister, F., Outsider or Frontrunner? Recent Developments under International and European Law on the Status of the European Union in International Organizations and Treaty Bodies', 44 CMLR, 2007, 41–68.

—— and Kuijper, P.J., The Status of the European Union at the United Nations: Institutional Ambiguities and Political Realities, *The United Nations and the European Union: An Ever Stronger Partnership* (J. Wouters, F. Hoffmeister, and T. Ruys (eds), The Hague: TMC Asser Press, 2006), 9–34.

Jørgensen, K.E. and Wessel, R.A., The Position of the European Union in (Other) International Organizations: Confronting Legal and Political Approaches, *European Foreign Policy—Legal and Political Perspectives* (P. Koutrakos (ed.), Cheltenham: Edward Elgar, 2011), 261–86.

Koutrakos, P., *EU International Relations Law* (Oxford and Portland, OR: Hart Publishing, 2006), 165–81.

Pedersen, J.M., FAO–EU Cooperation: An Ever Stronger Partnership, *The United Nations and the European Union: An Ever Stronger Partnership* (J. Wouters, F. Hoffmeister, and T. Ruys (eds), The Hague: TMC Asser Press, 2006), 63–91.

Serrano de Haro, P.A., *Participation of the EU in the Work of the UN: General Assembly Resolution 65/276* (The Hague: CLEER Working Papers 2012/4).

Wouters, J., Hoffmeister, F., and Ruys, T. (eds), *The United Nations and the European Union: An Ever Stronger Partnership* (The Hague: TMC Asser Press, 2006).

——, Odermatt, J., and Ramopoulos, T., *The Status of the European Union at the United Nations after the General Assembly Resolution of 3 May 2011* (Leuven: Leuven Centre for Global Governance Studies, 2011).

6

EU Sanctions and Countermeasures

6.1 Introduction

This chapter includes different kinds of the sanctions and countermeasures taken by the EU against third states and against natural or legal persons and groups or non-state entities. Since sanctions or restrictive measures comprise the most significant category of EU countermeasures, the legal basis for their adoption is briefly described first. Then, the implementation of Security Council sanctions under Chapter VII of the UN Charter is discussed. Subsequently, quasi-autonomous and autonomous EU countermeasures are examined. What distinguishes these from the former category, is that, though some of them are linked to binding decisions of the Security Council, they nevertheless have autonomous aspects insofar as, in addition to provisions implementing the Security Council resolution in question, they contain a large number of complementary measures that the Union has taken entirely on its own authority; or are the implementation of 'decisions' of international arrangements for export control, such as the Nuclear Suppliers Group or the Missile Technology Control Regime (MTCR), which are not formally binding. Others are taken in the framework of an elaborate system of countermeasures which may be taken, when certain fundamental bases of a treaty regime are not respected. This is the case with the special system of countermeasures authorized by the Cotonou Agreement.[1] Yet, others are purely autonomous in nature and not triggered by a breach of a treaty at all, but by other actions taken by third states; an example of this is the so-called Helms-Burton blocking regulation.

6.2 EU sanctions provisions

Within the framework of CFSP, the Council can impose restrictive measures against third countries and against natural or legal persons and groups or non-state entities.[2] As indicated above, these sanctions may implement UN Security Council resolutions

---

[1] 2000/483/EC: Partnership agreement between the members of the African, Caribbean, and Pacific Group of States of the one part, and the European Community and its Member States, of the other part, signed in Cotonou on 23 June 2000, OJ L 317, 15.12.2000, pp. 3–353 as first amended in Luxembourg on 25 June 2005, OJ L 209, 11.8.2005, pp. 27–53, and second in Burkina Faso on 22 June 2010, OJ L 287, 4.11.2010, pp. 3–49.

[2] Sanctions against terrorism can also be imposed on the basis of Art. 75 TFEU, which forms part of the Area of Freedom, Security and Justice. This article would seem to be directed at 'internal' terrorism, while Art. 215 concentrates on countermeasures and sanctions against third states and individuals in the area of CFSP. Given the scope of the book, Art. 75 is not discussed further here.

under Chapter VII of the UN Charter or constitute autonomous measures.[3] In both cases, the Council first adopts a Decision based on Chapter 2 Title V TEU (formerly this Union act was a Common Position pursuant to former Article 15 TEU). This CFSP act is implemented by the Union and/or at a national level. This depends on the nature of the imposed sanctions, which often cut across the vertical division of competences within the EU legal order. Thus, arms embargos or restrictions on admission are implemented directly by the Member States. On the contrary, economic and financial sanctions targeted at third states or individuals and non-state entities are implemented at the EU level. Grounded in the CFSP act, the Council adopts restrictive measures against third countries 'includ[ing] the rulers of such a country and also individuals and entities associated with or controlled, directly or indirectly, by them' pursuant to Article 215(1) TFEU (formerly Articles 60 and 301 TEC).[4] However, the scope of this article cannot be broadened further to include in the sanctions against 'third states' individuals 'on the sole ground of their family connection with persons associated with the leaders of the third country concerned, irrespective of the personal conduct of such natural persons'.[5] Rather, based on a CFSP act again, the Council can impose restrictive measures against natural or legal persons and groups or non-state entities pursuant to Article 215(2) TFEU (formerly Articles 60, 301, and 308 TEC).[6]

Treaty on the Functioning of the European Union
Article 215

1. Where a decision, adopted in accordance with Chapter 2 of Title V of the Treaty on European Union, provides for the interruption or reduction, in part or completely, of economic and financial relations with one or more third countries, the Council, acting by a qualified majority on a joint proposal from the High Representative of the Union for Foreign Affairs and Security Policy and the Commission, shall adopt the necessary measures. It shall inform the European Parliament thereof.

2. Where a decision adopted in accordance with Chapter 2 of Title V of the Treaty on European Union so provides, the Council may adopt restrictive measures under the procedure referred to in paragraph 1 against natural or legal persons and groups or non-State entities.

3. The acts referred to in this Article shall include necessary provisions on legal safeguards.

---

[3] For more detailed information, see: Council of the European Union, Basic Principles on the Use of Restrictive Measures (2004), Council doc. 10198/1/04 REV1; Council of the European Union, Restrictive measures (Sanctions)—Update of the EU Best Practices for the effective implementation of restrictive measures (2008), Council doc. 8666/1/08 REV 1; Council of the European Union, Guidelines on implementation and evaluation of restrictive measures (sanctions) in the framework of the EU Common Foreign and security Policy (2009), Council doc. 17464/09.

[4] Joined Cases C-402/05 P and C-415/05 P, *Kadi and Al Barakaat International Foundation v. Council and Commission* [2008] ECR I-6351, para. 166; although Arts 60 and 301 TEC only referred to 'third countries', the CJEU made a broad interpretation of this concept.

[5] Case C-376/10 P, *Pye Phyo Tay Za v. Council of the European Union*, not yet reported, para. 66.

[6] With regard to the question when Art. 215(2) TFEU constitutes the appropriate legal basis as opposed to Art. 75 TFEU for the adoption of sanctions, such as asset freezing, against individuals, see Opinion of Advocate General Bot in Case C-130/10, *European Parliament v. Council of the European Union*, not yet reported, paras 52–83.

6.3 The UN sanctions regime

The sanctions regime established by the UN Security Council Resolution 1267 (1999) is discussed here.[7] This regime is directed against al-Qaeda and the Taliban, and associated individuals and entities obliging all UN Member States to implement an asset freeze, travel ban, and arms embargo on them. It revolves around the function of a Sanctions Committee created pursuant to paragraph 6 of the said resolution, in order to oversee the implementation of these sanctions imposed by the UN Security Council. The difference between the 1267 regime and the one established by UN Security Council Resolution 1373 (2001), which is discussed further below, lies in the centralized and universal structure of the 1267 regime allowing for no autonomous action by individual states or the EU. It is the 1267 Sanctions Committee that on the basis of information from the UN Member States establishes and amends a list of persons related to al-Qaeda, on whom sanctions are to be imposed by the UN Member States. The Union adopted Common Position 2002/402/CFSP[8] in accordance with Resolution 1267 and implemented it with Council Regulation (EC) No. 881/2002. It is worth noting here that the Court found in this respect that the prohibition against providing the designated persons with funds (Article 2(2) Regulation No. 881/2002) does not apply 'to the provision by the State of social security or social assistance benefits to the spouse of a designated person on the grounds only that the spouse lives with the designated person and will or may use some of those payments to pay for goods and services which the designated person also will consume or from which he will benefit'.[9] Further, the centralized nature of the 1267 regime has raised issues within the EU with regard to the adequate protection of human rights of listed individuals. This has been particularly illustrated in the Kadi saga before the CJEU, which is discussed in detail in Chapter 12 on the Status of UN law within the EU legal order (see pp. 999–1023).

Security Council Resolution 1267 (1999) of 15 October 1999 on the situation in Afghanistan, UN Doc. S/RES/1267 (1999).

The Security Council,
Reaffirming its previous resolutions, in particular resolutions 1189 (1998) of 13 August 1998, 1193 (1998) of 28 August 1998 and 1214 (1998) of 8 December 1998, and the statements of its President on the situation in Afghanistan,

---

[7] This regime was amended subsequently by a number of UN Security Council Resolutions, including in particular Resolutions 1333 (2000), 1363 (2001), 1390 (2002), 1452 (2002), 1455 (2003), 1526 (2004), 1617 (2005), 1699 (2006), 1730 (2006), 1735 (2006), 1822 (2008), 1904 (2009), 1989 (2011), and 2083 (2012).

[8] As amended by Council Common Position 2003/140/CFSP of 27 February 2003 concerning exceptions to the restrictive measures imposed by Common Position 2002/402/CFSP, OJ L 53, 28.02.2003, p. 62, and Council Common Position 2011/487/CFSP of 1 August 2011 amending Common Position 2002/402/CFSP concerning restrictive measures against Usama bin Laden, members of the Al-Qaida organisation and the Taliban, and other individuals, groups, undertakings and entities associated with them, OJ L 199, 2.8.2011, p. 73.

[9] Case C-340/08, *M and Others v. Her Majesty's Treasury* [2010] ECR I-3913, para. 74.

Reaffirming its strong commitment to the sovereignty, independence, territorial integrity and national unity of Afghanistan, and its respect for Afghanistan's cultural and historical heritage,

Reiterating its deep concern over the continuing violations of international humanitarian law and of human rights, particularly discrimination against women and girls, and over the significant rise in the illicit production of opium, and stressing that the capture by the Taliban of the Consulate-General of the Islamic Republic of Iran and the murder of Iranian diplomats and a journalist in Mazar-e-Sharif constituted flagrant violations of established international law,

Recalling the relevant international counter-terrorism conventions and in particular the obligations of parties to those conventions to extradite or prosecute terrorists,

Strongly condemning the continuing use of Afghan territory, especially areas controlled by the Taliban, for the sheltering and training of terrorists and planning of terrorist acts, and reaffirming its conviction that the suppression of international terrorism is essential for the maintenance of international peace and security,

Deploring the fact that the Taliban continues to provide safe haven to Usama bin Laden and to allow him and others associated with him to operate a network of terrorist training camps from Taliban-controlled territory and to use Afghanistan as a base from which to sponsor international terrorist operations,

Noting the indictment of Usama bin Laden and his associates by the United States of America for, inter alia, the 7 August 1998 bombings of the United States embassies in Nairobi, Kenya, and Dar es Salaam, Tanzania and for conspiring to kill American nationals outside the United States, and noting also the request of the United States of America to the Taliban to surrender them for trial (S/1999/1021),

Determining that the failure of the Taliban authorities to respond to the demands in paragraph 13 of resolution 1214 (1998) constitutes a threat to international peace and security,

Stressing its determination to ensure respect for its resolutions,

Acting under Chapter VII of the Charter of the United Nations,

1. Insists that the Afghan faction known as the Taliban, which also calls itself the Islamic Emirate of Afghanistan, comply promptly with its previous resolutions and in particular cease the provision of sanctuary and training for international terrorists and their organizations, take appropriate effective measures to ensure that the territory under its control is not used for terrorist installations and camps, or for the preparation or organization of terrorist acts against other States or their citizens, and cooperate with efforts to bring indicted terrorists to justice;

2. Demands that the Taliban turn over Usama bin Laden without further delay to appropriate authorities in a country where he has been indicted, or to appropriate authorities in a country where he will be returned to such a country, or to appropriate authorities in a country where he will be arrested and effectively brought to justice;

3. Decides that on 14 November 1999 all States shall impose the measures set out in paragraph 4 below, unless the Council has previously decided, on the basis of a report of the Secretary-General, that the Taliban has fully complied with the obligation set out in paragraph 2 above;

4. Decides further that, in order to enforce paragraph 2 above, all States shall:

(a) Deny permission for any aircraft to take off from or land in their territory if it is owned, leased or operated by or on behalf of the Taliban as designated by the Committee established by paragraph 6 below, unless the particular flight has been approved in advance by the Committee on the grounds of humanitarian need, including religious obligation such as the performance of the Hajj;

(b) Freeze funds and other financial resources, including funds derived or generated from property owned or controlled directly or indirectly by the Taliban, or by any undertaking owned or controlled by the Taliban, as designated by the Committee established by paragraph 6 below, and ensure that neither they nor any other funds or financial resources so designated are made available, by their nationals or by any persons within their territory, to or for the benefit of the Taliban or any undertaking owned or controlled, directly or indirectly, by the Taliban, except as may be authorized by the Committee on a case-by-case basis on the grounds of humanitarian need;

5. Urges all States to cooperate with efforts to fulfil the demand in paragraph 2 above, and to consider further measures against Usama bin Laden and his associates;

6. Decides to establish, in accordance with rule 28 of its provisional rules of procedure, a Committee of the Security Council consisting of all the members of the Council to undertake the following tasks and to report on its work to the Council with its observations and recommendations:

(a) To seek from all States further information regarding the action taken by them with a view to effectively implementing the measures imposed by paragraph 4 above;

(b) To consider information brought to its attention by States concerning violations of the measures imposed by paragraph 4 above and to recommend appropriate measures in response thereto;

(c) To make periodic reports to the Council on the impact, including the humanitarian implications, of the measures imposed by paragraph 4 above;

(d) To make periodic reports to the Council on information submitted to it regarding alleged violations of the measures imposed by paragraph 4 above, identifying where possible persons or entities reported to be engaged in such violations;

(e) To designate the aircraft and funds or other financial resources referred to in paragraph 4 above in order to facilitate the implementation of the measures imposed by that paragraph;

(f) To consider requests for exemptions from the measures imposed by paragraph 4 above as provided in that paragraph, and to decide on the granting of an exemption to these measures in respect of the payment by the International Air Transport Association (IATA) to the aeronautical authority of Afghanistan on behalf of international airlines for air traffic control services;

(g) To examine the reports submitted pursuant to paragraph 9 below;

7. Calls upon all States to act strictly in accordance with the provisions of this resolution, notwithstanding the existence of any rights or obligations conferred or imposed by any international agreement or any contract entered into or any licence or permit granted prior to the date of coming into force of the measures imposed by paragraph 4 above;

8. Calls upon States to bring proceedings against persons and entities within their jurisdiction that violate the measures imposed by paragraph 4 above and to impose appropriate penalties;

9. Calls upon all States to cooperate fully with the Committee established by paragraph 6 above in the fulfilment of its tasks, including supplying such information as may be required by the Committee in pursuance of this resolution;

10. Requests all States to report to the Committee established by paragraph 6 above within 30 days of the coming into force of the measures imposed by paragraph 4 above on the steps they have taken with a view to effectively implementing paragraph 4 above;

11. Requests the Secretary-General to provide all necessary assistance to the Committee established by paragraph 6 above and to make the necessary arrangements in the Secretariat for this purpose;

12. Requests the Committee established by paragraph 6 above to determine appropriate arrangements, on the basis of recommendations of the Secretariat, with competent international organizations, neighbouring and other States, and parties concerned with a view to improving the monitoring of the implementation of the measures imposed by paragraph 4 above;

13. Requests the Secretariat to submit for consideration by the Committee established by paragraph 6 above information received from Governments and public sources on possible violations of the measures imposed by paragraph 4 above;

14. Decides to terminate the measures imposed by paragraph 4 above once the Secretary-General reports to the Security Council that the Taliban has fulfilled the obligation set out in paragraph 2 above;

15. Expresses its readiness to consider the imposition of further measures, in accordance with its responsibility under the Charter of the United Nations, with the aim of achieving the full implementation of this resolution;

16. Decides to remain actively seized of the matter.

Council Common Position 2002/402/CFSP of 27 May 2002 concerning restrictive measures against Usama bin Laden, members of the Al-Qaida organisation and the Taliban and other individuals, groups, undertakings and entities associated with them and repealing Common Positions 96/746/CFSP, 1999/727/CFSP, 2001/154/CFSP and 2001/771/CFSP, Official Journal L 139, 29.5.2002, pp. 4–5.

THE COUNCIL OF THE EUROPEAN UNION,
Having regard to the Treaty on European Union, and in particular Article 15 thereof,

Whereas:
(1) On 19 October 2001, the European Council declared that it is determined to combat terrorism in every form throughout the world and that it will continue its efforts to strengthen the coalition of the international community to combat terrorism in every shape and form.
(2) On 16 January 2002 the United Nations Security Council adopted Resolution 1390(2002), hereinafter referred to as 'UNSCR 1390(2002)', setting out measures to be imposed against Usama bin Laden, members of the Al-Qaida organisation and the Taliban and other individuals, groups, undertakings and entities associated with them.

(3) UNSCR 1390(2002) adjusts the scope of the sanctions concerning the freezing of funds, the visa ban and the embargo on supply, sale or transfer of arms as well as on technical advice, assistance or training related to military activities imposed by UNSCR 1267(1999) and 1333(2000).

(4) In accordance with paragraph 3 of UNSCR 1390(2002), the above measures will be reviewed by the UN Security Council 12 months after adoption of the resolution and at the end of this period the Security Council will either allow the measures to continue or decide to improve them.

(5) UNSCR 1390(2002) imposes a travel ban on Usama bin Laden, members of the Al-Qaida organisation and the Taliban and other individuals associated with them.

(6) The sanctions concerning the flight ban and the embargo on acetic anhydride sale imposed by UNSCR 1267(1999) and 1333(2000) are no longer in force in accordance with paragraph 23 of UNSCR 1333(2000) and paragraph 1 of UNSCR 1390(2002). Moreover, all restrictive measures against Ariana Afghan Airlines were terminated by UNSCR 1388(2002) of 15 January 2002.

(7) Therefore, the European Union restrictive measures adopted pursuant to UNSCR and 1333(2000) should be adjusted in accordance with UNSCR 1390(2002).

(8) For the sake of clarity and transparency, those European Union restrictive measures as referred to in the relevant Council Common Positions should be compiled in one legal instrument and therefore Common Positions 96/746/CFSP, 1999/727/CFSP, 2001/154/CFSP and 2001/771/CFSP should be repealed.

(9) Action by the Community is needed in order to implement certain measures,

HAS ADOPTED THIS COMMON POSITION:

Article 1

This Common Position applies to Usama bin Laden, members of the Al-Qaida organisation and the Taliban and other individuals, groups, undertakings and entities associated with them, as referred to in the list drawn up pursuant to UNSCR 1267(1999) and 1333(2000) to be updated regularly by the Committee established pursuant to UNSCR 1267(1999).

Article 2

1. The direct or indirect supply, sale and transfer to the individuals, groups, undertakings and entities referred to in Article 1 of arms and related materiel of all types including weapons and ammunition, military vehicles and equipment, paramilitary equipment, and spare parts for the aforementioned, from the territories of the Member States, or using their flag vessels or aircraft, or by nationals of Member States outside their territories, under the conditions set out in UNSCR 1390(2002), shall be prohibited.

2. Without prejudice to the powers of Member States in the exercise of their public authority, the European Community, acting within the limits of the powers conferred on it by the Treaty establishing the European Community, shall prevent the direct or indirect supply, sale and transfer to the individuals, groups, undertakings and entities referred to in Article 1 of technical advice, assistance, or training related to military activities from the territories of the Member States, or using their flag vessels or

aircraft, or by nationals of Member States outside their territories, under the conditions set out in UNSCR 1390(2002).

Article 3

The European Community, acting within the limits of the powers conferred on it by the Treaty establishing the European Community:
— shall order the freezing of the funds and other financial assets or economic resources of the individuals, groups, undertakings and entities referred to in Article 1,
— shall ensure that funds, financial assets or economic resources will not be made available, directly or indirectly, to or for the benefit of the individuals, groups, undertakings and entities referred to in Article 1.

Article 4

Member States shall take the necessary measures to prevent the entry into, or transit through, their territories of the individuals referred to in Article 1 under the conditions set out in paragraph 2(b) of UNSCR 1390(2002).

Article 5

Common Positions 96/746/CFSP, 1999/727/CFSP, 2001/154/ CFSP and 2001/771/ CFSP are hereby repealed.

Article 6

This Common Position shall take effect on the date of its adoption.
This Common Position shall be kept under constant review.

Article 7

This Common Position shall be published in the Official Journal.

Council Regulation (EC) No 881/2002 of 27 May 2002 imposing certain specific restrictive measures directed against certain persons and entities associated with Usama bin Laden, the Al-Qaida network and the Taliban, and repealing Council Regulation (EC) No 467/2001 prohibiting the export of certain goods and services to Afghanistan, strengthening the flight ban and extending the freeze of funds and other financial resources in respect of the Taliban of Afghanistan.

THE COUNCIL OF THE EUROPEAN UNION,
Having regard to the Treaty establishing the European Community, and in particular Articles 60, 301 and 308 thereof,
Having regard to Common Position 2002/402/CFSP concerning restrictive measures against Usama bin Laden, members of the Al-Qaida organisation and the Taliban and other individuals, groups, undertakings and entities associated with them and repealing Common Positions 96/746/CFSP, 1999/727/CFSP, 2001/154/CFSP and 2001/771/CFSP,
Having regard to the proposal from the Commission,
Having regard to the opinion of the European Parliament,

Whereas:

(1) On 16 January 2002, the Security Council of the United Nations adopted Resolution 1390(2002) determining that the Taliban had failed to respond to its demands made in a number of previous resolutions and condemning the Taliban for allowing Afghanistan to be used as a base for terrorist training and activities and also condemning the Al-Qaida network and other associated terrorist groups for their terrorist acts and destruction of property.

(2) The Security Council decided, inter alia, that the flight ban and certain export restrictions imposed on Afghanistan further to its Resolutions 1267(1999) and 1333(2000) should be repealed and that the scope of the freezing of funds and the prohibition on funds being made available, which were imposed further to these Resolutions, should be adjusted. It also decided that a prohibition on providing the Taliban and the Al-Qaida organisation with certain services related to military activities should be applied. In accordance with paragraph 3 of Resolution 1390(2002), those measures will be reviewed by the Security Council 12 months after adoption of the resolution and at the end of this period the Security Council will either allow the measures to continue or decide to improve them.

(3) In this regard, the Security Council recalled the obligation to implement in full its Resolution 1373(2001) with regard to any member of the Taliban and the Al-Qaida organisation, but also with regard to those who are associated with them and have participated in the financing, planning, facilitation, preparation or perpetration of terrorist acts.

(4) These measures fall under the scope of the Treaty and, therefore, notably with a view to avoiding distortion of competition, Community legislation is necessary to implement the relevant decisions of the Security Council as far as the territory of the Community is concerned. For the purpose of this Regulation, the territory of the Community is deemed to encompass the territories of the Member States to which the Treaty is applicable, under the conditions laid down in that Treaty.

(5) In order to create maximum legal certainty within the Community, the names and other relevant data with regard to natural or legal persons, groups or entities whose funds should be frozen further to a designation by the UN authorities, should be made publicly known and a procedure should be established within the Community to amend these lists.

(6) The competent authorities of the Member States should, where necessary, be empowered to ensure compliance with the provisions of this Regulation.

(7) UN Security Council Resolution 1267(1999) provides that the relevant UN Sanctions Committee may grant exemptions from the freezing of funds on grounds of humanitarian need. Therefore, provision needs to be made to render such exemptions applicable throughout the Community.

(8) For reasons of expediency, the Commission should be empowered to amend the Annexes to this Regulation on the basis of pertinent notification or information by the UN Security Council, the relevant UN Sanctions Committee and Member States, as appropriate.

(9) The Commission and Member States should inform each other of the measures taken under this Regulation and of other relevant information at their disposal in connection

with this Regulation, and cooperate with the relevant UN Sanctions Committee, in particular by supplying it with information.

(10) Member States should lay down rules on sanctions applicable to infringements of the provisions of this Regulation and ensure that they are implemented. Those sanctions must be effective, proportionate and dissuasive.

(11) Taking into account that the freezing of funds is to be adjusted, it is necessary to ensure that sanctions for breaches of this Regulation can be imposed as of the date of entry into force of this Regulation.

(12) In view of the measures imposed under Resolution 1390(2002) it is necessary to adjust the measures imposed in the Community by repealing Council Regulation (EC) No 467/2001 and adopting a new Regulation,

HAS ADOPTED THIS REGULATION:

Article 1

For the purpose of this Regulation, the following definitions shall apply:

1. 'funds' means financial assets and economic benefits of every kind, including but not limited to cash, cheques, claims on money, drafts, money orders and other payment instruments; deposits with financial institutions or other entities, balances on accounts, debts and debt obligations; publicly and privately traded securities and debt instruments, including stocks and shares, certificates presenting securities, bonds, notes, warrants, debentures, derivatives contracts; interest, dividends or other income on or value accruing from or generated by assets; credit, right of set-off, guarantees, performance bonds or other financial commitments; letters of credit, bills of lading, bills of sale; documents evidencing an interest in funds or financial resources, and any other instrument of export-financing;

2. 'economic resources' means assets of every kind, whether tangible or intangible, movable or immovable, which are not funds but can be used to obtain funds, goods or services;

3. 'freezing of funds' means preventing any move, transfer, alteration, use of or dealing with funds in any way that would result in any change in their volume, amount, location, ownership, possession, character, destination or other change that would enable the use of the funds, including portfolio management;

4. 'freezing of economic resources' means preventing their use to obtain funds, goods or services in any way, including, but not limited to, by selling, hiring or mortgaging them.

Article 2

1. All funds and economic resources belonging to, or owned or held by, a natural or legal person, group or entity designated by the Sanctions Committee and listed in Annex I shall be frozen.

2. No funds shall be made available, directly or indirectly, to, or for the benefit of, a natural or legal person, group or entity designated by the Sanctions Committee and listed in Annex I.

3. No economic resources shall be made available, directly or indirectly, to, or for the benefit of, a natural or legal person, group or entity designated by the Sanctions

Committee and listed in Annex I, so as to enable that person, group or entity to obtain funds, goods or services.

Article 3

Without prejudice to the powers of Member States in the exercise of their public authority, it shall be prohibited to grant, sell, supply or transfer, directly or indirectly, technical advice, assistance or training related to military activities, including in particular training and assistance related to the manufacture, maintenance and use of arms and related materiel of all types, to any natural or legal person, group or entity designated by the Sanctions Committee and listed in Annex I.

Article 4

1. The participation, knowingly and intentionally, in activities, the object or effect of which is, directly or indirectly, to circumvent Article 2 or to promote the transactions referred to in Article 3, shall be prohibited.
2. Any information that the provisions of this Regulation are being, or have been, circumvented shall be notified to the competent authorities of the Member States and, directly or through these competent authorities, to the Commission.

Article 5

1. Without prejudice to the applicable rules concerning reporting, confidentiality and professional secrecy and to the provisions of Article 284 of the Treaty, natural and legal persons, entities and bodies shall:
(a) provide immediately any information which would facilitate compliance with this Regulation, such as accounts and amounts frozen in accordance with Article 2, to the competent authorities of the Member States listed in Annex II where they are resident or located, and, directly or through these competent authorities, to the Commission. In particular, available information in respect of funds, financial assets or economic resources owned or controlled by persons designated by the Sanctions Committee and listed in Annex 1 during the period of six months before the entry into force of this Regulation shall be provided;
(b) cooperate with the competent authorities listed in Annex II in any verification of this information.
2. Any information provided or received in accordance with this Article shall be used only for the purposes for which it was provided or received.
3. Any additional information directly received by the Commission shall be made available to the competent authorities of the Member States concerned.

Article 6

The freezing of funds, other financial assets and economic resources, in good faith that such action is in accordance with this Regulation, shall not involve the natural or legal person, group or entity implementing it, or its directors or employees, in liability of any kind unless it is proved that the freezing was due to negligence.

Article 7

1. The Commission shall be empowered to:

— amend or supplement Annex I on the basis of determinations made by either the United Nations Security Council or the Sanctions Committee, and
— amend Annex II on the basis of information supplied by Member States.
2. Without prejudice to the rights and obligations of the Member States under the Charter of the United Nations, the Commission shall maintain all necessary contacts with the Sanctions Committee for the purpose of the effective implementation of this Regulation.

Article 8

The Commission and the Member States shall immediately inform each other of the measures taken under this Regulation and shall supply each other with relevant information at their disposal in connection with this Regulation, in particular information received in accordance with Article 5 and in respect of violation and enforcement problems and judgements handed down by national courts.

Article 9

This Regulation shall apply notwithstanding any rights conferred or obligations imposed by any international agreement signed or any contract entered into or any licence or permit granted before the entry into force of this Regulation.

Article 10

1. Each Member State shall determine the sanctions to be imposed where the provisions of this Regulation are infringed. Such sanctions shall be effective, proportionate and dissuasive.
2. Pending the adoption, where necessary, of any legislation to this end, the sanctions to be imposed where the provisions of this Regulation are infringed, shall be those determined by the Member States in accordance with Article 13 of Regulation (EC) No 467/2001.
3. Each Member State shall be responsible for bringing proceedings against any natural or legal person, group or entity under its jurisdiction, in cases of violation of any of the prohibitions laid down in this Regulation by any such person, group or entity.

Article 11

This Regulation shall apply
— within the territory of the Community, including its airspace,
— on board any aircraft or any vessel under the jurisdiction of a Member State,
— to any person elsewhere who is a national of a Member State,
— to any legal person, group or entity which is incorporated or constituted under the law of a Member State,
— to any legal person, group or entity doing business within the Community.

Article 12

Regulation (EC) No 467/2001 is hereby repealed.

Article 13

This Regulation shall enter into force on the day following that of its publication in the Official Journal of the European Communities.

This Regulation shall be binding in its entirety and directly applicable in all Member States.

6.4 The UN system authorizing terrorist listings by states

This section contains first of all UN Security Council (SC) Resolution 1373 (2001). The structure of this resolution demonstrates why sanctions taken against individuals in its implementation, frequently in the form of asset freezing, are considered to be of an autonomous nature, unlike the listing of persons pursuant to the SC Resolution directed against al-Qaeda, discussed above. In the case of Resolution 1373 (2001), the UN Member States, though enjoined to take certain actions, such as ratifying a number of existing anti-terrorism conventions, had the possibility to indicate which persons they considered to be terrorists on the basis of their own legislation. Regulation (EC) No. 2580/2001 established precisely such a system, in particular through Article 2(3), which laid down the criteria according to which a person can be branded a terrorist so that restrictive measures can be taken against him. The Court of First Instance interpreted and applied in case T-341/07 these provisions, arriving at the conclusion that the different judgments handed down in the Dutch procedures concerning Mr Sison's request for asylum did not constitute sufficient indications that the Dutch authorities had decided to prosecute him for terrorist crimes; to the contrary, they had decided not to open an investigation in this respect. In referring back to the *OMPI*, *PMOI I* and *PMOI II* cases,[10] the Court set here once more the threshold for the safeguard of human rights when imposing autonomous EU sanctions on individuals and entities. Finally, parts of Case C-27/09 (*PMOI II* Appeal case) are included here, constituting the most recent judicial developments in the field of human rights protection in the EU autonomous sanctions regime.

Security Council Resolution 1373 (2001) of 28 September 2001 on International Terrorism, UN Doc. S/RES/1373 (2001).

Resolution 1373 (2001)
Adopted by the Security Council at its 4385th meeting, on
28 September 2001

The Security Council,

Reaffirming its resolutions 1269 (1999) of 19 October 1999 and 1368 (2001) of 12 September 2001,

Reaffirming also its unequivocal condemnation of the terrorist attacks which took place in New York, Washington, D.C. and Pennsylvania on 11 September 2001, and expressing its determination to prevent all such acts,

---

[10] Case T-228/02 *Organisation des Modjahedines du peuple d'Iran v. Council* [2006] ECR II-5665 (OMPI); Case T-256/07 *People's Mojahedin Organization of Iran v. Council* [2008] ECR II-3019 (PMOI I); Case T-284/08 *People's Mojahedin Organization of Iran v. Council* [2008] ECR II-3487 (PMOI II).

Reaffirming further that such acts, like any act of international terrorism, constitute a threat to international peace and security,

Reaffirming the inherent right of individual or collective self-defence as recognized by the Charter of the United Nations as reiterated in resolution 1368 (2001),

Reaffirming the need to combat by all means, in accordance with the Charter of the United Nations, threats to international peace and security caused by terrorist acts,

Deeply concerned by the increase, in various regions of the world, of acts of terrorism motivated by intolerance or extremism,

Calling on States to work together urgently to prevent and suppress terrorist acts, including through increased cooperation and full implementation of the relevant international conventions relating to terrorism,

Recognizing the need for States to complement international cooperation by taking additional measures to prevent and suppress, in their territories through all lawful means, the financing and preparation of any acts of terrorism,

Reaffirming the principle established by the General Assembly in its declaration of October 1970 (resolution 2625 (XXV)) and reiterated by the Security Council in its resolution 1189 (1998) of 13 August 1998, namely that every State has the duty to refrain from organizing, instigating, assisting or participating in terrorist acts in another State or acquiescing in organized activities within its territory directed towards the commission of such acts,

Acting under Chapter VII of the Charter of the United Nations,

1. Decides that all States shall:

(a) Prevent and suppress the financing of terrorist acts;

(b) Criminalize the wilful provision or collection, by any means, directly or indirectly, of funds by their nationals or in their territories with the intention that the funds should be used, or in the knowledge that they are to be used, in order to carry out terrorist acts;

(c) Freeze without delay funds and other financial assets or economic resources of persons who commit, or attempt to commit, terrorist acts or participate in or facilitate the commission of terrorist acts; of entities owned or controlled directly or indirectly by such persons; and of persons and entities acting on behalf of, or at the direction of such persons and entities, including funds derived or generated from property owned or controlled directly or indirectly by such persons and associated persons and entities;

(d) Prohibit their nationals or any persons and entities within their territories from making any funds, financial assets or economic resources or financial or other related services available, directly or indirectly, for the benefit of persons who commit or attempt to commit or facilitate or participate in the commission of terrorist acts, of entities owned or controlled, directly or indirectly, by such persons and of persons and entities acting on behalf of or at the direction of such persons;

2. Decides also that all States shall:

(a) Refrain from providing any form of support, active or passive, to entities or persons involved in terrorist acts, including by suppressing recruitment of members of terrorist groups and eliminating the supply of weapons to terrorists;

(b) Take the necessary steps to prevent the commission of terrorist acts, including by provision of early warning to other States by exchange of information;

(c) Deny safe haven to those who finance, plan, support, or commit terrorist acts, or provide safe havens;

(d) Prevent those who finance, plan, facilitate or commit terrorist acts from using their respective territories for those purposes against other States or their citizens;

(e) Ensure that any person who participates in the financing, planning, preparation or perpetration of terrorist acts or in supporting terrorist acts is brought to justice and ensure that, in addition to any other measures against them, such terrorist acts are established as serious criminal offences in domestic laws and regulations and that the punishment duly reflects the seriousness of such terrorist acts;

(f) Afford one another the greatest measure of assistance in connection with criminal investigations or criminal proceedings relating to the financing or support of terrorist acts, including assistance in obtaining evidence in their possession necessary for the proceedings;

(g) Prevent the movement of terrorists or terrorist groups by effective border controls and controls on issuance of identity papers and travel documents, and through measures for preventing counterfeiting, forgery or fraudulent use of identity papers and travel documents;

3. Calls upon all States to:

(a) Find ways of intensifying and accelerating the exchange of operational information, especially regarding actions or movements of terrorist persons or networks; forged or falsified travel documents; traffic in arms, explosives or sensitive materials; use of communications technologies by terrorist groups; and the threat posed by the possession of weapons of mass destruction by terrorist groups;

(b) Exchange information in accordance with international and domestic law and cooperate on administrative and judicial matters to prevent the commission of terrorist acts;

(c) Cooperate, particularly through bilateral and multilateral arrangements and agreements, to prevent and suppress terrorist attacks and take action against perpetrators of such acts;

(d) Become parties as soon as possible to the relevant international conventions and protocols relating to terrorism, including the International Convention for the Suppression of the Financing of Terrorism of 9 December 1999;

(e) Increase cooperation and fully implement the relevant international conventions and protocols relating to terrorism and Security Council resolutions 1269 (1999) and 1368 (2001);

(f) Take appropriate measures in conformity with the relevant provisions of national and international law, including international standards of human rights, before granting refugee status, for the purpose of ensuring that the asylum-seeker has not planned, facilitated or participated in the commission of terrorist acts;

(g) Ensure, in conformity with international law, that refugee status is not abused by the perpetrators, organizers or facilitators of terrorist acts, and that claims of political motivation are not recognized as grounds for refusing requests for the extradition of alleged terrorists;

4. Notes with concern the close connection between international terrorism and trans-national organized crime, illicit drugs, money-laundering, illegal armstrafficking, and illegal movement of nuclear, chemical, biological and other potentially deadly materials, and in this regard emphasizes the need to enhance coordination of efforts on national, subregional, regional and international levels in order to strengthen a global response to this serious challenge and threat to international security;

5. Declares that acts, methods, and practices of terrorism are contrary to the purposes and principles of the United Nations and that knowingly financing, planning and inciting terrorist acts are also contrary to the purposes and principles of the United Nations;

6. Decides to establish, in accordance with rule 28 of its provisional rules of procedure, a Committee of the Security Council, consisting of all the members of the Council, to monitor implementation of this resolution, with the assistance of appropriate expertise, and calls upon all States to report to the Committee, no later than 90 days from the date of adoption of this resolution and thereafter according to a timetable to be proposed by the Committee, on the steps they have taken to implement this resolution;

7. Directs the Committee to delineate its tasks, submit a work programme within 30 days of the adoption of this resolution, and to consider the support it requires, in consultation with the Secretary-General;

8. Expresses its determination to take all necessary steps in order to ensure the full implementation of this resolution, in accordance with its responsibilities under the Charter;

9. Decides to remain seized of this matter.

Council Common Position 2001/931/CFSP of 27 December 2001 on the application specific measures to combat terrorism, Official Journal L 344, 28.12.2001, pp. 93–6.

THE COUNCIL OF THE EUROPEAN UNION,
Having regard to the Treaty on European Union, and in particular Articles 15 and 34 thereof,

Whereas:
(1) At its extraordinary meeting on 21 September 2001, the European Council declared that terrorism is a real challenge to the world and to Europe and that the fight against terrorism will be a priority objective of the European Union.
(2) On 28 September 2001, the United Nations Security Council adopted Resolution 1373(2001) laying out wide-ranging strategies to combat terrorism and in particular the fight against the financing of terrorism.
(3) On 8 October 2001, the Council reiterated the Union's determination to attack the sources which fund terrorism, in close cooperation with the United States.
(4) On 26 February 2001, pursuant to UNSC Resolution 1333(2000), the Council adopted Common Position 2001/154/CFSP which provides inter alia for the

freezing of funds of Usama bin Laden and individuals and entities associated with him. Consequently, those persons, groups and entities are not covered by this Common Position.

(5) The European Union should take additional measures in order to implement UNSC Resolution 1373(2001).

(6) Member States have transmitted to the European Union the information necessary to implement some of those additional measures.

(7) Action by the Community is necessary in order to implement some of those additional measures; action by the Member States is also necessary, in particular as far as the application of forms of police and judicial cooperation in criminal matters is concerned,

HAS ADOPTED THIS COMMON POSITION:

Article 1

1. This Common Position applies in accordance with the provisions of the following Articles to persons, groups and entities involved in terrorist acts and listed in the Annex.

2. For the purposes of this Common Position, 'persons, groups and entities involved in terrorist acts' shall mean:

– persons who commit, or attempt to commit, terrorist acts or who participate in, or facilitate, the commission of terrorist acts,

– groups and entities owned or controlled directly or indirectly by such persons; and persons, groups and entities acting on behalf of, or under the direction of, such persons, groups and entities, including funds derived or generated from property owned or controlled directly or indirectly by such persons and associated persons, groups and entities.

3. For the purposes of this Common Position, 'terrorist act' shall mean one of the following intentional acts, which, given its nature or its context, may seriously damage a country or an international organisation, as defined as an offence under national law, where committed with the aim of:

(i) seriously intimidating a population, or

(ii) unduly compelling a Government or an international organisation to perform or abstain from performing any act, or

(iii) seriously destabilising or destroying the fundamental political, constitutional, economic or social structures of a country or an international organisation:

(a) attacks upon a person's life which may cause death;

(b) attacks upon the physical integrity of a person;

(c) kidnapping or hostage taking;

(d) causing extensive destruction to a Government or public facility, a transport system, an infrastructure facility, including an information system, a fixed platform located on the continental shelf, a public place or private property, likely to endanger human life or result in major economic loss;

(e) seizure of aircraft, ships or other means of public or goods transport;

(f) manufacture, possession, acquisition, transport, supply or use of weapons, explosives or of nuclear, biological or chemical weapons, as well as research into, and development of, biological and chemical weapons;

(g) release of dangerous substances, or causing fires, explosions or floods the effect of which is to endanger human life;

(h) interfering with or disrupting the supply of water, power or any other fundamental natural resource, the effect of which is to endanger human life;

(i) threatening to commit any of the acts listed under (a) to (h);

(j) directing a terrorist group;

(k) participating in the activities of a terrorist group, including by supplying information or material resources, or by funding its activities in any way, with knowledge of the fact that such participation will contribute to the criminal activities of the group.

For the purposes of this paragraph, 'terrorist group' shall mean a structured group of more than two persons, established over a period of time and acting in concert to commit terrorist acts. 'Structured group' means a group that is not randomly formed for the immediate commission of a terrorist act and that does not need to have formally defined roles for its members, continuity of its membership or a developed structure.

4. The list in the Annex shall be drawn up on the basis of precise information or material in the relevant file which indicates that a decision has been taken by a competent authority in respect of the persons, groups and entities concerned, irrespective of whether it concerns the instigation of investigations or prosecution for a terrorist act, an attempt to perpetrate, participate in or facilitate such an act based on serious and credible evidence or clues, or condemnation for such deeds. Persons, groups and entities identified by the Security Council of the United Nations as being related to terrorism and against whom it has ordered sanctions may be included in the list.

For the purposes of this paragraph 'competent authority' shall mean a judicial authority, or, where judicial authorities have no competence in the area covered by this paragraph, an equivalent competent authority in that area.

5. The Council shall work to ensure that names of natural or legal persons, groups or entities listed in the Annex have sufficient particulars appended to permit effective identification of specific human beings, legal persons, entities or bodies, thus facilitating the exculpation of those bearing the same or similar names.

6. The names of persons and entities on the list in the Annex shall be reviewed at regular intervals and at least once every six months to ensure that there are grounds for keeping them on the list.

Article 2

The European Community, acting within the limits of the powers conferred on it by the Treaty establishing the European Community, shall order the freezing of the funds and other financial assets or economic resources of persons, groups and entities listed in the Annex.

Article 3

The European Community, acting within the limits of the powers conferred on it by the Treaty establishing the European Community, shall ensure that funds, financial assets or economic resources or financial or other related services will not be made available, directly or indirectly, for the benefit of persons, groups and entities listed in the Annex.

Article 4

Member States shall, through police and judicial cooperation in criminal matters within the framework of Title VI of the Treaty on European Union, afford each other the widest possible assistance in preventing and combating terrorist acts. To that end they shall, with respect to enquiries and proceedings conducted by their authorities in respect of any of the persons, groups and entities listed in the Annex, fully exploit, upon request, their existing powers in accordance with acts of the European Union and other international agreements, arrangements and conventions which are binding upon Member States.

Article 5

This Common Position shall take effect on the date of its adoption.

Article 6

This Common Position shall be kept under constant review.

Article 7

This Common Position shall be published in the Official Journal.

[...]

Council Regulation (EC) No 2580/2001 of 27 December 2001 on specific restrictive measures directed against certain persons and entities with a view to combating terrorism, Official Journal L 344, 28.12.2001, pp. 70–5.[11]

THE COUNCIL OF THE EUROPEAN UNION,

Having regard to the Treaty establishing the European Community, and in particular Articles 60, 301 and 308 thereof,

Having regard to Common Position 2001/931/CFSP on the application of specific measures to combat terrorism, adopted by the Council on 27 December 2001,

Having regard to the proposal from the Commission,

Having regard to the opinion of the European Parliament,

Whereas:

(1) At its extraordinary meeting on 21 September 2001, the European Council declared that terrorism is a real challenge to the world and to Europe and that the fight against terrorism will be a priority objective of the European Union.

(2) The European Council declared that combating the funding of terrorism is a decisive aspect of the fight against terrorism and called upon the Council to take the necessary measures to combat any form of financing for terrorist activities.

---

[11] It has since been amended by Commission Regulation (EC) No. 745/2003 OJ L 106, 28.4.2003, pp. 22–3; Commission Regulation (EC) No. 1207/2005 OJ L 197, 28.7.2005, pp. 16–18; Commission Regulation (EC) No. 1957/2005 OJ L 314, 30.11.2005, pp. 16–17; Commission Regulation (EC) No. 1461/2006 OJ L 272, 3.10.2006, pp. 11–12; Council Regulation (EC) No. 1791/2006 OJ L 363, 20.12.2006, pp. 1–80.

(3) In its Resolution 1373(2001), the United Nations Security Council decided on 28 September 2001 that all States should implement a freezing of funds and other financial assets or economic resources as against persons who commit, or attempt to commit, terrorist acts or who participate in or facilitate the commission of such acts.

(4) In addition, the Security Council decided that measures should be taken to prohibit funds and other financial assets or economic resources from being made available for the benefit of such persons, and to prohibit financial or other related services from being rendered for the benefit of such persons.

(5) Action by the Community is necessary in order to implement the CFSP aspects of Common Position 2001/931/CFSP.

(6) This Regulation is a measure needed at Community level and complementary to administrative and judicial procedures regarding terrorist organisations in the European Union and third countries.

(7) Community territory is deemed to encompass, for the purposes of this Regulation, all the territories of the Member States to which the Treaty is applicable, under the conditions laid down in that Treaty.

(8) With a view to protecting the interests of the Community, certain exceptions may be granted.

(9) As regards the procedure for establishing and amending the list referred to in Article 2(3) of this Regulation, the Council should exercise the corresponding implementing powers itself in view of the specific means available to its members for that purpose.

(10) Circumvention of this Regulation should be prevented by an adequate system of information and, where appropriate, remedial measures, including additional Community legislation.

(11) The competent authorities of the Member States should, where necessary, be empowered to ensure compliance with the provisions of this Regulation.

(12) Member States should lay down rules on sanctions applicable to infringements of the provisions of this Regulation and ensure that they are implemented. Those sanctions must be effective, proportionate and dissuasive.

(13) The Commission and the Member States should inform each other of the measures taken under this Regulation and of other relevant information at their disposal in connection with this Regulation.

(14) The list referred to in Article 2(3) of this Regulation may include persons and entities linked or related to third countries as well as those who otherwise are the focus of the CFSP aspects of Common Position 2001/931/CFSP. For the adoption of provisions in this Regulation concerning the latter, the Treaty does not provide powers other than those under Article 308.

(15) The European Community has already implemented UNSCR 1267(1999) and 1333(2000) by adopting Regulation (EC) No 467/2001 freezing the assets of certain persons and groups and therefore those persons and groups are not covered by this Regulation,

HAS ADOPTED THIS REGULATION:

Article 1

For the purpose of this Regulation, the following definitions shall apply:

1. 'Funds, other financial assets and economic resources' means assets of every kind, whether tangible or intangible, movable or immovable, however acquired, and legal documents or instruments in any form, including electronic or digital, evidencing title to, or interest in, such assets, including, but not limited to, bank credits, travellers' cheques, bank cheques, money orders, shares, securities, bonds, drafts and letters of credit.

2. 'Freezing of funds, other financial assets and economic resources' means the prevention of any move, transfer, alteration, use of or dealing with funds in any way that would result in any change in their volume, amount, location, ownership, possession, character, destination or other change that would enable the funds to be used, including portfolio management.

3. 'Financial services' means any service of a financial nature, including all insurance and insurance-related services, and all banking and other financial services (excluding insurance) as follows:

Insurance and insurance-related services

(i) Direct insurance (including co-insurance):

    (A) life assurance;

    (B) non-life;

(ii) Reinsurance and retrocession;

(iii) Insurance intermediation, such as brokerage and agency;

(iv) Services auxiliary to insurance, such as consultancy, actuarial, risk assessment and claim settlement services.

Banking and other financial services (excluding insurance)

(v) Acceptance of deposits and other repayable funds;

(vi) Lending of all types, including consumer credit, mortgage credit, factoring and financing of commercial transaction;

(vii) Financial leasing;

(viii) All payment and money transmission services, including credit, charge and debit cards, travellers' cheques and bankers' drafts;

(ix) Guarantees and commitments;

(x) Trading for own account or for account of customers, whether on an exchange, in an over-the-counter market or otherwise, the following:

    (A) money market instruments (including cheques, bills, certificates of deposits);

    (B) foreign exchange;

    (C) derivative products including, but not limited to, futures and options;

    (D) exchange rate and interest rate instruments, including products such as swaps and forward rate agreements;

    (E) transferable securities;

    (F) other negotiable instruments and financial assets, including bullion;

(xi) Participation in issues of all kinds of securities, including underwriting and placement as agent (whether publicly or privately) and provision of services related to such issues;

(xii) Money brokering;

(xiii) Asset management, such as cash or portfolio management, all forms of collective investment management, pension fund management, custodial, depository and trust services;

(xiv) Settlement and clearing services for financial assets, including securities, derivative products, and other negotiable instruments;

(xv) Provision and transfer of financial information, and financial data processing and related software by suppliers of other financial services;

(xvi) Advisory, intermediation and other auxiliary financial services on all the activities listed in subparagraphs (v) to (xv), including credit reference and analysis, investment and portfolio research and advice, advice on acquisitions and on corporate restructuring and strategy.

4. For the purposes of this Regulation, the definition of 'terrorist act' shall be the one contained in Article 1(3) of Common Position 2001/931/CFSP.

5. 'Owning a legal person, group or entity' means being in possession of 50% or more of the proprietary rights of a legal person, group or entity, or having a majority interest therein.

6. 'Controlling a legal person, group or entity' means any of the following:

(a) having the right to appoint or remove a majority of the members of the administrative, management or supervisory body of such legal person, group or entity;

(b) having appointed solely as a result of the exercise of one's voting rights a majority of the members of the administrative, management or supervisory bodies of a legal person, group or entity who have held office during the present and previous financial year;

(c) controlling alone, pursuant to an agreement with other shareholders in or members of a legal person, group or entity, a majority of shareholders' or members' voting rights in that legal person, group or entity;

(d) having the right to exercise a dominant influence over a legal person, group or entity, pursuant to an agreement entered into with that legal person, group or entity, or to a provision in its Memorandum or Articles of Association, where the law governing that legal person, group or entity permits its being subject to such agreement or provision;

(e) having the power to exercise the right to exercise a dominant influence referred to in point (d), without being the holder of that right;

(f) having the right to use all or part of the assets of a legal person, group or entity;

(g) managing the business of a legal person, group or entity on a unified basis, while publishing consolidated accounts;

(h) sharing jointly and severally the financial liabilities of a legal person, group or entity, or guaranteeing them.

Article 2

1. Except as permitted under Articles 5 and 6:

(a) all funds, other financial assets and economic resources belonging to, or owned or held by, a natural or legal person, group or entity included in the list referred to in paragraph 3 shall be frozen;

(b) no funds, other financial assets and economic resources shall be made available, directly or indirectly, to, or for the benefit of, a natural or legal person, group or entity included in the list referred to in paragraph 3.

2. Except as permitted under Articles 5 and 6, it shall be prohibited to provide financial services to, or for the benefit of, a natural or legal person, group or entity included in the list referred to in paragraph 3.

3. The Council, acting by unanimity, shall establish, review and amend the list of persons, groups and entities to which this Regulation applies, in accordance with the provisions laid down in Article 1(4), (5) and (6) of Common Position 2001/931/CFSP; such list shall consist of:

(i) natural persons committing, or attempting to commit, participating in or facilitating the commission of any act of terrorism;

(ii) legal persons, groups or entities committing, or attempting to commit, participating in or facilitating the commission of any act of terrorism;

(iii) legal persons, groups or entities owned or controlled by one or more natural or legal persons, groups or entities referred to in points (i) and (ii); or

(iv) natural legal persons, groups or entities acting on behalf of or at the direction of one or more natural or legal persons, groups or entities referred to in points (i) and (ii).

Article 3

1. The participation, knowingly and intentionally, in activities, the object or effect of which is, directly or indirectly, to circumvent Article 2 shall be prohibited.

2. Any information that the provisions of this Regulation are being, or have been, circumvented shall be notified to the competent authorities of the Member States listed in the Annex and to the Commission.

Article 4

1. Without prejudice to the applicable rules concerning reporting, confidentiality and professional secrecy and to the provisions of Article 284 of the Treaty, banks, other financial institutions, insurance companies, and other bodies and persons shall:

– provide immediately any information which would facilitate compliance with this Regulation, such as accounts and amounts frozen in accordance with Article 2 and transactions executed pursuant to Articles 5 and 6:

  – to the competent authorities of the Member States listed in the Annex where they are resident or located, and

  – through these competent authorities, to the Commission,

– cooperate with the competent authorities listed in the Annex in any verification of this information.

2. Any information provided or received in accordance with this Article shall be used only for the purposes for which it was provided or received.

3. Any information directly received by the Commission shall be made available to the competent authorities of the Member States concerned and to the Council.

Article 5

1. Article 2(1)(b) shall not apply to the addition to frozen accounts of interest due on those accounts. Such interest shall also be frozen.

2. The competent authorities of the Member States listed in the Annex may grant specific authorisations, under such conditions as they deem appropriate, in order to prevent the financing of acts of terrorism, for

1. the use of frozen funds for essential human needs of a natural person included in the list referred to in Article 2(3) or a member of his family, including in particular payments for foodstuffs, medicines, the rent or mortgage for the family residence and fees and charges concerning medical treatment of members of that family, to be fulfilled within the Community;

2. payments from frozen accounts for the following purposes:

(a) payment of taxes, compulsory insurance premiums and fees for public utility services such as gas, water, electricity and telecommunications to be paid in the Community; and

(b) payment of charges due to a financial institution in the Community for the maintenance of accounts;

3. payments to a person, entity or body person included in the list referred to in Article 2(3), due under contracts, agreements or obligations which were concluded or arose before the entry into force of this Regulation provided that those payments are made into a frozen account within the Community.

3. Requests for authorisations shall be made to the competent authority of the Member State in whose territory the funds, other financial assets or other economic resources have been frozen.

Article 6

1. Notwithstanding the provisions of Article 2 and with a view to the protection of the interests of the Community, which include the interests of its citizens and residents, the competent authorities of a Member State may grant specific authorisations:

– to unfreeze funds, other financial assets or other economic resources,

– to make funds, other financial assets or other economic resources available to a person, entity or body included in the list referred to in Article 2(3), or

– to render financial services to such person, entity or body,

after consultation with the other Member States, the Council and the Commission in accordance with paragraph 2.

2. A competent authority which receives a request for an authorisation referred to in paragraph 1 shall notify the competent authorities of the other Member States, the Council and the Commission, as listed in the Annex, of the grounds on which it intends to either reject the request or grant a specific authorisation, informing them of the conditions that it considers necessary in order to prevent the financing of acts of terrorism.

The competent authority which intends to grant a specific authorisation shall take due account of comments made within two weeks by other Member States, the Council and the Commission.

Article 7

The Commission shall be empowered, on the basis of information supplied by Member States, to amend the Annex.

Article 8

The Member States, the Council and the Commission shall inform each other of the measures taken under this Regulation and supply each other with the relevant information at their disposal in connection with this Regulation, notably information received in accordance with Articles 3 and 4, and in respect of violation and enforcement problems or judgments handed down by national courts.

Article 9

Each Member State shall determine the sanctions to be imposed where the provisions of this Regulation are infringed. Such sanctions shall be effective, proportionate and dissuasive.

Article 10

This Regulation shall apply:
1. within the territory of the Community, including its airspace,
2. on board any aircraft or any vessel under the jurisdiction of a Member State,
3. to any person elsewhere who is a national of a Member State,
4. to any legal person, group or entity incorporated or constituted under the law of a Member State,
5. to any legal person, group or entity doing business within the Community.

Article 11

1. This Regulation shall enter into force on the day of its publication in the Official Journal of the European Communities.
2. Within a period of one year from the entry into force of this Regulation, the Commission shall present a report on the impact of this Regulation and, if necessary, make proposals to amend it.

This Regulation shall be binding in its entirety and directly applicable in all Member States.

[...]

Judgment of the Court of First Instance (Seventh Chamber) of 30 September 2009, Jose Maria Sison v Council of the European Union, Case T-341/07, European Court Reports 2009, p. II-3625, paras. 1–10, 67–71, 87–123 and 133–8.

The case taken up below is one of the many cases concerning Mr Sison, a Philippine politician with a leadership role in the Communist Party and guerilla movement, whose presence in the Netherlands was tolerated for many years, but never fully recognized as refugee status. After the end of the Marcos regime, he even played a role in negotiations between the government and the Communist Party, but was quickly placed on the list of terrorists of Resolution 1373 by the Netherlands under pressure of the Philippine and US governments, when the opportunity presented itself. Consequently, he was put on an EU list of persons whose assets had to be frozen. This is the judgment in the interlocutory proceedings in Case T-341/07. It demonstrates that the European Courts are much more at ease in criticizing listings under Resolution 1373, since the Member States governments play an important role in these listings, than those under the 1267 al-Qaeda and Taliban listings regime.

The final stage of Case T-341/07 concerned Sison's claim for damages on the basis of non-contractual liability on the part of the Council, the EU institution that had taken the freezing measure against him. This part of Sison's claims, however, was rejected. The Court ruled that though the illegality of the Council's actions had been clearly established, in the particular circumstances of the case, this illegality did not amount to a sufficiently serious breach of a rule of law conferring rights to individuals.[12]

Background to the case

1. For a summary of the early background to this case, reference is made to the judgment of the Court of First Instance of 11 July 2007 in Case T-47/03 *Sison v Council*, not published in the European Court Reports ('*Sison*'), in particular to paragraphs 46 to 70, describing the administrative and judicial proceedings relating to the applicant, Mr Jose Maria Sison, in the Netherlands which gave rise to the judgments of the Raad van State (Council of State, Netherlands) of 17 December 1992 ('the judgment of the Raad van State of 1992') and of 21 February 1995 ('the judgment of the Raad van State of 1995') and also to the decision of the Arrondissementsrechtbank te's-Gravenhage (The Hague District Court, 'the Rechtbank'), Sector Bestuursrecht, Rechtseenheidskamer Vreemdelingenzaken (Administrative Law Section, Chamber responsible for the uniform applica-tion of the law, cases involving aliens) of 11 September 1997 ('the decision of the Rechtbank').

2. In *Sison* the Court of First Instance annulled Council Decision 2006/379/EC of 29 May 2006 implementing Article 2(3) of Regulation (EC) No 2580/2001 on specific restrictive measures directed against certain persons and entities with a view to combating terrorism and repealing Decision 2005/930/EC (OJ 2006 L 144, p. 21), in so far as it concerned the applicant, on the grounds that no statement of reasons had been given for the decision, that it had been adopted in the course of a pro-cedure during which the applicant's rights of defence had not been observed and that the Court of First Instance itself was not in a position to undertake the judicial review of the lawfulness of that decision (see *Sison*, paragraph 226).

3. After the hearing in *Sison*, which was held on 30 May 2006, but before judgment was delivered, the Council of the European Union adopted Decision 2007/445/EC of 28 June 2007 implementing Article 2(3) of Regulation No 2580/2001 and repealing Decisions 2006/379/EC and 2006/1008/EC (OJ 2007 L 169, p. 58). By that decision, the Council maintained the applicant's name in the list in the Annex to Council Regulation (EC) No 2580/2001 of 27 December 2001 on specific restric-tive measures directed against certain persons and entities with a view to combat-ing terrorism (OJ 2001 L 344, p. 70, corrigendum in OJ 2007 L 164, p. 36, 'the list at issue').

4. Before that decision was adopted, by letter of 23 April 2007 the Council informed the applicant that, in its view, the reasons for including him in the list at issue were still valid, and that it therefore intended to maintain him in that list. Enclosed with that letter was the Council's statement of reasons. The applicant was also informed

---

[12] See Case T-341/07, *Sison v. Council*, Judgment of 23 November 2011, not yet reported, points 72–5.

that he could submit observations to the Council on the latter's intention to continue to maintain him in the list and on the reasons stated in that regard, and any supporting documents, within a period of one month.

5. In the statement of reasons enclosed with that letter, the Council noted the following:

'SISON, Jose Maria (alias Armando Liwanag, alias Joma, head of the Communist Party of the Philippines, including the NPA) born on 8.2.1939 in Cabugao, Philippines

Jose Maria Sison is the founder and leader of the Philippine Communist Party, including the New People's Army (NPA) (Philippines), which is put in the list of groups involved in terrorist acts in the meaning of Article 1, paragraph 2, of the Common Position 2001/931/CFSP. He has repeatedly advocated the use of violence for the realisation of political aims and has given leadership to the NPA, which is responsible for a number of terrorist attacks in the Philippines. These acts fall under Article 1, paragraph 3, point iii,...(i) and (j) of Common Position 2001/931/CFSP (hereafter 'the Common Position') and have been perpetrated with the intention as meant in Article 1, paragraph 3, point iii) of the Common Position.

The [Rechtbank] confirmed on 11 September 1997...[the judgment of the Raad van State]. The Administrative Law Division of the Raad van State came to the decision that the status of asylum seeker in the Netherlands was legitimately refused, because the proof was delivered that he gave leadership—or has tried to give—to the armed wing of the CPP, the NPA, which is responsible for a number of terrorist attacks in the Philippines, and because it also turned out that he maintains contacts with terrorist organisations throughout the whole world.

The Minister of Foreign Affairs and the Minister of Finance [of the Netherlands] decided, through ministerial ruling ('regeling') No DJZ/BR/749-02 of 13 August 2002 (Sanction regulation terrorism 2002 III), which was published in the Netherlands Gazette on 13 August 2002, that all means which belong to Jose Maria Sison and the Philippine Communist Party, including the Philippine New People's Army (NPA) be frozen.

The American Government named Jose Maria Sison as 'Specially Designated Global Terrorist' (specifically named as a world ['mondial'] terrorist person pursuant to US Executive Order 13224. This decision can be reviewed according to American law.

Thus with regards to Jose Maria Sison, decisions have been taken by competent authorities in the meaning of Article 1, paragraph 4, of the Common Position.

The Council is convinced that the reasons to put Jose Maria Sison on the list of persons and entities to which the stated measures in Article 2, paragraphs 1 and 2 of Regulation (EC) No 2580/2001 are applicable, remain valid.'

6. By letter of 22 May 2007 the applicant submitted to the Council its observations in response. He claimed, inter alia, that neither the judgment of the Raad van State of 1995 nor the decision of the Rechtbank satisfied the requirements laid down by the relevant Community legislation to serve as a basis for a decision to freeze funds. He also requested that the Council should, first, give him an opportunity to be heard before a new decision to freeze funds was adopted and, secondly, send a

copy of his written observations and all the procedural documents in Case T-47/03 to all the Member States.

7. Decision 2007/445 was notified to the applicant under cover of a letter from the Council of 29 June 2007. Enclosed with that letter was a statement of reasons identical to that enclosed with the letter from the Council of 23 April 2007.

8. By Decision 2007/868/EC of 20 December 2007 implementing Article 2(3) of Regulation No 2580/2001 and repealing Decision 2007/445 (OJ 2007 L 340, p. 100), the Council adopted a new updated list of the persons, groups and entities to whom and to which that regulation applies. The names of the applicant and of the NPA are repeated in that list, in the same terms as those used in the Annex to Decision 2007/445.

9. Decision 2007/868 was notified to the applicant under cover of a letter from the Council of 3 January 2008. Enclosed with that letter was a statement of reasons identical to that enclosed with the letters from the Council of 23 April and 29 June 2007.

10. By Decision 2008/343/EC of 29 April 2008 amending Decision 2007/868 (OJ 2008 L 116, p. 25), the Council maintained the applicant in the list at issue, although it amended the entries for the applicant and the Communist Party of the Philippines in the Annex to Decision 2007/868.

[...]

Findings of the Court

[...]

67. In so far as the applicant complains that the Council relied on clearly incorrect reasoning, it is to be borne in mind that, according to settled case-law, the obligation to state reasons constitutes an essential procedural requirement which must be distinguished from the issue of the validity of the reasoning, the latter falling within the ambit of the substantive lawfulness of the contested act (Case C-66/02 *Italy* v *Commission* [2005] ECR I-10901, paragraph 26; Case T-303/02 *Westfalen Gassen Nederland* v Commission [2006] ECR II-4567, paragraph 72, and *PMOI I*, paragraph 85). Thus, a challenge to the merits of that reasoning may not be examined at the stage of verifying whether the obligation laid down by Article 253 EC has been performed (*Italy* v *Commission*, paragraph 55).

68. That complaint must, therefore, be rejected as ineffective in relation to this plea in law. It will, however, be taken into consideration in the examination of the plea alleging contravention of Article 2(3) of Regulation No 2580/2001 and of Article 1(4) of Common Position 2001/931, with regard to which it might be relevant (see paragraph 87 below).

69. Inasmuch as the applicant complains that the Council failed to answer his written observations, it is to be recalled that although, by virtue of Article 253 EC, the Council is required to state all the factual circumstances justifying the measures it adopts and the legal considerations leading it to take them, that provision does not require the Council to discuss all the points of fact and law which may have been raised by the persons concerned during the administrative procedure (*PMOI I*, paragraph 101 and the case-law cited).

70. That complaint must, therefore, be rejected as ineffective in relation to this plea in law. It will, however, be taken into consideration in the examination of the plea alleging breach of the rights of defence.

71. It follows from the foregoing that the alleged breach of the obligation to state reasons has not, in the circumstances of this case, been established, with the result that the first plea in law must be rejected.

[...]

87. The applicant's complaint that the allegations as to fact contained in the statements of reasons annexed to the Council's letters of 23 April and 29 June 2007 and of 21 January 2008 are incorrect and baseless must be examined first. This complaint is essentially the same as that, put forward in relation to the first plea in law, alleging that the reasons annexed to the letters of notification were plainly incorrect (see paragraph 55 above).

88. It must be stated that the allegations in question—other than that claiming the applicant to be Armando Liwanag, which is in any case quite irrelevant in the circumstances—are substantiated in due fashion by the material in the file produced before the Court and, more particularly, by the findings of fact made by the Raad van State and repeated by the Rechtbank, which possess the force of *res judicata*. It is sufficient, here, to refer to paragraphs 46 to 70 of *Sison*, reproduced in paragraph 106 below.

89. In the circumstances, the applicant's complaints alleging an error, indeed, even a manifest error, in the assessment of the facts must be dismissed as unfounded.

90. The second subject of examination must be the applicant's complaints, taken together, that it is not possible to identify in the judgment of the Raad van State of 1995, or the decision of the Rechtbank, or the Sanctieregeling or the American decision a decision taken by a competent authority for the purpose of Article 2(3) of Regulation No 2580/2001 or of Article 1(4) of Common Position 2001/931.

91. The Court notes that in its judgments in *OMPI* and *PMOI I* and in Case T-284/08 *People's Mojahedin Organization of Iran v Council* [2008] ECR II-0000 ('*PMOI II*'), it clarified: (a) the conditions for implementing Article 1(4) of Common Position 2001/931 and Article 2(3) of Regulation No 2580/2001; (b) the burden of proof incumbent on the Council in that context; and (c) the scope of judicial review in such matters.

92. As the Court pointed out in paragraphs 115 and 116 of *OMPI*, in paragraph 130 of *PMOI I* and in paragraph 50 of *PMOI II*, the matters of fact and law capable of affecting the application of a fund-freezing measure to a person, group or entity are determined by Article 2(3) of Regulation No 2580/2001. In the words of that provision, the Council, acting by unanimity, is to establish, review and amend the list of persons, groups and entities to whom and to which that regulation applies, in accordance with the provisions laid down in Article 1(4) to (6) of Common Position 2001/931. The list in question must, therefore, be drawn up, in accordance with Article 1(4) of Common Position 2001/931, on the basis of precise information or material in the relevant file which indicates that a decision has been taken by a competent authority in respect of the persons, groups and entities concerned, irrespective of whether it concerns the instigation of investigations or prosecution

for a terrorist act, or an attempt to perpetrate, participate in or facilitate such an act, based on serious and credible evidence or clues [sic], or condemnation [sic] for such deeds. 'Competent authority' means a judicial authority or, where judicial authorities have no competence in that area, an equivalent authority in that sphere. In addition, the names of the persons and entities appearing in that list must be reviewed at regular intervals and at least once every six months to ensure that there are still grounds for keeping them in the list, in accordance with Article 1(6) of Common Position 2001/931.

93. In paragraph 117 of *OMPI*, paragraph 131 of *PMOI I* and paragraph 51 of *PMOI II*, the Court inferred from those provisions that the procedure which may culminate in a measure to freeze funds under the relevant legislation takes place at two levels, one national, the other Community. In the first stage, a competent national authority, as a rule judicial, must take in respect of the party concerned a decision satisfying the definition in Article 1(4) of Common Position 2001/931. If it is a decision to instigate investigations or to prosecute, it must be based on serious and credible evidence or 'clues'. In the second stage, the Council, acting by unanimity, must decide whether to include the party concerned in the disputed list, on the basis of precise information or material in the relevant file which indicates that such a decision has been taken. Next, the Council must, at regular intervals, and at least once every six months, be satisfied that there are grounds for continuing to include the party concerned in the list at issue. Verification that there is a decision of a national authority meeting that definition is an essential precondition for the adoption, by the Council, of an initial decision to freeze funds, whereas verification of the consequences of that decision at the national level is imperative in the context of the adoption of a subsequent decision to freeze funds.

94. In paragraph 123 of *OMPI*, paragraph 132 of *PMOI I* and paragraph 52 of *PMOI II*, the Court noted, inter alia, that under Article 10 EC, relations between the Member States and the Community institutions are governed by reciprocal duties to cooperate in good faith (see Case C-339/00 *Ireland* v *Commission* [2003] ECR I-11757, paragraphs 71 and 72 and the case-law cited). That principle is of general application and is binding in, inter alia, the area of police and judicial cooperation in criminal matters (commonly known as 'Justice and Home Affairs') (JHA) governed by Title VI of the EU Treaty, which is moreover entirely based on cooperation between the Member States and the institutions (Case C-105/03 *Pupino* [2005] ECR I-5285, paragraph 42).

95. In paragraph 124 of *OMPI*, paragraph 133 of *PMOI I* and paragraph 53 of *PMOI II*, the Court found that, in a case of application of Article 1(4) of Common Position 2001/931 and Article 2(3) of Regulation No 2580/2001, provisions which introduce a specific form of cooperation between the Council and the Member States in the context of combating terrorism, that principle entails, for the Council, the obligation to defer as far as possible to the assessment conducted by the competent national authority, at least where it is a judicial authority, in particular in respect of the existence of 'serious and credible evidence or clues' on which its decision is based.

96. As the Court ruled in paragraph 134 of *PMOI I* and in paragraph 54 of *PMOI II*, it follows from the foregoing that, although it is indeed for the Council to prove that freezing of the funds of a person, group or entity is or remains legally justified, in the light of the relevant legislation, that burden of proof has a relatively limited purpose in respect of the Community procedure for freezing funds. In the case of an initial decision to freeze funds, the burden of proof essentially relates to the existence of precise information or material in the relevant file which indicates that a decision by a national authority meeting the definition laid down in Article 1(4) of Common Position 2001/931 has been taken with regard to the person concerned. Furthermore, in the case of a subsequent decision to freeze funds, after review, the burden of proof essentially relates to whether the freezing of funds is still justified, having regard to all the relevant circumstances of the case and, most particularly, to the action taken following that decision of the competent national authority.

97. With regard to the review carried out by the Court, the latter has recognised, in paragraph 159 of *OMPI*, paragraph 137 of *PMOI I* and paragraph 55 of *PMOI II*, that the Council has broad discretion as to what matters to take into consideration for the purpose of adopting economic and financial sanctions on the basis of Articles 60 EC, 301 EC and 308 EC, consistent with a common position adopted on the basis of the common foreign and security policy. This discretion concerns, in particular, the assessment of the considerations of appropriateness on which such decisions are based.

98. However, although the Court acknowledges that the Council possesses some latitude in that sphere, that does not mean that the Court is not to review the interpretation made by the Council of the relevant facts (see *PMOI I*, paragraph 138, *PMOI II*, paragraph 55). The Community judicature must not only establish whether the evidence relied on is factually accurate, reliable and consistent, but must also ascertain whether that evidence contains all the relevant information to be taken into account in order to assess the situation and whether it is capable of substantiating the conclusions drawn from it. However, when conducting such a review, it must not substitute its own assessment of what is appropriate for that of the Council (see, by analogy, Case C-525/04 P *Spain* v *Lenzing* [2007] ECR I-9947, paragraph 57 and the case-law cited).

99. In the instant case, it is first of all to be ascertained, in accordance with that case-law, whether the contested decisions were taken on the basis of precise information or material in the file indicating that a decision meeting the definition laid down in Article 1(4) of Common Position 2001/931 had been taken with regard to the applicant.

100. In this respect, the statements of reasons annexed to the Council's letters of 23 April and 29 June 2007 and of 21 January 2008 addressed to the applicant make reference to four decisions which could be presumed to have been taken by competent authorities for the purpose of Article 1(4) of Common Position 2001/931, namely: the judgment of the Raad van State of 1995, the decision of the Rechtbank, the Sanctieregeling and the American decision.

101. In its defence (paragraph 31) the Council asserted, however, that for the purposes of these proceedings, and although it considered that it was entitled to treat the

Sanctieregeling and the US decision as decisions of competent authorities within the meaning of that provision on which it could have based its own decision, it relied on the judgment of the Raad van State of 1995 and the decision of the Rechtbank alone as constituting such decisions.

102. At the hearing the Council and the Kingdom of the Netherlands expressly confirmed that point in answer to a question put by the Court, making it clear that the judgment of the Raad van State of 1995 and the decision of the Rechtbank were indeed the only two decisions taken by competent authorities, within the meaning of Article 1(4) of Common Position 2001/931, on which the contested decisions were based. The Council went on to state that it had taken the Sanctieregeling and the US decision into consideration, in exercising its discretion, only as facts intended to bear out the findings made in the two decisions in question, concerning the applicant's continuing involvement in the CPP and the NPA.

103. Those explanations, in keeping moreover with those previously given by the Council and the Kingdom of the Netherlands in Case T-47/03 (see *Sison*, paragraphs 211 and 222), are tantamount to a formal admission which must benefit the applicant, given that they are not clearly inconsistent with the actual wording of the decisions contested in this action.

104. Furthermore, it has not been established, or even claimed, that the contested decisions were taken on the basis of another decision of a competent authority, within the meaning of Article 1(4) of Common Position 2001/931. In particular, it has not been argued that the applicant is or was the subject of any decision to investigate or of any prosecution or of any conviction and sentence whatsoever in the Philippines, in connection with the alleged terrorist activities of the CPP and the NPA.

105. In consequence, the Court must confine its review of the lawfulness of the contested decisions, in the light of the requirements recalled above laid down in Article 1(4) of Common Position 2001/931 and in Article 2(3) of Regulation No 2580/2001, exclusively to the examination of the judgment of the Raad van State of 1995 and of the decision of the Rechtbank.

106. In this regard it is appropriate to begin by recalling the context in which the judgment of the Raad van State of 1995 was delivered and the decision of the Rechtbank made, and the exact content and significance of that judgment and of that decision, as they were defined by the Court in *Sison*, paragraphs 46 to 70:

    '46   The papers before the Court indicate that the applicant, who has Filipino nationality, has resided in the Netherlands since 1987. In September 1988, after the Philippine Government withdrew his passport, he applied for refugee status and a residence permit in the Netherlands on humanitarian grounds. That application was refused by decision of the State Secretary for Justice ("the State Secretary") of 13 July 1990, on the basis of Article 1F of the Geneva Convention...

    47   His request for a review of that decision having been impliedly rejected by the State Secretary, the applicant brought an action before the Raad van State (Netherlands Council of State) against that implied decision to reject.

    48   By judgment of 17 December 1992 ("the judgment of the Raad van State of 1992"), the Raad van State annulled the implied decision to reject. It held

essentially that the State Secretary had not demonstrated to the requisite legal standard which of the acts allegedly committed by the applicant had led him to conclude that the applicant fell within the scope of Article 1F of the Geneva Convention. The Raad van State stated in that regard that the documents supplied to it on a confidential basis by the State Secretary were not sufficiently clear on the point. Since the confidential nature of the documents in question meant that that lack of clarity could not be remedied by an inter partes hearing, the Raad van State held that the information contained in those documents, in so far as it was unclear, could not be construed in a manner which was unfavourable to the applicant.

49 By decision of 26 March 1993, the State Secretary again rejected the applicant's request for a review of his decision of 13 July 1990. That decision to reject was taken primarily on the basis of Article 1F of the Geneva Convention and in the alternative on the basis of the second paragraph of Article 15 of the Vreemdelingenwet (Netherlands Law on Aliens), by reason of the overriding interests of the Netherlands State, that is to say the integrity and credibility of the Netherlands as a sovereign State, particularly with regard to its responsibilities towards other States.

50 In an action to challenge that [decision] brought by the applicant, the Raad van State annulled the State Secretary's decision of 26 March 1993 by judgment of 21 February 1995 ("the judgment of the Raad van State of 1995").

51 In that judgment, the Raad van State held that the State Secretary had reached his decision on the basis of the following factors:

  – a letter from the Binnenlandse Veiligheidsdienst (Netherlands internal security service, "the BVD") of 3 March 1993, which stated, first, that the applicant held the post of chairman and was the head of the Communist Party of the Philippines ("the CPP") and, second, that the military wing of the CPP, the NPA, was under the Central Committee of the CPP and, accordingly, the applicant;

  – the findings of the BVD, first, that the applicant was, in fact, the head of the NPA and, second, that the NPA—and thus the applicant—was responsible for a large number of terrorist acts in the Philippines.

52 The Raad van State noted the following examples of such terrorist acts, given by the State Secretary in his decision of 26 March 1993:

  – the murder of 40 inhabitants (mostly defenceless women and children) of the village of Digos, on the Island of Mindanao (Philippines) on 25 June 1989;

  – the shooting of 14 people, including six children, in the village of Dipalog (Philippines) in August 1989;

  – the execution of four inhabitants of the village of Del Monte (Philippines) on 16 October 1991.

53 The Raad van State also noted that the State Secretary had mentioned the purges carried out in 1985 in the CPP and the NPA, in the course of which it was estimated that 800 of their members were assassinated without any form of trial taking place.

54   Lastly, the Raad van State noted that, according to the State Secretary, the BVD had also determined that the CPP and the NPA maintained contacts with terrorist organisations throughout the world and that personal contacts between the applicant and representatives of those organisations had also been observed.

55   The Raad van State next examined by special procedure certain confidential evidence in the State Secretary's file together with the "operational material" on which the letter sent to him by the BVD on 3 March 1993 (paragraph 51 above) was based.

56   Taking the above matters into account, the Raad van State went on to rule as follows:

"In the light of the above evidence, the [Raad van State] holds there to be sufficient indication that the [applicant] was, at the time the decision [of 26 March 1993] was taken, the chairman and the head of the CPP. In addition, the evidence supports the conclusion that the NPA is subject to the Central Committee of the CPP and the conclusion that, at the time the decision [of 26 March 1993] was taken, the [applicant] had at least attempted to effectively direct the NPA from the Netherlands. The [Raad van State] also holds there to be sufficient indication based on public sources alone, such as reports by Amnesty International, that the NPA is responsible for a large number of terrorist acts in the Philippines. The evidence also provides support for the conclusion that the [applicant] has at least attempted to direct the abovementioned activities carried out under the control of the NPA in the Philippines. The evidence supplied also provides support for the [State Secretary's] contention that the CPP/NPA maintain contacts with terrorist organisations throughout the world and that there have been personal contacts between the [applicant] and representatives of such organisations. However, the evidence does not provide support for the conclusion that the [applicant] directed the operations in question and is responsible for them to such an extent that it may be held that there are serious reasons to suppose that the [applicant] has actually committed the serious crimes referred to in [Article 1F of the Geneva Convention]. In that regard, the [Raad van State] has expressly taken into account the fact that, as it has already held in its judgment of 17 December 1992, Article 1F of the Geneva Convention must be narrowly construed.

The [Raad van State] considers accordingly that the [State Secretary] was not entitled to conclude, on the basis of the abovementioned evidence, that the [applicant] should be denied the protection afforded by the [Geneva] Convention."

57   The Raad van State also held that the applicant had sound reasons to fear that he would be persecuted if he was sent back to the Philippines and that he should accordingly be treated as a refugee for the purposes of Article 1(A)(2) of the Geneva Convention.

58   The Raad van State then considered the merits of the State Secretary's alternative reason for refusing the applicant admission to the Netherlands on

grounds of public interest, on the basis of the second paragraph of Article 15 of the Netherlands Law on Aliens.

59   In that regard, the Raad van State held in particular as follows:
     "While the [Raad van State] acknowledges the importance of the [State Secretary's] concern, particularly in view of the indications he has recorded of personal contacts between the [applicant] and representatives of terrorist organisations, that cannot justify recourse to the second paragraph of Article 15 of the Law on Aliens if there is no guarantee that the [applicant] will be permitted to enter a country other than the Philippines. It is precluded by the fact that such a refusal to admit the [applicant] must be regarded as being contrary to Article 3 of the European Convention for the Protection of Human Rights and Fundamental Freedoms."

60   Following that judgment, the State Secretary, by decision of 4 June 1996, again rejected the applicant's request for review of his decision of 13 July 1990. He ordered the applicant to leave the Netherlands, but decided at the same time that the applicant should not be deported to the Philippines for so long as he had a well-founded fear of being persecuted within the meaning of the Geneva Convention or of treatment contrary to Article 3 of the European Convention for the Protection of Human Rights and Fundamental Freedoms ("the ECHR").

61   By decision of 11 September 1997...[the Rechtbank] dismissed the action brought by the applicant against the State Secretary's decision of 4 June 1996 on the basis that it was unfounded.

62   In the course of the proceedings before the Rechtbank, all the documents relating to the investigation carried out by the BVD into the applicant's activities in the Netherlands, and in particular the letter from that organisation to the State Secretary of 3 March 1993 (paragraph 51 above), as well as the operational material on which that letter is based, were produced in confidence to the Rechtbank. The President of the Rechtbank examined them under a special procedure. On the basis of the report prepared by its President, the Rechtbank decided that the restriction on making those documents available to the applicant was justified. As the latter had given the consent to that effect required by the legislation, the Rechtbank none the less took account of the content of those documents in order to decide the case.

63   The Rechtbank then considered whether the decision contested before it could be upheld, in so far as it refused the applicant admission as a refugee and the granting to him of a residence permit.

64   With regard to the facts on which the decision was based, the Rechtbank referred back to the judgment of the Raad van State of 1995.

65   On the basis of that judgment, the Rechtbank considered that it must be regarded as settled in law that Article 1F of the Geneva Convention could not be invoked against the applicant, that the latter had a well-founded fear of being persecuted within the meaning of Article 1A of that Convention and of Article 15 of the Netherlands Law on Aliens and that Article 3 of the

ECHR prevented the applicant from being deported, directly or indirectly, to his country of origin.

66 The Rechtbank next considered the question whether the judgment of the Raad van State of 1995 entitled the State Secretary to refuse the applicant admission as a refugee, pursuant to the second paragraph of Article 15 of the Netherlands Law on Aliens, which provides that "admission can be refused only on important grounds of public interest if that refusal would compel the alien to go immediately to a country referred to in the first paragraph", when the State Secretary had failed to guarantee the applicant admission to a country other than the Philippines.

67 In that regard the Rechtbank quoted in full the paragraph of the judgment of the Raad van State of 1995 set out in paragraph 59 above.

68 The Rechtbank then ruled on the question whether the State Secretary had properly exercised his power to derogate from the rule that an alien is normally to be admitted to the Netherlands as a refugee where he can establish a well-founded fear of being persecuted within the meaning of Article 1A of the Geneva Convention and no other country will admit him as an asylum seeker, as, in the Rechtbank's opinion, was the position in that case. In that regard, the Rechtbank held as follows:

"In the opinion of the Rechtbank, it cannot be argued that the [State Secretary] has not used this power reasonably in respect of the [applicant], taking into account the 'essential interests of the Netherlands State, namely the integrity and credibility of the Netherlands as a sovereign State, particularly with regard to its responsibilities towards other States', also recognised by the [Raad van State]. The facts on which the [Raad van State] based that assessment are also of overriding importance as far as the Rechtbank is concerned. It has not been shown that a different significance should have been attributed to those facts by the [State Secretary] at the time the decision [at issue in the case] was taken. The [applicant's] observations on the changed political situation in the Philippines and on his role in the negotiations between the Philippine authorities and the [CPP] do not affect that, since the important reasons—as is clear from the judgment of the [Raad van State]—are based on other facts."

69 The Rechtbank accordingly dismissed as unfounded the applicant's appeal against the refusal to admit him to the Netherlands as a refugee.

70 The Rechtbank also dismissed as unfounded the applicant's challenge to the refusal to grant him a residence permit. Ruling more particularly on the question whether the State Secretary had taken his decision after a reasonable weighing up of interests, the Rechtbank referred to its findings quoted in paragraph 68 above and added that the State Secretary had acted reasonably in attaching less weight to the interests invoked by the applicant in that regard.'

107. Having regard to their content, significance and context, the Court considers that neither the judgment of the Raad van State of 1995 nor the decision of the Rechtbank constitutes a decision taken by a competent authority within the

meaning of Article 1(4) of Common Position 2001/931 and of Article 2(3) of Regulation No 2580/2001.

108. On the one hand, that judgment and that decision contain no evidence at all of any 'condemnation' [sic] of the applicant, within the meaning of those provisions.

109. Nor, on the other hand, do that judgment and that decision constitute decisions for the 'instigation of investigations or prosecution for a terrorist act' etc., within the meaning of those provisions.

110. It should be borne in mind that, in determining the purport of a provision of Community law, its wording, context and objectives must all be taken into account (see Case C-280/04 *Jyske Finans* [2005] ECR I-10683, paragraph 34 and the case-law cited).

111. The Court considers that, having regard both to the wording, context and objectives of the provisions at issue in this case (see, especially, the first recital in the preamble to Common Position 2001/931) and to the major part played by the national authorities in the fund-freezing process provided for in Article 2(3) of Regulation No 2580/2001 (see *Sison*, paragraph 164 et seq.), a decision to 'instigat[e] ... investigations or prosecut[e]' must, if the Council is to be able validly to invoke it, form part of national proceedings seeking, directly and chiefly, the imposition on the person concerned of measures of a preventive or punitive nature, in connection with the combating of terrorism and by reason of that person's involvement in terrorism. That requirement is not satisfied by a decision of a national judicial authority ruling only incidentally and indirectly on the possible involvement of the person concerned in such activity, in relation to a dispute concerning, for example, rights and duties of a civil nature.

112. That narrow interpretation of the concept of 'instigation of investigations or prosecution' is confirmed, in particular, by the various language versions of Article 1(4) of Common Position 2001/931.

113. In the present case, the applicant correctly emphasises that the procedures before the Raad van State and the Rechtbank were in no way directed at punishing his possible participation in past acts of terrorism, but were solely concerned with the review of the lawfulness of the decision of the Secretary of State for Justice refusing to grant him refugee status and a residence permit in the Netherlands, principally on the basis of Article 1F of the Geneva Convention or, alternatively, on the basis of the second subparagraph of Article 15 of the Vreemdelingenwet.

114. While it is true that the Raad van State and the Rechtbank, in the course of those procedures, studied the file of the Netherlands internal security service ('the BVD') relating to the applicant's alleged involvement in certain terrorist activities in the Philippines, they did not decide for that reason to open an investigation into those facts, still less to instigate a prosecution against the applicant.

115. It follows that the judgment of the Raad van State of 1995 and the decision of the Rechtbank could not be considered to satisfy the requirements of Article 1(4) of Common Position 2001/931 and could not, accordingly, alone justify the adoption of a decision to freeze the applicant's funds pursuant to Article 2(3) of Regulation No 2580/2001.

116. In any event, it is to be stressed that the Council, when contemplating adopting or maintaining, after review, a fund-freezing measure pursuant to Regulation No 2580/2001, on the basis of a national decision for the 'instigation of investigations or prosecution' for an act of terrorism, may not disregard subsequent developments arising out of those investigations or that prosecution (see, to that effect, *PMOI I* and *PMOI II*). It may thus happen that police or security enquiries are closed without giving rise to any judicial consequences, because it proved impossible to gather sufficient evidence, or that measures of investigation ordered by the investigating judge do not lead to proceedings going to judgment for the same reasons. Similarly, a decision to prosecute may end in the abandoning of the prosecution or in acquittal in the criminal proceedings. It would be unacceptable for the Council not to take account of such matters, which form part of the body of information having to be taken into account in order to assess the situation (see paragraph 98 above). To decide otherwise would be tantamount to giving the Council and the Member States the excessive power to freeze a person's funds indefinitely, beyond review by any court and whatever the result of any judicial proceedings taken.

117. In the circumstances of the case, account must also be taken of the Raad van State and the Rechtbank's evaluation of the seriousness and credibility of the evidence or factors gathered by the BVD in the course of its enquiries. It is not obvious that that evaluation supports the approach followed by the Council and the Netherlands. It is true that those judicial bodies regarded as 'plausible enough' or as 'giving a factual basis for...the Secretary of State's view' certain information in the BVD file, particularly in connection with the allegations that the applicant had 'at least attempted to direct the [terrorist] activities carried out under the control of the NPA in the Philippines' and the allegations relating to the 'personal contacts' that he had supposedly maintained with representatives of terrorist organisations throughout the world. However, those judicial bodies considered, ultimately, that the evidence in question 'd[id] not provide support for the conclusion that the [applicant had] directed the operations in question and [wa]s responsible for them to such an extent that it may be held that there [we]re serious reasons to suppose that the [applicant] ha[d] actually committed...serious crimes' as referred to in Article 1(F) of the Geneva Convention. Furthermore, although the Rechtbank accepted the Secretary of State's alternative argument that he could refuse to allow the applicant into the Netherlands as a refugee and to issue him with a residence permit for reasons relating to the public interest, on the basis of the second subparagraph of Article 15 of the Vreemdelingenwet, the applicant has rightly noted that the concept of 'public interest' under that provision, especially the integrity and credibility of the Netherlands as a sovereign State, particularly with regard to its responsibilities towards other States, hardly corresponds to the criterion of 'terrorism' used by the Council in Common Position 2001/931 and in Regulation No 2580/2001.

118. But there is still more, for it is clear from the file before the Court that, on the basis of information gathered by the BVD, the Netherlands prosecuting authority considered that there was no evidence justifying the opening in the Netherlands of a criminal investigation relating to the applicant.

119. The latter puts forward, to that effect, an official statement made by the Netherlands Minister for Foreign Affairs at that time, Mr J. de Hoop Scheffer, in reply to a parliamentary question put on 16 August 2002 in the following terms: 'Have the Netherlands conducted an independent investigation into the accusations of terrorism [made against the CPP, the NPA and Mr Sison]? If so, how long ago and in what form?' Answering that question, Mr de Hoop Scheffer informed the Dutch Parliament (Tweede Kamer der Staten-Generaal) on 8 October 2002 that:
'The Netherlands have conducted an investigation into the activities of the CPP [and of the] NPA and of Mr Sison in the Netherlands. That is apparent from the 2001 annual report of the [BVD, which has in the meantime become the Algemene Inlichtingen- en Veiligsheidsdienst or AIVD (General Information and Security Service)]...On the basis, in particular, of AIVD evidence that the CPP [and the] NPA [are] guided from the Netherlands, enquiries were made, under the supervision of the prosecuting authority, to ascertain whether there was sufficient evidence to warrant opening a criminal investigation. It was clear that such was not the case.'

120. Thus, it has been declared officially that, on 8 October 2002, that is to say, less than three weeks before the applicant was first included in the list at issue on 28 October 2002, the prosecuting authority, stated by the Kingdom of the Netherlands at the hearing to be an independent judicial authority, considered that the BVD and AIVD file did not contain evidence or information sufficiently serious to warrant the opening of criminal investigations into or prosecutions of the applicant in the Netherlands in respect of an act of terrorism relating to his involvement in the activities of the CPP and/or the NPA.

121. In those circumstances, and on any view, the Court considers that neither the judgment of the Raad van State of 1995 nor the decision of the Rechtbank could be considered, at the date on which the contested decisions were adopted, to satisfy the requirements of Article 1(4) of Common Position 2001/931. They could not, therefore, lawfully justify the adoption at that date of the decisions in question, pursuant to Article 2(3) of Regulation No 2580/2001.

122. Having regard to all the foregoing considerations, it is appropriate to reject the applicant's complaints alleging an error, indeed, even a manifest error, in the assessment of the facts, while allowing, so far as it concerns the judgment of the Raad van State of 1995 and the decision of the Rechtbank, his principal complaint that the legal conditions laid down in Article 2(3) of Regulation No 2580/2001 and in Article 1(4) of Common Position 2001/931 have not been satisfied.

123. In the light of what has been set out in paragraphs 100 to 105 above, the acknowledgement that that complaint is well founded cannot but bring about the annulment of Decisions 2007/445 and 2007/868, in so far as they concern the applicant, and there is, therefore, no need to examine the other pleas in law raised by him.

[...]

133. It is to be borne in mind that the judgments of the Rechtbank of 13 September 2007 and of the Court of Appeal of the Hague of 3 October 2007 constitute decisions taken in connection with a preliminary criminal investigation instigated with respect to the applicant in the Netherlands on 28 August 2007 for

taking part in, or inciting the commission of, certain murders or attempted murders in the Philippines in 2003 and 2004, following internal dissension in the CPP.

134. None the less, it has not been established, or even alleged, that those murders or attempted murders, even if they could be ascribed to the applicant, may be regarded as acts of terrorism, for the purpose of Article 1(3) of Common Position 2001/931.

135. The inevitable conclusion is thus that the judgments of the Rechtbank of 13 September 2007 and of the Court of Appeal of the Hague of 3 October 2007 do not satisfy the requirements of Article 1(4) of Common Position 2001/931 any more than do the judgment of the Raad van State of 1995 and the decision of the Rechtbank.

136. Irrespective of the action taken with regard to the preliminary criminal investigation in question, and in particular of the decision of the rechter-commissaris of 21 November 2007 closing that investigation for want of serious evidence, those two judgments cannot, therefore, on any view constitute legal justification for the adoption of the decisions and the regulation contested pursuant to Article 2(3) of Regulation No 2580/2001.

137. Moreover, as the Council has stated in its written pleadings and as it expressly confirmed at the hearing, the judgments of the Rechtbank of 13 September 2007 and of the Court of Appeal of the Hague of 3 October 2007 were not invoked in the statements of reasons annexed to its letters of 25 February, 29 April and 15 July 2008 and of 27 January 2009 as decisions of competent authorities for the purpose of Article 1(4) of Common Position 2001/931, but as matters of fact intended as corroboration of the findings made by the Raad van State in its judgment of 1995 and by the Rechtbank in its decision, concerning the applicant's continuing involvement in the CPP and the NPA. The same must be found in respect of the statement of reasons annexed to the Council's letter of 16 June 2009.

138. Having regard to what has been set out above, in connection with the examination of the second plea for annulment of Decisions 2007/445 and 2007/868, those considerations cannot but bring about the annulment of Decisions 2008/343, 2008/583 and 2009/62 and also of Regulation No 501/2009, in so far as they concern the applicant, and there is no need to examine the other pleas in law raised by him.

Judgment of the Court (Grand Chamber) of 21 December 2011 (Appeal), French Republic v People's Mojahedin Organization of Iran, Case C-27/09 P, not yet reported, paras. 59–76.

Findings of the Court

59. At paragraphs 36 and 37 of the judgment under appeal, the General Court held that, by adopting the contested decision without first informing the PMOI of the new information or new material in the file which, in its view, justified maintaining

it in the list referred to in Article 2(3) of Regulation No 2580/2001 and, *a fortiori*, by failing to give it the opportunity of making known to advantage its views on the matter, the Council breached the principles relating to the observance of the rights of the defence set forth, in particular, in paragraphs 120, 126 and 131 of *Organisation des Modjahedines du peuple d'Iran v Council*.

60. The principles thus referred to by the General Court, and not challenged by the French Republic, may also be found in the Court of Justice's case-law (see, in connection with Council Regulation (EC) No 881/2002 of 27 May 2002 imposing certain specific restrictive measures directed against certain persons and entities associated with Usama bin Laden, the Al-Qaida network and the Taliban, and repealing Council Regulation (EC) No 467/2001 prohibiting the export of certain goods and services to Afghanistan, strengthening the flight ban and extending the freeze of funds and other financial resources in respect of the Taliban of Afghanistan (OJ 2002 L 139, p. 9), *Kadi and Al Barakaat v Council and Commission*, paragraphs 338 to 341).

61. It is to be borne in mind that, in the case of an initial decision to freeze funds, the Council is not obliged to inform the person or entity concerned beforehand of the grounds on which that institution intends to rely in order to include that person or entity's name in the list referred to in Article 2(3) of Regulation No 2580/2001. So that its effectiveness may not be jeopardised, such a measure must be able to take advantage of a surprise effect and to apply immediately. In such a case, it is as a rule enough if the institution notifies the person or entity concerned of the grounds and affords it the right to be heard at the same time as, or immediately after, the decision is adopted.

62. In contrast, in the case of a subsequent decision to freeze funds by which the inclusion of the name of a person or entity already appearing in the list referred to in Article 2(3) of Regulation No 2580/2001 is maintained, that surprise effect is no longer necessary in order to ensure that the measure is effective, with the result that the adoption of such a decision must, in principle, be preceded by notification of the incriminating evidence and by allowing the person or entity concerned an opportunity of being heard.

63. In the judgment under appeal, the General Court applied those principles to the facts of the case and rightly concluded that, given that the PMOI's name had been maintained, by the contested decision, in the list referred to in Article 2(3) of Regulation No 2580/2001, a list in which it had appeared ever since its original inclusion on 3 May 2002 pursuant to Decision 2002/334, the Council might not, as it did in that case, communicate the new incriminating evidence against the PMOI at the same time as it adopted the contested decision. The Council was bound, imperatively, to ensure that the PMOI's rights of defence were observed, that is to say, notification of the incriminating evidence against it and the right to be heard, before that decision was adopted.

64. In this regard, it is to be stressed, as the Advocate General did in point 103 of her Opinion, that the element of protection afforded by the requirement of notification of incriminating evidence and the right to make representations before the adoption of a measure, such as the contested decision, that sets in motion the

application of restrictive measures is fundamental and essential to the rights of defence. This is all the more the case because such measures have a considerable effect on the rights and freedoms of the persons and groups concerned.

65. The purpose of the rule that the addressee of a decision affecting him adversely must be placed in a position to submit his observations before that decision is adopted is to enable the authority concerned effectively to take into account all relevant information. In order to ensure that the addressee is in fact protected, the object of that rule is, in particular, to enable him to correct an error or produce such information relating to his personal circumstances as will tell in favour of the decision's being adopted or not, or of its having this content or that (see, to this effect, Case C-349/07 *Sopropé* [2008] ECR I-10369, paragraph 49).

66. That right, fundamental to observance of the rights of defence during a procedure preceding the adoption of a restrictive measure such as the contested decision, is moreover expressly affirmed in Article 41(2)(a) of the Charter of Fundamental Rights of the European Union, recognised by Article 6(1) TEU as having the same legal value as the Treaties.

67. If, as has been noted at paragraph 61 above, an exception to that fundamental right has been allowed with regard to initial decisions to freeze funds, that is justified by the need to ensure that the freezing measures are effective and, in short, by overriding considerations to do with safety or the conduct of the international relations of the Union and of its Member States (see, to this effect, *Kadi and Al Barakaat International Foundation* v *Council and Commission*, paragraph 342).

68. In paragraphs 39 to 44 of the judgment under appeal, the General Court nevertheless considered the Council's argument that that institution was justified in communicating the new incriminating evidence against the PMOI at the same time as the contested decision was adopted and not before, despite the fact that it was not an initial decision to freeze funds, because of the particular situation in which the Council found itself in that case, more specifically, the urgency with which the contested decision had to be adopted.

69. That line of argument is in substance repeated by the French Republic in this appeal.

70. The General Court held, first, that as of 7 May 2008, the date on which the Court of Appeal delivered its judgment, it became once and for all impossible for the Council to rely on the order of the Home Secretary of 28 March 2001 as a decision of a competent authority for the purpose of Article 1(4) of Common Position 2001/931 in order to maintain the inclusion of the PMOI in the list referred to in Article 2(3) of Regulation No 2580/2001. In addition, by order of 23 June 2008, which entered into force the following day, the Home Secretary acted on that judgment, striking the PMOI's name from the list of organisations proscribed under the Terrorism Act 2000.

71. Secondly, it is not disputed that on 9 June 2008 the Council received from the French Republic new information relating to legal proceedings brought in France against alleged members of the PMOI, which that Member State considered could warrant the continued inclusion of the organisation in the list referred to in Article 2(3) of Regulation No 2580/2001.

72. It must be pointed out here that the Council had, therefore, within a very short period of time, to examine that new material in order to decide whether it could constitute the decision of a competent authority for the purpose of Article 1(4) of Common Position 2001/931 in order to justify the continued inclusion of the PMOI in that list or whether that group must be removed forthwith from the list.

73. While it is indeed true, as the French Republic has maintained, that, at the very least as from 24 June 2008, the Council could not possibly allow a situation to continue in which Decision 2007/868 lacked any basis, but had as soon as possible to take appropriate action, the fact nevertheless remains, as indeed that Member State accepts and as the General Court rightly pointed out at paragraph 42 of the judgment under appeal, that neither the judgment of the Court of Appeal nor the Home Secretary's order of 23 June 2008 had an automatic, immediate effect on Decision 2007/868, then applicable.

74. In fact, that latter decision remained in force by reason of the presumption that acts of the institutions of the European Union are lawful, which, according to the Court's settled case-law, means that those acts produce legal effects until such time as they are withdrawn, annulled in an action for annulment or declared invalid following a reference for a preliminary ruling or a plea of illegality (see, inter alia, Case C-199/06 *CELF and Ministre de la Culture et de la Communication* [2008] ECR I-469, paragraph 60 and case-law cited).

75. In consequence, having regard too to the fundamental importance that must attach, as indicated in paragraphs 64 and 65 above, to observance of the rights of the defence in the procedure preceding the adoption of a decision such as the contested decision, the General Court did not err in law in holding, at paragraphs 39 and 43 of the judgment under appeal, that the Council had not established that the contested decision had so urgently to be adopted that it was impossible for that institution to notify the PMOI of the new evidence adduced against it and to allow the PMOI to be heard before the contested decision was adopted.

76. It follows from all those considerations that the first ground of appeal is unfounded.

6.5 Sanctions against third states and natural or legal persons and groups or non-state entities

EU sanctions against third states and natural or legal persons and groups or non-state entities can constitute the implementation of a UN Security Council resolution or are completely autonomous in nature.[13] The 2010 Council decision and regulation imposing sanctions against Somalia are included here since they put into force in the EU legal order restrictive measures previously mandated by the UN Security Council,

---

[13] Sanctions against the Democratic Republic of Congo, Ivory Coast, Eritrea, Haiti, Iran, Iraq, the Democratic People's Republic of Korea, Lebanon, Liberia, Libya, Somalia, and South Sudan have been mandated by UN Security Council resolutions. On the contrary, sanctions against Belarus, Bosnia and Herzegovina, China, Egypt, the Republic of Guinea, Moldova, Myanmar, Syria, Tunisia, the USA (see Section 6.8), Serbia, and Zimbabwe have been autonomously imposed by the EU.

while striving to take account of the Court's judgment in the *Kadi* case.[14] It is important to note that in the case of sanctions adopted in implementation of UN Security
Council resolutions, reference must be made to the relevant resolution, as is the case
in the included documents below. However, nothing prevents the Union from applying sanctions that go beyond or are stricter than those foreseen by the UN Security
Council resolution. Although they belong to this category, the sanctions against Iran
are discussed in a separate section below since they are further informed by the work
of informal fora, such as the Nuclear Suppliers Group and the MTCR. Finally, a significant part of the Judgment of the Court of Justice of the EU in the *Bosphorus v. Ireland*
case of the 1990s is also included here. In that case, the Court assessed and confirmed
the legality of sanctions imposed on the Federal Republic of Yugoslavia in light of the
obligation of the EU to safeguard fundamental rights, such as the right to property and
the right to exercise a commercial activity.

Council Decision 2010/231/CFSP of 26 April 2010 concerning restrictive measures against Somalia and repealing Common Position 2009/138/CFSP, Official Journal L 105, 27.4.2010, pp. 17–21.[15]

THE COUNCIL OF THE EUROPEAN UNION,

Having regard to the Treaty on European Union, and in particular Article 29 thereof,

Whereas:

(1) On 10 December 2002, the Council adopted Common Position 2002/960/CFSP
concerning restrictive measures against Somalia following United Nations Security
Council Resolutions (UNSCR) 733 (1992), 1356 (2001) and 1425 (2002) relating to an
arms embargo against Somalia.

(2) On 16 February 2009, the Council adopted Common Position 2009/138/CFSP
concerning restrictive measures against Somalia and repealing Common Position
2002/960/CFSP, implementing UNSCR 1844 (2008) which introduced restrictive measures against those who seek to prevent or block a peaceful political process, or those
who threaten the Transitional Federal Institutions (TFIs) of Somalia or the African
Union Mission in Somalia (AMISOM) by force, or take action that undermines stability in Somalia or in the region.

(3) On 1 March 2010, the Council adopted Council Decision 2010/126/CFSP amending Common Position 2009/138/CFSP and implementing UNSCR 1907 (2009) which
called upon all States to inspect, in accordance with their national authorities and

---

[14] On the other hand, Council Decision 2011/782/CFSP of 1 December 2011 concerning restrictive
measures against Syria and repealing Decision 2011/273/CFSP, OJ L 319, 2.12.2011, pp. 56–70, and Council
Regulation (EU) No. 36/2012 of 18 January 2012 concerning restrictive measures in view of the situation in
Syria and repealing Regulation (EU) No. 442/201, OJ L 16, 19.1.2012, pp. 1–32, constitute prime examples
of sanctions imposed autonomously by the EU.

[15] As amended by Council Decision 2011/635/CFSP of 26 September 2011 amending Decision 2010/231/
CFSP concerning restrictive measures against Somalia, OJ L 249, 27.9.2011, pp. 12–17.

legislation and consistent with international law, all cargoes to and from Somalia, in their territory, including seaports and airports, if the State concerned has information that provides reasonable grounds to believe that the cargo contains items whose supply, sale, transfer or export is prohibited under the general and complete arms embargo to Somalia established pursuant to paragraph 5 of UNSCR 733 (1992) and elaborated and amended by subsequent resolutions.

(4) On 19 March 2010, the United Nations Security Council (hereinafter referred to as the 'Security Council') adopted UNSCR 1916 (2010) which, inter alia, extended the mandate of the monitoring group referred to in paragraph 3 of UNSCR 1558 (2004) and decided to ease some restrictions and obligations under the sanctions regime to enable the delivery of supplies and technical assistance by international, regional and sub-regional organisations and to ensure the timely delivery of urgently needed humanitarian assistance by the United Nations (UN).

(5) On 12 April 2010, the Sanctions Committee established by paragraph 11 of UNSCR 751 (1992) concerning Somalia (hereinafter referred to as the 'Sanctions Committee') adopted the list of persons and entities which are subject to restrictive measures.

(6) For the sake of clarity, the measures imposed by Common Position 2009/138/CFSP as amended by Council Decision 2010/126/CFSP and the exemptions provided for in UNSCR 1916 (2010) should be integrated into a single legal instrument.

(7) Common Position 2009/138/CFSP should therefore be repealed.

(8) This Decision respects the fundamental rights and observes the principles recognised in particular by the Charter of Fundamental Rights of the European Union and notably the right to an effective remedy and to a fair trial, the right to property and the right to the protection of personal data. This Decision should be applied in accordance with those rights and principles.

(9) This Decision also fully respects the obligations of Member States under the Charter of the United Nations and the legally binding nature of Security Council Resolutions.

(10) The procedure for amending the Annex to this Decision should include providing to designated persons and entities the reasons for their listing as transmitted by the Sanctions Committee, so as to give them an opportunity to present observations. Where observations are submitted or where substantial new evidence is presented, the Council should review its decision in the light of those observations and inform the person or entity concerned accordingly.

(11) Further action by the Union is needed in order to implement certain measures,

HAS ADOPTED THIS DECISION:

Article 1

1. The direct or indirect supply, sale or transfer of arms and related material of all types, including weapons and ammunition, military vehicles and equipment, paramilitary equipment and spare parts for the aforementioned to Somalia by nationals of Member States or from the territories of Member States shall be prohibited whether originating or not in their territories.

2. The direct or indirect supply to Somalia of technical advice, financial and other assistance and training related to military activities, including in particular technical

training and assistance related to the provision, manufacture, maintenance or use of the items mentioned in paragraph 1, by nationals of Member States or from the territories of the Member States, shall be prohibited.

3. Paragraphs 1 and 2 shall not apply to:

(a) the supply, sale or transfer of arms and related material of all types and the direct or indirect supply of technical advice, financial and other assistance and training related to military activities intended solely for the support of or use by AMISOM as stipulated in paragraph 4 of UNSCR 1744 (2007) or for the sole use of States and regional organisations undertaking measures in accordance with paragraph 6 of UNSCR 1851 (2008) and paragraph 10 of UNSCR 1846 (2008);

(b) the supply, sale or transfer of arms and related material of all types and to the direct or indirect supply of technical advice intended solely for the purpose of helping to develop security sector institutions, consistent with the political process set out in paragraphs 1, 2 and 3 of UNSCR 1744 (2007) and in the absence of a negative decision by the Sanctions Committee within five working days of receiving the relevant notification;

(c) the supply, sale or transfer of non-lethal military equipment intended solely for humanitarian or protective use, or of material intended for institution building programmes of the Union, or Member States, including in the field of security, carried out within the framework of the Peace and reconciliation Process, as approved in advance by the Sanctions Committee, and to protective clothing, including flak jackets and military helmets, temporarily exported to Somalia by UN personnel, representatives of the media and humanitarian and development workers and associated personnel for their personal use only.

Article 2

Restrictive measures as provided for in Articles 3, 5(1) and 6(1) and (2) shall be imposed against persons and entities designated by the Sanctions Committee as:

— engaging in or providing support for acts that threaten the peace, security or stability of Somalia, including acts that threaten the Djibouti Agreement of 18 August 2008 or the political process, or threaten the TFIs or AMISOM by force,

— having acted in violation of the arms embargo and related measures as referred to in Article 1,

— obstructing the delivery of humanitarian assistance to Somalia, or access to, or distribution of, humanitarian assistance in Somalia,

— being political or military leaders recruiting or using children in armed conflicts in Somalia in violation of applicable international law,

— being responsible for violations of applicable international law in Somalia involving the targeting of civilians including children and women in situations of armed conflict, including killing and maiming, sexual and gender-based violence, attacks on schools and hospitals and abduction and forced displacement.

The relevant persons and entities are listed in the Annex.

Article 3

Member States shall take the necessary measures to prevent the direct and indirect supply, sale or transfer of weapons and military equipment and the direct or indirect supply of technical assistance or training, financial and other assistance including investment, brokering or other financial services, related to military activities or to the supply, sale, transfer, manufacture, maintenance or use of weapons and military equipment, to persons or entities referred to in Article 2.

Article 4

1. Member States shall inspect, in accordance with their national authorities and legislation and consistent with international law, all cargo to and from Somalia in their territory, including at their airports and seaports, if they have information that provides reasonable grounds to believe that the cargo contains items the supply, sale, transfer or export of which is prohibited under Article 3.

2. Aircrafts and vessels transporting cargo to and from Somalia shall be subject to the requirement of additional pre-arrival or pre-departure information for all goods brought into or out of a Member State.

3. Member States shall, upon discovery, seize and dispose of (either by destroying or rendering inoperable) items the supply, sale, transfer or export of which is prohibited under Article 3.

Article 5

1. Member States shall take the necessary measures to prevent the entry into, or transit through, their territories of the persons referred to in Article 2.

2. Paragraph 1 shall not oblige a Member State to refuse its own nationals entry into its territory.

3. Paragraph 1 shall not apply where the Sanctions Committee:

(a) determines on a case-by-case basis that such entry or transit is justified on the grounds of humanitarian need, including religious obligation,

(b) determines on a case-by-case basis that an exemption would otherwise further the objectives of peace and national reconciliation in Somalia and stability in the region.

4. In cases where, pursuant to paragraph 3, a Member State authorises the entry into, or transit through, its territory of persons designated by the Sanctions Committee, the authorisation shall be limited to the purpose for which it is given and to the persons concerned thereby.

Article 6

1. All funds and economic resources owned or controlled directly or indirectly by the persons or entities referred to in Article 2 or held by entities owned or controlled directly or indirectly by them or by any persons or entities acting on their behalf or at their direction, as designated by the Sanctions Committee, shall be frozen. The persons and entities concerned are identified in the Annex.

2. No funds or economic resources shall be made available, directly or indirectly, to or for the benefit of the persons or entities referred to in paragraph 1.

3. Member States may allow for exemptions from the measures referred to in paragraphs 1 and 2 in respect of funds and economic resources which are:

(a) necessary for basic expenses, including payments for foodstuffs, rent or mortgage, medicines and medical treatment, taxes, insurance premiums, and public utility charges;

(b) intended exclusively for the payment of reasonable professional fees and reimbursement of incurred expenses associated with the provision of legal services;

(c) intended exclusively for the payment of fees or service charges, in accordance with national laws, for routine holding or maintenance of frozen funds and economic resources;

(d) necessary for extraordinary expenses, after notification by the Member State concerned to, and approval by, the Sanctions Committee;

(e) the subject of a judicial, administrative or arbitral lien or judgment, in which case the funds and economic resources may be used to satisfy that lien or judgment provided that the lien or judgment was entered before designation by the Sanctions Committee of the person or entity concerned, and is not for the benefit of a person or entity referred to in Article 2, after notification by the Member State concerned to the Sanctions Committee.

4. The exemptions referred to in paragraph 3(a), (b) and (c) may be made after notification to the Sanctions Committee by the Member State concerned of its intention to authorise, where appropriate, access to such funds and economic resources, and in the absence of a negative decision by the Sanctions Committee within three working days of such notification.

5. Paragraph 2 shall not apply to the addition to frozen accounts of:

(a) interest or other earnings on those accounts; or

(b) payments due under contracts, agreements or obligations that were concluded or arose before the date on which those accounts became subject to restrictive measures, provided that any such interest, other earnings and payments remain subject to paragraph 1.

6. Paragraphs 1 and 2 shall not apply to the making available of funds, other financial assets or economic resources necessary to ensure the timely delivery of urgently needed humanitarian assistance in Somalia, by the United Nations, its specialised agencies or programmes, humanitarian organisations having observer status with the United Nations General Assembly that provide humanitarian assistance, and their implementing partners, including bilaterally or multilaterally funded NGOs participating in the UN Consolidated Appeal for Somalia.

Article 7

The Council shall establish the list contained in the Annex and amend it in accordance with determinations made by either the Security Council or the Sanctions Committee.

Article 8

1. Where the Security Council or the Sanctions Committee lists a person or entity and has provided a statement of reasons for the designation, the Council shall include such person or entity in the Annex. The Council shall communicate its decision and the statement of reasons to the person or entity concerned, either directly, if the address is known, or through the publication of a notice, providing such person or entity an opportunity to present observations.

2. Where observations are submitted, or where substantial new evidence is presented, the Council shall review its decision and inform the person or entity accordingly.

Article 9

The Annex shall include, where available, information provided by the Security Council or by the Sanctions Committee necessary to identify the persons or entities concerned. With regard to persons, such information may include names including aliases, date and place of birth, nationality, passport and ID card numbers, gender, address, if known and function or profession. With regard to entities such information may include names, place and date of registration, registration number and place of business. The Annex shall also include the date of designation by the Security Council or by the Sanctions Committee.

Article 10

This Decision shall be reviewed, amended or repealed, as appropriate, in accordance with relevant decisions of the Security Council.

[...]

Council Regulation (EU) No 356/2010 of 26 April 2010 imposing certain specific restrictive measures directed against certain natural or legal persons, entities or bodies, in view of the situation in Somalia (consolidated version including the amendments of September 2011 and July 2012), Official Journal L 105, 27.4.2010, pp. 1–19.

THE COUNCIL OF THE EUROPEAN UNION,
Having regard to the Treaty on the Functioning of the European Union, and in particular Article 215 (1) and (2) thereof,
Having regard to Council Decision 2010/231/CFSP of 26 April 2010 concerning restrictive measures against Somalia and repealing Common Position 2009/138/CFSP,
Having regard to the joint proposal from the High Representative of the Union for Foreign Affairs and Security Policy and the European Commission,

Whereas:
(1) On 20 November 2008, the United Nations Security Council (hereinafter referred to as the 'Security Council'), acting under Chapter VII of the Charter of the United Nations, adopted Resolution 1844 (2008) confirming the general and complete arms embargo against Somalia imposed by the United Nations Security Council Resolution (UNSCR) 733 (1992) and introducing additional restrictive measures.
(2) The additional restrictive measures concern restrictions on admission and financial restrictive measures against individuals and entities designated by the Security Council or by the United Nations Sanctions Committee established pursuant to UNSCR 751 (1992) concerning Somalia (hereinafter referred to as the 'Sanctions Committee'). In addition to the general arms embargo, the Resolution introduces a specific prohibition on the direct and indirect supply, sale or transfer, of weapons and military equipment and a specific prohibition on the provision of related assistance and services, to individuals and entities listed by the Sanctions Committee.
(3) The restrictive measures are aimed at individuals and entities designated by the United Nations (UN) as engaging in or providing support for acts that threaten

the peace, security or stability of Somalia, including acts that threaten the Djibouti Agreement of 18 August 2008 or the political process, or threaten the Transitional Federal Institutions (TFIs) or the African Union Mission in Somalia (AMISOM) by force, as having acted in violation of the arms embargo and related measures, or as obstructing the delivery of humanitarian assistance to Somalia, or access to, or distribution of, humanitarian assistance in Somalia.

(4) On 16 February 2009, the Council of the European Union adopted Common Position 2009/138/CFSP concerning restrictive measures against Somalia which provides, inter alia, for financial restrictive measures concerning natural or legal persons, entities or bodies listed by the UN, as well as for a prohibition on the direct and indirect provision of assistance and services related to weapons and military equipment to such persons, entities or bodies.

(5) On 19 March 2010, the Security Council adopted UNSCR 1916 (2010) which, inter alia, decided to ease some restrictions and obligations under the sanctions regime to enable the delivery of supplies and technical assistance by international, regional and sub-regional organisations and to ensure the timely delivery of urgently needed humanitarian assistance by the UN.

(6) On 12 April 2010, the Sanctions Committee adopted the list of persons and entities which are subject to restrictive measures.

(7) On that basis, on 26 April 2010 the Council adopted Decision 2010/231/CFSP.

(8) These measures fall within the scope of the Treaty on the Functioning of the European Union and, therefore, notably with a view to ensuring their uniform application by economic operators in all Member States, an act of the Union is necessary in order to implement them as far as the Union is concerned.

(9) Council Regulation (EC) No 147/2003 of 27 January 2003 concerning certain restrictive measures in respect of Somalia imposed a general prohibition on the provision of technical advice, assistance, training, financing or financial assistance related to military activities, to any person, entity or body in Somalia. A new Council Regulation should be adopted to implement the measures concerning natural or legal persons, entities or bodies listed by the UN.

(10) This Regulation respects the fundamental rights and observes the principles recognised in particular by the Charter of Fundamental Rights of the European Union and notably the right to an effective remedy and to a fair trial, the right to property and the right to the protection of personal data. This Regulation should be applied in accordance with those rights and principles.

(11) This Regulation also fully respects the obligations of Member States under the Charter of the United Nations and the legally binding nature of Security Council Resolutions.

(12) The power to amend the list in Annex I to this Regulation should be exercised by the Council, in view of the specific threat to international peace and security in the region posed by the situation in Somalia and in order to ensure consistency with the process for amending and reviewing the Annex to Council Decision 2010/231/CFSP.

(13) The procedure for amending the list in Annex I to this Regulation should include providing to designated natural or legal persons, entities or bodies the reasons

for their listing as transmitted by the Sanctions Committee, so as to give them an opportunity to present observations. Where observations are submitted or substantial new evidence is presented, the Council should review its decision in the light of those observations and inform the person, entity or body concerned accordingly.

(14) In order to create maximum legal certainty within the Union, the names and other relevant data for identifying natural or legal persons, entities or bodies whose funds and economic resources are frozen in accordance with this Regulation should be published.

(15) Any processing of personal data of natural persons under this Regulation should respect Regulation (EC) No 45/2001 of the European Parliament and of the Council of 18 December 2000 on the protection of individuals with regard to the processing of personal data by the Community institutions and bodies and on the free movement of such data and Directive 95/46/EC of the European Parliament and of the Council of 24 October 1995 on the protection of individuals with regard to the processing of personal data and on the free movement of such data.

(16) Member States should determine the penalties applicable to infringements of the provisions of this Regulation. The penalties provided for should be proportionate, effective and dissuasive,

HAS ADOPTED THIS REGULATION:

Article 1

For the purposes of this Regulation, the following definitions shall apply:

(a) 'funds' means financial assets and benefits of every kind, including but not limited to:

(i) cash, cheques, claims on money, drafts, money orders and other payment instruments;

(ii) deposits with financial institutions or other entities, balances on accounts, debts and debt obligations;

(iii) publicly and privately traded securities and debt instruments, including stocks and shares, certificates representing securities, bonds, notes, warrants, debentures and derivatives contracts;

(iv) interest, dividends or other income on or value accruing from or generated by assets;

(v) credit, right of set-off, guarantees, performance bonds or other financial commitments;

(vi) letters of credit, bills of lading, bills of sale;

(vii) documents evidencing an interest in funds or financial resources;

(b) 'freezing of funds' means preventing any move, transfer, alteration, use of, access to, or dealing with funds in any way that would result in any change in their volume, amount, location, ownership, possession, character, destination or other change that would enable the funds to be used, including portfolio management;

(c) 'economic resources' means assets of every kind, whether tangible or intangible, movable or immovable, which are not funds but may be used to obtain funds, goods or services;

(d) 'freezing of economic resources' means preventing their use to obtain funds, goods or services in any way, including, but not limited to, by selling, hiring or mortgaging them;

(e) 'Sanctions Committee' means the Committee of the Security Council established pursuant to UNSCR 751 (1992) concerning Somalia;

(f) 'technical assistance' means any technical support related to repairs, development, manufacture, assembly, testing, maintenance, or any other technical service, and may take forms such as instruction, advice, training, transmission of working knowledge or skills or consulting services; including verbal forms of assistance;

(g) 'investment services' means:

(i) reception and transmission of orders in relation to one or more financial instruments;

(ii) execution of orders on behalf of clients;

(iii) dealing on own account;

(iv) portfolio management;

(v) investment advice;

(vi) underwriting of financial instruments and/or placing of financial instruments on a firm commitment basis;

(vii) placing of financial instruments without a firm commitment basis; or

(viii) operating of multilateral trading facilities,

provided that the activity relates to any of the financial instruments listed in Section C of Annex I to Directive 2004/39/EC of the European Parliament and of the Council of 21 April 2004 on markets in financial instruments;

(h) 'territory of the Union' means the territories to which the Treaties are applicable, under the conditions laid down in the Treaties;

(i) 'statement of reasons' means the publicly releasable portion of the statement of case and/or, where applicable, the narrative summary of reasons for listing as provided by the Sanctions Committee.

Article 2

1. All funds and economic resources belonging to, owned, held or controlled by natural or legal persons, entities, or bodies listed in Annex I, shall be frozen.

2. No funds or economic resources shall be made available, directly or indirectly, to or for the benefit of natural or legal persons, entities or bodies listed in Annex I.

3. Annex I shall consist of natural or legal persons, entities or bodies designated by the Security Council or the Sanctions Committee in accordance with UNSCR 1844 (2008) as:

(a) engaging in or providing support for acts that threaten the peace, security or stability of Somalia, including acts that threaten to infringe the Djibouti Agreement of 18 August 2008 or the political process, or threaten the TFIs or AMISOM by force;

(b) having acted in violation of the arms embargo and related measures as reaffirmed in paragraph 6 of UNSCR 1844 (2008);

(c) obstructing the delivery of humanitarian assistance to Somalia, or access to, or distribution of, humanitarian assistance in Somalia;

(d) being political or military leaders recruiting or using children in armed conflicts in Somalia in violation of the applicable international law; or

(e) being responsible for violations of applicable international law in Somalia involving the targeting of civilians, including children and women, in situations of armed conflict, including killing and maiming, sexual and gender-based violence, attacks on schools and hospitals and abduction and forced displacement.

4. The participation, knowingly and intentionally, in activities the object or effect of which is, directly or indirectly, to circumvent the measures referred to in paragraphs 1 and 2 shall be prohibited.

5. The prohibition set out in paragraph 2 shall not give rise to liability of any kind on the part of the natural or legal persons, entities or bodies which made funds or economic resources available, where they did not know, and had no reasonable cause to suspect, that their actions would infringe this prohibition.

Article 3

1. Article 2(2) shall not apply to the addition to frozen accounts of:
(a) interest or other earnings on those accounts; or
(b) payments due under contracts, agreements or obligations that were concluded or arose before the date on which the natural or legal person, entity or body referred to in Article 2 was designated by the Sanctions Committee or the Security Council,
provided that any such interest, other earnings and payments continue to be subject to Article 2(1).

2. Article 2(2) shall not prevent financial or credit institutions in the Union from crediting frozen accounts where they receive funds transferred to the account of a listed natural or legal person, entity or body, provided that any additions to such accounts will also be frozen. The financial or credit institution shall inform the competent authorities in the Member States, as indicated in the websites listed in Annex II, about such transactions without delay.

Article 4

1. Article 2(1) and (2) shall not apply to the making available of funds or economic resources necessary to ensure the timely delivery of urgently needed humanitarian assistance in Somalia by the UN, its specialised agencies or programmes, humanitarian organisations having observer status with the United Nations General Assembly that provide humanitarian assistance, and their implementing partners, including bilaterally or multilaterally funded NGOs participating in the UN Consolidated Appeal for Somalia.

2. The exemption set out in paragraph 1 shall not give rise to liability of any kind on the part of the natural or legal persons, entities or bodies which made funds or economic resources available, where they did not know, and had no reasonable cause to suspect, that their actions would not be covered by this exemption.

Article 5

1. By way of derogation from Article 2, the competent authorities in the Member States, as indicated in the websites listed in Annex II, may authorise, under such conditions as they deem appropriate, the release of certain frozen funds or economic resources, or the making available of certain funds or economic resources, if the following conditions are met:

(a) the competent authority concerned has determined that the funds or economic resources are:

(i) necessary to satisfy the basic needs of the persons listed in Annex I, and their dependent family members, including payments for foodstuffs, rent or mortgage, medicines and medical treatment, taxes, insurance premiums, and public utility charges;

(ii) intended exclusively for payment of reasonable professional fees and reimbursement of incurred expenses associated with the provision of legal services; or

(iii) intended exclusively for payment of fees or service charges for routine holding or maintenance of frozen funds or economic resources; and

(b) the Member State concerned has notified the Sanctions Committee of that determination and its intention to grant an authorisation, and the Sanctions Committee has not objected to that course of action within three working days of the notification.

2. By way of derogation from Article 2, the competent authorities in the Member States, as listed in Annex II, may authorise the release of certain frozen funds or economic resources or the making available of certain funds or economic resources, after having determined that these are necessary to cover extraordinary expenses, provided that the Sanctions Committee has been notified of this determination by the Member State concerned and that the determination has been approved by that Committee.

3. The relevant Member State shall inform the other Member States and the Commission of any authorisation granted under paragraphs 1 and 2.

Article 6

By way of derogation from Article 2, the competent authorities in the Member States, as indicated in the websites listed in Annex II, may authorise the release of certain frozen funds or economic resources, if the following conditions are met:

(a) the funds or economic resources are the subject of a judicial, administrative or arbitral lien established before the date on which the natural or legal person, entity or body referred to in Article 2 has been designated by the Sanctions Committee or the Security Council or of a judicial, administrative or arbitral judgment rendered prior to that date;

(b) the funds or economic resources will be used exclusively to satisfy claims secured by such a lien or recognised as valid in such a judgment, within the limits set by applicable laws and regulations governing the rights of persons having such claims;

(c) the lien or judgment is not for the benefit of a natural or legal person, entity or body listed in Annex I;

(d) the lien or judgment is not contrary to public policy in the Member State concerned; and

(e) the Sanctions Committee has been notified by the Member State of the lien or judgment.

Article 7

The freezing of funds and economic resources or the refusal to make funds or economic resources available, carried out in good faith on the basis that such action is in accordance with this Regulation, shall not give rise to liability of any kind on the part of the natural or legal person or entity implementing it, or its directors or employees, unless it is proved that the funds and economic resources were frozen as a result of negligence.

Article 8

1. It shall be prohibited to provide, directly or indirectly, any of the following to any natural or legal person, entity or body listed in Annex I:

(a) technical assistance related to military activities or to the supply, sale, transfer, manufacture, maintenance or use of goods and technology included in the Common Military List of the European Union;

(b) financing or financial assistance related to military activities or to the supply, sale, transfer, manufacture, maintenance or use of goods and technology included in the Common Military List of the European Union;

(c) investment services related to military activities or to the supply, sale, transfer, manufacture, maintenance or use of goods and technology included in the Common Military List of the European Union.

2. The participation knowingly and intentionally, in activities the object or effect of which is, directly or indirectly, to circumvent the prohibition referred to in paragraph 1 shall be prohibited.

3. The prohibition set out in paragraph 1(b) shall not give rise to liability of any kind on the part of the natural or legal persons, entities or bodies which provided financing or financial assistance, where they did not know, and had no reasonable cause to suspect, that their actions would infringe this prohibition.

Article 9

1. Without prejudice to the applicable rules concerning reporting, confidentiality and professional secrecy, natural or legal persons, entities or bodies shall:

(a) supply immediately the competent authorities, as indicated on the websites listed in Annex II for the country where they are resident or located, with any information which would facilitate compliance with this Regulation, such as accounts and amounts frozen in accordance with Article 2, and shall forward such information, directly or through these competent authorities, to the Commission; and

(b) cooperate with the competent authorities as indicated on the websites listed in Annex II in any verification of this information.

2. Any information provided or received in accordance with this Article shall be used only for the purposes for which it was provided or received.

Article 10

The Commission and Member States shall immediately inform each other of the measures taken under this Regulation and shall supply each other with any other relevant information at their disposal in connection with this Regulation, in particular information in respect of violation and enforcement problems and judgments handed down by national courts.

Article 11

The Commission shall be empowered to amend Annex II on the basis of information supplied by Member States.

Article 12

1. Where the Security Council or the Sanctions Committee lists a natural or legal person, entity or body and has provided a statement of reasons for the designation, the Council shall include such natural or legal person, entity or body in Annex I. The Council shall communicate its decision and the statement of reasons to the natural or legal person, entity or body concerned, either directly, if the address is known, or through the publication of a notice, providing such natural or legal person, entity or body an opportunity to present observations.

2. Where observations are submitted, or where substantial new evidence is presented, the Council shall review its decision and inform the person, entity or body accordingly.

Article 13

Where the UN decides to de-list a person, entity or body, or to amend the identifying data of a listed person, entity or body, the Council shall amend Annex I accordingly.

Article 14

Annex I shall include, where available, information provided by the Security Council or by the Sanctions Committee necessary to identify the natural or legal persons, entities or bodies concerned. With regard to natural persons, such information may include names including aliases, date and place of birth, nationality, passport and ID card numbers, gender, address, if known, and function or profession. With regard to legal persons, entities or bodies, such information may include names, place and date of registration, registration number and place of business. Annex I shall also include the date of designation by the Security Council or by the Sanctions Committee.

Article 15

1. Member States shall lay down the rules on penalties applicable to infringements of the provisions of this Regulation and shall take all measures necessary to ensure that they are implemented. The penalties provided for must be effective, proportionate and dissuasive.

2. Member States shall notify the Commission of those rules without delay after the entry into force of this Regulation and shall notify it of any subsequent amendment.

Article 16

1. Member States shall designate the competent authorities referred to in this Regulation and identify them in, or through, the websites listed in Annex II.

2. Member States shall notify the Commission of their competent authorities without delay after the entry into force of this Regulation, and shall notify it of any subsequent amendment thereto.

3. Where this Regulation sets out a requirement to notify, inform or otherwise communicate with the Commission, the address and other contact details to be used for such communication shall be those indicated in Annex II.

Article 17

This Regulation shall apply:

(a) within the territory of the Union, including its airspace;

(b) on board any aircraft or any vessel under the jurisdiction of a Member State;

(c) to any person inside or outside the territory of the Union who is a national of a Member State;

(d) to any legal person, entity or body which is incorporated or constituted under the law of a Member State;

(e) to any legal person, entity or body in respect of any business done in whole or in part within the Union.

Article 18

This Regulation shall enter into force on the day following that of its publication in the *Official Journal of the European Union.*

This Regulation shall be binding in its entirety and directly applicable in all Member States.

ANNEX I

LIST OF NATURAL AND LEGAL PERSONS, ENTITIES OR BODIES
REFERRED TO IN ARTICLES 2 AND 8

I. Persons

[...]

II. Entities

[...]

Judgment of the Court of 30 July 1996, Bosphorus Hava Yollari Turizm ve Ticaret AS v. Minister for Transport, Energy and Communications and others, Case C-84/95, European Court Reports 1996, p. I-3953, paras. 19–26.

This case deals with the conformity of the embargo measures against the then Federal Republic of Yugoslavia (Serbia and Montenegro) with fundamental rights. After recalling its well-established case law that 'the fundamental rights invoked by Bosphorus Airways [i.e. the right to peaceful enjoyment of property and the freedom to pursue a commercial activity] are not absolute and their exercise may be subject to restrictions justified by objectives of general interest pursued by the Community' (paragraph 21), the Court broadly held that in the light of the enormous importance of stopping internecine killing in Yugoslavia, the embargo measures did not impose disproportionate restraints on the enjoyment of these fundamental rights. The case should now be read in the light of the *Kadi* case (see Chapter 12, pp. 999–1023), but is still significant because of the method of conforming interpretation of the Community act in the light of the UN Security Council resolution that the Court applied.

Fundamental rights and the principle of proportionality

19. Bosphorus Airways submits, in the second place, that to interpret the first paragraph of Article 8 of Regulation No 990/93 as meaning that an aircraft whose

day-to-day operation and control are carried out under a lease by a person or undertaking not based in or operating from the Federal Republic of Yugoslavia must nevertheless be impounded because it belongs to an undertaking based in that republic, would infringe Bosphorus's fundamental rights, in particular its right to peaceful enjoyment of its property and its freedom to pursue a commercial activity, in that it would have the effect of destroying and obliterating its air charter and travel organization business.

20. That interpretation, according to Bosphorus Airways, would also infringe the principle of proportionality, since the owner of the aircraft in question has already been penalized by the rent being held in blocked accounts and the impounding of the aircraft was therefore a manifestly unnecessary penalty, disproportionate with respect to a wholly innocent party.

21. It is settled case-law that the fundamental rights invoked by Bosphorus Airways are not absolute and their exercise may be subject to restrictions justified by objectives of general interest pursued by the Community (see Case 44/79 *Hauer v Land Rheinland-Pfalz* [1979] ECR 3727; Case 5/88 *Wachauf v Bundesamt für Ernährung und Forstwirtschaft* [1989] ECR 2609; and Case C-280/93 *Germany v Council* [1994] ECR I-4973).

22. Any measure imposing sanctions has, by definition, consequences which affect the right to property and the freedom to pursue a trade or business, thereby causing harm to persons who are in no way responsible for the situation which led to the adoption of the sanctions.

23. Moreover, the importance of the aims pursued by the regulation at issue is such as to justify negative consequences, even of a substantial nature, for some operators.

24. The provisions of Regulation No 990/93 contribute in particular to the implementation at Community level of the sanctions against the Federal Republic of Yugoslavia adopted, and later strengthened, by several resolutions of the Security Council of the United Nations. The third recital in the preamble to Regulation No 990/93 states that 'the prolonged direct and indirect activities of the Federal Republic of Yugoslavia (Serbia and Montenegro) in, and with regard to, the Republic of Bosnia-Herzegovina are the main cause for the dramatic developments in the Republic of Bosnia-Herzegovina'; the fourth recital states that 'a continuation of these activities will lead to further unacceptable loss of human life and material damage and to a further breach of international peace and security in the region'; and the seventh recital states that 'the Bosnian Serb party has hitherto not accepted, in full, the peace plan of the International Conference on the Former Yugoslavia in spite of appeals thereto by the Security Council'.

25. It is in the light of those circumstances that the aim pursued by the sanctions assumes especial importance, which is, in particular, in terms of Regulation No 990/93 and more especially the eighth recital in the preamble thereto, to dissuade the Federal Republic of Yugoslavia from 'further violating the integrity and security of the Republic of Bosnia-Herzegovina and to induce the Bosnian Serb party to cooperate in the restoration of peace in this Republic'.

26. As compared with an objective of general interest so fundamental for the international community, which consists in putting an end to the state of war in the

region and to the massive violations of human rights and humanitarian international law in the Republic of Bosnia-Herzegovina, the impounding of the aircraft in question, which is owned by an undertaking based in or operating from the Federal Republic of Yugoslavia, cannot be regarded as inappropriate or disproportionate.

6.6 The case of the non-proliferation sanctions against Iran

The non-proliferation sanctions presently in force against Iran are, even more than the anti-terrorist measures under Security Council Resolution 1373 (2001), a true mixture of UN-imposed measures and measures taken at the behest of informal export control groups, such as the Nuclear Suppliers Group and the MTCR.[16] This becomes clear in comparing the measures laid down in Resolution 1737 (2006),[17] included immediately below, to the measures the Union is prepared to take, in both the CFSP and in other areas of Union competence, which refer in part to the informal export control groups mentioned above.

In the past few years there has been a proliferation of cases brought before EU courts by Iranian banks and their subsidiaries established in EU Member States. As the jurisprudence with regard to the freezing of assets of Bank Melli Iran and its subsidiary registered in the UK, Melli Bank plc, indicates, if the Member States and the Union institutions do their work carefully, meticulously, dispose of information that can be shown to the Court, and produce a well-reasoned Union act, restrictive measures directed at an individual or a specific company will be upheld by the Court, and need not share the fate of many earlier such cases.[18] On the contrary, failure by the Council to state sufficiently detailed reasons justifying the imposition of restrictive measures, or to notify 'in good time' the affected entity of the measures, or to conduct a genuine assessment of the information and evidence against that entity, have been found by the General Court to infringe that entity's rights of defence and effective judicial protection. Also, a manifest error of assessment of the reasons for imposing restrictive measures on an entity has been found to taint such a measure with illegality. Excerpts from the judgments of the

---

[16] The EU has also autonomously imposed sanctions against individuals in Iran in view of the deteriorating situation of human rights in the country. These fall within the ambit of the previous section of this chapter; see Council Decision 2011/235/CFSP of 12 April 2011 concerning restrictive measures directed against certain persons and entities in view of the situation in Iran, OJ L 100, 14.4.2011, pp. 51–7, and Council Regulation (EU) No. 359/2011 of 12 April 2011 concerning restrictive measures directed against certain persons, entities and bodies in view of the situation in Iran, OJ L 100, 14.4.2011, pp. 1–11.

[17] The scope of this resolution as well as that of UN Security Council Resolutions 1747 (2007) and 1803 (2008) have since been widened by UN Security Council Resolution 1929 (2010) whereas the latter resolution imposed further restrictive measures against Iran.

[18] See Joined Cases T-246/08 and T-332/08 *Melli Bank plc v. Council of the European Union* [2009] ECR II-2629; Case T-390/08 *Bank Melli Iran v. Council of the European Union* [2009] ECR II-3967; Case C-548/09 P *Bank Melli Iran v. Council of the European Union*, not yet reported; Case C-380/09 P *Melli Bank plc v. Council of the European Union*, not yet reported; Case T-492/10 *Melli Bank plc v. Council of the European Union*, not yet reported.

General Court in Case T-496/10 concerning Bank Mellat, an Iranian bank, and in Case T-495/10 concerning Bank Saderat plc, a bank registered in the UK but wholly owned by Bank Saderat Iran, an Iranian Bank, are introduced below. Before the case law, however, Council Decision 2010/413/CFSP and the preamble of Council Regulation (EU) No. 267/2012 are included to give an overview of the current EU framework concerning restrictive measures against Iran.

Security Council Resolution 1737 (2006) of 23 December 2006 on Non-Proliferation, UN Doc. S/RES/1737 (2006).

The Security Council,

Recalling the Statement of its President, S/PRST/2006/15, of 29 March 2006, and its resolution 1696 (2006) of 31 July 2006,

Reaffirming its commitment to the Treaty on the Non-Proliferation of Nuclear Weapons, and recalling the right of States Party, in conformity with Articles I and II of that Treaty, to develop research, production and use of nuclear energy for peaceful purposes without discrimination,

Reiterating its serious concern over the many reports of the IAEA Director General and resolutions of the IAEA Board of Governors related to Iran's nuclear programme, reported to it by the IAEA Director General, including IAEA Board resolution GOV/2006/14,

Reiterating its serious concern that the IAEA Director General's report of 27 February 2006 (GOV/2006/15) lists a number of outstanding issues and concerns on Iran's nuclear programme, including topics which could have a military nuclear dimension, and that the IAEA is unable to conclude that there are no undeclared nuclear materials or activities in Iran,

Reiterating its serious concern over the IAEA Director General's report of 28 April 2006 (GOV/2006/27) and its findings, including that, after more than three years of Agency efforts to seek clarity about all aspects of Iran's nuclear programme, the existing gaps in knowledge continue to be a matter of concern, and that the IAEA is unable to make progress in its efforts to provide assurances about the absence of undeclared nuclear material and activities in Iran,

Noting with serious concern that, as confirmed by the IAEA Director General's reports of 8 June 2006 (GOV/2006/38), 31 August 2006 (GOV/2006/53) and 14 November 2006 (GOV/2006/64), Iran has not established full and sustained suspension of all enrichment-related and reprocessing activities as set out in resolution 1696 (2006), nor resumed its cooperation with the IAEA under the Additional Protocol, nor taken the other steps required of it by the IAEA Board of Governors, nor complied with the provisions of Security Council resolution 1696 (2006) and which are essential to build confidence, and *deploring* Iran's refusal to take these steps,

Emphasizing the importance of political and diplomatic efforts to find a negotiated solution guaranteeing that Iran's nuclear programme is exclusively for peaceful purposes, and *noting* that such a solution would benefit nuclear nonproliferation elsewhere, and *welcoming* the continuing commitment of China, France, Germany, the Russian Federation, the United Kingdom and the United States, with the support of the European Union's High Representative to seek a negotiated solution,

Determined to give effect to its decisions by adopting appropriate measures to persuade Iran to comply with resolution 1696 (2006) and with the requirements of the IAEA, and also to constrain Iran's development of sensitive technologies in support of its nuclear and missile programmes, until such time as the Security Council determines that the objectives of this resolution have been met,

Concerned by the proliferation risks presented by the Iranian nuclear programme and, in this context, by Iran's continuing failure to meet the requirements of the IAEA Board of Governors and to comply with the provisions of Security Council resolution 1696 (2006), *mindful* of its primary responsibility under the Charter of the United Nations for the maintenance of international peace and security,

Acting under Article 41 of Chapter VII of the Charter of the United Nations,

1. *Affirms* that Iran shall without further delay take the steps required by the IAEA Board of Governors in its resolution GOV/2006/14, which are essential to build confidence in the exclusively peaceful purpose of its nuclear programme and to resolve outstanding questions;

2. *Decides*, in this context, that Iran shall without further delay suspend the following proliferation sensitive nuclear activities:

(a) all enrichment-related and reprocessing activities, including research and development, to be verified by the IAEA; and

(b) work on all heavy water-related projects, including the construction of a research reactor moderated by heavy water, also to be verified by the IAEA;

3. *Decides* that all States shall take the necessary measures to prevent the supply, sale or transfer directly or indirectly from their territories, or by their nationals or using their flag vessels or aircraft to, or for the use in or benefit of, Iran, and whether or not originating in their territories, of all items, materials, equipment, goods and technology which could contribute to Iran's enrichment-related, reprocessing or heavy water-related activities, or to the development of nuclear weapon delivery systems, namely:

(a) those set out in sections B.2, B.3, B.4, B.5, B.6 and B.7 of INFCIRC/254/Rev.8/Part 1 in document S/2006/814;

(b) those set out in sections A.1 and B.1 of INFCIRC/254/Rev.8/Part 1 in document S/2006/814, except the supply, sale or transfer of:

(i) equipment covered by B.1 when such equipment is for light water reactors;

(ii) low-enriched uranium covered by A.1.2 when it is incorporated in assembled nuclear fuel elements for such reactors;

(c) those set out in document S/2006/815, except the supply, sale or transfer of items covered by 19.A.3 of Category II;

(d) any additional items, materials, equipment, goods and technology, determined as necessary by the Security Council or the Committee established by paragraph 18 below (herein 'the Committee'), which could contribute to enrichment-related, or reprocessing, or heavy water-related activities, or to the development of nuclear weapon delivery systems;

4. *Decides* that all States shall take the necessary measures to prevent the supply, sale or transfer directly or indirectly from their territories, or by their nationals or using their flag vessels or aircraft to, or for the use in or benefit of, Iran, and whether or not originating in their territories, of the following items, materials, equipment, goods and technology:

(a) those set out in INFCIRC/254/Rev.7/Part2 of document S/2006/814 if the State determines that they would contribute to enrichment-related, reprocessing or heavy water-related activities;

(b) any other items not listed in documents S/2006/814 or S/2006/815 if the State determines that they would contribute to enrichment-related, reprocessing or heavy water-related activities, or to the development of nuclear weapon delivery systems;

(c) any further items if the State determines that they would contribute to the pursuit of activities related to other topics about which the IAEA has expressed concerns or identified as outstanding;

5. *Decides* that, for the supply, sale or transfer of all items, materials, equipment, goods and technology covered by documents S/2006/814 and S/2006/815 the export of which to Iran is not prohibited by subparagraphs 3 (b), 3 (c) or 4 (a) above, States shall ensure that:

(a) the requirements, as appropriate, of the Guidelines as set out in documents S/2006/814 and S/2006/985 have been met; and

(b) they have obtained and are in a position to exercise effectively a right to verify the end-use and end-use location of any supplied item; and

(c) they notify the Committee within ten days of the supply, sale or transfer; and

(d) in the case of items, materials, equipment, goods and technology contained in document S/2006/814, they also notify the IAEA within ten days of the supply, sale or transfer;

6. *Decides* that all States shall also take the necessary measures to prevent the provision to Iran of any technical assistance or training, financial assistance, investment, brokering or other services, and the transfer of financial resources or services, related to the supply, sale, transfer, manufacture or use of the prohibited items, materials, equipment, goods and technology specified in paragraphs 3 and 4 above;

7. *Decides* that Iran shall not export any of the items in documents S/2006/814 and S/2006/815 and that all Member States shall prohibit the procurement of such items from Iran by their nationals, or using their flag vessels or aircraft, and whether or not originating in the territory of Iran;

8. *Decides* that Iran shall provide such access and cooperation as the IAEA requests to be able to verify the suspension outlined in paragraph 2 and to resolve all outstanding issues, as identified in IAEA reports, and *calls upon* Iran to ratify promptly the Additional Protocol;

9. *Decides* that the measures imposed by paragraphs 3, 4 and 6 above shall not apply where the Committee determines in advance and on a case-by-case basis that such supply, sale, transfer or provision of such items or assistance would clearly not contribute to the development of Iran's technologies in support of its proliferation sensitive nuclear activities and of development of nuclear weapon delivery systems, including where such items or assistance are for food, agricultural, medical or other humanitarian purposes, provided that:

(a) contracts for delivery of such items or assistance include appropriate end-user guarantees; and

(b) Iran has committed not to use such items in proliferation sensitive nuclear activities or for development of nuclear weapon delivery systems;

10. *Calls upon* all States to exercise vigilance regarding the entry into or transit through their territories of individuals who are engaged in, directly associated with or providing support for Iran's proliferation sensitive nuclear activities or for the development of nuclear weapon delivery systems, and *decides* in this regard that all States shall notify the Committee of the entry into or transit through their territories of the persons designated in the Annex to this resolution (herein 'the Annex'), as well as of additional persons designated by the Security Council or the Committee as being engaged in, directly associated with or providing support for Iran's proliferation sensitive nuclear activities and for the development of nuclear weapon delivery systems, including through the involvement in procurement of the prohibited items, goods, equipment, materials and technology specified by and under the measures in paragraphs 3 and 4 above, except where such travel is for activities directly related to the items in subparagraphs 3 (b) (i) and (ii) above;

11. *Underlines* that nothing in the above paragraph requires a State to refuse its own nationals entry into its territory, and that all States shall, in the implementation of the above paragraph, take into account humanitarian considerations as well as the necessity to meet the objectives of this resolution, including where Article XV of the IAEA Statute is engaged;

12. *Decides* that all States shall freeze the funds, other financial assets and economic resources which are on their territories at the date of adoption of this resolution or at any time thereafter, that are owned or controlled by the persons or entities designated in the Annex, as well as those of additional persons or entities designated by the Security Council or by the Committee as being engaged in, directly associated with or providing support for Iran's proliferation sensitive nuclear activities or the development of nuclear weapon delivery systems, or by persons or entities acting on their behalf or at their direction, or by entities owned or controlled by them, including through illicit means, and that the measures in this paragraph shall cease to apply in respect of such persons or entities if, and at such time as, the Security Council or the Committee removes them from the Annex, and *decides further* that all States shall ensure that any funds, financial assets or economic resources are prevented from being made available by their nationals or by any persons or entities within their territories, to or for the benefit of these persons and entities;

13. *Decides* that the measures imposed by paragraph 12 above do not apply to funds, other financial assets or economic resources that have been determined by relevant States:

(a) to be necessary for basic expenses, including payment for foodstuffs, rent or mortgage, medicines and medical treatment, taxes, insurance premiums, and public utility charges or exclusively for payment of reasonable professional fees and reimbursement of incurred expenses associated with the provision of legal services, or fees or service charges, in accordance with national laws, for routine holding or maintenance of frozen funds, other financial assets and economic resources, after notification by the relevant

States to the Committee of the intention to authorize, where appropriate, access to such funds, other financial assets or economic resources and in the absence of a negative decision by the Committee within five working days of such notification;

(b) to be necessary for extraordinary expenses, provided that such determination has been notified by the relevant States to the Committee and has been approved by the Committee;

(c) to be the subject of a judicial, administrative or arbitral lien or judgement, in which case the funds, other financial assets and economic resources may be used to satisfy that lien or judgement provided that the lien or judgement was entered into prior to the date of the present resolution, is not for the benefit of a person or entity designated pursuant to paragraphs 10 and 12 above, and has been notified by the relevant States to the Committee;

(d) to be necessary for activities directly related to the items specified in subparagraphs 3 (b) (i) and (ii) and have been notified by the relevant States to the Committee;

14. *Decides* that States may permit the addition to the accounts frozen pursuant to the provisions of paragraph 12 above of interests or other earnings due on those accounts or payments due under contracts, agreements or obligations that arose prior to the date on which those accounts became subject to the provisions of this resolution, provided that any such interest, other earnings and payments continue to be subject to these provisions and are frozen;

15. *Decides* that the measures in paragraph 12 above shall not prevent a designated person or entity from making payment due under a contract entered into prior to the listing of such a person or entity, provided that the relevant States have determined that:

(a) the contract is not related to any of the prohibited items, materials, equipment, goods, technologies, assistance, training, financial assistance, investment, brokering or services referred to in paragraphs 3, 4 and 6 above;

(b) the payment is not directly or indirectly received by a person or entity designated pursuant to paragraph 12 above;

and after notification by the relevant States to the Committee of the intention to make or receive such payments or to authorize, where appropriate, the unfreezing of funds, other financial assets or economic resources for this purpose, ten working days prior to such authorization;

16. *Decides* that technical cooperation provided to Iran by the IAEA or under its auspices shall only be for food, agricultural, medical, safety or other humanitarian purposes, or where it is necessary for projects directly related to the items specified in subparagraphs 3 (b) (i) and (ii) above, but that no such technical cooperation shall be provided that relates to the proliferation sensitive nuclear activities set out in paragraph 2 above;

17. *Calls upon* all States to exercise vigilance and prevent specialized teaching or training of Iranian nationals, within their territories or by their nationals, of disciplines which would contribute to Iran's proliferation sensitive nuclear activities and development of nuclear weapon delivery systems;

18. *Decides* to establish, in accordance with rule 28 of its provisional rules of procedure, a Committee of the Security Council consisting of all the members of the Council, to undertake the following tasks:

(a) to seek from all States, in particular those in the region and those producing the items, materials, equipment, goods and technology referred to in paragraphs 3 and 4 above, information regarding the actions taken by them to implement effectively the measures imposed by paragraphs 3, 4, 5, 6, 7, 8, 10 and 12 of this resolution and whatever further information it may consider useful in this regard;

(b) to seek from the secretariat of the IAEA information regarding the actions taken by the IAEA to implement effectively the measures imposed by paragraph 16 of this resolution and whatever further information it may consider useful in this regard;

(c) to examine and take appropriate action on information regarding alleged violations of measures imposed by paragraphs 3, 4, 5, 6, 7, 8, 10 and 12 of this resolution;

(d) to consider and decide upon requests for exemptions set out in paragraphs 9, 13 and 15 above;

(e) to determine as may be necessary additional items, materials, equipment, goods and technology to be specified for the purpose of paragraph 3 above;

(f) to designate as may be necessary additional individuals and entities subject to the measures imposed by paragraphs 10 and 12 above;

(g) to promulgate guidelines as may be necessary to facilitate the implementation of the measures imposed by this resolution and include in such guidelines a requirement on States to provide information where possible as to why any individuals and/or entities meet the criteria set out in paragraphs 10 and 12 and any relevant identifying information;

(h) to report at least every 90 days to the Security Council on its work and on the implementation of this resolution, with its observations and recommendations, in particular on ways to strengthen the effectiveness of the measures imposed by paragraphs 3, 4, 5, 6, 7, 8, 10 and 12 above;

19. *Decides* that all States shall report to the Committee within 60 days of the adoption of this resolution on the steps they have taken with a view to implementing effectively paragraphs 3, 4, 5, 6, 7, 8, 10, 12 and 17 above;

20. *Expresses* the conviction that the suspension set out in paragraph 2 above as well as full, verified Iranian compliance with the requirements set out by the IAEA Board of Governors, would contribute to a diplomatic, negotiated solution that guarantees Iran's nuclear programme is for exclusively peaceful purposes, *underlines* the willingness of the international community to work positively for such a solution, *encourages* Iran, in conforming to the above provisions, to re-engage with the international community and with the IAEA, and *stresses* that such engagement will be beneficial to Iran;

21. *Welcomes* the commitment of China, France, Germany, the Russian Federation, the United Kingdom and the United States, with the support of the European Union's High Representative, to a negotiated solution to this issue and encourages Iran to engage with their June 2006 proposals (S/2006/521), which were endorsed by the Security Council in resolution 1696 (2006), for a long-term comprehensive agreement which would allow for the development of relations and cooperation with Iran based on mutual respect and the establishment of international confidence in the exclusively peaceful nature of Iran's nuclear programme;

22. *Reiterates* its determination to reinforce the authority of the IAEA, strongly supports the role of the IAEA Board of Governors, *commends* and *encourages* the Director

General of the IAEA and its secretariat for their ongoing professional and impartial efforts to resolve all remaining outstanding issues in Iran within the framework of the IAEA, *underlines* the necessity of the IAEA continuing its work to clarify all outstanding issues relating to Iran's nuclear programme;

23. *Requests* within 60 days a report from the Director General of the IAEA on whether Iran has established full and sustained suspension of all activities mentioned in this resolution, as well as on the process of Iranian compliance with all the steps required by the IAEA Board and with the other provisions of this resolution, to the IAEA Board of Governors and in parallel to the Security Council for its consideration;

24. *Affirms* that it shall review Iran's actions in the light of the report referred to in paragraph 23 above, to be submitted within 60 days, and:

(a) that it shall suspend the implementation of measures if and for so long as Iran suspends all enrichment-related and reprocessing activities, including research and development, as verified by the IAEA, to allow for negotiations;

(b) that it shall terminate the measures specified in paragraphs 3, 4, 5, 6, 7, 10 and 12 of this resolution as soon as it determines that Iran has fully complied with its obligations under the relevant resolutions of the Security Council and met the requirements of the IAEA Board of Governors, as confirmed by the IAEA Board;

(c) that it shall, in the event that the report in paragraph 23 above shows that Iran has not complied with this resolution, adopt further appropriate measures under Article 41 of Chapter VII of the Charter of the United Nations to persuade Iran to comply with this resolution and the requirements of the IAEA, and underlines that further decisions will be required should such additional measures be necessary;

25. *Decides* to remain seized of the matter.

[...]

Council Decision 2010/413/CFSP of 26 July 2010 concerning restrictive measures against Iran and repealing Common Position 2007/140/CFSP, Official Journal of the European Union L 195, 27.7.2010, pp. 39–73.

THE COUNCIL OF THE EUROPEAN UNION,
Having regard to the Treaty on European Union, and in particular Article 29 thereof,

Whereas:

(1) On 27 February 2007, the Council of the European Union adopted Common Position 2007/140/CFSP concerning restrictive measures against Iran which implemented United Nations Security Council Resolution (UNSCR) 1737 (2006).

(2) On 23 April 2007, the Council adopted Common Position 2007/246/CFSP which implemented UNSCR 1747 (2007).

(3) On 7 August 2008, the Council adopted Common Position 2008/652/CFSP which implemented UNSCR 1803 (2008).

(4) On 9 June 2010, the United Nations Security Council ('the Security Council') adopted UNSCR 1929 (2010) which widened the scope of the restrictive measures imposed by UNSCR 1737 (2006), UNSCR 1747 (2007), and UNSCR 1803 (2008) and introduced additional restrictive measures against Iran.

(5) On 17 June 2010, the European Council underlined its deepening concern about Iran's nuclear programme and welcomed the adoption of UNSCR 1929 (2010). Recalling its Declaration of 11 December 2009, the European Council invited the Council to adopt measures implementing those contained in UNSCR 1929 (2010) as well as accompanying measures, with a view to supporting the resolution of all outstanding concerns regarding Iran's development of sensitive technologies in support of its nuclear and missile programmes, through negotiation. These should focus on the areas of trade, the financial sector, the Iranian transport sector, key sectors in the oil and gas industry and additional designations in particular for the Islamic Revolutionary Guards Corps (IRGC).

(6) UNSCR 1929 (2010) prohibits investment by Iran, its nationals and entities incorporated in Iran or subject to its jurisdiction, or by persons or entities acting on their behalf or at their direction, or by entities owned or controlled by them in any commercial activity involving uranium mining, production or use of nuclear materials and technology.

(7) UNSCR 1929 (2010) extends the financial and travel restrictions imposed by UNSCR 1737 (2006) to additional persons and entities, including IRGC individuals and entities as well as entities of the Islamic Republic of Iran Shipping Lines (IRISL).

(8) In accordance with the European Council Declaration, the restrictions on admission and the freezing of funds and economic resources should be applied to further persons and entities, in addition to those designated by the Security Council or the Committee established pursuant to paragraph 18 of UNSCR 1737 (2006) ('the Committee'), using the same criteria as those applied by the Security Council or the Committee.

(9) In accordance with the European Council Declaration, it is appropriate to prohibit the supply, sale or transfer to Iran of further items, materials, equipment, goods and technology, in addition to those determined by the Security Council or the Committee, that could contribute to Iran's enrichment-related, reprocessing or heavy water-related activities, to the development of nuclear weapon delivery systems or to the pursuit of activities related to other topics about which the International Atomic Energy Agency (IAEA) has expressed concerns or identified as outstanding, or to other weapons of mass destruction programmes. This prohibition should include dual-use goods and technology.

(10) In accordance with the European Council Declaration, Member States should exercise restraint in entering into new short term commitments for public and private provided financial support for trade with Iran with a view to reducing outstanding amounts, in particular to avoid any financial support contributing to proliferation-sensitive nuclear activities, or to the development of nuclear weapon delivery systems, and should prohibit any medium and long-term commitment for public and private provided financial support for trade with Iran.

(11) UNSCR 1929 (2010) calls upon all States to inspect, in accordance with their national authorities and legislation, and consistent with international law, all cargoes to and from Iran, in their territory, including seaports and airports, if the State concerned has information that provides reasonable grounds to believe that the cargo contains items the supply, sale, transfer or export of which is prohibited under UNSCR 1737 (2006), UNSCR 1747 (2007), UNSCR 1803 (2008) or UNSCR 1929 (2010).

(12) UNSCR 1929 (2010) also notes that Member States, consistent with international law, in particular the law of the sea, may request inspections of vessels on the high seas

with the consent of the flag State, if they have information that provides reasonable grounds to believe that the vessels carry items the supply, sale, transfer or export of which is prohibited under UNSCR 1737 (2006), UNSCR 1747 (2007), UNSCR 1803 (2008) or UNSCR 1929 (2010).

(13) UNSCR 1929 (2010) also provides that UN Member States are to seize and dispose of items the supply, sale, transfer or export of which is prohibited under UNSCR 1737 (2006), UNSCR 1747 (2007), UNSCR 1803 (2008) or UNSCR 1929 (2010) in a manner that is not inconsistent with their obligations under the applicable Security Council Resolutions and international conventions.

(14) UNSCR 1929 (2010) further provides that UN Member States are to prohibit the provision by their nationals or from their territory of bunkering services, or other servicing of vessels, to Iran vessels if they have information that provides reasonable grounds to believe they are carrying items the supply, sale, transfer or export of which is prohibited under UNSCR 1737 (2006), UNSCR 1747 (2007), UNSCR 1803 (2008) or UNSCR 1929 (2010).

(15) In accordance with the European Council Declaration, Member States, in accordance with their national legal authorities and legislation and consistent with international law, in particular relevant international civil aviation agreements, should take the necessary measures to prevent the access to the airports under their jurisdiction of all cargo flights from Iran with the exception of mixed passengers and cargo flights.

(16) Moreover, the provision by nationals of Member States or from the territory of Member States of engineering and maintenance services to Iranian cargo aircrafts should be prohibited if the State concerned has information that provides reasonable grounds to believe that they are carrying items the supply, sale, transfer or export of which is prohibited under UNSCR 1737 (2006), UNSCR 1747 (2007), UNSCR 1803 (2008) or UNSCR 1929 (2010).

(17) UNSCR 1929 (2010) also calls upon all UN Member States to prevent the provision of financial services, including insurance and re-insurance, or the transfer to, through, or from their territory, or to or by their nationals or entities organised under their laws, or persons of financial institutions in their territory, of any financial or other assets or resources that could contribute to Iran's proliferation-sensitive nuclear activities or the development of nuclear weapon delivery systems.

(18) In accordance with the European Council Declaration, Member States should prohibit the provision of insurance and re-insurance to the Government of Iran, to entities incorporated in Iran or subject to Iran's jurisdiction or to individuals and entities acting on their behalf or at their direction, or to entities owned and controlled by them, including through illicit means.

(19) Moreover, the sale or purchase of, or brokering or assistance in the issuance of public or public-guaranteed bonds to and from the Government of Iran, the Central Bank of Iran or Iranian banks, including branches and subsidiaries, and financial entities controlled by persons and entities domiciled in Iran should be prohibited.

(20) In accordance with the European Council Declaration and in order to fulfil the objectives of UNSCR 1929 (2010), the opening of new branches, subsidiaries, or representative offices of Iranian banks in the territory of Member States, and the establishment of new joint ventures, or the taking of an ownership interest by Iranian banks in

banks within the jurisdiction of Member States, should be prohibited. Furthermore, Member States should take the appropriate measures to prohibit financial institutions within their territories or under their jurisdiction from opening representatives offices or subsidiaries or banking accounts in Iran.

(21) UNSCR 1929 (2010) also provides for States to require their nationals, persons subject to their jurisdiction or firms incorporated in their territories or subject to their jurisdiction to exercise vigilance when doing business with entities incorporated in Iran or subject to Iran's jurisdiction, if they have reasonable grounds to believe that such business could contribute to Iran's proliferation-sensitive nuclear activities or the development of nuclear weapon delivery system or to violations of UNSCR 1737 (2006), UNSCR 1747 (2007), UNSCR 1803 (2008) or UNSCR 1929 (2010).

(22) UNSCR 1929 (2010) notes the potential connection between Iran's revenues derived from its energy sector and the funding of Iran's proliferation-sensitive nuclear activities and further notes that chemical process equipment and materials required for the petrochemical industry have much in common with those required for certain sensitive nuclear fuel cycle activities.

(23) In accordance with the European Council Declaration, Member States should prohibit the sale, supply or transfer to Iran of key equipment and technology as well as related technical and financial assistance, which could be used in key sectors in the oil and natural gas industries. Moreover, Member States should prohibit any new investment in these sectors in Iran.

(24) The procedure for amending Annexes I and II to this Decision should include providing to designated persons and entities the grounds for listing so as to give them an opportunity to present observations.

Where observations are submitted or where substantial new evidence is presented, the Council should review its decision in the light of those observations and inform the person or entity concerned accordingly.

(25) This Decision respects the fundamental rights and observes the principles recognised in particular by the Charter of Fundamental Rights of the European Union and notably the right to an effective remedy and to a fair trial, the right to property and the right to the protection of personal data. This Decision should be applied in accordance with those rights and principles.

(26) This Decision also fully respects the obligations of Member States under the Charter of the United Nations and the legally binding nature of Security Council Resolutions.

(27) Further action by the Union is needed in order to implement certain measures,

HAS ADOPTED THIS DECISION:

CHAPTER 1
EXPORT AND IMPORT RESTRICTIONS
Article 1

1. The direct or indirect supply, sale or transfer of the following items, materials, equipment, goods and technology, including software, to, or for the use in, or benefit of, Iran, by nationals of Member States, or through the territories of Member States, or

using their flag vessels or aircraft, shall be prohibited whether or not originating in their territories:

(a) items, materials, equipment, goods and technology contained in the Nuclear Suppliers Group and Missile Technology Control Regime lists;

(b) any additional items, materials, equipment, goods and technology, determined by the Security Council or the Committee, which could contribute to enrichment-related, reprocessing or heavy water-related activities, or to the development of nuclear weapon delivery systems;

(c) arms and related materiel of all types, including weapons and ammunition, military vehicles and equipment, paramilitary equipment and spare parts for such arms and related materiel, as well as equipment which might be used for internal repression. This prohibition shall not apply to non-combat vehicles which have been manufactured or fitted with materials to provide ballistic protection, intended solely for protective use of personnel of the EU and its Member States in Iran;

(d) certain other items, materials, equipment, goods and technology that could contribute to enrichment-related, reprocessing or heavy water-related activities, to the development of nuclear weapon delivery systems or to the pursuit of activities related to other topics about which the IAEA has expressed concerns or identified as outstanding. The Union shall take the necessary measures in order to determine the relevant items to be covered by this provision;

(e) other dual-use goods and technology listed in Annex I to Council Regulation (EC) No 428/2009 of 5 May 2009 setting up a Community regime for the control of exports, transfer, brokering and transit of dual-use items and not covered by point (a) except for category 5—Part 1 and category 5—Part 2 in Annex I to Council Regulation (EC) No 428/2009.

2. The prohibition in paragraph 1 shall not apply to the direct or indirect transfer to, or for use in, or the benefit of Iran through the territories of Member States of items referred to in subparagraphs 3(b)(i) and (ii) of UNSCR 1737 (2006) for light water reactors begun before December 2006.

3. It shall also be prohibited to:

(a) provide technical assistance or training, investment, or brokering services related to items, materials, equipment, goods and technology set out in paragraph 1 and to the provision, manufacture, maintenance and use of these items, materials, equipment, goods and technology, directly or indirectly to any person, entity or body in, or for use in Iran;

(b) provide financing or financial assistance related to items and technologies referred to in paragraph 1, including in particular grants, loans and export credit insurance, for any sale, supply, transfer or export of these items and technologies, or for the provision of related technical training, services or assistance, directly or indirectly to any person, entity or body in, or for use in Iran;

(c) participate, knowingly or intentionally, in activities the object or effect of which is to circumvent the prohibition referred to in points (a) and (b).

4. The procurement by nationals of Member States, or using their flagged vessels or aircraft, of the items, materials, equipment, goods and technology referred to in

paragraph 1 from Iran shall be prohibited, whether or not originating in the territory of Iran.

Article 2

1. The direct or indirect supply, sale or transfer to, or for use in, or the benefit of Iran, by nationals of Member States or through the territories of Member States, or using vessels or aircraft under their jurisdiction, of items, materials, equipment, goods and technology, including software, not covered by Article 1, that could contribute to enrichment-related, reprocessing or heavy water-related activities, to the development of nuclear weapon delivery systems or to the pursuit of activities related to other topics about which the IAEA has expressed concerns or identified as outstanding, shall be subject to authorisation on a case-by-case basis by the competent authorities of the exporting Member State. The Union shall take the necessary measures in order to determine the relevant items to be covered by this provision.

2. The provision of:

(a) technical assistance or training, investment, or brokering services related to items, materials, equipment, goods and technology set out in paragraph 1 and to the provision, manufacture, maintenance and use of these items, directly or indirectly, to any person, entity or body in, or for use in, Iran;

(b) financing or financial assistance related to items and technologies referred to in paragraph 1, including in particular grants, loans and export credit insurance, for any sale, supply, transfer or export of these items, or for the provision of related technical training, services or assistance, directly or indirectly to any person, entity or body in, or for use in, Iran;

shall also be subject to an authorisation of the competent authority of the exporting Member State.

3. The competent authorities of the Member States shall not grant any authorisation for any supply, sale or transfer of the items, materials, equipment, goods and technology referred to in paragraph 1 if they determine that the sale, supply, transfer or export concerned or the provision of the service concerned would contribute to the activities referred to in paragraph 1.

Article 3

1. The measures imposed by Article 1(1)(a), (b) and (c) and (3) shall not apply, as appropriate, where the Committee determines in advance and on a case-by-case basis that such supply, sale, transfer or provision of such items or assistance would clearly not contribute to the development of Iran's technologies in support of its proliferation-sensitive nuclear activities and of development of nuclear weapon delivery systems, including where such items or assistance are for food, agricultural, medical or other humanitarian purposes, provided that:

(a) contracts for delivery of such items or assistance include appropriate end-user guarantees; and

(b) Iran has committed not to use such items in proliferation-sensitive nuclear activities or for development of nuclear weapon delivery systems.

2. The measures imposed by Article 1(1)(e) and (3) shall not apply where the competent authority in the relevant Member State determines in advance and on a case-by-case basis that such supply, sale, transfer or provision of such items or assistance would clearly not contribute to the development of Iran's technologies in support of its proliferation-sensitive nuclear activities and of development of nuclear weapon delivery systems, including where such items or assistance are for medical or other humanitarian purposes, provided that:

(a) contracts for delivery of such items or assistance include appropriate end-user guarantees; and

(b) Iran has committed not to use such items in proliferation-sensitive nuclear activities or for development of nuclear weapon delivery systems.

The relevant Member State shall inform the other Member States of any exemption rejected.

Article 4

1. The sale, supply or transfer of key equipment and technology for the following key sectors of the oil and natural gas industry in Iran, or to Iranian or Iranian-owned enterprises engaged in those sectors outside Iran, by nationals of Member States, or from the territories of Member States, or using vessels or aircraft under the jurisdiction of Member States shall be prohibited whether or not originating in their territories:

(a) refining;

(b) liquefied natural gas;

(c) exploration;

(d) production.

The Union shall take the necessary measures in order to determine the relevant items to be covered by this provision.

2. It shall be prohibited to provide the following to enterprises in Iran that are engaged in the key sectors of the Iranian oil and gas industry referred to in paragraph 1 or to Iranian, or Iranian-owned enterprises engaged in those sectors outside Iran:

(a) technical assistance or training and other services related to key equipment and technology as determined according to paragraph 1;

(b) financing or financial assistance for any sale, supply, transfer or export of key equipment and technology as determined according to paragraph 1 or for the provision of related technical assistance or training.

3. It shall be prohibited to participate, knowingly or intentionally, in activities the object or effect of which is to circumvent the prohibitions referred to in paragraphs 1 and 2.

RESTRICTIONS ON FINANCING OF CERTAIN ENTERPRISES

Article 5

Investment in the territories under the jurisdiction of Member States by Iran, its nationals, or entities incorporated in Iran or subject to its jurisdiction, or by persons or entities acting on their behalf or at their direction, or by entities owned or controlled by them in any commercial activity involving uranium mining, production or use of nuclear materials and technology, in particular uranium enrichment and reprocessing activities, all heavy-water related activities or technologies related to ballistic missiles capable of delivering nuclear weapons, shall be prohibited. The Union shall take the necessary measures in order to determine the relevant items to be covered by this Article.

Article 6

The following shall be prohibited:

(a) the granting of any financial loan or credit to enterprises in Iran that are engaged in the sectors of the Iranian oil and gas industry referred to in Article 4(1) or to Iranian or Iranian-owned enterprises engaged in those sectors outside Iran;

(b) the acquisition or extension of a participation in enterprises in Iran that are engaged in the sectors of the Iranian oil and gas industry referred to in Article 4(1), or to Iranian or Iranian-owned enterprises engaged in those sectors outside Iran, including the acquisition in full of such enterprises and the acquisition of shares and securities of a participating nature;

(c) the creation of any joint venture with enterprises in Iran that are engaged in the industries in the oil and gas sectors referred to in Article 4(1) and with any subsidiary or affiliate under their control.

Article 7

1. The prohibition in Article 4(1) shall be without prejudice to the execution of an obligation relating to the delivery of goods provided for in contracts concluded before the date of adoption of this Decision.

2. The prohibitions in Article 4 shall be without prejudice to the execution of an obligation arising from contracts concluded before the date of adoption of this Decision and relating to investments made in Iran before the same date by enterprises established in Member States.

3. The prohibitions in Article 6(a) and (b) respectively:

(i) shall be without prejudice to the execution of an obligation arising from contracts or agreements concluded before the date of adoption of this Decision;

(ii) shall not prevent the extension of a participation, if such extension is an obligation under an agreement concluded before the date of adoption of this Decision.

RESTRICTIONS ON FINANCIAL SUPPORT FOR TRADE
Article 8

1. Member States shall exercise restraint in entering into new short term commitments for public and private provided financial support for trade with Iran, including the granting of export credits, guarantees or insurance, to their nationals or entities involved in such trade, with a view to reducing their outstanding amounts, in particular to avoid any financial support contributing to proliferation-sensitive nuclear activities, or to the development of nuclear weapon delivery systems. In addition, Member States shall not enter into new medium and long-term commitments for public and private provided financial support for trade with Iran.

2. Paragraph 1 shall not affect commitments established prior to the entry into force of this Decision.

3. Paragraph 1 shall not concern trade for food, agricultural, medical or other humanitarian purposes.

CHAPTER 2

FINANCIAL SECTOR

Article 9

Member States shall not enter into new commitments for grants, financial assistance and concessional loans to the Government of Iran, including through their participation in international financial institutions, except for humanitarian and developmental purposes.

Article 10

1. In order to prevent the provision of financial services, or the transfer to, through, or from the territories of Member States, or to or by nationals of Member States or entities organised under their laws (including branches abroad), or persons or financial institutions in the territories of Member States, of any financial or other assets or resources that could contribute to Iran's proliferation-sensitive nuclear activities, or the development of nuclear weapon delivery systems, Member States shall exercise enhanced monitoring over all the activities of financial institutions within their jurisdiction with:

(a) banks domiciled in Iran, in particular the Central Bank of Iran;

(b) branches and subsidiaries within the jurisdiction of the Member States of banks domiciled in Iran;

(c) branches and subsidiaries outside the jurisdiction of the Member States of banks domiciled in Iran;

(d) financial entities that are not domiciled in Iran, but are controlled by persons and entities domiciled in Iran.

2. For the purposes of paragraph 1, financial institutions shall be required, in their activities with banks and financial institutions as set out in paragraph 1, to:

(a) exercise continuous vigilance over account activity including through their programmes on customer due diligence and under their obligations relating to money-laundering and financing of terrorism;

(b) require that all information fields of payment instructions which relate to the originator and beneficiary of the transaction in question be completed; and if that information is not supplied, refuse the transaction;

(c) maintain all records of transactions for a period of five years and make them available to national authorities on request;

(d) if they suspect or have reasonable grounds to suspect that funds are related to proliferation financing, promptly report their suspicions to the Financial Intelligence Unit (FIU) or another competent authority designated by the Member State concerned. The FIU or such other competent authority shall have access, directly or indirectly, on a timely basis to the financial, administrative and law enforcement information that it requires to properly undertake this function, including the analysis of suspicious transaction reports.

3. Transfers of funds to and from Iran shall be processed as follows:

(a) transfers due on transactions regarding foodstuffs, healthcare, medical equipment, or for humanitarian purposes shall be carried out without any prior authorisation; the transfer shall be notified to the competent authority of the Member State concerned if above 10 000 euros;

(b) any other transfer below 40 000 euros shall be carried out without any prior authorisation; the transfer shall be notified to the competent authority of the Member State concerned if above 10 000 euros;

(c) any other transfer above 40 000 euros shall require the prior authorisation from the competent authority of the Member State concerned. The authorisation shall be deemed granted within four weeks unless the competent authority of the Member State concerned has objected within this time-limit. The relevant Member State shall inform the other Member States of any authorization rejected.

4. Branches and subsidiaries of banks domiciled in Iran within the jurisdiction of the Member States shall also be required to notify the competent authority of the Member State where they are established, of all transfers of funds carried out or received by them, within five working days after carrying out or receiving the respective transfer of funds. Subject to information-sharing arrangements, notified competent authorities shall without delay transmit this data, as appropriate, to the competent authorities of other Member States, where the counterparts to such transactions are established.

Article 11

1. The opening of new branches, subsidiaries, or representative offices of Iranian banks in the territories of Member States, and the establishment of new joint ventures, or the taking of an ownership interest, or the establishment of new correspondent banking relationships by Iranian banks, including the Central Bank of Iran, its branches and subsidiaries and other financial entities referred to in Article 10(1), with banks in the jurisdiction of Member States, shall be prohibited.

2. Financial institutions within the territories of Member States or under their jurisdiction shall be prohibited from opening representative offices, subsidiaries or banking accounts in Iran.

Article 12

1. The provision of insurance and re-insurance to the Government of Iran, or to entities incorporated in Iran or subject to Iran's jurisdiction, or to any individuals or entities acting on their behalf or at their direction, or to entities owned or controlled by them, including through illicit means, shall be prohibited.

2. Paragraph 1 shall not apply to the provision of health and travel insurances to individuals.

3. It shall be prohibited to participate, knowingly or intentionally, in activities the object or effect of which is to circumvent the prohibition referred to in paragraph 1.

Article 13

The direct or indirect sale or purchase of, or brokering or assistance in the issuance of public or public-guaranteed bonds issued after the entry into force of this Decision to and from the Government of Iran, the Central Bank of Iran, or banks domiciled in Iran, or branches and subsidiaries within and outside the jurisdiction of Member States of banks domiciled in Iran, or financial entities that are neither domiciled in Iran nor within the jurisdiction of the Member States, but are controlled by persons and entities domiciled in Iran as well as any individuals and entities acting on their behalf or at their direction, or entities owned or controlled by them, shall be prohibited.

Article 14

Member States shall require their nationals, persons subject to their jurisdiction and firms incorporated in their territories or subject to their jurisdiction to exercise vigilance when doing business with entities incorporated in Iran or subject to Iran's jurisdiction, including those of the IRGC and IRISL and any individuals and entities acting on their behalf or at their direction, and entities owned or controlled by them including through illicit means in order to ensure such business does not contribute to Iran's proliferation-sensitive nuclear activities or the development of nuclear weapon delivery systems or to violations of UNSCR 1737 (2006), UNSCR 1747 (2007), UNSCR 1803 (2008) or UNSCR 1929 (2010).

CHAPTER 3
TRANSPORT SECTOR
Article 15

1. Member States shall inspect, in accordance with their national authorities and legislation and consistent with international law, in particular the law of the sea and relevant international civil aviation agreements, all cargo to and from Iran in their territories, including seaports and airports, if they have information that provides reasonable grounds to believe that the cargo contains items the supply, sale, transfer or export of which is prohibited under this Decision.

2. Member States, consistent with international law, in particular the law of the sea, may request inspections of vessels on the high seas with the consent of the flag State, if they have information that provides reasonable grounds to believe that the vessels carry items the supply, sale, transfer or export of which is prohibited under this Decision.

3. Member States shall cooperate, in accordance with their national legislation, with inspections undertaken pursuant to paragraph 2.

4. Aircrafts and vessels transporting cargo to and from Iran shall be subject to the requirement of additional pre-arrival or pre-departure information for all goods brought into or out of a Member State.

5. In cases where an inspection referred to in paragraphs 1 or 2 is undertaken, Member States shall seize and dispose of (such as through destruction, rendering inoperable, storage or transferring to a State other than the originating or destination States for disposal) items the supply, sale, transfer or export of which is prohibited under this Decision in accordance with paragraph 16 of UNSCR 1929 (2010). Such seizure and disposal will be carried out at the expense of the importer or, if it is not possible to recover these expenses from the importer, they may, in accordance with national legislation, be recovered from any other person or entity responsible for the attempted illicit supply, sale, transfer or export.

6. The provision by nationals of Member States or from the territories under the jurisdiction of Member States of bunkering or ship supply services, or other servicing of vessels, to Iranian-owned or -contracted vessels, including chartered vessels, shall be prohibited if they have information that provides reasonable grounds to believe that the vessels carry items the supply, sale, transfer or export of which is prohibited under this Decision unless the provision of such services is necessary for humanitarian purposes or until the cargo has been inspected, and seized and disposed of if necessary, in accordance with paragraphs 1, 2 and 5.

Article 16

Member States shall communicate to the Committee any information available on transfers or activity by Iran's Air's cargo division or vessels owned or operated by the IRISL to other companies, that may have been undertaken in order to evade the sanctions of, or in violation of the provisions of UNSCR 1737 (2006), UNSCR 1747 (2007), UNSCR 1803 (2008) or UNSCR 1929 (2010), including the renaming or re-registering of aircraft, vessels or ships.

Article 17

Member States, in accordance with their national legal authorities and legislation and consistent with international law, in particular relevant international civil aviation agreements, shall take the necessary measures to prevent access to the airports under their jurisdiction of all cargo flights operated by Iranian carriers or originating from Iran with the exception of mixed passenger and cargo flights.

Article 18

The provision by nationals of Member States, or from the territories of Member States, of engineering and maintenance services to Iranian cargo aircraft shall be prohibited if they have information that provides reasonable grounds to believe that the cargo aircraft carry items the supply, sale, transfer or export of which is prohibited under this Decision unless the provision of such services is necessary for humanitarian and safety purposes or until the cargo has been inspected, and seized and disposed of if necessary, in accordance with Article 15 (1) and (5).

CHAPTER 4
RESTRICTIONS ON ADMISSION
Article 19

1. Member States shall take the necessary measures to prevent the entry into, or transit through their territories of:
(a) persons listed in the Annex to UNSCR 1737 (2006), and additional persons designated by the Security Council or by the Committee in accordance with paragraph 10 of UNSCR 1737 (2006) as well as IRGC individuals designated by the Security Council or by the Committee, as listed in Annex I;
(b) other persons not covered by Annex I that are engaged in, directly associated with, or providing support for Iran's proliferation-sensitive nuclear activities or for the development of nuclear weapon delivery systems, including through the involvement in

procurement of the prohibited items, goods, equipment, materials and technology, or persons acting on their behalf or at their direction, or persons that have assisted designated persons or entities in evading or violating the provisions of UNSCR 1737 (2006), UNSCR 1747 (2007), UNSCR 1803 (2008) and UNSCR 1929 (2010) or this Decision as well as other senior members of the IRGC, as listed in Annex II.

2. The prohibition in paragraph 1 shall not apply to the transit through the territories of Member States for the purposes of activities directly related to the items specified in subparagraphs 3(b)(i) and (ii) of UNSCR 1737 (2006) for light water reactors begun before December 2006.

3. Paragraph 1 shall not oblige a Member State to refuse its own nationals entry into its territory.

4. Paragraph 1 shall be without prejudice to cases where a Member State is bound by an obligation of international law, namely:

(i) as a host country of an international intergovernmental organisation;

(ii) as a host country to an international conference convened by, or under the auspices of, the United Nations;

(iii) under a multilateral agreement conferring privileges and immunities;

(iv) under the 1929 Treaty of Conciliation (Lateran pact) concluded by the Holy See (State of the Vatican City) and Italy.

5. Paragraph 4 shall be considered as applying also in cases where a Member State is host country of the Organisation for Security and Cooperation in Europe (OSCE).

6. The Council shall be duly informed in all cases where a Member State grants an exemption pursuant to paragraph 4 or 5.

7. Member States may grant exemptions from the measures imposed in paragraph 1 where they determine that travel is justified on the grounds of:

(i) urgent humanitarian need, including religious obligations;

(ii) the necessity to meet the objectives of UNSCR 1737 (2006) and UNSCR 1929 (2010), including where Article XV of the IAEA Statute is engaged;

(iii) attending intergovernmental meetings, including those promoted by the Union, or hosted by a Member State holding the Chairmanship in office of the OSCE, where a political dialogue is conducted that directly promotes democracy, human rights and the rule of law in Iran.

8. A Member State wishing to grant exemptions referred to in paragraph 6 shall notify the Council thereof in writing. The exemption shall be deemed to be granted unless one or more of the Council Members raises an objection in writing within two working days of receiving notification of the proposed exemption. Should one or more of the Council members raise an objection, the Council, acting by a qualified majority, may decide to grant the proposed exemption.

9. In cases where, pursuant to paragraphs 4, 5 and 7, a Member State authorises the entry into, or transit through, its territory of persons listed in Annex I or II, the authorisation shall be limited to the purpose for which it is given and to the persons concerned thereby.

10. Member States shall notify the Committee of the entry into, or transit through, their territories of the persons set out in Annex I, if an exemption has been granted.

CHAPTER 5

FREEZING OF FUNDS AND ECONOMIC RESOURCES

Article 20

1. All funds and economic resources which belong to, are owned, held or controlled, directly or indirectly by the following, shall be frozen:

(a) persons and entities designated in the Annex to UNSCR 1737 (2006), additional persons and entities designated by the Security Council or by the Committee in accordance with paragraph 12 of UNSCR 1737 (2006) and paragraph 7 of UNSCR 1803 (2008) as well as IRGC individuals and entities and IRISL entities designated by the Security Council or by the Committee, as listed in Annex I;

(b) persons and entities not covered by Annex I that are engaged in, directly associated with, or providing support for, Iran's proliferation-sensitive nuclear activities or for the development of nuclear weapon delivery systems, including through the involvement in procurement of the prohibited items, goods, equipment, materials and technology, or persons or entities acting on their behalf or at their direction, or entities owned or controlled by them, including through illicit means, or persons and entities that have assisted designated persons or entities in evading or violating the provisions of UNSCR 1737 (2006), UNSCR 1747 (2007), UNSCR 1803 (2008) and UNSCR 1929 (2010) or this Decision as well as other senior members and entities of IRGC and IRISL and entities owned or controlled by them or acting on their behalf, as listed in Annex II.

2. No funds or economic resources shall be made available, directly or indirectly, to or for the benefit of persons and entities referred to in paragraph 1.

3. Exemptions may be made for funds and economic resources which are:

(a) necessary to satisfy basic needs, including payment for foodstuffs, rent or mortgage, medicines and medical treatment, taxes, insurance premiums, and public utility charges;

(b) intended exclusively for payment of reasonable professional fees and reimbursement of incurred expenses associated with the provision of legal services;

(c) intended exclusively for payment of fees or service charges, in accordance with national laws, for routine holding or maintenance of frozen funds and economic resources;

after notification by the Member State concerned to the Committee of the intention to authorise, where appropriate, access to such funds and economic resources and in the absence of a negative decision by the Committee within five working days of such notification.

4. Exemptions may also be made for funds and economic resources which are:

(a) necessary for extraordinary expenses, after notification by the Member State concerned to, and approval by, the Committee;

(b) the subject of a judicial, administrative or arbitral lien or judgement, in which case the funds and economic resources may be used to satisfy that lien or judgement provided that the lien or judgement was entered before the date of UNSCR 1737 (2006), and is not for the benefit of a person or entity referred to in paragraph 1, after notification by the Member State concerned to the Committee;

(c) necessary for activities directly related to the items specified in subparagraphs 3(b)(i) and (ii) of UNSCR 1737 (2006) for light water reactors begun before December 2006.

5. Paragraph 2 shall not apply to the addition to frozen accounts of:

(a) interest or other earnings on those accounts; or

(b) payments to frozen accounts due under contracts, agreements or obligations that were concluded or arose before the date on which those accounts became subject to restrictive measures;

provided that any such interest, other earnings and payments continue to be subject to paragraph 1.

6. Paragraph 1 shall not prevent a designated person or entity from making payment due under a contract entered into before the listing of such a person or entity, provided that the relevant Member State has determined that:

(a) the contract is not related to any of the prohibited items, materials, equipment, goods, technologies, assistance, training, financial assistance, investment, brokering or services referred to in Article 1;

(b) the payment is not directly or indirectly received by a person or entity referred to in paragraph 1;

and after notification by the relevant Member State to the Committee of the intention to make or receive such payments or to authorize, where appropriate, the unfreezing of funds or economic resources for this purpose, 10 working days prior to such authorisation.

CHAPTER 6
OTHER RESTRICTIVE MEASURES
Article 21

Member States shall, in accordance with their national legislation, take the necessary measures to prevent specialised teaching or training of Iranian nationals, within their territories or by their nationals, of disciplines which would contribute to Iran's proliferation-sensitive nuclear activities and development of nuclear weapon delivery systems.

CHAPTER 7
GENERAL AND FINAL PROVISIONS
Article 22

No claims, including for compensation or for other claim of this kind, such as a claim of set-off or a claim under a guarantee, in connection with any contract or transaction the performance of which was affected, directly or indirectly, wholly or in part, by reason of measures decided on pursuant to UNSCR 1737 (2006), UNSCR 1747 (2007), UNSCR 1803 (2008) or UNSCR 1929 (2010), including measures of the Union or any Member State in accordance with, as required by or in any connection with, the implementation of the relevant decisions of the Security Council or measures covered by the present Decision, shall be granted to the designated persons or entities listed in Annexes I or II, or any other person or entity in Iran, including the Government of Iran, or any person or entity claiming through or for the benefit of any such person or entity.

Article 23

1. The Council shall implement modifications to Annex I on the basis of the determinations made by the Security Council or by the Committee.

2. The Council, acting by unanimity on a proposal from Member States or from the High Representative of the Union for Foreign Affairs and Security Policy, shall establish the list in Annex II and adopt modifications to it.

Article 24

1. Where the Security Council or the Committee lists a person or entity, the Council shall include such person or entity in Annex I.

2. Where the Council decides to subject a person or entity to the measures referred to in Articles 19(1)(b) and 20(1)(b), it shall amend Annex II accordingly.

3. The Council shall communicate its decision to the person or entity referred to in paragraphs 1 and 2, including the grounds for listing, either directly, if the address is known, or through the publication of a notice, providing such person or entity an opportunity to present observations.

4. Where observations are submitted, or where substantial new evidence is presented, the Council shall review its decision and inform the person or entity accordingly.

Article 25

1. Annexes I and II shall include the grounds for listing of listed persons and entities, as provided by the Security Council or by the Committee with regard to Annex I.

2. Annexes I and II shall also include, where available, information necessary to identify the persons or entities concerned, as provided by the Security Council or by the Committee for Annex I. With regard to persons, such information may include names including aliases, date and place of birth, nationality, passport and ID card numbers, gender, address, if known and function or profession. With regard to entities such information may include names, place and date of registration, registration number and place of business. Annex I shall also include the date of designation by the Security Council or by the Committee.

Article 26

1. This Decision shall be reviewed, amended or repealed as appropriate, notably in the light of relevant decisions by the Security Council.

2. The measures on banking relationships with Iranian banks in Articles 10 and 11 shall be reviewed within six months of the adoption of this Decision.

3. The measures referred to in Articles 19(1)(b) and 20(1)(b) shall be reviewed at regular intervals and at least every 12 months. They shall cease to apply in respect of the persons and entities concerned if the Council determines, in accordance with the procedure referred in Article 24, that the conditions for their application are no longer met.

Article 27

Common Position 2007/140/CFSP is hereby repealed.

Article 28

This Decision shall enter into force on the date of its adoption.

ANNEX I

List of persons referred to in Article 19(1)(a) and of persons and entities referred to in Article 20(1)(a)

[...]

COUNCIL REGULATION (EU) No 267/2012 of 23 March 2012 concerning restrictive measures against Iran and repealing Regulation (EU) No 961/2010, Official Journal of the European Union L 88, 24.3.2012, pp. 1–112.

THE COUNCIL OF THE EUROPEAN UNION,

Having regard to the Treaty on the Functioning of the European Union, and in particular Article 215 thereof,

Having regard to Council Decision 2012/35/CFSP of 23 January 2012 amending Decision 2010/413/CFSP concerning restrictive measures against Iran,

Having regard to the joint proposal from the High Representative of the Union for Foreign Affairs and Security Policy and the European Commission,

Whereas:

(1) On 25 October 2010, the Council adopted Regulation (EU) No 961/2010 on restrictive measures against Iran and repealing Regulation (EC) No 423/2007, in order to give effect to Council Decision 2010/413/CFSP.

(2) On 23 January 2012, the Council approved Decision 2012/35/CFSP providing for additional restrictive measures against the Islamic Republic of Iran ('Iran') as requested by the European Council on 9 December 2011.

(3) Those restrictive measures comprise, in particular, additional restrictions on trade in dual-use goods and technology, as well as on key equipment and technology which could be used in the petrochemical industry, a ban on the import of Iranian crude oil, petroleum products and petrochemical products, as well as a prohibition of investment in the petrochemical industry. Moreover, trade in gold, precious metals and diamonds with the Government of Iran, as well as the delivery of newly printed banknotes and coinage to or for the benefit of the Central Bank of Iran, should be prohibited.

(4) Certain technical amendments to existing measures have also become necessary. In particular, the definition of 'brokering services' should be clarified. In cases where the purchase, sale, supply, transfer or export of goods and technology or of financial and technical services may be authorised by a competent authority no separate authorisation of related brokering services will be required.

(5) The definition of 'transfers of funds' should be broadened to non-electronic transfers so as to counter attempts at circumventing the restrictive measures.

(6) The revised restrictive measures concerning dual-use goods should cover all goods and technology set out in Annex I to Council Regulation (EC) No 428/2009 of 5 May 2009 setting up a Community regime for the control of exports, transfer, brokering and transit of dual-use items, with the exception of certain items in Part 2 of category 5 thereof in view of their use in public communication services in Iran. However, the prohibitions in Article 2 of this Regulation do not apply to the sale, supply, transfer or export of goods

and technology newly listed in Annex I or II of this Regulation for which an authorisation has already been granted by the competent authorities of the Member States pursuant to Article 3 of Regulation (EU) No 961/2010 prior to the entry into force of this Regulation.

(7) In order to ensure the effective implementation of the prohibition on the sale, supply, transfer or export to Iran of certain key equipment or technology which could be used in the key sectors of the oil, natural gas and petrochemical industries, lists of such key equipment and technology should be provided.

(8) For the same reason, lists of items subject to trade restrictions on crude oil and petroleum products, petrochemical products, gold, precious metals and diamonds should also be provided.

(9) In addition, to be effective, restrictions on investment in the Iranian oil and gas sector should cover certain key activities, such as bulk gas transmission services for the purpose of transit or delivery to directly interconnected grids, and, for the same reason, should apply to joint ventures as well as other forms of associations and cooperation with Iran in the sector of the transmission of natural gas.

(10) Effective restrictions on Iranian investment in the Union require that measures be taken to prohibit natural or legal persons, entities and bodies subject to the jurisdiction of the Member States from enabling or authorising such investment.

(11) Decision 2012/35/CFSP also extends the freezing of assets to additional persons, entities or bodies providing support to the Government of Iran, including financial, logistical and material support, or associated with them. The Decision also extends the freezing measures to other members of the Islamic Revolutionary Guard Corps (IRGC).

(12) Decision 2012/35/CFSP also provides for the freezing of the assets of the Central Bank of Iran. However, in consideration of possible involvement of the Central Bank of Iran in the financing of foreign trade, derogations are deemed necessary as this targeted financial measure should not prevent trade operations, including contracts relating to foodstuffs, healthcare, medical equipment or for humanitarian purposes in accordance with the provisions of this Regulation. The exemptions in Articles 12 and 14 of this Regulation concerning contracts for the import, purchase or transport of Iranian crude oil, petroleum products and petrochemical products concluded before 23 January 2012 also apply to ancillary contracts, including transport, insurance or inspections contracts necessary for the execution of such contracts. Furthermore, Iranian crude oil, petroleum products and petrochemical products which are legally imported into a Member State pursuant to the exemptions in Articles 12 and 14 of this Regulation are to be considered as being in free circulation within the Union.

(13) It is prohibited, pursuant to the obligation to freeze the assets of Islamic Republic of Iran Shipping Line (IRISL) and of entities owned or controlled by IRISL to load and unload cargoes on and from vessels owned or chartered by IRISL or by such entities in ports of Member States.

Moreover, the transfer of ownership of vessels owned, controlled or chartered by IRISL companies to other entities is also prohibited pursuant to the freezing of IRISL's assets. However, the obligation to freeze the funds and economic resources of IRISL and of entities owned or controlled by IRISL does not require the impounding or detention of vessels owned by such entities or the cargoes carried by them insofar as such cargoes belong to third parties, nor does it require the detention of the crew contracted by them.

(14) In consideration of Iran's attempts at circumventing the sanctions, it should be clarified that all funds and economic resources belonging to, owned, held or controlled by persons, entities or bodies listed in Annexes I or II to Decision 2010/413/CFSP are to be frozen without delay, including those of successor entities established to circumvent the measures set out in this Regulation.

(15) It should also be clarified that submitting and forwarding the necessary documents to a bank for the purpose of their final transfer to a person, entity or body that is not listed, to trigger payments allowed under this Regulation, does not constitute making funds available within the meaning of this Regulation.

(16) It should be clarified that funds or economic resources should be able to be released for the official purposes of diplomatic or consular missions or international organisations enjoying immunities in accordance with international law, in conformity with the provisions of this Regulation.

(17) The application of targeted financial measures by providers of specialised financial messaging services should be further developed, in conformity with the provisions of this Regulation.

It should be clarified that the assets of non-designated persons, entities or bodies held at designated credit and financial institutions should not remain frozen in application of the targeted financial measures and should be able to be released under the conditions provided for in this Regulation.

In consideration of Iran's attempts at using its financial system for the purpose of circumventing the sanctions, it is necessary to require enhanced vigilance in relation to the activities of Iran's credit and financial institutions so as to prevent circumvention of this Regulation, including the freezing of the assets of the Central Bank of Iran. These enhanced vigilance requirements for credit and financial institutions should be complementary to existing obligations deriving from Regulation (EC) 1781/2006 of the European Parliament and of the Council of 15 November 2006 on information on the payer accompanying transfers of funds and from the implementation of Directive 2005/60/EC of the European Parliament and of the Council of 26 October 2005 on the prevention of the use of the financial system for the purpose of money laundering and terrorist financing.

(18) Certain provisions regarding the controls of funds transfers should be reviewed in order to facilitate their application by competent authorities and operators and to prevent circumvention of the provisions of this Regulation, including the freezing of the assets of the Central Bank of Iran.

(19) Furthermore, the restrictions on insurance should be adjusted, in particular with a view to clarifying that the insurance of diplomatic and consular missions within the Union is permitted, and to allow for the provision of third party liability insurance or environmental liability insurance.

(20) Moreover, the requirement to submit pre-arrival and pre-departure information should be updated, since this obligation has become generally applicable to all goods entering or leaving the customs territory of the Union following the full implementation as from 1 January 2012 of the customs security measures laid down in the relevant provisions concerning entry and exit summary declarations in Regulation (EEC) No 2913/92 and in Regulation (EEC) No 2454/93.

(21) Adjustments should also be made concerning the provision of bunkering and ship supply services, the liability of operators and the prohibition of the circumvention of the relevant restrictive measures.

(22) The mechanisms for exchange of information between Member States and the Commission should be reviewed so as to ensure the effective implementation and uniform interpretation of this Regulation.

(23) In consideration of its objectives, the ban on internal repression equipment should be provided for under Regulation (EU) No 359/2011 concerning restrictive measures directed against certain persons, entities and bodies in view of the situation in Iran, rather than under this Regulation.

(24) For the sake of clarity, Regulation (EU) No 961/2010 should be repealed and replaced by this Regulation.

(25) The restrictive measures provided for in this Regulation fall within the scope of the Treaty on the Functioning of the European Union and legislation at the level of the Union is therefore necessary in order to implement them, in particular with a view to ensuring their uniform application by economic operators in all Member States.

(26) This Regulation respects the fundamental rights and observes the principles recognised in particular by the Charter of Fundamental Rights of the European Union and in particular the right to an effective remedy and to a fair trial, the right to property and the right to protection of personal data. This Regulation should be applied in accordance with those rights and principles.

(27) This Regulation also respects the obligations of Member States under the Charter of the United Nations and the legally binding nature of Resolutions of the United Nations Security Council.

(28) The procedure for the designation of persons subject to freezing measures under this Regulation should include providing designated natural or legal persons, entities or bodies with the grounds for listing, so as to give them an opportunity to submit observations. Where observations are submitted, or substantial new evidence is presented, the Council should review its decision in the light of those observations and inform the person, entity or body concerned accordingly.

(29) For the implementation of this Regulation, and to create maximum legal certainty within the Union, the names and other relevant data concerning natural and legal persons, entities and bodies whose funds and economic resources must be frozen in accordance with the Regulation, should be made public. Any processing of personal data of natural persons under this Regulation should be in conformity with Regulation (EC) No 45/2001 of the European Parliament and of the Council of 18 December 2000 on the protection of individuals with regard to the processing of personal data by the Community institutions and bodies and on the free movement of such data and Directive 95/46/EC of the European Parliament and of the Council of 24 October 1995 on the protection of individuals with regard to the processing of personal data and on the free movement of such data.

(30) In order to ensure that the measures provided for in this Regulation are effective, it should enter into force on the day of its publication.

[...]

Judgment of the Court of First Instance (Second Chamber) of 9 July 2009, Melli Bank v. Council of the European Union, Joined cases T-246/08 and T-332/08, European Court Reports 2009, p. II-2629, paras. 1–11, 61–77, 98–114, 135–139, and 143–152.

In the included extracts of this judgment of the Court of First Instance (CFI), the Court interpreted Article 7(2)(d) of Regulation No 423/2007 and determined its compatibility with the principle of proportionality. It, further, dismissed the plea that the Decision imposing restrictive measures on Melli Bank plc is in breach of the principle of non-discrimination. Finally, the Council was found to have complied with its obligation to state reasons for the freezing of the funds of the applicant. In the Appeal Case C-380/09 P, the CJEU upheld the judgment on first instance but found that the CFI erred in the application of the 'ownership' test of Article 7(2)(d) of Regulation No. 423/2007. That test is satisfied when an entity is fully owned by a person, entity, or body engaged in, directly associated with, or providing support for Iran's nuclear activities, without the need for further review by the Court.[19]

Background to the case

1. The applicant, Melli Bank plc, is a public limited company registered and having its registered office in the United Kingdom, authorised and regulated by the Financial Services Authority ('the FSA'). It began to carry on its banking activities in the United Kingdom on 1 January 2002, following the transformation of the branch of Bank Melli Iran ('BMI') in that country. BMI, the parent company wholly owning the applicant, is an Iranian bank controlled by the Iranian State.

The restrictive measures adopted against the Islamic Republic of Iran

2. These cases have been brought in connection with the restrictive measures introduced in order to apply pressure on the Islamic Republic of Iran to end proliferation-sensitive nuclear activities and the development of nuclear weapon delivery systems ('nuclear proliferation').

3. The origin of the regime at issue is to be found in the United Nations. On 23 December 2006 the United Nations Security Council ('the Security Council') adopted Resolution 1737 (2006), the annex to which lists a series of persons and entities involved in nuclear proliferation whose funds and economic resources ('funds') were to be frozen. The list contained in the annex to Resolution 1737 (2006) has subsequently been updated by several resolutions, in particular by Security Council Resolution 1747 (2007) by which the funds of the Iranian Bank Sepah and its subsidiary in the United Kingdom, Bank Sepah International plc, were frozen. Neither BMI nor the applicant has been subject to fund-freezing measures adopted by the Security Council.

4. Furthermore, under paragraph 10 of Security Council Resolution 1803 (2008) of 3 March 2008, the Security Council called upon 'all States to exercise vigilance over the activities of financial institutions in their territories with all banks domiciled

---

[19] Case C-380/09 P *Melli Bank plc v. Council of the European Union*, not yet reported, para. 79.

in Iran, in particular with Bank Melli and Bank Saderat, and their branches and subsidiaries abroad, in order to avoid such activities contributing to [nuclear proliferation]'.

5. So far as the European Union is concerned, Resolution 1737 (2006) was given effect by Council Common Position 2007/140/CFSP of 27 February 2007 concerning restrictive measures against Iran (OJ 2007 L 61, p. 49). Article 5(1) thereof provides for the freezing of all funds belonging to the persons or entities designated in Security Council Resolution 1737 (2006), in subsequent resolutions or pursuant to them, and also all funds owned, held or controlled, directly or indirectly, by those persons or entities. Article 5(1)(b) of Common Position 2007/140 provides, moreover, that those measures are to apply to persons or entities owned or controlled by persons or entities engaged in, directly associated with, or providing support for nuclear proliferation. According to Article 7(2) of Common Position 2007/140, the list of persons or entities to whom and to which the fund-freezing measures apply, by virtue of Article 5(1)(b) of that Common Position, is to be established and amended by the Council, acting by unanimity.

6. In so far as the powers of the European Community are concerned, Resolution 1737 (2006) was given effect by Council Regulation (EC) No 423/2007 of 19 April 2007 concerning restrictive measures against Iran (OJ 2007 L 103, p. 1), the content of which is substantially the same as that of Common Position 2007/140. Thus, Article 7(1) of Regulation No 423/2007 provides for the freezing of the funds of the persons, entities and bodies ('entities') designated by the Security Council. Article 7(2) of that regulation lays down the same provisions with regard to the entities identified as being engaged in nuclear proliferation as provided in Article 5(1)(b) of Common Position 2007/140. In particular, Article 7(2)(d) of the regulation provides for the freezing of the funds of entities owned or controlled by entities identified as engaged in, directly associated with or providing support for nuclear proliferation as referred to in Article 7(2)(a) or (b) of Regulation No 423/2007. The entities to which a measure freezing funds pursuant to Article 7(2) of Regulation No 423/2007 applies are listed in Annex V to that document.

7. By way of derogation from Article 7 of Regulation No 423/2007, Articles 9 and 10 thereof authorise the competent authorities of the Member States, in essence, to release frozen funds in order to enable entities listed in Annex V to honour obligations arising from contracts concluded before the fund-freezing measure was adopted and to cover essential expenses.

8. Article 15(2) of Regulation No 423/2007 provides, first, that the Council, acting by qualified majority, is to establish, review and amend the list in Annex V in full accordance with the determinations made by the Council pursuant to Article 5(1)(b) of Common Position 2007/140 and, second, that the list in Annex V is to be reviewed at regular intervals and at least every 12 months.

9. Article 15(3) of Regulation No 423/2007 requires the Council to state individual and specific reasons for decisions taken pursuant to Article 15(2) of that regulation, and to make them known to the entities concerned.

The contested decision

10. On 23 June 2008 the Council adopted Decision 2008/475/EC implementing Article 7(2) of Regulation No 423/2007 (OJ 2008 L 163, p. 29, 'the contested decision'). As set out in paragraph 4 of Table B in the annex to the contested decision, both BMI and its subsidiaries, including the applicant, were entered in the list in Annex V to the regulation, with the consequence that their funds were frozen.

11. The Council gave the following reasons:

'Providing or attempting to provide financial support for companies which are involved in or procure goods for Iran's nuclear and missile programmes (AIO, SHIG, SBIG, AEOI, Novin Energy Company, Mesbah Energy Company, Kalaye Electric Company and DIO). Bank Melli serves as a facilitator for Iran's sensitive activities. It has facilitated numerous purchases of sensitive materials for Iran's nuclear and missile programmes. It has provided a range of financial services on behalf of entities linked to Iran's nuclear and missile industries, including opening letters of credit and maintaining accounts. Many of the above companies have been designated by [Security Council] Resolutions 1737 and 1747.'

[...]

Interpretation of Article 7(2)(d) of Regulation No 423/2007

[...]

Findings of the Court

61. The first point to be borne in mind is that, in interpreting a provision of Community law, it is necessary to consider not only its wording but also the context in which it occurs and the objects of the rules of which it is part (Case 292/82 *Merck* [1983] ECR 3781, paragraph 12).

62. With regard to the wording of Article 7(2)(d) of Regulation No 423/2007, that provision states that '[a]ll funds...belonging to entities...identified, in accordance with Article 5(1)(b) of Common Position 2007/140...as being [an entity] owned or controlled by [an entity identified as engaged in nuclear proliferation] shall be frozen'. This wording calls for two comments.

63. First, by reason of the use of the words 'shall be frozen', extension of the fund-freezing measure to entities owned or controlled is obligatory, the Council enjoying no leeway in this respect. Indeed, if the legislature had intended to give the Council such leeway, it would have given expression to its intention by the use of explicit words such as 'may be frozen'.

64. Secondly, when adopting a decision pursuant to Article 7(2)(d) of Regulation No 423/2007, the Council must undertake an evaluation of the facts of the case in order to ascertain which entities are entities owned or controlled.

65. The context of which Article 7(2)(d) of Regulation No 423/2007 forms part, and in particular the broad logic of Article 7(2), bears out the textual analysis of that provision. Inasmuch as the expression 'have been identified' appears in the introductory part of that provision, it must be considered that, like each of the four hypotheses set out in (a) to (d), classification as an entity 'owned or controlled' is the subject of a case-by-case evaluation by the Council.

66. Finally, the interpretation suggested by the textual and contextual analyses is in line with the objective sought by Regulation No 423/2007, namely, the intention of preventing nuclear proliferation and, more generally, to maintain international peace and security, given the seriousness of the risk posed by nuclear proliferation.

67. Having regard to all the foregoing, it must be concluded that Article 7(2)(d) of Regulation No 423/2007 requires the Council to freeze the funds of an entity 'owned or controlled' by an entity identified as engaged in nuclear proliferation as provided for in Article 7(2)(a) or (b) of that regulation, the Council assessing case by case whether the entities concerned are entities 'owned or controlled'.

68. The arguments put forward by the applicant cannot shake that conclusion.

69. First, inasmuch as the Council is called upon to evaluate the classification of an entity 'owned or controlled', it is led to take into account all the relevant aspects of the specific case, such as the degree of operational independence of the entity in question or the possible effect of the supervision to which it is subjected by public authorities. In contrast, the nature of that entity's activities and the possible lack of any link between those activities and nuclear proliferation are not, in this context, a relevant criterion, for the reason for the adoption of a measure freezing funds applying to the entity owned or controlled is not, as paragraph 103 below makes clear, that the latter itself is engaged in nuclear proliferation. Likewise, the fact that the purpose of the restrictive measures adopted by virtue of Regulation No 423/2007 is to stop all financial and technical assistance for the nuclear and missile-development activities of the Islamic Republic of Iran, which pose the risk of nuclear proliferation, necessarily means that those measures were adopted vis-à-vis a third State, with the result that they must be regarded as being compatible with the interpretation of Articles 60 EC and 301 EC given in *Kadi and Al Barakaat International Foundation* v *Council and Commission*.

70. So far as concerns the obligation to state reasons imposed on the Council by Article 15(3) of Regulation No 423/2007, it is apparent from paragraphs 143 to 146 below that the Council is required to indicate the reasons that prompted it to consider that an entity is 'owned or controlled' by an entity identified as engaged in nuclear proliferation and that its funds must, in consequence, be frozen pursuant to Article 7(2)(d) of Regulation No 423/2007. That obligation is, however, without prejudice to the fact that, once it considers that the conditions laid down in that provision have been satisfied, the Council is bound to adopt a measure freezing the funds of the entity concerned.

71. Secondly, the provisions of Regulation No 423/2007 cited by the applicant first prohibit carrying out transactions with entities identified as engaged in nuclear proliferation or engaging in such transactions, next impose a duty of transparency and cooperation with the competent authorities and, lastly, oblige the Member States to provide for sanctions applicable in the case of infringement of that regulation. Those provisions were, it is true, adopted so that the objectives sought by the Council might be attained. None the less, the mere existence of rules prohibiting the carrying-out of transactions with entities identified as engaged in nuclear proliferation and providing for obligations entailing sanctions does not guarantee that such transactions will not be performed, should the occasion arise, by an entity

owned or controlled by an entity identified as engaged in nuclear proliferation. Consequently, that fact does not permit the inference that any additional measure, such as the freezing of the funds of entities owned or controlled by entities identified as engaged in nuclear proliferation, is redundant.

72. Thirdly, the argument drawn from the applicant's particular situation does not concern the interpretation to be made of Article 7(2)(d) of Regulation No 423/2007 but rather an error supposedly made by the Council in applying that provision to the applicant. Those arguments are not, therefore, relevant at this stage of the analysis. They will be examined, as a separate plea in law, later on in this judgment (paragraphs 119 to 129 below).

73. Fourthly, as regards the argument that it is not the Council's practice automatically to freeze the funds of all subsidiaries of entities identified as being engaged in nuclear proliferation as provided for Article 7(2)(a) or (b) of Regulation No 423/2007, it is to be observed, first, that the Council may legitimately, as paragraph 123 below makes clear, not apply Article 7(2)(d) of the regulation to entities which, in its opinion, do not fulfil the conditions for the application of that provision, despite the fact that they are subsidiaries of entities identified as engaged in nuclear proliferation.

74. Next, as the Council and the French Republic observe, it is impossible to identify, in every case, all the entities owned or controlled by an entity identified as engaged in nuclear proliferation.

75. Lastly, even on the assumption that the Council had omitted to adopt measures to freeze the funds of certain entities owned or controlled by entities identified as engaged in nuclear proliferation as provided for in Article 7(2)(a) or (b) of Regulation No 423/2007, it must be stated, on the one hand, that because the Council is bound to comply with the regulation, any divergent practice of that institution's cannot properly derogate from that act and cannot, with all the more reason, give rise to any legitimate expectations on the part of the entities concerned. On the other hand, while the argument at issue alleges breach of the principle of equal treatment, it is to be borne in mind that the latter must be reconciled with the principle of legality, according to which no one may rely, to his own benefit, on an unlawful act committed in favour of another (Case T-327/94 *SCA Holding* v *Commission* [1998] ECR II-1373, paragraph 160; Case T-347/94 *Mayr-Melnhof* v *Commission* [1998] ECR II-1751, paragraph 334; and Case T-23/99 *LR AF 1998* v *Commission* [2002] ECR II-1705, paragraph 367). Any unlawful conduct by the Council in other cases, supposing it to have been established, cannot, therefore, be relied on to advantage in support of the applicant's position.

76. In those circumstances, the case-law holding that, when the wording of secondary legislation is open to more than one interpretation, preference is to be given to that which renders the provision consistent with the Treaty rather than that which leads to its being incompatible with the Treaty (Case 218/82 *Commission* v *Council* [1983] ECR 4063, paragraph 15) is not relevant. In fact, in the circumstances of this case there is no doubt as to the interpretation of Article 7(2)(d) of Regulation No 423/2007.

77. The applicant's arguments relating to the supposed incompatibility of the interpretation set out in paragraph 67 above with the principle of proportionality will, however, be evaluated later in this judgment, in connection with the examination of the plea of illegality raised against Article 7(2)(d) of Regulation No 423/2007 by the applicant in Case T-332/08.

The plea of illegality raised against Article 7(2)(d) of Regulation No 423/2007

[...]

Findings of the Court

98. A preliminary point to be noted here is that this plea of illegality consists of denying the compatibility with the principle of proportionality of one of the general rules determining the procedure for implementing the restrictive measures laid down by Regulation No 423/2007, namely, Article 7(2)(d) of the regulation, which requires the Council, as shown in paragraphs 61 to 67 above, to freeze the funds of entities owned or controlled by an entity identified as being engaged in nuclear proliferation, as provided for by Article 7(2)(a) or (b) of the regulation. It follows, first, that the considerations set out in paragraph 45 above are applicable so far as concerns the rigour of the review carried out by the Court and, second, that, by analogy with what has been held in paragraph 72 above, the arguments in respect of the relationship between the applicant and BMI, and of the applicant's particular position as a United Kingdom bank, are not relevant to the examination of this plea of illegality. They must, however, be taken into account in the examination of the claim that there was no justification for applying Article 7(2)(d) of Regulation No 423/2007 to the applicant. Those arguments will therefore be considered in paragraphs 119 to 129 below.

99. It must also be found that the reference to Security Council Resolution 1803 (2008) has no bearing on the issue. Application of Article 7(2) of Regulation No 423/2007, unlike Article 7(1), is independent of the adoption of fund-freezing measures by the Security Council. The actual aim of Article 7(2) is to enable the Council to adopt, if it considers it warranted, under its powers conferred by Articles 60 EC and 301 EC, fund-freezing measures directed against entities that are not the subject of similar measures decided on by the Security Council. In consequence, contrary to what the applicant argues, Article 7(2) does not give effect to Resolution 1803 (2008), which means that the content of that resolution does not constitute a criterion having regard to which the compatibility of Article 7(2)(d) of Regulation No 423/2007 with the principle of proportionality must be assessed.

100. According to the case-law, by virtue of the principle of proportionality, which is one of the general principles of Community law, the lawfulness of the prohibition of an economic activity is subject to the condition that the prohibitory measures should be appropriate and necessary in order to achieve the objectives legitimately pursued by the legislation in question; when there is a choice between several appropriate measures recourse must be had to the least onerous, and the disadvantages caused must not be disproportionate to the aims pursued (Case C-331/88 *Fedesa and Others* [1990] ECR I-4023, paragraph 13). It is therefore in the light of those criteria that the applicant's other arguments are to be examined.

101. First, in so far as the applicant's reasoning concerning the interpretation of Article 7(2)(d) of Regulation No 423/2007, summarised in paragraphs 48 to 54 above, is relevant to the examination of that provision's compatibility with the principle of proportionality, it must be rejected for the reasons set out in paragraphs 69 to 76 above.

102. Secondly, with regard to the existence of a link between Article 7(2)(d) of Regulation No 423/2007 and the objective pursued, it is to be observed that the purpose of Regulation No 423/2007 is to stop nuclear proliferation and its funding and so to bring pressure to bear upon the Islamic Republic of Iran to put an end to the activities concerned. That objective forms part of a more general framework of endeavours linked to the maintenance of international peace and security and is, therefore, legitimate, which the applicant does not, moreover, deny.

103. Contrary to what the applicant argues, the freezing of the funds of entities owned or controlled by an entity identified as being engaged in nuclear proliferation, as provided for by Article 7(2)(a) or (b) of Regulation No 423/2007 is linked to the objective defined in the previous paragraph. When the funds of an entity identified as being engaged in nuclear proliferation are frozen, there is a not insignificant danger that that entity may exert pressure on the entities it owns or controls in order to circumvent the effect of the measures applying to it, by encouraging them either to transfer their funds to it, directly or indirectly, or to carry out transactions which it cannot itself perform by reason of the freezing of its funds. That being so, it must be considered that the freezing of the funds of entities owned or controlled by an entity identified as being engaged in nuclear proliferation is necessary and appropriate in order to ensure the effectiveness of the measures adopted vis-à-vis that entity and to ensure that those measures are not circumvented.

104. The existence of the danger just described makes it possible to explain, furthermore, the fact, argued at the hearing, that Regulation No 423/2007 applies to the entities owned or controlled, even though they are not expressly mentioned in recitals 2 and 6 in its preamble, which set out the various restrictive measures at issue. It also makes it possible to explain that the question whether the entity owned or controlled itself engages in nuclear proliferation is irrelevant.

105. The other matters referred to by the applicant cannot alter that conclusion. So, the facts that the entity owned or controlled has not been the subject of disciplinary or regulatory measures in the past and that it has complied with the sanctions regimes and the restrictive measures in force are not relevant in that connection for, so long as a fund-freezing measure did not apply to the parent entity, the latter could, subject to observance of other rules applicable, have the funds of the entities it owns or controls transferred to it and carry out transactions which are from now on incompatible with the restrictive measures adopted. It had, therefore, no reason to put pressure on those entities. Likewise, a declaration by the entity owned or controlled to the effect that it would abide by the consequences of the freezing of its parent entity's funds does not carry sufficient guarantees that any pressure brought to bear by the parent entity would not be effective.

106. On the other hand, the argument advanced by the United Kingdom has to be rejected, that the freezing of the funds of entities owned or controlled also

pursues the objective of putting economic pressure on the Islamic Republic of Iran through BMI, by stopping the latter benefiting from the applicant's profits, reputation and position on the market. It is not, in point of fact, the object of the restrictive measures imposed by Regulation No 423/2007 to bring such economic pressure to bear. It may be observed that, while it is indeed the aim of those measures, set out in recitals 2 and 6 in the preamble to Regulation No 423/2007, to put pressure on the Islamic Republic of Iran, they are, nevertheless, precautionary measures designed to prevent nuclear proliferation and its funding. However, nothing in Regulation No 423/2007 permits the inference that those measures are intended to affect the economic situation of the entities concerned, beyond what is essential in order to prevent nuclear proliferation and its funding.

107. Third, as regards the existence of other measures, less restrictive than the freezing of funds, that could be applied either separately or cumulatively in order to attain the objective pursued, it has not been established that the supervision and control measures existing at the time the contested decision was adopted are adequate, in relation to the danger described in paragraph 103 above.

108. Next, the reinforcement of supervision by the competent authorities of compliance with the restrictive measures and greater cooperation with those authorities, the requirement of particular transparency with regard to the applicant's activities and the adoption of measures to ensure that its situation is regularly reviewed are ex post measures concerning transactions already performed and are not, therefore, capable of preventing possible future transactions incompatible with the restrictive measures enacted. Such is all the more the case because if they are to be effective the competent authorities must be able to determine whether the other party to a transaction is linked to BMI or to another entity identified as being engaged in nuclear proliferation.

109. Lastly, as regards the measures mentioned for the first time at the hearing, it must be considered that they cannot be taken into consideration. It was contrary to Articles 48(2) and 76a(3) of the Rules of Procedure that they were referred to during the proceedings without any justification whatsoever being offered. In any event, the practicability of a system of prior authorisation and supervision by an independent agent has not been demonstrated by the applicant. In its opinion, the total prohibition of transactions with Iran is not, on any view, effective in preventing transactions with intermediaries not situated in that country and not known to be associated with BMI.

110. In those circumstances, it must be concluded that the alternative measures suggested by the applicant are not apt to attain the objective pursued.

111. Fourthly, as regards the difficulties caused to the applicant, the case-law makes it clear that the fundamental rights relied on by the latter, namely, the right to property and the right to carry on economic activity, are not absolute rights and that their exercise may be subject to restrictions justified by objectives of public interest pursued by the Community. Thus, any restrictive economic or financial measure entails, ex hypothesi, consequences affecting the right to property and the right to the free exercise of economic activity, so causing harm to parties who have not been found to be responsible for the situation giving rise to the measures in

question. The importance of the aims pursued by the legislation at issue is such as to justify negative consequences, even of a substantial nature, for some operators (see, to this effect, Case C-84/95 *Bosphorus* [1996] ECR I-3953, paragraphs 21 to 23, and *Kadi and Al Barakaat International Foundation*, paragraphs 354 to 361).

112. In this regard, it is to be noted that the freedom to carry on economic activity and the right to property of a bank established in the territory of the Community are to a considerable extent restricted by the freezing of its funds. The entity concerned cannot enter into new transactions with its customers or, unless it has received specific authorisation, make any transfer of its funds. None the less, given the prime importance of the preservation of international peace and security, the Court considers that the difficulties caused are not disproportionate to the ends sought.

113. With regard, lastly, to the interference with the free movement of capital and payments pleaded by the applicant, it is to be observed that Article 60 EC, which is one of the measures governing this sphere, expressly authorises the Council to take the necessary urgent measures on the movement of capital and on payments as regards third countries, in accordance with the procedure provided for in Article 301. It is precisely on the basis of those two provisions of the EC Treaty that Regulation No 423/2007 was adopted, which implies that the restrictions entailed by that act form part of the rules circumscribing the free movement of capital and payments guaranteed by the Treaty and cannot, therefore, be incompatible with it.

114. Having regard to all the foregoing, it must be concluded that it has not been established that Article 7(2)(d) of Regulation No 423/2007 is incompatible with the principle of proportionality. Accordingly, the plea of illegality raised by the applicant against that provision must be rejected.

The plea in law alleging breach of the principle of non-discrimination

[...]

Findings of the Court

135. According to the case-law, the principle of equal treatment, which constitutes a fundamental principle of law, prohibits comparable situations from being treated differently or different situations from being treated in the same way, unless such difference in treatment is objectively justified (Joined Cases T-222/99, T-327/99 and T-329/99 *Martinez and Others* v *Parliament* [2001] ECR II-2823, paragraph 150).

136. The examination of the previous pleas in law shows that the decisive criterion for giving effect to Article 7(2)(d) of Regulation No 423/2007, and therefore the criterion for comparison applicable in determining whether there has been any breach of the principle of equal treatment, is whether the entity in question is owned or controlled by an entity identified as being engaged in nuclear proliferation, as provided for in Article 7(2)(a) or (b) of that regulation.

137. In this case, BMI has been identified, in the contested decision, as an entity engaged in nuclear proliferation and it has been concluded in paragraph 30 above that the validity of that finding does not form part of the subject-matter of these cases. In the same way, as is apparent from the considerations in paragraphs 119 to 129 above, the applicant is an entity 'owned or controlled' within the meaning of Article 7(2)(d) of Regulation No 423/2007. In those circumstances, even if the

Council had in fact omitted to adopt measures to freeze the funds of certain entities owned or controlled by entities identified as being engaged in nuclear proliferation, such as Persia International Bank or Bank Saderat, that fact cannot be relied on with advantage by the applicant, for the reasons explained in paragraph 75 above. The applicant's first head of claim must therefore be rejected.

138. With regard to the second head of claim, it is to be observed that whereas the applicant's funds were frozen pursuant to Article 7(2) of Regulation No 423/2007, the measure applying to the Bank Sepah International was adopted under Article 7(1) of that regulation. That means that this head of claim is of no consequence, for it relates to an alleged breach of the principle of equal treatment in the application of Article 7(2)(d) of Regulation No 423/2007, the provision at issue having been given effect in only one of the two situations presented by the applicant. Furthermore, the latter has not even claimed that Bank Sepah International's parent entity was not engaged in nuclear proliferation. It has, accordingly, not established that it was in this connection in a factual situation different from that of Bank Sepah International.

139. This plea in law must therefore be rejected.

The plea in law alleging breach of the obligation to state reasons

[...]

Findings of the Court

143. The purpose of the obligation to state the reasons for an act adversely affecting a person, as provided for in Article 253 EC and, in this case, more particularly in Article 15(3) of Regulation No 423/2007, is, first, to provide the person concerned with sufficient information to make it possible to determine whether the act is well founded or whether it is vitiated by an error permitting its validity to be contested before the Community courts and, second, to enable the Community judicature to review the lawfulness of the act. The obligation to state reasons thus laid down constitutes an essential principle of Community law which may be derogated from only for overriding reasons. The statement of reasons must therefore in principle be notified to the person concerned at the same time as the act adversely affecting him, for failure to do so cannot be remedied by the fact that the person concerned learns the reasons for the measure during the proceedings before the Community courts. Furthermore, observance of the obligation to state reasons is all the more important in the case of an initial decision to freeze an entity's funds because it constitutes the sole safeguard enabling the party concerned to make effective use of the legal remedies available to it to challenge the lawfulness of the decision in question, given that that person has no right to be heard before the decision is adopted (see, to this effect, *Organisation des Modjahedines du peuple d'Iran* v *Council*, paragraphs 138 to 140 and the case-law cited).

144. Consequently, unless overriding considerations involving the security of the Community and its Member States or the conduct of their international relations militate against it, the Council is required, by virtue of Article 15(3) of Regulation No 423/2007, to advise the entity concerned of the actual specific reasons when it adopts a fund-freezing decision such as the contested decision. It must thus

mention the matters of fact and law on which the legal justification for the measure depends and the considerations which led it to adopt that measure. So far as is possible, those reasons must be communicated either when the measure at issue is adopted or as soon as may be after it has been adopted (see, to this effect and by analogy, *Organisation des Modjahedines du peuple d'Iran* v *Council*, paragraphs 143 and 148 and the case-law cited).

145. However, the statement of reasons must be appropriate to the measure at issue and the context in which it was adopted. The requirement of a statement of reasons must be assessed in the light of the circumstances of the case, in particular of the content of the measure, the nature of the reasons given and the interest which the addressees of the measure, or other parties to whom it is of direct and individual concern, may have in obtaining explanations. It is not necessary for the reasoning to specify all the relevant matters of fact and law, inasmuch as the adequacy or otherwise of the reasoning is to be evaluated with regard not only to its wording but also to its context and to all the legal rules governing the matter in question. In particular, the reasons given for a measure adversely affecting a person are sufficient if it was adopted in circumstances known to that person which enable him to understand the scope of the measure concerning him (*Organisation des Modjahedines du peuple d'Iran* v *Council*, paragraph 141 and the case-law cited).

146. As is made apparent in paragraphs 61 to 67 above, application of Article 7(2)(d) of Regulation No 423/2007, at issue in these proceedings, requires the entity concerned to be owned or controlled by an entity identified as being engaged in nuclear proliferation as provided for in Article 7(2)(a) or (b) of that regulation, the Council determining case by case whether the entity concerned is an entity 'owned or controlled'. In consequence, in addition to indicating the legal basis of the measure adopted, the obligation to state reasons incumbent on the Council relates to that very circumstance. In this context, the French Republic's argument that there is no need to mention, in decisions applying Article 7(2) of the regulation, the names of the entities owned or controlled to which the fund-freezing measures apply must be rejected. If that interpretation were upheld, the entities concerned would be unable either to ascertain by official means that the fund-freezing measures were applicable to them or to know why the Council considered that they were classified as an entity 'owned or controlled'. In the same way, third parties could not determine the ambit *ratione personae* of the measures taken. Such a situation would be incompatible both with the obligation to state reasons binding on the Council and with the principles of legal certainty and of transparency.

147. In the instant case, the Council has indicated, both in the title of the contested decision and in recital 2 in the preamble thereto, that the measures taken were based on Article 7(2) of Regulation No 423/2007. In point 4 of Table B in the Annex to the contested decision, it found that BMI engaged in nuclear proliferation, relying on the grounds set out in paragraph 11 above. Lastly, in point 4 of Table B in the Annex to the contested decision, it mentioned the applicant among the 'branches and subsidiaries' of BMI.

148. In those circumstances, the Court considers that the statement of reasons for the contested decision, although exceptionally concise, is sufficient having regard to the case-law cited in paragraphs 143 to 145 above. First, the applicant could in the contested decision identify Article 7(2)(d) of Regulation No 423/2007 as the legal basis for the fund-freezing measure affecting it, for, on the one hand, Article 7(2) of that regulation had been mentioned as being the provision implemented and, on the other, the applicant was identified in it as being one of BMI's 'branches and subsidiaries', which signifies that Article 7(2)(d) of the regulation, specifically applicable to entities owned or controlled, and in particular therefore to subsidiaries, had been given effect with regard to the applicant.

149. Secondly, in the contested decision the Council makes plain the reasons why it considered that BMI engaged in nuclear proliferation, as provided for in Article 7(2)(a) or (b) of Regulation No 423/2007.

150. Thirdly, the fact that the applicant was identified as one of BMI's 'branches and subsidiaries' in the contested decision implies that the Council considered that the applicant, because its capital was wholly owned by BMI, was 'owned' by the latter for the purpose of Article 7(2)(d) of Regulation No 423/2007.

151. The conclusion that the reasons stated for the contested decision are sufficient is, furthermore, borne out by the subject-matter of the application in Case T-246/08. In that application, Melli Bank claimed that it was legally and operationally distinct from BMI and that it could not be held responsible for the latter's supposed engagement in nuclear proliferation. It also maintained that the freezing of its funds would not impinge on nuclear proliferation, given that it would in any case comply with the contested decision by freezing all the BMI funds it held and by ceasing all operations with BMI. It follows from that line of argument that the applicant, when it brought its first action, was aware of the link between the freezing of its funds and the engagement in nuclear proliferation laid to the charge of its parent entity, BMI.

152. Having regard to the foregoing, this plea must be rejected and, in consequence, the actions must be dismissed in their entirety.

Judgment of the Court (Grand Chamber) of 16 November 2011, Bank Melli Iran v. Council of the European Union, Case C-548/09 P, not yet reported, paras. 35, 45–57.

In the selected passages the Court of Justice discussed whether the obligation to notify the applicant 'in good time' of the reasons for imposing restrictive measures against him, had been fulfilled. The Court found that although the Council had failed to give an individual notification to the applicant, the latter's rights of defence and effective judicial protection had not been violated. This was the case since a national authority, namely the French banking commission, communicated sufficient information to the applicant in a timely manner.

The first principal ground of appeal, alleging an infringement of the obligation of individual notification and erroneous grounds in the judgment under appeal

35. The present ground of appeal concerns paragraphs 86 to 90 of the judgment under appeal, which state the following:

'86 In contrast, the Council's assertion, supported by the interveners, that the obligation to apprise the applicant of the reasons was satisfied by the publication of the contested decision in the Official Journal cannot be accepted. A decision such as the contested decision, which adopts an amended version of Annex V to Regulation No 423/2007, produces its effects *erga omnes*, in that it is addressed to a body of addressees determined in a general and abstract manner, which are required to freeze the funds of the entities designated by name in the list in that annex. Such a decision, however, is not of an exclusively general nature, for the freezing of funds applies to entities designated by name, directly and individually concerned by the individual restrictive measures adopted in respect of them (see, to that effect and by analogy, [Joined Cases C-402/05 P and C-415/05 P *Kadi and Al Barakaat International Foundation* v *Council and Commission* [2008] I-6351, paragraphs 241 to 244, and Case T-228/02 *Organisation des Modjahedines du peuple d'Iran* v *Council* [2006] ECR II-4665], paragraph 98). Furthermore, the freezing of funds has considerable consequences for the entities concerned, for it may restrict the exercise of their fundamental rights. In the circumstances, given the need…to ensure that those rights, both substantive and procedural, are respected, it must be considered that the Council is bound, in so far as may be possible, to apprise the entities concerned of the fund-freezing measures by making individual notification.

87 The arguments put forward by the Council are not such as to alter that conclusion. First, the fact that individual notification proves impossible in certain cases is without prejudice to the interest of those entities in receiving such notification and is therefore irrelevant in those cases in which the address of the entity concerned is known. Secondly, the rule that ignorance of the law is no defence cannot be relied on against the applicant, for in its regard the contested decision has the nature of an individual measure. Thirdly, the distinction drawn by the Council in relation to fund-freezing measures adopted in the campaign against terrorism is misplaced, for whether or not the reasons invoked are defamatory can be of relevance only if it should be necessary to determine whether the publication of the statement of reasons in the Official Journal was appropriate. On the other hand, the requirement of individual notification of fund-freezing measures stems from the fact that those measures affect the rights of the entities concerned individually and to a considerable extent. The effects of the fund-freezing measures adopted pursuant to Regulation No 423/2007 and of those adopted as part of the campaign against terrorism being comparable, in both cases the entities affected must be apprised of the measures adopted.

88 In the light of the foregoing, the Council must be considered not to have fulfilled its obligation, stemming from Article 15(3) of Regulation No 423/2007, to apprise the applicant of the grounds of the contested decision, inasmuch as it did not make individual notification, even though it is clear from the actual content of the decision that it knew the address of the applicant's headquarters.

89 However, the annexes to the application for interim measures, lodged by the applicant in Case T-390/08 R, make it clear that by letter of 24 June 2008 the French banking commission informed the applicant's branch in Paris of the adoption of the contested decision and of its publication in the Official Journal that same day. Thus the applicant was informed, timeously and officially, of the adoption of the contested decision, and that it might consult the statement of reasons for that decision in the Official Journal. What is more, it is apparent that it did actually consult the content of that decision, a copy of which is annexed to the application.

90 In those exceptional circumstances, it must be held that the fact that the Council did not apprise the applicant by individual notification of the statement of reasons for the contested decision did not have the effect of depriving the applicant of an opportunity of knowing, in good time, the reasons for the contested decision or of assessing the validity of the fund-freezing measure adopted in its regard. In consequence, the Council's omission does not justify annulment of the contested decision.'

[...]

Findings of the Court

45. The Court of Justice notes, first, that, in spite of its title, the contested decision is of the same nature as a regulation. It contains just one annex, which replaces Annex V to Regulation No 423/2007. The effect of that annex is determined in the second paragraph of Article 19 of that regulation, which provides that the regulation is to be binding in its entirety and directly applicable in all Member States, which corresponds to the effects of a regulation as provided for in Article 249 EC.

46. In principle, therefore, the Treaty does not require such a measure to be notified, but to be published, in accordance with Article 254(1) and (2) EC.

47. Second, as regards Article 15(3) of Regulation No 423/2007 more specifically, it must be borne in mind that the principle of effective judicial review means that the European Union authority which adopts an act imposing restrictive measures against a person or entity is bound to communicate the grounds on which it is based, so far as possible, either when that measure is adopted or, at the very least, as swiftly as possible after it has been adopted in order to enable those persons or entities to exercise their right to bring an action (see, to that effect, *Kadi and Al Barakaat International Foundation v Council and Commission*, paragraph 336).

48. It is with a view to ensuring observance of that principle that Article 15(3) of Regulation No 423/2007 requires the Council to state individual and specific reasons for decisions taken pursuant to Article 7(2) of the regulation and make them known to the persons, entities and bodies concerned.

49. As the General Court noted in paragraph 86 of the judgment under appeal, the freezing of funds has considerable consequences for the entities concerned, for it may restrict the exercise of their fundamental rights.

50. Although Regulation No 423/2007 does not state how reasons are 'to be made known' to the persons, entities and bodies concerned, the claim made by the United Kingdom that publication in the *Official Journal of the European Union* is sufficient cannot be upheld.

51. Indeed, if the communication of individual and specific reasons could be regarded as accomplished through publication in the *Official Journal of the European Union*, it is difficult to imagine why express reference is made to such communication, as in Article 15(3) of Regulation No 423/2007, since that decision must be published in any event, in accordance with Article 254(1) and (2) EC, having regard to its prescriptive nature, as pointed out in paragraph 45 above.

52. It follows that the Council is required to communicate a decision individually to satisfy the obligation imposed on it by that provision.

53. That conclusion is not called into question by Article 254(3) EC, to which the appellant refers, concerning the notification of a decision in the narrow sense; besides, the appellant did not allege an infringement of that provision before the General Court.

54. The same is true of paragraphs 68 to 73 of the judgment in *Hoechst v Commission*, to which the appellant refers and which need to be understood in the light of the parties' arguments to which they respond and their context. As is apparent from paragraphs 44 to 53 of the judgment in *Hoechst v Commission*, and paragraphs 21 to 24 of the Opinion of Advocate General Cosmos in that case, Hoechst AG relied on the lack of authentification of the contested decision and the fact that the text sent to it was not that adopted on the date indicated. In paragraph 69 of that judgment, the Court of Justice answered that line of argument by referring to paragraphs 48 and 49 of the judgment in Case C-137/92 P *Commission v BASF and Others* [1994] ECR I-2555, which relate to irregularities such as that at issue in that case, namely the lack of authentification of the measure. In so far as concerns paragraph 72 of the judgment in *Hoechst v Commission*, reference is clearly made to the issue ruled upon in *Commission v BASF and Others*, namely, the legal consequences of the lack of authentification of a measure.

55. In the present case, the individual and specific reasons for the freezing of funds provided for in Article 15(3) of Regulation No 423/2007 have not been communicated by the Council, but sufficient information was communicated to the appellant's branch by the French banking commission and the appellant was able to bring an action. In the light of those factors, nor did the General Court commit an error of law, in paragraph 90 of the judgment under appeal, in holding that the fact that the Council did not apprise the appellant of the statement of reasons for the contested decision did not have the effect of depriving it of an opportunity of knowing, in good time, the reasons for the contested decision or of assessing the validity of the fund-freezing measure adopted in its regard.

56. Although, as just pointed out, an individual communication is necessary in principle, it is sufficient to note that Article 15(3) of Regulation No 423/2007 does not require communications to take a specific form, and refers only to the obligation to 'make them known'. What matters is that useful effect should have been given to that provision, namely, effective judicial protection of the persons and entities concerned by the restrictive measures adopted pursuant to Article 7(2) of the regulation, which was the case in this instance.

57. It follows from all of the above considerations that the first ground of appeal is unfounded.

Judgment of the General Court (Fourth Chamber) of 29 January 2013, Bank Mellat v. Council of the European Union, Case T-496/10, not yet reported, paras. 35–140.

Bank Mellat is an Iranian Bank against which the Council imposed restrictive measures. Having brought a case before the General Court asking for the annulment of these measures, it gave the latter the opportunity to pronounce itself in detail on a number of issues. A substantial part of this judgment is included here since it gives a clear view of the current interpretation of the General Court of the EU legal framework regarding restrictive measures on entities engaged in nuclear proliferation in Iran, and its interplay with the protection of procedural rights in the EU legal order.

Whether it is open to the applicant to rely on fundamental rights protection and guarantees

35. The Council and the Commission contend that, under European Union law, legal persons who are emanations of non-Member countries cannot rely on fundamental rights protection and guarantees. They claim that since the applicant is an emanation of the Iranian State, that rule applies to it.

36. In that regard, it must first be observed that neither in the Charter of Fundamental Rights of the European Union (OJ 2010, C 83, p. 389) nor in European Union primary law are there any provisions which state that legal persons who are emanations of States are not entitled to the protection of fundamental rights. On the contrary, the provisions of the Charter which are relevant to the pleas raised by the applicant, and in particular Articles 17, 41 and 47, guarantee the rights of 'everyone', a wording which includes legal persons such as the applicant.

37. Nonetheless, the Council and the Commission rely, in this context, on Article 34 of the Convention for the Protection of Human Rights and Fundamental Freedoms, signed at Rome on 4 November 1950 ('ECHR'), the effect of which is that applications submitted by governmental organisations to the European Court of Human Rights are not admissible.

38. First, Article 34 of the ECHR is a procedural provision which is not applicable to procedures before the Courts of the European Union. Secondly, according to the case-law of the European Court of Human Rights, the aim of that provision is to ensure that a State which is a party to the ECHR is not both applicant and defendant before that court (see, to that effect, judgment of the European Court of Human Rights of 13 December 2007, *Islamic Republic of Iran Shipping Lines* v *Turkey*, No 40998/98, § 81, ECHR 2007-V). That argument is not applicable to the present case.

39. The Council and the Commission also argue that the justification of the rule on which they rely is that a State is the guarantor of respect for fundamental rights in its territory but cannot qualify for such rights.

40. However, even if that justification were applicable in relation to an internal situation, the fact that a State is the guarantor of respect for fundamental rights in its own territory is of no relevance as regards the extent of the rights to which legal

persons which are emanations of that same State may be entitled in the territory of other States.

41. In the light of the foregoing, it must be held that European Union law contains no rule preventing legal persons which are emanations of non-Member countries from taking advantage of fundamental rights protection and guarantees. Those rights may therefore be relied upon by those persons before the Courts of the European Union in so far as those rights are compatible with their status as legal persons.

42. Further, and in any event, the Council and the Commission have not put forward any evidence capable of proving that the applicant was in fact an emanation of the Iranian State, that is, an entity which participated in the exercise of governmental powers or which ran a public service under governmental control (see, to that effect, judgment of the European Court of Human Rights *Islamic Republic of Iran Shipping Lines* v *Turkey*, cited above in paragraph 38, § 79).

43. In that regard, first, the Council maintains that the applicant runs a public service under the control of the Iranian government since it provides financial services which are essential for the operation of the Iranian economy. The Council does not however contest the applicant's claims that those services represent commercial activities carried out in a competitive sector and subject to the ordinary law. In those circumstances, the fact that those activities are essential for the operation of a State's economy cannot, by itself, confer on them the status of a public service.

44. Next, the Commission maintains that the fact that the applicant is involved in nuclear proliferation demonstrates that it participates in the exercise of governmental powers. However, in adopting that approach the Commission assumes the truth of a premiss which the applicant denies is true and which is a question of fact at the very core of the dispute before the Court. Further, the claimed involvement of the applicant in nuclear proliferation, as set out in the contested measures, cannot be assimilated to the exercise of State powers, but to commercial transactions entered into with entities engaged in nuclear proliferation. Consequently, that claim cannot justify the classification of the applicant as an emanation of the Iranian State.

45. Lastly, the Commission considers that the applicant is an emanation of the Iranian State because of the latter's participation in its share capital. Leaving aside the fact that, according to the information provided by the applicant, which is not disputed by the Council and the Commission, the holding concerned is only a minority shareholding, that participation does not by itself imply that the applicant participates in the exercise of governmental powers or that it runs a public service.

46. In the light of all the foregoing, it must be concluded that the applicant may take advantage of fundamental rights protection and guarantees.

The first plea in law: infringement of the obligation to state reasons, the applicant's rights of defence and its right to effective judicial protection

47. By its first plea in law, the applicant claims that the Council infringed the obligation to state reasons, the applicant's rights of defence and its right to effective judicial protection since, first, the Council did not provide it with sufficient information to enable it to make effective representations regarding the adoption of

restrictive measures against it and to guarantee it a fair hearing and, secondly, both the assessment prior to the adoption of the restrictive measures affecting it and the regular review of those measures are vitiated by a number of errors.

48. The Council, supported by the Commission, contends that the applicant's arguments are unfounded. It submits, in particular, that the applicant cannot plead the principle of respect for the rights of the defence.

49. Firstly, it must be recalled that the purpose of the obligation to state the reasons for an act adversely affecting a person, as provided for by the second paragraph of Article 296 TFEU and, more particularly in this case, by Article 24(3) of Decision 2010/413, Article 15(3) of Regulation No 423/2007, Article 36(3) of Regulation No 961/2010 and Article 46(3) of Regulation No 267/2012, is, first, to provide the person concerned with sufficient information to make it possible to determine whether the measure is well founded or whether it is vitiated by an error which may permit its validity to be contested before the Courts of the European Union and, secondly, to enable the latter to review the lawfulness of that measure. The obligation to state reasons therefore constitutes an essential principle of European Union law which may be derogated from only for compelling reasons. The statement of reasons must therefore in principle be notified to the person concerned at the same time as the act adversely affecting him, for failure to state the reasons cannot be remedied by the fact that the person concerned learns the reasons for the act during the proceedings before the Courts of the European Union (see, to that effect, Case T-390/08 *Bank Melli Iran* v *Council* [2009] ECR II-3967, paragraph 80 and case-law cited).

50. Consequently, unless there are compelling reasons touching on the security of the European Union or of its Member States or the conduct of their international relations which prevent the disclosure of certain information, the Council is required to inform the entity covered by restrictive measures of the actual and specific reasons why it considers that those measures had to be adopted. It must thus state the matters of fact and law which constitute the legal basis of the measures concerned and the considerations which led it to adopt them (see, to that effect, *Bank Melli Iran* v *Council*, cited above in paragraph 49, paragraph 81 and case-law cited).

51. Moreover, the statement of reasons must be appropriate to the measure at issue and to the context in which it was adopted. The requirements to be satisfied by the statement of reasons depend on the circumstances of each case, in particular the content of the measure in question, the nature of the reasons given and the interest which the addressees of the measure, or other parties to whom it is of direct and individual concern, may have in obtaining explanations. It is not necessary for the statement of reasons to specify all the relevant matters of fact and law, since the question whether the statement of reasons is adequate must be assessed with regard not only to its wording but also to its context and to all the legal rules governing the matter in question. In particular, the reasons given for a decision are sufficient if it was adopted in circumstances known to the party concerned which enable him to understand the scope of the measure adversely affecting him (see *Bank Melli Iran* v *Council*, cited above in paragraph 49, paragraph 82 and case-law cited).

52. Secondly, according to settled case-law, observance of the rights of the defence, especially the right to be heard, in all proceedings initiated against an entity which may lead to a measure adversely affecting that entity, is a fundamental principle of European Union law which must be guaranteed, even when there are no rules governing the procedure in question (*Bank Melli Iran v Council*, cited above in paragraph 49, paragraph 91).

53. The principle of respect for the rights of the defence requires, first, that the entity concerned must be informed of the evidence adduced against it to justify the measure adversely affecting it. Secondly, it must be afforded the opportunity effectively to make known its view on that evidence (see, by analogy, Case T-228/02 *Organisation des Modjahedines du peuple d'Iran v Council* [2006] ECR II-4665, paragraph 93).

54. Consequently, as regards an initial measure whereby the funds of an entity are frozen, unless there are compelling reasons touching on the security of the European Union or of its Member States or the conduct of their international relations which preclude it, the evidence adduced against that entity should be disclosed to it either concomitantly with or as soon as possible after the adoption of the measure concerned. At the request of the entity concerned, it also has the right to make known its view on that evidence after the adoption of the measure. Subject to the same proviso, any subsequent decision to freeze funds must as a general rule be preceded by disclosure of further evidence adduced against the entity concerned and a further opportunity for it to make known its view (see, by analogy, *Organisation des Modjahedines du peuple d'Iran v Council*, cited above in paragraph 53, paragraph 137).

55. It must also be observed that, when sufficiently precise information has been disclosed, enabling the entity concerned effectively to state its point of view on the evidence adduced against it by the Council, the principle of respect for the rights of the defence does not mean that the institution is obliged spontaneously to grant access to the documents in its file. It is only on the request of the party concerned that the Council is required to provide access to all non-confidential official documents concerning the measure at issue (see *Bank Melli Iran v Council*, cited above in paragraph 49, paragraph 97 and case-law cited).

56. Thirdly, the principle of effective judicial protection is a general principle of European Union law, stemming from the constitutional traditions common to the Member States, which has been enshrined in Articles 6 and 13 of the ECHR and in Article 47 of the Charter of Fundamental Rights of the European Union. The effectiveness of judicial review means that the European Union authority in question is bound to disclose the grounds for a restrictive measure to the entity concerned, so far as possible, either when that measure is adopted or, at the very least, as swiftly as possible after that decision, in order to enable the entity concerned to exercise, within the periods prescribed, its right to bring an action. Observance of that obligation to disclose the grounds is necessary both to enable the persons to whom restrictive measures are addressed to defend their rights in the best possible conditions and to decide, with full knowledge of the relevant facts, whether there is any point in their applying to the Courts of the European Union, and also to put the latter fully in a position to carry out the review of the lawfulness of the measure in question which

is the duty of those courts (see, to that effect and by analogy, Joined Cases C-402/05 P and C-415/05 P *Kadi and Al Barakaat International Foundation* v *Council and Commission* [2008] ECR I-6351, paragraphs 335 to 337 and case-law cited).

57. In the light of that case-law, the Court considers that the arguments submitted by the parties in respect of the first plea in law should be examined in five stages, as follows. First, the Court must examine the preliminary argument of the Council and the Commission that the applicant cannot rely on the principle of respect for the rights of the defence. Secondly, the Court must examine the arguments relating to (i) the obligation to state reasons and (ii) the claimed infringement of the applicant's rights of defence as regards the initial disclosure of the evidence adduced against it. Thirdly, the Court must examine the arguments on the claimed infringement of the rights of the defence in relation to access to the Council's file. Fourthly, the Court will examine the arguments dealing with (i) the claimed infringement of the applicant's rights of defence as regards whether it had the opportunity to state its point of view and (ii) the claimed infringement of its right to effective judicial protection. Fifthly, the arguments relating to the claimed errors vitiating the assessment and review carried out by the Council will be considered.

Whether the applicant may rely on the principle of respect for the rights of the defence

58. The Council and the Commission dispute the applicability of the principle of respect for the rights of the defence to the present case. Referring to Case T-181/08 *Tay Za* v *Council* [2010] ECR II-1965, paragraphs 121 to 123, they claim that the applicant was not the subject of restrictive measures because of its own activities, but because of its membership of a general category of persons and entities which had supported nuclear proliferation. Consequently, the procedure for the adoption of the restrictive measures was not initiated against the applicant within the meaning of the case-law cited in paragraph 52 above and the applicant can consequently not rely on the rights of the defence or can do so to only a limited extent.

59. That argument cannot be accepted.

60. First, the judgment of the General Court in *Tay Za* v *Council*, cited above in paragraph 58, was set aside on appeal, in its entirety, by the judgment of the Court of Justice of 13 March 2012 in Case C-376/10 P *Tay Za* v *Council*. Consequently, what is stated in that judgment is no longer part of the legal order of the European Union and cannot validly be relied on by the Council and the Commission.

61. Secondly, Article 24(3) and (4) of Decision 2010/413, Article 15(3) of Regulation No 423/2007, Article 36(3) and (4) of Regulation No 961/2010 and Article 46(3) and (4) of Regulation No 267/2012 set out provisions to safeguard the rights of defence of entities which are subject to restrictive measures adopted under those acts. Respect for those rights is subject to review by the Courts of the European Union (see, to that effect, *Bank Melli Iran* v *Council*, cited above in paragraph 49, paragraph 37).

62. In those circumstances, it must be concluded that the principle of respect for the rights of the defence, as stated in paragraphs 52 to 55 above, may be relied on by the applicant in this case.

The obligation to state reasons and the initial disclosure of inculpatory evidence

63. It must be observed at the outset that in order to assess whether the obligation to state reasons and the obligation to disclose to the entity concerned the evidence considered to inculpate it have been fulfilled, there must be taken into consideration not only the reasons stated in the contested measures, but the three proposals for the adoption of restrictive measures sent by the Council to the applicant.

64. First, it is apparent from those proposals, as disclosed to the applicant, that they were submitted to the delegations of the Member States in the context of adoption of the restrictive measures affecting the applicant and that those proposals constitute, consequently, evidence on which those measures are based.

65. Secondly, it is true that the third proposal was disclosed to the applicant both after the action was brought and after the adaptation of claims following adoption of Decision 2010/644 and Regulation No 961/2010. Consequently, it cannot validly supplement the reasons stated for Decision 2010/413, Implementing Regulation No 668/2010, Decision 2010/644 and Regulation No 961/2010. It may, however, be taken into consideration for the assessment of the legality of the later measures, namely Decision 2011/783, Implementing Regulation No 1245/2011 and Regulation No 267/2012.

66. The contested measures state the following four reasons as regards the applicant:
    – according to Decision 2010/413 and Implementing Regulation No 668/2010, the applicant is a State-owned Bank ('the first reason');
    – the applicant engages in a pattern of conduct which supports and facilitates Iran's nuclear and ballistic missile programmes ('the second reason');
    – the applicant has provided banking services to UN and EU listed entities, to entities acting on their behalf or at their direction, or to entities owned or controlled by them ('the third reason');
    – the applicant is the parent bank of First East Export [Bank] ('FEE'), which is designated under [United Nations Security Council Resolution] 1929 [2010] ('the fourth reason').

67. The first of the two proposals for adoption of restrictive measures notified on 13 September 2010 partly overlaps the second reason provided in the contested measures. It adds the following reasons:
    – the applicant provides banking services to the Atomic Energy Organisation of Iran ('AEOI') and to Novin Energy Company ('Novin') which are subject to restrictive measures adopted by the United Nations Security Council ('the fifth reason');
    – the applicant manages the accounts of officials of the Aerospace Industries Organisation and an Iranian procurement agent ('the sixth reason').

68. The second proposal notified on 13 September 2010 essentially overlaps the statement of reasons in the contested measures. There is one additional reason: that since at least 2003 the applicant has facilitated the movement of millions of dollars for the Iranian nuclear programme ('the seventh reason').

69. The third proposal for the adoption of restrictive measures, which is annexed to the rejoinder, contains no additional information as compared with the contested measures and the two proposals notified on 13 September 2010.

70. The applicant maintains that such a statement of reasons does not explain in sufficient detail why restrictive measures against it were adopted. It considers that that deficiency implies, further, an infringement of its rights of defence.

71. The Council, supported by the Commission, contends that the applicant's argument is unfounded.

72. The first reason is sufficiently detailed since it enables the applicant to appreciate that the allegation made against it by the Council is that part of its share capital is held by the Iranian State.

73. On the other hand, the second and third reasons are excessively vague in that they give no details of the nature of the conduct alleged on the part of either the applicant or the other entities concerned.

74. The fourth reason is set out in sufficient detail, since it enables the applicant to appreciate that the allegation made against it by the Council concerns the control it exercises over FEE.

75. The same is true of the fifth reason, which identifies the entities to which the financial services at issue were allegedly supplied.

76. Lastly, the sixth and seventh reasons are not sufficiently detailed, since the sixth does not identify the persons concerned and the seventh contains no details of the entities and transactions concerned.

77. In the light of the foregoing, it must be held that the Council is in breach of the obligation to state reasons and the obligation to disclose to the applicant, as the entity concerned, the evidence adduced against it as regards the second, third, sixth and seventh reasons. On the other hand, those obligations were fulfilled as regards the other reasons.

Access to the file

78. As stated in paragraphs 9 and 15 above, the Council notified the applicant on 13 September 2010 of two proposals for the adoption of restrictive measures submitted by Member States and subsequently of a third proposal as an annex to the rejoinder.

79. The applicant considers that that access was not sufficient to enable it effectively to make known its point of view.

80. The Council, supported by the Commission, contends that the applicant's arguments are unfounded.

81. In that regard, in relation to the extent of the access granted, it must be observed that it is not apparent from the information in the Court file that the Council relied, when the contested measures were adopted, on material other than the three proposals submitted by the Member States. In those circumstances, the Council cannot be criticised for not having notified the applicant of additional evidence.

82. On the other hand, unlike the two proposals for the adoption of restrictive measures annexed to the letter of 13 September 2010, the applicant was notified of the third proposal only as an annex to the rejoinder, in other words after the expiry of the period within which the applicant was required by the Council to submit its observations following the adoption of Decision 2010/413 and Implementing Regulation No 668/2010, after the lodging of the action and after the adoption of Decision 2010/644 and Regulation No 961/2010.

83. The Council maintains, in that regard, that it notified the applicant of the third proposal as soon as it obtained the agreement of the Member State which submitted the proposal.

84. That argument cannot be accepted. Where the Council intends to rely on information submitted by a Member State in order to adopt restrictive measures affecting an entity, it is obliged to ensure, before the adoption of those measures, that the entity concerned can be notified of the information in question in good time so that it is able effectively to make known its point of view.

85. In those circumstances, it must be concluded that, since the Council notified the applicant of the third proposal for the adoption of restrictive measures only as an annex to the rejoinder, it did not give the applicant access to that information in its file in good time, and thereby infringed the rights of the defence.

Whether the applicant had the opportunity effectively to make known its point of view and the right to effective judicial protection

86. First, the applicant claims that it did not have an opportunity effectively to make known its point of view and that, in any event, the observations which it was able to present were not taken into consideration by the Council.

87. The Council, supported by the Commission, contends that the applicant's arguments are unfounded.

88. First, it is clear that, following the adoption of the first measures whereby the applicant's funds were frozen, on 26 July 2010, the applicant sent a letter to the Council on 24 September 2010 setting out its point of view and asking for the restrictive measures against it to be lifted. The Council replied by letter of 28 October 2010. Next, before the adoption of Decision 2011/783 and Implementing Regulation No 1245/2011, the applicant submitted its observations to the Council by letter of 29 August 2011, to which the Council replied on 5 December 2011. Lastly, no argument is put forward by the applicant to suggest that it was not in a position to submit further observations to the Council, in a similar fashion, before the adoption of Regulation No 267/2012.

89. Accordingly, it must be held that the applicant had the opportunity effectively to make known its point of view, except as regards (i) the second, third, sixth and seventh reasons provided by the Council, which are excessively vague (see paragraph 77 above) and (ii) the proposal for the adoption of restrictive measures notified as an annex to the rejoinder, since that proposal was not known to the applicant when it submitted its observations (see paragraph 82 above).

90. As regards whether the observations submitted were taken into consideration, it is admittedly true that the reply to the applicant's arguments in the Council's letters of 28 October 2010 and 5 December 2011 is brief. The fact remains that the Council made clear, in the letter of 28 October 2010, that it considered, contrary to the position of the applicant, that there was no adequate guarantee that the applicant would not in the future supply banking services to persons and entities engaged in nuclear proliferation. The Council reiterated that position in its letter of 5 December 2011.

91. Further, it is common ground that the Council removed, in Decision 2010/644 and in Regulation No 961/2010, the statement that the applicant was a State-owned bank, which the applicant denied was the case.

92. In the light of those circumstances, it must be held that the applicant's observations were taken into consideration by the Council during its review, contrary to what is claimed by the applicant.

93. Secondly, the applicant claims that the inadequacy of the information and evidence disclosed to it affected its right to effective judicial protection.

94. The Council, supported by the Commission, contends that that argument is unfounded.

95. It follows from paragraph 89 above that it must be held that, in so far as there was individual notification to the applicant of reasons which were sufficiently detailed, namely the first, fourth and fifth reasons relied on by the Council, the applicant's right to effective judicial protection was respected.

96. On the other hand, the vagueness of the second, third, sixth and seventh reasons provided by the Council and the late notification of the third proposal for the adoption of restrictive measures constitute an infringement of the applicant's right to effective judicial protection.

The defects in the Council's assessment

97. The applicant claims that the Council did not carry out a genuine assessment of the circumstances of the case, but did no more than adopt the proposals submitted by Member States. That defect affects both the assessment prior to the adoption of the restrictive measures against and the regular review of those measures.

98. Further, according to the applicant, it is clear from diplomatic cables, made public through the Wikileaks organisation ('the diplomatic cables'), that Member States, in particular the United Kingdom, were subject to pressure from the United States Government to ensure the adoption of restrictive measures against Iranian entities. That fact, it is claimed, casts doubt on the lawfulness of the measures adopted and of the procedure for their adoption.

99. The Council, supported by the Commission, contends that the applicant's argument is unfounded. It contends, in particular, that no account should be taken of the diplomatic cables.

100. First, it must be observed that acts which establish restrictive measures against entities allegedly involved in nuclear proliferation are acts of the Council, which must, therefore, ensure that their adoption is justified. Consequently, when adopting an initial act establishing such measures, the Council must assess the relevance and the validity of the information and evidence submitted to it, pursuant to Article 23(2) of Decision 2010/413, by a Member State or by the High Representative of the Union for Foreign Affairs and Security Policy. When adopting subsequent acts affecting the same entity, the Council is required, in accordance with Article 24(4) of that decision, to review the need to maintain those measures in the light of observations submitted by that entity.

101. In the present case, there is nothing in the Court file to suggest that the Council checked the relevance and the validity of the evidence concerning the applicant submitted to it before the adoption of Decision 2010/413 and Implementing Regulation No 668/2010. On the contrary, the incorrect statement, in those acts, that the applicant was a State-owned bank, the inaccuracy of which is not denied by the Council, is an indication that no such checking took place.

102. Further, it is clear from paragraphs 90 to 92 above that, when adopting the subsequent contested measures, the Council reviewed the circumstances of the case in the light of the applicant's observations, since it removed the statement that

the applicant was a State-owned bank and expressed its view on the applicant's arguments relating to financial services supplied to entities involved in nuclear proliferation.

103. Secondly, as regards the diplomatic cables, the fact that some Member States were subject to diplomatic pressure, even if proved, does not imply, by itself, that such pressure affected the contested measures which were adopted by the Council or the assessment carried out by the Council when they were adopted.

104. In those circumstances, the Court must uphold the applicant's arguments relating to the defects affecting the assessment carried out by the Council in relation to Decision 2010/413 and Implementing Regulation No 668/2010, but must reject those arguments for the remainder.

105. In the light of paragraphs 47 to 104 above, it must be observed that, first, the Council infringed the applicant's rights of defence and its right to effective judicial protection in that it did not notify the applicant, in good time, of the proposal for the adoption of restrictive measures annexed to the rejoinder. Since that proposal was relied on by the Council as justification of all the contested measures against the applicant, and taking into account the date when it was notified, that defect affects the lawfulness of Decision 2010/413, Implementing Regulation No 668/2010, Decision 2010/644 and Regulation No 961/2010, in so far as those measures concern the applicant.

106. Next, the Council did not, when adopting Decision 2010/413 and Implementing Regulation No 668/2010, comply with the obligation to assess the relevance and the validity of the information and evidence against the applicant submitted to it, with the consequence that those measures are tainted by illegality.

107. Lastly, the Council infringed the obligation to state reasons as regards the second, third, sixth and seventh reasons relied on against the applicant. Nonetheless, taking into account the fact that the various reasons relied on by the Council are independent of each other and that other reasons are sufficiently detailed, that fact does not justify the annulment of Decision 2011/783, Implementing Regulation No 1245/2011 and Regulation No 267/2012. It implies only that the second, third, sixth and seventh reasons cannot be taken into consideration for the purposes of assessment of the second plea in law concerning the question whether the restrictive measures against the applicant are well founded.

108. In the light of all the foregoing, the Court must uphold the first plea in law to the extent that it concerns the annulment of Decision 2010/413, Implementing Regulation No 668/2010, Decision 2010/644 and Regulation No 961/2010 in so far as those acts concern the applicant, and reject that plea for the remainder.

The second plea in law: manifest error of assessment in relation to the adoption of restrictive measures against the applicant

109. The applicant claims that the reasons relied on against it by the Council, set out in paragraphs 66 to 69 above, do not satisfy the conditions laid down by Decision 2010/413, Regulation No 423/2007, Regulation No 961/2010 and Regulation No 267/2012 and are not substantiated by evidence. Consequently, the Council made a manifest error of assessment by adopting restrictive measures against it on the basis of those reasons.

110. The Council, supported by the Commission, disputes the applicant's arguments.

111. In accordance with the case-law, the judicial review of the lawfulness of a measure whereby restrictive measures are imposed on an entity extends to the assessment of the facts and circumstances relied on as justifying it, and to the evidence and information on which that assessment is based. In the event of challenge, it is for the Council to present that evidence for review by the Courts of the European Union (see, to that effect, *Bank Melli Iran v Council*, cited above in paragraph 49, paragraphs 37 and 107).

112. Having regard to that case-law, taking into consideration the fact that the second, third, sixth and seventh reasons relied on by the Council against the applicant do not constitute an adequate statement of reasons (see paragraph 107 above), the Court need be concerned only with the determination of whether the first, fourth and fifth reasons relied on are well founded.

113. As regards the first reason, relied on solely in Decision 2010/413 and Implementing Regulation No 668/2010, it has now been established that the applicant is not a State-owned bank. Consequently, the first reason is based on a mistaken factual premiss and cannot therefore justify the restrictive measures imposed on the applicant by Decision 2010/413 and Implementing Regulation No 668/2010.

114. As regards the fourth reason, it is certainly the case that FEE, a wholly owned subsidiary of the applicant, was the subject of United Nations Security Council Resolution 1929 (2010).

115. First, it is apparent from that resolution that the adoption of restrictive measures against FEE was justified solely by the alleged involvement of the applicant in nuclear proliferation.

116. Secondly, that involvement was described in Resolution 1929 (2010) in imprecise terms which correspond, essentially, to the seventh reason provided by the Council, namely that '[o]ver the last seven years, [the applicant] has facilitated hundreds of millions of dollars in transactions for Iranian nuclear, missile and defense entities'.

117. In those circumstances, it must be concluded that the fourth reason is not only based on mere allegations but also does not constitute an autonomous reason distinct from those directly concerning the applicant. Consequently, it cannot justify the adoption of restrictive measures against the applicant.

118. As regards the fifth reason, the applicant denies having supplied services to AEOI. The Council has produced no evidence or information to establish that such services were supplied. Consequently, it must be concluded that the allegations concerning AEOI also do not justify the adoption of restrictive measures against the applicant.

119. On the other hand, the applicant admits having supplied account operation services to Novin, which has been the subject of restrictive measures adopted by the United Nations Security Council since 24 March 2007, by reason of its alleged engagement in nuclear proliferation. The applicant explains however, first, that it was not informed of Novin's involvement in nuclear proliferation, inter alia because the services supplied were not connected thereto. Secondly, the applicant claims that it gradually ran down, then completely ended, its relationship with Novin after the adoption of restrictive measures against Novin.

120. The response of the Council, supported by the Commission, is that the services supplied by the applicant to Novin justify the adoption of restrictive measures against the applicant, taking account of the risk that the applicant may in the future supply similar support to other listed entities. In that context, it is of no relevance whether the applicant knew or might have known that Novin was in fact involved in nuclear proliferation or that the transactions concerned were connected thereto.

121. Having regard to the parties' arguments, it is necessary to examine whether, as maintained by the Council, the services supplied by the applicant to Novin constitute support to nuclear proliferation within the meaning of Decision 2010/413, Regulation No 423/2007, Regulation No 961/2010 and Regulation No 267/2012.

122. In that regard, it must be recalled, first, that, under Article 18 of Regulation No 423/2007, Article 39 of Regulation No 961/2010 and Article 49 of Regulation No 267/2012, those regulations are applicable within the territory of the European Union, including its airspace, on board any aircraft or any vessel under the jurisdiction of a Member State, to any person inside or outside the territory of the European Union who is a national of a Member State, to any legal person, entity or body which is incorporated or constituted under the law of a Member State and to any legal person, entity or body in respect of any business done in whole or in part within the European Union.

123. Accordingly, as regards transactions carried out outside the European Union, Regulation No 423/2007, Regulation No 961/2010 and Regulation No 267/2012 are not capable of imposing legal obligations on a financial institution established in a non-Member country and constituted under the law of that country (a 'foreign financial institution') such as the applicant. Consequently, such a financial institution is not obliged, under those regulations, to freeze the funds of entities involved in nuclear proliferation.

124. The fact remains however that if a foreign financial institution is engaged in, is directly associated with or is providing support to nuclear proliferation, its funds and economic resources which are located within the European Union, involved in business carried out wholly or in part within the European Union or held by nationals of Member States or by any legal persons, entities or bodies which are incorporated or constituted under the law of a Member State, can be struck at by restrictive measures adopted pursuant to Regulation No 423/2007, Regulation No 961/2010 and Regulation No 267/2012.

125. It follows that it is very much in the interests of a foreign financial institution to ensure that it is not engaged in, is not directly associated with and is not providing support to nuclear proliferation, in particular by supplying financial services to an entity involved in nuclear proliferation. Consequently, where it knows or may reasonably suspect that one of its clients is involved in nuclear proliferation, it should bring to an end the supply of financial services to that client without delay, taking into account the applicable legal obligations, and should not supply any further services.

126. In the present case, it is not disputed by the Council that the services supplied to Novin by the applicant were supplied in Iran, and their relationship is governed by Iranian law.

127. Accordingly, it is necessary to examine whether the applicant acted without delay to bring to an end the supply of financial services to Novin, taking into account the applicable obligations laid down by Iranian law, as soon as it knew or might reasonably have suspected that Novin was involved in nuclear proliferation.

128. In that regard, the applicant denies having been aware of the involvement of Novin in nuclear proliferation before Novin became the subject of restrictive measures adopted by the United Nations Security Council. Since the Council has not submitted, pursuant to the case-law cited in paragraph 111 above, detailed and specific evidence or information to suggest that the applicant knew or might reasonably have suspected that Novin was involved in nuclear proliferation at an earlier date, the applicant's claim on that point must be accepted.

129. As regards the period subsequent to the adoption of restrictive measures against Novin, the applicant explains that it issued without delay an internal circular requesting that its employees inform Novin that it could no longer supply services to it. Thereafter, no further services were supplied and no further instructions were accepted. The applicant confined itself to effecting payments from Novin's accounts, which were due under instructions, cheques and promissory notes issued before the date of the adoption of restrictive measures against Novin, taking into account that none of those payments were linked to nuclear proliferation or to the acquisition of goods in general. As soon as the balance in any account was extinguished as a result of payments made, the accounts were closed by the applicant. Any residual balances, which were negligible, were returned to Novin.

130. The Council and the Commission do not dispute the accuracy of that factual account, which is substantiated by the written statements of the applicant's director.

131. As regards whether those measures are sufficient when judged by the test set out in paragraph 124 above, it must be held that, taking into account the specific features of services related to the operation of accounts, the applicant demonstrates that it acted without delay to bring to an end the supply of financial services to Novin as soon as it learned of Novin's involvement in nuclear proliferation.

132. In that regard, it is true that payments were effected by the applicant from Novin's accounts after the adoption of the restrictive measures concerned.

133. However, the applicant explains, and is not contradicted by the Council or the Commission, that it was required, by virtue of its obligations to Novin, to effect the payments in compliance with instructions, cheques and promissory notes issued previously.

134. In that regard, it must be observed that Article 20(6) of Decision 2010/413, Article 9 of Regulation No 423/2007, Article 18 of Regulation No 961/2010 and Article 25 of Regulation No 267/2012 permit, in essence, the unfreezing of funds of entities subject to restrictive measures in order to make payments due under obligations entered into by them prior to their being listed, provided that those payments are not linked to nuclear proliferation. In those circumstances, the applicant, which was in this case under no obligation, as is clear from paragraphs 123 to 126 above, to freeze Novin's funds pursuant to the abovementioned measures, should not be required to apply stricter rules in respect of Novin.

135. Yet the Council and the Commission do not even claim that the payments at issue were linked to nuclear proliferation.

136. Further, the applicant admits that it paid back to Novin any residual balances in closed accounts. The applicant states, however, and this is not disputed by either the Council or the Commission, that it was not entitled to retain the balances concerned.

137. In those circumstances, it must be held that neither the services supplied by the applicant to Novin before the adoption of restrictive measures against Novin nor the arrangements for the termination of the applicant's commercial relationship with Novin constitute support to nuclear proliferation within the meaning of Decision 2010/413, Regulation No 423/2007, Regulation No 961/2010 and Regulation No 267/2012.

138. Consequently, those circumstances do not justify the adoption of restrictive measures against the applicant.

139. Since none of the first, fourth or fifth reasons relied on by the Council against the applicant justify the adoption of the restrictive measures against it, the second plea in law must be upheld.

140. In the light of all the foregoing, the contested measures must be annulled in so far as they concern the applicant, and there is no need to examine the third plea in law, claiming an infringement of the principle of proportionality.

Judgment of the General Court (Fourth Chamber) of 20 March 2013, Bank Saderat plc v. Council of the European Union, Case T-495/10, not yet reported, paras. 39–41.

A very short excerpt from this case is to be found here. In these three paragraphs the General Court dismisses rather summarily a plea made by the applicant, which illustrates an obvious inconsistency that may occur in the application of now Article 23(2) Council Regulation No. 267/2012. Restrictive measures on subsidiaries of Iranian entities engaged in nuclear proliferation, are imposed on them solely on the grounds of their being 'owned or controlled' by the latter and not due to their own activity. Still, it is conceivable that these measures may continue being in force even if the parent entity has been successful in an action for annulment before European Courts. This is presently the case with Bank Saderat Iran and Bank Saderat plc.[20]

Admissibility of the fourth plea in law: error of assessment as regards the involvement of BSI in nuclear proliferation

39. By its fourth plea, the applicant maintains that the adoption of restrictive measures with respect to BSI is not justified. The applicant refers, in that regard, to actions brought before the Courts of the European Union by BSI and states that, if BSI is no longer the subject of restrictive measures at the time when judgment

[20] See Case T-494/10 *Bank Saderat Iran v. Council of the European Union,* not yet reported.

in this case is delivered, the measures to which it itself is subject ought to be annulled.

40. That said, the applicant pleads no specific ground of complaint in order to challenge the lawfulness of the restrictive measures against BSI. In particular the applicant expresses no view, with a sufficient degree of detail, on the reasons concerning the alleged involvement of BSI in nuclear proliferation, since the applicant does not even indicate whether it disputes the truth of what BSI is accused of having done or the classification of such conduct as support for nuclear proliferation.

41. In those circumstances, the Court is not in a position to rule on the fourth plea in law, in the absence of sufficiently detailed argument from the applicant. Consequently, that plea in law must be declared to be inadmissible pursuant to Article 44(1)(c) of the Rules of Procedure, as contended by the Commission.

6.7 The regulated countermeasures of the Cotonou agreement

Many Cooperation Agreements of the EU with third countries contain among their first provisions clauses that proclaim the importance of the values inherent in democracy, the rule of law, and human rights as a basis for the cooperation between the parties (see also the Euro-Mediterranean Agreement with Egypt, Chapter 9, pp. 730–55). Note that these values are also said to be undergirding the external relations of the Union (Articles 3(5) and 21(1) TEU) and, in particular, its development policy (Article 208 TFEU, formerly Article 180 EC, see Chapter 8). In the final provisions of such Cooperation Agreements, one is likely to find a provision which enables either party to suspend the agreement in whole or in part, if the other side no longer acts in conformity with the basic underpinnings of the agreement. This is an implicit reference to the human rights and democracy clause among the opening articles and enables either party (but in reality primarily the Union) to suspend parts of the cooperation and, thus, to exercise pressure on the other party. In the Partnership Agreement ACP-EC (Cotonou 23 June 2000, revised first in Luxembourg on 25 June 2005 and second in Burkina Faso on 22 June 2010), these two provisions are particularly elaborate. They are reproduced below. The Commission proposal concerning Fiji is an example of how these provisions are applied after a *coup d'état* and how, after the modifications introduced in the revision of 2005, there is a tendency to obtain improvements through negotiation rather than immediate suspension or through a combination between suspension and negotiation.

Cotonou Agreement
Article 9

Essential elements *regarding human rights, democratic principles and the rule of law,* **and fundamental element** *regarding good governance*

1. Cooperation shall be directed towards sustainable development centred on the human person, who is the main protagonist and beneficiary of development; this entails respect for and promotion of all human rights.

Respect for all human rights and fundamental freedoms, including respect for fundamental social rights, democracy based on the rule of law and transparent and accountable governance are an integral part of sustainable development.

2. The Parties refer to their international obligations and commitments concerning respect for human rights. They reiterate their deep attachment to human dignity and human rights, which are legitimate aspirations of individuals and peoples. Human rights are universal, indivisible and inter related. The Parties undertake to promote and protect all fundamental freedoms and human rights, be they civil and political, or economic, social and cultural. In this context, the Parties reaffirm the equality of men and women.

The Parties reaffirm that democratisation, development and the protection of fundamental freedoms and human rights are interrelated and mutually reinforcing. Democratic principles are universally recognised principles underpinning the organisation of the State to ensure the legitimacy of its authority, the legality of its actions reflected in its constitutional, legislative and regulatory system, and the existence of participatory mechanisms. On the basis of universally recognised principles, each country develops its democratic culture.

The structure of government and the prerogatives of the different powers shall be founded on rule of law, which shall entail in particular effective and accessible means of legal redress, an independent legal system guaranteeing equality before the law and an executive that is fully subject to the law.

Respect for human rights, democratic principles and the rule of law, which underpin the ACP-EU Partnership, shall underpin the domestic and international policies of the Parties and constitute the essential elements of this Agreement.

3. In the context of a political and institutional environment that upholds human rights, democratic principles and the rule of law, good governance is the transparent and accountable management of human, natural, economic and financial resources for the purposes of equitable and sustainable development. It entails clear decision-making procedures at the level of public authorities, transparent and accountable institutions, the primacy of law in the management and distribution of resources and capacity building for elaborating and implementing measures aiming in particular at preventing and combating corruption.

Good governance, which underpins the ACP-EU Partnership, shall underpin the domestic and international policies of the Parties, and constitute a fundamental element of this Agreement. The Parties agree that serious cases of corruption, including acts of bribery leading to such corruption, as referred to in Article 97 constitute a violation of that element.

4. The Partnership shall actively support the promotion of human rights, processes of democratisation, consolidation of the rule of law, and good governance.

These areas will be an important subject for the political dialogue. In the context of this dialogue, the Parties shall attach particular importance to the changes underway and to the continuity of the progress achieved. This regular assessment shall take into account each country's economic, social, cultural and historical context.

These areas will also be a focus of support for development strategies. The Community shall provide support for political, institutional and legal reforms and for building the capacity of public and private actors and civil society in the framework of strategies agreed jointly between the State concerned and the Community.

The principles underlying the essential and fundamental elements as defined in this Article shall apply equally to the ACP States on the one hand, and to the European Union and its Member States, on the other hand.

Article 96

Essential elements: consultation procedure and appropriate measures as regards human rights, democratic principles and the rule of law

1. Within the meaning of this Article, the term 'Party' refers to the Community and the Member States of the European Union, of the one part, and each ACP State, of the other part.

1a. Both Parties agree to exhaust all possible options for dialogue under Article 8, except in cases of special urgency, prior to commencement of the consultations referred to in paragraph 2(a) of this Article.

2. a) If, despite the political dialogue on the essential elements *as provided for under Article 8 and paragraph 1a of this Article*, a Party considers that the other Party *fails* to fulfil an obligation stemming from respect for human rights, democratic principles and the rule of law referred to in Article 9(2), it shall, except in cases of special urgency, supply the other Party and the Council of Ministers with the relevant information required for a thorough examination of the situation with a view to seeking a solution acceptable to the Parties. To this end, it shall invite the other Party to hold consultations that focus on the measures taken or to be taken by the Party concerned to remedy the situation *in accordance with Annexe VII.*

The consultations shall be conducted at the level and in the form considered most appropriate for finding a solution.

The consultations shall begin no later than *30* days after the invitation and shall continue for a period established by mutual agreement, depending on the nature and gravity of the violation. In no case shall *the dialogue under* the consultations procedure last longer than *120* days.

If the consultations do not lead to a solution acceptable to both Parties, if consultation is refused or in cases of special urgency, appropriate measures may be taken. These measures shall be revoked as soon as the reasons for taking them no longer prevail.

b) The term 'cases of special urgency' shall refer to exceptional cases of particularly serious and flagrant violation of one of the essential elements referred to in paragraph 2 of Article 9, that require an immediate reaction.

The Party resorting to the special urgency procedure shall inform the other Party and the Council of Ministers separately of the fact unless it does not have time to do so.

c) The 'appropriate measures' referred to in this Article are measures taken in accordance with international law, and proportional to the violation. In the selection of these measures, priority must be given to those which least disrupt the application of this agreement. It is understood that suspension would be a measure of last resort.

If measures are taken in cases of special urgency, they shall be immediately notified to the other Party and the Council of Ministers. At the request of the Party concerned, consultations may then be called in order to examine the situation thoroughly and, if possible, find solutions. These consultations shall be conducted according to the arrangements set out in the second and third subparagraphs of paragraph (a).

Proposal for a Council Decision on the conclusion of consultations with the Republic of the Fiji Island under Article 96 of the ACP-EC Partnership Agreement and Article 37 of the Development Cooperation Instrument, Brussels, 10.8.2007, COM (2007) 467 final.

THE COUNCIL OF THE EUROPEAN UNION,

Having regard to the Treaty establishing the European Community,

Having regard to the ACP-EC Partnership Agreement signed in Cotonou on 23 June 2000 and revised in Luxemburg on 25 June 2005, and in particular Article 96 thereof,

Having regard to the Internal Agreement on measures to be taken and procedures to be followed for the implementation of the ACP-EC Partnership Agreement, and in particular Article 3 thereof,

Having regard to the Development Cooperation Instrument, and in particular Article 37 thereof,

Having regard to the proposal from the Commission,

Whereas:

(1) The essential elements referred to in Article 9 of the Cotonou Agreement have been violated.

(2) The values referred to in Article 3 of the Development Cooperation Instrument have been violated.

(3) On 18 April 2007, pursuant to Article 96 of the Cotonou Agreement and Article 37 of the Development Cooperation Instrument, formal consultations began with the ACP countries and the Republic of the Fiji Islands during which the Fijian authorities gave specific commitments to remedy the problems identified by the European Union and to implement them.

(4) Some substantive initiatives have been taken in respect of some of the commitments referred to above; nevertheless many important commitments concerning essential elements of the Cotonou Agreement and the Development Cooperation Instrument have yet to be implemented,

HAS DECIDED AS FOLLOWS:

Article 1

Consultations with the Republic of the Fiji Islands under Article 96 of the Cotonou Agreement and Article 37 of the Development Cooperation Instrument are hereby concluded.

Article 2

The appropriate measures set out in the annexed letter are hereby adopted as appropriate measures under Article 96(2)(c) of the Cotonou Agreement and Article 37 of the Development Cooperation Instrument.

Article 3

This Decision shall enter into force on the day of its adoption. It shall be published in the *Official Journal of the European Union.*

It shall be valid for 24 months from the date of its adoption by the Council. It shall be reviewed regularly at least once every six months

[…]

ANNEX

Draft letter
H.E. Ratu Josefa ILOILO
President of the Republic of the Fiji Islands
Suva
Fiji

Excellency,

The European Union attaches great importance to the provisions of Article 9 of the Cotonou Agreement and Article 3 of the Development Cooperation Instrument. The ACP-EC partnership is founded on respect for human rights, democratic principles and the rule of law, which form the essential elements of the Cotonou Agreement, and form the basis of our relations.

On 11 December 2006 the Council of the European Union condemned the military takeover in Fiji.

Under Article 96 of the Cotonou Agreement, and considering that the military take-over which took place on 5 December 2006 constituted a violation of the essential elements listed in Article 9 of that Agreement, the EU invited Fiji to consultations in order, as provided for in the Agreement, to thoroughly examine the situation and, where necessary, take steps to remedy it.

The formal part of these consultations began in Brussels on 18 April 2007. The Interim Government of Fiji made a presentation based on a submission dated 18 April 2007 on the reasons for the military takeover of 5th December 2006, on developments in the country's situation since the takeover, and on the Interim Government's programme for the transitional period.

The EU took note of the Interim Government's submission of 18 April 2007 to the EU.

For its part, the EU was pleased that the Interim Government confirmed a number of key commitments regarding human rights and fundamental freedoms, respect for democratic principles and the rule of law, as noted below, and proposed positive steps regarding their implementation. Fiji also agreed to close cooperation regarding the monitoring and verification of the commitments.

Most of the commitments made in the context of the consultations will be imple-mented over an extended period, and it is consequently necessary to monitor and verify their implementation closely over time. The EU underlines that, following the credible general elections held in Fiji as recently as May 2006 and in the light of the findings and recommendations of the EU Election Monitoring Mission, and notably the final report from the EU Chief Observer, MEP Istvan Szent-Ivanyi, the EU is of the view that new and credible elections can be held well within the agreed deadline of 28 February 2009.

The EU stresses the importance of early and full compliance with the agreed commitments listed in annex.

The EU notes that the Interim Government, in accordance with the agreed commitments, has lifted the Public Emergency Regulations on 31 May 2007 and accepted the findings and recommendations of the Pacific Islands Forum independent election experts on 19 June 2007.

In the spirit of partnership that underlies the Cotonou Agreement, and in the light of the positive outcome of the consultations, the EU expressed its readiness to support implementation of Fiji's commitments.

The EU has adopted the following appropriate measures under Article 96(2)(c) of the revised Cotonou Agreement and Article 37 of the Development Cooperation Instrument:

– humanitarian aid as well as direct support to civil society may continue;
– cooperation activities under way and/or in preparation, in particular under the 8th and 9th EDFs may continue;
– the 9th EDF End-of-term Review may proceed;
– cooperation activities, which would help the return to democracy and improve governance, may be pursued, save under very exceptional circumstances;
– implementation of the sugar reform accompanying measures for 2006 may proceed. The financing agreement was signed at the technical level by Fiji on 19 June 2007. It is noted that the financing agreement includes a suspension clause;
– the Interim Government's acceptance on 19 June 2007 of the report of 7 June 2007 by the Pacific Islands Forum's independent election experts is in line with Commitment n° 1 agreed on 18 April 2007 between the Interim Government and the EU. Consequently, the preparation and eventual signing of the multi-annual indicative programme for sugar reform accompanying measures for 2008–2010 can proceed;
– the finalisation, signing at the technical level and implementation of the Country Strategy Paper and National Indicative Programme for the 10th EDF with an indicative financial envelope, as well as the possible allocation of an incentive tranche of up to 25% of this sum, will be subject to respect of the commitments made with regard to human rights and the rule of law; notably that the Interim Government upholds the Constitution; that the independence of the judiciary is fully respected; that all allegations of human rights infringements are investigated or dealt with in accordance with the various procedures and forums under the laws of the Fiji Islands and that the Interim Government shall use best endeavours to prevent statements by security agencies destined to intimidate;
– the 2007 sugar allocation will be zero;
– the 2008 sugar allocation, will become available subject to evidence of credible and timely preparation of elections in accordance with the agreed commitments; notably regarding census, redrafting of boundaries and electoral reform in accordance with the Constitution;

that measures will be taken to ensure the functioning of the Elections Office, including the appointment by a Supervisor of Elections by 30 September 2007 in accordance with the Constitution;

– the 2009 sugar allocation will become available subject to a legitimate government being in place;

– the 2010 sugar allocation will depend on progress made in implementing the 2009 sugar allocation and the continuation of the democratic process;

– additional support for the preparation and implementation of key commitments, in particular in support of the preparation and/or holding of elections, could be considered over and above what is described in this letter;

– regional cooperation, and Fiji's participation in it, is unaffected;

– cooperation with the European Investment Bank and the Centre for the Development of Enterprise may continue subject to the timely fulfilment of commitments made.

Follow-up of the commitments will be in accordance with the commitments on monitoring in terms of regular dialogue, cooperation with missions and reporting, as referred to in annex.

Furthermore, the EU expects Fiji to cooperate fully with the Pacific Islands Forum regarding the implementation of the recommendations by the Eminent Persons' Group, as endorsed by the Forum Foreign Ministers at their meeting in Vanuatu on 16 March 2007.

The European Union will continue to follow the situation in Fiji closely. Under Article 8 of the Cotonou Agreement, an enhanced political dialogue will be conducted with Fiji to ensure the respect for human rights, restoration of democracy and respect for the rule of law.

If there is a slowing down, breakdown or reversal in the implementation by the Interim Government of the commitments made, the EU reserves the right to adjust the appropriate measures.

The EU stresses that Fiji's privileges in its cooperation with the EU depend on respect for the essential elements of the Cotonou Agreement and for the values referred to in the Development Cooperation Instrument. In order to convince the EU that the interim government is fully prepared to follow-up on the commitments given, it is essential that early and substantial progress is made in the fulfilment of the agreed commitments.

ANNEX TO THE ANNEX
AGREED COMMITMENTS WITH THE REPUBLIC OF THE FIJI ISLANDS

A. Respect for Democratic Principles

Commitment No. 1

That free and fair parliamentary elections take place within 24 months from 1 March 2007 subject to the findings of the assessment to be carried out by the independent auditors appointed by the Pacific Islands Forum Secretariat. The processes leading to and the holding of the elections shall be jointly monitored, adapted and revised as necessary on the basis of mutually agreed benchmarks. This implies in particular:

• That by 30 June 2007 the Interim Government will adopt a schedule setting out dates for the completion of the various steps to be taken in preparation for the new Parliamentary Elections;

• That the schedule specifies the timing of census, redrafting of boundaries and electoral reform;

• That determination of boundaries and electoral reform shall be carried out in accordance with the Constitution;

• That measures will be taken to ensure the functioning of the Elections Office including the appointment of a Supervisor of Elections by 30 September 2007 in accordance with the Constitution;

• That the appointment of the Vice President shall be made in accordance with the Constitution.

Commitment No. 2
That the Interim Government, when adopting major legislative, fiscal and other policy initiatives and changes, shall take into account consultations with civil society and all other relevant stakeholders.

B. Rule of Law
Commitment No. 1
That the Interim Government shall use best endeavours to prevent statements by security agencies destined to intimidate.

Commitment No. 2
That the Interim Government upholds the 1997 Constitution, and guarantees the normal and independent functioning of Constitutional institutions such as the Fiji Human Rights Commission, Public Service Commission, Constitutional Offices Commission. The substantial independence and functioning of the Great Council of Chiefs will be preserved.

Commitment No. 3
That the independence of the judiciary is fully respected, that it is allowed to work freely and that its rulings are respected by all concerned parties, in particular:

• That the Interim Government undertakes that the tribunal pursuant to Section 138 (3) of the Constitution be appointed by 15 July 2007;

• That any appointment and/or dismissal of judges is henceforth carried out in strict conformity with Constitutional provisions and procedural rules;

• That no instances whatsoever occur, of whatever form, of interference by the military and the police or by the Interim Government with the judicial process, including full respect for the legal profession.

Commitment No. 4
That all criminal proceedings linked to corruption are dealt with through the appropriate judicial channels and that any other bodies that may be set up to investigate alleged cases of corruption will operate within constitutional boundaries.

C. Human Rights and Fundamental Freedoms
Commitment No. 1
The Interim Government will take all necessary steps to facilitate that all allegations of human rights infringements are investigated or dealt with in accordance with the various procedures and forums under the laws of the Fiji Islands.

Commitment No. 2
The Interim Government intends to lift the Public Emergency Regulations in May 2007
subject to any threats to national security, public order and safety.

Commitment No. 3
The Interim Government is committed to ensuring that the Fiji Human Rights Commission functions with full independence and in accordance with the Constitution.

Commitment No. 4
That the freedom of expression and the freedom of the media, in all its forms are fully
respected as provided in the Constitution.

D. Follow-up of Commitments
Commitment No. 1
That the Interim Government undertakes to maintain a regular dialogue to allow verification of progress made and gives EU and EC authorities/representatives full access to
information on all matters linked to human rights, the peaceful restoration of democracy and the rule of law in Fiji.

Commitment No. 2
That the Interim Government cooperates fully with eventual missions from the EU and
the EC for assessing and monitoring progress.

Commitment No. 3
That the Interim Government sends progress reports every three (3) months starting 30 June 2007 regarding the essential elements of the Cotonou Agreement and the
commitments.
It is noted that certain issues can only be effectively addressed through a pragmatic
approach which acknowledges the realities of the present and which focuses on the
future.

6.8 Classical countermeasures under international law

In March 1996, the US Congress passed the so-called Cuban Liberty and Democratic
Solidarity (Libertad) Act, also known as the Helms/Burton Act, after its two sponsors.
The thrust of the Act was to expand US sanctions against Cuba and also to apply these
sanctions against certain foreign companies that allegedly profited from Cuban nation-
alizations of US property. These extraterritorial effects of the law were strongly resisted
by the EC at the time. The EC undertook two counteractions. One was demanding
consultations and later demanding and obtaining the establishment of a panel on certain aspects of the Act that were considered to be contrary to the WTO Agreement, in
particular in the field of Trade-Related Intellectual Property Rights (TRIPs). The other
was a true countermeasure within the meaning of Article 49 ff. of the Draft Articles on
State Responsibility, namely the so-called blocking statute reproduced below. After
long-drawn-out negotiations between US and EC delegations, the result of which was

never fully made public, the EC first suspended the panel procedure in the WTO and then let it lapse, but the 'blocking regulation' is still being applied to the US legislation, as is the Helms-Burton Act itself, although certain specific aspects of it, concerning travel restrictions, are routinely suspended.

So-called 'blocking legislation' is a technique that was first developed by the UK in the 1960s in response to far-reaching claims of extraterritorial authority for US antitrust law. It applies to nationals of the state enacting it and to those within the territory of that state (in this case the EU). Essentially, it tries to counter the extraterritorial effects of foreign legislation by prohibiting the individuals and entities within its scope of application from obeying the foreign legislation.

Council Regulation (EC) No 2271/96 of 22 November 1996 protecting against the effects of the extra-territorial application of legislation adopted by a third country, and actions based thereon or resulting therefrom, Official Journal L 309, 29.11.1996, pp. 1-6 (Helms/Burton blocking legislation).

THE COUNCIL OF THE EUROPEAN UNION,
Having regard to the Treaty establishing the European Community, and in particular Articles 73c, 113 and 235 thereof,
Having regard to the proposal from the Commission,
Having regard to the opinion of the European Parliament,
Whereas the objectives of the Community include contributing to the harmonious development of world trade and to the progressive abolition of restrictions on international trade;
Whereas the Community endeavours to achieve to the greatest extent possible the objective of free movement of capital between Member States and third countries, including the removal of any restrictions on direct investment—including investment in real estate—establishment, the provision of financial services or the admission of securities to capital markets;
Whereas a third country has enacted certain laws, regulations, and other legislative instruments which purport to regulate activities of natural and legal persons under the jurisdiction of the Member State;
Whereas by their extra-territorial application such laws, regulations and other legislative instruments violate international law and impede the attainment of the aforementioned objectives;
Whereas such laws, including regulations and other legislative instruments, and actions based thereon or resulting therefrom affect or are likely to affect the established legal order and have adverse effects on the interests of the Community and the interests of natural and legal persons exercising rights under the Treaty establishing the European Community;
Whereas, under these exceptional circumstances, it is necessary to take action at Community level to protect the established legal order, the interests of the Community and the interests of the said natural and legal persons, in particular by removing, neutralising, blocking or otherwise countering the effects of the foreign legislation concerned;

Whereas the request to supply information under this Regulation does not preclude a Member State from requiring information of the same kind to be provided to the authorities of that State;

Whereas the Council has adopted the Joint Action 96/668/CFSP of 22 November 1996 in order to ensure that the Member States take the necessary measures to protect those natural and legal persons whose interests are affected by the aforementioned laws and actions based thereon, insofar as those interests are not protected by this Regulation;

Whereas the Commission, in the implementation of this Regulation, should be assisted by a committee composed of representatives of the Member States;

Whereas the actions provided for in this Regulation are necessary to attain objectives of the Treaty establishing the European Community;

Whereas for the adoption of certain provisions of this Regulation the Treaty does not provide powers other than those of Article 235,

HAS ADOPTED THIS REGULATION:

Article 1

This Regulation provides protection against and counteracts the effects of the extra-territorial application of the laws specified in the Annex of this Regulation, including regulations and other legislative instruments, and of actions based thereon or resulting therefrom, where such application affects the interests of persons, referred to in Article 11, engaging in international trade and/or the movement of capital and related commercial activities between the Community and third countries.

Acting in accordance with the relevant provisions of the Treaty and notwithstanding the provisions of Article 7(c), the Council may add or delete laws to or from the Annex to this Regulation.

Article 2

Where the economic and/or financial interests of any person referred to in Article 11 are affected, directly or indirectly, by the laws specified in the Annex or by actions based thereon or resulting therefrom, that person shall inform the Commission accordingly within 30 days from the date on which it obtained such information; insofar as the interests of a legal person are affected, this obligation applies to the directors, managers and other persons with management responsibilities.

At the request of the Commission, such person shall provide all information relevant for the purposes of this Regulation in accordance with the request from the Commission within 30 days from the date of the request.

All information shall be submitted to the Commission either directly or through the competent authorities of the Member States. Should the information be submitted directly to the Commission, the Commission will inform immediately the competent authorities of the Member States in which the person who gave the information is resident or incorporated.

Article 3

All information supplied in accordance with Article 2 shall only be used for the purposes for which it was provided.

Information which is by nature confidential or which is provided on a confidential basis shall be covered by the obligation of professional secrecy. It shall not be disclosed by the Commission without the express permission of the person providing it.

Communication of such information shall be permitted where the Commission is obliged or authorized to do so, in particular in connection with legal proceedings. Such communication must take into account the legitimate interests of the person concerned that his or her business secrets should not be divulged.

This article shall not preclude the disclosure of general information by the Commission. Such disclosure shall not be permitted if this is incompatible with the original purpose of such information.

In the event of a breach of confidentiality, the originator of the information shall be entitled to obtain that it be deleted, disregarded or rectified, as the case may be.

Article 4

No judgment of a court or tribunal and no decision of an administrative authority located outside the Community giving effect, directly or indirectly, to the laws specified in the Annex or to actions based thereon or resulting there from, shall be recognized or be enforceable in any manner.

Article 5

No person referred to in article 11 shall comply, whether directly or through a subsidiary or other intermediary person, actively or by deliberate omission, with any requirement or prohibition, including requests of foreign courts, based on or resulting, directly or indirectly, from the laws specified in the Annex or from actions based thereon or resulting therefrom.

Persons may be authorized, in accordance with the procedures provided in Articles 7 and 8, to comply fully or partially to the extent that non-compliance would seriously damage their interests or those of the Community. The criteria for the application of this provision shall be established in accordance with the procedure set out in Article 8. When there is sufficient evidence that non-compliance would cause serious damage to a natural or legal person, the Commission shall expeditiously submit to the committee referred to in Article 8 a draft of the appropriate measures to be taken under the terms of the Regulation.

Article 6

Any person referred to in Article 11, who is engaging in an activity referred to in Article 1 shall be entitled to recover any damages, including legal costs, caused to that person by the application of the laws specified in the Annex or by actions based thereon or resulting therefrom.

Such recovery may be obtained from the natural or legal person or any other entity causing the damages or from any person acting on its behalf or intermediary.

The Brussels Convention of 27 September 1968 on jurisdiction and the enforcement of judgments in civil and commercial matters shall apply to proceedings brought and judgments given under this article. Recovery may be obtained on the basis of the provisions of Sections 2 to 6 of Title II of that Convention, as well as, in accordance with

Article 57(3) of that Convention, through judicial proceedings instituted in the Courts of any Member State where that person, entity, person acting on its behalf or intermediary holds assets.

Without prejudice to other means available and in accordance with applicable law, the recovery could take the form of seizure and sale of assets held by those persons, entities, persons acting on their behalf or intermediaries within the Community, including shares held in a legal person incorporated within the Community.

Article 7

For the implementation of this Regulation the Commission shall:

(a) inform the European Parliament and the Council immediately and fully of the effects of the laws, regulations and other legislative instruments and ensuing actions mentioned in Article 1, on the basis of the information obtained under this Regulation, and make regularly a full public report thereon;

(b) grant authorization under the conditions set forth in Article 5 and, when laying down the time limits with regard to the delivery by the Committee of its opinion, take fully into account the time limits which have to be complied with by the persons which are to be subject of an authorization;

(c) add or delete, where appropriate, references to regulations or other legislative instruments deriving from the laws specified in the Annex, and falling under the scope of this Regulation;

(d) publish a notice in the Official Journal of the European Communities on the judgments and decisions to which Articles 4 and 6 apply;

(e) publish in the Official Journal of the European Communities the names and addresses of the competent authorities of the Member States referred to in Article 2.

Article 8

For the purposes of the implementation of Article 7(b) and (c), the Commission shall be assisted by a Committee composed of the representatives of the Member States and chaired by the representative of the Commission.

The representative of the Commission shall submit to the committee a draft of the measures to be taken. The committee shall deliver its opinion on the draft within a time limit which the chairman may lay down according to the urgency of the matter. The opinion shall be delivered by the majority laid down in Article 148(2) of the Treaty in the case of decisions which the Council is required to adopt on a proposal from the Commission. The votes of the representatives of the Member States within the committee shall be weighted in the manner set out in that article. The chairman shall not vote.

The Commission shall adopt the measures envisaged if they are in accordance with the opinion of the committee.

If the measures envisaged are not in accordance with the opinion of the committee, or if no opinion is delivered, the Commission shall, without delay, submit to the Council a proposal relating to the measures to be taken. The Council shall act by a qualified majority.

If, on the expiry of a period of two weeks from the date of referral to the Council, the Council has not acted, the proposed measures shall be adopted by the Commission.

Article 9

Each Member State shall determine the sanctions to be imposed in the event of breach of any relevant provisions of this Regulation. Such sanctions must be effective, proportional and dissuasive.

Article 10

The Commission and the Member States shall inform each other of the measures taken under this Regulation and of all other relevant information pertaining to this Regulation.

Article 11

This Regulation shall apply to:

1. any natural person being a resident in the Community and a national of a Member State,
2. any legal person incorporated within the Community,
3. any natural or legal person referred to in Article 1(2) of Regulation (EEC) No 4055/86,
4. any other natural person being a resident in the Community, unless that person is in the country of which he is a national,
5. any other natural person within the Community, including its territorial waters and air space and in any aircraft or on any vessel under the jurisdiction or control of a Member State, acting in a professional capacity.

Article 12

This Regulation shall enter into force on the day of its publication in the Official Journal of the European Communities.

This Regulation shall be binding in its entirety and directly applicable in all Member States.

ANNEX

LAWS, REGULATIONS AND OTHER LEGISLATIVE INSTRUMENTS referred to in Article 1

COUNTRY: UNITED STATES OF AMERICA
ACTS

1. 'National Defense Authorization Act for Fiscal Year 1993', Title XVII 'Cuban Democracy Act 1992', sections 1704 and 1706

Required compliance:
The requirements are consolidated in Title I of the 'Cuban Liberty and Democratic Solidarity Act of 1996', see below.

Possible damages to EU interests:
The liabilities incurred are now incorporated within the 'Cuban Liberty and Democratic Solidarity Act of 1996', see below.

2. 'Cuban Liberty and Democratic Solidarity Act of 1996'

Title I

Required compliance:
To comply with the economic and financial embargo concerning Cuba by the USA, by, inter alia, not exporting to the USA any goods or services of Cuban origin or containing materials or goods originating in Cuba either directly or through third countries, dealing in merchandise that is or has been located in or transported from or through Cuba, re-exporting to the USA sugar originating in Cuba without notification by the competent national authority of the exporter or importing into the USA sugar products without assurance that those products are not products of Cuba, freezing Cuban assets, and financial dealings with Cuba.

Possible damages to EU interests:
Prohibition to load or unload freight from a vessel in any place in the USA or to enter a USA port; refusal to import any goods or services originating in Cuba and to import into Cuba goods or services originating in the USA, blocking of financial dealings involving Cuba.

Title III and Title IV

Required compliance:
To terminate 'trafficking' in property, formerly owned by US persons (including Cubans who have obtained US citizenship) and expropriated by the Cuban regime. (Trafficking includes: use, sale, transfer, control, management and other activities to the benefit of a person).

Possible damages to EU interests:
Legal proceedings in the USA, based upon liability already accruing, against EU citizens or companies involved in trafficking, leading to judgments/decisions to pay (multiple) compensation to the USA party. Refusal of entry into the USA for persons involved in trafficking, including the spouses, minor children and agents thereof.
3. 'Iran and Libya Sanctions Act of 1996'

Required compliance:
Not to invest in Iran or Libya any amount greater than USD 40 million during a period of 12 months that directly and significantly contributes to the enhancement of the Iranian or Libyan ability to develop their petroleum resources. (Investment covering the entering into a contract for the said development, or the guaranteeing of it, or the profiting therefrom or the purchase of a share of ownership therein.)
NB: Investments under contracts existing before 5 August 1996 are exempted.
Respect of embargo concerning Libya established by Resolutions 748 (1992) and 883 (1993) of the Security Council of the United Nations.

Possible damages to EU interests:
Measures taken by the US President to limit imports into USA or procurement to USA, prohibition of designation as primary dealer or as repository of USA Government funds, denial of access to loans from USA financial institutions, export restrictions by USA, or refusal of assistance by EXIM-Bank.

REGULATIONS

1. 1 CFR (Code of Federal Regulations) Ch. V (7-1-95 edition) Part 515 – Cuban Assets Control Regulations, subpart B (Prohibitions), E (Licenses, Authorizations and Statements of Licensing Policy) and G (Penalties)

Required compliance:
The prohibitions are consolidated in Title I of the 'Cuban Liberty and Democratic Solidarity Act of 1996', see above. Furthermore, requires the obtaining of licences and/ or authorizations in respect of economic activities concerning Cuba.

Possible damages to EU interests:
Fines, forfeiture, imprisonment in cases of violation.

Select Bibliography

de Búrca, G., The European Court of Justice and the International Legal Order After *Kadi*, *Harvard International Law Journal*, vol. 51, no. 1, 2010, 1–49.

Eckes, C., *EU Counter-Terrorist Policies and Fundamental Rights: The Case of Individual Sanctions* (Oxford: Oxford University Press, 2009).

Halberstam, D. and Stein, E., The United Nations, the European Union, and the King of Sweden: Economic Sanctions and Individual Rights in a Plural World Order, *Common Market Law Review*, vol. 46, 2009, 13–72.

Hoffmeister, F. and Kuijper, P.J., The Status of the European Union at the United Nations: Institutional Ambiguities and Political Realities, *The United Nations and the European Union: An Ever Stronger Partnership* (J. Wouters, F. Hoffmeister, and T. Ruys (eds), The Hague: T.M.C. Asser Press, 2006), 9–34.

7

Common Commercial Policy

7.1 Introduction

The common commercial policy was originally the core of the EU's external relations powers. It was included immediately in the Treaty of Rome (Articles 111–114) and from the beginning it was also embedded in international economic law, professing the liberalization of trade on a world scale as one of its goals. In practice, this meant that at the same time that the Community was evolving towards the goal of establishing a customs union with a common external tariff at the end of the transitional period of twelve years (1970), it was negotiating externally, represented by the Commission, the level of this tariff in the so-called Dillon and Kennedy rounds in the framework of the General Agreement on Tariffs and Trade (GATT). Ever since, there have been, roughly speaking, two trends that have dominated the evolution of the common commercial policy. Externally, the EC/EU has functioned, initially unofficially in the GATT, and later officially in the WTO, as a full Member. Although the Member States remained members in the GATT and the WTO, their powers were in reality very limited, even perfunctory. As a consequence, nearly all autonomous trade legislation of the EC is firmly embedded in the various WTO agreements. The origins of such basic regulations, as those on safeguards, anti-dumping, subsidized imports, and so on have their roots in the relevant WTO texts.

Internally, ever since the completion of first the customs union and later the internal market, epic legal battles have been fought over the question whether the common commercial policy was merely intended to be the external face of the customs union or of the internal market. This determination was of great significance, since the former approach was rather restrictive, limiting the common commercial policy to trade in goods. On the contrary, the latter approach kept pace with both the internal development of the EC/EU and with the evolution of the nature of international trade, just as in the internal market, trade in services, intellectual property, and the protection of human, animal, and plant health and life and environmental protection became more and more important. The Council, often representing the view of the Member States, pushed for the rather restrictive interpretation, whereas the Commission advocated in favour of the broader interpretation of the scope of the common commercial policy.

7.2 Commercial policy powers and the WTO

In order to gain a proper perspective on the common commercial policy and to understand the case law included below, it is necessary to be aware not just of Article 207 TFEU, the current article spelling out the scope of that policy, but also of some of its predecessors, such as Article 133 of the EC Treaty in the Nice version, as well as the original version of Article 113 in the Rome Treaty.[1] In addition, Article XI:1 of the WTO Agreement shows that the 'European Communities'—at the time still all three of them—are Members of the WTO. In the meantime, of course, they have been succeeded by the EU after the entry into force of the Lisbon Treaty.

Treaty establishing the European Economic Community (Treaty of Rome)
Article 113

1. After the transitional period has ended, the common commercial policy shall be based on uniform principles, particularly in regard to changes in tariff rates, the conclusion of tariff and trade agreements, the achievement of uniformity in measures of liberalisation, export policy and measures to protect trade such as those to be taken in case of dumping or subsidies.

2. The Commission shall submit proposals to the Council for implementing the common commercial policy.

3. Where agreements with third countries need to be negotiated, the Commission shall make recommendations to the Council, which shall authorise the Commission to open the necessary negotiations.

The Commission shall conduct these negotiations in consultation with a special committee appointed by the Council to assist the Commission in this task and within the framework of such directives as the Council may issue to it.

4. In exercising the powers conferred upon it by this Article, the Council shall act by a qualified majority.

Treaty establishing the European Community (Treaty of Nice)
Article 133

1. The common commercial policy shall be based on uniform principles, particularly in regard to changes in tariff rates, the conclusion of tariff and trade agreements, the achievement of uniformity in measures of liberalisation, export policy and measures to protect trade such as those to be taken in the event of dumping or subsidies.

2. The Commission shall submit proposals to the Council for implementing the common commercial policy.

3. Where agreements with one or more States or international organisations need to be negotiated, the Commission shall make recommendations to the Council, which shall authorise the Commission to open the necessary negotiations. The Council and the Commission shall be responsible for ensuring that the agreements negotiated are compatible with internal Community policies and rules.

The Commission shall conduct these negotiations in consultation with a special committee appointed by the Council to assist the Commission in this task and within the

---

[1] Article 133 of the Treaty of Amsterdam is not included here, since it merely provided for the possibility that the Council decide that trade in services and TRIPs would become part of the Community's exclusive competence; a possibility that was never used.

framework of such directives as the Council may issue to it. The Commission shall report regularly to the special committee on the progress of negotiations.

The relevant provisions of Article 300 shall apply.

4. In exercising the powers conferred upon it by this Article, the Council shall act by a qualified majority.

5. Paragraphs 1 to 4 shall also apply to the negotiation and conclusion of agreements in the fields of trade in services and the commercial aspects of intellectual property, in so far as those agreements are not covered by the said paragraphs and without prejudice to paragraph 6.

By way of derogation from paragraph 4, the Council shall act unanimously when negotiating and concluding an agreement in one of the fields referred to in the first subparagraph, where that agreement includes provisions for which unanimity is required for the adoption of internal rules or where it relates to a field in which the Community has not yet exercised the powers conferred upon it by this Treaty by adopting internal rules.

The Council shall act unanimously with respect to the negotiation and conclusion of a horizontal agreement insofar as it also concerns the preceding subparagraph or the second subparagraph of paragraph 6.

This paragraph shall not affect the right of the Member States to maintain and conclude agreements with third countries or international organisations in so far as such agreements comply with Community law and other relevant international agreements.

6. An agreement may not be concluded by the Council if it includes provisions which would go beyond the Community's internal powers, in particular by leading to harmonisation of the laws or regulations of the Member States in an area for which this Treaty rules out such harmonisation.

In this regard, by way of derogation from the first subparagraph of paragraph 5, agreements relating to trade in cultural and audiovisual services, educational services, and social and human health services, shall fall within the shared competence of the Community and its Member States. Consequently, in addition to a Community decision taken in accordance with the relevant provisions of Article 300, the negotiation of such agreements shall require the common accord of the Member States. Agreements thus negotiated shall be concluded jointly by the Community and the Member States.

The negotiation and conclusion of international agreements in the field of transport shall continue to be governed by the provisions of Title V and Article 300.

7. Without prejudice to the first subparagraph of paragraph 6, the Council, acting unanimously on a proposal from the Commission and after consulting the European Parliament, may extend the application of paragraphs 1 to 4 to international negotiations and agreements on intellectual property in so far as they are not covered by paragraph 5.

Treaty on the Functioning of the European Union

Article 207

1. The common commercial policy shall be based on uniform principles, particularly with regard to changes in tariff rates, the conclusion of tariff and trade agreements relating to trade in goods and services, and the commercial aspects of intellectual property, foreign direct investment, the achievement of uniformity in measures of liberalisation,

export policy and measures to protect trade such as those to be taken in the event of dumping or subsidies. The common commercial policy shall be conducted in the context of the principles and objectives of the Union's external action.

2. The European Parliament and the Council, acting by means of regulations in accordance with the ordinary legislative procedure, shall adopt the measures defining the framework for implementing the common commercial policy.

3. Where agreements with one or more third countries or international organisations need to be negotiated and concluded, Article 218 shall apply, subject to the special provisions of this Article.

The Commission shall make recommendations to the Council, which shall authorise it to open the necessary negotiations. The Council and the Commission shall be responsible for ensuring that the agreements negotiated are compatible with internal Union policies and rules.

The Commission shall conduct these negotiations in consultation with a special committee appointed by the Council to assist the Commission in this task and within the framework of such directives as the Council may issue to it. The Commission shall report regularly to the special committee and to the European Parliament on the progress of negotiations.

4. For the negotiation and conclusion of the agreements referred to in paragraph 3, the Council shall act by a qualified majority.

For the negotiation and conclusion of agreements in the fields of trade in services and the commercial aspects of intellectual property, as well as foreign direct investment, the Council shall act unanimously where such agreements include provisions for which unanimity is required for the adoption of internal rules.

The Council shall also act unanimously for the negotiation and conclusion of agreements:

(a) in the field of trade in cultural and audiovisual services, where these agreements risk prejudicing the Union's cultural and linguistic diversity;

(b) in the field of trade in social, education and health services, where these agreements risk seriously disturbing the national organisation of such services and prejudicing the responsibility of Member States to deliver them.

5. The negotiation and conclusion of international agreements in the field of transport shall be subject to Title VI of Part Three and to Article 218.

6. The exercise of the competences conferred by this Article in the field of the common commercial policy shall not affect the delimitation of competences between the Union and the Member States, and shall not lead to harmonisation of legislative or regulatory provisions of the Member States in so far as the Treaties exclude such harmonisation.

Agreement establishing the World Trade Organization
Article XI:1

Original Membership

1. The contracting parties to GATT 1947 as of the date of entry into force of this Agreement, and the European Communities, which accept this Agreement and the Multilateral Trade Agreements and for which Schedules of Concessions and

Commitments are annexed to GATT 1994 and for which Schedules of Specific Commitments are annexed to GATS shall become original Members of the WTO.

Opinion of the Court of 11 November 1975 (OECD Understanding on a Local Cost Standard), Opinion 1/75, European Court Reports 1975, p. 1355 (Extracts).

This was the first request for an Opinion of the Court based on Article 228 TEC (now Article 218(11) TFEU). It was inescapable, therefore, that questions of the admissibility of the request would arise, especially since the request was formulated not in terms of 'conformity with the Treaty' or 'constitutionality', but in terms of the scope of the powers granted to the Community by (then) Article 113 and their exclusive character. The Court addresses all these issues, admissibility, scope of the common commercial policy, and exclusivity in turn.

The admissibility question is answered on the basis of a functional interpretation of Article 218(11) TFEU. This leads to a broad interpretation of the provision so as to include questions of the scope of external relations powers of the Union and their exclusive character. This has made this Treaty provision the favourite vehicle for disputes between the institutions as well as between Member States and the institutions on matters of external relations powers.

The answer on the scope of the common commercial policy is not surprising in the light of the fact that the Understanding of the Organization for Economic Cooperation and Development (OECD) was directly linked to export credit insurance so that its falling into the ambit of the common commercial policy was virtually undeniable.

The crucial issue of the case was, of course, the exclusive character of the powers of the Community in the field of the common commercial policy. With the benefit of hindsight EU lawyers have a tendency to regard this as self-evident, but at the time it was not (the Treaty did not say a word about it, unlike Article 3(1)(e) TFEU now). Hence it is useful to recall the reasons why the Court took this step, as well as to realize that this decision ensured that all the later legal fights would be about the scope of the common commercial policy. Because of the Court's ruling on exclusivity, the only way in which the Member States individually could retain some grip on the common commercial policy, at least in part, was to limit its scope. That battle has gone on ever since 1975.

[...]

[The question of admissibility]
It is the purpose of the second subparagraph of Article 228(1) to forestall complications which would result from legal disputes concerning the compatibility with the Treaty of international agreements binding upon the Community. In fact, a possible decision of the Court to the effect that such an agreement is, either by reason of its content or of the procedure adopted for its conclusion, incompatible with the provisions

of the Treaty could not fail to provoke, not only in a Community context but also in that of international relations, serious difficulties and might give rise to adverse consequences for all interested parties, including third countries.

For the purpose of avoiding such complications the Treaty had recourse to the exceptional procedure of a prior reference to the Court of Justice for the purpose of elucidating, before the conclusion of the agreement, whether the latter is compatible with the Treaty. This procedure must therefore be open for all questions capable of submission for judicial consideration, either by the Court of Justice or possibly by national courts, in so far as such questions give rise to doubt either as to the substantive or formal validity of the agreement with regard to the Treaty.

The question whether the conclusion of a given agreement is within the power of the Community and whether, in a given case, such power has been exercised in conformity with the provisions of the Treaty is, in principle a question which may be submitted to the Court of Justice, either directly, under Article 169 or Article 173 of the Treaty, or in accordance with the preliminary procedure, and it must therefore be admitted that the matter may be referred to the Court in accordance with the preliminary procedure of Article 228.

Similarly, the fact that discussions concerning the substance of the understanding in question are now at an end cannot constitute a valid argument on which to base a finding that the request for an opinion is out of time, since the Treaty, by reason of the non-contentious character of the procedure contained in the second subparagraph of Article 228(1), does not lay down a time-limit for the submission of such a request.

There is therefore no reason why the request for an opinion should not be admitted.

b—The reply to be given to the questions submitted

1. The existence of a Community power to conclude the OECD understanding on a Local Cost Standard

Articles 112 and 113 of the Treaty must be borne in mind in formulating a reply to this question.

The first of these provisions provides that:

'...Member States shall, before the end of the transitional period, progressively harmonize the systems whereby they grant aid for exports to third countries, to the extent necessary to ensure that competition between undertakings of the Community is not distorted'.

Since there is no doubt that the grant of export credits falls within the system of aids granted by member states for exports, it is already clear from Article 112 that the subject-matter of the standard laid down in the understanding in question relates to a field in which the provisions of the Treaty recognize a Community power.

Furthermore, Article 113 of the Treaty lays down, in paragraphs (1) and (2), that:

'...the common commercial policy shall be based on uniform principles, particularly in regard to...export policy...'.

The field of the common commercial policy, and more particularly that of export policy, necessarily covers systems of aid for exports and more particularly measures concerning credits for the financing of local costs linked to export operations. In fact, such measures constitute an important element of commercial policy, that concept having the same content whether it is applied in the context of the international action of a state or to that of the Community.

Directives concerning credit insurance, adopted by the Council towards the end of 1970 and the beginning of 1971 expressly recognize the important role played by export credits in international trade, as a factor of commercial policy.

For these reasons the subject-matter covered by the standard contained in the understanding in question, since it forms part not only of the sphere of the system of aids for exports laid down at Article 112 of the Treaty but also, in a more general way, of export policy and, by reason of that fact, of the sphere of the common commercial policy defined in Article 113 of the Treaty, falls within the ambit of the Community's powers.

In the course of the measures necessary to implement the principles laid down in the abovementioned provisions, particularly those covered by Article 113 of the Treaty, concerning the common commercial policy, the Community is empowered, pursuant to the powers which it possesses, not only to adopt internal rules of Community law, but also to conclude agreements with third countries pursuant to Article 113(2) and Article 114 of the Treaty.

A commercial policy is in fact made up by the combination and interaction of internal and external measures, without priority being taken by one over the others. Sometimes agreements are concluded in execution of a policy fixed in advance, sometimes that policy is defined by the agreements themselves.

Such agreements may be outline agreements, the purpose of which is to lay down uniform principles. Such is the case with the understanding on local costs: it does not have a specific content adapted to particular export credit transactions; it merely lays down a standard, sets out certain exceptions, provides, in exceptional circumstances, for derogations and, finally, lays down general provisions. Furthermore, the implementation of the export policy to be pursued within the framework of a common commercial policy does not necessarily find expression in the adoption of general and abstract rules of internal or Community law. The common commercial policy is above all the outcome of a progressive development based upon specific measures which may refer without distinction to 'autonomous' and external aspects of that policy and which do not necessarily presuppose, by the fact that they are linked to the field of the common commercial policy, the existence of a large body of rules, but combine gradually to form that body.

2. The exclusive nature of the Community's powers

The reply to this question depends, on the one hand, on the objective of the understanding in question and, on the other hand, on the manner in which the common commercial policy is conceived in the Treaty.

At Nos I and II the understanding itself defines the transactions to which the common standard applies, and those which, on the other hand, are excluded from its field of application because they are directed to specifically military ends or because they have been entered into with developing countries.

It is to be understood from this definition that the subject-matter of the standard, and therefore of the understanding, is one of those measures belonging to the common commercial policy prescribed by Article 113 of the Treaty.

Such a policy is conceived in that article in the context of the operation of the common market, for the defence of the common interests of the Community, within which the particular interests of the member states must endeavour to adapt to each other.

Quite clearly, however, this conception is incompatible with the freedom to which the member states could lay claim by invoking a concurrent power, so as to ensure that their own interests were separately satisfied in external relations, at the risk of compromising the effective defence of the common interests of the Community.

In fact any unilateral action on the part of the Member States would lead to disparities in the conditions for the grant of export credits, calculated to distort competition between undertakings of the various Member States in external markets. Such distortion can be eliminated only by means of a strict uniformity of credit conditions granted to undertakings in the Community, whatever their nationality.

It cannot therefore be accepted that, in a field such as that governed by the understanding in question, which is covered by export policy and more generally by the common commercial policy, the Member States should exercise a power concurrent to that of the Community, in the Community sphere and in the international sphere. The provisions of Articles 113 and 114 concerning the conditions under which, according to the Treaty, agreements on commercial policy must be concluded show clearly that the exercise of concurrent powers by the Member States and the Community in this matter is impossible.

To accept that the contrary were true would amount to recognizing that, in relations with third countries, Member States may adopt positions which differ from those which the Community intends to adopt, and would thereby distort the institutional framework, call into question the mutual trust within the Community and prevent the latter from fulfilling its task in the defence of the common interest.

It is of little importance that the obligations and financial burdens inherent in the execution of the agreement envisaged are borne directly by the Member States. The 'internal' and 'external' measures adopted by the Community within the framework of the common commercial policy do not necessarily involve, in order to ensure their compatibility with the treaty, a transfer to the institutions of the Community of the obligations and financial burdens which they may involve: such measures are solely concerned to substitute for the unilateral action of the member states, in the field under consideration, a common action based upon uniform principles on behalf of the whole of the Community.

Similarly, in relation to products subject to the ECSC Treaty, it is of little importance to note that the power of the member states to conclude the understanding envisaged is safeguarded by Article 71 of that Treaty, according to which:

'The powers of the governments of Member States in matters of commercial policy shall not be affected by this Treaty...'.

The matter under discussion has been referred to the Court pursuant to the second subparagraph of Article 228(1) of the EEC Treaty. The opinion which it has been called upon to give therefore bears upon the problem of the compatibility of the agreement envisaged with the provisions of the EEC Treaty and will define the power of the Community to conclude that agreement solely in relation to those provisions.

Independently of the question whether, in view of the necessity of ensuring that international transactions to which the Communities are party should have as uniform a character as possible, Article 71 of the ECSC Treaty retains its former force follow-ing the entry into force of the EEC Treaty, that provision cannot in any event render inoperative Articles 113 and 114 of the EEC Treaty and affect the vesting of power in the Community for the negotiation and conclusion of international agreements in the realm of common commercial policy.

Accordingly,
the Court
gives the following opinion:
The Community has exclusive power to participate in the understanding on a Local Cost Standard referred to in the request for an opinion

---

Opinion of the Court of 4 October 1979 (Commodity Agreement on Natural Rubber), Opinion 1/78, European Court Reports 1979, p. 2871, paras. 41–49 and 52–60.

This Opinion dates from the time when there were strong tendencies to bring about a change in international economic policy: the so-called New International Economic Order, embodied, together with the Charter of Economic Rights and Duties of States, in (non-binding) UN resolutions. In line with these ideas, the United Nations Conference on Trade and Development (UNCTAD) developed a plan for Commodity Agreements for many primary products, both agricultural and mineral, with a view to combat the large price fluctuations on the markets for these products. Such agreements were to be equipped with a fund and a buffer stock that would put them in a position to dampen these fluctuations and to aim for a broadly stable and remunerative price level in the interest of the developing countries. The Natural Rubber Agreement was one of these agreements being negotiated at the time.

Again, the question was related to the scope of the common commercial policy: was the common commercial policy as a concept flexible and broad enough to accommo-date new measures such as mechanisms for stabilizing world markets in commodities? Did it matter that such new policies had to be accompanied by considerable financing for the funds and buffer stocks involved? The answer to the first question is positive, but the Court is much more ambiguous on the second question. There is, therefore, reason to question whether the Court still fully adheres to its views on the evolutionary nature of the notion of commercial policy (see in particular Opinion 1/94 below), but it has never openly disavowed them.

(a) Consideration of the agreement's links with commercial policy and development problems
41. By its special machinery as much as by certain aspects of its legal structure, the International Agreement on Natural Rubber which it is proposed to conclude stands apart from ordinary commercial and tariff agreements which are based primarily on the operation of customs duties and quantitative restrictions. The

agreement in question is a more structured instrument in the form of an organization of the market on a world scale and in this way it is distinguished from classical commercial agreements. An answer to the question which is the subject of the request for an opinion requires a reference to the scope and consequences of these specific characteristics in relation to the concept of common commercial policy as referred to in Article 113 of the Treaty. At the same time consideration must be given to the question whether the link which exists between the agreement envisaged and the development problems to which the Council refers may perhaps exclude the agreement from the sphere of the common commercial policy as defined by the Treaty.

42. The Nairobi Resolution, which is the basis of the negotiations in progress on natural rubber, shows that commodity agreements have complex objectives. Whilst stressing the needs of the developing countries the resolution includes many references to mechanisms of a commercial nature and does not overlook the needs of the industrialized countries. As regards, more particularly, the interests of the developing countries, it is true that commodity agreements may involve the granting of advantages which are characteristic of development aid; it must however be acknowledged also that for those countries such agreements respond more fundamentally to the preoccupation of bringing about an improvement in the 'terms of trade' and thus of increasing their export earnings. This characteristic is particularly brought out in the agreement in question, which seeks to establish a fair balance between the interests of the producer countries and those of the consumer countries. It is natural that, in negotiating an agreement of this type, the industrialized countries, whilst seeking to defend their own interests, should be obliged to recognize the situation of the producer countries which are negotiating from an economic standpoint which is very different from their own and that a reasonable compromise must be found between these points of view so as to make an agreement possible.

43. The link between the various agreements on commodities which were emphasized by the Nairobi Resolution must also be taken into account. As an increasing number of products which are particularly important from the economic point of view are concerned, it is clear that a coherent commercial policy would no longer be practicable if the Community were not in a position to exercise its powers also in connexion with a category of agreements which are becoming, alongside traditional commercial agreements, one of the major factors in the regulation of international trade.

44. Following the impulse given by UNCTAD to the development of this type of control it seems that it would no longer be possible to carry on any worthwhile common commercial policy if the Community were not in a position to avail itself also of more elaborate means devised with a view to furthering the development of international trade. It is therefore not possible to lay down, for Article 113 of the EEC Treaty, an interpretation the effect of which would be to restrict the common commercial policy to the use of instruments intended to have an effect only on the traditional aspects of external trade to the exclusion of more highly developed

mechanisms such as appear in the agreement envisaged. A 'commercial policy' understood in that sense would be destined to become nugatory in the course of time. Although it may be thought that at the time when the Treaty was drafted liberalization of trade was the dominant idea, the treaty nevertheless does not form a barrier to the possibility of the Community's developing a commercial policy aiming at a regulation of the world market for certain products rather than at a mere liberalization of trade.

45. Article 113 empowers the Community to formulate a commercial 'policy', based on 'uniform principles' thus showing that the question of external trade must be governed from a wide point of view and not only having regard to the administration of precise systems such as customs and quantitative restrictions. The same conclusion may be deduced from the fact that the enumeration in Article 113 of the subjects covered by commercial policy (changes in tariff rates, the conclusion of tariff and trade agreements, the achievement of uniformity in measures of liberalization, export policy and measures to protect trade) is conceived as a non-exhaustive enumeration which must not, as such, close the door to the application in a Community context of any other process intended to regulate external trade. A restrictive interpretation of the concept of common commercial policy would risk causing disturbances in intra-Community trade by reason of the disparities which would then exist in certain sectors of economic relations with non-member countries.

46. Moreover, when the whole canvas of existing and planned agreements is considered it appears that as far as the Community is concerned a wide range of interests is involved in the negotiation of those agreements and that there are connexions with the most varied spheres in which the Community has undertaken responsibilities. Thus, alongside agreements dealing, like the rubber agreement, with products with regard to which (always excepting of course the problem of substitution products) the Community appears only in the position of a consumer, there are other agreements, for example those concerning products such as wheat, oils and fats and sugar, in which the Community is interested also as a producer and by which its export policy, expressly mentioned in Article 113 as being amongst the objectives of the common commercial policy, is affected at the same time import policy. Several of the agreements belonging to this category are furthermore directly related to the execution of the common agricultural policy.

(b) The agreement's links with general economic policy

47. In its arguments the Council has raised the problem of the interrelation within the structure of the Treaty of the concepts of 'economic policy' and 'commercial policy'. In certain provisions economic policy is indeed considered primarily as a question of national interest; such is the meaning of that concept in Articles 6 and 145 which, for that reason, prescribe for the Member States nothing more than a duty to ensure co-ordination. In other provisions economic policy is envisaged as being a matter of common interest as is the case with Articles 103 to 116, which are grouped together in a title devoted to the 'economic policy' of the

Community. The chapter devoted to the common commercial policy forms part of that title.

48. The considerations set out above already form to some extent an answer to the arguments relating to the distinction to be drawn between the spheres of general economic policy and those of the common commercial policy since international co-operation, inasmuch as it does not belong to commercial policy, would be confused with the domain of general economic policy. If it appears that it comes, at least in part, under the common commercial policy, as has been indicated above, it follows clearly that it could not, under the name of general economic policy, be withdrawn from the competence of the Community.

49. Having regard to the specific nature of the provisions relating to commercial policy in so far as they concern relations with non-member countries and are founded, according to Article 113, on the concept of a common policy, their scope cannot be restricted in the light of more general provisions relating to economic policy and based on the idea of mere co-ordination. Consequently, where the organization of the Community's economic links with non-member countries may have repercussions on certain sectors of economic policy such as the supply of raw materials to the community or price policy, as is precisely the case with the regulation of international trade in commodities, that consideration does not constitute a reason for excluding such objectives from the field of application of the rules relating to the common commercial policy. Similarly, the fact that a product may have a political importance by reason of the building up of security stocks is not a reason for excluding that product from the domain of the common commercial policy.

v – Problems raised by the financing of the agreement and by other specific provisions

52. Consideration must still be given, having regard to what has been stated above as regards correspondence between the objective and purposes of the agreement envisaged and the concept of common commercial policy, whether the detailed arrangements for financing the buffer stock, or certain specific clauses of the agreement, concerning technological assistance, research programmes, the maintenance of fair conditions of labour in the rubber industry and consultations relating to national tax policies which may have an effect on the price of rubber lead to a negation of the Community's exclusive competence.

53. As regards the question of financing, the Council and those of the governments which have supported its views state that since those negotiating the agreement have opted for financing by means of public funds, the finances of the Member States will be involved in the execution of the agreement so that it cannot be accepted that such undertakings should be entered into without their participation. The Commission, for its part, takes the view that the question of competence precedes that of financing and that the question of Community powers cannot therefore be made dependent on the choice of financial arrangements.

54. As regards the specific clauses mentioned above, the Council states that provisions of this kind lie in any case outside the sphere of commercial policy with the consequence that the negotiation of the agreement envisaged comes from point of view also under Article 116 relating to common action by Member States within international organization.

55. The Court feels that a distinction should be made in this respect between the specific clauses referred to by the Council and the financial provisions which occupy a central position in the structure of the agreement and which, for that reason, raise a more fundamental difficulty as regards the demarcation between the powers of the Community and those of the Member States.

56. The Court takes the view that the fact that the agreement may cover subjects such as technological assistance, research programmes, labour conditions in the industry concerned or consultations relating to national tax policies which may have an effect on the price of rubber cannot modify the description of the agreement which must be assessed having regard to its essential objective rather than in terms of individual clauses of an altogether subsidiary or ancillary nature. This is the more true because the clauses under consideration are in fact closely connected with the objective of the agreement and the duties of the bodies which are to operate in the framework of the International Natural Rubber Organization which it is planned to set up. The negotiation and execution of these clauses must therefore follow the system applicable to the agreement considered as a whole.

57. With regard to the system of financing it should be borne in mind in the first place that, in its recommendation to the Council on 5 October 1978 under Article 113, the Commission had proposed that the application of the financial clauses of the agreement on Natural Rubber should be effected by the Community itself with a direct contribution from the Community budget. Whilst accepting that this method of financing would be possible having regard to the financial provisions of the EEC Treaty, the Council expressed its preference for financing by the Member States. However, no formal decision has yet been taken on this question. Moreover, there is no certainty as regards the attitude of the various Member States on this particular question and its implications for the apportionment of the financial burdens.

58. Having regard to the uncertainty which exists as regards the final solution to be adopted for this problem, the Court feels bound to have regard to two possible situations: one in which the financial burdens envisaged by the agreement would be entered in the Community budget and one in which the burdens would be directly charged to the budgets of the Member States. The Court itself is in no position, within the limits of the present proceedings, to make any choice between the two alternatives.

59. In the first case no problem would arise as regards the exclusive powers of the Community to conclude the agreement in question. As has been indicated above, the mechanism of the buffer stock has the purpose of regulating trade and from this point of view constitutes an instrument of the common commercial policy.

It follows that Community financing of the charges arising would have to be regarded as a solution in conformity with the Treaty.

60. The facts of the problem would be different if the second alternative were to be preferred. It cannot in fact be denied that the financing of the buffer stock constitutes an essential feature of the scheme for regulating the market which it is proposed to set up. The extent of and the detailed arrangements for the financial undertakings which the Member States will be required to satisfy will directly condition the possibilities and the degree of efficiency of intervention by the buffer mechanism whilst the decisions to be taken as regards the level of the central reference price and the margins of fluctuation to be permitted either upwards or downwards will have immediate repercussions on the use of the financial means put at the disposal of the International Rubber Council which is to be set up and on the extent of the financial means to be put at its disposal. Furthermore sight must not be lost of the fact that the financial structure which it is proposed to set up will make necessary, as is mentioned in the documents submitted to the Court and reflecting the most recent stage of negotiations, co-ordination between the use of the specific financial means put at the disposal of the future International Rubber Council and those which it might find in the common fund which is to be set up. If the financing of the agreement is a matter for the Community the necessary decisions will be taken according to the appropriate Community procedures. If on the other hand the financing is to be by the Member States that will imply the participation of those states in the decision-making machinery or, at least, their agreement with regard to the arrangements for financing envisaged and consequently their participation in the agreement together with the Community. The exclusive competence of the Community could not be envisaged in such a case.

[...]

In conclusion,
the Court
gives the following opinion:

1. The Community's powers relating to commercial policy within the meaning of Article 113 of the Treaty establishing the European Economic Community extend to the International Agreement on Natural Rubber which is in the course of negotiation within the United Nations Conference on Trade and Development.

2. The question of the exclusive nature of the Community's powers depends in this case on the arrangements for financing the operations of the buffer stock which it is proposed to set up under that agreement.

   If the burden of financing the stock falls upon the Community budget the Community will have exclusive powers.

   If on the other hand the charges are to be borne directly by the Member States that will imply the participation of those states in the agreement together with the Community.

3. As long as that question has not been settled by the competent Community authorities the Member States must be allowed to participate in the negotiation of the agreement.

Opinion of the Court of 15 November 1994 (WTO Agreement), Opinion 1/94, European Court Reports 1994, p. I-5267, paras. 4–6, 19–21, 35–71 and 106–10.

The negotiations of the Uruguay Round were characterized for the EC by virtually constant disagreement between the Commission and the Member States about the power of the Community to conclude the final package to come out of the negotiations and consequently of the power of the Commission to negotiate for the Community. The latter problem was fortunately glossed over in practice by appointing the Commission as sole negotiator for the Community in respect of trade in goods and for the Member States in the domains of trade in services (General Agreement on Trade in Services (GATS)) and of Trade-Related Intellectual Property Rights (TRIPs). The two last mentioned agreements did not fall under the common commercial policy according to the Member States. The Commission, however, maintained that GATS and TRIPs belonged to the common commercial policy, if a proper evolutionary approach to this policy was followed in line with Opinion 1/78, or, in the alternative, if the ERTA doctrine was applied.[2]

It was so obvious that no agreement with the Member States on the Community's powers under the common commercial policy was possible in respect to the WTO Agreement that the Commission, immediately after full agreement on the text of the results of the Uruguay Round was reached in December 1993, started preparing a request for an Opinion on the matter. The request was filed just before the signature of the WTO Agreement and the Final Act at Marrakech in April 1994. The Court rendered its Opinion in record time before the deadline set for ratification by the participants at the Conference of Marrakech (31 December 1994). This resulted in a resounding defeat of the Commission and opened up the domain of commercial policy, as it had developed during the Uruguay Round, for mixed competence. The only counterweight that the Court could offer in order to maintain minimal coherence in the conduct of commercial policy was the so-called duty of cooperation between the Community and Member States.

In the extracts from Opinion 1/94 below, the preliminary issues have been omitted, except the question of budgetary powers. The section related to trade in goods was largely devoted to rearguard actions by the Member States pleading for a restrictive interpretation of the notion of common commercial policy even in this domain and has been left out. Similarly, the attempt by the Commission to argue that the application of the ERTA doctrine ought to lead to exclusive powers in the field of GATS and TRIPs is now largely of historical and anecdotic interest and it is therefore omitted as well.

4. On 15 December 1993, the Trade Negotiations Committee, a body specially set up by the Punta del Este Conference to conclude the Uruguay Round negotiations, meeting at the level of senior officials, approved the Final Act embodying the results of the Uruguay Round multilateral trade negotiations.

---

[2] For the ERTA doctrine, see Chapter 1.

5. At its meeting on 7 and 8 March 1994, the Council decided to proceed to the signature of the Final Act and the WTO Agreement. It authorized the President of the Council and Commissioner Sir Leon Brittan to sign the Final Act and the WTO Agreement at Marrakesh on 15 April 1994 on behalf of the Council of the European Union. The representatives of the Member States, who took the view that those acts 'also cover[ed] matters of national competence', agreed on the same date that they would proceed to sign the Final Act and the WTO Agreement. The Commission, for its part, had recorded in the minutes its view that 'the Final Act (…) and the agreements annexed thereto fall exclusively within the competence of the European Community'.

6. The Commission submitted its request for an Opinion on 6 April 1994. It asked the following questions:

'As regards the results of the Uruguay Round GATT trade talks contained in the Final Act of 15 December 1993:

(1) Does the European Community have the competence to conclude all parts of the Agreement establishing the WTO concerning trade in Services (GATS) and the trade-related aspects of intellectual property rights including trade in counterfeit goods (TRIPs) on the basis of the EC Treaty, more particularly on the basis of Article 113 EC alone, or in combination with Article 100a EC and/or Article 235 EC?

(2) Does the European Community have the competence to conclude alone also those parts of the WTO Agreement which concern products and/or services falling exclusively within the scope of application of the ECSC and the EAEC Treaties?

(3) If the answer to the above two questions is in the affirmative, does this affect the ability of Member States to conclude the WTO Agreement, in the light of the agreement already reached that they will be original Members of the WTO?'

[…]

V. Budgetary and financial matters

19. The Portuguese Government refers to Article VII of the WTO Agreement, which provides that each member is to contribute to the expenses of the WTO, and submits that, given that the Member States of the Community are to acquire the status of original members of the WTO (see Article XI(1)), that is enough to justify the participation of the Member States in the conclusion of the agreement, even though financing is not as crucially important as it was in the International Agreement on Natural Rubber which gave rise to Opinion 1/78, cited above. The Portuguese Government also advances a reason based on its own constitutional law, under which the national parliament is required to approve international treaties providing for the participation of the Portuguese Republic in international organizations.

20. In reply to that latter argument, suffice it to say that internal rules of law, even of a constitutional nature, cannot alter the division of international powers between the Member States and the Community as laid down by the Treaty.

21. Nor can the first argument be accepted. Given that the WTO is an international organization which will have only an operating budget and not a financial policy

instrument, the fact that the Member States will bear some of its expenses cannot, on any view, of itself justify participation of the Member States in the conclusion of the WTO Agreement.

[...]

VII. Article 113 of the EC Treaty, GATS and TRIPs

35. The Commission's main contention is that the conclusion of both GATS and TRIPs falls within the exclusive competence conferred on the Community in commercial policy matters by Article 113 of the EC Treaty. That point of view has been vigorously disputed, as to its essentials, by the Council, by the Member States which have submitted observations and by the European Parliament, which has been permitted, at its request, to submit observations. It is therefore appropriate to begin by examining the Commission's main contention, with reference to GATS and to TRIPs respectively.

A. GATS

36. Relying essentially on the non-restrictive interpretation applied by the Court's case-law to the concept of the common commercial policy (see Opinion 1/78, paragraphs 44 and 45), the links or overlap between goods and services, the purpose of GATS and the instruments used, the Commission concludes that services fall within the common commercial policy, without any need to distinguish between the different modes of supply of services and, in particular, between the direct, cross-frontier supply of services and the supply of services through a commercial presence in the country of the person to whom they are supplied. The Commission also maintains that international agreements of a commercial nature in relation to transport (as opposed to those relating to safety rules) fall within the common commercial policy and not within the particular title of the Treaty on the common transport policy.

37. It is appropriate to consider, first, services other than transport and, subsequently, the particular services comprised in transport.

38. As regards the first category, it should be recalled at the outset that in Opinion 1/75 the Court, which had been asked to rule on the scope of Community competence as to the arrangements relating to a local cost standard, held that 'the field of the common commercial policy, and more particularly that of export policy, necessarily covers systems of aid for exports and more particularly measures concerning credits for the financing of local costs linked to export operations' ([1975] ECR 1362). The local costs in question concerned expenses incurred for the supply of both goods and services. Nevertheless, the Court recognized the exclusive competence of the Community, without drawing a distinction between goods and services.

39. In its Opinion 1/78, cited above (paragraph 44), the Court rejected an interpretation of Article 113 'the effect of which would be to restrict the common commercial policy to the use of instruments intended to have an effect only on the traditional aspects of external trade'. On the contrary, it considered that 'the question of external trade must be governed from a wide point of view', as is confirmed

by 'the fact that the enumeration in Article 113 of the subjects covered by commercial policy...is conceived as a non-exhaustive enumeration' (Opinion 1/78, cited above, paragraph 45).

40. The Commission points out in its request for an opinion that in certain developed countries the services sector has become the dominant sector of the economy and that the global economy has been undergoing fundamental structural changes. The trend is for basic industry to be transferred to developing countries, whilst the developed economies have tended to become, in the main, exporters of services and of goods with a high value-added content. The Court notes that this trend is borne out by the WTO Agreement and its annexes, which were the subject of a single process of negotiation covering both goods and services.

41. Having regard to this trend in international trade, it follows from the open nature of the common commercial policy, within the meaning of the Treaty, that trade in services cannot immediately, and as a matter of principle, be excluded from the scope of Article 113, as some of the Governments which have submitted observations contend.

42. In order to make that conclusion more specific, however, one must take into account the definition of trade in services given in GATS in order to see whether the overall scheme of the Treaty is not such as to limit the extent to which trade in services can be included within Article 113.

43. Under Article I(2) of GATS, trade in services is defined, for the purposes of that agreement, as comprising four modes of supply of services: (1) cross-frontier supplies not involving any movement of persons; (2) consumption abroad, which entails the movement of the consumer into the territory of the WTO member country in which the supplier is established; (3) commercial presence, i.e. the presence of a subsidiary or branch in the territory of the WTO member country in which the service is to be rendered; (4) the presence of natural persons from a WTO member country, enabling a supplier from one member country to supply services within the territory of any other member country.

44. As regards cross-frontier supplies, the service is rendered by a supplier established in one country to a consumer residing in another. The supplier does not move to the consumer's country; nor, conversely, does the consumer move to the supplier's country. That situation is, therefore, not unlike trade in goods, which is unquestionably covered by the common commercial policy within the meaning of the Treaty. There is thus no particular reason why such a supply should not fall within the concept of the common commercial policy.

45. The same cannot be said of the other three modes of supply of services covered by GATS, namely, consumption abroad, commercial presence and the presence of natural persons.

46. As regards natural persons, it is clear from Article 3 of the Treaty, which distinguishes between 'a common commercial policy' in paragraph (b) and 'measures concerning the entry and movement of persons' in paragraph (d), that the treatment of nationals of non-member countries on crossing the external frontiers

of Member States cannot be regarded as falling within the common commercial policy. More generally, the existence in the Treaty of specific chapters on the free movement of natural and legal persons shows that those matters do not fall within the common commercial policy.

47. It follows that the modes of supply of services referred to by GATS as 'consumption abroad', 'commercial presence' and the 'presence of natural persons' are not covered by the common commercial policy.

48. Turning next to the particular services comprised in transport, these are the subject of a specific title (Title IV) of the Treaty, distinct from Title VII on the common commercial policy. It was precisely in relation to transport policy that the Court held for the first time that the competence of the Community to conclude international agreements 'arises not only from an express conferment by the Treaty—as is the case with Articles 113 and 114 for tariff and trade agreements and with Article 238 for association agreements—but may equally flow from other provisions of the Treaty and from measures adopted, within the framework of those provisions, by the Community institutions' (Case 22/70 *Commission* v *Council* [1971] ECR 263, paragraph 16, the 'AETR judgment'). The idea underlying that decision is that international agreements in transport matters are not covered by Article 113.

49. The scope of the AETR judgment cannot be cut down by drawing a distinction between agreements on safety rules, such as those relating to the length of driving periods of professional drivers, with which the AETR judgment was concerned, and agreements of a commercial nature.

50. The AETR judgment draws no such distinction. The Court confirmed that analysis in Opinion 1/76 ([1977] ECR 741) concerning an agreement intended to rationalize the economic situation in the inland waterways sector—in other words, an economic agreement not concerned with the laying down of safety rules. Moreover, numerous agreements have been concluded with non-member countries on the basis of the Transport Title; a long list of such agreements was given by the United Kingdom in its observations.

51. In support of its view the Commission has further cited a series of embargoes based on Article 113 and involving the suspension of transport services: measures against Iraq: Council Regulation (EEC) No 2340/90 of 8 August 1990 preventing trade by the Community as regards Iraq and Kuwait (OJ 1990 L 213, p. 1), Council Regulation (EEC) No 3155/90 of 29 October 1990 extending and amending Regulation (EEC) No 2340/90 preventing trade by the Community as regards Iraq and Kuwait (OJ 1990 L 304, p. 1) and Council Regulation (EEC) No 1194/91 of 7 May 1991 amending Regulations (EEC) No 2340/90 and (EEC) No 3155/90 preventing trade by the Community as regards Iraq and Kuwait (OJ 1991 L 115, p. 37); measures against the Federal Republic of Yugoslavia (Serbia and Montenegro): Council Regulation (EEC) No 990/93 of 26 April 1993 concerning trade between the European Economic Community and the Federal Republic of Yugoslavia (Serbia and Montenegro) (OJ 1993 L 102, p. 14); measures against Haiti: Council Regulation (EEC) No 1608/93 of 23 June 1993 introducing an

embargo concerning certain trade between the European Economic Community and Haiti (OJ 1993 L 155, p. 2). Those precedents are not conclusive. As the European Parliament has rightly observed, since the embargoes related primarily to the export and import of products, they could not have been effective if it had not been decided at the same time to suspend transport services. Such suspension is to be seen as a necessary adjunct to the principal measure. Consequently, the precedents are not relevant to the question whether the Community has exclusive competence pursuant to Article 113 to conclude international agreements in the field of transport.

52. In any event, the Court has consistently held that a mere practice of the Council cannot derogate from the rules laid down in the Treaty and cannot, therefore, create a precedent binding on Community institutions with regard to the correct legal basis (see Case 68/86 *United Kingdom* v *Council* [1988] ECR 855, paragraph 24).

53. It follows that only cross-frontier supplies are covered by Article 113 of the Treaty and that international agreements in the field of transport are excluded from it.

B. TRIPs

54. The Commission's argument in support of its contention that the Community has exclusive competence under Article 113 is essentially that the rules concerning intellectual property rights are closely linked to trade in the products and services to which they apply.

55. It should be noted, first, that Section 4 of Part III of TRIPs, which concerns the means of enforcement of intellectual property rights, contains specific rules as to measures to be applied at border crossing points. As the United Kingdom has pointed out, that section has its counterpart in the provisions of Council Regulation (EEC) No 3842/86 of 1 December 1986 laying down measures to prohibit the release for free circulation of counterfeit goods (OJ 1986 L 357, p. 1). Inasmuch as that regulation concerns the prohibition of the release into free circulation of counterfeit goods, it was rightly based on Article 113 of the Treaty: it relates to measures to be taken by the customs authorities at the external frontiers of the Community. Since measures of that type can be adopted autonomously by the Community institutions on the basis of Article 113 of the EC Treaty, it is for the Community alone to conclude international agreements on such matters.

56. However, as regards matters other than the provisions of TRIPs on the release into free circulation of counterfeit goods, the Commission's arguments cannot be accepted.

57. Admittedly, there is a connection between intellectual property and trade in goods. Intellectual property rights enable those holding them to prevent third parties from carrying out certain acts. The power to prohibit the use of a trade mark, the manufacture of a product, the copying of a design or the reproduction of a book, a disc or a videocassette inevitably has effects on trade. Intellectual property rights are moreover specifically designed to produce such effects. That is not enough to bring them within the scope of Article 113. Intellectual property rights do not

relate specifically to international trade; they affect internal trade just as much as, if not more than, international trade.

58. As the French Government has rightly observed, the primary objective of TRIPs is to strengthen and harmonize the protection of intellectual property on a world-wide scale. The Commission has itself conceded that, since TRIPs lays down rules in fields in which there are no Community harmonization measures, its conclusion would make it possible at the same time to achieve harmonization within the Community and thereby to contribute to the establishment and functioning of the common market.

59. It should be noted here that, at the level of internal legislation, the Community is competent, in the field of intellectual property, to harmonize national laws pursuant to Articles 100 and 100a and may use Article 235 as the basis for creating new rights superimposed on national rights, as it did in Council Regulation (EC) No 40/94 of 20 December 1993 on the Community trade mark (OJ 1994 L 11, p. 1). Those measures are subject to voting rules (unanimity in the case of Articles 100 and 235) or rules of procedure (consultation of the Parliament in the case of Articles 100 and 235, the joint decision-making procedure in the case of Article 100a) which are different from those applicable under Article 113.

60. If the Community were to be recognized as having exclusive competence to enter into agreements with non-member countries to harmonize the protection of intellectual property and, at the same time, to achieve harmonization at Community level, the Community institutions would be able to escape the internal constraints to which they are subject in relation to procedures and to rules as to voting.

61. Institutional practice in relation to autonomous measures or external agreements adopted on the basis of Article 113 cannot alter this conclusion.

62. The Commission cites three cases in which, by virtue of the 'new commercial policy instrument' (Council Regulation (EEC) No 2641/84 of 17 September 1984 on the strengthening of the common commercial policy with regard in particular to protection against illicit commercial practices (OJ 1984 L 252, p. 1), which was itself based on Article 113 of the Treaty), procedures were opened to defend the Community's intellectual property interests: Commission Decision 87/251/EEC of 12 March 1987 on the initiation of an international consultation and disputes settlement procedure concerning a United States measure excluding imports of certain aramid fibres into the United States of America (OJ 1987 L 117, p. 18); notice of initiation of an 'illicit commercial practice' procedure concerning the unauthorized reproduction of sound recordings in Indonesia (OJ 1987 C 136, p. 3); notice of initiation of an examination procedure concerning an illicit commercial practice, within the meaning of Council Regulation (EEC) No 2641/84, consisting of piracy of Community sound recordings in Thailand (OJ 1991 C 189, p. 26).

63. The measures which may be taken pursuant to that regulation in response to a lack of protection in a non-member country of intellectual property rights held by Community undertakings (or to discrimination against them in that field) are

unrelated to the harmonization of intellectual property protection which is the primary objective of TRIPs. According to Article 10(3) of Regulation No 2641/84, cited above, those measures are: the suspension or withdrawal of any concession resulting from commercial policy negotiations; the raising of existing customs duties or the introduction of any other charge on imports; and the introduction of quantitative restrictions or any other measures modifying import or export conditions in trade with the non-member country concerned. All those measures fall, by their very nature, within the ambit of commercial policy.

64. The Commission also relies on measures adopted by the Community in relation to Korea within the framework of Council Regulation (EEC) No 4257/88 of 19 December 1988 applying generalized tariff preferences for 1989 in respect of certain industrial products originating in developing countries (OJ 1988 L 375, p. 1). Since Korea had discriminated between its trading partners as regards protection of intellectual property (see the nineteenth recital in the preamble to the regulation), the Community suspended the generalized tariff preferences in respect of its products (Article 1(3) of the regulation).

65. That argument is no more convincing than the preceding one. Since the grant of generalized preferences is a commercial policy measure, as the Court has held (see the 'Generalized tariff preferences' judgment in Case 45/86 *Commission* v *Council* [1987] ECR 1493, paragraph 21), so too is their suspension. That does not in any way show that the Community has exclusive competence pursuant to Article 113 to conclude an agreement with non-member countries to harmonize the protection of intellectual property worldwide.

66. In support of its argument, the Commission has also cited provisions relating to the protection of intellectual property in certain agreements with non-member countries concluded on the basis of Article 113 of the Treaty.

67. It should be noted that those provisions are extremely limited in scope. The agreement between the European Economic Community and the People's Republic of China on trade in textile products, initialled on 9 December 1988 (OJ 1988 L 380, p. 2), and the agreement between the European Economic Community and the Union of Soviet Socialist Republics on trade in textile products, initialled on 11 December 1989 (OJ 1989 L 397, p. 2), merely provides for a consultation procedure in relation to the protection of trade marks or designs in respect of textile products. Moreover, the three interim agreements concluded between the Community and certain east European countries (Agreement with Hungary of 16 December 1991 (OJ 1992 L 116, p. 2); Agreement with the Czech and Slovak Federal Republic of 16 December 1991 (OJ 1992 L 115, p. 2); Agreement with the Republic of Bulgaria of 8 March 1993 (OJ 1993 L 323, p. 2)) all contain identically worded clauses (Articles 35, 36 and 37 respectively) calling upon those countries to improve the protection of intellectual property in order to provide, within a given time, 'a level of protection similar to that provided in the Community' by Community acts. As the French Government has rightly observed, clauses of that type are binding only on the non-member country which is party to the agreement.

68. The fact that the Community and its institutions are entitled to incorporate within external agreements otherwise falling within the ambit of Article 113 ancillary provisions for the organization of purely consultative procedures or clauses calling on the other party to raise the level of protection of intellectual property does not mean that the Community has exclusive competence to conclude an international agreement of the type and scope of TRIPs.

69. Lastly, it is indeed true, as the Commission states, that the Agreement with the Republic of Austria of 23 December 1988 on the control and reciprocal protection of quality wines and 'retsina' wine (OJ 1989 L 56, p. 2) and the Agreement with Australia of 26 and 31 January 1994 on trade in wine (OJ 1994 L 86, p. 3) contain provisions relating to the reciprocal protection of descriptions of wines. The names of Austrian wine-growing regions are reserved exclusively, within the territory of the Community, to the Austrian wines to which they apply and may be used only in accordance with the conditions laid down in the Austrian rules (Article 3(3) of the agreement). A similar provision is contained in the agreement with Australia (Article 7(3)).

70. However, as is plain from the preamble to Council Decision 94/184/EC of 24 January 1994 concerning the conclusion of an Agreement between the European Community and Australia on trade in wine (OJ 1994 L 86, p. 1), that agreement was reached at Community level, because its provisions are directly linked to measures covered by the common agricultural policy, and specifically by the Community rules on wine and winegrowing. Moreover, that precedent does not provide support for any argument in relation to patents and designs, the protection of undisclosed technical information, trade marks or copyright, which are also covered by TRIPs.

71. In the light of the foregoing, it must be held that, apart from those of its provisions which concern the prohibition of the release into free circulation of counterfeit goods, TRIPs does not fall within the scope of the common commercial policy.

[...]

IX. The duty of cooperation between the Member States and the Community institutions

106. At the hearing, the Commission drew the Court's attention to the problems which would arise, as regards the administration of the agreements, if the Community and the Member States were recognized as sharing competence to participate in the conclusion of the GATS and TRIPs agreements. While it is true that, in the negotiation of the agreements, the procedure under Article 113 of the Treaty prevailed subject to certain very minor adjustments, the Member States will, in the context of the WTO, undoubtedly seek to express their views individually on matters falling within their competence whenever no consensus has been found. Furthermore, interminable discussions will ensue to determine whether a given matter falls within the competence of the Community, so that the Community mechanisms laid down by the relevant provisions of the Treaty will apply, or whether it is within the competence of the Member

States, in which case the consensus rule will operate. The Community's unity of action vis-à-vis the rest of the world will thus be undermined and its negotiating power greatly weakened.

107. In response to that concern, which is quite legitimate, it must be stressed, first, that any problems which may arise in implementation of the WTO Agreement and its annexes as regards the coordination necessary to ensure unity of action where the Community and the Member States participate jointly cannot modify the answer to the question of competence, that being a prior issue. As the Council has pointed out, resolution of the issue of the allocation of competence cannot depend on problems which may possibly arise in administration of the agreements.

108. Next, where it is apparent that the subject-matter of an agreement or convention falls in part within the competence of the Community and in part within that of the Member States, it is essential to ensure close cooperation between the Member States and the Community institutions, both in the process of negotiation and conclusion and in the fulfilment of the commitments entered into. That obligation to cooperate flows from the requirement of unity in the international representation of the Community (Ruling 1/78 [1978] ECR 2151, paragraphs 34 to 36, and Opinion 2/91, cited above, paragraph 36).

109. The duty to cooperate is all the more imperative in the case of agreements such as those annexed to the WTO Agreement, which are inextricably interlinked, and in view of the cross-retaliation measures established by the Dispute Settlement Understanding. Thus, in the absence of close cooperation, where a Member State, duly authorized within its sphere of competence to take cross-retaliation measures, considered that they would be ineffective if taken in the fields covered by GATS or TRIPs, it would not, under Community law, be empowered to retaliate in the area of trade in goods, since that is an area which on any view falls within the exclusive competence of the Community under Article 113 of the Treaty. Conversely, if the Community were given the right to retaliate in the sector of goods but found itself incapable of exercising that right, it would, in the absence of close cooperation, find itself unable, in law, to retaliate in the areas covered by GATS or TRIPs, those being within the competence of the Member States.

110. The Commission's third question having been put only on the assumption that the Court recognized that the Community had exclusive competence, it does not call for reply.

In conclusion,

THE COURT,

[...]

gives the following opinion:

1. The Community has sole competence, pursuant to Article 113 of the EC Treaty, to conclude the Multilateral Agreements on Trade in Goods.

2. The Community and its Member States are jointly competent to conclude GATS.

3. The Community and its Member States are jointly competent to conclude TRIPs.

Opinion of the Court (Grand Chamber) of 30 November 2009 (Consolidated GATS Schedule) Opinion 1/08, European Court Reports 2009, p. I-11129, paras. 15–28, 114–120, 125–137 and 152–173.

The so-called GATS schedule of the Community and its Member States, containing all their commitments in the field of services had not been consolidated to take account of the new accessions since the conclusion of the WTO Agreement in 1994, when the Community consisted of only twelve Member States. It was, therefore urgently necessary to proceed to such a consolidation after the accession of the ten new Member States. The procedures that needed to be followed for that are clearly explained in paragraphs 15–28 of Opinion 1/08. The Commission had waited that long with proceeding to consolidation not only because the relevant WTO procedure is complicated, but also because the internal procedure for obtaining the agreement of all the Member States was seen as extremely onerous. After the entry into force of the Nice version of Article 133 on trade policy, the Commission perceived a chance to argue that the trade in services area had become virtually an exclusive competence. The Commission felt that the consolidation of Schedules of Commitments, which was a very technical procedure, could be performed by the Community alone, if the rules on ancillary competences could also be used not only to choose between different legal bases, but also to determine the division of powers between Community and Member States, and if the withdrawal of concessions by the Commission could be seen as *de minimis*.

However, the Court, as so often on earlier occasions, did not want to take into consideration what it essentially regarded as practical qualms in a legal packaging on the part of the Commission. If the Treaty leads to complicated or near-unmanageable situations on the international level between the Community and Member States, the Court invariably points to the duty of cooperation in order to come to a solution.

Given that the intricacies of the badly drafted paragraphs 5 and 6 of the Nice version of Article 133 are of less importance now than they seemed to be when the Treaty on the Constitution was rejected and the Treaty of Lisbon seemed in mortal peril, the selection from the Opinion below leaves these aspects out. However, it includes the full section of the Opinion on the exclusion of transport policy from the common commercial policy, which essentially refuses to apply the notion of ancillarity to transport services provisions in broad trade agreements, since this part remains of great importance for future trade agreements including transport services.

Purpose and origin of the proposed agreements

15. The Commission states that, since the establishment under the GATS of the Schedule of specific commitments of the Community and its Member States, then numbering 12, the enlargements which took place in 1995 and 2004 made it necessary to draw up a new schedule, including the 13 new Member States which until then had their own Schedules of commitments.

16. On 28 May 2004, the Commission notified, under Article V(5) of the GATS, the list of the modifications and withdrawals of commitments intended to be made to the Schedules of the 13 new Member States in order to merge those various Schedules with the existing Schedule of the Community and of its Member States ('Document S/SECRET/8'). That notification was followed by a second on 4 April 2005 concerning the withdrawal of certain commitments contained in the Schedules of the Republic of Malta and the Republic of Cyprus ('Document S/SECRET/9').

17. Following claims of interest submitted by various WTO members which considered themselves affected by the proposed modifications and withdrawals of commitments, negotiations with a view to agreeing on compensatory adjustments under Article XXI(2) of the GATS were conducted by the Commission acting on behalf of the Community and its 25 Member States.

18. Upon completion of those negotiations, the parties agreed on the compensation to be provided in consideration of the modifications and withdrawals of commitments mentioned in Document S/SECRET/8. In contrast, they were unable to agree on compensation in relation to the withdrawals of commitments listed in Document S/SECRET/9. No arbitration was initiated on that matter by the affected WTO members.

19. As is apparent from the Council's conclusions of 26 July 2006, the Commission was authorised to sign the agreements thus negotiated and to transmit the draft consolidated Schedule of commitments of the Community and of its Member States to the WTO Secretariat for certification.

20. Those conclusions stated in particular that, 'in circulating the consolidated schedule of specific commitments of the European Community and its Member States…, the Commission will indicate that the new schedule will enter into force following the completion of the internal decision-making procedures of the European Community and its Member States, where appropriate. In this respect, the Commission will submit a proposal to the Council'.

21. Agreements were thus signed with each of the following 17 States or territories: the Republic of Argentina, the Commonwealth of Australia, the Federative Republic of Brazil, Canada, the People's Republic of China, the Separate Customs Territory of Taiwan, Penghu, Kinmen and Matsu (Chinese Taipei), the Republic of Columbia, the Republic of Cuba, the Republic of Ecuador, Hong Kong (China), the Republic of India, Japan, the Republic of Korea, New Zealand, the Republic of the Philippines, the Swiss Confederation and the United States of America ('the agreements at issue').

22. The certification procedure was successfully completed on 15 December 2006.

23. On 27 March 2007, the Commission submitted to the Council a proposal for a decision to conclude the agreements at issue on the basis of Article 133(1) to (5) EC, in conjunction with Article 300(2) EC.

24. In the explanatory memorandum to that proposal, the Commission explained inter alia that it had negotiated the agreements at issue for and on behalf of the Community and its Member States on the premiss that it could not, from the outset, be ruled out that those agreements would require approval by Member States.

In view of the compensatory adjustments actually negotiated, the Commission was, however, of the opinion that they did not go beyond the Community's internal powers and did not lead to harmonisation of the laws of the Member States in an area for which the Treaty rules out such harmonisation, so that the second subparagraph of Article 133(6) EC would not be applicable and conclusion of the agreements at issue would therefore be within the exclusive competence of the Community.

25. However, the Council and the Member States meeting within it considered that competence to conclude the agreements at issue was shared between the Community and its Member States.

26. Consequently, the Member States initiated their own internal procedures with a view to approval of those agreements.

27. On 13 July 2007, the Council, for its part, consulted the Parliament regarding the abovementioned Commission proposal. On that occasion, the Council informed the Parliament that it envisaged basing the decision to conclude the agreements at issue both on Article 133(1) to (5) EC, in conjunction with Article 300(2) EC, and on Articles 71 EC 80(2) EC, and 133(6) EC, in conjunction with Article 300(3) EC.

28. In its legislative resolution of 11 October 2007, the Parliament approved the abovementioned proposal. The recitals in the preamble to that resolution refer, however, only to Articles 133(1) and (5) EC and 300(2) and (3) EC.

[...]

The competence of the Community to conclude the agreements at issue and the legal bases for such conclusion

114. As a preliminary point, it must be recalled that, in the present case, the agreements at issue amend the GATS and more specifically the Annex thereto which includes the Schedules of specific commitments of WTO members. The GATS is a mixed agreement concluded both by the Community and by its Member States. The single Schedule of commitments of the Community and its Member States—the modification of which is inter alia the purpose of the agreements at issue—sets out, like the Schedules of the other WTO members, a collection of specific commitments which contribute to the establishment of a multilateral balance between the commitments of the various WTO members.

115. In those circumstances, it is important to make clear from the outset that the Schedule of commitments of the Community and its Member States cannot be modified as the result of unilateral action by the Member States, whether they act individually or together. For such modifications, the Community's participation is essential.

116. However, it does not necessarily follow from those circumstances that the same is true as far as the participation of the Member States in the agreements at issue is concerned. Indeed, whether the participation of the Member States is necessary depends, in this instance, on, inter alia, whether, by virtue of the amendments made to Article 133 EC by the Treaty of Nice, external Community competence has evolved in such a way as to justify the Community alone concluding the agreements at issue—a question which will be examined in this Opinion.

Concerning recourse to Article 133(1) and (5) EC, relating to the common commercial policy

117. The competence of the Community to participate in conclusion of the agreements at issue under Article 133(1) and (5) EC is beyond doubt.

118. First, it is not in dispute that those agreements contain provisions which concern inter alia services supplied under mode 1. As the Court held in paragraph 44 of Opinion 1/94, such a mode which covers cross-frontier supplies of services falls within the concept of the common commercial policy referred to in Article 133(1) EC. That provision, which, as the Court has consistently held, confers exclusive competence on the Community, has not been amended.

119. Second, it follows from the first subparagraph of Article 133(5) EC, which was introduced by the Treaty of Nice, that the Community is now also competent to conclude, under the common commercial policy, international agreements relating to trade in services supplied under modes 2 to 4. Such modes of supply of services, which the GATS refers to as 'consumption abroad', 'commercial presence' and 'presence of natural persons' respectively and which were formerly outside the sphere of the common commercial policy (see Opinion 1/94, paragraph 47), now fall within it on the conditions laid down in Article 133(5) and (6) EC.

120. Contrary to the submission of the Kingdom of Spain, nothing permits the inference that only trade in services through supplies made under mode 2, within the meaning of the GATS, is covered by the external Community competence thus established in the first subparagraph of Article 133(5) EC.

[...]

Concerning recourse to Articles 71 EC and 80(2) EC, relating to the common transport policy

152. The Commission and the Parliament submit that Article 133(1) and (5) EC constitute the sole legal basis to which recourse must be had for the purposes of adoption of the Community act concluding the agreements at issue.

153. Conversely, the Council and all the Member States which have intervened in these proceedings and which have expressed a view on this point contend that, since the agreements cover inter alia transport services—in particular maritime and air transport services—the Community act concluding the agreements must, in addition to Article 133(1), (5) and (6) EC, also be based on Articles 71 EC and 80(2) EC.

154. In order to give an opinion on these divergent views, it is necessary, as all the governments and institutions which have submitted observations agree, to consider the third subparagraph of Article 133(6) EC, which specifically provides that the negotiation and conclusion of international agreements in the field of transport is to continue to be governed by the provisions of Title V of the Treaty and Article 300 EC.

155. According to the Commission and the Parliament, the third subparagraph of Article 133(6) EC must be interpreted as being applicable only in the case of agreements which are exclusively, or at the very least predominantly, concerned

with transport. In the view of those institutions, that is not the case of the agreements at issue, whose object is trade in services in general, transport services for their part being only ancillary or secondary within the agreements.

156. In order to clarify the scope of the third subparagraph of Article 133(6) EC, it should, in the first place, be recalled that the first subparagraph of Article 133(5) EC, which, as has been stated above, confers external competence on the Community in respect of the common commercial policy in the field of trade in services supplied under modes 2 to 4, expressly states that that competence is 'without prejudice to paragraph 6'.

157. Second, it is highly unusual that a Treaty provision conferring external Community competence in a given field should resolve, as the third subparagraph of Article 133(6) EC does, a potential conflict of Community legal bases by specifically stating that another provision of the Treaty is to be preferred to it so far as concerns the conclusion of certain types of international agreements which are prima facie liable to be covered by one or other legal basis.

158. Third, there is no doubt that the expression 'international agreements in the field of transport' covers, inter alia, the field of trade concerning transport services. It would make no sense to specify in the middle of a provision relating to the common commercial policy that agreements in the field of transport which are not related to trade in transport services fall within the transport policy and not the common commercial policy.

159. Fourth, the provision stating that the negotiation and conclusion of agreements in the field of transport 'shall continue' to be governed by the provisions of the Treaty relating to transport policy reflects the intention that a form of status quo ante should be preserved in that field.

160. It should be recalled in that regard that in Opinion 1/94, given precisely in relation to the conclusion of the GATS which the agreements at issue are to modify, the Court held that international agreements in transport matters were not covered by Article 113 of the EC Treaty (now, after amendment, Article 133 EC) making clear that that was the case irrespective of the fact that such agreements concern safety rules such as those at issue in Case 22/70 *Commission v Council* ('*ERTA*') [1971] ECR 263 or that they constitute, like the GATS, agreements of a commercial nature (see Opinion 1/94, paragraphs 48 to 53; see also, to that effect, Opinion 2/92, paragraph 27).

161. In order to arrive at that conclusion, the Court pointed out, in particular, (in paragraph 48 of Opinion 1/94) that transport was the subject of a specific title of the Treaty, distinct from the title on the common commercial policy, and recalled in that regard that it followed from settled case-law that the Community has an implied external competence under the common transport policy.

162. It follows from the foregoing that, before the entry into force of the Treaty of Nice, trade in services in transport matters remained wholly outside the common commercial policy. Even if supplied under mode 1, trade in such services thus continued, unlike other types of services, to be covered by the title of the Treaty relating to the common transport policy (Opinion 1/94, paragraph 53).

163. Fifth, the interpretation proposed by the Commission, by virtue of which only agreements exclusively or predominantly relating to trade in transport services are covered by the third subparagraph of Article 133(6) EC, would to a large extent deprive that provision of its effectiveness. Indeed, the consequence of that interpretation would be that international provisions with strictly the same object and contained in an agreement would fall in some cases within transport policy and in some cases within commercial policy depending solely on whether the parties to the agreement decided to deal only with trade in transport services or whether they agreed to deal at the same time with that trade and with trade in some other type of services or in services as a whole.

164. It is apparent, however, from all the foregoing that the third subparagraph of Article 133(6) EC seeks to maintain, with regard to international trade in transport services, a fundamental parallelism between internal competence whereby Community rules are unilaterally adopted and external competence which operates through the conclusion of international agreements, each competence remaining—as previously—anchored in the title of the Treaty specifically relating to the common transport policy.

165. It may, moreover, be observed that the particularity of Community action in respect of transport policy is underlined in Article 71(1) EC, which specifies that the Council is required to establish the common transport policy taking into account 'the distinctive features of transport'. Similarly, it may be noted that, with regard more specifically to the field of trade in services, Article 71(1)(b) EC expressly confers competence on the Community to lay down, for the purpose of implementing that policy, 'the conditions under which non-resident carriers may operate transport services within a Member State'.

166. As regards the case-law concerning the choice of legal basis by reference to the criterion of the principal and the incidental purpose of a Community act, to which the Commission has also referred in order to justify recourse to Article 133(1) and (5) EC alone when concluding the agreements at issue, it is sufficient, in this instance, to state that the provisions of the agreements at issue relating to trade in transport services cannot be held to constitute a necessary adjunct to ensure the effectiveness of the provisions of those agreements concerning other service sectors (see, in that regard, Opinion 1/94, paragraph 51) or to be extremely limited in scope (see, in that regard, Opinion 1/94, paragraph 67, and Case C-268/94 *Portugal* v *Council* [1996] ECR I-6177, paragraph 75).

167. First, trade in transport services, like trade in the other types of services covered by the GATS or by the agreements at issue, falls within the very purpose of the GATS and of those agreements, which, moreover, have a direct and immediate effect on trade in each of the types of services thus affected, no distinction being possible in that regard between those types of services.

168. Second, it is established that the agreements at issue include, in this instance, a relatively high number of provisions whose effect is to modify both horizontal and sectoral commitments made by the Community and its Member States under the GATS, as regards the terms, conditions and limitations on which the Member States grant (i) access to transport services markets, in particular air or

maritime, to suppliers of services from other WTO members and (ii) national treatment.

169. It is clear for example from paragraph 34 of this Opinion that Annex I(A) to the agreements at issue extends to various new Member States the horizontal limitation relating to access under mode 3 to services regarded as public utilities at a national or local level which may be subject to public monopolies or to exclusive rights granted to private operators. As is specifically made clear by the explanatory note relating to that horizontal limitation in the existing Schedule of commitments of the Community and its Member States, that limitation may affect, inter alia, transport services and services related and auxiliary to all modes of transport. Likewise, the horizontal restrictions relating in some cases to national treatment and in others to market access, with which paragraph 34 of this Opinion is also concerned, are as a rule applicable in the service sectors covered by that Schedule of the Community and its Member States, which include, for example, certain air transport services such as services for the repair and maintenance of aircraft, sales and marketing of transport services or computer reservations systems as well as road transport services for passengers or freight.

170. Furthermore, as is clear from paragraphs 36 and 37 of this Opinion, Annex I(A) to the agreements at issue also includes a number of provisions relating to sectoral commitments concerning transport services, which in some cases involve extension of sectoral limitations to certain new Member States and in some cases introduce such limitations in their regard.

171. Annex I(B) to the agreements at issue effects, as can be seen from paragraph 38 of this Opinion, various withdrawals of horizontal commitments previously given by the Republic of Malta and the Republic of Cyprus in relation to national treatment under mode 4, as well as the withdrawal of a sectoral commitment given by the Republic of Malta concerning maritime transport services for passengers and freight.

172. With regard, finally to the legislative practice invoked by the Commission, it is sufficient to recall that a mere practice on the part of the Council cannot derogate from rules laid down in the Treaty and cannot therefore create a precedent binding on the Community institutions with regard to the correct legal basis (Opinion 1/94, paragraph 52). According to settled case-law, the choice of the legal basis for a Community measure must rest on objective factors amenable to judicial review and not on the legal basis used for the adoption of other Community measures which might, in certain cases, display similar characteristics (see, inter alia, Case C-155/07 *Parliament* v *Council* [2008] ECR I-0000, paragraph 34 and case-law cited).

173. On the basis of all the foregoing it must be concluded, in the context of the answer to be given to the second question raised in the request for an Opinion, that the 'transport' aspect of the agreements at issue falls, in accordance with the third subparagraph of Article 133(6) EC, within the sphere of transport policy and not that of the common commercial policy.

In conclusion, the Court (Grand Chamber) gives the following opinion:

1. The conclusion of the agreements with the affected members of the World Trade Organisation, pursuant to Article XXI of the General Agreement on Trade in Services (GATS), as described in the request for an Opinion, falls within the sphere of shared competence of the European Community and the Member States.
2. The Community act concluding the abovementioned agreements must be based both on Article 133(1), (5) and (6), second subparagraph, EC and on Articles 71 EC and 80(2) EC, in conjunction with Article 300(2) and (3), first subparagraph, EC.

Council Decision 94/800/EC of 22 December 1994 concerning the conclusion on behalf of the European Community, as regards matters within its competence, of the agreements reached in the Uruguay Round multilateral negotiations (1986–1994), 23.12.94, Official Journal L 336, 23.12.1994, pp. 1–2.

This is the decision on the conclusion of the WTO Agreement and all its annexes, including even its Final Act. (The conclusion or ratification of Final Acts is not common practice everywhere, since they do not have the same rank as the treaty of which they constitute the record of negotiation. The Community/EU, however, has made a habit of it.) The preamble and the text clearly bear the marks of Opinion 1/94. The final clause of the preamble is remarkable in connection with the Court's later case law on the lack of direct effect of the WTO Agreements (see Chapter 12, pp. 964–96) and reflects the pre-existing case law on the GATT in this respect.

THE COUNCIL OF THE EUROPEAN UNION,
Having regard to the Treaty establishing the European Community, and in particular Articles 43, 54, 57, 66, 75, 84(2), 99, 100, 100a, 113, and 235, in conjunction with the second subparagraph of Article 228 (3), thereof,
Having regard to the proposal from the Commission,
Having regard to the opinion of the Economic and Social Committee,
Having regard to the assent of the European Parliament,
Whereas the multilateral trade negotiations opened under the GATT, pursuant to the Declaration by Ministers adopted at Punta del Este on 20 September 1986, have led to the Final Act embodying the results of the Uruguay Round of multilateral trade negotiations;
Whereas the representatives of the Community and of the Member States signed the Final Act embodying the results of the Uruguay Round of multilateral trade negotiations and, subject to conclusion, the Agreement establishing the World Trade Organization in Marrakesh on 15 April 1994;
Whereas the reciprocal concessions and commitments negotiated by the Commission on behalf of the European Community and its Member States, as embodied in the multilateral agreements in the Final Act, represent a satisfactory and balanced outcome overall;
Whereas a number of the reciprocal concessions and commitments negotiated by the Commission on behalf of the European Community and its Member States and

certain countries party to the negotiations are furthermore set out in the special plurilateral agreements in Annex 4 to the Agreement establishing the World Trade Organization;

Whereas some of these concessions and commitments were negotiated bilaterally with Uruguay on bovine meat in parallel to the Uruguay Round;

Whereas the competence of the Community to conclude international agreements does not derive only from explicit conferral by the Treaty but may also derive from other provisions of the Treaty and from acts adopted pursuant to those provisions by Community institutions;

Whereas where Community rules have been adopted in order to achieve the aims of the Treaty, Member States may not, outside the framework of the common institutions, enter into commitments liable to affect those rules or alter their scope;

Whereas a portion of the commitments contained in the Agreement establishing the World Trade Organization, including the Annexes thereto, falls within the competence of the Community under Article 113 of the Treaty; whereas, furthermore, of the remainder of the said commitments some affect Community rules adopted on the basis of Articles 43, 54, 57, 66, 75, 84(2), 99, 100, 100a and 235 and may therefore only be entered into by the Community alone;

Whereas, in particular, the use of Articles 100 and 235 of the Treaty as legal bases for this Decision is justified to the extent that the Agreement establishing the World Trade Organization, including the Annexes thereto, affects Council Directive 90/434/EEC of 23 July 1990 on the common system of taxation applicable to mergers, divisions, transfers of assets and exchanges of shares concerning companies of different Member States, Council Directive 90/435/EEC of 23 July 1990 on the common system of taxation applicable in the case of parent companies and subsidiaries of different Member States, which are based on Article 100 of the Treaty, and Council Regulation (EC) No 40/94 of 20 December 1993 on the Community trade mark, which is based on Article 235 of the Treaty;

Whereas no act in Community law has yet been adopted on the basis of Article 73c of the Treaty;

Whereas, by its nature, the Agreement establishing the World Trade Organization, including the Annexes thereto, is not susceptible to being directly invoked in Community or Member State courts,

HAS DECIDED AS FOLLOWS:

Article 1

1. The following multilateral agreements and acts are hereby approved on behalf of the European Community with regard to that portion of them which falls within the competence of the European Community:

– the Agreement establishing the World Trade Organization, and also the Agreements in Annexes 1, 2 and 3 to that Agreement;

– the ministerial decisions and declarations and the Understanding on Commitment in Financial Services which appear in the Uruguay Round Final Act.

2. The texts of the agreements and acts referred to in this Article are attached to this Decision.

3. The President of the Council is hereby authorized to designate the person empowered to take the measure provided for in Article XIV of the Agreement establishing the World Trade Organization in order to bind the European Community with regard to that portion of the Agreement falling within its competence.

Article 2

1. The plurilateral agreements in Annex 4 to the Agreement establishing the World Trade Organization are hereby approved on behalf of the European Community with regard to that portion of them which falls within the competence of the European Community.
2. The texts of the agreements referred to in this Article are attached to this Decision.
3. The President of the Council is hereby authorized to designate the person empowered to take the measures provided for by the agreements referred to in this Article in order to bind the European Community with regard to that portion of the agreements which falls within its competence.

Article 3

1. The Agreement on bovine meat concluded with Uruguay is hereby approved on behalf of the European Community.
2. The text of the said Agreement is attached to this Decision.
3. The President of the Council is hereby authorized to designate the person empowered to sign the Agreement in order to bind the European Community.

Scope of the Common Commercial Policy: Foreign Direct Investment.

The reference to Foreign Direct Investment (FDI) was incorporated for the first time in the article on the common commercial policy by the Treaty of Lisbon. This was a logical step to take. Trade in services had been declared to be part of the common commercial policy by the Treaty of Nice. As the WTO had made clear, trade in services included establishment in the field of services (Article 1 of GATS). This meant that investment in the services sector was already part of the common commercial policy. Excluding FDI in manufacturing of goods from the common commercial policy thus became an anomaly. The EU Constitutional Convention duly noted this and included FDI in general in what was to become eventually Article 207 TFEU.

However, the term Foreign *Direct* Investment is generally believed to exclude portfolio investment. Therefore, such investment is not part of the exclusive competence of the Union in the field of the common commercial policy (Article 3(1)(e) TFEU) and since there was no thorough legislation of it at the internal Union level either, trade agreements encompassing both direct and portfolio investment would inevitably need to be mixed. Thus there is a considerable chance that the common commercial policy will function in future as a mixed policy. This is obviously contrary to the intention of the drafters of the Treaty of Lisbon. They were primarily concerned with the coherence and effectiveness of the Union's external action. The Commission is, however, of the view that such a mixed common commercial policy is not necessary in light of the fact that portfolio investment falls under Article 63 and following TFEU on the freedom of movement of capital, also with third countries.

After the entry into force of the Lisbon Treaty, the first matter that the Commission chose to deal with with respect to FDI was the continuing validity of Member States existing agreements with third countries in the field of investment and investment protection, and their eventual succession by Union trade agreements covering the same subject matter. Long discussions between the Commission, the Council and the European Parliament in the end led to the adoption of Regulation No. 1219/2012 of 12 December 2012, of which extracts are included below. The scope of FDI and its possible coverage of portfolio investment is left undecided by this regulation.

The Commission has furthermore made a proposal for a Regulation establishing a framework for managing financial responsibility linked to investor-state dispute settlement tribunals established by international agreements to which the European Union is party.[3] It is certainly of great importance that such matters are settled before a case would arise in the framework of a Union agreement covering FDI and investment protection. However, for the moment the Council does not seem very eager to deal with the matter.

The proposed regulation is concerned with the agreements on FDI and investment protection that have been concluded by Member States and that may be concluded by the Union within the framework of the common commercial policy with third countries. A related problem is the continued existence of bilateral investment agreements between Member States *inter se* and their compatibility with Union law. This problem will not be discussed here. It merely suffices to point out that the most international arbitration cases affecting the Union in the field of investment and investment protection thus far deal with such disputes.[4]

Regulation (EU) No 1219/2012 of the European Parliament and of the Council of 12 December 2012 establishing transitional arrangements for bilateral investment agreements between Member States and third countries, Official Journal L 351, 20.12.2012, pp. 40–46.

THE EUROPEAN PARLIAMENT AND THE COUNCIL OF
THE EUROPEAN UNION,

Having regard to the Treaty on the Functioning of the European Union, and in particular Article 207(2) thereof,

Having regard to the proposal from the European Commission,

After transmission of the draft legislative act to the national parliaments,

Acting in accordance with the ordinary legislative procedure,

---

[3] COM(2012) 335 final.

[4] *Achmea B.V. v The Slovak Republic* (formerly *Eureko B.V. v The Slovak Republic*), PCA Case No. 2008–13 (UNCITRAL Arbitration Rules); *Eastern Sugar v The Czech Republic*, SCC Case No. 088/2004. *AES v The Republic of Hungary*, ICSID Case No. ARB/07/22 and *Electrabel v The Republic of Hungary*, ICSID Case No. ARB/07/19 deserve special mention, since they were based on an agreement, the Energy Charter Treaty, to which the Union is also a party. In these two cases, the Commission submitted briefs as a non-disputing third party to the arbitral panel.

Whereas:

(1) Following the entry into force of the Treaty of Lisbon, foreign direct investment is included in the list of matters falling under the common commercial policy. In accordance with Article 3(1)(e) of the Treaty on the Functioning of the European Union ('TFEU'), the European Union has exclusive competence with respect to the common commercial policy. Accordingly, only the Union may legislate and adopt legally binding acts within that area. The Member States are able to do so themselves only if so empowered by the Union, in accordance with Article 2(1) TFEU.

(2) In addition, Chapter 4 of Title IV of Part Three TFEU lays down common rules on the movement of capital between Member States and third countries, including in respect of capital movements involving investments. Those rules can be affected by international agreements relating to foreign investment concluded by Member States.

(3) This Regulation is without prejudice to the allocation of competences between the Union and its Member States in accordance with the TFEU.

[...]

HAVE ADOPTED THIS REGULATION:

CHAPTER I
SCOPE
Article 1
Subject matter and scope

1. Without prejudice to the division of competences established by the TFEU, this Regulation addresses the status of the bilateral investment agreements of the Member States under Union law, and establishes the terms, conditions and procedures under which the Member States are authorised to amend or conclude bilateral investment agreements.

2. For the purpose of this Regulation the term 'bilateral investment agreement' means any agreement with a third country that contains provisions on investment protection. This Regulation covers only those provisions of bilateral investment agreements dealing with investment protection.

CHAPTER II
MAINTENANCE IN FORCE OF EXISTING BILATERAL INVESTMENT AGREEMENTS
Article 2
Notification to the Commission

By 8 February 2013 or within 30 days of the date of their accession to the Union, the Member States shall notify the Commission of all bilateral investment agreements with third countries signed before 1 December 2009 or before the date of their accession, whichever is later, that they either wish to maintain in force or permit to enter into force under this Chapter. The notification shall include a copy of those bilateral investment agreements. Member States shall also notify the Commission of any subsequent changes to the status of those agreements.

Article 3

Maintenance in force

Without prejudice to other obligations of the Member States under Union law, bilateral investment agreements notified pursuant to Article 2 of this Regulation may be maintained in force, or enter into force, in accordance with the TFEU and this Regulation, until a bilateral investment agreement between the Union and the same third country enters into force.

[...]

Article 5

Assessment

The Commission may assess the bilateral investment agreements notified pursuant to Article 2, by evaluating whether one or more of their provisions constitute a serious obstacle to the negotiation or conclusion by the Union of bilateral investment agreements with third countries, with a view to the progressive replacement of the bilateral investment agreements notified pursuant to Article 2.

Article 6

Duty of cooperation

1. The Member States shall take any appropriate measures to ensure that the provisions of the bilateral investment agreements notified pursuant to Article 2 do not constitute a serious obstacle to the negotiation or conclusion by the Union of bilateral investment agreements with third countries, with a view to the progressive replacement of the bilateral investment agreements notified pursuant to Article 2.

2. If the Commission establishes that one or more of the provisions of a bilateral investment agreement notified pursuant to Article 2 constitute a serious obstacle to the negotiation or conclusion by the Union of bilateral investment agreements with third countries, with a view to the progressive replacement of the bilateral investment agreements notified pursuant to Article 2, the Commission and the Member State concerned shall enter into consultations expeditiously and cooperate with a view to identifying the appropriate actions to resolve the matter. Those consultations shall take no longer than 90 days.

3. Without prejudice to paragraph 1, the Commission may, within 60 days of the end of consultations, indicate the appropriate measures to be taken by the Member State concerned in order to remove the obstacles referred to in paragraph 2.

CHAPTER III

AUTHORISATION TO AMEND OR CONCLUDE BILATERAL
INVESTMENT AGREEMENTS

Article 7

Authorisation to amend or conclude a bilateral investment agreement

Subject to the conditions laid down in Articles 8 to 11, a Member State shall be authorised to enter into negotiations with a third country to amend an existing or to conclude a new bilateral investment agreement.

Article 8
Notification to the Commission

1. Where a Member State intends to enter into negotiations with a third country in order to amend or conclude a bilateral investment agreement, it shall notify the Commission of its intentions in writing.

2. The notification referred to in paragraph 1 shall include relevant documentation and an indication of the provisions to be addressed in the negotiations or to be renegotiated, the objectives of the negotiations and any other relevant information.

3. The notification referred to in paragraph 1 shall be transmitted at least five months before formal negotiations are to commence.

4. Where the information transmitted by the Member State is not sufficient for the purposes of authorising the opening of formal negotiations in accordance with Article 9, the Commission may request additional information.

5. The Commission shall make the notification referred to in paragraph 1 of this Article and, on request, the accompanying documentation, available to the other Member States subject to the requirements of confidentiality laid down in Article 14.

Article 9
Authorisation to open formal negotiations

1. The Commission shall authorise the Member States to open formal negotiations with a third country to amend or conclude a bilateral investment agreement unless it concludes that the opening of such negotiations would:

(a) be in conflict with Union law other than the incompatibilities arising from the allocation of competences between the Union and its Member States;

(b) be superfluous, because the Commission has submitted or has decided to submit a recommendation to open negotiations with the third country concerned pursuant to Article 218(3) TFEU;

(c) be inconsistent with the Union's principles and objectives for external action as elaborated in accordance with the general provisions laid down in Chapter 1 of Title V of the Treaty on European Union; or

(d) constitute a serious obstacle to the negotiation or conclusion of bilateral investment agreements with third countries by the Union.

2. As part of the authorisation referred to in paragraph 1, the Commission may require the Member State to include or remove from such negotiations and prospective bilateral investment agreement any clauses where necessary to ensure consistency with the Union's investment policy or compatibility with Union law.

3. The authorisation referred to in paragraph 1 of this Article shall be granted in accordance with the advisory procedure referred to in Article 16(2). The Commission shall take its decision within 90 days of receipt of the notification referred to in Article 8. Where additional information is needed to take a decision, the 90-day period shall run from the date of receipt of the additional information.

4. The Commission shall inform the European Parliament and the Council about the decisions taken pursuant to paragraph 3.

5. In the event that the Commission does not grant an authorisation pursuant to paragraph 1, it shall inform the Member State concerned thereof and state the reasons therefor.

[…]

Article 11
Authorisation to sign and conclude a bilateral investment agreement

1. Before signing a bilateral investment agreement, the Member State concerned shall notify the Commission of the outcome of negotiations and shall transmit the text of such an agreement to the Commission.

2. This Article shall also apply to bilateral investment agreements which were negotiated before 9 January 2013, but are not subject to the obligation to notify under Article 2 or under Article 12.

3. Upon notification the Commission shall make an assessment as to whether the negotiated bilateral investment agreement conflicts with the requirements of Article 9(1) and (2).

4. Where the Commission finds that the negotiations have resulted in a bilateral investment agreement which fulfils the requirements of Article 9(1) and (2), it shall authorise the Member State to sign and conclude such an agreement. Articles 3, 5 and 6 apply to such agreements, as if they had been notified under Article 2.

5. Decisions pursuant to paragraph 4 of this Article shall be taken in accordance with the advisory procedure referred to in Article 16(2). The Commission shall take its decision within 90 days of receipt of the notifications referred to in paragraphs 1 and 2 of this Article. Where additional information is needed to take the decision, the 90-day period shall run from the date of receipt of the additional information.

6. Where the Commission grants an authorisation pursuant to paragraph 4, the Member State concerned shall notify the Commission of the conclusion and entry into force of the bilateral investment agreement, and of any subsequent changes to the status of that agreement.

7. The Commission shall inform the European Parliament and the Council about the decisions taken pursuant to paragraph 4.

8. In the event that the Commission does not grant the authorisation pursuant to paragraph 4, it shall inform the Member State concerned thereof and state the reasons therefore.

CHAPTER IV
FINAL PROVISIONS
Article 12
Agreements signed by the Member States between
1 December 2009 and 9 January 2013

1. Where between 1 December 2009 and 9 January 2013, a Member State has signed a bilateral investment agreement, that Member State shall notify the Commission of such an agreement which it wishes to maintain in force or permit to enter into force by 8 February 2013. The notification shall include a copy of such an agreement.

2. Upon notification the Commission shall make an assessment as to whether the bilateral investment agreement notified pursuant to paragraph 1 of this Article conflicts with the requirements of Article 9(1) and (2).

3. Where the Commission finds that a bilateral investment agreement notified pursuant to paragraph 1 of this Article fulfils the requirements of Article 9(1) and (2), it shall authorise the maintenance or entry into force of such an agreement under Union law.

[...]

STATEMENT BY THE EUROPEAN PARLIAMENT, THE COUNCIL
AND THE COMMISSION

The fact that this Regulation, including recitals 17, 18 and 19, provides for the use of the procedures referred to in Regulation (EU) No 182/2011 does not constitute a precedent as to future regulations allowing the Union to empower the Member States under Article 2(1) TFEU to legislate and adopt legally binding acts in areas of Union exclusive competence. Furthermore, in this Regulation, the use of the advisory as opposed to the examination procedure shall not be considered as setting a precedent for future regulations establishing the framework for the common commercial policy.

7.3 Common rules for imports and safeguards

Council Regulation (EC) No 260/2009 of 26 February 2009 on the common rules for imports, Official Journal L 84, 31.3.2009, pp. 1–17 (Codified version).

The regulation below is a codification of the original regulation that was part of the 'Uruguay Round package' and establishes the quota-free import into the Community of third (market economy) countries' imports, at least in principle. The exception for textiles in Article 1 is largely irrelevant, as the so-called Textiles Agreement of the WTO has run its course and trade in textiles is now nearly completely quota-free as between WTO Members. The Regulation also contains the rules on the so-called surveillance and safeguards measures. The procedures for these measures are designed so as to be in conformity with the WTO Agreement on Safeguards. That agreement, briefly summarized, provides for a restraint on imports and an adjustment period for national producers for a maximum of three years, if the tariff concessions of the importing country have unexpected consequences and lead to a sudden increase of imports, which threatens the existence of a national industry. In short, it grants a brief period of protection during which a national industry can adjust to the consequences of reduced tariffs. It is thus supposed to protect the willingness of WTO Members to continue to make tariff concessions. However, keeping safeguard measures within the bounds of that agreement has proved extremely difficult, as is attested by the imposition and withdrawal regulations on safeguard measures against imports of farmed salmon, reproduced further below.

THE COUNCIL OF THE EUROPEAN UNION,

Having regard to the Treaty establishing the European Community, and in particular Article 133 thereof,

Having regard to the instruments establishing the common organisation of agricultural markets and the instruments concerning processed agricultural products adopted in pursuance of Article 308 of the Treaty, in particular in so far as they provide for derogation from the general principle that quantitative restrictions or measures having equivalent effect may be replaced solely by the measures provided for in the said instruments,

Having regard to the proposal from the Commission,

Whereas:

(1) Council Regulation (EC) No 3285/94 of 22 December 1994 on the common rules for imports and repealing Regulation (EC) No 518/94 has been substantially amended several times. In the interests of clarity and rationality the said Regulation should be codified.

(2) The common commercial policy should be based on uniform principles.

(3) The Community has concluded the Agreement establishing the World Trade Organisation, hereinafter referred to as the 'WTO'. Annex 1A to that Agreement contains inter alia the General Agreement on Tariffs and Trade 1994 (GATT 1994) and an Agreement on Safeguards.

(4) The Agreement on Safeguards meets the need to clarify and reinforce the disciplines of GATT 1994, and specifically those of Article XIX. That Agreement requires the elimination of safeguard measures which escape those rules, such as voluntary export restraints, orderly marketing arrangements and any other similar import or export arrangements.

(5) The Agreement on Safeguards also covers coal and steel products. The common rules for imports, especially as regards safeguard measures, therefore also apply to those products without prejudice to any possible measures to apply an agreement specifically concerning coal and steel products.

(6) The textile products covered by Council Regulation (EC) No 517/94 of 7 March 1994 on common rules for imports of textile products from certain third countries not covered by bilateral agreements, protocols or other arrangements, or by other specific Community import rules are subject to special treatment at Community and international level. They should therefore be excluded from the scope of this Regulation.

(7) The Commission should be informed by the Member States of any danger created by trends in imports which might call for Community surveillance or the application of safeguard measures.

(8) In such instances the Commission should examine the terms and conditions under which imports occur, the trend in imports, the various aspects of the economic and trade situations and, where appropriate, the measures to be applied.

(9) If prior Community surveillance is applied, release for free circulation of the products concerned should be made subject to presentation of a surveillance document meeting uniform criteria. That document should, on simple application by the importer,

be issued by the authorities of the Member States within a certain period but without the importer thereby acquiring any right to import. The surveillance document should therefore be valid only during such period as the import rules remain unchanged.

(10) The Member States and the Commission should exchange the information resulting from Community surveillance as fully as possible.

(11) It falls to the Commission and the Council to adopt the safeguard measures required by the interests of the Community. Those interests should be considered as a whole and should in particular encompass the interests of Community producers, users and consumers.

(12) Safeguard measures against a member of the WTO may be considered only if the product in question is imported into the Community in such greatly increased quantities and on such terms or conditions as to cause, or threaten to cause, serious injury to Community producers of like or directly competing products, unless international obligations permit derogation from this rule.

(13) The terms 'serious injury', 'threat of serious injury' and 'Community producers' should be defined and precise criteria for determining injury should be established.

(14) An investigation should precede the application of any safeguard measure, subject to the reservation that the Commission be allowed in urgent cases to apply provisional measures.

(15) There should be detailed provisions on the opening of investigations, the checks and inspections required, access by exporter countries and interested parties to the information gathered, hearings for the parties involved and the opportunities for those parties to submit their views.

(16) The provisions on investigations introduced by this Regulation are without prejudice to Community or national rules concerning professional secrecy.

(17) It is also necessary to set time limits for the initiation of investigations and for determinations as to whether or not measures are appropriate, with a view to ensuring that such determinations are made quickly, in order to increase legal certainty for the economic operators concerned.

(18) In cases in which safeguard measures take the form of a quota the level of the latter should be set in principle no lower than the average level of imports over a representative period of at least three years.

(19) In cases in which a quota is allocated among supplier countries each country's quota may be determined by agreement with the countries themselves or by taking as a reference the level of imports over a representative period. Derogations from these rules should nevertheless be possible where there is serious injury and a disproportionate increase in imports, provided that due consultation under the auspices of the WTO Committee on Safeguards takes place.

(20) The maximum duration of safeguard measures should be determined and specific provisions regarding extension, progressive liberalisation and reviews of such measures be laid down.

(21) The circumstances in which products originating in a developing country which is a member of the WTO are to be exempt from safeguard measures should be established.

(22) Surveillance or safeguard measures confined to one or more regions of the Community may prove more suitable than measures applying to the whole Community. However, such measures should be authorised only exceptionally and where no alternative exists. It is necessary to ensure that such measures are temporary and cause the minimum of disruption to the operation of the internal market.

(23) In the interest of uniformity in rules for imports, the formalities to be carried out by importers should be simplified and made identical regardless of the place where the goods clear customs. It is therefore desirable to provide that any formalities should be carried out using forms corresponding to the specimen annexed to the Regulation.

(24) Surveillance documents issued in connection with Community surveillance measures should be valid throughout the Community irrespective of the Member State of issue,

HAS ADOPTED THIS REGULATION:

CHAPTER I

General principles

Article 1

1. This Regulation applies to imports of products originating in third countries, except for:

(a) textile products subject to specific import rules under Regulation (EC) No 517/94;

(b) the products originating in certain third countries listed in Council Regulation (EC) No 519/94 of 7 March 1994 on common rules for imports from certain third countries.

2. The products referred to in paragraph 1 shall be freely imported into the Community and accordingly, without prejudice to the safeguard measures which may be taken under Chapter V, shall not be subject to any quantitative restrictions.

CHAPTER II

Community information and consultation procedure

Article 2

Member States shall inform the Commission if trends in imports appear to call for surveillance or safeguard measures. This information shall contain the evidence available, as determined on the basis of the criteria laid down in Article 10. The Commission shall immediately pass this information on to all the Member States.

Article 3

1. Consultations may be held either at the request of a Member State or on the initiative of the Commission.

2. Consultations shall take place within eight working days of the Commission receiving the information provided for in Article 2 and, in any event, before the introduction of any Community surveillance or safeguard measure.

Article 4

1. Consultations shall take place within an Advisory Committee, hereinafter called 'the Committee', made up of representatives of each Member State with a representative of the Commission as chairman.

2. The Committee shall meet when convened by its chairman. He shall provide the Member States with all relevant information as promptly as possible.

3. Consultations shall cover in particular:

(a) terms and conditions of import, import trends and the various aspects of the economic and commercial situation with regard to the product in question;

(b) the measures, if any, to be taken.

4. Consultations may be conducted in writing if necessary.

The Commission shall in this event inform the Member States, which may express their opinion or request oral consultations within a period of five to eight working days, to be decided by the Commission.

CHAPTER III
Community investigation procedure
Article 5

1. Without prejudice to Article 8, the Community investigation procedure shall be implemented before any safeguard measure is applied.

2. Using as a basis the factors referred to in Article 10, the investigation shall seek to determine whether imports of the product in question are causing or threatening to cause serious injury to the Community producers concerned.

3. The following definitions shall apply:

(a) 'serious injury' means a significant overall impairment in the position of Community producers;

(b) 'threat of serious injury' means serious injury that is clearly imminent;

(c) 'Community producers' means the producers as a whole of the like or directly competing products operating within the territory of the Community, or those whose collective output of the like or directly competing products constitutes a major proportion of the total Community production of those products.

Article 6

1. Where, after the consultations referred to in Articles 3 and 4, it is apparent to the Commission that there is sufficient evidence to justify the initiation of an investigation, the Commission shall initiate an investigation within one month of receipt of information from a Member State and publish a notice in the Official Journal of the European Union. This notice shall:

(a) give a summary of the information received, and require that all relevant information is to be communicated to the Commission;

(b) state the period within which interested parties may make known their views in writing and submit information, if such views and information are to be taken into account during the investigation;

(c) state the period within which interested parties may apply to be heard orally by the Commission in accordance with paragraph 4.

The Commission shall commence the investigation, acting in cooperation with the Member States.

2. The Commission shall seek all information it deems to be necessary and, where it considers it appropriate, after consulting the Committee, endeavour to check this information with importers, traders, agents, producers, trade associations and organisations.

The Commission shall be assisted in this task by staff of the Member State on whose territory these checks are being carried out, provided that Member State so wishes.

3. The Member States shall supply the Commission, at its request and following procedures laid down by it, with the information at their disposal on developments in the market of the product being investigated.

4. Interested parties which have come forward pursuant to the first subparagraph of paragraph 1 and representatives of the exporting country may, upon written request, inspect all information made available to the Commission in connection with the investigation other than internal documents prepared by the authorities of the Community or its Member States, provided that that information is relevant to the presentation of their case and not confidential within the meaning of Article 9 and that it is used by the Commission in the investigation.

Interested parties which have come forward may communicate their views on the information in question to the Commission. Those views may be taken into consideration where they are backed by sufficient evidence.

5. The Commission may hear the interested parties. Such parties must be heard where they have made a written application within the period laid down in the notice published in the Official Journal of the European Union, showing that they are actually likely to be affected by the outcome of the investigation and that there are special reasons for them to be heard orally.

6. When information is not supplied within the time limits set by this Regulation or by the Commission pursuant to this Regulation, or the investigation is significantly impeded, findings may be made on the basis of the facts available.

Where the Commission finds that any interested party or third party has supplied it with false or misleading information, it shall disregard the information and may make use of facts available.

7. Where it appears to the Commission, after the consultations referred to in Articles 3 and 4, that there is insufficient evidence to justify an investigation, it shall inform the Member States of its decision within one month of receipt of the information from the Member States.

Article 7

1. At the end of the investigation, the Commission shall submit a report on the results to the Committee.

2. Where the Commission considers, within nine months of the initiation of the investigation, that no Community surveillance or safeguard measures are necessary, the investigation shall be terminated within a month, the Committee having first been consulted.

The decision to terminate the investigation, stating the main conclusions of the investigation and a summary of the reasons therefore, shall be published in the Official Journal of the European Union.

3. If the Commission considers that Community surveillance or safeguard measures are necessary, it shall take the necessary decisions in accordance with Chapters IV and V, no later than nine months from the initiation of the investigation. In exceptional circumstances, this time limit may be extended by a further maximum period of two months; the Commission shall then publish a notice in the Official Journal of the European Union setting forth the duration of the extension and a summary of the reasons therefore.

Article 8

1. The provisions of this Chapter shall not preclude the use, at any time, of surveillance measures in accordance with Articles 11 to 15 or provisional safeguard measures in accordance with Articles 16, 17 and 18.

Provisional safeguard measures shall be applied:

(a) in critical circumstances where delay would cause damage which would be difficult to repair, making immediate action necessary; and

(b) where a preliminary determination provides clear evidence that increased imports have caused or are threatening to cause serious injury.

The duration of such measures shall not exceed 200 days.

2. Provisional safeguard measures shall take the form of an increase in the existing level of customs duty, whether the latter is zero or higher, if such action is likely to prevent or repair the serious injury.

3. The Commission shall immediately conduct whatever investigation measures are still necessary.

4. Should the provisional safeguard measures be repealed because no serious injury or threat of serious injury exists, the customs duties collected as a result of the provisional measures shall be automatically refunded as soon as possible. The procedure laid down in Article 235 et seq. of Council Regulation (EEC) No 2913/92 of 12 October 1992 establishing the Community Customs Code shall apply.

Article 9

1. Information received pursuant to this Regulation shall be used only for the purpose for which it was requested.

2. Neither the Council, nor the Commission, nor the Member States, nor the officials of any of these shall reveal any information of a confidential nature received pursuant to this Regulation, or any information provided on a confidential basis without specific permission from the supplier of such information.

3. Each request for confidentiality shall state the reasons why the information is confidential. However, if it appears that a request for confidentiality is unjustified and if the supplier of the information wishes neither to make it public nor to authorise its disclosure in general terms or in the form of a summary, the information concerned may be disregarded.

4. Information shall in any case be considered to be confidential if its disclosure is likely to have a significantly adverse effect upon the supplier or the source of such information.

5. Paragraphs 1 to 4 shall not preclude reference by the Community authorities to general information and in particular to reasons on which decisions taken pursuant to this Regulation are based. Those authorities shall, however, take into account the legitimate

interest of legal and natural persons concerned that their business secrets should not be divulged.

Article 10

1. Examination of the trend in imports, of the conditions in which they take place and of serious injury or threat of serious injury to Community producers resulting from such imports shall cover in particular the following factors:

(a) the volume of imports, in particular where there has been a significant increase, either in absolute terms or relative to production or consumption in the Community;

(b) the price of imports, in particular where there has been a significant price under-cutting as compared with the price of a like product in the Community;

(c) the consequent impact on Community producers as indicated by trends in certain economic factors such as:

– production,

– capacity utilisation,

– stocks,

– sales,

– market share,

– prices (i.e. depression of prices or prevention of price increases which would normally have occurred),

– profits,

– return on capital employed,

– cash flow,

– employment;

(d) factors other than trends in imports which are causing or may have caused injury to the Community producers concerned.

2. Where a threat of serious injury is alleged, the Commission shall also examine whether it is clearly foreseeable that a particular situation is likely to develop into actual injury. In this regard account may be taken of factors such as:

(a) the rate of increase of the exports to the Community;

(b) export capacity in the country of origin or export, as it stands or is likely to be in the foreseeable future, and the likelihood that that capacity will be used to export to the Community.

CHAPTER IV
Surveillance
Article 11

1. Where the trend in imports of a product originating in a third country covered by this Regulation threatens to cause injury to Community producers, and where the interests of the Community so require, import of that product may be subject, as appropriate, to:

(a) retrospective Community surveillance carried out in accordance with the provisions laid down in the decision referred to in paragraph 2;

(b) prior Community surveillance carried out in accordance with Article 12.

2. The decision to impose surveillance shall be taken by the Commission according to the procedure laid down in the second subparagraph of Article 16(6) and Article 16(7).

3. The surveillance measures shall have a limited period of validity. Unless otherwise provided, they shall cease to be valid at the end of the second six-month period following the six months in which the measures were introduced.

Article 12

1. Products under prior Community surveillance may be put into free circulation only on production of a surveillance document. Such document shall be issued by the competent authority designated by Member States, free of charge, for any quantity requested and within a maximum of five working days of receipt by the national competent authority of an application by any Community importer, regardless of his place of business in the Community. This application shall be deemed to have been received by the national competent authority no later than three working days after submission, unless it is proved otherwise.

2. The surveillance document shall be made out on a form corresponding to the model in Annex I.

Except where the decision to impose surveillance provides otherwise, the importer's application for surveillance documents shall contain only the following:

(a) the full name and address of the applicant (including telephone and fax numbers and any number identifying the applicant to the competent national authority), plus the applicant's VAT registration number if he is liable for VAT;

(b) where appropriate, the full name and address of the declarant or of any representative appointed by the applicant (including telephone and fax numbers);

(c) a description of the goods giving:

– their trade name,

– their combined nomenclature code,

– their place of origin and place of consignment;

(d) the quantity declared, in kilograms and, where appropriate, any other additional unit (pairs, items, etc.);

(e) the value of the goods, cif at Community frontier, in euro;

(f) the following statement, dated and signed by the applicant, with the applicant's name spelt out in capital letters:

'I, the undersigned, certify that the information provided in this application is true and given in good faith, and that I am established in the Community.'

3. The surveillance document shall be valid throughout the Community, regardless of the Member State of issue.

4. A finding that the unit price at which the transaction is effected exceeds that indicated in the surveillance document by less than 5 % or that the total value or quantity of the products presented for import exceeds the value or quantity given in the surveillance document by less than 5 % shall not preclude the release for free circulation of the product in question. The Commission, having heard the opinions expressed in the Committee and taking account of the nature of the products and other special features of the transactions concerned, may fix a different percentage, which, however, should not normally exceed 10 %.

5. Surveillance documents may be used only for such time as arrangements for liberalisation of imports remain in force in respect of the transactions concerned. Such surveillance documents may not in any event be used beyond the expiry of a period which shall be laid down at the same time and by means of the same procedure as the

imposition of surveillance, and shall take account of the nature of the products and other special features of the transactions.

6. Where the decision taken pursuant to Article 11 so requires, the origin of products under Community surveillance must be proved by a certificate of origin. This paragraph shall not affect other provisions concerning the production of any such certificate.

7. Where the product under prior Community surveillance is subject to regional safeguard measures in a Member State, the import authorisation granted by that Member State may replace the surveillance document.

[...]

Article 13

Where import of a product has not been made subject to prior Community surveillance within eight working days of the end of the consultations referred to in Articles 3 and 4, the Commission, in accordance with Article 18, may introduce surveillance confined to imports into one or more regions of the Community.

Article 14

1. Products under regional surveillance may be put into free circulation in the region concerned only on production of a surveillance document. Such document shall be issued by the competent authority designated by the Member State(s) concerned, free of charge, for any quantity requested and within a maximum of five working days of receipt by the national competent authority of an application by any Community importer, regardless of his place of business in the Community. This application shall be deemed to have been received by the national competent authority no later than three working days after submission, unless it is proved otherwise. Surveillance documents may be used only for such time as arrangements for imports remain liberalised in respect of the transactions concerned.

2. Article 12(2) shall apply.

Article 15

1. Member States shall communicate to the Commission within the first 10 days of each month in the case of Community or regional surveillance:

(a) in the case of prior surveillance, details of the sums of money (calculated on the basis of cif prices) and quantities of goods in respect of which surveillance documents were issued during the preceding period;

(b) in every case, details of imports during the period preceding the period referred to in point (a).

The information supplied by Member States shall be broken down by product and by country.

Different provisions may be laid down at the same time and by the same procedure as the surveillance arrangements.

2. Where the nature of the products or special circumstances so require, the Commission may, at the request of a Member State or on its own initiative, amend the timetables for submitting this information.

3. The Commission shall inform the Member States accordingly.

CHAPTER V
Safeguard measures
Article 16

1. Where a product is imported into the Community in such greatly increased quantities and/or on such terms or conditions as to cause, or threaten to cause, serious injury to Community producers, the Commission, in order to safeguard the interests of the Community, may, acting at the request of a Member State or on its own initiative:

(a) limit the period of validity of surveillance documents within the meaning of Article 12 to be issued after the entry into force of this measure;

(b) alter the import rules for the product in question by making its release for free circulation conditional on production of an import authorisation, the granting of which shall be governed by such provisions and subject to such limits as the Commission shall lay down.

The measures referred to in (a) and (b) shall take effect immediately.

2. As regards members of the WTO, the measures referred to in paragraph 1 shall be taken only when the two conditions indicated in the first subparagraph of that paragraph are met.

3. If establishing a quota, account shall be taken in particular of:

(a) the desirability of maintaining, as far as possible, traditional trade flows;

(b) the volume of goods exported under contracts concluded on normal terms and conditions before the entry into force of a safeguard measure within the meaning of this Chapter, where such contracts have been notified to the Commission by the Member State concerned;

(c) the need to avoid jeopardising achievement of the aim pursued in establishing the quota.

Any quota shall not be set lower than the average level of imports over the last three representative years for which statistics are available unless a different level is necessary to prevent or remedy serious injury.

4. In cases in which a quota is allocated among supplier countries, allocation may be agreed with those of them having a substantial interest in supplying the product concerned for import into the Community.

Failing this, the quota shall be allocated among the supplier countries in proportion to their share of imports into the Community of the product concerned during a previous representative period, due account being taken of any specific factors which may have affected or may be affecting the trade in the product.

Provided that its obligation to see that consultations are conducted under the auspices of the WTO Committee on Safeguards is not disregarded, the Community may nevertheless depart from this method of allocation in the case of serious injury if imports originating in one or more supplier countries have increased in disproportionate percentage in relation to the total increase of imports of the product concerned over a previous representative period.

5. The measures referred to in this Article shall apply to every product which is put into free circulation after their entry into force. In accordance with Article 18 they may be confined to one or more regions of the Community.

However, such measures shall not prevent the release for free circulation of products already on their way to the Community provided that the destination of such products cannot be changed and that those products which, pursuant to Articles 11 and 12, may be put into free circulation only on production of a surveillance document are in fact accompanied by such a document.

6. Where intervention by the Commission has been requested by a Member State, the Commission shall take a decision within a maximum of five working days of receipt of such a request.

Any decision taken by the Commission pursuant to this Article shall be communicated to the Council and to the Member States. Any Member State may, within one month following the day of such communication, refer the decision to the Council.

7. If a Member State refers the Commission's decision to the Council, the Council, acting by a qualified majority, may confirm, amend or revoke that decision.

If, within three months of the referral of the matter to the Council, the Council has not taken a decision, the decision taken by the Commission shall be deemed revoked.

Article 17

Where the interests of the Community so require, the Council, acting by a qualified majority on a proposal from the Commission drawn up in accordance with the terms of Chapter III, may adopt appropriate measures to prevent a product being imported into the Community in such greatly increased quantities and/or on such terms or conditions as to cause, or threaten to cause, serious injury to Community producers of like or directly competing products.

Article 16(2) to (5) shall apply.

Article 18

Where it emerges, primarily on the basis of the factors referred to in Article 10, that the conditions laid down for the adoption of measures pursuant to Articles 11 and 16 are met in one or more regions of the Community, the Commission, after having examined alternative solutions, may exceptionally authorise the application of surveillance or safeguard measures limited to the region(s) concerned if it considers that such measures applied at that level are more appropriate than measures applied throughout the Community.

These measures must be temporary and must disrupt the operation of the internal market as little as possible.

The measures shall be adopted in accordance with the provisions laid down in Articles 11 and 16.

Article 19

No safeguard measure may be applied to a product originating in a developing country member of the WTO as long as that country's share of Community imports of the product concerned does not exceed 3 %, provided that developing country members of the WTO with less than a 3 % import share collectively account for not more than 9 % of total Community imports of the product concerned.

Article 20

1. The duration of safeguard measures must be limited to the period of time necessary to prevent or remedy serious injury and to facilitate adjustment on the part of Community producers. The period must not exceed four years, including the duration of any provisional measure.

2. Such initial period may be extended, except in the case of the measures referred to in the third subparagraph of Article 16(4) provided it is determined that:

(a) the safeguard measure continues to be necessary to prevent or remedy serious injury;

(b) there is evidence that Community producers are adjusting.

3. Extensions shall be adopted in accordance with the terms of Chapter III and using the same procedures as the initial measures. A measure so extended shall not be more restrictive than it was at the end of the initial period.

4. If the duration of the measure exceeds one year, the measure must be progressively liberalised at regular intervals during the period of application, including the period of extension.

5. The total period of application of a safeguard measure, including the period of application of any provisional measures, the initial period of application and any prorogation thereof, may not exceed eight years.

Article 21

1. While any surveillance or safeguard measure applied in accordance with Chapters IV and V is in operation, consultations shall be held within the Committee, either at the request of a Member State or on the initiative of the Commission. If the duration of a safeguard measure exceeds three years, the Commission shall seek such consultations no later than the mid-point of the period of application of that measure. The purpose of such consultations shall be:

(a) to examine the effects of the measure;

(b) to determine whether and in what manner it is appropriate to accelerate the pace of liberalisation;

(c) to ascertain whether application of the measure is still necessary.

2. Where, as a result of the consultations referred to in paragraph 1, the Commission considers that any surveillance or safeguard measure referred to in Articles 11, 13, 16, 17 and 18 should be revoked or amended, it shall proceed as follows:

(a) where the measure was enacted by the Council, the Commission shall propose to the Council that it be revoked or amended. The Council shall act by a qualified majority;

(b) in all other cases, the Commission shall amend or revoke Community safeguard and surveillance measures.

Where the decision relates to regional surveillance measures, it shall apply from the sixth day following its publication in the Official Journal of the European Union.

Article 22

1. Where imports of a product have already been subject to a safeguard measure, no further measure shall be applied to that product until a period equal to the duration of the previous measure has elapsed. Such period shall not be less than two years.

2. Notwithstanding paragraph 1, a safeguard measure of 180 days or less may be re-imposed for a product if:

(a) at least one year has elapsed since the date of introduction of a safeguard measure on the import of that product; and

(b) such a safeguard measure has not been applied to the same product more than twice in the five-year period immediately preceding the date of introduction of the measure.

CHAPTER VI

Final provisions

Article 23

Where the interests of the Community so require, the Council, acting by a qualified majority on a proposal from the Commission, may adopt appropriate measures to allow the rights and obligations of the Community or of all its Member States, in particular those relating to trade in commodities, to be exercised and fulfilled at international level.

Article 24

1. This Regulation shall not preclude the fulfilment of obligations arising from special rules contained in agreements concluded between the Community and third countries.

2. Without prejudice to other Community provisions, this Regulation shall not preclude the adoption or application by Member States:

(a) of prohibitions, quantitative restrictions or surveillance measures on grounds of public morality, public policy or public security; the protection of health and life of humans, animals or plants, the protection of national treasures possessing artistic, historic or archaeological value, or the protection of industrial and commercial property;

(b) of special formalities concerning foreign exchange;

(c) of formalities introduced pursuant to international agreements in accordance with the Treaty.

The Member States shall inform the Commission of the measures or formalities they intend to introduce or amend in accordance with the first subparagraph.

In the event of extreme urgency, the national measures or formalities in question shall be communicated to the Commission immediately upon their adoption.

Article 25

1. This Regulation shall be without prejudice to the operation of the instruments establishing the common organisation of agricultural markets or of Community or national administrative provisions derived therefrom or of the specific instruments applicable to goods resulting from the processing
of agricultural products. It shall operate by way of complement to those instruments.

2. In the case of products covered by the instruments referred to in paragraph 1, Articles 11 to 15 and Article 22 shall not apply to those in respect of which the Community rules on trade with third countries require the production of a licence or other import document.

Articles 16, 18 and 21 to 24 shall not apply to those products in respect of which such rules provide for the application of quantitative import restrictions.

Article 26

Regulation (EC) No 3285/94, as amended by the acts listed in Annex II, is repealed. References to the repealed Regulation shall be construed as references to this Regulation and shall be read in accordance with the correlation table in Annex III.

Article 27

This Regulation shall enter into force on the 20th day following its publication in the Official Journal of the European Union.
This Regulation shall be binding in its entirety and directly applicable in all Member States.

[...]

Commission Regulation (EC) No 206/2005 of 4 February 2005 imposing definitive safeguard measures against imports of farmed salmon; and Commission Regulation (EC) No 627/2005 of 22 April 2005 revoking Regulation (EC) No 206/2005 imposing definitive safeguard measures against import of farmed salmon.

These two Commission regulations are testimony to the difficulty of imposing safeguard regulations that fully conform to the requirements of the WTO Safeguards Agreement. Since these safeguards measures were essentially directed against imports of farmed salmon from Norway, their application on a most-favoured nation basis in accordance with the Safeguards Agreement caused considerable difficulties, as did the requirement of unforeseen circumstances, since Norway's imports of salmon into the Community had always been somewhat problematic for the European (primarily Scottish) salmon farms. Under the threat of a Norwegian WTO complaint (DS 328, request for consultations 17 March 2005) the safeguard measures were very quickly replaced by anti-dumping duties. This is remarkable, since safeguard measures are a temporary defence against fair trade, while dumping is considered unfair trade. (For the anti-dumping measures on Norwegian farmed salmon, see pp. 478–95.)

Commission Regulation (EC) No 206/2005 of 4 February 2005 imposing definitive safeguard measures against imports of farmed salmon, Official Journal L 33, 5.2.2005, pp. 8–29.

THE COMMISSION OF THE EUROPEAN COMMUNITIES,
Having regard to Council Regulation (EC) No 3285/94 of 22 December 1994 on common rules for imports and repealing Regulation (EC) No 518/94, as last amended by Regulation (EC) No 2474/2000, and in particular Article 16 thereof,

Having regard to Council Regulation (EC) No 519/94 of 7 March 1994 on common rules for imports from certain third countries and repealing Regulations (EEC) No 1765/82, (EEC) No 1766/82 and (EEC) No 3420/83, as last amended by Regulation (EC) No 427/2003, and in particular Article 15 thereof,

After consultations within the Advisory Committee established under Article 4 of Regulation (EC) No 3285/94 and of Regulation (EC) No 519/94 respectively,

Whereas:

1. PROCEDURE

(1) On 6 February 2004, Ireland and the United Kingdom informed the Commission that trends in imports of farmed Atlantic salmon appeared to call for safeguard measures under Regulations (EC) No 3285/94 and 519/94; submitted information containing the evidence available as determined on the basis of Article 10 of Regulation (EC) No 3285/94 and Article 8 of Regulation (EC) No 519/94; and requested the Commission to take safeguard measures under those instruments.

(2) Ireland and the United Kingdom provided evidence that imports into the European Community of farmed Atlantic salmon are increasing rapidly both in absolute terms, and relative to Community production and consumption.

(3) They alleged that the increase in the volume of imports of farmed Atlantic salmon has, among other consequences, had a negative impact on the prices of like or directly competitive products in the Community, and on the market share held by the Community producers, resulting in damage to the Community producers.

(4) Ireland and the United Kingdom further advised that, based on the information submitted by the Community producers, any delay in the adoption of safeguard measures by the European Community would cause damage which it would be difficult to repair, and that measures should therefore be adopted as a matter of urgency.

(5) The Commission informed all Member States of the situation and consulted with them on the terms and conditions of imports, import trends and the evidence as to serious injury, and the various aspects of the economic and commercial situation with regard to the Community product in question.

(6) On 6 March 2004, the Commission initiated an investigation relating to serious injury or threat thereof to the Community producers of the product like or directly competitive with the imported product, which has been defined as farmed salmon, whether or not filleted, fresh, chilled or frozen ('the product concerned') as explained below. The investigation period (IP) is 2003, and the period under examination in the investigation is from the beginning of 2000 to the end of 2003.

(7) The Commission officially advised the exporting producers and importers as well as their representative associations known to be concerned, the representatives of exporting countries and the Community producers of the investigation. The Commission sent questionnaires to all these parties, to representative associations of salmon farmers in the Community, and to those parties who made themselves known within the time limits set in the Notice of Initiation. Pursuant to Articles 5 of Council Regulation (EC) No 519/94 and 6 of Council Regulation (EC) No 3285/94 the Commission also gave parties directly concerned the opportunity to make their views known in writing and to request a hearing.

(8) On 13 August 2004, the Commission imposed provisional safeguard measures. These were referred to the Council under Articles 15(5) of Council Regulation (EC) No 519/94 and 16(7) of Council Regulation (EC) No 3285/94 and subsequently lapsed on 6 December 2004.

(9) Following the publication of the provisional measures, the Commission continued its investigation with a view to reaching definitive findings. Certain governments, certain exporting producers and their representative associations, the Community producers, suppliers, processors and importers and their representative associations submitted comments in writing. The oral and written comments submitted by the parties were considered and taken into account in reaching the definitive findings. All the information which was deemed necessary for the purpose of a final determination was sought and verified. Verification visits were carried out at the premises of eight Community producers.

(10) All cooperating parties were informed of the essential facts and considerations on the basis of which it was intended to impose definitive safeguard measures and the form of the proposed measures. They were granted the opportunity to submit comments and these were considered, and, where deemed appropriate, taken into account in the definitive findings.

2. LIST OF COOPERATING PARTIES

[...]

3. PRODUCT CONCERNED

(11) The product in respect of which the Commission was informed that trends in imports appear to call for safeguard measures is farmed Atlantic salmon, whether or not filleted, fresh, chilled or frozen.

[...]

4. LIKE OR DIRECTLY COMPETITIVE PRODUCTS

(18) An examination has been undertaken to establish whether the product produced by the Community producers—i.e. farmed salmon (hereinafter referred to as 'the like product') is like or directly competitive with the imported product concerned.

(19) In reaching a determination, the following findings in particular were taken into account.

(a) the imported product and the Community product share the same international classification for tariff purposes at HS code level (6 digits). Furthermore, they share the same or similar physical properties such as taste, size, shape and texture. The domestic product is often marketed as a premium quality product and often enjoys a price premium at the retail level. However, 'likeness' does not require products to be completely identical, and the minor variations in quality are not sufficient to change the overall finding of likeness between the imported and domestic products;

(b) the imported product and the Community product were sold via similar or identical sales channels, price information was readily available to buyers and the product concerned and the product of the Community producers competed mainly on price;

(c) the imported product and the Community product both serve the same or similar end-uses, they were, therefore, alternative or substitute products and were easily interchangeable;

(d) the imported product and the Community product were both perceived by consumers as alternatives to satisfy a particular want or demand, in this respect the differences identified by certain exporters and importers were simply minor variations.

(20) Therefore, the conclusion reached is that the imported product and the Community product are 'like or directly competitive'.

5. IMPORTS

[…]

6. DEFINITION OF THE COMMUNITY PRODUCERS

(33) Almost all production of the product concerned in the Community was in Scotland and Ireland, although there are also two producers in France and at least one in Latvia.

(34) In the year 2003, total Community production of the product concerned was 190 903 tonnes, of which the producers which co-operated fully in the provisional stage of the investigation accounted for 85 231 tonnes, equivalent to 45% of the total Community production. They therefore represent a major proportion of total Community production within the meaning of Article 5(3)(c) of Regulation (EC) No 3285/94 and Article 15(1) of Regulation (EC) No 519/94. They are accordingly considered as the Community producers.

7. UNFORESEEN DEVELOPMENTS

[…]

(42) Therefore it is concluded that the unforeseen development which caused the increase in imports was significant over-production in Norway (despite lower forecasts), exacerbated by the failure of the Norwegian industry to achieve forecast growth in exports to markets outwith the Community, the unexpected extent of the effects of the termination of trade defence measures against Norway and the operation of the Norwegian banking system as described above, together with the rise in the value of the euro which made the Community market an unusually attractive destination for Norwegian exports.

8. SERIOUS INJURY

8.1. Introduction

(43) In order to make a determination of serious injury to the Community producers of the like product, an evaluation of all relevant factors of an objective and quantifiable nature having a bearing on their situation has been undertaken. In particular, for the product concerned, an evaluation has been carried out of the development of global Community data for consumption, production capacity, production, capacity utilisation, employment, productivity, overall sales and market share. These global data are based on statistical information gathered by the United Kingdom and Ireland through comprehensive industry surveys. As concerns company specific data, these are based upon data provided by the co-operating Community producers on cash flow, return on capital employed, stocks, price, undercutting and profitability for the years 2000 to 2003.

(44) It should be noted at the outset that in the Community salmon farming industry, as elsewhere, there is a long and relatively inflexible production cycle leading to

harvesting and that, once harvested, the farmed salmon must be sold immediately since they can only be stored for a few days unless frozen. Freezing is expensive, and in any event, there is limited freezing capacity in the Community. In consequence, the level of production must be planned at least two years in advance and, once planned, cannot be altered except at the margins. Therefore, oversupply has a delayed effect on production, but an immediate and severe effect on prices.

8.2. Analysis of the situation of the Community Producers
[...]
(73) Taking account of all of these factors the conclusion reached is that the Community producers have suffered serious injury in terms of a significant overall impairment of the situation in their position.

9. CAUSATION
(74) In order to examine the existence of a causal link between the increased imports and the serious injury, and ensure that injury caused by other factors is not attributed to increased imports, the injurious effects of factors considered to be causing injury have been distinguished from each other, the injurious effects have been attributed to the factors which are causing them, and, after having attributed injury to all causal factors present, it has been determined whether increased imports are a 'genuine and substantial' cause of serious injury.

9.1. Analysis of causation factors
[...]
9.3. Conclusion
(98) Therefore, having determined that no material injurious effects resulted from the other known factors, it is concluded that there is a genuine and substantial link between increased low priced imports and serious injury to the Community producers.

10. THE SAFEGUARD MEASURES
(99) Analysis of the findings of the investigation confirms that there is serious injury and the need for definitive safeguard measures in order to remedy the serious injury suffered by the Community producers and prevent further injury to the Community producers.

10.1. Form and level of definitive safeguard measures
(100) Community production of farmed salmon is insufficient to meet demand and it is therefore necessary to ensure that the measures taken are not such as to deny export-ing producers access to the Community market. As the main cause of damage to the Community producers is the large volume imports leading to low price and causing price depression and suppression, the measures taken should be designed to remedy the serious injury and facilitate adjustment. To achieve these aims, the measures should lead to a temporary stabilisation of prices that does not unnecessarily limit supply and provides for a period during which the Community producers may adjust to future conditions of increased competition from cheap imported products.

(101) The provisional safeguard measures took the form of tariff quotas alone. Even in the period during which the provisional measures were in force, imports of farmed salmon were continuing to enter the Community at prices which were substantially below the cost of production of the Community producers. Measures should therefore be taken which will have the effect of increasing prices to a level at which there is at least full cost recovery by the Community producers. This should facilitate adjustment by ensuring that during the period of the present measures the Community producers do not continue to sustain losses the effect of which would be to prevent them raising finance so as to take the measures necessary for adjustment and restructuring. In order to achieve an upward impact on prices, it was considered whether tariff quotas should be installed, albeit with very small safeguard tariff-free volumes. However, while this could arguably have been expected to impact on prices, such an approach was considered inappropriate since the growing market for farmed salmon should not be unduly restricted. Therefore, a price element should be established for all imports of farmed salmon to the Community. The Community producers' average cost of production has been found to be EUR 3.10 per kilo in 2003. However, the Community producers' product normally commands a price premium over the imported product of up to around 10%. It is therefore concluded that the import price level should be established at EUR 2850 per tonne for fresh salmon. This should permit Community producers, despite the low price element, to sell at around break-even. It was argued that minimum price undertakings in previous cases had not been respected. Whilst that may be the case, these measures do not involve undertakings but the establishment of an import price level below which duty is payable, and circumvention of which is customs fraud. In addition, some parties expressed a preference for a specific or ad valorem duty instead of the establishment of a minimum price for imports. However, the imposition of such a duty would take money out of the market and it is therefore considered that the establishment of a minimum price for imports represents a better solution in the medium term. Nevertheless, in order to facilitate the adaptation, it is considered appropriate that during the phasing-in as described below, a specific duty should be applied.

(102) It has been argued that as frozen salmon commands a lower price than fresh salmon because of a slight difference in the structure of the cost of production, applying the same import price level would effectively exclude frozen salmon from the Community market. On that basis, it is argued that a lower import price level should be established for frozen salmon to take account of these different cost elements and that any price element should be lower for frozen than for fresh salmon. As there appears to be a price difference of around 4% on the market, it is considered that a lower import price level should be established for frozen salmon which reflects that difference. The import price level for frozen farmed salmon should therefore be EUR 2736.

(103) One party argued that having two price levels would lead to complexity for authorities and increase the likelihood of fraud at the point of entry, but these claims are not practically substantiated given the existence of penalties for customs fraud. On the other hand, it was argued that a different price regime should apply to farmed salmon depending on its intended end use (whether for processing or eventual retail sale). This would be much more difficult to control and so, for practical reasons, it was found not to be feasible in the circumstances.

(104) As market prices are currently lower and in order to prevent market disturbances, especially for the processing industry, the price element should be phased-in
over a period of time. This will allow the market to gradually adapt to the import
price to be established. In this respect, it was argued both that a long period was
necessary to allow processors to adapt to the price increase, and that a short period
should be set given the difficult situation of the Community producers. It is considered that the phase-in period should be from the date of entry into force of definitive
safeguard measures until 15 April 2005, during which period a minimum import
price of EUR 2700 per tonne for fresh salmon and EUR 2592 for frozen salmon
should apply.

(105) It is considered that the price element, during the definitive stage, should take the
form of a variable duty. If imports are undertaken at a CIF Community border price
equal to or above the import price established, no duty would be payable. If imports
are undertaken at a lower price, the difference between the actual price and the import
price established would become payable. This minimum price element shall be applicable at all times, both within the tariff quota as set out below, and when the threshold
of the tariff quota is reached.

(106) In order to ensure that importers respect the price element, it is considered that
within a specified time limit, importers should be required to provide satisfactory evidence to the national customs authorities of the actual import price per tonne paid for
imports of farmed salmon. In order to ensure that all importers respect the condition
to provide satisfactory evidence and do so within the time limit, importers should be
required to provide adequate security to the national customs authorities upon the
importation of farmed salmon. Given the level of the proposed price element, both
phase-in and definitive, for fresh and frozen farmed salmon, a security of EUR 290
per tonne (WFE) of farmed salmon imported (Group 1—EUR 320 per tonne, Group
2—EUR 450 per tonne) is considered to be appropriate. It was argued that this level of
security is too expensive and burdensome for importers. However, it is considered that
a lower level of security would not achieve its purpose given the difference between
current market prices and the import price level to be established. Given the nature of
the information to be provided and considerations of administrative convenience, it is
considered that the time limit within which to provide satisfactory evidence should be
a period of 1 year from the date of acceptance of the relevant customs declaration. The
security should be released at the moment that the importer provides satisfactory evidence provided that this is done within the specified time limit. If an importer fails to
provide satisfactory evidence within the time limit, the security should be definitively
collected as import duties.

(107) In order to ensure that, beyond the traditional level of imports, the Community
producers can operate at a reasonable level of profitability whilst keeping the Community
market open and ensuring the availability of supply to meet demand, it is in addition
considered appropriate to establish tariff quotas reflecting traditional levels of imports.
Beyond those quotas, an additional duty should be payable on imports. Traditional
levels of imports of farmed salmon which respect the price element established can
then continue without payment of any additional duty, and unlimited quantities can be
imported albeit upon payment of the additional duty.

(108) In order to preserve traditional trade flows and ensure that the Community market also remains open to minor players, the tariff quota should be divided amongst those countries/regions having a substantial interest in supplying the product concerned, and a part should be reserved to other countries. After consultation with Norway, Chile and the Faeroes which have such a substantial interest and represent substantial import shares, it is considered appropriate to assign a specific tariff quota to each of these countries. In principle, the tariff quota should be divided up based on the proportions of the total quantity of the product supplied by that country during the three year period 2001 to 2003. However, it is noted that imports from Chile fell substantially (to below 3% of imports to the Community) in the second semester 2003 due to technical reasons concerning border controls, which is approximately half of their normal share of imports to the Community. For this reason imports from Chile in 2003 are not representative and the country specific quota for Chile should instead be based on average imports in 2001, 2002 and an adjusted figure for 2003 (based on 2002 plus average import growth rates in 2003 excluding Chile) so as not to distort traditional flows of trade. In order to avoid an unnecessary administrative burden, the tariff quotas should operate on a first come first served basis.

(109) It appears that in normal circumstances Community consumption of farmed salmon had been growing at between around 4% to 5% annually taking into account growth levels observed in the new Member States. However, data for the first semester 2004 indicates that market growth in the Community salmon market is in fact increasing, and that whilst the size of the market in the new Member States is small relative to that in the EU-15, there is evidence that the annual growth rates in the new Member States (which were of the order of 30%) have increased as a result of enlargement and are now materially higher (around 50%). In order to take account of this growth, the tariff quotas (based on average imports in 2001 to 2003) should be increased by 10%. As the salmon market is seasonal, with higher imports and sales in the second semester than the first, the tariff quotas should be seasonally adjusted. The quotas have been calculated on a whole fish equivalent basis (WFE) and conversion ratios to fillets and non-fillets actually imported are 1:0.65 and 1:0.9 respectively. If, during the application of the measures, it becomes apparent that the conversion ratio for non fillets (1:0.9) ceases to be appropriate taking account of the presentation of farmed salmon imported, currently mainly gutted head-on, the measures may be reviewed.

(110) The additional duty should be set at a level such as to provide adequate relief to the Community producers but at the same time should not constitute an unnecessarily onerous burden on importers and users. An ad valorem duty is considered unsuitable as it would act as an incentive to lower import prices free of duty, and would increase in real terms if a price increase occurs. Therefore a fixed amount of duty should be set.

(111) A minimum price element as outlined above will always be applicable to enable Community producers to sell at break-even. As also mentioned above, the minimum price element is set below the Community producers' cost of production, but as they have been able to sell at a premium of around 10% in the past, it is expected that they will continue to be able to do so and thus recover their costs of production. Should traditional trade levels be surpassed, and an additional duty thus become payable, it is considered appropriate, in application of the Community institution's traditional

'underselling' approach, to base this additional duty on the difference between the level of the non-injurious target price of the Community producers and the minimum price element. This difference, which reflects the extent to which the price of the imported product is lower than the price which the Community producers could be expected to achieve in a non-injurious situation, after adjustment for price differences as between the imported product and the Community product, is thus considered to be a reasonable basis for fixing the level of duty. This difference was calculated on the basis of the weighted average non-injurious price per tonne of the Community product, based on the cost of production of the Community product plus a profit on turnover of 14%. This is consistent with the level of profit established as necessary in previous trade defence cases relating to salmon and reflects the meteorological, biological and escape risks faced by this industry. This non-injurious price was compared with the minimum price element. The difference between these two prices results in an initial duty payable of EUR 330 euro per tonne (WFE), which, based on the conversion ratios shown above, is equivalent to EUR 366 per tonne for other than fillets and EUR 508 per tonne for fillets.

(112) Provision should be made for review of the measures by the Commission if circumstances should change. In order to properly take into account market developments after the imposition of the present safeguard measures, if any, it is considered to undertake a monitoring of the market and the development of prices. If the data or other information collected indicates that a definitive import price level of EUR 2850 or EUR 2736, as the case may be, would be inappropriate, an early review would be initiated so as to change this definitive import price level before its entry into force. Regular meetings with interested parties should take place every six months or as requested by interested parties on the basis of relevant substantiated evidence.

(113) In conformity with Community legislation and the international obligations of the Community, the definitive safeguard measures should not apply to any product originating in a developing country as long as its share of imports of that product into the Community does not exceed 3%. In this regard, in Regulation (EC) No 1447/2004 special account was taken of the particular situation of Chile as a developing country to the effect that imports from Chile were not covered by the provisional measures since, in the second semester of 2003, imports originating in Chile were below the 3% threshold. Under that Regulation it was stated that the development of these imports would be closely monitored in order to ascertain whether the downward trend observed would prove to be a lasting phenomenon. However, following further investigation it is apparent that imports from Chile have now returned to around 6% of Community imports and that the reduced level of imports in the second semester 2003 appears to have been only a temporary phenomenon. Therefore, and having regard to the fact that overall imports originating in Chile during the year 2003 exceeded the mentioned level of 3%, the definitive safeguard measures should also apply to imports from Chile. The developing countries to which the definitive measures do not apply are specified in Annex 2.

10.2. Duration

(114) The definitive measures should not last more than four years including the period of the provisional measures. The measures should enter into force on 6 February 2005 and should remain in force until 13 August 2008.

10.3. Liberalisation

(115) In order to induce adjustment, the measures should be subject to liberalisation on a regular basis following their imposition, thereby ensuring that there is a strong incentive for the Community producers to progressively undertake the necessary restructuring and adjustment. It is considered that liberalisation should commence one year after the imposition of provisional measures, and be undertaken annually thereafter.

(116) Liberalisation should be designed to allow the importation of increasing quantities of farmed salmon which respect the price element without the payment of additional duty thereby increasing the competitive pressure to which the Community producers are subject during the course of the measures. Similarly, in order that imports beyond the level of the tariff quota gradually become subject to a lower duty, the rate of the additional duty should be gradually reduced. Liberalisation must also take account of the expectation of market growth. Liberalisation should therefore take the form of an increase in the tariff quota together with a decrease in the level of the additional duty payable beyond the level of the tariff quota. On each occasion it is considered that the tariff quota should be increased by 10% and the additional duty decreased by 5% but this may be reviewed upon cause shown.

10.4. Restructuring

(117) The purpose of definitive safeguard measures is to provide the Community producers with a limited period of time in which to restructure so as to more effectively compete with imports. In this regard, reference is made to Article 20(2) of Commission Regulation (EC) No 3285/94 which prohibits any possible extension of measures if there is no evidence that the Community producers are adjusting.

(118) The Community producers are already in the process of restructuring as a result of heavy losses which have resulted in some operators leaving the industry, as well as bankruptcies and receiverships, which have forced others to close. Significant improvements in productivity and efficiency have also been made in recent years. However, if the industry is to develop so as to maximise its competitiveness both now and in the future, it requires a period of time in which to implement an organised restructuring plan.

(119) Key elements of the restructuring strategy developed by the relevant national authorities in collaboration with the industry include (1) implementation of site optimisation plans to relocate or merge fish farm sites to increase the size of farms over the next two to three years thereby increasing efficiency and reducing costs; (2) diversification into other species with the emergence of cod and halibut farming with sites being stocked with white fish species and increasing shellfish growing (however, due to their current financial situation these changes are being severely hampered through lack of funding); (3) the development of more sophisticated environmental carrying capacity tools so as to allow better assessment of the maximum level of consented fish farm biomass which can be permitted whilst maintaining a healthy marine ecosystem, thereby facilitating a move towards larger single farms and greater economies of scale; (4) further use of synchronised fallowing of fish farms within hydrologically linked areas together with co-ordinated sea lice treatment thereby better protecting farmed fish from sea lice infestation and disease, and enhancing smolt survival rates thereby reducing costs, (5) establishment of coordination amongst producer organisations in

Ireland, the United Kingdom and Norway with a view to avoiding future problems of severe over-production.

(120) Some progress has already been made in implementing parts of this strategy, in particular, in pursuing synchronised fallowing and co-ordinated sea lice treatment, and substantial further progress is anticipated during the period of these measures. In the event that such adjustment fails to progress sufficiently during the period of these measures, the Commission may consider such failure to be a change of circumstances within the meaning of Article 1(6) of this Regulation, requiring the review of the continued need for the measures.

11. COMMUNITY INTEREST

11.1. Preliminary remarks

(121) In addition to unforeseen developments, increased imports, serious injury, causation and critical circumstances, it has been examined whether any compelling reasons exist which could lead to the conclusion that it is not in the Community interest to impose definitive measures. For this purpose, the impact of definitive measures on all parties involved in the proceedings and the likely consequences of taking or not taking such measures were considered on the basis of the evidence available after taking contact with the Community producers, other producers of farmed salmon in the Community, importers and processors.

11.2. Interest of the Community producers

(122) The Community producers have a combined annual turnover of over EUR 500 million, and, in addition to the direct employment of around 1450 which they create, are estimated to indirectly support a further 8000 jobs in the processing and other sectors. They are part of a major growth industry which has seen production double between 1995 and 2001. They are achieving increasing efficiency in the production of a product for which there is a growing market both in the Community and globally. They are viable and competitive in normal market conditions, and show increasing productivity.

(123) The Community producers' position is clearly in jeopardy unless the current level of low priced imports is corrected. This is evidenced by continuing reports of impending bankruptcies. The proposed measures will apply to all imports of the product concerned other than those from developing countries whose exports to the European Community are no more than 3% of imports to the Community. They would therefore apply to over 95% of such imports. Although it was argued that the price element of the measures may be difficult to enforce having regard to previous experience with price undertakings in relation to farmed salmon, it is recalled that the price element is not based on undertakings but on a variable duty to be collected by national customs authorities. Therefore, it can be anticipated that the measures would be effective and allow the Community producers prices to rise to a fair level.

11.3. Interest of the dependent industries

(124) The areas in which salmon farming is undertaken tend to be remote—mainly on coastal areas of Western and Northern Scotland and the West coast of Ireland. There

are limited employment opportunities and the economic activity generated by salmon farming makes an important contribution to these local economies. Without that contribution, many of the small local business which supply goods and services to the Community producers and their employees would cease to be viable. It is therefore in the interests of dependent industries that effective definitive measures are taken.

11.4. Interests of producers of smolt and feed

(125) Although one party argued the contrary, it is clearly in the interests of the major suppliers to the Community producers (such as smolt and feed producers) to have strong and predictable demand for their product at a price which allows them to make a reasonable profit.

11.5. Interest of users, processors and importers in the Community

(126) In order to evaluate the impact on importers, processors and users of taking or not taking measures questionnaires were sent to the known importers, processors and users of the product concerned on the Community market. Importers/processors/users are normally one and the same and many are in fact related to exporting producers outside the Community, particularly in Norway. Responses were received from 6 importers/processors/users and from an association of processors. In addition, a number of processors' associations made representations to the Commission and contact was taken with certain processors and their associations.

(127) Some argued that no measures should be taken because there had been only a short temporary fall in farmed salmon prices in the two to three months following the termination of anti-dumping measures against Norway in May 2003, and prices had since returned to normal. Processors stressed that any increase in prices would increase their cost base, reduce their sales and profitability and may lead to job losses and even de-localisation, stressing that employment in the fish processing sector is far higher than in the fish farming industry and in some cases provides employment in areas of low employment.

(128) However, it is clear that prices have not recovered in the first semester of 2004. Import prices increased between Q4 2003 and early Q1 2004 but then fell steadily in the latter part of Q1 2004 and in Q2 2004, and the Community producers' prices followed the same trends. The Community producers' prices remain substantially below a non-injurious price. Further, the latest information indicates that prices are still following a downward trend.

(129) The main costs incurred by processors are the cost of the raw material and employment costs, and it is true that an increase in raw material prices would increase the processors' costs. However, according to the information provided by processors, the cost of their raw material fell by 10% between 2002 and 2003, having already fallen by 18% between 2000 and 2002. In 2003, it was 26% cheaper than in 2000. At the same time, the information provided by them indicates that their selling prices have remained about the same in 2002 and 2003. All processors which provided information as to the profitability of their salmon processing operations have profitable salmon processing operations and it is considered that they can absorb a modest cost increase without any job losses or de-localisation. It is clear that current price levels of farmed

salmon are unsustainable in the medium to long term. The processing industry will therefore face an increase in the cost of their raw material in the medium to long term, in any event.

(130) As to employment, around 100 000 workers are employed in the fish processing sector in the Community although only a small proportion of those are concerned in processing farmed salmon. No evidence was found that the possible measures would lead to a decrease in the level of employment in the Community.

(131) Processors also stressed the need for traders in the principal European markets and consumers to continue to have access to good quality product at low prices. They expressed particular concern about the possibility of speculative buying immediately after the introduction of a tariff quota, and claimed that if the tariff quota is reached they might have to stop production. Finally, they stated that if measures were to be taken, they should be such as to maintain adequacy of supply and help bring price stability to the market in order that their costs could better be predicted. In this regard, whilst some maintained outright opposition to any form of measures, others indicated that if measures were to be imposed they would prefer a tariff quota system, certain expressing preference for a licensing system.

(132) It should be noted that the measures consist of a price element which reflects cost recovery for the Community producers and tariff quotas based on average imports to the Community (including the new Member States) in the period 2001 to 2003 plus 10%, beyond which an additional duty applies. Therefore, the processing industry throughout the Community should continue to have access to an adequate supply of raw material. Although some parties argued that the measures would constitute a heavy administrative burden for the Community processors, this claim was not substantiated and it is considered that the measures constitute the minimum administrative burden consistent with efficient application.

(133) Therefore, the disadvantages likely to be suffered by processors/users and import- ers, if any, are not considered such as to outweigh the benefits expected to accrue to the Community producers as a consequence of the definitive measures, which are consid- ered the minimum necessary to remedy the serious injury suffered and prevent further serious deterioration in the situation of the Community producers.

11.6. Interest of consumers in the Community

(134) As the product concerned is a consumer product, the Commission informed vari- ous consumer organisations of the opening of an investigation. A response was received from one party to the effect that the beneficial effects of salmon are widely recognised and that artificially increasing the price would make good nutrition choices more difficult for consumers and damage the economic viability of importers, processors and retailers of farmed salmon. Another claimed that the measures may prevent them from import- ing and continuing to sell frozen farmed salmon. Concern was also expressed that any increase in prices would make farmed salmon less affordable and stifle market growth in those Member States with a lower than average gross domestic product per head (GDP).

(135) However, as noted above, it is considered that the current market price is so low as to be unsustainable in the medium to long term, and economic operators will continue to have access to unlimited quantities of imports subject to the price element and above

the level of the tariff quota, additional duty. Further, given the magnitude of the margins between the whole fish ex-farm and the retail price of processed salmon products, it is considered that the measures are unlikely to have a material effect on retail prices and the impact on consumers is therefore considered to be minimal. Nevertheless, the Commission will carefully monitor the effect of the measures on affordability and market growth in those Member States with a lower than average GDP,

HAS ADOPTED THIS REGULATION:

Article 1

System of tariff quotas and their additional duties

1. A system of tariff quotas is hereby opened for the period 6 February 2005 to 13 August 2008 in relation to imports into the Community of farmed (other than wild) salmon, whether or not filleted, fresh, chilled or frozen, classified within CN codes ex03021200, ex03031100, ex03031900, ex03032200, ex03041013 and ex03042013 (hereinafter 'farmed salmon'). The volume of the tariff quotas and the countries to which they apply are specified in Annex 1. The quotas have been calculated on a whole fish equivalent basis (WFE) and conversion ratios to non-fillets (Group 1) and fillets (Group 2) actually imported are 1:0.9 and 1:0.65 respectively.

2. Wild salmon shall not be subject, or allocated, to the tariff quotas. For the purpose of this Regulation, wild salmon shall be that in respect of which the competent authorities of the Member State where the customs declaration for free circulation is accepted are satisfied, by means of all appropriate documents to be provided by interested parties, that it was caught at sea for Atlantic or Pacific salmon or in rivers for Danube salmon.

3. Subject to Article 4, imports of farmed salmon beyond the level of the tariff quota shall be subject to the additional duty specified in Annex 1 for the group to which they belong.

4. For the purposes of determining the level of additional duty payable, farmed salmon falling within CN codes ex03021200, ex03031100, ex03031900, ex03032200 shall fall within Group 1 in Annex 1, whilst those falling within ex03041013 and ex03042013 shall fall within Group 2.

5. The conventional rate of duty provided in Council Regulation (EC) No 2658/87, or any preferential rate of duty, shall continue to apply to imports of farmed salmon.

6. If circumstances should change, these measures may be reviewed by the Commission.

7. Upon cause shown, the rate of liberalisation of these measures may be reviewed.

Article 2

Minimum import price

1. Both within and beyond the tariff quota mentioned in Article 1 above, imports of farmed salmon are subject to a minimum import price ('MIP') which may be reviewed from time to time having regard to relevant factors including supply, demand and cost of production.

2. Imports of farmed salmon sold at a price which is less than the MIP shall be subject to a duty equivalent to the difference between the MIP for the respective products listed in annex 1 and the actual import price of those products (CIF Community border excluding customs duty).

3. From the entry into force of this Regulation until 15 April 2005, the MIP shall be EUR 2700 per tonne whole fish equivalent (CIF Community border excluding customs duty) for fresh farmed salmon and EUR 2592 for frozen farmed salmon. The MIP for imports in Group 1 shall be EUR 3000 per tonne fresh and EUR 2880 frozen, and that for imports in Group 2 shall be EUR 4154 per tonne fresh and EUR 3988 frozen.

4. From 16 April 2005 until 13 August 2008, the MIP shall be EUR 2850 per tonne whole fish equivalent (CIF Community border excluding customs duty) for fresh farmed salmon and EUR 2736 for frozen farmed salmon. The MIP for imports in Group 1 shall be EUR 3170 per tonne fresh and EUR 3040 frozen, and that for imports in Group 2 shall be EUR 4385 per tonne fresh and EUR 4209 frozen.

5. In cases where goods have been damaged before entry into free circulation and, therefore, the price is apportioned as for the determination of the customs value pursuant to Article 145 of Commission Regulation (EEC) No 2454/93, the MIP set out in paragraph (3) or (4) as appropriate, shall be reduced by a percentage which corresponds to the apportioning of the price actually paid or payable. The duty payable will then be equal to the difference between the reduced MIP and the reduced net, free-at-Community-frontier price.

Article 3

Security to be provided on importation

1. For the purpose of this regulation, 'importer' shall mean the person lodging the declaration for release for free circulation, or the person on whose behalf that declaration is lodged, and 'satisfactory evidence' shall be provided by the production to the customs authority of evidence of payment of the actual import price for the salmon imported, or by results of appropriate controls carried out by customs authorities.

2. Importers of farmed salmon shall provide satisfactory evidence to the customs authorities of the actual import price per tonne paid for imports of farmed salmon.

3. Pending the provision of satisfactory evidence, the release of the goods shall be conditional upon the provision of a security to the customs authorities of EUR 290 per tonne (WFE) of farmed salmon imported (Group 1—EUR 320 per tonne, Group 2—EUR 450 per tonne).

4. If, within 1 year of the date of acceptance of the customs declaration for release for free circulation or within 3 months following the foreseen date of payment for the goods, whichever date is the later, the importer has not supplied satisfactory evidence as required by paragraph (2) above, the customs authorities shall immediately enter in the accounts, as duties to which the goods in question are subject, the amount of the security provided in accordance with the provisions of paragraph (3) above.

5. If on verification the customs authorities establish that the price actually paid for the goods is below the MIP as indicated in Article 2, they shall recover the difference between that price and the respective MIP in accordance with Article 220(1) of Regulation (EEC) No 2913/92. In order to prevent the wrongful acquisition of financial advantage, compensatory interests shall be applied in accordance with the provisions in force.

6. The security provided shall be released at the moment the importer provides satisfactory evidence as required in paragraph (2) above.

Article 4

Developing countries
Imports of farmed salmon originating in one of the developing countries specified in
Annex 2 shall not be subject, or allocated, to the tariff quotas laid down in Article 1 or
subject to the requirements under Articles 2 or 3.

Article 5

General provisions
1. The origin of the farmed salmon to which this Regulation applies shall be determined in accordance with the provisions in force in the Community.
2. Subject to paragraph (3), any release into free circulation in the Community of
farmed salmon originating in a developing country shall be subject to:
(a) presentation of a certificate of origin issued by the competent national authorities
of that country meeting the conditions laid down in Article 47 of Regulation (EEC) No
2454/93, and
(b) the condition that the product has been transported directly, within the meaning of
Article 6, from that country to the Community.
3. The certificate of origin referred to in paragraph (2)(a) shall not be required for
imports of farmed salmon covered by a proof of origin issued or made out in accordance with the relevant rules established in order to qualify for preferential tariff
measures.
4. Proof of origin shall be accepted only if the farmed salmon meet the criteria for
determining origin set out in the provisions in force in the Community.

Article 6

Direct transport
1. The following shall be considered as transported direct to the Community from a
third country:
(a) products transported without passing through the territory of any third country;
(b) products transported through one or more third countries other than the country
of origin, with or without trans-shipment or temporary warehousing in those countries, provided that such passage is justified for geographical reasons or exclusively on
account of transport requirements and provided that the products:
– have remained under the supervision of the customs authorities of the country or
countries of transit or warehousing,
– have not entered into commerce or been released for consumption there, and
– have not undergone operations there other than unloading and reloading.
2. Proof that the conditions referred to in paragraph (1)(b) have been satisfied shall be
submitted to the Community authorities. That proof may be provided, in particular, in
the form of one of the following documents:
(a) a single transport document issued in the country of origin covering passage
through the country or countries of transit;
(b) a certificate issued by the customs authorities of the country or countries of transit
containing:
– a precise description of the goods;

– the dates of their unloading and reloading or their lading or unlading, identifying the vessels used.

Article 7

Imports in the process of shipment to the Community

1. This Regulation shall not apply to products in the process of shipment to the Community within the meaning of paragraph (2).

2. Products shall be deemed to be in the process of shipment to the Community if they:

– left the country of origin before the date this Regulation begins to apply, and

– are shipped from the place of loading in the country of origin to the place of unloading in the Community under cover of a valid transport document issued before the date this Regulation begins to apply.

3. The parties concerned shall provide, to the satisfaction of the customs authorities, proof that the conditions laid down in paragraph (2) have been met.

However, the authorities may regard the products as having left the country of origin before the date this Regulation begins to apply if one of the following documents is provided:

– in the case of transport by sea, the bill of lading showing that loading took place before that date,

– in the case of transport by rail, the consignment note that was accepted by the railway authorities in the country of origin before that date,

– in the case of transport by road, the CMR contract for the carriage of goods or any other transport document issued in the country of origin before that date,

– in the case of transport by air, the air consignment note showing that the airline took the products over before that date.

Article 8

The Member States and the Commission shall co-operate closely to ensure compliance with this Regulation.

Article 9

This Regulation shall enter into force on the day following that of its publication in the Official Journal of the European Union and apply until 13 August 2008.

This Regulation shall be binding in its entirety and directly applicable in all Member States.

ANNEX I

[...]

ANNEX II
LIST OF DEVELOPING COUNTRIES
(referred to in Article 4)

[...]

Commission Regulation (EC) No 627/2005 of 22 April 2005 revoking Regulation (EC) No 206/2005 imposing definitive safeguard measures against imports of farmed salmon, Official Journal L 104, 23.4.2005, p. 4.

THE COMMISSION OF THE EUROPEAN COMMUNITIES,

[...]

PROCEDURE

(1) On 6 March 2004, the Commission initiated a safeguard investigation on imports of farmed salmon into the Community. On 4 February 2005, the Commission imposed definitive safeguard measures by Commission Regulation (EC) No 206/2005.

(2) On 23 October 2004, the Commission initiated an anti-dumping investigation on imports of farmed salmon originating in Norway. On 22 April 2005, the Commission adopted provisional anti-dumping measures by Commission Regulation (EC) No 628/2005.

CONSIDERATIONS

(3) The imposition of definitive safeguard measures on imports of farmed salmon of all origins followed an investigation covering the period 2000 to 2003. Having reached a provisional determination that, in the period from 1 October 2003 to 30 September 2004, imports from Norway have continued to increase and that there is injurious dumping, the Commission adopted provisional anti-dumping measures against imports of farmed salmon from Norway.

(4) Imports of farmed salmon from Norway in the year ending 30 September 2004 represent around 60% of the Community market and around 75% of overall imports into the Community. In Regulation (EC) No 206/2005, the Commission had found that the considerable increase in imports had a devastating effect on the profitability of the Community producers, given the accompanying price drop. The provisional anti-dumping measures in relation to imports of farmed salmon originating in Norway would eliminate the unfair price element in these imports. It can also be expected that they will slow down the quantitative import increase originating in Norway, the largest source of imports into the Community. Therefore, in the particular circumstances of this case, it is considered that anti-dumping measures are sufficient to address the injury which the community industry is suffering, and it is no longer necessary to maintain the safeguard measures, which should therefore be repealed at the same time as the anti-dumping measures enter into force,

HAS ADOPTED THIS REGULATION:

Sole Article

Regulation (EC) No 206/2005 is hereby revoked.

This Regulation shall enter into force on 27 April 2005.

This Regulation shall be binding in its entirety and directly applicable in all Member States.

7.4 Anti-dumping

Council Regulation (EC) No 1225/2009 of 30 November 2009 on protection against dumped imports from countries not members of the European Community, Official Journal L 343, 22.12.2009, pp. 51–73.

This is the codified version of the anti-dumping regulation that was originally adopted after the Uruguay Round as an implementation of the WTO Anti-Dumping Agreement (ADA), and was modified a year later. In the meantime it has been amended many times. Contrary to the Safeguards Agreement, which provides brief protection against surges in imports that are considered 'fair' in that they result from normal tariff concessions, the ADA is regarded as being directed against unfair trade. It is supposed to give, if necessary, unlimited protection against surges in imports that are considered the result of unfair pricing. In the absence of tariff barriers, 'unfairly' priced goods for export would flow back to the home market of the producer and thus limit the capacity of the producer to continue selling against 'unfair' or 'dumped' prices. In the absence of such a natural limitation, protective measures against such 'dumping' are indispensable, according to the line of thinking behind the ADA.

The Regulation is particularly interesting for the peculiar voting arrangements in the Council for the adoption of definitive anti-dumping measures, laid down in Article 9(4). This article limits the possibility of using a blocking minority under the qualified majority voting system applicable under Article 133 TEC (now Article 207 TFEU). Another controversial provision of the Regulation is Article 13 on circumvention. A somewhat similar provision had been attacked by Japan during the GATT years and its application had been condemned by the panel.[5] However, since the entry into force of the WTO Agreement, this provision or its application has not yet been subjected to scrutiny in a dispute settlement procedure.

THE COUNCIL OF THE EUROPEAN UNION,
Having regard to the Treaty establishing the European Community, and in particular Article 133 thereof,
Having regard to Council Regulation (EC) No 1234/2007 of 22 October 2007 establishing a common organisation of agricultural markets and on specific provisions for certain agricultural products (Single CMO Regulation),
Having regard to the proposal from the Commission,

Whereas:
(1) Council Regulation (EC) No 384/96 of 22 December 1995 on protection against dumped imports from countries not members of the European Community, has been substantially amended several times. In the interests of clarity and rationality the said Regulation should be codified.

---

[5] GATT Panel Report, *European Economic Community—Regulation on Imports of Parts and Components*, L/6657, adopted 16 May 1990, BISD 375/132.

(2) The multilateral trade negotiations concluded in 1994 led to new Agreements on the implementation of Article VI of the General Agreement on Tariffs and Trade (hereinafter referred to as 'GATT'). In the light of the different nature of the new rules for dumping and subsidies respectively, it is also appropriate to have a separate body of Community rules in each of those two areas. Consequently, the rules on protection against subsidies and countervailing duties are contained in a separate Regulation.

(3) The agreement on dumping, namely, the Agreement on Implementation of Article VI of the General Agreement on Tariffs and Trade 1994 (hereinafter referred to as 'the 1994 Anti-Dumping Agreement'), contains detailed rules, relating in particular to the calculation of dumping, procedures for initiating and pursuing an investigation, including the establishment and treatment of the facts, the imposition of provisional measures, the imposition and collection of anti-dumping duties, the duration and review of anti-dumping measures and the public disclosure of information relating to anti-dumping investigations. In order to ensure a proper and transparent application of those rules, the language of the agreement should be brought into Community legislation as far as possible.

(4) In applying the rules it is essential, in order to maintain the balance of rights and obligations which the GATT Agreement establishes, that the Community take account of how they are interpreted by the Community's major trading partners.

(5) It is desirable to lay down clear and detailed rules on the calculation of normal value. In particular such value should in all cases be based on representative sales in the ordinary course of trade in the exporting country. It is expedient to give guidance as to when parties may be considered as being associated for the purpose of determining dumping. It is expedient to define the circumstances in which domestic sales may be considered to be made at a loss and may be disregarded, and in which recourse may be had to remaining sales, or to constructed normal value, or to sales to a third country. It is also appropriate to provide for a proper allocation of costs, even in start-up situations, and to lay down guidance as to the definition of start-up and the extent and method of allocation. It is also necessary, when constructing normal value, to indicate the methodology to be applied in determining the amounts for selling, general and administrative costs and the profit margin that should be included in such value.

(6) When determining normal value for non-market economy countries, it appears prudent to set out rules for choosing the appropriate market-economy third country to be used for such purpose and, where it is not possible to find a suitable third country, to provide that normal value may be established on any other reasonable basis.

(7) It is appropriate for the Community's anti-dumping practice to take account of the changed economic conditions in Kazakhstan. In particular, it is appropriate to specify that normal value may be determined in accordance with the rules applicable to market economy countries in cases where it can be shown that market conditions prevail for one or more producers, subject to investigation in relation to the manufacture and sale of the product concerned.

(8) It is also appropriate to grant similar treatment to imports from such countries which are members of the World Trade Organisation (WTO) at the date of the initiation of the relevant anti-dumping investigation.

(9) It is appropriate to specify that an examination of whether market conditions prevail will be carried out on the basis of properly substantiated claims by one or more producers subject to investigation who wish to avail themselves of the possibility to have normal value determined on the basis of rules applicable to market economy countries.

(10) It is expedient to define the export price and to enumerate the adjustments which are to be made in those cases where a reconstruction of this price from the first open-market price is deemed necessary.

(11) For the purpose of ensuring a fair comparison between export price and normal value, it is advisable to list the factors which may affect prices and price comparability and to lay down specific rules as to when and how the adjustments should be made, including the fact that any duplication of adjustments should be avoided. It is also necessary to provide that comparison may be made using average prices although individual export prices may be compared to an average normal value where the former vary by customer, region or time period.

(12) It is necessary to lay down clear and detailed guidance as to the factors which may be relevant for the determination of whether the dumped imports have caused material injury or are threatening to cause injury. In demonstrating that the volume and price levels of the imports concerned are responsible for injury sustained by a Community industry, attention should be given to the effect of other factors and in particular prevailing market conditions in the Community.

(13) It is advisable to define the term 'Community industry' and to provide that parties related to exporters may be excluded from such industry, and to define the term 'related'. It is also necessary to provide for anti-dumping action to be taken on behalf of producers in a region of the Community and to lay down guidelines on the definition of such region.

(14) It is necessary to lay down who may lodge an anti-dumping complaint, including the extent to which it should be supported by the Community industry, and the information on dumping, injury and causation which such complaint should contain. It is also expedient to specify the procedures for the rejection of complaints or the initiation of proceedings.

(15) It is necessary to lay down the manner in which interested parties should be given notice of the information which the authorities require, and should have ample opportunity to present all relevant evidence and to defend their interests. It is also desirable to set out clearly the rules and procedures to be followed during the investigation, in particular the rules whereby interested parties are to make themselves known, present their views and submit information within specified time-limits, if such views and information are to be taken into account. It is also appropriate to set out the conditions under which an interested party may have access to, and comment on, information presented by other interested parties. There should also be cooperation between the Member States and the Commission in the collection of information.

(16) It is necessary to lay down the conditions under which provisional duties may be imposed, including the condition that they may be imposed no earlier than 60 days from initiation and no later than nine months thereafter. For administrative reasons, it is also necessary to provide that such duties may in all cases be imposed by the Commission, either directly for a nine-month period or in two stages of six and three months.

(17) It is necessary to specify procedures for accepting undertakings which eliminate dumping and injury instead of imposing provisional or definitive duties. It is also appropriate to lay down the consequences of breach or withdrawal of undertakings and that provisional duties may be imposed in cases of suspected violation or where further investigation is necessary to supplement the findings. In accepting undertakings, care should be taken that the proposed undertakings, and their enforcement, do not lead to anti-competitive behaviour.

(18) It is necessary to provide that the termination of cases should, irrespective of whether definitive measures are adopted or not, normally take place within 12 months, and in no case later than 15 months, from the initiation of the investigation. Investigations or proceedings should be terminated where the dumping is de minimis or the injury is negligible, and it is appropriate to define those terms. Where measures are to be imposed, it is necessary to provide for the termination of investigations and to lay down that measures should be less than the margin of dumping if such lesser amount would remove the injury, as well as to specify the method of calculating the level of measures in cases of sampling.

(19) It is necessary to provide for retroactive collection of provisional duties if that is deemed appropriate and to define the circumstances which may trigger the retroactive application of duties to avoid the undermining of the definitive measures to be applied. It is also necessary to provide that duties may be applied retroactively in cases of breach or withdrawal of undertakings.

(20) It is necessary to provide that measures are to lapse after five years unless a review indicates that they should be maintained. It is also necessary to provide, in cases where sufficient evidence is submitted of changed circumstances, for interim reviews or for investigations to determine whether refunds of anti-dumping duties are warranted. It is also appropriate to lay down that in any recalculation of dumping which neces- sitates a reconstruction of export prices, duties are not to be treated as a cost incurred between importation and resale where the said duty is being reflected in the prices of the products subject to measures in the Community.

(21) It is necessary to provide specifically for the reassessment of export prices and dumping margins where the duty is being absorbed by the exporter through a form of compensatory arrangement and the measures are not being reflected in the prices of the products subject to measures in the Community.

(22) The 1994 Anti-Dumping Agreement does not contain provisions regarding the cir- cumvention of anti-dumping measures, though a separate GATT Ministerial Decision recognises circumvention as a problem and has referred it to the GATT Anti-dumping Committee for resolution. Given the failure of the multilateral negotiations so far and pending the outcome of the referral to the WTO Anti-Dumping Committee, it is necessary that Community legislation should contain provisions to deal with practices, including mere assembly of goods in the Community or a third country, which have as their main aim the circumvention of anti-dumping measures.

(23) It is also desirable to clarify which practices constitute circumvention of the measures in place. Circumvention practices may take place either inside or outside the Community. It is consequently necessary to provide that exemptions from the extended duties which may already be granted to importers may also be granted to

exporters when duties are being extended to address circumvention taking place outside the Community.

(24) It is expedient to permit suspension of anti-dumping measures where there is a temporary change in market conditions which makes the continued imposition of such measures temporarily inappropriate.

(25) It is necessary to provide that imports under investigation may be made subject to registration upon importation in order to enable measures to be applied subsequently against such imports.

(26) In order to ensure proper enforcement of measures, it is necessary that Member States monitor, and report to the Commission, the import trade of products subject to investigation or subject to measures, and also the amount of duties collected under this Regulation.

(27) It is necessary to provide for consultation of an Advisory Committee at regular and specified stages of the investigation. The Committee should consist of representatives of Member States with a representative of the Commission as chairman.

(28) Information provided to Member States in the Advisory Committee is often of a highly technical nature and involves an elaborate economic and legal analysis. In order to provide Member States with sufficient time to consider this information, it should be sent at an appropriate time before the date of a meeting set by the Chairman of the Advisory Committee.

(29) It is expedient to provide for verification visits to check information submitted on dumping and injury, such visits being, however, conditional on proper replies to questionnaires being received.

(30) It is essential to provide for sampling in cases where the number of parties or transactions is large in order to permit completion of investigations within the appointed time-limits.

(31) It is necessary to provide that where parties do not cooperate satisfactorily other information may be used to establish findings and that such information may be less favourable to the parties than if they had cooperated.

(32) Provision should be made for the treatment of confidential information so that business secrets are not divulged.

(33) It is essential that provision be made for proper disclosure of essential facts and considerations to parties which qualify for such treatment and that such disclosure be made, with due regard to the decision-making process in the Community, within a time-limit which permits parties to defend their interests.

(34) It is prudent to provide for an administrative system under which arguments can be presented as to whether measures are in the Community interest, including the consumers' interest, and to lay down the time-limits within which such information has to be presented as well as the disclosure rights of the parties concerned,

HAS ADOPTED THIS REGULATION:

Article 1

Principles

1. An anti-dumping duty may be applied to any dumped product whose release for free circulation in the Community causes injury.

2. A product is to be considered as being dumped if its export price to the Community is less than a comparable price for the like product, in the ordinary course of trade, as established for the exporting country.

3. The exporting country shall normally be the country of origin. However, it may be an intermediate country, except where, for example, the products are merely transhipped through that country, or the products concerned are not produced in that country, or there is no comparable price for them in that country.

4. For the purpose of this Regulation, 'like product' means a product which is identical, that is to say, alike in all respects, to the product under consideration, or in the absence of such a product, another product which, although not alike in all respects, has characteristics closely resembling those of the product under consideration.

Article 2

Determination of dumping

A. NORMAL VALUE

1. The normal value shall normally be based on the prices paid or payable, in the ordinary course of trade, by independent customers in the exporting country.

However, where the exporter in the exporting country does not produce or does not sell the like product, the normal value may be established on the basis of prices of other sellers or producers.

Prices between parties which appear to be associated or to have a compensatory arrangement with each other may not be considered to be in the ordinary course of trade and may not be used to establish normal value unless it is determined that they are unaffected by the relationship.

In order to determine whether two parties are associated account may be taken of the definition of related parties set out in Article 143 of Commission Regulation (EEC) No 2454/93 of 2 July 1993 laying down provisions for the implementation of Council Regulation (EEC) No 2913/92 establishing the Community Customs Code.

2. Sales of the like product intended for domestic consumption shall normally be used to determine normal value if such sales volume constitutes 5% or more of the sales volume of the product under consideration to the Community. However, a lower volume of sales may be used when, for example, the prices charged are considered representative for the market concerned.

3. When there are no or insufficient sales of the like product in the ordinary course of trade, or where because of the particular market situation such sales do not permit a proper comparison, the normal value of the like product shall be calculated on the basis of the cost of production in the country of origin plus a reasonable amount for selling, general and administrative costs and for profits, or on the basis of the export prices, in the ordinary course of trade, to an appropriate third country, provided that those prices are representative.

A particular market situation for the product concerned within the meaning of the first subparagraph may be deemed to exist, inter alia, when prices are artificially low, when there is significant barter trade, or when there are non-commercial processing arrangements.

4. Sales of the like product in the domestic market of the exporting country, or export sales to a third country, at prices below unit production costs (fixed and variable) plus selling, general and administrative costs may be treated as not being in the ordinary course of trade by reason of price, and may be disregarded in determining normal value, only if it is determined that such sales are made within an extended period in substantial quantities, and are at prices which do not provide for the recovery of all costs within a reasonable period of time.

If prices which are below costs at the time of sale are above weighted average costs for the period of investigation, such prices shall be considered to provide for recovery of costs within a reasonable period of time.

The extended period of time shall normally be one year but shall in no case be less than six months, and sales below unit cost shall be considered to be made in substantial quantities within such a period when it is established that the weighted average selling price is below the weighted average unit cost, or that the volume of sales below unit cost is not less than 20% of sales being used to determine normal value.

5. Costs shall normally be calculated on the basis of records kept by the party under investigation, provided that such records are in accordance with the generally accepted accounting principles of the country concerned and that it is shown that the records reasonably reflect the costs associated with the production and sale of the product under consideration.

If costs associated with the production and sale of the product under investigation are not reasonably reflected in the records of the party concerned, they shall be adjusted or established on the basis of the costs of other producers or exporters in the same country or, where such information is not available or cannot be used, on any other reasonable basis, including information from other representative markets.

Consideration shall be given to evidence submitted on the proper allocation of costs, provided that it is shown that such allocations have been historically utilised. In the absence of a more appropriate method, preference shall be given to the allocation of costs on the basis of turnover. Unless already reflected in the cost allocations under this subparagraph, costs shall be adjusted appropriately for those non-recurring items of cost which benefit future and/or current production.

Where the costs for part of the period for cost recovery are affected by the use of new production facilities requiring substantial additional investment and by low capacity utilisation rates, which are the result of start-up operations which take place within or during part of the investigation period, the average costs for the start-up phase shall be those applicable, under the abovementioned allocation rules, at the end of such a phase, and shall be included at that level, for the period concerned, in the weighted average costs referred to in the second subparagraph of paragraph 4. The length of a start-up phase shall be determined in relation to the circumstances of the producer or exporter concerned, but shall not exceed an appropriate initial portion of the period for cost recovery. For this adjustment to costs applicable during the investigation period, information relating to a start-up phase which extends beyond that period shall be taken into account where it is submitted prior to verification visits and within three months of the initiation of the investigation.

6. The amounts for selling, for general and administrative costs and for profits shall be based on actual data pertaining to production and sales, in the ordinary course of trade, of the like product, by the exporter or producer under investigation. When such amounts cannot be determined on this basis, the amounts may be determined on the basis of:

(a) the weighted average of the actual amounts determined for other exporters or producers subject to investigation in respect of production and sales of the like product in the domestic market of the country of origin;

(b) the actual amounts applicable to production and sales, in the ordinary course of trade, of the same general category of products for the exporter or producer in question in the domestic market of the country of origin;

(c) any other reasonable method, provided that the amount for profit so established shall not exceed the profit normally realised by other exporters or producers on sales of products of the same general category in the domestic market of the country of origin.

7. (a) In the case of imports from non-market economy countries, normal value shall be determined on the basis of the price or constructed value in a market economy third country, or the price from such a third country to other countries, including the Community, or where those are not possible, on any other reasonable basis, including the price actually paid or payable in the Community for the like product, duly adjusted if necessary to include a reasonable profit margin.

An appropriate market economy third country shall be selected in a not unreasonable manner, due account being taken of any reliable information made available at the time of selection. Account shall also be taken of time-limits; where appropriate, a market economy third country which is subject to the same investigation shall be used.

The parties to the investigation shall be informed shortly after its initiation of the market economy third country envisaged and shall be given 10 days to comment.

(b) In anti-dumping investigations concerning imports from Kazakhstan and any non-market-economy country which is a member of the WTO at the date of the initiation of the investigation, normal value shall be determined in accordance with paragraphs 1 to 6, if it is shown, on the basis of properly substantiated claims by one or more producers subject to the investigation and in accordance with the criteria and procedures set out in subparagraph (c), that market economy conditions prevail for this producer or producers in respect of the manufacture and sale of the like product concerned. When this is not the case, the rules set out under subparagraph (a) shall apply.

(c) A claim under subparagraph (b) must be made in writing and contain sufficient evidence that the producer operates under market economy conditions, that is if:

– decisions of firms regarding prices, costs and inputs, including for instance raw materials, cost of technology and labour, output, sales and investment, are made in response to market signals reflecting supply and demand, and without significant State interference in this regard, and costs of major inputs substantially reflect market values,

– firms have one clear set of basic accounting records which are independently audited in line with international accounting standards and are applied for all purposes,

– the production costs and financial situation of firms are not subject to significant distortions carried over from the former non-market economy system, in particular in relation to depreciation of assets, other write-offs, barter trade and payment via compensation of debts,

– the firms concerned are subject to bankruptcy and property laws which guarantee legal certainty and stability for the operation of firms, and

– exchange rate conversions are carried out at the market rate.

A determination whether the producer meets the abovementioned criteria shall be made within three months of the initiation of the investigation, after specific consultation of the Advisory Committee and after the Community industry has been given an opportunity to comment. This determination shall remain in force throughout the investigation.

B. EXPORT PRICE

8. The export price shall be the price actually paid or payable for the product when sold for export from the exporting country to the Community.

9. In cases where there is no export price or where it appears that the export price is unreliable because of an association or a compensatory arrangement between the exporter and the importer or a third party, the export price may be constructed on the basis of the price at which the imported products are first resold to an independent buyer, or, if the products are not resold to an independent buyer, or are not resold in the condition in which they were imported, on any reasonable basis.

In these cases, adjustment for all costs, including duties and taxes, incurred between importation and resale, and for profits accruing, shall be made so as to establish a reliable export price, at the Community frontier level.

The items for which adjustment shall be made shall include those normally borne by an importer but paid by any party, either inside or outside the Community, which appears to be associated or to have a compensatory arrangement with the importer or exporter, including usual transport, insurance, handling, loading and ancillary costs; customs duties, any anti-dumping duties, and other taxes payable in the importing country by reason of the importation or sale of the goods; and a reasonable margin for selling, general and administrative costs and profit.

C. COMPARISON

10. A fair comparison shall be made between the export price and the normal value. This comparison shall be made at the same level of trade and in respect of sales made at, as closely as possible, the same time and with due account taken of other differences which affect price comparability. Where the normal value and the export price as established are not on such a comparable basis due allowance, in the form of adjustments, shall be made in each case, on its merits, for differences in factors which are claimed, and demonstrated, to affect prices and price comparability. Any duplication when making adjustments shall be avoided, in particular in relation to discounts, rebates, quantities and level of trade. When the specified conditions are met, the factors for which adjustment can be made are listed as follows:

(a) Physical characteristics
An adjustment shall be made for differences in the physical characteristics of the product concerned. The amount of the adjustment shall correspond to a reasonable estimate of the market value of the difference.

(b) Import charges and indirect taxes
An adjustment shall be made to normal value for an amount corresponding to any import charges or indirect taxes borne by the like product and by materials physically incorporated therein, when intended for consumption in the exporting country and not collected or refunded in respect of the product exported to the Community.

(c) Discounts, rebates and quantities
An adjustment shall be made for differences in discounts and rebates, including those given for differences in quantities, if these are properly quantified and are directly linked to the sales under consideration. An adjustment may also be made for deferred discounts and rebates if the claim is based on consistent practice in prior periods, including compliance with the conditions required to qualify for the discount or rebates.

(d) Level of trade
(i) An adjustment for differences in levels of trade, including any differences which may arise in OEM (Original Equipment Manufacturer) sales, shall be made where, in relation to the distribution chain in both markets, it is shown that the export price, including a constructed export price, is at a different level of trade from the normal value and the difference has affected price comparability which is demonstrated by consistent and distinct differences in functions and prices of the seller for the different levels of trade in the domestic market of the exporting country. The amount of the adjustment shall be based on the market value of the difference.
(ii) However, in circumstances not envisaged under point (i), when an existing difference in level of trade cannot be quantified because of the absence of the relevant levels on the domestic market of the exporting countries, or where certain functions are shown clearly to relate to levels of trade other than the one which is to be used in the comparison, a special adjustment may be granted.

(e) Transport, insurance, handling, loading and ancillary costs
An adjustment shall be made for differences in the directly related costs incurred for conveying the product concerned from the premises of the exporter to an independent buyer, where such costs are included in the prices charged. Those costs shall include transport, insurance, handling, loading and ancillary costs.

(f) Packing
An adjustment shall be made for differences in the directly related packing costs for the product concerned.

(g) Credit
An adjustment shall be made for differences in the cost of any credit granted for the sales under consideration, provided that it is a factor taken into account in the determination of the prices charged.

(h) After-sales costs

An adjustment shall be made for differences in the direct costs of providing warranties, guarantees, technical assistance and services, as provided for by law and/or in the sales contract.

(i) Commissions

An adjustment shall be made for differences in commissions paid in respect of the sales under consideration.

The term 'commissions' shall be understood to include the mark-up received by a trader of the product or the like product if the functions of such a trader are similar to those of an agent working on a commission basis.

(j) Currency conversions

When the price comparison requires a conversion of currencies, such conversion shall be made using the rate of exchange on the date of sale, except when a sale of foreign currency on forward markets is directly linked to the export sale involved, in which case the rate of exchange in the forward sale shall be used. Normally, the date of sale shall be the date of invoice but the date of contract, purchase order or order confirmation may be used if these more appropriately establish the material terms of sale. Fluctuations in exchange rates shall be ignored and exporters shall be granted 60 days to reflect a sustained movement in exchange rates during the investigation period.

(k) Other factors

An adjustment may also be made for differences in other factors not provided for under subparagraphs (a) to (j) if it is demonstrated that they affect price comparability as required under this paragraph, in particular that customers consistently pay different prices on the domestic market because of the difference in such factors.

D. DUMPING MARGIN

11. Subject to the relevant provisions governing fair comparison, the existence of margins of dumping during the investigation period shall normally be established on the basis of a comparison of a weighted average normal value with a weighted average of prices of all export transactions to the Community, or by a comparison of individual normal values and individual export prices to the Community on a transaction-to-transaction basis. However, a normal value established on a weighted average basis may be compared to prices of all individual export transactions to the Community, if there is a pattern of export prices which differs significantly among different purchasers, regions or time periods, and if the methods specified in the first sentence of this paragraph would not reflect the full degree of dumping being practised. This paragraph shall not preclude the use of sampling in accordance with Article 17.

12. The dumping margin shall be the amount by which the normal value exceeds the export price. Where dumping margins vary, a weighted average dumping margin may be established.

Article 3

Determination of injury

1. Pursuant to this Regulation, the term 'injury' shall, unless otherwise specified, be taken to mean material injury to the Community industry, threat of material injury to the Community industry or material retardation of the establishment of such an industry and shall be interpreted in accordance with the provisions of this Article.

2. A determination of injury shall be based on positive evidence and shall involve an objective examination of both:

(a) the volume of the dumped imports and the effect of the dumped imports on prices in the Community market for like products; and

(b) the consequent impact of those imports on the Community industry.

3. With regard to the volume of the dumped imports, consideration shall be given to whether there has been a significant increase in dumped imports, either in absolute terms or relative to production or consumption in the Community. With regard to the effect of the dumped imports on prices, consideration shall be given to whether there has been significant price undercutting by the dumped imports as compared with the price of a like product of the Community industry, or whether the effect of such imports is otherwise to depress prices to a significant degree or prevent price increases, which would otherwise have occurred, to a significant degree. No one or more of these factors can necessarily give decisive guidance.

4. Where imports of a product from more than one country are simultaneously subject to anti-dumping investigations, the effects of such imports shall be cumulatively assessed only if it is determined that:

(a) the margin of dumping established in relation to the imports from each country is more than de minimis as defined in Article 9(3) and that the volume of imports from each country is not negligible; and

(b) a cumulative assessment of the effects of the imports is appropriate in light of the conditions of competition between imported products and the conditions of competition between the imported products and the like Community product.

5. The examination of the impact of the dumped imports on the Community industry concerned shall include an evaluation of all relevant economic factors and indices having a bearing on the state of the industry, including the fact that an industry is still in the process of recovering from the effects of past dumping or subsidisation, the magnitude of the actual margin of dumping, actual and potential decline in sales, profits, output, market share, productivity, return on investments, utilisation of capacity; factors affecting Community prices; actual and potential negative effects on cash flow, inventories, employment, wages, growth, ability to raise capital or investments. This list is not exhaustive, nor can any one or more of these factors necessarily give decisive guidance.

6. It must be demonstrated, from all the relevant evidence presented in relation to paragraph 2, that the dumped imports are causing injury within the meaning of this Regulation. Specifically, this shall entail a demonstration that the volume and/or price levels identified pursuant to paragraph 3 are responsible for an impact on the Community industry as provided for in paragraph 5, and that this impact exists to a degree which enables it to be classified as material.

7. Known factors other than the dumped imports which at the same time are injuring the Community industry shall also be examined to ensure that injury caused by these

other factors is not attributed to the dumped imports under paragraph 6. Factors which may be considered in this respect include the volume and prices of imports not sold at dumping prices, contraction in demand or changes in the patterns of consumption, restrictive trade practices of, and competition between, third country and Community producers, developments in technology and the export performance and productivity of the Community industry.

8. The effect of the dumped imports shall be assessed in relation to the production of the Community industry of the like product when available data permit the separate identification of that production on the basis of such criteria as the production process, producers' sales and profits. If such separate identification of that production is not possible, the effects of the dumped imports shall be assessed by examination of the production of the narrowest group or range of products, which includes the like product, for which the necessary information can be provided.

9. A determination of a threat of material injury shall be based on facts and not merely on an allegation, conjecture or remote possibility. The change in circumstances which would create a situation in which the dumping would cause injury must be clearly foreseen and imminent.

In making a determination regarding the existence of a threat of material injury, consideration should be given to such factors as:

(a) a significant rate of increase of dumped imports into the Community market indicating the likelihood of substantially increased imports;

(b) sufficient freely disposable capacity of the exporter or an imminent and substantial increase in such capacity indicating the likelihood of substantially increased dumped exports to the Community, account being taken of the availability of other export markets to absorb any additional exports;

(c) whether imports are entering at prices that would, to a significant degree, depress prices or prevent price increases which otherwise would have occurred, and would probably increase demand for further imports; and

(d) inventories of the product being investigated.

No one of the factors listed above by itself can necessarily give decisive guidance but the totality of the factors considered must lead to the conclusion that further dumped exports are imminent and that, unless protective action is taken, material injury will occur.

Article 4

Definition of Community industry

1. For the purposes of this Regulation, the term 'Community industry' shall be interpreted as referring to the Community producers as a whole of the like products or to those of them whose collective output of the products constitutes a major proportion, as defined in Article 5(4), of the total Community production of those products, except that:

(a) when producers are related to the exporters or importers or are themselves importers of the allegedly dumped product, the term 'Community industry' may be interpreted as referring to the rest of the producers;

(b) in exceptional circumstances the territory of the Community may, for the production in question, be divided into two or more competitive markets and the producers within each market may be regarded as a separate industry if:

(i) the producers within such a market sell all or almost all of their production of the product in question in that market; and

(ii) the demand in that market is not to any substantial degree supplied by producers of the product in question located elsewhere in the Community. In such circumstances, injury may be found to exist even where a major portion of the total Community industry is not injured, provided there is a concentration of dumped imports into such an isolated market and provided further that the dumped imports are causing injury to the producers of all or almost all of the production within such a market.

2. For the purpose of paragraph 1, producers shall be considered to be related to exporters or importers only if:

(a) one of them directly or indirectly controls the other; or

(b) both of them are directly or indirectly controlled by a third person; or

(c) together they directly or indirectly control a third person provided that there are grounds for believing or suspecting that the effect of the relationship is such as to cause the producer concerned to behave differently from non-related producers.

For the purpose of this paragraph, one shall be deemed to control another when the former is legally or operationally in a position to exercise restraint or direction over the latter.

3. Where the Community industry has been interpreted as referring to the producers in a certain region, the exporters shall be given an opportunity to offer undertakings pursuant to Article 8 in respect of the region concerned. In such cases, when evaluating the Community interest of the measures, special account shall be taken of the interest of the region. If an adequate undertaking is not offered promptly or the situations set out in Article 8(9) and (10) apply, a provisional or definitive duty may be imposed in respect of the Community as a whole. In such cases, the duties may, if practicable, be limited to specific producers or exporters.

4. The provisions of Article 3(8) shall be applicable to this Article.

Article 5

Initiation of proceedings

1. Except as provided for in paragraph 6, an investigation to determine the existence, degree and effect of any alleged dumping shall be initiated upon a written complaint by any natural or legal person, or any association not having legal personality, acting on behalf of the Community industry.

The complaint may be submitted to the Commission, or to a Member State, which shall forward it to the Commission. The Commission shall send Member States a copy of any complaint it receives. The complaint shall be deemed to have been lodged on the first working day following its delivery to the Commission by registered mail or the issuing of an acknowledgement of receipt by the Commission.

Where, in the absence of any complaint, a Member State is in possession of sufficient evidence of dumping and of resultant injury to the Community industry, it shall immediately communicate such evidence to the Commission.

2. A complaint under paragraph 1 shall include evidence of dumping, injury and a causal link between the allegedly dumped imports and the alleged injury. The complaint shall contain such information as is reasonably available to the complainant on the following:

(a) the identity of the complainant and a description of the volume and value of the Community production of the like product by the complainant. Where a written complaint is made on behalf of the Community industry, the complaint shall identify the industry on behalf of which the complaint is made by a list of all known Community producers of the like product (or associations of Community producers of the like product) and, to the extent possible, a description of the volume and value of Community production of the like product accounted for by such producers;

(b) a complete description of the allegedly dumped product, the names of the country or countries of origin or export in question, the identity of each known exporter or foreign producer and a list of known persons importing the product in question;

(c) information on prices at which the product in question is sold when destined for consumption in the domestic markets of the country or countries of origin or export (or, where appropriate, information on the prices at which the product is sold from the country or countries of origin or export to a third country or countries or on the constructed value of the product) and information on export prices or, where appropriate, on the prices at which the product is first resold to an independent buyer in the Community;

(d) information on changes in the volume of the allegedly dumped imports, the effect of those imports on prices of the like product on the Community market and the consequent impact of the imports on the Community industry, as demonstrated by relevant factors and indices having a bearing on the state of the Community industry, such as those listed in Article 3(3) and (5).

3. The Commission shall, as far as possible, examine the accuracy and adequacy of the evidence provided in the complaint to determine whether there is sufficient evidence to justify the initiation of an investigation.

4. An investigation shall not be initiated pursuant to paragraph 1 unless it has been determined, on the basis of an examination as to the degree of support for, or opposition to, the complaint expressed by Community producers of the like product, that the complaint has been made by or on behalf of the Community industry. The complaint shall be considered to have been made by or on behalf of the Community industry if it is supported by those Community producers whose collective output constitutes more than 50% of the total production of the like product produced by that portion of the Community industry expressing either support for or opposition to the complaint. However, no investigation shall be initiated when Community producers expressly supporting the complaint account for less than 25% of total production of the like product produced by the Community industry.

5. The authorities shall avoid, unless a decision has been made to initiate an investigation, any publicising of the complaint seeking the initiation of an investigation. However, after receipt of a properly documented complaint and before proceeding to initiate an investigation, the government of the exporting country concerned shall be notified.

6. If in special circumstances, it is decided to initiate an investigation without having received a written complaint by or on behalf of the Community industry for the initiation of such investigation, this shall be done on the basis of sufficient evidence of dumping, injury and a causal link, as described in paragraph 2, to justify such initiation.

7. The evidence of both dumping and injury shall be considered simultaneously in the decision on whether or not to initiate an investigation. A complaint shall be rejected where there is insufficient evidence of either dumping or of injury to justify proceeding with the case. Proceedings shall not be initiated against countries whose imports represent a market share of below 1%, unless such countries collectively account for 3% or more of Community consumption.

8. The complaint may be withdrawn prior to initiation, in which case it shall be considered not to have been lodged.

9. Where, after consultation, it is apparent that there is sufficient evidence to justify initiating a proceeding, the Commission shall do so within 45 days of the lodging of the complaint and shall publish a notice in the Official Journal of the European Union. Where insufficient evidence has been presented, the complainant shall, after consultation, be so informed within 45 days of the date on which the complaint is lodged with the Commission.

10. The notice of initiation of the proceedings shall announce the initiation of an investigation, indicate the product and countries concerned, give a summary of the information received, and provide that all relevant information is to be communicated to the Commission; it shall state the periods within which interested parties may make themselves known, present their views in writing and submit information if such views and information are to be taken into account during the investigation; it shall also state the period within which interested parties may apply to be heard by the Commission in accordance with Article 6(5).

11. The Commission shall advise the exporters, importers and representative associations of importers or exporters known to it to be concerned, as well as representatives of the exporting country and the complainants, of the initiation of the proceedings and, with due regard to the protection of confidential information, provide the full text of the written complaint received pursuant to paragraph 1 to the known exporters and to the authorities of the exporting country, and make it available upon request to other interested parties involved. Where the number of exporters involved is particularly high, the full text of the written complaint may instead be provided only to the authorities of the exporting country or to the relevant trade association.

12. An anti-dumping investigation shall not hinder the procedures of customs clearance.

Article 6

The investigation

1. Following the initiation of the proceeding, the Commission, acting in cooperation with the Member States, shall commence an investigation at Community level. Such investigation shall cover both dumping and injury and these shall be investigated simultaneously. For the purpose of a representative finding, an investigation period shall be selected which, in the case of dumping shall, normally, cover a period of no

less than six months immediately prior to the initiation of the proceeding. Information relating to a period subsequent to the investigation period shall, normally, not be taken into account.

2. Parties receiving questionnaires used in an anti-dumping investigation shall be given at least 30 days to reply. The time-limit for exporters shall be counted from the date of receipt of the questionnaire, which for this purpose shall be deemed to have been received one week from the day on which it was sent to the exporter or transmitted to the appropriate diplomatic representative of the exporting country. An extension to the 30 day period may be granted, due account being taken of the time-limits of the investigation, provided that the party shows due cause for such extension, in terms of its particular circumstances.

3. The Commission may request Member States to supply information, and Member States shall take whatever steps are necessary in order to give effect to such requests. They shall send to the Commission the information requested together within the results of all inspections, checks or investigations carried out. Where this information is of general interest or where its transmission has been requested by a Member State, the Commission shall forward it to the Member States, provided it is not confidential, in which case a non-confidential summary shall be forwarded.

4. The Commission may request Member States to carry out all necessary checks and inspections, particularly amongst importers, traders and Community producers, and to carry out investigations in third countries, provided that the firms concerned give their consent and that the government of the country in question has been officially notified and raises no objection. Member States shall take whatever steps are necessary in order to give effect to such requests from the Commission. Officials of the Commission shall be authorised, if the Commission or a Member State so requests, to assist the officials of Member States in carrying out their duties.

5. The interested parties which have made themselves known in accordance with Article 5(10) shall be heard if they have, within the period prescribed in the notice published in the Official Journal of the European Union, made a written request for a hearing showing that they are an interested party likely to be affected by the result of the proceeding and that there are particular reasons why they should be heard.

6. Opportunities shall, on request, be provided for the importers, exporters, representatives of the government of the exporting country and the complainants, which have made themselves known in accordance with Article 5(10), to meet those parties with adverse interests, so that opposing views may be presented and rebuttal arguments offered. Provision of such opportunities must take account of the need to preserve confidentiality and of the convenience to the parties. There shall be no obligation on any party to attend a meeting, and failure to do so shall not be prejudicial to that party's case. Oral information provided under this paragraph shall be taken into account in so far as it is subsequently confirmed in writing.

7. The complainants, importers and exporters and their representative associations, users and consumer organisations, which have made themselves known in accordance with Article 5(10), as well as the representatives of the exporting country may, upon written request, inspect all information made available by any party to an investigation, as distinct from internal documents prepared by the authorities of the Community or

its Member States, which is relevant to the presentation of their cases and not confidential within the meaning of Article 19, and that it is used in the investigation. Such parties may respond to such information and their comments shall be taken into consideration, wherever they are sufficiently substantiated in the response.

8. Except in the circumstances provided for in Article 18, the information which is supplied by interested parties and upon which findings are based shall be examined for accuracy as far as possible.

9. For proceedings initiated pursuant to Article 5(9), an investigation shall, whenever possible, be concluded within one year. In any event, such investigations shall in all cases be concluded within 15 months of initiation, in accordance with the findings made pursuant to Article 8 for undertakings or the findings made pursuant to Article 9 for definitive action.

Article 7

Provisional measures

1. Provisional duties may be imposed if proceedings have been initiated in accordance with Article 5, if a notice has been given to that effect and interested parties have been given adequate opportunities to submit information and make comments in accordance with Article 5(10), if a provisional affirmative determination has been made of dumping and consequent injury to the Community industry, and if the Community interest calls for intervention to prevent such injury. The provisional duties shall be imposed no earlier than 60 days from the initiation of the proceedings but no later than nine months from the initiation of the proceedings.

2. The amount of the provisional anti-dumping duty shall not exceed the margin of dumping as provisionally established, but it should be less than the margin if such lesser duty would be adequate to remove the injury to the Community industry.

3. Provisional duties shall be secured by a guarantee, and the release of the products concerned for free circulation in the Community shall be conditional upon the provision of such guarantee.

4. The Commission shall take provisional action after consultation or, in cases of extreme urgency, after informing the Member States. In this latter case, consultations shall take place 10 days, at the latest, after notification to the Member States of the action taken by the Commission.

5. Where a Member State requests immediate intervention by the Commission and where the conditions in paragraph 1 are met, the Commission shall within a maximum of five working days of receipt of the request, decide whether a provisional anti-dumping duty shall be imposed.

6. The Commission shall forthwith inform the Council and the Member States of any decision taken under paragraphs 1 to 5. The Council, acting by a qualified majority, may decide differently.

7. Provisional duties may be imposed for six months and extended for a further three months or they may be imposed for nine months. However, they may only be extended, or imposed for a nine-month period, where exporters representing a significant percentage of the trade involved so request or do not object upon notification by the Commission.

Article 8

Undertakings

1. Upon condition that a provisional affirmative determination of dumping and injury has been made, the Commission may accept satisfactory voluntary undertaking offers submitted by any exporter to revise its prices or to cease exports at dumped prices, if, after specific consultation of the Advisory Committee, it is satisfied that the injurious effect of the dumping is thereby eliminated. In such a case and as long as such undertakings are in force, provisional duties imposed by the Commission in accordance with Article 7(1) or definitive duties imposed by the Council in accordance with Article 9(4) as the case may be shall not apply to the relevant imports of the product concerned manufactured by the companies referred to in the Commission decision accepting undertakings, as subsequently amended. Price increases under such undertakings shall not be higher than necessary to eliminate the margin of dumping and they should be less than the margin of dumping if such increases would be adequate to remove the injury to the Community industry.

2. Undertakings may be suggested by the Commission, but no exporter shall be obliged to enter into such an undertaking. The fact that exporters do not offer such undertakings, or do not accept an invitation to do so, shall in no way prejudice consideration of the case. However, it may be determined that a threat of injury is more likely to be realised if the dumped imports continue. Undertakings shall not be sought or accepted from exporters unless a provisional affirmative determination of dumping and injury caused by such dumping has been made. Save in exceptional circumstances, undertakings may not be offered later than the end of the period during which representations may be made pursuant to Article 20(5).

3. Undertakings offered need not be accepted if their acceptance is considered impractical, if such as where the number of actual or potential exporters is too great, or for other reasons, including reasons of general policy. The exporter concerned may be provided with the reasons for which it is proposed to reject the offer of an undertaking and may be given an opportunity to make comments thereon. The reasons for rejection shall be set out in the definitive decision.

4. Parties which offer an undertaking shall be required to provide a non-confidential version of such undertaking, so that it may be made available to interested parties to the investigation.

5. Where undertakings are, after consultation, accepted and where there is no objection raised within the Advisory Committee, the investigation shall be terminated. In all other cases, the Commission shall submit to the Council forthwith a report on the results of the consultation, together with a proposal that the investigation be terminated. The investigation shall be deemed terminated if, within one month, the Council, acting by a qualified majority, has not decided otherwise.

6. If the undertakings are accepted, the investigation of dumping and injury shall normally be completed. In such a case, if a negative determination of dumping or injury is made, the undertaking shall automatically lapse, except in cases where such a determination is due in large part to the existence of an undertaking. In such cases it may be required that an undertaking be maintained for a reasonable period. In the event that an affirmative determination of dumping and injury is

made, the undertaking shall continue consistent with its terms and the provisions of this Regulation.

7. The Commission shall require any exporter from which an undertaking has been accepted to provide, periodically, information relevant to the fulfilment of such undertaking, and to permit verification of pertinent data. Non-compliance with such requirements shall be construed as a breach of the undertaking.

8. Where undertakings are accepted from certain exporters during the course of an investigation, they shall, for the purpose of Article 11, be deemed to take effect from the date on which the investigation is concluded for the exporting country.

9. In case of breach or withdrawal of undertakings by any party to the undertaking, or in case of withdrawal of acceptance of the undertaking by the Commission, the acceptance of the undertaking shall, after consultation, be withdrawn by Commission Decision or Commission Regulation, as appropriate, and the provisional duty which has been imposed by the Commission in accordance with Article 7 or the definitive duty which has been imposed by the Council in accordance with Article 9(4) shall automatically apply, provided that the exporter concerned has, except where he himself has withdrawn the undertaking, been given an opportunity to comment.

Any interested party or Member State may submit information showing prima facie evidence of a breach of an undertaking. The subsequent assessment of whether or not a breach of an undertaking has occurred shall normally be concluded within six months, but in no case later than nine months following a duly substantiated request. The Commission may request the assistance of the competent authorities of the Member States in the monitoring of undertakings.

10. A provisional duty may, after consultation, be imposed in accordance with Article 7 on the basis of the best information available, where there is reason to believe that an undertaking is being breached, or in case of breach or withdrawal of an undertaking where the investigation which led to the undertaking has not been concluded.

Article 9

Termination without measures; imposition of definitive duties

1. Where the complaint is withdrawn, the proceeding may be terminated unless such termination would not be in the Community interest.

2. Where, after consultation, protective measures are unnecessary and there is no objection raised within the Advisory Committee, the investigation or proceeding shall be terminated. In all other cases, the Commission shall submit to the Council forthwith a report on the results of the consultation, together with a proposal that the proceeding be terminated. The proceeding shall be deemed terminated if, within one month, the Council, acting by a qualified majority, has not decided otherwise.

3. For a proceeding initiated pursuant to Article 5(9), injury shall normally be regarded as negligible where the imports concerned represent less than the volumes set out in Article 5(7). For the same proceeding, there shall be immediate termination where it is determined that the margin of dumping is less than 2%, expressed as a percentage of the export price, provided that it is only the investigation that shall be terminated where the margin is below 2% for individual exporters and they shall remain subject to

the proceeding and may be reinvestigated in any subsequent review carried out for the country concerned pursuant to Article 11.

4. Where the facts as finally established show that there is dumping and injury caused thereby, and the Community interest calls for intervention in accordance with Article 21, a definitive anti-dumping duty shall be imposed by the Council, acting on a proposal submitted by the Commission after consultation of the Advisory Committee. The proposal shall be adopted by the Council unless it decides by a simple majority to reject the proposal, within a period of one month after its submission by the Commission. Where provisional duties are in force, a proposal for definitive action shall be submitted no later than one month before the expiry of such duties. The amount of the anti-dumping duty shall not exceed the margin of dumping established but it should be less than the margin if such lesser duty would be adequate to remove the injury to the Community industry.

5. An anti-dumping duty shall be imposed in the appropriate amounts in each case, on a non-discriminatory basis on imports of a product from all sources found to be dumped and causing injury, except for imports from those sources from which undertakings under the terms of this Regulation have been accepted. The Regulation imposing the duty shall specify the duty for each supplier or, if that is impracticable, and in general where Article 2(7)(a) applies, the supplying country concerned.

Where Article 2(7)(a) applies, an individual duty shall, however, be specified for the exporters which can demonstrate, on the basis of properly substantiated claims that:

(a) in the case of wholly or partly foreign owned firms or joint ventures, exporters are free to repatriate capital and profits;

(b) export prices and quantities, and conditions and terms of sale are freely determined;

(c) the majority of the shares belong to private persons; state officials appearing on the board of directors or holding key management positions shall either be in minority or it must be demonstrated that the company is nonetheless sufficiently independent from State interference;

(d) exchange rate conversions are carried out at the market rate; and

(e) State interference is not such as to permit circumvention of measures if individual exporters are given different rates of duty.

6. When the Commission has limited its examination in accordance with Article 17, any anti-dumping duty applied to imports from exporters or producers which have made themselves known in accordance with Article 17 but were not included in the examination shall not exceed the weighted average margin of dumping established for the parties in the sample. For the purpose of this paragraph, the Commission shall disregard any zero and de minimis margins, and margins established in the circumstances referred to in Article 18. Individual duties shall be applied to imports from any exporter or producer which is granted individual treatment, as provided for in Article 17.

Article 10

Retroactivity

1. Provisional measures and definitive anti-dumping duties shall only be applied to products which enter free circulation after the time when the decision taken pursuant

to Article 7(1) or 9(4), as the case may be, enters into force, subject to the exceptions set out in this Regulation.

2. Where a provisional duty has been applied and the facts as finally established show that there is dumping and injury, the Council shall decide, irrespective of whether a definitive anti-dumping duty is to be imposed, what proportion of the provisional duty is to be definitively collected. For this purpose, 'injury' shall not include material retardation of the establishment of a Community industry, nor threat of material injury, except where it is found that this would, in the absence of provisional measures, have developed into material injury. In all other cases involving such threat or retardation, any provisional amounts shall be released and definitive duties can only be imposed from the date that a final determination of threat or material retardation is made.

3. If the definitive anti-dumping duty is higher than the provisional duty, the difference shall not be collected. If the definitive duty is lower than the provisional duty, the duty shall be recalculated. Where a final determination is negative, the provisional duty shall not be confirmed.

4. A definitive anti-dumping duty may be levied on products which were entered for consumption no more than 90 days prior to the date of application of provisional measures but not prior to the initiation of the investigation, provided that imports have been registered in accordance with Article 14(5), the Commission has allowed the importers concerned an opportunity to comment, and:

(a) there is, for the product in question, a history of dumping over an extended period, or the importer was aware of, or should have been aware of, the dumping as regards the extent of the dumping and the injury alleged or found; and

(b) in addition to the level of imports which caused injury during the investigation period, there is a further substantial rise in imports which, in the light of its timing and volume and other circumstances, is likely to seriously undermine the remedial effect of the definitive anti-dumping duty to be applied.

5. In cases of breach or withdrawal of undertakings, definitive duties may be levied on goods entered for free circulation no more than 90 days before the application of provisional measures, provided that imports have been registered in accordance with Article 14(5), and that any such retroactive assessment shall not apply to imports entered before the breach or withdrawal of the undertaking.

Article 11

Duration, reviews and refunds

1. An anti-dumping measure shall remain in force only as long as, and to the extent that, it is necessary to counteract the dumping which is causing injury.

2. A definitive anti-dumping measure shall expire five years from its imposition or five years from the date of the conclusion of the most recent review which has covered both dumping and injury, unless it is determined in a review that the expiry would be likely to lead to a continuation or recurrence of dumping and injury. Such an expiry review shall be initiated on the initiative of the Commission, or upon request made by or on behalf of Community producers, and the measure shall remain in force pending the outcome of such review.

An expiry review shall be initiated where the request contains sufficient evidence that the expiry of the measures would be likely to result in a continuation or recurrence of dumping and injury. Such likelihood may, for example, be indicated by evidence of continued dumping and injury or evidence that the removal of injury is partly or solely due to the existence of measures or evidence that the circumstances of the exporters, or market conditions, are such that they would indicate the likelihood of further injurious dumping.

In carrying out investigations under this paragraph, the exporters, importers, the representatives of the exporting country and the Community producers shall be provided with the opportunity to amplify, rebut or comment on the matters set out in the review request, and conclusions shall be reached with due account taken of all relevant and duly documented evidence presented in relation to the question as to whether the expiry of measures would be likely, or unlikely, to lead to the continuation or recurrence of dumping and injury.

A notice of impending expiry shall be published in the Official Journal of the European Union at an appropriate time in the final year of the period of application of the measures as defined in this paragraph. Thereafter, the Community producers shall, no later than three months before the end of the five-year period, be entitled to lodge a review request in accordance with the second subparagraph. A notice announcing the actual expiry of measures pursuant to this paragraph shall also be published.

3. The need for the continued imposition of measures may also be reviewed, where warranted, on the initiative of the Commission or at the request of a Member State or, provided that a reasonable period of time of at least one year has elapsed since the imposition of the definitive measure, upon a request by any exporter or importer or by the Community producers which contains sufficient evidence substantiating the need for such an interim review.

An interim review shall be initiated where the request contains sufficient evidence that the continued imposition of the measure is no longer necessary to offset dumping and/or that the injury would be unlikely to continue or recur if the measure were removed or varied, or that the existing measure is not, or is no longer, sufficient to counteract the dumping which is causing injury.

In carrying out investigations pursuant to this paragraph, the Commission may, inter alia, consider whether the circumstances with regard to dumping and injury have changed significantly, or whether existing measures are achieving the intended results in removing the injury previously established under Article 3. In these respects, account shall be taken in the final determination of all relevant and duly documented evidence.

4. A review shall also be carried out for the purpose of determining individual margins of dumping for new exporters in the exporting country in question which have not exported the product during the period of investigation on which the measures were based.

The review shall be initiated where a new exporter or producer can show that it is not related to any of the exporters or producers in the exporting country which are subject to the anti-dumping measures on the product, and that it has actually exported to the Community following the investigation period, or where it can demonstrate that it has entered into an irrevocable contractual obligation to export a significant quantity to the Community.

A review for a new exporter shall be initiated, and carried out on an accelerated basis, after consultation of the Advisory Committee and after Community producers have been given an opportunity to comment. The Commission regulation initiating a review shall repeal the duty in force with regard to the new exporter concerned by amending the Regulation which has imposed such duty, and by making imports subject to registration in accordance with Article 14(5) in order to ensure that, should the review result in a determination of dumping in respect of such an exporter, anti-dumping duties can be levied retroactively to the date of the initiation of the review.

The provisions of this paragraph shall not apply where duties have been imposed under Article 9(6).

5. The relevant provisions of this Regulation with regard to procedures and the conduct of investigations, excluding those relating to time-limits, shall apply to any review carried out pursuant to paragraphs 2, 3 and 4. Reviews carried out pursuant to paragraphs 2 and 3 shall be carried out expeditiously and shall normally be concluded within 12 months of the date of initiation of the review. In any event, reviews pursuant to paragraphs 2 and 3 shall in all cases be concluded within 15 months of initiation. Reviews pursuant to paragraph 4 shall in all cases be concluded within nine months of the date of initiation. If a review carried out pursuant to paragraph 2 is initiated while a review under paragraph 3 is ongoing in the same proceeding, the review pursuant to paragraph 3 shall be concluded at the same time as the review pursuant to paragraph 2.

The Commission shall submit a proposal for action to the Council no later than one month before the expiry of the deadlines specified in the first subparagraph.

If the investigation is not completed within the deadlines specified in the first subparagraph, the measures shall:

– expire in investigations pursuant to paragraph 2,

– expire in the case of investigations carried out pursuant to paragraphs 2 and 3 in parallel, where either the investigation pursuant to paragraph 2 was initiated while a review under paragraph 3 was ongoing in the same proceeding or where such reviews were initiated at the same time, or

– remain unchanged in investigations pursuant to paragraphs 3 and 4.

A notice announcing the actual expiry or maintenance of the measures pursuant to this paragraph shall then be published in the Official Journal of the European Union.

6. Reviews pursuant to this Article shall be initiated by the Commission after consultation of the Advisory Committee. Where warranted by reviews, measures shall be repealed or maintained pursuant to paragraph 2, or repealed, maintained or amended pursuant to paragraphs 3 and 4, by the Community institution responsible for their introduction. Where measures are repealed for individual exporters, but not for the country as a whole, such exporters shall remain subject to the proceeding and may, automatically, be reinvestigated in any subsequent review carried out for that country pursuant to this Article.

7. Where a review of measures pursuant to paragraph 3 is in progress at the end of the period of application of measures as defined in paragraph 2, such review shall also cover the circumstances set out in paragraph 2.

8. Notwithstanding paragraph 2, an importer may request reimbursement of duties collected where it is shown that the dumping margin, on the basis of which duties were paid, has been eliminated, or reduced to a level which is below the level of the duty in force.

In requesting a refund of anti-dumping duties, the importer shall submit an application to the Commission. The application shall be submitted via the Member State of the territory in which the products were released for free circulation, within six months of the date on which the amount of the definitive duties to be levied was duly determined by the competent authorities or of the date on which a decision was made definitively to collect the amounts secured by way of provisional duty. Member States shall forward the request to the Commission forthwith.

An application for refund shall only be considered to be duly supported by evidence where it contains precise information on the amount of refund of anti-dumping duties claimed and all customs documentation relating to the calculation and payment of such amount. It shall also include evidence, for a representative period, of normal values and export prices to the Community for the exporter or producer to which the duty applies. In cases where the importer is not associated with the exporter or producer concerned and such information is not immediately available, or where the exporter or producer is unwilling to release it to the importer, the application shall contain a statement from the exporter or producer that the dumping margin has been reduced or eliminated, as specified in this Article, and that the relevant supporting evidence will be provided to the Commission. Where such evidence is not forthcoming from the exporter or producer within a reasonable period of time the application shall be rejected.

The Commission shall, after consultation of the Advisory Committee, decide whether and to what extent the application should be granted, or it may decide at any time to initiate an interim review, whereupon the information and findings from such review carried out in accordance with the provisions applicable for such reviews, shall be used to determine whether and to what extent a refund is justified. Refunds of duties shall normally take place within 12 months, and in no circumstances more than 18 months after the date on which a request for a refund, duly supported by evidence, has been made by an importer of the product subject to the anti-dumping duty. The payment of any refund authorised should normally be made by Member States within 90 days of the Commission's decision.

9. In all review or refund investigations carried out pursuant to this Article, the Commission shall, provided that circumstances have not changed, apply the same methodology as in the investigation which led to the duty, with due account being taken of Article 2, and in particular paragraphs 11 and 12 thereof, and of Article 17.

10. In any investigation carried our pursuant to this Article, the Commission shall examine the reliability of export prices in accordance with Article 2. However, where it is decided to construct the export price in accordance with Article 2(9), it shall calculate it with no deduction for the amount of anti-dumping duties paid when conclusive evidence is provided that the duty is duly reflected in resale prices and the subsequent selling prices in the Community.

Article 12

Reinvestigation

1. Where the Community industry or any other interested party submit, normally within two years from the entry into force of the measures, sufficient information showing that, after the original investigation period and prior to or following the imposition of measures, export prices have decreased or that there has been no movement, or insufficient movement in the resale prices or subsequent selling prices of the imported product in the Community, the investigation may, after consultation, be reopened to examine whether the measure has had effects on the above-mentioned prices.

The investigation may also be reopened, under the conditions set out above, at the initiative of the Commission or at the request of a Member State.

2. During a reinvestigation pursuant to this Article, exporters, importers and Community producers shall be provided with an opportunity to clarify the situation with regard to resale prices and subsequent selling prices: if it is concluded that the measure should have led to movements in such prices, then, in order to remove the injury previously established in accordance with Article 3, export prices shall be reassessed in accordance with Article 2 and dumping margins shall be recalculated to take account of the reassessed export prices.

Where it is considered that the conditions of Article 12(1) are met due to a fall in export prices which has occurred after the original investigation period and prior to or following the imposition of measures, dumping margins may be recalculated to take account of such lower export prices.

3. Where a reinvestigation pursuant to this Article shows increased dumping, the measures in force may, after consultation, be amended by the Council, acting on a proposal from the Commission in accordance with the new findings on export prices. The proposal shall be adopted by the Council unless it decides by a simple majority to reject the proposal, within a period of one month after its submission by the Commission. The amount of the anti-dumping duty imposed pursuant to this Article shall not exceed twice the amount of the duty imposed initially by the Council.

4. The relevant provisions of Articles 5 and 6 shall apply to any reinvestigation carried out pursuant to this Article, except that such reinvestigation shall be carried out expeditiously and shall normally be concluded within six months of the date of initiation of the reinvestigation. In any event, such reinvestigations shall in all cases be concluded within nine months of initiation of the reinvestigation.

The Commission shall submit a proposal for action to the Council no later than one month before the expiry of the deadlines specified in the first subparagraph.

If the reinvestigation is not completed within the deadlines specified in the first subparagraph, measures shall remain unchanged. A notice announcing the maintenance of the measures pursuant to this paragraph shall be published in the Official Journal of the European Union.

5. Alleged changes in normal value shall only be taken into account under this Article where complete information on revised normal values, duly substantiated by evidence, is made available to the Commission within the time-limits set out in the notice of

initiation of an investigation. Where an investigation involves a re-examination of normal values, imports may be made subject to registration in accordance with Article 14(5) pending the outcome of the reinvestigation.

Article 13

Circumvention

1. Anti-dumping duties imposed pursuant to this Regulation may be extended to imports from third countries, of the like product, whether slightly modified or not, or to imports of the slightly modified like product from the country subject to measures, or parts thereof, when circumvention of the measures in force is taking place. Anti-dumping duties not exceeding the residual anti-dumping duty imposed in accordance with Article 9(5) may be extended to imports from companies benefiting from individual duties in the countries subject to measures when circumvention of the measures in force is taking place. Circumvention shall be defined as a change in the pattern of trade between third countries and the Community or between individual companies in the country subject to measures and the Community, which stems from a practice, process or work for which there is insufficient due cause or economic justification other than the imposition of the duty, and where there is evidence of injury or that the remedial effects of the duty are being undermined in terms of the prices and/or quantities of the like product, and where there is evidence of dumping in relation to the normal values previously established for the like product, if necessary in accordance with the provisions of Article 2.

The practice, process or work referred to in the first subparagraph includes, inter alia, the slight modification of the product concerned to make it fall under customs codes which are normally not subject to the measures, provided that the modification does not alter its essential characteristics, the consignment of the product subject to measures via third countries, the reorganisation by exporters or producers of their patterns and channels of sales in the country subject to measures in order to eventually have their products exported to the Community through producers benefiting from an individual duty rate lower than that applicable to the products of the manufacturers, and, in the circumstances indicated in paragraph 2, the assembly of parts by an assembly operation in the Community or a third country.

2. An assembly operation in the Community or a third country shall be considered to circumvent the measures in force where:

(a) the operation started or substantially increased since, or just prior to, the initiation of the anti-dumping investigation and the parts concerned are from the country subject to measures, and

(b) the parts constitute 60% or more of the total value of the parts of the assembled product, except that in no case shall circumvention be considered to be taking place where the value added to the parts brought in, during the assembly or completion operation, is greater than 25% of the manufacturing cost, and

(c) the remedial effects of the duty are being undermined in terms of the prices and/or quantities of the assembled like product and there is evidence of dumping in relation to the normal values previously established for the like or similar products.

3. Investigations shall be initiated pursuant to this Article on the initiative of the Commission or at the request of a Member State or any interested party on the basis of sufficient evidence regarding the factors set out in paragraph 1. Initiations shall be made, after consultation of the Advisory Committee, by Commission Regulation which may also instruct the customs authorities to make imports subject to registration in accordance with Article 14(5) or to request guarantees. Investigations shall be carried out by the Commission, which may be assisted by customs authorities and shall be concluded within nine months. When the facts as finally ascertained justify the extension of measures, this shall be done by the Council, acting on a proposal submitted by the Commission, after consultation of the Advisory Committee. The proposal shall be adopted by the Council unless it decides by a simple majority to reject the proposal, within a period of one month after its submission by the Commission. The extension shall take effect from the date on which registration was imposed pursuant to Article 14(5) or on which guarantees were requested. The relevant procedural provisions of this Regulation with regard to initiations and the conduct of investigations shall apply pursuant to this Article.

4. Imports shall not be subject to registration pursuant to Article 14(5) or measures where they are traded by companies which benefit from exemptions. Requests for exemptions duly supported by evidence shall be submitted within the time-limits established in the Commission regulation initiating the investigation. Where the circumventing practice, process or work takes place outside the Community, exemptions may be granted to producers of the product concerned that can show that they are not related to any producer subject to the measures and that are found not to be engaged in circumvention practices as defined in paragraphs 1 and 2 of this Article. Where the circumventing practice, process or work takes place inside the Community, exemptions may be granted to importers that can show that they are not related to producers subject to the measures.

These exemptions shall be granted by decision of the Commission after consultation of the Advisory Committee or decision of the Council imposing measures and shall remain valid for the period and under the conditions set down therein.

Provided that the conditions set in Article 11(4) are met, exemptions may also be granted after the conclusion of the investigation leading to the extension of the measures.

Provided that at least one year has lapsed from the extension of the measures, and in case the number of parties requesting or potentially requesting an exemption is significant, the Commission may decide to initiate a review of the extension of the measures. Any such review shall be conducted in accordance with the provisions of Article 11(5) as applicable to reviews pursuant to Article 11(3).

5. Nothing in this Article shall preclude the normal application of the provisions in force concerning customs duties.

Article 14

General provisions

1. Provisional or definitive anti-dumping duties shall be imposed by Regulation, and collected by Member States in the form, at the rate specified and according to the other criteria laid down in the Regulation imposing such duties. Such duties shall also

be collected independently of the customs duties, taxes and other charges normally imposed on imports. No product shall be subject to both anti-dumping and counter-vailing duties for the purpose of dealing with one and the same situation arising from dumping or from export subsidisation.

2. Regulations imposing provisional or definitive anti-dumping duties, and regulations or decisions accepting undertakings or terminating investigations or proceedings, shall be published in the Official Journal of the European Union. Such regulations or deci-sions shall contain in particular and with due regard to the protection of confidential information, the names of the exporters, if possible, or of the countries involved, a description of the product and a summary of the material facts and considerations rel-evant to the dumping and injury determinations. In each case, a copy of the regulation or decision shall be sent to known interested parties. The provisions of this paragraph shall apply mutatis mutandis to reviews.

3. Special provisions, in particular with regard to the common definition of the con-cept of origin, as contained in Council Regulation (EEC) No 2913/92 of 12 October 1992 establishing the Community Customs Code, may be adopted pursuant to this Regulation.

4. In the Community interest, measures imposed pursuant to this Regulation may, after consultation of the Advisory Committee, be suspended by a decision of the Commission for a period of nine months. The suspension may be extended for a fur-ther period, not exceeding one year, if the Council so decides, acting on a proposal from the Commission. The proposal shall be adopted by the Council unless it decides by a simple majority to reject the proposal, within a period of one month after its sub-mission by the Commission. Measures may only be suspended where market condi-tions have temporarily changed to an extent that injury would be unlikely to resume as a result of the suspension, and provided that the Community industry has been given an opportunity to comment and these comments have been taken into account. Measures may, at any time and after consultation, be reinstated if the reason for sus-pension is no longer applicable.

5. The Commission may, after consultation of the Advisory Committee, direct the cus-toms authorities to take the appropriate steps to register imports, so that measures may subsequently be applied against those imports from the date of such registration. Imports may be made subject to registration following a request from the Community industry which contains sufficient evidence to justify such action. Registration shall be introduced by regulation which shall specify the purpose of the action and, if appropri-ate, the estimated amount of possible future liability. Imports shall not be made subject to registration for a period longer than nine months.

6. Member States shall report to the Commission every month, on the import trade in products subject to investigation and to measures, and on the amount of duties col-lected pursuant to this Regulation.

7. Without prejudice to paragraph 6, the Commission may request Member States, on a case-by-case basis, to supply information necessary to monitor efficiently the appli-cation of measures. In this respect, the provisions of Article 6(3) and (4) shall apply. Any data submitted by Member States pursuant to this Article shall be covered by the provisions of Article 19(6).

Article 15

Consultations

1. Any consultations provided for in this Regulation shall take place within an Advisory Committee, which shall consist of representatives of each Member State, with a representative of the Commission as chairman. Consultations shall be held immediately at the request of a Member State or on the initiative of the Commission and in any event within a period which allows the time-limits set by this Regulation to be adhered to.

2. The Committee shall meet when convened by its chairman. He shall provide the Member States, as promptly as possible, but no later than 10 working days before the meeting, with all relevant information.

3. Where necessary, consultation may be in writing only; in that event, the Commission shall notify the Member States and shall specify a period within which they shall be entitled to express their opinions or to request an oral consultation which the chairman shall arrange, provided that such oral consultation can be held within a period which allows the time-limits set by this Regulation to be adhered to.

4. Consultation shall cover, in particular:

(a) the existence of dumping and the methods of establishing the dumping margin;

(b) the existence and extent of injury;

(c) the causal link between the dumped imports and injury;

(d) the measures which, in the circumstances, are appropriate to prevent or remedy the injury caused by dumping and the ways and means of putting such measures into effect.

Article 16

Verification visits

1. The Commission shall, where it considers it appropriate, carry out visits to examine the records of importers, exporters, traders, agents, producers, trade associations and organisations and to verify information provided on dumping and injury. In the absence of a proper and timely reply, a verification visit may not be carried out.

2. The Commission may carry out investigations in third countries as required, provided that it obtains the agreement of the firms concerned, that it notifies the representatives of the government of the country in question and that the latter does not object to the investigation. As soon as the agreement of the firms concerned has been obtained the Commission should notify the authorities of the exporting country of the names and addresses of the firms to be visited and the dates agreed.

3. The firms concerned shall be advised of the nature of the information to be verified during verification visits and of any further information which needs to be provided during such visits, though this should not preclude requests made during the verification for further details to be provided in the light of information obtained.

4. In investigations carried out pursuant to paragraphs 1, 2 and 3, the Commission shall be assisted by officials of those Member States who so request.

Article 17

Sampling

1. In cases where the number of complainants, exporters or importers, types of product or transactions is large, the investigation may be limited to a reasonable number

of parties, products or transactions by using samples which are statistically valid on the basis of information available at the time of the selection, or to the largest representative volume of production, sales or exports which can reasonably be investigated within the time available.

2. The final selection of parties, types of products or transactions made under these sampling provisions shall rest with the Commission, though preference shall be given to choosing a sample in consultation with, and with the consent of, the parties concerned, provided such parties make themselves known and make sufficient information available, within three weeks of initiation of the investigation, to enable a representative sample to be chosen.

3. In cases where the examination has been limited in accordance with this Article, an individual margin of dumping shall, nevertheless, be calculated for any exporter or producer not initially selected who submits the necessary information within the time-limits provided for in this Regulation, except where the number of exporters or producers is so large that individual examinations would be unduly burdensome and would prevent completion of the investigation in good time.

4. Where it is decided to sample and there is a degree of non-cooperation by some or all of the parties selected which is likely to materially affect the outcome of the investigation, a new sample may be selected. However, if a material degree of non-cooperation persists or there is insufficient time to select a new sample, the relevant provisions of Article 18 shall apply.

Article 18

Non-cooperation

1. In cases in which any interested party refuses access to, or otherwise does not provide, necessary information within the time-limits provided in this Regulation, or significantly impedes the investigation, provisional or final findings, affirmative or negative, may be made on the basis of the facts available. Where it is found that any interested party has supplied false or misleading information, the information shall be disregarded and use may be made of facts available. Interested parties should be made aware of the consequences of non-cooperation.

2. Failure to give a computerised response shall not be deemed to constitute non-cooperation, provided that the interested party shows that presenting the response as requested would result in an unreasonable extra burden or unreasonable additional cost.

3. Where the information submitted by an interested party is not ideal in all respects it should nevertheless not be disregarded, provided that any deficiencies are not such as to cause undue difficulty in arriving at a reasonably accurate finding and that the information is appropriately submitted in good time and is verifiable, and that the party has acted to the best of its ability.

4. If evidence or information is not accepted, the supplying party shall be informed forthwith of the reasons therefor and shall be granted an opportunity to provide further explanations within the time-limit specified. If the explanations are considered unsatisfactory, the reasons for rejection of such evidence or information shall be disclosed and given in published findings.

5. If determinations, including those regarding normal value, are based on the provisions of paragraph 1, including the information supplied in the complaint, it shall, where practicable and with due regard to the time-limits of the investigation, be checked by reference to information from other independent sources which may be available, such as published price lists, official import statistics and customs returns, or information obtained from other interested parties during the investigation.

Such information may include relevant data pertaining to the world market or other representative markets, where appropriate.

6. If an interested party does not cooperate, or cooperates only partially, so that relevant information is thereby withheld, the result may be less favourable to the party than if it had cooperated.

Article 19

Confidentiality

1. Any information which is by nature confidential (for example, because its disclosure would be of significant competitive advantage to a competitor or would have a significantly adverse effect upon a person supplying the information or upon a person from whom he has acquired the information) or which is provided on a confidential basis by parties to an investigation, shall, if good cause is shown, be treated as such by the authorities.

2. Interested parties providing confidential information shall be required to furnish non-confidential summaries thereof. Those summaries shall be in sufficient detail to permit a reasonable understanding of the substance of the information submitted in confidence. In exceptional circumstances, such parties may indicate that such information is not susceptible of summary. In such exceptional circumstances, a statement of the reasons why such summary is not possible must be provided.

3. If it is considered that a request for confidentiality is not warranted and if the supplier of the information is either unwilling to make the information available or to authorise its disclosure in generalised or summary form, such information may be disregarded unless it can be satisfactorily demonstrated from appropriate sources that the information is correct. Requests for confidentiality shall not be arbitrarily rejected.

4. This Article shall not preclude the disclosure of general information by the Community authorities and in particular of the reasons on which decisions taken pursuant to this Regulation are based, or disclosure of the evidence relied on by the Community authorities in so far as is necessary to explain those reasons in court proceedings. Such disclosure must take into account the legitimate interests of the parties concerned that their business secrets should not be divulged.

5. The Council, the Commission and Member States, or the officials of any of these, shall not reveal any information received pursuant to this Regulation for which confidential treatment has been requested by its supplier, without specific permission from the supplier. Exchanges of information between the Commission and Member States, or any information relating to consultations made pursuant to Article 15, or any internal documents prepared by the authorities of the Community or its Member States, shall not be divulged except as specifically provided for in this Regulation.

6. Information received pursuant to this Regulation shall be used only for the purpose for which it was requested. This provision shall not preclude the use of information received in the context of one investigation for the purpose of initiating other investigations within the same proceeding in relation to the product concerned.

Article 20

Disclosure

1. The complainants, importers and exporters and their representative associations, and representatives of the exporting country, may request disclosure of the details underlying the essential facts and considerations on the basis of which provisional measures have been imposed. Requests for such disclosure shall be made in writing immediately following the imposition of provisional measures, and the disclosure shall be made in writing as soon as possible thereafter.

2. The parties mentioned in paragraph 1 may request final disclosure of the essential facts and considerations on the basis of which it is intended to recommend the imposition of definitive measures, or the termination of an investigation or proceedings without the imposition of measures, particular attention being paid to the disclosure of any facts or considerations which are different from those used for any provisional measures.

3. Requests for final disclosure, as defined in paragraph 2, shall be addressed to the Commission in writing and be received, in cases where a provisional duty has been applied, no later than one month after publication of the imposition of that duty. Where a provisional duty has not been applied, parties shall be provided with an opportunity to request final disclosure within time-limits set by the Commission.

4. Final disclosure shall be given in writing. It shall be made, due regard being had to the protection of confidential information, as soon as possible and, normally, no later than one month prior to a definitive decision or the submission by the Commission of any proposal for final action pursuant to Article 9. Where the Commission is not in a position to disclose certain facts or considerations at that time, these shall be disclosed as soon as possible thereafter. Disclosure shall not prejudice any subsequent decision which may be taken by the Commission or the Council but where such decision is based on any different facts and considerations, these shall be disclosed as soon as possible.

5. Representations made after final disclosure is given shall be taken into consideration only if received within a period to be set by the Commission in each case, which shall be at least 10 days, due consideration being given to the urgency of the matter.

Article 21

Community interest

1. A determination as to whether the Community interest calls for intervention shall be based on an appreciation of all the various interests taken as a whole, including the interests of the domestic industry and users and consumers, and a determination pursuant to this Article shall only be made where all parties have been given the opportunity to make their views known pursuant to paragraph 2. In such an examination, the need to eliminate the trade distorting effects of injurious dumping and to restore effective competition shall be given special consideration. Measures, as determined on

the basis of the dumping and injury found, may not be applied where the authorities, on the basis of all the information submitted, can clearly conclude that it is not in the Community interest to apply such measures.

2. In order to provide a sound basis on which the authorities can take account of all views and information in the decision as to whether or not the imposition of measures is in the Community interest, the complainants, importers and their representative associations, representative users and representative consumer organisations may, within the time-limits specified in the notice of initiation of the anti-dumping investigation, make themselves known and provide information to the Commission. Such information, or appropriate summaries thereof, shall be made available to the other parties specified in this Article, and they shall be entitled to respond to such information.

3. The parties which have acted in conformity with paragraph 2 may request a hearing. Such requests shall be granted when they are submitted within the time-limits set in paragraph 2, and when they set out the reasons, in terms of the Community interest, why the parties should be heard.

4. The parties which have acted in conformity with paragraph 2 may provide comments on the application of any provisional duties imposed. Such comments shall be received within one month of the application of such measures if they are to be taken into account and they, or appropriate summaries thereof, shall be made available to other parties who shall be entitled to respond to such comments.

5. The Commission shall examine the information which is properly submitted and the extent to which it is representative and the results of such analysis, together with an opinion on its merits, shall be transmitted to the Advisory Committee. The balance of views expressed in the Committee shall be taken into account by the Commission in any proposal made pursuant to Article 9.

6. The parties which have acted in conformity with paragraph 2 may request the facts and considerations on which final decisions are likely to be taken to be made available to them. Such information shall be made available to the extent possible and without prejudice to any subsequent decision taken by the Commission or the Council.

7. Information shall only be taken into account where it is supported by actual evidence which substantiates its validity.

Article 22

Final provisions

This Regulation shall not preclude the application of:

(a) any special rules laid down in agreements concluded between the Community and third countries;

(b) the Community Regulations in the agricultural sector and Council Regulation (EC) No 3448/93 of 6 December 1993 laying down the trade arrangements applicable to certain goods resulting from the processing of agricultural products, Council Regulation (EC) No 1667/2006 of 7 November 2006 on glucose and lactose and Council Regulation (EEC) No 2783/75 of the Council of 29 October 1975 on the common system of trade for ovalbumin and lactalbumin. This Regulation shall operate by way of complement to those Regulations and in derogation from any provisions thereof which preclude the application of anti-dumping duties;

(c) special measures, provided that such action does not run counter to obligations pursuant to the GATT.

Article 23

Repeal

Regulation (EC) No 384/96 is repealed.

However, the repeal of Regulation (EC) No 384/96 shall not prejudice the validity of proceedings initiated thereunder.

References to the repealed Regulation shall be construed as references to this Regulation and shall be read in accordance with the correlation table in Annex II.

Article 24

Entry into force

This Regulation shall enter into force on the twentieth day following its publication in the Official Journal of the European Union.

This Regulation shall be binding in its entirety and directly applicable in all Member States.

Council Regulation (EC) No 85/2006 of 17 January 2006 imposing a definitive anti-dumping duty and collecting definitively the provisional duty imposed on imports of farmed salmon originating in Norway, Official Journal L 15, 20.1.2006, pp. 1–23.

This is the anti-dumping regulation that succeeded the safeguard measures against Norwegian farmed salmon. It was considered equally dubious as to its conformity with the ADA, not only by Norway, but also by certain Member States. However, a simple majority for rejection of the Commission proposal could obviously not be mustered under Article 9(4) of the basic anti-dumping regulation. Norway again started a WTO dispute settlement procedure (DS 337, request for consultations 27 March 2006). On 15 January 2008 the WTO Dispute Settlement Body adopted the Panel report that was broadly negative for the Community. Shortly afterward the EU announced that it would not appeal the report and intended to implement it. The period of time allowed for that according to an agreement between the parties expired on 15 November 2008. Before then the Commission, however, had started a partial interim review of the anti-dumping duties at the request of a number of Member States, which resulted in a repeal of the anti-dumping duties for the products concerned. The relevant regulation is also included below.

THE COUNCIL OF THE EUROPEAN UNION,

Having regard to the Treaty establishing the European Community,

Having regard to Council Regulation (EC) No 384/96 of 22 December 1995 on protection against dumped imports from countries not members of the European Community (the basic Regulation), and in particular Article 9 thereof,

Having regard to the proposal submitted by the Commission after consulting the Advisory Committee,

Whereas:

1. PROCEDURE

1.1. Provisional measures

(1) Following the initiation of an anti-dumping investigation on 23 October 2004, the Commission, by Regulation (EC) No 628/2005, imposed provisional anti-dumping duties on imports of farmed salmon originating in Norway (Regulation imposing a provisional anti-dumping duty or provisional Regulation). The provisional anti-dumping duties which took the form of ad valorem duties ranging between 6.8% and 24.5% for the imported products applied as of 27 April 2005.

(2) On 1 July 2005, by Regulation (EC) No 1010/2005 (amending Regulation), the Commission changed the form of the provisional measures by replacing the ad valorem duties by a minimum import price (MIP) of EUR 2.81 per kilogram whole fish equivalent (WFE) and extended the duration of the provisional measures for a further three months, by amending the Regulation imposing a provisional anti-dumping duty.

1.2. Subsequent procedure

(3) Following the publication of the Regulation imposing a provisional anti-dumping duty, parties received disclosure of facts and considerations on which the provisional Regulation was based. Some parties submitted comments in writing. All interested parties who so requested were granted an opportunity to be heard by the Commission.

(4) Following the publication of the amending Regulation, all parties were informed of the essential facts and considerations on which the amendment of the provisional Regulation was based. Some parties submitted comments in writing. All interested parties who so requested were granted an opportunity to be heard by the Commission.

(5) Similarly, all parties were informed of the essential facts and considerations on the basis of which it is intended to recommend the imposition of definitive anti-dumping measures and the modalities on the collection of amounts secured by way of provisional duties. They were also granted a period within which to make representations subsequent to this disclosure.

(6) The oral and written comments submitted by the interested parties were considered and, where appropriate, taken into account for the definitive findings.

(7) The Commission continued to seek all information it deemed necessary for the purpose of its definitive findings. In addition to the verification visits undertaken at the premises of the companies mentioned in recital 7 of the Regulation imposing a provisional anti-dumping duty, it should be noted that after the imposition of provisional measures, additional on-spot visits were carried out at the premises of the following Community users and associations of Community users:

[…]

3. DUMPING

[…]

4. INJURY

4.1. Definition of Community production and Community industry

(34) Following disclosure of the provisional findings, a large number of claims and allegations concerning the assessment of Community production, the definition of the

Community industry and the selection of the sample of Community producers was received. The Commission thus deepened the injury investigation and carried out additional analysis on data provided by all Community producers. In addition, where necessary, more detailed information was requested from all the companies forming the Community industry at provisional stage. This has allowed to establish the final determinations for the Community production, the Community industry and to strengthen the accuracy and consistency of the data used for assessing all the injury indicators.

(35) Several exporting producers and producers related to Norwegian exporters repeated their claim that they should be included in the definition of the Community production.

(36) The Commission re-examined all the arguments, which were already raised at provisional stage, in support of the claim. However, in the light of the provisions of Article 4(1) of the basic Regulation, it was considered, that the relationship between these related producers and the exporters or importers of the dumped product was such as to cause the related producers concerned to behave differently from non-related producers.

[…]

5. CAUSATION

5.1. Effect of imports originating in other third countries

(83) Several interested parties questioned the interpretation of the figures relating to the imports originating in third countries, as presented in recitals 94 to 99 of the provisional Regulation. They stated that the figures did show a causal link between the low-priced imports from some third countries and the situation of the Community industry. These parties claimed that the total average import price from all third countries other than Norway and the average import prices of some countries were below the import price from Norway. It was further alleged that the Commission failed to prove that wild salmon did not have any impact on the situation of the Community industry and that wild and farmed salmon are not interchangeable.

(84) It is noted that none of the interested parties questioned the figures relating to the prices and absolute quantities of imports originating in other third countries, but rather their interpretation. It was also not disputed that the import statistics do not distinguish between farmed salmon and wild salmon and that the price of wild salmon is lower than that of farmed salmon.

(85) It is thus important to recall that there is no distinction between farmed salmon and wild salmon in the import statistics. However, it has been found that the taste of wild salmon is significantly different from that of farmed salmon. More importantly, the investigation showed that contrary to farmed salmon, wild salmon is practically not offered in the market for sale as a fresh product but it is mostly sold in tins and cans. It is clear that these products are not directly competing with each other on the market. This explains why the price of wild salmon is lower compared to farmed salmon and why these products are not interchangeable for users and consumers. Finally, it is noted that none of these interested parties submitted evidence with regard to the alleged interchangeability of wild and farmed salmon. On this basis, their claims had to be rejected.

(86) When looking at the overall average prices of some countries in isolation, e.g. USA and Canada, they seem to be below the import price from Norway. However, on the basis of information gathered during the investigation, the majority of imports from the USA and Canada consists of wild salmon, which, as explained above, is cheaper than and not interchangeable with farmed salmon. In view of the findings made in

recital 85 above, it is unlikely that imports from these two countries could have had a significant impact on the situation of the Community industry.

(87) As regards other exporting countries not concerned, it was observed that whilst the average import price from Chile was above the level of those of the Community industry, during the IP import price from the Faeroe Islands was lower than those charged by the Norwegian exporting producers on the Community market. This, however, should not hide the fact that the import volumes from Chile and the Faeroe Islands have decreased by 7% (or –1895 tonnes) and 8% (or –3397 tonnes) respectively during the period considered, whereas imports from Norway increased by 35% (or +93 366 tonnes). These developments should also be seen in the light of the development of consumption which increased by 15% during the same period.

(88) In addition, in the period between 2001 and 2003, when the situation of the Community industry deteriorated the most, the development of imports from Chile and the Faeroe Islands showed some similarities to the development of the fortunes of the Community industry. Whilst the import volumes from Chile have significantly decreased by 26% (or –6987 tonnes) and imports from the Faeroe Island only increased by 2%, namely much less than the increase in consumption (16%), imports from Norway increased by 31% (or +82 631 tonnes) during the same period. In view of the above, it is to be noted that whilst it cannot be entirely excluded that the presence of low-priced salmon from these two countries affected the Community market, it does not breach the causal link between the increased presence of high volumes of dumped imports from Norway and the injury suffered by the Community industry.

[...]

6. COMMUNITY INTEREST

[...]

6.2. Interest of the Community industry

(103) Some interested parties argued that given the low employment in the Community industry on the one hand and the high employment in the user industries on the other hand, alternative options of supporting the Community industry other than imposing anti-dumping measures should be taken.

(104) In this context, it is noted that possible alternative options and anti-dumping measures have different legal contexts and different purposes. It is recalled that the Community industry has been suffering from low-priced dumped imports of farmed salmon from Norway. In view of the nature of the injury suffered by the Community industry, it is considered that, in the absence of measures, a further deterioration in the situation of the Community industry is unavoidable. Not adopting measures will most likely entail further injury and in the medium term potentially the disappearance of that industry, bearing in mind the losses occurred during the period considered. Therefore, on the basis of the findings in the IP, the Community industry is considered to be in jeopardy unless the low level of the dumped import prices is corrected. Given that a finding of injurious dumping has been made, the appropriate action is the imposition of anti-dumping measures and alternative options are therefore not relevant.

(105) If no anti-dumping measures are imposed, the threat of having large quantities of dumped Norwegian salmon on the Community market will increase. This situation will not provide the required long-term stability which is essential for the salmon

farmers in the Community to recover from current dumping practices and will jeopardise all restructuring efforts undertaken by the Community industry so far. In view of the large number of farms which closed down in recent years in the EU, it is considered that, without any measures to eliminate injurious dumping, there is a high risk that the Community industry will disappear in the medium term.

(106) If definitive anti-dumping measures are imposed, those would reinstate fair trading conditions on the market and allow the Community industry to benefit from its restructuring efforts made in recent years. Under these conditions, the Community industry will be able to remain a viable producer offering high quality farmed salmon and will likely be able to expand. In particular, it is also expected that the Community industry will return to a profitable situation as was the case in 2001. In the meantime, in view of the capacities left over by farms which were forced to close down during the period considered, it should not be excluded that the Community industry could double its market share.

(107) The viability of the Community industry will have several positive effects for users and consumers of salmon. The high quality products offered by the Community industry will continue to be available to all users and consumers. It is also reasonable to assume that after restructuring and with an increased market share the Community industry will also be able to better control its costs and profit from economies of scale, which it has not been able to do in view of the pressure it has been facing from dumped imports. This will materialise into a strengthening of the financial situation of the Community industry, more effective competition and stable salmon prices to the benefit of all parties on the Community market.

(108) It should finally be borne in mind that a number of Community producers are located in remote and rural areas of the EU where the direct and indirect employment of salmon producers is extremely important for the local Community. This employment is likely to disappear if the Community industry is not protected against low-priced dumped imports from Norway. Should measures be imposed, to the contrary, it is to be expected that with the expected improvement in the situation of the Community industry as outlined above, employment levels will also increase.

(109) In the absence of any further substantiated comments submitted with respect to the interest of the Community industry, the findings as set out in recitals 113 to 116 of the provisional Regulation are hereby confirmed.

6.3. Interest of unrelated importers and processors (users)

(110) Following disclosure of the provisional findings and further investigation as mentioned above in recital 100, a number of claims were received from processors of farmed salmon. Some additional cooperation was received from importers and processors as a result of the further investigation. The companies now submitting meaningful replies at the definitive stage of the proceeding represent around 18% of total imports from Norway during the IP and roughly 11% of consumption (compared with 9% and 6% respectively at provisional stage).

(111) Importers and processors (users) considered that ad valorem duties would increase their costs, reduce their sales volume and profitability and may lead to job losses and even delocalisation. They also argued that employment in the fish processing

sector is far higher than in the fish farming industry, which nevertheless in some cases provides employment in regions of low employment. Processors also stressed the need for consumers and traders to continue to have access to good quality farmed salmon at low prices. However, they generally considered the MIP as a more acceptable form of the measure compared to an ad valorem duty.

(112) The main costs incurred in smoking or otherwise processing salmon are those related to the purchase of salmon and employment. As to employment, during the further investigation different figures have been presented to the Commission in a number of studies or submissions. These studies and submissions are only of limited use for the purpose of this investigation. In this context, it should be noted that the studies submitted refer to periods of time other than the IP, do not exactly cover the product concerned and partly use different parameters not covered by this investigation. Therefore, the Commission also undertook to carry out on-spot visits to relevant associations. On the basis of all the information gathered, the best estimate indicates that around 7500 workers are employed directly in the salmon processing sector in the Community.

(113) Following the further investigation it was found that farmed salmon represents around 48–54% and wages around 6–12% of the total costs of processors. Under normal market conditions (i.e. reasonable raw material price and good retail price), processors expect operating profits ranging between 5 and 12%. This has been confirmed by the cooperating processors which reported data on profitability. The further investigation showed that profit can be even higher in good times. At the end of the distribution chain, retailers may expect a profit margin ranging between 6 and 11%.

(114) The worries expressed by the users industry are legitimate as they fear a negative impact of the proposed measures on their costs leading to a reduced profitability. However, under the current circumstances and in view of the proposed MIP, any impact on the users' costs is likely to be small or non-existent.

(115) In a best case scenario, market conditions will remain as they are currently, i.e. prices will remain at a level well above the MIP. In such a case the MIP will have no impact at all on the costs of users. Where imports are undertaken at a CIF Community border price equal to or above the MIP established, no duty would be payable.

(116) In a worst case scenario with the imposition of measures, the cost of users' raw material will be set at the level of the MIP, namely at the level of the actual costs incurred by producers plus reasonable profit for deliveries on the Community market. Although this scenario does not reflect current market conditions, it is considered that in such a case it cannot be excluded that the imposition of anti-dumping duties will have some negative impact on importers and processors as duties, if any, would be directly payable at the time of import whatever the level of the import price. However, in this context it is recalled that the measure proposed is in the form of a MIP which is a floor price intended only to ensure that Community producers can sell their salmon in the Community at prices, on the basis of the lesser duty rule, that will allow them to cover their costs and allow for a margin of profit that they could normally expect in the absence of dumped imports. Duties will only be collected, in possible exceptional cases, when the free-at-Community-frontier price of Norwegian imports falls below the MIP and then only at a level equivalent to the difference between the import price and the MIP. In addition, the whole salmon market from production to deliveries to

consumers will be governed by fair competition. These conditions will allow for costs to be duly reflected on the sales prices at each level of the distribution chain. Users may also expect an increased possibility of supplies from EU sources and from other third countries, once the market will be recovering from the effects of injurious dumping. Indeed, when all operators in the market enjoy sound market conditions governed by fair trade, the largest choices of products and qualities are available from various sources of supply. Prices being set according to market signals should have a positive impact on the production and distribution chains, allowing more price and cost stability and predictability.

(117) If no measures are imposed and if the price for Norwegian exports were permitted to drop back to previously dumped low levels, users may be allowed to profit from unfairly dumped imports for a while. The market, however, will not sustain this situation for a long time. Salmon prices to users will be below the costs of producers for deliveries on the Community market. If dumping is allowed to recur, Norwegian imports representing around 60% of Community consumption will prevent exports from non-dumped third country sources. Users will not have the choice of obtaining alternative supplies and quality. The fact that prices will not be set according to market signals will lead to price volatility and negative influence on final products to consumers. This may ultimately affect processors' profitability.

(118) Therefore, the application of a MIP will on the one hand have only minor cost implications for importers and processors. Indeed, whilst market prices remain above the MIP, there will be no financial implications at all. On the other hand, it is considered that such market conditions should also prevent any delocalisation as import duties on processed salmon are high. Therefore, the processing industry in the Community should continue to have access to an adequate supply of raw material.

(119) As set out in recital 140 below, the Commission undertakes to monitor the developments in the farmed salmon market in the Community. Where on the basis of this monitoring, there is prima facie evidence that the existing measure is no longer necessary or sufficient to counteract injurious dumping, the Commission may consider initiating a review on the basis of Article 11(3) of the basic Regulation and conducting the investigation expeditiously. This will allow the Commission to react quickly, should market prices fall for a longer period of time below the level of the MIP.

(120) There has been some debate with interested parties on the question of future employment levels. However, as with the analysis of the cost implication of the measures, there is no evidence that the impact on employment in this sector by any anti-dumping measure on imports of salmon from Norway will be anything other than small.

(121) The further investigation confirmed that the MIP and its proposed level is the most appropriate form of the measure (see below at recital 128). Therefore, with a MIP the disadvantages likely to be suffered by importers/processors/users, if any, are not considered such as to outweigh the benefits expected to accrue to the Community producers as a consequence of the anti-dumping measures which are considered the minimum necessary to remedy the serious injury suffered and prevent further serious deterioration in the situation of the Community producers. In addition, it should be noted that separate sources of supply from other third countries also remain available.

(122) In the absence of any further substantiated comments submitted with respect to the interest of unrelated importers and processors (users), the findings as set out in recital 128 of the provisional Regulation are hereby confirmed.

6.4. Interest of producers of smolt and feed, suppliers and producers in the EC related to Norwegian producers/importers
(123) In the absence of any substantiated comments submitted with respect to the interests of producers of smolt and feed, suppliers and producers in the EC related to Norwegian producers/importers, the findings as set out in recitals 117 to 121 of the provisional Regulation are hereby confirmed.

6.5. Interest of consumers
(124) As the product concerned is a consumer product, the Commission informed various consumer organisations of the opening of an investigation. A response was received from one party which claimed that the nutritional beneficial effects of salmon are widely recognised and that artificially increasing the price would make good nutrition choices more difficult for consumers. Concern was also expressed that any increase in prices would make farmed salmon less affordable and stifle market growth in those Member States with a lower than average gross domestic product per head (GDP).
(125) It is considered that if anti-dumping measures are imposed, economic operators will continue to have access to unlimited quantities of imports, albeit at fair prices. Further, given the magnitude of the margins between the whole fish ex-farm and the retail price of processed salmon products, it is considered that the measures are unlikely to have a material effect on retail prices, since it is unlikely that the full price increase, if any, will be passed on to consumers. Indeed, at current market prices which are well above the MIP, there would be no impact at all. The impact on consumers, even in a worst case scenario, is therefore likely to be small. In addition, loss-making price levels are probably not sustainable in the medium to long term. On that basis, it is not expected that anti-dumping measures would have any significant negative consequences for consumers.

6.6. Conclusion on Community interest
(126) In view of the conclusions drawn in the provisional Regulation and taking into account the submissions made by the various parties and the results of the further investigation, it is concluded that there are no compelling reasons not to impose definitive anti-dumping measures against dumped imports of farmed salmon originating in Norway. The conclusion as set out in recital 131 of the provisional Regulation is therefore confirmed.

7. DEFINITIVE ANTI-DUMPING MEASURES
7.1. Form of the definitive measures
(127) In view of the definitive conclusions reached with regard to dumping, injury, causation and Community interest, anti-dumping measures should be imposed in order to prevent further injury being caused to the Community industry by the dumped imports. Account has been taken of both the dumping margins found and the amounts of duty necessary to eliminate the injury sustained by the Community industry. It

has been found that all injury margins were above 2.0% and could therefore not be considered as de minimis. The weighted average injury margin, which was below the weighted average dumping margin, was found to be 14.6%.

(128) However, following disclosure of facts leading to the adoption of the amending Regulation, some interested parties explicitly rejected ad valorem duties and welcomed the introduction of a MIP. Therefore, in light of these comments received and the findings of the further investigation, the MIP as the appropriate form of the measure is confirmed.

7.2. Injury elimination level

(129) In accordance with Article 9(4) of the basic Regulation, the definitive duty should be set at the level of the dumping or injury margins, whichever is the lower. In order to apply this rule, a non-injurious MIP was established. In order to verify this method, company specific non-dumped MIPs were also calculated on the basis of normal value, adjusted to the net free-at-Community-border price. These were compared with the non-injurious MIP calculated according to the methodology set out at recital 131. In all cases it was found that the non-injurious MIP was lower than the non-dumped MIP.

(130) In calculating non-dumped MIPs, a conversion from Norwegian kroner to euro had to be made. At the provisional stage, the Commission used three-year average currency exchange rates for this conversion. Several companies claimed that the correct rate should be that which applied during the IP. In response to this claim, the Commission again notes that three years is the average production cycle for salmon. As a number of important costs which are included in the normal value are incurred over this production cycle, the Commission considers that three-year average rates are appropriate when calculating non-dumped MIPs. The claim is, therefore, rejected.

(131) As regards the level of the non-injurious price necessary to remove the effects of the injurious dumping, the findings of the further investigation had to be taken into account. When calculating the amount of duty necessary to remove the effects of the injurious dumping, it was considered that any measures should allow the Community industry to cover its costs of production and obtain overall a profit before tax that could be reasonably achieved by an industry of this type in the sector under normal conditions of competition, i.e. in the absence of dumped imports, on the sales of the like product in the Community. On this basis, a non-injurious price was calculated for the Community industry of the like product. The non-injurious price has been obtained by adding a profit margin of 8% on turnover to the cost of production. The cost of production was cross-checked on the basis of the average unit sales price of the sampled Community industry (2.77 EUR/kg) and the average loss of sampled Community industry (5% loss) during the IP. The profit margin of 8% was established on the basis of the profit achieved during the year 2001 (see Table 3) and is a strict minimum which the Community industry could expect to obtain in the absence of injurious dumping.

(132) Farmed salmon is commonly traded in different presentations (gutted head on, gutted head off, whole fish fillets, other fillets or fillet portions). Therefore, a non-injurious minimum import price level had to be established for each of these presentations, to reflect the added costs incurred in preparing each of them. In this respect, the different minimum import prices are based on the findings in this investigation. They are

essentially derived from the conversion factors, as contained in Council Regulation (EC) No 772/1999, and also used in this investigation. With regard to the whole fish fillets and fillets cut in pieces, processing costs were taken into account.

(133) Where imports are undertaken at a CIF Community border price equal to or above the minimum import price established, no duty would be payable. If imports are undertaken at a lower price, the difference between the actual price and the minimum import price established would become payable. As imports from Norway made at prices at or above the MIP will remove the effects of the injurious dumping, it is appropriate that the MIP should apply to all imports from Norway except for one company, for which a de minimis dumping margin has been found as outlined in recital 33 above.

8. DEFINITIVE COLLECTION OF THE PROVISIONAL DUTY

(134) In view of the magnitude of the dumping margins found for the exporting producers in Norway and in light of the level of the injury caused to the Community industry, it is considered necessary that the amounts secured by way of provisional anti-dumping duties imposed by the provisional Regulation, as amended by Regulation (EC) No 1010/2005, should be definitively collected to the extent of the amount of definitive duties imposed. In so far as the definitive duties are lower than the provisional duties, only amounts secured up to the level of the definitive duties should be definitely collected.

(135) The provisional anti-dumping duties which took the form of ad valorem duties, ranging between 6.8% and 24.5%, for the imported products which were imposed by Regulation (EC) No 628/2005 and applied during the period from 27 April 2005 to 4 July 2005 shall however be released. The collection of the ad valorem duties would be disproportionate to the removal of injurious dumping given that during this period market prices were significantly above the MIP which was introduced in view of unprecedented and unforeseeable market developments. The amounts secured by way of provisional anti-dumping duties pursuant to Regulation (EC) No 1010/2005 on imports of farmed salmon originating in Norway shall be definitively collected, by taking account of the MIP finally imposed. The amounts secured by way of provisional anti-dumping duties pursuant to Regulation (EC) No 1010/2005 on imports of farmed salmon originating in Norway in excess of the definitive rate shall be released.

9. ENFORCEABILITY OF THE MIP

(136) Following disclosure, it was argued that a MIP may be more difficult to enforce and more open to misdeclaration of the customs value of the goods than other forms of the measure. Indeed, in view of indications that some circumvention of the MIP occurred since it was imposed on 1 July 2005 and the potential which exists for compensatory arrangements in this market sector, it is necessary to introduce a double system of measures. This double system is composed of a MIP (see recitals 129 to 133 above) and a fixed duty. In accordance with Article 9(4) of the basic Regulation, the fixed duty was calculated on the basis of the weighted average injury margin as this was found to be lower than the weighted average dumping margin. To ensure the effective respect of the MIP, importers should be made aware that when it is found following a post-importation verification that (i) the net free-at-Community-frontier price

actually paid by the first independent customer in the Community (post-importation price) is below the net free-at-Community-frontier price, before duty, as resulted from the customs declaration; and (ii) the post-importation price is lower than the MIP, a fixed duty shall apply retrospectively for the relevant transactions, unless the application of the fixed duty plus the post-importation price lead to an amount (price actually paid plus fixed duty) which remains below the MIP. In such a case, an amount of duty equivalent to the difference between the MIP and the post-importation price shall apply. Customs authorities should inform the Commission immediately whenever indications of a misdeclaration are found.

(137) In this context, and in order to address the concerns raised, the Commission intends to put in place three specific pillars to ensure that the measures continue to be relevant whilst also being fully respected. Firstly, reference is made to Council Regulation (EEC) No 2913/92 of 12 October 1992 establishing the Community Customs Code, inter alia, to Article 78, according to which the customs authorities may inspect the commercial documents and data relating to the import or export operations in respect of the goods concerned or to subsequent commercial operations involving those goods. Such inspections may be carried out at the premises of the declarant, of any other person directly or indirectly involved in the said operations in a business capacity or of any other person in possession of the said document and data for business purposes. Those authorities may also examine the goods.

(138) Secondly, in order to best guard against any possible absorption of the measures, particularly between related companies, the Community institutions hereby notify their intention to immediately initiate a review under Article 12(1) of the basic Regulation and to subject importations to registration in accordance with Article 14(5) of the basic Regulation, should any evidence of such behaviour be provided.

(139) The Community institutions will rely, inter alia, on import surveillance information provided by national customs authorities, as well as information provided by Member States pursuant to Article 14(6) of the basic Regulation.

(140) Finally, the Commission undertakes to monitor the developments in the farmed salmon market in the Community. Where on the basis of this monitoring, there is prima facie evidence that the existing measure is no longer necessary or sufficient to counteract injurious dumping, the Commission may consider initiating a review on the basis of Article 11(3) of the basic Regulation and conducting the investigation expeditiously,

HAS ADOPTED THIS REGULATION:

Article 1

1. A definitive anti-dumping duty is hereby imposed on imports of farmed (other than wild) salmon, whether or not filleted, fresh, chilled or frozen, falling within CN codes ex03021200, ex03031100, ex03031900, ex03032200, ex03041013 and ex03042013 (hereinafter farmed salmon) originating in Norway.

2. Wild salmon shall not be subject to the definitive anti-dumping duty. For the purpose of this Regulation, wild salmon shall be that in respect of which the competent authorities of the Member State, where the customs declaration for free circulation is accepted, are satisfied, by means of all appropriate documents to be provided by interested parties, that it was caught at sea for Atlantic or Pacific salmon or in rivers for Danube salmon.

3. The amount of the definitive anti-dumping duty in respect of Nordlaks Oppdrett AS shall be:

Company | Definitive duty | TARIC additional code |

Nordlaks Oppdrett AS, Boks 224, N-8455 Stokmarknes | 0.0% | A707 |

4. For all other companies (TARIC additional code A999), the amount of the definitive anti-dumping duty shall be the difference between the minimum import price fixed in paragraph 5 and the net free-at-Community-frontier price, before duty, if the latter is lower than the former. No duty shall be collected where the net free-at-Community-frontier price is equal to or higher than the corresponding minimum import price fixed in paragraph 5.

5. For the purpose of paragraph 4, the minimum import price set out in column 2 in the table below shall apply. Where it is found following post-importation verification that the net free-at-Community-frontier price actually paid by the first independent customer in the Community (post-importation price) is below the net free-at-Community-frontier price, before duty, as resulted from the customs declaration and the post-importation price is lower than the minimum import price, the fixed anti-dumping duty set out in column 3 of the table below shall apply, unless the application of the fixed duty set out in column 3 plus the post-importation price lead to an amount (price actually paid plus fixed duty) which remains below the minimum import price set out in column 2 in the table below. In such a case, an amount of duty equivalent to the difference between the minimum import price set out in column 2 in the table below and the post-importation price shall apply. Where such fixed anti-dumping duty is collected retrospectively, it shall be collected net of any anti-dumping duty previously paid, calculated on the basis of the minimum import price.

Presentation of farmed salmon | Minimum import price EUR/kg net product weight | Fixed duty EUR/kg net product weight | TARIC code |

[...]

6. In cases where goods have been damaged before entry into free circulation and, therefore, the price actually paid or payable is apportioned for the determination of the customs value pursuant to Article 145 of Commission Regulation (EEC) No 2454/93, the amount of anti-dumping duty, calculated on the basis of paragraph 4 and 5 above, shall be reduced by a percentage which corresponds to the apportioning of the price actually paid or payable.

7. Unless otherwise specified, the provisions in force concerning customs duties shall apply.

Article 2

The amounts secured by way of provisional anti-dumping duties pursuant to Regulation (EC) No 628/2005, prior to the entry into force of Regulation (EC) No 1010/2005, on imports of farmed salmon originating in Norway shall be released.

The amounts secured by way of provisional anti-dumping duties pursuant to Regulation (EC) No 1010/2005 on imports of farmed salmon originating in Norway shall be definitively collected in accordance with the following rules:

(a) the amounts secured in excess of the definitive duties shall be released;

(b) where the definitive duties are higher than the provisional duties, only the amounts secured at the level of the provisional duties shall be definitively collected.

Article 3

This Regulation shall enter into force on the day following its publication in the Official Journal of the European Union.

This Regulation shall be binding in its entirety and directly applicable in all Member States.

Council Regulation (EC) No 685/2008 of 17 July 2008, repealing the anti-dumping duties imposed by Regulation (EC) No 85/2006 on imports of farmed salmon originating in Norway, Official Journal L 192, 19.7.2008, pp. 5–17.

It is interesting to note that the Commission and the Council did not have recourse to a special instrument adopted in 2001, which laid down procedures and fixed the measures that the Council may take if anti-dumping duties or Countervailing measures need to be brought into conformity with the recommendations and rulings contained in a Panel or Appellate Body report adopted by the Dispute Settlement Body of the WTO. The regulation repealing the anti-dumping duties did not refer to this special instrument, namely Regulation No. 1515/2001 (reproduced below). The Community institutions preferred to rely on the results of the interim review, which had indeed started before the Panel report was adopted. Although a notice regarding the implementation of the Panel report based on Regulation No 1515/2001 was published in the Official Journal on 24 May 2008 (see OJ C127/32), the process concerning the implementation of the Panel report was terminated by another notice which referred to the repeal resulting from the interim review. Both Regulation No. 1515/2001 and the second notice are reproduced below.

THE COUNCIL OF THE EUROPEAN UNION,

Having regard to the Treaty establishing the European Community,

Having regard to Council Regulation (EC) No 384/96 of 22 December 1995 on protection against dumped imports from countries not members of the European Community (the basic Regulation), and in particular Article 9 and 11(3) thereof,

Having regard to the proposal submitted by the Commission after having consulted the Advisory Committee,

Whereas:

A. PROCEDURE

1. Measures in force

(1) The Council, following an anti-dumping investigation (the original investigation), by Regulation (EC) No 85/2006 imposed a definitive anti-dumping duty on imports of farmed salmon originating in Norway. The definitive duty was imposed in the form of a minimum import price (MIP).

2. Request for review and initiation

(2) On 20 February 2007, the Commission received a request for a partial interim review lodged by the following Member States: Italy, Lithuania, Poland, Portugal and Spain (the applicants) pursuant to Article 11(3) of the basic Regulation.

(3) The applicants have provided prima facie evidence that the basis on which the measures were established has changed and that these changes are of a lasting nature. The applicants alleged and provided prima facie evidence showing that a comparison between a constructed normal value and export prices would lead to a reduction of dumping significantly below the level of the current measures. Therefore, the continued imposition of measures at the existing levels is no longer necessary to offset dumping. This evidence was considered sufficient to justify the opening of a proceeding.

(4) Accordingly, after having consulted the Advisory Committee, the Commission on 21 April 2007 initiated, by the publication of a notice in the Official Journal of the European Union, a partial interim review of anti-dumping measures in force on imports of farmed salmon originating in Norway in accordance with Article 11(3) of the basic Regulation (the notice of initiation).

(5) This review was limited in scope to the aspects of dumping with the objective of assessing the need for the continuation, removal or amendment of the existing measures.

[...]

HAS ADOPTED THIS REGULATION:

Sole Article

The partial interim review of the anti-dumping measures applicable to imports of farmed (other than wild) salmon, whether or not filleted, fresh, chilled or frozen, currently classifiable within CN codes ex03021200, ex03031100, ex03031900, ex03032200, ex03041913 and ex03042913, originating in Norway, initiated pursuant to Article 11(3) of Regulation (EC) No 384/96, is hereby terminated.

The definitive anti-dumping duty imposed by Regulation (EC) No 85/2006 on the abovementioned imports is hereby repealed.

This Regulation shall enter into force on the day following its publication in the Official Journal of the European Union.

This Regulation shall be binding in its entirety and directly applicable in all Member States.

Council Regulation (EC) No 1515/2001 of 23 July 2001 on the measures that may be taken by the Community following a report adopted by the WTO Dispute Settlement Body concerning anti-dumping and anti-subsidy matters, Official Journal L 201, 26.7.2001, pp. 10–11.

A few things are noteworthy about this Regulation. First, Article 1 allows the Council to take the appropriate measures for the implementation of a Panel or Appellate Body report by simple majority. Second, the appropriate measures may go beyond a mere repeal or amendment of the disputed measure and may consist in the adoption of any other special measure deemed appropriate in the circumstances (see Article 1(1) (a) and (b)). This enables the Council to find a generic solution to a problem with the basic anti-dumping regulation or its application policy, rather than restrict itself to the punctual correction of the individual measure. Third, in conformity with long-standing GATT and WTO law and practice, retro-active remedies are not allowed (Article 3).

THE COUNCIL OF THE EUROPEAN UNION,

Having regard to the Treaty establishing the European Community, and in particular Article 133 thereof,

Having regard to the proposal from the Commission,

Whereas:

(1) By Regulation (EC) No 384/96, the Council adopted common rules for protection against dumped imports from countries which are not members of the European Community.

(2) By Regulation (EC) No 2026/97 the Council adopted common rules for protection against subsidised imports from countries which are not members of the European Community.

(3) Under the Marrakesh Agreement establishing the World Trade Organisation ('WTO'), an Understanding on Rules and Procedures Governing the Settlement of Disputes ('DSU') was reached. Pursuant to the DSU, the Dispute Settlement Body ('DSB') was established.

(4) With a view to permitting the Community, where it considers this appropriate, to bring a measure taken under Regulation (EC) No 384/96 or Regulation (EC) No 2026/97 into conformity with the recommendations and rulings contained in a report adopted by the DSB, specific provisions must be introduced.

(5) The Community institutions may consider it appropriate to repeal, amend or adopt any other special measures with respect to measures taken under Regulation (EC) No 384/96 or Regulation (EC) No 2026/97, including measures which have not been the subject of dispute settlement under the DSU, in order to take account of the legal interpretations made in a report adopted by the DSB. In addition, the Community institutions should be able, where appropriate, to suspend or review such measures.

(6) Recourse to the DSU is not subject to time limits. The recommendations in reports adopted by the DSB only have prospective effect. Consequently, it is appropriate to specify that any measures taken under this Regulation will take effect from the date of their entry into force, unless otherwise specified, and, therefore, do not provide any basis for the reimbursement of the duties collected prior to that date,

HAS ADOPTED THIS REGULATION:

Article 1

1. Whenever the DSB adopts a Report concerning a Community measure taken pursuant to Council Regulation (EC) No 384/96, Regulation (EC) No 2026/97 or to this Regulation ('disputed measure'), the Council may, acting by simple majority on a

proposal submitted by the Commission after consultation of the Advisory Committee established pursuant to Article 15 of Regulation (EC) No 384/96 or Article 25 of Regulation (EC) No 2026/97 ('Advisory Committee'), take one or more of the following measures, whichever it considers appropriate:

(a) repeal or amend the disputed measure or;

(b) adopt any other special measures which are deemed to be appropriate in the circumstances.

2. For the purpose of taking measures under paragraph 1, the Commission may request interested parties to provide all necessary information in order to complete the information obtained during the investigation that resulted in the adoption of the disputed measure.

3. Insofar as it is appropriate to conduct a review before or at the same time as taking any measures under paragraph 1, such review shall be initiated by the Commission, after consultation of the Advisory Committee.

4. Insofar as it is appropriate to suspend the disputed or amended measure, such suspension shall be granted for a limited period of time by the Council, acting by simple majority on a proposal submitted by the Commission after consultation of the Advisory Committee.

Article 2

1. The Council may also take any of the measures mentioned in Article 1(1) in order to take into account the legal interpretations made in a report adopted by the DSB with regard to a non-disputed measure, if it considers this appropriate.

2. For the purpose of taking measures under paragraph 1, the Commission may request interested parties to provide all necessary information in order to complete the information obtained during the investigation that resulted in the adoption of the non-disputed measure.

3. Insofar as it is appropriate to conduct a review before or at the same time as taking any measures under paragraph 1, such review shall be initiated by the Commission after consultation of the Advisory Committee.

4. Insofar as it is appropriate to suspend the non-disputed or amended measure, such suspension shall be granted for a limited period of time by the Council, acting by simple majority on a proposal submitted by the Commission after consultation of the Advisory Committee.

Article 3

Any measures adopted pursuant to this Regulation shall take effect from the date of their entry into force and shall not serve as basis for the reimbursement of the duties collected prior to that date, unless otherwise provided for.

Article 4

This Regulation shall enter into force on the day of its publication in the Official Journal of the European Communities.

It applies to reports adopted after 1 January 2001 by the DSB.

This Regulation shall be binding in its entirety and directly applicable in all Member States.

Notice regarding the termination of the process concerning implementation of the Panel report adopted by the WTO Dispute Settlement Body concerning the anti-dumping measure applicable on imports of farmed salmon originating in Norway, (2008/C 298/04), Official Journal C 298, 21.11.2008, pp. 7–8.

This Notice clearly demonstrates how the procedure under ex Regulation 1515/2001 for the implementation of the Panel report started slightly over a year after the interim review called for by the Member States. The latter (interim review) procedure led to a repeal two months after the former (implementation) procedure had started, which was thereupon terminated.

1. Background

In January 2006, the Council, by Regulation (EC) No 85/2006, imposed a definitive anti-dumping duty and collected definitively the provisional duty imposed on imports of farmed salmon originating in Norway ('the original measure'). Subsequently, Norway lodged a World Trade Organisation ('WTO' dispute settlement proceeding challenging certain aspects of this Regulation ('the measure') and the report of the WTO Panel, which had been established by the WTO Dispute Settlement Body (DSB), was circulated to WTO members on 16 November 2007. At its meeting on 15 January 2008, the DSB adopted the Panel report ('the report'). An implementation process was initiated in order to bring the original measure into conformity with the recommendations and rulings contained in the report ('the implementation').

2. Termination of the implementation

In May 2008, the Commission published a notice ('the notice') in the Official Journal providing all the details concerning the implementation of the report recommendations and rulings. Questionnaires were sent to all relevant parties and to parties which made themselves known within the time limits provided under point 5(b) of the notice ('interested parties').

However, in April 2007, certain Member States of the European Union (the applicants) provided prima facie evidence that the basis on which the measures were established had changed. The applicants alleged and provided prima facie evidence showing that dumping from Norwegian exporters was reduced significantly and that therefore, the continued imposition of measures would not be justified. The Commission thus initiated a partial interim review (the review) pursuant to Article 11(3) of the basic Regulation.

The review showed that Norwegian exporters were not dumping their products on the Community market. Accordingly, in July 2008, by Council Regulation (EC) No 685/2008, the Council repealed the original measures in force on farmed salmon originating in Norway.

As a consequence, the implementation proceeding referred to in the notice is terminated.

All interested parties were given an opportunity to comment on the termination and or to address any claim concerning their rights of defence to the Hearing Officer. No party made comments or referred to the Hearing Officer.

Council Regulation (EC) No 655/2006 of 27 April 2006 extending the definitive anti-dumping duty imposed by Regulation (EC) No 964/2003 on imports of tube or pipe fittings, of iron or steel, originating in the People's Republic of China to imports of tube or pipe fittings, of iron or steel, consigned from the Philippines, whether declared as originating in the Philippines or not, Official Journal L 116, 29.4.2006, pp. 1–6.

This regulation is an example of a measure pursuant to the non-circumvention provision (Article 13) of the basic anti-dumping regulation (see pp. 470–1).

THE COUNCIL OF THE EUROPEAN UNION,
Having regard to the Treaty establishing the European Community,
Having regard to Council Regulation (EC) No 384/96 of 22 December 1995 on protection against dumped imports from countries not members of the European Community (the basic Regulation) and in particular Article 13 thereof,
Having regard to the proposal submitted by the Commission after consulting the Advisory Committee,

Whereas:
A. PROCEDURE
1. Existing measures
(1) Following an expiry review, by Regulation (EC) No 964/2003 (the original Regulation), the Council imposed definitive anti-dumping duties of 58.6% on imports of tube or pipe fittings (other than cast fittings, flanges and threaded fittings) of iron or steel (not including stainless steel) with a greatest external diameter not exceeding 609.6 mm, of a kind used for butt-welding or other purposes (tube or pipe fittings or the product concerned), originating, inter alia, in the People's Republic of China (the PRC) and extended the measures to imports of the same fittings consigned from Taiwan, with the exception of those produced by three specific Taiwanese companies.
(2) In December 2004, by Regulations (EC) No 2052/2004 and No 2053/2004, the Council extended the above-mentioned definitive anti-dumping duties to imports of the same tube or pipe fittings consigned from Indonesia and Sri Lanka respectively.

2. Request
(3) On 23 June 2005, the Commission received a request pursuant to Article 13(3) of the basic Regulation to investigate the alleged circumvention of the anti-dumping measures imposed on imports of tube or pipe fittings originating in the PRC by means of the transhipment and incorrect declaration of origin via the Philippines. The request was submitted by the Defence Committee of the Steel Butt-Welding Fittings Industry

of the European Union on behalf of four Community producers, representing a major proportion of the Community production of certain tube and pipe fittings.

(4) The request alleged and submitted sufficient prima facie evidence that there had been a change in the pattern of trade following the imposition of the anti-dumping measures on imports of tube or pipe fittings originating in the PRC, as shown by a significant increase in imports of the same product from the Philippines.

(5) This change in the pattern of trade was alleged to stem from the transhipment of tube or pipe fittings originating in the PRC via the Philippines. It was further alleged that there was insufficient due cause or economic justification for these practices other than the existence of the anti-dumping duties on tube or pipe fittings originating in the PRC.

(6) Finally, the applicant alleged and submitted prima facie evidence showing that the remedial effects of the existing anti-dumping duties on tube or pipe fittings originating in the PRC were being undermined both in terms of quantities and prices and that dumping was taking place in relation to the normal values previously established for the tube or pipe fittings originating in the PRC.

3. Initiation

(7) By Regulation (EC) No 1288/2005 (the initiating Regulation), the Commission initiated an investigation into the alleged circumvention of the anti-dumping measures imposed on imports of tube or pipe fittings originating in the PRC by imports of tube or pipe fittings consigned from the Philippines, whether declared as originating in the Philippines or not and, pursuant to Articles 13(3) and 14(5) of the basic Regulation, directed the customs authorities to register imports into the Community of tube or pipe fittings consigned from the Philippines, whether declared as originating in the Philippines or not, as from 6 August 2005.

4. Investigation

(8) The Commission officially advised the authorities of the PRC and of the Philippines, the producers/exporters and the importers in the Community known to be concerned as well as the Community industry of the initiation of the investigation. Questionnaires were sent to producers/exporters in the PRC and in the Philippines as well as to importers in the Community named in the request or known to the Commission from the investigation which lead to the imposition of the existing measures on imports of tube or pipe fittings originating in the PRC (the original investigation). Interested parties were given the opportunity to make their views known in writing and to request a hearing within the time limit set in the initiating Regulation. All parties were informed that non-cooperation might lead to the application of Article 18 of the basic Regulation and to findings being made on the basis of facts available.

(9) No questionnaire replies were received from exporters/producers in the Philippines, even though the authorities of the Philippines had contacted several companies possibly involved in producing tube or pipe fittings. Moreover, no questionnaire replies were received from exporters/producers in the PRC.

(10) Two importers in the Community cooperated and submitted replies to the questionnaire.

(11) Verification visits took place at the premises of the following companies:
Importers
– Valvorobica Industriale SpA, Italy,
– General Commercial & Industrial SA, Greece.

5. Investigation period
(12) The investigation period covered the period from 1 July 2004 to 30 June 2005 (the IP). Data were collected from 2001 up to the end of the IP to investigate the alleged change in the pattern of trade.

B. RESULTS OF THE INVESTIGATION
1. General considerations/degree of cooperation
(13) As mentioned in recital 9, no producer/exporter in the PRC or the Philippines cooperated in the investigation. Three Philippine companies came forward and stated that they did not produce nor export the tube or pipe fittings as defined in the original Regulation, but only stainless steel fittings, a product which is not covered by the current investigation. Accordingly, findings in respect of tube or pipe fittings consigned from the Philippines to the Community had partially to be based on facts available in accordance with Article 18 of the basic Regulation.

2. Product concerned and like product
(14) The product concerned by the alleged circumvention is, as defined in the original investigation, tube or pipe fittings (other than cast fittings, flanges and threaded fittings) of iron or steel (not including stainless steel), with a greatest external diameter not exceeding 609.6 mm, of a kind used for butt-welding or other purposes, currently classifiable within CN codes ex73079311 (TARIC code 7307931195), ex73079319 (TARIC code 7307931995), ex73079930 (TARIC code 7307993095) and ex73079990 (TARIC code 7307999095), originating in the PRC.
(15) On the basis of the information available and the data supplied by the Philippine authorities and considering the change in the pattern of trade as described in the following section, it must be inferred, in the absence of any contrary evidence, that the tube or pipe fittings exported to the Community from the PRC and those consigned from the Philippines to the Community have the same basic physical and chemical characteristics and have the same uses. They are therefore to be considered as like products within the meaning of Article 1(4) of the basic Regulation.

3. Change in the pattern of trade
(16) Due to the non-cooperation of any Philippine company, the volume and the value of exports of the like product from the Philippines to the Community had to be established on the basis of the facts available pursuant to Article 18 of the basic Regulation. Eurostat data were the most appropriate information available and were therefore used to establish the export quantities and prices from the Philippines to the Community.
Imports into the Community
Source: Eurostat.
(in tonnes) |
| 2001 | 2002 | 2003 | 2004 | IP |

Philippines | 0 | 3 | 700 | 2445 | 2941 |
The PRC | 1324 | 772 | 677 | 1153 | 1411 |
Indonesia | 0 | 983 | 1294 | 0 | 0 |
Sri Lanka | 0 | 332 | 302 | 39 | 0 |
Total EU imports | 17 422 | 15 111 | 16 085 | 16 050 | 18 900 |

(17) As this table shows, imports of tube or pipe fittings from the Philippines into the Community increased from 0 tonnes in 2001 to almost 3000 tonnes during the IP. The imports from the Philippines commenced in 2002, at a time when the original investigation was ongoing. In 2003, however the imports from the Philippines increased significantly to 700 tonnes. In 2004, imports from the Philippines to the Community more than tripled to 2445 tonnes. It should be noted that following the extension of the original anti-dumping measures to imports of the like product consigned from Indonesia and Sri Lanka in December 2004, imports from these countries came to a complete stop. This complete halt of imports from Indonesia and Sri Lanka to the Community in 2004 coincided with the most substantial increase of imports from the Philippines.

(18) At the same time, exports from the PRC to the Philippines remained at a low but stable level.

Exports from the PRC to the Philippines
Source: Chinese export statistics.
(in tonnes) |
| 2001 | 2002 | 2003 | 2004 | IP |
Philippines | 466 | 604 | 402 | 643 | 694 |

(19) It must be noted, however, that the data used to establish the change in the pattern of trade, with special regard to those relating to exports from the PRC to the Philippines, should be seen in the light of the likelihood of false declarations of origin (see recital 22) and might therefore not give a complete picture of the situation.

(20) From the figures shown above, it is concluded that there has been a clear change in the pattern of trade which started after the conclusion of the original investigation and became apparent after the extension of the measures to imports of the like product from Indonesia and Sri Lanka. The pattern consisted of a sharp increase of imports of tube or pipe fittings from the Philippines into the Community, especially in 2004 and the IP, coinciding with a stop of imports from the two countries to which the original measures were extended.

(21) It is clear from the above that due to the coincidence in time the Chinese exports transhipped via Indonesia and Sri Lanka have been redirected at least partly via the Philippines when the original anti-dumping measures were extended to imports from Indonesia and Sri Lanka. This was the case in particular during the year 2004 and during the IP.

4. Insufficient due cause or economic justification

(22) As already mentioned in recital 9, no Philippine producer/exporter cooperated in the investigation. Indeed, no evidence has been found during the investigation that any such producer would actually exist. Moreover, evidence collected during the investigation shows that tubes or pipe fittings have been in some cases declared as produced by Philippine companies that have submitted never having been involved

in the manufacturing of the like product. This is corroborated by the information contained in the request for the initiation of anti-circumvention investigation, e.g. offers to potential importers containing the proposal of falsifying the documents of origin.

(23) From the information referred to in recitals 17 and 20, it can be concluded that exports of tubes or pipes fittings produced in the PRC and channelled to the Community through Indonesia and Sri Lanka during the years 2002 until 2004 have been redirected to a large extent via the Philippines, starting in the year 2003 and continuing until the end of IP.

(24) Moreover, although the volume of imports of the product concerned from the PRC to the Philippines did by far not reach the increase of imports consigned from the Philippines to the Community (see recital 18), the steep increase of exports from the Philippines to the Community also has to be seen in the light of the evidence found concerning false declarations or falsification of certificates of origin (see recital 22), the lack of genuine Philippine producers of tube or pipe fittings and the decrease of exports from Sri Lanka and Indonesia to the Community. It is the totality of these elements which explain the absence of an economic justification for the change in the pattern of trade observed.

(25) In the absence of cooperation by any exporting producer in the Philippines and the PRC and of any contrary evidence, it is therefore concluded that, given the coincidence in time with the investigations which lead to the extension of the original measures to imports from Indonesia and Sri Lanka, the change in the pattern of trade stemmed from the existence of the anti-dumping duty rather than from any other sufficient due cause or economic justification within the meaning of Article 13(1), third sentence of the basic Regulation.

5. Undermining of the remedial effects of the duty in terms of the prices and/or the quantities of the like product

(26) Based on the trade flow analysis made in recital 17, a clear quantitative change in the pattern of Community imports of tube or pipe fittings occurred. Imports declared as originating in the Philippines were negligible on the Community market until June 2003. After the said date imports declared as originating in the Philippines suddenly emerged and increased rapidly to 2941 tonnes during the IP. This volume represents 3% of the Community consumption calculated on production figures submitted by the applicants and imports based on Eurostat data. It is therefore clear that the marked change in trade flows undermined the remedial effects of the anti-dumping measures in terms of the quantities imported into the Community market.

(27) With regard to prices of the products consigned from the Philippines and in the absence of cooperation and of any contrary evidence, Eurostat data show that average export prices of imports from the Philippines during the IP were lower than the average export prices established for the PRC in the original investigation. It has been established that prices of imports from the Philippines are around one third lower than those of imports originating in the PRC both during 2004 and the IP. Moreover, it was found that the average export prices of the Philippine exports to the Community were below the injury elimination level of Community prices as established in the original investigation. Hence, the remedial effects of the anti-dumping duty imposed are undermined in terms of prices. Detailed information can be found in the table below:

(EUR/kg) |

| 2004 | IP |

Philippines | 0.97 | 1.07 |

PRC | 1.57 | 1.50 |

Difference | –38% | –29% |

(28) On the basis of the above, it is concluded that the change in trade flows, together with the substantial increase in imports made at very low prices from the Philippines have undermined the remedial effects of the anti-dumping measures in terms of both quantities and prices of the like product.

6. Evidence of dumping in relation to the normal values previously established for the like product

(29) In order to determine whether evidence of dumping could be found with respect to the product concerned exported to the Community from the Philippines during the IP, export prices established on the basis of Eurostat data were used pursuant to Article 18 of the basic Regulation.

(30) In accordance with Article 13(1) of the basic Regulation, these export prices were compared with the normal value previously established for the like product. In the original investigation, Thailand was found to be an appropriate market economy analogue country for the PRC for the purpose of establishing normal value.

(31) For the purpose of a fair comparison between the normal value and the export price, due allowance, in the form of adjustments, was made for differences which affect prices and price comparability. These adjustments were made in accordance with Article 2(10) of the basic Regulation in respect of transport costs, on the basis of the information contained in the request.

(32) In accordance with Article 2(11) of the basic Regulation, the comparison of a weighted average normal value as established in the original investigation and the weighted average of export prices during this investigation's IP, expressed as a percentage of the cif price at the Community frontier, duty unpaid, showed dumping for the imports of tube or pipe fittings consigned from the Philippines. The dumping margin found, expressed as a percentage of the cif price at the Community frontier, duty unpaid, was in excess of 60%.

C. MEASURES

(33) In view of the above finding of circumvention within the meaning of Article 13(1), third sentence of the basic Regulation and in accordance with Article 13(1), first sentence of the basic Regulation, the existing anti-dumping measures on imports of the product concerned originating in the PRC should be extended to imports of the same product consigned from the Philippines, whether declared as originating in the Philippines or not.

(34) The duty extended should be the one established in Article 1(2) of the original Regulation.

(35) In accordance with Articles 13(3) and 14(5) of the basic Regulation, which provides that any extended measures shall be applied on registered imports from the date of registration, the anti-dumping duty should be collected on imports of tube or pipe fittings consigned from the Philippines which entered the Community under registration imposed by the initiating Regulation.

(36) Although during this investigation no genuine exporting producer of tube or pipe fittings was found to exist in the Philippines or made itself known to the Commission, new exporting producers which would consider lodging a request for an exemption from the extended anti-dumping duty pursuant to Article 13(4) of the basic Regulation will be required to complete a questionnaire in order to enable the Commission to determine whether an exemption may be warranted. Such exemption may be granted after the assessment of, for instance, the market situation of the product concerned, production capacity and capacity utilisation, procurement and sales, the likelihood of continuation of practices for which there is insufficient due cause or economic justification and the evidence of dumping. The Commission would normally also carry out an on-the-spot verification visit. The request would have to be addressed to the Commission forthwith, with all relevant information, in particular any modification in the company's activities linked to production and sales.

(37) Importers could still benefit from exemption for registration or measures to the extent that their imports are from exporting producers, which are granted such an exemption, and in accordance with Article 13(4) of the basic Regulation.

(38) Where an exemption is warranted, the Commission will, after consultation of the Advisory Committee, propose the amendment of this Regulation accordingly. Subsequently, any exemptions granted will be monitored to ensure compliance with the conditions set therein.

D. PROCEDURE

(39) Interested parties were informed of the essential facts and considerations on the basis of which the Council intended to extend the definitive anti-dumping duty in force and were given the opportunity to comment. No comments which were of a nature to change the above-mentioned conclusions were received,

HAS ADOPTED THIS REGULATION:

Article 1

1. The definitive anti-dumping duty imposed by Regulation (EC) No 964/2003 on imports of tube or pipe fittings (other than cast fittings, flanges and threaded fittings), of iron or steel (not including stainless steel), with a greatest external diameter not exceeding 609.6 mm, of a kind used for butt-welding or other purposes, falling within CN codes [...] originating in the People's Republic of China is hereby extended to imports of tube or pipe fittings (other than cast fittings, flanges and threaded fittings), of iron or steel (not including stainless steel), with a greatest external diameter not exceeding 609.6 mm, of a kind used for butt-welding or other purposes falling within CN codes [...] consigned from the Philippines, whether declared as originating in the Philippines or not.

2. The duty extended by paragraph 1 of this Article shall be collected on imports registered in accordance with Article 2 of Regulation (EC) No 1288/2005 and Articles 13(3) and 14(5) of Regulation (EC) No 384/96.

3. The provisions in force concerning customs duties shall apply.

Article 2

1. Requests for exemption from the duty extended by Article 1 shall be made in writing in one of the official languages of the European Union must be signed by a

person authorised to represent the applicant. The request shall be sent to the following address: [...]

2. The Commission, after consulting the Advisory Committee, may authorise, by decision, the exemption of imports from companies which do not circumvent the anti-dumping measures imposed by Regulation (EC) No 964/2003 from the duty extended by Article 1, and propose the amendment of this Regulation accordingly.

Article 3

Customs authorities are hereby directed to discontinue the registration of imports established in accordance with Article 2 of Regulation (EC) No 1288/2005.

Article 4

This Regulation shall enter into force on the day following its publication in the Official Journal of the European Union.

This Regulation shall be binding in its entirety and directly applicable in all Member States.

7.5 Protection against subsidized imports

Council Regulation (EC) No 597/2009 of 11 June 2009 on protection against subsidized imports from countries not members of the European Community, (codified version), Official Journal L 188, 18.7.2009, pp. 93–126.

This is the codified version of the post-Uruguay Round regulation on subsidized imports. It serves as implementation of the WTO Agreement on Subsidies and Countervailing Measures (SCM Agreement). It is less frequently resorted to than the anti-dumping regulation, but in many ways the system and procedures of both basic regulations run in parallel and they are being applied by the same division in the Commission's Directorate-General for Trade. Regulation (EC) No 1515/2001 on the measures that may be taken by the Community following a report adopted by the WTO DSB (see pp. 491–3) is equally applicable to the area of the protection against subsidized imports. Regulation (EC) No. 598/09 (not included here) is a good example of the application of countervailing duty law to a product, even if it may be said that such product has certain (environmentally) desirable aspects.[6]

THE COUNCIL OF THE EUROPEAN UNION,

Having regard to the Treaty establishing the European Community, and in particular Article 133 thereof,

Having regard to the Regulations establishing the common organisation of agricultural markets and the Regulations adopted pursuant to Article 308 of the Treaty applicable

---

[6] Council Regulation (EC) No. 598/2009 of 7 July 2009 imposing a definitive countervailing duty and collecting definitively the provisional duty imposed on imports of biodiesel originating in the United States of America, OJ L 179, 10.7.2009, pp. 1–25.

to goods manufactured from agricultural products, and in particular the provisions of those Regulations which allow for derogation from the general principle that protective measures at frontiers may be replaced solely by the measures provided for in those Regulations,
Having regard to the proposal from the Commission,

Whereas:

(1) Council Regulation (EC) No 2026/97 of 6 October 1997 on protection against subsidised imports from countries not members of the European Community has been substantially amended several times. In the interests of clarity and rationality the said Regulation should be codified.

(2) The conclusion of the Uruguay Round of multilateral trade negotiations led to the establishment of the World Trade Organisation (WTO).

(3) Annex 1A to the Agreement establishing the WTO (hereinafter referred to as the WTO Agreement), approved by Council Decision 94/800/EC of 22 December 1994 concerning the conclusion on behalf of the European Community, as regards matters within its competence, of the agreements reached in the Uruguay Round multilateral negotiations (1986 to 1994), contains, inter alia, the General Agreement on Tariffs and Trade 1994 (hereinafter referred to as the GATT 1994), an Agreement on Agriculture (hereinafter referred to as the Agreement on Agriculture), an Agreement on implementation of Article VI of the GATT 1994 (hereinafter referred to as the 1994 Anti-Dumping Agreement) and an Agreement on Subsidies and Countervailing Measures (hereinafter referred to as the Subsidies Agreement).

(4) In order to reach greater transparency and effectiveness in the application by the Community of the rules laid down in the 1994 Anti-Dumping Agreement and the Subsidies Agreement respectively, the adoption of two separate Regulations which would lay down in sufficient detail the requirements for the application of each of these commercial defence instruments has been considered as necessary.

(5) In order to ensure an adequate and transparent implementation of the rules provided for in those two Agreements, it is appropriate to transpose their language into Community legislation to the best extent possible.

(6) Furthermore, it seems advisable to explain, in adequate detail, when a subsidy shall be deemed to exist, according to which principles it shall be countervailable (in particular whether the subsidy has been granted specifically), and according to which criteria the amount of the countervailable subsidy is to be calculated.

(7) In determining the existence of a subsidy, it is necessary to demonstrate that there has been a financial contribution by a government or any public body within the territory of a country, or that there has been some form of income or price support within the meaning of Article XVI of the GATT 1994, and that a benefit has thereby been conferred on the recipient enterprise.

(8) For the calculation of the benefit to the recipient, in cases where a market benchmark does not exist in the country concerned the benchmark should be determined by adjusting the terms and conditions prevailing in the country concerned on the basis of actual factors available in that country. If this is not practicable because, inter alia, such

prices or costs do no exist or are unreliable, then the appropriate benchmark should be determined by resorting to terms and conditions in other markets.

(9) It is desirable to lay down clear and detailed guidance as to the factors which may be relevant for the determination of whether the subsidised imports have caused material injury or are threatening to cause injury. In demonstrating that the volume and price levels of the imports concerned are responsible for injury sustained by a Community industry, attention should be given to the effect of other factors and in particular prevailing market conditions in the Community.

(10) It is advisable to define the term 'Community industry' and to provide that parties related to exporters may be excluded from such industry, and to define the term 'related'. It is also necessary to provide for countervailing duty action to be taken on behalf of producers in a region of the Community and to lay down guidelines on the definition of such region.

(11) It is necessary to lay down who may lodge a countervailing duty complaint, including the extent to which it should be supported by the Community industry, and the information on countervailable subsidies, injury and causation which such complaint should contain. It is also expedient to specify the procedures for the rejection of complaints or the initiation of proceedings.

(12) It is necessary to lay down the manner in which interested parties should be given notice of the information which the authorities require, and should have ample opportunity to present all relevant evidence and to defend their interests. It is also desirable to set out clearly the rules and procedures to be followed during the investigation, in particular the rules whereby interested parties are to make themselves known, present their views and submit information within specified time limits, if such views and information are to be taken into account. It is also appropriate to set out the conditions under which an interested party may have access to, and comment on, information presented by other interested parties. There should also be cooperation between the Member States and the Commission in the collection of information.

(13) It is necessary to lay down the conditions under which provisional duties may be imposed, including conditions whereby they may be imposed no earlier than 60 days from initiation and no later than nine months thereafter. Such duties may in all cases be imposed by the Commission only for a four-month period.

(14) It is necessary to specify procedures for the acceptance of undertakings eliminating or offsetting the countervailable subsidies and injury in lieu of the imposition of provisional or definitive duties. It is also appropriate to lay down the consequences of breach or withdrawal of undertakings and that provisional duties may be imposed in cases of suspected violation or where further investigation is necessary to supplement the findings. In accepting undertakings, care should be taken that the proposed undertakings, and their enforcement, do not lead to anti-competitive behaviour.

(15) It is considered appropriate to allow withdrawal of an undertaking and application of the duty by one single legal act. It is also necessary to ensure that the withdrawal procedure is terminated within a time limit of normally six months and in no case more than nine months in order to ensure a proper enforcement of the measure in force.

(16) It is necessary to provide that the termination of cases should, irrespective of whether definitive measures are adopted or not, normally take place within 12 months and in no case later than 13 months, from the initiation of the investigation.

(17) An investigation or proceedings should be terminated whenever the amount of the subsidy is found to be de minimis or if, particularly in the case of imports originating in developing countries, the volume of subsidised imports or the injury is negligible, and it is appropriate to define those criteria. Where measures are to be imposed, it is necessary to provide for the termination of investigations and to lay down that measures should be less than the amount of countervailable subsidies if such lesser amount would remove the injury, and also to specify the method of calculating the level of measures in cases of sampling.

(18) It is necessary to provide for the retroactive collection of provisional duties if that is deemed appropriate and to define the circumstances which may trigger the retroactive application of duties in order to avoid the undermining of the definitive measures to be applied. It is also necessary to provide that duties may be applied retroactively in cases of breach or withdrawal of undertakings.

(19) It is necessary to provide that measures are to lapse after five years unless a review indicates that they should be maintained. It is also necessary to provide, in cases where sufficient evidence is submitted of changed circumstances, for interim reviews or for investigations to determine whether refunds of countervailing duties are warranted.

(20) Even though the Subsidies Agreement does not contain provisions concerning circumvention of countervailing measures, the possibility of such circumvention exists, in terms similar, albeit not identical, to the circumvention of anti-dumping measures. It appears therefore appropriate to enact an anti-circumvention provision in this Regulation.

(21) It is desirable to clarify which parties have the right to request the initiation of anti-circumvention investigations.

(22) It is also desirable to clarify which practices constitute circumvention of the measures in place. Circumvention practices may take place either inside or outside the Community. It is consequently necessary to provide that exemptions from the extended duties which may be granted to importers may also be granted to exporters when duties are being extended to address circumvention taking place outside the Community.

(23) It is expedient to permit the suspension of countervailing measures where there is a temporary change in market conditions which makes the continued imposition of such measures temporarily inappropriate.

(24) It is necessary to provide that imports under investigation may be made subject to registration upon importation in order to enable measures to be subsequently applied against such imports.

(25) In order to ensure proper enforcement of measures, it is necessary that Member States monitor, and report to the Commission, the import trade in products subject to investigation or subject to measures, and also the amount of duties collected under this Regulation. It is also necessary to provide for the possibility for the Commission to request Member States to supply, subject to the respect of confidentiality rules, information to be used for monitoring price undertakings and verifying the level of effectiveness of the measures in force.

(26) It is necessary to provide for consultation of an Advisory Committee at regular and specified stages of the investigation. The Committee should consist of representatives of Member States with a representative of the Commission as chairman.

(27) It is expedient to provide for verification visits to check information submitted on countervailable subsidies and injury, such visits being, however, conditional on proper replies to questionnaires being received.

(28) It is essential to provide for sampling in cases where the number of parties or transactions is large in order to permit completion of investigations within the appointed time limits.

(29) It is necessary to provide that, where parties do not cooperate satisfactorily, other information may be used to establish findings and that such information may be less favourable to the parties than if they had cooperated.

(30) Provision should be made for the treatment of confidential information so that business or governmental secrets are not divulged.

(31) It is essential that provision be made for proper disclosure of essential facts and considerations to parties which qualify for such treatment and that such disclosure be made, with due regard to the decision-making process in the Community, within a time period which permits parties to defend their interests.

(32) It is prudent to provide for an administrative system under which arguments can be presented as to whether measures are in the Community interest, including the interests of consumers, and to lay down the time periods within which such information has to be presented, together with the disclosure rights of the parties concerned.

(33) In applying the rules of the Subsidies Agreement it is essential, in order to maintain the balance of rights and obligations which this Agreement sought to establish, that the Community take account of their interpretation by the Community's major trading partners, as reflected in legislation or established practice,

HAS ADOPTED THIS REGULATION:

Article 1

Principles

1. A countervailing duty may be imposed for the purpose of offsetting any subsidy granted, directly or indirectly, for the manufacture, production, export or transport of any product whose release for free circulation in the Community causes injury.

2. Notwithstanding paragraph 1, where products are not directly imported from the country of origin but are exported to the Community from an intermediate country, the provisions of this Regulation shall be fully applicable and the transaction or transactions shall, where appropriate, be regarded as having taken place between the country of origin and the Community.

Article 2

Definitions

For the purpose of this Regulation:

(a) a product is considered to be subsidised if it benefits from a countervailable subsidy as defined in Articles 3 and 4. Such subsidy may be granted by the government of the country of origin of the imported product, or by the government of an intermediate country from which the product is exported to the Community, known for the purpose of this Regulation as 'the country of export';

(b) 'government' means a government or any public body within the territory of the country of origin or export;

(c) 'like product' shall be interpreted to mean a product which is identical, that is to say, alike in all respects, to the product under consideration, or in the absence of such a product, another product which, although not alike in all respects, has characteristics closely resembling those of the product under consideration;

(d) 'injury', unless otherwise specified, means material injury to the Community industry, threat of material injury to the Community industry or material retardation of the establishment of such an industry, and shall be interpreted in accordance with the provisions of Article 8.

Article 3

Definition of a subsidy
A subsidy shall be deemed to exist if:

1. (a) there is a financial contribution by a government in the country of origin or export, that is to say, where:

(i) a government practice involves a direct transfer of funds (for example, grants, loans, equity infusion), potential direct transfers of funds or liabilities (for example, loan guarantees);

(ii) government revenue that is otherwise due is forgone or not collected (for example, fiscal incentives such as tax credits). In this regard, the exemption of an exported product from duties or taxes borne by the like product when destined for domestic consumption, or the remission of such duties or taxes in amounts not in excess of those which have been accrued, shall not be deemed to be a subsidy, provided that such an exemption is granted in accordance with the provisions of Annexes I, II and III;

(iii) a government provides goods or services other than general infrastructure, or purchases goods;

(iv) a government:

– makes payments to a funding mechanism, or

– entrusts or directs a private body to carry out one or more of the type of functions illustrated in points (i), (ii) and (iii) which would normally be vested in the government, and the practice, in no real sense, differs from practices normally followed by governments;

or

(b) there is any form of income or price support within the meaning of Article XVI of the GATT 1994; and

2. a benefit is thereby conferred.

Article 4

Countervailable subsidies
1. Subsidies shall be subject to countervailing measures only if they are specific, as defined in paragraphs 2, 3 and 4.

2. In order to determine whether a subsidy is specific to an enterprise or industry or group of enterprises or industries (hereinafter referred to as certain enterprises) within the jurisdiction of the granting authority, the following principles shall apply:

(a) where the granting authority, or the legislation pursuant to which the granting authority operates, explicitly limits access to a subsidy to certain enterprises, such subsidy shall be specific;

(b) where the granting authority, or the legislation pursuant to which the granting authority operates, establishes objective criteria or conditions governing the eligibility for, and the amount of, a subsidy, specificity shall not exist, provided that the eligibility is automatic and that such criteria and conditions are strictly adhered to;

(c) if, notwithstanding any appearance of non-specificity resulting from the application of the principles laid down in points (a) and (b), there are reasons to believe that the subsidy may in fact be specific, other factors may be considered. Such factors are: use of a subsidy programme by a limited number of certain enterprises; predominant use by certain enterprises; the granting of disproportionately large amounts of subsidy to certain enterprises; and the manner in which discretion has been exercised by the granting authority in the decision to grant a subsidy. In this regard, information on the frequency with which applications for a subsidy are refused or approved and the reasons for such decisions shall, in particular, be considered.

For the purpose of point (b), 'objective criteria or conditions' means criteria or conditions which are neutral, which do not favour certain enterprises over others, and which are economic in nature and horizontal in application, such as number of employees or size of enterprise.

The criteria or conditions must be clearly set out by law, regulation, or other official document, so as to be capable of verification.

In applying point (c) of the first subparagraph, account shall be taken of the extent of diversification of economic activities within the jurisdiction of the granting authority, as well as of the length of time during which the subsidy programme has been in operation.

3. A subsidy which is limited to certain enterprises located within a designated geographical region within the jurisdiction of the granting authority shall be specific. The setting or changing of generally applicable tax rates by all levels of government entitled to do so shall not be deemed to be a specific subsidy for the purposes of this Regulation.

4. Notwithstanding paragraphs 2 and 3, the following subsidies shall be deemed to be specific:

(a) subsidies contingent, in law or in fact, whether solely or as one of several other conditions, upon export performance, including those illustrated in Annex I;

(b) subsidies contingent, whether solely or as one of several other conditions, upon the use of domestic over imported goods.

For the purposes of point (a), subsidies shall be considered to be contingent in fact upon export performance when the facts demonstrate that the granting of a subsidy, without having been made legally contingent upon export performance, is in fact tied to actual or anticipated exportation or export earnings. The mere fact that a subsidy is accorded to enterprises which export shall not, for that reason alone, be considered to be an export subsidy within the meaning of this provision.

5. Any determination of specificity under the provisions of this Article shall be clearly substantiated on the basis of positive evidence.

Article 5

Calculation of the amount of the countervailable subsidy

The amount of countervailable subsidies shall be calculated in terms of the benefit conferred on the recipient which is found to exist during the investigation period for subsidisation. Normally this period shall be the most recent accounting year of the beneficiary, but may be any other period of at least six months prior to the initiation of the investigation for which reliable financial and other relevant data are available.

Article 6

Calculation of benefit to the recipient

As regards the calculation of benefit to the recipient, the following rules shall apply:

(a) government provision of equity capital shall not be considered to confer a benefit, unless the investment can be regarded as inconsistent with the usual investment practice, including for the provision of risk capital, of private investors in the territory of the country of origin and/or export;

(b) a loan by a government shall not be considered to confer a benefit, unless there is a difference between the amount that the firm receiving the loan pays on the government loan and the amount that the firm would pay for a comparable commercial loan which the firm could actually obtain on the market. In that event the benefit shall be the difference between these two amounts;

(c) a loan guarantee by a government shall not be considered to confer a benefit, unless there is a difference between the amount that the firm receiving the guarantee pays on a loan guaranteed by the government and the amount that the firm would pay for a comparable commercial loan in the absence of the government guarantee. In this case the benefit shall be the difference between these two amounts, adjusted for any differences in fees;

(d) the provision of goods or services or purchase of goods by a government shall not be considered to confer a benefit, unless the provision is made for less than adequate remuneration or the purchase is made for more than adequate remuneration. The adequacy of remuneration shall be determined in relation to prevailing market conditions for the product or service in question in the country of provision or purchase, including price, quality, availability, marketability, transportation and other conditions of purchase or sale.

If there are no such prevailing market terms and conditions for the product or service in question in the country of provision or purchase which can be used as appropriate benchmarks, the following rules shall apply:

(i) the terms and conditions prevailing in the country concerned shall be adjusted, on the basis of actual costs, prices and other factors available in that country, by an appropriate amount which reflects normal market terms and conditions; or

(ii) when appropriate, the terms and conditions prevailing in the market of another country or on the world market which are available to the recipient shall be used.

Article 7

General provisions on calculation

1. The amount of the countervailable subsidies shall be determined per unit of the subsidised product exported to the Community.

In establishing this amount the following elements may be deducted from the total subsidy:

(a) any application fee, or other costs necessarily incurred in order to qualify for, or to obtain, the subsidy;

(b) export taxes, duties or other charges levied on the export of the product to the Community specifically intended to offset the subsidy.

Where an interested party claims a deduction, it must prove that the claim is justified.

2. Where the subsidy is not granted by reference to the quantities manufactured, produced, exported or transported, the amount of countervailable subsidy shall be determined by allocating the value of the total subsidy, as appropriate, over the level of production, sales or exports of the products concerned during the investigation period for subsidisation.

3. Where the subsidy can be linked to the acquisition or future acquisition of fixed assets, the amount of the countervailable subsidy shall be calculated by spreading the subsidy across a period which reflects the normal depreciation of such assets in the industry concerned.

The amount so calculated which is attributable to the investigation period, including that which derives from fixed assets acquired before this period, shall be allocated as described in paragraph 2.

Where the assets are non-depreciating, the subsidy shall be valued as an interest-free loan, and be treated in accordance with Article 6(b).

4. Where a subsidy cannot be linked to the acquisition of fixed assets, the amount of the benefit received during the investigation period shall in principle be attributed to this period, and allocated as described in paragraph 2, unless special circumstances arise justifying attribution over a different period.

Article 8

Determination of injury

1. A determination of injury shall be based on positive evidence and shall involve an objective examination of:

(a) the volume of the subsidised imports and the effect of the subsidised imports on prices in the Community market for like products; and

(b) the consequent impact of those imports on the Community industry.

2. With regard to the volume of the subsidised imports, consideration shall be given to whether there has been a significant increase in subsidised imports, either in absolute terms or relative to production or consumption in the Community. With regard to the effect of the subsidised imports on prices, consideration shall be given to whether there has been significant price undercutting by the subsidised imports as compared with

the price of a like product of the Community industry, or whether the effect of such imports is otherwise to depress prices to a significant degree or prevent price increases which would otherwise have occurred, to a significant degree. No one or more of these factors can necessarily give decisive guidance.

3. Where imports of a product from more than one country are simultaneously subject to countervailing duty investigations, the effects of such imports shall be cumulatively assessed only if it is determined that:

(a) the amount of countervailable subsidies established in relation to the imports from each country is more than de minimis as defined in Article 14(5) and that the volume of imports from each country is not negligible; and

(b) a cumulative assessment of the effects of the imports is appropriate in light of the conditions of competition between imported products and the conditions of competition between the imported products and the like Community product.

4. The examination of the impact of the subsidised imports on the Community industry concerned shall include an evaluation of all relevant economic factors and indices having a bearing on the state of the industry, including: the fact that an industry is still in the process of recovering from the effects of past subsidisation or dumping; the magnitude of the amount of countervailable subsidies; actual and potential decline in sales, profits, output, market share, productivity, return on investments, utilisation of capacity; factors affecting Community prices; actual and potential negative effects on cash flow, inventories, employment, wages, growth, ability to raise capital or investments and, in the case of agriculture, whether there has been an increased burden on government support programmes. This list is not exhaustive, nor can any one or more of these factors necessarily give decisive guidance.

5. It must be demonstrated, from all the relevant evidence presented in relation to paragraph 1, that the subsidised imports are causing injury. Specifically, this shall entail a demonstration that the volume and/or price levels identified pursuant to paragraph 2 are responsible for an impact on the Community industry as provided for in paragraph 4, and that this impact exists to a degree which enables it to be classified as material.

6. Known factors, other than the subsidised imports which are injuring the Community industry at the same time, shall also be examined to ensure that injury caused by these other factors is not attributed to the subsidised imports pursuant to paragraph 5. Factors which may be considered in this respect include the volume and prices of non-subsidised imports, contraction in demand or changes in the patterns of consumption, restrictive trade practices of, and competition between, third country and Community producers, developments in technology and the export performance and productivity of the Community industry.

7. The effect of the subsidised imports shall be assessed in relation to the production of the Community industry of the like product when available data permit the separate identification of that production on the basis of such criteria as the production process, producers' sales and profits. If such separate identification of that production is not possible, the effects of the subsidised imports shall be assessed by examination of the production of the narrowest group or range of products including the like product, for which the necessary information can be provided.

8. A determination of a threat of material injury shall be based on facts and not merely on allegations, conjecture or remote possibility. The change in circumstances which would create a situation in which the subsidy would cause injury must be clearly foreseen and imminent.

In making a determination regarding the existence of a threat of material injury, consideration should be given to, inter alia, such factors as:

(a) the nature of the subsidy or subsidies in question and the trade effects likely to arise there from;

(b) a significant rate of increase of subsidised imports into the Community market indicating the likelihood of substantially increased imports;

(c) sufficient freely disposable capacity of the exporter or an imminent substantial increase in such capacity indicating the likelihood of substantially increased subsidised exports to the Community, account being taken of the availability of other export markets to absorb any additional exports;

(d) whether imports are entering at prices that would, to a significant degree, depress prices or prevent price increases which otherwise would have occurred, and would probably increase demand for further imports; and

(e) inventories of the product being investigated.

Not one of the factors listed above by itself can necessarily give decisive guidance but the totality of the factors considered must lead to the conclusion that further subsidised exports are imminent and that, unless protective action is taken, material injury will occur.

Article 9

Definition of Community industry

1. For the purposes of this Regulation, the term 'Community industry' shall be interpreted as referring to the Community producers as a whole of the like products or to those of them whose collective output of the products constitutes a major proportion, as defined in Article 10(6), of the total Community production of those products, except that:

(a) when producers are related to the exporters or importers, or are themselves importers of the allegedly subsidised product, the term 'Community industry' may be interpreted as referring to the rest of the producers;

(b) in exceptional circumstances the territory of the Community may, for the production in question, be divided into two or more competitive markets and the producers within each market may be regarded as a separate industry if:

(i) the producers within such a market sell all or almost all of their production of the product in question in that market; and

(ii) the demand in that market is not to any substantial degree met by producers of the product in question located elsewhere in the Community.

In such circumstances, injury may be found to exist even where a major portion of the total Community industry is not injured, provided that there is a concentration of subsidised imports into such an isolated market and provided further that the subsidised imports are causing injury to the producers of all or almost all of the production within such a market.

2. For the purpose of paragraph 1, producers shall be considered to be related to exporters or importers only if:

(a) one of them directly or indirectly controls the other; or

(b) both of them are directly or indirectly controlled by a third person; or

(c) together they directly or indirectly control a third person, provided that there are grounds for believing or suspecting that the effect of the relationship is such as to cause the producer concerned to behave differently from non-related producers.

For the purpose of this paragraph, one producer shall be deemed to control another when the former is legally or operationally in a position to exercise restraint or direction over the latter.

3. Where the Community industry has been interpreted as referring to the producers in a certain region, the exporters or the government granting countervailable subsidies shall be given an opportunity to offer undertakings pursuant to Article 13 in respect of the region concerned. In such cases, when evaluating the Community interest of the measures, special account shall be taken of the interest of the region. If an adequate undertaking is not offered promptly or if the situations set out in Article 13(9) and (10) apply, a provisional or definitive countervailing duty may be imposed in respect of the Community as a whole. In such cases the duties may, if practicable, be limited to specific producers or exporters.

4. The provisions of Article 8(7) shall apply to this Article.

Article 10

Initiation of proceedings

1. Except as provided for in paragraph 8, an investigation to determine the existence, degree and effect of any alleged subsidy shall be initiated upon a written complaint by any natural or legal person, or any association not having legal personality, acting on behalf of the Community industry.

The complaint may be submitted to the Commission, or to a Member State, which shall forward it to the Commission. The Commission shall send Member States a copy of any complaint it receives. The complaint shall be deemed to have been lodged on the first working day following its delivery to the Commission by registered mail or the issuing of an acknowledgement of receipt by the Commission.

Where, in the absence of any complaint, a Member State is in possession of sufficient evidence of subsidisation and of resultant injury to the Community industry, it shall immediately communicate such evidence to the Commission.

2. A complaint, as referred to in paragraph 1, shall include sufficient evidence of the existence of countervailable subsidies (including, if possible, of their amount), injury and a causal link between the allegedly subsidised imports and the alleged injury. The complaint shall contain such information as is reasonably available to the complainant on the following:

(a) the identity of the complainant and a description of the volume and value of the Community production of the like product by the complainant. Where a written complaint is made on behalf of the Community industry, the complaint shall identify the industry on behalf of which the complaint is made by a list of all known Community producers of the like product (or associations of Community producers of the like product) and, to the extent possible, a description of the volume and value of Community production of the like product accounted for by such producers;

(b) a complete description of the allegedly subsidised product, the names of the country or countries of origin and/or export in question, the identity of each known exporter or foreign producer and a list of known persons importing the product in question;

(c) evidence with regard to the existence, amount, nature and countervailability of the subsidies in question;

(d) information on changes in the volume of the allegedly subsidised imports, the effect of those imports on prices of the like product in the Community market and the consequent impact of the imports on the Community industry, as demonstrated by relevant factors and indices having a bearing on the state of the Community industry, such as those listed in Article 8(2) and (4).

3. The Commission shall, as far as possible, examine the accuracy and adequacy of the evidence provided in the complaint, in order to determine whether there is sufficient evidence to justify the initiation of an investigation.

4. An investigation may be initiated in order to determine whether or not the alleged subsidies are 'specific' within the meaning of Article 4(2) and (3).

5. An investigation may also be initiated in respect of measures of the type listed in Annex IV, to the extent that they contain an element of subsidy as defined by Article 3, in order to determine whether the measures in question fully conform to the provisions of that Annex.

6. An investigation shall not be initiated pursuant to paragraph 1 unless it has been determined, on the basis of an examination as to the degree of support for, or opposition to, the complaint expressed by Community producers of the like product, that the complaint has been made by or on behalf of the Community industry. The complaint shall be considered to have been made by or on behalf of the Community industry if it is supported by those Community producers whose collective output constitutes more than 50% of the total production of the like product produced by that portion of the Community industry expressing either support for or opposition to the complaint. However, no investigation shall be initiated when Community producers expressly supporting the complaint account for less than 25% of total production of the like product produced by the Community industry.

7. The authorities shall, unless a decision has been made to initiate an investigation, avoid any publicising of the complaint seeking the initiation of an investigation. However, as soon as possible after receipt of a properly documented complaint pursuant to this Article, and in any event before the initiation of an investigation, the Commission shall notify the country of origin and/or export concerned, which shall be invited for consultations with the aim of clarifying the situation as to matters referred to in paragraph 2 and arriving at a mutually agreed solution.

8. If, in special circumstances, the Commission decides to initiate an investigation without having received a written complaint by or on behalf of the Community industry for the initiation of such investigation, this shall be done on the basis of sufficient evidence of the existence of countervailable subsidies, injury and causal link, as described in paragraph 2, to justify such initiation.

9. The evidence both of subsidies and of injury shall be considered simultaneously in the decision on whether or not to initiate an investigation. A complaint shall be rejected where there is insufficient evidence of either countervailable subsidies or of injury to justify proceeding with the case. Proceedings shall not be initiated against countries whose imports represent a market share of below 1%, unless such countries collectively account for 3% or more of Community consumption.

10. The complaint may be withdrawn prior to initiation, in which case it shall be considered not to have been lodged.

11. Where, after consultation, it is apparent that there is sufficient evidence to justify initiating proceedings, the Commission shall do so within 45 days of the lodging of the complaint and shall publish a notice in the Official Journal of the European Union. Where insufficient evidence has been presented, the complainant shall, after consultation, be so informed within 45 days of the date on which the complaint is lodged with the Commission.

12. The notice of initiation of the proceedings shall announce the initiation of an investigation, indicate the product and countries concerned, give a summary of the information received, and provide that all relevant information is to be communicated to the Commission.

It shall state the periods within which interested parties may make themselves known, present their views in writing and submit information, if such views and information are to be taken into account during the investigation. It shall also state the period within which interested parties may apply to be heard by the Commission in accordance with Article 11(5).

13. The Commission shall advise the exporters, importers and representative associations of importers or exporters known to it to be concerned, as well as the country of origin and/or export and the complainants, of the initiation of the proceedings and, with due regard to the protection of confidential information, provide the full text of the written complaint referred to in paragraph 1 to the known exporters and to the authorities of the country of origin and/or export, and make it available upon request to other interested parties involved. Where the number of exporters involved is particularly high, the full text of the written complaint may instead be provided only to the authorities of the country of origin and/or export or to the relevant trade association.

14. A countervailing duty investigation shall not hinder the procedures of customs clearance.

Article 11

The investigation

1. Following the initiation of the proceedings, the Commission, acting in cooperation with the Member States, shall commence an investigation at Community level. Such investigation shall cover both subsidisation and injury, and these shall be investigated simultaneously.

For the purpose of a representative finding, an investigation period shall be selected which, in the case of subsidisation shall, normally, cover the investigation period provided for in Article 5.

Information relating to a period subsequent to the investigation period shall not, normally, be taken into account.

2. Parties receiving questionnaires used in a countervailing duty investigation shall be given at least 30 days to reply. The time limit for exporters shall be counted from the date of receipt of the questionnaire, which for this purpose shall be deemed to have been received one week from the day on which it was sent to the respondent or transmitted to the appropriate diplomatic representative of the country of origin and/or export. An extension to the 30-day period may be granted, due account being taken of the time limits of the investigation, provided that the party shows due cause for such extension, in terms of its particular circumstances.

3. The Commission may request Member States to supply information, and Member States shall take whatever steps are necessary in order to give effect to such requests.

They shall send to the Commission the information requested together with the results of all inspections, checks or investigations carried out.

Where this information is of general interest or where its transmission has been requested by a Member State, the Commission shall forward it to the Member States, provided it is not confidential, in which case a non-confidential summary shall be forwarded.

4. The Commission may request Member States to carry out all necessary checks and inspections, particularly amongst importers, traders and Community producers, and to carry out investigations in third countries, provided that the firms concerned give their consent and that the government of the country in question has been officially notified and raises no objection.

Member States shall take whatever steps are necessary in order to give effect to such requests from the Commission.

Officials of the Commission shall be authorised, if the Commission or a Member State so requests, to assist the officials of Member States in carrying out their duties.

5. The interested parties which have made themselves known in accordance with the second subparagraph of Article 10(12), shall be heard if they have, within the period prescribed in the notice published in the Official Journal of the European Union, made a written request for a hearing showing that they are an interested party likely to be affected by the result of the proceedings and that there are particular reasons why they should be heard.

6. Opportunities shall, on request, be provided for the importers, exporters and the complainants, which have made themselves known in accordance with the second subparagraph of Article 10(12), and the government of the country of origin and/or export, to meet those parties having adverse interests, so that opposing views may be presented and rebuttal arguments offered.

Provision of such opportunities must take account of the need to preserve confidentiality and of the convenience to the parties.

There shall be no obligation on any party to attend a meeting, and failure to do so shall not be prejudicial to that party's case.

Oral information provided under this paragraph shall be taken into account by the Commission in so far as it is subsequently confirmed in writing.

7. The complainants, the government of the country of origin and/or export, importers and exporters and their representative associations, users and consumer organisations, which have made themselves known in accordance with the second subparagraph of Article 10(12), may, upon written request, inspect all information made available to the Commission by any party to an investigation, as distinct from internal documents prepared by the authorities of the Community or its Member States, which is relevant to the presentation of their cases and is not confidential within the meaning of Article 29, and is used in the investigation.

Such parties may respond to such information and their comments shall be taken into consideration wherever they are sufficiently substantiated in the response.

8. Except in circumstances provided for in Article 28, the information which is supplied by interested parties and upon which findings are based shall be examined for accuracy as far as possible.

9. For proceedings initiated pursuant to Article 10(11), an investigation shall, whenever possible, be concluded within one year. In any event, such investigations shall in all cases be concluded within 13 months of their initiation, in accordance with the findings made pursuant to Article 13 for undertakings or the findings made pursuant to Article 15 for definitive action.

10. Throughout the investigation, the Commission shall afford the country of origin and/or export a reasonable opportunity to continue consultations with a view to clarifying the factual situation and arriving at a mutually agreed solution.

Article 12

Provisional measures

1. Provisional duties may be imposed if:

(a) proceedings have been initiated in accordance with Article 10;

(b) a notice has been given to that effect and interested parties have been given adequate opportunities to submit information and make comments in accordance with the second subparagraph of Article 10(12);

(c) a provisional affirmative determination has been made that the imported product benefits from countervailable subsidies and of consequent injury to the Community industry; and

(d) the Community interest calls for intervention to prevent such injury.

The provisional duties shall be imposed no earlier than 60 days from the initiation of the proceedings but no later than nine months from the initiation of the proceedings.

The amount of the provisional countervailing duty shall not exceed the total amount of countervailable subsidies as provisionally established but it should be less than this amount, if such lesser duty would be adequate to remove the injury to the Community industry.

2. Provisional duties shall be secured by a guarantee and the release of the products concerned for free circulation in the Community shall be conditional upon the provision of such guarantee.

3. The Commission shall take provisional action after consultation or, in cases of extreme urgency, after informing the Member States. In this latter case, consultations shall take place 10 days, at the latest, after notification to the Member States of the action taken by the Commission.

4. Where a Member State requests immediate intervention by the Commission and where the conditions of the first and second subparagraphs of paragraph 1 are met, the Commission shall, within a maximum of five working days from receipt of the request, decide whether a provisional countervailing duty shall be imposed.

5. The Commission shall forthwith inform the Council and the Member States of any decision taken under paragraphs 1 to 4. The Council, acting by a qualified majority, may decide differently.

6. Provisional countervailing duties shall be imposed for a maximum period of four months.

Article 13

Undertakings

1. Upon condition that a provisional affirmative determination of subsidisation and injury has been made, the Commission may accept satisfactory voluntary undertakings offers under which:

(a) the country of origin and/or export agrees to eliminate or limit the subsidy or take other measures concerning its effects; or

(b) any exporter undertakes to revise its prices or to cease exports to the area in question as long as such exports benefit from countervailable subsidies, so that the Commission, after specific consultation of the Advisory Committee, is satisfied that the injurious effect of the subsidies is thereby eliminated.

In such a case and as long as such undertakings are in force, the provisional duties imposed by the Commission in accordance with Article 12(3) and the definitive duties imposed by the Council in accordance with Article 15(1) shall not apply to the relevant imports of the product concerned manufactured by the companies referred to in the Commission decision accepting undertakings and in any subsequent amendment of such decision.

Price increases under such undertakings shall not be higher than is necessary to offset the amount of countervailable subsidies, and should be less than the amount of countervailable subsidies if such increases would be adequate to remove the injury to the Community industry.

2. Undertakings may be suggested by the Commission, but no country or exporter shall be obliged to enter into such an undertaking. The fact that countries or exporters do not offer such undertakings, or do not accept an invitation to do so, shall in no way prejudice consideration of the case.

However, it may be determined that a threat of injury is more likely to be realised if the subsidised imports continue. Undertakings shall not be sought or accepted from countries or exporters unless a provisional affirmative determination of subsidisation and injury caused by such subsidisation has been made.

Save in exceptional circumstances, undertakings may not be offered later than the end of the period during which representations may be made pursuant to Article 30(5).

3. Undertakings offered need not be accepted if their acceptance is considered impractical, such as where the number of actual or potential exporters is too great, or for other reasons, including reasons of general policy. The exporter and/or the country of origin

and/or export concerned may be provided with the reasons for which it is proposed to reject the offer of an undertaking and may be given an opportunity to make comments thereon. The reasons for rejection shall be set out in the definitive decision.

4. Parties which offer an undertaking shall be required to provide a non-confidential version of such undertaking, so that it may be made available to interested parties to the investigation.

5. Where undertakings are, after consultation, accepted, and where there is no objection raised within the Advisory Committee, the investigation shall be terminated. In all other cases, the Commission shall submit to the Council forthwith a report on the results of the consultation, together with a proposal that the investigation be terminated. The investigation shall be deemed terminated if, within one month, the Council, acting by qualified majority, has not decided otherwise.

6. If the undertakings are accepted, the investigation of subsidisation and injury shall normally be completed. In such a case, if a negative determination of subsidisation or injury is made, the undertaking shall automatically lapse, except in cases where such a determination is due in large part to the existence of an undertaking. In such cases, it may be required that an undertaking be maintained for a reasonable period.

In the event that an affirmative determination of subsidisation and injury is made, the undertaking shall continue consistent with its terms and the provisions of this Regulation.

7. The Commission shall require any country or exporter from whom undertakings have been accepted to provide, periodically, information relevant to the fulfilment of such undertaking, and to permit verification of pertinent data. Non-compliance with such requirements shall be construed as a breach of the undertaking.

8. Where undertakings are accepted from certain exporters during the course of an investigation, they shall, for the purpose of Articles 18, 19, 20 and 22, be deemed to take effect from the date on which the investigation is concluded for the country of origin and/or export.

9. In case of breach or withdrawal of undertakings by any party to the undertaking, or in case of withdrawal of acceptance of the undertaking by the Commission, the acceptance of the undertaking shall, after consultation, be withdrawn by Commission Decision or Commission Regulation, as appropriate, and the provisional duty which has been imposed by the Commission in accordance with Article 12 or the definitive duty which has been imposed by the Council in accordance with Article 15(1), shall apply, provided that the exporter concerned, or the country of origin and/or export has, except in the case of withdrawal of the undertaking by the exporter or such country, been given an opportunity to comment.

Any interested party or Member State may submit information, showing prima facie evidence of a breach of an undertaking. The subsequent assessment of whether or not a breach of an undertaking has occurred shall normally be concluded within six months, but in no case later than nine months following a duly substantiated request.

The Commission may request the assistance of the competent authorities of the Member States in the monitoring of undertakings.

10. A provisional duty may, after consultation, be imposed in accordance with Article 12 on the basis of the best information available, where there is reason to believe that

an undertaking is being breached, or in case of breach or withdrawal of an undertaking where the investigation which led to the undertaking has not been concluded.

Article 14

Termination without measures

1. Where the complaint is withdrawn, the proceedings may be terminated unless such termination would not be in the Community interest.

2. Where, after consultation, protective measures are unnecessary and there is no objection raised within the Advisory Committee, the investigation or proceedings shall be terminated. In all other cases, the Commission shall submit to the Council forthwith a report on the results of the consultation, together with a proposal that the proceedings be terminated. The proceedings shall be deemed terminated if, within one month, the Council, acting by a qualified majority, has not decided otherwise.

3. There shall be immediate termination of the proceedings where it is determined that the amount of countervailable subsidies is de minimis, in accordance with paragraph 5, or where the volume of subsidised imports, actual or potential, or the injury, is negligible.

4. For proceedings initiated pursuant to Article 10(11), injury shall normally be regarded as negligible where the market share of the imports is less than the amounts set out in Article 10(9). With regard to investigations concerning imports from developing countries, the volume of subsidised imports shall also be considered negligible if it represents less than 4% of the total imports of the like product in the Community, unless imports from developing countries whose individual shares of total imports represent less than 4% collectively account for more than 9% of the total imports of the like product in the Community.

5. The amount of the countervailable subsidies shall be considered to be de minimis if such amount is less than 1% ad valorem, except where, as regards investigations concerning imports from developing countries, the de minimis threshold shall be 2% ad valorem, provided that it is only the investigation that shall be terminated where the amount of the countervailable subsidies is below the relevant de minimis level for individual exporters, which shall remain subject to the proceedings and may be reinvestigated in any subsequent review carried out for the country concerned pursuant to Articles 18 and 19.

Article 15

Imposition of definitive duties

1. Where the facts as finally established show the existence of countervailable subsidies and injury caused thereby, and the Community interest calls for intervention in accordance with Article 31, a definitive countervailing duty shall be imposed by the Council, acting on a proposal submitted by the Commission after consultation of the Advisory Committee.

The proposal shall be adopted by the Council unless it decides by a simple majority to reject the proposal, within a period of one month after its submission by the Commission.

Where provisional duties are in force, a proposal regarding definitive action shall be submitted no later than one month before the expiry of such duties.

No measures shall be imposed if the subsidy or subsidies are withdrawn or it has been demonstrated that the subsidies no longer confer any benefit on the exporters involved.

The amount of the countervailing duty shall not exceed the amount of countervailable subsidies established but it should be less than the total amount of countervailable subsidies if such lesser duty would be adequate to remove the injury to the Community industry.

2. A countervailing duty shall be imposed in the appropriate amounts in each case, on a non-discriminatory basis, on imports of a product from all sources found to benefit from countervailable subsidies and causing injury, except for imports from those sources from which undertakings under the terms of this Regulation have been accepted. The regulation imposing the duty shall specify the duty for each supplier, or, if that is impracticable, the supplying country concerned.

3. When the Commission has limited its examination in accordance with Article 27, any countervailing duty applied to imports from exporters or producers which have made themselves known in accordance with Article 27 but were not included in the examination shall not exceed the weighted average amount of countervailable subsidies established for the parties in the sample.

For the purpose of this paragraph, the Commission shall disregard any zero and de minimis amounts of countervailable subsidies and amounts of countervailable subsidies established in the circumstances referred to in Article 28.

Individual duties shall be applied to imports from any exporter or producer for which an individual amount of subsidisation has been calculated as provided for in Article 27.

Article 16

Retroactivity

1. Provisional measures and definitive countervailing duties shall only be applied to products which enter free circulation after the time when the measure taken pursuant to Article 12(1) or Article 15(1), as the case may be, enters into force, subject to the exceptions set out in this Regulation.

2. Where a provisional duty has been applied and the facts as finally established show the existence of countervailable subsidies and injury, the Council shall decide, irrespective of whether a definitive countervailing duty is to be imposed, what proportion of the provisional duty is to be definitively collected.

For this purpose, 'injury' shall not include material delay of the establishment of a Community industry, nor threat of material injury, except where it is found that this would, in the absence of provisional measures, have developed into material injury. In all other cases involving such threat or delay, any provisional amounts shall be released and definitive duties can only be imposed from the date on which a final determination of threat or material delay is made.

3. If the definitive countervailing duty is higher than the provisional duty, the difference shall not be collected. If the definitive duty is lower than the provisional duty, the duty shall be recalculated. Where a final determination is negative, the provisional duty shall not be confirmed.

4. A definitive countervailing duty may be levied on products which were entered for consumption no more than 90 days prior to the date of application of provisional measures but not prior to the initiation of the investigation.

The first subparagraph shall apply, provided that:

(a) the imports have been registered in accordance with Article 24(5);

(b) the importers concerned have been given an opportunity to comment by the Commission;

(c) there are critical circumstances where for the subsidised product in question injury which is difficult to repair is caused by massive imports in a relatively short period of a product benefiting from countervailable subsidies under the terms of this Regulation; and

(d) it is deemed necessary, in order to preclude the recurrence of such injury, to assess countervailing duties retroactively on those imports.

5. In cases of breach or withdrawal of undertakings, definitive duties may be levied on goods entered for free circulation no more than 90 days before the application of provisional measures, provided that the imports have been registered in accordance with Article 24(5) and that any such retroactive assessment shall not apply to imports entered before the breach or withdrawal of the undertaking.

Article 17

Duration

A countervailing measure shall remain in force only as long as, and to the extent that, it is necessary to counteract the countervailable subsidies which are causing injury.

Article 18

Expiry reviews

1. A definitive countervailing measure shall expire five years from its imposition or five years from the date of the most recent review which has covered both subsidisation and injury, unless it is determined in a review that the expiry would be likely to lead to a continuation or recurrence of subsidisation and injury. Such an expiry review shall be initiated on the initiative of the Commission, or upon a request made by or on behalf of Community producers, and the measure shall remain in force pending the outcome of such review.

2. An expiry review shall be initiated where the request contains sufficient evidence that the expiry of the measures would be likely to result in a continuation or recurrence of subsidisation and injury. Such a likelihood may, for example, be indicated by evidence of continued subsidisation and injury or evidence that the removal of injury is partly or solely due to the existence of measures or evidence that the circumstances of the exporters, or market conditions, are such that they would indicate the likelihood of further injurious subsidisation.

3. In carrying out investigations under this Article, the exporters, importers, the country of origin and/or export and the Community producers shall be provided with the opportunity to amplify, rebut or comment on the matters set out in the review request, and conclusions shall be reached with due account taken of all relevant and duly documented evidence presented in relation to the question as to whether the expiry of

measures would be likely, or unlikely, to lead to the continuation or recurrence of subsidisation and injury.

4. A notice of impending expiry shall be published in the Official Journal of the European Union at an appropriate time in the final year of the period of application of the measures as defined in this Article. Thereafter, the Community producers shall, no later than three months before the end of the five-year period, be entitled to lodge a review request in accordance with paragraph 2. A notice announcing the actual expiry of measures under this Article shall also be published.

Article 19

Interim reviews

1. The need for the continued imposition of measures may also be reviewed, where warranted, on the initiative of the Commission or at the request of a Member State or, provided that a reasonable period of time of at least one year has elapsed since the imposition of the definitive measure, upon a request by any exporter, importer or by the Community producers or the country of origin and/or export which contains sufficient evidence substantiating the need for such an interim review.

2. An interim review shall be initiated where the request contains sufficient evidence that the continued imposition of the measure is no longer necessary to offset the countervailable subsidy and/or that the injury would be unlikely to continue or recur if the measure were removed or varied, or that the existing measure is not, or is no longer, sufficient to counteract the countervailable subsidy which is causing injury.

3. Where the countervailing duties imposed are less than the amount of countervailable subsidies found, an interim review may be initiated if the Community producers or any other interested party submit, normally within two years from the entry into force of the measures, sufficient evidence that, after the original investigation period and prior to or following the imposition of measures, export prices have decreased or that there has been no movement, or insufficient movement of resale prices of the imported product in the Community. If the investigation proves the allegations to be correct, countervailing duties may be increased to achieve the price increase required to remove injury. However, the increased duty level shall not exceed the amount of the countervailable subsidies.

The interim review may also be initiated, under the conditions set out above, at the initiative of the Commission or at the request of a Member State.

4. In carrying out investigations pursuant to this Article, the Commission may, inter alia, consider whether the circumstances with regard to subsidisation and injury have changed significantly, or whether existing measures are achieving the intended results in removing the injury previously determined under Article 8. In these respects, account shall be taken in the final determination of all relevant and duly documented evidence.

Article 20

Accelerated reviews

Any exporter whose exports are subject to a definitive countervailing duty but which was not individually investigated during the original investigation for reasons other than a refusal to cooperate with the Commission, shall be entitled, upon request, to an accelerated review in order that the Commission may promptly establish an individual countervailing duty rate for that exporter.

Such a review shall be initiated after consultation of the Advisory Committee and after Community producers have been given an opportunity to comment.

Article 21

Refunds

1. Notwithstanding Article 18, an importer may request reimbursement of duties collected where it is shown that the amount of countervailable subsidies, on the basis of which duties were paid, has been either eliminated or reduced to a level which is below the level of the duty in force.

2. In requesting a refund of countervailing duties, the importer shall submit an application to the Commission. The application shall be submitted via the Member State in the territory of which the products were released for free circulation, within six months of the date on which the amount of the definitive duties to be levied was duly determined by the competent authorities or of the date on which a decision was made definitively to collect the amounts secured by way of provisional duty. Member States shall forward the request to the Commission forthwith.

3. An application for refund shall be considered to be duly supported by evidence only where it contains precise information on the amount of refund of countervailing duties claimed and all customs documentation relating to the calculation and payment of such amount. It shall also include evidence, for a representative period, of the amount of countervailable subsidies for the exporter or producer to which the duty applies. In cases where the importer is not associated with the exporter or producer concerned and such information is not immediately available, or where the exporter or producer is unwilling to release it to the importer, the application shall contain a statement from the exporter or producer that the amount of countervailable subsidies has been reduced or eliminated, as specified in this Article, and that the relevant supporting evidence will be provided to the Commission. Where such evidence is not forthcoming from the exporter or producer within a reasonable period of time the application shall be rejected.

4. The Commission shall, after consultation of the Advisory Committee, decide whether and to what extent the application should be granted, or it may decide at any time to initiate an interim review, whereupon the information and findings from such review, carried out in accordance with the provisions applicable for such reviews, shall be used to determine whether and to what extent a refund is justified.

Refunds of duties shall normally take place within 12 months and in no circumstances more than 18 months after the date on which a request for a refund, duly supported by evidence, has been made by an importer of the product subject to the countervailing duty. The payment of any refund authorised should normally be made by Member States within 90 days of the decision referred to in the first subparagraph.

Article 22

General provisions on reviews and refunds

1. The relevant provisions of this Regulation with regard to procedures and the conduct of investigations, excluding those relating to time limits, shall apply to any review carried out pursuant to Articles 18, 19 and 20.

Reviews carried out pursuant to Articles 18 and 19 shall be carried out expeditiously and shall normally be concluded within 12 months of the date of initiation of the review. In any event, reviews pursuant to Articles 18 and 19 shall in all cases be concluded within 15 months of initiation.

Reviews pursuant to Article 20 shall in all cases be concluded within nine months of the date of initiation.

If a review carried out pursuant to Article 18 is initiated while a review under Article 19 is ongoing in the same proceedings, the review pursuant to Article 19 shall be concluded at the same time as foreseen above for the review pursuant to Article 18.

The Commission shall submit a proposal for action to the Council no later than one month before the expiry of the above deadlines.

If the investigation is not completed within the above deadlines, the measures shall:

(a) expire in investigations pursuant to Article 18;

(b) expire in the case of investigations carried out pursuant to Articles 18 and 19 in parallel, where either the investigation pursuant to Article 18 was initiated while a review under Article 19 was ongoing in the same proceedings or where such reviews were initiated at the same time; or

(c) remain unchanged in investigations pursuant to Articles 19 and 20.

A notice announcing the actual expiry or maintenance of the measures pursuant to this paragraph shall be published in the Official Journal of the European Union.

2. Reviews pursuant to Articles 18, 19 and 20 shall be initiated by the Commission after consultation of the Advisory Committee.

3. Where warranted by reviews, measures shall be repealed or maintained pursuant to Article 18, or repealed, maintained or amended pursuant to Articles 19 and 20, by the Community institution responsible for their introduction.

4. Where measures are repealed for individual exporters, but not for the country as a whole, such exporters shall remain subject to the proceedings and may be reinvestigated in any subsequent review carried out for that country pursuant to this Article.

5. Where a review of measures pursuant to Article 19 is in progress at the end of the period of application of measures as defined in Article 18, the measures shall also be investigated under the provisions of Article 18.

6. In all review or refund investigations carried out pursuant to Articles 18 to 21, the Commission shall, provided that circumstances have not changed, apply the same methodology as in the investigation which led to the duty, with due account being taken of Articles 5, 6, 7 and 27.

Article 23

Circumvention

1. Countervailing duties imposed pursuant to this Regulation may be extended to imports from third countries, of the like product, whether slightly modified or not, or to imports of the slightly modified like product from the country subject to measures, or to parts thereof, when circumvention of the measures in force is taking place.

2. Countervailing duties not exceeding the residual countervailing duty imposed in accordance with Article 15(2) may be extended to imports from companies benefiting from individual duties in the countries subject to measures when circumvention of the measures in force is taking place.

3. Circumvention shall be defined as a change in the pattern of trade between third countries and the Community or between individual companies in the country subject to measures and the Community, which stems from a practice, process or work for which there is insufficient due cause or economic justification other than the imposition of the duty, and where there is evidence of injury or that the remedial effects of the duty are being undermined in terms of the prices and/or quantities of the like product and that the imported like product and/or parts thereof still benefit from the subsidy.

The practice, process or work referred to in the first subparagraph includes, inter alia:

(a) the slight modification of the product concerned to make it fall under customs codes which are normally not subject to the measures, provided that the modification does not alter its essential characteristics;

(b) the consignment of the product subject to measures via third countries; and

(c) the reorganisation by exporters or producers of their patterns and channels of sales in the country subject to measures in order to eventually have their products exported to the Community through producers benefiting from an individual duty rate lower than that applicable to the products of the manufacturers.

4. Investigations shall be initiated pursuant to this Article on the initiative of the Commission or at the request of a Member State or of any interested party on the basis of sufficient evidence regarding the factors set out in paragraphs 1, 2 and 3. Initiations shall be made, after consultation of the Advisory Committee, by Commission Regulation which may also instruct the customs authorities to make imports subject to registration in accordance with Article 24(5) or to request guarantees.

Investigations shall be carried out by the Commission, which may be assisted by customs authorities and shall be concluded within nine months.

If the facts as finally ascertained justify the extension of measures, this shall be done by the Council, acting on a proposal submitted by the Commission after consultation of the Advisory Committee. The proposal shall be adopted by the Council unless it decides by a simple majority to reject the proposal, within a period of one month after its submission by the Commission.

The extension shall take effect from the date on which registration was imposed pursuant to Article 24(5) or on which guarantees were requested. The relevant procedural provisions of this Regulation with regard to initiations and the conduct of investigations shall apply pursuant to this Article.

5. Imports shall not be subject to registration pursuant to Article 24(5) or measures where they are traded by companies which benefit from exemptions.

6. Requests for exemptions duly supported by evidence shall be submitted within the time limits established in the Commission Regulation initiating the investigation.

Where the circumventing practice, process or work takes place outside the Community, exemptions may be granted to producers of the product concerned that can show that they are not related to any producer subject to the measures and that are found not to be engaged in circumvention practices as defined in paragraph 3.

Where the circumventing practice, process or work takes place inside the Community, exemptions may be granted to importers that can show that they are not related to producers subject to the measures.

These exemptions are granted by decision of the Commission after consultation of the Advisory Committee or decision of the Council imposing measures and shall remain valid for the period and under the conditions set down therein.

Provided that the conditions set in Article 20 are met, exemptions may also be granted after the conclusion of the investigation leading to the extension of the measures.

7. Provided that at least one year has lapsed from the extension of the measures, and in case the number of parties requesting or potentially requesting an exemption is significant, the Commission may decide to initiate a review of the extension of the measures. Any such review shall be conducted in accordance with the provisions of Article 22(1) as applicable to reviews under Article 19.

8. Nothing in this Article shall preclude the normal application of the provisions in force concerning customs duties.

Article 24

General provisions

1. Provisional or definitive countervailing duties shall be imposed by Regulation, and collected by Member States in the form, at the rate specified and according to the other criteria laid down in the Regulation imposing such duties. Such duties shall also be collected independently of the customs duties, taxes and other charges normally imposed on imports.

No product shall be subject to both anti-dumping and countervailing duties for the purpose of dealing with one and the same situation arising from dumping or from export subsidisation.

2. Regulations imposing provisional or definitive countervailing duties, and Regulations or Decisions accepting undertakings or terminating investigations or proceedings, shall be published in the Official Journal of the European Union.

Such Regulations or Decisions shall contain in particular, and with due regard to the protection of confidential information, the names of the exporters, if possible, or of the countries involved, a description of the product and a summary of the facts and considerations relevant to the subsidy and injury determinations. In each case, a copy of the Regulation or Decision shall be sent to known interested parties. The provisions of this paragraph shall apply mutatis mutandis to reviews.

3. Special provisions, in particular with regard to the common definition of the concept of origin, as contained in Council Regulation (EEC) No 2913/92 of 12 October 1992 establishing the Community Customs Code, may be adopted pursuant to this Regulation.

4. In the Community interest, measures imposed pursuant to this Regulation may, after consultation of the Advisory Committee, be suspended by a decision of the Commission for a period of nine months. The suspension may be extended for a further period, not exceeding one year, if the Council so decides, acting on a proposal from the Commission.

The proposal shall be adopted by the Council unless it decides by a simple majority to reject the proposal, within a period of one month after its submission by the Commission.

Measures may only be suspended where market conditions have temporarily changed to an extent that injury would be unlikely to resume as a result of the suspension, and provided that the Community industry has been given an opportunity to comment and these comments have been taken into account. Measures may, at any time and after consultation, be reinstated if the reason for suspension is no longer applicable.

5. The Commission may, after consultation of the Advisory Committee, direct the customs authorities to take the appropriate steps to register imports, so that measures may subsequently be applied against those imports from the date of such registration.

Imports may be made subject to registration following a request from the Community industry which contains sufficient evidence to justify such action.

Registration shall be introduced by Regulation which shall specify the purpose of the action and, if appropriate, the estimated amount of possible future liability. Imports shall not be made subject to registration for a period longer than nine months.

6. Member States shall report to the Commission every month on the import trade of products subject to investigation and to measures, and on the amount of duties collected pursuant to this Regulation.

7. Without prejudice to paragraph 6, the Commission may request Member States, on a case-by-case basis, to supply information necessary to monitor efficiently the application of measures. In this respect, the provisions of Articles 11(3) and (4) shall apply. Any data submitted by Member States pursuant to this Article shall be covered by the provisions of Article 29(6).

Article 25

Consultations

1. Any consultations provided for in this Regulation, except those referred to in Articles 10(7) and 11(10), shall take place within an Advisory Committee, which shall consist of representatives of each Member State, with a representative of the Commission as chairman. Consultations shall be held immediately on request by a Member State or on the initiative of the Commission, and in any event within a period of time which allows the time limits set by this Regulation to be adhered to.

2. The Committee shall meet when convened by its chairman. He shall provide the Member States, as promptly as possible, but no later than 10 working days before the meeting, with all relevant information.

3. Where necessary, consultation may be in writing only. In that event, the Commission shall notify the Member States and shall specify a period within which they shall be entitled to express their opinions or to request an oral consultation which the chairman shall arrange, provided that such oral consultation can be held within a period of time which allows the time limits set by this Regulation to be adhered to.

4. Consultation shall cover, in particular:

(a) the existence of countervailable subsidies and the methods of establishing their amount;

(b) the existence and extent of injury;

(c) the causal link between the subsidised imports and injury;

(d) the measures which, in the circumstances, are appropriate to prevent or remedy the injury caused by the countervailable subsidies and the ways and means of putting such measures into effect.

Article 26

Verification visits

1. The Commission shall, where it considers it appropriate, carry out visits to examine the records of importers, exporters, traders, agents, producers, trade associations and organisations, to verify information provided on subsidisation and injury. In the absence of a proper and timely reply a verification visit may not be carried out.

2. The Commission may carry out investigations in third countries as required, provided that it obtains the agreement of the firms concerned, that it notifies the country in question and that the latter does not object to the investigation. As soon as the agreement of the firms concerned has been obtained the Commission should notify the country of origin and/or export of the names and addresses of the firms to be visited and the dates agreed.

3. The firms concerned shall be advised of the nature of the information to be verified during verification visits and of any further information which needs to be provided during such visits, though this should not preclude requests made during the verification for further details to be provided in the light of information obtained.

4. In investigations carried out pursuant to paragraphs 1, 2 and 3, the Commission shall be assisted by officials of those Member States which so request.

Article 27

Sampling

1. In cases where the number of complainants, exporters or importers, types of product or transactions is large, the investigation may be limited to:

(a) a reasonable number of parties, products or transactions by using samples which are statistically valid on the basis of information available at the time of the selection; or

(b) the largest representative volume of the production, sales or exports which can reasonably be investigated within the time available.

2. The selection of parties, types of products or transactions made under this Article shall rest with the Commission, though preference shall be given to choosing a sample in consultation with, and with the consent of, the parties concerned, provided that such parties make themselves known and make sufficient information available, within three weeks of initiation of the investigation, to enable a representative sample to be chosen.

3. In cases where the examination has been limited in accordance with this Article, an individual amount of countervailable subsidisation shall be calculated for any exporter or producer not initially selected who submits the necessary information within the time limits provided for in this Regulation, except where the number of exporters or producers is so large that individual examinations would be unduly burdensome and would prevent completion of the investigation in good time.

4. Where it is decided to sample and there is a degree of non-cooperation by some or all of the parties selected which is likely to materially affect the outcome of the investigation, a new sample may be selected.

However, if a material degree of non-cooperation persists or there is insufficient time to select a new sample, the relevant provisions of Article 28 shall apply.

Article 28

Non-cooperation

1. In cases in which any interested party refuses access to, or otherwise does not provide necessary information within the time limits provided in this Regulation, or significantly impedes the investigation, provisional or final findings, affirmative or negative, may be made on the basis of the facts available.

Where it is found that any interested party has supplied false or misleading information, the information shall be disregarded and use may be made of the facts available. Interested parties should be made aware of the consequences of non-cooperation.

2. Failure to give a computerised response shall not be deemed to constitute non-cooperation, provided that the interested party shows that presenting the response as requested would result in an unreasonable extra burden or unreasonable additional cost.

3. Where the information submitted by an interested party is not ideal in all respects it should nevertheless not be disregarded, provided that any deficiencies are not such as to cause undue difficulty in arriving at a reasonably accurate finding and that the information is appropriately submitted in good time and is verifiable, and that the party has acted to the best of its ability.

4. If evidence or information is not accepted, the supplying party shall be informed forthwith of the reasons therefore and shall be granted an opportunity to provide further explanations within the time limit specified. If the explanations are considered unsatisfactory, the reasons for rejection of such evidence or information shall be disclosed and given in published findings.

5. If determinations, including those regarding the amount of countervailable subsidies, are based on the provisions of paragraph 1, including the information supplied in the complaint, it shall, where practicable and with due regard to the time limits of the investigation, be checked by reference to information from other independent sources which may be available, such as published price lists, official import statistics and customs returns, or information obtained from other interested parties during the investigation. Such information may include relevant data pertaining to the world market or other representative markets, where appropriate.

6. If an interested party does not cooperate, or cooperates only partially, so that relevant information is thereby withheld, the result may be less favourable to the party than if it had cooperated.

Article 29

Confidentiality

1. Any information which is by nature confidential (for example, because its disclosure would be of significant competitive advantage to a competitor or would have a

significantly adverse effect upon a person supplying the information or upon a person from whom he has acquired the information), or which is provided on a confidential basis by parties to an investigation shall, if good cause is shown, be treated as such by the authorities.

2. Interested parties providing confidential information shall be required to furnish non-confidential summaries thereof. Those summaries shall be in sufficient detail to permit a reasonable understanding of the substance of the information submitted in confidence. In exceptional circumstances, such parties may indicate that such information is not susceptible of summary. In such exceptional circumstances, a statement of the reasons why summarisation is not possible must be provided.

3. If it is considered that a request for confidentiality is not warranted and if the supplier of the information is either unwilling to make the information available or to authorise its disclosure in generalised or summary form, such information may be disregarded unless it can be satisfactorily demonstrated from appropriate sources that the information is correct. Requests for confidentiality shall not be arbitrarily rejected.

4. This Article shall not preclude the disclosure of general information by the Community authorities, and in particular of the reasons on which decisions taken pursuant to this Regulation are based, nor disclosure of the evidence relied on by the Community authorities in so far as is necessary to explain those reasons in court proceedings. Such disclosure must take into account the legitimate interests of the parties concerned that their business or governmental secrets should not be divulged.

5. The Council, the Commission and the Member States, or the officials of any of these, shall not reveal any information received pursuant to this Regulation for which confidential treatment has been requested by its supplier, without specific permission from the supplier. Exchanges of information between the Commission and Member States, or any information relating to consultations made pursuant to Article 25, or consultations described in Articles 10(7) and 11(10), or any internal documents prepared by the authorities of the Community or its Member States, shall not be divulged except as specifically provided for in this Regulation.

6. Information received pursuant to this Regulation shall be used only for the purpose for which it was requested.

This provision shall not preclude the use of information received in the context of one investigation for the purpose of initiating other investigations within the same proceedings concerning the same like product.

Article 30

Disclosure

1. The complainants, importers and exporters and their representative associations, and the country of origin and/or export, may request disclosure of the details underlying the essential facts and considerations on the basis of which provisional measures have been imposed. Requests for such disclosure shall be made in writing immediately following the imposition of provisional measures, and the disclosure shall be made in writing as soon as possible thereafter.

2. The parties mentioned in paragraph 1 may request final disclosure of the essential facts and considerations on the basis of which it is intended to recommend the

imposition of definitive measures, or the termination of an investigation or proceedings without the imposition of measures, particular attention being paid to the disclosure of any facts or considerations which are different from those used for any provisional measures.

3. Requests for final disclosure shall be addressed to the Commission in writing and be received, in cases where a provisional duty has been applied, no later than one month after publication of the imposition of that duty. Where a provisional duty has not been imposed, parties shall be provided with an opportunity to request final disclosure within time limits set by the Commission.

4. Final disclosure shall be given in writing. It shall be made, with due regard to the protection of confidential information, as soon as possible and, normally, not later than one month prior to a definitive decision or the submission by the Commission of any proposal for final action pursuant to Articles 14 and 15. Where the Commission is not in a position to disclose certain facts or considerations at that time, they shall be disclosed as soon as possible thereafter.

Disclosure shall not prejudice any subsequent decision which may be taken by the Commission or the Council but where such decision is based on any different facts and considerations they shall be disclosed as soon as possible.

5. Representations made after final disclosure is given shall be taken into consideration only if received within a period to be set by the Commission in each case, which shall be at least 10 days, due consideration being given to the urgency of the matter.

Article 31

Community interest

1. A determination as to whether the Community interest calls for intervention should be based on an appraisal of all the various interests taken as a whole, including the interests of the domestic industry and users and consumers. A determination pursuant to this Article shall be made only where all parties have been given the opportunity to make their views known pursuant to paragraph 2. In such an examination, the need to eliminate the trade-distorting effects of injurious subsidisation and to restore effective competition shall be given special consideration. Measures, as determined on the basis of subsidisation and injury found, may not be applied where the authorities, on the basis of all the information submitted, can clearly conclude that it is not in the Community interest to apply such measures.

2. In order to provide a sound basis on which the authorities can take account of all views and information in the decision as to whether or not the imposition of measures is in the Community interest, the complainants, importers and their representative associations, representative users and representative consumer organisations may, within the time limits specified in the notice of initiation of the countervailing duty investigation, make themselves known and provide information to the Commission. Such information, or appropriate summaries thereof, shall be made available to the other parties specified in this paragraph, and they shall be entitled to respond to such information.

3. The parties which have acted in conformity with paragraph 2 may request a hearing. Such requests shall be granted when they are submitted within the time limits set in

paragraph 2, and when they set out the reasons, in terms of the Community interest, why the parties should be heard.

4. The parties which have acted in conformity with paragraph 2 may provide comments on the application of any provisional duties imposed. Such comments shall be received within one month of the application of such measures if they are to be taken into account and they, or appropriate summaries thereof, shall be made available to other parties who shall be entitled to respond to such comments.

5. The Commission shall examine the information which is properly submitted and the extent to which it is representative, and the results of such analysis, together with an opinion on its merits, shall be transmitted to the Advisory Committee. The balance of views expressed in the Committee shall be taken into account by the Commission in any proposal made pursuant to Articles 14 and 15.

6. The parties which have acted in conformity with paragraph 2 may request that the facts and considerations on which final decisions are likely to be taken be made available to them. Such information shall be made available to the extent possible and without prejudice to any subsequent decision taken by the Commission or the Council.

7. Information shall be taken into account only where it is supported by actual evidence which substantiates its validity.

Article 32

Relationships between countervailing duty measures and multilateral remedies

If an imported product is made subject to any countermeasures imposed following recourse to the dispute settlement procedures of the Subsidies Agreement, and such measures are appropriate to remove the injury caused by the countervailable subsidies, any countervailing duty imposed with regard to that product shall immediately be suspended, or repealed, as appropriate.

Article 33

Final provisions

This Regulation shall not preclude the application of:

(a) any special rules laid down in agreements concluded between the Community and third countries;

(b) the Community Regulations in the agricultural sector and Council Regulations (EEC) No 2783/75, (EC) No 3448/93 and (EC) No 1667/2006. This Regulation shall operate by way of complement to those regulations and in derogation from any provisions thereof which preclude the application of countervailing duties;

(c) special measures, provided that such action does not run counter to obligations under the GATT.

Article 34

Repeal

Regulation (EC) No 2026/97 is repealed.

References to the repealed Regulation shall be construed as references to this Regulation and be read in accordance with the correlation table set out in Annex VI.

Article 35

Entry into force

This Regulation shall enter into force on the 20th day following its publication in the Official Journal of the European Union.

This Regulation shall be binding in its entirety and directly applicable in all Member States.

ANNEX I

ILLUSTRATIVE LIST OF EXPORT SUBSIDIES

(a) The provision by governments of direct subsidies to a firm or an industry contingent upon export performance.

(b) Currency retention schemes or any similar practices which involve a bonus on exports.

(c) Internal transport and freight charges on export shipments, provided or mandated by governments, on terms more favourable than for domestic shipments.

(d) The provision by governments or their agencies either directly or indirectly through government-mandated schemes, of imported or domestic products or services for use in the production of exported goods, on terms or conditions more favourable than for provision of like or directly competitive products or services for use in the production of goods for domestic consumption, if (in the case of products) such terms or conditions are more favourable than those commercially available on world markets to their exporters.

(e) The full or partial exemption, remission, or deferral specifically related to exports, of direct taxes or social welfare charges paid or payable by industrial or commercial enterprises.

(f) The allowance of special deductions directly related to exports or export performance, over and above those granted in respect of production for domestic consumption, in the calculation of the base on which direct taxes are charged.

(g) The exemption or remission, in respect of the production and distribution of exported products, of indirect taxes in excess of those levied in respect of the production and distribution of like products when sold for domestic consumption.

(h) The exemption, remission or deferral of prior-stage cumulative indirect taxes on goods or services used in the production of exported products in excess of the exemption, remission or deferral of like prior-stage cumulative indirect taxes on goods or services used in the production of like products when sold for domestic consumption; provided, however, that prior-stage cumulative indirect taxes may be exempted, remitted or deferred on exported products even when not exempted, remitted or deferred on like products when sold for domestic consumption, if the prior-stage cumulative indirect taxes are levied on inputs that are consumed in the production of the exported product (making normal allowance for waste). This item shall be interpreted in accordance with the guidelines on consumption of inputs in the production process contained in Annex II.

(i) The remission or drawback of import charges in excess of those levied on imported inputs that are consumed in the production of the exported product (making normal allowance for waste); provided, however, that in particular cases a firm may use a quantity of home market inputs equal to, and having the same quality and characteristics as, the imported inputs as a substitute for them in order to benefit from this provision if the import and the corresponding export operations both occur within a reasonable time period, not to exceed two years. This item shall be interpreted in accordance with the guidelines on consumption of inputs in the production process contained in Annex II and the guidelines in the determination of substitution drawback systems as export subsidies contained in Annex III.

(j) The provision by governments (or special institutions controlled by governments) of export credit guarantee or insurance programmes, of insurance or guarantee programmes against increases in the cost of exported products or of exchange risk programmes, at premium rates which are inadequate to cover the long-term operating costs and losses of the programmes.

(k) The grant by governments (or special institutions controlled by and/or acting under the authority of governments) of export credits at rates below those which they actually have to pay for the funds so employed (or would have to pay if they borrowed on international capital markets in order to obtain funds of the same maturity and other credit terms and denominated in the same currency as the export credit), or the payment by them of all or part of the costs incurred by exporters or financial institutions in obtaining credits, in so far as they are used to secure a material advantage in the field of export credit terms.

Provided, however, that if a Member of the WTO is a party to an international undertaking on official export credits to which at least 12 original such Members are parties as of 1 January 1979 (or a successor undertaking which has been adopted by those original Members), or if in practice a Member of the WTO applies the interest rates provisions of the relevant undertaking, an export credit practice which is in conformity with those provisions shall not be considered an export subsidy.

ANNEX II
GUIDELINES ON CONSUMPTION OF INPUTS IN THE PRODUCTION PROCESS

I

1. Indirect tax rebate schemes can allow for exemption, remission or deferral of prior-stage cumulative indirect taxes levied on inputs that are consumed in the production of the exported product (making normal allowance for waste). Similarly, drawback schemes can allow for the remission or drawback of import charges levied on inputs that are consumed in the production of the exported product (making normal allowance for waste).

2. The illustrative list of export subsidies in Annex I makes reference to the term 'inputs that are consumed in the production of the exported product' in points (h) and (i). Pursuant to point (h), indirect tax rebate schemes can constitute an export subsidy to the extent that they result in exemption, remission or deferral of prior-stage cumulative indirect taxes in excess of the amount of such taxes actually levied on

inputs that are consumed in the production of the exported product. Pursuant to point (i), drawback schemes can constitute an export subsidy to the extent that they result in a remission or drawback of import charges in excess of those actually levied on inputs that are consumed in the production of the exported product. Both points stipulate that normal allowance for waste must be made in findings regarding consumption of inputs in the production of the exported product. Point (i) also provides for substitution, where appropriate.

II

3. In examining whether inputs are consumed in the production of the exported product, as part of a countervailing duty investigation pursuant to this Regulation, the Commission must normally proceed on the following basis.

4. Where it is alleged that an indirect tax rebate scheme, or a drawback scheme, conveys a subsidy by reason of over-rebate or excess drawback of indirect taxes or import charges on inputs consumed in the production of the exported product, the Commission must normally first determine whether the government of the exporting country has in place and applies a system or procedure to confirm which inputs are consumed in the production of the exported product and in what amounts. Where such a system or procedure is determined to be applied, the Commission must normally then examine the system or procedure to see whether it is reasonable, effective for the purpose intended, and based on generally accepted commercial practices in the country of export. The Commission may deem it necessary to carry out, in accordance with Article 26(2), certain practical tests in order to verify information or to satisfy itself that the system or procedure is being effectively applied.

5. Where there is no such system or procedure, where it is not reasonable, or where it is instituted and considered reasonable but is found not to be applied or not to be applied effectively, a further examination by the exporting country based on the actual inputs involved will normally need to be carried out in the context of determining whether an excess payment occurred. If the Commission deems it necessary, a further examination may be carried out in accordance with point 4.

6. The Commission must normally treat inputs as physically incorporated if such inputs are used in the production process and are physically present in the product exported. An input need not be present in the final product in the same form in which it entered the production process.

7. In determining the amount of a particular input that is consumed in the production of the exported product, a 'normal allowance for waste' must normally be taken into account, and such waste must normally be treated as consumed in the production of the exported product. The term 'waste' refers to that portion of a given input which does not serve an independent function in the production process, is not consumed in the production of the exported product (for reasons such as inefficiencies) and is not recovered, used or sold by the same manufacturer.

8. The Commission's determination of whether the claimed allowance for waste is 'normal' must normally take into account the production process, the average experience of the industry in the country of export, and other technical factors, as appropriate. The Commission must bear in mind that an important question is whether the authorities

in the exporting country have reasonably calculated the amount of waste, when such an amount is intended to be included in the tax or duty rebate or remission.

ANNEX III
GUIDELINES IN THE DETERMINATION OF SUBSTITUTION DRAWBACK SYSTEMS AS EXPORT SUBSIDIES

I

Drawback systems can allow for the refund or drawback of import charges on inputs which are consumed in the production process of another product and where the export of this latter product contains domestic inputs having the same quality and characteristics as those submitted for the imported inputs. Pursuant to point (i) of Annex I, substitution drawback systems can constitute an export subsidy to the extent that they result in an excess drawback of the import charges levied initially on the imported inputs for which drawback is being claimed.

II

In examining any substitution drawback system as part of a countervailing duty investigation pursuant to this Regulation, the Commission must normally proceed on the following basis:

1. point (i) of Annex I stipulates that home market inputs may be substituted for imported inputs in the production of a product for export provided such inputs are equal in quantity to, and have the same quality and characteristics as, the imported inputs being substituted. The existence of a verification system or procedure is important because it enables the government of the exporting country to ensure and demonstrate that the quantity of inputs for which drawback is claimed does not exceed the quantity of similar products exported, in whatever form, and that there is not drawback of import charges in excess of those originally levied on the imported inputs in question;

2. where it is alleged that a substitution drawback system conveys a subsidy, the Commission must normally first proceed to determine whether the government of the exporting country has in place and applies a verification system or procedure. Where such a system or procedure is determined to be applied, the Commission shall normally then examine the verification procedures to see whether they are reasonable, effective for the purpose intended, and based on generally accepted commercial practices in the country of export. To the extent that the procedures are determined to meet this test and are effectively applied, no subsidy will be presumed to exist. It may be deemed necessary by the Commission to carry out, in accordance with Article 26(2), certain practical tests in order to verify information or to satisfy itself that the verification procedures are being effectively applied;

3. where there are no verification procedures, where they are not reasonable, or where such procedures are instituted and considered reasonable but are found not to be actually applied or not to be applied effectively, there may be a subsidy. In such cases, further examination by the exporting country based on the actual transactions involved would need to be carried out to determine whether an excess payment occurred. If the

Commission deems it necessary, a further examination may be carried out in accordance with point 2;

4. the existence of a substitution drawback provision under which exporters are allowed to select particular import shipments on which drawback is claimed should not of itself be considered to convey a subsidy;

5. an excess drawback of import charges within the meaning of point (i) of Annex I would be deemed to exist where governments paid interest on any monies refunded under their drawback schemes, to the extent of the interest actually paid or payable.

ANNEX IV

(This Annex reproduces Annex 2 to the Agreement on Agriculture. Any terms or expressions which are not explained herein or which are not self-explanatory are to be interpreted in the context of that Agreement.)

DOMESTIC SUPPORT: THE BASIS OF EXEMPTION FROM THE REDUCTION COMMITMENTS

1. Domestic support measures for which exemption from the reduction commitments is claimed shall meet the fundamental requirement that they have no, or at most minimal, trade-distorting effects or effects on production. Accordingly, all measures for which exemption is claimed shall conform to the following basic criteria:

(a) the support in question shall be provided through a publicly-funded government programme (including government revenue foregone) not involving transfers from consumers; and

(b) the support in question shall not have the effect of providing price support to producers;

plus policy-specific criteria and conditions as set out below.

[...]

Council Regulation (EC) No 584/2006 of 10 April 2006 amending Regulation (EC) No 1480/2003 imposing a definitive countervailing duty and collecting definitely the provisional duty imposed on imports of certain electronic microcircuits known as DRAMs (dynamic random access memories) originating in the Republic of Korea, Official Journal L 103, 12.4.2006, pp. 1–26.

This regulation followed the WTO case on the countervailing duties imposed on certain Korean electronic microcircuits known as dynamic random access memories (DRAMs) (DS 299 EC—Countervailing duties on DRAM chips). The Panel report resulting from that case was not appealed by the EC and was adopted on 3 August 2005. The result was mixed. Korea won on a few points. On others the Community had been properly applying the provisions of the WTO Agreement on Subsidies and Countervailing

Duties, according to the Panel. This Regulation seeks to adapt the imposition of the countervailing duty on Korean DRAMs, in accordance with Regulation No. 1515/2001 (see pp. 491–3), to the recommendations and rulings of the Panel.

THE COUNCIL OF THE EUROPEAN UNION,
Having regard to the Treaty establishing the European Community,
Having regard to Council Regulation (EC) No 1515/2001 of 23 July 2001 on the measures that may be taken by the Community following a report adopted by the WTO Dispute Settlement Body concerning anti-dumping and anti-subsidy matters,
Having regard to Council Regulation (EC) No 2026/97 of 6 October 1997 on protection against subsidised imports from countries not members of the European Community (the basic Regulation),
Having regard to the proposal submitted by the Commission after consulting the Advisory Committee,

Whereas:
A. PROCEDURE
1. Existing measures
(1) By Regulation (EC) No 1480/2003 (the definitive Regulation), the Council imposed a definitive countervailing duty of 34.8% on imports of certain electronic microcircuits known as dynamic random access memories (DRAMs) originating in the Republic of Korea and manufactured by all companies other than Samsung Electronics Co., Ltd (Samsung), for which a 0% duty rate was established. The definitive Regulation was preceded by Commission Regulation (EC) No 708/2003 of 23 April 2003 imposing a provisional countervailing duty on imports of certain electronic microcircuits known as DRAMs (dynamic random access memories) originating in the Republic of Korea (provisional Regulation).
(2) Two exporting producers located in the Republic of Korea cooperated in the investigation which led to the imposition of the existing measures (the original investigation): Samsung, which was not found receiving subsidies, and Hynix Semiconductor Inc. (Hynix). The European Community (EC) industry in the original investigation consisted of two producers which accounted for the major proportion of the total Community production of DRAMs, Infineon Technologies AG, Munich, Germany (Infineon) and Micron Europe Ltd, Crowthorne, United Kingdom (Micron).
(3) The investigation of subsidisation and injury covered the period from 1 January 2001 to 31 December 2001 (IP). The examination of trends relevant for the assessment of injury covered the period from 1 January 1998 to the end of the IP (the period under consideration).

2. Report adopted by the Dispute Settlement Body of the WTO
(4) On 3 August 2005, the Dispute Settlement Body (DSB) of the World Trade Organisation (WTO) adopted a Panel report in 'European Communities— Countervailing measures on dynamic random access memory chips from Korea'.

(5) According to the Panel report, the EC acted in a manner inconsistent with its WTO obligations under:

(a) Article 1.1(a) of the Agreement on Subsidies and Countervailing Measures (the SCM Agreement) in determining that the May 2001 restructuring programme constituted a financial contribution by the government;

(b) Article 1.1(b) of the SCM Agreement in its determination of the existence of a benefit in the case of the syndicated loan;

(c) Articles 1.1(b) and 14 of the SCM Agreement in directly applying, for the purposes of the calculation of the amount of benefit, its grant methodology to all programmes found to constitute a subsidy;

(d) Article 15.4 of the SCM Agreement by not evaluating the factor 'wages' as a relevant factor affecting the state of the domestic industry; and

(e) Article 15.5 of the SCM Agreement by failing to make sure that the injury caused by certain other factors (in particular, decline in demand, overcapacity, and other (non-subsidised) imports) was not attributed to the subsidised imports.

(6) On the other hand, the EC was found to have acted consistently with its WTO obligations under:

(a) Article 1.1(a) of the SCM Agreement in determining that the syndicated loan, the KEIC guarantee, the KDB debenture programme and the October 2001 restructuring programme constituted a financial contribution by the Government of Korea (GOK);

(b) Article 1.1(b) of the SCM Agreement in determining that a benefit was conferred on Hynix by the KEIC guarantee, the KDB debenture programme, the May 2001 restructuring programme and the October 2001 restructuring programme;

(c) Articles 1.2 and 2 of the SCM Agreement in finding de facto specificity (two Korean claims);

(d) Article 15.2 of the SCM Agreement in assessing the significance of the volume and price effects of the subsidised imports (2 Korean claims);

(e) Article 15.4 of the SCM Agreement in considering all factors relevant to the overall condition of the domestic industry, except for the factor 'wages';

(f) Article 15.5 of the SCM Agreement in demonstrating the requisite causal link between the subsidised imports and injury; and

(g) Article 12.7 of the SCM Agreement in applying 'facts available' with respect to the subsidy investigation.

3. Reassessment to implement the DSB's recommendations

(7) In the light of the recommendations set out in the Panel report, the Commission conducted a thorough and objective reassessment of the relevant findings in the definitive Regulation on the basis of information on the record. The scope of the reassessment is appropriately limited to an examination of the five specific aspects of the existing measure, as described above, that were found to be inconsistent with the SCM Agreement. This examination is based on the re-evaluation of the existing evidence on the record of the original investigation in light of the relevant findings in the Panel report.

(8) The reassessment set out below shows that injurious subsidisation still exists, although at a slightly lower level.

B. PRODUCT UNDER CONSIDERATION AND LIKE PRODUCT

(9) The product under consideration and the like product are the same as that covered by the original investigation, i.e. certain electronic microcircuits known as dynamic random access memories (DRAMs), of all types, densities and variations, whether assembled, in processed wafer or chips (dies), manufactured using variations of metal oxide-semiconductors (MOS) process technology, including complementary MOS types (CMOS), of all densities (including future densities), irrespective of access speed, configuration, package or frame etc., originating in the Republic of Korea. The product concerned also includes DRAMs presented in (non-customised) memory modules or (non-customised) memory boards, or in some other kind of aggregate form, provided the main purpose of which is to provide memory.

(10) The product concerned is currently classifiable within CN codes 85422111, 85422113, 85422115, 85422117, ex85422101, ex85422105, ex85489010, ex84733010 and ex84735010.

(11) The Panel report did not cover any claims affecting the findings set out in the definitive Regulation concerning the product under consideration and the like product.

C. REVISED FINDINGS BASED ON THE PANEL REPORT

1. Subsidies

1.1. Introduction

(12) This part sets out the reassessed findings based on the conclusions and recommendations of the Panel report concerning:

(a) whether the May 2001 restructuring programme constituted a financial contribution by the GOK within the meaning of Article 2(1) of the basic Regulation;

(b) whether there was a benefit in the case of the syndicated loan within the meaning of Article 2(2) of the basic Regulation;

(c) the calculation of the amount of the benefit with regard to all subsidy programmes within the meaning of Articles 2(2) and 6 of the basic Regulation.

(13) All other findings concerning subsidies remain as established in the original investigation and set out in the provisional Regulation and the definitive Regulation.

[...]

2. Injury

2.1. Introduction

(90) This part sets out the reassessed findings based on the recommendation of the Panel report concerning the evaluation of the factor 'wages' as a relevant factor affecting the state of the Community industry within the meaning of Article 8(5) of the basic Regulation (which generally corresponds to Article 15.4 of the SCM Agreement).

(91) All other findings concerning injury remain as established in the original investigation and set out in the provisional Regulation and the definitive Regulation.

2.2. Wages

(92) In the original investigation the EC had considered and evaluated the wages factor, but found wages to be irrelevant to its injury determination. However, the Panel found that:

'without a written record of the analytical process undertaken by the investigating authority to evaluate "wages", we cannot examine whether an adequate and reasoned explanation has been provided of how the facts support the injury determination made by the EC and, consequently, whether that determination was consistent with Article 15.4. Without that written record, we would be forced to embark on post hoc speculation about the thought process by which the investigating authority arrived at its ultimate conclusions. We consider that the standard of review in Article 11 of the DSU prevents us from embarking upon this exercise'.

Consequently, the Panel concluded that the EC acted inconsistently with Article 15.4 of the SCM Agreement in not evaluating the 'wages' factor when examining the impact of the subsidised imports on the state of the domestic industry.

(93) In the light of the Panel's finding, the Commission, having again reviewed the information on the record concerning Community wages, both in isolation and together with the other injury factors set out in Article 8(5) of the basic Regulation, provides herein a written record of its evaluation of the wages factor.

[...]

2.3. Conclusion

(98) Based on the foregoing, the conclusion set out in recital 188 of the definitive Regulation that the Community industry suffered material injury within the meaning of Article 8 of the basic Regulation is hereby confirmed.

3. Causation
3.1. Introduction

(99) This part sets out the reassessed findings based on the recommendations of the Panel report concerning the non-attribution to the subsidised imports of any injury caused by other factors (in particular, decline in demand, overcapacity and other, non-subsidised imports) within the meaning of Article 8(7) of the basic Regulation. The Panel's determination in paragraph 7.437 of its report does not preclude a conclusion of a causal relationship between subsidised imports and the material injury suffered by the Community industry, but added that a satisfactory explanation of the nature and extent of the injurious effects of those other factors, preferably with quantitative analysis, as distinguished from the effects of the subsidised imports, is required.

3.2. Decline (contraction) in demand and economic downturn

(100) Article 8(7) of the basic Regulation (which generally corresponds to Article 15.5 of the SCM Agreement) requires examination of any known factors other than subsidised imports which at the same time are injuring the Community industry, and not to attribute injury caused by these other factors to subsidised imports. One of the factors referred to is 'contraction in demand'.

(101) The Panel found in paragraph 8.1(e) of its report that the EC had failed to make sure that the injury caused by 'decline in demand' was not attributed to the subsidised imports. This conclusion was reached in the light of the Panel's findings in paragraphs

7.411 to 7.414 of its report, which treat a 'decline in demand' as synonymous with a 'general economic downturn'.

[...]

(107) Accordingly, the Commission is of the view that its redetermination satisfies the non-attribution requirement under Article 8(7) of the basic Regulation (which generally corresponds to Article 15.5 of the SCM Agreement) in respect of demand growth by showing that, during the period under consideration, trends in demand growth were independent from trends in the sales prices of the Community industry. The Commission is also of the view that its redetermination satisfies the non-attribution requirement in respect of declines in the level of demand by showing that during the period under consideration no such demand declines took place.

3.3. Overcapacity

(108) The Panel noted in paragraph 7.421 of its report that the question of separating and distinguishing the effects of overcapacity in driving prices down should be addressed, irrespective of who is to blame for such overcapacity.

(109) The Commission notes that 'overcapacity' is not expressly referred to in Article 8(7) of the basic Regulation (which generally corresponds to Article 15.5 of the SCM Agreement). The concept is discussed in the provisional and definitive Regulations insofar as it is invoked by certain of the interested parties. It is a relative concept, insofar as it depends on how much capacity is available and how much capacity is being used—that is, on the level of demand. 'Overcapacity' may thus arise either because capacity is increased, or demand falls.

(110) 'Overcapacity' as a possible factor of injury can be examined in the context of the world market or in the context of the Community market. The Commission considers both situations below.

[...]

(118) As reviewed, there is no demonstrated causal relationship between overcapacity and either price declines or injury to the Community industry. In contrast, the Community industry suffered severe declines during 2001, which is the same period when subject import prices plummeted and when subject import volumes reached peak penetration in the Community market. This contrast establishes that subject import volumes and price effects are a separate and distinguishable cause of material injury to the Community industry as compared with overcapacity.

3.4. Other non-subsidised imports

(119) The Panel noted in paragraph 7.426 of its report that there is no requirement to consider non-subsidised imports on a country-per-country basis. The Panel also noted in paragraph 7.435 that a satisfactory explanation of the nature and extent of the injurious effects of non-subsidised imports, as distinguished from the injurious effects of the subsidised imports, should be provided. Accordingly, the effects of non-subsidised imports were examined by considering jointly imports from countries other than Korea (e.g. the United States, Japan, and Taiwan) and imports from Samsung. Recital 151 of the provisional Regulation and recitals 194 and 200 of the

definitive Regulation provide the growth rates of import volume, market share, and average prices of non-subsidised imports during the period under consideration. These data are re-stated below in aggregated index form. Given the very limited number of players in the DRAMs market, for reasons of confidentiality, indices are used to show the evolution of trends.

[...]

(123) Therefore, the Commission is of the view that its redetermination satisfies the non-attribution requirement under Article 8(7) of the basic Regulation (which generally corresponds to Article 15.5 of the SCM Agreement) in respect of non-subject imports by separating and distinguishing this other factor from subsidised imports and showing that, during the period under consideration, non-subject imports did not cause material injury to the Community industry, either in terms of their volume effects or in terms of their price effects.

3.5. Conclusion

(124) Having separated, where appropriate, and analysed further the effects, if any, of the decline in demand, overcapacity and other non-subsidised imports, it is considered that no injury caused by any of these factors has been attributed to the subsidised imports within the meaning of Article 8(7) of the basic Regulation. Furthermore, it is confirmed that the subsidised imports through the effects set out in recitals 144 to 149 of the provisional Regulation and recitals 191 and 192 of the definitive Regulation have caused material injury to the Community industry within the meaning of Article 8(6) of the basic Regulation.

4. Community interest

(125) The contents and conclusions reached in recitals 206 to 209 of the definitive Regulation remain unaffected by the Panel report.

D. REVISED MEASURES

(126) The Panel report and the reassessed findings do not concern Samsung which was not found to be subsidised and thus was attributed a 0% duty rate in the original investigation. The revised subsidy amount for Hynix was found to be lower than the injury elimination level established during the original investigation and, thus, the revised countervailing duty rate should be based on the revised subsidy amount expressed ad valorem, i.e. 32.9%.

(127) It is noted that the revised duty rate for Hynix should apply on the duty as specified by Regulation (EC) No 2116/2005.

(128) The GOK, Hynix and the Community producers Infineon and Micron received disclosure of the reassessed findings and were given an opportunity to comment and to be heard. They each submitted comments.

[...]

(133) Thus, all comments submitted by the interested parties were considered and taken into account where appropriate. However, certain comments were outside the scope of this Regulation which is only intended to implement the DSB recommendations. Thus, such comments have not resulted in any changes to this Regulation,

HAS ADOPTED THIS REGULATION:

Article 1

Council Regulation (EC) No 1480/2003 is hereby amended as follows:

1. Article 1(2) and (3) shall be replaced by the following:

'2. The rate of the definitive countervailing duty applicable to the net free-at-Community-frontier price, before duty, shall be as follows:

Korean producers | Rate of duty (%) | TARIC additional code |

Samsung Electronics Co., Ltd (Samsung) 24th Fl., Samsung Main Bldg 250, 2-Ga, Taepyeong-Ro Jung-Gu, Seoul | 0% | A437 |

Hynix Semiconductor Inc. 891, Daechidong Kangnamgu, Seoul | 32.9% | A693 |

All other companies | 32.9% | A999 |

3. Upon presentation to the Member State's customs authorities of the customs declaration for release into free circulation of multi-combinational forms of DRAMs, the declarant shall indicate in box 44 of the Single Administrative Document (SAD) the reference number corresponding to the below product/origin descriptions indicated in the following table. The rate of the definitive countervailing duty applicable to the net-free-at-Community-frontier price, before duty, shall be as follows: [...]

2. Article 1(5) shall be replaced by the following:

'5. In the case of no indication of any reference number in the SAD, as foreseen in paragraph 3, or if the customs declaration is not accompanied by any statement in the cases required in paragraph 4, the multi-combinational form of DRAM shall—unless the contrary is proved—be considered as originating in the Republic of Korea and as having been manufactured by all companies other than Samsung, and the countervailing duty rate of 32.9% shall apply.

In cases where some of the DRAM chips and/or mounted DRAMs incorporated in multi-combinational forms of DRAMs are not clearly marked and their manufacturers are not clearly identifiable from the statement required in paragraph 4, such DRAM chips and/or mounted DRAMs shall—unless the contrary is proved—be considered as originating in the Republic of Korea and as having been manufactured by companies subject to the countervailing duty. In such cases, the countervailing duty rate applicable to multi-combinational forms of DRAMs shall be calculated on the basis of the percentage represented by the net free-at-Community-frontier price of the DRAM chips and/or mounted DRAMs originating in the Republic of Korea out of the net free-at-Community-frontier price of the multi-combinational forms of DRAM, as established in the table contained in paragraph 3, numbers 2 to 7. Should, however, the value of the aforementioned DRAM chips and/or mounted DRAMs be such to determine that the multi-combinational forms of DRAMs in which they are incorporated becomes of Korean origin, the countervailing duty rate of 32.9% shall apply to the multi-combinational forms of DRAMs'.

Article 2

This Regulation shall enter into force on the day following its publication in the Official Journal of the European Union.

This Regulation shall be binding in its entirety and directly applicable in all Member States.

7.6 Trade barrier regulation

Council Regulation (EC) No 3286/94 of 22 December 1994 laying down Community procedures in the field of the common commercial policy in order to ensure the exercise of the Community's rights under international trade rules, in particular those established under the auspices of the World Trade Organization, Official Journal L 349, 31.12.1994, pp. 71–8. Consolidated version of 5 March 2008.

Many countries have legislation on the books that makes it possible for representatives of economic sectors or individual companies to launch complaints with their own authorities of the allegedly illegal or unfair legislation or application thereof of third countries. The term 'illegal', 'unfair', or 'contrary to the Community's rights' can be used in connection with any measure that is contrary to a third country's WTO obligations and rules of 'fair trade'. However, 'illicit' should be the qualification, if a third country is not a party to the WTO agreements or if the measures are not contrary to WTO obligations, but nevertheless lead to prejudice being inflicted on an economic sector of the Union. What is commonly called the Union's trade barrier regulation, is such an instrument. Application of this instrument can broadly lead to three kinds of outcomes: after discussion with the third country concerned, that country takes satisfactory measures and the procedure is suspended or terminated (Article 11); such satisfactory measures are not taken and, for instance, dispute settlement is resorted to by the Union, mostly in the framework of the WTO; and finally, the application by a branch of industry or individual enterprises may not be justified and their complaint will therefore be rejected. Examples of all these possibilities are included below.

THE COUNCIL OF THE EUROPEAN UNION

Having regard to the Treaty establishing the European Community, and in particular Article 113 thereof,

Having regard to the rules establishing the common organization of agricultural markets and the rules adopted pursuant to Article 235 of the Treaty, applicable to goods processed from agricultural products, and in particular those provisions thereof, which allow for derogation from the general principle that any quantitative restriction or measure having equivalent effect may be replaced solely by the measures provided for in those instruments,

Having regard to the proposal from the Commission,

Having regard to the opinion of the European Parliament,

Whereas the common commercial policy must be based on uniform principles, in particular with regard to commercial defence;

Whereas Council Regulation (EEC) No 2641/84 of 17 September 1984 on the strengthening of the common commercial policy with regard in particular to protection against illicit commercial practices provided the Community with procedures enabling it:

— to respond to any illicit commercial practice with a view to removing the injury resulting therefrom, and

— to ensure full exercise of the Community's rights with regard to the commercial practices of third countries;

Whereas experience in the application of Regulation (EEC) No 2641/84 has shown that the need to deal with obstacles to trade adopted or maintained by third countries remains, and whereas the approach followed in Regulation (EEC) No 2641/84 has not proved to be entirely effective;

Whereas it appears necessary, therefore, to establish new and improved Community procedures to ensure the effective exercise of the rights of the Community under international trade rules;

Whereas international trade rules are primarily those established under the auspices of the WTO and laid down in the Annexes to the WTO Agreement, but they can also be those laid down in any other agreement to which the Community is a party and which sets out rules applicable to trade between the Community and third countries, and whereas it is appropriate to give a clear idea of the types of agreements to which the term 'international trade rules' refers;

Whereas the abovementioned Community procedures should be based on a legal mechanism under Community law which would be fully transparent, and would ensure that the decision to invoke the Community's rights under international trade rules is taken on the basis of accurate factual information and legal analysis;

Whereas this mechanism aims to provide procedural means to request that the Community institutions react to obstacles to trade adopted or maintained by third countries which cause injury or otherwise adverse trade effects, provided that a right of action exists, in respect of such obstacles, under applicable international trade rules;

Whereas the right of Member States to resort to this mechanism should be without prejudice to their possibility to raise the same or similar matters through other existing Community procedures, and in particular before the committee established by Article 113 of the Treaty;

Whereas regard should be paid to the institutional role of the committee established by Article 113 of the Treaty in formulating advice for the institutions of the Community on all issues of commercial policy;

Whereas, therefore, this committee should be kept informed of the development of individual cases, in order to enable it to consider their broader policy implications;

Whereas, moreover, to the extent that an agreement with a third country appears to be the most appropriate means to resolve a dispute arising from an obstacle to trade, negotiations to this end shall be conducted according to the procedures established in Article 113 of the Treaty, in particular in consultation with the committee established thereby;

Whereas it is appropriate to confirm that the Community must act in compliance with its international obligations and, where such obligations result from agreements, maintain the balance of rights and obligations which it is the purpose of those agreements to establish;

Whereas it is also appropriate to confirm that any measures taken under the procedures in question should also be in conformity with the Community's international obligations, as well as being without prejudice to other measures in cases not covered by this Regulation which might be adopted directly pursuant to Article 113 of the Treaty;

Whereas the rules of procedures to be followed during the examination procedure provided for in this Regulation should also be confirmed, in particular as regards the rights and obligations of the Community authorities and the parties involved, and the conditions under which interested parties may have access to information and may ask to be informed of the essential facts and considerations resulting from the examination procedure;

Whereas in acting pursuant to this Regulation the Community has to bear in mind the need for rapid and effective action, through the application of the decision-making procedures provided for in the Regulation;

Whereas it is incumbent on the Commission and the Council to act in respect of obstacles to trade adopted or maintained by third countries, within the framework of the Community's international rights and obligations, only when the interests of the Community call for intervention, and whereas, when assessing such interests, the Commission and the Council should give due consideration to the views by all interested parties in the proceedings;

HAS ADOPTED THIS REGULATION:

Article 1

Aims

This Regulation establishes Community procedures in the field of the common commercial policy in order to ensure the exercise of the Community's rights under international trade rules, in particular those established under the auspices of the World Trade Organization which, subject to compliance with existing international obligations and procedures, are aimed at:

(a) responding to obstacles to trade that have an effect on the market of the Community, with a view to removing the injury resulting therefrom;

(b) responding to obstacles to trade that have an effect on the market of a third country, with a view to removing the adverse trade effects resulting therefrom.

These procedures shall be applied in particular to the initiation and subsequent conduct and termination of international dispute settlement procedures in the area of common commercial policy.

Article 2

Definitions

1. For the purposes of this Regulation, 'obstacles to trade' shall be any trade practice adopted or maintained by a third country in respect of which international trade rules establish a right of action. Such a right of action exists when international trade rules either prohibit a practice outright, or give another party affected by the practice a right to seek elimination of the effect of the practice in question.

2. For the purposes of this Regulation and subject to paragraph 8, 'the Community's rights' shall be those international trade rights of which it may avail itself under international trade rules. In this context, 'international trade rules' are primarily those established under the auspices of the WTO and laid down in the Annexes to the WTO Agreement, but they can also be those laid down in any other agreement to which

the Community is a party and which sets out rules applicable to trade between the Community and third countries.

3. For the purposes of this Regulation, 'injury' shall be any material injury which an obstacle to trade causes or threatens to cause, in respect of a product or service, to a Community industry on the market of the Community.

4. For the purposes of this Regulation, 'adverse trade effects' shall be those which an obstacle to trade causes or threatens to cause, in respect of a product or service, to Community enterprises on the market of any third country, and which have a material impact on the economy of the Community or of a region of the Community, or on a sector of economic activity therein. The fact that the complainant suffers from such adverse effects shall not be considered sufficient to justify, on its own, that the Community institutions proceed with any action.

5. The term 'Community industry' shall be taken to mean all Community producers or providers, respectively:

— of products or services identical or similar to the product or service which is the subject of an obstacle to trade, or

— of products or services competing directly with that product or service, or

— who are consumers or processors of the product or consumers or users of the service which is the subject of an obstacle to trade, or all those producers or providers whose combined output constitutes a major proportion of total Community production of the products or services in question; however:

(a) when producers or providers are related to the exporters or importers or are themselves importers of the product or service alleged to be the subject of obstacles to trade, the term 'Community industry' may be interpreted as referring to the rest of the producers or providers;

(b) in particular circumstances, the producers or providers within a region of the Community may be regarded as the Community industry if their collective output constitutes the major proportion of the output of the product or service in question in the Member State or Member States within which the region is located provided that the effect of the obstacle to trade is concentrated in that Member State or those Member States.

6. The term 'Community enterprise' shall be taken to mean a company or firm formed in accordance with the law of a Member State and having its registered office, central administration or principal place of business within the Community, directly concerned by the production of goods or the provision of services which are the subject of the obstacle to trade.

7. For the purposes of this Regulation, the notion of 'providers of services' in the context of both the term 'Community industry' as defined in paragraph 5, and the term 'Community enterprises' as defined in paragraph 6, is without prejudice to the non-commercial nature which the provision of any particular service may have according to the legislation or regulation of a Member State.

8. For the purposes of this Regulation, the term 'services' shall be taken to mean those services in respect of which international agreements can be concluded by the Community on the basis of Article 113 of the Treaty.

Article 3

Complaint on behalf of the Community industry

1. Any natural or legal person, or any association not having legal personality, acting on behalf of a Community industry which considers that it has suffered injury as a result of obstacles to trade that have an effect on the market of the Community may lodge a written complaint.

2. The complaint must contain sufficient evidence of the existence of the obstacles to trade and of the injury resulting therefrom. Evidence of injury must be given on the basis of the illustrative list of factors indicated in Article 10, where applicable.

Article 4

Complaint on behalf of Community enterprises

1. Any Community enterprise, or any association, having or not legal personality, acting on behalf of one or more Community enterprises, which considers that such Community enterprises have suffered adverse trade effects as a result of obstacles to trade that have an effect on the market of a third country may lodge a written complaint.

2. The complaint must contain sufficient evidence of the existence of the obstacles to trade and of the adverse trade effects, resulting therefrom. Evidence of adverse trade effects must be given on the basis of the illustrative list of factors indicated in Article 10, where applicable.

Article 5

Complaint procedures

1. The complaint shall be submitted to the Commission, which shall send a copy thereof to the Member States.

2. The complaint may be withdrawn, in which case the procedure may be terminated unless such termination would not be in the interests of the Community.

3. Where it becomes apparent after consultation that the complaint does not provide sufficient evidence to justify initiating an investigation, then the complainant shall be so informed.

4. The Commission shall take a decision as soon as possible on the opening of a Community examination procedure following any complaint made in accordance with Articles 3 or 4; the decision shall normally be taken within 45 days of the lodging of the complaint; this period may be suspended at the request, or with the agreement, of the complainant, in order to allow the provision of complementary information which may be needed to fully assess the validity of the complainant's case.

Article 6

Referral by a Member State

1. Any Member State may ask the Commission to initiate the procedures referred to in Article 1.

2. It shall supply the Commission with sufficient evidence to support its request, as regards obstacles to trade and of any effects resulting therefrom. Where evidence of injury or of adverse trade effects is appropriate, is must be given on the basis of the illustrative list of factors indicated in Article 10, where applicable.

3. The Commission shall notify the other Member States of the requests without delay.

4. Where it becomes apparent after consultation that the request does not provide sufficient evidence to justify initiating an investigation, then the Member State shall be so informed.

5. The Commission shall take a decision as soon as possible on the opening of a Community examination procedure following any referral by a Member State made in accordance with Article 6; the decision shall normally be taken with 45 days of the referral; this period may be suspended at the request, or with the agreement, of the referring Member State, in order to allow the provision of complementary information which may be needed to fully assess the validity of the case presented by the referring Member State.

Article 7

Consultation procedure

1. For the purpose of consultations pursuant to this Regulation, an Advisory Committee, hereinafter referred to as 'the Committee', is hereby set up and shall consist of representatives of each Member State, with a representative of the Commission as chairman.

2. Consultations shall be held immediately at the request of a Member State or on the initiative of the Commission, and in any event within a time frame which allows the time limits set by this Regulation to be respected. The chairman of the Committee shall provide the Member States, as promptly as possible, with all relevant information in his possession. The Commission shall also refer such information to the committee established by Article 113 of the Treaty so that it can consider any wider implications for the common commercial policy.

3. The Committee shall meet when convened by its chairman.

4. Where necessary, consultations may be in writing. In such case the Commission shall notify in writing the Member States who, within a period of eight working days from such notification, shall be entitled to express their opinions in writing or to request oral consultations which the chairman shall arrange, provided that such oral consultations can be held within a time frame which allows the time limits set by this Regulation to be respected.

Article 8

Community examination procedure

1. Where, after consultation, it is apparent to the Commission that there is sufficient evidence to justify initiating an examination procedure and that it is necessary in the interest of the Community, the Commission shall act as follows:

(a) it shall announce the initiation of an examination procedure in the Official Journal of the European Communities; such announcement shall indicate the product or service and countries concerned, give a summary of the information received, and provide that all relevant information is to be communicated to the Commission; it shall state the period within which interested parties may apply to be heard orally by the Commission in accordance with paragraph 5;

(b) it shall officially notify the representatives of the country or countries which are the subject of the procedure, with whom, where appropriate, consultations may be held;

(c) it shall conduct the examination at Community level, acting in cooperation with the Member States.

2. (a) If necessary the Commission shall seek all the information it deems necessary and attempt to check this information with the importers, traders, agents, producers, trade associations and organizations, provided that the undertakings or organizations concerned give their consent.

(b) Where necessary, the Commission shall carry out investigations in the territory of third countries, provided that the governments of the countries have been officially notified and raise no objection within a reasonable period.

(c) The Commission shall be assisted in its investigation by officials of the Member State in whose territory the checks are carried out, provided that the Member State in question so requests.

3. Member States shall supply the Commission, upon request, with all information necessary for the examination, in accordance with the detailed arrangements laid down by the Commission.

4. (a) The complainants and the exporters and importers concerned, as well as the representatives of the country or countries concerned, may inspect all information made available to the Commission except for internal documents for the use of the Commission and the administrations, provided that such information is relevant to the protection of their interests and not confidential within the meaning of Article 9 and that it is used by the Commission in its examination procedure. The persons concerned shall address a reasoned request in writing to the Commission, indicating the information required.

(b) The complainants and the exporters and importers concerned and the representatives of the country or countries concerned may ask to be informed of the principal facts and considerations resulting from the examination procedure.

5. The Commission may hear the parties concerned. It shall hear them if they have, within the period prescribed in the notice published in the Official Journal of the European Communities, made a written request for a hearing showing that they are a party primarily concerned by the result of the procedure.

6. Furthermore, the Commission shall, on request, give the parties primarily concerned an opportunity to meet, so that opposing views may be presented and any rebuttal argument put forward. In providing this opportunity the Commission shall take account of the wishes of the parties and of the need to preserve confidentiality. There shall be no obligation on any party to attend a meeting and failure to do so shall not be prejudicial to that party's case.

7. When the information requested by the Commission is not supplied within a reasonable time or where the investigation is significantly impeded, findings may be made on the basis of the facts available.

8. When it has concluded its examination the Commission shall report to the Committee. The report should normally be presented within five months of the announcement of initiation of the procedure, unless the complexity of the examination is such that the Commission extends the period to seven months.

Article 9

Confidentiality

1. Information received pursuant to this Regulation shall be used only for the purpose for which it was requested.

2. (a) Neither the Council, nor the Commission, nor Member States, nor the officials of any of these, shall reveal any information of a confidential nature received pursuant to this Regulation, or any information provided on a confidential basis by a party to an examination procedure, without specific permission from the party submitting such information.

(b) Each request for confidential treatment shall indicate why the information is confidential and shall be accompanied by a nonconfidential summary of the information or a statement of the reasons why the information is not susceptible of such summary.

3. Information will normally be considered to be confidential if its disclosure is likely to have a significantly adverse effect upon the supplier or the source of such information.

4. However, if it appears that a request for confidentiality is not warranted and if the supplier is either unwilling to make the information public or to authorize its disclosure in generalized or summary form, the information in question may be disregarded.

5. This article shall not preclude the disclosure of general information by the Community authorities and in particular of the reasons on which decisions taken pursuant to this Regulation are based. Such disclosure must take into account the legitimate interest of the parties concerned that their business secrets should not be divulged.

Article 10

Evidence

1. An examination of injury shall involve where applicable the following factors:

(a) the volume of Community imports or exports concerned, notably where there has been a significant increase or decrease, either in absolute terms or relative to production or consumption on the market in question;

(b) the prices of the Community industry's competitors, in particular in order to determine whether there has been, either in the Community or on third country markets, significant undercutting of the prices of the Community industry;

(c) the consequent impact on the Community industry and as indicated by trends in certain economic factors such as: production, utilization of capacity, stocks, sales, market share, prices (that is depression of prices or prevention of price increases which would normally have occurred), profits, return on capital, investment, employment.

2. Where a threat of injury is alleged, the Commission shall also examine whether it is clearly foreseeable that a particular situation is likely to develop into actual injury. In this regard, account may also be taken of factors such as:

(a) the rate of increase of exports to the market where the competition with Community products is taking place;

(b) export capacity in the country of origin or export, which is already in existence or will be operational in the foreseeable future, and the likelihood that the exports resulting from that capacity will be to the market referred to in point (a).

3. Injury caused by other factors which, either individually or in combination, are also adversely affecting Community industry must not be attributed to the practices under consideration.

4. Where adverse trade effects are alleged, the Commission shall examine the impact of such adverse effects on the economy of the Community or of a region of the

Community, or on a sector of economic activity therein. To this effect, the Commission may take into account, where relevant, factors of the type listed in paragraphs 1 and 2. Adverse trade effects may arise, inter alia, in situations in which trade flows concerning a product or service are prevented, impeded or diverted as a result of any obstacle to trade, or from situations in which obstacles to trade have materially affected the supply or inputs (e.g. parts and components or raw materials) to Community enterprises. Where a threat of adverse trade effects is alleged, the Commission shall also examine whether it is clearly foreseeable that a particular situation is likely to develop into actual adverse trade effects.

5. The Commission shall also, in examining evidence of adverse trade effects, have regard to the provisions, principles or practice which govern the right of action under relevant international rules referred to in Article 2 (1).

6. The Commission shall further examine any other relevant evidence contained in the complaint or in the referral. In this respect, the list of factors and the indications given in paragraphs 1 to 5 are not exhaustive, nor can one or several of such factors and indications necessarily give decisive guidance as to the existence of injury or of adverse trade effects.

Article 11

Termination and suspension of the procedure

1. When it is found as a result of the examination procedure that the interests of the Community do not require any action to be taken, the procedure shall be terminated in accordance with Article 14.

2. (a) When, after an examination procedure, the third country or countries concerned take(s) measures which are considered satisfactory, and therefore no action by the Community is required, the procedure may be suspended in accordance with the provisions of Article 14.

(b) The Commission shall supervise the application of these measures, where appropriate on the basis of information supplied at intervals, which it may request from the third countries concerned and check as necessary.

(c) Where the measures taken by the third country or countries concerned have been rescinded, suspended or improperly implemented or where the Commission has grounds for believing this to be the case or, finally, where a request for information made by the Commission as provided for by point (b) has not been granted, the Commission shall inform the Member States, and where necessary and justified by the results of the investigation and the new facts available any measures shall be taken in accordance with Article 13 (3).

3. Where, either after an examination procedure, or at any time before, during and after an international dispute settlement procedure, it appears that the most appropriate means to resolve a dispute arising from an obstacle to trade is the conclusion of an agreement with the third country or countries concerned, which may change the substantive rights of the Community and of the third country or countries concerned, the procedure shall be suspended according to the provisions of Article 14, and negotiations shall be carried out according to the provisions of Article 113 of the Treaty.

Article 12

Adoption of commercial policy measures

1. Where it is found (as a result of the examination procedure, unless the factual and legal situation is such that an examination procedure may not be required) that action is necessary in the interests of the Community in order to ensure the exercise of the Community's rights under international trade rules, with a view to removing the injury or the adverse trade effects resulting from obstacles to trade adopted or maintained by third countries, the appropriate measures shall be determined in accordance with the procedure set out in Article 13.

2. Where the Community's international obligations require the prior discharge of an international procedure for consultation or for the settlement of disputes, the measures referred to in paragraph 3 shall only be decided on after that procedure has been terminated, and taking account of the results of the procedure. In particular, where the Community has requested an international dispute settlement body to indicate and authorize the measures which are appropriate for the implementation of the results of an international dispute settlement procedure, the Community commercial policy measures which may be needed in consequence of such authorization shall be in accordance with the recommendation of such international dispute settlement body.

3. Any commercial policy measures may be taken which are compatible with existing international obligations and procedures, notably:

(a) suspension or withdrawal of any concession resulting from commercial policy negotiations;

(b) the raising of existing customs duties or the introduction of any other charge on imports;

(c) the introduction of quantitative restrictions or any other measures modifying import or export conditions or otherwise affecting trade with the third country concerned.

4. The corresponding decisions shall state the reasons on which they are based and shall be published in the Official Journal of the European Communities. Publication shall also be deemed to constitute notification to the countries and parties primarily concerned.

Article 13

Decision-making procedures

1. The decisions referred to in Article 11 (1) and (2) (a) shall be adopted in accordance with the provisions of Article 14.

2. Where the Community, as a result of a complaint pursuant to Articles 3 or 4, or of a referral pursuant to Article 6, follows formal international consultation or dispute settlement procedures, decisions relating to the initiation, conduct or termination of such procedures shall be taken in accordance with Article 14.

3. Where the Community, having acted in accordance with Article 12(2), has to take a decision on the measures of commercial policy to be adopted pursuant to Article 11 (2) (c) or pursuant to Article 12 the Council shall act, in accordance with Article 113 of the Treaty, by a qualified majority, not later than 30 working days after receiving the proposal.

Article 14

Committee procedure

1. Should reference be made to the procedure provided for in this Article, the matter shall be brought before the Committee by its chairman.

2. The Commission representative shall submit to the Committee a draft of the decision to be taken. The Committee shall discuss the matter within a period to be fixed by the chairman, depending on the urgency of the matter.

3. The Commission shall adopt a decision which it shall communicate to the Member States and which shall apply after a period of 10 days if during this period no Member State has referred the matter to the Council.

4. The Council may, at the request of a Member State and acting by a qualified majority revise the Commission's decision.

5. The Commission's decision shall apply after a period of 30 days if the Council has not given a ruling within this period, calculated from the day on which the matter was referred to the Council.

Article 15

General provisions

1. This Regulation shall not apply in cases covered by other existing rules in the common commercial policy field. It shall operate by way of complement to:
— the rules establishing the common organization of agricultural markets and their implementing provisions, and
— the specific rules adopted pursuant to Article 235 of the Treaty, applicable to goods processed from agricultural products.
It shall be without prejudice to other measures which may be taken pursuant to Article 113 of the Treaty, as well as to Community procedures for dealing with matters concerning obstacles to trade raised by Member States in the committee established by Article 113 of the Treaty.

2. Regulation (EEC) No 2641/84 is hereby repealed. References to the repealed Regulation shall be construed as references to this Regulation where appropriate.

Article 16

Entry into force

This Regulation shall enter into force on 1 January 1995.

It shall apply to proceedings initiated after that date as well as to proceedings pending at that date and in relation to which Community examination procedures have been completed.

This Regulation shall be binding in its entirety and directly applicable in all Member States.

The Notice below and the later Decision terminating the examination procedure in respect of the trade restrictive measures imposed on Scotch whisky imported into and traded in Uruguay together form an example of a long, but finally peacefully resolved, negotiation between the EU and Uruguay.

Notice of initiation of an examination procedure concerning obstacles to trade within the meaning of Council Regulation (EC) No 3286/94, consisting of measures imposed and practices followed by the Eastern Republic of Uruguay affecting trade in Scotch whisky (2004/C 261/03), Official Journal C 261, 21.10.2004, pp. 3–5.

On 2 September 2004, the Commission received a complaint pursuant to Article 4 of Council Regulation (EC) No 3286/94 (hereinafter 'the Regulation').

1. THE COMPLAINANT

The complaint was lodged by the Scotch Whisky Association (SWA) on behalf of the its 54 member companies, all of whom are distillers, blenders, brand owners, brokers and exporters of Scotch whisky, comprising together over 95% of Scotland's distilling and blending capacity.

The SWA is an association acting on behalf of one or more Community enterprises within the meaning of Articles 4(1) and 2(6) of the Regulation.

2. THE PRODUCT

The complaint concerns Scotch whiskies produced from cereals in Scotland, in accordance with the provisions of Council Regulation (EC) No 1576/89, and classified within Chapter 22 of the harmonised Customs Nomenclature under HS subheading 220830.

However, the examination which the Commission is initiating may also cover other products, particularly those which interested parties making themselves known within the time limits mentioned below (see Section 8), can show are affected by the alleged practices.

3. SUBJECT

The complaint concerns four separate aspects of Uruguay's tax arrangements concerning imported whiskies:

1. Ageing requirement for whisky

According to the complaint, Uruguay's excise taxes on spirits (IMESI) are based on a system of price bands and fictional prices in order to determine the taxable base for each spirit drink. A flat tax rate is then applied in order to establish the final tax liability.

The price bands for whisky are set at levels designed to ensure that all domestic brands benefit from the lowest taxation. At the same time, Uruguay excludes from the lowest price band all whiskies aged more than three years. Since EU regulations require that whisky be matured for at least three years, Uruguay's ageing requirement has the effect of excluding EU whiskies from the lowest tax category.

2. Prepayment of tax

According to the complaint, Uruguay requires that importers pre-pay the taxes on imports at a rate of 80% of the customs value of the goods. A similar requirement does not apply to domestic producers. Although the pre-payment is offset against the final tax liability, it nevertheless impacts adversely on importers' cash flow and renders imported spirits less competitive vis-à-vis their domestic counterparts.

3. Application of strip stamps

The complainant contends that there is also discrimination against imported products by virtue of the requirement for strip stamps to be affixed to them on arrival in the market, whereas strip stamps are not imposed on domestic products.

4. Lack of transparency

Finally, the complaint addresses the alleged lack of transparency and predictability of the IMESI system, due to the frequent changes in the price band thresholds and the fictional prices, and to the absence of any methodology or criteria to set those values.

4. ALLEGATIONS OF OBSTACLES TO TRADE

The SWA considers that the practices described in Section 3 constitute obstacles to trade within the meaning of Article 2(1) of the Regulation.

(a) Ageing requirement for whisky

The SWA contends that Uruguay's ageing requirement accords treatment to imported Scotch whiskies that is clearly less favourable than that accorded to 'like' products of national origin, in breach of GATT, Articles III.2 and III.4.

According to the SWA, the three-year ageing requirement has the effect of excluding from the lowest price band imported whiskies that would otherwise be included in such lowest band. Only imported whiskies are affected by such requirement, as Uruguay's standards for spirits require only two years of ageing for whisky. Moreover, the SWA claims that price bands for whisky are set at levels designed to ensure that all domestic brands benefit from the lowest taxation.

(b) Pre-payment of tax

The SWA claims that, in so far as Uruguay's pre-payment requirements for imported spirits constitute a restriction on the importation of spirit drinks from other WTO Members, they are in contravention of GATT, Article XI.1. Moreover, by applying internal taxation to imported products so as to provide protection for domestic production, the measures at issue are in breach of GATT Article III.2.

(c) Strip stamps

The SWA contends that Uruguay's strip stamp arrangements for imported spirits constitute a restriction on the importation of goods in contravention of GATT Article XI.1. In the alternative, the measures are in breach of GATT Article III.4 in so far as they accord to imported spirits treatment that is clearly less favourable than that accorded to 'like' products of national origin.

(d) Lack of transparency

The SWA claims that Uruguay's IMESI tax arrangements are in breach of GATT Article X.3(a) in so far as they are not administered in a uniform, impartial and reasonable manner, due to an alleged lack of transparency and predictability.

In the light of the factual information available and the evidence submitted, the Commission is satisfied that the complaint contains sufficient prima facie evidence of the existence of obstacles to trade within the meaning of Article 2(1) of the Regulation.

5. ALLEGATION OF ADVERSE TRADE EFFECTS

In 2002 SWA members exported Scotch whisky with a value of some EUR 20 million to Uruguay, making it the industry's fourth most important market in Latin America. Within the imported whiskies category, Scotch whisky represents some 90% of the total sales of imported whisky in Uruguay.

The complainant claims that the practices subject to the complaint have contributed to a considerable fall in consumption of Scotch whisky in Uruguay. By the end of 2003, Scotch whisky's share of the overall whisky market had fallen from a little over 40% (at the end of 2002) to just under 35% as consumers traded down to lower-priced and lower-taxed domestic products in a context of economic difficulties. According to the complainant, with price a significant factor in consumers' purchasing decisions, the discrimination against Scotch whiskies in the "value for money" segment has had a particularly negative effect.

The complainant has submitted estimates of the likely effect on the shelf prices of a selection of lower-cost Scotch whiskies if the current ageing requirement were to be eliminated. The shelf prices of a number of popular brands would fall by some 15%, thereby enhancing their competitiveness vis-à-vis many domestic brands. Moreover, there are several other brands of Scotch whisky which could also benefit from inclusion in the lowest price band. At present, there is no incentive to trim margins because all Scotch whiskies are automatically excluded from the lowest price band irrespective of their price at the point of first sale. Moreover, the alleged discriminatory application of the pre-payment and the strip stamps requirements also affects the retail price of imported whiskies, thereby adversely affecting their competitive position in the market place.

Finally, the complainant refers more generally to the market performance of imported spirits in Uruguay, where also the other types of internationally traded spirit drinks, such as brandy, gin, rum and vodka, have made little impact in the market, especially if compared with the market penetration achieved in neighbouring markets.

The Commission considers that the complaint contains sufficient prima facie evidence of adverse trade effects, within the meaning of Article 2(4) of the TBR.

6. COMMUNITY INTEREST

The Scotch whisky industry exports each year goods valued in excess of EUR 3.5 billion to some 200 world markets. Over 10 000 people are directly employed in the production of Scotch whisky, while a further 50 000 jobs across the United Kingdom are dependent in part on the industry.

The Commission considers it essential to ensure a level playing field in third-country markets for our export industries, particularly with regard to internal taxes. Tariff protection should not be replaced with other protectionist barriers in breach of international commitments. This is especially important in the case of alcoholic beverages, as they typically bear a high tax burden through the combination of excise duties and value added taxes.

In view of the above, it is considered to be in the Community's interest to initiate an examination procedure.

7. PROCEDURE

Having decided, after due consultation of the Advisory Committee established by the Regulation, that there is sufficient evidence to justify initiating an examination procedure for the purpose of considering the legal and factual issues involved, and that this is in the interest of the Community, the Commission has commenced an examination in accordance with Article 8 of the Regulation.

Interested parties may make themselves known and make known their views in writing on specific issues raised by the complaint, providing supporting evidence.

Furthermore, the Commission will hear the parties who so request in writing when they make themselves known, provided that they are primarily concerned by the result of the procedure.

This notice is published in accordance with Article 8(1)(a) of the Regulation.

8. TIME LIMIT

Any information relating to the matter and any request for a hearing should reach the Commission not later than 30 days following the date of publication of this notice and should be sent in writing to: [...]

Commission Decision of 5 October 2009 terminating the examination procedure concerning the measures imposed by the Eastern Republic of Uruguay affecting the importation and sale of whisky in Uruguay, Official Journal L 262, 6.10.2009, pp. 52–3.

THE COMMISSION OF THE EUROPEAN COMMUNITIES,

Having regard to the Treaty establishing the European Community,

Having regard to Council Regulation (EC) No 3286/94 of 22 December 1994 laying down Community procedures in the field of the common commercial policy in order to ensure the exercise of the Community's rights under international trade rules, in particular those established under the auspices of the World Trade Organisation and in particular Article 11(1) thereof,

Whereas:

A. PROCEDURAL BACKGROUND

(1) On 2 September 2004 SWA (the Scotch Whisky Association) lodged a complaint under Article 4 of Regulation (EC) No 3286/94 (hereinafter 'the Regulation') on behalf of its members representing the Scotch whisky industry.

(2) The complainant alleged that the Community sales of Scotch whisky in the Eastern Republic of Uruguay were hindered by various obstacles to trade within the meaning of Article 2(1) of the Regulation. The alleged obstacles to trade were all directly linked to the IMESI excise taxes in Uruguay (IMESI—Impuesto Especifico Interno), and they consisted in:

(a) the exclusion of whiskies matured for three or more years from the lowest category of taxation;

(b) a lack of transparency and predictability of the IMESI system;

(c) a requirement to affix strip stamps on imported whiskies;

(d) a requirement to pay taxes in advance on imports.

(3) The complainant also claimed that these practices were causing adverse trade effects within the meaning of Article 2(4) of the Regulation.

(4) The Commission decided therefore, after consultation of the Advisory Committee established by the Regulation, that there was sufficient evidence to justify initiating an examination procedure for the purpose of considering the legal and factual issues involved. Consequently, an examination procedure was initiated on 23 October 2004.

B. THE FINDINGS OF THE EXAMINATION PROCEDURE

(5) During the investigation procedure, the Uruguayan authorities expressed their willingness to explore the prospects for a mutually satisfactory solution. The Commission services agreed to discuss possible means of addressing the issues raised in the Complaint. On the basis of the discussion, the Uruguayan authorities proposed to settle the case on the basis of the following elements:

(a) in response to the first practice of the Uruguayan authorities consisting in excluding from the lowest tax category all whiskies aged more than three years (and EU regulations require that whiskies be matured for at least 3 years), Uruguay proposed to withdraw this requirement with effect from 1 July 2005;

(b) as regards the discriminatory requirement to affix strip stamps on imported whisky bottles, Uruguay committed to amend its regulations by 30 June 2005, with an entry force within 90 days;

(c) thirdly, SWA had also claimed that Uruguay's internal tax arrangements for spirits are in breach of GATT insofar as they are not administered in a uniform, impartial and reasonable manner. The Uruguayan authorities proposed to promote a change in the structure of the IMESI excise tax in order to 'bring it in line with the most usual tax systems at the international level' by 2006;

(d) concerning the fourth aspect, i.e. the requirement to pre-pay the import tax at a rate of 80% of the customs value of the goods, we agreed that Uruguay could maintain its system of advance payment of the IMESI tax in order to prevent cases of tax evasion.

C. DEVELOPMENTS AFTER THE END OF THE INVESTIGATION

(6) The first two steps envisaged by Uruguayan authorities were implemented within the agreed deadlines, but the change of the IMESI structure was delayed until 2007, when, with the Decree No 520/2007 of 27 December 2007, Uruguay introduced a new legislation on its excise taxes.

(7) In early 2008 the Commission requested Uruguay a number of clarifications as regards the revisions to the structure of the specific internal tax, which have been provided in May 2009. The clarifications provided by the government of Uruguay confirmed that the Uruguayan system is operating in a manner consistent with the relevant WTO obligations and Uruguay's engagements in the settlement.

D. CONCLUSION AND RECOMMENDATIONS

(8) In view of the above analysis, it is considered that the examination procedure has led to a satisfactory situation with regard to the obstacles that faced the trade as alleged in the complaint lodged by SWA. The examination procedure should therefore be terminated in accordance with Article 11(1) of the Regulation.

(9) The Advisory Committee has been consulted on the measures provided for in this Decision,

HAS DECIDED AS FOLLOWS:

Sole Article

The examination procedure concerning measures imposed by the Eastern Republic of Uruguay affecting the importation and sale of whisky in Uruguay is hereby terminated.

Commission Decision of 9 July 2002 terminating the examination procedure concerning obstacles to trade within the meaning of Council Regulation (EC) No 3286/94, consisting of trade practices maintained by the United States of America in relation to imports of prepared mustard (2002/604/EC), Official Journal L 195, 24.7.2002, pp. 72–3.

The trade practices of the United States (US) in relation to prepared mustard mentioned in the title of this decision, were part of the 'suspension of concessions and other obligations' authorized by the DSB of the WTO under Article 22(2) and (6) of the Dispute Settlement Understanding in response to the continued breach by the EC of its obligations in the so-called bananas case (DS 27). The US, like the EC on other occasions with regard to the US, had specifically targeted certain Member States and products with the aim to create pressure where it would be most effective, so as to incite the EC to comply with its WTO obligations. However, the Federation of French Mustard Producers (FICF) did not appreciate this and argued that by permitting this to happen, the EC contributed to discrimination and had the obligation to start a case in the WTO against the US on this basis, since such discrimination between Member States was contrary to the Community interest. The FICF therefore brought two cases before the Court of First Instance (CFI) for annulment of this Commission Decision, one of which is partially included below.

THE COMMISSION OF THE EUROPEAN COMMUNITIES,

Having regard to the Treaty establishing the European Community,

Having regard to Council Regulation (EC) No 3286/94 of 22 December 1994 (hereinafter 'the Regulation') laying down Community procedures in the field of the common commercial policy in order to ensure the exercise of the Community's rights under international trade rules, in particular those established under the auspices of the World Trade Organisation, as amended by Regulation (EC) No 356/95, and in particular Article 11(1) thereof,

After consulting the Advisory Committee,

Whereas:

A. PROCEDURAL BACKGROUND

(1) On 7 June 2001 the Federation of the French Condiment Industries (FICF) lodged a complaint pursuant to Article 4 of the Regulation.

(2) FICF alleged that Community exports of prepared mustard to the United States of America are hindered by an obstacle to trade within the meaning of Article 2(1) of the Regulation.

(3) The alleged obstacle to trade was constituted by the United States decision to apply the suspension of trade concessions imposed on prepared mustard, following the Hormones Case, only to exports originating in certain Community Member States (the United Kingdom is included).

(4) The Commission decided, after consultation of the Advisory Committee established by the Regulation, that the complaint contained sufficient evidence to justify the initiation of an examination procedure. Consequently, an examination procedure was initiated on 1 August 2001.

B. FINDINGS OF THE INVESTIGATION

(5) Article 1 of the Regulation states that 'this Regulation establishes Community procedures in the field of the common commercial policy in order to ensure the exercise of the Community's rights under international trade rules [...] which [...] are aimed at: (a) [...]; (b) responding to obstacles to trade that have an effect on the market of a third country, with a view to removing the adverse trade effects resulting therefrom'. Furthermore, Article 4(1) of the Regulation provides that a written complaint may be lodged by Community enterprises that are considered to 'have suffered adverse trade effects as a result of obstacles to trade that have an effect on the market of a third country'.

(6) The examination procedure led to the conclusion that the alleged adverse trade effects do not appear to stem from the obstacle to trade claimed in the complaint, i.e. the United States of America practice of applying withdrawal of concessions selectively against some but not all the Member States (selective sanctioning). In fact, the investigation did not provide any evidence of the fact that making the suspension of concessions also applicable to the United Kingdom would result in greater export opportunities for the complainant for prepared mustard to the United States market. Therefore, no adverse trade effect, as defined in the Regulation, can be attributed to the obstacle to trade claimed by the complaint, other than the trade effects resulting from the suspension of concessions which are authorised and lawfully applied by the United States of America under the WTO Agreement. Therefore, in accordance with Article 11, the examination procedure has demonstrated that the interests of the Community do not require that a specific action be taken against the alleged obstacle to trade under the Regulation.

C. CONCLUSIONS AND RECOMMENDATIONS

(7) The examination procedure did not provide sufficient evidence that the interests of the Community require a specific action to be taken under the Regulation against the adverse trade effects produced by the alleged obstacle to trade. The examination procedure should therefore be terminated.

(8) The measures provided for in this Decision are in accordance with the opinion of the Advisory Committee established by the Regulation.

HAS ADOPTED THIS DECISION:

Sole Article

The examination procedure concerning obstacles to trade, within the meaning of the Regulation, consisting of trade practices maintained by the United States of America in relation to imports of prepared mustard initiated on 1 August 2001 is hereby terminated.

Judgment of the Court of First Instance (First Chamber, extended composition) of 14 December 2004, FICF and others v Commission, Case T-317/02, European Court Reports 2004, II-4325, paras. 1–10, 48–58, 84–103, and 109–110.

This case concerns the request for annulment of the rather tersely drafted Commission decision reproduced above. In spite of its rather summary character, the CFI upheld the decision, finding that the essence of the decision was sufficiently reasoned and substantially broadly correct. Of particular interest, and reproduced below, are the parts of the judgment that relate to two core notions of the Trade Barrier regulation, namely what constitutes 'an obstacle to trade' and within which limits the 'interests of the Community' must be taken into account by the Commission.

Legal framework

1. Article 1 of Council Regulation (EC) No 3286/94 of 22 December 1994 laying down Community procedures in the field of the common commercial policy in order to ensure the exercise of the Community's rights under international trade rules, in particular those established under the auspices of the World Trade Organisation (WTO) (OJ 1994 L 349, p. 71), as amended by Council Regulation (EC) No 356/95 of 20 February 1995 (OJ 1995 L 41, p. 3) ('Regulation No 3286/94'), provides:

   'This Regulation establishes Community procedures in the field of the common commercial policy in order to ensure the exercise of the Community's rights under international trade rules, in particular those established under the auspices of the World Trade Organisation which, subject to compliance with existing international obligations and procedures, are aimed at:

   ...(b) responding to obstacles to trade that have an effect on the market of a third country, with a view to removing the adverse trade effects resulting therefrom.

   These procedures shall be applied in particular to the initiation and subsequent conduct and termination of international dispute settlement procedures in the area of common commercial policy.'

2. Article 2 of Regulation No 3286/94 states:

   '1. For the purposes of this Regulation, "obstacles to trade" shall be any trade practice adopted or maintained by a third country in respect of which international trade rules establish a right of action. Such a right of action exists when international trade rules either prohibit a practice outright, or give another party affected by the practice a right to seek elimination of the effect of the practice in question.

2. For the purposes of this Regulation and subject to paragraph 8, "the Community's rights" shall be those international trade rights of which it may avail itself under international trade rules. In this context, "international trade rules" are primarily those established under the auspices of the WTO and laid down in the Annexes to the WTO Agreement, but they can also be those laid down in any other agreement to which the Community is a party and which sets out rules applicable to trade between the Community and third countries.

...

4. For the purposes of this Regulation, "adverse trade effects" shall be those which an obstacle to trade causes or threatens to cause, in respect of a product or service, to Community enterprises on the market of any third country, and which have a material impact on the economy of the Community or of a region of the Community, or on a sector of economic activity therein. The fact that the complainant suffers from such adverse effects shall not be considered sufficient to justify, on its own, that the Community institutions proceed with any action.

...'

3. Article 4 of Regulation No 3286/94 provides:

'1. Any Community enterprise, or any association, having or not legal personality, acting on behalf of one or more Community enterprises, which considers that such Community enterprises have suffered adverse trade effects as a result of obstacles to trade that have an effect on the market of a third country may lodge a written complaint. Such complaint, however, shall only be admissible if the obstacle to trade alleged therein is the subject of a right of action established under international trade rules laid down in a multilateral or plurilateral trade agreement.

2. The complaint must contain sufficient evidence of the existence of the obstacles to trade and of the adverse trade effects resulting therefrom. Evidence of adverse trade effects must be given on the basis of the illustrative list of factors indicated in Article 10, where applicable.'

4. Article 5 of Regulation No 3286/94, headed 'Complaint procedures', reads as follows:

'1. The complaint shall be submitted to the Commission, which shall send a copy thereof to the Member States.

2. The complaint may be withdrawn, in which case the procedure may be terminated unless such termination would not be in the interests of the Community.

3. Where it becomes apparent after consultation that the complaint does not provide sufficient evidence to justify initiating an investigation, then the complainant shall be so informed.

4. The Commission shall take a decision as soon as possible on the opening of a Community examination procedure following any complaint made in accordance with Articles 3 or 4; the decision shall normally be taken within 45 days of the lodging of the complaint; this period may be suspended at the request, or with the agreement, of the complainant, in order to allow the provision of complementary information which may be needed to fully assess the validity of the complainant's case.'

5. Article 7(1) of Regulation No 3286/94 states:

'For the purpose of consultations pursuant to this Regulation, an Advisory Committee, hereinafter referred to as "the Committee", is hereby set up and shall consist of representatives of each Member State, with a representative of the Commission as chairman.'

6. Article 8 of Regulation No 3286/94 provides:

'1. Where, after consultation, it is apparent to the Commission that there is sufficient evidence to justify initiating an examination procedure and that it is necessary in the interest of the Community, the Commission shall act as follows:

(a) it shall announce the initiation of an examination procedure in the *Official Journal of the European Communities*; such announcement shall indicate the product or service and countries concerned, give a summary of the information received, and provide that all relevant information is to be communicated to the Commission; it shall state the period within which interested parties may apply to be heard orally by the Commission in accordance with paragraph 5;

(b) it shall officially notify the representatives of the country or countries which are the subject of the procedure, with whom, where appropriate, consultations may be held;

(c) it shall conduct the examination at Community level, acting in cooperation with the Member States.

...

4. (a) The complainants and the exporters and importers concerned, as well as the representatives of the country or countries concerned, may inspect all information made available to the Commission except for internal documents for the use of the Commission and the administrations, provided that such information is relevant to the protection of their interests and not confidential within the meaning of Article 9 and that it is used by the Commission in its examination procedure. The persons concerned shall address a reasoned request in writing to the Commission, indicating the information required.

(b) The complainants and the exporters and importers concerned and the representatives of the country or countries concerned may ask to be informed of the principal facts and considerations resulting from the examination procedure.

5. The Commission may hear the parties concerned. It shall hear them if they have, within the period prescribed in the notice published in the *Official Journal of the European Communities*, made a written request for a hearing showing that they are a party primarily concerned by the result of the procedure.

...

8. When it has concluded its examination the Commission shall report to the Committee. The report should normally be presented within five months of the announcement of initiation of the procedure, unless the complexity of the examination is such that the Commission extends the period to seven months.'

7. Article 10 of Regulation No 3286/94, which relates to evidence, states:

'...

4. Where adverse trade effects are alleged, the Commission shall examine the impact of such adverse effects on the economy of the Community or of a region of the Community, or on a sector of economic activity therein. To this effect, the

Commission may take into account, where relevant, factors of the type listed in paragraphs 1 and 2. Adverse trade effects may arise, inter alia, in situations in which trade flows concerning a product or service are prevented, impeded or diverted as a result of any obstacle to trade, or from situations in which obstacles to trade have materially affected the supply or inputs (e.g. parts and components or raw materials) to Community enterprises. Where a threat of adverse trade effects is alleged, the Commission shall also examine whether it is clearly foreseeable that a particular situation is likely to develop into actual adverse trade effects.

5. The Commission shall also, in examining evidence of adverse trade effects, have regard to the provisions, principles or practice which govern the right of action under relevant international rules referred to in Article 2(1).

...'

8. Article 11(1) of Regulation No 3286/94 states:

'When it is found as a result of the examination procedure that the interests of the Community do not require any action to be taken, the procedure shall be terminated in accordance with Article 14.'

9. Article 12 of Regulation No 3286/94 provides:

'1. Where it is found (as a result of the examination procedure, unless the factual and legal situation is such that an examination procedure may not be required) that action is necessary in the interests of the Community in order to ensure the exercise of the Community's rights under international trade rules, with a view to removing...the adverse trade effects resulting from obstacles to trade adopted or maintained by third countries, the appropriate measures shall be determined in accordance with the procedure set out in Article 13.

...'

10. Article 14 of Regulation No 3286/94 states:

'1. Should reference be made to the procedure provided for in this article, the matter shall be brought before the Committee by its chairman.

2. The Commission representative shall submit to the Committee a draft of the decision to be taken. The Committee shall discuss the matter within a period to be fixed by the chairman, depending on the urgency of the matter.

3. The Commission shall adopt a decision which it shall communicate to the Member States and which shall apply after a period of ten days if during this period no Member State has referred the matter to the Council.

4. The Council may, at the request of a Member State and acting by a qualified majority, revise the Commission's decision.

5. The Commission's decision shall apply after a period of 30 days if the Council has not given a ruling within this period, calculated from the day on which the matter was referred to the Council.'

[...]

Findings of the Court

48. It must be observed as a preliminary point that, under Regulation No 3286/94, exercise of the right of action by the Community under international trade rules against an obstacle to trade adopted or maintained by a third country and having an effect on the market of that country requires as a minimum that three cumulative

conditions be satisfied, namely the existence of an obstacle to trade, as defined in the regulation, the presence of adverse trade effects which result from that obstacle and the need to take action in the interests of the Community. Where, upon the conclusion of an examination procedure initiated under Regulation No 3286/94, the Commission finds that one of those conditions is not satisfied, the Community institutions are entitled to form the view that such an action should not be proceeded with.

49. As regards the concept of an obstacle to trade, it should be noted that Article 2(1) of Regulation No 3286/94 provides:

'For the purposes of this Regulation, "obstacles to trade" shall be any trade practice adopted or maintained by a third country in respect of which international trade rules establish a right of action. Such a right of action exists when international trade rules either prohibit a practice outright, or give another party affected by the practice a right to seek elimination of the effect of the practice in question.'

50. In the present case, it is not disputed that the Commission formed the view, in the contested decision, that the FICF was objecting to an obstacle to trade constituted by the suspension of tariff concessions by the United States against exporters of prepared mustard in the Member States of the Community, other than those in the United Kingdom, a sanction which the contested decision termed 'selective'.

51. The applicants maintain that in adopting that approach the Commission failed to have regard to the definition of obstacle to trade in Article 2(1) of Regulation No 3286/94, in so far as it had regard in the present case only to the 'illegality' element of that definition.

52. That argument cannot be accepted.

53. First of all, the elements of the definition of an obstacle to trade within the meaning of Regulation No 3286/94 cannot be artificially separated, as the applicants suggest. For there to be an obstacle to trade which may be relied upon for the purposes of the application of Regulation No 3286/94, there must be a right of action under international trade rules. That interpretation arises in particular from the reference in the first paragraph of Article 1 of the regulation to 'compliance with existing international obligations and procedures'. It is supported by the seventh recital in the preamble to Regulation No 3286/94, which states that '[the] mechanism [instituted by the regulation] aims to provide procedural means to request that the Community institutions react to obstacles to trade adopted or maintained by third countries..., provided that a right of action exists, in respect of such obstacles, under applicable international trade rules'. A different interpretation would mean that any trade practice adopted or maintained by a third country could be considered to be an obstacle to trade, even where no right of action existed under international trade rules.

54. As regards, next, the applicants' argument that the Commission's interpretation fails to have regard to the scope of the complaint lodged by the FICF with the Commission, contrary to what the applicants maintained before the Court, the complainant did not allege that the US measures suspending the tariff concessions, to the extent of USD 116.8 million, in relation to certain products from the

Community fell within the definition of 'obstacle to trade'. The complaint accepted that those measures had been authorised by the WTO on 26 July 1999. By contrast, in its arguments in relation to whether the measures adopted by the United States constituted an 'obstacle to trade' within the meaning of Regulation No 3286/94 (point IV of the complaint), the complainant took the view that there was a breach of the rules of the WTO in that 'the United States could not lawfully choose to apply retaliatory measures to certain members of the European Union and not to others' (point IV.1, p. 8 of the complaint) and that 'the selective application of retaliatory measures by the United States call[ed] into question the fixing by the arbitrators of a level of suspension of the concessions' (point IV.2, p. 11 of the complaint). Furthermore, it accepted that 'the conclusions and recommendations of the panel and the Appellate Body referred to the "European Communities" [and that] the United States were accordingly obliged to apply their measures to the "European Communities" and were not entitled to make any distinction between the Member States, all of which applied the contested Community measures' (p. 13 of the complaint). Lastly, it stated that 'the attitude of the United States had the effect of distorting the Community element of the trade policy provided for under the Treaty' in that the retaliatory measures related only to 14 of the 15 Member States (p. 14 of the complaint).

55. It follows that the obstacle to trade which the complaint attacks consisted only in the selective application of the US measures suspending the tariff concessions, and that the Commission did not misinterpret the scope of the complaint. Furthermore, in the present case, having regard to the definition of an obstacle to trade set out in paragraph 53 above, the obstacle to trade under Regulation No 3286/94 could consist only in the selective application of the US measures suspending the tariff concessions. As it is only obstacles to trade in relation to which a right of action under international trade rules exists which fall within the scope of Regulation No 3286/94, a procedure under that regulation could not be initiated in relation to the US measures suspending tariff concessions which had been authorised by the WTO, in that, as a matter of principle, no Community right of action under international trade rules existed in relation to those measures. That is why point 4 of the notice of initiation of the examination procedure, referred to at paragraph 20 above, stated that the obstacle to trade alleged in the complaint was constituted by the maintaining of 'trade measures...against several Member States rather than the whole of the Community' and the FICF considered, without the correctness of that view being challenged before the Court, that 'the practice of seeking measures against all the Member States, which are subsequently applied only in relation to some of them, failed to reflect the predictability which the dispute settlement system requires'. Moreover, it should also be noted that point 1.4 of the examination report drawn up by the Commission, headed 'The obstacle to trade', stated:

'...it is important to note that the obstacle to trade at issue in this investigation does not consist in the US suspension of the concessions following the Hormones case, but in the way in which this suspension has been enforced by the United States. Accordingly, the complainant does not question the US right under the

WTO DSU to suspend the above-mentioned concessions, but only its right to suspend them with regard to only several Community Member States, by excluding others.'

56. Contrary to what the applicants maintain, in stating that the obstacle to trade identified in the complaint consisted in the selective application of the US measures to Member States of the Community recitals (3) and (6) to the contested decision are consistent both with the definition of 'obstacle to trade' set out in Article 2(1) of Regulation No 3286/94 and with the definition arising from the complaint in the present case, which was followed in the notice of initiation of the procedure and the examination report.

57. It follows from all the above considerations that, contrary to what the applicants maintain, the Commission did not restrict itself in the present case only to the 'illegality' element of the definition of an obstacle to trade, but took account of all the essential and indissociable elements of the concept of an obstacle to trade, as defined in Article 2(1) of Regulation No 3286/94.

58. In those circumstances, the first plea is rejected.

[...]

The fourth plea, alleging breach of Article 11(1) of Regulation No 3286/94
Arguments of the parties

84. The applicants submit that the contested decision confused the 'interests of the Community', referred to in Article 11(1) of Regulation No 3286/94, with the interests of the complainant. In the applicants' opinion, such an approach not only contravenes that provision, but in this case also disregards the fact that other parties intervened during the examination procedure and that when the initiation of that procedure was announced on 1 August 2001 the Commission recognised the interest of the Community in 'tackling the US practices which can represent a systemic threat to the role of the Community in the WTO and severely affect the cohesion and solidarity of the [Community], since any exclusion of a Member State from suspension of trade concessions inevitably implies an increased burden for the others'.

85. In addition, the applicants take the view that the remarks made by the Commission in the procedure before the Court to the effect that an analysis of the interests of the complainant is a condition precedent to an analysis of the interests of the Community are not compatible with the contested decision inasmuch as, in order to terminate the examination procedure, the Commission relied on the absence of any Community interest and not the absence of any interest on the complainant's part. In any event, the applicants consider that the recognition by the Commission in the written procedure of the distinction between the interests of the complainant and those of the Community supports their claim that in this case the contested decision infringed Article 11(4) of Regulation No 3286/94.

86. The Commission maintains that Regulation No 3286/94 does not define the concept of 'interests of the Community' and that it has a wide discretion in that regard. Nevertheless, it claims, having regard to the general scheme of Regulation No 3286/94 that concept has a very precise role to play, which is to prevent an action

being proceeded with on principle or *in abstracto*. In other words, the Commission considers that a complainant cannot rely on Regulation No 3286/94 to urge the Community to take action on principle in defence of the general interests of the Community, if it has not itself suffered adverse trade effects. As, in the present case, the complainant has not suffered such effects other than those which the retaliatory measures could (lawfully) give rise to, the condition precedent to the examination of the Community interest in taking action was not satisfied. Furthermore, the conclusions of the examination report clearly show that the applicants had no interest in the measures being uniformly applied in relation to all the Member States of the Community.

87. In its rejoinder, the Commission also states that it took account of all the interests at issue, including those of the undertakings which intervened during the examination procedure, as is shown by the examination report, the conclusions of which were fully taken account of in the contested decision. In any event, the selective nature of the US measures principally affect prepared mustard, since, in the present case, only that product was exported by the United Kingdom, with Roquefort, foie gras and shallots accordingly being excluded.

88. In short, the Commission considers that it correctly took the view that, in the light of the conclusions of the examination report, it was not in the interests of the Community to continue the procedure.

Findings of the Court
– Preliminary remarks
89. Regulation No 3286/94 provides no definition of the 'interests of the Community', any more than it states the rules governing the examination of those interests. However, a number of provisions of Regulation No 3286/94 refer to that expression.

90. Article 8(1) of Regulation No 3286/94 thus states that the Commission is to initiate an examination procedure 'where, after consultation, it is apparent to [it] that there is sufficient evidence to justify initiating an examination procedure and that it is necessary in the interest of the Community'.

91. In addition, Article 11(1) of Regulation No 3286/94 provides that 'when it is found as a result of the examination procedure that the interests of the Community do not require any action to be taken, the procedure shall be terminated in accordance with Article 14'.

92. Moreover, Article 12(1) of Regulation No 3286/94 states that 'where it is found (as a result of the examination procedure, unless the factual and legal situation is such that an examination procedure may not be required) that action is necessary in the interests of the Community in order to ensure the exercise of the Community's rights under international trade rules, with a view to removing...the adverse trade effects resulting from obstacles to trade adopted or maintained by third countries, the appropriate measures shall be determined'.

93. Those provisions must be read in the light of the 15th recital in the preamble to Regulation No 3286/94, which states that 'it is incumbent on the Commission...to act in respect of obstacles to trade adopted or maintained by third countries, within the framework of the Community's international rights and obligations, only when

the interests of the Community call for intervention, and…when assessing such interests, the Commission…should give due consideration to the views [of] all interested parties in the proceedings'.

94. The question whether the interests of the Community require that action be taken involves appraisal of complex economic situations and judicial review of such an appraisal must be limited to verifying that the relevant procedural rules have been complied with, that the facts on which the choice is based have been accurately stated and that there has not been a manifest error of assessment of those facts or a misuse of powers (see, to that effect, Case C-179/87 *Sharp Corporation v Council* [1992] ECR I-1635, paragraph 58, and Case T-2/95 *Industrie des poudres sphériques v Council* [1998] ECR II-3939, paragraph 292). Where proceedings are brought before the Community judicature for the annulment of a Commission decision terminating an examination procedure relating to obstacles to trade for reasons relating to the absence of a Community interest under Regulation No 3286/94, the scope of judicial review includes verifying the absence of errors of law (see, by way of analogy, Case T-132/01 *Euroalliages and Others v Commission* [2003] ECR II-2359, paragraph 49). That restriction on judicial review in the context of the examination of anti-dumping measures applies a fortiori to proceedings having a much wider scope and which may, depending on the circumstances, result in an international complaint being brought.

95. It is in the light of those considerations that it should be determined whether, as the applicants maintain, first, the interest of the Community in taking action against an obstacle to trade which is the subject of a complaint has already been definitively examined and determined when the notice of initiation of the examination procedure is published and, secondly, whether the Commission has assimilated or reduced the interests of the Community to the individual interests of the complainant, without taking account of the interests of the other interested parties.

– The assessment of the interests of the Community when the notice of initiation of the examination procedure is published

96. At point 6 of the notice of initiation of the examination procedure, the Commission stated:

'There is a Community interest in tackling the US practices which can represent a systemic threat to the role of the Community in the WTO and severely affect the cohesion and solidarity of the [Community], since any exclusion of a Member State from suspension of trade concessions inevitably implies an increased burden for the others. Therefore, it is considered to be in the Community's interest to initiate an examination procedure.'

97. Generally speaking, it may be considered that the assessment of the interests of the Community carried out when the examination procedure is initiated, is, by definition, of a preparatory nature. It cannot therefore be compared with the assessment which must be carried out subsequently, that is to say on termination of the examination procedure, when deciding whether action is necessary in the interests of the Community.

98. A different interpretation would mean that, when the Commission decides to initiate an examination procedure, it is automatically obliged, when the decision as to whether the Community should act is taken, to assume that such action is necessary, provided that the other legal conditions for the application of Regulation No 3286/94, namely the existence of an obstacle to trade and the existence of adverse trade effects arising from it, are satisfied, thereby depriving the Commission of its power of discretion.

99. In the present case, the general terms in which point 6 of the notice of initiation of the examination procedure is expressed could not be interpreted as meaning that the Commission had abandoned all right to decide, on termination of the examination procedure, whether or not the interests of the Community required that action be taken in the case in question. It is sufficient to hold that point 6 of the notice of initiation merely found that it was in the interests of the Community to 'initiate an examination procedure'.

100. The applicants' first argument must accordingly be rejected.
    – The assimilation or reduction of the Community's interests to the individual interests of the complainant and the failure to take account of the interests of the other interested parties

101. The argument in question is based essentially on the following two complaints, namely, first, failure to take account of the interests of the interested parties other than the complainant and, secondly, the assimilation or reduction by the Commission of the interests of the Community to those of the complainant.

102. With respect to the first complaint, the contested decision does not refer in any way whatsoever to those parties.

103. However, that does not constitute a breach of Article 11(1) of Regulation No 3286/94 in the present case.

[...]

109. The complaint relative to the failure to take account of the interests of the interested parties other than the complainant must accordingly be rejected.

110. As regards the complaint relating to the alleged assimilation of the interests of the Community to those of the complainant, reference should first be made to recitals (6) and (7) to the contested decision.

111. In recital (6), the Commission, having stated that 'in fact, the investigation did not provide any evidence of the fact that making the suspension of [tariff] concessions also applicable to the United Kingdom would result in greater export opportunities for the complainant for prepared mustard to the [US] market' and then that 'therefore, no adverse trade effect, as defined in the regulation, can be attributed to the obstacle to trade claimed by the complaint', concluded that 'therefore, in accordance with Article 11 [of Regulation No 3286/94], the examination procedure has demonstrated that the interests of the Community do not require that a specific action be taken against the alleged obstacle to trade'.

112. In recital (7), the Commission concluded that 'the examination procedure did not provide sufficient evidence that the interests of the Community require a specific action to be taken under the Regulation' and that 'the examination procedure should therefore be terminated'.

113. The use of the conjunction 'therefore' in the last sentence of recital (6) shows that, in the Commission's opinion, the fact that the interests of the Community did not require that action be taken is, at least indirectly, the result of the finding that the complainant had no interest in the suspension of the tariff concessions being extended to the United Kingdom, inasmuch as it suffered no adverse trade effects as a result of the selective application of the US measures.

114. The requirement that the interest of the complainant should first be established before a Community interest may itself exist was, moreover, confirmed by the Commission in its written pleadings. It defended the idea that Regulation No 3286/94 cannot be used by a complainant to urge the Community to take action on principle in defence of the general interest of the Community, without itself having suffered adverse trade effects.

115. Accordingly, contrary to what the applicants claim, the arguments set out by the Commission in the written pleadings before the Court are not incompatible with the reasons for the contested decision.

116. Reference should next be made to the relevant passages of the examination report. At point 4 of the examination report (headed 'Community Interest'), the Commission stated:

'The findings of the investigation have demonstrated that there are no adverse trade effects to the applicant that are caused by the alleged obstacle to trade in this case. This finding already deprives the procedure of one basic condition for pursuing this action further under the [regulation]. None the less, the Commission has evaluated whether there are other courses of action that the Community could take to address the potential violations and trade effects identified in this report.'

117. It went on to observe:

'...a WTO dispute is not likely to eliminate or reduce the economic problems faced by the complainants. On the other hand, the legal and political significance of the US practice could hardly be underestimated. Indeed, the US appear to have adopted the practice of "selective sanctioning" as a trade "weapon" in order to undermine the internal cohesion of the EC and thus influence its relations with its major trade partner. In sum, the Commission is of the view that the broader and long-term Community interests would require an action aimed at avoiding that the US practice of suspending concessions only to some EC Member States and not to others (i.e. "selective sanctioning") takes place in the future. In this perspective, the Commission will pursue the discussions for a mutually satisfactory solution on the Hormones case and will discuss with the US authorities the systemic issues raised in this report.'

118. At point 6 of the examination report, headed 'Envisaged course of action', the Commission, having noted the three conditions required for Community action to be proceeded with (that is to say (a) that a Community right exist under international trade rules, (b) that there be adverse trade effects caused by the alleged obstacle to trade and (c) that the action be necessary in the interests of the Community), stated that 'on the basis of the above analysis and conclusions, notably as regards the absence of adverse trade effects, it is suggested to terminate the [examination] procedure in this case' and that 'the most appropriate way to

deal with the problems faced by the complainant would be to continue the talks with the US authorities aimed at finding a mutually satisfactory solution in the Hormones case'.

119. The examination procedure did not exclude the possibility of a long-term Community interest in taking action in the future against the potential breaches analysed in the examination report; by contrast, inasmuch as WTO proceedings could not eliminate or reduce the economic problems faced by the complainants, it was proposed to terminate the examination procedure, in particular because of the absence of adverse trade effects within the meaning of Regulation No 3286/94.

120. The Commission does not fail to have regard to Article 11(1) of Regulation No 3286/94 by requiring that any action by the Community be linked to the facts and legal bases underlying the examination procedure and, though faced with a general and long-term interest in acting in the future against potential breaches which might result from the practice of 'selective sanctions' adopted by the United States, such as those identified in the examination report, by deciding to terminate the examination procedure.

121. Article 11(1) of Regulation No 3286/94 must be read in the light of the sixth recital in the preamble to the regulation, which states that the legal mechanism established by Regulation No 3286/94 should 'ensure that the decision to invoke the Community's rights under international trade rules is taken on the basis of accurate factual information and legal analysis'. Accordingly, if the outcome of an examination procedure is that the matters of fact and law which gave rise to that procedure do not suffice to form the basis of any decision to invoke the rights of the Community, in particular because of the absence of one of the legal conditions precedent to the application of Regulation No 3286/94, in the present case that of the absence of adverse trade effects resulting from the alleged obstacle to trade, the Commission is entitled to hold that the conditions required by Regulation No 3286/94 have not been satisfied.

122. That interpretation is also supported by Article 12(1) of Regulation No 3286/94, which states that 'where it is found (as a result of the examination procedure, unless the factual and legal situation is such that an examination procedure may not be required) that action is necessary in the interests of the Community in order to ensure the exercise of the Community's rights under international trade rules, with a view to removing the... adverse trade effects resulting from obstacles to trade adopted or maintained by third countries, the appropriate measures shall be determined'. It is clear from the wording of Article 12(1) of Regulation No 3286/94 that the Community action must seek the cessation of adverse trade effects caused by an obstacle to trade and, accordingly, that that action cannot be initiated if it does not allow that objective to be addressed. In other words, Article 12(1) of Regulation No 3286/94 does not enable the regulation to be relied on by a complainant to urge the Community to take action in defence of the general interests of the Community, if the complainant has not itself suffered adverse trade effects. In any event, even if it has, it is not sufficient to hold that such an adverse trade effect exists for the Community to be required to act under

Regulation No 3286/94, as the Commission has a wide discretion when assessing the commercial interests of the Community, seen as a whole.

123. In the present case, the fact that the Commission considered it to be relevant, for the sake of completeness, to assess in the examination procedure whether a more general and long-term Community interest might exist cannot mean that the Commission was obliged to conclude that the examination procedure should result in action in the interests of the Community. Such an approach may be appropriate in particular because of the need to respond to all the arguments raised by the complainant and/or the interested parties and reflects compliance with the principle of sound administration. It cannot, however, be used against the Commission in order to show that it infringed Article 11(1) of Regulation No 3286/94.

124. Accordingly, contrary to what the applicants maintain, the Commission did not restrict the interests of the Community to those of the complainant, nor did it fail to have regard to Article 11(1) of Regulation No 3286/94.

125. For all those reasons, the fourth plea must be rejected in its entirety.

Select Bibliography

Adamantopoulos, K., and Pereyra-Friedrichsen, M.J., *EU Anti-subsidy Law and Practice* (2nd edn, London: Sweet & Maxwell, 2007).

Andersen, H., *EU Safeguards Applications and WTO Law, Liberalising Trade in the EU and the WTO: A Legal Comparison* (S.E. Gaines, B.E. Olse, and K.E. Sørensen (eds), Cambridge: Cambridge University Press, 2012, 467–89.

Bungenberg, M. and Herrmann, C. (eds.), Common Commercial Policy after Lisbon, *European Yearbook of International Economic Law/Special Issue*, 2013.

Kuijper, P.J., The Court and the Appellate Body: Between Constitutionalism and Dispute Settlement, *Liberalising Trade in the EU and the WTO: A Legal Comparison* (S.E. Gaines, B.E. Olse, and K.E. Sørensen (eds), Cambridge: Cambridge University Press, 2012), 99–138.

Messerlin, P.A., The Influence of the EU in the World Trade System, *The Oxford Handbook on the World Trade Organization* (A. Narlikar, M. Daunton, and R.M. Stern (eds), Oxford: Oxford University Press, 2012), 213–34.

Rovegno, L. and Vandenbussche, H., Anti-dumping Practices in the EU: A Comparative Analysis of Rules and Application in the Context of the WTO, *Liberalising Trade in the EU and the WTO: A Legal Comparison* (S.E. Gaines, B.E. Olse, and K.E. Sørensen (eds), Cambridge: Cambridge University Press, 2012), 440–66.

Rovetta, D. and Senduk, J.H., A Survey of EU Trade Devence Case Law in 2009, 5(6) *Global Trade and Customs Journal*, 2010, 213–22.

Van Bael, I. and Bellis, J.-F., *EU Anti-dumping and Other Trade Defence Instruments* (5th edn, The Hague: Kluwer Law International, 2011).

Vermulst, E.A., *EU Anti-dumping Law & Practice* (2nd edn, London: Sweet & Maxwell, 2010).

Woolcock, S., EU Trade Policy and the Treaty of Lisbon, *The European Union in International Fora: Lessons for the Union's External Representation after Lisbon* (J. Lieb, N. von Ondarza, and D. Schwarzer (eds), Baden-Baden: Nomos, 2011), 87–98.

8

Cooperation Policies and Humanitarian Aid

8.1 Historical evolution

Part Five of the Treaty on the Functioning of the European Union (TFEU) contains a new Title III on cooperation with third countries and humanitarian aid. It brings together the former Titles XX (Articles 177–181 EC) and XXI (Article 181a EC) of Part Three of the EC Treaty, which had empowered the Community to conduct cooperation policies, both with developing and developed countries. While development cooperation was inserted into the Treaty by the Maastricht Treaty (1992), only the Nice Treaty (2001) provided for a specific legal basis for economic, financial, and technical cooperation with third countries. Chapter 3 on humanitarian aid (Article 214 TFEU) is an innovation of the Lisbon Treaty. Development cooperation is examined first, followed by a section on economic, financial, and technical cooperation with developed countries. Subsequently, issues pertaining to thematic cooperation worldwide and humanitarian aid are addressed.

Treaty on the Functioning of the European Union

TITLE III

COOPERATION WITH THIRD COUNTRIES AND HUMANITARIAN AID

CHAPTER 1
DEVELOPMENT COOPERATION
Article 208
(ex Article 177 TEC)

1. Union policy in the field of development cooperation shall be conducted within the framework of the principles and objectives of the Union's external action. The Union's development cooperation policy and that of the Member States complement and reinforce each other.

Union development cooperation policy shall have as its primary objective the reduction and, in the long term, the eradication of poverty. The Union shall take account of the objectives of development cooperation in the policies that it implements which are likely to affect developing countries.

2. The Union and the Member States shall comply with the commitments and take account of the objectives they have approved in the context of the United Nations and other competent international organisations.

Article 209
(ex Article 179 TEC)

1. The European Parliament and the Council, acting in accordance with the ordinary legislative procedure, shall adopt the measures necessary for the implementation of development cooperation policy, which may relate to multiannual cooperation programmes with developing countries or programmes with a thematic approach.

2. The Union may conclude with third countries and competent international organisations any agreement helping to achieve the objectives referred to in Article 21 of the Treaty on European Union and in Article 208 of this Treaty.

The first subparagraph shall be without prejudice to Member States' competence to negotiate in international bodies and to conclude agreements.

3. The European Investment Bank shall contribute, under the terms laid down in its Statute, to the implementation of the measures referred to in paragraph 1.

Article 210
(ex Article 180 TEC)

1. In order to promote the complementarity and efficiency of their action, the Union and the Member States shall coordinate their policies on development cooperation and shall consult each other on their aid programmes, including in international organisations and during international conferences. They may undertake joint action. Member States shall contribute if necessary to the implementation of Union aid programmes.

2. The Commission may take any useful initiative to promote the coordination referred to in paragraph 1.

Article 211
(ex Article 181 TEC)

Within their respective spheres of competence, the Union and the Member States shall cooperate with third countries and with the competent international organisations.

CHAPTER 2

ECONOMIC, FINANCIAL AND TECHNICAL COOPERATION WITH THIRD COUNTRIES

Article 212
(ex Article 181a TEC)

1. Without prejudice to the other provisions of the Treaties, and in particular Articles 208 to 211, the Union shall carry out economic, financial and technical cooperation measures, including assistance, in particular financial assistance, with third countries other than developing countries. Such measures shall be consistent with the development policy of the Union and shall be carried out within the framework of the principles

and objectives of its external action. The Union's operations and those of the Member States shall complement and reinforce each other.

2. The European Parliament and the Council, acting in accordance with the ordinary legislative procedure, shall adopt the measures necessary for the implementation of paragraph 1.

3. Within their respective spheres of competence, the Union and the Member States shall cooperate with third countries and the competent international organisations. The arrangements for Union cooperation may be the subject of agreements between the Union and the third parties concerned.

The first subparagraph shall be without prejudice to the Member States' competence to negotiate in international bodies and to conclude international agreements.

Article 213

When the situation in a third country requires urgent financial assistance from the Union, the Council shall adopt the necessary decisions on a proposal from the Commission.

CHAPTER 3

HUMANITARIAN AID

Article 214

1. The Union's operations in the field of humanitarian aid shall be conducted within the framework of the principles and objectives of the external action of the Union. Such operations shall be intended to provide ad hoc assistance and relief and protection for people in third countries who are victims of natural or man-made disasters, in order to meet the humanitarian needs resulting from these different situations. The Union's measures and those of the Member States shall complement and reinforce each other.

2. Humanitarian aid operations shall be conducted in compliance with the principles of international law and with the principles of impartiality, neutrality and non-discrimination.

3. The European Parliament and the Council, acting in accordance with the ordinary legislative procedure, shall establish the measures defining the framework within which the Union's humanitarian aid operations shall be implemented.

4. The Union may conclude with third countries and competent international organisations any agreement helping to achieve the objectives referred to in paragraph 1 and in Article 21 of the Treaty on European Union.

The first subparagraph shall be without prejudice to Member States' competence to negotiate in international bodies and to conclude agreements.

5. In order to establish a framework for joint contributions from young Europeans to the humanitarian aid operations of the Union, a European Voluntary Humanitarian Aid Corps shall be set up. The European Parliament and the Council, acting by means of regulations in accordance with the ordinary legislative procedure, shall determine the rules and procedures for the operation of the Corps.

6. The Commission may take any useful initiative to promote coordination between actions of the Union and those of the Member States, in order to enhance the efficiency and complementarity of Union and national humanitarian aid measures.

7. The Union shall ensure that its humanitarian aid operations are coordinated and consistent with those of international organisations and bodies, in particular those forming part of the United Nations system.

8.2 Development cooperation

According to Article 208(1) TFEU (former Article 177(1) EC) Union policy in the sphere of development cooperation shall 'complement and reinforce' the policies pursued by the Member States and vice versa. It follows that this competence is not exclusive. Rather, the development cooperation policies of both the Union and the Member States exist in parallel and should be coordinated (Article 210 TFEU, former Article 180 EC). The Court has first described the nature of this competence for development cooperation in *Parliament v. Council*.

Judgment of the Court of 2 March 1994, European Parliament v. Council of the European Union, Case C-316/91, European Court Reports 1994, p. 625, paras. 20–42.

In this case, the European Parliament claimed that the European Development Funds, established for financing the development aid granted to a number of African, Caribbean, and Pacific (ACP) states in the framework of the Lomé-Conventions (a mixed agreement between the Community and its Member States, on the one hand, and the ACP states on the other hand), should be subject to the rules of the Community budget. The Court dismissed the claim, stressing the parallel competence of the Member States and their freedom to organize national development policy according to their preferences.

20. Title III of Part Three of the Convention governs development aid finance cooperation. For the purposes set out in that title a Financial Protocol to the Convention sets, in the words of Article 231 of the Convention, the overall amount of 'the Community' s financial assistance'.

21. The Parliament argues that it follows from the very words of Article 231 of the Convention, repeated in Article 1 of the Financial Protocol, that the Community as such has undertaken vis-à-vis the ACP States, in the framework of development finance cooperation, an obligation of international law distinct from those undertaken by the Member States.

22. In its view, the financial resources to be granted thus constitute Community expenditure which must be shown in the Community budget and which is subject to the provisions of the Treaty concerning its implementation, in particular Article 209.

23. That argument must be rejected.

24. The question as to who has entered into a commitment vis-à-vis the ACP States must be dissociated from the question whether it is for the Community or its Member States to perform the commitment entered into. The answer to the first question depends

on an interpretation of the Convention and on how in Community law powers are distributed between the Community and its Member States in the relevant field, while the answer to the second question depends only on how those powers are distributed.

25. It is appropriate first to consider the distribution of powers between the Community and its Member States in the field of development aid.

26. The Community's competence in that field is not exclusive. The Member States are accordingly entitled to enter into commitments themselves vis-à-vis non-member States, either collectively or individually, or even jointly with the Community.

27. As the Spanish Government has observed, that finding is supported by the new Title XVII of the EC Treaty, inserted by the Treaty on European Union, Article 130x of which provides for the Community and the Member States to coordinate their policies on development cooperation and to consult each other on their aid programmes and for the possibility of joint action.

28. It is appropriate next to interpret the Convention in order to identify the parties which have entered into commitments.

29. The Convention was concluded, according to its preamble and Article 1, by the Community and its Member States of the one part and the ACP States of the other part. It established an essentially bilateral ACP–EEC cooperation. In those circumstances, in the absence of derogations expressly laid down in the Convention, the Community and its Member States as partners of the ACP States are jointly liable to those latter States for the fulfilment of every obligation arising from the commitments undertaken, including those relating to financial assistance.

30. Although Article 231 of the Convention, like Article 1 of the Financial Protocol, uses the phrase 'the Community's financial assistance', it is nonetheless the case that several other provisions use the term 'Community' in order to denote the Community and its Member States considered together.

31. Thus, Article 338 of the Convention provides, without distinction depending on the subject-matter of the proceedings, that the Council of Ministers of the Association is to act by agreement between the Community, on the one hand, and the ACP States, on the other. Furthermore, Article 367 of the Convention provides that it may be denounced by the Community, without being more specific.

32. Finally, Article 223 of the Convention provides, in the very field of development finance cooperation, that, unless otherwise provided in the Convention, all decisions requiring the approval of either contracting party are to be approved, or be deemed approved, within 60 days of notification by the other party.

33. It follows from the above that, in accordance with the essentially bilateral character of the cooperation, the obligation to grant 'the Community's financial assistance' falls on the Community and on its Member States, considered together.

34. As for the question whether it is for the Community or for its Member States to perform that obligation, it should be noted, as stated above at paragraph 26, that the competence of the Community in the field of development aid is not exclusive, so that the Member States are entitled collectively to exercise their competence in that field with a view to bearing the financial assistance to be granted to the ACP States.

35. It follows that the competence to implement the Community's financial assistance provided for by Article 231 of the Convention and Article 1 of the Financial

Protocol is shared by the Community and its Member States and that it is for them to choose the source and methods of financing.

36. That choice was made by the abovementioned Internal Agreement 91/401 on the financing and administration of Community aid under the Fourth ACP-EEC Convention, the provisions for implementing which are the subject of the contested financial regulation, adopted by the Council pursuant to Article 32 thereof.

37. Article 1 of the Internal Agreement provides that the Member States set up the EDF and specifies the contribution of each Member State to that Fund. Article 10 makes the Commission responsible for administering the EDF, while Article 33(2) provides that the Court of Auditors is also to exercise its powers in respect of the EDF' s operations and Article 33(3) provides that the discharge for the financial management of the EDF is to be given to the Commission by the Parliament on the recommendation of the Council.

38. It follows that the expenditure necessary for the Community's financial assistance provided for in Article 231 of the Convention and Article 1 of the Financial Protocol is assumed directly by the Member States and distributed by a Fund which they have set up by mutual agreement, with the administration of which the Community institutions are associated by virtue of that agreement.

39. Consequently, that expenditure is not Community expenditure which must be entered in the Community budget and to which Article 209 of the Treaty must apply.

40. The Parliament has also argued before the Court that the fact that the expenditure is Community expenditure is apparent from all aspects of the procedure laid down for its administration and allocation. Thus, it appears from the origin, the external appearance, the decision-making procedure and the content of the financial regulation that it is very closely related to Community acts.

41. That argument cannot be accepted. No provision of the Treaty prevents Member States from using, outside its framework, procedural steps drawing on the rules applicable to Community expenditure and from associating the Community institutions with the procedure thus set up (see the judgment in Joined Cases C-181/91 and C-248/91 *Parliament v Council and Commission* [1993] ECR I-3685).

42. It follows from the foregoing that the financial regulation did not have to be adopted on the basis of Article 209 of the Treaty. Accordingly, no prerogative of the Parliament has been infringed. The application must therefore be dismissed as unfounded.

The Union has two main instruments at its disposal to conduct development policy. First, under Article 209(1) EC, the European Parliament and the Council may adopt unilateral measures in the ordinary legislative procedure which pursue the objectives of Article 208 TFEU (if the instrument is of a commercial character it must be adopted on the basis of Article 207 TFEU[1]). Second, the Union may conclude international agreements with a developing country under Article 209(2) TFEU (former Article 181 EC).

[1] See Case 45/86, *Commission v. Council (GSP)* [1987] ECR 1493.

Over time, certain model agreements have emerged, differing in the intensity of cooperation. If closer cooperation is sought, the Union might also opt for the conclusion of an association agreement under Article 217 TFEU (former Article 310 EC).

Regulation (EC) No 1905/2006 of the European Parliament and of the Council of 18 December 2006 establishing a financing instrument for development cooperation, Official Journal L 378, 27.12.2006, pp. 41–71.

This regulation is an example of a unilateral Union act in the field of development policy. It lays down the fundamental rules for providing development assistance to non-ACP countries. It defines the objectives and general principles for such aid, and entrusts the Commission with its implementation. The Commission is thus empowered to finance development projects for a wide array of beneficiaries and areas.

THE EUROPEAN PARLIAMENT AND THE COUNCIL OF
THE EUROPEAN UNION,
Having regard to the Treaty establishing the European Community, and in particular Article 179(1) thereof,
Having regard to the proposal from the Commission,
Acting in accordance with the procedure laid down in Article 251 of the Treaty,

Whereas:
(1) A new framework for planning and delivering assistance is proposed in order to make the Community's external assistance more effective. Council Regulation (EC) No 1085/2006 establishes an Instrument for Pre Accession (IPA) for Community assistance to candidate and potential candidate countries. Regulation (EC) No 1638/2006 lays down general provisions establishing a European Neighbourhood and Partnership Instrument (ENPI). Council Regulation (EC) No 1934/2006 establishes a financing instrument for cooperation with industrialised and other high-income countries and territories. Regulation (EC) No 1717/2006 establishes an instrument for stability. Regulation (EC) No .../2007 establishes an instrument for nuclear safety cooperation. Regulation (EC) No 1889/2006 establishes a financing instrument for the promotion of democracy and human rights worldwide. Council Regulation (EC) No 1257/96 concerns humanitarian aid. This Regulation establishes a financing instrument for development cooperation providing direct support for the Community's development cooperation policy.
(2) The Community pursues a development cooperation policy aimed at achieving the objectives of poverty reduction, sustainable economic and social development and the smooth and gradual integration of developing countries into the world economy.
(3) The Community pursues a cooperation policy that fosters cooperation, partnerships and joint undertakings between economic players in the Community and partner countries and regions, and promotes dialogue between political, economic and social partners in relevant sectors.

(4) The Community's development cooperation policy and international action are guided by the Millennium Development Goals (MDGs), such as the eradication of extreme poverty and hunger, adopted by the United Nations General Assembly on 8 September 2000, and the main development objectives and principles approved by the Community and its Member States in the context of the United Nations (UN) and other competent international organisations in the field of development cooperation.

(5) With a view to policy coherence for development, it is important that Community non-development policies assist developing countries' efforts in achieving the MDGs in line with Article 178 of the Treaty establishing the European Community.

(6) A political environment which guarantees peace and stability, respect for human rights, fundamental freedoms, democratic principles, the rule of law, good governance and gender equality is fundamental to long-term development.

(7) Sound and sustainable economic policies are a prerequisite for development.

(8) The members of the World Trade Organization (WTO) committed themselves at the 4th Ministerial Conference in Doha to mainstreaming trade in development strategies and to providing trade-related technical and capacity building assistance as well as the necessary measures seeking to facilitate the transfer of technology through and for trade, to enhance the relationship between foreign direct investment and trade, and the mutual interrelation of trade and environment, and to help developing countries take part in new trade negotiations and implement their results.

(9) The Joint Statement by the Council and the Representatives of the Governments of the Member States meeting within the Council, the European Parliament and the Commission on European Union Development Policy: 'The European Consensus', of 20 December 2005, and any subsequent modifications thereto, provides the general framework for action by the Community on development matters. It should steer the planning and implementation of the development assistance and cooperation strategies.

(10) Development cooperation should be implemented through geographic and thematic programmes. Geographic programmes should support the development of, and reinforce the cooperation with, countries and regions in Latin America, Asia, Central Asia, the Middle East and South Africa.

[...]

HAVE ADOPTED THIS REGULATION:

Article 1

Overall purpose and scope

1. The Community shall finance measures aimed at supporting cooperation with developing countries, territories and regions included in the list of aid recipients of the Development Assistance Committee of the Organization for Economic Cooperation and Development (OECD/DAC), and set out in Annex I (hereinafter referred to as 'partner countries and regions'). The Commission shall amend Annex I in accordance with regular OECD/DAC reviews of its list of aid recipients and inform the European Parliament and the Council thereof.

2. The Community shall finance thematic programmes in countries, territories and regions eligible for assistance under a geographic programme of this Regulation, set

out in Articles 5 to 10, for assistance under Regulation (EC) No 1638/2006 or for geographic cooperation under the European Development Fund (EDF).

3. For the purposes of this Regulation, a region is defined as a geographical entity comprising more than one developing country.

TITLE I

OBJECTIVES AND GENERAL PRINCIPLES

Article 2

Objectives

1. The primary and overarching objective of cooperation under this Regulation shall be the eradication of poverty in partner countries and regions in the context of sustainable development, including pursuit of the Millennium Development Goals (MDGs), as well as the promotion of democracy, good governance and respect for human rights and for the rule of law. Consistently with this objective, cooperation with partner countries and regions shall:

— consolidate and support democracy, the rule of law, human rights and fundamental freedoms, good governance, gender equality and related instruments of international law;

— foster the sustainable development—including political, economic, social and environmental aspects—of partner countries and regions, and more particularly the most disadvantaged among them;

— encourage their smooth and gradual integration into the world economy;

— help develop international measures to preserve and improve the quality of the environment and the sustainable management of global natural resources, in order to ensure sustainable development, including addressing climate change and biodiversity loss; and

— strengthen the relationship between the Community and partner countries and regions.

2. Community cooperation under this Regulation shall comply with the commitments and objectives in the field of development cooperation that the Community has approved in the context of the United Nations (UN) and other competent international organisations in the field of development cooperation.

3. Community development policy, as laid down in Title XX of the Treaty, shall provide the legal framework for cooperation with partner countries and regions. The Joint Statement by the Council and the Representatives of the Governments of the Member States meeting within the Council, the European Parliament and the Commission on European Union Development Policy: 'The European Consensus', of 20 December 2005, and any subsequent modifications thereto, shall provide the general framework, orientations and focus to steer the implementation of Community cooperation with partner countries and regions under this Regulation.

4. Measures referred to in Article 1(1) shall be designed so as to fulfil the criteria for Official Development Assistance (ODA) established by the OECD/DAC.

Programmes referred to in Article 1(2) shall be designed so as to fulfil the criteria for ODA established by the OECD/DAC, unless:

— the characteristics of the beneficiary require otherwise, or

— the programme implements a global initiative, a community policy priority or an international obligation or commitment of the Community, as referred to in Article 11(2), and the measure does not have the characteristics to fulfil such criteria.

At least 90% of the expenditure foreseen under thematic programmes shall be designed so as to fulfil the criteria for ODA established by the OECD/DAC, without prejudice to Article 2(4), second subparagraph, first indent.

5. Community assistance under this Regulation shall not be used to finance the procurement of arms or ammunition, and operations having military or defence implications.

6. Measures covered by Regulation (EC) No 1717/2006 and in particular Article 4 thereof, and eligible for funding thereunder shall not, in principle, be funded under this Regulation, except where there is a need to ensure continuity of cooperation from crisis to stable conditions for development.

Without prejudice to the need to ensure continuity of cooperation from crisis to stable conditions for development, measures covered by, and eligible for funding under, Council Regulation (EC) No 1257/96, shall not be funded under this Regulation.

Article 3

General principles

1. The Community is founded on the values of democracy, the rule of law, respect for human rights and fundamental freedoms and seeks to develop and consolidate commitment to these values in partner countries and regions through dialogue and cooperation.

2. In the implementation of this Regulation, a differentiated approach depending on development contexts and needs shall be pursued so that partner countries or regions are provided with specific, tailor-made cooperation, based on their own needs, strategies, priorities and assets.

Least developed countries and low income countries shall be given priority in terms of overall resource allocation in order to achieve the MDGs. Appropriate attention shall be given to support the pro-poor development of middle income countries, particularly the lower middle income countries many of which face problems similar to those of low income countries.

3. Mainstreaming of the following cross-cutting issues shall be undertaken in all programmes: the promotion of human rights, gender equality, democracy, good governance, the rights of the child and indigenous peoples' rights, environmental sustainability and combating HIV/AIDS. In addition, particular attention shall be given to strengthening the rule of law, improving access to justice and supporting civil society, as well as promoting dialogue, participation and reconciliation, and institution-building.

4. The Community shall take account of the objectives laid down in Title XX of the Treaty and in Article 2 of this Regulation, in all policies which are likely to affect partner countries and regions. For measures financed under this Regulation, the Community

shall also aim to ensure coherence with other areas of its external action. This shall be ensured in formulating policy, strategic planning and the programming and implementation of measures.

5. The Community and the Member States shall improve coordination and complementarity of their policies on development cooperation by responding to partner countries' and regions' priorities at country and regional level. Community policy in the sphere of development cooperation shall be complementary to the policies pursued by the Member States.

6. The Commission and the Member States shall seek regular and frequent exchanges of information, including with other donors, and promote better donor coordination and complementarity by working towards joint multiannual programming, based on partner countries' poverty reduction or equivalent strategies and partner countries' own budget processes, by common implementation mechanisms including shared analysis, by joint donor-wide missions and by the use of co-financing arrangements.

7. Within their respective spheres of competence, the Community and the Member States shall promote a multilateral approach to global challenges and foster cooperation with multilateral and regional organisations and bodies such as international financial institutions, UN agencies, funds and programmes, and other bilateral donors.

8. The Community shall promote effective cooperation with partner countries and regions in line with international best practice. It shall promote:

(a) a development process that is partner country led and owned. The Community shall increasingly align its support with partners' national development strategies, reform policies and procedures. The Community shall contribute to strengthening the process of mutual accountability between partner governments and donors and promote local expertise and local employment;

(b) inclusive and participatory approaches to development and a broad involvement of all segments of society in the development process and in national dialogue, including political dialogue;

(c) effective cooperation modalities and instruments as set out in Article 25 in line with OECD/DAC best practices, adapted to the particular circumstances of each partner country or region, with a focus on programme-based approaches, delivery of predictable aid funding, the development and use of country systems and on results-based approaches to development including, where appropriate, MDG targets and indicators;

(d) improved impact of policies and programming through coordination and harmonisation between donors to reduce overlap and duplication, to improve complementarity and to support donor-wide initiatives. Coordination shall take place in partner countries and regions using agreed guidelines and best practice principles on coordination and aid effectiveness;

(e) an MDG profile in Country Strategy Papers and in its multiannual programming.

9. The Commission shall inform and have regular exchanges of views with the European Parliament.

10. The Commission shall seek regular exchanges of information with civil society.

TITLE II

GEOGRAPHIC AND THEMATIC PROGRAMMES

[...]

Article 11

Thematic programmes

1. A thematic programme shall be subsidiary to programmes referred to in Articles 5 to 10 and shall encompass a specific area of activity of interest to a group of partner countries not determined by geography, or cooperation activities addressed to various regions or groups of partner countries, or an international operation that is not geographically specific.

2. Consistently with the overall purpose and scope, objectives and general principles of this Regulation, the actions undertaken through thematic programmes shall add value to and be additional to, and coherent with, actions funded under geographic programmes. The following principles shall apply to these actions:

(a) Community policy objectives cannot be achieved in an appropriate or effective manner through geographic programmes and the thematic programme is implemented by or through an intermediary organisation such as nongovernmental organisations, other non-State actors, international organisations or multilateral mechanisms. This includes global initiatives supporting the MDGs, sustainable development or global public goods and actions in Member States and acceding countries by way of derogation from Article 24 as envisaged in the relevant thematic programme,

and/or

(b) actions are of the following nature:

— multi-regional and/or cross-cutting actions, including pilot projects and innovatory policies;

— actions in cases where there is no agreement on the action with the partner government(s);

— actions relevant to the purpose of a specific thematic programme which respond to a Community policy priority or an international obligation or commitment of the Community;

— where appropriate, actions in cases where there is no geographic programme or it has been suspended.

[...]

Cooperation Agreement between the European Community and the Republic of India on partnership and development—Declaration of the Community concerning tariff adjustments—Declarations of the Community and India, Official Journal L 223, 27.8.1994, pp. 24–34.

The selected EC—India agreement is a standard model 'on cooperation and partnership'. Partners have agreed to cooperate in a variety of policy fields and have set up a 'light' institutional structure.

THE COUNCIL OF THE EUROPEAN UNION,

on the one part,

THE GOVERNMENT OF INDIA,

on the other part,

CONSIDERING the excellent relations and traditional links of friendship between the European Community and its Member States, hereinafter referred to as 'the Community', and the Republic of India, hereinafter referred to as 'India';

RECOGNIZING the importance of strengthening the links and enhancing the partnership between the Community and India;

HAVING REGARD to the foundations for close cooperation between India and the Community laid by the first Agreement between India and the Community signed on 17 December 1973 and later developed by the Agreement for Commercial and Economic Cooperation signed on 23 June 1981;

NOTING with satisfaction the achievements resulting from these Agreements;

REAFFIRMING the importance they attach to the principles of the United Nations Charter and the respect of democratic principles and human rights;

INSPIRED by their common will to consolidate, deepen and diversify their relations in areas of mutual interest on the basis of equality, non-discrimination and mutual benefit;

RECOGNIZING the positive consequences of the process of economic reforms for modernization of the economy undertaking in India for enhancing commercial and economic relations between India and the Community;

DESIROUS of creating favourable conditions for a substantial development and diversification of trade and industry between the Community and India, within the framework of the more dynamic relationship which both India and the Community desire, which will further, in their mutual interest and consistently with their developmental needs, investment flows, commercial and economic cooperation in areas of mutual interest including science and technology, and foster cultural cooperation;

HAVING REGARD TO the need to support Indian efforts for economic development especially improving the living conditions of the poor;

CONSIDERING the importance attached by the Community and India to the protection of the environment on a global and on a local level and to the sustainable use of natural resources and recognizing the linkage between the environment and development;

TAKING INTO ACCOUNT their membership of the General Agreement on Tariffs and Trade (GATT), the importance of its principles and of the need to uphold and reinforce the rules which promote free and unhindered trade in a stable, transparent and non-discriminatory manner;

BELIEVING that relations between them have developed beyond the scope of the Agreement concluded in 1981;

[...]

HAVE AGREED AS FOLLOWS:

Article 1

Basis and objectives

1. Respect for human rights and democratic principles is the basis for the cooperation between the Contracting Parties and for the provisions of this Agreement, and it constitutes an essential element of the Agreement.

2. The principal objective of this Agreement is to enhance and develop, through dialogue and partnership, the various aspects of cooperation between the Contracting Parties in order to achieve a closer and upgraded relationship.

This cooperation will focus in particular on:

– further development and diversification of trade and investment in their mutual interest, taking into account their respective economic situations;

– facilitation of better mutual understanding and strengthening of ties between the two regions in respect of technical, economic and cultural matters;

– building up of India's economic capability to interact more effectively with the Community;

– acceleration of the pace of India's economic development, supporting India's efforts in building up its economic capabilities, by way of provision of resources and technical assistance by the Community within the framework of its cooperation policies and regulations, in particular to improve the living conditions of the poorer sections of the population;

– development in their mutual interest of existing and new forms of economic cooperation directed at promoting and facilitating exchanges and connections between their business communities, taking into account the implementation of Indian economic reforms and opportunities for the creation of a suitable environment for investment;

– support of environmental protection and sustainable management of natural resources.

3. The Contracting Parties acknowledge the value in the light of the objectives of this Agreement of consulting each other on international, economic and commercial issues of mutual interest.

Article 2

Most-favoured-nation treatment

The Community and India shall grant each other most-favoured-nation treatment in their trade in accordance with the provisions of the General Agreement on Tariffs and Trade.

Article 3

Trade and commercial cooperation

1. In the interest of strengthening new relations in a dynamic and complementary way, thereby providing mutual benefits, the Contracting Parties undertake to develop and diversify their commercial exchanges and to improve market access, to the highest possible degree, in a manner compatible with their economic situations.

2. The Contracting Parties are committed to a policy for improving the terms of access for their products to each other's markets. In this context, they shall grant each other the highest degree of liberalization of imports and exports which they generally apply to third countries and they agree to examine ways and means of eliminating barriers

to trade between them, notably non-tariff barriers, taking account of the work already done in this connection by international organizations.

3. The Contracting Parties agree to promote the exchange of information about mutually beneficial market opportunities and to hold consultations in a constructive spirit on the issues of tariff, non-tariff, services, health, safety or environmental measures, and technical requirements.

4. The Contracting Parties agree to improve cooperation in customs matters between the respective authorities, especially in professional training, the simplification and harmonization of customs procedures, and the prevention, investigation and suppression of infractions of customs regulations.

5. The Contracting Parties also undertake to give consideration, each in accordance with its laws, to exempting from duty, tax and other charges, goods admitted temporarily to their territories for subsequent re-export unaltered or for goods which re-enter their territories after processing in the other Contracting Party which is not sufficient for the goods to be treated as originating from the territory of that Contracting Party.

6.1. The Contracting Parties agree to consult each other on any dispute which may arise in connection with trade. If the Community or India request such consultation, it shall take place at the earliest opportunity. The Contracting Party making the request shall provide the other Party with all information necessary for a detailed examination of the situation. Attempts shall be made through such consultations to resolve trade disputes as rapidly as possible.

6.2. In respect of anti-dumping or subsidies investigations, each Contracting Party agrees to examine submissions made by the other Contracting Party and to inform the interested parties concerned of the essential facts and considerations on the basis of which a decision is to be based. Before definitive anti-dumping and countervailing duties are imposed, the Contracting Parties shall do their utmost to bring about a constructive solution to the problem.

6.3. Paragraphs 6.1. and 6.2. shall be without prejudice to the Contracting Parties' rights and obligations under the GATT, which shall prevail in the event of any inconsistency.

Article 4

Economic cooperation

1. The Contracting Parties undertake, in their mutual interests and in accordance with their respective policies and objectives, to foster economic cooperation of the widest possible scope in order to contribute to the expansion of their respective economies and their developmental needs.

2. The Contracting Parties agree that economic cooperation will involve three broad fields of action:

(a) improving the economic environment in India by facilitating access to Community know-how and technology;

(b) facilitating contacts between economic operators and other measures designed to promote commercial exchanges and investments;

(c) reinforcing mutual understanding of their respective economic, social and cultural environment as a basis for effective cooperation.

3. In the broad fields described above, the aims shall be in particular to:
– improve the economic environment and business climate,
– cooperate in the protection of the environment and natural resources,
– cooperate in the field of energy and energy efficiency,
– cooperate in the field of telecommunications, information technology, and related matters,
– cooperate in all aspects of industrial standards and intellectual property,
– encourage technology transfer in other sectors of mutual benefit,
– exchange information on monetary matters and the macro-economic environment,
– reinforce and diversify economic links between them,
– encourage the two-way flow of Community-Indian trade and investments,
– activate industrial cooperation including agro-industry,
– promote cooperation in order to develop agriculture, fisheries, mining, transport and communication, health, banking and insurance, tourism and other services,
– encourage close cooperation between the private sectors of both regions,
– promote cooperation in industrial and urban ecology,
– promote support of undertaking by means of trade promotion and market development,
– promote scientific and technological development,
– promote training and specific training programmes,
– cooperate in the fields of information and culture.
Cooperation in a number of the abovementioned sectors is set out in more detail in Articles 5 to 15 included which follow.
4. The Contracting Parties shall consider in particular the following means to achieve these aims:
– exchange of information and ideas,
– preparation of studies,
– provision of technical assistance,
– training programmes,
– establishment of links between research and training centres, specialized agencies and business organizations,
– promotion of investment and joint ventures,
– institutional development of public and private agencies and administrations,
– access to each other's existing data bases and creation of new ones,
– workshops and seminars,
– exchanges of experts.
5. The Contracting Parties will determine together and to their mutual advantage the areas and priorities to be covered by concrete actions of economic cooperation, in conformity with their long-term objectives. In view of the importance of long-term enhancement of cooperation between the Community and India, no sector shall be excluded a priori from the field of economic cooperation.

Article 5

Industry and services
1. The Contracting Parties shall:

(a) identify sectors of industry on which cooperation will centre and the means to promote industrial cooperation with a heavy technological bias;

(b) promote the expansion and diversification of India's production base in the industrial and service sectors, including modernization and reform of the public sector, directing their cooperation activities at small and medium-sized enterprises in particular and taking steps to facilitate their access to sources of capital, markets and technology directed especially towards promoting trade between the Contracting Parties as well as at third country markets.

2. The Contracting Parties shall facilitate, within the relevant existing rules, access to available information and capital facilities in order to encourage projects and operations promoting cooperation between firms, such as joint ventures, sub-contracting, transfer of technology, licences, applied research and franchises.

Article 6

Private sector

The Contracting Parties agree to promote the involvement of the private sector in their cooperation programmes in order to strengthen economic and industrial cooperation between themselves.

The Contracting Parties shall take measures to:

(a) encourage the private sectors of both geographical regions to find effective ways of joint consultations, results of which could then be transmitted to the Joint Commission, referred to in Article 22 of this Agreement, for the required follow-up action;

(b) involve the private sectors of the Contracting Parties in activities developed within the framework of this Agreement.

Article 7

Energy

The Contracting Parties recognize the importance of the energy sector to economic and social development and undertake to step up cooperation relating particularly to the generation, saving and efficient use of energy. Such improved cooperation will include planning concerning energy, non-conventional energy including solar energy and the consideration of its environmental implications.

Article 8

Telecommunications, electronics, and information and satellite technologies

The Contracting Parties recognize the importance of cooperation in the fields of telecommunications, electronics, and information technologies which contribute to increased economic development and trade. Such cooperation may include:

(a) standardization, testing and certification;

(b) earth and space-based telecommunications;

(c) electronics and micro-electronics;

(d) information and automation;

(e) high definition television;

(f) research and development in new information technologies and telecommunications;

(g) promotion of investment and joint investment.

Article 9

Standards

Without prejudice to their international obligations, within the scope of their responsibilities and in accordance with their laws, the Contracting Parties shall take steps to reduce differences in respect of metrology, standardization and certification by promoting the use of compatible systems of standards and certification. To that end, they shall encourage the following in particular:

– establishing links between experts in order to facilitate exchanges of information and studies on metrology, standards, and quality control, promotion and certification,

– encouraging interchange and contact between bodies and institutions specializing in these fields including consultations to ensure that standards do not constitute a barrier to trade,

– promoting measures aimed at achieving mutual recognition of systems of quality certification,

– developing technical assistance in connection with metrology, standards and certification, and in connection with quality promotion programmes,

– providing technical assistance for institutional development to upgrade standards and quality certification organizations as well as for the setting up of a national accreditation scheme for conformity assessment in India.

Article 10

Intellectual property

The Contracting Parties undertake to ensure as far as their laws, regulations and policies allow that suitable and effective protection is provided for intellectual property rights, including patents, trade or service marks, copyright and similar rights, geographical designations (including marks of origin), industrial designs and integrated circuit topographics, reinforcing this protection where desirable. They also undertake, wherever possible, to facilitate access to the data bases of intellectual property organizations.

Article 11

Investment

1. The Contracting Parties shall encourage an increase in mutually beneficial investment by establishing a favourable climate for private investments including better conditions for the transfer of capital and exchange of information on investment opportunities.

2. Taking into account work done in this area in relevant international fora, and recognizing in particular the recent signing by India of the Multilateral Investments Guarantee Agency (MIGA) Convention, the Contracting Parties agree to support the promotion and protection of investments between the Member States of the Community and India on the basis of the principles of non-discrimination and reciprocity.

3. The Contracting Parties undertake to encourage cooperation between their respective financial institutions.

Article 12

Agriculture and fisheries
The Contracting Parties agree to promote cooperation in agriculture and fisheries, including horticulture and food processing. To this end, they undertake to examine:
(a) the opportunities for increasing trade in agricultural and fishery products;
(b) health, plant and animal health, environmental measures and any obstacles to trade which they might engender;
(c) the linkage between agriculture and the rural environment;
(d) agricultural and fishery research.

Article 13

Tourism
The Contracting Parties agree to contribute to cooperation on tourism, to be achieved through specific measures, including:
(a) interchange of information and the carrying out of studies;
(b) training programmes;
(c) promotion of investment and joint ventures.

Article 14

Science and technology
1. The Contracting Parties will, in accordance with their mutual interest and aims of their development strategy in this area, promote scientific and technological cooperation including in high-level fields, e.g. life-sciences, bio-technology, new materials, and geo and marine sciences, with a view to:
(a) fostering the transfer of know-how and stimulating innovation;
(b) disseminating information and expertise in science and technology;
(c) opening up opportunities for future economic, industrial and trade cooperation.
This will be implemented through:
(a) joint research projects between the Parties' research centres and other appropriate institutions;
(b) exchange and trading of scientists and researchers, particularly promoting the establishment of permanent links between the scientific and technical communities of the Parties;
(c) exchange of scientific information.
2. The Contracting Parties undertake to establish appropriate procedures to facilitate the greatest possible degree of participation by their scientists and research centres in the abovementioned cooperation.

Article 15

Information and culture
The Contracting Parties will cooperate in the fields of information and culture, both to create better mutual understanding and to strengthen cultural ties between the two regions. Such cooperation may include:
(a) exchange of information on matters of cultural interest;
(b) preparatory studies and technical assistance in the preservation of cultural heritage;

(c) cooperation in the field of media and audio-visual documentation;

(d) organizing cultural events and exchanges.

Article 16

Development cooperation

1. The Community recognizes India's need for development assistance and is prepared to strengthen its cooperation and enhance its efficiency in order to contribute to India's own efforts in achieving sustainable economic development and social progress of its people through concrete projects and programmes. Community support will be in accordance with Community policies, regulations and limits of the financial means available for cooperation and be in accordance with an elaborated development strategy.

2. Projects and programmes will be targeted towards the poorer sections of the population. Particular attention will be given to rural development with participation of the groups to be targeted and, where appropriate, the involvement of qualified non-governmental organizations. Cooperation in this area will also cover the promotion of employment in rural towns, and of the role of women in development, with appropriate emphasis on their education and family welfare.

3. Public health, especially in the form of primary health care including control of both communicable and non-communicable diseases will also be covered. The aim will be to increase the quality of health care in India of the most disadvantaged sections of the population both in urban and in rural areas.

4. The cooperation will concentrate on mutually agreed priorities and will pursue project and programme efficiency, sustainability and respect for the environment.

Article 17

Environment

1. The Contracting Parties recognize the need to take account of environmental protection as an integral part of economic and development cooperation. Moreover, they underline the importance of environmental issues and their will to establish cooperation in protecting and improving the environment with particular emphasis on water, soil and air pollution, erosion, deforestation and sustainable management of natural resources, taking into account the work done in international fora.

Particular attention will be paid to:

(a) the sustainable management of forest eco-systems;

(b) protection and conservation of natural forests;

(c) the strengthening of forestry institutes;

(d) the finding of practical solutions to rural energy problems;

(e) prevention of industrial pollution;

(f) protection of the urban environment.

2. Cooperation in this area will centre on:

(a) reinforcing and improving environmental protection institutions;

(b) developing legislation and upgrading standards;

(c) research, training and information;

(d) executing studies and pilot programmes and providing technical assistance.

Article 18

Human resource development

The Contracting Parties recognize the importance of human resource development in improving economic development and the living conditions of the disadvantaged sections of the population. They agree that human resource development should constitute an integral part of both economic and development cooperation.

In their mutual interest, particular attention should be paid to promoting cooperation between Community and Indian higher education and training institutes.

Article 19

Drug abuse control

1. The Contracting Parties affirm their resolve, in conformity with their respective competences, to increase the efficiency of policies and measures, to counter the supply and distribution of narcotics and psychotropic substances as well as preventing and reducing drug abuse, taking into account work done in this connection by international bodies.

2. Cooperation between the Parties shall comprise the following:

(a) training, education, health promotion and rehabilitation of addicts, including projects for the reintegration of addicts into work and social environments;

(b) measures to encourage alternative economic opportunities;

(c) technical, financial and administrative assistance in the monitoring of precursors trade, prevention, treatment and reduction of drug abuse;

(d) exchange of all relevant information, including that relating to money laundering.

Article 20

South-south and regional cooperation

The Contracting Parties recognize their mutual interest in furthering economic and trade relations with other developing countries within a concept of regional and south-south cooperation.

Article 21

Resources for undertaking cooperation

The Contracting Parties will, within the limits of their available financial means and within the framework of their respective procedures and instruments, make available funds to facilitate the achievement of the aims set out in this Agreement especially as concerns economic cooperation.

Concerning development aid, and within the framework of its programme in favour of Asian and Latin American (ALA) countries, the Community will support India's development programmes, through direct concessional transfers, as well as through institutional and other sources of finance in accordance with the rules and practices of such Community institutions.

[...]

Judgment of the Court of 3 December 1996, Portuguese Republic v. Council of the European Union, Case C-268/94, European Court Reports 1996, p. I-6177, paras. 13–14, 21–30, and 36–77.

Such development cooperation agreements may cover a wide area of subject matters. In particular, in *Portugal v. Council*, the Court accepted that a human rights and democracy clause may be inserted into a development cooperation agreement, which would allow the Union to suspend the agreement in cases of grave violations of human rights or the principles of democracy (paragraphs 24–9). Moreover, the Union may insert a number of policy areas into the agreement, such as energy, tourism, drug abuse control, and intellectual property, as long as they fit into the overall objective of development cooperation. This is so since the characterization of an agreement as cooperation agreement 'must be determined having regard to its essential object and not in terms of individual clauses, provided that those clauses do not impose such extensive obligations concerning the specific matters referred to that those obligations in fact constitute objectives distinct from those of development cooperation' (paragraph 39).

13. In its action, the Portuguese Government challenges the validity of the legal basis of Community competence and the corresponding procedure by which the Community concluded the Agreement. It considers that the legal basis of the contested decision does not confer on the Community the necessary powers to conclude the Agreement as regards, first, the provision therein relating to human rights and, second, the provisions relating to various specific fields of cooperation. It considers that recourse should also have been had to Article 235 of the Treaty and to participation of all the Member States in the conclusion of the Agreement.

Respect for human rights and democratic principles
14. The argument of the Portuguese Government to the effect that Article 1(1) of the Agreement required recourse to Article 235 of the Treaty as the legal basis of the contested decision must be considered first.

[...]

21. As a preliminary point, it should be borne in mind that the Court has consistently held that the use of Article 235 as the legal basis for a measure is justified only where no other provision of the Treaty gives the Community institutions the necessary power to adopt the measure in question (see, inter alia, Case 45/86 *Commission* v *Council* [1987] ECR 1493, paragraph 13, and Case C-271/94 *Parliament* v *Council* [1996] ECR I-1689, paragraph 13).

22. In the context of the organization of the powers of the Community, the choice of the legal basis for a measure must be based on objective factors which are amenable to judicial review. Those factors include in particular the aim and content of the measure (see in particular Case C-300/89 *Commission* v *Council* [1991] ECR I-2867, paragraph 10, and Case C-84/94 *United Kingdom* v *Council* [1996] ECR I-5755, paragraph 25).

23. By declaring that 'Community policy (...) shall contribute to the general objective of developing and consolidating democracy and the rule of law, and to that of respecting human rights and fundamental freedoms', Article 130u(2) requires the Community to take account of the objective of respect for human rights when it adopts measures in the field of development cooperation.

24. The mere fact that Article 1(1) of the Agreement provides that respect for human rights and democratic principles 'constitutes an essential element' of the Agreement does not justify the conclusion that that provision goes beyond the objective stated in Article 130u(2) of the Treaty. The very wording of the latter provision demonstrates the importance to be attached to respect for human rights and democratic principles, so that, amongst other things, development cooperation policy must be adapted to the requirement of respect for those rights and principles.

25. Moreover, as the Advocate General pointed out in paragraph 27 of his Opinion, the importance of human rights in the context of development cooperation was emphasized in various declarations and documents of the Member States and the Community institutions which had already been drawn up before the Treaty on European Union, and in consequence Title XVII of the EC Treaty, entered into force.

26. With regard, more particularly, to the argument of the Portuguese Government that the characterization of respect for human rights as an essential element in cooperation presupposes specific means of action, it must first be stated that to adapt cooperation policy to respect for human rights necessarily entails establishing a certain connection between those matters whereby one of them is made subordinate to the other.

27. In that regard, it should be borne in mind that a provision such as Article 1(1) of the Agreement may be, amongst other things, an important factor for the exercise of the right to have a development cooperation agreement suspended or terminated where the non-member country has violated human rights.

28. Furthermore, Article 1 of the Agreement, headed 'Basis and objectives', and the wording of the first paragraph of that provision, provide confirmation that the question of respect for human rights and democratic principles is not a specific field of cooperation provided for by the Agreement.

29. It must therefore be held that, so far as Article 1(1) of the Agreement is concerned, the contested decision could be validly based on Article 130y.

The provisions of the Agreement concerning specific cooperation matters

30. The Portuguese Government claims that the scope of some of the provisions of the Agreement, relating to specific matters falling within the sphere of cooperation, is such that the legal basis of the contested decision is inadequate.

[...]

36. It should first be observed that it is apparent from Title XVII of the Treaty, in particular from Articles 130u(1), 130w(1), 130x and 130y, that, on the one hand, the Community has specific competence to conclude agreements with non-member countries in the sphere of development cooperation and that, on the other hand, that competence is not exclusive but is complementary to that of the Member States.

37. In order to qualify as a development cooperation agreement for the purposes of Article 130y of the Treaty, an agreement must pursue the objectives referred to in Article 130u. Article 130u(1) in particular makes it clear that those are broad objectives in the sense that it must be possible for the measures required for their pursuit to concern a variety of specific matters. That is so in particular in the case of an agreement establishing the framework of such cooperation.

38. That being so, to require a development cooperation agreement concluded between the Community and a non-member country to be based on another provision as well as on Article 130y and, possibly, also to be concluded by the Member States whenever it touches on a specific matter would in practice amount to rendering devoid of substance the competence and procedure prescribed in Article 130y.

39. It must therefore be held that the fact that a development cooperation agreement contains clauses concerning various specific matters cannot alter the characterization of the agreement, which must be determined having regard to its essential object and not in terms of individual clauses, provided that those clauses do not impose such extensive obligations concerning the specific matters referred to that those obligations in fact constitute objectives distinct from those of development cooperation (see, in particular, to this effect, Opinion 1/78 [1979] ECR 2871, paragraph 56).

40. In the light of those considerations, the objectives of the Agreement and the general scheme of the provisions in question must first be examined in the case in point.

41. According to the first subparagraph of Article 1(2), the principal objective of the Agreement is to enhance and develop the various aspects of cooperation between the contracting parties. Both the second subparagraph of Article 1(2) of and the preamble to the Agreement emphasize inter alia, first, the development of relations between the contracting parties in the areas of common interests and, second, the need to support Indian efforts for development. The second subparagraph lays particular stresses on development of economic cooperation.

42. While Articles 2 to 4 of the Agreement are concerned in a general way with commercial relations and economic cooperation between the contracting parties, Articles 5 to 15 and 17 to 19 contain provisions on specific matters most of which are, however, linked to economic cooperation.

43. Article 16 of the Agreement governs development cooperation in general. According to Article 16(1), the Community 'is prepared to strengthen its cooperation and enhance its efficiency in order to contribute to India's own efforts in achieving sustainable economic development and social progress of its people through concrete proposals and programmes'. That paragraph continues: 'Community support will be in accordance with Community policies, regulations and limits of the financial means available for cooperation and be in accordance with an elaborated development strategy'. Article 16(2) provides inter alia that 'Projects and programmes will be targeted towards the poorer sections of the population'.

44. The examination thus carried out shows that the cooperation provided for by the Agreement is specified in terms that take particular account of the needs of a developing country and, consequently, amongst other things, contributes to furthering the pursuit of the objectives mentioned in Article 130u(1) of the Treaty.

45. As regards more particularly the provisions of the Agreement which relate to specific matters, those provisions establish the framework of cooperation between the contracting parties. Taken as a whole, they are limited to determining the areas for cooperation and to specifying certain of its aspects and various actions to which special importance is attached. By contrast, those provisions contain nothing that prescribes in concrete terms the manner in which cooperation in each specific area envisaged is to be implemented.

46. That finding is reinforced by the fact that some of the provisions of the Agreement contemplate extending and achieving cooperation by other measures. Thus, the fifth subparagraph of Article 22(2) provides that the joint commission referred to in that article is also to have the task of ensuring the proper functioning of any sectoral agreements concluded or which may be concluded between the Community and India. Similarly, under Article 24(1) it is possible for cooperation to be developed and added to by means of agreements on specific sectors or activities. Furthermore, according to Article 24(2), either of the contracting parties may, within the framework of the Agreement, put forward suggestions for expanding the scope of the cooperation. Finally, Article 25 states that neither the Agreement nor any action taken thereunder is in any way to affect the powers of the Member States to undertake bilateral activities with India in the framework of economic cooperation or to conclude, where appropriate, new economic cooperation agreements with India.

47. The mere inclusion of provisions for cooperation in a specific field does not therefore necessarily imply a general power such as to lay down the basis of a competence to undertake any kind of cooperation action in that field. It does not, therefore, predetermine the allocation of spheres of competence between the Community and the Member States or the legal basis of Community acts for implementing cooperation in such a field.

48. In order to verify whether that analysis is valid, the Court must go on to examine in more detail the objective and content of each of the provisions challenged by the Portuguese Government.

Energy, tourism and culture

49. The Portuguese Government contends that Article 7 of the Agreement relating to energy constitutes the basis for subsequent adoption of specific measures, especially legislative measures, in order to implement the objectives and give effect to the commitments laid down in the Agreement. The provisions of that article are not ancillary clauses or mere declarations of intent made by the contracting parties. Article 7 provides for a high degree of cooperation in such areas as non-conventional energy. In the absence of specific powers of action in that sphere, the applicant considers that the Community should have had recourse to Article 235 of the Treaty.

50. As regards Article 13 of the Agreement, the Portuguese Government points out that its actual wording provides for specific measures, in particular for training programmes. It claims that Articles 126(3) and 127(3) of the EC Treaty make it clear that the Community is not empowered to conclude a tourism agreement on its own.

51. As regards culture, the applicant government notes first that Article 128 of the EC Treaty is aimed only at encouraging cooperation between Member States and, if necessary, supporting and supplementing their action in a number of areas. What is concerned, therefore, is a Community competence clearly subordinate to an objective of coordinating cultural policies defined by each Member State within the sphere of its own competences. It is, admittedly, mentioned in Article 128(3) that the Community and the Member States are to foster cooperation with third countries, but that provision does not confer on the Community any external competence. The Portuguese Government stresses that, even if such competence were recognized, measures could be taken only by the Council acting unanimously and following the co-decision procedure. It concludes that the inclusion of provisions relating to culture in cooperation agreements necessitates at the very least recourse to Article 235 of the Treaty and to a joint agreement.

52. The Council and the Commission consider that the provisions of the Agreement relating to the fields of energy, tourism and culture are ancillary to the principal objectives of the Agreement. Those provisions are not therefore concerned with objectives separable from that of development cooperation and are, moreover, merely declaratory in nature. The Council adds that Article 7 of the Agreement does not provide for a high degree of cooperation in the field of non-conventional energy, but merely mentions that area as one of those in which cooperation may take place.

53. In the light of those considerations, it should be noted first of all that the Portuguese Government does not deny that the provisions of the Agreement relating to the fields of energy, tourism and culture pursue the objectives referred to in Article 130u.

54. In determining the scope of Articles 7, 13 and 15 of the Agreement, the examination carried out in paragraphs 45 to 47 of this judgment of the general scheme of the provisions of the Agreement concerning specific matters must be taken into account. Analysis of the wording of Articles 7, 13 and 15 bears out the conclusion that those provisions establish the framework of cooperation in regard to the matters to which those articles refer. The obligations laid down in the provisions in question in the spheres of energy, tourism and culture are obligations to take action which do not constitute objectives distinct from those of development cooperation.

55. From the point of view of the incorporation into the Agreement of Articles 7, 13 and 15, their scope having thus been defined, it must be concluded that it was possible for the contested decision to be validly adopted on the basis of Article 130y of the Treaty.

Drug abuse control

56. The Portuguese Government considers that Article 19 of the Agreement contains a specific reciprocal commitment in the matter of drug abuse control. However, that matter belongs to the sphere of cooperation in the fields of justice and home affairs (see Article K.1(4) and (9) of the Treaty on European Union). In its view, the Treaty on European Union merely confirms the previous Community practice under which competence was vested in the Member States themselves.

57. According to the applicant, Article 129 of the EC Treaty, which provides that in the sphere of public health the Community may take action towards the prevention of drug dependence, does not constitute a legal basis enabling the Community to assume powers of decision; Community action must be limited to measures of encouragement or to adopting recommendations.

58. The Council, for its part, refers to the existence of several Community acts which are concerned directly or indirectly with drug abuse control and which were adopted without any challenge as to their legal basis. Since those acts govern various aspects of drug abuse control, the Community possesses, by virtue of the principle of parallel competences, the same competence in external matters.

59. The Commission considers that Community actions in the field of drug abuse control are also intended to contribute to India's economic and social development and maintains that drug abuse control is an integral part of Community development aid. In that connection, it mentions Council Regulation (EEC) No 443/92 of 25 February 1992 on financial and technical assistance to, and economic cooperation with, the developing countries in Asia and Latin America (OJ 1992 L 52, p. 1), which contains a provision stating that the fight against drugs falls within the scope of development cooperation with those countries.

60. It must be held, in the first place, that drug abuse control cannot, as such, be excluded from the measures necessary for the pursuit of the objectives referred to in Article 130u, since production of narcotics, drug abuse and related activities can constitute serious impediments to economic and social development.

61. It must then be considered whether Article 19 of the Agreement remains within limits which do not necessitate recourse to a competence and to a legal basis specific to the sphere of drug abuse control.

62. In that regard, it should be noted that the text of Article 19(1) contains nothing more than a declaration of intent to cooperate in drug abuse control. In addition, it states that the contracting parties are to act in conformity with their respective competences.

63. Article 19(2) of the Agreement defines the substance of that cooperation by mentioning the actions which it comprises. It is apparent from an examination of those actions that they can constitute measures falling within the sphere of the development cooperation objectives. Training, education, treatment and rehabilitation of addicts, as well as actions intended to encourage the creation of alternative economic opportunities, mentioned in subparagraphs (a) and (b), can be linked to the social and economic objectives pursued by development cooperation. The technical, financial and administrative assistance in the prevention, treatment and reduction of drug abuse provided for in subparagraph (c) can be assimilated to those actions.

64. Assistance in the monitoring of precursors' trade, provided for in Article 19(2)(c), may, as the Advocate General pointed out in paragraph 61 of his Opinion, form part of the objectives defined in Article 130u, in so far as this represents the Community's contribution to the efforts of the other contracting party to combat drug trafficking.

65. As regards Article 19(2)(d), the Council's representative stated at the hearing that that provision did not concern individual items of information such as those

relating to specific persons, bank accounts or transactions, but only general information relating to the problems of money laundering.

66. It is in fact only in so far as that exchange of information makes a contribution that is intimately linked to the other measures provided for by Article 19 that subparagraph (d) can be included amongst the actions falling within the field of development cooperation. That restrictive interpretation is confirmed by the actual wording of the provision, which limits its scope to 'relevant' information. In that connection, Article 19(1) expressly refers to the respective competences of the contracting parties, namely, as regards the Community, the competence it possesses in the sphere of drug abuse control.

67. Finally, it must be held, as has already been pointed out in paragraphs 45 to 47 of this judgment, with respect to the general scheme of the provisions relating to specific matters, that even the provisions concerning the actions specified in Article 19(2) of the Agreement cannot, having regard to their wording and context, constitute general enabling powers for their implementation.

68. In the light of that definition of the scope of Article 19 of the Agreement, it must be concluded that that provision did not require the participation of the Member States in the conclusion of the Agreement.

Intellectual property

69. As regards Article 10 of the Agreement, the Portuguese Government maintains that it is clear from Opinion 1/94 of 15 November 1994 ([1994] ECR I-5267) that protection of intellectual property is an area in which the Community does not possess exclusive competence.

70. The Portuguese Government concludes that, in accordance with the principle of parallel competences, Articles 113 and 130y of the Treaty are insufficient to confer on the Community the powers necessary to perform the contractual obligation assumed by the Community in Article 10 of the Agreement.

71. The Council maintains that the fact that the Community's competence is not exclusive does not mean that the Community may not in any circumstances conclude on its own agreements which contain provisions affecting this sphere. It considers that the Community had the power to conclude the Agreement without the participation of the Member States since the clause in the Agreement concerning intellectual property has only limited scope and involves substantial obligations only on the part of India.

72. It should therefore be considered whether Article 10 of the Agreement can be founded on the legal basis referred to in the contested decision, namely Articles 113 and 130y of the Treaty.

73. It must first be observed that the improvement in protection of intellectual property rights sought by Article 10 is such as to contribute to the objective laid down in Article 130u(1) of smoothly and gradually integrating the developing countries into the world economy.

74. Secondly, the first sentence of Article 10 merely provides that the contracting parties undertake to ensure as far as their laws, regulations and policies allow

that suitable and effective protection is provided for intellectual property rights, reinforcing this protection where necessary.

75. The last sentence of Article 10 provides that the contracting parties 'also undertake, wherever possible, to facilitate access to the data bases of intellectual property organizations'. The obligation created by that provision has only a very limited scope and is ancillary in nature, even in relation to the substance of intellectual property protection.

76. In those circumstances, it must be concluded that the scope of the obligations arising from Article 10 of the Agreement is not such that those obligations constitute objectives distinct from those of development cooperation. Consequently, Article 130y of the Treaty is a sufficient basis for the incorporation of Article 10 in the Agreement.

77. Furthermore, with regard to the linking of Article 10 of the Agreement to commercial policy, it is sufficient to point out that the Community is entitled to include in external agreements otherwise falling within the ambit of Article 113 ancillary provisions for the organization of purely consultative procedures or clauses calling on the other party to raise the level of protection of intellectual property (see, to that effect, Opinion 1/94, cited above, paragraph 68).

Partnership Agreement between the members of the African, Caribbean and Pacific Group of states of the one part, and the European Community and its Member States, of the other part, signed in Cotonou on 23 June 2000, Official Journal L 317, 15.12.2000, pp. 3–353 as first amended in Luxembourg on 25 June 2005, OJ L 209, 11.8.2005, pp. 27–53, and second in Burkina Faso on 22 June 2010, OJ L 287, 4.11.2010, pp. 3–49 (Cotonou Agreement—Extracts).

Historically, the most elaborate text of an association agreement is the Partnership Agreement with the ACP states.[2] The latest agreement, the so-called Cotonou Agreement, dates from 2000 (partially revised in 2005 and 2010). Next, to a more elaborate institutional structure, the main difference to classical cooperation agreements is that the Community and its Member States undertook in the Cotonou Agreement a contractual commitment to deliver a precise amount of financial development assistance during the lifetime of the agreement, which is funded by the European Development Funds (see above Case C-316/91, pp. 580-2). Excerpts of the agreement are reproduced here.

---

[2] The EU–ACP relationship has been developing through consecutive association agreements since 1963 when the 'First Yaoundé Convention' (JO 93, 11.6.1964, p. 1431) was signed. Each new agreement repealed and replaced the previous one, changing the focus of the cooperation depending on developments on the ground in the ACP and the then EEC. Thus, successive EEC–ACP agreements were signed in 1969 ('Second Yaoundé Convention', OJ English Special Edition 1970(II), p. 7), 1975 ('First Lomé Convention', OJ L 25, 30.1.1976, p. 2), 1979 ('Second Lomé Convention', OJ L 347, 22.12.1980, p. 2), 1984 ('Third Lomé Convention', OJ L 86, 31.3.1986, p. 3), and 1989 ('Fourth Lomé Convention', OJ L 229, 17.8.1991, p. 3), which was revised by the Mauritius Agreement in 1995 (OJ L 156, 29.5.1998, p. 3).

PREAMBLE

HAVING REGARD TO the Treaty establishing the European Community, on the one hand, and the Georgetown Agreement establishing the Group of African, Caribbean and Pacific States (ACP), on the other;

AFFIRMING their commitment to work together towards the achievement of the objectives of poverty eradication, sustainable development and the gradual integration of the ACP countries into the world economy;

ASSERTING their resolve to make, through their cooperation, a significant contribution to the economic, social and cultural development of the ACP States and to the greater well-being of their population, helping them facing the challenges of globalisation and strengthening the ACP-EU Partnership in the effort to give the process of globalisation a stronger social dimension;

REAFFIRMING their willingness to revitalise their special relationship and to implement a comprehensive and integrated approach for a strengthened partnership based on political dialogue, development cooperation and economic and trade relations;

ACKNOWLEDGING that a political environment guaranteeing peace, security and stability, respect for human rights, democratic principles and the rule of law, and good governance is part and parcel of long-term development; acknowledging that responsibility for establishing such an environment rests primarily with the countries concerned;

ACKNOWLEDGING that sound and sustainable economic policies are prerequisites for development;

REFERRING to the principles of the Charter of the United Nations, and recalling the Universal Declaration of Human Rights, the conclusions of the 1993 Vienna Conference on Human Rights, the Covenants on Civil and Political Rights and on Economic, Social and Cultural Rights, the Convention on the Rights of the Child, the Convention on the Elimination of all forms of Discrimination against Women, the International Convention on the Elimination of all forms of Racial Discrimination, the 1949 Geneva Conventions and the other instruments of international humanitarian law, the 1954 Convention relating to the status of stateless persons, the 1951 Geneva Convention relating to the Status of Refugees and the 1967 New York Protocol relating to the Status of Refugees;

CONSIDERING the Convention for the Protection of Human Rights and Fundamental Freedoms of the Council of Europe, the African Charter on Human and Peoples' Rights and the American Convention on Human Rights as positive regional contributions to the respect of human rights in the European Union and in the ACP States;

REAFFIRMING that the most serious crimes of concern to the international community must not go unpunished and that their effective prosecution must be ensured by taking measures at national level and by enhancing global collaboration;

CONSIDERING that the establishment and effective functioning of the International Criminal Court constitutes an important development for peace and international justice;

RECALLING the declarations of the successive Summits of the Heads of State and Government of ACP States;

CONSIDERING that the Millennium Development Goals emanating from the Millennium Declaration adopted by the United Nations General Assembly in 2000, in particular the eradication of extreme poverty and hunger, as well as the development targets and principles agreed in the United Nations Conferences, provide for a clear vision and must underpin ACP-EU cooperation within this Agreement; acknowledging that the EU and the ACP States need to make a concerted effort to accelerate progress towards attaining the Millennium Development Goals;

SUBSCRIBING to the aid effectiveness agenda started in Rome, pursued in Paris and further developed in the Accra Agenda for Action;

PAYING particular attention to the pledges made and objectives agreed at major UN and other international conferences and acknowledging the need for further action to be taken in order to achieve the goals and implement the action programmes which have been drawn up in those fora;

AWARE of the serious global environmental challenge posed by climate change, and deeply concerned that the most vulnerable populations live in developing countries, in particular in Least Developed Countries and Small Island ACP States, where climate-related phenomena such as sea level rise, coastal erosion, flooding, droughts and desertification are threatening their livelihoods and sustainable development;

ANXIOUS to respect basic labour rights, taking account of the principles laid down in the relevant conventions of the International Labour Organisation;

RECALLING the commitments within the framework of the World Trade Organisation,

HAVE DECIDED TO CONCLUDE THIS AGREEMENT:

PART 1
GENERAL PROVISIONS

TITLE I
OBJECTIVES, PRINCIPLES AND ACTORS

CHAPTER 1
Objectives and principles
Article 1

Objectives of the partnership

The Community and its Member States, of the one part, and the ACP States, of the other part, hereinafter referred to as the "Parties" hereby conclude this Agreement in order to promote and expedite the economic, cultural and social development of the ACP States, with a view to contributing to peace and security and to promoting a stable and democratic political environment.

The partnership shall be centred on the objective of reducing and eventually eradicating poverty consistent with the objectives of sustainable development and the gradual integration of the ACP countries into the world economy.

These objectives and the Parties' international commitments, including the Millennium Development Goals, shall inform all development strategies and shall be tackled through an integrated approach taking account at the same time of the political, economic, social, cultural and environmental aspects of development. The partnership shall provide a coherent support framework for the development strategies adopted by each ACP State.

Sustained economic growth, developing the private sector, increasing employment and improving access to productive resources shall all be part of this framework. Support shall be given to the respect of the rights of the individual and meeting basic needs, the promotion of social development and the conditions for an equitable distribution of the fruits of growth. Regional and subregional integration processes which foster the integration of the ACP countries into the world economy in terms of trade and private investment shall be encouraged and supported. Building the capacity of the actors in development and improving the institutional framework necessary for social cohesion, for the functioning of a democratic society and market economy, and for the emergence of an active and organised civil society shall be integral to the approach. Systematic account shall be taken of the situation of women and gender issues in all areas—political, economic and social. The principles of sustainable management of natural resources and the environment, including climate change, shall be applied and integrated at every level of the partnership.

Article 2

Fundamental principles

ACP-EC cooperation, underpinned by a legally binding system and the existence of joint institutions, shall be guided by the internationally agreed aid effectiveness agenda regarding ownership, alignment, harmonisation, results-oriented aid management and mutual accountability, exercised on the basis of the following fundamental principles:

— equality of the partners and ownership of the development strategies: for the purposes of implementing the objectives of the partnership, the ACP States shall determine the development strategies for their economies and societies in all sovereignty and with due regard for the essential and fundamental elements described in Article 9; the partnership shall encourage ownership of the development strategies by the countries and populations concerned; EU development partners shall align their programmes with these strategies;

— participation: apart from central government as the main partner, the partnership shall be open to ACP parliaments, and local authorities in ACP States and different kinds of other actors in order to encourage the integration of all sections of society, including the private sector and civil society organisations, into the mainstream of political, economic and social life;

— the pivotal role of dialogue and the fulfilment of mutual obligations and accountability: the obligations assumed by the Parties in the framework of their dialogue shall be central to their partnership and cooperation relations; the Parties shall work closely together in determining and implementing the necessary processes of donor alignment and harmonisation, with a view to securing a key role for ACP States in these processes;

— differentiation and regionalisation: cooperation arrangements and priorities shall vary according to a partner's level of development, its needs, its performance and its long-term development strategy. Special treatment shall be given to the least-developed countries. The vulnerability of landlocked and island countries shall be taken into account. Particular emphasis shall be put on regional integration, including at continental level.

Article 3
Achievement of this Agreement's objectives
The Parties shall, each as far as it is concerned in the framework of this Agreement, take all appropriate measures, whether general or particular, to ensure the fulfilment of the obligations arising from this Agreement and to facilitate the attainment of the objectives thereof. They shall refrain from any measures liable to jeopardise these objectives.

CHAPTER 2
The actors of the partnership
Article 4

General approach
The ACP States shall determine the development principles, strategies and models of their economies and societies in all sovereignty. They shall establish, with the Community, the cooperation programmes provided for under this Agreement. However, the parties recognise the complementary role of and potential for contributions by non-State actors, ACP national parliaments and local decentralised authorities to the development process, particularly at the national and regional levels. To this end, under the conditions laid down in this Agreement, non-State actors, ACP national parliaments and local decentralised authorities, shall, where appropriate:
— be informed and involved in consultation on cooperation policies and strategies, on priorities for cooperation especially in areas that concern or directly affect them, and on the political dialogue,
— be provided with capacity-building support in critical areas in order to reinforce the capabilities of these actors, particularly as regards organisation and representation, and the establishment of consultation mechanisms including channels of communication and dialogue, and to promote strategic alliances.
Non-State actors and local decentralised authorities shall, where appropriate:
— be provided with financial resources, under the conditions laid down in this Agreement in order to support local development processes,
— be involved in the implementation of cooperation projects and programmes in areas that concern them or where these actors have a comparative advantage.

Article 5

Information
Cooperation will support operation to provide more information and create greater awareness of the basic features of ACP-EU Partnership.
Cooperation will also:
— encourage partnership and build links between ACP and EU actors;
— strengthen networking and exchange of expertise and experience among the actors.

Article 6

Definitions
1. The actors of cooperation will include:
(a) State (local, regional and national), including ACP national parliaments;

(b) ACP regional organisations and the African Union. For the purpose of this Agreement the notion of regional organisations or levels shall also include sub-regional organisations or levels;

(c) non-State:

— private sector,

— economic and social partners, including trade union organisations,

— civil society in all its forms according to national characteristics.

2. Recognition by the parties of non-State actors shall depend on the extent to which they address the needs of the population, on their specific competencies and whether they are organised and managed democratically and transparently.

Article 7

Capacity building

The contribution of civil society to development can be enhanced by strengthening community organisations and non-profit non-governmental organisations in all spheres of cooperation. This will require:

— encouraging and supporting the creation and development of such organisations;

— establishing arrangements for involving such organisations in the design, implementation and evaluation of development strategies and programmes.

TITLE II

THE POLITICAL DIMENSION

Article 8

Political dialogue

1. The Parties shall regularly engage in a comprehensive, balanced and deep political dialogue leading to commitments on both sides.

2. The objective of this dialogue shall be to exchange information, to foster mutual understanding and to facilitate the establishment of agreed priorities and shared agendas, in particular by recognising existing links between the different aspects of the relations between the Parties and the various areas of cooperation as laid down in this Agreement. The dialogue shall facilitate consultations and strengthen cooperation between the Parties within international fora as well as promote and sustain a system of effective multilateralism. The objectives of the dialogue shall also include preventing situations arising in which one Party might deem it necessary to have recourse to the consultation procedures envisaged in Articles 96 and 97.

3. The dialogue shall cover all the aims and objectives laid down in this Agreement as well as all questions of common, general or regional interest, including issues pertaining to regional and continental integration. Through dialogue, the Parties shall contribute to peace, security and stability and promote a stable and democratic political environment. It shall encompass cooperation strategies, including the aid effectiveness agenda, as well as global and sectoral policies, including environment, climate change, gender, migration and questions related to the cultural heritage. It shall also address global and sectoral policies of both Parties that might affect the achievement of the objectives of development cooperation.

4. The dialogue shall focus, inter alia, on specific political issues of mutual concern or of general significance for the attainment of the objectives of this Agreement, such as the arms trade, excessive military expenditure, drugs, organised crime or child labour, or discrimination of any kind, such as race, colour, sex, language, religion, political or other opinion, national or social origin, property, birth or other status. The dialogue shall also encompass a regular assessment of the developments concerning the respect for human rights, democratic principles, the rule of law and good governance.

5. Broadly based policies to promote peace and to prevent, manage and resolve violent conflicts shall play a prominent role in this dialogue, as shall the need to take full account of the objective of peace and democratic stability in the definition of priority areas of cooperation. The dialogue in this context shall fully involve the relevant ACP regional organisations and the African Union, where appropriate.

6. The dialogue shall be conducted in a flexible manner. The dialogue shall be formal or informal according to the need, and conducted within and outside the institutional framework, including the ACP Group, the Joint Parliamentary Assembly, in the appropriate format and at the appropriate level, including national, regional, continental or all ACP level.

7. Regional organisations and representatives of civil society organisations shall be associated with this dialogue, as well as ACP national parliaments, where appropriate.

8. Where appropriate, and in order to prevent situations arising in which one Party might deem it necessary to have recourse to the consultation procedure foreseen in Article 96, dialogue covering the essential elements shall be systematic and formalised in accordance with the modalities set out in Annex VII.

[...]

Article 10

Other elements of the political environment

1. The Parties consider the following elements as contributing to the maintenance and consolidation of a stable and democratic political environment:
— sustainable and equitable development involving, inter alia, access to productive resources, essential services and justice;
— greater involvement of ACP national parliaments, local decentralised authorities, where appropriate, and of an active and organised civil society and the private sector.

2. The Parties recognise that the principles of the social market economy, supported by transparent competition rules and sound economic and social policies, contribute to achieving the objectives of the partnership.

Article 11

Peace-building policies, conflict prevention and resolution, response to situations of fragility

1. The Parties acknowledge that without development and poverty reduction there will be no sustainable peace and security, and that without peace and security there can be no sustainable development. The Parties shall pursue an active, comprehensive and integrated policy of peace building and conflict prevention and resolution, and human security, and shall address situations of fragility within the framework of the

Partnership. This policy shall be based on the principle of ownership and shall in particular focus on building national, regional and continental capacities, and on preventing violent conflicts at an early stage by addressing their root-causes, including poverty, in a targeted manner, and with an adequate combination of all available instruments.

The Parties acknowledge that new or expanding security threats need to be addressed, such as organised crime, piracy and trafficking of, notably, people, drugs and weapons. The impacts of global challenges like international financial market shocks, climate change and pandemics also need to be taken into account.

The Parties emphasize the important role of regional organisations in peace building and conflict prevention and resolution and in tackling new or expanding security threats with, in Africa, a key responsibility for the African Union.

2. The interdependence between security and development shall inform the activities in the field of peace building, conflict prevention and resolution which shall combine short and long-term approaches, which encompass and go beyond crisis management. Activities to tackle new or expanding security threats shall, inter alia, support law enforcement, including cooperating on border controls, enhancing the security of the international supply chain, and improving air, maritime and road transport safeguards.

Activities in the field of peace building, conflict prevention and resolution shall in particular include support for balancing political, economic, social and cultural opportunities among all segments of society, for strengthening the democratic legitimacy and effectiveness of governance, for establishing effective mechanisms for the peaceful conciliation of group interests, for active involvement of women, for bridging dividing lines among different segments of society as well as support for an active and organised civil society. In this respect, particular attention shall be paid to developing early warning systems and peace-building mechanisms that would contribute to the prevention of conflicts.

3. Relevant activities shall also include, inter alia, support for mediation, negotiation and reconciliation efforts, for effective regional management of shared, scarce natural resources, for demobilisation and reintegration of former combatants into the society, for addressing the problems of child soldiers and of violence against women and children. Suitable action shall be taken to set responsible limits to military expenditure and arms trade, including through support for the promotion and application of agreed standards and codes of conduct, as well as to combat activities that fuel conflict.

3a. Particular emphasis shall be given to the fight against anti-personnel landmines and explosive remnants of war as well as to addressing the illicit manufacture, transfer, circulation and accumulation of small arms and light weapons and their ammunition, including inadequately secured and poorly managed stocks and stockpiles and their uncontrolled spread.

The Parties agree to coordinate, observe and fully implement their respective obligations under all relevant international conventions and instruments, and, to this end, they undertake to cooperate at the national, regional and continental levels.

3b. The Parties also undertake to cooperate in the prevention of mercenary activities in accordance with their obligations under all relevant international conventions and instruments, and their respective legislation and regulations.

4. In order to address situations of fragility in a strategic and effective manner, the Parties shall share information and facilitate preventive responses combining diplomatic, security and development cooperation tools in a coherent way. They shall agree on the best way to strengthen capabilities of States to fulfil their core functions and to stimulate political will for reform while respecting the principle of ownership. In situations of fragility, political dialogue is especially important and shall be further developed and reinforced.

5. In situations of violent conflict the Parties shall take all suitable action to prevent an intensification of violence, to limit its territorial spread, and to facilitate a peaceful settlement of the existing disputes. Particular attention shall be paid to ensuring that financial resources for cooperation are used in accordance with the principles and objectives of the Partnership, and to preventing a diversion of funds for belligerent purposes.

6. In post-conflict situations, the Parties shall take all suitable action to stabilise the situation during the transition in order to facilitate the return to a non-violent, stable and democratic situation. The Parties shall ensure the creation of the necessary links between emergency measures, rehabilitation and development cooperation.

7. In promoting the strengthening of peace and international justice, the Parties reaffirm their determination to:

— share experience in the adoption of legal adjustments required to allow for the ratification and implementation of the Rome Statute of the International Criminal Court; and

— fight against international crime in accordance with international law, giving due regard to the Rome Statute.

The Parties shall seek to take steps towards ratifying and implementing the Rome Statute and related instruments.

Article 11a

Fight against terrorism
The Parties reiterate their firm condemnation of all acts of terrorism and undertake to combat terrorism through international cooperation, in accordance with the Charter of the United Nations and international law, relevant conventions and instruments and in particular full implementation of UN Security Council Resolutions 1373 (2001) and 1456 (2003) and other relevant UN resolutions. To this end, the Parties agree to exchange:

— information on terrorist groups and their support networks; and

— views on means and methods to counter terrorist acts, including in technical fields and training, and experiences in relation to the prevention of terrorism.

Article 11b

Cooperation in countering the proliferation of weapons of mass destruction
1. The Parties consider that the proliferation of weapons of mass destruction and their means of delivery, both to State and non-State actors, represents one of the most serious threats to international stability and security

The Parties therefore agree to cooperate and to contribute to countering the proliferation of weapons of mass destruction and their means of delivery through full compliance with and national implementation of their existing obligations under international disarmament and non-proliferation treaties and agreements and other relevant international obligations.

The Parties agree that this provision constitutes an essential element of this Agreement.

2. The Parties furthermore agree to cooperate and to contribute to the objective of non-proliferation by:

— taking steps to sign, ratify or accede to, as appropriate, and fully implement all other relevant

international instruments,

— the establishment of an effective system of national export controls, controlling the export as well as transit of weapons of mass destruction related goods, including a weapons of mass destruction end-use control on dual-use technologies and containing effective sanctions for breaches of export controls.

Financial and technical assistance in the area of cooperation to counter the proliferation of weapons of mass destruction will be financed by specific instruments other than those intended for the financing of ACP-EC cooperation.

3. The Parties agree to establish a regular political dialogue that will accompany and consolidate their cooperation in this area.

4. If, after having conducted a strengthened political dialogue, a Party, informed in particular by reports by the International Atomic Energy Agency (IAEA), the Organisation for the Prohibition of Chemical Weapons (OPCW) and other relevant multilateral institutions, considers that the other Party has failed to fulfil an obligation stemming from paragraph 1, it shall, except in cases of special urgency, supply the other Party and both the ACP and the EU Councils of Ministers with the relevant information required for a thorough examination of the situation with a view to seeking a solution acceptable to the Parties. To this end, it shall invite the other Party to hold consultations that focus on the measures taken or to be taken by the Party concerned to remedy the situation.

5. The consultations shall be conducted at the level and in the form considered most appropriate for finding a solution.

The consultations shall begin no later than 30 days after the invitation and shall continue for a period established by mutual agreement, depending on the nature and gravity of the violation. In no case shall the dialogue under the consultation procedure last longer than 120 days.

6. If the consultations do not lead to a solution acceptable to both Parties, if consultation is refused or in cases of special urgency, appropriate measures may be taken. These measures shall be revoked as soon as the reasons for taking them no longer prevail.

Article 12

Coherence of Community policies and their impact on the implementation of this Agreement

The Parties are committed to addressing policy coherence for development in a targeted, strategic and partnership-oriented way, including strengthening dialogue on issues of policy coherence for development. The Union acknowledges that Union policies, other than development policy, can support the development priorities of ACP States in line with the objectives of this Agreement. On this basis the Union will enhance the coherence of those policies with a view to attaining the objectives of this Agreement.

Without prejudice to Article 96, where the Community intends, in the exercise of its powers, to take a measure which might affect the interests of the ACP States, as far as this Agreement's objectives are concerned, it shall inform in good time the ACP Group of its intentions. To this end, the Commission shall regularly inform the Secretariat of the ACP Group of planned proposals and communicate simultaneously its proposal for such measures. Where necessary, a request for information may also take place on the initiative of the ACP States.

At their request, consultations shall be held promptly so that account may be taken of their concerns as to the impact of those measures before any final decision is made.

After such consultations have taken place, the ACP States and the ACP Group may, in addition, transmit their concerns in writing to the Community as soon as possible and submit suggestions for amendments indicating the way their concerns should be met. If the Community does not accede to the ACP States' submissions, it shall advise them as soon as possible giving its reasons.

The ACP Group shall also be provided with adequate information on the entry into force of such decisions, in advance whenever possible.

Article 13

Migration

1. The issue of migration shall be the subject of in-depth dialogue in the framework of the ACP-EU Partnership.

The Parties reaffirm their existing obligations and commitments in international law to ensure respect for human rights and to eliminate all forms of discrimination based particularly on origin, sex, race, language and religion.

2. The Parties agree to consider that a partnership implies, with relation to migration, fair treatment of third country nationals who reside legally on their territories, integration policy aiming at granting them rights and obligations comparable to those of their citizens, enhancing non-discrimination in economic, social and cultural life and developing measures against racism and xenophobia.

3. The treatment accorded by each Member State to workers of ACP countries legally employed in its territory, shall be free from any discrimination based on nationality, as regards working conditions, remuneration and dismissal, relative to its own nationals. Further in this regard, each ACP State shall accord comparable non-discriminatory treatment to workers who are nationals of a Member State.

4. The Parties consider that strategies aiming at reducing poverty, improving living and working conditions, creating employment and developing training contribute in the long term to normalising migratory flows.

The Parties will take account, in the framework of development strategies and national and regional programming, of structural constraints associated with migratory flows with the purpose of supporting the economic and social development of the regions from which migrants originate and of reducing poverty.

The Community shall support, through national and regional Cooperation programmes, the training of ACP nationals in their country of origin, in another ACP country or in a Member State of the European Union. As regards training in a Member State, the Parties shall ensure that such action is geared towards the vocational integration of ACP nationals in their countries of origin.

The Parties shall develop cooperation programmes to facilitate the access of students from ACP States to education, in particular through the use of new communication technologies.

5. (a) In the framework of the political dialogue the Council of Ministers shall examine issues arising from illegal immigration with a view to establishing, where appropriate, the means for a prevention policy.

(b) In this context the Parties agree in particular to ensure that the rights and dignity of individuals are respected in any procedure initiated to return illegal immigrants to their countries of origin. In this connection the authorities concerned shall extend to them the administrative facilities necessary for their return.

(c) The Parties further agree that:

i) – each Member State of the European Union shall accept the return of and readmission of any of its nationals who are illegally present on the territory of an ACP State, at that State's request and without further formalities;

– each of the ACP States shall accept the return of and readmission of any of its nationals who are illegally present on the territory of a Member State of the European Union, at that Member State's request and without further formalities.

The Member States and the ACP States will provide their nationals with appropriate identity documents for such purposes.

In respect of the Member States of the European Union, the obligations in this paragraph apply only in respect of those persons who are to be considered their nationals for the Community purposes in accordance with Declaration No 2 to the Treaty establishing the European Community. In respect of ACP States, the obligations in this paragraph apply only in respect of those persons who are considered as their nationals in accordance with their respective legal system.

(ii) at the request of a Party, negotiations shall be initiated with ACP States aiming at concluding in good faith and with due regard for the relevant rules of international law, bilateral agreements governing specific obligations for the readmission and return of their nationals. These agreements shall also cover, if deemed necessary by any of the Parties, arrangements for the readmission of third country nationals and stateless persons. Such agreements will lay down the details about the categories of persons covered by these arrangements as well as the modalities of their readmission and return.

Adequate assistance to implement these agreements will be provided to the ACP States.

(iii) for the purposes of this point (c), the term 'Parties' shall refer to the Community, any of its Member States and any ACP State.

PART 2

INSTITUTIONAL PROVISIONS

Article 14

The joint institutions

1. The joint institutions of this Agreement are the Council of Ministers, the Committee of Ambassadors and the Joint Parliamentary Assembly.

2. The joint institutions and the institutions set up under the Economic Partnership Agreements, without prejudice to the relevant provisions of existing or future Economic Partnership Agreements, shall endeavour to ensure coordination, coherence and complementarity, as well as an effective and reciprocal flow of information.

Article 14a

Meetings of Heads of State or Government
The Parties shall meet at the level of Heads of State or Government, upon joint agreement, in an appropriate format.

Article 15

The Council of Ministers
1. The Council of Ministers shall comprise, on the one hand, the members of the Council of the European Union and members of the Commission of the European Communities and, on the other, a member of the government of each ACP State.
The office of the President of the Council of Ministers shall be held alternately by a member of the Council of the European Union and a member of the government of an ACP State.
The Council shall meet as a rule once a year on the initiative of the President and whenever it seems necessary, in a form and a geographical composition appropriate to the issues to be addressed. Such meetings will provide for high-level consultations on matters which are of specific concern to the Parties, complementing the work that is being done in the Joint Ministerial Trade Committee, as set out in Article 38, and in the ACP-EC Development Finance Cooperation Committee, as set out in Article 83, which feed into the annual regular Council of Ministers meetings.
2. The functions of the Council of Ministers shall be to:
(a) conduct the political dialogue;
(b) adopt the policy guidelines and take the decisions necessary for the implementation of the provisions of this Agreement, in particular as regards development strategies in the specific areas provided for by this Agreement or any other area that should prove relevant, and as regards procedures;
(c) examine and resolve any issue liable to impede the effective and efficient implementation of this Agreement or present an obstacle to achieving its objectives;
(d) ensure the smooth functioning of the consultation mechanisms.
3. The Council of Ministers shall take its decisions by common agreement of the Parties.
The proceedings of the Council of Ministers shall be valid only if half the members of the Council of the European Union, one member of the Commission and two-thirds of the members representing the governments of the ACP States are present. Any member of the Council of Ministers unable to attend may be represented. The representative shall exercise all the rights of that member.
It may take decisions that are binding on the Parties and frame resolutions, recommendations and opinions, during the annual regular meeting, or by written procedure. It shall report annually to the Joint Parliamentary Assembly on the implementation of this Agreement. It shall examine and take into consideration resolutions and recommendations adopted by the Joint Parliamentary Assembly.

The Council of Ministers shall conduct an ongoing dialogue with the representatives of the social and economic partners and other actors of civil society in the ACP and the EU. To that end, consultations may be held alongside its meetings.

4. The Council of Ministers may delegate powers to the Committee of Ambassadors.

5. The Council of Ministers shall adopt its rules of procedure within six months of the entry into force of this Agreement.

Article 16

The Committee of Ambassadors

1. The Committee of Ambassadors shall comprise, on the one hand, the permanent representative of each Member State to the European Union and a representative of the Commission and, on the other, the head of mission of each ACP State to the European Union.

The office of Chairman of the Committee of Ambassadors shall be held alternately by a Permanent Representative of a Member State designated by the Community, and a head of mission representing an ACP State, designated by the ACP States.

2. The Committee shall assist the Council of Ministers in the fulfilment of its tasks and carry out any mandate entrusted to it by the Council. In this context, it shall monitor implementation of this Agreement and progress towards achieving the objectives set therein.

The Committee of Ambassadors shall meet regularly, in particular to prepare the Council sessions and whenever it proves necessary.

3. The Committee shall adopt its rules of procedure within six months of the entry into force of this Agreement.

Article 17

The Joint Parliamentary Assembly

1. The Joint Parliamentary Assembly shall be composed of equal numbers of EU and ACP representatives. The members of the Joint Parliamentary Assembly shall be, on the one hand, members of the European Parliament and, on the other, members of parliament or, failing this, representatives designated by the parliament of each ACP State. In the absence of a parliament, the attendance of a representative from the ACP State concerned shall be subject to the prior approval of the Joint Parliamentary Assembly.

2. The role of the Joint Parliamentary Assembly, as a consultative body, shall be to:

— promote democratic processes through dialogue and consultation;

— facilitate greater understanding between the peoples of the European Union and those of the ACP States and raise public awareness of development issues;

— discuss issues pertaining to development and the ACP-EU Partnership, including the Economic Partnership Agreements, other trading arrangements, the European Development Fund and Country and Regional Strategy Papers. To this end, the Commission shall transmit such Strategy Papers for information to the Joint Parliamentary Assembly;

— discuss the annual report of the Council of Ministers on the implementation of this Agreement, and adopt resolutions and make recommendations to the Council of Ministers with a view to achieving the objectives of this Agreement;

— advocate for institutional development and capacity building of national parliaments in accordance with Article 33(1) of this Agreement.

3. The Joint Parliamentary Assembly shall meet twice a year in plenary session, alternately in the European Union and in an ACP State. With a view to strengthening regional integration and fostering cooperation between national parliaments meetings between EU and ACP members of parliament shall be arranged at regional level.

Such meetings at regional level will be organised in pursuance of the objectives laid down in Article 14(2) of this Agreement.

4. The Joint Parliamentary Assembly shall adopt its rules of procedure within six months of the entry into force of this Agreement.

[...]

ANNEX I

FINANCIAL PROTOCOL

1. For the purposes set out in this Agreement and for a period of five years commencing 1 March 2000, the overall amount of the Community's financial assistance to the ACP States shall be EUR 15 200 million.

2. The Community's financial assistance shall comprise an amount up to EUR 13 500 million from the 9th European Development Fund (EDF).

3. The 9th EDF shall be allocated between the instruments of cooperation as follows:

(a) EUR 10 000 million in the form of grants shall be reserved for an envelope for support for long-term development. This envelope shall be used to finance national indicative programmes in accordance with Articles 1 to 5 of Annex IV 'Implementation and management procedures' to this Agreement. From the envelope for support for long-term development:

(i) EUR 90 million shall be reserved for the financing of the budget of the Centre for the Development of Enterprise (CDE);

(ii) EUR 70 million shall be reserved for the financing of the budget of the Centre for the Development of Agriculture (CTA); and

(iii) an amount not exceeding EUR 4 million shall be reserved for the purposes referred to in Article 17 of this Agreement (Joint Parliamentary Assembly).

(b) EUR 1 300 million in the form of grants shall be reserved for the financing of support for regional cooperation and integration of the ACP States in accordance with Articles 6 to 14 of Annex IV 'Implementation and management procedures' to this Agreement.

(c) EUR 2 200 million shall be allocated to finance the Investment Facility according to the terms and conditions set out in Annex II 'Terms and conditions of financing' to this Agreement without prejudice to the financing of the interest rate subsidies provided for in Articles 2 and 4 of Annex II to this Agreement funded from the resources mentioned in paragraph 3(a) of this Annex.

4. An amount of up to EUR 1 700 million shall be provided from the European Investment Bank in the form of loans made from its own resources. These resources shall be granted for the purposes set out in Annex II 'Terms and conditions of financing' to this Agreement in accordance with the conditions provided for by its statutes

and the relevant provisions of the terms and conditions for investment financing as laid down in the aforementioned Annex. The Bank may, from the resources it manages, contribute to the financing of regional projects and programmes.

5. Any balances remaining from previous EDFs on the date of entry into force of this Financial Protocol, as well as any amounts that shall be decommitted at a later date from ongoing projects under these Funds, shall be transferred to the 9th EDF and shall be used in accordance with the conditions laid down in this Agreement. Any resources thus transferred to the 9th EDF that previously had been allocated to the indicative programme of an ACP State or region shall remain allocated to that State or region. The overall amount of this Financial Protocol, supplemented by the transferred balances from previous EDFs, will cover the period of 2000–2007.

6. The Bank shall administer the loans made from its own resources, as well as the operations financed under the Investment Facility. All other financial resources of this Agreement shall be administered by the Commission.

7. Before the expiry of this Financial Protocol, the Parties shall assess the degree of realisation of commitments and disbursements. This assessment shall constitute the basis for re-evaluating the overall amount of resources as well for evaluating the need for new resources to support financial cooperation under this Agreement.

8. In the event of the funds provided for in any of the instruments of the Agreement being exhausted before the expiry of this Financial Protocol, the joint ACP-EC Council of Ministers shall take the appropriate measures.

9. By derogation from Article 58 of this Agreement, an amount of EUR 90 million shall be transferred to the intra ACP envelope under the 9th EDF. This amount may be allocated to finance devolution for the period 2006 to 2007, and shall be managed directly by the Commission.

8.3 Economic, financial, and technical cooperation with developed countries

In contrast to Chapter 1 of the Treaty on developing countries, Chapter 2 on economic, financial, and technical cooperation deals with the cooperation with developed countries, as can be drawn from the opening phrase of Article 212(1) TFEU, which states that it is '[w]ithout prejudice to the other provisions of the Treaties, and in particular Articles 208 to 211'. Whereas the two chapters have thus to be distinguished according to the qualification of the third country as a developing country or not, they share a lot of similarities, not least because the former has served as a model for the latter. Again, under Article 212(1) TFEU, the Community enjoys an external competence in the area, which is complementary to the ones which the Member States retain. Article 212(2) TFEU foresees the adoption of unilateral measures of support and Article 212(3) TFEU empowers the Union to conclude agreements in the field. In practice, the Union concludes far less agreements than in the development cooperation field, but has adopted a general financial regulation in the field.

Council Regulation (EC) No 1934/2006 of 21 December 2006 establishing a financing instrument for cooperation with industrialised and other high-income countries and territories, Official Journal L 405, 30.12.2006, pp. 41–59.

THE COUNCIL OF THE EUROPEAN UNION,

Having regard to the Treaty establishing the European Community, and in particular Article 181a thereof,

Having regard to the proposal from the Commission,

Having regard to the opinion of the European Parliament,

Whereas:

(1) Over the past decade, the Community has consistently strengthened its bilateral relations with a broad range of industrialised and other high-income countries and territories across different regions of the world, primarily in North America, East Asia and Australasia, but also in South-East Asia and the Gulf region. Furthermore, these relations have developed to embrace a widening array of subjects and areas in the economic sphere and beyond.

(2) It is in the Community's interest to further deepen its relations with industrialised countries and territories with which it often shares similar political, economic and institutional structures and values and which are important bilateral political and trading partners as well as players in multilateral fora and in global governance. This will be an important factor in strengthening the European Union's role and place in the world, consolidating multilateral institutions and in contributing to balance and in developing the world economy and the international system.

(3) The European Union and industrialised and other high-income countries and territories have agreed to strengthen their relationship and to cooperate across the areas in which they have shared interests through a variety of bilateral instruments such as agreements, declarations, action plans and other similar documents.

(4) In accordance with the principles laid down in those bilateral instruments, the Community implements a cooperation policy aimed at creating an environment conducive to pursuing and developing its relations with those countries and territories. Cooperation activities will help to strengthen the European presence and visibility in these countries and encourage economic, commercial, academic, cultural and other exchanges and interaction between a diversified range of actors on each side.

(5) The European Union is founded on the principles of democracy, the rule of law, good governance, respect for human rights and fundamental freedoms. Community action under this Regulation should contribute to the general objective of developing and consolidating these principles in partner countries and regions through dialogue and cooperation.

(6) The promotion of diversified bilateral cooperation initiatives with industrialised and other high-income countries and territories within a single instrument will allow economies of scale, synergy effects, greater effectiveness and visibility for the Community action.

(7) In order to achieve the objectives of this Regulation it is necessary to pursue a differentiated approach and to design cooperation with partner countries taking account of their economic, social and political contexts as well as of the Community's specific interests, strategies and priorities.

(8) This Regulation makes it necessary to repeal Council Regulation (EC) No 382/2001 of 26 February 2001 concerning the implementation of projects promoting cooperation and commercial relations between the European Union and the industrialised countries of North America, the Far East and Australasia.

(9) Since the objectives of this Regulation, namely to promote enhanced cooperation between the Community and industrialised and other high-income countries and territories, cannot be sufficiently achieved by the Member States and can therefore, by reason of the scale of the action, be better achieved at Community level, the Community may adopt measures, in accordance with the principle of subsidiarity as set out in Article 5 of the Treaty. In accordance with the principle of proportionality, as set out in that article, this Regulation does not go beyond what is necessary in order to achieve those objectives.

(10) The measures necessary for the implementation of this Regulation should be adopted in accordance with Council Decision 1999/468/EC of 28 June 1999 laying down the procedures for the exercise of implementing powers conferred on the Commission,

HAS ADOPTED THIS REGULATION:

Article 1

Objective

1. Community financing shall support economic, financial and technical cooperation and other forms of cooperation falling within its spheres of competence, with industrialised and other high-income countries and territories.

2. The primary objective of cooperation with the countries and territories referred to in paragraph 1 shall be to provide a specific response to the need to strengthen links and to engage further with them on a bilateral, regional or multilateral basis in order to create a more favourable environment for the development of the relations of the Community with these countries and territories and promote dialogue while fostering Community's interests.

Article 2

Scope

1. The cooperation with industrialised and other high-income countries and territories shall be aimed at engaging with partners which share similar political, economic and institutional structures and values to the Community and which are important bilateral partners and players in multilateral fora and in global governance. The cooperation also covers newly industrialised or high-income countries and territories with which the Community has a strategic interest in promoting links.

2. For the purpose of this Regulation, industrialised and other high-income countries and territories shall comprise countries and territories listed in the Annex and are hereinafter referred to as 'partner countries'. However, in duly justified circumstances and in order to foster regional cooperation, the Commission may decide when

adopting action programmes referred to in Article 6 that countries not listed in the Annex are eligible, where the project or programme to be implemented is of regional or cross-border nature. Provisions may be made for this in the multi-annual cooperation programmes referred to in Article 5. The Commission shall amend the list in the Annex in accordance with regular OECD/DAC reviews of its List of developing countries and inform the Council thereof.

Article 3

General principles

1. The European Union is founded on the principles of liberty, democracy, respect for human rights and fundamental freedoms and the rule of law and seeks to promote commitment to these principles in partner countries through dialogue and cooperation.

2. In the implementation of this Regulation a differentiated approach in designing cooperation with partner countries shall be pursued, where appropriate, to take account of their economic, social and political contexts as well as of the Community's specific interests, strategies and priorities.

3. Measures financed under this Regulation shall cover areas of cooperation set out notably in the instruments, agreements, declarations and action plans between the Community and the partner countries as well as areas pertaining to the Community's specific interests.

4. For measures financed under this Regulation, the Community shall aim to ensure coherence with other areas of its external action as well as other relevant Community policies. This shall be ensured by formulating policy, strategic planning and the programming and implementation of measures.

5. Measures financed under this Regulation shall complement and bring added value to the efforts undertaken by Member States and Community public bodies, including in the area of commercial relations.

Article 4

Areas of cooperation

Community financing shall support cooperation actions in accordance with Article 1 and shall be consistent with the overall purpose, scope, objectives and general principles of this Regulation.

Specific attention shall be paid to actions, which may include a regional dimension, in the following areas of cooperation:

1) the promotion of cooperation, partnerships and joint undertakings between economic, academic and scientific actors in the Community and partner countries;

2) the stimulation of bilateral trade, investment flows and economic partnerships;

3) the promotion of dialogues between political, economic and social actors and other non-governmental organisations in relevant sectors in the Community and partner countries;

4) the promotion of people-to-people links, education and training programmes and intellectual exchanges and the enhancement of mutual understanding between cultures and civilisations;

5) the promotion of cooperative projects in areas such as research, science and technology, energy, transport and environmental matters—including climate change, customs and financial issues and any other matter of mutual interest between the Community and the partner countries;

6) the enhancement of awareness about and understanding of the European Union and of its visibility in partner countries;

7) support for specific initiatives, including research work, studies, pilot schemes or joint projects destined to respond in an effective and flexible manner to cooperation objectives arising from developments in the Community's bilateral relationship with the partner countries or aiming to provide impetus to the further deepening and broadening of bilateral relationships with them.

Article 5

Programming and allocation of funds

1. Actions to promote cooperation under this Regulation shall be carried out in the framework of multi-annual cooperation programmes covering cooperation with all or with a selection of the partner countries. The Commission shall draw-up the multi-annual cooperation programmes and specify their scope.

2. Multi-annual cooperation programmes shall cover no more than the period of validity of this Regulation. They shall set out the Community's strategic interests and priorities, the general objectives and the expected results. They shall also set out the areas selected for financing by the Community and outline the indicative financial allocation of funds, overall, per priority area and per partner country or group of partner countries for the period concerned. Where appropriate, this may be given in the form of a range. Multi-annual cooperation programmes shall be reviewed at mid-term, or ad hoc if necessary.

3. Multi-annual cooperation programmes and any reviews thereof shall be adopted by the Commission in accordance with the procedure set out in Article 15(2).

Article 6

Implementation

1. The Commission shall adopt annual action programmes based on the multi-annual cooperation programmes referred to in Article 5.

2. Annual action programmes shall specify, for all or for a selection of partner countries, the objectives pursued, the fields of intervention, the expected results, the management procedures and the total amount of financing planned. They shall contain a description of the operations to be financed, an indication of the amounts allocated for each operation and an indicative implementation timetable.

3. Annual action programmes shall be adopted by the Commission in accordance with the procedure set out in Article 15(2). This procedure needs not be used for amendments to action programmes, such as those making technical adjustments, extending the implementation period, reassigning funds between the planned operations within the forecast budget, or increasing or reducing the size of the budget by less than 20% of the initial budget, provided these amendments are consistent with the initial objectives set out in the action programmes.

Article 7

Eligibility

The following entities shall be eligible for funding under this Regulation for the purposes of implementing the action programmes referred to in Article 6:

(a) the following entities and bodies in the Member States and in the partner countries:

>   (i) public or parastatal bodies, local authorities and consortia thereof;

>   (ii) companies, firms and other private organisations and businesses;

>   (iii) non-governmental organisations; citizens' groups and sectoral organisations such as trade unions, organisations representing economic and social interests, consumer organisations, women's and youth organisations; teaching, training, cultural, media, research and scientific organisations; universities and other education institutions;

(b) partner countries and their regions, institutions and decentralised bodies;

(c) international organisations, including regional organisations, in so far as they contribute to the objectives of this Regulation;

(d) natural persons of the Member States and of partner countries or other third countries in so far as they contribute to the objectives of this Regulation;

(e) joint bodies set up by the partner countries and regions and the Community;

(f) Community institutions and bodies, insofar as they implement support measures specified in Article 9;

(g) European Union agencies.

Article 8

Types of financing

1. Cooperation projects and programmes will be financed by the general budget of the European Union either in totality or in the form of co-financing with other sources as specified in Article 10.

2. Financing for the implementation of action programmes may take in particular the following legal forms:

>   (a) grant agreements (including scholarships);

>   (b) procurement contracts;

>   (c) employment contracts;

>   (d) financing agreements.

3. Where the implementation of action programmes takes the form of financing agreements with partner countries, it shall be established that Community funding shall not be used to finance taxes, customs duties and other fiscal charges in the partner countries.

Article 9

Support measures

1. Community financing may cover expenditure associated with the preparation, follow up, monitoring, audit and evaluation activities directly necessary for the implementation of this Regulation and the achievement of its objectives, and any other administrative or technical assistance expenditure that the Commission, including at

its Delegations in the partner countries, may incur for the management of operations financed under this Regulation.

2. These support measures are not necessarily covered by multi-annual programmes and may therefore be financed outside their scope.

3. The Commission shall adopt support measures not covered by the multi-annual programmes and shall inform Member States thereof.

Article 10

Co-financing

1. Measures shall be eligible for co-financing inter alia with:

(a) Member States, their regional and local authorities, and in particular their public and parastatal agencies;

(b) partner countries, and in particular their public and parastatal agencies;

(c) international organisations and regional organisations, including international and regional financial institutions;

(d) companies, firms, other private organisations and businesses, and other non-state actors;

(e) partner countries in receipt of funding, and other bodies eligible for funding under Article 7.

2. In the case of parallel co-financing, the project or programme will be split into a number of clearly identifiable operations which are each financed by the different partners providing co-financing in such a way that the end-use of the financing can always be identified.

3. In the case of joint co-financing, the total cost of a project or programme will be shared between the partners providing the co-financing and the resources are pooled in such a way that it is not possible to identify the source of financing for any given activity undertaken as part of the project or programme.

4. The Commission may receive and manage funds for co-financed projects on behalf of the bodies referred to in paragraph 1(a) (b) and (c) for the purpose of implementing joint measures. Such funds shall be treated as assigned revenue, in accordance with Article 18 of Council Regulation (EC, Euratom) No 1605/2002 of 25 June 2002 on the Financial Regulation applicable to the general budget of the European Communities.

Article 11

Management procedures

1. The measures financed under this Regulation shall be implemented in accordance with Regulation (EC, Euratom) No 1605/2002 and in particular Part Two, Title IV thereof.

2. The Commission may entrust tasks of public authority, and in particular budget implementation tasks, to the bodies referred to in Article 54(2)(a) and (c) of Regulation (EC, Euratom) No 1605/2002. The bodies referred to in Article 54(2)(c) of that Regulation may be entrusted with tasks of public authority if they are of recognised international standing, comply with internationally recognised systems of management and control, and are supervised by a public authority.

Article 12

Protecting the Community's financial interests

1. Any agreements resulting from this Regulation shall contain provisions ensuring the protection of the Community's financial interests, in particular with respect to irregularities, fraud, corruption and any other illegal activity, in accordance with Council Regulations (EC, Euratom) No 2988/95 of 18 December 1995 on the protection of the European Communities financial interests and (Euratom, EC) No 2185/96 of 11 November 1996 concerning on-the-spot checks and inspections carried out by the Commission in order to protect the European Communities' financial interests against fraud and other irregularities and Regulation (EC) No 1073/1999 of the European Parliament and of the Council of 25 May 1999 concerning investigations conducted by the European Anti-Fraud Office (OLAF).

2. Agreements shall expressly entitle the Commission and the Court of Auditors to perform audits, including document audits or on-the-spot audits of any contractor or subcontractor who has received Community funds. They shall also expressly authorise the Commission to carry out on-the-spot checks and inspections in accordance with Regulation (Euratom, EC) No 2185/96.

3. All contracts resulting from the implementation of cooperation shall ensure the rights of the Commission and the Court of Auditors under paragraph 2 during and after the performance of the contracts.

Article 13

Evaluation

1. The Commission shall regularly evaluate the actions and programmes financed under this Regulation, where appropriate by means of independent external evaluations, in order to ascertain whether the objectives have been met and enable it to formulate recommendations with a view to improving future operations. The results shall feed back into programme design and resource allocation.

2. The Commission shall send its evaluation reports to the European Parliament and to the Committee referred to in Article 15 for information.

3. The Commission shall associate relevant stakeholders, including non-state actors, in the evaluation phase of the Community cooperation provided for under this Regulation.

Article 14

Annual report

The Commission shall examine the progress made on implementing the measures taken under this Regulation and shall submit to the European Parliament and the Council an annual report on the implementation of this Regulation. The report shall set out the results of implementation of the budget and present the actions and programmes financed, and as far as possible, set out the main outcomes and impacts of the cooperation actions and programmes.

Article 15

Committee

1. The Commission shall be assisted by a committee.

2. Where reference is made to this paragraph, Articles 4 and 7 of Decision 1999/468/EC shall apply.

The period laid down in Article 4(3) of Decision 1999/468/EC shall be set at 30 days.

3. The Committee shall adopt its rules of procedure.

Article 16

Financial provisions

The financial reference amount for the implementation of this Regulation for the period from 2007 to 2013 shall be EUR 172 million. The annual appropriations shall be authorised by the budgetary authority within the limits of the financial framework.

Article 17

Repeal

1. Regulation (EC) No 382/2001 shall be repealed as of the latest of the following dates:
– 1 January 2007;
– the date of entry into force of this Regulation.

2. The repealed Regulation shall continue to apply for legal acts and commitments of budget years preceding the year 2007. Any reference to the repealed Regulation shall be deemed to be a reference to this Regulation.

Article 18

Review

Not later than 31 December 2010, the Commission shall submit to the European Parliament and the Council a report evaluating the implementation of this Regulation in the first three years with, if appropriate, a legislative proposal introducing the necessary modifications.

Article 19

Entry into force

This Regulation shall enter into force on the day following its publication in the Official Journal of the European Union.

It shall apply from 1 January 2007 to 31 December 2013.

This Regulation shall be binding in its entirety and directly applicable in all Member States.

8.4 Thematic cooperation worldwide

In addition, the Community has adopted two important thematic instruments; one on the promotion of democracy and human rights, and one on crisis management. As they are designed to apply in cooperation worldwide, they neither fitted under Title XX nor under Title XXI of the EC Treaty, whereas the Lisbon Treaty has not changed this. Accordingly, the Community legislature based such thematic cooperation instruments on both Article 179(1) EC and 181a EC alike (now Articles 209(1) and 212 TFEU, respectively). The combination of Articles 179(1) EC and 181a EC as legal bases of the same instrument had certain procedural ramifications. Whereas the Parliament acted as co-legislator for measures adopted under Article 179(1) EC, it was (only) consulted for measures adopted under Article 181a(2) EC. Combining the two articles hence means giving the Parliament influence as co-legislator over the entire legal act. This possibility has been accepted by the Court in *Parliament v. Council*.[3] In that case, the Parliament attacked a decision of the Council adopted under Article 181a(2) EC granting a Community guarantee to the European Investment Bank against losses under loans and loan guarantees for projects outside the Community[4] although some beneficiaries were developing countries. The Court condemned the Council for not having added Article 179 EC as an additional legal basis. Nowadays, this procedural problem has disappeared, as both Articles 209(1) TFEU and 212(2) TFEU foresee the ordinary legislative procedure for the adoption of unilateral acts.

Regulation (EC) No 1889/2006 of the European Parliament and of the Council of 20 December 2006 on establishing a financing instrument for the promotion of democracy and human rights worldwide, Official Journal L 386, 29.12.2006, pp. 1–11.

This regulation is a flagship of the EU's external human rights and democracy policy. It allows the financing of projects worldwide, which help human rights defenders and democracy activists. Again, implementation is entrusted to the Commission.

THE EUROPEAN PARLIAMENT AND THE COUNCIL OF
THE EUROPEAN UNION,
Having regard to the Treaty establishing the European Community, and in particular Articles 179(1) and 181a(2) thereof,
Having regard to the proposal from the Commission,
Acting in accordance with the procedure referred to in Article 251 of the Treaty,
[...]

HAVE ADOPTED THIS REGULATION:

TITLE I
OBJECTIVES AND SCOPE
Article 1

Objectives
1. This Regulation establishes a European Instrument for Democracy and Human Rights under which the Community shall provide assistance, within the framework of the Community's policy on development cooperation, and economic, financial

---

[3] Case C-155/07 *European Parliament v. Council*, [2008] ECR I-8103.
[4] Council Decision 2006/1016/EC of 19 December 2006 granting a Community guarantee to the European Investment Bank against losses under loans and loan guarantees for projects outside the Community, OJ L 414, 30.12.2006, pp. 95–103.

and technical cooperation with third countries, consistent with the European Union's foreign policy as a whole, contributing to the development and consolidation of democracy and the rule of law, and of respect for all human rights and fundamental freedoms.

2. Such assistance shall aim in particular at:

(a) enhancing the respect for and observance of human rights and fundamental freedoms, as proclaimed in the Universal Declaration of Human Rights and other international and regional human rights instruments, and promoting and consolidating democracy and democratic reform in third countries, mainly through support for civil society organisations, providing support and solidarity to human rights defenders and victims of repression and abuse, and strengthening civil society active in the field of human rights and democracy promotion;

(b) supporting and strengthening the international and regional framework for the protection, promotion and monitoring of human rights, the promotion of democracy and the rule of law, and reinforcing an active role for civil society within these frameworks;

(c) building confidence in and enhancing the reliability of electoral processes, in particular through election observation missions, and through support for local civil society organisations involved in these processes.

Article 2

Scope

1. Having regard to Articles 1 and 3, Community assistance shall relate to the following fields:

(a) promotion and enhancement of participatory and representative democracy, including parliamentary democracy, and the processes of democratisation, mainly through civil society organisations, inter alia in:

 i) promoting freedom of association and assembly, unhindered movement of persons, freedom of opinion and expression, including artistic and cultural expression, independent media, unimpeded access to information, and measures to combat administrative obstacles to the exercise of these freedoms, including the fight against censorship;

 ii) strengthening the rule of law, promoting the independence of the judiciary, encouraging and evaluating legal and institutional reforms, and promoting access to justice;

 iii) promoting and strengthening the International Criminal Court, ad hoc international criminal tribunals and the processes of transitional justice and truth and reconciliation mechanisms;

 iv) supporting reforms to achieve effective and transparent democratic accountability and oversight, including that of the security and justice sectors, and encouraging measures against corruption;

 v) promoting political pluralism and democratic political representation, and encouraging political participation by citizens, in particular marginalised groups, in democratic reform processes at local, regional and national level;

vi) promoting the equal participation of men and women in social, economic and political life, and supporting equality of opportunity, and the participation and political representation of women;

vii) supporting measures to facilitate the peaceful conciliation of group interests, including support for confidence-building measures relating to human rights and democratisation.

(b) the promotion and protection of human rights and fundamental freedoms, as proclaimed in the Universal Declaration of Human rights and other international and regional instruments concerning civil, political, economic, social and cultural rights, mainly through civil society organisations, relating to inter alia:

i) the abolition of the death penalty, prevention of torture, ill-treatment and other cruel, inhuman and degrading treatment or punishment, and the rehabilitation of victims of torture;

ii) support for, protection of, and assistance to human rights defenders, in terms of Article 1 of the UN Declaration on the Right and Responsibility of Individuals, Groups and Organs of Society to Promote and Protect Universally Recognized Human Rights and Fundamental Freedoms;

iii) the fight against racism and xenophobia, and discrimination based on any ground including sex, race, colour, ethnic or social origin, genetic features, language, religion or belief, political or any other opinion, membership of a national minority, property, birth, disability, age or sexual orientation;

iv) the rights of indigenous peoples and the rights of persons belonging to minorities and ethnic groups;

v) the rights of women as proclaimed in the Convention on the Elimination of All Forms of Discrimination against Women and its Optional Protocols, including measures to combat female genital mutilation, forced marriages, crimes of honour, trafficking, and any other form of violence against women;

vi) the rights of the child, as proclaimed in the Convention on the Rights of the Child and its Optional Protocols, including the fight against child labour, child trafficking and child prostitution, and the recruitment and use of child soldiers;

vii) the rights of persons with disabilities;

viii) the promotion of core labour standards and corporate social responsibility;

ix) education, training and monitoring in the area of human rights and democracy, and in the area covered by paragraph 1(a)(vii);

x) support for local, regional, national or international civil society organisations involved in the protection, promotion or defence of human rights and in measures referred to in paragraph 1(a)(vii);

(c) the strengthening of the international framework for the protection of human rights, justice, the rule of law and the promotion of democracy, in particular by:

i) providing support for international and regional instruments concerning human rights, justice, the rule of law and democracy;

ii) fostering cooperation of civil society with international and regional intergovernmental organisations, and supporting civil society activities aimed at promoting and monitoring the implementation of international and regional instruments concerning human rights, justice, the rule of law and democracy;

iii) promoting observance of international humanitarian law;

(d) building confidence in and enhancing the reliability and transparency of democratic electoral processes, in particular:

i) through deployment of European Union Election Observation Missions;

ii) through other measures of monitoring electoral processes;

iii) by contributing to developing electoral observation capacity of civil society organisations at regional and local level, and supporting their initiatives to enhance participation in, and the follow-up to, the electoral process;

iv) by supporting measures aimed at implementing recommendations of European Union Election Observation Missions, in particular through civil society organisations.

2. The promotion and protection of gender equality, the rights of the child, rights of indigenous peoples, rights of persons with disabilities, and principles such as empowerment, participation, non-discrimination of vulnerable groups and accountability shall be taken into account whenever relevant by all assistance measures referred to in this Regulation.

3. The assistance measures referred to in this Regulation shall be implemented in the territory of third countries or shall be directly related to situations arising in third countries, or shall be directly related to global or regional actions.

Article 3

Complementarity and Coherence of Community
Assistance

1. Community assistance under this Regulation shall be consistent with the framework of the Community's policy on development cooperation and with the European Union's foreign policy as a whole, and complementary to that provided for under related Community instruments for external assistance and the Partnership Agreement between the Members of the African, Caribbean and Pacific Group of States, of the one part, and the European Community and its Member States, on the other part.

Complementary Community assistance under this Regulation shall be provided to reinforce action under the related external assistance instruments.

2. The Commission shall ensure that measures adopted under this Regulation are consistent with the Community's overall strategic policy framework and in particular with the objectives of the above instruments, as well as with other relevant Community measures.

3. In order to enhance the effectiveness and consistency of Community and Member States assistance measures, the Commission shall ensure close coordination between its own activities and those of the Member States, both at decision-making level and on the ground. Coordination shall involve regular consultations and frequent exchanges of relevant information, including with other donors, during the different phases of the assistance cycle, in particular at field level.

4. The Commission shall inform and have regular exchanges of views with the European Parliament.

5. The Commission shall seek regular exchanges of information with civil society, at all levels, including in third countries.

TITLE II

IMPLEMENTATION

Article 4

General framework for implementation

Community assistance under this Regulation shall be implemented through the following measures:

a) Strategy Papers and revisions thereof as appropriate;

b) Annual Action Programmes;

c) Special Measures;

d) Ad hoc Measures.

[...]

As we have seen with the field of human rights and democracy, thematic cooperation can touch a wide range of topics. This raises the issue of delimitation with the EU's CFSP. Is it possible for the EU to fund certain activities either as part of the EU's development policy or as a CFSP project? Does the Council have discretion to opt for a former 1st pillar or a 2nd pillar legal basis? These were the questions that the Commission put to the CJEU in the leading *ECOWAS* case. Here, the Council had adopted a CFSP action which was designed to foster peace and development in certain African countries through financing a number of partner institutions in collecting and destroying such arms. The Commission considered that such action should have been financed within the former Community's development cooperation envelope. The Court recalled that the former Article 47 EU gave precedence to the 1st pillar over the 2nd pillar. Today, the provision is kept in Article 40(1) EU, but a second paragraph has been added according to which the implementation of integrated EU external polices should not affect the CFSP.

Judgment of the Court (Grand Chamber) of 20 May 2008, Commission of the European Communities v. Council of the European Union, Case C-91/05, European Court Reports 2008, p. I-3651, paras. 1–24, 29–34, and 56–110.

1. By its action, the Commission of the European Communities asks the Court to annul Council Decision 2004/833/CFSP of 2 December 2004 implementing Joint Action 2002/589/CFSP with a view to a European Union contribution to ECOWAS in the framework of the Moratorium on Small Arms and Light Weapons (OJ 2004 L 359, p. 65; 'the contested decision') and to declare illegal and hence inapplicable the Council Joint Action 2002/589/CFSP of 12 July 2002 on the European Union's contribution to combating the destabilising accumulation and spread of small arms and light weapons and repealing Joint Action 1999/34/CFSP (OJ 2002 L 191, p. 1; 'the contested joint action'), in particular Title II thereof.

Legal context and background to the dispute

The Cotonou Agreement

2. On 23 June 2000 the Partnership Agreement between the members of the African, Caribbean and Pacific Group of States ('the ACP States') of the one part, and the European Community and its Member States, of the other part, was signed in Cotonou, Benin (OJ 2000 L 317, p. 3; 'the Cotonou Agreement'); it was approved on behalf of the Community by Council Decision 2003/159/EC of 19 December 2002 (OJ 2003 L 65, p. 27). It entered into force on 1 April 2003.

3. Article 1 of the Cotonou Agreement, entitled 'Objectives of the partnership', states:

'The Community and its Member States, of the one part, and the ACP States, of the other part, hereinafter referred to as the "Parties" hereby conclude this Agreement in order to promote and expedite the economic, cultural and social development of the ACP States, with a view to contributing to peace and security and to promoting a stable and democratic political environment.

The partnership shall be centred on the objective of reducing and eventually eradicating poverty consistent with the objectives of sustainable development and the gradual integration of the ACP countries into the world economy.

These objectives and the Parties' international commitments shall inform all development strategies and shall be tackled through an integrated approach taking account at the same time of the political, economic, social, cultural and environmental aspects of development. The partnership shall provide a coherent support framework for the development strategies adopted by each ACP State.

...'

4. Article 11 of the Cotonou Agreement, entitled 'Peace-building policies, conflict prevention and resolution', states:

'1. The Parties shall pursue an active, comprehensive and integrated policy of peace-building and conflict prevention and resolution within the framework of the Partnership. This policy shall be based on the principle of ownership. It shall in particular focus on building regional, sub-regional and national capacities, and on preventing violent conflicts at an early stage by addressing their root-causes in a targeted manner, and with an adequate combination of all available instruments.

2. The activities in the field of peace-building, conflict prevention and resolution shall in particular include support for balancing political, economic, social and cultural opportunities among all segments of society, for strengthening the democratic legitimacy and effectiveness of governance, for establishing effective mechanisms for the peaceful conciliation of group interests, for bridging dividing lines among different segments of society as well as support for an active and organised civil society.

3. Relevant activities shall also include, inter alia, support for mediation, negotiation and reconciliation efforts, for effective regional management of shared, scarce natural resources, for demobilisation and reintegration of former combatants into the society, for addressing the problem of child soldiers, as well as for suitable action to set responsible limits to military expenditure and the arms trade, including through support for the promotion and application of agreed standards and codes of conduct. In this context, particular emphasis shall be given to the fight against anti-personnel landmines as well as to addressing an excessive and

uncontrolled spread, illegal trafficking and accumulation of small arms and light weapons.
...'

5. Under Articles 6 to 10 of Annex IV of the Cotonou Agreement, entitled 'Implementation and Management Procedures', a regional support strategy and a regional indicative programme were drawn up in a document signed on 19 February 2003 by the Commission, of the one part, and by the Economic Community of West African States (ECOWAS) and the West African Economic and Monetary Union (WAEMU), of the other.

6. This document highlights, in section 2.3.1, entitled 'Security and conflict prevention', 'the importance of controlling the traffic in small arms', noting that 'there is a moratorium on export and import supported by the United Nations'. Section 6.4.1, entitled 'Support for a regional policy of conflict prevention and good governance', refers to support which may be given to back up the United Nations in carrying out priority measures under the action plan to implement a moratorium on the import, export and production of small arms.

7. Following a request from ECOWAS, in 2004 the Commission started preparing a financing proposal for conflict prevention and peace-building operations. According to the Commission, the largest single block of this financing was to be allocated to the ECOWAS Small Arms Control Programme.

The contested joint action

8. On 12 July 2002, the Council of the European Union adopted, on the basis of Article 14 EU, the contested joint action, which repealed and replaced Council Joint Action 1999/34/CFSP of 17 December 1998, adopted on the basis of Article J.3 of the Treaty on European Union, on the European Union's contribution to combating the destabilising accumulation and spread of small arms and light weapons (OJ 1999 L 9, p. 1).

9. According to Article 1(1) of the contested joint action, '[t]he objectives of this Joint Action are:
   – to combat, and contribute to ending, the destabilising accumulation and spread of small arms,
   – to contribute to the reduction of existing accumulations of these weapons and their ammunition to levels consistent with countries' legitimate security needs, and
   – to help solve the problems caused by such accumulations.'

10. Title I of the contested joint action, entitled 'Principles on preventive and reactive aspects', sets out the programme on the basis of which the European Union will aim to build consensus in the relevant regional and international forums. To this end, it sets out the principles and measures which must be realised in order to prevent the further destabilising accumulation of small arms (Article 3) and to reduce existing accumulations of small arms and their ammunition (Article 4).

11. Among the principles and measures which must be realised in order to prevent the further destabilising accumulation of small arms, Article 3 of the contested joint action refers to commitments by all the countries concerned regarding the production, export, import and holding of those arms, as well as the establishment and maintenance of national inventories of weapons and the establishment of restrictive national weapons legislation.

12. Among the principles and measures which must be realised in order to reduce existing accumulations of small arms and their ammunition, Article 4 of the contested joint action mentions the provision of assistance as appropriate to countries requesting support for controlling or eliminating surplus small arms on their territory, and the promotion of confidence-building measures and incentives to encourage the voluntary surrender of surplus or illegally-held small arms and their ammunition.

13. Title II of the contested joint action, headed 'Contribution by the Union to specific actions', provides, in particular, for financial and technical assistance to programmes and projects which make a direct contribution to the principles and measures referred to in Title I.

14. Article 6(2) of the joint action states:

    'In providing such assistance, the Union shall take into account in particular the recipients' commitments to comply with the principles mentioned in Article 3; their respect for human rights; their compliance with international humanitarian law and the protection of the rule of law; and their compliance with their international commitments, in particular with regard to existing peace treaties and international arms control agreements.'

15. Under Article 7(1) of the contested joint action, the Council is to decide on the allocation of the financial and technical assistance referred to in Article 6(1) of the joint action, on the priorities for the use of those funds and on the conditions for implementing specific actions of the Union. Article 7(2) provides that '[t]he Council shall decide on the principle, arrangements and financing of such projects on the basis of concrete and properly-costed project proposals and on a case-by-case basis, without prejudice to Member States' bilateral contributions and operation of the Community'.

16. Article 8 of the contested joint action provides:

    'The Council notes that the Commission intends to direct its action towards achieving the objectives and the priorities of this Joint Action, where appropriate by pertinent Community measures.'

17. Article 9(1) of the joint action provides:

    'The Council and the Commission shall be responsible for ensuring the consistency of the Union's activities in the field of small arms, in particular with regard to its development policies. For this purpose, Member States and the Commission shall submit any relevant information to the relevant Council bodies. The Council and the Commission shall ensure implementation of their respective action, each in accordance with its powers.'

The contested decision

18. On 2 December 2004, the Council adopted the contested decision, which implements the contested joint action with a view to a contribution by the Union to ECOWAS in the framework of the Moratorium on Small Arms and Light Weapons. As its legal basis, the contested decision refers to the contested joint action, in particular Article 3 thereof, in conjunction with Article 23(2) EU.

19. The preamble of the contested decision contains the following recitals:

'(1) The excessive and uncontrolled accumulation and spread of small arms and light weapons poses a threat to peace and security and reduces the prospects for sustainable development; this is particularly the case in West Africa.

(2) In pursuing the objectives set out in Article 1 of [the contested] Joint Action, the European Union envisages operating within the relevant international forums to promote confidence-building measures. This Decision is accordingly intended to implement the said Joint Action.

(3) The European Union considers that a financial contribution and technical assistance would help to consolidate the [ECOWAS] initiative concerning small arms and light weapons.

(4) The European Union therefore intends to offer financial support and technical assistance to ECOWAS in accordance with Title II of [the contested] Joint Action.'

20. Under Article 1 of the contested decision, the Union is to contribute towards implementing projects in the framework of the ECOWAS Moratorium on the Import, Export and Manufacture of Small Arms and Light Weapons. To that end, it is to offer a financial contribution and technical assistance in order to set up the Light Weapons Unit within the ECOWAS Technical Secretariat and to convert the Moratorium into a Convention on small arms and light weapons between the ECOWAS Member States.

21. Article 3 of the contested decision provides:

'The Commission shall be entrusted with the financial implementation of this Decision. To that end, it shall conclude a financing agreement with ECOWAS on the conditions for use of the European Union contribution, which shall take the form of a grant. Amongst other things, this grant shall cover, over a period of 12 months, salaries, travel expenses, supplies and equipment necessary for setting up the Light Weapons Unit within the ECOWAS Technical Secretariat and converting the Moratorium into a Convention on small arms and light weapons between the ECOWAS Member States....'

22. Article 4(2) of the decision provides:

'The Presidency and the Commission shall submit to the relevant Council bodies regular reports on the consistency of the European Union's activities in the field of small arms and light weapons, in particular with regard to its development policies, in accordance with Article 9(1) of [the contested] Joint Action. More particularly, the Commission shall report on the aspects referred to in the first sentence of Article 3. This information shall be based, amongst other things, on regular reports to be supplied by ECOWAS under its contractual relationship with the Commission.'

23. When the draft of the contested decision was discussed by the Committee of Permanent Representatives on 24 November 2004, the Commission made the following declaration to the minutes of the Council meeting (document No 15236/04 PESC 1039 of 25 November 2004):

'In the view of the Commission this Joint Action should not have been adopted and the project ought to have been financed from the 9th [European Development Fund—"EDF"] under the Cotonou Agreement. This is clearly borne out by Article 11(3) of the Cotonou Agreement which specifically mentions the fight against the accumulation of small arms and light weapons as a relevant activity. It is also reflected in the annotation to the relevant [Common Foreign and Security Policy—"CFSP"] budget line (19 03 02) in the 2004 budget, which excludes CFSP financing of such projects if they "are already covered by the provisions of the Cotonou Agreement...".

The Joint Action for financing under the CFSP would have been eligible under the 9th EDF and fully coherent with the regional indicative programme with ECOWAS. This is demonstrated by the fact that the Commission is already preparing a financing proposal for an indicative amount of EUR 1.5 million to support the implementation of the ECOWAS moratorium on small arms and light weapons (SALW).

Finally, the Joint Action falls within the shared competences on which Community development policy and the Cotonou Agreement are based. Such areas of shared competences are just as much protected by Article 47 [EU] as the areas of exclusive Community competence; otherwise Article 47 would be deprived of a large part of its useful effect. The Commission reserves its rights in this matter.'

24. Taking the view that the contested decision was not adopted on the correct legal basis, and that by virtue of that fact Article 47 EU was infringed, the Commission brought the present action.

[...]

Jurisdiction of the Court

29. By the present action for annulment, brought under Article 230 EC, the Commission is seeking a declaration that the Council, by adopting the contested decision, has encroached upon Community competences and, therefore, infringed Article 47 EU. In so far as the contested decision is based on the contested joint action, the Commission relies on Article 241 EC in order to invoke the inapplicability of that joint action, in particular Title II thereof, on the ground that it also infringes Article 47 EU.

30. Without thereby calling in question the jurisdiction of the Court to rule on the action, the Council, supported by the Spanish and United Kingdom governments, submits, in particular with regard to the plea based on the illegality of the contested joint action, that the Court has no jurisdiction to rule on the legality of a measure falling within the CFSP.

31. In that regard, it follows from Article 46(f) EU that the provisions of the EC Treaty concerning the powers of the Court and the exercise of those powers are applicable to Article 47 EU.

32. Under Article 47 EU, none of the provisions of the EC Treaty is to be affected by a provision of the Treaty on European Union (Case C-176/03 *Commission* v *Council* [2005] ECR I-7879, paragraph 38, and Case C-440/05 *Commission* v *Council* [2007] ECR I-0000, paragraph 52).

33. It is therefore the task of the Court to ensure that acts which, according to the Council, fall within the scope of Title V of the Treaty on European Union and which, by their nature, are capable of having legal effects, do not encroach upon the powers conferred by the EC Treaty on the Community (see, to that effect, Case C-170/96

Commission v *Council* [1998] ECR I-2763, paragraph 16; Case C-176/03 *Commission* v *Council*, paragraph 39; and Case C-440/05 *Commission* v *Council*, paragraph 53).

34. It follows that the Court has jurisdiction to consider the action for annulment brought by the Commission under Article 230 EC and, in that context, to consider the pleas invoked in accordance with Article 241 EC in so far as they allege an infringement of Article 47 EU.

The action

[...]

Findings of the Court

Application of Article 47 EU

56. As stated in paragraphs 31 to 33 of this judgment, under Article 47 EU, it is the task of the Court to ensure that the acts which, according to the Council, fall within the scope of Title V of the EU Treaty and which are capable of having legal effects do not encroach upon the powers conferred by provisions of the EC Treaty on the Community.

57. According to the Commission, the contested decision fails to respect the division of competences between the Community and the Union established by Article 47 EU as it could have been adopted on the basis of competences conferred on the Community in the area of development cooperation. The same applies to the provisions of Title II of the contested joint action, as implemented by the contested decision, which, it claims, fall either within Community competences concerning development cooperation or those concerning economic, financial and technical cooperation with third countries.

58. It is therefore necessary to determine whether the provisions of the contested decision affect competences enjoyed by the Community under the EC Treaty, on the ground that, as the Commission argues, they could have been adopted on the basis of that treaty (see, to that effect, Case C-176/03 *Commission* v *Council*, paragraph 40, and Case C-440/05 *Commission* v *Council*, paragraph 54).

59. In providing that nothing in the EU Treaty is to affect the Treaties establishing the European Communities or the subsequent Treaties and Acts modifying or supplementing them, Article 47 EU aims, in accordance with the fifth indent of Article 2 EU and the first paragraph of Article 3 EU, to maintain and build on the acquis communautaire.

60. Contrary to what is submitted by the United Kingdom Government, a measure having legal effects adopted under Title V of the EU Treaty affects the provisions of the EC Treaty within the meaning of Article 47 EU whenever it could have been adopted on the basis of the EC Treaty, it being unnecessary to examine whether the measure prevents or limits the exercise by the Community of its competences. It is apparent from the case-law of the Court that, if it is established that the provisions of a measure adopted under Titles V or VI of the EU Treaty, on account of both their aim and their content, have as their main purpose the implementation of a policy conferred by the EC Treaty on the Community, and if they could properly have been adopted on the basis of the EC Treaty, the Court must find that those provisions infringe Article 47 EU (see, to that effect, Case C-176/03 *Commission*

v *Council,* paragraphs 51 and 53, and Case C-440/05 *Commission* v *Council,* paragraphs 69 to 74).

61. Since the infringement of Article 47 EU arises from the fact that a measure having legal effects adopted by the Union on the basis of the EU Treaty could have been adopted by the Community, it is also not relevant whether in an area such as development cooperation—which does not fall within the exclusive competence of the Community and in which, therefore, the Member States are not precluded from exercising, individually or collectively, their competences (see, to that effect, Joined Cases C-181/91 and C-248/91 *Parliament* v *Council and Commission* [1993] ECR I-3685, paragraph 16, and C-316/91 *Parliament* v *Council* [1994] ECR I-625, paragraph 26)—such a measure could have been adopted by the Member States in exercise of their competences.

62. Moreover, the question whether the provisions of such a measure adopted by the Union fall within the competence of the Community relates to the attribution and, thus, the very existence of that competence, and not its exclusive or shared nature (see, to that effect, Case C-459/03 *Commission* v *Ireland* [2006] ECR I-4635, paragraph 93).

63. It is therefore necessary to determine whether the contested decision infringes Article 47 EU inasmuch as it could have been adopted on the basis of the provisions of the EC Treaty.

Demarcation of the areas of Community development cooperation policy and the CFSP respectively

64. With regard to Community development cooperation policy, the Court has held that the objectives pursued by Article 130u of the EC Treaty (now Article 177 EC) are broad in the sense that it must be possible for the measures required for their pursuit to concern various specific matters (Case C-268/94 *Portugal* v *Council* [1996] ECR I-6177, paragraph 37).

65. Articles 177 EC to 181 EC, which deal with cooperation with developing countries, refer not only to the sustainable economic and social development of those countries, their smooth and gradual integration into the world economy and the campaign against poverty, but also to the development and consolidation of democracy and the rule of law, as well as to respect for human rights and fundamental freedoms, in compliance also with commitments in the context of the United Nations and other international organisations (C-403/05 *Parliament* v *Commission* [2007] ECR I-0000, paragraph 56).

66. In addition, it follows from the Joint Statement by the Council and the representatives of the governments of the Member States meeting within the Council, the European Parliament and the Commission on European Union Development Policy, entitled 'The European Consensus [on Development]' (OJ 2006 C 46, p. 1) that there can be no sustainable development and eradication of poverty without peace and security and that the pursuit of the objectives of the Community's new development policy necessarily proceed via the promotion of democracy and respect for human rights (C-403/05 *Parliament* v *Commission,* paragraph 57).

67. While the objectives of current Community development cooperation policy should therefore not be limited to measures directly related to the campaign against

poverty, it is none the less necessary, if a measure is to fall within that policy, that it contributes to the pursuit of that policy's economic and social development objectives (see, to that effect, Case C-268/94 *Portugal* v *Council*, paragraphs 44, 60, 63 and 73).

68. In that regard, it is apparent from a number of documents emanating from the Union institutions and from the European Council that certain measures aiming to prevent fragility in developing countries, including those adopted in order to combat the proliferation of small arms and light weapons, can contribute to the elimination or reduction of obstacles to the economic and social development of those countries.

69. For example, on 21 May 1999, the 'development' Council of the European Union adopted a resolution on small arms in which it presented the proliferation of those weapons as a problem of global proportions which, in particular in crisis zones and countries where the security situation is unstable, has been an obstacle to peaceful economic and social development. More recently, in the European Union strategy to combat illicit accumulation and trafficking of small arms and light weapons adopted by the European Council on 15 and 16 December 2005 (Council document No 5319/06 PESC 31 of 13 January 2006), the European Council referred, among the consequences of the illicit spread of small arms and light weapons, in particular to those relating to the development of the countries concerned, that is, the weakening of State structures, displacement of persons, collapse of health and education services, declining economic activity, reduced government resources, the spread of pandemics, damage to the social fabric and, in the long term, the reduction or withholding of development aid, while adding that those consequences constitute, for sub-Saharan Africa, the region principally affected, a key factor in limiting development.

70. Equally, the Joint Statement by the Council and the representatives of the governments of the Member States meeting within the Council, the European Parliament and the Commission on European Union development policy, mentioned in paragraph 66 of the present judgment, refers, in paragraph 37, to insecurity and violent conflict as amongst the biggest obstacles to the achievement of the Millennium Development Goals, agreed by the United Nations, while mentioning, in that context, the fight against the uncontrolled proliferation of small arms and light weapons.

71. Nevertheless, a concrete measure aiming to combat the proliferation of small arms and light weapons may be adopted by the Community under its development cooperation policy only if that measure, by virtue both of its aim and its content, falls within the scope of the competences conferred by the EC Treaty on the Community in that field.

72. That is not the case if such a measure, even if it contributes to the economic and social development of the developing country, has as its main purpose the implementation of the CFSP.

73. If examination of a measure reveals that it pursues a twofold aim or that it has a twofold component and if one of those is identifiable as the main one, whereas the other is merely incidental, the measure must be based on a single legal basis,

namely that required by the main aim or component (see, to that effect, Case C-211/01 *Commission* v *Council* [2003] ECR I-8913, paragraph 39; Case C-338/01 *Commission* v *Council* [2004] ECR I-4829, paragraph 55, and Case C-94/03 *Commission* v *Council* [2006] ECR I-1, paragraph 35; and see, with regard to the application of Article 47 EU, Case C-176/03 *Commission* v *Council*, paragraphs 51 to 53, and Case C-440/05 *Commission* v *Council*, paragraphs 71 to 73).

74. It follows that measures combating the proliferation of small arms and light weapons do not fall within the competences conferred on the Community in the field of development cooperation policy if, on account of their main aim or component, they are part of the pursuit of the CFSP.

75. With regard to a measure which simultaneously pursues a number of objectives or which has several components, without one being incidental to the other, the Court has held, where various legal bases of the EC Treaty are therefore applicable, that such a measure will have to be founded, exceptionally, on the various corresponding legal bases (see, to that effect, Case C-211/03 *Commission* v *Council*, paragraph 40, and Case C-94/03 *Commission* v *Council*, paragraph 36).

76. However, under Article 47 EU, such a solution is impossible with regard to a measure which pursues a number of objectives or which has several components falling, respectively, within development cooperation policy, as conferred by the EC Treaty on the Community, and within the CFSP, and where neither one of those components is incidental to the other.

77. Since Article 47 EU precludes the Union from adopting, on the basis of the EU Treaty, a measure which could properly be adopted on the basis of the EC Treaty, the Union cannot have recourse to a legal basis falling within the CFSP in order to adopt provisions which also fall within a competence conferred by the EC Treaty on the Community.

78. In the light of the foregoing it must be established whether, as the Commission claims, the contested decision, which implements the contested joint action with a view to a European Union contribution to ECOWAS in the framework of the Moratorium on Small Arms and Light Weapons, falls, by virtue both of its aim and its content, within the policy on development cooperation conferred by the EC Treaty on the Community.

Aim of the contested decision

79. With regard to the aim of the contested decision, it follows both from its title, from the legal basis relied upon and from recitals 2 to 4 in its preamble that, by making a financial and technical contribution to an ECOWAS initiative concerning the fight against the proliferation of small arms and light weapons, the decision aims to implement the contested joint action which the Council adopted on the basis of Title V of the EU Treaty.

80. To the extent that the contested decision implements a measure falling within the CFSP, it is necessary at the outset to examine whether, because of that fact, the decision must be understood as aiming to achieve the objectives of the CFSP rather than those of Community development cooperation policy.

81. In that regard, and without it being necessary, at this stage, to examine the Commission's plea as to the alleged illegality of the contested joint action, it should

be pointed out that the joint action is presented, in its preamble, as a measure intended to replace Joint Action 1999/34, in order to include, where appropriate, ammunition for small arms and light weapons in the Union joint action.

82. Article 1(1) of the contested joint action sets out as objectives the combating of the destabilising accumulation and spread of small arms, the contribution to the reduction of existing accumulations of these weapons and their ammunition to levels consistent with countries' legitimate security needs and assistance in solving the problems caused by such accumulations.

83. Concrete expression is given to these objectives, first, in Title I of the contested joint action, which lists certain principles and measures around which the Union is aiming to build a consensus in order to combat the destabilising accumulation and spread of small arms and light weapons and, second, in Title II of the joint action, which deals with the financial and technical assistance provided by the Union to projects which contribute to those principles and measures.

84. However, it cannot be inferred from the contested joint action that the implementation of the campaign against the proliferation of small arms and light weapons which it sets out will necessarily take the form of measures which pursue CFSP objectives, such as the preservation of peace and the strengthening of international security, rather than objectives of Community development policy.

85. In that regard, it should be observed, first, that Joint Action 1999/34, of which the contested joint action is the successor and whose objectives, principles listed and type of contribution envisaged are fully reproduced by it, stated clearly, in the first recital to its preamble, that the excessive and uncontrolled accumulation and spread of small arms and light weapons poses a threat to peace and security and reduces the prospects for sustainable development in many regions of the world, thereby from the outset placing the fight against that phenomenon within a dual perspective, that is preservation of peace and international security, on the one hand, and safeguarding development perspectives, on the other.

86. Second, it follows from the provisions of Title II of the contested joint action— which, while reproducing the provisions of Joint Action 1999/34, specify the nature of the contribution the Union will make and how its tasks will be divided between the Council and the Commission—that the objectives and the programme of action laid down by it can be implemented not only by the Union, acting within the CFSP context, but equally by the Community, on the basis of its own competences.

87. Indeed, Article 7 of the contested joint action points out that it is for the Council to decide on the allocation of the financial and technical assistance referred to in Article 6 of the joint action, but explains, in Article 7(2), that the Council is to decide 'without prejudice to...operation of the Community', on a case-by-case basis, on the principle, arrangements and financing of the projects implementing the joint action. The fact that the contested joint action can be implemented both by the Community and the Union is confirmed in Article 8 thereof, in which the Council notes that the Commission intends to direct its action towards achieving the objectives and the priorities of the joint action, where appropriate by pertinent Community measures, and in Article 9 of the joint action, which places

in the hands of the Council and the Commission the responsibility for ensuring the consistency of the Union's activities in the field of small arms, 'in particular with regard to its development policies', and for ensuring implementation of their respective action, each in accordance with its powers. The need for consistency of the Union's activities in the field of small arms and light weapons is also stated, with an identical reference to 'development policies [of the Union]' in Article 4(2) of the contested decision.

88. The conclusion that the objectives of the contested joint action can be implemented both by the Union, under Title V of the EU Treaty, and by the Community, under its development cooperation policy, corresponds, in the end, to the approach advocated by the Union's institutions and by the European Council in numerous documents.

89. First, the Council itself, in the resolution on small arms referred to in paragraph 69 of this judgment, while alluding to the action undertaken by the Union in the CFSP framework and recalling the need to ensure coherence of Union activities in the field of small arms, inter alia in relation to the CFSP, nevertheless recommends, in the same document, that, in the field of development cooperation, the Community and the Member States devote particular attention to the following measures: 'inclusion of the small arms issue in the political dialogue with ACP and other development cooperation partner countries of the Union; development cooperation support for countries seeking assistance in the control or elimination of surplus small arms...; considering support, where necessary, to strengthen appropriate government institutions and legislation to better control small arms', while adding, concerning the last point, that '[t]he first interventions could be focused on Southern...and on West Africa (ECOWAS), where significant progress has been made and frameworks for combating small arms proliferation have been developed and agreed'.

90. Second, in the European Union strategy to combat illicit accumulation and trafficking of small arms and light weapons, referred to in paragraph 69 of this judgment, the European Council mentions, among the means at the disposal of the Union, the Community and the Member States to react to the threat of the illicit spread of those weapons, in particular, apart from civilian and military instruments for managing crises and other diplomatic tools, partnership and cooperation agreements with third countries and development and assistance programmes which fall within EC-ACP cooperation and include a chapter on small arms and light weapons and their ammunition. Having indicated, in paragraph 15, that, according to the European Council, the challenge for a Union strategy on small arms and light weapons is to respond to that threat and to ensure that its security policy and its development policy are consistent, the document mentions, as the final element of the action plan introduced in order to respond to the accumulation of such weapons, the need to '[e]nsure consistency and complementarity between Council decisions in the CFSP framework and actions implemented by the Commission in the field of development aid in order to promote a consistent approach for all [Union] activities in the...area [of small arms and light weapons]'.

91. Third, paragraph 37 of the joint statement of the Council and the representatives of the governments of the Member States meeting within the Council, the European Parliament and the Commission on European Union Development Policy, referred to in paragraph 66 of this judgment, announces concrete steps to limit the uncontrolled proliferation of small arms and light weapons which will be taken, in line with the European strategy against the accumulation and the illicit traffic of such weapons and their ammunition, by '[t]he EU, within the respective competences of the Community and the Member States'.

92. Therefore, since the measure falling within the CFSP which the contested decision is intended to implement does not exclude the possibility that its objectives can be achieved by measures adopted by the Community on the basis of its competences in the field of development cooperation, it is necessary to examine whether the contested decision, as such, must be regarded as a measure which pursues objectives falling within Community development cooperation policy.

93. In that regard, recital 1 in the preamble to the contested decision states that the excessive and uncontrolled accumulation and spread of small arms and light weapons not only poses a threat to peace and security, but also reduces the prospects for sustainable development, particularly in West Africa.

94. According to recital 2 in its preamble, the contested decision is intended to implement the contested joint action by which the Union envisages, in particular by promoting confidence-building measures, the pursuit of the objectives set out in Article 1 of that joint action, that is, the combating of the destabilising accumulation and spread of small arms and light weapons and the reduction of existing accumulations of these weapons.

95. Contrary to what is submitted by the Commission and the Parliament, it cannot be denied that the contested decision, to the extent that it aims to prevent further accumulation of small arms and light weapons in West Africa capable of destabilising that region, forms part of a general perspective of preserving peace and strengthening international security.

96. None the less, it cannot be inferred from the contested decision that in comparison with its objectives of preserving peace and strengthening international security its concern to eliminate or reduce obstacles to the development of the countries concerned is purely incidental.

97. As confirmed by recitals 3 and 4 in the preamble of the decision, the financial and technical contribution which the Union intends to make is designed to help consolidate the initiative taken in the field of small arms and light weapons by ECOWAS.

98. The contested decision therefore has the specific goal of strengthening the capacities of a group of African developing countries to combat a phenomenon which, according to recital 1 in the preamble to the decision, constitutes an obstacle to the sustainable development of those countries.

99. It follows that the contested decision pursues a number of objectives, falling within the CFSP and development cooperation policy respectively, without one of those objectives being incidental to the other.

Content of the contested decision

100. The conclusion drawn in the preceding paragraphs from the examination of the objective of the contested decision is not invalidated by the analysis of its content.

101. Article 1(2) of the contested decision provides for a financial contribution and technical assistance to set up a Light Weapons Unit within the ECOWAS Technical Secretariat and to convert into a convention the existing moratorium between the member states of that organisation concerning small arms and light weapons. To that end, Article 4(1) of the contested decision provides for a reference amount of EUR 515 000.

102. Under Article 3 of the contested decision, the financial implementation of that decision is entrusted to the Commission and, following conclusion by it of a financing agreement with ECOWAS, is to take the form of a grant which, amongst other things, is to cover, over a period of one year, the salaries, travel expenses, supplies and equipment necessary for setting up the Light Weapons Unit within the ECOWAS Technical Secretariat and for converting the abovementioned moratorium into a convention.

103. With regard to the technical assistance which must be afforded by the Union, the project which is detailed in the annex to the contested decision indicates that it involves the putting in place of experts responsible for carrying out the studies necessary to draw up a draft convention.

104. As pointed out by the Advocate General in point 211 of his Opinion, it is only in the light of the aims that they pursue that a financial contribution or technical assistance can be regarded as falling within the scope of the CFSP or of Community development cooperation policy.

105. While there may be some measures, such as the grant of political support for a moratorium or even the collection and destruction of weapons, which fall rather within action to preserve peace and strengthen international security or to promote international cooperation, being CFSP objectives stated in Article 11(1) EU, the decision to make funds available and to give technical assistance to a group of developing countries in order to draft a convention is capable of falling both under development cooperation policy and the CFSP.

106. The fact that the contested joint action was implemented by other decisions adopted under Title V of the EU Treaty, the legality of which the Commission has not challenged, cannot determine the outcome of the present case. For, according to settled case-law, the legal basis for an act must be determined having regard to its own aim and content and not to the legal basis used for the adoption of other Union measures which might, in certain cases, display similar characteristics (see, to that effect, Case C-94/03 *Commission v Council*, paragraph 50).

107. Moreover, as pointed out in paragraph 87 of this judgment, the contested joint action which the contested decision aims to implement does not itself exclude the possibility that the objective of the campaign against the proliferation of small arms and light weapons can be achieved by Community measures, when it refers, in Articles 8 and 9, to the Commission's intention to direct its action towards achieving that objective, where appropriate by pertinent Community measures, and to the obligation of the Council and the Commission to ensure the

consistency of the Union's activities in the field of small arms, in particular with regard to its development policies, and to ensure implementation of their respective action, each in accordance with its powers.

108. It follows from the foregoing that, taking account of its aim and its content, the contested decision contains two components, neither of which can be considered to be incidental to the other, one falling within Community development cooperation policy and the other within the CFSP.

109. Having regard to the reasoning contained in paragraphs 76 and 77 of this judgment, it must be concluded that the Council has infringed Article 47 EU by adopting the contested decision on the basis of Title V of the EU Treaty, since that decision also falls within development cooperation policy.

110. The contested decision must therefore be annulled.

[…]

On those grounds, the Court (Grand Chamber) hereby:

1. Annuls Council Decision 2004/833/CFSP of 2 December 2004 implementing Joint Action 2002/589/CFSP with a view to a European Union contribution to ECOWAS in the framework of the Moratorium on Small Arms and Light Weapons;

[…]

Regulation (EC) No 1717/2006 of the European Parliament and of the Council of 15 November 2006 establishing an Instrument for Stability, Official Journal L 327, 24.11.2006, pp. 1–11.

The tensions around the delimitation between the former pillars are also felt in the 'Stability Instrument', falling within the 1st pillar. Here, urgent measures can be financed, which are, however, not designed to replace the CFSP, as is clear from Article 1 of the regulation.

THE EUROPEAN PARLIAMENT AND THE COUNCIL OF THE EUROPEAN UNION,

Having regard to the Treaty establishing the European Community, and in particular Articles 179(1) and 181a thereof,

Having regard to the proposal from the Commission,

Acting in accordance with the procedure referred to in Article 251 of the Treaty,

[…]

TITLE I

OBJECTIVES AND SCOPE

Article 1

Objectives

1. The Community shall undertake development cooperation measures, as well as financial, economic and technical cooperation measures with third countries under the conditions set out in this Regulation.

2. In accordance with the objectives of such cooperation and within its limits as laid down in the EC Treaty, the specific aims of this Regulation shall be:

(a) in a situation of crisis or emerging crisis, to contribute to stability by providing an effective response to help preserve, establish or re-establish the conditions essential to the proper implementation of the Community's development and cooperation policies;

(b) in the context of stable conditions for the implementation of Community cooperation policies in third countries, to help build capacity both to address specific global and transregional threats having a destabilising effect and to ensure preparedness to address pre- and post-crisis situations.

3. Measures taken under this Regulation may be complementary to, and shall be consistent with, and without prejudice to, measures adopted under Title V and Title VI of the EU Treaty.

[...]

8.5 Humanitarian aid

The Treaty of Lisbon dedicated a new chapter to humanitarian aid. This remedies the precarious situation that Union action could hitherto only be based on former Article 308 EC (now Article 352 TFEU). Moreover, it demonstrates the increased importance of this policy field. Inside the Council this upgrading had already been achieved through the creation of a self-standing working party in 2009, whereas the European Community Humanitarian Assistance Office (ECHO) has been put under the auspices of a specialized portfolio in the Barroso II Commission since 2010.

In legal terms, Article 214(1) TFEU follows the structure of Articles 208 TFEU [...] and 212 TFEU, as Union competence is described as being complementary to the policies of the Member States. That, again, underlines the special nature of this Union competence, which does not prevent Member States from exercising their competence in the field (Article 4(4) TFEU).[5] The second paragraph recalls the long-standing substantive principles in the field, namely compliance with international law and with the principles of impartiality, neutrality, and non-discrimination. This means, in particular, that humanitarian aid cannot be delivered against the will of the legitimate government (or *de facto* regime) in a third country. Moreover, humanitarian aid shall not be used as political instrument to exercise influence in a given conflict, but shall be intended to provide help for the population of a third country that is victim of natural or man-made disasters. Under Article 214(3) TFEU, the ordinary legislative procedure applies for the adoption of a framework for the Union's humanitarian aid operation. The current regulation, however, stems from 1996, having been amended twice in 2003 and 2009, and may be replaced in the future.

---

[5] See also Joined Cases C-181/91 and C-248/91 *European Parliament v. Council* [1993] ECR I-3685, para. 16.

In addition, Article 214(5) foresees the setting up of a European voluntary Humanitarian Aid Corps, which shall allow young Europeans to contribute to the humanitarian aid operations of the Union. The relevant legal act has not yet been adopted in ordinary legislative procedure.[6]

Council Regulation (EC) No 1257/96 of 20 June 1996 concerning humanitarian aid, Official Journal L 163, 2.7.1996, pp. 1–6; as amended by Regulation (EC) No 1882/2003 of the European Parliament and of the Council of 29 September 2003, Official Journal L 284, 31.10.2003, pp. 1–53 and Regulation (EC) No 219/2009 of the European Parliament and of the Council of 11 March 2009, Official Journal L 87, 31/3/2009, pp. 109–154.

THE COUNCIL OF THE EUROPEAN UNION,

Having regard to the Treaty establishing the European Community, and in particular Article 130w thereof,

Having regard to the proposal from the Commission,

Acting in accordance with the procedure laid down in Article 189c of the Treaty,

Whereas people in distress, victims of natural disasters, wars and outbreaks of fighting, or other comparable exceptional circumstances have a right to international humanitarian assistance where their own authorities prove unable to provide effective relief;

Whereas civilian operations to protect the victims of fighting or of comparable exceptional circumstances are governed by international humanitarian law and should accordingly be considered part of humanitarian action;

Whereas humanitarian assistance encompasses not only relief operations to save and preserve life in emergencies or their immediate aftermath, but also action aimed at facilitating or obtaining freedom of access to victims and the free flow of such assistance;

Whereas humanitarian assistance may be a prerequisite for development or reconstruction work and must therefore cover the full duration of a crisis and its aftermath; whereas, in this context, it may include an element of short-term rehabilitation aimed at facilitating the arrival of relief, preventing any worsening in the impact of the crisis and starting to help those affected regain a minimum level of self-sufficiency;

Whereas there is a particular need for preventive action to ensure preparedness for disaster risks and, in consequence, for the establishment of an appropriate early-warning and intervention system;

Whereas the effectiveness and consistency of the Community, national and international prevention and intervention systems set up to meet the needs generated by natural or man-made disasters or comparable exceptional circumstances should therefore be ensured and strengthened;

Whereas humanitarian aid, the sole aim of which is to prevent or relieve human suffering, is accorded to victims without discrimination on the grounds of race, ethnic

---

[6] See Proposal for a Regulation of the European Parliament and of the Council Establishing the European Voluntary Humanitarian Aid Corps, EU Aid Volunteers, 19.9.2012, COM (2012) 514 final.

group, religion, sex, age, nationality or political affiliation and must not be guided by, or subject to, political considerations;

Whereas humanitarian aid decisions must be taken impartially and solely according to the victims' needs and interests;

Whereas close coordination between the Member States and the Commission both at decision-making level and on the ground constitutes the foundation for effective humanitarian action by the Community;

Whereas the Community, as part of its contribution to the effectiveness of international humanitarian aid, must endeavour to cooperate and coordinate its action with that of third countries;

Whereas, in pursuit of that same objective, criteria should be established for cooperation with non-governmental organizations and the international agencies and organizations specializing in the field of humanitarian aid;

Whereas the independence and impartiality of non-governmental organizations and other humanitarian institutions in the implementation of humanitarian aid must be preserved, respected and encouraged;

Whereas cooperation in the humanitarian sphere should be encouraged between non-governmental organizations in the Member States and other developed countries and their equivalents in the third countries concerned;

Whereas the very nature of humanitarian aid calls for the establishment of efficient, flexible, transparent and, where necessary, rapid decision-making procedures for the financing of humanitarian operations and projects;

Whereas procedures should be established for the implementation and administration of humanitarian aid financed by the European Community from the general budget, with emergency aid under the Fourth ACP-EC Convention signed at Lomé on 15 December 1989, amended by the Agreement amending the said Convention, signed at Mauritius on 4 November 1995 remaining subject to the procedures and arrangements laid down in that Convention,

HAS ADOPTED THIS REGULATION:

CHAPTER I
Objectives and general principles of humanitarian aid
Article 1

The Community's humanitarian aid shall comprise assistance, relief and protection operations on a non-discriminatory basis to help people in third countries, particularly the most vulnerable among them, and as a priority those in developing countries, victims of natural disasters, manmade crises, such as wars and outbreaks of fighting, or exceptional situations or circumstances comparable to natural or man-made disasters. It shall do so for the time needed to meet the humanitarian requirements resulting from these different situations.

Such aid shall also comprise operations to prepare for risks or prevent disasters or comparable exceptional circumstances.

Article 2

The principal objectives of the humanitarian aid operations referred to in Article 1 shall be:

(a) to save and preserve life during emergencies and their immediate aftermath and natural disasters that have entailed major loss of life, physical, psychological or social suffering or material damage;

(b) to provide the necessary assistance and relief to people affected by longer-lasting crises arising, in particular, from outbreaks of fighting or wars, producing the same effects as those described in subparagraph (a), especially where their own governments prove unable to help or there is a vacuum of power;

(c) to help finance the transport of aid and efforts to ensure that it is accessible to those for whom it is intended, by all logistical means available, and by protecting humanitarian goods and personnel, but excluding operations with defence implications;

(d) to carry out short-term rehabilitation and reconstruction work, especially on infrastructure and equipment, in close association with local structures, with a view to facilitating the arrival of relief, preventing the impact of the crisis from worsening and starting to help those affected regain a minimum level of self-sufficiency, taking long-term development objectives into account where possible;

(e) to cope with the consequences of population movements (refugees, displaced people and returnees) caused by natural and man-made disasters and carry out schemes to assist repatriation to the country of origin and resettlement there when the conditions laid down in current international agreements are in place;

(f) to ensure preparedness for risks of natural disasters or comparable exceptional circumstances and use a suitable rapid early-warning and intervention system;

(g) to support civil operations to protect the victims of fighting or comparable emergencies, in accordance with current international agreements.

Article 3

Community aid referred to in Articles 1, 2 and 4 may be used to finance the purchase and delivery of any product or equipment needed for the implementation of humanitarian operations, including the construction of housing or shelter for the victims, the costs associated with the outside staff, expatriate or local, employed for those operations, the storage, international or national transport, logistics and distribution of relief and any other action aimed at facilitating or obtaining freedom of access for aid recipients.

It may also be used to finance any other expenditure directly related to the implementation of humanitarian operations.

Article 4

Such Community aid referred to in Articles 1 and 2 may also be used to finance:

— preparatory and feasibility studies for humanitarian operations and the assessment of humanitarian projects and plans,

— operations to monitor humanitarian projects and plans,

— small-scale training schemes and general studies in the field of humanitarian operations, to be phased out gradually where funding is over several years,

— the cost of highlighting the Community nature of the aid,

— public awareness and information campaigns aimed at increasing understanding of humanitarian issues, especially in Europe and in third countries where the Community is funding major humanitarian operations,

— measures to strengthen the Community's coordination with the Member States, other donor countries, international humanitarian organizations and institutions, non-governmental organizations and organizations representing them,

— the technical assistance necessary for the implementation of humanitarian projects, including the exchange of technical know-how and experience by European humanitarian organizations and agencies or between such bodies and those of third countries,

— humanitarian mine-clearance operations, including campaigns to increase awareness of anti-personnel mines on the part of the local population.

Article 5

Community financing under this Regulation shall take the form of grants.

The operations covered by this Regulation shall be exempt from taxes, charges, duties and customs duties.

CHAPTER II

Procedures for the implementation of humanitarian aid

Article 6

Humanitarian aid operations financed by the Community may be implemented either at the request of international or non-governmental agencies and organizations from a Member State or a recipient third country or on the initiative of the Commission.

Article 7

1. Non-governmental organizations eligible for Community financing for the implementation of operations under this Regulation must meet the following criteria:

(a) be non-profit-making autonomous organizations in a Member State of the Community under the laws in force in that Member State;

(b) have their main headquarters in a Member State of the Community or in the third countries in receipt of Community aid. This headquarters must be the effective decision-making centre for all operations financed under this Regulation. Exceptionally, the headquarters may be in a third donor country.

2. When determining a non-governmental organization's suitability for Community funding, account shall be taken of the following factors:

(a) its administrative and financial management capacities;

(b) its technical and logistical capacity in relation to the planned operation;

(c) its experience in the field of humanitarian aid;

(d) the results of previous operations carried out by the organization concerned, and in particular those financed by the Community;

(e) its readiness to take part, if need be, in the coordination system set up for a humanitarian operation;

(f) its ability and readiness to work with humanitarian agencies and the basic communities in the third countries concerned;

(g) its impartiality in the implementation of humanitarian aid;

(h) where appropriate, its previous experience in the third country involved in the humanitarian operation concerned.

Article 8

The Community may also finance humanitarian operations by international agencies and organizations.

Article 9

Where necessary, the Community may also finance humanitarian operations by the Commission or the Member States' specialized agencies.

Article 10

1. In order to guarantee and enhance the effectiveness and consistency of Community and national humanitarian aid systems, the Commission may take any measure necessary to promote close coordination between its own activities and those of the Member States, both at decision-making level and on the ground. To that end, the Member States and the Commission shall operate a system for exchange of information.

2. The Commission shall ensure that humanitarian operations financed by the Community are coordinated and consistent with those of international organizations and agencies, in particular those which form part of the United Nations system.

3. The Commission shall endeavour to develop collaboration and cooperation between the Community and third-country donors in the field of humanitarian aid.

Article 11

1. The Commission shall lay down the conditions for allocating, mobilizing and implementing aid under this Regulation.

2. Aid shall not be implemented unless the recipient complies with these conditions.

Article 12

All financing contracts concluded under this Regulation shall provide in particular that the Commission and the Court of Auditors may conduct checks on the spot and at the headquarters of humanitarian partners according to the usual procedures established by the Commission under the rules in force, and in particular those of the Financial Regulation applicable to the general budget of the European Communities.

CHAPTER III

Procedures for the implementation of humanitarian operations

Article 13

The Commission shall decide on emergency action for an amount not in excess of ECU 10 million.

The following operations shall be deemed to necessitate emergency action:

— operations to meet immediate and unforeseeable humanitarian requirements generated by sudden natural or man-made disasters, such as floods, earthquakes and outbreaks of fighting or comparable situations,

— operations limited to the duration of the unforeseeable emergency response: the corresponding funds shall cover the response to the humanitarian needs referred to in the first indent for a period of not more than six months laid down in the decision on financing.

Where operations fulfil these conditions and are in excess of ECU 2 million:

— the Commission shall adopt its decision,

— it shall inform the Member States in writing within forty-eight hours,

— it shall account for its decision at the Committee's next meeting, in particular giving the reasons for its use of the emergency procedure.

Decisions to continue operations adopted by the emergency procedure shall be taken by the Commission, acting in accordance with the management procedure referred to in Article 17(2) and within the limits set in the second indent of Article 15(2).

Article 14

The Commission shall appraise, decide upon and administer, monitor and assess operations under this Regulation according to the budgetary and other procedures in force, and in particular those laid down in the Financial Regulation applicable to the general budget of the European Communities.

Article 15

1. The Commission shall adopt implementing measures for this Regulation. Those measures, designed to amend non-essential elements of this Regulation by supplementing it, shall be adopted in accordance with the regulatory procedure with scrutiny referred to in

Article 17(4)

2. Acting in accordance with the regulatory procedure referred to in Article 17(3), the Commission shall:

— decide on Community financing for the humanitarian-aid protection operations referred to in Article 2(c),

— decide to take direct Commission action or finance action by Member States' specialised agencies.

3. Acting in accordance with the management procedure referred to in Article 17(2), the Commission shall:

— approve global plans intended to provide for actions in a given country or region where the scale and complexity of the humanitarian crisis is such that it seems likely to continue, and the budgets for those plans. In this context, the Commission and the Member States shall examine the priorities to be established in the implementation of these global plans,

— decide on projects in excess of ECU 2 million, without prejudice to Article 13.

Article 16

1. Once a year the Committee referred to in Article 17 shall discuss general guidelines presented by a representative of the Commission for humanitarian operations to be undertaken in the year ahead and examine the whole question of the coordination of Community and national humanitarian aid and any general or specific issues concerning Community aid in that field.

2. The Commission shall also submit to the Committee referred to in Article 17 information on changes in the instruments for administering humanitarian aid, including the framework partnership agreement.

3. The Committee referred to in Article 17 shall also be notified of the Commission's intentions regarding the assessment of humanitarian operations, and, possibly, its timetable of work.

Article 17

1. The Commission shall be assisted by a Committee.

2. Where reference is made to this paragraph, Articles 4 and 7 of Decision 1999/468/EC shall apply, having regard to the provisions of Article 8 thereof. The period laid down in Article 4(3) of Decision 1999/468/EC shall be set at one month.

3. Where reference is made to this paragraph, Articles 5 and 7 of Decision 1999/468/EC shall apply, having regard to the provisions of Article 8 thereof. The period laid down in Article 5(6) of Decision 1999/468/EC shall be set at one month.

4. Where reference is made to this paragraph, Article 5a(1) to (4) and Article 7 of Decision 1999/468/EC shall apply, having regard to the provisions of Article 8 thereof.

Article 18

1. The Commission shall regularly assess humanitarian aid operations financed by the Community in order to establish whether they have achieved their objectives and to produce guidelines for improving the effectiveness of subsequent operations. The Commission shall submit to the Committee a summary, which shall also indicate the status of the experts employed, of the assessment exercises carried out that it might, if necessary, examine. The assessment reports shall be available to the Member States on request.

2. At the Member States' request, and with their participation, the Commission may also assess the results of the Community's humanitarian operations and plans.

Article 19

At the close of each financial year, the Commission shall submit an annual report to the European Parliament and to the Council with a summary of the operations financed in the course of that year.

The summary shall contain information concerning the agencies with which humanitarian operations have been implemented.

The report shall also include a review of any outside assessment exercises which may have been conducted on specific operations.

The Commission shall notify the Member States, within no more than one month of its decision and without prejudice to Article 13 of this Regulation, of the operations approved, indicating the amount granted, the nature of the operation, the people who have received aid and the partners involved.

Article 20

Three years after entry into force of this Regulation, the Commission shall submit an overall assessment of the operations financed by the Community under this Regulation to the European Parliament and to the Council, together with suggestions for the future of the Regulation and, as necessary, proposals for amendments to it.

Article 21

This Regulation shall enter into force on the third day following its publication in the Official Journal of the European Communities.

This Regulation shall be binding in its entirety and directly applicable in all Member States.

Select Bibliography

Bartels, L., The Trade and Development Policy of the European Union, *Developments in EU External Relations Law* (M. Cremona (ed.), Oxford: Oxford University Press, 2008), pp. 128–71.

Bartelt, S., The Legislative Architecture of EU External Assistance and Development Cooperation, *Europarecht—Beiheft* 2/2008, 9–35.

Hillion, C. and Wessel, R., Copmpetence Distribution in EU External Relations After Ecowas: Clarification or Continued Fuzziness?,' *Common Market Law Review* 46, (2009, pp. 551–86).

Hoffmeister, F., Inter-pillar Coherence in the European Union's Crisis Management, *The European Union and Crisis Management—Policy and Legal Aspects*, 2008, 157–80.

9

Enlargement and Neighbourhood Policy

9.1 Historical evolution

Originally, the Treaty establishing the European Economic Community (1957) did not contain a specific chapter for either the Union's enlargement or its neighbourhood policy. However, over time, treaty references were added to reflect and direct evolving practice.

With respect to enlargement, the treaties gave a right for any European state to apply for membership since the very beginning. However, after the end of the Cold War and in view of the pending applications from a number of East European states, the Treaty of Amsterdam added a reference to the principles of the Union as a political condition to join the Union. The Treaty of Lisbon replaced this reference to 'principles' as accession criteria by a reference to 'values' in Article 49 TEU. Moreover, the list of values enumerated in the current Article 2 TEU is longer than the previous set of principles enshrined in Article 6 EU (Amsterdam version).

Treaty on European Union
Article 49
(ex Article 49 TEU)

Any European State which respects the values referred to in Article 2 and is committed to promoting them may apply to become a member of the Union. The European Parliament and national Parliaments shall be notified of this application. The applicant State shall address its application to the Council, which shall act unanimously after consulting the Commission and after receiving the consent of the European Parliament, which shall act by a majority of its component members. The conditions of eligibility agreed upon by the European Council shall be taken into account.

The conditions of admission and the adjustments to the Treaties on which the Union is founded, which such admission entails, shall be the subject of an agreement between the Member States and the applicant State. This agreement shall be submitted for ratification by all the contracting States in accordance with their respective constitutional requirements.

Article 2

(ex Article 6 TEU)

The Union is founded on the values of respect for human dignity, freedom, democracy, equality, the rule of law and respect for human rights, including the rights of persons belonging to minorities. These values are common to the Member States in a society in which pluralism, non-discrimination, tolerance, justice, solidarity and equality between women and men prevail.

Similarly, the Union's neighbourhood policy developed lately on the basis of the former Article 181a EC introduced as late as the Treaty of Nice only. Whereas this provision relates to cooperation with all non-developing countries (including those located far away), the Treaty of Lisbon dedicated the new Article 8 TEU specifically to the relations with neighbours only. In addition, Article 212 TFEU remains relevant as legal basis for unilateral measures in the neighbourhood context (see Chapter 8). Here, the European Parliament has gained influence as the provision now falls under the ordinary legislative procedure, contrary to what was previously the case when the Parliament only had a right of consultation.

Article 8

1. The Union shall develop a special relationship with neighbouring countries, aiming to establish an area of prosperity and good neighbourliness, founded on the values of the Union and characterized by close and peaceful relations based on cooperation.
2. For the purposes of paragraph 1, the Union may conclude specific agreements with the countries concerned. These agreements may contain reciprocal rights and obligations as well as the possibility of undertaking activities jointly. Their implementation shall be the subject of periodic consultation.

9.2 Enlargement policy

9.2.1 Membership criteria

As reflected in today's Article 49(1) TEU, any European state which respects the values set out in Article 2(1) TEU (respect for human dignity, freedom, democracy, equality, the rule of law, and human rights, including the rights of persons belonging to minorities) may apply to become a member of the EU. The third sentence further refers to the 'conditions of eligibility agreed upon by the European Council'. Currently, these can be found in the historic Conclusions of the Presidency of the European Council of Copenhagen (21–22 June 1993).

Conclusions of the Presidency of the European Council, Copenhagen 21–22 June 1993, SN 180/1/93 REV 1 (extracts).

Accession will take place as soon as an associated country is able to assume the obligations of membership by satisfying the economic and political conditions required.

Membership requires that the candidate country has achieved stability of institutions guaranteeing democracy, the rule of law, human rights and respect for and protection of minorities, the existence of a functioning market economy as well as the capacity to cope with competitive pressure and market forces within the Union. Membership presupposes the candidate's ability to take on the obligations of membership including adherence to the aims of political, economic and monetary union.

9.2.2 **Enlargement process**

The enlargement process involves both the Union institutions and the Member States. According to Article 49(1) second sentence TEU, the application is sent to the Council. Before the latter acts upon it, it first requests from the Commission an opinion about the suitability of the candidate to start negotiations. Once the Commission has issued a favourable opinion, the Member States may (by unanimity) convene an intergovernmental conference with the candidate. During the negotiations, the Member States (acting upon drafts received from the Commission) put forward EU positions, whereas the candidate reacts by sending in position papers. The aim of those exchanges is to satisfy the Union that the candidate has properly taken over the existing Union legislation (*acquis communautaire*) and to grant, where necessary, transitional periods. Nowadays, following the Conclusions of the European Council of Brussels (16-17 December 2004), the Council lays down the principles of negotiation in a 'negotiating framework', adopted at the start of the negotiations. This has also been the case in the negotiations with Turkey, the framework of which is included below.

Presidency Conclusions of the Brussels European Council (16–17 December 2004), 16238/1/04 REV 1 (extracts).

Framework for negotiations
23. The European Council agreed that accession negotiations with individual candidate States will be based on a framework for negotiations. Each framework, which will be established by the Council on a proposal by the Commission, taking account of the experience of the fifth enlargement process and of the evolving acquis, will address the following elements according to their own merits and the specific situations and characteristics of each candidate State:

• As in previous negotiations, the substance of the negotiations, which will be conducted in an Intergovernmental Conference with the participation of all Member States on the one hand and the candidate State concerned on the other, where decisions require unanimity, will be broken down into a number of chapters, each covering a specific policy area. The Council, acting by unanimity on a proposal by the Commission, will lay down benchmarks for the provisional closure and, where appropriate, for the opening of each chapter; depending on the chapter concerned, these benchmarks will refer to legislative alignment and a satisfactory track record of implementation of the acquis as well as obligations deriving from contractual relations with the European Union.

• Long transitional periods, derogations, specific arrangements or permanent safe-guard clauses, i.e. clauses which are permanently available as a basis for safeguard measures, may be considered. The Commission will include these, as appropriate, in its proposals for each framework, for areas such as freedom of movement of persons, structural policies or agriculture. Furthermore, the decision-taking process regarding the eventual establishment of freedom of movement of persons should allow for a maximum role of individual Member States. Transitional arrangements or safeguards should be reviewed regarding their impact on competition or the functioning of the internal market.

• The financial aspects of accession of a candidate State must be allowed for in the applicable Financial Framework. Hence, accession negotiations yet to be opened with candidates whose accession could have substantial financial consequences can only be concluded after the establishment of the Financial Framework for the period from 2014 together with possible consequential financial reforms.

• The shared objective of the negotiations is accession.

These negotiations are an open-ended process, the outcome of which cannot be guaranteed beforehand.

While taking account of all Copenhagen criteria, if the candidate State is not in a position to assume in full all the obligations of membership it must be ensured that the candidate State concerned is fully anchored in the European structures through the strongest possible bond.

• In the case of a serious and persistent breach in a candidate State of the principles of liberty, democracy, respect for human rights and fundamental freedoms and the rule of law on which the Union is founded, the Commission will, on its own initiative or on the request of one third of the Member States, recommend the suspension of nego-tiations and propose the conditions for eventual resumption. The Council will decide by qualified majority on such a recommendation, after having heard the candidate State, whether to suspend the negotiations and on the conditions for their resump-tion. The Member States will act in the IGC in accordance with the Council decision, without prejudice to the general requirement for unanimity in the IGC. The European Parliament will be informed.

• Parallel to accession negotiations, the Union will engage with every candidate State in an intensive political and cultural dialogue. With the aim of enhancing mutual understanding by bringing people together, this inclusive dialogue also will involve civil society.

Negotiating Framework (for Turkey), (Luxembourg, 3 October 2005).

Principles governing the negotiations
1. The negotiations will be based on Turkey's own merits and the pace will depend on Turkey's progress in meeting the requirements for membership. The Presidency or the Commission as appropriate will keep the Council fully informed so that the Council can keep the situation under regular review. The Union side, for its part, will decide in due course whether the conditions for the conclusion of negotiations have been met;

this will be done on the basis of a report from the Commission confirming the fulfilment by Turkey of the requirements listed in point 6.

2. As agreed at the European Council in December 2004, these negotiations are
based on Article 49 of the Treaty on European Union. The shared objective of the
negotiations is accession. These negotiations are an open-ended process, the outcome of which cannot be guaranteed beforehand. While having full regard to all
Copenhagen criteria, including the absorption capacity of the Union, if Turkey is
not in a position to assume in full all the obligations of membership it must be
ensured that Turkey is fully anchored in the European structures through the strongest possible bond.

3. Enlargement should strengthen the process of continuous creation and integration
in which the Union and its Member States are engaged. Every effort should be made
to protect the cohesion and effectiveness of the Union. In accordance with the conclusions of the Copenhagen European Council in 1993, the Union's capacity to absorb
Turkey, while maintaining the momentum of European integration is an important
consideration in the general interest of both the Union and Turkey. The Commission
shall monitor this capacity during the negotiations, encompassing the whole range of
issues set out in its October 2004 paper on issues arising from Turkey's membership
perspective, in order to inform an assessment by the Council as to whether this condition of membership has been met.

4. Negotiations are opened on the basis that Turkey sufficiently meets the political criteria set by the Copenhagen European Council in 1993, for the most part later
enshrined in Article 6(1) of the Treaty on European Union and proclaimed in the
Charter of Fundamental Rights. The Union expects Turkey to sustain the process of
reform and to work towards further improvement in the respect of the principles of
liberty, democracy, the rule of law and respect for human rights and fundamental freedoms, including relevant European case law; to consolidate and broaden legislation
and implementation measures specifically in relation to the zero tolerance policy in the
fight against torture and ill-treatment and the implementation of provisions relating
to freedom of expression, freedom of religion, women's rights, ILO standards including trade union rights, and minority rights. The Union and Turkey will continue their
intensive political dialogue. To ensure the irreversibility of progress in these areas and
its full and effective implementation, notably with regard to fundamental freedoms
and to full respect of human rights, progress will continue to be closely monitored by
the Commission, which is invited to continue to report regularly on it to the Council,
addressing all points of concern identified in the Commission's 2004 report and recommendation as well as its annual regular report.

5. In the case of a serious and persistent breach in Turkey of the principles of liberty,
democracy, respect for human rights and fundamental freedoms and the rule of law
on which the Union is founded, the Commission will, on its own initiative or on the
request of one third of the Member States, recommend the suspension of negotiations
and propose the conditions for eventual resumption. The Council will decide by qualified majority on such a recommendation, after having heard Turkey, whether to suspend the negotiations and on the conditions for their resumption. The Member States
will act in the Intergovernmental Conference in accordance with the Council decision,

without prejudice to the general requirement for unanimity in the Intergovernmental Conference. The European Parliament will be informed.

6. The advancement of the negotiations will be guided by Turkey's progress in preparing for accession, within a framework of economic and social convergence and with reference to the Commission's reports in paragraph 4. This progress will be measured in particular against the following requirements:

– the Copenhagen criteria, which set down the following requirements for membership:

* the stability of institutions guaranteeing democracy, the rule of law, human rights and respect for and protection of minorities;

* the existence of a functioning market economy and the capacity to cope with competitive pressure and market forces within the Union;

* the ability to take on the obligations of membership, including adherence to the aims of political, economic and monetary union and the administrative capacity to effectively apply and implement the acquis;

– Turkey's unequivocal commitment to good neighbourly relations and its undertaking to resolve any outstanding border disputes in conformity with the principle of peaceful settlement of disputes in accordance with the United Nations Charter, including if necessary jurisdiction of the International Court of Justice;

– Turkey's continued support for efforts to achieve a comprehensive settlement of the Cyprus problem within the UN framework and in line with the principles on which the Union is founded, including steps to contribute to a favourable climate for a comprehensive settlement, and progress in the normalisation of bilateral relations between Turkey and all EU Member States, including the Republic of Cyprus.

– the fulfilment of Turkey's obligations under the Association Agreement and its Additional Protocol extending the Association Agreement to all new EU Member States, in particular those pertaining to the EU-Turkey customs union, as well as the implementation of the Accession Partnership, as regularly revised.

7. In the period up to accession, Turkey will be required to progressively align its policies towards third countries and its positions within international organisations (including in relation to the membership by all EU Member States of those organisations and arrangements) with the policies and positions adopted by the Union and its Member States.

8. Parallel to accession negotiations, the Union will engage with Turkey in an intensive political and civil society dialogue. The aim of the inclusive civil society dialogue will be to enhance mutual understanding by bringing people together in particular with a view to ensuring the support of European citizens for the accession process.

9. Turkey must accept the results of any other accession negotiations as they stand at the moment of its accession.

Substance of the negotiations

10. Accession implies the acceptance of the rights and obligations attached to the Union system and its institutional framework, known as the acquis of the Union. Turkey will have to apply this as it stands at the time of accession. Furthermore, in addition to legislative alignment, accession implies timely and effective implementation of the acquis. The acquis is constantly evolving and includes:

– the content, principles and political objectives of the Treaties on which the Union is founded;

– legislation and decisions adopted pursuant to the Treaties, and the case law of the Court of Justice;

– other acts, legally binding or not, adopted within the Union framework, such as interinstitutional agreements, resolutions, statements, recommendations, guidelines;

– joint actions, common positions, declarations, conclusions and other acts within the framework of the common foreign and security policy;

– joint actions, joint positions, conventions signed, resolutions, statements and other acts agreed within the framework of justice and home affairs;

– international agreements concluded by the Communities, the Communities jointly with their Member States, the Union, and those concluded by the Member States among themselves with regard to Union activities.

Turkey will need to produce translations of the acquis into Turkish in good time before accession, and will need to train a sufficient number of translators and interpreters required for the proper functioning of the EU institutions upon its accession.

11. The resulting rights and obligations, all of which Turkey will have to honour as a Member State, imply the termination of all existing bilateral agreements between Turkey and the Communities, and of all other international agreements concluded by Turkey which are incompatible with the obligations of membership. Any provisions of the Association Agreement which depart from the acquis cannot be considered as precedents in the accession negotiations.

12. Turkey's acceptance of the rights and obligations arising from the acquis may necessitate specific adaptations to the acquis and may, exceptionally, give rise to transitional measures which must be defined during the accession negotiations.

Where necessary, specific adaptations to the acquis will be agreed on the basis of the principles, criteria and parameters inherent in that acquis as applied by the Member States when adopting that acquis, and taking into consideration the specificities of Turkey.

The Union may agree to requests from Turkey for transitional measures provided they are limited in time and scope, and accompanied by a plan with clearly defined stages for application of the acquis. For areas linked to the extension of the internal market, regulatory measures should be implemented quickly and transition periods should be short and few; where considerable adaptations are necessary requiring substantial effort including large financial outlays, appropriate transitional arrangements can be envisaged as part of an ongoing, detailed and budgeted plan for alignment. In any case, transitional arrangements must not involve amendments to the rules or policies of the Union, disrupt their proper functioning, or lead to significant distortions of competition. In this connection, account must be taken of the interests of the Union and of Turkey.

Long transitional periods, derogations, specific arrangements or permanent safeguard clauses, i.e. clauses which are permanently available as a basis for safeguard measures, may be considered. The Commission will include these, as appropriate, in its proposals in areas such as freedom of movement of persons, structural policies or agriculture. Furthermore, the decision-taking process regarding the eventual establishment of freedom of movement of persons should allow for a maximum role of individual Member States. Transitional arrangements or safeguards should be reviewed regarding their impact on competition or the functioning of the internal market.

Detailed technical adaptations to the acquis will not need to be fixed during the accession negotiations. They will be prepared in cooperation with Turkey and adopted by the Union institutions in good time with a view to their entry into force on the date of accession.

13. The financial aspects of the accession of Turkey must be allowed for in the applicable Financial Framework. Hence, as Turkey's accession could have substantial financial consequences, the negotiations can only be concluded after the establishment of the Financial Framework for the period from 2014 together with possible consequential financial reforms. Any arrangements should ensure that the financial burdens are fairly shared between all Member States.

14. Turkey will participate in economic and monetary union from accession as a Member State with a derogation and shall adopt the euro as its national currency following a Council decision to this effect on the basis of an evaluation of its fulfilment of the necessary conditions. The remaining acquis in this area fully applies from accession.

15. With regard to the area of freedom, justice and security, membership of the European Union implies that Turkey accepts in full on accession the entire acquis in this area, including the Schengen acquis. However, part of this acquis will only apply in Turkey following a Council decision to lift controls on persons at internal borders taken on the basis of the applicable Schengen evaluation of Turkey's readiness.

16. The EU points out the importance of a high level of environmental protection, including all aspects of nuclear safety.

17. In all areas of the acquis, Turkey must bring its institutions, management capacity and administrative and judicial systems up to Union standards, both at national and regional level, with a view to implementing the acquis effectively or, as the case may be, being able to implement it effectively in good time before accession. At the general level, this requires a well-functioning and stable public administration built on an efficient and impartial civil service, and an independent and efficient judicial system.

Negotiating procedures

18. The substance of negotiations will be conducted in an Intergovernmental Conference with the participation of all Member States on the one hand and the candidate State on the other.

19. The Commission will undertake a formal process of examination of the acquis, called screening, in order to explain it to the Turkish authorities, to assess the state of preparation of Turkey for opening negotiations in specific areas and to obtain preliminary indications of the issues that will most likely come up in the negotiations.

20. For the purposes of screening and the subsequent negotiations, the acquis will be broken down into a number of chapters, each covering a specific policy area. A list of these chapters is provided in the Annex. Any view expressed by either Turkey or the EU on a specific chapter of the negotiations will in no way prejudge the position which may be taken on other chapters. Also, agreements reached in the course of negotiations

on specific chapters, even partial ones, may not be considered as final until an overall agreement has been reached for all chapters.

21. Building on the Commission's Regular Reports on Turkey's progress towards accession and in particular on information obtained by the Commission during screening, the Council, acting by unanimity on a proposal by the Commission, will lay down benchmarks for the provisional closure and, where appropriate, for the opening of each chapter. The Union will communicate such benchmarks to Turkey. Depending on the chapter, precise benchmarks will refer in particular to the existence of a functioning market economy, to legislative alignment with the acquis and to a satisfactory track record in implementation of key elements of the acquis demonstrating the existence of an adequate administrative and judicial capacity. Where relevant, benchmarks will also include the fulfilment of commitments under the Association Agreement, in particular those pertaining to the EU-Turkey customs union and those that mirror requirements under the acquis. Where negotiations cover a considerable period of time, or where a chapter is revisited at a later date to incorporate new elements such as new acquis, the existing benchmarks may be updated.

22. Turkey will be requested to indicate its position in relation to the acquis and to report on its progress in meeting the benchmarks. Turkey's correct transposition and implementation of the acquis, including effective and efficient application through appropriate administrative and judicial structures, will determine the pace of negotiations.

23. To this end, the Commission will closely monitor Turkey's progress in all areas, making use of all available instruments, including on-site expert reviews by or on behalf of the Commission. The Commission will inform the Council of Turkey's progress in any given area when presenting draft EU Common Positions. The Council will take this assessment into account when deciding on further steps relating to the negotiations on that chapter. In addition to the information the EU may require for the negotiations on each chapter and which is to be provided by Turkey to the Conference, Turkey will be required to continue to provide regularly detailed, written information on progress in the alignment with and implementation of the acquis, even after provisional closure of a chapter. In the case of provisionally closed chapters, the Commission may recommend the re-opening of negotiations, in particular where Turkey has failed to meet important benchmarks or to implement its commitments.

ANNEX
PRELIMINARY INDICATIVE LIST OF CHAPTER HEADINGS

(Note: This list in no way prejudices the decisions to be taken at an appropriate stage in the negotiations on the order in which the subjects will be dealt with.)

1. Free movement of goods
2. Freedom of movement for workers
3. Right of establishment and freedom to provide services
4. Free movement of capital
5. Public procurement
6. Company law
7. Intellectual property law
8. Competition policy

9. Financial services
10. Information society and media
11. Agriculture and rural development
12. Food safety, veterinary and phytosanitary policy
13. Fisheries
14. Transport policy
15. Energy
16. Taxation
17. Economic and monetary policy
18. Statistics
19. Social policy and employment
20. Enterprise and industrial policy
21. Trans-European networks
22. Regional policy and coordination of structural instruments
23. Judiciary and fundamental rights
24. Justice, freedom and security
25. Science and research
26. Education and culture
27. Environment
28. Consumer and health protection
29. Customs union
30. External relations
31. Foreign, security and defence policy
32. Financial control
33. Financial and budgetary provisions
34. Institutions
35. Other issues

Once the negotiations are finalized, an accession treaty is concluded between the old Member States and (one or more) new Member State(s) according to Article 49(2) TEU. The EU as such is not a party to this agreement. Accordingly, the treaty-making procedures under Article 218 TFEU do not apply. Rather, the European Parliament is asked to give its consent to each (individual) application of a candidate country, and the Commission writes (a second, but standardized) opinion on each (individual) candidate country at the end of the enlargement process according to Article 49(1) 2nd sentence TEU.

9.2.3 Pre-accession assistance

In order to support the efforts of a candidate country to harmonize its domestic legal system with the EU legal order, the Union provides pre-accession assistance. Next to providing advice and know-how in the negotiations also through a specialized office (TAIEX—Technical Assistance Information Exchange Instrument), it further earmarks considerable funds for harmonization projects.

Council Regulation (EC) No 1085/2006 of 17 July 2006 establishing an Instrument for Pre-Accession Assistance (IPA), Official Journal L 210, 31.7.2006, pp. 82–93.

This Regulation defines the amounts and applicable procedures for giving pre-accession assistance. It has been adopted under former Article 181a EC (today Article 212 TFEU) (see Chapter 8).

THE COUNCIL OF THE EUROPEAN UNION,

Having regard to the Treaty establishing the European Community, and in particular Article 181a thereof,

Having regard to the proposal from the Commission,

Having regard to the opinion of the European Parliament (1),

Having regard to the opinion of the Committee of the Regions (2),

Whereas:

(1) In order to improve the efficiency of the Community's External Aid, a new framework for programming and delivery of assistance has been envisaged. The present instrument constitutes one of the general instruments directly supporting European External Aid policies.

(2) Article 49 of the Treaty on European Union states that any European State which respects the principles of liberty, democracy, respect for human rights and fundamental freedoms, and the rule of law may apply to become a member of the Union.

(3) The Republic of Turkey's application for membership to the European Union was accepted by the European Council in Helsinki in 1999. Pre-accession assistance has been made available to the Republic of Turkey since 2002. The Brussels European Council on 16 and 17 December 2004 recommended that accession negotiations should be opened with Turkey.

(4) At its meeting at Santa Maria da Feira on 20 June 2000, the European Council stressed that the countries of the Western Balkans were potential candidates for membership of the European Union.

(5) At its meeting in Thessaloniki, on 19 and 20 June 2003, the European Council recalled the conclusions of its meetings in Copenhagen in December 2002 and Brussels in March 2003 and reiterated its determination to fully and effectively support the European perspective of the Western Balkan countries, indicating that they would become an integral part of the European Union, once they met the established criteria.

(6) The Thessaloniki European Council 2003 also indicated that the Stabilisation and Association Process would constitute the overall framework for the European course of the Western Balkan countries all the way to their future accession.

(7) In its resolution on the Thessaloniki European Council Conclusions, the European Parliament recognised that each of the Western Balkan countries was moving towards accession, but at the same time insisted that each country should be judged on its own merits.

(8) All the Western Balkan countries can therefore be considered as potential candidate countries; however, a clear distinction should be made between candidate countries and potential candidate countries.

(9) On 17 and 18 June 2004 the Brussels European Council recommended that accession negotiations should be opened with Croatia.

(10) On 15 and 16 December 2005 the Brussels European Council decided to grant candidate country status to the former Yugoslav Republic of Macedonia.

(11) Further, on 16 and 17 December 2004, the Brussels European Council recommended that parallel to accession negotiations, the European Union should engage an intensive political and cultural dialogue with every candidate country.

(12) In the interests of coherence and consistency of Community assistance, assistance for candidate countries as well as for potential candidate countries should be granted in the context of a coherent framework, taking advantage of the lessons learned from earlier pre-accession instruments as well as Council Regulation (EC) No 2666/2000 of 5 December 2000 on assistance for Albania, Bosnia and Herzegovina, Croatia, the Federal Republic of Yugoslavia and the Former Yugoslav Republic of Macedonia (3). The assistance should also be consistent with the development policy of the Community in accordance with Article 181a of the EC Treaty.

(13) Assistance for candidate countries as well as for potential candidate countries should continue to support them in their efforts to strengthen democratic institutions and the rule of law, reform public administration, carry out economic reforms, respect human as well as minority rights, promote gender equality, support the development of civil society and advance regional cooperation as well as reconciliation and reconstruction, and contribute to sustainable development and poverty reduction in these countries, and it should therefore be targeted at supporting a wide range of institution-building measures.

(14) Assistance for candidate countries should additionally focus on the adoption and implementation of the full acquis communautaire, and in particular prepare candidate countries for the implementation of the Community's agricultural and cohesion policy.

(15) Assistance for potential candidate countries may include some alignment with the acquis communautaire, as well as support for investment projects, aiming in particular at building management capacity in the areas of regional, human resources and rural development.

(16) Assistance should be provided on the basis of a comprehensive multi-annual strategy that reflects the priorities of the Stabilisation and Association Process, as well as the strategic priorities of the pre-accession process.

(17) In order to assist with the financial part of this strategy, and without prejudice to the prerogatives of the Budgetary Authority, the Commission should present its intentions for the financial allocations to be proposed for the three forthcoming years by means of a multi-annual indicative financial framework, as an integral part of its annual enlargement package.

(18) The Transition Assistance and Institution Building, and Cross-Border Cooperation Components should be accessible to all beneficiary countries, in order to assist them in the process of transition and approximation to the EU, as well as to encourage regional cooperation between them.

(19) The Regional Development Component, the Human Resources Development Component, and the Rural Development Component should be accessible only to candidate countries accredited to manage funds in a decentralised manner, in order to help them prepare for the time after accession, in particular for the implementation of the Community's cohesion and rural development policies.

(20) Potential candidate countries and candidate countries that have not been accredited to manage funds in a decentralised manner should however be eligible, under the Transition Assistance and Institution Building Component, for measures and actions of a similar nature to those which will be available under the Regional Development Component, the Human Resources Development Component and the Rural Development Component.

(21) Assistance should be managed in accordance with the rules for External Aid contained in Council Regulation (EC, Euratom) No 1605/2002 of 25 June 2002 on the Financial Regulation applicable to the general budget of the European Communities (1), making use of the structures that have proved their worth in the pre-accession process, such as decentralised management, twinning and TAIEX (Technical Assistance Information Exchange Instrument), but should also allow for innovative approaches such as the implementation through Member States via shared management in case of cross-border programmes on the external borders of the European Union. The transfer of knowledge and expertise regarding the implementation of the acquis communautaire, from Member States with relevant experience to the beneficiaries of this Regulation, should be particularly beneficial in this context.

(22) The actions necessary for the implementation of this Regulation are management measures relating to the implementation of programmes with substantial budgetary implications. They should therefore be adopted in accordance with Council Decision 1999/468/EC of 28 June 1999 laying down the procedures for the exercise of implementing powers conferred on the Commission (2), by submitting the multi-annual indicative planning documents to a Management Committee.

(23) The annual or multi-annual programmes on a horizontal and per country basis for the implementation of assistance under the Transition Assistance and Institution Building Component and the Cross-Border Cooperation Component should also be submitted to a Management Committee in accordance with Decision 1999/468/EC.

(24) The multi-annual programmes for the implementation of the Regional Development Component, the Human Resources Development Component, and the Rural Development Component should also be submitted to a Management Committee, in accordance with Decision 1999/468/EC. Since these actions will be closely aligned to Structural Fund and Rural Development practices, they should make use as far as possible of the existing Committees which are in place for Structural Funds and Rural Development.

(25) Where the Commission implements this Regulation through centralised management, it should take the utmost care to protect the financial interests of the Community, in particular by applying the rules and standards of the acquis communautaire in that respect, and where the Commission implements this Regulation through other forms of management, the financial interests of the Community should be safeguarded through the conclusion of appropriate agreements containing sufficient guarantees in that respect.

(26) Rules determining the eligibility of participation in tenders and grant contracts, as well as rules concerning the origin of supplies should be laid down in accordance with recent developments within the European Union concerning the untying of aid, but should leave the flexibility to react to new developments in this field.

(27) Where a beneficiary country violates the principles on which the European Union is founded, or makes insufficient progress with respect to the Copenhagen criteria and the priorities laid down in the European or Accession Partnership, the Council must, on the basis of a proposal from the Commission, be in a position to take the necessary measures. Full and immediate information to the European Parliament should be ensured.

(28) Provision should be made to enable the Council to amend this Regulation by way of a simplified procedure with respect to the status of a beneficiary country as defined in this Regulation.

(29) Countries which are beneficiaries under the other regional External Assistance Instruments should, on the basis of reciprocity, be able to participate in actions under this Regulation, where this offers an added value on account of the regional, cross-border, transnational or global nature of the action in question.

(30) Since the objective of this Regulation, namely the progressive alignment of the beneficiary countries with the standards and policies of the European Union, including where appropriate the acquis communautaire, with a view to membership, cannot sufficiently be achieved by the Member States and can therefore be better achieved at Community level, the Community may adopt measures in accordance with the principle of subsidiarity as set out in Article 5 of the EC Treaty. In accordance with the principle of proportionality as set out in that Article, this Regulation does not go beyond what is necessary in order to achieve this objective.

(31) Given that Article 181a of the EC Treaty stipulates that measures in the area of economic, financial and technical cooperation with third countries are to be complementary to those carried out by the Member States, the Commission and the Member States are committed to ensure coordination, coherence and complementarity of their assistance, in line with the established EU 2001 guidelines for strengthening operational coordination between the Community and the Member States in the field of external assistance, in particular through regular consultations and frequent exchanges of relevant information during the different phases of the assistance cycle.

(32) A financial reference amount, within the meaning of point 38 of the Interinstitutional Agreement of 17 May 2006 between the European Parliament, the Council and the Commission on budgetary discipline and sound financial management, is included in this Regulation for the entire duration of the instrument, without thereby affecting the powers of the budgetary authority as they are defined by the EC Treaty.

(33) The institution of the new system of Community preaccession assistance makes it necessary to repeal Council Regulation (EEC) No 3906/89 of 18 December 1989 on economic aid to the Republic of Hungary and the Polish People's Republic, Commission Regulation (EC) No 2760/98 of 18 December 1998 concerning the implementation of a programme for cross-border cooperation in the framework of the PHARE programme, Council Regulation (EC) No 1266/1999 of 21 June 1999 on coordinating aid to the applicant countries in the framework of the pre-accession strategy, Council Regulation (EC) No 1267/1999 of 21 June 1999 establishing an

Instrument for Structural Policies for Preaccession, Council Regulation (EC) No 1268/1999 of 21 June 1999 on Community support for pre-accession measures for agriculture and rural development in the applicant countries of central and eastern Europe in the pre-accession period, Council Regulation (EC) No 555/2000 of 13 March 2000 on the implementation of operations in the framework of the pre-accession strategy for the Republic of Cyprus and the Republic of Malta, Council Regulation (EC) No 2500/2001 of 17 December 2001 concerning pre-accession financial assistance for Turkey and Council Regulation (EC) No 2112/2005 of 21 November 2005 on access to Community external assistance. Equally, this Regulation should replace Regulation (EC) No 2666/2000, which expires on 31 December 2006,

HAS ADOPTED THIS REGULATION:

TITLE I
GENERAL PROVISIONS
Article 1

Beneficiaries and overall objective
The Community shall assist the countries listed in Annexes I and II in their progressive alignment with the standards and policies of the European Union, including where appropriate the acquis communautaire, with a view to membership.

Article 2

Scope
1. Assistance shall, where appropriate, be used in the beneficiary countries listed in Annexes I and II to support the following areas:
(a) strengthening of democratic institutions, as well as the rule of law, including its enforcement;
(b) the promotion and the protection of human rights and fundamental freedoms and enhanced respect for minority rights, the promotion of gender equality and non-discrimination;
(c) public administration reform, including the establishment of a system enabling decentralisation of assistance management to the beneficiary country in accordance with the rules laid down in Regulation (EC, Euratom) No 1605/2002;
(d) economic reform;
(e) the development of civil society;
(f) social inclusion;
(g) reconciliation, confidence-building measures and reconstruction;
(h) regional and cross-border cooperation.
2. In the case of countries listed in Annex I, assistance shall also be used to support the following areas:
(a) the adoption and implementation of the acquis communautaire;
(b) support for the policy development as well as preparation for the implementation and management of the Community's common agricultural and cohesion policies.
3. In the case of countries listed in Annex II, assistance shall also be used to support the following areas:

(a) progressive alignment with the acquis communautaire;

(b) social, economic and territorial development including, inter alia, infrastructure and investment related activities, in particular in the areas of regional, human resources and rural development.

Article 3

Components

1. Assistance shall be programmed and implemented according to the following components:

(a) Transition Assistance and Institution Building;

(b) Cross-Border Cooperation;

(c) Regional Development;

(d) Human Resources Development;

(e) Rural Development.

2. The Commission shall ensure coordination and coherence between assistance granted under the different components.

3. The Commission shall adopt rules for the implementation of this Regulation in accordance with the procedure laid down in Articles 4 and 7 of Decision 1999/468/EC. To that effect, the Commission shall be assisted by the IPA Committee referred to in Article 14(1).

The period laid down in Article 4(3) of Decision 1999/468/EC shall be set at two months.

Article 4

Political framework for assistance

Assistance under this Regulation shall be provided in accordance with the general policy framework for pre-accession, defined by the European and Accession Partnerships, and taking due account of the Reports and the Strategy Paper comprised in the annual Enlargement package of the Commission.

Article 5

Information on proposed indicative financial allocations

1. With a view to supporting the strategic planning as provided for in Article 6, the Commission shall present annually to the European Parliament and the Council its intentions for the financial allocations to be proposed for the three forthcoming years, in the form of a multi-annual indicative financial framework, taking into consideration the financial framework, as well as the European Partnerships, Accession Partnerships, Reports and Strategy Paper.

2. This multi-annual indicative financial framework shall present the Commission's intentions for the allocation of funds, broken down by component, country and multi-country action. It shall be elaborated on the basis of a set of objective and transparent criteria, including needs assessment, absorption capacity, respect of conditionalities and capacity of management. Due account shall also be taken of any exceptional assistance measures or interim response programmes adopted under a Regulation establishing the Stability Instrument.

3. The multi-annual indicative financial framework shall be included in the Commission's annual Enlargement package, while maintaining a three-year planning horizon.

Article 6

Planning of assistance

1. Assistance under this Regulation shall be provided on the basis of multi-annual indicative planning documents established by country in close consultation with the national authorities, so as to support national strategies and ensure the engagement and involvement of the country concerned. Civil society and other stakeholders shall be associated where appropriate. Other programmes of assistance will also be taken into account.

2. For countries listed in Annex I, assistance shall be based in particular on the Accession Partnerships. Assistance shall cover the priorities and overall strategy resulting from a regular analysis of the situation in each country and on which preparations for accession must concentrate. Assistance shall be planned in view of the criteria defined by the Copenhagen European Council of June 1993 and the progress made in the adoption and implementation of the acquis communautaire, as well as regional cooperation.

3. For countries listed in Annex II, assistance shall be based in particular on the European Partnerships. Assistance shall cover the priorities and overall strategy resulting from a regular analysis of the situation in each country and on which preparation for further integration into the European Union must concentrate. Assistance shall be planned in view of the criteria defined by the Copenhagen European Council of June 1993 and the progress made in implementing the stabilisation and association agreements, including regional cooperation.

4. Multi-annual indicative planning documents shall present indicative allocations for the main priorities within each component, taking into account the indicative breakdown per country and per component proposed in the multi-annual indicative financial framework. They shall also set out, as appropriate, any funding provided for multi-country programmes and horizontal initiatives.

5. Multi-annual indicative planning documents shall be established following a three-year perspective. They shall be reviewed annually.

6. The Commission shall adopt the multi-annual indicative planning documents and annual reviews thereof in accordance with the procedure referred to in Article 14(2)(a).

Article 7

Programming

1. Assistance under this Regulation shall be provided through multi-annual or annual programmes, established by country and by component, or, as appropriate, by group of countries or by theme in accordance with the priorities defined in the multi-annual indicative planning documents.

2. Programmes shall specify the objectives pursued, the fields of intervention, the expected results, the management procedures and total amount of financing planned. They shall contain a summary description of the type of operations to be financed, an indication of the amounts allocated for each type of operation and an indicative implementation timetable. Where relevant, they shall include the results of any lessons

learned from previous assistance. Objectives shall be specific, relevant and measurable and have time-bound benchmarks.

3. The Commission shall adopt the multi-annual and annual programmes, and any reviews thereof, in accordance with the procedures provided for in Article 14(2).

TITLE II
RULES CONCERNING SPECIFIC COMPONENTS
Article 8

Transition Assistance and Institution Building Component

1. The Transition Assistance and Institution Building Component shall assist the countries listed in Annexes I and II in the attainment of the objectives set out in Article 2.

2. It may, inter alia, be used to finance capacity and institution building as well as investment in as far as the latter is not covered by Articles 9 to 12.

3. Assistance under this component may also support the participation of countries listed in Annexes I and II in Community programmes and agencies. In addition, assistance may be provided for regional and horizontal programmes.

Article 9

Cross-Border Cooperation Component

1. The Cross-Border Cooperation Component may support the countries listed in Annexes I and II in cross-border, and, where appropriate, transnational and inter-regional cooperation among themselves and between them and the Member States.

2. Such cooperation shall have the objective of promoting good neighbourly relations, fostering stability, security and prosperity in the mutual interest of all countries concerned, and of encouraging their harmonious, balanced and sustainable development.

3. In the event of cross-border cooperation with Member States, the rules governing the financial contributions of the European Regional Development Fund and this Regulation shall be the relevant provisions of Article 21 of Council Regulation (EC) No 1083/2006 of 11 July 2006 laying down general provisions on the European Regional Development Fund, the European Social Fund and the Cohesion Fund (1).

4. Cooperation will be coordinated with other Community instruments for cross-border, trans-national and interregional cooperation. In case of cross-border cooperation with Member States, this component shall cover the regions on both sides of the respective border or borders, either terrestrial or maritime.

5. Within the objectives of this article, this component may inter alia be used to finance capacity and institution building as well as investment.

Article 10

Regional Development Component

1. The Regional Development Component shall support countries listed in Annex I in policy development as well as preparation for the implementation and management of the Community's cohesion policy, in particular in their preparation for the European Regional Development Fund and the Cohesion Fund.

2. It may in particular contribute towards the financing of the type of actions provided for under Regulation (EC) No 1080/2006 of the European Parliament and of the

Council of 5 July 2006 on the European Regional Development Fund (1) and Council Regulation (EC) No 1084/2006 of 11 July 2006 establishing a Cohesion Fund (2).

Article 11

Human Resources Development Component

1. The Human Resources Development Component shall support countries listed in Annex I in policy development as well as preparation for the implementation and management of the Community's cohesion policy, in particular in their preparation for the European Social Fund.

2. It may in particular contribute towards the financing of the type of actions provided for under Regulation (EC) No 1081/2006 of the European Parliament and of the Council of 5 July 2006 on the European Social Fund (3).

Article 12

Rural Development Component

1. The Rural Development Component shall support countries listed in Annex I in policy development as well as preparation for the implementation and management of the Community's common agricultural policy. It shall in particular contribute to the sustainable adaptation of the agricultural sector and rural areas and to the candidate countries' preparation for the implementation of the acquis communautaire concerning the Common Agricultural Policy and related policies.

2. It may in particular contribute towards the financing of the type of actions provided for under Regulation (EC) No 1698/2005 of 20 September 2005 on support for rural development by the European Agricultural Fund for Rural Development (EAFRD) (4).

TITLE III

MANAGEMENT AND IMPLEMENTATION

Article 13

Management of assistance, reporting

1. The Commission shall be responsible for the implementation of this Regulation, acting in accordance with the procedures referred to in Article 14 and the implementing rules referred to in Article 3(3).

2. Actions under this Regulation shall be managed, monitored, evaluated and reported on in accordance with Regulation (EC, Euratom) No 1605/2002. Community financing can take in particular the form of financing agreements between the Commission and the beneficiary country, procurement contracts or grant agreements with national or international public sector bodies or natural or legal persons responsible for carrying out the action, or employment contracts. For cross-border programmes with Member States according to Article 9 of this Regulation, implementation tasks may be delegated to Member States, in which case they shall be implemented through shared management in accordance with the relevant provisions of Regulation (EC, Euratom) No 1605/2002. In case of shared management, the managing authority shall operate in accordance with the principles and rules laid down in Regulation (EC) No 1083/2006.

3. The Commission may also receive and manage funds from other donors, as assigned revenue in accordance with Article 18 of Regulation (EC, Euratom) No 1605/2002, in order to implement actions with these donors.

4. In duly justified cases, the Commission may, in accordance with Article 54 of Regulation (EC, Euratom) No 1605/2002, decide to entrust tasks of public authority, and in particular budget implementation tasks, to the bodies listed in Article 54(2) of that Regulation. The bodies defined in Article 54(2)(c) of that Regulation may be entrusted with tasks of public authority if they are of recognised international standing, comply with internationally recognised systems of management and control, and are supervised by a public authority.

5. Budgetary commitments for actions extending over more than one financial year may be broken down over several years into annual instalments.

6. Each year the Commission shall send to the European Parliament and the Council a report on the implementation of Community assistance under this Regulation. The report shall contain information on the actions financed during the year and on the findings of monitoring work, and shall give an assessment of the results achieved in the implementation of the assistance.

Article 14

Committees

1. An IPA Committee shall be established, composed of the representatives of the Member States and chaired by a representative of the Commission. It shall assist the Commission in particular in its task to ensure the coordination and coherence between assistance granted under the different components as required by Article 3(2).

The IPA Committee shall adopt its rules of procedure.

2. (a) The Commission shall adopt the multi-annual indicative planning documents and annual reviews thereof referred to in Article 6 of this Regulation, and the programmes concerning assistance to be provided under Articles 8 and 9 of this Regulation, in accordance with the procedure laid down in Articles 4 and 7 of Decision 1999/468/EC. To that effect, the Commission shall be assisted by the IPA Committee.

The period laid down in Article 4(3) of Decision 1999/468/EC shall be set at one month.

(b) The Commission shall adopt the programmes concerning assistance to be provided under Article 10 of this Regulation, in accordance with the procedure laid down in Articles 4 and 7 of Decision 1999/468/EC. To that effect, the Commission shall be assisted by the Coordination Committee of the Funds referred to in Article 103 of Regulation (EC) No 1083/2006.

The period laid down in Article 4(3) of Decision 1999/468/EC shall be set at one month.

(c) The Commission shall, after having consulted the Committee provided for in Article 147 of the EC Treaty, adopt the programmes concerning assistance to be provided under Article 11 of this Regulation, in accordance with the procedure laid down in Articles 4 and 7 of Decision 1999/468/EC. To that effect, the Commission shall be assisted by the Coordination Committee of the Funds referred to in Article 103 of Regulation (EC) No 1083/2006.

The period laid down in Article 4(3) of Decision 1999/468/EC shall be set at one month.

(d) The Commission shall adopt the programmes concerning assistance to be provided under Article 12 of this Regulation, in accordance with the procedure laid down in Articles 4 and 7 of Decision 1999/468/EC. To that effect, the Commission shall be assisted by the Rural Development Committee established by Article 90 of Regulation (EC) No 1698/2005.

The period laid down in Article 4(3) of Decision 1999/468/EC shall be set at one month.

3. Financing decisions not covered by a multi-annual or annual programme shall be adopted by the Commission, in accordance with the procedure provided for in paragraph 2(a) of this Article.

4. The Commission shall adopt the amendments to the multi-annual and annual programmes and the decisions referred to in paragraph 3 where they do not comprise substantial changes to the nature of the original programmes and actions and, as regards the financial element, where they do not exceed 20% of the total amount allocated for the programme or action in question, subject to a limit of EUR 4 million. The Committee which gave an opinion on the original programme or action shall be informed of all amending decisions.

5. An observer from the European Investment Bank shall take part in the Committees' proceedings with regard to questions concerning the Bank.

Article 15

Types of assistance

1. Assistance under this Regulation may, inter alia, finance investments, procurement contracts, grants including interest rate subsidies, special loans, loan guarantees and financial assistance, budgetary support, and other specific forms of budgetary aid, and the contribution to the capital of international financial institutions or the regional development banks to the extent that the financial risk of the Community is limited to the amount of these funds. Budgetary support shall be exceptional, with precise objectives and related benchmarks, and be contingent on the administration of public finances of the beneficiary country being sufficiently transparent, reliable and efficient, and on well-defined sectoral or macroeconomic policies approved in principle by international financing institutions having been put in place. Disbursement of budgetary support shall be conditional on satisfactory progress towards achieving the objectives in terms of impact and results.

2. Assistance may be implemented through administrative cooperation measures involving public-sector experts dispatched from Member States. Such projects shall be implemented according to implementing rules laid down by the Commission.

3. Assistance may also be used to cover the costs of the Community's participation in international missions, initiatives or organisations active in the interest of the beneficiary country, including administrative costs.

4. Community financing shall in principle not be used for paying taxes, duties or charges in beneficiary countries listed in Annexes I and II.

Article 16

Support measures

Assistance may also be used to cover the costs of actions linked to preparation, follow-up, control, audit and evaluation directly necessary for the administration of the programme and the attainment of its objectives, in particular studies, meetings, information and publicity, expenses linked to informatics networks aiming at information exchange, as well as any other expenses for administrative and technical assistance of which the Commission can avail itself for the administration of the programme. It also covers the cost of the administrative support for the purposes of devolved programme management in the Commission delegations in third countries.

Article 17

Implementation of assistance

1. The Commission and the beneficiary countries shall conclude framework agreements on the implementation of the assistance.
2. Subsidiary agreements concerning implementation of assistance shall be concluded between the Commission and the beneficiary country or its implementing authorities as required.

Article 18

Protection of the Community's financial interests

1. Any agreements resulting from this Regulation shall contain provisions ensuring the protection of the Community's financial interest, in particular with respect to fraud, corruption and any other irregularities in accordance with Council Regulation (EC, Euratom) No 2988/95 of 18 December 1995 on the protection of the European Communities financial interests (1), Council Regulation (EC, Euratom) No 2185/96 of 11 November 1996 concerning on-the-spot checks and inspections carried out by the Commission in order to protect the European Communities' financial interests against fraud and other irregularities (2) and Regulation (EC) No 1073/1999 of the European Parliament and of the Council of 25 May 1999 concerning investigations conducted by the European Anti-Fraud Office (OLAF) (3).
2. Agreements shall expressly provide for the Commission and the Court of Auditors to have the power of audit, on the basis of documents and on the spot, over all contractors and subcontractors who have received Community funds. They shall also expressly authorise the Commission to carry out on-the-spot checks and inspections as laid down in Regulation (EC, Euratom) No 2185/96.
3. All contracts resulting from the implementation of assistance shall ensure the rights of the Commission and the Court of Auditors as provided for in paragraph 2, both during and after the implementation of contracts.

Article 19

Rules of participation and origin, eligibility for grants

1. Participation in the award of procurement or grant contracts financed under this Regulation shall be open to all natural persons who are nationals of and legal persons

who are established in a Member State, a country that is a beneficiary of this Regulation, a country that is a beneficiary of the European Neighbourhood and Partnership Instrument, or a Member State of the European Economic Area.

2. Participation in the award of procurement or grant contracts financed under this Regulation shall also be open to all natural persons who are nationals of and legal persons who are established in any country other than those referred to in paragraph 1, where reciprocal access to their external assistance has been established.

Reciprocal access to the Community's external assistance shall be established by means of a specific decision concerning a given country or a given regional group of countries. Such a decision shall be adopted by the Commission in accordance with the procedure laid down in Article 14(2)(a) and shall be in force for a minimum period of one year.

The granting of reciprocal access to the Community's external assistance shall be based on a comparison between the Community and other donors and shall proceed at sectoral level or entire country level, whether it be a donor or a recipient country. The decision of granting this reciprocity to a donor country shall be based on the transparency, consistency and proportionality of the aid provided by that donor, including its qualitative and quantitative nature. The beneficiary countries shall be consulted in the process described in this paragraph.

3. Participation in the award of procurement or grant contracts financed under this Regulation shall be open to international organisations.

4. Experts proposed in the context of procedures for the award of contracts are not required to comply with the nationality condition of paragraphs 1 and 2.

5. All supplies and materials purchased under a contract financed under this Regulation must originate from the Community or a country eligible according to paragraphs 1 or 2. The term 'origin' for the purpose of this Regulation is defined in the relevant Community legislation on rules of origin for customs purposes.

6. The Commission may, in duly substantiated exceptional cases, authorise the participation of natural persons who are nationals of and legal persons who are established in other countries than those referred to in paragraphs 1 and 2, or the purchase of supplies and materials of different origin from that set out in paragraph 5. Derogations may be justified on the basis of the unavailability of products and services in the markets of the countries concerned, for reasons of extreme urgency, or if the eligibility rules would make the realisation of a project, a programme or an action impossible or exceedingly difficult.

7. In conformity with Article 114 of Regulation (EC, Euratom) No 1605/2002 natural persons may receive grants.

8. Whenever Community funding covers an operation implemented through an international organisation, participation in the appropriate contractual procedures shall be open to all natural or legal persons who are eligible pursuant to paragraphs 1 and 2 as well as to all natural or legal persons who are eligible pursuant to the rules of that organisation, care being taken to ensure that equal treatment is afforded to all donors. The same rules shall apply in respect of supplies, materials and experts.

Whenever Community funding covers an operation co-financed with a Member State, with a third country, subject to reciprocity as defined in paragraph 2, or with a regional organisation, participation in the appropriate contractual procedures shall be open to all natural or legal persons who are eligible pursuant to paragraphs 1, 2 and 3 as well as to all natural or legal persons who are eligible under the rules of such Member State, third country or regional organisation. The same rules shall apply in respect of supplies, materials and experts.

Article 20

Coherence, compatibility and coordination

1. Programmes and projects financed under this Regulation shall be consistent with EU policies. They shall comply with the agreements concluded by the Community and its Member States with the beneficiary countries and respect commitments under multilateral agreements to which they are parties.

2. The Commission and the Member States shall ensure coherence between Community assistance provided under this Regulation and financial assistance provided by the Community and the Member States through other internal and external financial instruments and by the European Investment Bank.

3. The Commission and the Member States shall ensure coordination of their respective assistance programmes with the aim of increasing effectiveness and efficiency in the delivery of assistance in line with the established guidelines for strengthening operational coordination in the field of external assistance, and for the harmonisation of policies and procedures. Coordination shall involve regular consultations and frequent exchanges of relevant information during the different phases of the assistance cycle, in particular at field level and shall constitute a key step in the programming processes of the Member States and the Community.

4. The Commission will, in liaison with the Member States, take the necessary steps to ensure proper coordination and harmonisation and cooperation with multilateral and regional organisations and entities, such as international financial institutions, United Nations agencies, funds and programmes, and non-EU donors.

Article 21

Suspension of assistance

1. Respect for the principles of democracy, the rule of law and for human rights and minority rights and fundamental freedoms is an essential element for the application of this Regulation and the granting of assistance under it. Community assistance for Albania, Bosnia and Herzegovina, Croatia, the former Yugoslav Republic of Macedonia, Montenegro and Serbia, including Kosovo, shall also be subject to the conditions defined by the Council in its Conclusions of 29 April 1997, in particular as regards the recipients' undertaking to carry out democratic, economic and institutional reforms.

2. Where a beneficiary country fails to respect these principles or the commitments contained in the relevant Partnership with the EU, or where progress toward fulfilment of the accession criteria is insufficient, the Council, acting by qualified majority on a proposal from the Commission, may take appropriate steps with regard to any

assistance granted under this Regulation. The European Parliament shall be fully and immediately informed of any decisions taken in this context.

Article 22

Evaluation

The Commission shall regularly evaluate the results and efficiency of policies and programmes and the effectiveness of programming in order to ascertain whether the objectives have been met and enable it to formulate recommendations with a view to improving future operations. The Commission shall send relevant evaluation reports to the Committees referred to in Article 14 for discussion. These results shall feed back into programme design and resource allocation.

TITLE IV

TRANSITIONAL AND FINAL PROVISIONS

Article 23

Status of Beneficiary Country

If a beneficiary country listed in Annex II is granted candidate status for accession to the EU, the Council, acting by qualified majority on the basis of a proposal from the Commission will transfer that country from Annex II to Annex I.

Article 24

Cross-instrument provision

In order to ensure consistency and efficiency of Community assistance, the Commission can decide, in accordance with the procedure referred to in Article 14(2)(a), that other third countries, territories and regions can benefit from actions under this Regulation, if the project or programme in question has a regional, cross-border, transnational or global character. In so doing, the Commission shall strive to avoid duplication with regard to other instruments of external financial assistance.

Article 25

Transitional provisions

1. Regulations (EEC) No 3906/89, (EC) No 2760/98, (EC) No 1266/1999, (EC) No 1267/1999, (EC) No 1268/1999, (EC) No 555/2000, (EC) No 2500/2001 and (EC) No 2112/2005 shall be repealed with effect from 1 January 2007.

These Regulations, as well as Regulation (EC) No 2666/2000, shall continue to apply for legal acts and commitments implementing the budget years preceding 2007, and for the implementation of Article 31 of the Act concerning the conditions of accession of the Republic of Bulgaria and Romania and the adjustments to the Treaties on which the European Union is founded.

2. Should specific measures be necessary to facilitate the transition from the system established by Regulations (EEC) No 3906/89, (EC) No 2760/98, (EC) No 1266/1999, (EC) No 1267/1999, (EC) No 1268/1999, (EC) No 555/2000, (EC) No 2666/2000 or (EC) No 2500/2001 to the one established by this Regulation, such measures shall be adopted by the Commission in accordance with the procedures referred to in Article 14 of this Regulation.

Article 26

Financial reference amount

The financial reference amount for the implementation of this Regulation for the period from 2007 to 2013 shall be EUR 11 468 million. The annual appropriations shall be authorised by the budgetary authority within the limits of the financial framework.

Article 27

Review

The Commission shall submit to the European Parliament and the Council, by 31 December 2010, a report evaluating the implementation of this Regulation in the first three years, if appropriate with a legislative proposal introducing the necessary modifications to this Regulation.

Article 28

Entry into force

This Regulation shall enter into force on the day following its publication in the Official Journal of the European Union. It shall apply from 1 January 2007 to 31 December 2013.

This Regulation shall be binding in its entirety and directly applicable in all Member States.

ANNEX I

— Croatia
— Turkey
— The former Yugoslav Republic of Macedonia.

ANNEX II

— Albania
— Bosnia
— Montenegro
— Serbia, including Kosovo

Council Decision 2008/119/EC of 12 February 2008 on the principles, priorities and conditions contained in the Accession Partnership with Croatia and repealing Decision 2006/145/EC, Official Journal L 42, 16.2.2008, pp. 51–62.

Moreover, the Union lays down priorities for the reform process in the candidate countries. These are included in so-called 'Accession Partnerships' (APs), which serve as a checklist for progress. Technically, the APs are adopted by a Council Decision (after consultation with the candidate country) and are updated every two years. The legal basis for these Council Decisions is a general regulation establishing the AP with the respective country.

THE COUNCIL OF THE EUROPEAN UNION,

Having regard to the Treaty establishing the European Community,

Having regard to Council Regulation (EC) No 533/2004 of 22 March 2004 on the establishment of partnerships in the framework of the stabilisation and association process, and in particular Article 2 thereof,

Having regard to the proposal from the Commission,

Whereas:

(1) The Thessaloniki European Council of 19 and 20 June 2003 endorsed the introduction of the Partnerships as a means to materialise the European perspective of the Western Balkan countries.

(2) Regulation (EC) No 533/2004 provides that the Council is to decide on the principles, priorities and conditions to be contained in the Partnerships, as well as any subsequent adjustments. It also states that the follow-up to the Accession Partnerships will be ensured through the mechanisms established under the stabilisation and association process, notably by the annual progress reports.

(3) Following the European Partnership of 2004, the Council adopted on 20 February 2006 the first Accession Partnership with Croatia.

(4) On 3 October 2005 the Member States started negotiations with Croatia on its accession to the European Union. The progress of the negotiations will be guided by Croatia's progress in preparing for accession, which will be measured, inter alia, against the implementation of the Accession Partnership, as regularly revised.

(5) The Commission's Communication on Enlargement Strategy and Main Challenges 2006–2007 indicated that the Partnerships would be updated at the end of 2007.

(6) On 17 July 2006 the Council adopted Regulation (EC) No 1085/2006 establishing an instrument for Pre-Accession Assistance (IPA), which renews the framework for financial assistance to pre-accession countries.

(7) It is therefore appropriate to adopt a revised Accession Partnership which updates the current Partnership in order to identify renewed priorities for further work, on the basis of the findings of the 2007 Progress Report on Croatia's preparations for further integration with the European Union.

(8) In order to prepare for membership, Croatia is expected to develop a plan with a timetable and specific measures to address the priorities of the Accession Partnership.

(9) Decision 2006/145/EC should be repealed,

HAS DECIDED AS FOLLOWS:

Article 1

In accordance with Article 2 of Regulation (EC) No 533/2004, the principles, priorities and conditions contained in the Accession Partnership with Croatia are set out in the Annex hereto.

Article 2

The implementation of the Accession Partnership shall be examined and monitored through the mechanisms established under the stabilisation and association process, and by the Council on the basis of annual reports presented by the Commission.

Article 3

Decision 2006/145/EC shall be repealed.

Article 4

This Decision shall take effect on the third day following its publication in the Official Journal of the European Union.

ANNEX
CROATIA 2007 ACCESSION PARTNERSHIP

1. INTRODUCTION

The proposed revised Accession Partnership updates the first one, on the basis of the findings of the 2007 Commission's Progress Report on Croatia. It identifies new as well as remaining priorities for action. The new priorities are adapted to the country's specific needs and stage of preparation and will be updated as necessary. Croatia is expected to develop a plan including a timetable and specific measures intended to address the Accession Partnership priorities. The Accession Partnership also provides guidance for financial assistance to the country.

2. PRINCIPLES

The Stabilisation and Association Process remains the framework for the European course of the Western Balkan countries, all the way to their future accession. The main priorities identified for Croatia relate to its capacity to meet the criteria defined by the Copenhagen European Council of 1993 and the conditions set for the Stabilisation and Association Process, notably the conditions defined by the Council in its Conclusions of 29 April 1997 and of 21 and 22 June 1999, the final declaration of the Zagreb Summit of 24 November 2000 and the Thessaloniki Agenda, and the requirements of the negotiating framework adopted by the Council on 3 October 2005.

3. PRIORITIES

The priorities listed in this Accession Partnership have been selected on the basis that it is realistic to expect that Croatia can complete them or take them substantially forward over the next few years. The priorities concern both legislation and the implementation thereof.

In view of the need to set priorities, it is clear that there are other tasks for Croatia to complete which may become priorities in any future partnership, also taking into account future progress made by Croatia.

Among the priorities, the key priorities have been identified and grouped together at the beginning of the section below. The order of these key priorities does not imply a ranking of their importance.

Key Priorities
— Ensure proper implementation of all commitments undertaken in the Stabilisation
and Association Agreement,
— update and implement the strategy and action plan for judicial reform,
— rapidly adopt and implement a strategic framework for public administration reform,
— update and accelerate implementation of the anti-corruption programme and related
action plans and ensure more coordinated and proactive efforts to prevent, detect and
effectively prosecute corruption, especially at high level,
— implement the Constitutional Law on National Minorities, with particular attention
to its provisions guaranteeing proportional representation of minorities in employment. Tackle discrimination more widely in the public sector,
— complete the process of refugee return; definitively settle all cases of housing care for
former occupancy/tenancy rights holders; complete reconstruction and repossession
of property and reopen the possibility for convalidation claims,
— pursue efforts aimed at reconciliation among citizens in the region,
— enhance efforts to find definitive solutions to pending bilateral issues, in particular
border issues, with Slovenia, Serbia, Montenegro, and Bosnia and Herzegovina; and
resolve the Ecological and Fisheries Protection Zone issue,
— maintain full cooperation with the International Criminal Tribunal for the former
Yugoslavia and ensure integrity of domestic war crimes proceedings,
— improve the business environment and economic growth potential, in particular
by reducing subsidies, restructuring large loss-making enterprises and increasing the
efficiency of public spending.

Political Criteria

Democracy and the rule of law

Public administration
— Fully implement public administration reform measures on administrative procedures and on recruitment, promotion, training and de-politicisation; improve human
resource management in areas of public administration.

Judicial system
— Substantially reduce the case backlog in courts and ensure an acceptable length of
judicial proceedings,
— rationalise the organisation of courts, including the introduction of modern information technology systems,
— establish an open, fair and transparent system of recruitment, evaluation, promotion and
disciplinary measures in the judiciary and enhance professionalism through high-quality
training supported by adequate financing of the Justice Academy, including in EU law,
— take measures to ensure proper and full execution of court rulings.

Anti-corruption policy
— Continue to develop and implement Codes of Conduct/ethics for officials and
elected representatives as well as action plans to prevent corruption in the relevant
law enforcement agencies (border police, police, customs, judiciary) and other public
sector institutions and agencies; fully address public procurement related corruption.

Establish specialist units for combating corruption within the appropriate services with an appropriate coordination mechanism between them and provide them with adequate training and resources,

— take steps to ensure that the legal framework for tackling corruption is uniformly implemented and enforced including through the use of adequate statistics. Ensure that the standards set by international instruments are met, by putting in place the appropriate legislative and administrative measures,

— take concrete actions to raise public awareness of corruption as a serious criminal offence,

— ensure full cooperation of State authorities with the Office for Prevention of Corruption and Organised crime.

Human rights and the protection of minorities

— Ensure access to justice and legal aid and make available the corresponding budgetary resources,

— promote respect for and protection of minorities in accordance with international law and best practice in EU Member States,

(1) Some Member States underlined in this context the importance of accelerating the process of restitution of property, in line with the relevant Croatian Constitutional Court rulings.

— encourage a spirit of tolerance vis-à-vis the Serb and Roma minorities and take measures to protect persons belonging to minorities who may be subject to threats or acts of discrimination, hostility or violence,

— continue to implement the strategy and action plan for the protection and integration of Roma and ensure availability of the necessary means, especially as regards employment, education and housing,

— adopt and implement a comprehensive anti-discrimination strategy.

Regional issues and international obligations

— Fully respect the 4 June 2004 agreement concerning the Ecological and Fisheries Protected Zone referred to in the June 2004 European Council conclusions and the Negotiating Framework and do not apply any aspect of the Zone to the EU Member States until a common agreement in the EU spirit is found,

— ensure the integrity of proceedings as regards war crimes, in particular by ensuring an end to ethnic bias against Serbs, including application of a uniform standard of criminal responsibility and improved security of witnesses and informants,

— secure adequate coordination and cooperation between all relevant authorities at central and local level on refugee return matters,

— make headway in settling with neighbours all issues arising from lost occupancy and tenancy rights,

— create the social and economic conditions to improve the climate for reintegration of returnees and the acceptance of returnees by receiving communities, including through regional development programmes in affected areas,

— contribute to strengthening regional cooperation, including by promoting the transition process from the Stability Pact to a more regionally-owned cooperation framework and the effective implementation of the Central European Free Trade Agreement (CEFTA),

— fully implement agreements with neighbouring countries, notably the fight against organised crime, border management and readmission, cross-border cooperation, and judicial and police cooperation, including on war crimes, and conclude such agreements where they are still outstanding.

Economic criteria

— Continue to implement prudent fiscal, monetary and financial sector policies with a view to sustaining macroeconomic stability, including low inflation, exchange rate stability and a further reduction of general government's spending-to-GDP ratio as well of its deficit and debt ratio,

— continue institutional reforms in public finance with a view to enhancing fiscal transparency, and improving the efficiency and transparency of public debt management, and completing the planned change of budget reporting to ESA 95 principles,

— continue the implementation of comprehensive health care reforms to avoid the accumulation of new payment arrears in the health system and to improve the efficiency of health spending. Continue the reform of social security. Ensure the financial sustainability of the pension system's first pillar through adequate parametric reforms,

— continue to facilitate business entry by further reducing the time and procedures needed and the costs for establishing a business. Improve bankruptcy procedures to speed up market exit,

— improve the institutional framework for privatisation with a view to significantly advancing the privatisation of companies held under the State Privatisation Fund. Continue with the restructuring of loss-making state-owned enterprises and of the railway system to reduce the amount of subsidies to the enterprise sector as a share of GDP,

— improve incentive structures and flexibility in the labour market to increase participation and employment rates.

Ability to assume the obligations of membership

Chapter 1: Free movement of goods

— Adopt and implement horizontal framework legislation to complete the necessary infrastructure, and ensure segregation of tasks between the various functions (regulation, standardisation, accreditation, metrology, conformity assessment and market surveillance),

— adopt and implement a comprehensive strategy for the transposition and implementation of EC legislation for relevant horizontal organisations (standardisation, accreditation, metrology and market surveillance) and in individual sectors, and enhance administrative capacity,

— adopt and implement an Action Plan for compliance with Articles 28–30 of the EC Treaty, including the introduction of mutual recognition clauses,

— continue adoption of European standards. Continue preparations towards meeting membership criteria for standardisation bodies,

— complete transposition of the new and old Approach directives, particularly with regard to pharmaceutical products.

Chapter 2: Freedom of movement of workers

— Abolish any discriminatory measures towards EU migrant workers and EU citizens,

— reinforce administrative structures for the coordination of social security schemes.

Chapter 3: Right of establishment and freedom to provide services

— Complete alignment of legislation with the acquis on the recognition of professional qualifications for EU citizens and amend existing legislation to repeal remaining requirements in respect of nationality, language, establishment or business permits for EU service providers, remove other administrative and technical barriers to the right of establishment and the freedom to provide services and ensure even handling of applications for business permits, including building permits.

Chapter 4: Free movement of capital

— Complete the establishment of an effective anti-money-laundering regime, in particular by ensuring that enforcement agencies are fully operational, adequately resourced and well coordinated with domestic and international counterparts,

— make further progress in the removal of remaining restrictions on capital movements; remove all restrictions on the purchase of real estate by EU citizens in line with the SAA and ensure that all applications for permission to purchase real estate submitted in the meantime by EU citizens are handled expeditiously.

Chapter 5: Public procurement

— Give an organisation for procurement the task of guaranteeing a coherent and transparent policy and steering its implementation, in all areas related to public procurement,

— adopt and implement a comprehensive strategy, with time schedules and milestones for legislative alignment and capacity building, in all areas of public procurement (public contracts, concessions, public-private partnerships) as well as for review procedures and bodies. Strengthen enforcement mechanisms of review bodies.

Chapter 6: Company law

— Align the Companies Act with the acquis and complete alignment with the directive on takeover bids,

— align accounting and auditing legislation with the acquis. Strengthen the relevant institutional framework.

Chapter 7: Intellectual property law

— Complete the alignment with the acquis concerning copyright and related rights and ensure the enforcement of intellectual property rights by strengthening the administrative capacity of the relevant bodies,

— provide a satisfactory track record of investigation, prosecution and judicial treatment of cases of piracy and counterfeiting.

Chapter 8: Competition policy

— Adopt a National Restructuring Programme for the steel sector that ensures the viability and respect for EU rules on State aids. Adopt individual restructuring plans

for each of the shipyards in difficulties and incorporate such plans in a National Restructuring Programme, in line with EU rules on State aids,
— complete legislative alignment with EU State aid rules in the area of fiscal aid and align all other remaining aid schemes identified in the State aid inventory as being incompatible with EU rules. Adopt the regional aid map,
— adopt legislative measures allowing for effective anti-trust control, in particular as regards fine setting and judicial control.

Chapter 9: Financial services
— Complete the transposition of the acquis on banking licences, capital requirements, electronic money institutions, financial conglomerates, winding-up and reorganisation, bank accounts, branch accounts and deposit guarantee schemes,
— complete legislative alignment with regard to solvency margins, insurance supervision, reinsurance and insurance mediation, financial market infrastructure, investment and securities markets,
— establish an investor compensation scheme in line with the acquis. Demonstrate enforcement of prudential requirements by establishing a track record.

Chapter 10: Information society and media
— Complete the alignment with the acquis concerning electronic communications, commerce, signatures and media, information security and the Television without Frontiers Directive,
— ensure sufficient administrative capacity to enforce the acquis, in particular in the field of electronic communications and provide a track record of the enforcement of obligations on operators with significant market power and the rights of new entrants on the electronic communications market, including rights of way, co-location and facility sharing,
— complete the planned review of audiovisual media legislation on the basis of public consultation, to ensure regulatory independence and guard against undue political interference.

Chapter 11: Agriculture and rural development
— Strengthen the administrative structures and capacity needed to implement market and rural development policies, including collection and processing of agricultural data,
— establish a vineyard register in line with EU standards,
— continue preparations to establish effective and financially sound paying bodies for the management and control of agricultural funds, in line with EU requirements and international auditing standards.

Chapter 12: Food safety, veterinary and phytosanitary policy
— Substantially improve the alignment of legislation in the food safety, veterinary and phytosanitary domain and strengthen the necessary implementing structures including control and inspection services,
— ensure the setting up of compliant regimes in the food safety, veterinary and phytosanitary sectors, including a system for animal identification and registration of

movements, treatment of animal by-products, upgrading of agri-food establishments, animal welfare and programmes of control of animal diseases, control of animals and animal products at border inspection posts, control of plant health, authorisation of plant protection products and control of their residues as well as quality of seeds and plant propagating material.

Chapter 13: Fisheries
— Strengthen administrative and, in particular, inspection structures for fisheries policy and improve the collection of catch and landing data,
— complete the computerised fishing vessel register and establish a satellite-based vessel monitoring system.

Chapter 14: Transport policy
— Complete alignment with the EU acquis and enhance administrative capacity in the area of road transport (including the implementation of the digital tachograph) aviation and maritime transport and in the area of inland waterway transport, in particular as regards the safety of navigation and River Information Services,
— adopt implementing legislation for rail transport, in particular interoperability provisions and independent allocation of capacity. Publish a finalised network statement,
— implement the first transitional phase of the European Common Aviation Area Agreement and ratify it.

Chapter 15: Energy
— Fulfil obligations arising from the Energy Community Treaty,
— strengthen administrative capacity and complete alignment with the EU acquis in the fields of security of supply, energy efficiency and renewable energy sources, the internal energy market (electricity and gas) and nuclear energy, as well as ensure a high level of nuclear safety and radiation protection.

Chapter 16: Taxation
— Accelerate alignment of tax legislation with the acquis with particular attention to including free zones in the territorial application of the VAT regime, abolishing the existing zero rates of VAT, eliminating the discriminatory taxation of cigarettes and further harmonising the system of excise duties,
— significantly strengthen the enforcement capacity of the tax and customs administrations, particularly regarding collection and control functions and developing the necessary IT systems; continue the work on building a functioning and adequately staffed excise duty service; simplify procedures and reinforce controls to effectively prosecute tax fraud,
— commit to the principles of the Code of Conduct for business taxation and ensure that new tax measures are in conformity with these principles.

Chapter 17: Economic and monetary union
— Align the legal framework in order to ensure full central bank independence, to ensure alignment as regards prohibition of privileged access of the public sector to

financial institutions and to allow for the full integration of its central bank into the European System of Central Banks.

Chapter 18: Statistics
— Strengthen the administrative capacity of the Bureau of Statistics, reform its regional offices and improve coordination with other producers of official statistics,
— continue developing agricultural, macroeconomic and business statistics.

Chapter 19: Social policy and employment
— Further align with the acquis and strengthen the related administrative and enforcement structures, including the labour inspectorates, in association with social partners,
— implement effectively the Joint Inclusion Memorandum (JIM) and, once adopted, the Joint Assessment Paper on Employment Policy Priorities (JAP).

Chapter 20: Enterprise and industrial policy
— Implement a comprehensive industrial policy strategy, with particular emphasis on the restructuring of key lossmaking sectors and individual companies, including steel and shipbuilding.

Chapter 21: Trans-European Networks
— Increase gas and electricity interconnections with neighbouring countries.

Chapter 22: Regional policy and coordination of structural instruments
— Adopt and begin implementing an action plan setting out clear objectives and a related timetable in order to meet regulatory and operational requirements deriving from Community cohesion policy, including strengthening capacity at central, regional and local level,
— ensure a clear distribution of responsibilities and strengthen the capacity of, and coordination between, designated implementing authorities/structures, including local authorities.
— adopt a Regional Development Act,
— reinforce capacity for programming, project preparation, monitoring, evaluation and financial management and control, particularly of line Ministries, to implement EU pre-accession programmes as a preparation for Community cohesion policy.

Chapter 23: Judiciary and fundamental rights
— Continue to implement the national law on personal data protection in line with the acquis and ensure an efficient monitoring and enforcement,
— see for other priorities the section on political criteria.

Chapter 24: Justice, freedom and security
— Complete the revision of key legislation to align with the Schengen acquis and extend investments at local level in terms of IT equipment and further training for the police,
— continue preparations to implement the Schengen acquis by increasing staffing levels and training for border guards, further investing in equipment including the extension of the National Border Management Information System and ensuring

its compatibility with the second-generation Schengen Information System (SIS II). Improve administrative and enforcement capacity of the border police by enhancing inter-agency cooperation,
— continue alignment to EU visa policy, including the introduction of biometric iden- tifiers in travel documents and preparations for the Visa Information system,
— introduce secondary legislation for implementation of the Asylum Act and Aliens Act,
— ensure compatibility of legislation with the acquis in judicial cooperation in civil and criminal matters and strengthen the capacity of the judiciary to apply the acquis.

Chapter 25: Science and research
— Ensure adequate capacity to take up EU-funded research projects,
— continue to take and implement actions to facilitate the integration into the European Research Area.

Chapter 26: Education and culture
— Ensuring adequate capacity to manage the Lifelong Learning and Youth in Action programmes,
— align with the acquis on non-discrimination between EU and Croatian nationals as regards access to education as well as the directive on the education of the children of migrant workers.

Chapter 27: Environment
— Continue work on transposition and implementation of the EU acquis, with par- ticular emphasis on waste management, water quality, air quality, nature protection and integrated pollution prevention and control,
— adopt and implement, in a well coordinated manner, a comprehensive plan for put- ting in place the necessary administrative capacity and required financial resources to implement the environment acquis,
— increase investments in environmental infrastructure, with particular emphasis on waste water collection and treatment, drinking water supply and waste management,
— start implementing the Kyoto Protocol,
— ensure integration of environmental protection requirements into the definition and implementation of other sectoral policies and promote sustainable development.

Chapter 28: Consumer and health protection
— Further align with the consumer and health acquis, including in the areas of tissues and cells and tobacco, and ensure adequate administrative structures and enforce- ment capacity,
— in the area of mental health, develop community-based services as an alternative to institutionalisation, and ensure allocation of sufficient financial resources for mental health care.

Chapter 29: Customs union
— Continue to adopt legislation in the limited remaining areas requiring further align- ment, in particular on the nonpreferential rules of origin and the application of fees,

— apply customs rules in a consistent and homogeneous manner across customs offices, notably in the areas of declaration processing, origin, simplified procedures, counterfeiting, selectivity of controls; ensure the application of modern and consistent risk analysis procedures in all offices,
— on the basis of a comprehensive and coherent strategy, make sufficient progress in developing all IT interconnectivity systems.

Chapter 30: External relations
— Prepare for the alignment of all relevant international agreements with third countries and strengthen administrative and control capacities for the common commercial policy.

Chapter 31: Foreign, security and defence policy
— Strengthen implementation and enforcement of arms control and further improve capacity for full implementation of the Common Foreign Security Policy and European Security and Defence Policy.

Chapter 32: Financial control
— Adopt and implement public internal financial control legislation and inherent policies supported by adequate implementation capacity,
— safeguard the functional and financial independence of the State Audit Institution by means of amended constitutional provisions or national legislation having equivalent effect, adoption and implementation of necessary accompanying legislation,
— align the Criminal Code with the acquis on protection of the EU's financial interests as well as with the convention on the protection of financial interests and its protocols,
— set up an effective and efficient coordination service to guarantee fulfilment of the obligations arising from Article 280(3) of the EC Treaty and application of the acquis concerning on-the-spot checks and inspections carried out by the Commission, in particular the obligation of assistance to Commission inspectors,
— take legislative and administrative measures to comply with the acquis on the protection of the euro against counterfeiting.

Chapter 33: Financial and budgetary provisions
— Increase administrative capacity and prepare procedural rules to ensure, from accession, the correct calculation, forecasting, collection, payment, control and reporting to the EU on own resources.

4. PROGRAMMING

Community assistance will be provided through the instrument for pre-accession (IPA) and, for programmes adopted before 2007, Council Regulation (EC) No 2666/2000 of 5 December 2000 on assistance for Albania, Bosnia and Herzegovina, Croatia, the Federal Republic of Yugoslavia and the former Yugoslav Republic of Macedonia (CARDS regulation). Accordingly, this Decision will have no financial implications. The financing agreements serve as legal basis for the implementation of the concrete programmes.

Croatia can also have access to funding from multi-country and horizontal programmes.

5. CONDITIONALITY

Assistance to the Western Balkan countries is conditional on further progress on satis-fying the Copenhagen criteria and on meeting the requirements of the Stabilisation and Association Agreement and specific priorities of this Accession Partnership. Failure to respect these conditions could lead the Council to take appropriate measures on the basis of Article 21 of Council Regulation (EC) No 1085/2006 or, in the case of pre-2007 programmes, on the basis of Article 5 of Regulation (EC) No 2666/2000. The assistance is also subject to the conditions defined by the Council in its conclusions of 29 April 1997, in particular as regards the recipients' undertaking to carry out democratic, eco-nomic and institutional reforms. Specific conditions are also included in individual annual programmes. The financing decisions will be followed by a financing agreement signed with Croatia.

6. MONITORING

The implementation of the Accession Partnership shall be examined in the framework of the Stabilisation and Association Process, including through the annual Reports presented by the Commission, in the context of the political and economic dialogues, as well as on the basis of information provided to the accession conference.

9.3 Neighbourhood policy

9.3.1 Historical evolution

Following a communication on 'Wider Europe' (2003), the Commission presented the outline for the EU's neighbourhood policy (ENP) in 2004. This document, an excerpt of which is included below, sets out common principles on how the EU should engage with Algeria, Armenia, Azerbaijan, Belarus, Egypt, Georgia, Israel, Jordan, Lebanon, Libya, Moldova, Morocco, Occupied Palestinian Territory, Syria, Tunisia, and Ukraine. In light of the cascading developments in the Arab world that started unfolding in December 2010, the EU launched 'A Partnership for Democracy and Shared Prosperity with the Southern Mediterranean'. A Joint Communication by the European Commission and the High Representative of the EU followed to reflect the EU's new approach to developments on the ground. The reorientation of the ENP has brought three priority goals: (1) support efforts to build deep and sustainable democracies; (2) support inclusive economic development; and (3) strengthen the two regional dimensions of the ENP (i.e. the Eastern and the Southern Partnerships). The EU aims to achieve these goals through a differentiated and flexible approach with each neighbour, whereas it has adopted a 'more for more' policy, which signifies a strict conditionality between internal reforms in the neighbours of the Union and more funds from the latter.

Communication from the Commission, European Neighbourhood Policy, Strategy Paper, 12.5.2004, COM(2004) 373 final, (introduction and summary only).

This Communication is at the origin of the EU's current neighbourhood policy and sets out its main political objectives.

INTRODUCTION AND SUMMARY

With its historic enlargement earlier this month, the European Union has taken a big step forward in promoting security and prosperity on the European continent. EU enlargement also means that the external borders of the Union have changed. We have acquired new neighbours and have come closer to old ones. These circumstances have created both opportunities and challenges. The European Neighbourhood Policy is a response to this new situation. It will also support efforts to realise the objectives of the European Security Strategy.

In March 2003 the Commission presented its Communication 'Wider Europe—Neighbourhood: A new Framework for relations with our Eastern and Southern Neighbours', following a joint letter to the Council by the High Representative Mr Javier Solana and Commissioner Patten in August 2002.

In June 2003 the Council welcomed this Communication as a good basis for developing a new range of policies towards these countries, defined overall goals and principles and identified possible incentives. The Thessaloniki European Council in June 2003 endorsed the Council conclusions and looked forward to the work to be undertaken by the Council and Commission in putting together the various elements of these policies.

In July 2003 the Commission tabled a Communication 'Paving the Way for a New Neighbourhood Instrument' and established a Wider Europe Task Force and a Wider Europe Inter-Service Group. In October 2003, the Council 'invited the Commission with the contribution, where appropriate, of the High Representative to present in the light of the conclusions of June detailed proposals for the relevant action plans early in 2004 in order to take this matter forward by June 2004'. The Council also welcomed the communication on the new neighbourhood instrument. The European Council of October 2003 welcomed the progress made on this initiative and urged the Council and the Commission to take it forward, with a view to ensuring a comprehensive, balanced and proportionate approach, including a financial instrument.

On this basis the Commission has made a detailed analysis of the elements which could be included in this initiative, both with respect to substance and procedure. The Commission has made two oral progress reports to the Council, in October 2003 and February 2004, and contributed to detailed discussions in the Permanent Representatives Committee and the relevant Council working groups, concerning the possible elements to be included in European Neighbourhood Policy (ENP) Actions Plans with a number of countries in Eastern Europe and the Mediterranean region. The parts of these Action Plans related to enhanced political co-operation and the Common Foreign and Security Policy have been worked on and agreed jointly by the services of the Commission and the High Representative.

The Commission has held exploratory talks with partners in Eastern Europe and the Southern Mediterranean which have Partnership and Cooperation Agreements or Association Agreements in force. These talks have confirmed their interest in ENP and ascertained their views on the priorities to be addressed in Action Plans. The intention is progressively to extend the process to other countries, which are at present within the scope of this initiative, as their agreements advance from the signature to the ratification stage.

At the same time the Commission has made an evaluation of the present situation in these countries, with respect to their political and economic systems and their co-operation with the European Union. The present Communication is designed to convey, to the Council and the European Parliament, the results of this work and to map out the next steps in carrying forward the European Neighbourhood Policy.

Since this policy was launched, the EU has emphasised that it offers a means to reinforce relations between the EU and partner countries, which is distinct from the possibilities available to European countries under Article 49 of the Treaty on European Union. The objective of the ENP is to share the benefits of the EU's 2004 enlargement with neighbouring countries in strengthening stability, security and well-being for all concerned. It is designed to prevent the emergence of new dividing lines between the enlarged EU and its neighbours and to offer them the chance to participate in various EU activities, through greater political, security, economic and cultural co-operation.

The method proposed is, together with partner countries, to define a set of priorities, whose fulfilment will bring them closer to the European Union. These priorities will be incorporated in jointly agreed Action Plans, covering a number of key areas for specific action: political dialogue and reform; trade and measures preparing partners for gradually obtaining a stake in the EU's Internal Market; justice and home affairs; energy, transport, information society, environment and research and innovation; and social policy and people-to-people contacts.

The privileged relationship with neighbours will build on mutual commitment to common values principally within the fields of the rule of law, good governance, the respect for human rights, including minority rights, the promotion of good neighbourly relations, and the principles of market economy and sustainable development. Commitments will also be sought to certain essential aspects of the EU's external action, including, in particular, the fight against terrorism and the proliferation of weapons of mass destruction, as well as abidance by international law and efforts to achieve conflict resolution.

The Action Plans will draw on a common set of principles but will be differentiated, reflecting the existing state of relations with each country, its needs and capacities, as well as common interests. The level of ambition of the EU's relationships with its neighbours will take into account the extent to which these values are effectively shared.

Progress in meeting the agreed priorities will be monitored in the bodies established by the Partnership and Cooperation Agreements or Association Agreements. The Commission will report periodically on progress accomplished. On the basis of this evaluation, the EU, together with partner countries, will review the content of the Action Plans and decide on their adaptation and renewal. Decisions may also be taken, on this basis, on the next step in the development of bilateral relations, including the possibility of new contractual links. These could take the form of European Neighbourhood Agreements whose scope would be defined in the light of progress in meeting the priorities set out in the Action Plans.

The Action Plans will be put forward by the Commission, with the contribution of the High Representative on issues related to political co-operation and the CFSP, following exploratory talks with the countries concerned. It is suggested that they be approved by the respective Cooperation or Association Councils. If any of the Actions proposed imply the need for legal acts or formal negotiations, the Commission will put forward the necessary proposals or recommendations.

The Action Plans will provide a point of reference for the programming of assistance to the countries concerned. Assistance from existing sources will be complemented in the future by support from the European Neighbourhood Instrument. The present communication puts forward for discussion an outline of this instrument, building on the Commission's communication of July 2003. Meanwhile Neighbourhood Programmes are being developed through existing support mechanisms. The Commission seeks to offer neighbouring countries additional support through instruments such as technical assistance and twinning. It is also conducting a survey of EU programmes and agencies where the participation of neighbouring countries may be in the interests of the enlarged EU and of neighbouring countries.

Russia is a key partner of the EU in its immediate neighbourhood. Together, Russia and the EU have decided to develop further their strategic partnership through the creation of four common spaces, as defined at the St Petersburg summit in May 2003.

Belarus and the EU will be able to develop contractual links when Belarus has established a democratic form of government, following free and fair elections. It will then be possible to extend the full benefits of the European Neighbourhood Policy to Belarus. Meanwhile the EU will consider ways of strengthening support to civil society in ways described below.

The EU looks forward to Libya's entry into the Barcelona process on the basis of Libya's full acceptance of the Barcelona acquis and of the resolution of outstanding bilateral issues. This will pave the way to the establishment of normal relations so that Libya will be able to benefit from the European Neighbourhood Policy.

The present Communication contains recommendations concerning the inclusion of the countries of the Southern Caucasus in the European Neighbourhood Policy.

The European Neighbourhood Policy will reinforce existing forms of regional and sub-regional cooperation and provide a framework for their further development. The ENP will reinforce stability and security and contribute to efforts at conflict resolution. This document contains recommendations on the development of regional cooperation and integration, as a means to address certain issues arising at the enlarged EU's external borders. By further developing various forms of cross-border co-operation, involving local and regional authorities, as well as non-governmental actors, the EU and its partners can work together to ensure that border regions benefit from the EU's 2004 enlargement. In the south, the ENP will also encourage the participants to reap the full benefits of the Euro-Mediterranean Partnership (the Barcelona process), to promote infrastructure interconnections and networks, in particular energy, and to develop new forms of cooperation with their neighbours. The ENP will contribute to develop further regional integration, building on the achievements of the Euro-Mediterranean partnership, notably in the area of trade. It will reinforce efforts to meet the objectives of the European security strategy in the Mediterranean and the Middle East.

The European Neighbourhood Policy's vision involves a ring of countries, sharing the EU's fundamental values and objectives, drawn into an increasingly close relationship, going beyond co-operation to involve a significant measure of economic and political integration.

This will bring enormous gains to all involved in terms of increased stability, security and well being. The Action Plans, which are to be developed on the basis of the principles set out in this Communication, constitute a first major step towards realising this vision. The Action Plans will define the way ahead over the next three to five years. The next step could consist in the negotiation of European Neighbourhood Agreements, to replace the present generation of bilateral agreements, when Action Plan priorities are met. Progress made in this way will enable the EU and its partners to agree on longer-term goals for the further development of relations in the years ahead.

The Commission invites the Council to consider the approach outlined in the present Communication and to draw up conclusions on the way to carry this initiative forward, addressing the substance of potential Action Plans and the countries with which they should be drawn up, bearing in mind the commitment to shared values. On this basis, the Commission, with the participation of representatives of the Presidency and the High Representative, is ready to complete exploratory talks with the countries identified and to present draft Action Plans. It suggests that these Action Plans be approved by the respective Cooperation or Association Councils. It is also ready to begin preparations with certain other countries, referred to in this Communication, to which this initiative applies.

[...]

Joint Communication to the European Council, the European Parliament, the Council, the European Economic and Social Committee and the Committee of the Regions, A Partnership for Democracy and Shared Prosperity with the Southern Mediterranean, 8.3.2011, COM(2011) 200 final.

After the Arab Spring, the High Representative for Foreign and Security Policy, Lady Ashton, as well as the EU Commissioner for Enlargement and Neighbourhood, Mr Füle, formulated together the first EU political response to the changes. The document sums up how the traditional EU instruments have been mobilized and which adjustments were thought of to further sustain the democratic development in those countries.

INTRODUCTION
The events unfolding in our southern neighbourhood are of historic proportions. They reflect a profound transformation process and will have lasting consequences not only for the people and countries of the region but also for the rest of the world and the EU in particular. The changes now underway carry the hope of a better life for the people

of the region and for greater respect of human rights, pluralism, rule of law and social justice—universal values that we all share. Movement towards full democracy is never an easy path—there are risks and uncertainties associated with these transitions. While acknowledging the difficulties the EU has to take the clear and strategic option of supporting the quest for the principles and values that it cherishes. For these reasons the EU must not be a passive spectator. It needs to support wholeheartedly the wish of the people in our neighbourhood to enjoy the same freedoms that we take as our right. European countries have their own experience of democratic transition. The European Union has a proud tradition of supporting countries in transition from autocratic regimes to democracy, first in the South and more recently in Central and Eastern Europe. While respecting what are primarily internal transformation processes, the EU can offer expertise—that of governments, the European Institutions (European Commission and European Parliament), local and regional authorities, political parties, foundations, trade unions and civil society organizations. There is a shared interest in a democratic, stable, prosperous and peaceful Southern Mediterranean.

We believe that now is the time for a qualitative step forward in the relations between the EU and its Southern neighbours. This new approach should be rooted unambiguously in a joint commitment to common values. The demand for political participation, dignity, freedom and employment opportunities expressed in recent weeks can only be addressed through faster and more ambitious political and economic reforms. The EU is ready to support all its Southern neighbours who are able and willing to embark on such reforms through a 'Partnership for Democracy and Shared Prosperity'. The commitment to democracy, human rights, social justice, good governance and the rule of law must be shared. The Partnership must be based on concrete progress in these areas. It must be a differentiated approach. Despite some commonalities, no country in the region is the same so we must react to the specificities of each of them.

A 'Partnership for Democracy and Shared Prosperity' should be built on the following three elements:

• democratic transformation and institution-building, with a particular focus on fundamental freedoms, constitutional reforms, reform of the judiciary and the fight against corruption

• a stronger partnership with the people, with specific emphasis on support to civil society and on enhanced opportunities for exchanges and people-to-people contacts with a particular focus on the young

• sustainable and inclusive growth and economic development, especially support to Small and Medium Enterprises (SMEs), vocational and educational training, improving health and education systems and development of the poorer regions.

This Communication explains what the EU has done to address the short-term consequences of recent events in North Africa. It then spells out our approach to the longer-term process of turning into reality the tremendous hopes that have been voiced in the region. It will be developed by listening, not only to requests for support from partner governments, but also to demands expressed by civil society.

A radically changing political landscape in the Southern Mediterranean requires a change in the EU's approach to the region—the underlying themes of differentiation, conditionality and of a partnership between our societies are part of the ongoing review of the European Neighbourhood Policy on which we will present a joint Communication in April.

1. OUR IMMEDIATE RESPONSE
• Humanitarian aid (EUR 30 million)
• Facilitating consular cooperation and evacuation
• Frontex joint operations
• Drawing on the EUR 25 million EU External Borders Fund and European Refugee Fund
• High Representative/Vice President (HR/VP) visits to Tunisia and Egypt; international co-ordination meeting in Brussels
• Support for Democratic transition

Our first concern has been to respond rapidly and effectively to the immediate challenges of the evolving situation in our Southern Neighbourhood and to address and pre-empt the risks of further bloodshed and hardship.

EUR 30 million has been made available in humanitarian aid by the Commission to tackle the most immediate humanitarian needs in Libya and of displaced persons at the Tunisian and Egyptian borders. With this aid, we are providing medical and food aid, shelter and other necessities. Commission experts are on the ground and contingency planning is taking place to ensure a rapid response in case the situation deteriorates further. Vigilance is necessary as the humanitarian crisis threatens to escalate to neighbouring countries both in the Maghreb and sub Saharan Africa as people flee from Libya. The Commission will increase financial support if needs on the ground so require it and we encourage EU Member States to continue to respond in a similar fashion.

Close consular cooperation has been maintained between all Member States and the EU and appropriate EU mechanisms, including the Situation Centre in the EEAS, have been activated to allow rapid exchange of information and most effective use of resources. The EU Civil Protection Mechanism (MIC) was activated on 23 February to facilitate the evacuation of EU citizens by way of an air and sea bridge. The EU Military Staff has been supporting this overall effort. The Commission is cooperating with international organisations (UNHCR, International Organisation for Migration, IOM) to help people who want to leave Libya get back to their home countries. Use of Common Security and Defence Policy (CSDP) instruments for strengthening the short-term action could be considered.

The Commission has mobilised its instruments to support Italy, and other Member States if needed, in case a massive influx of migrants from North Africa were to materialise. This response includes operational measures and financial assistance. The Frontex joint operation HERMES 2011 was launched on 20 February, with assets and experts from a number of Member States. If required, Frontex operations could be strengthened to help deal with possible new inflows. The Commission is ready to mobilise i.a. financial assistance from funds such as the External Borders Fund and European Refugee Fund which amount to EUR 25 million in total.

In Tunisia, EUR 17 million was allocated for immediate and short-term support for democratic transition and assistance to impoverished inland areas. This includes support to establish an appropriate legal framework for the holding of elections and for an EU Election Observation Mission in support of the work of the National Commission for Constitutional Reform and Elections. It also covers additional support for civil society. Further support for democratic reform will be provided through the Instrument for Stability. Following her visits to Tunisia and Egypt, the HR/VP convened an international meeting on 23 February providing the opportunity to compare notes with main partners and major International Financial Institutions (IFIs) on developments in the region. The meeting reconfirmed that the efforts of the international community must be closely coordinated and aligned with and guided by the priorities expressed by the Tunisians and the Egyptians themselves.

For Egypt, it would be premature to announce a support package until the authorities are ready to make a request for assistance and define priority needs. The EU is ready to mobilise support in line with those priorities when they are ready.

In Libya, the EU has been firm in its condemnation of the acts perpetrated by the Gaddafi regime. It immediately suspended negotiations of the EU–Libya framework agreement and all technical cooperation. In addition to the UN sanctions, on 28 February the EU adopted further restrictive measures such as an embargo on equipment which might be used for internal repression and autonomous designations under the travel restrictions and assets freeze. Additional measures have been proposed.

2. ADAPTING OUR APPROACH
• Reviewing and adjusting EU Neighbourhood Policy
• Moving towards advanced status in Association Agreements
• Enhancing political dialogue

The EU response to the changes taking place in the region needs to be more focused, innovative and ambitious, addressing the needs of the people and the realities on the ground. Political and economic reforms must go hand-in-hand and help deliver political rights and freedoms, accountability and participation. The EU should be ready to offer greater support to those countries ready to work on such a common agenda, but also reconsider support when countries depart from this track.

This new approach, a 'Partnership for Democracy and Shared Prosperity' represents a fundamental step change in the EU's relationship with those partners that commit themselves to specific, measurable reforms. It is an incentive-based approach based on more differentiation ('more for more'): those that go further and faster with reforms will be able to count on greater support from the EU. Support will be reallocated or refocused for those who stall or retrench on agreed reform plans.

More concretely, closer political co-operation means advancing towards higher standards of human rights and governance based on a set of minimum benchmarks against which performance will be assessed. A commitment to adequately monitored, free and fair elections should be the entry qualification for the Partnership. It also means closer cooperation in the context of the Common Foreign and Security Policy (CFSP) and more joint work in international fora on issues of common interest. The EU will continue to offer its commitment and support to the peaceful resolution of disputes within and between States in the region. The Partnership should be underpinned by enhanced political dialogue. The EU will step up bilateral political dialogue at all levels, as soon as local conditions allow, with a strong focus on human rights and political accountability.

Partner countries carrying out the necessary reforms can expect to resume negotiations on Association Agreements with the aim of achieving 'advanced status' which allows for significantly strengthened political dialogue and increased links between the partner country and EU institutions. This will encompass deeper engagement on mobility and improved market access to the EU.

3. DEMOCRACY AND INSTITUTION BUILDING

• Expanding support to civil society
• Establishing a Civil Society Neighbourhood Facility
• Support Social Dialogue Forum

The EU is ready to support the democratic and constitutional reform processes. Judicial reform, enhanced transparency and the fight against corruption are of particular importance in this process, both to encourage foreign and domestic economic investment and to demonstrate to people a visible change in their daily lives. We are ready to make expertise available, through instruments such as twinning and TAIEX, to support capacity building with a particular focus on strengthening government institutions that can ensure the consolidation of change, including at regional and local level. Our expertise in electoral assistance will also be fully mobilised to accompany the electoral processes in Tunisia and, if requested by the authorities in Egypt.

A thriving civil society can help uphold human rights and contribute to democracy building and good governance, playing an important role in checking government excesses. A range of non-government (NGOs) and civil society organisations (CSOs) can provide much-needed support for the reforms and involvement in areas close to citizens' concerns such as human rights, the environment, social and economic development. This is an area where we should seek to maximize the assistance that Member States can offer at short notice to develop a platform for civil society, political parties, trade unions and associations. This could be set up with EU funding and with the support of EU political parties, trade unions, foundations and relevant NGOs. Women have played an important role in the changes in the region and gender aspects will play an important role in future EU support.

The April review of the European Neighbourhood Policy will make proposals for the reinforcement of the EU's support to civil society organisations in our neighbourhood. This will include dedicated support for civil society (a Civil Society Neighbourhood Facility) aimed at developing the advocacy capacity of CSOs and increasing their ability to monitor reform and participate effectively in policy dialogues.

Social dialogue between trade unions and employers plays an important role in sustaining reform efforts. New trade unions and employers associations are now emerging. This provides an opportunity for more effective social dialogue. It should be supported through the EuroMediterranean Social Dialogue Forum which will facilitate exchange between the Mediterranean social partners on key employment and social issues and will support capacity building.

The EU is already supporting public administration reform aimed at streamlining and strengthening of basic policy processes, budget formulation and the capacity to raise domestic funding through efficient, fair and sustainable tax systems and administrations. With a view to supporting better the fight against corruption and illicit financial flows and to improving sound financial management, these programmes should also target transparency and accountability in public administration.

4. TACKLING THE CHALLENGES OF MOBILITY
• Conclude Mobility Partnerships
• Reinforce local Schengen cooperation
• Make full use of improvements in EU Visa Code

People-to-people contacts are important to promote mutual understanding as well as business, which will benefit the cultural and economical development of the entire Mediterranean region and the integration of migrants in the EU.

A key element in this is the strengthening of capacity building in the Mediterranean countries on borders/migration/asylum and more effective law enforcement cooperation to improve security throughout the Mediterranean.

Mobility Partnerships should be launched with partner countries. They aim to provide a comprehensive framework to ensure that the movement of persons between the EU and a third country is well-managed. They cover initiatives such as visa and legal migration arrangements; legal frameworks for (economic) migration; capacity building to manage remittances and for efficient matching of labour demands and needs, return and reintegration programmes, upgrading of the asylum systems to EU standards etc. In return for increased mobility, partners must be ready to undertake increasing capacity building and provide appropriate financial support for border management, preventing and fighting against irregular migration and trafficking in human beings, including through enhanced maritime surveillance; the return of irregular migrants (return arrangements and readmission agreements) and for enhancing the capacity and abilities of law enforcement authorities to effectively fight trans-border organised crime and corruption.

In the short-term, the Commission will work with Member States on legal migration legislation and visa policy to support the goal of enhanced mobility, in particular for students, researchers and business persons. Cooperation under Local Schengen Cooperation should be reinforced and full use should be made of practical improvements and flexibilities for visa applicants within the EU Visa Code, including the issuing of multiple entry visas to bona fide travellers and specific groups (such as researchers, students and business persons). The negotiation of short stay visa facilitation agreements with Southern Mediterranean Countries should be envisaged following a differentiated, evidence-based approach. Financial support will be provided, if needed. The Commission calls on the colegislators to adopt rapidly the Directives on third country seasonal workers and intracorporate transferees, which will also contribute to enhancing mobility to the EU.

In the long-term, provided that visa facilitation and readmission agreements are effectively implemented, gradual steps towards visa liberalisation for individual partner countries could be considered on a case-by-case basis, taking into account the overall relationship with the partner country concerned and provided that conditions for well-managed and secure mobility are in place.

5. PROMOTING INCLUSIVE ECONOMIC DEVELOPMENT
• Promote Small and Medium Size Enterprises (SMEs) and Job Creation
• Seek agreement of Member States to increase EIB lending by EUR 1 billion
• Work with other shareholders to extend the EBRD mandate to countries of the region
• Promote job creation and training

The unrest in several Southern Mediterranean countries is clearly linked to economic weaknesses. Many of the economies are characterised by an unequal distribution of wealth, insufficient social and economic reform, limited job creation, weak education and training systems which do not produce the skills needed on the labour market, as well as low level of regional trade integration.

There is a need for the countries of the region to re-invigorate their economies to deliver sustainable and inclusive growth, development of poorer regions and job creation. Small and medium size enterprises (SMEs) have a critical role to play in job creation. To thrive, they need a sound regulatory framework, conducive to business and entrepreneurship. The EU is ready to support this through policy dialogue and cooperation under the Euro Med industrial work programme. This should be accompanied by integrated employment and social policies, including matching of training initiatives and labour market needs, social dialogue, provision of social safety-nets and transformation of the informal sector.

The International Financing Institutions (IFIs) can contribute to this effort. Funding could come from the European Investment Bank (EIB) and, if other non-EU shareholders agree, the European Bank for Reconstruction and Development (EBRD). The EIB has been active in the region for over 30 years, its operations being implemented under the umbrella of the Facility for Euro-Mediterranean Investment and Partnership (FEMIP). FEMIP is active in nine countries in the Southern Mediterranean, focussing on investments in infrastructure and support for the private sector. In addition to accelerating the implementation and approval of projects currently in the pipeline, the EIB could provide around EUR 6 billion to the Mediterranean region in the coming three years if the Council approves the additional lending envelope of EUR 1 billion which was recently proposed by the European Parliament. The Commission supports this increase in the lending mandate and calls on the Council to reach an agreement rapidly on the increase.

The Council is also invited to adopt the Commission proposal of May 2008 on EIB reflows. This would allow the EIB and other financial intermediaries to re-invest funds under FEMIP reflowing from previous financing operations in favour of the private sector. In the immediate future this arrangement would generate approximately EUR 120 million now and up to EUR 200 million by 2013.

The EBRD, not currently active in the Southern Mediterranean, could extend operations if the Bank's statutes were amended. If agreed by all shareholders this could allow an annual EBRD business activity of an initial EUR 1 billion to be reached with the Bank's existing resources. The Commission supports the extension of EBRD operations and calls on EU Member States and other shareholder governments to support it urgently.

These initiatives will not come at the expense of lending to other countries of operation in the Eastern neighbourhood for example.

6. ENSURING MAXIMUM IMPACT OF TRADE AND INVESTMENT
• Adopt Pan-Euro-Mediterranean preferential rules of origin
• Approve rapidly agreements on agricultural and fisheries products
• Speed up negotiations on trade in services
• Negotiate Deep Free Trade Areas

Trade and investment are engines for growth and help to reduce poverty. They bring people together, securing ties between nations and contributing to political stability. However, for trade and Foreign Direct Investment (FDI) to deliver their potential, they must be embedded in a sound business climate, which, in turn, requires a strengthening of the rule of law and the judiciary, tackling corruption and overhauling administrative procedures.

The countries in the region are at different stages in their trade and investment relations with the EU. Some (Tunisia, Morocco, Egypt, Jordan) are relatively well advanced; others (Syria, Algeria, Libya) much less. The EU has free trade agreements with the whole of the region except for Syria and Libya. These agreements provide free market access for industrial products. The EU has recently upgraded preferential market access for agricultural and fisheries products, with Egypt and Jordan in particular, and several other agreements in this field are being negotiated or at the approval stage, for example, with Morocco. With Morocco, there has also been an exchange of offers to liberalise services, but the issue of labour mobility is a major stumbling block.

The EU's measures in support of trade and investment should best be calibrated to the situation in each country, including the pace and breadth of reforms more generally, also given the current level of volatility in the region.

In the short to medium term, the EU could set itself the following goals to:
• accelerate the conclusion and EU approval of trade liberalisation agreements, notably on agricultural and fisheries products with Tunisia and Morocco;
• launch negotiations on agreements on conformity assessment and acceptance of industrial products;
• accelerate on-going bilateral negotiations on the liberalisation of trade in services (including visa facilitation for persons from specific professional categories);
• conclude the single regional Convention on pan-Euro-Mediterranean preferential rules of origin in 2011. This should be accompanied by a rapid revision of the rules of origin themselves. A point of reference for these reforms is the recently adopted regime for GSP beneficiaries. The Commission calls on the Council to adopt urgently its pending proposals on the single regional Convention, after consultation with the European Parliament.

In the medium to long term, the common objective which has been agreed in both regional and bilateral discussions with Southern Mediterranean partners is the establishment of Deep and Comprehensive Free Trade Areas, building on the current Euro-Mediterranean Association Agreements and on the European Neighbourhood

Policy Action Plans. They should form part of a broader comprehensive package in support of democratic and economic reforms. Negotiations should be started with countries that are clearly engaged in such a process of political and economic transformation. Beyond the mere elimination of import duties, these agreements should foster, in a progressive manner, closer integration between the economies of our Southern Mediterranean partners and the EU single market and would include actions such as regulatory convergence. Particular priority should be given to measures in areas such as competition policy, public procurement, investment protection, sanitary and phytosanitary measures.

7. ENHANCING SECTORAL CO-OPERATION
• Establish an EU–South Mediterranean Energy Community
• Launch an Agricultural/rural development support programme
• Increase participation in education programmes
• Develop the Internet and other communication technologies
The Southern Mediterranean is strategically important for the EU in terms of security of gas and oil supplies from some of the countries but also more broadly in terms of transit from the region and beyond. There is clear potential for building an EU–Mediterranean partnership in the production and management of renewables, in particular solar and wind energy, and in having a joined-up approach to ensuring energy security. Joint renewable energy investments in the Southern Mediterranean in line with the EU's 2050 decarbonisation scenario could offer the possibility of a new partnership provided that the right market perspective is created for electricity imports.

It is desirable to open a credible perspective for the integration of the Southern Mediterranean in the EU internal energy market based on a differentiated and gradual approach. In the mid to long term, this would mean establishing a form of 'EU–Southern Mediterranean Energy Community' starting with the Maghreb countries and possibly expanding progressively to the Mashreq. Extending the Energy Community Treaty with the Union's Eastern and South-Eastern neighbours, or building on its experience, this community should cover relevant parts of the EU's energy legislation with a view to promoting a real and reliable convergence of South Mediterranean partners' energy policies with EU policy.

Education should be a key focus of EU activities in the region. Tackling high levels of illiteracy is key to promoting democracy and ensuring a qualified workforce to help modernise the Southern Mediterranean economies. Exchanges at university level are valuable, and fuller use should be made of Erasmus Mundus, Euromed Youth and Tempus to increase substantially the number of persons from Southern Mediterranean partner countries participating in these programmes. Vocational Education and Training (VET) also has an important role to play in addressing disparities. This should include the identification of the key strategic components on an integrated VET policy by organising national debates with key stakeholders. Exchanges of best practices on programmes enhancing the skills of unemployed people should also be encouraged.

Tourism is a key component of GDP in many of the countries in the South Mediterranean. The EU should seek to extend its existing initiatives 'European Destinations of Excellence (EDEN)', promoting sustainable tourism models and Calypso, promoting off-season tourism to these countries. The protection and promotion of cultural diversity is important and the EU is committed to further develop cultural initiatives with the South Mediterranean region.

Recent events in the Southern Mediterranean combined with rising food prices have demonstrated the urgency for the EU to help its partner countries to improve the efficiency and productivity of its agricultural sector and assuring the security of food supply. The Commission could support rural development through a new initiative—a European Neighbourhood Facility for Agriculture and Rural Development. The programme would build on EU best practice in developing rural areas. It would integrate investment support and building up of administrative capacities so as to facilitate the modernisation of the agricultural production aligned to EU quality and food safety standards. It could be developed in close cooperation with the FAO, World Bank and possibly EIB.

In the area of transport, cooperation should focus on modernising air traffic management and on improving aviation safety and security to create a Euro-Mediterranean Aviation Area. This will include extending the European Geostationary Navigation Overlay System (EGNOS) to the Mediterranean partners. Cooperation with the Mediterranean partners in the implementation of a Mediterranean Maritime Strategy should enhance maritime safety, security and surveillance.

The use of electronic communications technologies—on top of satellite broadcasting—greatly facilitated the wave of upheavals in the Mediterranean countries. The widespread use of mobile phones combined with social networking via internet—showed the importance of information society tools and technologies to the circulation of information. In countries where the circulation of information is partially restricted such tools can greatly contribute to the democratisation of societies and the creation of public opinion through the promotion of freedom of expression.

While some regulatory reforms have been undertaken, in many of the southern Mediterranean countries the regulatory environment is still insufficiently developed to exploit the full growth and productivity potentialities of the Information and Communications Technology sector. The main critical factors which remain to be addressed are the creation of truly open markets (which often remain quasi monopolies), the establishment of independent regulators, the creation of a level playing field and of competitive conditions for market players, efficient management of spectrum and safeguards of users' privacy and security.

Moreover, ensuring the security, stability and resilience of the Internet and of other electronic communication technologies is a fundamental building block in democracy. It is necessary to avoid arbitrarily depriving or disrupting citizen's access to them. Given the trans-border and interconnected nature of electronic communications technologies, including the Internet, any unilateral domestic intervention can have severe effects on other parts of the world. The Commission will develop tools to allow the EU, in appropriate cases, to assist civil society organisations or individual citizens to circumvent such arbitrary disruptions.

8. REGIONAL AND SUB-REGIONAL IMPLICATIONS

The dramatic events unfolding in the region may not be necessarily spread evenly across the region and effects of change may vary significantly. The regional dimension has taken on increased importance and regional cooperation will be important in mitigating negative spillovers.

Now, more than ever, changing dynamics in the region mean that urgent progress on the Middle East peace process is vital. The EU should also work in close co-operation with its partners in assisting political and social change in the region. Turkey in particular has a crucial role to play both as an important regional player and as a compelling case of multiparty democracy in a country with a predominantly Muslim population. A fresh view of the regional situation demands that the positive elements of the Barcelona process together with those of the Union for the Mediterranean be integrated in a new approach. The regional co-operation which proved to be most effective was on projects that delivered concrete benefits—in environment, energy, in transport, in trade and in social dialogue.

Regional economic integration should be encouraged. The EU will support projects which promote freer trade between the countries of the region, regulatory approximation, a strengthening of economic governance as well as the infrastructures needed for increased regional trade.

The idea behind the establishment of the Union for the Mediterranean was a positive one—that of a high level partnership between the two shores of the Mediterranean. However we have to recognise that its implementation did not deliver the results we expected. The UfM needs to reform to fully realise its potential. It needs to work more as a catalyst bringing States, International Financial Institutions and the private sector together around concrete projects generating the jobs, innovation and growth that are so badly needed in the region. It should help create the right conditions for progress in the Middle East Peace Process. But, one should not be conditional on the other. Partner countries' participation in these projects could follow the principle of variable geometry depending on their needs and interests. The High Representative and the Commission are ready to play a bigger role in the Union for the Mediterranean in line with the Lisbon Treaty.

9. EU FINANCIAL ASSISTANCE

• Refocusing bilateral programmes of the European Neighbourhood Partnership Instrument

• Providing additional funding

Approximately EUR 4 billion is currently available for the period to the end of 2013 to support our Southern neighbours under the European Neighbourhood and Partnership Instrument. The largest part of this assistance is delivered through bilateral assistance programmes. While many of the programmes underway or in the pipeline address the three priorities in the 'Partnership', the magnitude of recent changes in the region requires an extensive screening and the possible re-focussing of EU aid, in discussion with partner countries.

We have already made clear to both Tunisia and Egypt that we are ready to consider carefully full re-focussing of our bilateral programmes for 2011–13 (respectively EUR 240 and EUR 445 million) to better meet the current challenges and to ensure that our response meets peoples' legitimate aspirations. More generally, throughout the region, programmes will be screened in close cooperation and partnership with the beneficiary countries. We call on Member States to follow a similar screening exercise for their bilateral programmes to achieve maximum impact of EU aid. Within the present budgetary situation, we also consider that the present events will require unprecedented efforts to achieve maximum co-ordination and consistency between Member States' efforts, as well as with the EU. We will also continue to seek maximum interaction and co-ordination with International Financial Institutions.

The screening and re-focussing of assistance is the first step in providing support to help partner governments to consolidate reform and socio-economic development. While no meaningful needs assessment is yet possible, the reform process will require considerable support. This will come from the current EU budget.

Specific attention will also be paid to the encouragement of private sector investment from the EU into the southern Mediterranean. To this end, the Commission will continue to leverage loans from the EIB's FEMIP as well as from other IFIs, through the Neighbourhood Investment Facility (NIF) which provides grant support for infrastructure investment and private sector development. In view of the considerable contribution by the Commission to the Neighbourhood Investment Facility, Member States are encouraged to contribute to replenishing this instrument.

Private foreign direct investment supported through such financial instruments should also benefit from strong investment protection provisions and the Commission will provide an information tool and develop an investment protection framework for European companies interested in investment in the southern Mediterranean.

Finally, macroeconomic assistance may be necessary for some countries which are likely to face short-term difficulties, resulting from the impact of the crisis on trade, investment and tourism flows as well as the disruption of domestic production. Should the IMF have lending programmes in place and provided that external financing needs are confirmed, the countries covered by the European Neighbourhood Policy would be eligible for EU Macro-Financial Assistance (MFA).

10. CONCLUSIONS

These are first proposals to build a new partnership to support change in the Southern Mediterranean. Immediate and short-term help should be accompanied by longer-term assistance when each country is ready to indicate what it needs from its EU partners.

The European Union in its dual dimension of a community of democratic member states and a union of peoples has had to overcome historical hurdles. This success story was possible when hope triumphed over fear and freedom triumphed over repression. This is why there is deep understanding in the EU for the aspirations of the peoples in the Southern Neighbourhood. The EU wants to support them in building real democracies and peaceful and prosperous societies. Each country and people will of course choose their own path and make their own choices. It is rightly for them to decide and not for us to seek to impose solutions. This Communication underlines the determination of the EU in supporting them on their journey to a better future.

[…]

Joint Communication to the European Council, the European Parliament, the Council, the European Economic and Social Committee and the Committee of the Regions, A new response to a changing Neighbourhood, 25.5.2011, COM(2011) 303 final.[1]

Soon after the Arab Spring communication, the impact on the EU's neighbourhood policy at large was discussed in the following communication.

To the East and South of the European Union (EU) lie sixteen countries whose hopes and futures make a direct and significant difference to us. Recent events have brought this into sharper relief, highlighting the challenges we face together. The overthrow of long-standing repressive regimes in Egypt and Tunisia; the ongoing military conflict in Libya, the recent violent crackdown in Syria, continued repression in Belarus and the lingering protracted conflicts in the region, including in the Middle East, require us to look afresh at the EU's relationship with our neighbours. The encouraging progress made by other neighbours, for example by Republic of Moldova in its reform efforts, Ukraine in the negotiations of the Association Agreement or Morocco and Jordan in their announcement of constitutional reform, need also to be supported. The Lisbon Treaty has allowed the EU to strengthen the delivery of its foreign policy: co-operation with neighbouring countries can now be broadened to cover the full range of issues in an integrated and more effective manner. This was a key driver for initiating a review, in consultation with partner countries and other stakeholders, of the European Neighbourhood Policy (ENP) in summer 2010. Recent events throughout the Southern Mediterranean have made the case for this review even more compelling. The EU needs to rise to the historical challenges in our neighbourhood.

Since its inception in 2004, the ENP has promoted a variety of important initiatives, particularly on the trade and economic front, which have allowed the EU and its neighbours to develop stronger relationships in virtually all policy fields, from energy to education, from transport to research. These are now the subject of exchanges and co-operation between the EU and its neighbours. EU assistance has increased and is better targeted. But there is room for improvement on all sides of the relationship. Recent events and the results of the review have shown that EU support to political reforms in neighbouring countries has met with limited results. There is for example a need for greater flexibility and more tailored responses in dealing with rapidly evolving partners and reform needs—whether they are experiencing fast regime change or a prolonged process of reform and democratic consolidation. Coordination between the EU, its Member States and main international partners is essential and can be improved.

A new approach is needed to strengthen the partnership between the EU and the countries and societies of the neighbourhood: to build and consolidate healthy democracies, pursue sustainable economic growth and manage cross-border links.

---

[1] See further Joint Communication to the European Parliament, the Council, the European Economic and Social Committee and the Committee of the Regions, Delivering on a new European Neighbourhood Policy, 15.5.2012, JOIN(2012) 14 final.

The ENP should be a policy of the Union with the Member States aligning their own bilateral efforts in support of its overall political objectives. Equally, the European Parliament has a central role to play in helping to deliver some of its central objectives. And beyond that, the ENP should serve as a catalyst for the wider international community to support democratic change and economic and social development in the region.

This partnership with our neighbours is mutually beneficial. The EU is the main trading partner for most of its neighbours. Sustainable economic development and job creation in partner countries benefits the EU as well. Likewise, managed movement of people is positive for the entire neighbourhood, facilitating the mobility of students, workers and tourists, while discouraging irregular migration and human trafficking. Active engagement between the EU and its neighbours in areas such as education, strengthening and modernising social protection systems and advancing women's rights will do much to support our shared objectives of inclusive growth and job creation.

The new approach must be based on mutual accountability and a shared commitment to the universal values of human rights, democracy and the rule of law. It will involve a much higher level of differentiation allowing each partner country to develop its links with the EU as far as its own aspirations, needs and capacities allow. For those southern and eastern neighbours able and willing to take part, this vision includes closer economic integration and stronger political co-operation on governance reforms, security, conflict-resolution matters, including joint initiatives in international fora on issues of common interest. In the context of the southern Mediterranean, the Commission and the High Representative have already laid out their proposal for a Partnership for Democracy and Shared Prosperity with such partners.

The new approach, as described above, aims to:

(1) provide greater support to partners engaged in building deep democracy—the kind that lasts because the right to vote is accompanied by rights to exercise free speech, form competing political parties, receive impartial justice from independent judges, security from accountable police and army forces, access to a competent and noncorrupt civil service—and other civil and human rights that many Europeans take for granted, such as the freedom of thought, conscience and religion;

(2) support inclusive economic development—so that EU neighbours can trade, invest and grow in a sustainable way, reducing social and regional inequalities, creating jobs for their workers and higher standards of living for their people;

(3) strengthen the two regional dimensions of the European Neighbourhood Policy, covering respectively the Eastern Partnership and the Southern Mediterranean, so that we can work out consistent regional initiatives in areas such as trade, energy, transport or migration and mobility complementing and strengthening our bilateral co-operation;

(4) provide the mechanisms and instruments fit to deliver these objectives.

The partnership will develop with each neighbour on the basis of its needs, capacities and reform objectives. Some partners may want to move further in their integration effort, which will entail a greater degree of alignment with EU policies and rules leading progressively to economic integration in the EU Internal Market. The EU does not seek to impose a model or a ready-made recipe for political reform, but it will insist that each partner country's reform process reflect a clear commitment to universal values that form the basis of our renewed approach. The initiative lies with the partner and EU support will be tailored accordingly.

Increased EU support to its neighbours is conditional. It will depend on progress in building and consolidating democracy and respect for the rule of law. The more and the faster a country progresses in its internal reforms, the more support it will get from the EU. This enhanced support will come in various forms, including increased funding for social and economic development, larger programmes for comprehensive institution-building (CIB), greater market access, increased EIB financing in support of investments; and greater facilitation of mobility. These preferential commitments will be tailored to the needs of each country and to the regional context. They will recognise that meaningful reform comes with significant upfront costs. It will take the reform track record of partners during the 2010–12 period (based on the annual progress reports) into account when deciding on country financial allocations for 2014 and beyond. For countries where reform has not taken place, the EU will reconsider or even reduce funding.

The EU will uphold its policy of curtailing relations with governments engaged in violations of human rights and democracy standards, including by making use of targeted sanctions and other policy measures. Where it takes such measures, it will not only uphold but strengthen further its support to civil society. In applying this more differentiated approach, the EU will keep channels of dialogue open with governments, civil society and other stakeholders. At the same time and in line with the principle of mutual accountability, the EU will ensure that its resources are used in support of the central objectives of the ENP.

The resources that the EU and its international partners are mobilising in support of the democratic transitions in the neighbourhood must cover both the immediate and urgent needs as well as the medium- and longer-term requirements.

1. TO SUPPORT PROGRESS TOWARDS DEEP DEMOCRACY
We shall:

• adapt levels of EU support to partners according to progress on political reforms and building deep democracy

1.1. Supporting 'deep democracy'
A functioning democracy, respect for human rights and the rule of law are fundamental pillars of the EU partnership with its neighbours. There is no set model or a ready-made recipe for political reform. While reforms take place differently from one country to another, several elements are common to building deep and sustainable democracy and require a strong and lasting commitment on the part of governments. They include:

– free and fair elections;
– freedom of association, expression and assembly and a free press and media;
– the rule of law administered by an independent judiciary and right to a fair trial;
– fighting against corruption;
– security and law enforcement sector reform (including the police) and the establishment of democratic control over armed and security forces.

Reform based on these elements will not only strengthen democracy but help to create the conditions for sustainable and inclusive economic growth, stimulating trade and investment. They are the main benchmarks against which the EU will assess progress and adapt levels of support.

1.2. A partnership with societies
We shall:
• establish partnerships in each neighbouring country and make EU support more accessible to civil society organisations through a dedicated Civil Society Facility
• support the establishment of a European Endowment for Democracy to help political parties, non-registered NGOs and trade unions and other social partners
• promote media freedom by supporting civil society organisations' (CSOs') unhindered access to the internet and the use of electronic communications technologies
• reinforce human rights dialogues
A thriving civil society empowers citizens to express their concerns, contribute to policymaking and hold governments to account. It can also help ensure that economic growth becomes more inclusive. Key to making any of this happen is the guarantee of the freedoms of expression, association and assembly. Another challenge is to facilitate the emergence of democratic political parties that represent the broad spectrum of the views and approaches present in society so that they can compete for power and popular support. This challenge of fostering civil society and pluralism is felt throughout the neighbourhood but is particularly acute for countries engaged in fast political change or where repressive political regimes continue to stifle pluralism and diversity.

In order to address this situation and support political actors striving for democratic change in their countries (especially political parties and non-registered NGOs or trade unions and other social partners), the High Representative and the Commission support the establishment of a European Endowment for Democracy. This Endowment will seek to bring greater influence and consistency to the efforts of the EU, its Member States and several of the large European political foundations that are already active in this field.

Civil society plays a pivotal role in advancing women's rights, greater social justice and respect for minorities as well as environmental protection and resource efficiency. The EU will support this greater political role for non-state actors through a partnership with societies, helping CSOs to develop their advocacy capacity, their ability to monitor reform and their role in implementing and evaluating EU programmes. In-country EU Delegations will seek to bring partner countries' governments and civil society together in a structured dialogue on key areas of our co-operation. EU funding for such actions could be delivered through the establishment of a dedicated Civil Society Facility for the neighbourhood.

Media freedom and free access to information are key elements of functioning democracies. Social networks and new technologies play a significant role in promoting democratic change. EU support is already available through the European Instrument for Democracy and Human Rights (EIDHR). Additional tools may be developed to allow the EU, in appropriate cases, to assist civil society organisations or individual citizens to have unhindered access to the internet and other forms of electronic communications technologies, as well as independent media in print, radio and television.

Commitment to human rights and fundamental freedoms through multilateral treaties and bilateral agreements is essential. But these commitments are not always matched by action. Ratification of all the relevant international and regional instruments and full compliance with their provisions, should underpin our partnership. This includes a strong commitment to promoting gender equality, in line with the major role once again played by women in recent events in the South, fighting against all forms of discrimination, respecting freedom of religion and protecting the rights of refugees and beneficiaries of international protection. Reinforced human rights dialogues will allow monitoring of commitments in this area, including addressing cases of human rights violations. Boosting cooperation with the Council of Europe could also help in promoting compliance.

Parliaments can build links between our societies. The EuroNest Parliamentary Assembly (the joint Assembly of the European Parliament and counterparts from Eastern Partnership countries), the Euro-Mediterranean Parliamentary Assembly and Joint Parliamentary Committees between the European Parliament and partner countries' Parliaments constitute an essential forum for dialogue and increased mutual understanding between decision-makers. Parliamentarians can also bring a meaningful contribution to enhancing reform efforts and monitoring commitments in each country's ENP Action Plan, including on major political and human rights issues.

1.3. Intensifying our political and security co-operation
We shall:
• enhance EU involvement in solving protracted conflicts
• make joined-up use of the Common Foreign and Security Policy and other EU instruments
• promote joint action with European Neighbourhood Policy partners in international fora on key security issues

The Lisbon Treaty provides the EU with a unique opportunity to become a more effective actor. Nowhere is this more relevant than in our neighbourhood. But rising to the challenge requires that EU and Member States policies be much more closely aligned than in the past, in order to deliver the common message and the coherence that will make our actions effective. EU instruments and policies will be effective only if properly backed by Member States policies. Business as usual is no longer an option if we want to make our neighbourhood a safer place and protect our interests.

The persistence of protracted conflicts affecting a number of partner countries is a serious security challenge to the whole region. EU geopolitical, economic and security interests are directly affected by continuing instability. The Israeli-Palestinian conflict and other conflicts in the Middle East, the South Caucasus, the Republic of Moldova and Western Sahara continue to affect sizeable populations, feed radicalisation, drain considerable local and international resources, and act as powerful impediments to reform.

The EU is already active in seeking to resolve several of these conflicts. The EU is part of the Quartet on the Middle East. It co-chairs the Geneva talks directed at peace and security in Georgia. It participates as an observer in the '5+2' talks on the

Transnistrian conflict in the Republic of Moldova. It would be ready to step up its involvement in formats where it is not yet represented, e.g. the OSCE Minsk Group on the Nagorno-Karabakh conflict. The EU intends to enhance its support for confidence-building and outreach to breakaway territories, for international efforts and structures related to the conflicts, and, once that stage is reached, for the implementation of settlements. It will also continue to oppose border changes brought about through use of military force. Many of the instruments we use everywhere in the neighbourhood to promote economic integration and sectoral co-operation could also be mobilised to support confidence-building and conflict-resolution objectives. The EU is also ready to develop, together with the relevant international organisations and key partners, postconflict reconstruction scenarios which could act as a further incentive in the resolution of conflicts by showing the tangible benefits of peaceful settlements.

Where the EU is already engaged operationally on the ground, e.g. with the EU Monitoring Mission in Georgia, the EU Border Assistance Mission in Republic of Moldova/Ukraine, or the EU Police Mission and the EU Border Assistance Mission Rafah in the occupied Palestinian territories, further steps will be taken to exploit the synergies between this operational presence and the efforts to promote reforms. In particular, wherever it is appropriate, the EU will offer to back partner countries' efforts to reform their justice and security sector reforms with rule of law missions or other Common Foreign and Security Policy (CFSP) instruments that they will consider useful.

Looking beyond conflict resolution, the EU will make full use of the Lisbon Treaty's provisions in addressing other security concerns and specific common interests, e.g. energy and resource security, climate change, non-proliferation, combating international terrorism and trans-border organised crime, and the fight against drugs. It will engage with ENP partner countries to undertake joint actions in international fora (e.g. UN, international conferences) on CFSP issues, as well as other global issues.

2. TO SUPPORT SUSTAINABLE ECONOMIC AND SOCIAL DEVELOPMENT

We shall:

• support partner countries' adoption of policies conducive to stronger, sustainable and more inclusive growth, to the development of micro, small and medium-sized companies and to job creation

• strengthen industrial cooperation and support improvements to the business environment

• help to organise events to promote investment

• promote direct investment from EU SMEs and micro-credit

• build on the pilot regional development programmes to tackle economic disparities between regions

• launch pilot programmes to support agricultural and rural development

• enhance the macro-economic policy dialogue with partners making the most advanced economic reforms

• improve the effectiveness of Macro-Financial Assistance by streamlining its decision-making process

• enhance dialogue on employment and social policies

2.1. Sustainable economic growth and job creation

Economic and social challenges in our neighbourhood are immense. Poverty is rife, life expectancy is often low, youth unemployment is high and the participation of women in political and economic life is low in several countries of the region. Natural capital is being eroded and the rising food and energy prices have severe effects across the neighbourhood. Most partner countries have weak and poorly diversified economies that remain vulnerable to external economic shocks. The immediate objectives are therefore creating jobs, boosting growth, improving social protection and revitalising sectors affected by recent crises (such as tourism). Tackling these challenges is crucial to ensure the sustainability of political reforms and can also contribute to reaching the Millennium Development Goals. Feeble growth, rising unemployment and an increased gap between rich and poor are likely to fuel instability.

The ENP will continue encouraging partner countries' adoption of policies conducive to stronger and more inclusive growth. This includes support for efforts to improve the business environment such as simplifying procedures and catering to small and medium-sized businesses and to promote employability. Partner countries' efforts to strengthen respect for the rule of law and to fight corruption will also have a positive impact on the business environment, facilitating increased foreign direct investment and technology transfer which in turn stimulate innovation and job creation. The EU will pay particular attention to the challenge faced by countries emerging from political change—helping to organise initiatives such as investors' conferences to clarify national investment priorities and seek to build investors' confidence. A powerful signal for investors and traders would also be an enhanced investment protection scheme. The Commission will explore options to provide legal security to investors in neighbouring countries.

To provide additional support for SMEs the Commission will also discuss with the EIB and other stakeholders the possible role for the European Investment Fund in partner countries and will examine measures, including guarantees to promote direct investment from EU SMEs and micro-credits.

The Commission can also contribute to addressing high unemployment and poverty through pilot programmes supporting agricultural and rural development, as well as pilot regional development programmes, drawing on the EU's extensive experience in these fields.

The regional development programmes can contribute to addressing economic imbalances and disparities between regions that undermine the capacity of a country's economy as a whole. The current pilot programmes will help members of the Eastern Partnership identify appropriate structures and activities to address these challenges, within their territories and if appropriate cross-border with their neighbours in the region. A similar approach will be explored for the southern neighbourhood.

Policy dialogue will continue on macro-economic governance and budgetary sustainability. This macro-economic dialogue will be enhanced with those partners that go furthest in their economic integration with the EU and be based on a review of macro-economic policies and key structural reforms. This will be accompanied by an enhanced dialogue on employment and social policies.

The Macro-Financial Assistance (MFA) instrument may be mobilised to assist partner countries to address short-term balance-of-payments difficulties. In the short term this is most relevant to those dealing with the immediate economic and social impact of the recent political changes. The Commission will propose a Framework Regulation in order to make the decision-making process of MFA allocation more efficient, provide a more transparent legal basis for this instrument and refine some of its criteria.

2.2. Strengthening trade ties
We shall:
• negotiate Deep and Comprehensive Free Trade Areas with willing and able partners
• further develop trade concessions, especially in those sectors most likely to offer an immediate boost to partners' economies
Most of our neighbours rely on the EU as their main export market and import source. Trade in goods and services is a powerful instrument to stimulate economic growth, enhance competitiveness and support economic recovery. It is therefore essential that we establish with each of them mutually beneficial and ambitious trade arrangements matching their needs and their economic capacities.

The main and most effective vehicle for developing closer trade ties is the Deep and Comprehensive Free Trade Area (DCFTA). DCFTAs provide for the gradual dismantling of trade barriers and aim for regulatory convergence in areas that have an impact on trade, in particular sanitary and phytosanitary rules (SPS), animal welfare, customs and border procedures, competition and public procurement. They are designed to be dynamic in order to keep pace with regulatory developments in the EU's Internal Market. For the most advanced partners, a DCFTA can lead to a progressive economic integration with the EU Internal Market. Through progressive approximation of EU rules and practices, DCFTAs require a high degree of commitment to complex and broad-ranging reforms. This requires strong institutional capacity. The reforms can be politically challenging and require the involvement of the business community as well as other interested parties. To embark on negotiations, partner countries must be WTO members and address key recommendations enabling them to comply with the resulting commitments. They must also have made sufficient progress towards common values and principles.

Trade mostly relies on a bilateral approach between the EU and each partner. This allows the most advanced countries to move faster and is consistent with the differentiation principle. The principle is also consistent with the long-term vision of an economic community emerging between the EU and its ENP partners. Regional economic integration is important to boost trade between partners and develop wider economic networks. In the longer term, such a community would be based on a common regulatory framework and improved market access for goods and services among ENP partners and the EU. Such an approach would consider allowing partners that have a fully functioning independent judiciary, an efficient public administration and have made significant progress towards eradicating corruption, into the non-regulated area of the Internal Market for goods. This could only happen once participating countries have reached a sufficient level of administrative and legal reliability.

In the shorter term, for those partners not ready or willing to embark on DCFTA negotiations, other measures can be taken to boost and facilitate trade. Taking into account the circumstances and level of ambition of each partner country, the EU will seek to extend trade concessions in existing agreements or ongoing negotiations, notably in those sectors best positioned to provide an immediate boost to partners' economies including asymmetry in the pace of liberalisation to take into account the circumstances of each partner country. Greater market access for goods can be achieved through Agreements on Conformity Assessment and Acceptance of industrial products (ACAAs), which will allow free movement of industrial products in specific sectors through mutual acceptance of conformity certificates. The ACAAs aim to cover all sectors where the legislation is harmonised at EU level. A partner having reached that stage would in fact become part of a free trade area for industrial products between the EU, the EEA and Turkey. Close cooperation with European bodies and organisations in the areas of standardisation, conformity assessment, and metrology can facilitate ACAAs' implementation. In order to speed the preparation of ACAAs, the Commission is ready to enhance the technical support given to our partners. ACAAs are likely to be signed with Tunisia and Egypt already in 2011.

Further progress could also be made to encourage trade flows between partner countries as well as with the EU. The rapid implementation of the new Convention on pan-Euro-Mediterranean preferential rules of origin will be one important element for the partners in the South. The Commission will examine how the Convention can be extended to other ENP partners and will make appropriate proposals.

The EU will continue to support reforms to help partners build their capacities, through providing public sector expertise, including through Comprehensive Institution-Building programmes or other mechanisms such as twinning and TAIEX. This will help partners meet standards for food safety, animal and plant health and animal welfare and hence enhance their export potential. Likewise, in order to assist the agricultural sectors to modernise, the EU will offer rural development programmes so as to assist inter alia in improving agricultural and food product quality.

2.3. Enhancing sector cooperation

We shall:

• enhance sector co-operation, with a particular focus on knowledge and innovation, climate change and the environment, energy, transport and technology

• facilitate partner countries' participation in the work of selected EU agencies and programmes

Enhanced cooperation can take place in all sectors relevant to the Internal Market, ranging from social policy and public health to consumer protection, statistics, company law, research and technological development, maritime policy, tourism, space and many others. Cooperation and exchange will be stepped up significantly, in line with the more-for-more approach, in the following areas:

• The EU will propose to neighbouring partners to work towards the development of a Common Knowledge and Innovation Space. This would pull together several existing strands of cooperation: policy dialogue, national and regional capacity-building, co-operation in research and innovation, and increased mobility opportunities for students, researchers and academics. In parallel co-operation in the area of higher education will be expanded through increased support for student and academic staff mobility within university partnerships (under Erasmus Mundus) and structured cooperation for university modernisation (through Tempus).

• The EU will join up efforts with its neighbours on climate change by enhanced cooperation to address low-carbon development and improve resilience to climate impacts (adaptation), with a view to implementing the Cancun agreement and moving towards a comprehensive global climate regime. The EU and partner countries should also pursue a higher level of environment protection aimed at enforcing higher standards of air and water quality, improved environmental governance, higher resource efficiency, protection of biodiversity and ecosystems and supporting the necessary infrastructure investments.

• Energy co-operation will be stepped up through increased energy policy dialogue aiming at further market integration, improved energy security based on converging regulatory frameworks, including on safety and environmental standards, the development of new partnerships on renewable energy sources and energy efficiency, and nuclear safety. In the medium term this could lead to extending the Energy Community Treaty to neighbours not yet party to it or, building on its experience, establishing a complementary 'EU–Southern Mediterranean Energy Community'.

• The Commission will propose a new framework for transport co-operation, aiming at closer market integration in the transport sector, notably extending trans-European transport networks (TEN-Ts) to partner countries, addressing administrative bottlenecks with a focus on safety and security issues (including issues such as air and rail traffic management and maritime transport), and enhancing co-operation with various EU transport agencies.

• The Commission also supports a more strategic approach and cooperation on maritime affairs, aiming at enhancing cooperation across maritime sectors and allowing for sustainable economic development.

• Recent developments in the South Mediterranean countries have shown the importance of information and communication technologies as tools for political and social change. Cooperation with partner countries will therefore be stepped up to support the development of a digital economy, using ICT to tackle national and global challenges. Finally, the EU will further facilitate partner countries' participation in the work of EU agencies and the EU programmes which are open to them. This has been on offer for some years and has led to some co-operation in areas such as drugs monitoring or aviation safety. The Commission will put together a list of programmes in which partners may participate as a matter of priority, with a focus on those offering opportunities for youth and people-to-people contacts. It will also support partner countries in fulfilling the legislative pre-requisites for participating in EU agencies and provide support for covering some of the associated costs of participation.

2.4. Migration and mobility
We shall:
• pursue the process of visa facilitation for selected ENP partners and visa liberalisation for those most advanced
• develop existing Mobility Partnerships and establish new ones
• support the full use by Member States of opportunities offered by the EU Visa Code
Mobility and people-to-people contacts are fundamental to promoting mutual understanding and economic development. They are indispensable for trade, especially in

services, as well as for exchanging ideas, spreading innovation, tackling employment and social issues, establishing strong relationships between companies, universities and civil society organisations.

Labour mobility is an area where the EU and its neighbours can complement each other. The EU's workforce is ageing and labour shortages will develop in specific areas. Our neighbourhood has well-educated, young and talented workers who can fill these gaps. In attracting this talent, the EU is conscious of the risks of brain drain, which could require additional mitigating support measures.

Partner countries are also important countries of origin and transit for irregular migrants. Cooperation on fighting irregular migration is essential to reduce the human suffering and diminished security that is generated. Such cooperation will be one of the conditions on which Mobility partnerships will be based.

The ENP aims to develop a mutually beneficial approach where economic development in partner countries and in the EU, well-managed legal migration, capacity-building on border management, asylum and effective law-enforcement co-operation go hand in hand. This approach is in line with the three pillars of the EU Global Approach and the recently adopted Communication on migration: better organising legal migration, maximising the positive impact of migration on development, enhancing capacity-building in border and migration management. The promotion and respect of migrants' rights are also an integral part of the approach.

Mobility Partnerships provide the comprehensive frameworks to ensure that the movement of persons between the EU and a third country is well-managed. These partnerships bring together all the measures which ensure that mobility is mutually beneficial. They provide for better access to legal migration channels and to strengthen capacities for border management and handle irregular migration. They can include initiatives to assist partner countries to establish or improve labour migration management, including recruitment, vocational and language training, development and recognition of skills, and return and reintegration of migrants. With a view to enhancing the mobility of citizens between partner countries and the EU, in particular for students, researchers and businesspeople, the Commission calls on Member States to make full use of the opportunities offered by the EU Visa Code. It will examine ways to support them in this process and to monitor implementation. In this context the possibilities to waive the visa fee and to issue multi-entry visa to the categories of visa applicants referred to should be underlined.

So far amongst our neighbours, Mobility Partnerships have been established with the Republic of Moldova and Georgia. The Commission believes that various countries in our neighbourhood would be good candidates for such partnerships. The Commission will seek to conclude negotiations with Armenia and prepare for the launch of negotiations with e.g. Morocco, Tunisia and Egypt.

The EU will continue to assist Ukraine and Republic of Moldova in their efforts to implement visa liberalisation action plans. Along with the visa facilitation and readmission agreements in force or under elaboration with Eastern Partnership countries, the EU should also seek to conclude visa facilitation agreements, simultaneously with readmission agreements, with partner countries in the South. All such agreements will require co-operation with the EU on migration, mobility and security. Specific measures will need to be taken to prevent irregular migration, manage their borders effectively, ensure document security and fight organised crime, including trafficking in human beings and smuggling of migrants. In the long-term, gradual steps towards visa liberalisation should be considered on a case-by-case basis, where conditions for well-managed and secure mobility are in place.

Concerning asylum, the EU will contribute to strengthening international protection in the region by continuing the implementation of the Regional Protection Programme for Belarus, Republic of Moldova and Ukraine. Circumstances allowing, it will also start implementing the Regional Protection Programme for Egypt, Libya and Tunisia. Other initiatives by individual ENP partners in this area will also be supported. Resettlement of refugees in the EU must be an integral part of the EU's efforts to support neighbouring countries confronted with significant refugee flows.

3. TO BUILD EFFECTIVE REGIONAL PARTNERSHIPS WITHIN THE EUROPEAN NEIGHBOURHOOD POLICY

While fully recognising their diversity, the EU offers partnership to each individual neighbour through a single policy, based on mutual accountability. The eastern and southern dimensions of the ENP seek to complement that single policy by fostering regional cooperation and developing regional synergies and responses to the specific geographic, economic and social challenges of each region. They build on the different historical legacies of past EU policies towards the regions. In the South, fifteen years of Euro-Mediterranean cooperation across all areas of the relationship have been complemented recently by the Union for the Mediterranean. The Eastern Partnership has significantly boosted relations between the EU and its eastern neighbours over the past two years.

3.1. Strengthening the Eastern Partnership
We shall:
• move to conclude and implement Association Agreements including DCFTAs
• pursue democratisation
• pursue the visa facilitation and liberalisation process
• enhance sectoral cooperation, notably in the area of rural development
• promote benefits of the Eastern Partnership to citizens
• increase work with civil society and social partners.

The establishment of the Eastern Partnership (EaP) has strengthened mutual relations with partner countries in Eastern Europe and the Southern Caucasus. It has helped to initiate and consolidate a difficult process of change. The region has seen general progress towards democracy over the past decade, including situations of regime change. The region continues to face major economic challenges—it is poor, with significant differences between individual countries, and susceptible to external factors and influences.

The degree to which the partners have addressed key elements of the Eastern Partnership varies (for example respect for universal values of democracy, human rights and the rule of law; continuous efforts to reform; and a strengthened focus on the resolution of protracted conflicts). While some are clearly committed to reaching its full potential, others have only made piecemeal progress. The EU will ensure that partners most advanced and committed to the democratic reforms that underpin the Eastern Partnership benefit the most from it. At the same time, Eastern Partnership instruments need to be better tailored to the situations of individual countries, based on experience following this first phase of implementation—notably by identifying tools to bridge the long period required to negotiate far-reaching and complex Association Agreements.

Association Agreements (AAs), most of which include DCFTAs, offer each Eastern Partnership country the opportunity to choose the level of ambition it wishes to pursue in driving forward integration and reform. With sustained commitment and support by the EU, partner countries can use the Agreement for regulatory and institutional convergence. They include alignment with EU laws, norms and standards leading progressively to economic integration in the internal market.

Association Agreement negotiations have started with five partner countries and provide a sound political basis for advancing relations. DCFTA negotiations within the framework of the AA have started with Ukraine and will start with other partners as relevant conditions are met. In spite of their relatively small size, and therefore the limited trade exchanges between Eastern Partnership countries and the EU, DCFTAs are of high priority for the EU as efficient tools to reinforce the political and economic links between the EU and its Eastern neighbours. In order to help partner countries develop the administrative capacity required for in-depth reforms, the Eastern Partnership also provides for Comprehensive Institution-Building (CIB) programmes. To complement this, Pilot Regional Development Programmes are the newest EU instrument to assist partners in addressing economic, social and regional imbalances. They will help partners to establish appropriate structures and activities to address regional challenges.

Some EaP countries attach great importance to their European identity and the development of closer relations with the EU enjoys strong public support. The values on which the European Union is built—namely freedom, democracy, respect for human rights and fundamental freedoms, and the rule of law—are also at the heart of the process of political association and economic integration which the Eastern Partnership offers. These are the same values that are enshrined in article 2 of the European Union Treaty and on which articles 8 and 49 are based.

People-to-people contacts are an important part of the partnership. The EU will continue to assist Ukraine and the Republic of Moldova in their efforts to implement visa liberalisation action plans. These Plans could become models for other Eastern Partnership countries. In the meantime, Eastern Partnership countries should fully exploit opportunities offered by visa facilitation.

Eastern partners have benefited from five flagship initiatives in the areas of border management, SME development, energy cooperation, civil protection and environmental governance. These programmes will now be adapted to better support bilateral partnership objectives. For example, work under the Integrated Border Management flagship initiative is increasingly geared towards supporting partners in fulfilling the conditions for visa facilitation and liberalisation. Boosting the visibility of the Eastern Partnership's bilateral and multilateral activities is important to explain their benefits to the general public. To help increase regional solidarity, the EU should develop its support for sub-regional cooperation that concentrates on specific subjects involving fewer partners. The multilateral framework has to be used more strategically to advance bilateral relations between our partners, including in the area of conflict resolution.

In line with the aim of the renewed ENP to focus on links between societies, the EU will promote more intensive engagement with stakeholders, including parliaments in the framework of EURONEST, established by the European Parliament; regional actors in cooperation with the Committee of the Regions; business leaders, in the frame of an Eastern Partnership Business Forum; and civil society and social partners building on the Eastern Partnership Civil Society Forum and its national platforms.

Co-operation under the Eastern Partnership will continue with policy dialogue in areas such as:

• education, youth and culture: expanding participation in programmes such as Erasmus Mundus, Tempus, Youth in Action and eTwinning; opening of future new EU programmes such as Lifelong Learning to Eastern Partnership countries; follow-up of the Special Action Culture Programme 2009–10 and of the Eastern Partnership Culture Programme;

• transport: connecting infrastructure networks of the EU and its Eastern partners;

• energy, environment, climate change: intensified dialogue, following the establishment of the Eastern Europe Energy Efficiency and Environment Partnership (E5P), and accession to the European Energy Community Treaty by Ukraine and Republic of Moldova in order to strengthen co-operation on energy security;

• knowledge sharing, research and information society: full integration of the research and education communities in the region within the e-infrastructure (e.g. the GÉANT pan-European data network for networking, and the European Grid Infrastructure for grids and distributed computing).

• customs and law enforcement issues on the basis of Strategic Frameworks for Customs Cooperation with Ukraine, Republic of Moldova and Belarus as well as cooperation in the area of fight against smuggling;

• rural development measures (in line with the European Neighbourhood Programme for Agriculture and Rural Development);

• employment and social policies;

• justice, freedom and security on the basis of the Justice and Home Affairs Eastern Partnership Action Plan to be presented later this year under the Stockholm Programme, including mobility partnerships;

• Common Security and Defence Policy (CSDP).

EU Member States, third countries and International Financial Institutions (IFIs) have shown interest in furthering the goals of the Eastern Partnership and supporting projects of strategic importance. Additional resources are being mobilised from the Neighbourhood Investment Facility (NIF), bilateral partners and IFIs, in particular the EIB, the EBRD and the World Bank. Such co-operation should be pursued dynamically, building on the establishment of the SME Facility, the EIB's Eastern Partners Facility and its Eastern Partnership Technical Assistance Trust Fund to which the EU and Member States are invited to contribute.

The Eastern Partnership Information and Co-ordination Group gathers IFIs and third countries interested in donor coordination and more generally in the development of Eastern Partnership, including Canada, Japan, Norway, Russia, Switzerland, Turkey and the USA. This informal co-operation will be intensified in line with the interests of Eastern Partnership partners.

The second Eastern Partnership Summit will take place in September 2011 in Warsaw. The European Commission and the High Representative will subsequently put forward a roadmap to guide the future implementation of the Eastern Partnership, drawing on the results of the Summit.

3.2. Building the Partnership for Democracy and Shared Prosperity in the Southern Mediterranean

We shall:

• undertake Comprehensive Institution-Building programmes similar to those implemented with the eastern partners

• launch a dialogue on migration, mobility and security with Tunisia, Morocco and Egypt (as a first step towards a Mobility Partnership)

• strengthen Euro-Mediterranean industrial cooperation

• launch pilot programmes to support agricultural and rural development

• focus the Union for the Mediterranean on concrete projects with clear benefits to populations of the Mediterranean region

• advance sub-regional cooperation

• enhance dialogue on employment and social policies

The ENP must provide an ambitious response to the momentous changes currently ongoing in the Southern Mediterranean region. The joint Communication on a Partnership for Democracy and Shared Prosperity in the Southern Mediterranean, issued on 8 March outlined first elements of the EU's offer of a new partnership with partners engaged in building democracies and extensive reforms. The three main directions along which the EU intends to further develop its relations with its Mediterranean partners are carried over into this communication: democratic transformation and institution-building; a stronger partnership with the people; and sustainable and inclusive economic development. Through its different policies and instruments, the partnership will be comprehensive and wide, but will be more clearly differentiated according to the specific needs as well as the level of ambition of each partner. The EU is already engaged in a process of strengthening relations with a number of partners, notably through granting 'advanced status'.

Those partners that want to establish a Partnership for Democracy and Shared Prosperity with the EU are expected to make progress on the key elements highlighted in section 1.1. The long-term vision for our most advanced Mediterranean partners is close political association with the EU and economic integration into the Internal Market. In the short term, the following options will be available to partners making progress on reforms.

To support democratic transformation, Comprehensive Institution-Building programmes similar to those implemented with its Eastern neighbours will be set up: they will provide substantial expertise and financial support to build the capacity of key administrative bodies (customs, enforcement agencies, justice) and will be targeted in priority towards those institutions most needed to sustain democratisation.

To build a stronger partnership with people, the Commission will launch a dialogue on migration, mobility and security with e.g. Tunisia, Morocco and Egypt (as a first step towards a Mobility Partnership). These proposals are further detailed in the Communication on migration, mobility and security in the southern neighbourhood. School co-operation (eTwinning), student and academic staff mobility within university partnerships (Erasmus Mundus), structured cooperation for university modernisation (Tempus), and mobility of Young People (Youth in Action) will also be expanded to provide a better support to the youth. New initiatives may also be promoted in the field of culture.

In the short term, to build sustainable and inclusive economic development, the EU will step up efforts to enhance the trade provisions of the existing Association Agreements by concluding the ongoing negotiations on agriculture and those on services and the right of establishment. Selected southern neighbours will also be given the opportunity to enter into preparations for future DCFTA negotiations. To accompany the structural adjustments linked to market opening and promote inclusive growth, the Commission will finance pilot programmes for agricultural and rural development and, drawing on the experience of the Eastern Partnership, pilot regional development programmes.

The Commission will promote industrial cooperation at Euro-Mediterranean level by continuing to implement the Euro-Mediterranean Charter for Enterprise, by adapting the Charter to the needs of SMEs in line with the EU's Small Business Act and by sharing good practices and opening activities and networks in priority sectors (textiles, tourism, raw materials). It will enhance dialogue on employment and social policy and encourage effective social dialogue including through the Euro-Mediterranean Social Dialogue Forum. Regulatory cooperation on a regional level could facilitate trade exchanges and improve the investment climate. The development of an efficient, safe, secure and sustainable multi-modal Trans-Mediterranean Transport Network will also contribute to sustainable and inclusive economic development. The Commission is already working with the EIB and the International Maritime Organisation to identify pilot actions to improve cooperation between maritime sectors in the Mediterranean.

The Union for the Mediterranean (UfM) which complements the bilateral relations between EU and partners should enhance its potential to organise effective and result-oriented regional cooperation. It further ensures the inclusive character of regional cooperation in the Mediterranean by including actors such as Turkey and the Western Balkan countries. The High Representative and the Commission are ready to play a bigger role in the UfM in line with the Lisbon Treaty. Revitalising the UfM requires a switch to a more pragmatic and project-based approach. The UfM Secretariat must operate as a catalyst to bring states, the EIB, International Financial Institutions and the private sector together around concrete economic projects of strategic importance and generating jobs, innovation and growth throughout the region. Partner countries' participation in these projects could follow the principle of variable geometry depending on their needs and interests. Co-financing for specific infrastructure projects from the EU budget could be provided through the Neighbourhood Investment Facility. In the current economic and political context, flagship projects identified at the Paris Summit remain fully relevant, notably the Mediterranean Solar Plan, the de-pollution of the Mediterranean or the development of Motorways of the Sea and land highways, the

Mediterranean Business Development Initiative. To support sustainable development, implementation of existing regional agreements such as the Barcelona Convention for the Protection of the Marine Environment and Coastal Region of the Mediterranean should be given greater priority.

Finally, sub-regional co-operation involving fewer neighbours and concentrating on specific subjects can bring benefits and can create greater solidarity. Sub-regional coop-eration in the Maghreb could be advanced, for example through supporting greater physical interconnection. The EU will put forward specific proposals in the near future, including on ways to support the possible opening of borders in the region.

4. A SIMPLIFIED AND COHERENT POLICY AND PROGRAMME FRAMEWORK
4.1. Clearer priorities through stronger political steering
We shall:

• Focus ENP Action Plans and EU assistance on a smaller number of priorities, backed with more precise benchmarks:

Bilateral relations between the EU and each of its neighbours have become stronger in recent years. Close and intensive dialogue has developed not only on general polit-ical matters but on all specific areas of our co-operation. These very close relation-ships and a higher level of commitment call for much stronger political dialogue and co-operation. The Lisbon Treaty provides the means for the European Union to deliver coherent and consistent policies and programmes by bringing together strands of EU foreign and assistance policy that were previously run by different institutions.

There is a consensus among partner countries and Member States that more substan-tive Association Councils would allow for more in-depth discussion at political level. But political dialogue need not be reduced to a yearly discussion in the Association Council: more frequent and more ad hoc opportunities should be envisaged when conditions so require. A more continuous and more intimate political dialogue is key to establish the confidence and trust required to tackle our common challenges. In addition, the Commission intends to enhance dialogue on sectoral policies (such as energy, education, youth, migration and transport) with their Ministerial counterparts in partner countries.

While ENP Action Plans remain the framework for our general cooperation, the EU will suggest to partners that they focus on a limited number of short and medium-term priorities, incorporating more precise benchmarks and a clearer sequencing of actions. The EU will adapt the priorities for its financial assistance accordingly. This list of pri-orities will set the political pace and help both the EU and each neighbour to produce key deliverables, within a mutually agreed timeframe. This will also allow better linking of policy objectives and assistance programming. Building on that basis programming documents can be simplified and focus on identifying Action Plan priorities requiring particular EU assistance.

Further simplification of provision of financial assistance will also be sought in drafting the new European Neighbourhood Instrument (ENI) regulation in the context of the next multiannual financial framework, in order to translate the need for a more flexible and more focused delivery of financial assistance into practice.

In parallel, the EU will continue to report on an annual basis on progress in line with the Action Plans. Reports will put greater focus on democracy and a stronger link between the outcomes measured in these reports, assistance and levels of financial support will be developed over time.

4.2. Funding

We shall:

• re-focus and target foreseen and programmed funds in the ENPI as well as other relevant external policy instruments in the light of this new approach

• provide additional resources of over EUR 1 billion until 2013 to address the urgent needs of our neighbourhood

• mobilize budgetary reinforcement from various sources

• swiftly proceed with submitting concurring budget proposals to the Budget Authority (transfers for 2011, Amending Letter for 2012, re-programming for 2013).

Implementing the new approach of the neighbourhood policy based on mutual accountability and a shared commitment to the universal values of human rights, democracy and the rule of law requires additional resources of up to EUR 1242 million until 2013. These resources are in addition to the EUR 5700 million provided under the European Neighbourhood and Partnership Instrument for 2011–2013. In the event of new emergencies, funding of actions targeted at the region under thematic instruments and crisis intervention mechanisms in the EU budget constitute fresh resources. Financial support will be provided to further reinforce the partnership with people across the region, support sustainable and inclusive growth, cover the additional needs stemming from the democratic transformation of partner countries, advance the achievement of Millennium Development Goals and fund the new initiatives stemming from this review, notably in the areas of partnership with societies, rural and regional development (see sections 3.1 and 3.2 above). This includes an amount of up to EUR 250 million stemming from reflows from older loan and risk-capital operations to be made available to the Facility for Euro-Mediterranean Investment and Partnership (FEMIP) to promote growth and employment by financing new operations and to support the long-term financing needs of SMEs. To that effect, the Council should adopt the Commission proposal to amend Article 23 of the ENPI regulation.

These additional resources will be provided through reallocations from within Heading 4 of the 2007–2013 multi-annual financial framework, and by making use of the unallocated margin under the expenditure ceiling in 2012 and—to the extent necessary—through the Flexibility Instrument. The Commission will submit an Amending Letter to Draft Budget 2012 shortly.

The Commission is currently reflecting on how best to integrate the overall country situation regarding democracy, accountability, the rule of law and sound financial management into its decisions on budget support arrangements, and will outline its approach in the upcoming Communication on budget support. This should also provide the necessary flexibility to tailor levels and types of support to each partner's reform track record.

4.3. Involving the EIB and EBRD
We shall:

• secure additional loan possibilities by the EIB and the EBRD, including an extension of the latter's mandate to selected Southern partners

To support large infrastructure projects that can help connect the EU with its neighbourhood, boost development and address key energy, environment and transport challenges, it is important to ensure that the European Investment Bank and other regional development banks such as the European Bank for Reconstruction and Development have sufficient financial resources. The Commission supports the increase in the external mandate of the EIB for both eastern and southern neighbours as well as the extension of the EBRD mandate to selected southern Mediterranean countries. The EIB and EBRD can deliver on EU policy objectives together by maximising their comparative advantages. EBRD operations in the Southern Mediterranean countries should support EU policy objectives and should not lead to a transfer of resources from operations in the EU Eastern Neighbourhood.

The adoption of the revised EIB external mandate would provide for increased EIB lending under EU guarantee across the EU Neighbourhood. In particular, if the Council approves the additional lending envelope of EUR 1 billion proposed by the European Parliament, the EIB could provide almost EUR 6 billion to the Mediterranean countries over 2011–2013. The necessary funds up to 90 million will be mobilised to provide the budgetary guarantees needed to match the increase in EIB loans towards the Mediterranean region.

4.4. Planning for 2013 and beyond
We shall:

• promote more flexible and simpler aid delivery under the post-2013 successor to the present ENPI;

• step up efforts of co-ordination between the EU, its Member States and other key IFIs and bilateral donors.

In its July 2010 conclusions on the ENP the Council acknowledged 'the need to accompany market opening, economic integration and regulatory convergence as well as the process of strengthening bilateral relations, throughout the neighbourhood, with appropriate financial support, technical assistance and capacity building' and indicated that it 'will return to the issue of financial support in the context of discussions on the next multi-annual financial framework'. The Commission will reflect the renewed ENP vision and medium term objectives in its proposals for the post-2013 EU Multi-annual Financial Framework. The key source of funding, the new European Neighbourhood Instrument (ENI), will provide the bulk of financial support to partner countries, essentially through bilateral, regional and cross border co-operation programmes. Its level of funding will need to reflect the ambitions of the revised ENP. It should be increasingly policy-driven and provide for increased differentiation, more flexibility, stricter conditionality and incentives for best performers, reflecting the ambition of each partnership (e.g. DCFTA negotiations). EU assistance could also be increasingly implemented by devolving it to partner countries provided that the financial rules of the Union are respected and EU financial interests protected.

To maximise external support for the reform agenda agreed in the context of ENP the EU will step up efforts of co-ordination with EU Member States, other bilateral donors, the EIB, the EBRD and the international finance institutions. This can take the form of joint programming, joint co-operation initiatives and co-financing programmes and projects. To improve EU assistance co-ordination, the EEAS and Commission services will consider the possibility of launching pilot joint programming exercises with interested Member States in the countries of the southern neighbourhood undergoing democratic transition.

CONCLUSIONS

Our neighbourhood offers great opportunities for mutually beneficial integration and cooperation, for example large and well-educated working populations, sizeable markets still to be developed, and win-win solutions in energy security. Cooperation with our neighbours is the only means to take on the challenges and threats that do not respect borders—such as terrorism, irregular migration, pollution of our common seas and rivers. It allows us to tackle sources of instability and conflict in the region.

Several neighbours in the East and in the South have embarked on an ambitious path of transition during the last decade. They need support to consolidate these processes. Others have joined the process only recently. They also need our urgent assistance and they can benefit from the lessons learnt by other partners. It is in the EU's own interest to support these transformation processes, working together with our neighbours to anchor the essential values and principles of human rights, democracy and the rule of law, a market economy and inclusive, sustainable development in their political and economic fabric.

The new approach to the ENP set out in this Communication is a step in this direction. The Commission and the High Representative call on the Council and the European Parliament to endorse both its overall thrust and the concrete proposals it puts forward. We now intend to pursue our consultations with our neighbours on the best way to translate this new approach into each individual partnership.

The challenges are many, and fully meeting them may take time. What we are aiming for together is a democratic, prosperous and stable region where more than 800 million people can live, work and shape their own country's future, confident that their freedom, their dignity and their rights will be respected.

9.3.2 Neighbourhood policy instruments

Practically, the neighbourhood policy uses three instruments. First, the Union (and its Member States) have concluded cooperation or association agreements with the neighbouring countries. The southern neighbours are usually co-contractors of the European–Mediterranean Association Agreement, whereas the eastern neighbours (Armenia, Azerbaijan, Belarus, Georgia, Moldova, and Ukraine) have concluded a cooperation or association agreement. Relations with the eastern neighbours are guided by the Eastern Partnership launched in 2009 at a summit held in Prague.[2] Second, the Union provides financial assistance for all its neighbours through one basic regulation, which is implemented by the Commission with individual strategy papers and action plans for each country. Third, the EU and the third country agree on action plans to foster common objectives and projects. Such action plans resemble to a certain degree the accession partnerships; however, with a lesser emphasis on harmonization with the *acquis*. They are formally adopted as a recommendation by the Association Council established under the existing agreement between the neighbour and the Union and its Member States.

Euro-Mediterranean Agreement establishing an Association between the European Communities and their Member States, of the one part, and the Arab Republic of Egypt, of the other part, Official Journal L 304, 30.9.2004, pp. 39–53 (extracts).

A typical example of a neighbourhood agreement is the Euro-Med Agreement with Egypt (concluded a long time before the Arab Spring).

[...]

CONSIDERING the importance of the existing traditional links between the Community, its Member States and Egypt, and the common values that they share,

CONSIDERING that the Community, its Member States and Egypt wish to strengthen those links and to establish lasting relations based on partnership and reciprocity,

CONSIDERING the importance which the Parties attach to the principles of the United Nations Charter, particularly the observance of human rights, democratic principles and political and economic freedoms which form the very basis of the Association,

DESIROUS of establishing and developing regular political dialogue on bilateral and international issues of mutual interest,

CONSIDERING the difference in economic and social development existing between Egypt and the Community and the need to strengthen the process of economic and social development in Egypt,

DESIROUS of enhancing their economic relations and, in particular, the development of trade, investment and technological cooperation, supported by a regular dialogue, on economic, scientific, technological, cultural, audiovisual and social matters with a view to improving mutual knowledge and understanding,

CONSIDERING the commitment of the Community and Egypt to free trade, and in particular to compliance with the rights and obligations arising out of the

---

[2] Joint Declaration of the Prague Eastern Partnership Summit, Prague, 7.5.2009; see further Joint Communication to the European Parliament, the Council, the European Economic and Social Committee and the Committee of the Regions, Eastern Partnership: A Roadmap to the autumn 2013 Summit, 15.5.2012, JOIN(2012) 13 final.

provisions of the General Agreement on Tariffs and Trade of 1994 and of the other multilateral agreements annexed to the agreement establishing the World Trade Organisation,

CONSCIOUS of the need to associate their efforts to strengthen political stability and economic development in the region through the encouragement of regional cooperation,

CONVINCED that the Association Agreement will create a new climate for their relations,

HAVE AGREED AS FOLLOWS:

Article 1

1. An Association is hereby established between the Community and its Member States of the one part and Egypt of the other part.

2. The aims of this Agreement are:

— to provide an appropriate framework for political dialogue, allowing the development of close political relations between the Parties,

— to establish conditions for the progressive liberalisation of trade in goods, services and capital,

— to foster the development of balanced economic and social relations between the Parties through dialogue and cooperation,

— to contribute to the economic and social development of Egypt,

— to encourage regional cooperation with a view to the consolidation of peaceful co-existence and economic and political stability,

— to promote cooperation in other areas which are of mutual interest.

Article 2

Relations between the Parties, as well as all the provisions of the Agreement itself, shall be based on respect of democratic principles and fundamental human rights as set out in the Universal Declaration on Human Rights, which guides their internal and international policy and constitutes an essential element of this Agreement.

TITLE I

POLITICAL DIALOGUE

Article 3

1. A regular political dialogue shall be established between the Parties. It shall strengthen their relations, contribute to the development of a lasting partnership and increase mutual understanding and solidarity.

2. The political dialogue and cooperation shall aim, in particular, to:

— develop better mutual understanding and an increasing convergence of positions on international issues, and in particular on those issues likely to have substantial effects on one or the other Party,

— enable each Party to consider the position and interests of the other,

— enhance regional security and stability,

— promote common initiatives.

Article 4

The political dialogue shall cover all subjects of common interest, and, in particular peace, security, democracy and regional development.

Article 5

1. The political dialogue shall take place at regular intervals and whenever necessary, in particular:

(a) at ministerial level, mainly in the framework of the Association Council;

(b) at senior official level of Egypt of the one part, and of the Presidency of the Council and of the Commission of the other;

(c) by taking full advantage of all diplomatic channels including regular briefings by officials, consultations on the occasion of international meetings and contacts between diplomatic representatives in third countries;

(d) by any other means which would make a useful contribution to consolidating, developing and stepping up this dialogue.

2. There shall be a political dialogue between the European Parliament and the Egyptian People's Assembly.

TITLE II
FREE MOVEMENT OF GOODS
BASIC PRINCIPLES

Article 6

The Community and Egypt shall gradually establish a free trade area over a transitional period not exceeding 12 years from the entry into force of this Agreement, according to the modalities set out in this Title and in conformity with the provisions of the General Agreement on Tariffs and Trade of 1994 and of the other multilateral agreements on trade in goods annexed to the Agreement establishing the World Trade Organisation (WTO), hereinafter referred to as the GATT.

CHAPTER 1
Industrial products

Article 7

The provisions of this Chapter shall apply to products originating in the Community and Egypt falling within Chapters 25 to 97 of the Combined Nomenclature and of the Egyptian Customs tariff with the exception of the products listed in Annex I.

Article 8

Imports into the Community of products originating in Egypt shall be allowed free of customs duties and of any other charge having equivalent effect and free of quantitative restrictions and of any other restriction having equivalent effect.

Article 9

1. Customs duties and charges having equivalent effect applicable on import into Egypt of products originating in the Community listed in Annex II shall be gradually abolished in accordance with the following schedule:

— on the date of entry into force of this Agreement each duty and charge shall be reduced to 75% of the basic duty,

— one year after the date of entry into force of this Agreement each duty and charge shall be reduced to 50% of the basic duty,

— two years after the date of entry into force of this Agreement each duty and charge shall be reduced to 25% of the basic duty,

— three years after the date of entry into force of this Agreement any remaining duty and charge shall be abolished.

2. Customs duties and charges having equivalent effect applicable on import into Egypt of the products originating in the Community listed in Annex III shall be gradually abolished in accordance with the following schedule:

— three years after the date of entry into force of this Agreement each duty and charge shall be reduced to 90% of the basic duty,

— four years after the date of entry into force of this Agreement each duty and charge shall be reduced to 75% of the basic duty,

— five years after the date of entry into force of this Agreement each duty and charge shall be reduced to 60% of the basic duty,

— six years after the date of entry into force of this Agreement each duty and charge shall be reduced to 45% of the basic duty,

— seven years after the date of entry into force of this Agreement each duty and charge shall be reduced to 30% of the basic duty,

— eight years after the date of entry into force of this Agreement each duty and charge shall be reduced to 15% of the basic duty,

— nine years after the date of entry into force of this Agreement any remaining duty and charge shall be abolished.

3. Customs duties and charges having equivalent effect applicable on import into Egypt of the products originating in the Community listed in Annex IV shall be gradually abolished in accordance with the following schedule:

— five years after the date of entry into force of this Agreement each duty and charge shall be reduced to 95% of the basic duty,

— six years after the date of entry into force of this Agreement each duty and charge shall be reduced to 90% of the basic duty,

— seven years after the date of entry into force of this Agreement each duty and charge shall be reduced to 75% of the basic duty,

— eight years after the date of entry into force of this Agreement each duty and charge shall be reduced to 60% of the basic duty,

— nine years after the date of entry into force of this Agreement each duty and charge shall be reduced to 45% of the basic duty,

— 10 years after the date of entry into force of this Agreement each duty and charge shall be reduced to 30% of the basic duty,

— 11 years after the date of entry into force of this Agreement each duty and charge shall be reduced to 15% of the basic duty,

— 12 years after the date of entry into force of this Agreement any remaining duty and charge shall be abolished.

4. Customs duties and charges having equivalent effect applicable on import into Egypt of the products originating in the Community listed in Annex V shall be gradually abolished in accordance with the following schedule:

— six years after the date of entry into force of this Agreement each duty and charge shall be reduced to 90% of the basic duty,

— seven years after the date of entry into force of this Agreement each duty and charge shall be reduced to 80% of the basic duty,

— eight years after the date of entry into force of this Agreement each duty and charge shall be reduced to 70% of the basic duty,

— nine years after the date of entry into force of this Agreement each duty and charge shall be reduced to 60% of the basic duty,

— 10 years after the date of entry into force of this Agreement each duty and charge shall be reduced to 50% of the basic duty,

— 11 years after the date of entry into force of this Agreement each duty and charge shall be reduced to 40% of the basic duty,

— 12 years after the date of entry into force of this Agreement each duty and charge shall be reduced to 30% of the basic duty,

— 13 years after the date of entry into force of this Agreement each duty and charge shall be reduced to 20% of the basic duty,

— 14 years after the date of entry into force of this Agreement each duty and charge shall be reduced to 10% of the basic duty,

— 15 years after the date of entry into force of this Agreement any remaining duty and charge shall be abolished.

5. Customs duties and charges having equivalent effect applicable to imports into Egypt of products originating in the Community, other than those in Annexes II, III, IV and V shall be abolished in accordance with the relevant schedule on the basis of a decision of the Association Committee.

6. In the event of serious difficulties for a given product, the relevant timetables in accordance with paragraphs 1, 2, 3 and 4 may be reviewed by the Association Committee by common accord on the understanding that the schedule for which the review has been requested may not be extended in respect of the product concerned beyond the maximum transitional period. If the Association Committee has not taken a decision within 30 days of its application to review the timetable, Egypt may suspend the timetable provisionally for a period that may not exceed one year.

7. For each product concerned, the basic duty to be gradually reduced as provided for in paragraphs 1, 2, 3 and 4 shall be the rates referred to in Article 18.

Article 10

The provisions concerning the abolition of customs duties on imports shall also apply to customs duties of a fiscal nature.

Article 11

1. By way of derogation from the provisions of Article 9, Egypt may take exceptional measures of limited duration to increase or re-introduce customs duties.

2. Such measures may only apply to new and infant industries or to sectors undergoing restructuring or experiencing serious difficulties, particularly where those difficulties entail severe social problems.

3. Customs duties on import into Egypt of products originating in the Community that are introduced by such exceptional measures may not exceed 25% ad valorem, and must retain a preferential margin for products originating in the Community. The total value of imports of the products subjected to such measures may not exceed 20% of total imports of industrial products from the Community during the last year for which statistics are available.

4. Such measures shall be applied for no longer than five years, except where a longer duration is authorised by the Association Committee. They shall cease to apply at the latest on expiry of the maximum transitional period.

5. Such measures may not be introduced for a given product if more than three years have elapsed since the abolition of all duties, quantitative restrictions and charges and measures having equivalent effect on the product concerned.

6. Egypt shall inform the Association Committee of any exceptional measures it intends to adopt and, at the Community's request, consultations shall be held on the measures and sectors concerned before they are implemented. When adopting such measures, Egypt shall provide the Committee with a schedule for the abolition of the customs duties introduced pursuant to this Article. Such schedule shall provide for the phasing out of the duties concerned by equal annual instalments, starting no later than the end of the second year following their introduction. The Association Committee may decide on a different schedule.

7. By way of derogation from the provisions of paragraph 4, the Association Committee may exceptionally, in order to take into account the difficulties involved in setting up new industries, endorse the measures already taken by Egypt pursuant to paragraph 1 for a maximum period of four years beyond the 12 years transitional period.

CHAPTER 2
Agricultural, fisheries and processed agricultural products
Article 12

The provisions of this Chapter shall apply to products originating in the Community and Egypt falling within Chapters 1 to 24 of the Combined Nomenclature and of the Egyptian Customs tariff and to the products listed in Annex I.

Article 13

The Community and Egypt shall progressively establish a greater liberalisation of their trade in agricultural, fisheries and processed agricultural products of interest to both parties.

Article 14

1. Agricultural products originating in Egypt listed in Protocol 1 on importation into the Community shall be subject to the arrangements set out in that Protocol.

2. Agricultural products originating in the Community listed in Protocol 2 on importation into Egypt shall be subject to the arrangements set out in that Protocol.

3. Trade for processed agricultural products falling under this chapter shall be subject to the arrangements set out in Protocol 3.

Article 15

1. During the third year of implementation of the Agreement, the Community and Egypt shall examine the situation in order to determine the measures to be applied by the Community and Egypt from the beginning of the fourth year after the entry into force of the Agreement, in accordance with the objective set out in Article 13.

2. Without prejudice to the provisions of paragraph 1 and taking account of the volume of trade in agricultural, fisheries and processed agricultural products between them and of their particular sensitivity, the Community and Egypt shall examine in the Association Council, product by product and on an orderly and reciprocal basis, the possibility of granting each other further concessions.

Article 16

1. In the event of specific rules being introduced as a result of the implementation of its agricultural policy or of any alteration of the current rules or in the event of any alteration or extension of the provisions relating to the implementation of its agricultural policy, the Party concerned may amend the arrangements resulting from the Agreement in respect of the products concerned.

2. In such cases, the Party concerned shall inform the Association Committee. At the request of the other Party, the Association Committee shall meet to take due account of the interests of the other Party.

3. If the Community or Egypt, in applying paragraph 1, modifies the arrangements made by this Agreement for agricultural products, they shall accord imports originating in the other Party an advantage comparable to that provided for in this Agreement.

4. The application of this Article should be the subject of consultations in the Association Council.

CHAPTER 3
Common provisions
Article 17

1. No new quantitative restrictions on imports or any other restriction having equivalent effect shall be introduced in trade between the Community and Egypt.

2. Quantitative restrictions on imports and any other restriction having equivalent effect in trade between the Community and Egypt shall be abolished from the entry into force of this Agreement.

3. The Community and Egypt shall not apply to exports between themselves either customs duties or charges having equivalent effect, or quantitative restrictions or measures having equivalent effect.

Article 18

1. The applicable rates for imports between the Parties shall be the WTO bound rate or lower applied rate enforced as of 1 January 1999. If, after 1 January 1999, a tariff reduction is applied on an erga omnes basis, the reduced rate shall apply.

2. No new customs duties on imports or exports, or charges having equivalent effect, shall be introduced, nor shall those already applied be increased, in trade between the Community and Egypt, unless this Agreement provides otherwise.

3. The Parties shall communicate to each other their respective applied rates on 1 January 1999.

Article 19

1. Products originating in Egypt shall not, on importation into the Community, be accorded a treatment more favourable than that which the Member States apply among themselves.

2. Application of the provisions of this Agreement shall be without prejudice to the special provisions for the application of the Community law to the Canary Islands.

Article 20

1. The Parties shall refrain from any measure or practice of an internal fiscal nature establishing, whether directly or indirectly, discrimination between the products of one Party and like products originating in the territory of the other Party.

2. Products exported to the territory of one of the Parties may not benefit from repayment of indirect internal taxation in excess of the amount of indirect taxation imposed on them either directly or indirectly.

Article 21

1. This Agreement shall not preclude the maintenance or establishment of customs unions, free trade areas or arrangements for frontier trade, except in so far as they alter the trade arrangements provided for in this Agreement.

2. Consultation between the Parties shall take place within the Association Council concerning agreements establishing customs unions or free trade areas and, where requested, on other major issues related to their respective trade policy with third countries. In particular, in the event of a third country acceding to the Union, such consultation shall take place so as to ensure that account can be taken of the mutual interests of the Parties.

Article 22

If one of the Parties finds that dumping is taking place in trade with the other Party within the meaning of the provisions of Article VI of the GATT 1994, it may take appropriate measures against this practice in accordance with the WTO Agreement on the Implementation of Article VI of the GATT 1994 and related internal legislation.

Article 23

Without prejudice to Article 34, the WTO Agreement on Subsidies and Countervailing Measures shall apply between the Parties.

Until the necessary rules referred to in Article 34(2) are adopted, if either Party finds that subsidy is taking place in trade with the other party within the meanings of Articles VI and XVI of the GATT 1994, it may invoke appropriate measures against this practice in accordance with the WTO Agreement on Subsidies and Countervailing Measures and related internal legislation.

Article 24

1. The provisions of the Article XIX GATT 1994 and the WTO Agreement on Safeguards shall apply between the Parties.

2. Before applying safeguard measures pursuant to the provisions of the Article XIX GATT 1994 and the WTO Agreement on Safeguards, the Party intending to apply such measures shall supply the Association Committee with all relevant information required for a thorough examination of the situation with a view to seeking a solution acceptable to the Parties.

In order to find such a solution, the Parties shall immediately hold consultations within the Association Committee. If, as a result of the consultations, the Parties do not reach an agreement within 30 days of the initiation of the consultations on a solution to avoid the application of the safeguard measures, the Party intending to apply safeguard measures may apply the provisions of the Article XIX GATT 1994 and the WTO Agreement on Safeguards.

3. In the selection of safeguard measures pursuant to this Article, the Parties shall give priority to those which cause least disturbance to the achievement of the objectives of this Agreement.

4. Safeguard measures shall be notified immediately to the Association Committee and shall be the subject of periodic consultations within the Committee, particularly with a view to their abolition as soon as circumstances permit.

Article 25

1. Where compliance with the provisions of Article 17(3) leads to:

(i) re-export towards a third country against which the exporting Party maintains, for the product concerned, quantitative export restrictions, export duties, or measures having equivalent effect, or

(ii) a serious shortage, or threat thereof, of a product essential to the exporting Party;

and where the situations referred to above give rise, or are likely to give rise, to major difficulties for the exporting Party, that Party may take appropriate measures, according to the procedures laid down in paragraph 2.

2. The difficulties arising from the situations referred to in paragraph 1 shall be submitted for examination to the Association Committee. The Committee may take any decision needed to put an end to the difficulties. If it has not taken such a decision within 30 days of the matter being referred to it, the exporting Party may apply appropriate measures on the exportation of the product concerned. The measures shall be nondiscriminatory and be eliminated when conditions no longer justify their maintenance.

Article 26

Nothing in this Agreement shall preclude prohibitions or restrictions on imports, exports or goods in transit justified on grounds of public morality, public policy or public security, of the protection of health and life of humans, animals or plants, of the protection of national treasures possessing artistic, historic or archaeological value, of the protection of intellectual property or of regulations concerning gold and silver. Such prohibitions or restrictions shall not, however, constitute a means of arbitrary discrimination or a disguised restriction on trade between the Parties.

Article 27

The concept of 'originating products' for the application of the provisions of this Title and the methods of administrative cooperation relating to them are set out in Protocol 4.

Article 28

The Combined Nomenclature of goods shall be applied to the classification of goods for imports into the Community. The Egyptian customs tariff shall be applied to the classification of goods for imports into Egypt.

TITLE III

RIGHT OF ESTABLISHMENT AND SUPPLY OF SERVICES

Article 29

1. The Parties reaffirm their respective commitments under the terms of the General Agreement on Trade in Services (GATS) annexed to the Agreement establishing the WTO, and in particular the commitment to accord each other most favoured-nation treatment in trade in service sectors covered by these commitments.

2. In accordance with the GATS, this treatment shall not apply to:

(a) advantages accorded by either Party under the provisions of an agreement as defined in Article V of the GATS or under measures adopted on the basis of such an agreement;

(b) other advantages accorded pursuant to the list of most favoured-nation exemptions annexed by either Party to the GATS.

Article 30

1. The Parties will consider extending the scope of the Agreement to include the right of establishment of companies of one Party in the territory of another Party and the liberalisation of the supply of services by companies of one Party to service consumers in another Party.

2. The Association Council shall make the necessary recommendations for the implementation of the objective set out in paragraph 1.

When formulating these recommendations, the Association Council shall take into account the experience gained by the implementation of the MFN treatment granted to each other by the Parties in accordance with their respective obligations under the GATS, and in particular Article V thereof.

3. The objective set out in paragraph 1 of this Article shall be subject to a first examination by the Association Council at the latest five years after the entry into force of this Agreement.

TITLE IV
CAPITAL MOVEMENTS AND OTHER ECONOMIC MATTERS

CHAPTER 1
Payments and capital movements
Article 31

Subject to the provisions of Article 33, the Parties undertake to authorise, in fully convertible currency, any payments to the current account.

Article 32

1. The Community and Egypt will ensure, from the entry into force of the Agreement, the free circulation of capital for direct investments made in companies formed in accordance with the laws of the host country, and the liquidation or repatriation of these investments and of any profit stemming therefrom.

2. The Parties will hold consultations with a view to facilitating the movement of capital between the Community and Egypt and achieve its complete liberalisation as soon as conditions are met.

Article 33

Where one or several Member States of the Community or Egypt face, or risk facing, serious difficulties concerning balance of payments, the Community or Egypt respectively may, in conformity with the conditions laid down within the framework of the GATT and Articles VIII and XIV of the Statutes of the International Monetary Fund, take restrictive measures with regard to current payments if such measures are strictly necessary. The Community or Egypt, as appropriate, shall inform the other Party immediately thereof and shall provide as soon as possible a timetable for the removal of such measures.

CHAPTER 2
Competition and other economic matters
Article 34

1. The following are incompatible with the proper functioning of the Agreement, in so far as they may affect trade between the Community and Egypt:

(i) all agreements between undertakings, decisions by associations of undertakings and concerted practices between undertakings which have as their object or effect the prevention, restriction or distortion of competition;

(ii) abuse by one or more undertakings of a dominant position in the territories of the Community or Egypt as a whole or in a substantial part thereof;

(iii) any public aid which distorts, or threatens to distort, competition by favouring certain undertakings or the production of certain goods.

2. The Association Council shall, within five years of the entry into force of the Agreement, adopt by decision the necessary rules for the implementation of paragraph 1.

Until these rules are adopted, the provisions of Article 23 shall be applied as regards the implementation of paragraph 1(iii).

3. Each Party shall ensure transparency in the area of public aid, inter alia, by reporting annually to the other Party on the total amount and the distribution of the aid given and by providing, upon request, information on aid schemes. Upon request by one Party, the other Party shall provide information on particular individual cases of public aid.

4. With regard to agricultural products referred to in Title II, Chapter 2, paragraph 1(iii) does not apply. The WTO Agreement on Agriculture and the relevant provisions on WTO Agreement on Subsidies and Countervailing Duties shall apply with regard to these products.

5. If the Community or Egypt considers that a particular practice is incompatible with the terms of paragraph 1, and:

— is not adequately dealt with under the implementing rules referred to in paragraph 2, or

— in the absence of such rules, and if such practice causes, or threatens to cause, serious prejudice to the interest of the other Party or material injury to its domestic industry, including its services industry.

It may take appropriate measures after consultation within the Association Committee or after 30 working days following referral for such consultation.

With reference to practices incompatible with paragraph 1(iii), such appropriate measures, when the WTO rules are applicable to them, may only be adopted in accordance with the procedures and under the conditions laid down by the WTO or by any other relevant instrument negotiated under its auspices and applicable to the Parties.

6. Notwithstanding any provisions to the contrary adopted in conformity with paragraph 2, the Parties shall exchange information taking into account the limitations imposed by the requirements of professional and business secrecy.

Article 35

The Member States and Egypt shall progressively adjust, without prejudice to their commitments to the GATT, any State monopolies of a commercial character, so as to ensure that, by the end of the fifth year following the entry into force of this Agreement, no discrimination regarding the conditions under which goods are procured and marketed exists between nationals of the Member States and Egypt. The Association Committee will be informed of the measures adopted to implement this objective.

Article 36

With regard to public enterprises and enterprises to which special or exclusive rights have been granted, the Association Council shall ensure that, as from the fifth year following the date of entry into force of this Agreement, there is neither enacted nor maintained any measure distorting trade between the Community and Egypt contrary to the Parties' interests. This provision should not obstruct the performance in law or in fact of the particular tasks assigned to these enterprises.

Article 37

1. Pursuant to the provisions of this Article and of Annex VI, the Parties shall grant and ensure adequate and effective protection of intellectual property rights in accordance

with the prevailing international standards, including effective means of enforcing such rights.

2. The implementation of this Article and of Annex VI shall be regularly reviewed by the Parties. If problems in the area of intellectual property affecting trading conditions were to occur, urgent consultations shall be undertaken, at the request of either Party, with a view to reaching mutually satisfactory solutions.

Article 38

The Parties agree on the objective of a progressive liberalisation of public procurement. The Association Council will hold consultations on the implementation of this objective.

TITLE V

ECONOMIC COOPERATION

Article 39

Objectives

1. The Parties undertake to intensify economic cooperation in their mutual interest.
2. The aim of economic cooperation shall be to:
— encourage the implementation of the overall objectives of this Agreement,
— promote balanced economic relations between the Parties,
— support Egypt's own efforts to achieve sustainable economic and social development.

Article 40

Scope

1. Cooperation shall focus primarily on sectors suffering from internal difficulties or affected by the overall process of liberalisation of the Egyptian economy, and in particular by the liberalisation of trade between Egypt and the Community.
2. Similarly, cooperation shall focus on areas likely to bring the economies of the Community and Egypt closer together, particularly those which will generate growth and employment.
3. Cooperation shall encourage the implementation of measures designed to develop intra-regional cooperation.
4. Conservation of the environment and ecological balance shall be taken into account in the implementation of the various sectors of economic cooperation to which it is relevant.
5. The Parties may agree to extend the economic cooperation to other sectors not covered by the provisions of this Title.

Article 41

Methods and modalities

Economic cooperation shall be implemented in particular by:

(a) a regular economic dialogue between the Parties, which covers all areas of macro-economic policy;

(b) regular exchange of information and ideas in every sector of cooperation including meetings of officials and experts;

(c) transfer of advice, expertise and training;

(d) implementation of joint actions such as seminars and workshops;

(e) technical, administrative and regulatory assistance.

Article 42

Education and training

The Parties shall cooperate with the objective of identifying and employing the most effective means to improve significantly education and vocational training, in particular with regard to public and private enterprises, trade-related services, public administrations and authorities, technical agencies, standardisation and certification bodies and other relevant organisations. In this context, the access of women to higher education and training will receive special attention.

Cooperation shall also encourage the establishment of links between specialised bodies in the Community and in Egypt and shall promote the exchange of information and experience and the pooling of technical resources.

Article 43

Scientific and technological cooperation

Cooperation shall have the objective of:

(a) encouraging the establishment of durable links between the scientific communities of the Parties, notably through:

— the access of Egypt to Community R & D programmes, in conformity with existing provisions concerning the participation of third countries,

— the participation of Egypt in networks of decentralised cooperation,

— the promotion of synergy between training and research;

(b) strengthening research capacity in Egypt;

(c) stimulating technological innovation, transfer of new technologies, and dissemination of know-how.

Article 44

Environment

1. Cooperation shall aim at preventing deterioration of the environment, controlling pollution and ensuring the rational use of natural resources, with a view to ensuring sustainable development.

2. Cooperation shall focus, in particular, on:

— desertification,

— quality of Mediterranean water and the control and prevention of marine pollution,

— water resource management,

— energy management,

— waste management,

— salinisation,

— environmental management of sensitive coastal areas,

— the impact of industrial development and the safety of industrial plant in particular,

— the impact of agriculture on soil and water quality,

— environmental education and awareness.

Article 45

Industrial cooperation

Cooperation shall promote and encourage in particular:

— the debate regarding industrial policy and competitiveness in an open economy,

— industrial cooperation between economic operators in the Community and in Egypt, including access for Egypt to the Community's networks for the rapprochement of businesses and to networks created in the context of decentralised cooperation,

— modernisation and restructuring of Egyptian industry,

— the establishment of an environment favourable to the development of private enterprise, in order to stimulate the growth and the diversification of industrial production,

— technology transfer, innovation and R & D,

— the enhancement of human resources,

— access to the capital market for the financing of productive investments.

Article 46

Investments and promotion of investments

Cooperation shall aim at increasing the flow of capital, expertise and technology to Egypt through, inter alia:

— appropriate means of identifying investment opportunities and information channels on investment regulations,

— providing information on European investment regimes (such as technical assistance, direct financial support, fiscal incentives and investment insurance) related to outward investments and enhancing the possibility for Egypt to benefit from them,

— a legal environment conducive to investment between the two Parties, where appropriate through the conclusion by the Member States and Egypt of investment protection agreements, and agreements to prevent double taxation,

— examining the creation of joint ventures, especially for SMEs and, when appropriate, the conclusion of agreements between the Member States and Egypt,

— establishing mechanisms for encouraging and promoting investments.

Cooperation may extend to the planning and implementation of projects demonstrating the effective acquisition and use of basic technologies, the use of standards, the development of human resources and the creation of jobs locally.

Article 47

Standardisation and conformity assessment

The Parties shall aim to reduce differences in standardisation and conformity assessment. Cooperation in this field shall focus in particular on:

(a) rules in the field of standardisation, metrology, quality standards, and recognition of conformity, in particular as regards sanitary and phytosanitary standards for agricultural products and foodstuffs;

(b) upgrading the level of Egyptian conformity assessment bodies, with a view to the establishment, in due time, of mutual recognition agreements in the area of conformity assessment;

(c) developing structures for the protection of intellectual, industrial and commercial property rights, for standardisation and for setting quality standards.

Article 48

Approximation of laws
The Parties shall use their best endeavours to approximate their respective laws in order to facilitate the implementation of this Agreement.

Article 49

Financial services
The Parties shall cooperate with a view to the rapprochement of their standards and rules, in particular:
(a) to encourage the strengthening and restructuring of the financial sector in Egypt;
(b) to improve accounting and supervisory and regulatory systems of banking, insurance and other parts of the financial sector in Egypt.

Article 50

Agriculture and fisheries
Cooperation shall be aimed at:
(a) the modernisation and restructuring of agriculture and fisheries, including: the modernisation of infrastructures and of equipment; the development of packaging, storage and marketing techniques; the improvement of private distribution channels;
(b) the diversification of production and of external outlets, inter alia, through the encouragement of joint ventures in the agri-business sector;
(c) the promotion of cooperation in veterinary and phytosanitary matters and in growing techniques, with the objective of facilitating trade between the Parties. In this regard, the Parties shall exchange information.

Article 51

Transport
Cooperation shall be aimed at:
— the restructuring and modernisation of road, port and airport infrastructures linked to the main trans-European lines of communication of common interest,
— the establishment and enforcement of operating standards comparable to those prevailing in the Community,
— the upgrading of technical equipment for road/rail transport, container traffic and transhipment,
— the improvement of management of airports, railways and air traffic control, including cooperation between the relevant national bodies,
— the improvement of navigation aids.

Article 52

Information society and telecommunications
The Parties recognise that information and communication technologies constitute a key element of modern society, vital to economic and social development and a cornerstone of the emerging information society.

The cooperation activities between the Parties in this field shall aim at:
— a dialogue on issues related to the different aspects of the information society, including telecommunications policies,
— the exchanges of information and eventual technical assistance with regulatory matters, standardisation, conformity testing and certification in relation to information technologies and telecommunications,
— the diffusion of new information and communications technologies and the refinement of new applications in these fields,
— the implementation of joint projects for research, technical development or industrial applications in information technologies, communications, telematics and information society,
— the participation of Egyptian organisations in pilot projects and European programmes within the established frameworks,
— interconnection between networks and the interoperability of telematic services in the Community and Egypt.

Article 53

Energy
The priority areas of cooperation shall be:
— the promotion of renewable energies,
— the promotion of energy-saving and energy efficiency,
— applied research into data bank networks in the economic and social sectors, linking Community and Egyptian operators in particular,
— support for the modernisation and development of energy networks and for their linking to European Community networks.

Article 54

Tourism
Priorities for cooperation shall be:
— promoting investments in tourism,
— improving the knowledge of the tourist industry and ensuring greater consistency of policies affecting tourism,
— promoting a good seasonal spread of tourism,
— promoting cooperation between regions and cities of neighbouring countries,
— highlighting the importance of the cultural heritage for tourism,
— ensuring that the interaction between tourism and the environment is suitably maintained,
— making tourism more competitive through support for increased professionalism.

Article 55

Customs
1. The Parties shall develop customs cooperation to ensure that the provisions on trade are observed. Cooperation will focus in particular on:
(a) the simplification of controls and procedures concerning the customs clearance of goods;

(b) the introduction of the single administrative document and a system to link up the Community's and Egypt's transit arrangements.

2. Without prejudice to other forms of cooperation envisaged in this Agreement, notably for the fight against drugs and money laundering, the Parties' administrations will provide mutual assistance in accordance with the provisions of Protocol 5.

Article 56

Cooperation on statistics

The main objective of cooperation in this field shall be to harmonise methodology in order to create a reliable basis for handling statistics in all the fields that are covered by this Agreement and lend themselves to the establishment of statistics.

Article 57

Money laundering

1. The Parties shall cooperate with a view in particular to preventing the use of their financial systems to launder the proceeds arising from criminal activities in general and drug trafficking in particular.

2. Cooperation in this field shall include, in particular, technical and administrative assistance aimed at establishing effective standards relating to the fight against money laundering in line with international standards.

Article 58

Fight against drugs

1. The Parties shall cooperate with a view in particular to:
— improving the effectiveness of policies and measures to counter the supply of, and illicit trafficking in, narcotic drugs and psycho-tropic substances and the reduction of the abuse of these products,
— encouraging a joint approach to reducing demand.

2. The Parties shall determine together, in accordance with their respective legislation, the strategies and cooperation methods appropriate for attaining these objectives. Their operations, other than joint operations, shall form the subject of consultations and close coordination.

The relevant governmental and non-governmental sector bodies, in accordance with their own powers, working with the competent bodies of Egypt, the Community and its Member States, may take part in these operations.

3. Cooperation shall take the form of exchanges of information and, where appropriate, joint activities on:
— establishment or extension of social and health institutions and information centres for the treatment and rehabilitation of drug addicts,
— implementation of projects in the areas of prevention, training and epidemiological research,
— establishment of effective standards relating to the prevention of the diversion of precursors and other essential substances used for the illicit production of narcotic drugs and psychotropic substances, in line with international standards.

Article 59

Fight against terrorism

In accordance with international conventions and with their respective national legislations, the Parties shall cooperate in this field and focus in particular on:

— exchange of information on means and methods used to counter terrorism,

— exchange of experiences in respect of terrorism prevention,

— joint research and studies in the area of terrorism prevention.

Article 60

Regional cooperation

Regional cooperation shall focus on:

— development of economic infrastructures,

— scientific and technological research,

— intra-regional trade,

— customs matters,

— cultural matters,

— environmental issues.

Article 61

Consumer protection

Cooperation in this field should be geared to making consumer protection schemes in
the European Community and Egypt compatible and should, as far as possible, involve:

— increasing the compatibility of consumer legislation in order to avoid barriers to trade,

— establishment and development of systems of mutual information on dangerous
food and industrial products and interconnecting them (rapid alert systems),

— exchanges of information and experts,

— organising training schemes and supplying technical assistance.

TITLE VI

CHAPTER 1

Dialogue and cooperation on social matters

Article 62

The Parties reaffirm the importance they attach to the fair treatment of their workers
legally residing and employed in the territory of the other Party. The Member States
and Egypt, at the request of any of them, agree to initiate talks on reciprocal bilateral
agreements related to the working conditions and social security rights of Egyptian
and Member State workers legally resident and employed in their respective territory.

Article 63

1. The Parties shall conduct regular dialogue on social matters which are of interest to
them.

2. This dialogue shall be used to find ways to achieve progress in the field of movement
of workers and equal treatment and social integration of Egyptian and Community
nationals legally residing in the territories of their host countries.

3. The dialogue shall notably cover all issues related to:

(a) migrant communities' living and working conditions;

(b) migration;

(c) illegal migration;

(d) actions to encourage equal treatment between Egyptian and Community nationals, mutual knowledge of cultures and civilizations, the furthering of tolerance and the removal of discrimination.

Article 64

Dialogue on social matters shall be conducted in accordance with the same procedures as those provided for in Title I of this Agreement.

Article 65

With a view to consolidating cooperation between the Parties in the social field, projects and programmes shall be carried out in any area of interest to them.

Priority will be given to:

(a) reducing migratory pressures, notably by improving living conditions, creating jobs, and income generating activities and developing training in areas from which emigrants come;

(b) promoting the role of women in economic and social development;

(c) bolstering and developing Egyptian family planning and mother and child protection programmes;

(d) improving the social protection system;

(e) improving the health care system;

(f) improving living conditions in poor areas;

(g) implementing and financing exchange and leisure programmes for mixed groups of Egyptian and European young people residing in the Member States, with a view to promoting mutual knowledge of their respective cultures and fostering tolerance.

Article 66

Cooperation schemes may be carried out in cooperation with the Member States and the relevant international organisations.

Article 67

A working group shall be set up by the Association Council by the end of the first year following the entry into force of this Agreement. It shall be responsible for the continuous and regular evaluation of the implementation of Chapters 1 to 3.

CHAPTER 2

Cooperation for the prevention and control of illegal immigration and other consular issues

Article 68

The Parties agree to cooperate in order to prevent and control illegal immigration. To this end:

— each of the Member States agrees to readmit any of its nationals illegally present on the territory of Egypt, upon request by the latter and without further formalities once such persons have been positively identified as such,

— Egypt agrees to readmit any of its nationals illegally present on the territory of a Member State, upon request by the latter and without further formalities once such persons have been positively identified as such.

The Member States and Egypt will also provide their nationals with appropriate identity documents for such purposes.

In respect of the Member States of the European Union, the obligations in this Article shall apply only in respect of those persons who are to be considered their nationals for Community purposes.

In respect of Egypt, the obligation in this Article shall apply only in respect of those persons who are considered nationals of Egypt in accordance to the Egyptian legal system and all the relevant laws concerning citizenship.

Article 69

After the entry into force of the Agreement, the Parties, at the request of any of them, shall negotiate and conclude bilateral agreements with each other, regulating specific obligations for the readmission of their nationals. These agreements shall also cover, if deemed necessary by any of the Parties, arrangements for the readmission of third country nationals. Such agreements will lay down the details about the categories of persons covered by these arrangements as well as the modalities of their readmission.

Adequate financial and technical assistance to implement these agreements will be provided to Egypt.

Article 70

The Association Council shall examine what other joint efforts can be made to prevent and control illegal immigration as well as deal with other consular issues.

CHAPTER 3

Cooperation in cultural matters, audiovisual media and information

Article 71

1. The Parties agree to promote cultural cooperation in fields of mutual interest and in a spirit of respect for each other's cultures. They shall establish a sustainable cultural dialogue. This cooperation shall promote in particular:

— conservation and restoration of historic and cultural heritage (such as monuments, sites, artefacts, rare books and manuscripts),

— exchange of art exhibitions, troupes of performing arts, artists, men of letters, intellectuals and cultural events,

— translations,

— training of persons working in the cultural field.

2. Cooperation in the field of audiovisual media shall seek to encourage cooperation in such areas as co-production and training. The Parties shall seek ways to encourage Egyptian participation in Community initiatives in this sector.

3. The Parties agree that existing cultural programmes of the Community and of one or more of the Member States and further activities of interest to both sides can be extended to Egypt.

4. The Parties shall, in addition, work to promote cultural cooperation of a commercial nature, particularly through joint projects (production, investment and marketing), training and exchange of information.

5. The Parties shall, in identifying cooperation projects, programmes and joint activities, give special attention to young people, self-expression, heritage conservation issues, the dissemination of culture, and communication skills using written and audiovisual media.

6. Cooperation shall be implemented in particular through:

— a regular dialogue between the Parties,

— regular exchange of information and ideas in every sector of cooperation including meetings of officials and experts,

— transfer of advice, expertise and training,

— implementation of joint actions such as seminars and workshops,

— technical, administrative and regulatory assistance,

— dissemination of information on cooperation initiatives.

TITLE VII
FINANCIAL COOPERATION
Article 72

In order to achieve the objectives of this Agreement, a financial cooperation package shall be made available to Egypt in accordance with the appropriate procedures and the financial resources required.

Financial cooperation shall focus on:

— promoting reforms designed to modernise the economy,

— upgrading economic infrastructure,

— promoting private investment and job-creating activities,

— responding to the economic repercussions for Egypt of the gradual introduction of a free trade area, notably by upgrading and restructuring industry and enhancing Egypt's export capacity,

— accompanying measures for policies implemented in the social sector,

— promoting Egypt's capacity and capabilities in the field of the protection of intellectual property rights,

— where appropriate, supplementary measures for the implementation of bilateral agreements to prevent and control illegal immigration,

— accompanying measures for the establishment and implementation of competition legislation.

Article 73

In order to ensure that a coordinated approach is adopted to any exceptional macro-economic and financial problems that might arise as a result of the implementation of this Agreement, the Parties shall use the regular economic dialogue provided for in

Title V to give particular attention to monitoring trade and financial trends in relations between the Community and Egypt.

TITLE VIII

INSTITUTIONAL, GENERAL AND FINAL PROVISIONS

Article 74

An Association Council is hereby established which shall meet at ministerial level once a year and when circumstances require, at the initiative of its President and in accordance with the conditions laid down in its rules of procedure.

It shall examine any major issues arising within the framework of this Agreement and any other bilateral or international issues of mutual interest.

Article 75

1. The Association Council shall consist of the members of the Council of the European Union and of the Commission of the European Communities, on the one hand, and members of the Government of Egypt, on the other.

2. Members of the Association Council may arrange to be represented in accordance with the provisions laid down in its rules of procedure.

3. The Association Council shall establish its rules of procedure.

4. The Association Council shall be presided in turn by a member of the Council of the European Union and a member of the Government of Egypt, in accordance with the provisions laid down in its rules of procedure.

Article 76

The Association Council shall, for the purpose of attaining the objectives of the Agreement, have the power to take decisions in the cases provided for therein.

The decisions taken shall be binding on the Parties, which shall take the measures necessary to implement them. The Association Council may also make appropriate recommendations.

The Association Council shall draw up its decisions and recommendations by agreement between the two Parties.

Article 77

1. Subject to the powers of the Association Council, an Association Committee is hereby established which shall be responsible for the implementation of the Agreement.

2. The Association Council may delegate to the Association Committee, in full or in part, any of its powers.

Article 78

1. The Association Committee, which shall meet at official level, shall consist of representatives of members of the Council of the European Union and of the Commission of the European Communities, on the one hand, and of representatives of the Government of Egypt, on the other.

2. The Association Committee shall establish its rules of procedure.

3. The Association Committee shall be presided in turn by a representative of the Presidency of the Council of the European Union and by a representative of the Government of Egypt.

Article 79

1. The Association Committee shall have the power to take decisions for the management of the Agreement as well as in the areas in which the Association Council has delegated its powers to it.

2. The Association Committee shall draw up its decisions by agreement between the two Parties. These decisions shall be binding on the Parties which shall take the measures necessary to implement the decisions taken.

Article 80

The Association Council may decide to set up any working group or body necessary for the implementation of the Agreement. It shall define the terms of reference of any such working group or body that shall be subordinate to it.

Article 81

The Association Council shall take all appropriate measures to facilitate cooperation and contacts between the European Parliament and the Egyptian People's Assembly.

Article 82

1. Each of the Parties may refer to the Association Council any dispute relating to the application or interpretation of this Agreement.

2. The Association Council may settle the dispute by means of a decision.

3. Each Party shall be bound to take the measures involved in carrying out the decision referred to in paragraph 2.

4. In the event of it not being possible to settle the dispute in accordance with paragraph 2, either Party may notify the other of the appointment of an arbitrator; the other Party must then appoint a second arbitrator within two months. For the application of this procedure, the Community and the Member States shall be deemed to be one party to the dispute.

The Association Council shall appoint a third arbitrator.

The arbitrators' decisions shall be taken by majority vote.

Each party to the dispute must take the steps required to implement the decision of the arbitrators.

Article 83

Nothing in this Agreement shall prevent a Party from taking any measures:
(a) which it considers necessary to prevent the disclosure of information contrary to its essential security interests;
(b) which relate to the production of, or trade in, arms, munitions or war materials or to research, development or production indispensable for defence purposes, provided that such measures do not impair the conditions of competition in respect of products not intended for specifically military purposes;

(c) which it considers essential to its own security in the event of serious internal disturbances affecting the maintenance of law and order, in time of war or serious international tension constituting threat of war or in order to carry out obligations it has accepted for the purpose of maintaining peace and international security.

Article 84

In the fields covered by this Agreement and without prejudice to any special provisions contained therein:

— the arrangements applied by Egypt in respect of the Community shall not give rise to any discrimination between the Member States, their nationals or their companies or firms,

— the arrangements applied by the Community in respect of Egypt shall not give rise to discrimination between Egyptian nationals or its companies or firms.

Article 85

As regards direct taxation, nothing in this Agreement shall have the effect of:

— extending the fiscal advantages granted by either Party in any international agreement or arrangement by which it is bound,

— preventing the adoption or application by either Party of any measure aimed at preventing the avoidance or evasion of taxes,

— opposing the right of either Party to apply the relevant provisions of its tax legislation to taxpayers who are not in identical situation, in particular as regards their place of residence.

Article 86

1. The Parties shall take any general or specific measures required to fulfil their obligations under this Agreement. They shall see to it that the objectives set out in this Agreement are attained.

2. If either Party considers that the other Party has failed to fulfil an obligation under this Agreement, it may take appropriate measures. Before so doing, except in cases of a material breach of this Agreement by the other Party, it shall supply the Association Council with all relevant information required for a thorough examination of the situation with a view to seeking a solution acceptable to the Parties.

A material breach of this Agreement shall consist of the repudiation of this Agreement not sanctioned by the general rules of international law or a grave violation of an essential element of this Agreement, creating an environment not conducive for consultations or where a delay would be detrimental to the objectives of this Agreement.

3. In the selection of the appropriate measures referred to in paragraph 2, priority must be given to those which least disturb the functioning of this Agreement. The Parties also agree that these measures shall be taken in accordance with international law and shall be proportional to the violation.

The measures shall be notified immediately to the Association Council and shall be the subject of consultations within the Association Council if the other Party so requests. If one Party takes a measure as a result of a material breach of this

Agreement referred to in paragraph 2, the other Party may invoke the dispute settlement procedure.

Article 87

Protocols 1 to 5 and Annexes I to VI shall form an integral part of this Agreement.

Article 88

For the purpose of this Agreement the term 'Parties' shall mean Egypt on the one hand and the Community, or the Member States, or the Community and the Member States, in accordance with their respective powers, on the other hand.

Article 89

This Agreement is concluded for an unlimited period.
Each of the Parties may denounce this Agreement by notifying the other Party. This Agreement shall cease to apply six months after the date of such notification.

Article 90

This Agreement shall apply, on the one hand, to the territories in which the Treaties establishing the European Community, and the European Coal and Steel Community are applied and under the conditions laid down in those Treaties and, on the other hand, to the territory of Egypt.

Article 91

This Agreement shall be drawn up in duplicate in the Arabic, Danish, Dutch, English, Finnish, French, German, Greek, Italian, Portuguese, Spanish, and Swedish languages, each of these texts being equally authentic.

Article 92

1. This Agreement will be approved by the Parties in accordance with their own procedures.
This Agreement shall enter into force on the first day of the second month following the date on which the Parties notify each other that the procedures referred to in the first subparagraph have been completed.
2. Upon its entry into force, this Agreement shall replace the Agreement between the European Economic Community and Egypt, and the Agreement between the European Coal and Steel Community and Egypt, signed in Brussels on 18 January 1977.

Regulation (EC) No 1638/2006 of the European Parliament and of the Council of 24 October 2006 laying down general provisions establishing a European Neighbourhood and Partnership Instrument, Official Journal L 310, 9.11.2006, pp. 1–14.

The European Neighbourhood and Partnership Instrument (ENPI) regulation is a typical example of a unilateral act in the EU's neighbourhood policy. It was adopted on the joint bases of Articles 179 EC and 181a EC (today Articles 208 and 212 TFEU).[3] In accordance with the new approach adopted by the EU to the European Neighbourhood Policy in May 2011, the ENPI will be replaced by the European Neighbourhood Instrument (ENI) as of January 2014.[4] The ENI will reflect the new directions of the ENP as delineated in the Joint Communication of 25 May 2011 included above.

THE EUROPEAN PARLIAMENT AND THE COUNCIL OF THE EUROPEAN UNION,

Having regard to the Treaty establishing the European Community, and in particular Articles 179 and 181a thereof,

Having regard to the proposal from the Commission,

Acting in accordance with the procedure laid down in Article 251of the Treaty,

Whereas:

(1) A new framework for planning and delivering assistance is proposed in order to make the Community's external assistance more effective. This Regulation constitutes one of the general instruments providing direct support for the European Union's external policies.

(2) The Copenhagen European Council of 12 and 13 December 2002 confirmed that enlargement of the European Union presents an important opportunity to take forward relations with neighbouring countries based on shared political and economic values, and that the European Union remains determined to avoid new dividing lines in Europe and to promote stability and prosperity within and beyond the new borders of the European Union.

(3) The Brussels European Council of 17 and 18 June 2004 reiterated the importance it attached to strengthening cooperation with those neighbours, on the basis of partnership and joint ownership and building on shared values of democracy and respect for human rights.

(4) The privileged relationship between the European Union and its neighbours should build on commitments to common values, including democracy, the rule of law, good governance and respect for human rights, and to the principles of market economy, open, rule-based and fair trade, sustainable development and poverty reduction.

(5) It is important that Community assistance under this Regulation be provided in compliance with the international agreements and international conventions to which the Community, the Member States and the partner countries are parties and that it be delivered taking into account the general principles of international law commonly accepted by the parties.

(6) In eastern Europe and the southern Caucasus, the Partnership and Cooperation Agreements provide the basis for contractual relations. In the Mediterranean, the Euro-Mediterranean Partnership (the Barcelona Process) provides a regional

---

[3] For more details, see Chapter 8.

[4] As at the time of writing the new ENI regulation has not been enacted; see Proposal for a Regulation of the European Parliament and of the Council establishing a European Neighbourhood Instrument, 7.12.2011, COM(2011) 839 final.

framework for cooperation which is complemented by a network of Association Agreements.

(7) Under the European Neighbourhood Policy, a set of priorities are defined together by the European Union and the partner countries, to be incorporated in a series of jointly agreed Action Plans, covering a number of key areas for specific action, including political dialogue and reform, trade and economic reform, equitable social and economic development, justice and home affairs, energy, transport, information society, environment, research and innovation, the development of civil society and people-to-people contacts. Progress towards meeting these priorities will contribute to realising the full potential of the Partnership and Cooperation Agreements and the Association Agreements.

(8) In order to support the partner countries' commitment to common values and principles and their efforts in the implementation of the action plans, the Community should be in a position to provide assistance to those countries and to support various forms of cooperation among them and between them and the Member States with the aim of developing a zone of shared stability, security and prosperity involving a significant degree of economic integration and political cooperation.

(9) Promotion of political, economic and social reforms across the neighbourhood is an important objective of Community assistance. In the Mediterranean this objective will be further pursued within the Mediterranean strand of the Strategic Partnership with the Mediterranean and the Middle East. The relevant elements of the European Union strategy for Africa will be taken into account in the relations with the Mediterranean neighbours from North Africa.

(10) It is important that support to be provided to neighbouring developing countries within the framework established by the European Neighbourhood Policy should be coherent with the objectives and principles of the European Community Development Policy, as outlined in the Joint Statement entitled 'The European Consensus on Development' adopted on 20 December 2005 by the Council and the Representatives of the Governments of the Member States meeting within the Council, the European Parliament and the Commission.

(11) The European Union and Russia have decided to develop their specific strategic partnership through the creation of four common spaces, and Community assistance will be used to support the development of this partnership and to promote cross-border cooperation at the border between Russia and its European Union neighbours.

(12) The Northern Dimension provides a framework for cooperation between the European Union, Russia, Norway and Iceland and it is important that Community assistance be also used to support activities contributing to the implementation of such a framework. The new objectives of this policy will be set out in a political declaration and a policy framework document to be prepared on the basis of the guidelines approved by the Northern Dimension ministerial meeting of 21 November 2005.

(13) For Mediterranean partners, assistance and cooperation should take place within the framework of the Euro-Mediterranean Partnership established by the Barcelona Declaration of 28 November 1995 and affirmed at the 10th anniversary Euro-Mediterranean Summit of 28 November 2005, and should take into account the

agreement reached in that context on establishing a free-trade area for goods by 2010 and beginning a process of asymmetric liberalisation.

(14) It is important to foster cooperation both at the European Union external border and among partner countries, especially those among them that are geographically close to each other.

(15) In order to avoid the creation of new dividing lines, it is particularly important to remove obstacles to effective cross-border cooperation along the external borders of the European Union. Cross-border cooperation should contribute to integrated and sustainable regional development between neighbouring border regions and harmonious territorial integration across the Community and with neighbouring countries. This aim can best be achieved by combining external policy objectives with environmentally sustainable economic and social cohesion.

(16) In order to assist neighbouring partner countries in achieving their objectives, and to promote cooperation between them and Member States, it is desirable to establish a single policy-driven instrument which will replace a number of existing instruments, ensuring coherence and simplifying assistance programming and management.

(17) This instrument should also support cross-border cooperation between partner countries and the Member States bringing substantial efficiency gains operating through a single management mechanism and with a single set of procedures. It should build on the experience acquired from the implementation of the Neighbourhood Programmes in the period 2004 to 2006 and operate on the basis of principles such as multi-annual programming, partnership and cofinancing.

(18) It is important that border regions which belong to countries of the European Economic Area (EEA) and which are currently taking part in cross-border cooperation involving Member States and partner countries may continue to do so on the basis of their own resources.

(19) This Regulation establishes for the period 2007 to 2013 a financial envelope which constitutes the prime reference amount for the budgetary authority according to point 37 of the Interinstitutional Agreement between the European Parliament, the Council and the Commission on budgetary discipline and sound financial management.

(20) The measures necessary for the implementation of this Regulation should be adopted in accordance with Council Decision 1999/468/EC of 28 June 1999 laying down the procedures for the exercise of implementing powers conferred on the Commission.

(21) The use of the management procedure should be applicable when defining the implementing rules which will govern the implementation of cross-border cooperation and when adopting strategy papers, action programmes and special measures not provided for in strategy papers whose value exceeds the threshold of EUR 10 000 000.

(22) Since the objectives of this Regulation, namely to promote enhanced cooperation and progressive economic integration between the European Union and neighbouring countries, cannot be sufficiently achieved by the Member States and can, by reason of the scale of the action, be better achieved at Community level, the Community may adopt measures, in accordance with the principle of subsidiarity as set out in Article 5 of the Treaty. In accordance with the principle of proportionality, as set out in that

article, this Regulation does not go beyond what is necessary in order to achieve those objectives.

(23) This Regulation makes it necessary to repeal Council Regulations (EEC) No 1762/92 of 29 June 1992 on the implementation of the Protocols on financial and technical cooperation concluded by the Community with Mediterranean non-member countries, (EC) No 1734/94 of 11 July 1994 on financial and technical cooperation with the West Bank and the Gaza Strip and (EC) No 1488/96 of 23 July 1996 on financial and technical measures to accompany (MEDA) the reform of economic and social structures in the framework of the Euro-Mediterranean partnership. Equally, this Regulation will replace Council Regulation (EC, Euratom) No 99/2000 of 29 December 1999 concerning the provision of assistance to the partner States in eastern Europe and central Asia, which expires on 31 December 2006,

HAVE ADOPTED THIS REGULATION:

TITLE I
OBJECTIVES AND PRINCIPLES
Article 1

Subject matter and scope

1. This Regulation establishes a Neighbourhood and Partnership Instrument to provide Community assistance for the development of an area of prosperity and good neighbourliness involving the European Union, and the countries and territories listed in the Annex (hereinafter partner countries).

2. Community assistance shall be used for the benefit of partner countries. Community assistance may be used for the common benefit of Member States and partner countries and their regions, for the purpose of promoting cross-border and trans-regional cooperation as defined in Article 6.

3. The European Union is founded on the values of liberty, democracy, respect for human rights and fundamental freedoms and the rule of law and seeks to promote commitment to these values in partner countries through dialogue and cooperation.

Article 2

Scope of Community assistance

1. Community assistance shall promote enhanced cooperation and progressive economic integration between the European Union and the partner countries and, in particular, the implementation of partnership and cooperation agreements, association agreements or other existing and future agreements. It shall also encourage partner countries' efforts aimed at promoting good governance and equitable social and economic development.

2. Community assistance shall be used to support measures within the following areas of cooperation:

(a) promoting political dialogue and reform;

(b) promoting legislative and regulatory approximation towards higher standards in all relevant areas and in particular to encourage the progressive participation of partner countries in the internal market and the intensification of trade;

(c) strengthening of national institutions and bodies responsible for the elaboration and the effective implementation of policies in areas covered in association agreements, partnership and cooperation agreements, and other multilateral agreements to which the Community and/or its Member States and partner countries are parties, whose purpose is the achievement of objectives as defined in this Article;

(d) promoting the rule of law and good governance, including strengthening the effectiveness of public administration and the impartiality and effectiveness of the judiciary, and supporting the fight against corruption and fraud;

(e) promoting sustainable development in all aspects;

(f) pursuing regional and local development efforts, in both rural and urban areas, in order to reduce imbalances and improve regional and local development capacity;

(g) promoting environmental protection, nature conservation and sustainable management of natural resources including fresh water and marine resources;

(h) supporting policies aimed at poverty reduction, to help achieve the UN Millennium Development Goals;

(i) supporting policies to promote social development, social inclusion, gender equality, non-discrimination, employment and social protection including protection of migrant workers, social dialogues, and respect for trade union rights and core labour standards, including on child labour;

(j) supporting policies to promote health, education and training, including not only measures to combat the major communicable diseases and non-communicable diseases and disorders, but also access to services and education for good health, including reproductive and infant health for girls and women;

(k) promoting and protecting human rights and fundamental freedoms, including women's rights and children's rights;

(l) supporting democratisation, inter alia, by enhancing the role of civil society organisations and promoting media pluralism, as well as through electoral observation and assistance;

(m) fostering the development of civil society and of nongovernmental organisations;

(n) promoting the development of a market economy, including measures to support the private sector and the development of small and medium-sized enterprises, to encourage investment and to promote global trade;

(o) promoting cooperation in the sectors of energy, telecommunication and transport, including on interconnections, networks and their operations, enhancing the security and safety of international transport and energy operations and promoting renewable energy sources, energy efficiency and clean transport;

(p) providing support for actions aimed at increasing food safety for citizens, in particular in the sanitary and phytosanitary domains;

(q) ensuring efficient and secure border management;

(r) supporting reform and strengthening capacity in the field of justice and home affairs, including issues such as asylum, migration and readmission, and the fight against, and prevention of, trafficking in human beings as well as terrorism and organised crime, including its financing, money laundering and tax fraud;

(s) supporting administrative cooperation to improve transparency and the exchange of information in the area of taxation in order to combat tax avoidance and evasion;

(t) promoting participation in Community research and innovation activities;

(u) promoting cooperation between the Member States and partner countries in higher education and mobility of teachers, researchers and students;

(v) promoting multicultural dialogue, people-to-people contacts, including links with communities of immigrants living in Member States, cooperation between civil societies, cultural institutions and exchanges of young people;

(w) supporting cooperation aimed at protecting historical and cultural heritage and promoting its development potential, including through tourism;

(x) supporting participation of partner countries in Community programmes and agencies;

(y) supporting cross-border cooperation through joint local initiatives to promote sustainable economic, social and environmental development in border regions and integrated territorial development across the Community's external border;

(z) promoting regional and sub-regional cooperation and integration, including, where appropriate, with countries not eligible for Community assistance under this Regulation;

(aa) providing support in post-crisis situations, including support to refugees and displaced persons, and assisting in disaster preparedness;

(bb) encouraging communication and promoting exchange among the partners on the measures and activities financed under the programmes;

(cc) addressing common thematic challenges in fields of mutual concern and any other objectives consistent with the scope of this Regulation.

Article 3

Policy framework

1. The partnership and cooperation agreements, the association agreements and other existing or future agreements which establish a relationship with partner countries, and the relevant Commission communications and Council conclusions laying down guidelines for European Union policy towards these countries, shall provide an overall policy framework for the programming of Community assistance under this Regulation. Jointly agreed action plans or other equivalent documents shall provide a key point of reference for setting Community assistance priorities.

2. Where no agreements, as mentioned in paragraph 1, between the European Union and partner countries exist, Community assistance may be provided when it proves useful to pursue European Union policy objectives, and shall be programmed on the basis of such objectives.

Article 4

Complementarity, partnership and cofinancing

1. Community assistance under this Regulation shall normally complement or contribute to corresponding national, regional or local strategies and measures.

2. Community assistance under this Regulation shall normally be established in partnership between the Commission and the beneficiaries. The partnership shall involve, as appropriate, national, regional and local authorities, economic and social partners, civil society and other relevant bodies.

3. The beneficiary countries shall involve, as appropriate, the relevant partners at the appropriate territorial level, in particular at regional and local level, in the preparation, implementation and monitoring of programmes and projects.

4. Community assistance under this Regulation shall normally be co-financed by the beneficiary countries through public funds, contributions from the beneficiaries or other sources. Co-financing requirements may be waived in duly justified cases and when this is necessary to support the development of civil society and non-state actors for measures aimed at promoting human rights and fundamental freedoms and supporting democratisation.

Article 5
Coherence, compatibility and coordination

1. Programmes and projects financed under this Regulation shall be consistent with European Union policies. They shall comply with the agreements concluded by the Community and its Member States with the partner countries and respect commitments under multilateral agreements and international conventions to which they are parties, including commitments on human rights, democracy and good governance.

2. The Commission and the Member States shall ensure coherence between Community assistance provided under this Regulation and financial assistance provided by the Community and the Member States through other internal and external financial instruments and by the European Investment Bank (EIB).

3. The Commission and the Member States shall ensure coordination of their respective assistance programmes with the aim of increasing effectiveness and efficiency in the delivery of assistance in line with the established guidelines for strengthening operational coordination in the field of external assistance, and for the harmonisation of policies and procedures. Coordination shall involve regular consultations and frequent exchanges of relevant information during the different phases of the assistance cycle, in particular at field level, and shall constitute a key step in the programming processes of the Member States and the Community.

4. The Commission shall, in liaison with the Member States, take the necessary steps to ensure proper coordination and cooperation with multilateral and regional organisations and entities, such as international financial institutions, United Nations agencies, funds and programmes, and non-European Union donors.

TITLE II
PROGRAMMING AND ALLOCATION OF FUNDS
Article 6

Type of programmes

1. Community assistance under this Regulation shall be implemented through:

(a) country, multi-country and cross-border strategy papers and multi-annual indicative programmes referred to in Article 7, covering:

(i) country or multi-country programmes, which deal with assistance to one partner country or address regional and sub-regional cooperation between two or more partner countries, in which Member States may participate;

(ii) cross-border cooperation programmes, which deal with cooperation between one or more Member States and one or more partner countries, taking place in regions adjacent to their shared part of the external border of the Community;

(b) joint operational programmes for cross-border cooperation referred to in Article 9, annual action programmes referred to in Article 12 and special measures referred to in Article 13.

2. Multi-country programmes may include trans-regional cooperation measures. For the purposes of this Regulation, trans-regional cooperation shall mean cooperation between Member States and partner countries, addressing common challenges, intended for their common benefit, and taking place anywhere in the territory of the Member States and of partner countries.

Article 7

Programming and allocation of funds

1. For country or multi-country programmes, strategy papers shall be adopted in accordance with the procedure referred to in Article 26(2). Strategy papers shall reflect the policy framework and the action plans referred to in Article 3 and be consistent with the principles and modalities laid down in Articles 4 and 5.

Strategy papers shall be established for a period compatible with the priorities set in the policy framework and shall contain multiannual indicative programmes including indicative multi-annual financial allocations and priority objectives for each country or region consistent with those listed in Article 2(2). They shall be reviewed at mid-term or whenever necessary and may be revised in accordance with the procedure referred to in Article 26(2).

2. In establishing country or multi-country programmes, the Commission shall determine the allocations for each programme, using transparent and objective criteria and taking into account the specific characteristics and needs of the country or the region concerned, the level of ambition of the European Union's partnership with a given country, progress towards implementing agreed objectives, including on governance and on reform, and the capacity of managing and absorbing Community assistance.

3. For the sole purpose of cross-border cooperation, in order to establish the list of joint operational programmes referred to in Article 9(1), the indicative multi-annual allocations and the territorial units eligible to participate in each programme, one or, if necessary, more strategy papers shall be adopted in accordance with the procedure referred to in Article 26(2). Such strategy papers shall be drawn up taking into account the principles and modalities laid down in Articles 4 and 5 and shall, in principle, cover a period of up to seven years from 1 January 2007 to 31 December 2013.

4. The Commission shall determine the allocation of funds to the cross-border cooperation programmes, taking into account objective criteria, such as the population of the eligible areas and other factors affecting the intensity of cooperation, including the specific characteristics of the border areas and the capacity for managing and absorbing Community assistance.

5. The European Regional Development Fund (ERDF) shall contribute to cross-border cooperation programmes established and implemented under the provisions of this Regulation. The amount of the contribution from the ERDF for borders with partner

countries is set out in the relevant provisions of Council Regulation (EC) No 1083/2006 of 11 July 2006 laying down general provisions on the European Regional Development Fund, the European Social Fund and the Cohesion Fund.

6. In the event of crises or threats to democracy, the rule of law, human rights and fundamental freedoms, or of natural or man-made disasters, an emergency procedure may be used to conduct an ad hoc review of strategy papers. This review shall ensure coherence between Community assistance provided under this Regulation and assistance provided under other Community financial instruments, including Regulation (EC, Euratom) of the European Parliament and of…the Council of establishing an Instrument for Stability.

TITLE III
CROSS-BORDER COOPERATION
Article 8

Geographical eligibility

1. The cross-border cooperation programmes referred to in Article 6(1)(a)(ii) may cover all of the following border regions:

(a) all territorial units corresponding to NUTS level 3 or equivalent along the land borders between Member States and partner countries;

(b) all territorial units corresponding to NUTS level 3 or equivalent along sea crossings of significant importance;

(c) all coastal territorial units corresponding to NUTS level 2 or equivalent facing a sea basin common to Member States and partner countries.

2. In order to ensure the continuation of existing cooperation and in other justified cases, territorial units adjoining those referred to in paragraph 1 may be allowed to participate in cross-border cooperation programmes under the conditions laid down in the strategy papers referred to in Article 7(3).

3. When programmes are established pursuant to paragraph (1)(b), the Commission may, in agreement with the partners, propose that participation in cooperation be extended to the whole NUTS level 2 territorial unit in whose area the NUTS level 3 territorial unit is located.

4. The list of sea crossings of significant importance shall be defined by the Commission in the strategy papers referred to in Article 7(3) on the basis of distance and other relevant geographical and economic criteria.

Article 9

Programming

1. Cross-border cooperation under this Regulation shall be carried out in the framework of multi-annual programmes covering cooperation for a border or a group of borders and comprising multi-annual measures which pursue a consistent set of priorities and which may be implemented with the support of Community assistance (hereinafter joint operational programmes). The joint operational programmes shall be based on the strategy papers referred to in Article 7(3).

2. Joint operational programmes for land borders and sea crossings of significant importance shall be established for each border at the appropriate territorial level and

include eligible territorial units belonging to one or more Member States and one or more partner countries.

3. Joint operational programmes for sea basins shall be multilateral and include eligible territorial units facing a common sea basin belonging to several participating countries, including at least one Member State and one partner country, taking into account the institutional systems and the principle of partnership. They may include bilateral activities supporting cooperation between one Member State and one partner country. These programmes shall be closely coordinated with trans-national cooperation programmes having a partially overlapping geographical coverage and having been established in the European Union pursuant to Regulation (EC) No 1083/2006.

4. Joint operational programmes shall be established by the Member States and partner countries concerned at the appropriate territorial level, in accordance with their institutional system and taking into account the principle of partnership referred to in Article 4. They shall normally cover a period of seven years running from 1 January 2007 to 31 December 2013.

5. Countries, other than the participating countries, which face a common sea basin where a joint operational programme is being established may be associated with that joint operational programme and benefit from Community assistance under the conditions determined in the implementing rules referred to in Article 11.

6. Within one year of the approval of the strategy papers referred to in Article 7(3), the participating countries shall jointly submit proposals for joint operational programmes to the Commission. The Commission shall adopt each joint operational programme after assessing its consistency with this Regulation and the implementing rules.

7. Joint operational programmes may be revised at the initiative of the participating countries, participating border regions or the Commission to take into account changes in cooperation priorities, socio-economic developments, the results observed from implementation of the measures concerned and from the monitoring and evaluation process, and the need to adjust the amounts of aid available and reallocate resources.

8. Following the adoption of the joint operational programmes, the Commission shall conclude a financing agreement with the partner countries in accordance with the relevant provisions of Council Regulation (EC, Euratom) No 1605/2002 of 25 June 2002 on the Financial Regulation applicable to the general budget of the European Communities. The financing agreement shall include the legal provisions necessary for the implementation of the joint operational programme and should also be signed by the joint managing authority referred to in Article 10.

9. Participating countries shall, taking into account the principle of partnership, jointly select those actions consistent with the priorities and measures of the joint operational programme that will receive Community assistance.

10. In specific and duly justified cases, where:

(a) a joint operational programme cannot be established owing to problems arising in relations between participating countries or between the European Union and a partner country,

(b) by 30 June 2010, at the latest, the participating countries have not yet submitted to the Commission a joint operational programme,

(c) the partner country does not sign the financing agreement by the end of the year following the adoption of the programme,

(d) the joint operational programme cannot be implemented owing to problems arising in relations between participating countries, the Commission, following consultations with the Member State(s) concerned, shall take the necessary steps to allow the Member State concerned to use the ERDF contribution to the programme pursuant to Regulation (EC) No 1083/2006.

Article 10

Management of programmes

1. Joint operational programmes shall, in principle, be implemented through shared management by a joint managing authority located in a Member State. The joint managing authority may be assisted by a joint technical secretariat.

2. The participating countries may propose to the Commission that the joint managing authority should be located in a partner country, provided that the designated body is in a position to apply in full the criteria laid down in the relevant provisions of Regulation (EC, Euratom) No 1605/2002.

3. For the purpose of this Regulation 'joint managing authority' shall mean any public or private authority or body, including the state itself, at national, regional or local level, designated jointly by the Member State or States and the partner country or countries covered by a joint operational programme, having the financial and administrative capacity to manage Community assistance and having the legal capacity to conclude the agreements necessary for the purpose of this Regulation.

4. The joint managing authority shall be responsible for managing and implementing the joint operational programme in accordance with the principle of sound technical and financial management, and for ensuring the legality and regularity of its operations. To this end, it shall put in place appropriate management, control and accounting systems and standards.

5. The management and control system of a joint operational programme shall provide for proper separation of the management, certification and audit functions, either through a proper segregation of duties within the managing authority or through the designation of separate bodies for certification and audit.

6. In order to allow the joint operational programmes to prepare adequately for implementation, after the adoption of the joint operational programme and before the signature of the financing agreement, the Commission may allow the joint managing authority to use part of the programme budget to start financing programme activities such as the incurring of operational costs of the managing authority, technical assistance and other preparatory actions. The detailed modalities of such a preparatory phase shall be included in the implementing rules referred to in Article 11.

Article 11

Implementing rules

1. Implementing rules laying down specific provisions for the implementation of this Title shall be adopted in accordance with the procedure referred to in Article 26(2).

2. Matters covered by the implementing rules shall include issues such as the rate of cofinancing, preparation of joint operational programmes, the designation and functions of the joint authorities, the role and function of the monitoring and selection committees and of the joint secretariat, eligibility of expenditure, joint project selection, the preparatory phase, technical and financial management of Community assistance, financial control and audit, monitoring and evaluation, visibility and information activities for potential beneficiaries.

TITLE IV

IMPLEMENTATION

Article 12

Adoption of action programmes

1. Action programmes, drawn up on the basis of the strategy papers referred to in Article 7(1), shall be adopted in accordance with the procedure referred to in Article 26(2), normally on an annual basis.

Exceptionally, for instance where an action programme has not yet been adopted, the Commission may, on the basis of the strategy papers and multi-annual indicative programmes referred to in Article 7, adopt measures not provided for in an action programme under the same rules and procedures as apply to action programmes.

2. Action programmes shall specify the objectives pursued, the fields of intervention, the expected results, the management procedures and the total amount of financing planned. They shall take into account the lessons learned from past implementation of Community assistance. They shall contain a description of the operations to be financed, an indication of the amounts allocated for each operation and an indicative implementation timetable. They shall include a definition of the type of performance indicators that shall have to be monitored when implementing the measures financed under the programmes.

3. For cross-border cooperation, the Commission shall adopt joint programmes in accordance with the procedures referred to in Article 9.

4. The Commission shall present action programmes and joint cross-border cooperation programmes to the European Parliament and the Member States for their information within one month of their adoption.

Article 13

Adoption of special measures not provided for in the strategy papers or multi-annual indicative programmes

1. In the event of unforeseen and duly justified needs or circumstances, the Commission shall adopt special measures not provided for in the strategy papers or multi-annual indicative programmes (hereinafter special measures).

Special measures may also be used to fund activities to ease the transition from emergency aid to long-term development activities, including activities intended to ensure that the public is better prepared to deal with recurring crises.

2. Where the cost of such measures exceeds EUR 10 000 000, the Commission shall adopt them in accordance with the procedure referred to in Article 26(2).

The procedure referred to in Article 26(2) need not be used for amendments to special measures such as those making technical adjustments, extending the implementation period, reallocating appropriations within the forecast budget, or increasing the size of the budget by less than 20% of the initial budget, provided these amendments do not affect the initial objectives set out in the Commission decision.

3. Special measures shall specify the objectives pursued, the areas of activity, the expected results, the management procedures used and the total amount of financing planned. They shall contain a description of the operations to be financed, an indication of the amounts allocated for each operation and an indicative implementation timetable. They shall include a definition of the type of performance indicators that will have to be monitored when implementing the special measures.

4. The Commission shall send special measures the value of which does not exceed EUR 10 000 000 to the European Parliament and the Member States for their information within one month of adopting its decision.

Article 14

Eligibility
1. The following shall be eligible for funding under this Regulation for the purposes of implementing action programmes, joint cross-border cooperation programmes and special measures:
(a) partner countries and regions and their institutions;
(b) decentralised bodies in the partner countries, such as regions, departments, provinces and municipalities;
(c) joint bodies set up by the partner countries and regions and the Community;
(d) international organisations, including regional organisations, UN bodies, departments and missions, international financial institutions and development banks, in so far as they contribute to the objectives of this Regulation;
(e) Community institutions and bodies, but only for the purposes of implementing support measures of the type referred to in Article 16;
(f) European Union agencies;
(g) the following entities and bodies of the Member States, partner countries and regions and any other third country complying with the rules on access to the Community's external assistance referred to in Article 21, in so far as they contribute to the objectives of this Regulation:
(i) public or parastatal bodies, local authorities or administrations and consortia thereof;
(ii) companies, firms and other private organisations and businesses;
(iii) financial institutions that grant, promote and finance private investment in partner countries and regions;
(iv) non-state actors as defined in (h);
(v) natural persons;
(h) the following non-state actors:
(i) non-governmental organisations;
(ii) organisations representing national and/or ethnic minorities;
(iii) local citizens' groups and traders' associations;

(iv) cooperatives, trade unions, organisations representing economic and social interests;

(v) local organisations (including networks) involved in decentralised regional cooperation and integration;

(vi) consumer organisations, women's and youth organisations, teaching, cultural research and scientific organisations;

(vii) universities;

(viii) churches and religious associations and communities;

(ix) the media;

(x) cross-border associations, non-governmental associations and independent foundations.

2. When essential to achieve the objectives of this Regulation, Community assistance may be granted to bodies or actors which are not explicitly referred to in this Article.

Article 15

Types of measures

1. Community assistance shall be used to finance programmes, projects and any type of measure contributing to the objectives of this Regulation.

2. Community assistance may also be used:

(a) to finance technical assistance and targeted administrative measures, including those cooperation measures involving public-sector experts dispatched from the Member States and their regional and local authorities involved in the programme;

(b) to finance investments and investment-related activities;

(c) for contributions to the EIB or other financial intermediaries, in accordance with Article 23, for loan financing, equity investments, guarantee funds or investment funds;

(d) for debt relief programmes in exceptional cases, under an internationally agreed debt relief programme;

(e) for sectoral or general budget support if the partner country's management of public spending is sufficiently transparent, reliable and effective, and where it has put in place properly formulated sectoral or macroeconomic policies approved by its principal donors, including, where relevant, the international financial institutions;

(f) to provide interest-rate subsidies, in particular for environmental loans;

(g) to provide insurance against non-commercial risks;

(h) to contribute to a fund established by the Community, its Member States, international and regional organisations, other donors or partner countries;

(i) to contribute to the capital of international financial institutions or the regional development banks;

(j) to finance the costs necessary for the effective administration and supervision of projects and programmes by the countries benefiting from Community assistance;

(k) to finance microprojects;

(l) for food security measures.

3. In principle, Community assistance shall not be used to finance taxes, customs duties and other fiscal charges.

Article 16

Support measures

1. Community financing may also cover expenditure associated with the preparation, follow-up, monitoring, auditing and evaluation activities directly necessary for the implementation of this Regulation and for the achievement of its objectives, e.g. studies, meetings, information, awareness-raising, publication and training activities, including training and educational measures for partners enabling them to take part in the various stages of the programme, expenditure associated with computer networks for the exchange of information and any other administrative or technical assistance expenditure that the Commission may incur for the management of the programme. It shall also cover expenditure at Commission Delegations on the administrative support needed to manage operations financed under this Regulation.

2. These support measures are not necessarily covered by multi-annual programming and may therefore be financed outside the scope of strategy papers and multi-annual indicative programmes. However, they may also be financed under multiannual indicative programmes. The Commission shall adopt support measures not covered by multi-annual indicative programmes in accordance with Article 13.

Article 17

Co-financing

1. Measures financed under this Regulation shall be eligible for cofinancing from the following, inter alia:

(a) Member States, their regional and local authorities and their public and parastatal agencies;

(b) EEA countries, Switzerland and other donor countries, and in particular their public and parastatal agencies;

(c) international organisations, including regional organisations, and in particular international and regional financial institutions;

(d) companies, firms, other private organisations and businesses, and other non-state actors;

(e) partner countries and regions in receipt of funding.

2. In the case of parallel cofinancing, the project or programme is split into a number of clearly identifiable sub-projects which are each financed by the different partners providing cofinancing in such a way that the end-use of the financing can always be identified. In the case of joint cofinancing, the total cost of the project or programme is shared between the partners providing the cofinancing, and resources are pooled in such a way that it is not possible to identify the source of funding for any given activity undertaken as part of the project or programme.

3. In the case of joint cofinancing, the Commission may receive and manage funds on behalf of the bodies referred to in paragraph 1(a), (b) and (c) for the purpose of implementing joint measures. Such funds shall be treated as assigned revenue, in accordance with Article 18 of Regulation (EC, Euratom) No 1605/2002.

Article 18

Management procedures

1. The Commission shall implement operations under this Regulation in accordance with Regulation (EC, Euratom) No 1605/2002.

2. The Commission may entrust tasks of public authority, and in particular budget implementation tasks, to the bodies indicated in Article 54(2)(c) of Regulation (EC, Euratom) No 1605/2002 if they are of recognised international standing, comply with internationally recognised systems of management and control and are supervised by a public authority.

3. The Commission may conclude framework agreements with partner countries which shall provide for all measures necessary to ensure the effective implementation of Community assistance and protection of the Community's financial interests.

4. In the case of decentralised management, the Commission may decide to use the procurement or grant procedures of the beneficiary partner country or region, provided that:

(a) the procedures of the beneficiary partner country or region satisfy the principles of transparency, proportionality, equal treatment and non-discrimination and prevent any conflict of interests;

(b) the beneficiary partner country or region undertakes to check regularly that the operations financed by the Community budget have been properly implemented, to take appropriate measures to prevent irregularities and fraud, and, if necessary, to take legal action to recover unduly paid funds.

Article 19

Budget commitments

1. Budget commitments shall be made on the basis of decisions taken by the Commission in accordance with Articles 9(6), 12(1), 13(1) and 16(2).

2. Budget commitments for measures extending over a number of financial years may be split into annual instalments, spread over a number of years.

3. Community financing may take one of the following legal forms, inter alia: financing agreements, grant contracts, procurement contracts, employment contracts.

Article 20

Protecting the Community's financial interests

1. Any agreements resulting from this Regulation shall contain provisions ensuring the protection of the Community's financial interests, in particular with respect to irregularities, fraud, corruption and any other illegal activity, in accordance with Council Regulations (EC, Euratom) No 2988/95 of 18 December 1995 on the protection of the European Communities financial interests, and (Euratom, EC) No 2185/96 of 11 November 1996 concerning on-the-spot checks and inspections carried out by the Commission in order to protect the European Communities' financial interests against fraud and other irregularities and Regulation (EC) No 1073/1999 of the European Parliament and of the Council of 25 May 1999 concerning investigations conducted by the European Anti-Fraud Office (OLAF).

2. Agreements shall expressly entitle the Commission and the Court of Auditors to perform audits, including document audits or an on-the-spot audit of any contractor or subcontractor who has received Community funds. They shall also expressly authorise the Commission to carry out on-the-spot checks and inspections, as provided for in Regulation (Euratom, EC) No 2185/96.

3. All contracts resulting from the implementation of Community assistance shall ensure the rights of the Commission and the Court of Auditors under paragraph 2 during and after the performance of the contracts.

Article 21

Participation in tenders and contracts

1. Participation in the award of procurement or grant contracts financed under this Regulation shall be open to all natural persons who are nationals of, and legal persons established in, a Member State of the Community, a country that is a beneficiary of this Regulation, a country that is a beneficiary of an Instrument for Pre-Accession Assistance set up by Council Regulation (EC) No 1085/2006 of 17 July 2006 establishing an Instrument for Pre-Accession Assistance (IPA) or a Member State of the EEA.

2. The Commission may, in duly substantiated cases, authorise the participation of natural persons who are nationals of, and legal persons established in, a country having traditional economic, trade or geographical links with neighbouring countries, and the use of supplies and materials of different origin.

3. Participation in the award of procurement or grant contracts financed under this Regulation shall also be open to all natural persons who are nationals of, or legal persons established in, any country other than those referred to in paragraph 1, whenever reciprocal access to their external assistance has been established. Reciprocal access shall be granted whenever a country grants eligibility on equal terms to the Member States and to the recipient country concerned.

Reciprocal access to the Community's external assistance shall be established by means of a specific decision concerning a given country or a given regional group of countries. Such a decision shall be adopted by the Commission in accordance with the procedure referred to in Article 26(2) and shall be in force for a minimum period of one year.

The granting of reciprocal access to the Community's external assistance shall be based on a comparison between the Community and other donors and shall proceed at sectoral or entire country level, whether it be a donor or a recipient country. The decision to grant this reciprocity to a donor country shall be based on the transparency, consistency and proportionality of the aid provided by that donor, including its qualitative and quantitative nature. The beneficiary countries shall be consulted in the process described in this paragraph.

4. Participation in the award of procurement or grant contracts financed under this Regulation shall be open to international organisations.

5. Experts proposed in the context of procedures for the award of contracts need not comply with the nationality rules set out above.

6. All supplies and materials purchased under contracts financed under this Regulation shall originate in the Community or a country eligible under this Article. The term 'origin' for the purpose of this Regulation is defined in the relevant Community legislation on rules of origin for customs purposes.

7. The Commission may, in duly substantiated exceptional cases, authorise the participation of natural persons who are nationals of, and legal persons established in, countries other than those referred to in paragraphs 1, 2 and 3, or the purchase of supplies and materials of different origin from that set out in paragraph 6. Derogations may be justified on the basis of the unavailability of products and services in the markets of the countries concerned, for reasons of extreme urgency, or if the eligibility rules were to make the realisation of a project, a programme or an action impossible or exceedingly difficult.

8. Whenever Community funding covers an operation implemented through an international organisation, participation in the appropriate contractual procedures shall be open to all natural or legal persons who are eligible pursuant to paragraphs 1, 2 and 3 as well as to all natural or legal persons who are eligible pursuant to the rules of that organisation, care being taken to ensure that equal treatment is afforded to all donors. The same rules shall apply in respect of supplies, materials and experts.

Whenever Community funding covers an operation co-financed with a Member State, with a third country, subject to reciprocity as defined in paragraph 3, or with a regional organisation, participation in the appropriate contractual procedures shall be open to all natural or legal persons who are eligible pursuant to paragraphs 1, 2 and 3 as well as to all natural or legal persons who are eligible under the rules of such Member State, third country or regional organisation. The same rules shall apply in respect of supplies, materials and experts.

9. Where Community assistance under this Regulation is managed by a joint managing authority, as referred to in Article 10, the procurement rules shall be those laid down in the implementing rules referred to in Article 11.

10. Tenderers who have been awarded contracts under this Regulation shall respect core labour standards as defined in the relevant International Labour Organisation conventions.

11. Paragraphs 1 to 10 shall be without prejudice to the participation of categories of eligible organisations by nature or by localisation in regard to the objectives of the action.

Article 22

Prefinancing
Interest generated by prefinancing payments to beneficiaries shall be deducted from the final payment.

Article 23

Funds made available to the EIB or other financial intermediaries
1. The funds referred to in Article 15(2)(c) shall be managed by financial intermediaries, by the EIB or any other bank or organisation capable of managing them.
2. The Commission shall adopt implementing provisions for paragraph 1 on a case-by-case basis to cover risk-sharing, the remuneration of the intermediary responsible for implementation, the use and recovery of profits on funds, and the closure of the operation.

Article 24

Evaluation
1. The Commission shall regularly evaluate the results of geographical and cross-border policies and programmes and of sectoral policies and the effectiveness of programming

in order to ascertain whether the objectives have been met and enable it to formulate recommendations with a view to improving future operations.

2. The Commission shall send significant evaluation reports to the committee referred to in Article 26 for discussion. These reports and discussions shall feed back into programme design and resource allocation.

TITLE V
FINAL PROVISIONS
Article 25

Annual report

The Commission shall examine the progress made on implementing the measures taken under this Regulation and shall submit to the European Parliament and the Council an annual report on the implementation of Community assistance. This report shall also be submitted to the European Economic and Social Committee and to the Committee of the Regions. It shall contain information relating to the previous year on the measures financed, the results of monitoring and evaluation exercises, and the implementation of budget commitments and payments broken down by country, region and cooperation sector.

Article 26

Committee

1. The Commission shall be assisted by a committee.

2. Where reference is made to this paragraph, Articles 4 and 7 of Decision 1999/468/ EC shall apply.

The period laid down in Article 4(3) of Decision 1999/468/EC shall be set at 30 days.

3. The committee shall adopt its rules of procedure.

4. An observer from the EIB shall take part in the committee's proceedings with regard to questions concerning the EIB.

5. In order to facilitate the dialogue with the European Parliament, the Commission shall regularly inform the European Parliament of the committee proceedings and provide the relevant documents including agenda, draft measures and summary records of the meetings in accordance with Article 7(3) of Decision 1999/468/EC.

Article 27

Participation by a third country not listed in the Annex

1. To ensure the coherence and effectiveness of Community assistance, the Commission may decide, when adopting action programmes of the type referred to in Article 12 or the special measures referred to in Article 13, that countries, territories and regions eligible for assistance under other Community external assistance instruments and the European Development Fund are eligible for measures under this Regulation where the project or programme implemented is of a global, regional or cross-border nature.

2. Provision may be made for this method of financing possibility in the strategy papers referred to in Article 7.

3. The provisions of Article 14 concerning eligibility and the provisions of Article 21 concerning participation in procurement procedures shall be adapted to allow the countries, territories or regions concerned to take part.

4. In the case of programmes financed under the provisions of different Community external assistance instruments, participation in procurement procedures may be open to all natural and legal persons of the countries eligible under the different instruments.

Article 28

Suspension of Community assistance

1. Without prejudice to the provisions on the suspension of aid in partnership and cooperation agreements and association agreements with partner countries and regions, where a partner country fails to observe the principles referred to in Article 1, the Council, acting by a qualified majority on a proposal from the Commission, may take appropriate steps in respect of any Community assistance granted to the partner country under this Regulation.

2. In such cases, Community assistance shall primarily be used to support non-state actors for measures aimed at promoting human rights and fundamental freedoms and supporting the democratisation process in partner countries.

Article 29

Financial envelope

1. The financial envelope for implementation of this Regulation over the period 2007 to 2013 shall be EUR 11 181 000 000, broken down as follows:

(a) a minimum of 95% of the financial envelope shall be allocated to the country and multi-country programmes referred to in Article 6(1)(a)(i);

(b) up to 5% of the financial envelope shall be allocated to the cross-border cooperation programmes referred to in Article 6(1)(a)(ii).

2. Annual appropriations shall be authorised by the budgetary authority within the limits of the financial framework.

Article 30

Review

The Commission shall submit to the European Parliament and the Council by 31 December 2010 a report evaluating the implementation of this Regulation in the first three years with, if appropriate, a legislative proposal introducing the necessary modifications to it, including to the financial breakdown referred to in Article 29(1).

Article 31

Repeal

1. As from 1 January 2007, Regulations (EEC) No 1762/92, (EC) No 1734/94 and (EC) No 1488/96 shall be repealed.

2. The repealed Regulations shall continue to apply for legal acts and commitments of pre-2007 budget years.

Article 32

Entry into force

This Regulation shall enter into force 20 days after its publication in the Official Journal of the European Union.

It shall apply from 1 January 2007 to 31 December 2013.

This Regulation shall be binding in its entirety and directly applicable in all Member States.

ANNEX

Partner countries referred to in Article 1

Algeria
Armenia
Azerbaijan
Belarus
Egypt
Georgia
Israel
Jordan
Lebanon
Libya
Moldova
Morocco
Palestinian Authority of the West Bank and Gaza Strip
Russian Federation
Syria
Tunisia
Ukraine

EU/EGYPT ACTION PLAN (2007).

This Action Plan is an example of how the EU tries to steer reform in the neighbourhood countries. The Plan identifies areas and key actions for which EU funding may be mobilized. It was adopted as a recommendation by the EU–Egypt Association Council in 2007.

1. Introduction

The Arab Republic of Egypt and the European Union as key partners and, near neighbours, reaffirm their commitment to deepen their political, economic and social relations on the basis of their close cooperation and strategic partnership that has developed in the last few decades and within the framework of the Euro-Mediterranean Partnership and the Association Agreement embodying the objectives and principles of the Barcelona Declaration, and complementing its multilateral process.

The evolving regional and international context of Egypt–EU relations has fostered greater scope for cooperation. On the one hand, the enlargement of the EU on 1 May 2004 which has brought a historical shift for the Union in political, geographic and economic terms, paved the way for the European Neighbourhood Policy that aims to deepen the EU's relations with its neighbouring countries to the East and South. On the other hand, Egypt continues to pursue its dynamic foreign policy aiming to strengthen its relations with its international partners in particular the EU, its commitment to further integration with the global economy, and its efforts for further political and economic development and modernization. Thus, a major opportunity has evolved for Egypt and the EU to further develop their strategic partnership through an increasingly close and enhanced relationship. This will involve a significant degree of economic integration and deepening of political, cultural and social co-operation, aiming to promote peace, stability, security, growth, development and prosperity in the Euro-Mediterranean region as well as modernization of the Egyptian economy and society.

In this regard, the Action Plan between Egypt and the EU within the European Neighbourhood Policy sets ambitious objectives based on joint ownership, common interests, reciprocal commitments, differentiation, shared values and implementation of national plans and reform programmes, politically, economically, socially and institutionally.

Egypt and the EU agree, through the current Action Plan, to enter into intensified political, security, economic, trade, investment, scientific, technological and cultural relations, and shared responsibility in establishing an area of peace and stability including the prevention and settlement of conflicts in the region and to reinvigorate regional and sub-regional cooperation.

The level of ambition of the EU–Egypt relationship, leading to continuing trade liberalization including in agriculture and services, a stake in the EU's internal market, increased financial support and enhanced political cooperation, will depend on the degree of commitment to common values as well as the implementation of jointly agreed priorities to mutual benefits. The pace of progress of the relationship will acknowledge fully the efforts and concrete achievements in meeting those commitments.

Recognizing Egypt's efforts and reform priorities to further develop and modernise all sectors of the Egyptian society and economy based on the respect of her identity, specificities and national priorities, the Action Plan aims to support such efforts and priorities as reflected in the National Development Plan 2002–2007, President Mubarak's Electoral Platform for 2005 and the Government's statement to the parliament in January 2006.

These include national priorities aiming to: improve quality of life and standard of living; increase employment opportunities and reduce unemployment; reduce poverty and expand the coverage of social security; eradicate illiteracy and develop education and higher education; consolidate the role of institutions, promote the protection of human rights and fundamental freedoms; continue maintaining and ensuring judiciary independence; expand the participation in political life; enhance human resources and institutional capacity building; increase rates of economic growth and investments; increase female participation in development; achieve a significant expansion in the production and exports capacities; improve industrial potentials; promote innovation, scientific research and technological development and preserve the environment.

This Action Plan is a first step in a process covering a timeframe of three to five years. Its implementation will help fulfil the provisions and aims of the Association Agreement (AA) and will encourage and support Egypt's national development, modernization and reform objectives. It will furthermore help to devise and implement policies and measures to promote economic growth, employment and social cohesion, to reduce poverty and protect the environment, thereby contributing to the long-term objective of sustainable development. Implementation of the Action Plan will also help, where appropriate, further integration into European Union economic, social and technological structures and significantly increase the possibility to advance the approximation of Egyptian legislation, norms and standards to those of the European Union in appropriate areas, thereby enhancing prospects for trade, investment and growth.

The Action Plan will take into account the balance between the acceleration necessary for dynamic implementation and modernization of the Egyptian economy and the imperatives of a sustainable socio-economic development.

Egypt's unique geographical position and her historical and strategic relations with the Arab and African countries, and her key role for peace and stability in the Middle East, as well as the EU's increasing role on the global arena and its enhanced contribution to peace, security and economic development in the Mediterranean and the Middle East, enable Egypt and EU, through this Action Plan to further develop their cooperation on regional and international issues, particularly referring to the Middle East Peace Process, disarmament and arms control, non proliferation of weapons of mass destruction and their delivery systems in the Middle East and elsewhere, and the fight against terrorism; to enhance and to promote dialogue between cultures and civilizations and to promote South-South trade and cooperation.

In order to contribute to the realization of the ambitious objectives of this Action Plan, the EU will provide appropriate financial support through the different available financial instruments.

The AA is the legal framework governing the bilateral relations between Egypt and the EU.

New Partnership Perspectives

The European Neighbourhood Policy and Egypt's policy to deepen its relationship with the EU open New Partnership Perspectives:

• The perspective of moving beyond the existing relationship to a significant degree of economic integration including through a stake in the EU's Internal Market, which aims to promote the free movements of goods, services, capitals and persons and the possibility for Egypt to participate progressively in key aspects of EU policies and programmes.

• An upgrade in the scope and intensity of political cooperation.

• Deepening trade and economic relations through the continued reduction of trade barriers on both sides, increased access to each others' markets including in agriculture and services and continuous upgrading of economic legislations. This will stimulate trade and foreign direct investment and accelerate economic growth accompanied by a sufficient strengthening of the private sector and business conditions leading to a greater economic integration between Egypt and the European Union.

• Increased financial support: EU financial assistance for Egypt will be better targeted to support the implementation of the actions identified in the present document, as well as the implementation of the Association Agreement and development, modernization and reform agenda of the Government of Egypt, in particular developing human resources and enhancing the business climate to increase investment and employment. The European Commission is furthermore proposing a new European Neighbourhood and Partnership Instrument (ENPI) for this purpose, also covering cross-border and transnational cooperation between Egypt and EU Member States. There will also be support for infrastructure investment as well as for the development of the private sector and partnership through the European Investment Bank and FEMIP.

• Prospect of gradual opening of or reinforced co-operation in relevant European Community programmes, promoting i.a. cultural, educational, environmental, technological and scientific links.

• Support for meeting EU and international norms and standards and for modernization efforts including through technical assistance and twinning, as well as targeted support and advise for legislative approximation through mechanisms such as TAIEX.

• Enhanced direct cooperation between administrations based on the bodies set up by the Association Agreement in particular institutionalised thematic sub-committees.

In light of the fulfilment of the objectives of this Action Plan and of the overall evolution of EU–Egypt relations, consideration will be given to the possibility of a new contractual relationship.

Priorities for Action

This Action Plan sets out a comprehensive set of priorities in areas within the scope of the Association Agreement. Among these priorities, all of which are important, particular attention should be given to:

• Enhance political dialogue and co-operation, based on shared values, including on issues such as continued commitment and efforts to achieve a just, comprehensive and lasting settlement to the Middle East conflict based on relevant UNSC resolutions and the terms of reference of the Madrid Conference and the principle of 'land for peace'.

• Enhance dialogue on security issues such as disarmament and arms control; non proliferation of weapons of mass destruction and their delivery systems, including the objective of establishing a zone free of WMD and their delivery systems in the Middle East; strengthening the fight against terrorism; peacekeeping.

• Enhance the effectiveness of institutions entrusted with strengthening democracy and the rule of law and consolidate the independent and effective administration of justice.

• Promote the protection of human rights in all its aspects; improve the dialogue between cultures and religions, cooperate in the fight against intolerance, discrimination, racism and xenophobia and in the promotion of respect for religions and cultures. Such priorities would be pursued based on the principles of respect, understanding and equality.

• Increase economic integration with the EU, particularly by taking steps to the gradual liberalization of trade in services and on the right of establishment and to liberalize trade in agriculture, processed agricultural products and fisheries, and enhance Egypt's export potential to the EU market by upgrading the quality of Egypt's agricultural production through improving sanitary and phytosanitary standards and rural development.

• Improving macroeconomic governance, reforming the financial sector, strengthening the role of the private sector, enhancing the business climate, in particular for SMEs, eliminating institutional, regulatory and administrative obstacles with a view to attract increasing national and foreign investments and to create job opportunities, consequently alleviating poverty.

• Boost industrial development and enterprises capabilities and competitiveness through improved skills, better access to finance, promotion of new technologies, encouraging entrepreneurship and innovation, and development of efficient business support services and increase labour force productivity.

• Deepen and enhance the existing economic dialogue and identify areas suitable for gradual regulatory upgrading and approximation with EU technical legislation, standards and conformity assessment procedures.

• Proceed in reforming the tax system, improving public finance management, and upgrading public institutions.

• Promote south-south trade, through encouraging FDI participation in regional projects such as: infrastructure, trade facilitation, energy and transport.

• Strengthen cooperation on poverty reduction and social development, in particular in the areas of combating illiteracy, education reforms, upgrading the vocational training, training systems, quality assurance, as well as better socio-economic inclusion and social insurance and developing the health sector reform, with a particular focus on increasing the level of health security, health information and knowledge. Reforms of the education and higher education systems aim among other issues at enhancing overall quality and relevance to the labour market.

• Promote cooperation in the area of science and technology, develop national capabilities of technical, scientific and technological research and innovation, the development of R&D and transfer of technology, promote links in scientific research, strengthen efforts to implement the EU–Egypt Agreement on Scientific and Technological cooperation, strengthen links between higher research institutes and education institutions.

• Promote cooperation in the area of information technology and communications through promoting information society and its sustainability, including the use of ICT in development, the development of the ICT industry, innovation, in addition to the use of new technologies and electronic means of communications by businesses, government and citizens, as well as strengthening scientific and business links.

• Strengthen co-operation on migration-related issues, including the effective joint management of migration flows, legal and illegal migration, readmission, facilitation of the legal movement of individuals, equal treatment and social integration for legal migrants, and asylum issues.

• Promote cooperation on fight against organised crime, including trafficking in human beings, fight against drugs, fight against money laundering, and police and judicial cooperation.

• Promote co-operation in the transport field, in particular on developing infrastructure policies, implementing the sector reform programme aiming at separating regulatory, management and operation tasks; promoting the involvement of the private sector in transport projects and services; applying air, maritime, and road safety measures, and developing a Civil Global Navigation Satellite System (GALILEO).

• Enhance cooperation in the energy sector, in particular through energy policy exchanges, the gradual convergence towards the principles of the EU internal electricity and gas markets, the development of energy networks including facilitation of natural gas transportation between Egypt and the EU via the Arab gas pipeline, regional cooperation, and enhancing energy efficiency and the use of renewable energy as well as cooperation in the oil and gas industry.

• Strengthen the environmental dimension of public policy and EU–Egypt co-operation: promotion of sustainable development policies and actions, including on climate change, desertification and air, soil and water pollution.

• Strengthen links and co-operation in 'people-to-people' contacts in youth and sports, culture and audiovisual areas and civil society.

Cooperation and actions under this Plan shall be consistent with national laws and legislations.

Progress in meeting these priorities will be jointly evaluated in sub-committees established by the Association Agreement. On this basis, the EU and Egypt will review the content of the Action Plan and decide on its adaptation and renewal. After three years, Egypt and the EU will consider future prospect of the development of bilateral relations, including the possibility of new contractual links.

2. Actions

2.1. Enhanced political dialogue, economic and social development and reform

2.1.1. Enhanced political dialogue and reform

a) Democracy and rule of law

Enhance the effectiveness of institutions entrusted with strengthening democracy and the rule of law

– Strengthen participation in political life, including the promotion of public awareness and participation in elections.

– Exchange experience in the field of elections and jointly develop cooperation in areas of shared interest including through providing assistance on registering electors and capacity building.

– Foster the role of civil society and enhance its capacity to contribute more effectively to the democratic and political process as well as to the economic and social progress in accordance with national legislation.

– Pursue and support the efforts Government of Egypt towards decentralization and the reform of local administration.

– Enhance the ongoing political dialogue between the Egyptian and the European Parliaments.

– Establish a formal and regular dialogue on Human Rights and Democracy in the framework of the Association Agreement in the context of the relevant subcommittee.
– Pursue and support the Government of Egypt in the further modernization and development of public services rendered to citizens, promoting accountability, transparency and contestability.

Consolidate the independent and effective administration of justice and improve prison conditions.
– In the context of political and democratic reform, continue the ongoing process of strengthening, maintaining and ensuring the independence of the judiciary.
– Further develop measures to increase the capacity and efficiency of the justice administration (including prison) and access to justice, including capacity building of bodies entrusted with the implementation of the law.
– Support Egyptian government policies and programmes aiming at improving places of detention and prison conditions, especially the placement of minors.

b) Human rights and fundamental freedoms
– Support Egyptian government efforts to protect human rights and fundamental freedoms in line with international conventions to which Egypt is party and to elaborate a human rights strategy in partnership with the NCHR and with appropriate consultation of other relevant organizations.
– Strengthen the culture of respect for human rights and fundamental freedoms in Egypt and in the EU.
– Support Egyptian efforts to strengthen the capacity and effectiveness of competent Egyptian public institutions and councils.
– Continue the review of respective national legislations to further align their laws and practices with international human rights instruments to which they are party and taking into account relevant UN recommendations.
– Examine the possibility of accession to the optional protocols to international human rights conventions to which Egypt is a party.
– Continue and enhance cooperation with UN and African human rights treaty mechanisms, as well as with the newly established UN Human Rights Council.
– Examine the possibility for the EU Member States to sign the UN Convention on the Rights of Migrant Workers and Members of their Families.
– Promote dialogue on policies for physically and mentally disabled.
– Promote a dialogue on Rome Statute of International Criminal Court.
– Examine the relevant UN recommendations and the recommendations of the Egyptian National Council for Human Rights pertaining to security, detention conditions and prison staff with a view to their practical implementation in order to protect the human rights and integrity of detainees and to fight impunity.
– Initiate a review of laws and regulations dealing with pre-trial and administrative detention systems taking into consideration the relevant UN recommendations, particularly in order to ensure the prompt access of detainees to legal counsel and family.
– Ensure the possibility of legal recourse against death sentences for all types of courts, in accordance with the UN Safeguards guaranteeing protection of the rights

of those facing the death penalty and taking into account Article 4 and article 6 of the International Covenant on Civil and Political Rights.
– Engage in a dialogue on the death penalty.
– Co-operate to promote the achievement of the right to development in bilateral and multilateral fora.

Rights of women and children
– Promote the enhancement of women's participation in political, economic and social life as well as their role in the political decision-making process by supporting the formulation and implementation of Egypt's government policies and programmes.
– Support Egypt's efforts to promote gender equality and reinforce the fight against discrimination and gender-based violence, including strengthening the activities of the National Council for Women including its periodic review of the relevant existing legislation and recommendations for new legislation.
– Consolidate the rights of the child through the application of the relevant UN Convention on the Rights of the Child and consider revising existing legislation taking into account the recommendations of the relevant UN Committee.
– Support the efforts of the Government of Egypt to eradicate the practice of female genital mutilation including through appropriate legislative actions and the raising of public awareness.

Freedom of association and of expression and pluralism of the media
– Implement measures that promote the right of assembly and association in accordance with the International Covenant on Civil and Political Rights.
– Assert freedom of expression and independence of the media by facilitating the work of independent information providers including through appropriate legislative action.
– Examine the possibility for developing specific legislation on the protection of private data.
– Pursue the liberalisation process in the information sector and further increase access to information for all citizens including by reviewing the legal and administrative frameworks.
– Establish joint cooperation activities on media issues including capacity building.

Fight against discrimination, intolerance, racism and xenophobia
– Cooperate to combat all forms of discrimination, intolerance, racism and xenophobia and in particular hate or defamatory discourse based on religion, beliefs, race or origin, inter alia through exchange of best practices and legislative action, as required.
– Strengthen the role of media in combating xenophobia and discrimination on the grounds of religious belief or culture and assume its responsibilities in this regard.
– Promote efforts, in Egypt and the EU, towards increasing tolerance, understanding and respect of all religions and cultures.

Fundamental social rights and core labour standards
– Develop a dialogue on fundamental social rights and core labour standards.

– Support measures that enhance the development and independence of trade unions and their role in economic and social life.

– Enhance the effective implementation of core labour standards as defined in the 1998 ILO Declaration on Fundamental Principles and Rights at Work and related ILO Conventions.

c) Co-operation on foreign and security policy

CFSP

Strengthen the Political dialogue and co-operation on foreign and security policy

– Enhance political dialogue and cooperation in jointly agreed areas of Common Foreign and Security Policy (CFSP) and European Security and Defence Policy (ESDP) through the current frameworks or through new mutually agreed frameworks.

– Engage a dialogue through their respective missions in UN/multilateral institutions on issues of common interest, including peacekeeping operations conducted within the framework of the UNSC resolutions, and cooperate where appropriate.

– Cooperation on promoting disarmament efforts, in particular, those aimed at enhancing regional stability and on further coordinating their efforts in international fora to this end, in accordance with respective membership of relevant international instruments, including working together against the illicit trade of small arms and light weapons in all its aspects.

– Dialogue and cooperation on regional issues (advancement of the Middle East Peace Process, the stability and territorial integrity of Iraq and Sudan, other regional initiatives aimed at economic and social development particularly in Africa, NEPAD, Nile Basin Initiative).

– Cooperation aiming at strengthening the application of international law and of principles of the UN Charter and cooperation for the promotion, dissemination and ensuring the respect of international humanitarian law at the regional and international levels.

– Cooperation in conflict prevention and crisis management, including cooperating with the Cairo Centre for Training on Conflict Prevention and Peacekeeping in Africa and within the framework of the Bridge Project for the creation of Euro-Mediterranean system of mitigation, prevention and management of natural and man-made disasters.

– Develop an Egyptian national strategy on disaster management and reduction.

– Develop trilateral cooperation in areas of mutual interest taking into consideration their respective development cooperation mechanisms.

d) Combating terrorism

terrorism

– Ensure respect for human rights in the fight against terrorism in accordance with international law.

– Work on elaborating appropriate legislation to address the phenomenon of terrorism serving as a legal substitute to the application of the current state of emergency taking into account Egyptian national security considerations.

– Strengthen EU–Egypt co-operation on preventing and combating terrorism, including implementing the Code of Conduct on Countering Terrorism agreed at the Barcelona Summit in November 2005 as well as the initiatives identified in this Action Plan which will be discussed in the relevant sub-committees.

– Cooperate to reinforce the role of the UN in the fight against terrorism through the full implementation of the UNSC resolution 1373 (2001) and through the ratification and implementation of the 13 UN conventions and protocols on terrorism including the recently agreed Convention for the Suppression of Acts of Nuclear Terrorism.
– Pursue efforts to arrive at a Comprehensive UN Convention on International Terrorism and promote, following agreement on the Convention, President Mubarak's initiative to hold an international conference on terrorism.
– Cooperate to ensure the implementation of the standards laid down in the FATF's recommendations on terrorist financing.
– Exchange information on terrorist groups and their support networks in accordance with international and national law.
– Exchange views on means and methods used to counter terrorism, including in technical fields and training, and by exchange of experiences in respect of terrorism prevention.
– Foster international cooperation in the fight against and the prevention of terrorism by addressing all its causes.

e) Non-proliferation of weapons of mass destruction and their means of delivery   *weapons*
– Co-operate on non-proliferation of weapons of mass destruction as well as their means of delivery including through implementing UNSC Resolution 1540/04, ensuring full compliance with and national implementation of existing international obligations and consider promoting the accession to and implementation of other relevant international instruments.
– Further develop cooperation in the prevention of and fight against the illicit trafficking of WMD-related materials.
– Cooperate on developing effective systems of national export control, controlling export and transit of WMD-related materials, including WMD end-use control on dual use of technologies, and effective sanctions for breaches of these export controls.
– Improve overall coordination in the non-proliferation area and examine specific threats related to WMD which undermine regional security and the scope of cooperation in addressing them.
– Promote the relevant provisions on the political and security partnership of the Barcelona Declaration with the objective to pursue a mutually and effectively verifiable Middle East zone free of weapons of mass destruction and their delivery systems in consonance both with President Mubarak's initiative in this regard and the principles of the EU Strategy against the proliferation of WMD.

2.1.2. Economic development and reform
a) Monetary, exchange rate and fiscal policies
Consolidate progress made with a view to improving macroeconomic stability and to promoting growth and employment.
– Continue to pursue macroeconomic stability by reducing the inflation rate and gradually achieving price stability.
– Complete the preparations for the new monetary policy strategy based on inflation targeting and representative price indicators and further strengthen central bank

independence. Continue efforts to achieve sustainable public finances by reducing the central government deficit and the consolidated public deficit. Examine the scope for an increase of public investment in key budget areas—such as education and key infrastructure projects—through further rationalization of current government spending.

– Continue efforts for further progress in transparency and accountability of government finances, by publishing complete and timely information on the budget, fiscal outcomes and audit reports. Improve further the public finance management system, in particular by ensuring the comprehensiveness of the budget, by introducing a medium-term budget planning and a single treasury account.

b) Functioning of market economy

– Increase the capacity to create sustainable growth and employment by further improving the conditions of private sector development, enhancing the investment climate, and accelerating the privatisation programme. These measures should be accompanied by improving education and training including through EU support.

– Work to reduce gradually economic distortions as well as to better target subsidies to eligible groups of the population and upgrade the social safety net.

– Accelerate the reform of the financial sector, the restructuring and the privatisation of state banks and the introduction of strong financial market supervision.

– Improve the efficiency of public services and accelerate and streamline the procedures which are necessary to set up a new company.

– Reduce and accelerate judicial procedures which are necessary to enforce contracts.

– Develop co-operation in promoting and developing dispute resolution and exchange of expertise in the arbitration of commercial disputes.

c) Sustainable development

Promotion of sustainable development

– Take steps to prepare a comprehensive national sustainable development strategy and to complete administrative structures and procedures to ensure strategic planning of sustainable development at the central level, as co-ordinated by the Ministry of Environment including through EU support where appropriate.

– Take steps to strengthen and develop the institutional setup for the integration of sustainable development considerations into other sectoral policies and plans, such as industry, energy, transport, regional development and agriculture.

– Share experiences between the Commission and Egypt about sustainable development strategies.

d) Agriculture and fisheries

Pursue the modernization and restructuring of agriculture and fisheries

Agriculture

– Cooperate in the implementation of the reforms in sectoral agricultural policies in line with the provisions of art. 50 of the Association Agreement.

– Identify and adopt accompanying measures providing for the structural, institutional, legal and administrative support necessary in order to ease access to export markets, inter alia, by approximation of technical legislation; and in particular increase

co-operation in the field of international marketing standards for all agricultural and processed agricultural products.
– Identify and adopt measures in the sector of rural development, and at the level of the development of quality production (local products, food safety, organic products, geographical indications, etc., within the scope of the national rules), which would encourage the diversification of activity and the creation of new remunerative and sustainable trade flows and enhance the efficiency of water use.
– Identify and develop measures to create a framework to encourage private investment.
– Exchange expertise to strengthen the administrative capacity of the Land cadastre.
– Strengthen the role of agricultural research centres in improving the productivity, food safety and quality of agricultural products, and promote cooperation with European Research Centres, particularly in the areas of genetic engineering and biotechnology.
– Promote the use of modern technology in the agricultural sector and in different production phases.
– Promote the distribution and exchange of information on the agricultural policies and contribute to the transfer of expertise and experiences.

Fisheries
– Reinforce the cooperation in order to implement the actions identified in the Declaration of the Ministerial Conference for the Sustainable Development of Fishery in the Mediterranean (Venice, 25–26 November 2003) in the framework of the relevant international instruments.
– Take steps to promote further the creation of fishermen associations with a view of implementing responsible fisheries and improve their capacity to be represented into international and multilateral organisations.
– Increase the scientific and technical capacity to monitoring fisheries and evaluate the state of the exploited marine resources and marine environment.
– Improve scientific cooperation with the Regional Fisheries Body and in particular the GFCM with a view to strengthening a concerted and regional approach suited to the needs of sustainable fisheries and based on dialogue and coordination.
– Undertake necessary marketing infrastructure upgrading to cope with market demands and standards.

e) Mineral resources
– Encourage cooperation between EU Member States and Egypt to develop the mineral resources sector including through the establishment of a database on mineral resources, promoting relevant investment in Egypt and building human resources capacity.

2.1.3. Social development
a) Social situation, employment and poverty reduction
Enhance social development in particular through dialogue and co-operation
– Strengthen measures for poverty alleviation through the Poverty Reduction Strategy and the anti-poverty action plan.

– Engage in a dialogue on employment and social issues including the social consequences of economic reforms with a view to develop a joint analysis of the situation and identify possible measures in this field.

– Develop and implement market driven strategies for addressing the problem of unemployment; modernize the Public Employment Services.

– Support the implementation of the new labour code including through institutional capacity building. Continue the adoption of implementing regulations and build enforcement capacity.

– Strengthen the social dialogue at all levels (tripartite and bipartite).

– Ensure and develop the institutional capacity building of the social partners to take the suitable measures according to the International Labour conventions.

– Implement the relevant International Labour Conventions to which both Egypt and the EU Member States are parties.

– Strengthen the efficiency, targeting and coverage of social expenditures with a particular attention to the enlargement of the base of the targeted groups and to the improvement of social statistics.

– Engage in a dialogue on programmes and initiatives aimed at fostering social inclusion on the basis of the principle of non discrimination, with particular attention to the integration of disadvantaged, the disabled groups, the marginalised groups and people with special needs.

– Ensure equal opportunities for women and men, including in the field of employment. Further enhance the role of women in economic and social progress.

– Enhance protection of rights of the children at risk, particularly working children, street children and children with disabilities, and intensify efforts to progressively eliminate child labour.

– Engage in a dialogue with a view to promote equal treatment of Egyptian and Community nationals who are legally residing and working in the territory of the Community or Egypt.

– Promote exchanges of experiences, dialogue and cooperation on matters of social security, notably on issues such as the reform of pension systems, the introduction of new instruments and the extension of the coverage of social protection and the improvement and enforcement of social security institutions.

Strengthening socio-economic cohesion of Egyptian regions
– Strengthen the regional development management structures. Implement the decentralisation of programme of services delivery and management at governorates level.

– Support the reduction of regional disparities in social and economic development, in particular in rural areas.

– Support policies that aim at ensuring access to basic health, education and social services for all.

b) Education and training
Support and enhance cooperation in reforming and upgrading the education and training systems and work within the framework of Egyptian plans towards convergence with EU and international standards and practice.

– Combat illiteracy and achieve education for all, especially for women and girls, by continuing the reform of the education systems, and pre-school education aiming at early childhood development.

– Continue and enhance a policy dialogue between EU and Egyptian authorities in the field of education and training.

– Continue to reform primary and secondary education to improve quality, especially through continuing decentralization and community involvement and human resources development for teachers and professors, as well as technical vocational education and training (TVET) to make it more responsive to market needs in the context of the Egyptian national educational standards.

– Reform higher education in line with the principles of Bologna process to improve internal and external efficiency. Foster the development of human resources and human capital, and promote the reform of higher education through the TEMPUS programme; ensure the integration of the social dimension in educational planning and programmes.

– Promote the use of ICT in education.

– Enhance the quality and the capacity of institutions and organisations involved in the quality assurance of education and training provision, in particular Egyptian Agency for Quality Assurance and Accreditation.

– Take steps to increase the involvement of civil society stakeholders and social partners in higher and adult education and TVET reform.

– Encourage participation in the TEMPUS programme.

– Encourage participation in the Erasmus Mundus programme.

– Encourage the participation of Egyptian students in the forthcoming EC scholarship programme and in similar schemes of EU Member States.

c) Public health
Support and cooperate in the development of health sector reform
– Continue the development of the health sector through:
– implement re-organization and decentralization of the health sector;
– improve accessibility and affordability including in rural areas and with a focus on women/children including those with disabilities;
– elaborate a system for Social Health Insurance covering the whole population;
– ensure the efficiency of institutions including laboratories;
– enhance human resources capacity;
– enhance health security and epidemiological safety;
– strengthen family health models, including maternal mortality and reproductive health issues.

Increase the level of health security, health information and knowledge
– Exchange of information and know-how on health indicators and data collection.
– Invite Egypt as observer in the meetings of the Network of Competent Authorities.

Communicable Disease Surveillance and Health Security (Epidemiological Surveillance and Control)

– Participation in Communicable Disease Networks and dedicated surveillance networks.

– Enhance response to infectious diseases, such as HIV/AIDS and hepatitis C.

2.2. Trade-related issues, market and regulatory reform
2.2.1. Movement of goods
a) Trade relations

– Identify areas with export potential to the EU and further enhance Egypt's export capability by increasing quality of Egyptian products and their competitiveness on international markets.

– Reduce substantially non-tariff barriers of a regulatory and bureaucratic nature to trade and investments.

– Strengthen the capacity building in the Egyptian administration on international trade relations.

– Enhance Egypt's participation in and capacity to benefit from regional and sub regional trade arrangements including conclusion and implementation of Free Trade Agreements.

– Establish rules of procedure to ensure the effective implementation of dispute settlement provisions under the Association Agreement on economic/trade matters based on the principles of the dispute settlement understanding of the WTO.

– Continue liberalisation of trade in agricultural, processed agricultural and fishery products as developed in the agricultural roadmap taking into account the conclusions of the Luxembourg Ministerial Meeting of May 2005.

b) Customs

– Further modernization of the customs administration and simplification of customs legislation and procedures, including computerization; rolling out of Egyptians' pilot projects on model tax and customs centres and ports' automated one-stop-shop procedures.

– Develop an Integrated Border Management Strategy by strengthening cooperation between customs and other agencies working at the border and by implementing a single-window approach at all entry points.

– Adopt and implement the new protocol on Pan-Euro-Mediterranean cumulation of origin and exchange experience and information on the smooth implementation of the new protocol and consult on the future development of rules of origin, including systems of cumulation.

– Strengthen the capacity building of the customs administration by providing further training to customs officials, including in the areas of origin and custom valuation.

– Increase transparency of customs rules and tariffs and promote further public access to customs-related information and complaint procedures.

– Exchange experience and know-how with a view to strengthening measures against pirated or counterfeit goods through the reinforcement of customs controls.

– Strengthen administrative co-operation with the EU to combat irregularities and fraud in customs and related matters.

– Develop EU–Egypt co-operation with regard to risk based customs control ensuring safety and security of goods imported, exported or in transit, and define standards for certification of operators (exporters and transporters) intervening in commercial exchanges.
– Examine possibility of further convergence of customs related legislation.
– Take steps to adopt and implement a Customs Ethics Policy.

c) Standards and conformity assessment (EU-harmonized areas)
– Continuation of work on the implementation of the Palermo Action Plan for the Free Movement of Industrial Products approved by the July 2003 Euro-Mediterranean Conference of Trade Ministers. Take the necessary steps, with the support of continuing assistance, to complete and upgrade the quality infrastructure and to start negotiating an Agreement on Conformity Assessment and Acceptance of Industrial Products (ACAA).
– Adapt the Egyptian institutions in charge of implementing product legislation and train the various stakeholders.
– Harmonize the remaining national standards with European and international standards for industrial products.
– Co-operation in the field of legislation on liability for defective products and general product safety, including market surveillance.
– Explore the scope for co-operation between EU and Egyptian accreditation bodies.

d) Restrictions and streamlined administration (EU non-harmonized areas)
– Analyse legislation and administrative procedures with a view to identifying and progressively removing discrimination and restrictions against imported products.
– Strengthen and upgrade the performance of the central contact point to facilitate information flows and co-operation with economic operators.

e) Sanitary and phytosanitary issues
Increase food safety for Egyptian and European consumers. Reforms and modernization of the sanitary and phytosanitary sectors.
– Pursue efforts towards full implementation of the WTO agreement on the application of Sanitary and Phytosanitary measures and active participation in relevant international bodies such as OIE, IPPC, Codex Alimentarius.
– Enhance cooperation between Egypt and the EU in the field of sanitary and phytosanitary issues and explore possible areas of cooperation (e.g. legislation, implementing practices), while taking into account the different conditions prevailing on both sides.
– Develop an Egyptian policy on food safety and an action plan.
– Cooperate on modalities to develop animal and plant identification and traceability systems in Egypt.

2.2.2. Right of establishment, company law and services
a) Establishment and company law
– Co-operate to facilitate the establishment of companies and foreign investment and progressively remove obstacles to establishment.
– Improve the environment for business operation, e.g. adopt and implement effectively bankruptcy legislation.

– Work towards the adoption of key principles of international accounting standards for listed companies and consolidated accounts.
– Establish a qualified and independent audit profession and work towards the adoption of international standards on auditing for all statutory audits.
– Implement a code of corporate governance.

b) Services
– Facilitate the supply of services according to the parties' commitments under GATS including by the development of the necessary administrative structures and the removal of identified barriers.
– Prepare for negotiating progressive liberalization of trade in services and right of establishment taking into account the Euromed Framework Protocol adopted in Istanbul in 2004 and the Marrakech declaration of March 2006.
– Develop a strategy to enhance the competitiveness of the Egyptian services sector including regulatory simplification and administrative facilitation.
– Establish a list of EU Member States contact points on services to provide information to the Egyptian services suppliers/providers who seek to access the European market.

Financial services
– Full implementation of the Financial Sector Reform Program (FSRP).
– Enhance the prudential regulatory framework for financial services.
– Develop the capacity building of independent authorities to ensure effective supervision including through training.

2.2.3. Regional co-operation
– Further develop existing regional cooperation arrangements and support the development of new initiatives and policies promoting regional integration and cooperation, based on the priorities of the relevant regional partners.
– Develop south-south trade including support for the implementation of the Agadir agreement, and promote trade and investment among the regional partners.

2.2.4. Other key areas
a) Taxation
– Support tax strategy for the modernization and simplification of the tax administration. Define the necessary administrative structures and procedures, including a fiscal control strategy, audit and investigation methods, co-operation with the tax payers and tax compliance. Identify all objectives in terms of financial, human, logistic and IT resources.
– Support on-going efforts to complete the network of bilateral agreements between Egypt and EU Member States on avoidance of double taxation including the improvement of transparency and the exchange of information in accordance with international standards.
– Support the Egyptian efforts to modernise and improve the general sales tax system currently in force with a view to moving, in the medium term, towards a standard VAT system. Initiate a dialogue on international and EU tax standard including the

principles related to transparency and exchange of information for tax purposes and to OECD principles on harmful tax practices.

b) Competition policy and state aid
– Adoption of implementing rules on competition (Association Agreement, article 34.2), for which the deadline is five years after the entry into force of the Association Agreement (1/6/2009).

Antitrust
– Enforce the competition law in line with that of the EU and establish an independent and adequately-resourced competition authority.

State aids
– Agree on a definition of state aid and develop a national mechanism for collecting information on state aid in order to ensure implementation of article 34.3 of the Association Agreement by exchanging with the EU an annual report on the total amount and distribution of State aid.
– Exchange experience and know how at the appropriate time on the conditions to be met with reference to state aid control regimes in order to prepare Egypt's participation in the internal market.

c) Intellectual property rights
– Accede to the conventions within the timeframe stipulated in the Association Agreement and apply the standards of protection stated in such conventions or other conventions and agreements to which Egypt is party. Strengthen enforcements of IPR legislation within TRIPS requirements.
– Reinforce the fight against piracy and counterfeiting and promote cooperation between the authorities involved, police, judiciary and customs. Significantly reduce circulation and trafficking of counterfeit/pirated goods.
– Increase awareness at both public and private level and encourage the establishment and effective functioning of associations of rights holders and consumers.
– Explore the possibility of enhanced interaction with other Euromed partners.
– Initiate a policy dialogue covering all aspects of IPR, including further legal/administrative improvements and possible membership of additional relevant conventions etc.

d) Statistics
Adoption of statistical methods compatible with European and international standards in relevant statistical areas
– Elaborate a short and middle term development strategy for harmonisation with European and international standards in the relevant statistical areas covered by this Action Plan.
– Ensure that legislation on official statistics is based on the fundamental UN principles.
– First steps to develop economic, environmental and social statistics in conformity with European and international standards.
– Adoption of an Egyptian National Statistical Master Plan.

e) Public procurement
– Initiate a process of gradual approximation with, and implementation of key international principles, transparency, competition and access to legal recourse. In order to help enhance access to each other's public procurement markets, and to ensure effective communication, task the relevant sub-committee to identify obstacles hindering public procurement access inter alia through dialogue with relevant operators and authorities.
– Improve the functioning of the current system through increased transparency, information and training.
– Improve information and awareness among contracting authorities and the business community about public procurement procedures.
– Strengthen the administrative capacity of the Central Complaints Resolution Office at the Ministry of Finance.

f) Enterprise policy
– Support Small and Medium enterprises (SMEs) (encouraging investment climate, enhancing the activity of the Social Fund for Development, contributing to improve access to finance for SMEs, promoting youth and women entrepreneurship, enhancing productivity and competitiveness including through a better access to market).
– Adapt the priorities of the Industrial Modernization Programme (IMP) to the Objectives of the Egyptian strategy for Industrial Modernization and Competitiveness and of the Euro-Med Charter for Enterprise.
– Modernize and improve the competitiveness of Egyptian industry including through the implementation of the Egyptian strategy for Industrial modernization and competitiveness.
– Improve the business environment including through the implementation of the Euro-Mediterranean Charter for Enterprise.
– Work towards implementation of the October 2004 Euro-Mediterranean Work Programme on Industrial Cooperation.
– Create a dialogue between business, administration and academic institutions for the identification of priority actions for business improvement and the exchange of best practice.

g) Public Internal Financial Control and related issues
– Exchange of information on the concepts and legislative framework for public internal financial control in Egypt and EU Member States, taking into account EU best practices.
– Cooperate in view of establishing, and implementing a policy for upgrading the Public Internal Financial Control system on the basis of a gap analysis of the current internal control systems as compared to the relevant internationally agreed standards and best EU practice.
– Exchange of expertise and cooperation in order to upgrade the institutional capacity of the public internal control system to internationally agreed standards and methodologies as well as EU best practices in the area of internal control and internal audit, covering all income, expenditure, assets and liabilities, of the general Government and budget entities and economic authorities.

– Ensure effective cooperation with the relevant EU Institutions and bodies in the case of on-the-spot checks, audits and investigations related to the management and control of EU funds.

2.3. Transport, energy and environment
a) Transport
Cooperation in the transport sector (maritime, aviation, road, rail and inland waterway)
Implement a national transport strategy, including transport infrastructure development and transport sector reforming.
– Support the development and implementation of the national sustainable transport policy for the development of all modes of transport and related infrastructure, focusing in particular on strengthening safety and security; integration of environmental considerations in transport; as well as intermodality.
– Develop procedures to identify and help implement priority infrastructure projects. Such procedures should address financing strategies focusing on activating and promoting the participation of the private sector in transport projects; capacity constraints; lack of inter-modal equipment and missing link infrastructure.
– Continue the development of a comprehensive regulatory framework.
– Continue with the reform of the transport sector including institutional building, organizational restructuring; capacity building; Strengthen and if necessary establish strategic planning units and develop better asset management procedures for different sectors.
– Promote the use of intelligent transport systems and information technology in managing and operating all modes of transport as well as supporting intermodality.
– Take steps to negotiate a cooperation agreement between EU and Egypt on the development of a Civil Global Navigation Satellite System (GALILEO).

Regional element
– Participate in the regional transport planning activities, including the Euro-Med cooperation aimed at proposing an action plan for transport in the Mediterranean region, as well as a basic regional infrastructure network and interconnection of this network with the trans-European transport network.
– Continue participation in the development of Global Navigation Satellite System (Galileo) in the Mediterranean region, in particular by giving an active role to the Galileo Euromed Cooperation Office based in Cairo; take part in particular in the new regional cooperation activities on satellite navigation systems.

Implement selected measures and reforms in the road and rail transport sectors
– Introduce a transparent regulatory process for the issuing of freight and passenger transport licences and for granting access to the profession.
– Implement the relevant international conventions, notably on dangerous goods transport.
– Develop an integrated action plan on road safety including the technical control/road worthiness testing of vehicles.

– Develop and implement the railway sector restructuring policy and reorganise the administration to separate regulatory responsibilities from operational interests.
– Improve efficiency of rail freight transport services which might eventually lead the Egyptian rail system to be utilised as a gateway to Africa;
– Develop intermodality and multi-modal services, address issues of interoperability.

Regional element
– Explore the benefits of regional cooperation in order to improve the safety, speed and effectiveness (interoperability) of rail services.

Implement selected measures and reforms in the maritime and inland water transport sectors
– Develop and implement the existing comprehensive national maritime policy aiming at promoting and developing the maritime industry increasing its competitiveness and promoting the participation of private sector in all aspects of maritime industry, including ports and port activities; strengthen maritime safety and develop the fleet; continue to implement the relevant international conventions; and when possible approximate standards.
– Continue reform of the ports sector with a view to introduction of an independent port authority responsible for regulation and control and adoption of the 'Land Lord' management system. Ensure, in the context of the up-coming negotiations on liberalization of trade in services, on the basis of the Marrakech ministerial declaration in March 2006, the elimination of discriminatory treatment to Community vessels in Egyptian Ports.
– Assess and examine the possibility of extending VTMIS to the Mediterranean.
– Effectively enforce maritime safety standards and ensure effective enforcement in the areas of Port State Control and Flag State implementation. Step up cooperation on maritime security with a view to combating terrorism, in the context of implementing the SOLAS/ISPS code.
– Speed up the phasing-out of single-hull oil tankers and apply the changes recently agreed in the IMO Marpol Convention taking into consideration the relevant recommendation of the High Level Group on the extension of the trans-European transport network to neighbouring countries and regions.
– Establish an infrastructure and services development policies and strategies to activate the inland water transport role in freight transport as potential cheaper and environmentally friendlier mode of transport that could provide access to other African countries.

Regional element
– Maritime safety and security: take part in improving the Euromed framework for cooperation within the IMO; take part in regional cooperation on maritime safety (SAFEMED).
– Take part in regional cooperation on maritime policy, ports and short-sea shipping.

Implement selected measures and reforms in the aviation sector
– Implement the existing national aviation policy including as regards the development of the airports and further reinforce administrative capacity (including the foreseen separation of regulatory and management functions of the ECAA).

– Explore the possibility of extending to all airports open competition in groundhandling services.

– Assess the possibility of extending to all airports the liberalization of charter flights and examine the specific situation of Cairo airport.

– Negotiate a horizontal aviation agreement with the EC. Exchange of information on the possibility of developing a Euro-Mediterranean Aviation agreement.

– Enhance administrative and technical capacity to fully implement jointly agreed JAA standards. Explore possibilities to involve Egypt in the work of EASA and for involvement in the Single European Sky.

– Co-operate on aviation security matters (common rules to combat international terrorism) in accordance with international conventions to which Egypt and the EU Member States are party.

– Explore the possibilities of cooperation in establishing a Safety Management System Programmer.

Regional element

– Take part in regional cooperation on safety, security and air traffic management.

b) Energy

Cooperate in the development of an overall long-term energy strategy converging towards EU energy policy objectives.

– Take steps to prepare (under the auspices of the Ministry of Petroleum and the Ministry of Electricity and Energy) an overall Egyptian energy strategy converging towards EU energy policy objectives (security of supply, competitiveness and environmental protection) and covering, inter alia, all subsectors, the strengthening of institutions and financing.

– Enhance energy policy cooperation through information exchange (e.g. workshops on general energy policy; energy statistics, data mining and forecast systems; energy investments; energy technologies transfer and industrial cooperation; and electricity and gas markets and interconnections.

– Adoption and start of implementation of energy strategy documents.

– Continue energy policy cooperation.

Cooperation on electricity and gas markets

– Explore possibilities for gradual legal and regulatory convergence towards the principles of the EU internal electricity and gas markets.

– Further develop energy pricing methodologies and exchange of views on gas pricing and transit gas fee policies in view of the relevant EU experience.

– Cooperate to build the capacity of the Electric Utilities and Consumer Protection Regulatory Agency including its development towards an electricity regulator independent from market operators.

– Cooperate to develop an oil and gas Regulatory Agency.

– Cooperate to study the different models of electricity markets for establishing a local and regional electricity market and setting the rules and procedures in cooperation with the electricity sector.

– Continue sector restructuring; to explore possibilities for gradual convergence towards the principles of the EU internal electricity and gas markets and the Euro-Mashrek-Maghreb gas cooperation.

Regional element
– Cooperate, in the context of the Declaration of Intent of 2 December 2003 on the Euro-Mashrek cooperation in the field of natural gas including as regards the development of a regional Gas Master Plan expected to facilitate the transportation of natural gas in particular between Egypt and the EU.
– Cooperate in the field of the EU-Mashrek-Maghreb electricity market.

Progress on energy networks
– Reduce electricity network losses.
– Further develop regional energy infrastructures including upgrading the electricity link with Jordan and Libya.
– Improve the safety and security of energy infrastructure.
– Further develop electricity networks in rural areas.

Progress on energy efficiency and the use of renewable energy sources
– Take steps to develop an Action Plan including a financial plan for improving energy efficiency and enhancing the use of renewable energy.
– Reinforce the institutions dealing with energy efficiency and renewable energy sources.
– Cooperate to develop mechanisms for effective introduction of renewable energy into the Egyptian Electricity Market and promote technology transfer and knowhow in this area.
– Pursue measures in energy efficiency and renewable energy sources.
– Progress to reach Egypt's target to ensure that 3% of the electric energy needs are covered by the year 2010 by renewable energy sources.

c) Environment
Improve environmental performance and enhance good environmental governance
– Implement national priorities in the field of environment protection as specified in the national environmental action plan 2002–2017, with particular attention to the establishment of administrative structures and procedures to ensure strategic planning of environment issues by the Ministry of State for Environmental Affairs; to the environmental policy implementation framework and to coordination between relevant actors.
– Enhance coordination with line ministries through development of Policy Implementation Framework (an initiative to assess adopted environmental policies; prioritization for their integration into sectoral policies and activate their implementation).
– Establish procedures regarding access to environmental information and public participation.
– Reinforce structures and procedures to carry out environmental impact assessments.
– Exchange of experiences in the implementation of strategic environmental impact assessment.

– Improve co-operation between different Ministries to implement the national strategies on cleaner production and air quality.
– Implement the environmental communication strategy.
– Support civil society actors and local authorities, in order to implement the decentralised environmental management policy.

Take active action for prevention of deterioration of the environment, protection of human health, and achievement of rational use of natural resources, in line with the Johannesburg Plan of Implementation
– Implement national priorities in the field of environment protection with particular attention to legislation and its implementation as specified in the national environmental action plan 2002–2017.
– Take steps towards adoption of plans and programmes related to air quality, water quality and biodiversity.
– Implement the national plan for combating desertification.
– Exchange of experience on protection of biological diversity and rural landscape, with special attention to the relevant migratory species.
– Carry out strategic environmental impact assessment of industrial and tourist facilities.

Enhance co-operation on environmental issues
– Develop modalities for co-operation with the EU to implement multilateral environmental agreements with particular emphasis on climate change, desertification, biodiversity and waste management.
– Enhance co-operation to achieve the commitments by the parties with regard provisions under the Kyoto Protocol and the UN Framework Convention on Climate Change.
– Complete the ratification process of the new Emergency Protocol and the amendments to the Land-Based Sources Protocol of Barcelona Convention.
– Possible participation in selected European Environment Agency activities.
– Identify possibilities to enhance regional cooperation in the field of environment.
– Initiate actions which will contribute to the implementation of the objectives of the De-pollution Initiative for the Mediterranean Sea (Horizon 2020), and promote Egyptian efforts in this regard.
– Promote technology transfer and know-how in the following areas: waste management, including recycling and treatment of industrial and agricultural wastes.
– Enhance co-operation between Egypt and EU for protecting marine environment through the adoption of specific actions, and taking into consideration activities within the Mediterranean Action Plan (MAP).
– Enhance Euromed co-operation regarding the integrated coastal zone management.

2.4. Migration, social integration, justice and security
Further develop co-operation between Egypt and EU Member States judicial and law enforcement authorities

a) Judicial cooperation in criminal and civil matters
– Exchange information on ratification as well as implementation of relevant international conventions related to co-operation in criminal and civil matters to which either side is a party.
– Develop further judicial cooperation on criminal, commercial and civil matters.
– Facilitate solutions to problems arising from mixed marriage disputes and child custody cases and encourage cooperation in accordance with the principles of the UN convention of 1989 on the Rights of the Child and national legislation.
– Promote judicial cooperation through strengthening the capacity of law enforcement and assistant bodies as well as through the training of judges and prosecutors.

b) Law enforcement cooperation
– Explore the possibilities for co-operation between Egyptian and EU law enforcement agencies, in particular Europol and Eurojust.
– Establish a network of contact points with EU Member States law enforcement authorities with a view to exchange technical, strategic and operational information.
– Promote cooperation between law enforcement agencies of the EU Member States and Egypt.

c) Promoting transparency
Exchange information on ratification and implementation of the UN Convention against Corruption and other relevant international instruments to which either side is party
– Develop dialogue, exchange information and strengthen cooperation between law enforcement agencies on fighting corruption and further promote transparency, including exchanges on best practices, methods and standards in these areas.
– Strengthen measures against corruption through preventive anti-corruption policies and practices in accordance with the UN Convention against Corruption.

d) Border management
Enhance border management cooperation between Egypt and the EU Member States
– Develop co-operation between relevant law enforcement bodies in Egypt and in the EU, and initiate appropriate technical contacts with FRONTEX (European Border Agency).
– Cooperation in reinforcing organisational capacities of controlling and surveillance of entry and exit points, including ad hoc training.

e) Migration issues (legal and illegal migration, readmission, visa, asylum)
– Develop a comprehensive and balanced dialogue with Egypt on various migration-related issues, including legal migration, seasonal migration, status of Egyptian migrants and workers residing legally in Europe, brain drain, asylum, movement of people, control of illegal migration and return, visa.
– Monitoring and analysis of the migration phenomenon: synergy with the Euro-Med initiatives on research on migration and the Consortium on Applied Research on International Migration (CARIM) in particular.
– Promote the possibilities of Egypt to benefit from the Community programs and the AENEAS program aimed at providing technical and financial assistance to third countries in the areas of migration and asylum in particular.

– Promote the discussion between Egypt and the EU and its Member States on the economic, political, social and cultural dimensions of the migration issues, in addition to its security dimension.

Ensure an effective management of migration flows
– Exchange of information and experiences on legal migration, entry and stay, integration, reunification of family, inventory of existing routes and commitments made by Member States.
– Enhance cooperation to facilitate the legal movement of people between Egypt and the EU through strengthening of the concerned institutions dealing with the promotion of employment, capacity building, as well as providing information about the employment opportunities for labour migrants in the EU, risks of smuggling and trafficking of migrants; ensuring fair treatment of legal Egyptian migrants, and facilitate the flow of remittance transfers.
– Exchange of information and promotion of co-operation on transit migration.

Cooperate in combating illegal immigration into Egypt and the European Union
– Exchange of information and experiences on migratory movements, illegal migration including the scale of illegal immigration into and via Egypt.
– Pursue and support effort to prevent and counter illegal migration into Egypt and the European Union.
– Develop a dialogue and cooperation to curb illegal migration flows, including in the regional context.

Improve cooperation regarding readmission
– Develop the cooperation between Egypt and EU on readmission, including negotiating readmission agreements between the parties, building on Article 69 of the Association Agreement, taking into account the human dimension, socioeconomic aspects and accompanying measures.
– Cooperation on consular affairs and issuing of travel documents.

Facilitate the movement of persons
– Cooperate in the field of improving the movement of persons, including to facilitate the uniform visa issuing procedures for certain agreed categories of persons as stated in the Association Agreement and in accordance with the acquis.
– Cooperate to improve security of travel documents and visa in conformity with ICAO standards.

Asylum issues
– Exchange information and best practices in the field of asylum policy, refugee status determination, and legislation, and cooperate on the inter-linkages between migration and asylum.

f) Fight against organised crime (including trafficking in human beings)
Enhance international co-operation in accordance with the UN Convention against Transnational Organised Crime and its protocols on smuggling of migrants and trafficking in persons and on illicit manufacturing and trafficking of firearms.

– Implementation of the UN Convention against Trans-national Organised Crime and its Protocols.
– Exchange expertise and experiences, also through appropriate training on best practices in combating organised crime, including security and legal aspects.

Cooperate in the fight against cyber crime
– Work together to fight cyber crime.

Reinforce the fight against trafficking in human beings, especially women and children, and smuggling of illegal migrants, as well as activities to prevent trafficking in human beings and to reintegrate victims
– Promote co-operation between relevant law enforcement bodies in Egypt and in the EU on this issue.
– Develop legal, social and psychological support to victims aiming at their reintegration.

g) Fight against drugs
Continue the fight against drug trafficking, including the trafficking of essential chemicals and precursors, and against drug abuse in particular through prevention and rehabilitation, in accordance with the 1988 UN Convention on Illicit Traffic of Narcotic and Psychotropic Substances and with Article 58 of the AA.
– Develop international cooperation in fight against trafficking narcotics and drug addiction, in particular prevention of drugs abuse, treatment and rehabilitation of drug addicts.
– Cooperate in the implementation of the relevant UN Conventions.
– Support national efforts in the fight against trafficking and smuggling of narcotics and drug addiction as well as enhancing the capacity of the Egyptian Fund for the control and treatment of addiction, and supporting civil society organisations in this field.

h) Fight against money laundering, financial and economic crime
Strengthen efforts and co-operation in the fight against money laundering, financial and economic crime
– Intensify co-operation and promote exchange of information among law enforcement agencies and co-operation between Egypt and international organisations, such as FATF, as well as with corresponding services of EU Member States.
– Exchange information on the existing European structures (Financial Intelligence Unit (FIU)) and the existing system in Egypt as regards money laundering.
– Strengthen Egypt's system of financial and security information.
– Identify administrative/technical support and training requirements especially for the Egyptian Unit on combating money laundering.

i) Fight against terrorism
In the framework of the counter-terrorism-related UN resolutions and conventions
– Strengthen cooperation on measures to tackle the financing of terrorism.

– Develop cooperation between Egypt and EU Member States counter-terrorism and law enforcement agencies including through effective measures to preclude the access of terrorist elements to Egypt and EU Member States.
– Develop judicial cooperation on combating terrorism.
– Work together to fight cyber crime and to fight the use of the Internet for terrorist purposes.
– Cooperate in the fight against terrorist crimes in conformity with national legislation.
– Support the institutional capacity building and the development of human resources and technological capabilities of law enforcement institutions.

2.5. Science and technology, research and development, information society and audio-visual cooperation
a) Science and technology, research and development
Accelerate the integration of Egypt into the European Research Area and the Community Framework Programme
– Start implementation of the agreement on Scientific and Technological Cooperation.
– Put into place and ensure the well-functioning of a network of national contact points for the 6/7th Framework programme and link them up with the national RDT and innovation operators as well as with other EU Science and Technology activities.
– Pursue EU–Egypt cooperation in RDT-I, identifying the priority sectors of mutual interest, the instruments and means of cooperation and implementation policies and strategies, including the promotion of links between centers of excellence on both sides.
– Disseminate research results to all potential users, develop a 'patent culture' and set up intellectual property offices in technology parks and universities, including support for the introduction of a doctoral level programme in intellectual property law in the framework of the Agreement on Scientific and Technological Cooperation.
Develop the scientific and technological capacity with a focus on the use of RTD results by the industrial and SME sector
– Strengthen human, material and institutional resources in order to improve the capacities of RDT-I operators, including quality evaluation and management processes.
– Adopt a strategy for regional technopoles with a view to organising a dialogue between all those involved in research and end-users (industry, SMEs) and implementing interaction mechanisms between research and industry, public and private sector.
– Explore possibilities for EU support in the setting up and running of a National Fund for Scientific Research and Development.

Promote the integration of Egypt into scientific high-level exchanges
– Reinforce Egypt's participation in international exchange and mobility programmes, in particular the Marie Curie scholarships; foresee appropriate mechanisms for return and integration to Egypt.
– Reinforce the exchange of personnel in the joint projects and Centres of Excellence as well as promote and facilitate the participation of Egyptian scientists in international scientific debates and fora.

– Promote the access of Egyptian scientists to European scientific databases.
– Promote the participation of Egyptian scientists in European research groups also in the field of innovation.

b) Information society
Further progress in electronic communications policy and regulation
– Pursue and support the implementation of the national policy on the development of the information society sector.
– Pursue and support the development of a comprehensive regulatory framework that would fulfil effectively all aspects of its mandate. Areas of interest would include: number portability, privacy protection and information security, a state-of-art cost accounting system and subsequent cost-orientation of tariffs, users' rights, and universal service obligations and management.
– Liberalise the fixed telephony market and continue the liberalisation of the mobile telephony market according to national priorities.
– Improve the efficiency of the National Telecommunications Regulatory Authority by providing capacity building in areas of competition and regulation to ensure fair competition in a de-regulated market.

Further progress in the development and use of Information Society applications
– Promote the use of new technologies and electronic means of communications by businesses, government and citizens in areas such as e-Business, e-Government, e-Health, e-Learning, e-Culture and e-content.
– Cooperate in regional eStrategies such as EUMEDIS, New Approaches on telecommunications Policies (NATP) and similar programs.
– Adopt a specific plan to promote the participation of Egypt in the IST part of the Framework Programmes as well as other EU science and technology activities.
– Continue broadband development in order to increase internet penetration.
– Reinforce the skills of citizens and their access to ICT in order to overcome the digital divide.
– Encourage the different stakeholders to contribute efficiently to the implementation of the Information Society in Egypt.
– Exchange experience and cooperate on Information Society policies of global relevance, such as Internet Governance, information security and combat against cyber crime, convergence between electronic communications and media.
– Promote the transfer of know-how in the introduction of Information Society networks and services.
– Improve connectivity between Egypt and Europe.

c) Audio-visual cooperation
Create conditions for an environment favouring co-operation in the audio-visual area. Work towards the development of a transparent, efficient and predictable regulatory system including through the establishment of an independent regulatory authority in the audio-visual sector
– Promote an exchange of views on audiovisual policy.

– Encourage the exchange of information and experience with regard to regulatory aspects of the audio-visual sector.
– Strengthen human resource capacities and exchange of experience in the domains of audio-visual.

2.6. People-to-people contacts
a) Culture
Enhance cultural co-operation between Egypt and EU and its Member States
– Enhance cooperation through exchange of information, experience and expertise, in cultural sectors in line with Article 71 of the AA, in particular as regards the protection of historic monuments and cultural heritage, promotion of translations as well as capacity building and communication skills development.
– Enhance Egypt's participation in the relevant EC cultural cooperation programmes of the Euro-Med partnership inter alia by developing appropriate structures.

Dialogue between cultures
– Enhance dialogue between cultures, taking into consideration the principles embodied in the Action Programme for the Dialogue between Cultures and Civilizations, adopted by the Valencia Ministerial Meeting in April 2002 and taking advantage of Egypt's hosting Anna Lindh Euro-Mediterranean Foundation for the dialogue between cultures.
– Exchange views on the UNESCO Convention on the protection and promotion of the diversity of cultural expressions including its development aspects, and promote its ratification and cooperate in its implementation.
– Promote initiatives aiming at bringing closer cultures and civilizations.

b) Youth and sport issues
Enhance co-operation in the field of youth and sport
– Enhance youth exchanges and co-operation in the field of non-formal education and intercultural dialogue.
– Promote mutual knowledge among Egyptian and European youths of their respective cultures and fostering tolerance.
– Provide the best practices in establishing national councils for youth in EU Member States and on drafting youth policies.
– Promote a dialogue between EU and Egypt on sport issues.
– Exchange of experience with the EU Member States on the management of various sports sectors.
– Ensure the continued successful implementation of the Euro-Med Youth programme by developing an effective national management structure.

c) Civil society co-operation
– Examine the scope for further improving the legal and administrative framework for the operation of civil society organizations.
– Support the Egyptian Non-Governmental Organizations in contributing effectively in the economic, political and social development process in accordance with national legislation.

3. Joint monitoring

The Action Plan will be submitted for formal adoption to the EU–Egypt Association Council.

The Action Plan will give orientation for the cooperation between the EU and Egypt. The joint bodies established under the Association Agreement will advance and monitor the implementation of the Action Plan on the basis of regular reports on its implementation.

A first review of the implementation of the Action Plan will be undertaken within two years of its adoption.

The Action Plan can be regularly amended and/or updated jointly to reflect progress in addressing the priorities.

[...]

Select Bibliography

Blockmans, S. and Lazowski, A. (eds), *The European Union and its Neighbours: A Legal Appraisal of the EU's Policies of Stabilisation, Partnership and Integration* (The Hague: Asser Press, 2006).

Cornelli, M., Eralp, A., and Ustun, C. (eds), *The European Neighbourhood Policy and the Southern Mediterranean* (Ankara: METU Press, 2009).

Cremona, M., The European Neighbourhood Policy: More than a Partnership?, *Developments in EU External Relations Law* (M. Cremona (ed.), Oxford: Oxford University Press, 2008), 244–300.

Hoffmeister, F., Changing Requirements for Membership, *Handbook on European Enlargement* (A. Ott and K. Inglis (eds), The Hague: T.M.C. Asser Institute, 2002), 90–102.

Inglis, K., The Union's Fifth Enlargement Treaty: New Means to Make Enlargement Possible, *Common Market Law Review*, vol. 41(4), 2004, 937–73.

Wichmann, N., *Rule of Law Promotion in the European Neighbourhood Policy: Normative or Strategic Power Europe?* (Baden-Baden: Nomos, 2010).

10

External Environmental Policy

10.1 Objectives and competences

Environmental protection features prominently among the Union's aims and objectives. It is first mentioned in the ninth recital in the preamble to the EU Treaty, intended to reassure EU citizens that economic integration within the Union must not come at the cost of other societal goals, notably those of social progress, sustainable development, and environmental protection. That commitment is repeated in Article 3 TEU, which lists the aims of the Union. With respect to EU external relations, the protection of the environment is twice mentioned among the basic objectives of the Union's external action.

Treaty on European Union

Preamble

[…]

DETERMINED to promote economic and social progress for their peoples, taking into account the principle of sustainable development and within the context of the accomplishment of the internal market and of reinforced cohesion and environmental protection, and to implement policies ensuring that advances in economic integration are accompanied by parallel progress in other fields,

[…]

Article 3

(ex Article 2 TEU)

[…]

3. The Union shall establish an internal market. It shall work for the sustainable development of Europe based on balanced economic growth and price stability, a highly competitive social market economy, aiming at full employment and social progress, and a high level of protection and improvement of the quality of the environment. It shall promote scientific and technological advance.

[…]

Article 21

[…]

2. The Union shall define and pursue common policies and actions, and shall work for a high degree of cooperation in all fields of international relations, in order to:

[…]

(d) foster the sustainable economic, social and environmental development of developing countries, with the primary aim of eradicating poverty;

[...]

(f) help develop international measures to preserve and improve the quality of the environment and the sustainable management of global natural resources, in order to ensure sustainable development;

[...]

'Environment' is listed as a shared competence under Article 4(2)(e) TFEU, which implies, pursuant to Article 2(2) TFEU, that the Union and the Member States may legislate and adopt legally binding acts in that area. The Member States are to exercise their competence to the extent that the Union has not exercised its competence. The Member States are again to exercise their competence to the extent that the Union has decided to cease exercising its competence.

The legal bases for EU external environmental law are to be found in Articles 191 and 192 in Title XX of Part Three of the TFEU. Article 193 TFEU further makes clear that measures taken on the basis of Article 192 TFEU are to be minimum requirements.

Treaty on the Functioning of the European Union

TITLE XX
ENVIRONMENT
Article 191
(ex Article 174 TEC)

1. Union policy on the environment shall contribute to pursuit of the following objectives:
— preserving, protecting and improving the quality of the environment,
— protecting human health,
— prudent and rational utilisation of natural resources,
— promoting measures at international level to deal with regional or worldwide environmental problems, and in particular combating climate change.

2. Union policy on the environment shall aim at a high level of protection taking into account the diversity of situations in the various regions of the Union. It shall be based on the precautionary principle and on the principles that preventive action should be taken, that environmental damage should as a priority be rectified at source and that the polluter should pay.

In this context, harmonisation measures answering environmental protection requirements shall include, where appropriate, a safeguard clause allowing Member States to take provisional measures, for non-economic environmental reasons, subject to a procedure of inspection by the Union.

3. In preparing its policy on the environment, the Union shall take account of:
— available scientific and technical data,
— environmental conditions in the various regions of the Union,
— the potential benefits and costs of action or lack of action,

— the economic and social development of the Union as a whole and the balanced development of its regions.

4. Within their respective spheres of competence, the Union and the Member States shall cooperate with third countries and with the competent international organisations. The arrangements for Union cooperation may be the subject of agreements between the Union and the third parties concerned.

The previous subparagraph shall be without prejudice to Member States' competence to negotiate in international bodies and to conclude international agreements.

Article 192

(ex Article 175 TEC)

1. The European Parliament and the Council, acting in accordance with the ordinary legislative procedure and after consulting the Economic and Social Committee and the Committee of the Regions, shall decide what action is to be taken by the Union in order to achieve the objectives referred to in Article 191.

2. By way of derogation from the decision-making procedure provided for in paragraph 1 and without prejudice to Article 114, the Council acting unanimously in accordance with a special legislative procedure and after consulting the European Parliament, the Economic and Social Committee and the Committee of the Regions, shall adopt:

(a) provisions primarily of a fiscal nature;

(b) measures affecting:

— town and country planning,

— quantitative management of water resources or affecting, directly or indirectly, the availability of those resources,

— land use, with the exception of waste management;

(c) measures significantly affecting a Member State's choice between different energy sources and the general structure of its energy supply.

The Council, acting unanimously on a proposal from the Commission and after consulting the European Parliament, the Economic and Social Committee and the Committee of the Regions, may make the ordinary legislative procedure applicable to the matters referred to in the first subparagraph.

3. General action programmes setting out priority objectives to be attained shall be adopted by the European Parliament and the Council, acting in accordance with the ordinary legislative procedure and after consulting the Economic and Social Committee and the Committee of the Regions.

The measures necessary for the implementation of these programmes shall be adopted under the terms of paragraph 1 or 2, as the case may be.

4. Without prejudice to certain measures adopted by the Union, the Member States shall finance and implement the environment policy.

5. Without prejudice to the principle that the polluter should pay, if a measure based on the provisions of paragraph 1 involves costs deemed disproportionate for the public authorities of a Member State, such measure shall lay down appropriate provisions in the form of:

— temporary derogations, and/or

— financial support from the Cohesion Fund set up pursuant to Article 177.

Article 193

(ex Article 176 TEC)

The protective measures adopted pursuant to Article 192 shall not prevent any Member State from maintaining or introducing more stringent protective measures. Such measures must be compatible with the Treaties. They shall be notified to the Commission.

There is therefore an explicit legal basis for EU external relations in Article 191(4) TFEU. As is clear from its second subparagraph, measures based on Article 191(4) TFEU leave the Member States' competence to act internationally intact, which implies a parallel competence. However, in Opinion 2/00, the Court severely limited the applicability of that article as a legal basis. As a consequence, Article 174(4) TEC was abandoned as the default legal basis for external environmental agreements, as is, for example, clear from comparing the Commission proposal regarding the Kyoto Protocol and the eventual Council decision. The Commission had proposed Article 174(4) TEC as legal basis for the conclusion of the Kyoto Protocol. However, that legal basis was changed to Article 175(1) TEC for the adoption of the relevant Council decision. Most substantive measures were based on Article 175 TEC and will now presumably be based on Article 192 TFEU. As the Court appears to have held in Opinion 2/00, the *ERTA* doctrine (see Chapter 1) in principle applies to such measures. However, concluding from the above that Article 191(4) TFEU is virtually defunct as a legal basis for international environmental agreements would be premature, as the recently concluded Framework Agreement on Partnership and Cooperation with the Philippines demonstrates.[1] Excerpts of Opinion 2/00 and the aforementioned documents are included below.

Opinion of the Court of 6 December 2001, Cartagena Protocol on Biosafety, Opinion 2/00, European Court Reports 2001, p. I-9713, paras. 43–47.

43. As the Court has already held (see Peralta, cited above, paragraph 57, and Safety Hi-Tech, cited above, paragraph 43), Article 174 EC defines the objectives to be

---

[1] Note, however, that the Commission has brought an action for annulment of Decision 2012/272/EU of the Council of 14 May 2012 on the signing, on behalf of the Union, of the Framework Agreement on Partnership and Cooperation between the European Union and its Member States, of the one part, and the Republic of the Philippines, of the other part ('the PCA'), insofar as the Council has added the legal bases relating to transport (Articles 91 and 100 TFEU), readmission (Article 79(3) TFEU) and environment (Article 191(4) TFEU). The Commission takes the view that the addition of these legal bases was unnecessary and illegal. Indeed, the provisions of the PCA which have triggered the addition of these legal bases by the Council relate to cooperation on specific policy matters that form an integral part of the development cooperation policy of the EU and do not impose extensive obligations distinct from those of development cooperation. Therefore, according to the Commission, all these provisions of the PCA are covered by Article 209 TFEU: see Case C-377/12, Chapter 2, p. 106, fn 2.

pursued in the context of environmental policy, while Article 175 EC constitutes the legal basis on which Community measures are adopted. It is true that Article 174(4) EC specifically provides that the arrangements for Community cooperation with non-member countries and international organisations may be the subject of agreements...negotiated and concluded in accordance with Article 300. However, in the present case, the Protocol does not merely establish arrangements for cooperation regarding environmental protection, but lays down, in particular, precise rules on control procedures relating to transboundary movements, risk assessment and management, handling, transport, packaging and identification of LMOs.

44. Consequently, Article 175(1) EC is the appropriate legal basis for conclusion of the Protocol on behalf of the Community.

45. It is thus also necessary to consider whether the Community holds exclusive competence under Article 175 EC to conclude the Protocol because secondary legislation adopted within the framework of the Community covers the subject of biosafety and is liable to be affected if the Member States participate in the procedure for concluding the Protocol (see the ERTA judgment, paragraph 22).

46. It need only be observed in that regard that, as the United Kingdom Government and the Council correctly stated, the harmonisation achieved at Community level in the Protocol's field of application covers in any event only a very small part of such a field (see Directive 90/219, Directive 90/220 and Directive 2001/18/EC of the European Parliament and of the Council of 12 March 2001 on the deliberate release into the environment of genetically modified organisms (OJ 2001 L 106, p. 1), Article 36 of which repeals Directive 90/220).

47. It follows from the foregoing considerations that the Community and its Member States share competence to conclude the Protocol.

Proposal for a Council Decision concerning the approval, on behalf of the European Community, of the Kyoto Protocol to the United Nations Framework Convention on Climate Change and the joint fulfilment of commitments thereunder, COM/2001/0579 final, Official Journal C 75E, 26.3.2002, pp. 17–32.

[...]

EXPLANATORY MEMORANDUM

[...]

Legal basis

(11) The subject matter of the Kyoto Protocol comes under the heading of Community environment policy. This proposal is based on Article 174(4) of the Treaty establishing the European Community, in conjunction with the first sentence of Article 300(2) and the first subparagraph of Article 300(3). Article 174(4) confers express competence on the Community to conclude the Kyoto Protocol, while Article 300 lays down the procedural requirements. The Commission's proposal is subject to approval by a qualified majority in the Council after consultation of the European Parliament.

[...]

THE COUNCIL OF THE EUROPEAN UNION,
Having regard to the Treaty establishing the European Community, and in particular Article 174(4) in conjunction with Article 300(2), first sentence of the first subparagraph, and Article 300(3), first subparagraph, thereof,

[...]

Council Decision of 25 April 2002 concerning the approval, on behalf of the European Community, of the Kyoto Protocol to the United Nations Framework Convention on Climate Change and the joint fulfilment of commitments thereunder (2002/358/EC), Official Journal L 130, 15.5.2002, pp. 1–3.

THE COUNCIL OF THE EUROPEAN UNION,
Having regard to the Treaty establishing the European Community, and in particular Article 175(1) in conjunction with Article 300(2), first sentence of the first subparagraph, and Article 300(3), first subparagraph, thereof,

[...]

Whereas:

[...]

(11) The legal base of any further Decision in relation to the approval by the Community of future commitments in respect of emission reductions will be determined by the content and effect of that Decision.

Council Decision of 14 May 2012 on the signing, on behalf of the Union, of the Framework Agreement on Partnership and Cooperation between the European Union and its Member States, of the one part, and the Republic of the Philippines, of the other part (2012/272/EU), Official Journal L 134, 24.5.2012, p. 3.

THE COUNCIL OF THE EUROPEAN UNION,
Having regard to the Treaty on the Functioning of the European Union, and in particular Article 79(3), Articles 91 and 100, Article 191(4) and Articles 207 and 209 in conjunction with Article 218(5) thereof,

[...]

With regard to Article 193 TFEU, the Court has held in Opinion 2/91 that such minimum requirements could not form the basis of exclusive Union competences. However, the mere fact that the internal Union rules in question are minimum requirements does not necessarily justify the conclusion that the competence in question is non-exclusive, as is evident from Opinion 1/03.[2]

The Court further clarified the scope of Article 193 TFEU (ex-Article 176 EC) and the environmental minimum standards to be enacted pursuant to that provision in

---

[2] See Chapter 1, Opinion 1/03, paras. 123–7.

the *PFOS* case. Thus, a Member State is free to adopt measures providing for a higher level of protection within its own jurisdiction. Proposing such measures within the framework of an international agreement to which the Union is a party, which would imply that the Union may be bound by a more stringent measure with which it did not express its agreement, is quite a different thing and does not fall within the scope of Article 193 TFEU. That does *a contrario* seem to mean that, if the Union were *not* to be bound by a more stringent measure, the Member States would be free to adopt it or propose it in the relevant international fora. Such a situation would typically occur with respect to an international agreement to which the Union has not acceded, often because the international agreement in question does not permit international organizations to become a party.

An example of this would be the participation of the Member States in the International Whaling Commission (IWC), the international organization competent for the conservation and management of whale stocks. It was set up by the International Convention for the Regulation of Whaling ('the Whaling Convention').[3] Membership of the IWC is only open to governments that adhere to the Whaling Convention. An amendment to the Whaling Convention allowing the EU to become a member would require the ratification of a protocol by all IWC members. The Commission adopted a proposal in 1992 to negotiate the accession of the Community to the Whaling Convention,[4] but the Council has not followed up on this proposal.[5] The EU is therefore not a party, but merely an observer to the Whaling Convention.[6] EU regulatory activity as regards matters pertaining to whaling does not come under the exclusive common fisheries policy (Article 3(1)(d) TFEU), but under the shared competence on the environment (Article 4(2)(e) TFEU).[7] While Union action on whaling has been taken,[8] it would go too far to

---

[3] Signed in Washington DC on 2 December 1946 (62 Stat. 1716; 161 UNTS 72).

[4] Draft Council Decision authorizing the Commission to negotiate, on behalf of the Community, a protocol amending the international Convention on the regulation of whaling, Washington, 2 December 1946, COM(92) 316.

[5] See Proposal for a Council decision establishing the position to be adopted on behalf of the European Community with regard to proposals for amendments to the International Convention on the Regulation of Whaling and its Schedule, 6.11.2008, COM(2008) 711 final, Point 6 of the Explanatory Memorandum.

[6] However, in the context of the current talks about the reform of the IWC the Commission proposes to support proposals for revision of the Convention, including the possibility for the EU to become a party to the IWC: Proposal for a Council Decision establishing the position to be adopted on behalf of the European Union at the next five meetings of the International Whaling Commission including the related inter-sessional meetings with regard to proposals for amendments to the International Convention on the Regulation of Whaling and its Schedule, 25.8.2011, COM(2011) 495 final.

[7] Annex I to the TFEU lists the products coming under Art. 38 TFEU on the common agriculture and fisheries policy. Chapter 3 mentions 'Fish, crustaceans and molluscs', but not marine mammals. The latter are only mentioned in Chapter 15.04: 'Fats and oil, of fish and marine mammals, whether or not refined'. At any rate, EU action on whaling has, as a rule, been taken under environmental competence.

[8] See, for example, Council Regulation (EEC) No. 348/81 of 20 January 1981 on common rules for imports of whales or other cetacean products, OJ L 39, 12.2.1981, pp. 1–3, adopted on the basis of then Art. 235 EEC (now Art. 352 TFEU), as no specific legal basis for environmental protection was available at the time; Council Directive 92/43/EEC of 21 May 1992 on the conservation of natural habitats and of wild fauna and flora, OJ L 206, 22.7.1992, pp. 7–50, adopted on the basis of Art. 130s EEC (now Art. 192 TFEU); Council Regulation (EC) No. 338/97 of 9 December 1996 on the protection of species of wild fauna and flora by regulating trade therein, OJ L 61, 3.3.1997, pp. 1–69, adopted on the basis of Art. 130s EEC (now Art. 192 TFEU).

say that the Union has exercised its competence to such an extent that it has replaced the Member States within the IWC. Indeed, the Court has put the threshold for that to happen rather high, as was recently reaffirmed in the judgment in *Air Transport Association of America*.[9]

It would therefore seem perfectly legitimate for a Member State to vote in favour of any measure proposed within the IWC that would strengthen the protection of whales beyond and above the protection agreed within the Union institutions. That would quite clearly be the case if no position on such a proposal could be reached within the Council. Would the same conclusion apply, if a position had been reached? Given that the EU is not a Party to the Whaling Convention and cannot be bound by the decisions taken by the IWC, it would seem that it must follow from Article 193 TFEU that Member States ought to remain free to support measures enhancing the protection of whales, while being prevented from supporting any measure lowering such protection.[10]

At any rate, the Court of Justice made it clear in *Mox Plant* that the Union can choose the extent to which it exercises its shared competence in external environmental matters.[11]

Opinion of the Court of 19 March 1993, Convention No 170 of the International Labour Organization concerning safety in the use of chemicals at work, Opinion 2/91, European Court Reports 1993, p. I-1061, paras. 15–21.

15. The field covered by Convention No 170 falls within the 'social provisions' of the EEC Treaty which constitute Chapter 1 of Title III on social policy.

16. Under Article 118a of the Treaty, Member States are required to pay particular attention to encouraging improvements, especially in the working environment, as regards the health and safety of workers, and to set as their objective the harmonization of conditions in this area, while maintaining the improvements made. In order to help achieve this objective, the Council has the power to adopt minimum requirements by means of directives. It follows from Article 118a(3) that the provisions adopted pursuant to that article are not to prevent any Member State from maintaining or introducing more stringent measures for the protection of working conditions compatible with the Treaty.

17. The Community thus enjoys an internal legislative competence in the area of social policy. Consequently, Convention No 170, whose subject-matter coincides, moreover, with that of several directives adopted under Article 118a, falls within the Community's area of competence.

18. For the purpose of determining whether this competence is exclusive in nature, it should be pointed out that the provisions of Convention No 170 are not of such a kind as to affect rules adopted pursuant to Article 118a. If, on the one hand, the

---

[9] See Chapters 12 and 13.

[10] See in that sense also L. Krämer, *Negotiating and Voting on Whale Protection within the International Whaling Commission (IWC)*, (International Fund for Animal Welfare, 2010), 6–7.

[11] See Chapter 5.

Community decides to adopt rules which are less stringent than those set out in an ILO convention, Member States may, in accordance with Article 118a(3), adopt more stringent measures for the protection of working conditions or apply for that purpose the provisions of the relevant ILO convention. If, on the other hand, the Community decides to adopt more stringent measures than those provided for under an ILO convention, there is nothing to prevent the full application of Community law by the Member States under Article 19(8) of the ILO Constitution, which allows Members to adopt more stringent measures than those provided for in conventions or recommendations adopted by that organization.

19. The Commission notes, however, that it is sometimes difficult to determine whether a specific measure is more favourable to workers than another. Thus, in order to avoid being in breach of the provisions of an ILO convention, Member States may be tempted not to adopt provisions better suited to the social and technological conditions which are specific to the Community. The Commission therefore takes the view that, in so far as this attitude risks impairing the development of Community law, the Community itself ought to have exclusive competence to conclude Convention No 170.

20. That argument cannot be accepted. Difficulties, such as those referred to by the Commission, which might arise for the legislative function of the Community cannot constitute the basis for exclusive Community competence.

21. Nor, for the same reasons, can exclusive competence be founded on the Community provisions adopted on the basis of Article 100 of the Treaty, such as, in particular, Council Directive 80/1107/EEC of 27 November 1980 on the protection of workers from the risks related to exposure to chemical, physical and biological agents at work (OJ 1980 L 327, p. 8) and individual directives adopted pursuant to Article 8 of Directive 80/1107, all of which lay down minimum requirements.

Judgment of the Court (Grand Chamber) of 20 April 2010, European Commission v. Kingdom of Sweden (PFOS case), Case C-246/07, European Court Reports 2010, p. 3317, paras. 58, 67, and 102.

[...]

58. The Commission disputes the argument that Member States are entitled to adopt national rules which are more stringent than the POPs regulation on the ground that that regulation constitutes only minimum Community rules, which has the consequence, pursuant to Article 176 EC, that Member States are entitled to submit proposals for amendments to the Annexes to the Stockholm Convention. According to the Commission, the purpose of such a proposal is necessarily the introduction of a more stringent international legal rule, with effects not only with regard to the Member State which has made that proposal, but also with regard to the Community.

[...]

67. The Kingdom of Sweden, also supported on this point by the interveners, further maintains that the legal position resulting from its unilateral proposal to

list PFOS in Annex A to the Stockholm Convention is comparable to that which could arise if it decided, on the basis of Article 176 EC, to adopt national rules for the protection of the environment that were more stringent than those stemming from Community law. The Republic of Finland states that there is nothing in the Court's case-law to substantiate the Commission's view that a Member State may not, in the context of an international agreement, adopt protective measures that are more stringent than the Community rules.

[...]

102. In that regard, the assertion by the Kingdom of Sweden and the interveners that a proposal to list a substance in the Annex to an international convention which is binding on the Union is equivalent to a national measure that is more stringent than a minimum Union measure and is permitted by Article 176 EC cannot be accepted. The Union could be bound by an amendment to an Annex to the Stockholm Convention whereas it is not bound by such a national measure.

Moreover, while Articles 206 and 207 TFEU, which provide the legal basis for the Union's common commercial policy, do not explicitly mention the environment, there is a growing body of measures taken by the Union and international agreements to which the Union wishes to become a party that affect both external trade and the environment. The relevant case law on that topic will be explored in the next section.

10.2 The interaction between the external environmental policy and the common commercial policy

In contrast to the shared nature of EU environmental policy, the common commercial policy is an exclusive competence of the EU, pursuant to Article 3(1)(e) TFEU.[12] Given the increasing overlaps between the two policy areas and the obvious stakes involved in the choice between a shared competence and an exclusive competence, it comes as no surprise that the Court of Justice has had to adjudicate on a series of disputes over the choice between a legal basis in environmental protection or in the common commercial policy.

The Court of Justice first addressed the choice between EU environmental policy and the common commercial policy in the first *Chernobyl* case, in which Greece challenged the legal basis of an import measure taken in the wake of the 1986 nuclear disaster. In that case, the Court sketched out a fairly comprehensive approach to the possibility to take measures under the common commercial policy that are broadly inspired by environmental concerns. The concerns that moved the Court were probably quite accurately expressed in the Opinion of Advocate General Darmon in the case (point 32): 'In order to avoid any change in patterns of trade and any distortion of competition in dealings with non-member countries, the Community must be able, under the common commercial policy, to adopt uniform rules regarding the conditions under which

---

[12] See Chapter 7.

products from non-member countries may be imported into its territory. Those conditions may include in particular compliance with maximum permitted levels of radioactivity without the measure in question thereby being of a different nature or not capable of adoption under Article [207 TFEU].' The measure at issue in the first *Chernobyl* case was, therefore, quite clearly to be situated within the sphere of trade policy.

The factual and legal constellation was different in the second instance, at which the Court faced the question of choosing between trade and environment, the Cartagena Protocol on Biosafety to the Convention on Biological Diversity.

Judgment of the Court of 29 March 1990, Hellenic Republic v. Council of the European Communities, Case 62/88, European Court Reports 1990, p. I-1527, paras. 10–22.

10. As regards the choice of legal basis, it must first be pointed out that that choice may influence the content of the contested measure in so far as the procedural requirements connected with the enabling provisions in question are not the same from one piece of legislation to the next.

11. In the present case, Article 113(2) and (4) provide that in matters of common commercial policy the Council, on a proposal from the Commission, is to act by a qualified majority without the need for the Parliament or the Economic and Social Committee to be involved. By contrast, Article 31 of the EAEC Treaty, although providing that the Commission is to have the right to make proposals and providing for the same majority in Council deliberations as Article 113, requires an opinion to be obtained from the Economic and Social Committee and the Parliament to be consulted. According to Article 130s of the EEC Treaty, the Council, acting unanimously on a proposal from the Commission and after consulting the Parliament and the Economic and Social Committee, is to decide what action is to be taken by the Community regarding environmental matters, subject to the Council being entitled to define those matters on which decisions are to be taken by a qualified majority. Article 235 of the EEC Treaty for its part provides that, if action by the Community should prove necessary to attain, in the course of the operation of the common market, one of the objectives of the Community and the Treaty has not provided the necessary powers, the Council, acting unanimously on a proposal from the Commission and after consulting the Parliament, is to take the appropriate measures.

12. Since the procedural requirements of Article 113 of the EEC Treaty are thus different from those of Article 31 of the EAEC Treaty and from those of Articles 130s and 235 of the EEC Treaty, the Council's decision to adopt as the legal basis for the contested regulation Article 113 of the EEC Treaty rather than Article 31 of the EAEC Treaty or Article 130s of the EEC Treaty, possibly in conjunction with Article 235 of the latter Treaty, is capable of influencing the content of the measure. An incorrect choice of legal basis, if established, would not therefore constitute a purely formal defect. In those circumstances, it is necessary to decide whether the regulation in question could be validly adopted on the basis of Article 113 of the EEC Treaty.

13. The Court held in its judgment of 26 March 1987 in Case 45/86 *Commission* v *Council* ((1987)) ECR 1493, paragraph 11, that in the context of the organization of the powers of the Community the choice of the legal basis for a measure must be based on objective factors which are amenable to judicial review.

14. As far as the objective pursued is concerned, the preamble to Regulation No 3955/87 indicates that 'the Community must continue to ensure that agricultural products and processed agricultural products intended for human consumption and likely to be contaminated are introduced into the Community only according to common arrangements' and that those 'common arrangements should safeguard the health of consumers, maintain, without having unduly adverse effects on trade between the Community and third countries, the unified nature of the market and prevent deflections of trade'.

15. Regulation No 3955/87 establishes uniform rules regarding the conditions under which agricultural products likely to be contaminated may be imported into the Community from non-member countries.

16. It follows that, according to its objective and its content, as they appear from the very terms of the regulation, the regulation is intended to regulate trade between the Community and non-member countries; accordingly it comes within the common commercial policy within the meaning of Article 113 of the EEC Treaty.

17. Recourse to Article 113 as the legal basis for the contested regulation cannot be excluded on the ground that Article 30 et seq. of the EAEC Treaty lay down specific rules governing the basic standards for protection of the health of the general public against the dangers arising from ionizing radiation. Those provisions, which appear in a chapter entitled 'Health and Safety', which forms part of the second title of the EAEC Treaty entitled 'Provisions for the encouragement of progress in the field of nuclear energy', are intended to provide for the protection of public health in the nuclear sector. They are not intended to regulate trade between the Community and non-member countries.

18. The fact that maximum permitted levels of radioactive contamination are fixed in response to a concern to protect public health and that the protection of public health is also one of the objectives of Community action in environmental matters, in accordance with the Article 130r(1), likewise cannot remove Regulation No 3955/87 from the sphere of the common commercial policy.

19. Articles 130r and 130s are intended to confer powers on the Community to undertake specific action on environmental matters. However, those articles leave intact the powers held by the Community under other provisions of the Treaty, even if the measures to be taken under the latter provisions pursue at the same time any of the objectives of environmental protection.

20. Moreover, that interpretation is confirmed by the second sentence of Article 130r(2), pursuant to which 'environmental protection requirements shall be a component of the Community's other policies'. That provision, which reflects the principle whereby all Community measures must satisfy the requirements of environmental protection, implies that a Community measure cannot be part of Community action on environmental matters merely because it takes account of those requirements.

21. As regards the Greek Government's reference to the need to base Regulation No 3955/87 also on Article 235, it need merely be stated that, as the Court has held, use of that article as the legal basis for a measure is justified only where no other provision of the Treaty gives the Community institutions the necessary power to adopt the measure in question (see most recently the judgment of 30 May 1989 in Case 242/87 *Commission* v *Council* ((1989)) ECR 1425, paragraph 6).

22. Since the contested regulation comes within the sphere of the common commercial policy and thus has an appropriate legal basis in Article 113, as is apparent from the foregoing, recourse to Article 235 is excluded.

Opinion of the Court of 6 December 2001, Cartagena Protocol on Biosafety, Opinion 2/00, European Court Reports 2001, p. I-9713, paras. 20–42.

20. According to the Commission, the Protocol essentially falls within the scope of Article 133(3) EC, but it does not rule out that certain matters more specifically related to environmental protection fall outside that provision. It therefore maintains that Articles 133 and 174(4) EC constitute the appropriate legal basis for concluding the Protocol.

21. That interpretation is contested by the Council and by the Member States which have submitted observations. They argue that, principally on account of its purpose and content, the Protocol can be concluded only on the basis of Article 175(1) EC. The Parliament also contends that this provision constitutes the appropriate legal basis for the measure concluding the Protocol, but it does not rule out referring in addition to Article 133 EC in so far as it is established that the Protocol's effects on trade in LMOs are a significant additional factor over and above environmental protection, which is its primary objective.

22. It is settled case-law that the choice of the legal basis for a measure, including one adopted in order to conclude an international agreement, does not follow from its author's conviction alone, but must rest on objective factors which are amenable to judicial review. Those factors include in particular the aim and the content of the measure (see *Portugal* v *Council*, cited above, paragraph 22, Case C-269/97 *Commission* v *Council* [2000] ECR I-2257, paragraph 43, and *Spain* v *Council*, cited above, paragraph 58).

23. If examination of a Community measure reveals that it pursues a twofold purpose or that it has a twofold component and if one is identifiable as the main or predominant purpose or component, whereas the other is merely incidental, the measure must be founded on a single legal basis, namely that required by the main or predominant purpose or component (see the Waste Directive judgment, paragraphs 19 and 21, Case C-42/97 *Parliament* v *Council* [1999] ECR I-869, paragraphs 39 and 40, and *Spain* v *Council*, cited above, paragraph 59). By way of exception, if it is established that the measure simultaneously pursues several objectives which are inseparably linked without one being secondary and indirect in relation to the other, the measure may be founded on the corresponding legal bases (see, to that

effect, the Titanium Dioxide judgment, paragraphs 13 and 17, and Case C-42/97 *Parliament* v *Council*, paragraph 38).

24. Since interpretation of an international agreement is at issue, it should also be recalled that, under Article 31 of the Vienna Convention on the Law of Treaties, a treaty shall be interpreted in good faith in accordance with the ordinary meaning to be given to the terms of the treaty in their context and in the light of its object and purpose.

25. In the present case, application of those criteria amounts to asking whether the Protocol, in the light of its context, its aim and its content, constitutes an agreement principally concerning environmental protection which is liable to have incidental effects on trade in LMOs, whether, conversely, it is principally an agreement concerning international trade policy which incidentally takes account of certain environmental requirements, or whether it is inextricably concerned both with environmental protection and with international trade.

26. It is established, first of all, that the Protocol was drawn up pursuant to decision II/5 of the Conference of the Parties to the Convention, held in accordance with Article 19(3) of the Convention which calls on the parties to consider the desirability of adopting measures, in particular of a procedural nature, in the field of the safe transfer, handling and use of any living modified organism resulting from biotechnology that may have adverse effect on the conservation and sustainable use of biological diversity.

27. It is not in dispute that the Convention, concluded by the Community on the basis of Article 130s of the Treaty, is an instrument falling within the field of environmental protection. It results from the United Nations Conference on Environment and Development (UNCED), held in Rio de Janeiro in June 1992. Article 1 of the Convention states, in particular, that its objectives are the conservation of biological diversity, the sustainable use of its components and the fair and equitable sharing of the benefits arising out of the utilisation of genetic resources.

28. In accordance with Article 31 of the Vienna Convention on the Law of Treaties, it is by reference to that context relating to the Convention on Biological Diversity that it is necessary to identify the purpose and define the subject-matter of the Protocol, in whose preamble the second and third recitals refer to certain provisions of the Convention, in particular Article 19(3), and to decision II/5 of the Conference of the Parties to the Convention. Numerous provisions of the Protocol, in particular Articles 3, 7, 16, 18, 20, 22, 27 to 35 and 37, also refer to the Convention or to the Conference of the Parties to the Convention.

29. Next, as regards the Protocol's purpose, it is clear beyond doubt from Article 1 of the Protocol, which refers to Principle 15 of the Rio Declaration on Environment and Development, that the Protocol pursues an environmental objective, highlighted by mention of the precautionary principle, a fundamental principle of environmental protection referred to in Article 174(2) EC.

30. The objective of ensuring an adequate level of protection in the field of the safe transfer, handling and use of LMOs also emerges clearly from the Protocol's title, which expressly refers to biosafety, and from the fifth to eighth recitals in its preamble, which draw attention to risks to human health from biotechnology, the

need for biotechnology to be used with adequate safety measures for the environment and human health, and the crucial importance to humankind of centres of origin and centres of genetic diversity.

31. Finally, as to the Protocol's content, there is a clear reflection of the Protocol's environmental aim in the fundamental obligation imposed on the parties by Article 2(2) thereof to prevent or reduce the risks to biological diversity in the development, handling, transport, use, transfer and release of any LMO.

32. It may also be inferred from Article 4 of the Protocol that the Protocol intrinsically concerns environmental protection since that article provides, with regard to the Protocol's scope, that it applies to all LMOs that may have adverse effects on … biological diversity, taking also into account risks to human health.

33. Similarly, in order to enable the parties to fulfil their fundamental obligation, laid down in Article 2(2), the Protocol sets up various control procedures (see Articles 7 to 13), including the advance informed agreement procedure which is a typical instrument of environmental policy (see, in relation to the introduction of a system of prior notification and authorisation concerning shipments of waste between Member States, Case C-187/93 *Parliament* v *Council*, cited above, paragraphs 23, 25 and 26). The Protocol also deals with the assessment and management of risks associated with the use, handling and transboundary movement of LMOs (Articles 15 and 16), unintentional transboundary movements and emergency measures (Article 17) and the handling, transport, packaging and identification of LMOs (Article 18). Finally, Articles 19 to 28 of the Protocol, whose subject-matter has been outlined in the background to the request for an Opinion, apply to any kind of transboundary movement and are also essentially intended to enable the parties to comply with their fundamental obligation laid down in Article 2(2) of the Protocol.

34. It follows from the examination carried out in paragraphs 26 to 33 of this Opinion, relating to the context, aim and content of the Protocol, that its main purpose or component is the protection of biological diversity against the harmful effects which could result from activities that involve dealing with LMOs, in particular from their transboundary movement.

35. The Commission contends, however, that the Protocol essentially falls within the field of regulation of international trade. It refers in this connection to the case-law of the Court which, in its submission, has for a long time taken a broad view of the concept of common commercial policy (see Opinion 1/78, cited above, paragraph 45). The fact that provisions governing international trade in certain products pursue objectives which are not primarily commercial—such as protection of the environment or of human health, development cooperation, foreign and security policy objectives, or agricultural policy objectives—cannot, according to the Commission, have the effect of excluding the Community's exclusive competence and justifying recourse to, for example, Article 175 EC where the measures in question are intended specifically to govern the Community's external trade (see, to this effect, Case 45/86 *Commission* v *Council*, paragraphs 16 to 20, the Chernobyl judgment, paragraphs 17 to 20, Werner, cited above, paragraphs 8 to 11, Leifer and Others cited above, paragraphs 8 to 11, Centro-Com, cited above,

paragraphs 26 to 29, Opinion 1/78, cited above, paragraphs 41 to 46, and Opinion 1/94, cited above, paragraphs 28 to 34). In reality, measures regulating international trade often pursue a wide range of different objectives, but this does not mean that they must be adopted on the basis of the various Treaty provisions relating to those objectives.

36. The Commission adds that non-commercial considerations have already been integrated into the WTO Agreement and its annexes, in particular in Article XX of the GATT and in the SPS and TBT Agreements, without the Court nevertheless rejecting, in paragraph 34 of Opinion 1/94, exclusive Community competence under Article 113 of the Treaty to conclude all the Multilateral Agreements on Trade in Goods.

37. As to that point, it is true that, in the very words of Article 1 of the Protocol, the adequate level of protection sought concerns in particular the transfer of LMOs and that the focus must be placed on transboundary movements of LMOs. It is also true that numerous provisions of the Protocol relate specifically to control of those movements, in particular where LMOs are intended for direct use as food or animal feed or for processing, in order to enable the national authorities to prevent or reduce the risks which they entail for biological diversity or human health. However, even if, as the Commission maintains, the control procedures set up by the Protocol are applied most frequently, or at least in terms of market value preponderantly, to trade in LMOs, the fact remains that, as is shown by the examination carried out in paragraphs 26 to 33 of this Opinion, the Protocol is, in the light of its context, its aim and its content, an instrument intended essentially to improve biosafety and not to promote, facilitate or govern trade.

38. First of all, as stated in Article 3(k) of the Protocol, the term transboundary movement means the movement of a living modified organism from one Party to another Party, save that for the purposes of Articles 17 and 24 transboundary movement extends to movement between Parties and non-Parties. Such a definition, which is particularly wide, is intended to cover any form of movement of LMOs between States, whether or not the movements are for commercial purposes. It encompasses not only movements of LMOs of an agricultural nature, intended for direct use as food or feed, or for processing, but also illegal and unintentional transboundary movements, movements for charitable or scientific purposes and movements serving the public interest.

39. Likewise, the juxtaposition of the terms transfer, handling and use of LMOs in Articles 1 and 2(2) of the Protocol indicates the parties' wish to cover any manner in which LMOs are dealt with in order to ensure an adequate level of protection of biodiversity.

40. Second, the fact that numerous international trade agreements pursue multiple objectives and the broad interpretation of the concept of common commercial policy under the Court's case-law are not such as to call into question the finding that the Protocol is an instrument falling principally within environmental policy, even if the preventive measures are liable to affect trade relating to LMOs. The Commission's interpretation, if accepted, would effectively render the specific provisions of the Treaty concerning environmental protection policy largely

nugatory, since, as soon as it was established that Community action was liable to have repercussions on trade, the envisaged agreement would have to be placed in the category of agreements which fall within commercial policy. It should be noted that environmental policy is expressly referred to in Article 3(1)(l) EC, in the same way as the common commercial policy, to which reference is made in Article 3(1)(b).

41. Third, whatever their scale, the practical difficulties associated with the implementation of mixed agreements, which are relied on by the Commission to justify recourse to Article 133 EC—conferring exclusive competence on the Community so far as concerns common commercial policy—cannot be accepted as relevant when selecting the legal basis for a Community measure (see Opinion 1/94, cited above, paragraph 107).

42. On the other hand, it follows from all of the foregoing considerations that conclusion of the Protocol on behalf of the Community must be founded on a single legal basis, specific to environmental policy.

It was for a while unclear whether Opinion 2/00 hailed a new restrictive approach by the Court to the scope of the common commercial policy, or merely a nuanced balancing exercise between the potential legal bases under environmental policy and common commercial policy, respectively. The Court further clarified its approach in the *Energy Star Agreement* case, which seemed to indicate that the latter interpretation was more accurate:

Judgment of the Court of 12 December 2002, Commission of the European Communities v. Council of the European Union, Case C-281/01, European Court Reports 2002, p. I-12049, paras. 36–49.

36. In the present case, it is not in dispute that, as is clear from its title, the Energy Star Agreement is designed to coordinate energy-efficient labelling programmes for office equipment.

37. As the Commission points out, such coordination necessarily facilitates trade inasmuch as manufacturers henceforth need to refer to just one standard as regards labelling and to comply with just one registration procedure with a single management entity in order to sell equipment bearing the Energy Star logo on the European and American markets. That coordination therefore undoubtedly constitutes a commercial-policy measure.

38. However, it is also clear, on reading the preamble to the Energy Star Agreement and Article I thereof, that, by stimulating the supply of and demand for energy-efficient products, the labelling programme in question is intended to promote energy savings and therefore in itself constitutes an environmental-policy measure.

39. It follows that the Energy Star Agreement simultaneously pursues a commercial-policy objective and an environmental-protection objective. Thus, in order to determine the appropriate legal basis for the measure concluding the Agreement,

it must be established whether either objective is the Agreement's main or predominant aim, in which case the measure should be founded on a single legal basis, or whether the objectives pursued are inseparable without one being secondary and indirect in relation to the other, in which case the measure should be founded on a dual legal basis.

40. It is clear from the terms in which the Energy Star Agreement is couched, in particular from Articles I and V, that the Energy Star labelling program is essentially intended to enable manufacturers to use, in accordance with a procedure for the mutual recognition of registrations, a common logo to identify for consumers certain products complying with a common set of energy-efficiency specifications which they intend to sell on the American and Community markets. An instrument having a direct impact on trade in office equipment is therefore involved.

41. It is true that in the long term, depending on how manufacturers and consumers in fact behave, the programme should have a positive environmental effect as a result of the reduction in energy consumption which it should achieve. However, that is merely an indirect and distant effect, in contrast to the effect on trade in office equipment which is direct and immediate.

42. Furthermore, while it is not in dispute, first, that the American Energy Star Program was devised in order to stimulate the supply of, and demand for, energy-efficient products and therefore to promote energy conservation, and second, that its extension to the Community undoubtedly helps to achieve that objective, the fact remains that the Energy Star Agreement itself does not contain new energy-efficiency requirements. It merely renders the specifications initially adopted by the EPA applicable on both the American market and the European market and makes their amendment subject to the agreement of both contracting parties.

43. The commercial-policy objective pursued by the Energy Star Agreement must therefore be regarded as predominant, so that the decision approving the Agreement should have been based on Article 133 EC, in conjunction with Article 300(3) EC.

44. The fact that participation in the Energy Star labelling program is not mandatory cannot affect that conclusion. The Agreement is none the less designed to have a direct impact on trade in office equipment by facilitating such trade for manufacturers and enabling consumers to choose the products which use the least energy.

45. In addition, as the Advocate General has pointed out in point 62 of his Opinion, it is clear from the Agreement on Technical Barriers to Trade which is annexed to the Agreement establishing the World Trade Organisation, approved on behalf of the European Community, as regards matters within its competence, by Council Decision 94/800/EC of 22 December 1994 (OJ 1994 L 336, p. 1), that non-binding labelling provisions may constitute an obstacle to international trade.

46. Furthermore, the fact that the Treaty provisions relating to environmental policy have been chosen as the legal basis for the adoption of internal measures such as Regulations No 880/92 and No 1980/2000 is not sufficient to establish that the same basis must be used when approving an international agreement with similar subject-matter. Suffice it to state that, as observed by the Advocate General in point 78 of his Opinion, since Article 133 EC relates to external trade, it could not

in any event serve as legal basis for a measure whose effects are purely internal to the Community. With regard specifically to completion of the internal market, recourse should be had, where appropriate, to Article 95 EC. It was, moreover, Article 100a of the EC Treaty (now, after amendment, Article 95 EC) that was chosen as the legal basis for the adoption of Council Directive 92/75/EEC of 22 September 1992 on the indication by labelling and standard product information of the consumption of energy and other resources by household appliances (OJ 1992 L 297, p. 16).

47. Nor does the fact that certain Member States have adopted their own eco-label prevent the Energy Star Agreement from being regarded as a commercial-policy measure covered by Article 133 EC which therefore falls within a field in which the Community has exclusive competence. The eco-labels adopted by the Member States, to which the Council has referred, do not in fact concern the external trade of the Community.

48. It follows from the foregoing considerations that the Council should have chosen Article 133 EC, in conjunction with Article 300(3) EC, as the legal basis for the decision concluding the Energy Star Agreement on behalf of the Community.

49. Since Article 175(1) EC, in conjunction with the first sentence of the first subparagraph of Article 300(2), the first subparagraph of Article 300(3) and Article 300(4) EC, is the only legal basis referred to in that measure, Decision 2001/469 must be annulled.

Nevertheless, the Court's judgments in the *Rotterdam Convention* cases also indicated that it was willing to contemplate that trade and environment were inextricably linked within one single measure, and that a joint legal basis was therefore required:

Judgment of the Court of 10 January 2006, Commission of the European Communities v. Council of the European Union, Case C-178/03, European Court Reports 2006, p. I-107, paras. 40–60.[13]

40. It must be noted, at the outset, that the applicant and the defendants do not deny that the contested regulation contains elements both of a commercial nature and of an environmental nature. However, they differ as to the centre of gravity of the regulation. Whilst the Commission maintains that, although the contested regulation does have beneficial effects on human health and the environment, its main objective is to govern trade in hazardous chemicals, the Parliament and the Council, and all the interveners, contend, on the other hand, that the latter aspect is incidental, the primary aim of the contested regulation being to lay down rules and procedures conducive to ensuring a high level of protection of human health and the environment.

41. In that connection, it must be borne in mind that, according to settled case-law, the choice of the legal basis for a Community measure must be based on objective

---

[13] See also Case C-94/03 *Commission v. Council* [2006] ECR I-1.

factors which are amenable to judicial review and include in particular the aim and content of the measure (see Case 45/86 *Commission* v *Council* [1987] ECR 1493, paragraph 11; Case C-300/89 *Commission* v *Council* (Titanium Dioxide) [1991] ECR I-2867, paragraph 10; Case C-268/94 *Portugal* v *Council* [1996] ECR I-6177, paragraph 22; and Case C-176/03 *Commission* v *Council* [2005] ECR I-0000, paragraph 45).

42. If examination of a Community measure reveals that it pursues a twofold purpose or that it has a twofold component and if one of those is identifiable as the main or predominant purpose or component, whereas the other is merely incidental, the act must be based on a single legal basis, namely that required by the main or pre-dominant purpose or component (see Case C-36/98 *Spain* v *Council* [2001] ECR I-779, paragraph 59; Case C-211/01 *Commission* v *Council* [2003] ECR I-8913, paragraph 39; and Case C-338/01 *Commission* v *Council* [2004] ECR I-4829, paragraph 55).

43. Exceptionally, if on the other hand it is established that the act simultaneously pursues a number of objectives or has several components that are indissociably linked, without one being secondary and indirect in relation to the other, such an act will have to be founded on the various corresponding legal bases (see, to that effect, Case C-336/00 *Huber* [2002] ECR I-7699, paragraph 31; Case C-281/01 *Commission* v *Council* [2002] ECR I-12049, paragraph 35; and Case C-211/01 *Commission* v *Council*, cited above, paragraph 40).

44. That is precisely the case here. Both the purposes and the terms of the contested regulation contain commercial and environmental components which are so indissociably linked that recourse to both Article 133 EC and Article 175(1) EC was required for the adoption of that measure.

45. In that connection, it must be borne in mind, first, that, as moreover is clear from both the preamble and Article 1(1)(a) of the contested regulation, its primary objective is to implement the Convention. As the Court has held in paragraph 51 of its judgment of today's date in Case C-94/03 *Commission* v *Council*, that Convention specifically includes two components regulating trade and protecting human health and the environment, which are linked so closely that the decision approving that Convention on behalf of the Community should have been based on Articles 133 EC and Article 175(1) EC.

46. It is true that the fact that one or more provisions of the Treaty have been chosen as legal bases for the approval of an international agreement is not suf-ficient to show that those same provisions must also be used as legal bases for the adoption of measures intended to implement that agreement at Community level.

47. In this case, however, use of the same legal bases both for the decision approving the Convention on behalf of the Community and for the contested regulation, which implements the Convention at Community level, is necessary in any event, in view of the clear convergence of the provisions of those two measures, reflect-ing both the concern to regulate trade in hazardous chemicals and the concern to ensure sound management of those products and/or to protect human health and the environment against the harmful effects of trade in such products.

48. That applies, in particular, to Articles 1(1) and 2 of the contested regulation, which lay down the objectives pursued by its authors and the substantive scope of the regulation in terms very close to those used in Articles 1 and 3, respectively, of the Convention and, moreover, the definitions contained in Article 2 of the Convention correspond to a considerable extent to those appearing in Article 3 of the contested regulation.

49. That applies also, and above all, to Articles 6 to 13 of the contested regulation, which lay down rules and procedures applicable to trade in hazardous chemicals in terms which in numerous respects reflect the rules and procedures provided for in the Convention. Articles 7 and 8 of the contested regulation thus clearly refer to Article 12 of the Convention, concerning export notifications, whilst Articles 12 and 13 of the contested regulation, concerning obligations associated with imports and exports of chemicals, directly echo Articles 10 and 11 of the Convention, setting out the same obligations.

50. Second, it must be observed that, as well as purporting to operate in parallel with the Convention, which it is intended to implement at Community level, the contested regulation goes beyond the scope of the Convention since, as moreover is apparent from the express terms of the fourth recital in its preamble, the Community legislature displays a clear intention to 'go further than the provisions of the Convention in certain respects'. The provisions included, to that end, in the contested regulation fully justify recourse to Article 133 EC in addition to recourse to Article 175(1) EC.

51. That applies, for example, to Articles 14(2) and 16(1) of the contested regulation. In so far as the first imposes a total ban on exports of the chemicals and articles listed in Annex V to the regulation and the second, read in conjunction with Articles 1(2) and 2(1)(c) of the regulation, requires compliance, in the case of exports, with the relevant Community rules on classification, packaging and labelling of dangerous substances and preparations, without prejudice to the specific requirements imposed by the importing party or country, those two articles in fact directly regulate commerce and trade in those products.

52. In that context, the defendants contend in particular that recourse to Article 133 EC was not necessary because, first, no major distortion had been observed in intra-Community trade in previous years and, second, in the exercise of their competences, the Member States are in any event required to comply with the relevant Community legislation, as moreover is apparent from Article 10(7) of the contested regulation.

53. In that connection, it need merely be observed that, even if it were assumed to be correct, the fact that no major distortion has been observed in intra-Community trade in the products concerned is not such as to call in question recourse in this case to Article 133 EC. The well-foundedness of recourse to that article as a legal basis for a Community measure depends on the specific characteristics of the measure and on whether those characteristics meet the objective criteria determining the applicability of that legal basis. As observed earlier, the contested regulation specifically meets those criteria.

54. As regards the argument that, in the exercise of their competences, the Member States are in all circumstances required to comply with the relevant Community

legislation, such an argument, the correctness of which cannot in itself be contested, is nevertheless irrelevant as regards choice of the appropriate legal basis for a Community measure.

55. As regards the fact, referred to by the defendants, that other Community measures, such as Regulations Nos 259/93 and 338/97, or Regulation No 2455/92, which preceded the contested regulation, have a legal basis relating to environmental policy, it is entirely irrelevant in the context of the present case. In fact, according to settled case-law, the legal basis for an act must be determined having regard to its own aim and content and not to the legal basis used for the adoption of other Community measures which might, in certain cases, display similar characteristics (see, in particular, Case C-187/93 *Parliament* v *Council* [1994] ECR I-2857, paragraph 28, regarding, specifically, the choice of legal basis for Regulation No 259/93).

56. In view of all the foregoing considerations, it must be concluded that the contested regulation includes, as regards both the aims pursued by its authors and its content, two indissociably linked components, neither of which can be regarded as secondary or indirect as compared with the other, one relating to the common commercial policy and the other to the policy of protection of human health and the environment. In accordance with the case-law cited in paragraph 43 of this judgment, that regulation should therefore have been founded on the two corresponding legal bases, namely, in this case, Articles 133 EC and 175(1) EC.

57. Admittedly, and as the Court held, in substance, in paragraphs 17 to 21 of the Titanium dioxide judgment, cited above, recourse to a dual legal basis is not possible where the procedures laid down for each legal basis are incompatible with each other or where the use of two legal bases is liable to undermine the rights of the Parliament (see also, to that effect, Joined Cases C-164/97 and C-165/97 *Parliament* v *Council* [1999] ECR I-1139, paragraph 14; and Case C-338/01 *Commission* v *Council*, cited above, paragraph 57). In this case, however, neither of those consequences follows from recourse to both Articles 133 EC and 175(1) EC.

58. First, recourse to Article 133 EC as an additional basis could not in this case have had any impact on the voting rules applicable within the Council because, in the same way as Article 175(1) EC, Article 133(4) EC provides that the Council, in exercising the powers conferred upon it by that provision, is to act by a qualified majority.

59. Second, recourse to Article 133 EC jointly with Article 175(1) EC is likewise not liable to undermine the Parliament's rights because, although the first-mentioned article does not formally provide for the participation of that institution in the adoption of a measure of the kind at issue in this case, the second article, on the other hand, expressly refers to the procedure provided for in Article 251 EC. In contrast to the situation at issue in the abovementioned Titanium dioxide case, the use of a combination of legal bases does not therefore in this case involve any encroachment upon the Parliament's rights since recourse to Article 175(1) EC enables that institution to adopt the measure under the co-decision procedure.

60. In view of all the foregoing, it is therefore necessary to annul the contested measure inasmuch as it is based solely on Article 175(1) EC.

> The Court was therefore willing to accept a rather broad reading of its *Titanium Dioxide* case law[14] in order to make measures based on a dual legal basis in environment and the common commercial policy possible. Another example of an accession decision based on a plural legal basis in the common commercial policy and in environmental policy is the decision pertaining to the Energy Community Treaty:

Council Decision of 29 May 2006 on the conclusion by the European Community of the Energy Community Treaty (2006/500/EC), Official Journal L 198, 20.7.2006, pp. 15–17.

THE COUNCIL OF THE EUROPEAN UNION,

Having regard to the Treaty establishing the European Community and in particular Articles 47(2), 55, 83, 89, 95, 133 and 175, in conjunction with the first sentence of the first subparagraph of Article 300(2) and the second subparagraph of Article 300(3) thereof,

[...]

Whereas:

[...]

(3) The Energy Community Treaty provides for the creation of an integrated market in natural gas and electricity in South-East Europe which will create a stable regulatory and market framework capable of attracting investment in gas networks, power generation and transmission networks, so that all Parties have access to the stable and continuous gas and electricity supply that is essential for economic development and social stability. It enables a regulatory framework to be set up, permitting the efficient operation of energy markets in the region, including issues such as congestion management, cross-border flows, power exchanges and others. It therefore aims at promoting high levels of gas and electricity supply to all citizens based on public service obligations, and achieving economic and social progress and a high level of employment.

(4) 'The Thessaloniki Agenda for the Western Balkans: moving towards European integration', endorsed by the European Council in June 2003 aims at further strengthening the privileged relations between the European Union and the Western Balkans. By creating favourable economic conditions and imposing the implementation of the relevant acquis communautaire, the Energy Community Treaty contributes to the economic integration of the other parties to that Treaty.

(5) The Energy Community Treaty enhances the security of supply of the parties to that Treaty by connecting Greece to the continental European Union gas and electricity markets, and providing incentives to connect the Balkans to the Caspian, North African and Middle East gas reserves.

---

[14] Case C-300/89 *Commission v. Council (Titanium dioxide)* [1991] ECR I-2867, paras 17–21.

(6) The Energy Community Treaty makes possible the development of energy market competition in a broader scale and the exploitation of economies of scale.

(7) The Energy Community Treaty improves the environmental situation in relation to gas and electricity, and promotes energy efficiency and renewable energy sources.

[...]

When the Cartagena Protocol was amended, the Commission proposed Article 192(1) TFEU as the only applicable substantive legal basis:

Proposal for a Council Decision on signing the Nagoya-Kuala Lumpur Supplementary Protocol on Liability and Redress to the Cartagena Protocol on Biosafety, 21.3.2011, COM(2011) 130 final.

EXPLANATORY MEMORANDUM

1. The Cartagena Protocol on Biosafety to the Convention on Biological Diversity entered into force on 11 September 2003. The Protocol provides a framework, based on the precautionary principle, for the safe transfer, handling and use of living modified organisms resulting from modern biotechnology that may have adverse effects on the conservation and sustainable use of biological diversity, or pose risks to human health. The Protocol focuses specifically on transboundary movements.

2. The Council adopted a Decision on the conclusion, on behalf of the European Community, of the Protocol on 25 June 2002. The instrument for Community ratification was deposited on 27 August 2002.

[...]

6. The Commission acted as the EU negotiator for the legally binding instrument on the basis of a formal authorisation adopted by the Council in June 2007 and extended in time after COP/MOP4. The negotiating directives were refined various times in response to developments in the negotiations, last by the Environment Council on 11 June 2010. They instructed the Commission to ensure that the results of the negotiation are consistent with relevant Union legislation and with the basic principles of Member States' law on liability and redress and that they could be implemented in the EU without introducing or amending substantive rules on civil liability. The Commission conducted the negotiations in close consultation with experts from Member States.

[...]

11. In view of the above, it is appropriate for a representative of the Union to sign, subject to subsequent conclusion, the Nagoya-Kuala Lumpur Supplementary Protocol on Liability and Redress to the Cartagena Protocol on Biosafety.

Proposal for a
COUNCIL DECISION
on signing the Nagoya-Kuala Lumpur Supplementary Protocol on Liability and Redress to the Cartagena Protocol on Biosafety

THE COUNCIL OF THE EUROPEAN UNION,

Having regard to the Treaty on the Functioning of the European Union, and in particular Article 192(1) in conjunction with Article 218 (5), thereof,

Having regard to the proposal from the European Commission,

Whereas:

12. Article 27 of the Cartagena Protocol on Biosafety bound the first meeting of the Conference of the Parties serving as the Meeting of the Parties to the Protocol to initiate a process with respect to the elaboration of international rules and procedures in the field of liability and redress for damage resulting from transboundary movements of living modified organisms.

13. In June 2007, the Council adopted a Decision authorising the Commission to participate in the liability and redress negotiations on behalf of the Union with respect to matters falling within Union competence, in accordance with certain negotiating directives. That authorisation was extended in October 2008 to cover the final stages of the negotiations.

14. The Union coordination meeting held on 11 October 2010 during the fifth Conference of the Parties serving as the Meeting of the Parties to the Protocol in Nagoya, Japan resulted in unanimous support for the final compromise reached on the Nagoya-Kuala Lumpur Supplementary Protocol on Liability and Redress to the Cartagena Protocol on Biosafety, following consideration that it was within the limits of the agreed EU positions and the negotiating directives addressed to the Commission.

15. On 15 October 2010, the final plenary of the fifth Conference of the Parties serving as the Meeting of the Parties to the Protocol successfully adopted the Nagoya-Kuala Lumpur Supplementary Protocol on Liability and Redress to the Cartagena Protocol on Biosafety.

[...]

18. The Agreement should be signed on behalf of the Union, subject to its conclusion at a later date.

HAS ADOPTED THIS DECISION:

Article 1

The President of the Council is hereby authorised to designate the person or persons empowered to sign the Nagoya-Kuala Lumpur Supplementary Protocol on Liability and Redress to the Cartagena Protocol on Biosafety on behalf of the Union.

[...]

By contrast, the *Shipments of waste* case demonstrates that the Court remains of the view that such dual legal bases should be the exception rather than the rule.

Judgment of the Court (Grand Chamber) of 8 September 2009, Commission of the European Communities v. European Parliament and Council of the European Union, Case C-411/06, European Court Reports 2009, p. I-7585, paras. 48–78.

48. In the present case, it is not disputed that the contested regulation pursues the objective of protection of the environment and that, consequently, it was, at least in

part, validly founded on Article 175(1) EC. The dispute relates solely to the question whether that regulation also pursues a common commercial policy objective and has components falling within that policy which are indissociably linked to environmental protection-related components of such importance that the act ought to have had a dual legal basis, namely Articles 133 EC and 175(1) EC.

49. In those circumstances, it is necessary to examine whether the objective and components of the contested regulation relating to the protection of the environment must be regarded as being the main or predominant objective and component.

50. That is indeed the case.

51. First, as regards the objective of the contested regulation, recital 1 in the preamble thereto states that '[t]he main and predominant objective and component of this Regulation is the protection of the environment'. Although disputed by the Commission, that statement is reiterated in recital 42 in the preamble to that regulation, which was contained in the Commission's proposal for that same regulation and which states that the objective of the contested regulation is 'to ensure protection of the environment when waste is subject to shipment'.

52. The other recitals in the preamble to the contested regulation confirm the environmental purpose thereof. As stated by the Advocate General in point 18 of his Opinion, apart from recitals 16 and 19, which refer to the proper functioning of the internal market, all of the recitals, albeit some more directly than others, bespeak environmental concerns.

53. By way of example, recital 33 in the preamble to the contested regulation states that necessary steps should be taken to ensure that waste shipped within the Community and waste imported into the Community is managed, throughout the period of shipment and including recovery or disposal in the country of destination, 'without endangering human health and without using processes or methods which could harm the environment' and that, as regards exports from the Community, 'efforts should be made to ensure that the waste is managed in an environmentally sound manner throughout the period of shipment and including recovery or disposal in the third country of destination'.

54. By contrast, and as observed by the Parliament and the Council, the preamble to the contested regulation does not make any reference to the pursuit of objectives falling within the common commercial policy.

55. As regards, secondly, the content of the contested regulation, Article 1 thereof states that that regulation 'establishes procedures and control regimes for the shipment of waste, depending on the origin, destination and route of the shipment, the type of waste shipped and the type of treatment to be applied to the waste at its destination'. As is clear from the summary of the content of the Regulation given in paragraphs 12 to 19 of this judgment, the principal instrument established by it is the prior written notification and consent procedure, the details of which are set out at length in Title II of the Regulation, relating to shipments of waste within the Community. That procedure is applicable, pursuant to Article 3(1) of the contested regulation, to shipments within the Community of all wastes destined for disposal, and also to shipments of specific categories of wastes destined for recovery.

56. The prior written notification and consent procedure is characterised by a number of elements aimed at ensuring that shipments of waste are carried out in a manner which respects the need to protect the environment. Thus, in the context of that procedure, under Articles 4(4), 5 and 22 to 24 of the contested regulation, the notifier of a shipment of waste must supply evidence of a contract concluded between him and the recipient, laying down obligations with respect to the recovery or disposal of the notified waste, as well as the obligation for the notifier to take back waste when a shipment cannot be completed or when a shipment is illegal.

57. Moreover, under Articles 4(5) and (6) of the contested regulation, the notifier must establish a financial guarantee or equivalent insurance covering the costs of shipment, recovery or disposal operations and storage of the waste in question.

58. When a shipment of notified waste is to be carried out, the competent authorities, when they opt to impose conditions for their consent to a notified shipment or to raise reasoned objections to such a shipment, as provided for in Articles 9 to 12 of the contested regulation, must base them primarily on grounds relating to compliance with environmental protection legislation.

59. It follows that, like the prior informed consent procedure established by the Cartagena Protocol on Biosafety, the prior written notification and consent procedure provided for by the contested regulation may be described as a typical instrument of environmental policy (see, to that effect, Opinion 2/00 [2001] ECR I-9713, paragraph 33).

60. As pointed out in paragraphs 17 and 18 of this judgment, the prior written notification and consent procedure provided for in Title II of the contested regulation and applicable to shipments of waste within the Community is also to apply mutatis mutandis, with adaptations and additions provided for by the relevant provisions of that regulation, to shipments of waste between the Community and third countries in cases where exports from the Community or imports into the Community are not prohibited under the provisions of Titles IV and V of that regulation. This is the case, pursuant to Articles 35 and 42 of the Regulation, of exports of waste destined for disposal from the Community to EFTA countries which are parties to the Basel Convention, and also imports into the Community of such waste originating from countries which are parties to that convention. The same is true, under Articles 38 and 44 of the contested regulation, of exports and imports of waste destined for recovery between the Community and the countries to which the OECD Decision applies. The same regime applies, under Articles 47 and 48 of the Regulation, in conjunction with Articles 42 and 44 thereof, in Title VI thereof, to shipments of waste through the Community from and to third countries.

61. It is also important to bear in mind the obligation imposed by Article 49 of the contested regulation on the producer, the notifier and other undertakings involved in a shipment of waste and/or its recovery or disposal to take 'the necessary steps to ensure that any waste they ship is managed without endangering human health and in an environmentally sound manner throughout the period of shipment and during its recovery and disposal'. That obligation, which is general in nature, applies to all shipments of waste, both within the Community and, mutatis mutandis pursuant to Article 49(2) and (3), between the Community and third countries.

62. Consequently, it is evident from the above analysis of the contested regulation that, both by its objective and content, it is aimed primarily at protecting human health and the environment against the potentially adverse effects of cross-border shipments of waste.

63. More specifically, in so far as the prior written notification and consent procedure clearly pursues an environmental protection purpose in the field of shipments of waste between the Member States and, consequently, was correctly based on Article 175(1) EC, it would not be coherent to consider that that same procedure, when it applies to shipments of waste between Member States and third countries with the same environmental protection objective, as confirmed by recital 33 in the preamble to the contested regulation, is in the nature of an instrument of common commercial policy and must, on that ground, be based on Article 133 EC.

64. That conclusion is corroborated by an analysis of the legislative context of the contested regulation.

65. First, that regulation replaces Regulation No 259/93, which, whilst providing inter alia in Titles IV to VI for a scheme similar to that provided for in Titles IV to VI of the contested regulation for imports and exports of waste between the Community and third countries, and also for transit through the Community of waste originating from third countries, was adopted on the basis of Article 130s of the EEC Treaty. The choice of that legal basis was endorsed by the Court in Case C-187/93 *Parliament v Council* [1994] ECR I-2857, as opposed to Article 100a of the EEC Treaty (subsequently 100a of the EC Treaty, now, after amendment, Article 95 EC). The Court has also found that the supervision and control established by Regulation No 259/93 are intended to protect the environment, not only within the Community but also in third countries to which waste is exported from the Community (see Case C-259/05 *Omni Metal Service* [2007] ECR I-4945, paragraph 30).

66. Secondly, like its predecessor Regulation No 259/93, the contested regulation, as evidenced by recital 3 in the preamble thereto, aims to implement the obligations under the Basel Convention. The environmental purpose of that convention is clear from the preamble thereto, which states that 'transboundary movements of [hazardous wastes and other wastes] from the State of their generation to any other State should be permitted only when conducted under conditions which do not endanger human health and the environment' and emphasises the need for 'their environmentally sound management'. In keeping with those objectives, that convention which, as observed by the Parliament and the Council, was characterised as a multilateral environmental agreement by the WTO, was approved on behalf of the Community by Decision 93/98, adopted on the sole basis of Article 130s of the EEC Treaty.

67. As regards the Commission's argument that the contested regulation is broader in scope than the Basel Convention, since it applies to all waste destined for disposal and recovery, whereas the Convention covers only hazardous waste for disposal, and that that difference denotes a commercial policy dimension to the Regulation, it must be pointed out that it is clear from Article 2(4) of that convention, read in conjunction with Section B of Annex IV thereto, that the term 'disposal' used in

that convention covers '[o]perations which may lead to resource recovery, recycling, reclamation, direct reuse or alternative uses'. As observed by the Advocate General in point 33 of his Opinion, the fact that the contested regulation also applies to non-hazardous waste and to waste intended for recovery does not make it commercial or weaken its environmental dimension since waste, of whatever type it may be, is inherently harmful to the environment (see, to that effect, Case C-9/00 *Palin Granit and Vehmassalon kansanterveystyön kuntayhtymän hallitus* [2002] ECR I-3533, paragraphs 36 and 45 to 51).

68. The foregoing analysis is not invalidated by the Commission's line of argument that Titles IV to VI of the contested regulation, concerning exports, imports and transit of waste, must be based on Article 133 EC because waste constitutes goods which may be the object of commercial transactions and that the notion of common commercial policy should be interpreted broadly, since it encompasses commercial measures which also pursue objectives in other areas, including environmental protection. Nor can it be affected by the fact that, according to the terminology used in Article 1(2) of that regulation, shipments of waste between the Community and third countries are categorised as 'imports' and 'exports'.

69. It should be borne in mind in that regard that the prior written notification and consent procedure applies to all shipments of waste, irrespective of any commercial context in which they might take place. The term 'shipment' is defined in Article 2(34) of the contested regulation in a neutral manner as 'the transport of waste destined for recovery or disposal...'. The term 'transport', in turn, is defined in Article 2(33) of that regulation as 'the carriage of waste by road, rail, air, sea or inland waterways'. 'Import' and 'export' are also defined, in Article 2(30) and (31) of the Regulation, in neutral terms, as 'any entry of waste into the Community...' and 'the action of waste leaving the Community...' respectively. The contested regulation thus emphasises the carriage of waste with a view to its treatment rather than carriage thereof for commercial purposes. Even if waste is shipped in the context of commercial trade, the fact remains that the prior written notification and consent procedure is aimed solely at protecting against risks to human health and the environment arising from such shipments and not to promote, facilitate or govern commercial trade (see, by analogy, Opinion 2/00, paragraphs 37 and 38).

70. Moreover, a broad interpretation of the concept of common commercial policy is not such as to call into question the finding that the contested regulation is an instrument falling principally under environmental protection policy. As the Court has held, a Community act may fall within that area, even when the measures provided for by that act are liable to affect trade (see, to that effect, Opinion 2/00, paragraph 40).

71. A Community act falls within the exclusive competence in the field of the common commercial policy provided for in Article 133 EC only if it relates specifically to international trade in that it is essentially intended to promote, facilitate or govern trade and has direct and immediate effects on trade in the products concerned (see Case C-347/03 *Regione autonoma Friuli-Venezia Giulia and ERSA* [2005] ECR I-3785, paragraph 75 and case-law cited).

72. That is clearly not the situation in the present case. As with its predecessor, the aim of the contested regulation is not to define those characteristics of waste which will enable it to circulate freely within the internal market or as part of commercial trade with third countries, but to provide a harmonised set of procedures whereby movements of waste can be limited in order to secure protection of the environment (see, to that effect, Case C-187/93 *Parliament* v *Council*, paragraph 26).

73. As to the Commission's argument that the Court should, in the present case, take the same approach as in Case C-178/03 *Commission* v *Parliament and Council*, suffice it to note that Regulation No 304/2003 concerning the export and import of dangerous chemicals, which was at issue in that case, is not comparable to the contested regulation.

74. The principal objective of Regulation No 304/2003 is to implement the Rotterdam Convention on the Prior Informed Consent Procedure for Certain Hazardous Chemicals and Pesticides in International Trade, approved, on behalf of the European Community, by Council Decision 2003/106/EC of 19 December 2002 (OJ 2003 L 63, p. 27) ('the Rotterdam Convention'). Given the clear convergence between the provisions of that convention and those of the Regulation, which implements the latter at Community level, the Court found that use of the same legal bases both for the decision approving that convention and for that regulation was necessary (see Case C-178/03 *Commission* v *Parliament and Council*, paragraphs 45 and 47).

75. In that regard, in Case C-94/03 *Commission* v *Council* [2006] ECR I-1, paragraph 43, the Court inferred from a detailed analysis of the Rotterdam Convention that it also aimed to promote shared responsibility and cooperative efforts in the international trade of certain hazardous chemicals and that it was through the adoption of measures of a commercial nature, relating to trade in certain hazardous chemicals or pesticides, that the parties to that convention sought to attain the objective of protecting human health and the environment. The Court concluded that the commercial components of that convention could not be regarded as merely incidental to the objective of environmental protection pursued thereby (see, to that effect, Case C-94/03 *Commission* v *Council*, paragraphs 37 and 42), and that the two components falling within the scope of the common commercial policy and protection of human health and the environment are indissociably linked and neither of them can be regarded as secondary or indirect as compared with the other. The decision approving that convention on behalf of the Community thus ought to have been based on Articles 133 EC and 175(1) EC, in conjunction with the relevant provisions of Article 300 EC (see Case C-94/03 *Commission* v *Council*, paragraph 51). Similarly, the Court has held that Regulation No 304/2003 implementing the Rotterdam Convention ought to have been founded on Articles 133 EC and 175(1) EC (Case C-178/03 *Commission* v *Parliament and Council*).

76. As shown by the analysis in paragraphs 51 to 67 of this judgment, the contested regulation does not contain such components of common commercial policy as to justify recourse to a dual legal basis. Accordingly, the Commission may not rely on

Case C-178/03 *Commission* v *Parliament and Council* in order to justify a finding to the contrary.

77. Moreover, the Commission's line of argument intended to demonstrate, by reference to the Community acts referred to in paragraph 35 of this judgment, the existence of a practice of adopting acts using a dual legal basis consisting of Articles 133 EC and 175(1) EC cannot be accepted. The legal basis for an act must be determined having regard to its own aim and content and not to the legal basis used for the adoption of other Community acts which might, in certain cases, display similar characteristics (see Case C-178/03 *Commission* v *Parliament and Council*, paragraph 55 and case-law cited).

78. In the light of all the above considerations, the Commission's action must be dismissed.

10.3 External representation and international negotiations in external environmental policy

Pursuant to the procedural rules contained in Article 218 TFEU, the Commission will submit recommendations to the Council if an international agreement in the field of environmental law needs to be negotiated, unless the external environmental aspects only form a minor part of an agreement that relates principally to the CFSP (which would appear possible after Lisbon), in which case the High Representative submits these recommendations. If it deems the negotiation of the environmental agreement in question to be opportune, the Council adopts a decision authorising the opening of negotiations and, depending on the subject of the agreement envisaged, nominating the Union negotiator or the head of the Union's negotiating team.[15] While under the first subparagraph of Article 300(1) TEC, the Commission was to 'conduct these negotiations', Article 218(3) TFEU appears to give the Council a choice.[16] Nonetheless, by virtue of the rule as regards the Union's external representation spelled out in Article 17(1) TEU, it could perhaps be assumed that, absent any contrary indication in Article 218 TFEU, the Commission will continue to act as negotiator for external environmental agreements.

The Council can also address directives to the negotiator and designate a special committee in consultation with which the negotiations must be conducted. On a proposal by the negotiator, the Council adopts a decision authorizing the signing of the agreement and, if necessary, its provisional application before entry into force.[17]

---

[15] Art. 218(3) TFEU.

[16] However, pursuant to Art. 207(3) TFEU, the Commission is the only possible negotiator in the field of the common commercial policy. Conversely, where agreements concerning monetary or foreign exchange regime matters need to be negotiated by the Union with one or more third states or international organizations, Art. 219(3) TFEU provides that the Council, on a recommendation from the Commission and after consulting the European Central Bank, is to decide the arrangements for the negotiation and for the conclusion of such agreements. These arrangements are to ensure that the Union expresses a single position. The Commission is to be merely 'fully associated with the negotiations'.

[17] Art. 218(4)–(5) TFEU.

Unless the agreement covers areas that internally require decision-making by unanimity, which is the case for the limited set of environmental matters listed in Article 191(2) TFEU,[18] the Council acts by qualified majority throughout the procedure.[19] If the environmental agreement falls under Article 192(1) TFEU, which prescribes the ordinary legislative procedure for the adoption of internal measures, its conclusion will require the consent of the European Parliament pursuant to Article 218(6)(a)(v) TFEU. If, however, the agreement falls under Article 192(2) TFEU, consent of the European Parliament will only be required if the agreement establishes a specific institutional framework by organizing cooperation procedures or has important budgetary implications for the Union.[20] In all other cases, the European Parliament will need to be consulted.[21]

International agreements regularly set up some form of institutional structure, which may be more or less developed. The Council adopts decisions establishing the positions to be adopted on the Union's behalf in a body set up by such an agreement, when that body is called upon to adopt acts having legal effects, with the exception of acts supplementing or amending the institutional framework of the agreement. It does so on a proposal from the Commission or the High Representative.[22] However, even before the Council has adopted a formal decision, the principle of sincere cooperation requires the Member States to take the interests of the Union into account when acting within bodies set up by international agreements. That was clearly illustrated by the *PFOS* case, in which Sweden proposed the addition of PFOS to the relevant annex of the Stockholm Convention even though a strategy had been agreed within the Council's Working Party on International Environmental Issues temporarily not to propose that addition.[23]

The complexity of EU external environmental competences being what it is, whether and, if so, to what extent a specific issue that forms the subject of international negotiations falls within the competence of the Union or of the Member States is often less than clear. That situation will inevitably lead to competence quarrels between the Union and the Member States and between the institutions of the Union. The latter, it should be recalled, are also bound by the duty of sincere cooperation in Article 4(3) TEU, a specific application of which is now explicitly contained in Article 13(2) TEU, according to which the institutions are to 'practice mutual sincere cooperation'.

A particularly unseemly example of how things can go awry regardless is the saga surrounding the negotiations for an international binding instrument on mercury, the most important publicly available documents of which are included here. In its recommendation of 15 July 2009, the Commission suggested that mercury was a substance

---

[18] '(a) provisions primarily of a fiscal nature; (b) measures affecting: [(i)] town and country planning, [ii] quantitative management of water resources or affecting, directly or indirectly, the availability of those resources, [iii] land use, with the exception of waste management; (c) measures significantly affecting a Member State's choice between different energy sources and the general structure of its energy supply.'

[19] Art. 218(8) TFEU.

[20] Art. 218(6)(a)(iii)–(iv) TFEU.

[21] Art. 218(6)(b) TFEU.

[22] Art. 218(9) TFEU.

[23] See Chapter 5.

already regulated to a large extent by existing legislation at Community level. It requested that the Council authorize it to participate, on behalf of the Community in the intergovernmental negotiating committee (INC) negotiations, in consultation with the special committee designated by the Council in accordance with the negotiating directives.

However, the Presidency prepared a revised compromise text that, as far as the Council was concerned, took into account views expressed by the Commission and by Member States, and provided for the EU and its Member States to be represented by the Commission and the rotating Presidency. The decision proposed by the Council was not well received by the Commission, as is clear from the contribution of the Council Legal Service on the situation.

Following the opinion of the Council Legal Service on the withdrawal by the Commission of its recommendation, the Council Presidency prepared a set of draft conclusions of the Council and the Representatives of the Governments of the Member States, meeting within the Council, in order to set out a common broad political framework for the EU and its Member States for the forthcoming INC-1 meeting.

What emerges from these documents, at least to the extent that they are publicly available, is that the withdrawal by the Commission of its recommendation led to an unprecedented institutional crisis. The first session of the INC took place in Stockholm on 7–11 June 2010. In the absence of a decision authorizing the Commission to participate in the negotiations, the EU was unable to negotiate, which gave rise to a bewilderingly paralytic performance by the EU, as can be gleaned from the Commission's explanation of the background to its later compromise proposal.

After letting the matter rest for a while and after having tried various methods and combinations as regards other international negotiations, a compromise was finally reached in December 2010. The Commission was authorized to participate, on behalf of the Union, as regards matters falling within the Union's competence and in respect of which the Union has adopted rules, in the negotiations on a legally binding instrument on mercury, further to Decision 25/5 of the Governing Council of the United Nations Environment Programme (UNEP).

Recommendation from the Commission to the Council on the participation of the European Community in negotiations on a legally binding instrument on mercury further to Decision 25/5 of the Governing Council of the United Nations Environment Programme (UNEP), 4.10.2010, SEC(2009) 983 final.

EXPLANATORY MEMORANDUM

[…]

4. EXISTING COMMUNITY PROVISIONS

Pursuant to Art. 174 (1) EC Treaty, the Community environmental policy contributes to promoting measures at international level to deal with regional or worldwide environmental problems. In accordance with Articles 174(4) and 175(1) EC Treaty, as interpreted by the Court of Justice [...], the Community may enter into agreements with third Parties. Mercury is a substance already regulated to a large extent by existing legislation at Community level. The mercury related acquis consists of some ten Directives and Decisions limiting the content of mercury in certain products, from cosmetics to batteries, or restricting the marketing and use of mercury containing products. An overview list of mercury related Community legislation is given in chapter 5.3 of the Impact Assessment accompanying the proposal of a Regulation on the banning of exports and the safe storage of metallic mercury [...]. This legislative Proposal has in the meantime been adopted as Regulation (EC) No 1102/2008 on the banning of exports of metallic mercury and certain mercury compounds and mixtures and the safe storage of metallic mercury [...]. Another legal act of major importance to be added to the overview list is Directive 2007/51/EC relating to restrictions on the marketing of certain measuring devices containing mercury [...]

B. RECOMMENDATION

In the light of the above, the Commission recommends: a) that the Council authorizes the Commission to participate, on behalf of the European Community in the negotiations on a legally binding instrument on mercury at the sessions of the Intergovernmental Negotiating Committee;

b) that the Council authorizes the Commission to conduct these negotiations on behalf of the European Community, in consultation with the special committee designated by the Council in accordance with the negotiating directives set out in the Annex;

c) that, when the negotiations deal with matters falling within the shared competence of the Community and of the Member States, the Commission and the Member States should cooperate closely during the negotiation process, with a view to aiming for unity in the international representation of the European Community.

ANNEX
NEGOTIATING DIRECTIVES

1. In the assessment and negotiation process under the auspices of UNEP the Commission will ensure that the full range of measures and available options for a global risk management of mercury are considered, in accordance with the mandate given by UNEP GC Decision 25/5 to the intergovernmental negotiating committee.

2. The Commission shall ensure that the provisions of the future legally binding instrument are consistent with relevant Community legislation, with international commitments and with the objectives of Community policies, in particular of the Community Strategy Concerning Mercury.

3. The Commission shall ensure that the draft legally binding instrument on mercury contains appropriate provisions enabling the Community to become a Contracting Party thereto.

4. The Commission shall report to the Council on the outcome of the negotiations and, where appropriate, on any problem that may arise during the negotiation.

Note from the General Secretariat to COREPER on the Draft Council Decision on the participation of the European Union in the negotiations on a legally binding instrument on mercury further to Decision 25/5 of the Governing Council of the United Nations Environment Programme (UNEP)—Adoption, 9504/10, 10.5.2010.

The first session of the International Negotiating Committee mandated by the UNEP Governing Council to prepare an international legally binding instrument on mercury will be held in Stockholm, Sweden, from 7 to 11 June 2010.

Coreper, at its last meeting on this matter, on 5 May, considered the options for a draft Council decision in a view of these negotiations. The majority of Member States expressed a preference for the Presidency's approach (a 'joint mandate' included in a Decision by the Council and the representatives of the governments of the Member States). Some delegations preferred the Commission's option (which foresaw 2 separate decisions, one by the Council and one by the Council and the representatives of the governments), but also indicated some flexibility on the issue.

Following these discussions, the Presidency prepared a revised compromise text set out in the Annex to this note. The proposal takes into account views expressed by the Commission and by Member States; it further clarifies the role of the negotiators to ensure an efficient participation and representation of the European Union and its Member States in the upcoming negotiations.

The Committee of Permanent Representatives is invited to agree on the text of the draft Decision in the Annex with a view to its adoption by the Council.

ANNEX

DRAFT DECISION BY THE COUNCIL AND THE REPRESENTATIVES
OF THE GOVERNMENTS OF THE MEMBER STATES, MEETING
WITHIN THE COUNCIL

on the participation of the European Union and of its Member States in the negotiations on a legally-binding instrument on mercury further to Decision 25/5 of the Governing Council of the United Nations Environment Programme (UNEP)

THE COUNCIL OF THE EUROPEAN UNION AND REPRESENTATIVES OF THE GOVERNMENTS OF THE MEMBER STATES, MEETING WITHIN THE COUNCIL,

Having regard to the Treaty on the Functioning of the European Union, and in particular Article 218(3) thereof concerning the authorisation to negotiate on behalf of the European Union,

Having regard to the recommendation from the European Commission of 15 July 2009, WHEREAS negotiations should be opened with a view to prepare an international legally-binding instrument on mercury,

HAVE ADOPTED THIS DECISION:

(a) The European Union and its Member States shall be represented by the Commission and the rotating Presidency of the Council of the European Union (hereinafter 'the

Presidency') in the negotiations on a global legally-binding instrument on mercury at the sessions of the Intergovernmental Negotiating Committee set up pursuant to UNEP Governing Council Decision 25/5.

(b) In the context of these particular negotiations, at the sessions of the Intergovernmental Negotiating Committee set up pursuant to UNEP Governing Council Decision 25/5, the Commission shall [...] negotiate on the provisions of the future global legally-binding instrument on mercury to:

– [...]

– reduce the supply of mercury and enhance the capacity for its environmentally sound storage;

– reduce the demand for mercury in products and processes;

– reduce international trade in mercury;

– reduce atmospheric emissions of mercury;

– address mercury-containing waste and remediation of contaminated sites, in accordance with the mandate given by UNEP GC Decision 25/5 to the Intergovernmental Negotiating Committee. A representative of the Presidency will accompany the Commission in the negotiations for these matters.

(c) In the context of these particular negotiations, at the sessions of the Intergovernmental Negotiating Committee set up pursuant to UNEP Governing Council Decision 25/5, the Presidency and the Commission shall [...] conduct together the negotiations on the provisions of the future global legally-binding instrument on mercury to:

– specify the objectives of the instrument;

– address compliance;

– increase knowledge through awareness-raising and scientific information exchange;

– specify arrangements for capacity-building and technical and financial assistance, in accordance with the mandate given by UNEP GC Decision 25/5 to the Intergovernmental Negotiating Committee.

The negotiators will determine on the spot, acting in accordance with the Treaties, the proper arrangements to achieve the most efficient defence of the positions of the Union and of the Member States. Unless the negotiators agree otherwise, the Commission should lead the negotiating team on the issues falling under the first and second indents and the Presidency should lead the negotiating team on the issues falling under the third and fourth indents.

(d) The Commission and the Presidency shall act in consultation with a special committee of representatives of Member States and in accordance with the negotiating directives set out in the Annex. [...]

In the course of negotiations, the [...] negotiators may delegate, as appropriate, certain specific tasks to each other, or to other designated representatives of Member States.

The Commission, the Presidency and the Member States shall cooperate closely during the negotiation process, with a view to aiming for unity in the international representation of the European Union.

(e) The Council and the Representatives of the Governments of the Member States, meeting within the Council, may at any time review the content of the negotiating directives set out in the Annex in connection with relevant developments and will do so in any case no later than 2011.

(e bis) Nothing in the present decision or in the negotiating directives in Annex shall affect in any way the respective competences of the European Union and the Member States or prejudge the exercise of these competences when a legally binding instrument on mercury is signed and concluded.

(e ter) The responsibility of the Commission to negotiate on matters of exclusive European Union competence in accordance with the Treaties is unaffected by the present decision.

(f) The appended negotiating directives are issued.

Participation of the European Union and the Member States in the negotiations on a legally binding instrument on mercury further to Decision 25/5 of the Governing Council of the United Nations Environment Programme (UNEP)— Withdrawal of the Commission recommendation, 9963/10, 19.5.2010.

At its meeting on 12 May 2010 Coreper (Part I) agreed by common accord to send for adoption to the Council and the Representatives of the Governments of the Member States meeting within the Council, a draft Decision authorising the Union and its Member States to participate in the negotiation of a legally binding international agreement on mercury.

At the end of the meeting, the Commission representative announced that in view of the position adopted by Coreper, the Commission would be withdrawing the recommendation which had given rise to the Decision now being sent to the Council. The representative of the Council Legal Service was asked to comment on the legality of such withdrawal and its impact on the way forward.

[...]

'A' ITEM NOTE from the General Secretariat to the Council, Addressing global mercury challenges—Adoption of conclusions by the Council and the Representatives of the Governments of the Member States, meeting within the Council, 4.6.2010, 10564/10.

The Commission submitted to the Council on 15 July 2009 a Recommendation on the participation of the European Community in the negotiations on a legally binding instrument on mercury further to Decision 25/5 of the Governing Council of the United Nations Environment Programme (UNEP).

The Committee of Permanent Representatives examined thoroughly the recommendation at its four meetings, for the last time on 12 May 2010. At that meeting, all delegations could accept the text of the Decision by the Council and the Representatives of the Governments of the Member States, meeting within the Council, as prepared by the Presidency, in order to give effect to the Commission's recommendation. The

Commission however announced that the proposed Decision was not acceptable and that it would withdraw its Recommendation. The Commission confirmed the withdrawal of its Recommendation by a letter addressed to the Council later that same day.

The Council Legal Service, at the request of the Presidency, issued a written opinion on the withdrawal by the Commission of its recommendation. The Committee of Permanent Representatives reverted further to the matter at its meeting on 21 May 2010, taking also into account that opinion.

Following the discussions in the Committee and the opinion of the Council Legal Service, the Presidency prepared a set of draft Conclusions of the Council and the Representatives of the Governments of the Member States, meeting within the Council, in order to set out a common broad political framework for the EU and its Member States for the forthcoming INC-1 meeting. The Committee of Permanent Representatives examined these Conclusions at its meetings on 2 and 4 June 2010.

The Annex to this note contains the text of the Conclusions as agreed by all delegations and the Commission.

Since the Intergovernmental Negotiating Committee to prepare a global legally binding instrument on mercury (INC-1) will be meeting on 7–11 June 2010 in Stockholm, the Committee of Permanent Representatives recommends that the Council and the Representatives of the Governments of the Member States, meeting within the Council adopt the annexed Conclusions as soon as possible as an 'A' item at one of its next sessions.

ANNEX
ADDRESSING GLOBAL MERCURY CHALLENGES
– DRAFT CONCLUSIONS –

THE COUNCIL OF THE EUROPEAN UNION AND THE REPRESENTATIVES OF THE GOVERNMENTS OF THE MEMBER STATES, MEETING WITHIN THE COUNCIL:

1. REAFFIRM their commitment to the overall objective of protecting human health and the environment from the release of mercury and its compounds by minimising and, where feasible, ultimately eliminating global anthropogenic mercury releases to air, water and land.

2. RECALL that the Council conclusions of 4 December 2008 regarded a multilateral environmental agreement as the most appropriate instrument to address the global challenges posed by mercury and emphasised that such a comprehensive multilateral environmental agreement should consider the whole life cycle of mercury and include a broad range of elements representing specific commitments and actions to accomplish the overall objective.

3. REITERATE that the future agreement on mercury should address in its core provisions the aspects of supply and environmentally sound storage and disposal alongside with provisions on demand for mercury products and processes, international trade, atmospheric emissions, environmentally sound management of mercury-containing wastes and remediation of existing contaminated sites.

4. BELIEVE that the future agreement should also contain provisions on compli-ance, increased knowledge and information exchange, technical assistance and capacity-building, as well as financial assistance which will play an important role in contributing to the full implementation of the agreement by all Parties; further BELIEVE that information exchange is a clear issue where, as in the case of technical assistance and capacity building, a synergistic approach should be taken from the out-set by deriving benefits from existing information exchange mechanisms.

5. STRESS that the new agreement on mercury should bring benefits to all; UNDERLINE therefore that a country-driven approach and effective use of resources devoted to the management of chemicals and waste are essential and all possible sources of financing, including from the private sector, should be explored in order to mobilize adequate resources for implementation.

6. ARE OF THE VIEW that a robust and successful multilateral agreement needs the involvement of all relevant stakeholders from the outset in the negotiations, as well as in the implementation phase.

7. RECALL that on 16 July 2009 the Commission submitted to the Council a rec-ommendation on the Community participation in UNEP negotiations on an international agreement on mercury; further RECALL that, following this recom-mendation, the preparatory bodies of the Council completed their work on a draft decision on the participation of the European Union and its Member States in the negotiations.

8. REGRET that the Commission has subsequently communicated to the Council, its decision to withdraw the recommendation on the participation of the European Union in these negotiations and URGE the Commission to submit, as soon as possible, a new recommendation for a Council Decision pursuant to Article 218 paragraph 3 of the Treaty on the Functioning of the European Union.

9. UNDERLINE the importance, for the European Union and its Member States, of the upcoming negotiations on an international legally binding agreement on mercury, pursuant to the UNEP Governing Council Decision 25/5, at INC-1 (First Intergovernmental Negotiating Committee, Stockholm, 7–11 June 2010).

10. HAVE NOT RETAINED, in the present instance, the option of going ahead, despite the withdrawal of the Commission's recommendation, with the adoption of the decision referred to in paragraph 7 above to formally authorise the opening of negotiations; ARE OF THE VIEW, that the practical arrangements described in this draft decision represent a viable solution for an effective coordination on the spot in order to achieve unity of representation and a successful defence of the common objectives of the European Union and of its Member States; REMAIN CONFIDENT that all parties concerned will loyally cooperate at the forthcoming INC-1 meeting.

11. NOTE that Member States agree to designate the Presidency of the Council as their representative in these negotiations on matters falling within their competence.

12. INVITE the Commission, on behalf of the European Union, and the Presidency, on behalf of the Member States, to work at INC-1 in a coordinated manner and in close and regular consultation with the Representatives of the Member States, towards the achievement of the common overall objective set out in paragraph 1.

Recommendation from the Commission to the Council on the participation of the European Union in negotiations on a legally binding instrument on mercury further to Decision 25/5 of the Governing Council of the United Nations Environment Programme (UNEP), 30.9.2010, SEC(2010) 1145 final.

A. EXPLANATORY MEMORANDUM
[...]

3. RECENT DEVELOPMENTS

On 15 July 2009, the Commission adopted a Recommendation to the Council on the participation of the European Community in negotiations on a legally binding instrument on mercury further to Decision 25/5 of the GC UNEP2. On 12 May 2010, COREPER reached an agreement on a draft Council Decision that was considered by the Commission not to be in line with the Treaties. The Commission therefore decided to withdraw its Recommendation on the same day.

The first session of the INC took place in Stockholm, 7–11 June 2010. In the absence of a Decision authorising the Commission to participate in the negotiations, the EU was unable to negotiate. In addition to an opening statement by the Commission explaining that it was not in a position to negotiate, statements made in Stockholm, partly by the Commission on behalf of the EU, partly by the Presidency on behalf of the Member States remained limited to general aspects and experience within the EU, in line with the 'common understanding' set out in Council conclusions adopted on 4 June 2013.

Four more INC sessions are scheduled: INC-2, 24–28 January 2011 (Chiba, Japan), INC-3 (end October 2011, Africa), INC-4 (June 2012, South America) and INC-5 (January 2013).

[...]

B. RECOMMENDATION

In the light of the above, the Commission recommends that:

(a) The Council authorises the Commission to participate, on behalf of the European Union for matters falling within Union competence, in the negotiations on a global legally binding instrument on mercury at the sessions of the Intergovernmental Negotiating Committee set up pursuant to UNEP Governing Council Decision 25/5.

(b) In the context of these particular negotiations, at the sessions of the Intergovernmental Negotiating Committee set up pursuant to UNEP Governing Council Decision 25/5, the Commission shall negotiate the provisions of the future global legally binding instrument on mercury to:

– specify the objectives of the instrument;

– reduce the supply of mercury and enhance the capacity for its environmentally sound storage;

– reduce the demand for mercury in products and processes;

– reduce international trade in mercury;

– reduce atmospheric emissions of mercury;

– address mercury-containing waste and remediation of contaminated sites;

– increase knowledge through awareness-raising;

– address compliance,

in accordance with the mandate given by UNEP GC Decision 25/5 to the Intergovernmental Negotiating Committee.

(c) In the context of these negotiations the Commission shall also negotiate the following matters relating to the EU competence covered by Articles 4(3) and 4(4) TFEU:

– scientific information exchange,

– provisions to specify arrangements for capacity building and technical and financial assistance.

(d) The Commission shall act in consultation with a special committee of representatives of Member States and in accordance with the negotiating directives set out in the Annex.

(e) The Commission and the Member States shall cooperate closely during the negotiating process, with a view to aiming for unity in the international representation of the European Union, notably in the matters referred to under (c).

(f) Upon an initiative of the Commission the Council may review the content of the negotiating directives in connection with relevant developments.

(g) The negotiating directives shall not affect in any way the respective competences of the European Union and the Member States, nor shall they prejudge the exercise of these competences when a legally binding instrument on mercury is signed and concluded.

(h) The Commission shall immediately and fully inform the European Parliament at all stages of the procedure.

ANNEX
NEGOTIATING DIRECTIVES

1. In the negotiation process under the auspices of the UNEP, the Commission shall endeavour to ensure that the global legally-binding instrument on mercury contains provisions to protect human health and the global environment from the release of mercury and its compounds by minimising and, where feasible, ultimately eliminating, global, anthropogenic mercury releases to air, water and land, in line with the overall goal of the UNEP Global Mercury Partnership and in accordance with the mandate given by UNEP GC Decision 25/5 to the Intergovernmental Negotiating Committee.

2. In the course of negotiations, the Commission shall be permanently in contact with the special committee of representatives of Member States to provide regular updates on the progress of negotiations and to coordinate the EU position accordingly, as needed.

3. The Commission shall ensure that the provisions of the future legally binding instrument are consistent with relevant European legislation and with international commitments, as well as with agreed EU positions, taking also into account the objectives of relevant European Union policies, in particular the Community Strategy Concerning Mercury.

4. The Commission shall consult Member States on the potential implications for their programmes of all negotiating proposals where developing countries would require financial and technical assistance or scientific information exchange to comply with obligations under the future instrument. The Commission shall take into account those implications in the negotiation process.

5. The Commission shall ensure that the future legally binding instrument on mercury contains appropriate provisions enabling the European Union to become a Contracting Party thereto.

6. The Commission shall report to the Council on the outcome of the negotiations at regular intervals after each session of the International Negotiating Committee and, where appropriate, on any problem that may arise during the negotiation.

Council Decision on the participation of the Union in negotiations on a legally binding instrument on mercury further to Decision 25/5 of the Governing Council of the United Nations Environment Programme (UNEP), 6.12.2010, 16632/10.

THE COUNCIL OF THE EUROPEAN UNION,

Having regard to the Treaty on the Functioning of the European Union, and in particular Article 218(3) thereof,

Having regard to the recommendation from the European Commission,

Whereas the Commission should be authorised to participate, on behalf of the Union, in negotiations on a legally binding instrument on mercury, further to Decision 25/5 of the Governing Council of the United Nations Environment Programme (UNEP),

HAS ADOPTED THIS DECISION:

Article 1

1. The Commission is hereby authorised to participate, on behalf of the Union, as regards matters falling within the Union's competence and in respect of which the Union has adopted rules, in the negotiations on a legally binding instrument on mercury, further to Decision 25/5 of the Governing Council of UNEP.

2. The Commission shall conduct these negotiations on behalf of the Union, as regards matters falling within the Union's competence and in respect of which the Union has adopted rules, in consultation with a special committee of representatives of Member States, and in accordance with the negotiating directives set out in the Addendum to this Decision.

3. To the extent that the subject matter of the agreement falls within the shared competence of the Union and of its Member States, the Commission and the Member States should cooperate closely during the negotiating process, with a view to aiming for unity in the international representation of the Union and its Member States.

4. The Council may review the content of the negotiating directives at any time. To this end, the Commission shall report in writing to the Council on the outcome of the negotiations at regular intervals.

Article 2

This Decision is addressed to the Commission.

[...]

Select Bibliography

Corthaut, T. and Van Eeckhoutte, D., Legal Aspects of EU Participation in Global Environmental Governance under the UN Umbrella, *The European Union and Multilateral Governance: Assessing EU Participation in United Nations Human Rights and Environmental Fora* (J. Wouters, H. Bruyninckx, S. Basu, and S. Schunz (eds), Basingstoke: Palgrave Macmillan, 2012), 145–70.

De Baere, G., 'O, Where is Faith? O, Where is Loyalty?' Some Thoughts on the Duty of Loyal Co-operation and the Union's External Environmental Competences in the Light of the PFOS Case, 36 *ELR*, 2011, 405–19.

——, *Mercury Rising*: The European Union and the International Negotiations for a Globally Binding Instrument on Mercury, 37 *ELR*, 2012, 640–55.

—— and Ryngaert, C., The ECJ's Judgment in *Air Transport Association of America* and the International Legal Context of the EU's Climate Change Policy, 18 *EFA Rev*, forthcoming.

De Jong, S. and Schunz, S., Coherence in European Union External Policy before and after the Lisbon Treaty: The Cases of Energy Security and Climate Change, 17 *EFA Rev*, 2012, 165–87.

Eeckhout, P., *EU External Relations Law* (2nd edn, Oxford: Oxford University Press, 2011), 39–57 and 141–4.

Inglis, K., EU Environmental Law and its Green Footprints in the World, *Law and Practice of EU External Relations: Salient Features of a Changing Landscape* (A. Dashwood and M. Maresceau (eds), Cambridge: Cambridge University Press, 2008), 429–64.

Jans, J.H. and Vedder, H.H.B., *European Environmental Law After Lisbon* (4th edn, Groningen: Europa Law Publishing, 2012).

Krämer, L., *Negotiating and Voting on Whale Protection within the International Whaling Commission (IWC)* (International Fund for Animal Welfare, 2010).

——, *EU Environmental Law* (7th edn, London: Sweet & Maxwell, 2012).

Morgera, E. (ed.), *The External Environmental Policy of the European Union: EU and International Law Perspectives* (Cambridge: Cambridge University Press, 2012).

Pagh, P., The Battle on Environmental Policy Competences; Challenging the Stricter Approach: Stricter Might Lead to Weaker Protection, *Reflections on 30 Years of EU Environmental Law* (R. Macrory (ed.), Groningen: Europa Law Publishing, 2006), 3–16.

Scott, J., The Multi-Level Governance of Climate Change, *The Evolution of EU Law* (2nd edn, P. Craig and G. de Búrca (eds), Oxford: Oxford University Press, 2011), 805–35.

11

Common Foreign and Security Policy

11.1 Historical evolution

The Common Foreign and Security Policy (CFSP) was introduced in the EU institutional framework with the Treaty of Maastricht in 1993. It replaced the European Political Cooperation (EPC), which had been developed since the 1970s but had remained outside the institutional framework of the European Communities. The Treaty of Amsterdam further created the post of the High Representative for the CFSP. As opposed to the former first or 'Community pillar', CFSP was, and is, characterized by its more intergovernmental decision-making processes and the dominant role of the institutions representing Member States, that is the European Council and the Council of Ministers. Decisions in the area of CFSP are in principle adopted by unanimity. The role of the European Commission and the European Parliament is marginal and the Court of Justice of the European Union (CJEU) has in principle no jurisdiction in this area, as is discussed below.

Prior to the Treaty of Lisbon the objectives of CFSP were laid down in the former Article 11 TEU and this policy had its own specific instruments such as 'common strategies', 'joint actions', 'common positions', and 'decisions', provided for in former Articles 12 and 13 TEU. The European Council defined the principles and general guidelines (former Article 13(1) TEU) and decided on common strategies 'in areas where the Member States have important interests in common' (former Article 13(2) TEU). These common strategies were recommended by the Council and were subsequently implemented by the same institution through the adoption of joint actions and common positions (former Article 13(3) second subparagraph TEU). The Council also adopted decisions in CFSP (former Article 13(3) first subparagraph TEU), whereas it was tasked to 'ensure the unity, consistency and effectiveness' of CFSP (former Article 13(3), third subparagraph TEU). The aim of joint actions was to 'address specific situations where operational action by the Union is deemed to be required' (former Article 14(1) TEU). Further, common positions were about 'defin[ing] the approach of the Union to a particular matter of a geographical or thematic nature', whereby Member States had to ensure their national policies would conform to such common positions (former Article 15 TEU). Thus, whereas joint actions had an operational dimension, common positions had a policy purpose.[1] However clear this appeared

---

[1] See, for instance, Council Common Position 2001/443/CFSP of 11 June 2001 on the International Criminal Court, OJ L 155, 12.6.2001, pp. 19–20.

on paper, in practice the concrete distinction between joint actions and common positions was never easy to make, especially since they often covered similar or even identical subjects. Next to these three instruments, other instruments have been developed and used in the CFSP area, such as political statements, declarations and guidelines by the Council,[2] *sui generis* decisions, and international agreements concluded under the former Article 24 TEU.

It was not always obvious which elements of the EU's external action fell under the first or under the second pillar. Consequently, in some cases it was not easy to determine which method (the 'Community' as opposed to the 'intergovernmental' method) and which instruments and legal bases had to be used. Former Article 47 TEU stipulated that 'nothing in this Treaty shall affect the Treaties establishing the European Communities or the subsequent Treaties and Acts modifying or supplementing them'. This provision made clear that CFSP could not affect Community competences. Importantly, this provision fell within the jurisdiction of the ECJ (former Article 46(f) TEU) and the latter, thus, could and did interpret it in the *ECOWAS* case examined in Chapter 8. It is sufficient to recall here the Court's finding that according to former Article 47 TEU the Community policies had priority over CFSP. This, however, is no longer the case since the entry into force of the Lisbon Treaty, raising new questions as regards the appropriate legal basis of legal instruments that are at the intersection between CFSP and non-CFSP policies. These issues are analysed here together with the wording of the new Article 40 TEU that replaced former Article 47 TEU.

Treaty on European Union (Treaty of Maastricht)

Preamble

[...]

RESOLVED to implement a common foreign and security policy including the eventual framing of a common defence policy, which might in time lead to a common defence, thereby reinforcing the European identity and its independence in order to promote peace, security and progress in Europe and in the world.

[...]

TITLE I

COMMON PROVISIONS

[...]

---

[2] See EU Guidelines on (1) death penalty, (2) torture and other cruel, inhuman or degrading treatment or punishment, (3) human rights dialogues with third countries, (4) children and armed conflict, (5) human rights defenders, (6) promotion and protection of the rights of the child, (7) violence against women and girls and combating all forms of discrimination against them, and (8) international humanitarian law; the Council has adopted a number of guidelines on human rights and international humanitarian law that are legally non-binding but constitute strong political statements that help streamline relevant EU policies as well as actions on the ground.

Article B

The Union shall set itself the following objectives:

[...]

— to assert its identity on the international scene, in particular through the implementation of a common foreign and security policy including the eventual framing of a common defence policy, which might in time lead to a common defence;

[...]

Treaty on European Union (Treaty of Nice)

TITLE V

PROVISIONS ON A COMMON FOREIGN AND SECURITY POLICY

Article 11

1. The Union shall define and implement a common foreign and security policy covering all areas of foreign and security policy, the objectives of which shall be:

— to safeguard the common values, fundamental interests, independence and integrity of the Union in conformity with the principles of the United Nations Charter,

— to strengthen the security of the Union in all ways,

— to preserve peace and strengthen international security, in accordance with the principles of the United Nations Charter, as well as the principles of the Helsinki Final Act and the objectives of the Paris Charter, including those on external borders,

— to promote international cooperation,

— to develop and consolidate democracy and the rule of law, and respect for human rights and fundamental freedoms.

2. The Member States shall support the Union's external and security policy actively and unreservedly in a spirit of loyalty and mutual solidarity.

The Member States shall work together to enhance and develop their mutual political solidarity.

They shall refrain from any action which is contrary to the interests of the Union or likely to impair its effectiveness as a cohesive force in international relations.

The Council shall ensure that these principles are complied with.

Article 12

The Union shall pursue the objectives set out in Article 11 by:

— defining the principles of and general guidelines for the common foreign and security policy,

— deciding on common strategies,

— adopting joint actions,

— adopting common positions,

— strengthening systematic cooperation between Member States in the conduct of policy.

[...]

TITLE VIII

FINAL PROVISIONS

Article 46

The provisions of the Treaty establishing the European Community, the Treaty establishing the European Coal and Steel Community and the Treaty establishing the European Atomic Energy Community concerning the powers of the Court of Justice of the European Communities and the exercise of those powers shall apply only to the following provisions of this Treaty:

[...]

(f) Articles 46 to 53.

Article 47

Subject to the provisions amending the Treaty establishing the European Economic Community with a view to establishing the European Community, the Treaty establishing the European Coal and Steel Community and the Treaty establishing the European Atomic Energy Community, and to these final provisions, nothing in this Treaty shall affect the Treaties establishing the European Communities or the subsequent Treaties and Acts modifying or supplementing them.

> Another significant step in the development of CFSP before Lisbon has been the adoption in December 2003 by the European Council of the European Security Strategy (ESS) on the implementation of which a report was submitted to the European Council in 2008.[3] The ESS was drafted in order to give CFSP some orientation, leaving behind the cacophony of EU Member States' voices over the war against Saddam Hussein's Iraq. The agreement on the ESS is believed to be a significant achievement, whereas it has arguably given impetus to the adoption of operational CFSP instruments that refer back to it.[4] The ESS gives an overview of the main global challenges and lists five key security threats for the EU, namely terrorism, the proliferation of weapons of mass destruction, regional conflicts, failed states, and organized crime. In its latter part, the ESS clarifies the strategic objectives of the Union. These include the focus on the European Neighbourhood Policy (ENP) and on upholding and developing 'an international order based on effective multilateralism'. In order to achieve its goals the EU has to become more active, more capable, and more coherent, whereas it also has to invest in its partnerships with third states. It is pertinent to note here that despite the changes brought about by Lisbon in CFSP as well as the historic developments in the immediate vicinity of the Union with the so-called Arab Spring that have changed significantly the international security environment, the ESS has yet to be updated.

[3] European Security Strategy: A Secure Europe in a Better World, 12.12.2003; Report on the Implementation of the European Security Strategy: Providing Security in a Changing World, 11.12.2008, S407/08.

[4] See Council Decision 2009/1012/CFSP of 22 December 2009 on support for EU activities in order to promote the control of arms exports and the principles and criteria of Common Position 2008/944/CFSP among third countries, OJ L 348, 29.12.2009, pp. 16–20; Council Decision 2010/336/CFSP of 14 June 2010 on EU activities in support of the Arms Trade Treaty, in the framework of the European Security Strategy, OJ L 152, 18.6.2010, pp. 14–20.

11.2 The Common Foreign and Security Policy in the scheme of the Treaties after Lisbon

Under the Treaty of Lisbon the pillar structure is formally abandoned. The Treaty of Lisbon recognizes the definition and implementation of CFSP as a competence of the Union (Article 2(4) TFEU). However, CFSP defies a simple categorization with regard to its nature as a Union competence. It is rather a non-exclusive, *sui generis* EU competence running in parallel with national competences in the same field. Thus, despite the competence of the EU in CFSP being formulated very broadly 'cover[ing] all areas of foreign policy and all questions relating to the Union's security, including the progressive framing of a common defence policy that might lead to a common defence' (Article 24(1), first subparagraph TEU), Member States agreed, on the insistence of the UK,[5] on two largely identical Declarations (Declarations no. 13 and 14 concerning the CFSP, included below) in the Intergovernmental Conference (IGC) of 2007, which stressed once more that CFSP does not affect national competences in the field.

Treaty on the Functioning of the European Union

Article 2

[...]

4. The Union shall have competence, in accordance with the provisions of the Treaty on European Union, to define and implement a common foreign and security policy, including the progressive framing of a common defence policy.

[...]

Treaty on European Union

Article 24

(ex Article 11 TEU)

1. The Union's competence in matters of common foreign and security policy shall cover all areas of foreign policy and all questions relating to the Union's security, including the progressive framing of a common defence policy that might lead to a common defence.

[...]

Declarations no. 13 and 14 annexed to the Final Act of the Intergovernmental Conference which adopted the Treaty of Lisbon, signed on 13 December 2007, Official Journal C 115, 9.5.2008, p. 343.

13. Declaration concerning the common foreign and security policy

The Conference underlines that the provisions in the Treaty on European Union covering the Common Foreign and Security Policy, including the creation of the office

---

[5] See House of Commons, Foreign Affairs Committee (2008) Foreign Affairs Policy Aspects of the Lisbon Treaty, Third Report of Session 2007–8, London, 16 January 2008.

of High Representative of the Union for Foreign Affairs and Security Policy and the establishment of an External Action Service, do not affect the responsibilities of the Member States, as they currently exist, for the formulation and conduct of their foreign policy nor of their national representation in third countries and international organisations.

The Conference also recalls that the provisions governing the Common Security and Defence Policy do not prejudice the specific character of the security and defence policy of the Member States.

It stresses that the European Union and its Member States will remain bound by the provisions of the Charter of the United Nations and, in particular, by the primary responsibility of the Security Council and of its Members for the maintenance of international peace and security.

14. Declaration concerning the common foreign and security policy

In addition to the specific rules and procedures referred to in paragraph 1 of Article 24 of the Treaty on European Union, the Conference underlines that the provisions covering the Common Foreign and Security Policy including in relation to the High Representative of the Union for Foreign Affairs and Security Policy and the External Action Service will not affect the existing legal basis, responsibilities, and powers of each Member State in relation to the formulation and conduct of its foreign policy, its national diplomatic service, relations with third countries and participation in international organisations, including a Member State's membership of the Security Council of the United Nations.

The Conference also notes that the provisions covering the Common Foreign and Security Policy do not give new powers to the Commission to initiate decisions nor do they increase the role of the European Parliament.

The Conference also recalls that the provisions governing the Common Security and Defence Policy do not prejudice the specific character of the security and defence policy of the Member States.

Under the Lisbon Treaty, nearly all Treaty provisions concerning the Union's external action, which previously were spread over the TEU and the TEC, are brought together in Part V of the TFEU, 'External Action by the Union'. Remarkably, CFSP is not part of this title, retaining its different position in the scheme of the Treaties contrary to other legal bases for EU action. It is dealt with in the TEU, where it is 'subject to specific rules and procedures' (Article 24(1), second subparagraph TEU). Thus, the decision-making process remains strongly intergovernmental in CFSP, whereas decisions are taken unanimously except for where the Treaties provide otherwise.[6] In addition, the role of the Commission, the European Parliament (Article 36 TEU), and the CJEU remain limited—though that of the Court in CFSP

---

[6] See Art. 31 TEU.

has expanded after Lisbon. The differences of CFSP from the normal 'Community method' applying to most other Union policies are discussed below, shedding further light on the remaining procedural and legal duality between non-CFSP and CFSP external actions of the Union.

The drafters of the Treaties attempted to overcome this duality through possibly the most important innovation of Lisbon in the field of EU external action, the creation of the post of the High Representative of the Union for Foreign Affairs and Security Policy, who is simultaneously a Vice-President of the Commission. In this dual capacity, the High Representative is expected to ensure consistency in the entirety of EU external action falling within non-CFSP and CFSP policies (Articles 18(4) and 26(2) TEU).[7] With particular regard to CFSP, the role of the High Representative is pivotal throughout the development and implementation of the policy. The High Representative 'conduct[s] the Union's common foreign and security policy' (Article 18(2) TEU). Still, the Member States retain some role in putting into effect this policy (Article 26(3) TEU). The High Representative not only represents the Union abroad in CFSP, as discussed in detail in Chapter 2, but also makes 'proposals to the development of that policy' (Article 18(2) TEU) and 'preside[s] over the Foreign Affairs Council' (Article 18(3) TEU; see also Article 16(6) TEU). What is more, the High Representative ensures the 'implementation of the decisions adopted by the European Council and the Council' (Article 27(1) TEU), and together with the Council the 'unity, consistency and effectiveness of action by the Union' (Article 26(2), second subparagraph TEU).

The High Representative is supported in fulfilling this broad mandate by the European External Action Service (EEAS), which was also established by the Treaty of Lisbon (Article 27(3) TEU). Chapter 2 contains the EEAS Decision establishing this Service and determining its legal status within the Union, as well as its role and function in the external relations of the EU, and in particular in CFSP. Suffice it to say here that the EEAS is tasked to support the High Representative in carrying out the entirety of his mandate pertaining to CFSP, including Common Security and Defence Policy (CSDP), and in ensuring the consistency of the external action of the EU (Article 2(1) EEAS Decision). The Service also has to assist 'the President of the European Council, the President of the Commission, and the Commission in the exercise of their respective functions in the area of external relations' (Article 2(2) EEAS Decision). Thus, the role of the EEAS in CFSP after Lisbon is crucial, whereas it is further expected to help bridge any gap between that policy and the non-CFSP policies of the Union abroad through its engagement in the latter, though in a secondary supportive role not prejudicing the allocation of powers. In order to fulfil its mandate, the EEAS has integrated units that covered these policy areas in the past and belonged to the General Secretariat of the Council and to the Commission.

---

[7] See also Art. 21(3) TEU.

Treaty on European Union
Article 18
[...]

2. The High Representative shall conduct the Union's common foreign and security policy. He shall contribute by his proposals to the development of that policy, which he shall carry out as mandated by the Council. The same shall apply to the common security and defence policy.

3. The High Representative shall preside over the Foreign Affairs Council.

4. The High Representative shall be one of the Vice-Presidents of the Commission. He shall ensure the consistency of the Union's external action. He shall be responsible within the Commission for responsibilities incumbent on it in external relations and for coordinating other aspects of the Union's external action. In exercising these responsibilities within the Commission, and only for these responsibilities, the High Representative shall be bound by Commission procedures to the extent that this is consistent with paragraphs 2 and 3.

Article 24
(ex Article 11 TEU)

1. [...]

The common foreign and security policy is subject to specific rules and procedures. It shall be defined and implemented by the European Council and the Council acting unanimously, except where the Treaties provide otherwise. The adoption of legislative acts shall be excluded. The common foreign and security policy shall be put into effect by the High Representative of the Union for Foreign Affairs and Security Policy and by Member States, in accordance with the Treaties. The specific role of the European Parliament and of the Commission in this area is defined by the Treaties. The Court of Justice of the European Union shall not have jurisdiction with respect to these provisions, with the exception of its jurisdiction to monitor compliance with Article 40 of this Treaty and to review the legality of certain decisions as provided for by the second paragraph of Article 275 of the Treaty on the Functioning of the European Union.

[...]

Article 26
(ex Article 13 TEU)

[...]

2. [...]The Council and the High Representative of the Union for Foreign Affairs and Security Policy shall ensure the unity, consistency and effectiveness of action by the Union.

3. The common foreign and security policy shall be put into effect by the High Representative and by the Member States, using national and Union resources.

Article 27

1. The High Representative of the Union for Foreign Affairs and Security Policy, who shall chair the Foreign Affairs Council, shall contribute through his proposals to the development of the common foreign and security policy and shall ensure implementation of the decisions adopted by the European Council and the Council.

The compilation of the 'general provisions on the Union's external action' in one chapter under Title V of the TEU constitutes another attempt of the Treaty of Lisbon to overcome the duality between CFSP and non-CFSP external actions of the Union. Article 21 lists the principles and objectives generally applicable to the EU's external action. Thus, former Article 11 TEU, which described the objectives of the EU in CFSP, has disappeared. These objectives are included in the aforementioned Article 21 TEU as well as in Article 3(5) TEU, which apply to all external action of the Union. The fact that the Treaties no longer contain specific provisions detailing the objectives of CFSP, makes the determination of the scope of CFSP based on its objectives a far more difficult exercise. Nonetheless, such a determination may prove crucial in light of the still existing divide between CFSP and non-CFSP policies. If different interpretations among EU institutions and Member States surface and persist, it will eventually be up to the Court to set the boundaries between CFSP and the rest of the EU external action, as it has jurisdiction to do so according to Articles 40 TEU and 275 TFEU, discussed below. Finally, with regard to Chapter 1 of Title V TEU, Article 22 TEU tasks the European Council to identify, and adopt by unanimity decisions on, the EU's strategic interests and objectives regarding 'the common foreign and security policy and [...] other areas of the external action of the Union'.

Chapter 2 of Title V of the TEU contains specific provisions on CFSP. Confirming the contention that there remains after Lisbon a procedural and legal duality between CFSP and non-CFSP policies, Article 24(3) TEU continues to impose—as it was the case with former Article 11(2) TEU—a CFSP-specific duty of loyalty on Member States. The compliance with Article 24(3) is to be ensured by the Council and the High Representative, whereas neither the Commission nor the CJEU has any role in it. At the same time, although it remains different from the rest of the EU, the landscape of CFSP legal instruments has been simplified. Now there is only one CFSP instrument—decisions—adopted by the European Council (Article 26(1) TEU) and the Council (Article 26(2) TEU), whereas the European Council is always responsible for 'identify[ing] the Union's strategic interests, determine the objectives of and define general guidelines' for CFSP.[8]

The procedure for negotiating international agreements has been unified under Article 218 TFEU,[9] including CFSP agreements (Article 37 TEU), which like any other international agreement of the Union are binding both on Union institutions and Member States (Article 216(2) TFEU). Some differences persist for CFSP agreements though. When 'the agreement envisaged relates exclusively or principally to the common foreign and security policy', it is the High Representative who submits recommendations to the Council to authorize the opening of negotiations (Article 218(3) TFEU), and makes proposals to the same institution to suspend application of an agreement concluded by the Union or to establish EU positions 'in a body set up

---

[8] See Council Decision 2010/212/CFSP of 29 March 2010 relating to the position of the European Union for the 2010 Review Conference of the Parties to the Treaty on the Non-Proliferation of Nuclear Weapons, OJ L 90, 10.4.2010, pp. 8-14; this is a typical example of an legal instrument that before the Lisbon Treaty would have been a Common Position.

[9] See Chapter 3.

by an agreement, when that body is called upon to adopt acts having legal effects, with the exception of acts supplementing or amending the institutional framework of the agreement (Article 218(9) TFEU). Thus, in the Council Decision, included below, authorizing the opening of negotiations with Kazakhstan for an enhanced Partnership and Cooperation Agreement, the High Representative is nominated as Union negotiator for issues pertaining to CFSP. Finally, all decisions regarding agreements in the field of CFSP are still to be taken unanimously (Article 218(8) TFEU combined with Articles 24(1) and 31(1) TEU).

Treaty on European Union

Article 24

(ex Article 11 TEU)

[...]

3. The Member States shall support the Union's external and security policy actively and unreservedly in a spirit of loyalty and mutual solidarity and shall comply with the Union's action in this area.

The Member States shall work together to enhance and develop their mutual political solidarity. They shall refrain from any action which is contrary to the interests of the Union or likely to impair its effectiveness as a cohesive force in international relations. The Council and the High Representative shall ensure compliance with these principles.

Article 26

(ex Article 13 TEU)

1. The European Council shall identify the Union's strategic interests, determine the objectives of and define general guidelines for the common foreign and security policy, including for matters with defence implications. It shall adopt the necessary decisions. If international developments so require, the President of the European Council shall convene an extraordinary meeting of the European Council in order to define the strategic lines of the Union's policy in the face of such developments.

2. The Council shall frame the common foreign and security policy and take the decisions necessary for defining and implementing it on the basis of the general guidelines and strategic lines defined by the European Council.

The Council and the High Representative of the Union for Foreign Affairs and Security Policy shall ensure the unity, consistency and effectiveness of action by the Union.

[...]

Article 31

(ex Article 23 TEU)

1. Decisions under this Chapter shall be taken by the European Council and the Council acting unanimously, except where this Chapter provides otherwise. The adoption of legislative acts shall be excluded.

When abstaining in a vote, any member of the Council may qualify its abstention by making a formal declaration under the present subparagraph. In that case, it shall not be obliged to apply the decision, but shall accept that the decision commits the Union. In a spirit of mutual solidarity, the Member State concerned shall refrain from any action likely to conflict with or impede Union action based on that decision and the other Member States shall respect its position. If the members of the Council qualifying their abstention in this way represent at least one third of the Member States comprising at least one third of the population of the Union, the decision shall not be adopted.

2. By derogation from the provisions of paragraph 1, the Council shall act by qualified majority:

— when adopting a decision defining a Union action or position on the basis of a decision of the European Council relating to the Union's strategic interests and objectives, as referred to in Article 22(1),

— when adopting a decision defining a Union action or position, on a proposal which the High Representative of the Union for Foreign Affairs and Security Policy has presented following a specific request from the European Council, made on its own initiative or that of the High Representative,

— when adopting any decision implementing a decision defining a Union action or position,

— when appointing a special representative in accordance with Article 33.

If a member of the Council declares that, for vital and stated reasons of national policy, it intends to oppose the adoption of a decision to be taken by qualified majority, a vote shall not be taken. The High Representative will, in close consultation with the Member State involved, search for a solution acceptable to it. If he does not succeed, the Council may, acting by a qualified majority, request that the matter be referred to the European Council for a decision by unanimity.

3. The European Council may unanimously adopt a decision stipulating that the Council shall act by a qualified majority in cases other than those referred to in paragraph 2.

4. Paragraphs 2 and 3 shall not apply to decisions having military or defence implications.

5. For procedural questions, the Council shall act by a majority of its members.

[...]

Article 37

(ex Article 24 TEU)

The Union may conclude agreements with one or more States or international organisations in areas covered by this Chapter.

Council Decision of 13 April 2011 authorising the opening of negotiations with the Republic of Kazakhstan for an enhanced Partnership and Cooperation Agreement between the European Union and its Member States, of the one part, and the Republic of Kazakhstan, of the other part, 8282/11.

THE COUNCIL OF THE EUROPEAN UNION,

Having regard to the Treaty on the Functioning of the European Union, and in particular Article 218(3) and (4) thereof,

Having regard to the recommendation from the European Commission,

Whereas negotiations should be opened with a view to concluding an enhanced Partnership and Cooperation Agreement between the European Union and its Member States, of the one part, and the Republic of Kazakhstan, of the other part,

HAS ADOPTED THIS DECISION:

Article 1

1. The Commission and the High Representative of the Union for Foreign Affairs and Security Policy ('the High Representative') are hereby authorised to negotiate, on behalf of the European Union, the provisions of an enhanced Partnership and Cooperation Agreement with the Republic of Kazakhstan ('the Agreement'), that fall within the competence of the European Union. The Agreement shall replace the Partnership and Cooperation Agreement between the European Communities and their Member States and the Republic of Kazakhstan.

2. The negotiations shall be conducted on the basis of the negotiating directives of the Council set out in the addendum to this Decision.

Article 2

1. The Commission shall be the head of the Union's negotiating team.

The Commission shall negotiate the provisions of the Agreement as set out in the negotiating directives and which, in accordance with the Treaties, fall within the competences of the Union, either as matters falling within the Union's exclusive competence or as matters in respect of areas of supporting or shared competence to the extent that the Union has exercised its competence, except for those relating to the field of the common foreign and security policy.

For the purpose of the second subparagraph, exercised shared competence shall include measures adopted by the Union from the date of adoption of this Decision until the conclusion of the negotiations by the initialling of the text representing the outcome of the negotiations.

2. The High Representative shall negotiate, in relation to matters within the common foreign and security policy as set out in the negotiating directives, the provisions of the Agreement concerning the general principles and essential elements of the Agreement and the provisions relating to political dialogue and cooperation.

Article 3

The negotiations shall be conducted in consultation with the Council Working Party on Eastern Europe and Central Asia acting as the special committee designated by the Council, in accordance with Article 218(4) of the Treaty. The Commission shall report regularly to the special committee on the progress of the negotiations. Additionally, as regards the negotiations on trade, negotiations shall be conducted in consultation with the Trade Policy Committee.

Article 4

This Decision is addressed to the Commission and to the High Representative.

The role of the CJEU in CFSP remains very limited, even though it has been slightly expanded since the Lisbon Treaty came into force. Thus, according to Article 275 TFEU, the Court has no jurisdiction in CFSP with two exceptions. First, it can review cases of alleged encroachment of non-CFSP areas of Union competence from CFSP decisions, and vice versa. This constitutes an expansion of the jurisdiction of the Court in comparison with the period before the coming into force of the Treaty of Lisbon, when the latter could only protect the integrity of the then first pillar from CFSP instruments but not the other way round. This is a significant development, especially in light of the fact that the former first pillar no longer enjoys any precedence over CFSP. Thus, in cases of disputed legal basis of a Union instrument between CFSP and non-CFSP, the jurisprudence of the Court from the *ECOWAS* case will have to be amended since the Court will have to decide based on the aim and content of the provisions of the disputed legal instrument whether its main purpose falls within CFSP or non-CFSP polices. At the same time the possibility of having dual legal bases (CFSP and non-CFSP) has been discussed and dismissed by the Court in Case C-130/10, included below. Still, it is unclear whether the Court will exclude the possibility of having dual legal bases in all such instances. In light of this, EU institutions continue bringing cases before the Court disputing the legal basis of instruments in an effort to safeguard their powers in the internal decision-making procedure. One such case currently pending is Case C-658/11, where the European Parliament made an application for annulment of a CFSP decision for lack of further legal bases, although the instrument allegedly pertains to judicial cooperation in criminal matters, police cooperation, and development cooperation.

The second exception provided for in Article 275 TFEU is when the Court is called upon to decide on 'the legality of decisions providing for restrictive measures against natural or legal persons adopted by the Council on the basis of Chapter 2 of Title V of the Treaty on European Union'. The General Court only recently attempted an interpretation of this provision in Case T-509/10, the relevant excerpt of which is included below. An appeal against this judgment is currently pending before the Court of Justice.

Treaty on the Functioning of the European Union
Article 275

The Court of Justice of the European Union shall not have jurisdiction with respect to the provisions relating to the common foreign and security policy nor with respect to acts adopted on the basis of those provisions.

However, the Court shall have jurisdiction to monitor compliance with Article 40 of the Treaty on European Union and to rule on proceedings, brought in accordance with the conditions laid down in the fourth paragraph of Article 263 of this Treaty, reviewing the legality of decisions providing for restrictive measures against natural or legal persons adopted by the Council on the basis of Chapter 2 of Title V of the Treaty on European Union.

Treaty on European Union
Article 40
(ex Article 47 TEU)

The implementation of the common foreign and security policy shall not affect the application of the procedures and the extent of the powers of the institutions laid down by the Treaties for the exercise of the Union competences referred to in Articles 3 to 6 of the Treaty on the Functioning of the European Union.

Similarly, the implementation of the policies listed in those articles shall not affect the application of the procedures and the extent of the powers of the institutions laid down by the Treaties for the exercise of the Union competences under this Chapter.

Judgment of the Court of 19 July 2012, European Parliament v. Council of the European Union, Case C-130/10, not yet reported, paras. 42–82.

Following the coming into force of the Lisbon Treaty, the European Parliament sought with this action for annulment to secure a more prominent role in the adoption of restrictive measures against certain persons and entities associated with the al-Qaeda network and the Taliban. The Parliament argued in its first plea, which is of interest here, that according to both the aim and content of the contested regulation, and to the general scheme of the Treaties, the appropriate legal basis for the regulation is Article 75 TFEU and not Article 215 TFEU, which the Council had opted for. The Court disagreed, upholding the regulation and finding that a dual legal basis of these two articles is not possible since they are incompatible.

42. According to settled case-law, the choice of the legal basis for a Community measure must rest on objective factors amenable to judicial review, which include the aim and content of that measure (see, in particular, *Parliament* v *Council*, paragraph 34 and case-law cited).

43. If examination of a measure reveals that it pursues two aims or that it has two components and if one of those aims or components is identifiable as the main one, whereas the other is merely incidental, the measure must be founded on a single legal basis, namely, that required by the main or predominant aim or component (see, in particular, *Parliament* v *Council*, paragraph 35 and case-law cited).

44. With regard to a measure that simultaneously pursues a number of objectives, or that has several components, which are inseparably linked without one's being incidental to the other, the Court has held that, where various provisions of the Treaty are therefore applicable, such a measure will have to be founded, exceptionally, on the various corresponding legal bases (see, in particular, *Parliament* v *Council*, paragraph 36 and case-law cited).

45. None the less, the Court has held also, in particular in paragraphs 17 to 21 of Case C-300/89 *Commission* v *Council* [1991] ECR I-2867 ('*Titanium dioxide*'), that recourse to a dual legal basis is not possible where the procedures laid down for each legal basis are incompatible with each other (see, in particular, *Parliament* v *Council*, paragraph 37 and case-law cited).

46. If it was in the context of the cooperation procedure that the Court found, in *Titanium dioxide*, an incompatibility between that procedure, provided for by one of the two legal bases concerned in that judgment, and the Council's acting unanimously after merely consulting the European Parliament, provided for by the

other, the Court has, nevertheless, in its subsequent decisions adopted a similar approach in connection with the procedure under Article 251 EC, known as 'the co-decision procedure' (see, to this effect, Case C-178/03 *Commission v Parliament and Council* [2006] ECR I-107, paragraphs 58 and 59, and *Parliament v Council*, paragraphs 76 to 79). Such an approach is still valid, after the entry into force of the Treaty of Lisbon, in the context of the ordinary legislative procedure.

47. In this instance, while Article 75 TFEU provides for application of the ordinary legislative procedure, which entails qualified majority voting in the Council and the Parliament's full participation in the procedure, Article 215(2) TFEU, for its part, entails merely informing the Parliament. In addition, recourse to Article 215(2) TFEU, unlike recourse to Article 75 TFEU, requires a previous decision in the sphere of the CFSP, namely, a decision adopted in accordance with Chapter 2 of Title V of the EU Treaty, providing for the adoption of restrictive measures such as those referred to in that provision. As a general rule, adoption of such a decision calls for unanimous voting in the Council acting alone.

48. Differences of that kind are such as to render those procedures incompatible.

49. It follows from the foregoing that, even if the contested regulation does pursue several objectives at the same time or have several components indissociably linked, without one's being secondary to the other, the differences in the procedures applicable under Articles 75 TFEU and 215(2) TFEU mean that it is not possible for the two provisions to be cumulated, one with the other, in order to serve as a twofold legal basis for a measure such as the contested regulation.

– The relationship between Articles 60 EC, 301 EC and 308 EC and Articles 75 TFEU and 215 TFEU

50. The parties are at one in considering that the legal basis of the contested regulation must, theoretically, correspond to that of Regulation No 881/2002, adopted on the basis of Articles 60 EC, 301 EC and 308 EC.

51. In this regard, it must be held that, as a result of the amendments made to primary law after the Treaty of Lisbon entered into force, the content of Articles 60 EC, relating to restrictive measures with regard to capital movements and payments, and 301 EC on the interruption or reduction, in part or completely, of economic relations with one or more third countries, is mirrored in Article 215 TFEU.

52. Indeed, that last article, included in the part of the FEU Treaty on external action by the Union, provides, like Article 301 EC, for the interruption or reduction, in part or completely, of economic relations with one or more third countries. It may be noted here that Articles 301 EC and 215(1) TFEU are worded in the same way. As regards Article 60 EC, which was applicable in those cases mentioned in Article 301 EC and which provided for the application of the procedure under that same article, Article 215(1) TFEU contains a reference to financial relations to cover the areas previously within the ambit of Article 60.

53. Furthermore, Article 215(2) TFEU allows the Council to adopt restrictive measures against natural or legal persons and groups or non-State entities, namely, measures that, before the Treaty of Lisbon entered into force, required Article 308 EC too to be included in their legal basis if their addressees were not linked to

the governing regime of a third country (see, to that effect, *Kadi and Al Barakaat International Foundation* v *Council and Commission*, paragraph 216).

54. As regards Article 75 TFEU, its context and tenor differ from those of Articles 60 EC and 301 EC. Article 75 TFEU does not, in fact, refer to the interruption or reduction, in part or completely, of economic relations with one or more third countries. Incorporated in Part Three of the FEU Treaty on Union policies and internal actions, and more specifically in Title V thereof, entitled 'Area of freedom, security and justice', that article simply refers to the definition, for the purpose of preventing terrorism and related activities and combating the same, of a framework for administrative measures with regard to capital movements and payments, when this is necessary to achieve the objectives set out in Article 67 TFEU.

– The ambit of Article 215 TFEU

55. It is necessary to examine the wording of Article 215 TFEU, the context of which that provision forms part and the objectives it pursues, in relation to those pursued by Article 75 TFEU, before determining, in the light of the purpose and content of the contested regulation, whether Article 215(2) TFEU constitutes the correct legal basis for the regulation.

56. Article 215 TFEU appears in Title IV, entitled 'Restrictive measures', of Part Five of the FEU Treaty on external action by the Union.

57. Article 215(1) concerns the adoption of measures necessary for the interruption or reduction, in part or completely, of economic and financial relations with one or more third countries. In this context, Article 215(2) concerns the adoption by the Council of 'restrictive measures [...] against natural or legal persons and groups or non-State entities', without specifically referring to the combating of terrorism and without limiting those measures to those measures alone that concern capital movements and payments.

58. Moreover, Article 215(2) TFEU, unlike Article 75 TFEU, provides, as mentioned at paragraph 47 above, that it may not be used until a decision under the CFSP has provided for the adoption of restrictive measures against natural or legal persons, groups or non-State entities. For its part, Article 75 TFEU states that it may be used where necessary to achieve the objectives set out in Article 67 TFEU, that is to say, in connection with creating an area of freedom, security and justice.

59. In this regard, it is to be borne in mind that, at paragraph 197 of *Kadi and Al Barakaat International Foundation* v *Council and Commission*, the Court considered that a bridge had been constructed between the actions of the Community involving economic measures under Articles 60 EC and 301 EC and the objectives of the EU Treaty, as it stood before the Treaty of Lisbon entered into force, in the sphere of external relations, including the CFSP. Article 215 TFEU expressly provides such a bridge, but this is not the case with Article 75 TFEU, which creates no link with decisions taken under the CFSP.

60. As regards combating terrorism and its funding, it is to be noted that there is nothing in Article 215 TFEU to indicate that measures designed to combat them, taken against natural or legal persons, groups or non-State entities, could not constitute restrictive measures provided for in subparagraph 2 of that article. It is to

be observed here that, although neither Article 60 EC nor Article 301 EC referred expressly to combating terrorism, those two provisions did, none the less, constitute the legal basis for the adoption, before the Treaty of Lisbon entered into force, of restrictive measures designed to combat that phenomenon (see, inter alia, in this respect, the measures at issue in *Kadi and Al Barakaat International Foundation* v *Council and Commission*).

61. While admittedly the combating of terrorism and its financing may well be among the objectives of the area of freedom, security and justice, as they appear in Article 3(2) TEU, the objective of combating international terrorism and its financing in order to preserve international peace and security corresponds, nevertheless, to the objectives of the Treaty provisions on external action by the Union.

62. Article 21(2)(c) TEU, which forms part of Chapter 1 laying down general provisions on the Union's external action in Title V of the EU Treaty, provides: 'The Union shall define and pursue common policies and actions, and shall work for a high degree of cooperation in all fields of international relations, in order to ... preserve peace, prevent conflicts and strengthen international security, in accordance with the purposes and principles of the United Nations Charter'. With more specific regard to the CFSP, it is to be noted that, according to the first subparagraph of Article 24(1) TEU, '[t]he Union's competence in matters of [the CFSP] shall cover all areas of foreign policy and all questions relating to the Union's security, including the progressive framing of a common defence policy that might lead to a common defence'.

63. Given that terrorism constitutes a threat to peace and international security, the object of actions undertaken by the Union in the sphere of the CFSP, and the measures taken in order to give effect to that policy in the Union's external actions, in particular, restrictive measures for the purpose of Article 215(2) TFEU, can be to combat terrorism.

64. That assertion is borne out by, in particular, the tenor of Article 43(1) TEU, which makes it clear that all the tasks covered by the common security and defence policy 'may contribute to the fight against terrorism, including by supporting third countries in combating terrorism in their territories'.

65. It follows from the foregoing that Article 215(2) TFEU may constitute the legal basis of restrictive measures, including those designed to combat terrorism, taken against natural or legal persons, groups or non-State entities by the Union when the decision to adopt those measures is part of the Union's action in the sphere of the CFSP.

66. As the Advocate General observed in point 69 of his Opinion, in so far as Articles 75 TFEU and 215 TFEU relate to different European Union policies that pursue objectives which, although complementary, do not have the same scope, it would not seem possible to regard Article 75 TFEU as a more specific legal basis than Article 215(2) TFEU.

– The purpose and tenor of the contested regulation

67. As is made clear in paragraphs 3 to 5 above, Regulation No 881/2002, amended by the contested regulation, constitutes one of the instruments by which the European

Union put into effect an action decided upon within the Security Council and intended to preserve international peace and security (see, to this effect, the penultimate sentence in the preamble to Resolution 1390 (2002)), namely: the adoption of measures freezing the funds and economic resources of persons designated by the Sanctions Committee, with regard to whom the Union simply reproduces the list. It is common ground that terrorism involving persons and entities associated with Usama ben Laden, the Al-Qaeda network and the Taliban is a phenomenon of international proportions.

68. As the Court stated at paragraphs 169 and 184 of *Kadi and Al Barakaat International Foundation* v *Council and Commission*, the essential purpose and object of the contested regulation is to combat international terrorism. This objective of Regulation No 881/2002 is recalled in recital 11 in the preamble to the contested regulation, which states that '[t]he purpose of Regulation … No 881/2002 is to prevent terrorist crimes, including terrorist financing, in order to maintain international peace and security'.

69. As the Parliament has itself stressed, the contested regulation for the most part merely reformulates or clarifies provisions of Regulation No 881/2002 or makes them easier to apply, but does not in any way change the nature of the latter regulation's content.

70. It is clear from recitals 4 to 9 in the preamble to the contested regulation that the latter falls within the same line of action as Regulation No 881/2002, supplementing that measure by having the more specific purpose of reconciling the fight against international terrorism with respect for fundamental rights, in accordance with *Kadi and Al Barakaat International Foundation* v *Council and Commission*.

71. To that end, the contested regulation introduces a listing procedure ensuring that the fundamental rights of the defence, in particular the right to be heard, are respected. Together with Common Position 2002/402, Regulation No 881/2002 and the contested regulation thus establish a system of interaction between the Security Council and the Union.

72. It follows from the foregoing that, in the light of its objectives and of its content, the contested regulation relates to a decision taken by the Union under the CFSP.

73. Contrary to what is maintained by the Parliament, the inclusion of Article 308 EC in the legal basis of Regulation No 881/2002 does not shake that conclusion. While it is true that a measure under the CFSP could not have had Article 308 EC for its sole basis, the fact remains that that article could, as held at paragraph 53 above, supplement the legal basis of a measure adopted in reliance on Articles 60 EC and 301 EC in order to cover the adoption of restrictive measures whose addressees were natural or legal persons, groups or non-State entities not linked to the governing regime of a third country. A supplementary legal foundation of such a kind is, however, no longer necessary since Article 215(2) TFEU has expressly made it possible to adopt measures directed to such addressees on the basis of that provision.

74. Moreover, the Parliament's argument that it is impossible to distinguish the combating of 'internal' terrorism, on the one hand, from the combating of 'external'

terrorism, on the other, does not appear capable of calling in question the choice of Article 215(2) TFEU as a legal basis of the contested regulation.

75. As is made clear at paragraph 65 above, Article 215(2) TFEU provides a sufficient legal basis for adopting, in response to a decision taken under the CFSP, restrictive measures taken in order to apply that policy to natural or legal persons, groups or non-State entities involved in acts of terrorism.

76. In the present case, it is to be emphasised that the contested regulation amends Regulation No 881/2002 which, as found at paragraph 67 above, constitutes one of the instruments by which the European Union put into effect an action decided upon within the Security Council and intended to preserve international peace and security. In addition, as observed at paragraph 72 above, in the light of both its objectives and its content, the contested regulation relates to a decision taken by the Union under the CFSP.

77. What is more, although, in connection with the second plea in law, the Parliament denies that Common Position 2002/402 can possibly amount to a decision under the CFSP for the purpose of Article 215(2) TFEU, it has not, however, called in question whether it was possible for that Common Position, having enabled adoption of Regulation No 881/2002 in accordance with Articles 60 EC and 301 EC, to be validly based on Title V of the EU Treaty, as it stood before the Treaty of Lisbon, that is to say, the title of that treaty concerning the CFSP.

78. Having regard to those factors, it suffices to find that Article 215(2) TFEU constitutes the appropriate legal basis for measures, such as those at issue in the present case, directed to addressees implicated in acts of terrorism who, having regard to their activities globally and to the international dimension of the threat they pose, affect fundamentally the Union's external activity.

– The consequences for the Parliament's prerogatives of the choice between Articles 75 TFEU and 215 TFEU

79. While it is true that choosing between Articles 75 TFEU and 215 TFEU as the legal basis for the contested regulation has consequences for the Parliament's prerogatives, inasmuch as the former provides for recourse to the ordinary legislative procedure whereas, under the latter, the Parliament is merely informed, that fact cannot, however, determine the choice of legal basis.

80. As the Council argues, it is not procedures that define the legal basis of a measure but the legal basis of a measure that determines the procedures to be followed in adopting that measure.

81. Admittedly, participation by the Parliament in the legislative process is the reflection, at Union level, of the fundamental democratic principle that the people should participate in the exercise of power through the intermediary of a representative assembly (see, to that effect, Case 138/79 *Roquette Frères* v *Council* [1980] ECR 3333, paragraph 33, and *Titanium dioxide*, paragraph 20).

82. Nevertheless, the difference between Article 75 TFEU and Article 215 TFEU, so far as the Parliament's involvement is concerned, is the result of the choice made by the framers of the Treaty of Lisbon conferring a more limited role on the Parliament with regard to the Union's action under the CFSP.

Judgment of the General Court of 25 April 2012, Manufacturing Support & Procurement Kala Naft Co., Tehran v. Council of the European Union, Case T-509/10, not yet reported, paras. 28–39.

The applicant asked the Court to annul a decision and an implementing regulation inasmuch as they concerned him. Of interest here are the Court's findings when discussing the second part of the first plea with regard to the scope of the second paragraph of Article 275 TFEU.

28. The applicant puts forward nine pleas in law. The first plea alleges illegality in connection with the entry into force of Decision 2010/413. This plea consists in essence of two parts. The first part alleges that the decision entered into force retroactively. The second part alleges that Article 4 of the decision is illegal when read in conjunction with Article 28. [...]
29. The Council and the Commission consider that the applicant's pleas are unfounded.
30. In addition, the Council and the Commission submit that the Court has no jurisdiction to give a ruling on the second part of the first plea. Furthermore, at the hearing, they contended that the action was inadmissible in so far as it was based on alleged violation of the applicant's fundamental rights.
31. First of all, it is necessary to examine the submissions of the Council and the Commission concerning the Court's jurisdiction, then their submissions concerning the admissibility of certain pleas and, finally, the admissibility of the application for the annulment of Decision 2010/644 and Regulation No 961/2010, this application having been made in the applicant's observations of 6 December 2011.

The Court's jurisdiction to rule on the second part of the first plea

32. In the second part of the first plea, the applicant submits, in essence, that Article 4 of Decision 2010/413 is illegal in that it provides for prohibition measures the scope of which is not specified with sufficient precision.
33. In order to reach a decision on that plea, it is necessary to give a ruling on the Court's jurisdiction.
34. Under Article 275 TFEU:
'The Court of Justice of the European Union shall not have jurisdiction with respect to the provisions relating to the common foreign and security policy nor with respect to acts adopted on the basis of those provisions.
However, the Court shall have jurisdiction to monitor compliance with Article 40 of the Treaty on European Union and to rule on proceedings, brought in accordance with the conditions laid down in the fourth paragraph of Article 263 of this Treaty, reviewing the legality of decisions providing for restrictive measures against natural or legal persons adopted by the Council on the basis of Chapter 2 of Title V of the Treaty on European Union.'
35. Article 4 of Decision 2010/413 provides as follows:
'1. The sale, supply or transfer of key equipment and technology for the following key sectors of the oil and natural gas industry in Iran, or to Iranian or Iranian-owned enterprises engaged in those sectors outside Iran, by nationals of

Member States, or from the territories of Member States, or using vessels or air-craft under the jurisdiction of Member States shall be prohibited whether or not originating in their territories:

(a) refining;

(b) liquefied natural gas;

(c) exploration;

(d) production.

The Union shall take the necessary measures in order to determine the relevant items to be covered by this provision.

2. It shall be prohibited to provide the following to enterprises in Iran that are engaged in the key sectors of the Iranian oil and gas industry referred to in paragraph 1 or to Iranian, or Iranian-owned enterprises engaged in those sectors outside Iran:

(a) technical assistance or training and other services related to key equipment and technology as determined according to paragraph 1;

(b) financing or financial assistance for any sale, supply, transfer or export of key equipment and technology as determined according to paragraph 1 or for the pro-vision of related technical assistance or training.

3. It shall be prohibited to participate, knowingly or intentionally, in activities the object or effect of which is to circumvent the prohibitions referred to in para-graphs 1 and 2.'

36. Decision 2010/413 was adopted on the basis of Article 29 EU, which is a provision concerning the common foreign and security policy within the meaning of Article 275 TFEU. It is therefore necessary to ascertain whether Article 4 of the decision fulfils the conditions set out in the second paragraph of Article 275 TFEU.

37. First, the prohibition measures laid down by Article 4 of Decision 2010/413 are of a general nature, their scope being determined by reference to objective criteria and not by reference to identified natural or legal persons. Consequently, as the Council and the Commission claim, Article 4 of Decision 2010/413 is not a deci-sion providing for restrictive measures against natural or legal persons within the meaning of the second paragraph of Article 275 TFEU.

38. Secondly, the restrictive measures adopted in relation to the applicant arise from the implementation of Article 20 of Decision 2010/413 and not from Article 4. Therefore the latter cannot, in the present case, be the subject of a plea of illegality under Article 277 TFEU, read in conjunction with Article 263 TFEU.

39. Therefore it must be concluded that, under the first paragraph of Article 275 TFEU, the Court does not have jurisdiction to take cognisance of an action seeking to assess the legality of Article 4 of Decision 2010/413 and, thereby, to give a ruling on the second part of the first plea.

11.3 The Common Security and Defence Policy after Lisbon

The Common Security and Defence Policy (CSDP) is an integral part of CFSP (Article 42(1) TEU). CSDP has reached its present state through a long non-linear process of development, which arguably started in the early 1950s with the abortive European Defence Community. Perhaps the most important events in this process before Lisbon have been the cautious provisions of the Maastricht Treaty on security and defence, the listing of the 'Petersberg tasks' in the Amsterdam Treaty in 1997, the St Malo Joint Declaration issued at a British–French Summit in December 1998,[10] the creation of the Political and Security Committee (PSC), the EU Military Committee (EUMC), and the EU Military Staff (EUMS) within the structures of the Council in 1999, and the 'Berlin Plus' Agreement between the EU and the North Atlantic Treaty Organization (NATO) in December 2002.[11]

Lisbon has introduced a number of innovations to CSDP acknowledging in practice the changing international security and defence needs while taking into account—at least to a certain extent—the growing number of Member States, which poses difficulties to having one concerted, effective, and flexible security and defence policy among all Member States. Thus, Lisbon renamed the previously called European Security and Defence Policy to CSDP, while Article 42(2) first subparagraph TEU suggests that CSDP 'will lead to a common defence'.[12] As a rule, decisions in CSDP continue to be taken unanimously on a proposal from the High Representative (Article 42(4) TEU) with some exceptions described below. Lisbon expressly distinguished between civilian and military means used by the EU in CSDP and broadened the Petersberg tasks to include 'peace-keeping, conflict prevention and strengthening international security in accordance with the principles of the United Nations Charter' (Article 42(1) TEU), as well as 'joint disarmament operations, humanitarian and rescue tasks, military advice and assistance tasks, conflict prevention and peace-keeping tasks, tasks of combat forces in crisis management, including peace-making and post-conflict stabilisation' (Article 43(1) TEU).

Two Council instruments launching military operations and one establishing a civilian CSDP mission are included below. The first instrument is the original Council Joint Action that authorized the so-called operation Atalanta against piracy off the coast of Somalia. This instrument can further be compared to the Council Decision adopted after Lisbon on the launch of an EU military mission to contribute to the training of Somali security forces (EUTM Somalia). Finally, the Decision on the EU CSDP mission in Niger (EUCAP Sahel Niger) is also reproduced here.

---

[10] Article 1 of the Declaration reads: 'The European Union needs to be in a position to play its full role on the international stage. [...] This includes the responsibility of the European Council to decide on the progressive framing of a common defence policy in the framework of CFSP. [...]' In addition, according to Article 2 '[t]o this end, the Union must have the capacity for autonomous action, backed up by credible military forces, the means to decide to use them, and a readiness to do so, in order to respond to international crises. [...] Europeans will operate within the institutional framework of the European Union (European Council, General Affairs Council, and meetings of Defence Ministers). [...]'

[11] This agreement gave the Union access to NATO's assets and capabilities for EU-led operations.

[12] Emphasis added. This formulation is different to the one former Art. 17(1) first subpara. TEU had as well as to that of Art. 24(1) first subpara. TEU, which reads that CSDP 'might lead to a common defence' (emphasis added).

Treaty on European Union
Article 42
(ex Article 17 TEU)

1. The common security and defence policy shall be an integral part of the common foreign and security policy. It shall provide the Union with an operational capacity drawing on civilian and military assets. The Union may use them on missions outside the Union for peace-keeping, conflict prevention and strengthening international security in accordance with the principles of the United Nations Charter. The performance of these tasks shall be undertaken using capabilities provided by the Member States.

2. The common security and defence policy shall include the progressive framing of a common Union defence policy. This will lead to a common defence, when the European Council, acting unanimously, so decides. It shall in that case recommend to the Member States the adoption of such a decision in accordance with their respective constitutional requirements.

The policy of the Union in accordance with this Section shall not prejudice the specific character of the security and defence policy of certain Member States and shall respect the obligations of certain Member States, which see their common defence realised in the North Atlantic Treaty Organisation (NATO), under the North Atlantic Treaty and be compatible with the common security and defence policy established within that framework.

[...]

4. Decisions relating to the common security and defence policy, including those initiating a mission as referred to in this Article, shall be adopted by the Council acting unanimously on a proposal from the High Representative of the Union for Foreign Affairs and Security Policy or an initiative from a Member State. The High Representative may propose the use of both national resources and Union instruments, together with the Commission where appropriate.

[...]

Article 43

1. The tasks referred to in Article 42(1), in the course of which the Union may use civilian and military means, shall include joint disarmament operations, humanitarian and rescue tasks, military advice and assistance tasks, conflict prevention and peace-keeping tasks, tasks of combat forces in crisis management, including peace-making and post-conflict stabilisation. All these tasks may contribute to the fight against terrorism, including by supporting third countries in combating terrorism in their territories.

2. The Council shall adopt decisions relating to the tasks referred to in paragraph 1, defining their objectives and scope and the general conditions for their implementation. The High Representative of the Union for Foreign Affairs and Security Policy, acting under the authority of the Council and in close and constant contact with the Political and Security Committee, shall ensure coordination of the civilian and military aspects of such tasks.

Council Joint Action 2008/851/CFSP of 10 November 2008 on a European Union military operation to contribute to the deterrence, prevention and repression of acts of piracy and armed robbery off the Somali coast, Official Journal L 301, 12.11.2008, pp. 33–7.

> This detailed instrument that dates back to the period before the Lisbon Treaty is still in force in its amended version. It is of particular interest as it authorized the launching of a UN Security Council-mandated operation, which is complex and entails high operational risks. The chain of command of the operation is of particular interest. Thus, the PSC is vested with the political control and strategic direction of the EU military operation. It is also authorized to take the relevant decisions in accordance with Article 25 TEU (now Article 38 TEU). However, the Council maintains the authority to alter the objectives of the operation or terminate it. The PSC, which will receive reports from the EUMC, will report regularly to the Council. The EUMC monitors the proper execution of the operation under the responsibility of the EU Operation Commander, who reports back to the EUMC.

THE COUNCIL OF THE EUROPEAN UNION,

Having regard to the Treaty on European Union, and in particular Article 14, the third subparagraph of Article 25 and Article 28(3) thereof,

Whereas:

(1) In its Resolution 1814 (2008) on the situation in Somalia, adopted on 15 May 2008, the United Nations Security Council (UNSC) has called on States and regional organisations, in close coordination with one another, to take action to protect shipping involved in the transport and delivery of humanitarian aid to Somalia and in activities authorised by the United Nations.

(2) In its Resolution 1816 (2008) on the situation in Somalia, adopted on 2 June 2008, the UNSC expressed its concern at the threat that acts of piracy and armed robbery against vessels pose to the delivery of humanitarian aid to Somalia, the safety of commercial maritime routes and international navigation. The UNSC encouraged, in particular, States interested in the use of commercial maritime routes off the coast of Somalia to increase and coordinate their efforts, in cooperation with the Transitional Federal Government of Somalia (TFG), to deter acts of piracy and armed robbery at sea. It authorised, for a period of six months from the date of the resolution, States cooperating with the TFG, of which advance notification had been given by the TFG to the UN Secretary-General, to enter the territorial waters of Somalia and to use, in a manner consistent with relevant international law, all necessary means to repress acts of piracy and armed robbery at sea.

(3) In its Resolution 1838 (2008) on the situation in Somalia, adopted on 7 October 2008, the UNSC commended the ongoing planning process towards a possible European Union (EU) naval operation, as well as other international or national initiatives taken with a view to implementing Resolutions 1814 (2008) and 1816 (2008), and urged States that have the capacity to do so, to cooperate with the TFG in the

fight against piracy and armed robbery at sea in conformity with the provisions of Resolution 1816 (2008). The UNSC also urged States and regional organisations, in conformity with the provisions of Resolution 1814 (2008), to continue to take action to protect the World Food Programme (WFP) maritime convoys, which is vital to bring humanitarian assistance to the affected populations in Somalia.

(4) In its conclusions of 26 May 2008, the Council expressed its concern at the upsurge of piracy attacks off the Somali coast, which affect humanitarian efforts and international maritime traffic in the region and contribute to continued violations of the UN arms embargo. The Council also commended the sequenced initiatives of some Member States to provide protection to WFP vessels. It stressed the need for wider participation by the international community in these escorts in order to secure the delivery of humanitarian aid to the Somali population.

(5) On 5 August 2008, the Council approved a crisis management concept for action by the EU to help implement UNSC Resolution 1816 (2008) and for peace and international security in the region.

(6) On 15 September 2008, the Council reaffirmed its serious concern at the acts of piracy and armed robbery off the Somali coast, deploring, in particular, their recent resurgence. As regards the EU's contribution to the implementation of UNSC Resolution 1816 (2008) on combating piracy off the Somali coast and to the protection, under Resolutions 1814 (2008) and 1816 (2008), of vessels chartered by the WFP and bound for Somalia, the Council decided to establish a coordination cell in Brussels with the task of supporting the surveillance and protection activities carried out by some Member States off the Somali coast. On the same day, it approved, on the one hand, a plan for the implementation of this military coordination action (EU NAVCO) and, on the other, a strategic military option for a possible EU naval operation for which those Member States wishing to cooperate with the TFG under Resolution 1816 (2008) would make available military resources for the deterrence and repression of acts of piracy and armed robbery off the Somali coast.

(7) On 19 September 2008, the Council adopted Joint Action 2008/749/CFSP on the European Union military coordination action in support of UN Security Council Resolution 1816 (2008) (EU NAVCO).

(8) On the launch of the Atalanta military operation, the tasks of the military coordination cell will be exercised under this Joint Action. The coordination cell should then be closed.

(9) The Political and Security Committee (PSC) should exercise political control over the EU military operation in order to help deter acts of piracy off the Somali coast, provide it with strategic direction and take the relevant decisions in accordance with third subparagraph of Article 25 of the Treaty.

(10) Under Article 28(3) of the Treaty, the operational expenditure, arising from this Joint Action, which has military or defence implications, should be borne by the Member States in accordance with Council Decision 2007/384/CFSP of 14 May 2007 establishing a mechanism to administer the financing of the common costs of European Union operations having military or defence implications (Athena) (hereinafter referred to as 'Athena').

(11) Article 14(1) of the Treaty calls for Joint Actions to lay down the means to be made available to the European Union. The financial reference amount, for a twelve-month period, for the common costs of the EU military operation constitutes the best current estimate and is without prejudice to the final figures to be included in a budget to be approved in accordance with the rules laid down in the decision regarding Athena.

(12) By letter dated 30 October 2008, the EU made an offer to the TFG, pursuant to point 7 of Resolution 1816 (2008), which contains proposals for States other than Somalia to exercise jurisdiction over persons captured in Somali territorial waters who have committed, or are suspected of having committed, acts of piracy or armed robbery.

(13) In accordance with Article 6 of the Protocol on the position of Denmark annexed to the Treaty on European Union and to the Treaty establishing the European Community, Denmark does not participate in the elaboration and implementation of decisions and actions of the European Union which have defence implications. Denmark does not participate in the implementation of this Joint Action and therefore does not participate in the financing of the operation,

HAS ADOPTED THIS JOINT ACTION:

Article 1

Mission

1. The European Union (EU) shall conduct a military operation in support of Resolutions 1814 (2008), 1816 (2008) and 1838 (2008) of the United Nations Security Council (UNSC), in a manner consistent with action permitted with respect to piracy under Article 100 et seq. of the United Nations Convention on the Law of the Sea signed in Montego Bay on 10 December 1982 (hereinafter referred to as 'the United Nations Convention on the Law of the Sea') and by means, in particular, of commitments made with third States, hereinafter called 'Atalanta' in order to contribute to:

— the protection of vessels of the WFP delivering food aid to displaced persons in Somalia, in accordance with the mandate laid down in UNSC Resolution 1814 (2008),

— the protection of vulnerable vessels cruising off the Somali coast, and the deterrence, prevention and repression of acts of piracy and armed robbery off the Somali coast, in accordance with the mandate laid down in UNSC Resolution 1816 (2008),

2. The forces deployed to that end shall operate, up to 500 nautical miles off the Somali coast and neighbouring countries, in accordance with the political objective of an EU maritime operation, as defined in the crisis management concept approved by the Council on 5 August 2008.

Article 2

Mandate

Under the conditions set by the relevant international law and by UNSC Resolutions 1814 (2008), 1816 (2008) and 1838 (2008), Atalanta shall, as far as available capabilities allow:

(a) provide protection to vessels chartered by the WFP, including by means of the presence on board those vessels of armed units of Atalanta, in particular when cruising in Somali territorial waters;

(b) provide protection, based on a case-by-case evaluation of needs, to merchant vessels cruising in the areas where it is deployed;

(c) keep watch over areas off the Somali coast, including Somalia's territorial waters, in which there are dangers to maritime activities, in particular to maritime traffic;

(d) take the necessary measures, including the use of force, to deter, prevent and intervene in order to bring to an end acts of piracy and armed robbery which may be committed in the areas where it is present;

(e) in view of prosecutions potentially being brought by the relevant States under the conditions in Article 12, arrest, detain and transfer persons who have committed, or are suspected of having committed, acts of piracy or armed robbery in the areas where it is present and seize the vessels of the pirates or armed robbers or the vessels caught following an act of piracy or an armed robbery and which are in the hands of the pirates, as well as the goods on board;

(f) liaise with organisations and entities, as well as States, working in the region to combat acts of piracy and armed robbery off the Somali coast, in particular the 'Combined Task Force 150' maritime force which operates within the framework of 'Operation Enduring Freedom'.

Article 3
Appointment of the EU Operation Commander
Rear Admiral Phillip Jones is hereby appointed EU Operation Commander.

Article 4
Designation of the EU Operational Headquarters
The EU Operational Headquarters shall be located at Northwood, United Kingdom.

Article 5
Planning and launch of the operation
The Decision to launch the EU military operation shall be adopted by the Council following approval of the Operation Plan and the Rules of Engagement and in the light of the notification by the TFG to the Secretary-General of the United Nations of the offer of cooperation made by the EU pursuant to point 7 of UNSC Resolution 1816 (2008).

Article 6
Political control and strategic direction
1. Under the responsibility of the Council, the Political and Security Committee (hereinafter referred to as the 'PSC') shall exercise the political control and strategic direction of the EU military operation. The Council hereby authorises the PSC to take the relevant decisions in accordance with Article 25 of the EU Treaty. This authorisation shall include the powers to amend the planning documents, including the Operation Plan, the Chain of Command and the Rules of Engagement. It shall also include the powers to take decisions on the appointment of the EU Operation Commander and/or EU Force Commander. The powers of decision with respect

to the objectives and termination of the EU military operation shall remain vested in the Council, assisted by the Secretary-General/High Representative (hereinafter referred to as the 'SG/HR').

2. The PSC shall report to the Council at regular intervals.

3. The PSC shall receive reports from the chairman of the EU Military Committee (EUMC) regarding the conduct of the EU military operation, at regular intervals. The PSC may invite the EU Operation Commander and/or EU Force Commander to its meetings, as appropriate.

Article 7

Military direction

1. The EUMC shall monitor the proper execution of the EU military operation conducted under the responsibility of the EU Operation Commander.

2. The EUMC shall receive reports from the EU Operation Commander at regular intervals. It may invite the EU Operation Commander and/or EU Force Commander to its meetings as appropriate.

3. The chairman of the EUMC shall act as the primary point of contact with the EU Operation Commander.

Article 8

Coherence of EU response

The Presidency, the SG/HR, the EU Operation Commander and the EU Force Commander shall closely coordinate their respective activities regarding the implementation of this Joint Action.

Article 9

Relations with the United Nations, neighbouring countries and other actors

1. The SG/HR, in close coordination with the Presidency, shall act as the primary point of contact with the United Nations, the Somali authorities, the authorities of neighbouring countries, and other relevant actors. Within the context of his contact with the African Union, the SG/HR shall be assisted by the EU Special Representative (EUSR) to the African Union, in close coordination with the presidency.

2. At operational level, the EU Operation Commander shall act as the contact point with, in particular, ship-owners' organisations, as well as with the relevant departments of the UN General Secretariat and the WFP.

Article 10

Participation by third States

1. Without prejudice to the decision-making autonomy of the EU or to the single institutional framework, and in accordance with the relevant guidelines of the European Council, third States may be invited to participate in the operation.

2. The Council hereby authorises the PSC to invite third States to offer contributions and to take the relevant decisions on acceptance of the proposed contributions, upon the recommendation of the EU Operation Commander and the EUMC.

3. Detailed modalities for the participation by third States shall be the subject of agreements concluded in accordance with the procedure laid down in Article 24 of

the Treaty. The SG/HR, who shall assist the Presidency, may negotiate such agreements on behalf of the Presidency. Where the EU and a third State have concluded an agreement establishing a framework for the latter's participation in EU crisis management operations, the provisions of such an agreement shall apply in the context of this operation.

4. Third States making significant military contributions to the EU military operation shall have the same rights and obligations in terms of day-to-day management of the operation as Member States taking part in the operation.

5. The Council hereby authorises the PSC to take relevant decisions on the setting-up of a Committee of Contributors, should third States provide significant military contributions.

6. The conditions for the transfer to a State participating in the operation of persons arrested and detained, with a view to the exercise of jurisdiction of that State, shall be established when the participation agreements referred to in paragraph 3 are concluded or implemented.

Article 11

Status of EU-led forces
The status of the EU-led forces and their personnel, including the privileges, immunities and further guarantees necessary for the fulfilment and smooth functioning of their mission, who:

— are stationed on the land territory of third States,

— operate in the territorial or internal waters of third States, shall be agreed in accordance with the procedure laid down in Article 24 of the Treaty. The SG/HR, who shall assist the Presidency, may negotiate such arrangements on behalf of the Presidency.

Article 12

Transfer of persons arrested and detained with a view to their prosecution

1. On the basis of Somalia's acceptance of the exercise of jurisdiction by Member States or by third States, on the one hand, and Article 105 of the United Nations Convention on the Law of the Sea, on the other hand, persons having committed, or suspected of having committed, acts of piracy or armed robbery in Somali territorial waters or on the high seas, who are arrested and detained, with a view to their prosecution, and property used to carry out such acts, shall be transferred:

— to the competent authorities of the flag Member State or of the third State participating in the operation, of the vessel which took them captive, or

— if this State cannot, or does not wish to, exercise its jurisdiction, to a Member State or any third State which wishes to exercise its jurisdiction over the aforementioned persons and property.

2. No persons referred to in paragraphs 1 and 2 may be transferred to a third State unless the conditions for the transfer have been agreed with that third State in a manner consistent with relevant international law, notably international law on human rights, in order to guarantee in particular that no one shall be subjected to the death penalty, to torture or to any cruel, inhuman or degrading treatment.

Article 13

Relations with the flag States of protected vessels

The conditions governing the presence on board merchant ships, particularly those chartered by the WFP, of units belonging to Atalanta, including privileges, immunities and other guarantees relating to the proper conduct of the operation, shall be agreed with the flag States of those vessels.

Article 14

Financial arrangements

1. The common costs of the EU military operation shall be administered by Athena.
2. The financial reference amount for the common costs of the EU military operation shall be EUR 8 300 000. The percentage of the reference amount referred to in Article 33(3) of Athena shall be 30%.

Article 15

Release of information to the United Nations and other third parties

1. The SG/HR is hereby authorised to release to the United Nations and to other third parties associated with this Joint Action, classified EU information and documents generated for the purposes of the EU military operation up to the level of classification appropriate for each of them and in accordance with the Council's security regulations.
2. The SG/HR is hereby authorised to release to the United Nations and to other third parties associated with this Joint Action, unclassified EU documents relating to Council deliberations on the operation which are covered by the obligation of professional secrecy pursuant to Article 6(1) of the Council's Rules of Procedure.

Article 16

Entry into force and termination

1. This Joint Action shall enter into force on the date of its adoption.
2. Joint Action 2008/749/CFSP shall be repealed as from the date of closure of the coordination cell put in place by that Joint Action. It shall be closed on the launch date of the operation referred to in Article 6 of this Joint Action.
3. The EU military operation shall terminate 12 months after the initial operating capability is declared, subject to the prolongation of UNSC Resolutions 1814 (2008) and 1816 (2008).
4. This Joint Action shall be repealed following the withdrawal of the EU force, in accordance with the plans approved for the termination of the EU military operation, and without prejudice to the relevant provisions of Athena.

Article 17

Publication

1. This Joint Action shall be published in the Official Journal of the European Union.
2. The PSC's decisions on the appointment of an EU Operation Commander and/or EU Force Commander, as well as the PSC's decisions on the acceptance of contributions from third States and the setting-up of a Committee of Contributors shall likewise be published in the Official Journal of the European Union.

Council Decision 2010/197/CFSP of 31 March 2010 on the launch of a European Union military mission to contribute to the training of Somali security forces (EUTM Somalia), Official Journal L 87, 7.4.2010, p. 33.

The Decision on EUTM Somalia was adopted on a proposal from the High Representative and its task is rather simpler than Operation Atalanta. EUTM Somalia has to participate in the training of Somali security forces taking place in Uganda.

THE COUNCIL OF THE EUROPEAN UNION,

Having regard to the Treaty on European Union, and in particular Articles 28 and 43(2) thereof,

Having regard to Council Decision 2010/96/CFSP of 15 February 2010 on a European Union military mission to contribute to the training of Somali security forces, and in particular Article 4 thereof,

Having regard to the proposal by the High Representative of the Union for Foreign Affairs and Security Policy,

Whereas:

(1) In its Resolution 1872 (2009) on the situation in Somalia, adopted on 26 May 2009, the United Nations Security Council (UNSC) stressed the importance of the re-establishment, training, equipping and retention of Somali security forces, and urged Member States and regional and international organisations to offer technical assistance for the training and equipping of the Somali security forces. In its Resolution 1897 (2009), adopted on 30 November 2009, the UNSC recalled its previous resolutions and reaffirmed its respect for the sovereignty, territorial integrity, political independence and unity of Somalia.

(2) By letter dated 5 January 2010, the Minister of Defence of Uganda welcomed the Union's envisaged mission in support of the Somali security sector and invited the Union to participate in the training of Somali security forces in Uganda for a period of at least one year.

(3) In accordance with Article 5 of the Protocol on the position of Denmark, annexed to the Treaty on European Union and to the Treaty on the Functioning of the European Union, Denmark does not participate in the elaboration and implementation of decisions and actions of the Union which have defence implications. Denmark does not, therefore, participate in the financing of this mission,

HAS ADOPTED THIS DECISION:

Article 1

The Mission Plan for the EU military mission to contribute to the training of Somali security forces, hereinafter referred to as 'EUTM Somalia', is approved.

Article 2

EUTM Somalia shall be launched on 7 April 2010.

Article 3

The EU Mission Commander of EUTM Somalia is hereby authorised with immediate effect to release the activation order (ACTORD) in order to execute the deployment of the forces and start execution of the mission.

Article 4

This Decision shall enter into force on the day of its adoption.

Council Decision 2012/392/CFSP of 16 July 2012 on the European Union CSDP mission in Niger (EUCAP Sahel Niger), Official Journal L 187, 17.7.2012, pp. 48–51.

The Council adopted by unanimity this instrument launching a civilian operation on a proposal by the High Representative. This EU crisis management operation has a supporting role in the reform and capacity-building of the Nigerian security actors to fight terrorism and organized crime, and in the strengthening of the rule of law. As usual, the command and responsibility structures are described in an elaborate manner in the Decision. There is a unified chain of command. The PSC exercises political control and strategic direction, under the responsibility of the Council and of the High Representative, and is authorized to take the relevant decisions in accordance with Article 38 third paragraph TEU. Command and control at the *strategic* level is in the hands of the Civilian Operation Commander, under the political control of the PSC and the overall authority of the High Representative. He can issue instructions at strategic level to the Head of Mission. The latter exercises command and control of the Mission at *theatre* level and is directly responsible to the Civilian Operation Commander. The Civilian Operation Commander reports to the Council through the High Representative. The Head of Mission also exercises disciplinary control over the staff. However, for seconded staff, disciplinary action must be exercised by the national authority or Union institution concerned. Such seconded staff remain 'under the full command of the national authorities of the seconding State in accordance with national rules, or the Union institution concerned or of the European External Action Service (EEAS)'. The state or EU institution having seconded a staff member remains responsible for answering any claims linked to the secondment, from or concerning the staff member, and is responsible for bringing any action against that person.

THE COUNCIL OF THE EUROPEAN UNION,

Having regard to the Treaty on European Union and in particular Article 28, Article 42(4) and Article 43(2) thereof,

Having regard to the proposal from the High Representative of the Union for Foreign Affairs and Security Policy,

Whereas:

(1) On 21 March 2011, the Council welcomed the European Union Strategy for Security and Development in the Sahel, underlining that the Union has a longstanding interest

in reducing insecurity and improving development in the Sahel region. More recently, the intensification of terrorist actions and the consequences of the conflict in Libya have increased the urgency of protecting Union citizens and interests in the region and preventing the extension of those threats to the Union, while helping to reduce regional security threats.

(2) On 23 March 2012, the Council approved the Crisis Management Concept for a possible common security and defence policy (CSDP) civilian mission in the Sahel.

(3) On 1 June 2012, the Prime Minister of Niger addressed to the High Representative of the Union for Foreign Affairs and Security Policy (HR) an invitation letter with regard to the planned CSDP mission, welcoming the Union's CSDP deployment with the aim of reinforcing the capacities of the Nigerien Security Forces, in particular to fight terrorism and organised crime in an effective, coherent and coordinated manner.

(4) The Watch-Keeping Capability should be activated for EUCAP Sahel Niger.

(5) EUCAP Sahel Niger will be conducted in the context of a situation which may deteriorate and could impede the achievement of the objectives of the Union's external action as set out in Article 21 of the Treaty on European Union (TEU),

HAS ADOPTED THIS DECISION:

Article 1

Mission
The Union hereby establishes a European Union CSDP mission in Niger to support the capacity building of the Nigerien security actors to fight terrorism and organised crime (EUCAP Sahel Niger).

Article 2

Objectives
In the context of the implementation of the European Union Strategy for Security and Development in the Sahel, EUCAP Sahel Niger shall aim at enabling the Nigerien authorities to implement the security dimension of their own Strategy for Security and Development, as well as at improving regional coordination in tackling common security challenges. In particular, EUCAP Sahel Niger shall aim at contributing to the development of an integrated, multidisciplinary, coherent, sustainable, and human rights-based approach among the various Nigerien security actors in the fight against terrorism and organised crime.

Article 3

Tasks
1. In order to fulfil the objectives set out in Article 2, EUCAP Sahel Niger shall:
(a) advise and assist in the implementation of the security dimension of the Nigerien Strategy for Security and Development at national level, complementary to other actors,
(b) support the development of comprehensive regional and international coordination in the fight against terrorism and organised crime,
(c) strengthen the rule of law through the development of the criminal investigation capacities, and in this context develop and implement adequate training programmes,

(d) support the development of Nigerien Security Forces' sustainability,

(e) contribute to the identification, planning and implementation of projects in the security field.

2. EUCAP Sahel Niger shall initially focus on the activities mentioned in paragraph 1 which contribute to improving the control of the territory of Niger, including in coordination with the Nigerien Armed Forces.

3. EUCAP Sahel Niger shall not carry out any executive function.

Article 4

Chain of command and structure

1. EUCAP Sahel Niger shall have a unified chain of command as a crisis management operation.

2. EUCAP Sahel Niger shall have its Headquarters in Niamey.

3. EUCAP Sahel Niger shall be structured as follows:

(a) Head of Mission;

(b) Planning and Operations component, including regional liaison officers;

(c) Mission Support component;

(d) Reporting, Security, Analytical and Advisory/Public Information elements;

(e) Brussels Support Element.

4. EUCAP Sahel Niger shall have a Project Cell for identifying and implementing projects. EUCAP Sahel Niger may, as appropriate, coordinate, facilitate and provide advice on projects implemented by Member States and third States under their responsibility, in areas related to EUCAP Sahel Niger and in support of its objectives.

Article 5

Civilian Operation Commander

1. The Civilian Planning and Conduct Capability (CPCC) Director shall be the Civilian Operation Commander for EUCAP Sahel Niger.

2. The Civilian Operation Commander, under the political control and strategic direction of the Political and Security Committee (PSC) and overall authority of the HR, shall exercise command and control of EUCAP Sahel Niger at the strategic level.

3. The Civilian Operation Commander shall ensure, with regard to the conduct of operations, the proper and effective implementation of the Council's decisions as well as the PSC's decisions, including by issuing instructions at the strategic level as required to the Head of Mission and providing him with advice and technical support.

4. The Civilian Operation Commander shall report to the Council through the HR.

5. All seconded staff shall remain under the full command of the national authorities of the seconding State in accordance with national rules, or the Union institution concerned or of the European External Action Service (EEAS). Those authorities shall transfer Operational Control (OPCON) of their personnel, teams and units to the Civilian Operation Commander.

6. The Civilian Operation Commander shall have overall responsibility for ensuring that the Union's duty of care is properly discharged.

7. The Civilian Operation Commander and the Head of Union delegation in Niamey shall consult each other as required.

Article 6

Head of Mission

1. The Head of Mission shall assume responsibility for, and exercise command and control of, EUCAP Sahel Niger at theatre level and shall be directly responsible to the Civilian Operation Commander.

2. The Head of Mission shall exercise command and control over personnel, teams and units from contributing States as assigned by the Civilian Operation Commander together with administrative and logistic responsibility including over assets, resources and information placed at the disposal of EUCAP Sahel Niger.

3. The Head of Mission shall issue instructions to all EUCAP Sahel Niger staff, including the Brussels Support Element and regional liaison officers, for the effective conduct of the EUCAP Sahel Niger in theatre, assuming its coordination and day-to-day management, and following the instructions at the strategic level of the Civilian Operation Commander.

4. The Head of Mission shall be responsible for the implementation of the budget of EUCAP Sahel Niger. For this purpose, the Head of Mission shall sign a contract with the Commission.

5. The Head of Mission shall be responsible for disciplinary control over the staff. For seconded staff, disciplinary action shall be exercised by the national authority in accordance with national rules, by the Union institution concerned or by the EEAS.

6. The Head of Mission shall represent EUCAP Sahel Niger in the operations area and shall ensure appropriate visibility of EUCAP Sahel Niger.

7. The Head of Mission shall coordinate, as appropriate, with other Union actors on the ground. The Head of Mission shall, without prejudice to the chain of command, receive local political guidance from the Head of Union Delegation in Niger.

8. In the context of the Project Cell, the Head of Mission shall be authorised to seek recourse to financial contributions from the Member States or third States to implement projects identified as supplementing in a consistent manner EUCAP Sahel Niger's other actions, if the project is:

(a) provided for in the Budgetary Impact Statement relating to this Decision; or

(b) included in the course of EUCAP Sahel Niger in the Budgetary Impact Statement at the request of the Head of Mission.

In such a case the Head of Mission shall conclude an arrangement with the States concerned, covering in particular the specific procedures for dealing with any complaint from third parties concerning damage caused as a result of acts or omissions by the Head of Mission in the use of the funds provided by the contributing States.

Under no circumstances shall the Union or the HR be held liable by contributing States as a result of acts or omissions by the Head of Mission in the use of funds from those States.

Article 7

Staff

1. EUCAP Sahel Niger shall consist primarily of staff seconded by Member States, Union institutions or the EEAS. Each Member State, Union institution, and the EEAS shall bear the costs related to any of the staff seconded by it, including travel expenses

to and from the place of deployment, salaries, medical coverage and allowances other than applicable daily allowances.

2. The Member State, Union institution, or the EEAS respectively shall be responsible for answering any claims linked to the secondment from or concerning the member of staff seconded, and for bringing any action against that person.

3. International and local staff shall be recruited on a contractual basis by EUCAP Sahel Niger if the functions required cannot be provided by personnel seconded by Member States. Exceptionally, in duly justified cases, where no qualified applicants from Member States are available, nationals from participating third States may be recruited on a contractual basis, as appropriate.

4. The conditions of employment and the rights and obligations of international and local staff shall be laid down in contracts between the Head of Mission and the members of staff.

Article 8
Status of EUCAP Sahel Niger and of its staff

The status of EUCAP Sahel Niger and its staff, including where appropriate the privileges, immunities and further guarantees necessary for the completion and smooth functioning of EUCAP Sahel Niger, shall be the subject of an agreement concluded pursuant to Article 37 TEU and in accordance with the procedure laid down in Article 218 of the Treaty on the Functioning of the European Union.

Article 9
Political control and strategic direction

1. The PSC shall exercise, under the responsibility of the Council and of the HR, political control and strategic direction of EUCAP Sahel Niger. The Council hereby authorises the PSC to take the relevant decisions in accordance with the third paragraph of Article 38 TEU. This authorisation shall include the powers to appoint a Head of Mission, upon a proposal of the HR, and to amend the Concept of Operations Plus (CONOPS Plus) and the Operation Plan (OPLAN). The powers of decision with respect to the objectives and termination of the EUCAP Sahel Niger shall remain vested in the Council.

2. The PSC shall report to the Council at regular intervals.

3. The PSC shall receive, on a regular basis and as required, reports by the Civilian Operation Commander and the Head of Mission on issues within their areas of responsibility.

Article 10
Participation of third States

1. Without prejudice to the decision-making autonomy of the Union and its single institutional framework, third States may be invited to contribute to EUCAP Sahel Niger, provided that they bear the cost of the staff seconded by them, including salaries, all risk insurance cover, daily subsistence allowances and travel expenses to and from Niger, and that they contribute to the running costs of EUCAP Sahel Niger, as appropriate.

2. Third States contributing to EUCAP Sahel Niger shall have the same rights and obligations in terms of the day-to-day management of EUCAP Sahel Niger as Member States.

3. The Council hereby authorises the PSC to take the relevant decisions on acceptance of the proposed contributions and to establish a Committee of Contributors.

4. Detailed arrangements regarding the participation of third States shall be covered by agreements concluded in accordance with Article 37 TEU and additional technical arrangements as necessary. Where the Union and a third State conclude or have concluded an agreement establishing a framework for the participation of that third State in Union crisis-management operations, the provisions of that agreement shall apply in the context of EUCAP Sahel Niger.

Article 11

Security

1. The Civilian Operation Commander shall direct the Head of Mission's planning of security measures and ensure their proper and effective implementation by EUCAP Sahel Niger in accordance with Article 5.

2. The Head of Mission shall be responsible for the security of EUCAP Sahel Niger and for ensuring compliance with minimum security requirements applicable to EUCAP Sahel Niger, in line with the policy of the Union on the security of personnel deployed outside the Union in an operational capacity under Title V TEU, and its supporting instruments.

3. The Head of Mission shall be assisted by a Mission Security Officer (MSO), who shall report to the Head of Mission and also maintain a close functional relationship with the EEAS.

4. The EUCAP Sahel Niger staff shall undergo mandatory security training before taking up their duties, in accordance with the OPLAN. They shall also receive regular in-theatre refresher training organised by the MSO.

5. The Head of Mission shall ensure the protection of EU classified information in accordance with Council Decision 2011/292/EU of 31 March 2011 on the security rules for protecting EU classified information.

Article 12

Watch-Keeping Capability

The Watch-Keeping Capability shall be activated for EUCAP Sahel Niger.

Article 13

Financial arrangements

1. The financial reference amount intended to cover the expenditure related to EUCAP Sahel Niger for the first 12 months shall be EUR 8 700 000. The financial reference amount for the subsequent periods shall be decided by the Council.

2. All expenditure shall be managed in accordance with the rules and procedures applicable to the general budget of the Union.

3. Nationals of participating third States and of host and neighbouring countries shall be allowed to tender for contracts. Subject to the Commission's approval, the Head of Mission may conclude technical arrangements with Member States, participating third States, and other international actors regarding the provision of equipment, services and premises to EUCAP Sahel Niger.

4. The financial arrangements shall respect the operational requirements of EUCAP Sahel Niger including compatibility of equipment and interoperability of its teams.

5. The Head of Mission shall report fully to, and be supervised by, the Commission on the activities undertaken in the framework of his/her contract.

6. The expenditure related to EUCAP Sahel Niger shall be eligible as of the date of adoption of this Decision.

Article 14

Consistency of the Union's response and coordination

1. The HR shall ensure the consistency of the implementation of this Decision with the Union's external action as a whole, including the Union's development programmes.

2. Without prejudice to the chain of command, the Head of Mission shall act in close coordination with the Union's delegation in Niamey to ensure the consistency of Union action in Niger.

3. The Head of Mission shall coordinate closely with Member States' Heads of Missions present in Niger.

Article 15

Release of information

1. The HR shall be authorised to release to the third States associated with this Decision, as appropriate and in accordance with the needs of EUCAP Sahel Niger, EU classified information up to 'CONFIDENTIEL UE/EU CONFIDENTIAL' level generated for the purposes of EUCAP Sahel Niger, in accordance with Decision 2011/292/EU.

2. In the event of a specific and immediate operational need, the HR shall also be authorised to release to the host State any EU classified information up to 'RESTREINT UE/ EU RESTRICTED' level which are generated for the purposes of EUCAP Sahel Niger, in accordance with Decision 2011/292/EU. Arrangements between the HR and the competent authorities of the host State shall be drawn up for this purpose.

3. The HR shall be authorised to release to the third States associated with this Decision any EU non-classified documents connected with the deliberations of the Council relating to EUCAP Sahel Niger and covered by the obligation of professional secrecy pursuant to Article 6(1) of the Council's Rules of Procedure.

4. The HR may delegate the powers referred to in paragraphs 1 to 3, as well as the ability to conclude the arrangements referred to in paragraph 2 to persons placed under his/her authority, to the Civilian Operations Commander and/or to the Head of Mission.

Article 16

Entry into force and duration

This Decision shall enter into force on the day of its adoption.

It shall apply for a period of 24 months.

The Council has concluded three types of international agreements in the field of CFSP that pertain directly to CSDP missions. These are, firstly, the so-called status of forces agreements (SOFAs) or status of mission agreements (SOMAs). SOMAs and SOFAs are concluded with the state hosting the EU forces and personnel, and regulate their legal status. Such is the EU–Uganda agreement on the status of EUTM Somalia included here. The second type consists of agreements with third states wishing to participate in a specific EU mission, such as the EU–Montenegro agreement on the participation of Montenegro in Operation Atalanta, or wishing to establish a prior framework governing possible participation in future EU crisis management operations, such as the recent EU–New Zealand agreement.[13] These agreements, thus, set the conditions for the engagement of third states in CSDP operations. Finally, there are agreements on security procedures for exchanging classified information such as the EU–Lichtenstein agreement regulating the exchange of classified information.

Agreement between the European Union and the Republic of Uganda on the Status of the European Union-led Mission in Uganda, Official Journal L 221, 24.8.2010, pp. 2–7.

THE EUROPEAN UNION,
hereinafter referred to as 'the Union',
of the one part, and
THE REPUBLIC OF UGANDA,
hereinafter referred to as 'the Host State',
of the other part,
together hereinafter referred to as the 'Parties',
TAKING INTO ACCOUNT:
— that in its Resolution 1897 (2009) on the situation in Somalia, adopted on 30 November 2009, the United Nations Security Council (UNSC) recalled its previous Resolutions in support of Somalia and reaffirmed its respect for the sovereignty, territorial integrity, political independence and unity of Somalia,
— that the UNSC further emphasised that Somalia's long-term security rests with the effective development by the Transitional Federal Government (TFG) of the National Security Force and Somali Police Force, in the framework of the Djibouti Agreement and in line with a national security strategy,
— the letter dated 5 January 2010, by which the Minister of Defence of the Host State welcomed the Union's envisaged mission in support of the Somali security sector and invited the Union to participate in the training of Somali security forces in the Host State for a period of at least one year,
— Council Decision 2010/96/CFSP of 15 February 2010 on a European Union military mission to contribute to the training of Somali security forces,
— that this mission is a non-executive mission which does not entail the right to take coercive measures independently from the consent of the Host State,

---

[13] Agreement between the European Union and New Zealand establishing a framework for the participation of New Zealand in European Union crisis management operation, OJ L 160, 21.6.2012, pp. 2–7.

— that this Agreement will not affect the Parties' rights and obligations under international agreements and other instruments establishing international courts and tribunals, including the Statute of the International Criminal Court,

HAVE AGREED AS FOLLOWS:

Article 1

Scope and definitions

1. This Agreement shall apply to the European Union-led Mission in Uganda (hereinafter referred to as 'EUTM Somalia') and to its personnel.

2. This Agreement shall apply only within the territory of the Host State.

3. For the purpose of this Agreement:

(a) 'EUTM Somalia' shall mean EU mission headquarters and national contingents contributing to the mission, their equipment and their means of transport;

(b) 'mission' shall mean the preparation, establishment, execution and support of EUTM Somalia;

(c) 'EU Mission Commander' shall mean the Commander in the theatre;

(d) 'EU mission headquarters' shall mean the military headquarters and elements thereof, whatever their location, under the authority of EU military commanders exercising the military command or control of the mission;

(e) 'national contingents' shall mean units and elements belonging to the Member States of the Union and to other States participating in the mission;

(f) 'EUTM Somalia personnel' shall mean the civilian and military personnel assigned to EUTM Somalia as well as personnel deployed for the preparation of the mission and personnel on mission for a Sending State or an institution of the Union in the framework of the mission, present, except as otherwise provided in this Agreement, within the territory of the Host State, with the exception of personnel employed locally and personnel employed by international commercial contractors;

(g) 'personnel employed locally' shall mean personnel who are nationals of, or permanently resident in, the Host State;

(h) 'facilities' shall mean all premises, accommodation and land areas required for EUTM Somalia and EUTM Somalia personnel;

(i) 'Sending State' shall mean a State providing a national contingent for EUTM Somalia, including Member States of the Union and third States participating in the mission;

(j) 'Host State' shall mean the Republic of Uganda;

(k) 'official correspondence' shall mean all correspondence relating to the mission and its functions.

Article 2

General provisions

1. EUTM Somalia and EUTM Somalia personnel shall respect the laws and regulations of the Host State and shall refrain from any action or activity incompatible with the objectives of the mission.

2. EUTM Somalia shall regularly inform the government of the Host State of the number of EUTM Somalia personnel stationed within the Host State's territory.

Article 3

Identification

1. EUTM Somalia personnel shall carry passports or military identity cards with them at all times.

2. EUTM Somalia vehicles, aircraft and other means of transport shall carry distinctive EUTM Somalia identification markings and/or registration plates, of which the relevant Host State authorities shall be notified.

3. EUTM Somalia shall have the right to display the flag of the Union and markings such as military insignia, titles and official symbols, on its facilities, vehicles and other means of transport. The uniforms of EUTM Somalia personnel shall carry a distinctive EUTM Somalia emblem. National flags or insignia of the constituent national contingents of the mission may be displayed on the EUTM Somalia facilities, vehicles and other means of transport and uniforms, as decided by the EU Mission Commander.

Article 4

Border crossing and movement within the Host State's territory

1. EUTM Somalia personnel shall enter the Host State's territory only on presentation of the documents provided for in Article 3(1) or, in the case of first entry, of an individual or collective movement order issued by EUTM Somalia. They shall be exempt from visa regulations, and the Host State shall facilitate EUTM Somalia personnel with immigration inspections and customs control requirements, on entering, leaving or within the Host State's territory.

2. EUTM Somalia personnel shall be exempt from the Host State's regulations on the registration and control of aliens, but shall not acquire any right to permanent residence or domicile within the Host State's territory.

3. The Host State shall be provided, for information purposes, with a general list of EUTM Somalia equipment entering its territory. This equipment shall carry EUTM Somalia identification markings. The procedure hereof shall be sufficient to satisfy all customs and inspection requirements.

4. EUTM Somalia personnel may drive motor vehicles and operate aircrafts within the Host State's territory provided they have valid national, international or military driving licences or pilot licences, as appropriate.

5. For the purpose of the mission, the Host State shall grant EUTM Somalia and EUTM Somalia personnel freedom of movement and freedom to travel within its territory, including its air space.

6. For the purpose of the mission, EUTM Somalia and the means of transport that it charters may use public roads, bridges, ferries and airports without the payment of duties, fees, tolls, taxes and similar charges. EUTM Somalia shall not be exempt from reasonable charges for services requested and received, under the conditions that apply to those provided to the Host State's armed forces.

Article 5

Privileges and immunities of EUTM Somalia granted by the Host State

1. EUTM Somalia's facilities shall be inviolable. The Host State's agents shall not enter them without the consent of the EU Mission Commander.

2. EUTM Somalia's facilities, their furnishings and other assets therein as well as its means of transport shall be immune from search, requisition, attachment or execution.

3. EUTM Somalia, its property and assets, wherever located and by whomsoever held as duly authorised by EUTM Somalia, shall enjoy immunity from every form of legal process.

4. EUTM Somalia's archives and documents shall be inviolable at any time, wherever they may be.

5. The official correspondence of EUTM Somalia shall be inviolable.

6. In respect of purchased and imported goods, services provided and facilities used by EUTM Somalia for the purposes of the mission, EUTM Somalia shall be exempt from all taxes and charges of a similar nature in the Host State. EUTM Somalia providers or contractors shall also be exempted from those taxes and charges of a similar nature concerning goods, services and facilities provided by them to EUTM Somalia. EUTM Somalia shall not be exempt from dues, taxes or charges that represent payment for services requested and rendered.

7. The Host State shall permit the entry and exit of articles for the mission and grant them exemption from all custom duties, fees, tolls, taxes and similar charges other than charges for storage, cartage and other services requested and rendered.

Article 6

Privileges and immunities of EUTM Somalia personnel granted by the Host State

1. EUTM Somalia personnel shall not be liable to any form of arrest or detention.

2. Papers, correspondence and property of EUTM Somalia personnel shall enjoy inviolability, except in case of measures of execution which are permitted pursuant to paragraph 6.

3. EUTM Somalia personnel shall enjoy immunity from the criminal jurisdiction of the Host State under all circumstances.

The immunity from criminal jurisdiction of EUTM Somalia personnel may be waived by the Sending State or the institution of the Union concerned, as the case may be. Such waiver shall always be in writing.

The immunity of EUTM Somalia personnel from the jurisdiction of the Host State shall not exempt them from the jurisdiction of the respective Sending State. In the event of an allegation of a criminal offence being committed by EUTM Somalia personnel, the Sending State shall inform the Host State of the outcome of such judicial procedure as it undertakes in connection with the alleged criminal offence.

4. EUTM Somalia personnel shall enjoy immunity from the civil and administrative jurisdiction of the Host State in respect of words spoken or written and all acts performed by them in the exercise of official functions. If any civil proceedings are instituted against EUTM Somalia personnel before any Host State court, the EU Mission Commander and the competent authority of the Sending State or the institution of the Union shall be notified immediately. Prior to initiation of civil proceedings before the court, the EU Mission Commander and the competent authority of the Sending State or the institution of the Union shall certify to the court whether the act in question was committed by EUTM Somalia personnel in the exercise of official functions.

If the act was committed in the exercise of official functions, civil proceedings shall not be initiated and the provisions of Article 15 shall apply. If the act was not committed in the exercise of official functions, civil proceedings may continue. The certification by the EU Mission Commander and the competent authority of the Sending State or the institution of the Union shall be binding upon the jurisdiction of the Host State which may not contest it.

The initiation of civil proceedings by EUTM Somalia personnel shall preclude them from invoking immunity from jurisdiction in respect of any counter-claim directly connected with the principal claim.

5. EUTM Somalia personnel shall not be obliged to give evidence as witnesses.

EUTM Somalia and the Sending State may produce statements of witnesses or affidavits by EUTM Somalia personnel about criminal acts witnessed in the context of training Somali security forces in Uganda.

6. No measures of execution may be taken in respect of EUTM Somalia personnel, except in the case where civil proceedings not related to official functions are instituted against them. Property of EUTM Somalia personnel, which is certified by the EU Mission Commander to be necessary for the fulfilment of official functions, shall be free from seizure for the satisfaction of a judgement, decision or order. In civil proceedings, EUTM Somalia personnel shall not be subject to any restrictions on their personal liberty or to any other measures of constraint.

7. EUTM Somalia personnel shall with respect to services rendered for EUTM Somalia be exempt from social security provisions which may be in force in the Host State.

8. EUTM Somalia personnel shall be exempt from any form of taxation in the Host State on the salary and emoluments paid to them by EUTM Somalia or the Sending States, as well as on any income received from outside the Host State.

9. The Host State shall, in accordance with such laws and regulations as it may adopt, permit entry of, and grant exemption from, all customs duties, indirect and direct taxes, excise duties, and related charges other than charges for storage, cartage and similar services, on articles for the personal use of EUTM Somalia personnel.

Any inspection of personal baggage of EUTM Somalia personnel shall be conducted only in the presence of the EUTM Somalia personnel concerned or of an authorised representative of EUTM Somalia.

Article 7

Personnel employed locally

Personnel employed locally shall enjoy privileges and immunities only to the extent admitted by the Host State. However, the Host State shall exercise its jurisdiction over that personnel in such a manner as not to interfere unduly with the performance of the functions of the mission.

Article 8

Criminal jurisdiction

The competent authorities of a Sending State shall have the right to exercise on the territory of the Host State all the criminal jurisdiction and disciplinary powers conferred on them by the law of the Sending State with regard to all EUTM Somalia personnel subject to the relevant law of the Sending State.

Article 9

Uniform and arms

1. The wearing of uniform shall be subject to rules adopted by the EU Mission Commander.

2. EUTM Somalia military personnel may carry arms and ammunition on condition that they are authorised to do so by their orders which shall be communicated to the Host State.

Article 10

Host State support and contracting

1. The Host State agrees, if requested, to assist EUTM Somalia in finding suitable facilities.

2. The Host State shall provide, free of charge, facilities of which it is the owner, in so far as such facilities are requested for the conduct of administrative and operational activities of EUTM Somalia.

3. Within its means and capabilities, the Host State shall assist in the preparation, establishment, and execution of, and support for, the mission. The Host State's assistance and support of the mission shall be provided under the same conditions as the assistance and support given to the Host State's armed forces.

4. The law applicable to contracts concluded by EUTM Somalia in the Host State shall be determined by the contract.

5. The contract may stipulate that the dispute settlement procedure referred to in Article 15(3) and (4) shall be applicable to disputes arising from the application of the contract.

6. The Host State shall facilitate the implementation of contracts concluded by EUTM Somalia with commercial entities for the purposes of the mission.

Article 11

Change to facilities

1. EUTM Somalia shall be authorised to construct, alter or otherwise modify facilities as requested for its operational requirements.

2. No compensation shall be requested from EUTM Somalia by the Host State for those constructions, alterations or modifications.

3. Prior to the withdrawal of EUTM Somalia, where appropriate, the EU Mission Commander will enter into negotiations on an arrangement in application of Article 18 with a view to seeking reasonable residual value for fixed and/or moveable facilities provided or improved with EUTM Somalia funds that will remain after withdrawal of EUTM Somalia. If EUTM Somalia is taken over by a successor mission, the Host State shall make the facilities available to this successor mission free of charge.

Article 12

Deceased EUTM Somalia personnel

1. The EU Mission Commander shall have the right to take charge of, and make suitable arrangements for, the repatriation of any deceased EUTM Somalia personnel, as well as that of their personal property.

2. No autopsy shall be performed on any deceased EUTM Somalia personnel without the agreement of the State of nationality of the deceased person concerned and the presence of a representative of EUTM Somalia and/or the State of nationality of the deceased person concerned.

3. The Host State and EUTM Somalia shall cooperate to the fullest extent possible with a view to early repatriation of deceased EUTM Somalia personnel.

Article 13

Security of EUTM Somalia and military police

1. The Host State shall take all appropriate measures to ensure the safety and security of EUTM Somalia and its personnel, including those necessary to protect its facilities against any external attack or intrusion.

2. The EU Mission Commander may establish a military police unit in order to maintain order in EUTM Somalia facilities.

3. The military police unit may also, in consultation and cooperation with the military police or the police of the Host State, act outside EUTM Somalia facilities to ensure the maintenance of good order and discipline among EUTM Somalia personnel.

Article 14

Communications

1. EUTM Somalia may install and operate radio sending and receiving stations, as well as satellite systems. It shall cooperate with the Host State's competent authorities with a view to avoiding conflicts in the use of appropriate frequencies. The Host State shall grant access to the frequency spectrum free of charge.

2. EUTM Somalia shall enjoy the right to unrestricted communication by radio (including satellite, mobile and hand-held radio), telephone, telegraph, facsimile and other means, as well as the right to install the equipment necessary for the maintenance of such communications within and between EUTM Somalia facilities, including the laying of cables and land lines for the purpose of the mission.

3. Within its own facilities EUTM Somalia may make the arrangements necessary for the conveyance of mail addressed to and from EUTM Somalia and/or EUTM Somalia personnel.

Article 15

Claims for death, injury, damage and loss

1. EUTM Somalia and EUTM Somalia personnel shall not be liable for any damage to or loss of civilian or government property which are related to operational necessities or caused by activities in connection with civil disturbances or protection of EUTM Somalia.

2. With a view to reaching an amicable settlement, claims for damage to or loss of civilian or government property not covered by paragraph 1, as well as claims for death of or injury to persons and for damage to or loss of EUTM Somalia property, shall be forwarded to EUTM Somalia via the competent authorities of the Host State, as far as claims brought by legal or natural persons from the Host State are concerned, or to the competent authorities of the Host State, as far as claims brought by EUTM Somalia are concerned.

3. Where no amicable settlement can be found, the claim shall be submitted to a claims commission composed on an equal basis of representatives of EUTM Somalia and representatives of the Host State. Settlement of claims shall be reached by common agreement.

4. Where no settlement can be reached within the claims commission, the dispute shall:

(a) for claims up to and including EUR 40 000, be settled by diplomatic means between representatives of the Host State and of the Union;

(b) for claims above the amount referred to in point (a), be submitted to an arbitration tribunal, the decisions of which shall be binding.

5. The arbitration tribunal shall be composed of three arbitrators, one arbitrator being appointed by the Host State, one arbitrator being appointed by EUTM Somalia and the third one being appointed jointly by the Host State and EUTM Somalia. Where one of the Parties does not appoint an arbitrator within two months or where no agreement can be found between the Host State and EUTM Somalia on the appointment of the third arbitrator, the arbitrator in question shall be appointed by the President of the Court of Justice of the European Union.

6. An administrative arrangement shall be concluded between EUTM Somalia and the administrative authorities of the Host State in order to determine the terms of reference of the claims commission and the arbitration tribunal, the procedure applicable within those bodies and the conditions under which claims are to be lodged.

Article 16

Liaison and disputes

1. All issues arising out of, or in connection with, the application of this Agreement shall be examined jointly by representatives of EUTM Somalia and of the Host State's competent authorities.

2. Failing any prior settlement, disputes concerning the interpretation or application of this Agreement shall be settled exclusively by diplomatic means between the representatives of the Host State and of the Union.

Article 17

Other provisions

1. Whenever this Agreement refers to the privileges, immunities and rights of EUTM Somalia and of EUTM Somalia personnel, the Government of the Host State shall be responsible for their implementation and for compliance with them on the part of the appropriate Host State local authorities.

2. Nothing in this Agreement is intended or may be construed as to derogate from any rights that may attach to a Member State of the Union or to any other State contributing to EUTM Somalia under other agreements.

Article 18

Implementing arrangements

For purposes of the application of this Agreement, operational, administrative and technical matters may be the subject of separate arrangements to be concluded between the EU Mission Commander and the Host State's administrative authorities.

Article 19

Entry into force and termination

1. This Agreement shall enter into force on the day on which it is signed and shall remain in force until the date of departure of the last EUTM Somalia element and of the last EUTM Somalia personnel, as notified by EUTM Somalia.

2. Notwithstanding paragraph 1, the provisions contained in Articles 4(6), 5(1) to (3), 5(6), 5(7), 6(1), 6(3), 6(4), 6(6), 6(7) to (9), 10(2), 11 and 15 shall be deemed to have applied from the date on which the first EUTM Somalia personnel were deployed if that date was earlier than the date of entry into force of this Agreement.

3. This Agreement may be amended by written agreement between the Parties.

4. Termination of this Agreement shall not affect any rights or obligations arising out of the execution of this Agreement before such termination.

Agreement between the European Union and Montenegro on the participation of Montenegro in the European Union military operation to contribute to the deterrence, prevention and repression of acts of piracy and armed robbery off the Somali coast (Operation Atalanta), Official Journal L 88, 8.4.2010, pp. 3–8.

THE EUROPEAN UNION (EU),

of the one part, and

MONTENEGRO,

of the other part,

hereinafter referred to as the 'Parties',

TAKING INTO ACCOUNT:

the adoption by the Council of the European Union of Joint Action 2008/851/CFSP on a European Union military operation to contribute to the deterrence, prevention and repression of acts of piracy and armed robbery off the Somali coast (operation Atalanta), as amended by Council Decision 2009/907/CFSP,

the invitation by the EU to Montenegro to participate in the EU-led operation,

the successful completion of the Force Generation process and the recommendation by the EU Operation Commander and the EU Military Committee to agree on the participation of Montenegro's forces in the EU-led operation,

the Political and Security Committee Decision ATALANTA/2/2009 of 21 April 2009 on the acceptance of third States' contributions to the European Union military operation to contribute to the deterrence, prevention and repression of acts of piracy and armed robbery off the Somali coast (Atalanta) and the Political and Security Committee Decision ATALANTA/3/2009 of 21 April 2009 on the setting up of the Committee of Contributors for the European Union military operation to contribute to the deterrence, prevention and repression of acts of piracy and armed robbery off the Somali coast (Atalanta), which were both amended by Political and Security Committee Decision ATALANTA/7/2009,

the decision by Montenegro of 13 August 2009 to participate in operation Atalanta,

HAVE AGREED AS FOLLOWS:

Article 1

Participation in the operation

1. Montenegro shall associate itself with Joint Action 2008/851/CFSP on a European Union military operation to contribute to the deterrence, prevention and repression of acts of piracy and armed robbery off the Somali coast (operation Atalanta), as amended by Decision 2009/907/CFSP, and with any further Decision by which the Council of the European Union decides to extend the operation, in accordance with the provisions of this Agreement and any required implementing arrangements.

2. The contribution of Montenegro to the European Union-led naval force (EUNAVFOR) is without prejudice to the decision-making autonomy of the European Union.

3. Montenegro shall ensure that its forces and personnel participating in operation Atalanta undertake their mission in conformity with:

– Joint Action 2008/851/CFSP and possible subsequent amendments,

– the Operation Plan,

– any implementing measures.

4. Forces and personnel seconded to the operation by Montenegro shall carry out their duties and conduct themselves solely with the interest of operation Atalanta in mind.

5. Montenegro shall inform the EU Operation Commander in due time of any change to its participation in the operation.

Article 2

Status of forces

1. The status of the forces and personnel contributed to operation Atalanta by Montenegro shall be governed by the agreement on the status of forces concluded between the European Union and Somalia, Djibouti or any other country in the region with which such an agreement will have been concluded for the purposes of the operation, or by the unilateral declaration on the status of forces issued by Kenya, the Seychelles or any country in the region which will have issued such a declaration for the purposes of the operation.

2. The status of the forces and personnel contributed to headquarters or command elements located outside the joint operation area, shall be governed by arrangements between the Host State of the headquarters and command elements concerned and Montenegro.

3. Without prejudice to the agreements and declarations on the status of forces referred to in paragraphs 1 and 2, Montenegro shall exercise jurisdiction over its forces and personnel participating in operation Atalanta.

4. Montenegro shall be responsible for answering any claims linked to the participation in operation Atalanta, from or concerning any of its forces and personnel. Montenegro shall be responsible for bringing any action, in particular legal or disciplinary, against any of its forces and personnel, in accordance with its laws and regulations.

5. Montenegro undertakes to make a declaration as regards the waiver of claims against any State participating in operation Atalanta, and to do so when signing this Agreement.

6. European Union Member States undertake to make a declaration as regards the waiver of claims, for the participation of Montenegro in operation Atalanta, and to do so when signing this Agreement.

Article 3

Conditions of transfer of persons arrested and detained with a view to their prosecution
If Montenegro exercises its jurisdiction upon persons having committed or suspected of having committed acts of piracy, or acts of armed robbery in a coastal State's territorial sea, within the area of the Operation, the transfer of persons arrested with a view to their prosecution and detained by EUNAVFOR and seized property in the possession of EUNAVFOR, from EUNAVFOR to Montenegro, shall be carried out under the conditions set out in the Annex, which forms an integral part of this Agreement.

Article 4

Classified information
1. Montenegro shall take appropriate measures to ensure that EU classified information is protected in accordance with the European Union Council's security regulations, contained in Council Decision 2001/264/EC of 19 March 2001 adopting the Council's security regulations, and in accordance with further guidance issued by competent authorities, including the EU Operation Commander.
2. Where the EU and Montenegro have concluded an agreement on security procedures for the exchange of classified information, the provisions of such an agreement shall apply in the context of operation Atalanta.

Article 5

Chain of command
1. All forces and personnel participating in operation Atalanta shall remain under the full command of their national authorities.
2. National authorities shall transfer the Operational and Tactical command and/ or control of their forces and personnel to the EU Operation Commander. The EU Operation Commander is entitled to delegate his authority.
3. Montenegro shall have the same rights and obligations in terms of the day-to-day management of the operation as participating European Union Member States.
4. The EU Operation Commander may—following consultations with Montenegro—at any time request the withdrawal of Montenegro's contribution.
5. A Senior Military Representative (SMR) shall be appointed by Montenegro to represent its national contingent in operation Atalanta. The SMR shall consult with the EU Force Commander on all matters affecting the operation and shall be responsible for day-to-day contingent discipline.

Article 6

Financial aspects
1. Montenegro shall assume all the costs associated with its participation in the operation unless the costs are subject to common funding as provided for in the legal instruments referred to in Article 1(1) of this Agreement, as well as in Council Decision

2008/975/CFSP of 18 December 2008 establishing a mechanism to administer the financing of the common costs of European Union operations having military or defence implications (Athena).

2. Operation Atalanta shall provide logistic support to the Montenegrin contingent on a cost reimbursement basis under the conditions provided in the implementing arrangements referred to in Article 7. Administrative management of related expenditure shall be entrusted to Athena.

3. In the event of death, injury, loss or damage to natural or legal persons from the State(s) in which the operation is conducted, Montenegro shall, when its liability has been established, pay compensation under the conditions foreseen in the agreement on status of forces, if available, as referred to in Article 2(1) of this Agreement.

Article 7

Arrangements to implement the Agreement

Any necessary technical and administrative arrangements in pursuance of the implementation of this Agreement shall be concluded between the High Representative of the Union for Foreign Affairs and Security Policy or the EU Operation Commander and the appropriate authorities of Montenegro.

Article 8

Non-compliance

Should one of the Parties fail to comply with its obligations laid down in the previous articles, the other Party shall have the right to terminate this Agreement by serving a notice of one month.

Article 9

Dispute settlement

Disputes concerning the interpretation or application of this Agreement shall be settled by diplomatic means between the Parties.

Article 10

Entry into force

1. This Agreement shall enter into force on the first day of the first month after the Parties have notified each other of the completion of the internal procedures necessary for this purpose.

2. This Agreement shall be provisionally applied from the date of signature.

3. This Agreement shall remain in force for the duration of Montenegro's contribution to the operation.

4. Termination of this Agreement will not affect any benefits or obligations arising out of the application of this Agreement before such termination, including the benefits to any transferred persons as long as they are held in custody or are prosecuted by Montenegro.

After the termination of the Operation, all benefits of EUNAVFOR under the Annex to this Agreement may be exercised by any person or entity designated by the State exercising the Presidency of the Council of the EU. A designated person or entity may, inter alia, be a diplomatic agent or consular official of that State accredited to Montenegro. After the termination of the Operation, all notifications that were to be made to EUNAVFOR under this Instrument will be made to the State exercising the Presidency of the Council of the EU.

Agreement between the European Union and the Principality of Liechtenstein on security procedures for exchanging classified information, Official Journal L 187, 21.7.2010, pp. 2–4.

The EUROPEAN UNION, hereinafter referred to as 'the EU', and
The PRINCIPALITY OF LIECHTENSTEIN, hereinafter referred to as 'Liechtenstein',
Hereinafter referred to as 'the Parties',
CONSIDERING THAT the Parties share the objectives to strengthen their own security in all ways and to provide their citizens with a high level of safety within an area of security,
CONSIDERING THAT the Parties agree that consultations and cooperation should be developed between them on questions of common interest relating to security,
CONSIDERING THAT, in this context, a permanent need therefore exists to exchange classified information between the Parties,
RECOGNISING THAT full and effective consultation and cooperation may require access to classified information and material of the EU and of Liechtenstein, as well as the exchange of classified information and related material between the Parties,
CONSCIOUS THAT such access to and exchange of classified information and related material require appropriate security measures,

HAVE AGREED AS FOLLOWS:

Article 1

In order to fulfil the objectives of strengthening the security of each of the Parties in all ways, this Agreement between the Principality of Liechtenstein and the European Union on security procedures for exchanging classified information (hereinafter referred to as the 'Agreement') shall apply to classified information or material in any form either provided or exchanged between the Parties.

Article 2

For the purposes of this Agreement, 'classified information' shall mean any information (i.e. knowledge that can be communicated in any form) or material determined by either of the Parties to require protection against unauthorised disclosure and which has been so designated by a security classification.

Article 3

The EU institutions and entities to which this Agreement shall apply are: the European Council, the Council of the European Union (hereinafter referred to as 'the Council'), the General Secretariat of the Council, the High Representative of the Union for Foreign Affairs and Security Policy, the European External Action Service (hereinafter:

'the EEAS') and the European Commission. For the purposes of this Agreement, these institutions and entities shall be referred to as 'the EU'.

Article 4

Each Party shall:

(a) protect and safeguard classified information provided or exchanged by the other Party under this Agreement;

(b) ensure that classified information provided or exchanged under this Agreement keeps the security classification marking given to it by the providing Party. The receiving Party shall protect and safeguard the classified information according to the provisions set out in its own security regulations for information or material holding an equivalent security classification, as specified in the security arrangements to be established pursuant to Article 11;

(c) not use such classified information for purposes other than those established by the originator or those for which the information is provided or exchanged;

(d) not disclose such classified information to third parties, or to any EU institution or entity not referred to in Article 3, without the prior written consent of the providing Party;

(e) not allow access to classified information to individuals unless they have a need to know and have been appropriately security-cleared.

Article 5

1. Classified information may be disclosed or released, in accordance with the principle of originator control, by one Party (the providing Party) to the other Party (the receiving Party).

2. For release to recipients other than the Parties, a decision on disclosure or release of classified information will be made by the receiving Party following the written consent of the providing Party, in accordance with the principle of originator control as defined in the latter's security regulations.

3. In implementing paragraphs 1 and 2, no generic release shall be possible unless procedures are established and agreed upon between the Parties regarding certain categories of information which are relevant to their operational requirements.

Article 6

Each of the Parties, and the institutions and entities referred to in Article 3 of this Agreement, shall ensure that they have a security system and security measures in place, based on the basic principles and minimum standards of security laid down in their respective laws or regulations, and reflected in the arrangements to be established pursuant to Article 11, in order to ensure that an equivalent level of protection is applied to classified information provided or exchanged under this Agreement.

Article 7

1. The Parties shall ensure that all persons who, in the conduct of their official duties, require access, or whose duties or functions may afford access, to classified information provided or exchanged under this Agreement are appropriately security-cleared before they are granted access to such information.

2. The security clearance procedures shall be designed to determine whether an individual may, taking into account his or her loyalty, trustworthiness and reliability, have access to classified information.

Article 8

The Parties shall provide mutual assistance with regard to the security of classified information provided or exchanged under this Agreement and matters of common security interest. Reciprocal security consultations and inspections shall be conducted by the authorities referred to in Article 11 to assess the effectiveness of the security arrangements within their respective responsibility to be established pursuant to that Article.

Article 9

1. For the purpose of this Agreement:
(a) as regards the EU, all correspondence shall be sent through the Chief Registry Officer of the Council and shall be forwarded by him to the Member States and to the institutions or entities referred to in Article 3, subject to paragraph 2;
(b) as regards Liechtenstein, all correspondence shall be sent to the Chief Registry Officer of the Ministry of Interior of Liechtenstein and forwarded, where appropriate, via the Mission of Liechtenstein to the EU.
2. Exceptionally, correspondence from one Party which is accessible to only specific competent officials, organs or services of that Party may, for operational reasons, be addressed and be accessible only to specific competent officials, organs or services of the other Party specifically designated as recipients, taking into account their competencies and according to the need-to-know principle. As far as the EU is concerned, such correspondence shall be transmitted through the Chief Registry Officer of the Council, the Chief Registry Officer of the European Commission or the Chief Registry Officer of the EEAS, as appropriate. As far as Liechtenstein is concerned, such correspondence shall be transmitted through the Mission of Liechtenstein to the EU.

Article 10

The Minister of Interior of Liechtenstein, the Secretary-General of the Council and the Member of the European Commission responsible for security matters shall oversee the implementation of this Agreement.

Article 11

1. In order to implement this Agreement, security arrangements shall be established between the three authorities designated in paragraphs 2, 3 and 4 in order to lay down the standards for the reciprocal security protection of classified information under this Agreement.
2. The Ministry of Interior of Liechtenstein shall develop the security arrangements for the protection and safeguarding of classified information provided to Liechtenstein under this Agreement.
3. The Security Office of the General Secretariat of the Council, under the direction and on behalf of the Secretary-General of the Council, acting in the name of the Council and under its authority, shall develop the security arrangements for the protection and safeguarding of classified information provided to the EU under this Agreement.

4. The European Commission Security Directorate, acting under the authority of the Member of the Commission responsible for security matters, shall develop the security arrangements for the protection of classified information provided or exchanged under this Agreement within the European Commission and its premises.

5. For the EU, the security arrangements mentioned in paragraph 1 shall be subject to approval by the Council Security Committee.

Article 12

The Authorities referred to in Article 11 shall establish procedures to be followed in the case of proven or suspected compromise of classified information provided or exchanged under this Agreement.

Article 13

Each Party shall bear its own costs incurred in implementing this Agreement.

Article 14

Before classified information is provided or exchanged between the Parties under this Agreement, the responsible security authorities referred to in Article 11 shall agree that the receiving Party is able to protect and safeguard the information in a way consistent with the arrangements to be established pursuant to that Article.

Article 15

This Agreement shall not prevent the Parties from concluding other agreements relating to the provision or exchange of classified information provided that they do not conflict with the provisions of this Agreement.

Article 16

Any disputes between Liechtenstein and the EU arising out of the interpretation or application of this Agreement shall be addressed by negotiation between the Parties.

Article 17

1. This Agreement shall enter into force on the first day of the first month after the Parties have notified each other of the completion of the internal procedures necessary for this purpose.

2. Each Party shall notify the other Party of any changes in its laws and regulations that could affect the protection of classified information referred to in this Agreement.

3. This Agreement may be reviewed for consideration of possible amendments at the request of either Party.

4. Any amendment to this Agreement shall be made in writing only and by common agreement of the Parties. It shall enter into force upon mutual notification as provided under paragraph 1.

Article 18

This Agreement may be denounced by one Party by written notice of denunciation given to the other Party. Such denunciation shall take effect six months after receipt of the notification by the other Party, but shall not affect obligations already entered into under this Agreement. In particular, all classified information provided or exchanged pursuant to this Agreement shall continue to be protected in accordance with the provisions set forth herein.

The EU Treaty now provides for entrusting a CSDP task to a group of Member States (Articles 42(5) and 44 TEU). It also allows for the establishment of a so-called 'permanent structured co-operation' among Member States that are politically willing and have the necessary military capabilities to move in this direction (Article 42(6) and 46 TEU together with Protocol no. 10). It is worth noting that the procedure to establish a permanent structured cooperation is far simpler and less demanding than the legal conditions for an enhanced cooperation in CFSP. This is the case since for the former there is no minimum number of participating Member States and the decision within the Council is taken with qualified majority contrary to the minimum condition of nine Member States (Article 20(2) TEU) and the unanimity requirement within the Council for enhanced cooperation (Article 329(2) and 331(2) TFEU). However, up to this point no permanent structured cooperation agreements have been concluded. Both the possibility to entrust a CSDP task to a group of Member States and the permanent structured cooperation reveal pragmatism from the side of the drafters of the Treaties but also contain a potential for further differing levels of integration within the EU architecture.

Treaty on European Union

Article 42

(ex Article 17 TEU)

[...]

5. The Council may entrust the execution of a task, within the Union framework, to a group of Member States in order to protect the Union's values and serve its interests. The execution of such a task shall be governed by Article 44.
6. Those Member States whose military capabilities fulfil higher criteria and which have made more binding commitments to one another in this area with a view to the most demanding missions shall establish permanent structured cooperation within the Union framework. Such cooperation shall be governed by Article 46. It shall not affect the provisions of Article 43.

[...]

Article 44

1. Within the framework of the decisions adopted in accordance with Article 43, the Council may entrust the implementation of a task to a group of Member States which are willing and have the necessary capability for such a task. Those Member States, in association with the High Representative of the Union for Foreign Affairs and Security Policy, shall agree among themselves on the management of the task.
2. Member States participating in the task shall keep the Council regularly informed of its progress on their own initiative or at the request of another Member State. Those

States shall inform the Council immediately should the completion of the task entail major consequences or require amendment of the objective, scope and conditions determined for the task in the decisions referred to in paragraph 1. In such cases, the Council shall adopt the necessary decisions.

[...]

Article 46

1. Those Member States which wish to participate in the permanent structured cooperation referred to in Article 42(6), which fulfil the criteria and have made the commitments on military capabilities set out in the Protocol on permanent structured cooperation, shall notify their intention to the Council and to the High Representative of the Union for Foreign Affairs and Security Policy.

2. Within three months following the notification referred to in paragraph 1 the Council shall adopt a decision establishing permanent structured cooperation and determining the list of participating Member States. The Council shall act by a qualified majority after consulting the High Representative.

3. Any Member State which, at a later stage, wishes to participate in the permanent structured cooperation shall notify its intention to the Council and to the High Representative.

The Council shall adopt a decision confirming the participation of the Member State concerned which fulfils the criteria and makes the commitments referred to in Articles 1 and 2 of the Protocol on permanent structured cooperation. The Council shall act by a qualified majority after consulting the High Representative. Only members of the Council representing the participating Member States shall take part in the vote.

A qualified majority shall be defined in accordance with Article 238(3)(a) of the Treaty on the Functioning of the European Union.

4. If a participating Member State no longer fulfils the criteria or is no longer able to meet the commitments referred to in Articles 1 and 2 of the Protocol on permanent structured cooperation, the Council may adopt a decision suspending the participation of the Member State concerned.

The Council shall act by a qualified majority. Only members of the Council representing the participating Member States, with the exception of the Member State in question, shall take part in the vote.

A qualified majority shall be defined in accordance with Article 238(3)(a) of the Treaty on the Functioning of the European Union.

5. Any participating Member State which wishes to withdraw from permanent structured cooperation shall notify its intention to the Council, which shall take note that the Member State in question has ceased to participate.

6. The decisions and recommendations of the Council within the framework of permanent structured cooperation, other than those provided for in paragraphs 2 to 5, shall be adopted by unanimity. For the purposes of this paragraph, unanimity shall be constituted by the votes of the representatives of the participating Member States only.

Another significant innovation brought about by Lisbon has been the introduction of a mutual assistance clause in Article 42(7) TEU. This article obliges Member States to aid and assist a Member State which is the victim of armed aggression on its territory. However, this obligation is to be complied with within the international security architecture and the regional defence structures, whereas it is without 'prejudice [to] the specific character of the security and defence policy of certain Member States'. Thus, the existence of this article is primarily of significant political value for the EU but in no way does it amount to a mutual defence provision or does it change the character of the Union into a defence union. Another observation that needs to be made here, is that the Treaty does not expressly oblige Member States to implement the mutual assistance clause within the EU framework, in contrast to the solidarity clause contained in Article 222 TFEU.[14] The solidarity clause obliges the EU and its Member States to 'act jointly' at the request of the Member State that has suffered a terrorist attack or a natural or man-made disaster, in order to prevent further threats and to protect and assist this Member State, its population, and its democratic institutions.

Treaty on European Union

Article 42

(ex Article 17 TEU)

[...]

7. If a Member State is the victim of armed aggression on its territory, the other Member States shall have towards it an obligation of aid and assistance by all the means in their power, in accordance with Article 51 of the United Nations Charter. This shall not prejudice the specific character of the security and defence policy of certain Member States.

Commitments and cooperation in this area shall be consistent with commitments under the North Atlantic Treaty Organisation, which, for those States which are members of it, remains the foundation of their collective defence and the forum for its implementation.

Treaty on the Functioning of the European Union

TITLE VII

SOLIDARITY CLAUSE

Article 222

1. The Union and its Member States shall act jointly in a spirit of solidarity if a Member State is the object of a terrorist attack or the victim of a natural or man-made disaster. The Union shall mobilise all the instruments at its disposal, including the military resources made available by the Member States, to:

(a) — prevent the terrorist threat in the territory of the Member States;

— protect democratic institutions and the civilian population from any terrorist attack;

---

[14] F. Naert, *International Law Aspects of the EU's Security and Defence Policy* (Antwerp: Intersentia, 2010), 222.

— assist a Member State in its territory, at the request of its political authorities, in the event of a terrorist attack;

(b) assist a Member State in its territory, at the request of its political authorities, in the event of a natural or man-made disaster.

2. Should a Member State be the object of a terrorist attack or the victim of a natural or man-made disaster, the other Member States shall assist it at the request of its political authorities. To that end, the Member States shall coordinate between themselves in the Council.

3. The arrangements for the implementation by the Union of the solidarity clause shall be defined by a decision adopted by the Council acting on a joint proposal by the Commission and the High Representative of the Union for Foreign Affairs and Security Policy. The Council shall act in accordance with Article 31(1) of the Treaty on European Union where this decision has defence implications. The European Parliament shall be informed.

For the purposes of this paragraph and without prejudice to Article 240, the Council shall be assisted by the Political and Security Committee with the support of the structures developed in the context of the common security and defence policy and by the Committee referred to in Article 71; the two committees shall, if necessary, submit joint opinions.

4. The European Council shall regularly assess the threats facing the Union in order to enable the Union and its Member States to take effective action.

Lisbon also allowed for the establishment of a European Defence Agency (EDA) by the Council with qualified majority voting (Article 42(3) and 45 TEU). The EDA already existed since 2004 but after Lisbon the Council repealed the joint action establishing the EDA, and amended the structure of this agency in order to bring it up to date with the novel institutional framework of the EU.

Treaty on European Union

Article 42

(ex Article 17 TEU)

[...]

3. Member States shall make civilian and military capabilities available to the Union for the implementation of the common security and defence policy, to contribute to the objectives defined by the Council. Those Member States which together establish multinational forces may also make them available to the common security and defence policy.

Member States shall undertake progressively to improve their military capabilities. The Agency in the field of defence capabilities development, research, acquisition and armaments (hereinafter referred to as 'the European Defence Agency') shall identify operational requirements, shall promote measures to satisfy those requirements, shall contribute to identifying and, where appropriate, implementing any measure needed to strengthen the industrial and technological base of the defence sector, shall participate in defining a European capabilities and armaments policy, and shall assist the Council in evaluating the improvement of military capabilities.

Article 45

1. The European Defence Agency referred to in Article 42(3), subject to the authority of the Council, shall have as its task to:

(a) contribute to identifying the Member States' military capability objectives and evaluating observance of the capability commitments given by the Member States;

(b) promote harmonisation of operational needs and adoption of effective, compatible procurement methods;

(c) propose multilateral projects to fulfil the objectives in terms of military capabilities, ensure coordination of the programmes implemented by the Member States and management of specific cooperation programmes;

(d) support defence technology research, and coordinate and plan joint research activities and the study of technical solutions meeting future operational needs;

(e) contribute to identifying and, if necessary, implementing any useful measure for strengthening the industrial and technological base of the defence sector and for improving the effectiveness of military expenditure.

2. The European Defence Agency shall be open to all Member States wishing to be part of it. The Council, acting by a qualified majority, shall adopt a decision defining the Agency's statute, seat and operational rules. That decision should take account of the level of effective participation in the Agency's activities. Specific groups shall be set up within the Agency bringing together Member States engaged in joint projects. The Agency shall carry out its tasks in liaison with the Commission where necessary.

Council Decision 2011/411/CFSP of 12 July 2011 defining the statute, seat and operational rules of the European Defence Agency and repealing Joint Action 2004/551/CFSP, Official Journal L 183, 13.7.2011, pp. 16–26.

THE COUNCIL OF THE EUROPEAN UNION,

Having regard to the Treaty on European Union, and in particular Articles 42 and 45 thereof,

Whereas:

(1) The European Defence Agency (hereinafter 'the Agency') was established by Council Joint Action 2004/551/CFSP (hereinafter 'Joint Action 2004/551/CFSP') to support the Council and Member States in their effort to improve the Union's defence capabilities in the field of crisis management and to sustain the European Security and Defence Policy.

(2) The European Security Strategy, endorsed by the European Council on 12 December 2003, identifies the establishment of a defence agency as an important element towards the development of more flexible and efficient European military resources.

(3) The report on the implementation of the European Security Strategy of 11 December 2008 endorses the Agency's leading role in the process of developing key defence capabilities for the Common Security and Defence Policy (CSDP).

(4) Joint Action 2004/551/CFSP should be repealed and replaced in order to take into account the amendments to the Treaty on European Union (TEU) introduced by the Treaty of Lisbon.

(5) Article 45 TEU provides for the adoption, by the Council, of a Decision defining the Agency's statute, seat and operational rules, which should take account of the level of effective participation of the Member States in the Agency's activities.

(6) The Agency should contribute to the implementation of the Common Foreign and Security Policy (CFSP), in particular the CSDP.

(7) The structure of the Agency should enable it to respond to the operational requirements of the Union and its Member States for the CSDP and, where necessary to fulfil its functions, to cooperate with third countries, organisations and entities.

(8) The Agency should develop close working relations with existing arrangements, groupings and organisations, such as those established under the Letter of Intent Framework Agreement (hereinafter 'LoI Framework Agreement'), as well as the Organisation Conjointe de Coopération en matière d'Armement (OCCAR) and the European Space Agency (ESA).

(9) The High Representative of the Union for Foreign Affairs and Security Policy (HR), in accordance with Article 18(2) TEU, should have a leading role in the Agency's structure and provide the essential link between the Agency and the Council.

(10) In the exercise of its role of political supervision and policy-making, the Council should issue guidelines to the Agency.

(11) In view of their nature, the adoption of the Financial Framework for the Agency, as referred to in Article 4(4), and the conclusion of administrative arrangements between the Agency and third countries, organisations and entities must be approved by the Council acting unanimously.

(12) When adopting guidelines and decisions in relation to the work of the Agency, the Council should meet at the level of Defence Ministers.

(13) Any guidelines or decisions adopted by the Council in relation with the Agency's work should be prepared in accordance with Article 240 TFEU.

(14) The competences of the Council's preparatory and advisory bodies, in particular those of the Committee of Permanent Representatives under Article 240 TFEU, the Political and Security Committee (PSC) under Article 38 TEU and the EU Military Committee (EUMC) should remain unaffected.

(15) The National Armaments Directors (NAD), Capability Directors, Research and Technology (R&T) Directors and Defence Policy Directors should receive reports and contribute on issues of their competence in preparation of Council decisions relating to the Agency.

(16) The Agency should have the legal personality necessary to perform its functions and attain its objectives, while maintaining close links with the Council and fully respecting the responsibilities of the European Union and its institutions.

(17) It should be provided that the budgets administered by the Agency may, on a case-by-case basis, receive contributions towards non-administrative costs, from the general budget of the European Union, in full respect of the rules, procedures and decision-making processes applicable to it, including Article 41(2) TEU.

(18) The Agency, while being open to participation by all Member States, should also provide for the possibility of specific groups of Member States establishing ad hoc projects or programmes.

(19) Subject to a Council decision on the establishment of permanent structured cooperation, in conformity with Articles 42(6) and 46 TEU and with Protocol (No 10) on permanent structured cooperation established by Article 42 TEU annexed to the TEU and to the TFEU, the Agency should support the implementation of permanent structured cooperation.

(20) The Agency should have decision-making procedures allowing it to fulfil its tasks efficiently, while respecting the national security and defence policies of participating Member States.

(21) The Agency should fulfil its mission in full respect of Article 40 TEU.

(22) The Agency should act in full compliance with the Council's security standards and rules.

(23) In accordance with Article 5 of Protocol (No 22) on the position of Denmark, annexed to the TEU and to the TFEU, Denmark does not participate in the elaboration and implementation of decisions and actions of the Union which have defence implications. Denmark will therefore not be bound by this Decision,

HAS ADOPTED THIS DECISION:

CHAPTER I
ESTABLISHMENT, MISSION AND TASKS OF THE AGENCY
Article 1

Establishment

1. An Agency in the field of defence capabilities development, research, acquisition and armaments (hereinafter the 'European Defence Agency' or the 'Agency'), as originally established by Joint Action 2004/551/CFSP, shall hereby continue in accordance with the following provisions.

2. The Agency shall act under the Council's authority, in support of the CFSP and the CSDP, within the single institutional framework of the European Union, and without prejudice to the responsibilities of the EU institutions and the Council bodies. The Agency's mission shall be without prejudice to other competences of the Union, in full respect of Article 40 TEU.

3. The Agency shall be open to participation by all EU Member States wishing to be part of it. Member States already participating in the Agency at the time of the adoption of this Decision shall continue as participating Member States.

4. Any Member State wishing to participate in the Agency after the entry into force of this Decision or wishing to withdraw from the Agency shall notify its intention to the Council and shall inform the HR. Any necessary technical and financial arrangements for such participation or withdrawal shall be determined by the Steering Board, referred to in Article 8.

5. The Agency shall have its seat in Brussels.

Article 2

Mission

1. The mission of the Agency is to support the Council and the Member States in their effort to improve the EU's defence capabilities in the field of crisis management and to sustain the CSDP as it stands now and develops in the future.

2. The Agency shall identify operational requirements, shall promote measures to satisfy those requirements, shall contribute to identifying and, where appropriate implementing any measure needed to strengthen the industrial and technological base of the defence sector, shall participate in defining a European capabilities and armaments policy, and shall assist the Council in evaluating the improvement of military capabilities.

3. The Agency's mission shall be without prejudice to the competences of Member States in defence matters.

Article 3

Definitions

For the purpose of this Decision, the following definitions shall apply:

(a) 'participating Member States' means the Member States of the European Union which participate in the Agency;

(b) 'contributing Member States' means the participating Member States of the European Union which contribute to a particular project or programme of the Agency.

Article 4

Political supervision and reporting arrangements to the Council

1. The Agency shall operate under the authority and the political supervision of the Council, to which it shall provide regular reports and from which it shall receive regular guidelines.

2. The Agency shall report regularly to the Council on its activities, and shall notably:

(a) submit to the Council in November each year a report on the Agency's activities for that year and provide elements for the Agency's work programme and budgets for the following year;

(b) subject to a Council decision on the establishment of permanent structured cooperation, submit to the Council at least once a year information on the Agency's contribution to the assessment activities in the context of permanent structured cooperation, referred to in Article 5(3)(f)(ii).

The Agency shall provide the Council in good time with information on important matters to be submitted to the Steering Board for decision.

3. The Council, acting by unanimity, and with advice from the PSC or other competent Council bodies as appropriate, shall issue guidelines annually in relation to the work of the Agency, notably with regard to its work programme. The Agency's work programme shall be established within the framework of these guidelines.

4. Every year, the Council, acting by unanimity, shall approve a Financial Framework for the Agency for the following 3 years. That Financial Framework shall set out agreed priorities associated with the Agency's 3-year Work Plan and shall constitute a legally binding ceiling for the first year and planning figures for the second and

third year. The Agency shall provide, no later than 31 March each year, a draft of the Financial Framework and its associated Work Plan to the Steering Board for consideration.

5. The Agency may make recommendations to the Council and to the Commission as necessary for the implementation of its mission.

Article 5

Functions and tasks

1. In fulfilling its functions and tasks, the Agency shall respect other competences of the Union and those of the EU institutions.

2. The Agency's fulfilment of its functions and tasks shall be without prejudice to the competences of Member States in defence matters.

3. The Agency, subject to the authority of the Council, shall have as its task to:

(a) contribute to identifying the Member States' military capability objectives and evaluating observance of the capability commitments given by the Member States, in particular by:

(i) identifying, in association with the competent Council bodies, including the EUMC, and utilising, inter alia, the Capability Development Mechanism (CDM) and any successor, the EU's future defence capability requirements;

(ii) coordinating the implementation of the Capability Development Plan (CDP) and any successor thereto;

(iii) evaluating, against criteria to be agreed by the Member States, the capability commitments given by the Member States, inter alia, through the CDP process and the CDM and any successor thereto;

(b) promote the harmonisation of operational needs and the adoption of effective, compatible procurement methods, in particular by:

(i) promoting and coordinating harmonisation of military requirements;

(ii) promoting cost-effective and efficient procurement by identifying and disseminating best practices;

(iii) providing appraisals on financial priorities for capabilities development and acquisition;

(c) propose multilateral projects to fulfil the objectives in terms of military capabilities, ensure coordination of the programmes implemented by the Member States and management of specific cooperation programmes, in particular by:

(i) promoting and proposing new multilateral cooperative projects;

(ii) identifying and proposing collaborative activities in the operational domain;

(iii) working for coordination of existing programmes implemented by Member States;

(iv) taking, at the request of Member States, responsibility for managing specific programmes;

(v) preparing, at the request of Member States, programmes to be managed by OCCAR or through other arrangements, as appropriate;

(d) support defence technology research, and coordinate and plan joint research activities and the study of technical solutions meeting future operational needs, in particular by:

(i) promoting, in liaison with the Union's research activities where appropriate, research aimed at fulfilling future security and defence capability requirements and thereby strengthening Europe's industrial and technological potential in this domain;

(ii) promoting more effectively targeted joint defence R&T;

(iii) catalysing defence R&T through studies and projects;

(iv) managing defence R&T contracts;

(v) working in liaison with the Commission to maximise complementarity and synergy between defence and civil or security-related research programmes;

(e) contribute to identifying and, if necessary, implementing any useful measure for strengthening the industrial and technological base of the defence sector and for improving the effectiveness of military expenditure, in particular by:

(i) contributing to the creation of an internationally competitive European defence equipment market, without prejudice to the internal market rules and the competences of the Commission in this field;

(ii) developing relevant policies and strategies in consultation with the Commission and, as appropriate, industry;

(iii) pursuing, in consultation with the Commission, EU-wide development and harmonisation of relevant procedures, within the tasks of the Agency;

(f) subject to a Council decision on the establishment of permanent structured cooperation, support this cooperation in particular by:

(i) facilitating major joint or European capability development initiatives;

(ii) contributing to the regular assessment of participating Member States' contributions with regard to capabilities, in particular contributions made in accordance with the criteria to be established, inter alia, on the basis of Article 2 of Protocol (No 10) on permanent structured cooperation annexed to the TEU and the TFEU and reporting thereon at least once a year.

Article 6

Legal personality

The Agency shall have legal personality in order to perform its functions and attain its objectives. Member States shall ensure that the Agency enjoys the most extensive legal capacity accorded to legal persons under their laws. The Agency may, in particular, acquire or dispose of movable and immovable property and be a party to legal proceedings. The Agency shall have the capacity to conclude contracts with private or public entities or organisations.

CHAPTER II

ORGANS AND STAFF OF THE AGENCY

Article 7

Head of the Agency

1. The Head of the Agency shall be the High Representative of the Union for Foreign Affairs and Security Policy (HR).

2. The Head of the Agency shall be responsible for the Agency's overall organisation and functioning and shall ensure that the guidelines issued by the Council and the

decisions of the Steering Board are implemented by the Chief Executive, who shall report to the Head of the Agency.

3. The Head of the Agency shall present the Agency's reports to the Council as referred to in Article 4(2).

4. The Head of the Agency shall be responsible for the negotiation of administrative arrangements with third countries and other organisations, groupings or entities in accordance with directives given by the Steering Board. Within such arrangements, as approved by the Steering Board, the Head of the Agency shall be responsible for establishing appropriate working relations with them.

Article 8

Steering Board

1. A Steering Board composed of one representative of each participating Member State, authorised to commit its government, and a representative of the Commission, shall be the decision-making body of the Agency. The Steering Board shall act within the framework of the guidelines issued by the Council.

2. The Steering Board shall meet at the level of Defence Ministers of the participating Member States or their representatives. The Steering Board shall, in principle, hold at least two meetings each year at the level of Defence Ministers.

3. The Head of the Agency shall convene and chair the Steering Board's meetings. If a participating Member State so requests, the Head of the Agency shall convene a meeting within 1 month.

4. The Head of the Agency may delegate the power to chair the Steering Board's meetings at the level of the representatives of the Ministers of Defence.

5. The Steering Board may meet in specific compositions (such as NADs, Capability Directors, R&T Directors or Defence Policy Directors).

6. The Steering Board meetings are attended by:

(a) the Chief Executive of the Agency, referred to in Article 10, or his/her representative;

(b) the Chairman of EUMC or his/her representative;

(c) representatives of the European External Action Service (EEAS).

7. The Steering Board may decide to invite, on matters of common interest:

(a) the NATO Secretary-General or his/her nominated representative;

(b) the Heads/Chairs of other arrangements, groupings or organisations whose work is relevant to that of the Agency (such as those established under the LoI Framework Agreement, as well as OCCAR and ESA);

(c) as appropriate, representatives of other third parties.

Article 9

Tasks and powers of the Steering Board

1. Within the framework of the guidelines of the Council referred to in Article 4(1), the Steering Board:

(a) shall approve the reports to be submitted to the Council;

(b) shall approve, on the basis of a draft submitted by the Head of the Agency, and no later than 31 December of each year, the Agency's annual work programme for the following year;

(c) shall adopt the Agency's general budget no later than 31 December of each year within the limits set in the Agency's Financial Framework as decided by the Council;

(d) shall approve the establishment within the Agency of ad hoc projects or programmes in accordance with Article 19;

(e) shall appoint the Chief Executive and up to two deputies;

(f) shall decide that the Agency may be entrusted by one or more Member States with the administrative and financial management of certain activities within its remit in accordance with Article 17;

(g) shall approve any recommendation to the Council or the Commission;

(h) shall adopt the Agency's rules of procedure;

(i) may amend the financial provisions for the implementation of the Agency's general budget;

(j) may amend the rules and regulations applicable to contractual staff and seconded national experts;

(k) shall determine the technical and financial arrangements regarding Member States' participation or withdrawal referred to in Article 1(4);

(l) shall adopt directives regarding the negotiation of administrative arrangements by the Head of the Agency;

(m) shall approve the ad hoc arrangements referred to in Article 22(1);

(n) shall conclude the administrative arrangement between the Agency and third parties referred to in Article 24(1);

(o) shall approve the annual accounts and balance sheet;

(p) shall adopt all other relevant decisions relating to the fulfilment of the Agency's mission.

2. Unless otherwise provided for in this Decision, the Steering Board shall take decisions by qualified majority. The votes of the participating Member States shall be weighted in accordance with paragraphs 4 and 5 of Article 16 TEU. Only the representatives of the participating Member States shall take part in the vote.

3. If a representative of a participating Member State in the Steering Board declares that, for important and stated reasons of national policy, it intends to oppose the adoption of a decision to be taken by qualified majority, a vote shall not be taken. That representative may refer the matter, through the Head of the Agency, to the Council with a view to issuing guidelines to the Steering Board, as appropriate. Alternatively, the Steering Board, acting by qualified majority, may decide to refer the matter to the Council for decision. The Council shall act by unanimity.

4. The Steering Board, on a proposal from the Chief Executive or from a participating Member State, may decide to set up:

(a) committees for the preparation of administrative and budgetary decisions of the Steering Board, composed of delegates of the participating Member States and a representative of the Commission;

(b) committees specialised in specific issues within the Agency's remit. These committees shall be composed of delegates of the participating Member States and, unless the Steering Board decides otherwise, a representative of the Commission.

The decision to establish such committees shall specify their mandate and duration.

Article 10

The Chief Executive

1. The Chief Executive, and his/her Deputy(ies), shall be appointed by the Steering Board on a proposal from the Head of the Agency for 3 years. The Steering Board may grant a 2-year extension. The Chief Executive and up to two Deputies shall act under the authority of the Head of the Agency and in accordance with the decisions of the Steering Board.

2. The Chief Executive, assisted by his/her Deputy(ies), shall take all necessary measures to ensure the efficiency and effectiveness of the Agency's work. The Chief Executive shall be responsible for the oversight and coordination of the functional units, in order to ensure the overall coherence of their work.

The Chief Executive shall be the head of the Agency's staff.

3. The Chief Executive is responsible for:

(a) ensuring the implementation of the Agency's annual work programme;

(b) preparing the work of the Steering Board, in particular the draft annual work programme of the Agency;

(c) preparing the draft annual general budget to be submitted to the Steering Board;

(d) preparing the 3-year Work Plan to be submitted to the Steering Board;

(e) preparing the 3-year Financial Framework to be submitted to the Council;

(f) ensuring close cooperation with, and providing information to, the Council preparatory bodies, notably the PSC and the EUMC;

(g) preparing the reports referred to in Article 4(2);

(h) preparing the statement of revenue and expenditure and implementing the Agency's general budget and the budgets of ad hoc projects or programmes entrusted to the Agency;

(i) the day-to-day administration of the Agency;

(j) all security aspects;

(k) all staff matters.

4. Within the work programme and the general budget of the Agency, the Chief Executive shall be empowered to enter into contracts and to recruit staff. The Chief Executive shall be the authorising officer responsible for the implementation of the budgets administered by the Agency.

5. The Chief Executive shall be accountable to the Steering Board.

6. The Chief Executive shall be the legal representative of the Agency.

Article 11

Staff

1. The staff of the Agency, including the Chief Executive, shall consist of contract and statutory staff members recruited from among candidates from all participating Member States on the broadest possible geographical basis, and from the EU institutions. The staff of the Agency shall be selected by the Chief Executive on the basis of relevant competence and expertise and through fair and transparent competition procedures. The Chief Executive shall publish in advance details of all available positions and the criteria relevant to the selection process. In all cases, recruitment shall be directed to securing for the Agency the services of staff of the highest standard of ability and efficiency.

2. The Head of the Agency, upon a proposal from the Chief Executive and following consultation with the Steering Board, shall appoint, and renew the contracts of, the staff of the Agency at senior management level.

3. The Agency staff shall consist of:

(a) personnel recruited directly by the Agency under fixed-term contracts, selected among nationals of participating Member States. The Council, acting by unanimity, has approved the regulations applicable to such staff. The Steering Board shall review and amend as necessary those regulations where they empower it to do so;

(b) national experts seconded by participating Member States either to posts within the Agency organisational structure or for specific tasks and projects. The Council, acting by unanimity, has approved the regulations applicable to such staff. The Steering Board shall review and amend as necessary those regulations, where they empower it to do so;

(c) Union officials seconded to the Agency for a fixed period and/or for specific tasks or projects as required.

4. The Court of Justice of the European Union shall have jurisdiction over any dispute between the Agency and any person to whom the regulations applicable to the staff of the Agency may apply.

CHAPTER III
BUDGET AND FINANCIAL RULES
Article 12

Budgetary principles

1. Budgets, drawn up in euro, are the acts which for each financial year lay down and authorise all the revenue and expenditure administered by the Agency.

2. The appropriations entered in a budget are authorised for the duration of a financial year which begins on 1 January and ends on 31 December of the same year.

3. For each budget, revenue and expenditure must be balanced. All revenue and expenditure shall be entered in full in the relevant budget without any adjustment against each other.

4. The budget shall contain differentiated appropriations, which shall consist of commitment appropriations and payment appropriations and non-differentiated appropriations.

5. Commitment appropriations shall cover the total cost of the legal commitments entered into during the current financial year. However, commitments may be made globally or in annual instalments. Commitments shall be entered into the accounts on the basis of the legal commitments entered into up to 31 December.

6. Payment appropriations shall cover payments made to honour the legal commitments entered into the current financial year and/or earlier financial years. Payments shall be entered in the accounts on the basis of the budget commitments up to 31 December.

7. The revenue of a financial year shall be entered in the accounts for the financial year on the basis of the amounts collected during that financial year.

8. Neither revenue nor expenditure may be implemented other than by allocation to a heading in the budget and within the limit of the appropriations entered therein.

9. Appropriations shall be used in accordance with the principles of sound financial management, namely in accordance with the principles of economy, efficiency and effectiveness.

Article 13

The general budget

1. The Head of the Agency shall provide the Steering Board, by 31 March each year, with an overall estimate of the draft general budget for the following year, with respect to the planning figures set down in the Financial Framework.

2. The Head of the Agency shall propose the draft general budget to the Steering Board by 30 June each year. The draft shall include:

(a) the appropriations deemed necessary:

(i) to cover the Agency's running, staffing and meeting costs;

(ii) for procuring external advice, notably operational analysis, essential for the Agency to discharge its tasks, and for specific research and technology activities for the common benefit of all participating Member States, notably technical case-studies and pre-feasibility studies;

(b) a forecast of the revenue needed to cover expenditure.

3. The Steering Board shall aim to ensure that the appropriations referred to in paragraph 2(a)(ii) represent a significant share of the total appropriations referred to in paragraph 2. These appropriations shall reflect actual needs and shall allow for an operational role for the Agency.

4. The draft general budget shall be accompanied by a detailed staff establishment plan and detailed justifications.

5. The Steering Board, acting by unanimity, may decide that the draft general budget shall, furthermore, cover a particular project or programme where this is clearly for the common benefit of all participating Member States.

6. The appropriations shall be classified in titles and chapters grouping expenditure by type or purpose, subdivided as necessary into articles.

7. Each title may include a chapter entitled 'provisional appropriations'. These appropriations shall be entered where there is uncertainty, based on serious grounds, about the amount of appropriations needed or the scope for implementing the appropriations entered.

8. Revenue shall consist of:

(a) contributions payable by the Member States participating in the Agency based on the gross national income (GNI) scale;

(b) other revenue.

The draft general budget shall carry lines to accommodate earmarked revenue and, wherever possible, shall indicate the amount foreseen.

9. The Steering Board shall adopt the draft general budget by 31 December of each year within the Agency's Financial Framework. When doing so, the Steering Board shall be chaired by the Head of the Agency, or by a representative appointed by the Head of the Agency, or by a member of the Steering Board invited to do so by the Head of the Agency. The Chief Executive shall declare that the budget has been adopted and shall notify the participating Member States.

10. If, at the beginning of a financial year, the draft general budget has not been adopted, a sum equivalent to not more than one twelfth of the budget appropriations for the preceding financial year may be spent each month in respect of any chapter or other subdivision of the budget. This arrangement shall not, however, have the effect of placing at the disposal of the Agency appropriations in excess of one twelfth of those provided for in the draft general budget in course of preparation. The Steering Board, acting by qualified majority on a proposal from the Chief Executive, may authorise expenditure in excess of one twelfth, provided that the overall budget appropriations for that financial year do not exceed those of the previous financial year. The Chief Executive may call for the contributions necessary to cover the appropriations authorised under this provision, which shall be payable within 30 days from dispatch of the call for contributions.

Article 14

Amending budgets
1. In the case of unavoidable, exceptional or unforeseen circumstances, the Chief Executive may propose a draft amending budget, within the limits set out in the Financial Framework.
2. The draft amending budget shall be drawn up, proposed, and adopted and notification given in accordance with the same procedure as the general budget, within the limits set out in the Financial Framework. The Steering Board shall act with due account to the urgency.
3. In the situation where the limits set down in the Financial Framework would be considered insufficient due to exceptional and unforeseen circumstances, taking also in full account rules set out in Article 13(2) and (3), the Steering Board will submit the amending budget for adoption by the Council, acting by unanimity.

Article 15

Earmarked revenue
1. The Agency may receive in its general budget as earmarked revenue for a specific purpose financial contributions to cover costs other than those referred to under Article 13(2)(a)(i):
(a) from the general budget of the European Union on a case-by-case basis, in full respect of the rules, procedures and decision-making processes applicable to it;
(b) from Member States, third countries or other third parties.
2. Earmarked revenue may only be used for the specific purpose to which it is assigned.

Article 16

Contributions and reimbursements
1. Determination of contributions where the GNI scale is applicable:
(a) Where the GNI scale is applicable, the breakdown of contributions between the Member States from which a contribution is required shall be determined in accordance with the gross national product scale as specified in Article 41(2) TEU and in

accordance with Council Decision 2007/436/EC, Euratom of 7 June 2007 on the system of the European Communities' own resources, or any other Council Decision which may replace it.

(b) The data for the calculation of each contribution shall be those set out in the 'GNI own resources' column in the 'Summary of financing of the general budget by type of own resource and by Member State' table appended to the latest budget of the European Union. The contribution of each Member State from which a contribution is due shall be proportional to the share of that Member State's GNI in the total GNI aggregate of the Member States from which a contribution is due.

2. Schedule for payment of contributions:

(a) The contributions intended to finance the Agency's general budget shall be paid by the participating Member States in three equal instalments, by 15 February, 15 June and 15 October of the financial year concerned.

(b) When an amending budget is adopted, the necessary contributions shall be paid by the Member States concerned within 60 days of dispatch of the call for contributions.

(c) Each Member State shall pay the bank charges relating to the payment of its own contributions.

(d) If the annual budget is not approved by the end of November, the Agency may issue upon request of a Member State an individual provisional call for contributions from that Member State.

Article 17

Management by the Agency of expenditure on behalf of Member States

1. The Steering Board, on a proposal from the Chief Executive or a Member State, may decide that the Agency may be entrusted by Member States with the administrative and financial management of certain activities within its remit.

2. The Steering Board, in its decision, may authorise the Agency to enter into contracts on behalf of certain Member States. It may authorise the Agency to collect the necessary funds from these Member States in advance to honour the contracts entered into.

Article 18

Implementation of the budget

1. The financial provisions applicable to the Agency's general budget have been adopted by the Council, by unanimity. The Steering Board, acting by unanimity, shall review and amend these provisions, as necessary.

2. The Steering Board, acting on a proposal from the Chief Executive, shall as necessary adopt the implementing rules regarding the implementation and control of the general budget, notably as regards public procurement, without prejudice to relevant EU rules. The Steering Board shall ensure, in particular, that security of supply and protection both of defence secret and intellectual property rights requirements are duly taken into account.

3. The financial provisions and rules referred to in this Article are not applicable to ad hoc projects and programmes as referred to in Articles 19 and 20.

CHAPTER IV

AD HOC PROJECTS OR PROGRAMMES AND ASSOCIATED BUDGETS

Article 19

Approval of Category A (opt out) ad hoc projects or programmes and ad hoc budgets associated thereto

1. One or more participating Member States or the Chief Executive may submit to the Steering Board an ad hoc project or programme within the Agency's remit, which shall presume general participation by the participating Member States. The Steering Board shall be informed of the ad hoc budget, if any, to be associated with the proposed project or programme, as well as of potential contributions by third parties.

2. All participating Member States shall in principle contribute. They shall inform the Chief Executive of their intentions in this regard.

3. The Steering Board shall approve the establishment of the ad hoc project or programme.

4. The Steering Board, on a proposal from the Chief Executive or from a participating Member State, may decide to set up a committee to supervise the management and implementation of the ad hoc project or programme. The committee shall be composed of delegates from each of the contributing Member States and, when the Union contributes to the project or programme, a representative of the Commission. The decision of the Steering Board shall specify the committee's mandate and duration.

5. For the ad hoc project or programme, the contributing Member States, meeting within the Steering Board, shall approve:

(a) the rules governing the management of the project or programme;

(b) where appropriate, the ad hoc budget associated with the project or programme, the key for contributions and the necessary implementing rules;

(c) participation of third parties in the committee referred to in paragraph 4. Their participation shall be without prejudice to the Union's decision-making autonomy.

6. Where the Union contributes to an ad hoc project or programme, the Commission shall participate in the decisions referred to in paragraph 5, in full compliance with the decision-making procedures applicable to the general budget of the European Union.

Article 20

Approval of Category B (opt in) ad hoc projects, or programmes and ad hoc budgets associated thereto

1. One or more participating Member States may inform the Steering Board that they intend to establish an ad hoc project or programme within the Agency's remit, and where appropriate the ad hoc budget associated with it. The Steering Board shall be informed of the ad hoc budget, if any, to be associated with the proposed project or programme and details, if relevant, on human resources for such project or programme, as well as of potential contributions by third parties.

2. In the interest of maximising opportunities for cooperation, all participating Member States shall be informed of the ad hoc project or programme, including the basis upon which participation might be expanded, in a timely manner so that any participating Member State may express an interest in joining. Moreover, the initiator(s) of the project or programme will endeavour to make their membership as wide as possible. Participation will be established on a case-by-case basis by the initiators.

3. The ad hoc project or programme shall then be regarded as an Agency project or programme, unless the Steering Board decides otherwise within 1 month of receiving the information referred to in paragraph 1.

4. Any participating Member State which, at a later stage, wishes to participate in the ad hoc project or programme shall notify the contributing Member States of its intentions. The contributing Member States, within 2 months of receipt of that notification, shall decide among themselves, having due regard to the basis set out when participating Member States are informed of the project or programme, on the participation of the Member State concerned.

5. The contributing Member States shall take the decisions necessary for the establishment and implementation of the ad hoc project or programme and, where appropriate, the budget associated with it. Where the Union contributes to such a project or programme, the Commission shall participate in the decisions referred to in this paragraph in full compliance with the decision-making procedures applicable to the general budget of the European Union. The contributing Member States shall keep the Steering Board informed, as appropriate, of developments relating to such project or programme.

Article 21

Contributions from the general budget of the European Union to ad hoc budgets
Contributions from the general budget of the European Union may be made to the ad hoc budgets established for ad hoc projects or programmes referred to in Articles 19 and 20.

Article 22

Participation of third parties

1. Third parties may contribute to a particular ad hoc project or programme, established in accordance with Articles 19 or 20, and to the budget associated with it. The Steering Board shall, acting by qualified majority, approve as necessary the ad hoc arrangements between the Agency and third parties for each particular project or programme.

2. For projects established under Article 19, the contributing Member States meeting within the Steering Board shall approve all necessary modalities with the relevant third parties relating to their contribution.

3. For projects established under Article 20, the contributing Member States shall decide all necessary arrangements with the relevant third parties relating to their contribution.

4. Where the Union contributes to an ad hoc project or programme, the Commission shall participate in the decisions referred to in paragraphs 2 and 3.

CHAPTER V
RELATIONS WITH THE COMMISSION
Article 23

Association with the Agency's work

1. The Commission is a member of the Steering Board without voting rights and shall be fully associated with the work of the Agency.

2. The Commission may also participate in projects and programmes of the Agency.

3. The Agency shall establish the necessary administrative arrangements and working relations with the Commission, in particular with a view to exchanging expertise and

advice in those areas where the activities of the Union have a bearing on the Agency's mission and where the activities of the Agency are relevant to those of the Union.

4. Necessary arrangements to cover a contribution, on a case-by-case basis, from the general budget of the European Union under Articles 15 and 21, shall be established between the Agency and the Commission by mutual agreement, or between the contributing Member States and the Commission by mutual agreement.

CHAPTER VI
RELATIONS WITH THIRD COUNTRIES, ORGANISATIONS AND ENTITIES

Article 24

Administrative arrangements and other matters

1. For the purpose of fulfilling its mission, the Agency may enter into administrative arrangements with third countries, organisations and entities. Such arrangements shall notably cover:

(a) the principle of a relationship between the Agency and the third party;

(b) provisions for consultation on subjects related to the Agency's work;

(c) security matters.

In so doing, the Agency shall respect the single institutional framework and the decision-making autonomy of the EU. Each such arrangement shall be concluded by the Steering Board upon approval by the Council acting by unanimity.

2. The Agency shall develop close working relations with the relevant elements of OCCAR and with those established under the LoI Framework Agreement, with a view to incorporating those elements or assimilating their principles and practices in due course, as appropriate and by mutual agreement.

3. Reciprocal transparency and coherent developments in the field of capabilities shall be ensured by the application of CDM procedures. Other working relations between the Agency and relevant NATO bodies shall be defined through an administrative arrangement referred to in paragraph 1, in full compliance with the established framework of cooperation and consultation between the EU and NATO.

4. Within the framework of arrangements referred to in paragraph 1, the Agency shall be entitled to establish working relations with organisations and entities other than those referred to in paragraphs 2 and 3, with a view to facilitating their possible participation in projects and programmes.

5. Within the framework of arrangements referred to in paragraph 1, the Agency shall be entitled to establish working relations with third countries, with a view to facilitating their possible participation in specific projects and programmes.

6. The former non-EU members of the Western European Armaments Group shall be provided with the fullest possible transparency regarding the Agency's specific projects and programmes with a view to their participation therein as appropriate. A consultative committee shall be set up for this purpose, and in order to provide a forum for exchanging views and information on matters of common interest falling within the scope of the Agency's mission. It shall be chaired by the Chief Executive or his/her representative. It shall include a representative of each participating Member State and a representative of the Commission, and representatives of the former non-EU WEAG members in accordance with arrangements to be agreed with them.

7. Upon request, other non-EU European NATO members may also participate in the Consultative Committee referred to in paragraph 6, in accordance with arrangements to be agreed with them.

8. The Consultative Committee referred to in paragraph 6 may also serve as a forum for dialogue with other third parties on specific matters of mutual interest within the Agency's remit, and may serve to ensure that they are kept fully informed of developments in matters of common interest and of opportunities for future cooperation.

CHAPTER VII
MISCELLANEOUS PROVISIONS
Article 25

Privileges and immunities

Privileges and immunities of the Chief Executive and the Agency's staff are provided for in the Decision of the representatives of the Governments of the Member States, meeting within the Council, on the privileges and immunities granted to the European Defence Agency and to its staff members, dated 10 November 2004.

Privileges and immunities of the Agency are provided for in Protocol (No 7) on the privileges and immunities of the European Union, annexed to the Treaty on European Union and to the Treaty on the Functioning of the European Union.

Article 26

Review clause

No later than 14 July 2014, the Head of the Agency shall present a report to the Steering Board on the implementation of this Decision, with a view to its possible review by the Council.

Article 27

Legal liability

1. The contractual liability of the Agency shall be governed by the law applicable to the contract concerned.

2. The Court of Justice of the European Union shall have jurisdiction pursuant to any arbitration clause contained in a contract concluded by the Agency.

3. The personal liability of staff towards the Agency shall be governed by the relevant rules applying to the Agency.

Article 28

Access to documents

The rules laid down in Regulation (EC) No 1049/2001 of the European Parliament and of the Council of 30 May 2001 regarding access to European Parliament, Council and Commission documents shall apply to documents held by the Agency.

Article 29

Security

1. The Agency shall apply the Council's security regulations as adopted by Council Decision 2001/264/EC.

2. The Agency shall ensure appropriate security in its external communications.

Article 30

Language Regime
The language regime of the Agency shall be established by the Council, acting by unanimity.

Article 31

Repeal of Joint Action 2004/551/CFSP
This Decision repeals and replaces Joint Action 2004/551/CFSP on the establishment of the European Defence Agency.

Article 32

Entry into force
This Decision shall enter into force on the day of its publication in the Official Journal of the European Union.

> The Lisbon Treaty has maintained the provisions detailing the sources of funding for civilian and military operations (Article 41(1) and (2) TEU) whereas the Council has amended the mechanism administering the financing of the common costs of EU operations having military or defence implications (Athena) in December 2011.[15] However, Article 41(3) TEU now allows also for the establishment of a start-up fund by qualified majority voting in the Council, which will facilitate the financing of preparatory activities for EU operations in CFSP, and in particular CSDP (Article 41(3) second, third, and fourth subparagraphs TEU) not financed through the Union budget. The adoption of the Council decision establishing this start-up fund is still pending, allowing for speculation as to its relationship to the Athena mechanism.

Treaty on European Union

Article 41

(ex Article 28 TEU)

[...]

3.[...]Preparatory activities for the tasks referred to in Article 42(1) and Article 43 which are not charged to the Union budget shall be financed by a start-up fund made up of Member States' contributions.
The Council shall adopt by a qualified majority, on a proposal from the High Representative of the Union for Foreign Affairs and Security Policy, decisions establishing:
(a) the procedures for setting up and financing the start-up fund, in particular the amounts allocated to the fund;
(b) the procedures for administering the start-up fund;
(c) the financial control procedures.
When the task planned in accordance with Article 42(1) and Article 43 cannot be charged to the Union budget, the Council shall authorise the High Representative to

---

[15] Council Decision 2011/871/CFSP of 19 December 2011 establishing a mechanism to administer the financing of the common costs of European Union operations having military or defence implications (Athena), OJ L 343, 23.12.2011, pp. 35–53.

use the fund. The High Representative shall report to the Council on the implementation of this remit.

Select Bibliography

Cremona, M., Defining Competence in EU External Relations: Lessons from the Treaty Reform Process, *Law and Practice of EU External Relations: Salient Features of a Changing Landscape* (A. Dashwood and M. Maresceau (eds), Cambridge: Cambridge University Press, 2008), 34–69.

Dashwood, A., The Law and Practice of CFSP Joint Actions, *EU Foreign Relations Law Constitutional Fundamentals* (M. Cremona and B. de Witte (eds), Oxford: Hart Publishing, 2008), 53–77.

Koutrakos, P., *The EU Common Security and Defence Policy* (Oxford: Oxford University Press, 2013).

Thym, D., Die völkerrechtlichen Verträge der Europäischen Union, *66 Zeitschrift für ausländisches öffentliches Recht und Völkerrecht*, 2006, 864–925.

Van Elsuwege, P., EU External Action After the Collapse of the Pillar Structure: In Search of a New Balance Between Delimitation and Consistency, *Common Market Law Review*, vol. 47, 2010, 987–1019.

Wouters, J., Coppens, D., and De Meester, B., The European Union's External Relations after the Lisbon Treaty, *The Lisbon Treaty: EU Constitutionalism Without a Constitutional Treaty?* (S. Griller and J. Ziller (eds), Vienna: Springer, 2008), 143–203.

——, Bijlmakers, S., and Meuwissen, K., The EU as a Multilateral Security Actor after the Treaty of Lisbon: Constitutional and Institutional Aspects, *The EU and Multilateral Security Governance* (S. Lucarelli, L. Van Langenhove, and J. Wouters (eds), Routledge, 2012), 72–103.

12

The Status of International Law in the EU

12.1 International agreements concluded by the EU

12.1.1 General framework

Once international agreements have been concluded by the Union, or by the Union and the Member States jointly, the question may arise what their status is under Union law and whether, therefore, international agreements may be interpreted and/or applied by the courts. Since the Member States' courts are, as it were, the first judicial line in the Union that is bound to apply Union law, such questions arise very often before national courts.

The issue is whether they can refer questions for a preliminary ruling on international agreements (co-)concluded by the EU. If that is indeed the case, does the question of interpretation include the question of direct effect of provisions of international agreements of the Union, or even of international agreements as a whole? Moreover, since most of the international agreements concluded by the Union are mixed, the issue of the scope of the powers of interpretation of the Court of Justice of the European Union (CJEU) may also arise.

All these different questions and problems are explored in the following European Court cases.

Judgment of the Court of 30 April 1974, Haegeman v. Belgian State, Case 181/73, European Court Reports 1974, p. 449, paras. 1–6.

This is the first judgment in which the Court of Justice decided that an international agreement concluded by the Council is an act of the Union (then Community) and forms an integral part of Community law. It can therefore be interpreted by the Court in the framework of the preliminary ruling procedure of Article 177 TEC (now Article 267 TFEU).

1. By judgment dated 17 October 1973, registered at the Court of Justice on 7 November 1973, the Tribunal de Premiere Instance of Brussels, under Article 177 of the EEC Treaty, referred preliminary questions on the interpretation of article 9(3) of Regulation no 816/70 of the Council dated 28 April 1970 (OJ 1970, L 99) and of

certain provisions of the 'Agreement creating an association between the European Economic Community and Greece', concluded in virtue of the Council's decision dated 25 September 1961 and published in the Official Journal dated 18 February 1963 (p. 293/63), hereinafter called the Athens Agreement.

2. Under the first paragraph of Article 177 of the EEC Treaty 'the Court of Justice shall have jurisdiction to give preliminary rulings concerning [...] the interpretation of acts of the institutions of the Community'.

3. The Athens Agreement was concluded by the Council under Articles 228 and 238 of the Treaty as appears from the terms of the decision dated 25 September 1961.

4. This agreement is therefore, in so far as concerns the Community, an act of one of the institutions of the Community within the meaning of subparagraph (b) of the first paragraph of Article 177.

5. The provisions of the Agreement, from the coming into force thereof, form an integral part of Community law.

6. Within the framework of this law, the Court accordingly has jurisdiction to give preliminary rulings concerning the interpretation of this agreement.

Judgment of the Court of 26 October 1982, Hauptzollamt Mainz v. Kupferberg, Case 104/81, European Court Reports 1982, p. 3641, paras. 1–46.

This case concerned the interpretation of a provision of the EEC–Portugal Free Trade Agreement—a pure Community agreement—that prohibited tax discrimination of imported goods in near-identical terms to Article 95 TEC (now Article 110 TFEU). The case should be contrasted with Case 270/80, *Polydor*, ECR 1982, p. 329, in which the Court decided that, in spite of the fact that the prohibition of quantitative restrictions and measures of equivalent effect was formulated in the EEC–Portugal Free Trade Agreement in terms identical to Article 30 TEC, the exhaustion theory of intellectual property did not operate in a Free Trade Agreement as it did within the common market of the EC, since the context was different. The *Kupferberg* case, however, is primarily known for its systematic and clear analysis of the question of direct effect of international agreements concluded by the Community. The Court observed that the fact that international agreements concluded by the Union form an integral part of EU law has consequences both for the legal orders of the Member States and of the Union. The Member States are under a duty to ensure that agreements concluded by the Union are duly complied with in their municipal legal orders. Further, if the effect of the agreement in the respective legal orders of the parties is not determined in the agreement itself, it is up to the courts of each legal order to perform this exercise. However, an existing divergence between the treaty partners as to the recognition of the direct effect of the treaty or the fact that the treaty establishes a mechanism for consultations and negotiations *inter se* in relation to the implementation of the agreement, is neither here nor there for the recognition of such an effect in the EU legal order. Only after having gone through this analysis does the Court proceed to the question whether tax discrimination fulfils the same function in a Free Trade Agreement as it does in a Customs Union and comes to the conclusion that it does, thus freeing the way for an implicit condemnation of the German method of taxing port wine in the light of the tax discrimination provision of the Free Trade Agreement.

Subject of the case

On the interpretation of the first paragraph of Article 21 of the Agreement made on 22 July 1972 between the EEC and the Portuguese Republic (Official Journal, English special edition (31 December) l301, p. 166) and Article 95 of the EEC Treaty.

Grounds

1. By order of 24 March 1981, received at the Court on 29 April 1981, the Bundesfinanzhof (Federal Finance Court) referred to the Court for a preliminary ruling under Article 177 of the EEC Treaty a number of questions on the interpretation of Article 95 of the Treaty and the first paragraph of Article 21 of the Agreement between the European Economic Community and the Portuguese Republic which was signed at Brussels on 22 July 1972 and concluded and adopted on behalf of the Community by Regulation no 2844/72 of the Council of 19 December 1972 (Official Journal, English special edition 1972 (31 December), l301, p. 165).

2. The main proceedings are between a German importer and the Hauptzollamt (Principal Customs Office) Mainz on the question of the rate of the duty known as 'monopoly equalization duty' (monopolausgleich) which was applied on the release for free circulation, on 26 August 1976, of a consignment of port wines from Portugal.

3. Monopoly equalization duty is levied under paragraph 151 (1) of the Branntweinmonopolgesetz (law on the monopoly in spirits) on imported spirits and spirituous products.

4. According to paragraph 151 (3) (paragraph 151 (2) at the time when the goods in question were released for free circulation) liqueur wines with an alcohol content of more than 14% by volume are among the products which are to be considered as spirituous products. Paragraph 152, point 2, of that law provides that monopoly equalization duty is to be calculated in respect of such wines according to the quantity of alcohol in excess of the aforesaid amount.

5. The monopoly equalization duty corresponds to the spirits surcharge (Branntweinaufschlag) levied under paragraph 73 of the Branntweinmonopolgesetz on national spirits exempt from the obligation of delivery to the monopoly. Paragraph 79 (2) however, provides for a reduction of 21% in the surcharge on spirits produced in limited quantities by certain distilleries. They included, at the material time, fruit farm cooperative distilleries which only produced a maximum of three hectolitres per member from the fruit of their own harvest.

6. Pursuant to the aforesaid paragraphs 151 and 152 the Hauptzollamt Mainz levied on the importation in question the sum of dm 18 103.80 per hectolitre of wine-spirit. The importer brought an action against that decision before the Finanzgericht Rheinland-pfalz (Finance Court, Rhineland-Palatinate) which varied the decision

by reducing the monopoly equalization duty on the basis of paragraph 79 (2) of the Branntweinmonopolgesetz and the first paragraph of Article 21 of the Agreement between the Community and Portugal which reads as follows:

'The contracting parties shall refrain from any measure or practice of an internal fiscal nature establishing, whether directly or indirectly, discrimination between the products of one contracting party and like products originating in the territory of the other contracting party.'

In doing so the finanzgericht treated the imported port wines in the same way as it would have treated domestic liqueur wines if there had been added to the latter spirits from fruit farm cooperative distilleries produced within the aforesaid limits.

7. The Hauptzollamt Mainz appealed on a point of law to the Bundesfinanzhof which referred the following questions to the Court:

1. Is the first paragraph of Article 21 of the Agreement between the European Economic Community and the Portuguese Republic of 22 July 1972, adopted and published by Regulation (EEC) no 2844/72 of the Council of 19 December 1972, directly applicable law and does it give rights to individual common market citizens? If so, does it contain a prohibition of discrimination in like terms to the first paragraph of Article 95 of the EEC Treaty and does it also apply to the importation of port wines?

2. If question (1) is answered in the affirmative:

(a) Is there discrimination, within the meaning of the prohibition of discrimination contained in the first paragraph of Article 95 of the EEC Treaty or the first paragraph of Article 21 of the EEC–Portugal Agreement, if under national tax provisions it is possible purely as a matter of legal theory for similar domestic products to be treated more favourably (potential discrimination), or does discrimination within the meaning of those provisions exist only if in an actual tax comparison similar domestic products are in practice found to be treated more favourably from the point of view of tax?

(b) Does Article 95 of the EEC Treaty or the first paragraph of Article 21 of the EEC–Portugal Agreement require a product from another Member State or Portugal, which on importation is taxed at the same rate as a directly similar domestic product, to be taxed at the lower rate of taxation which national law imposes on another product which is equally to be regarded as similar, within the meaning of the first paragraph of Article 95 of the EEC Treaty, to the imported product?

First question

8. The first question has three parts the first of which relates to the direct applicability of the first paragraph of Article 21 of the Agreement. In the event of an answer in the affirmative the second part raises the question whether the provision is analogous in scope to the first paragraph of Article 95 of the EEC Treaty and in the third part of the question it is asked whether the provision also applies to the importation of port wines.

First part of the question

9. In the first place the Bundesfinanzhof wishes to know whether the German importer may rely on the said Article 21 before the German court in the proceedings which it has brought against the decision of the tax authority.

10. In the observations which they have submitted to the Court, the governments of the kingdom of Denmark, the Federal Republic of Germany, the French Republic and the United Kingdom have laid the most stress on the question whether a provision which is part of one of the free-trade agreements made by the Community with the member countries of the European Free Trade Association is in principle capable of having direct effect in the Member States of the Community.

11. The Treaty establishing the Community has conferred upon the institutions the power not only of adopting measures applicable in the Community but also of making agreements with non-member countries and international organizations in accordance with the provisions of the Treaty. According to Article 228(2) these agreements are binding on the institutions of the Community and on Member States. Consequently, it is incumbent upon the Community institutions, as well as upon the Member States, to ensure compliance with the obligations arising from such agreements.

12. The measures needed to implement the provisions of an agreement concluded by the Community are to be adopted, according to the state of Community law for the time being in the areas affected by the provisions of the agreement, either by the Community institutions or by the Member States. That is particularly true of agreements such as those concerning free trade where the obligations entered into extend to many areas of a very diverse nature.

13. In ensuring respect for commitments arising from an agreement concluded by the Community institutions the Member States fulfil an obligation not only in relation to the non-member country concerned but also and above all in relation to the Community which has assumed responsibility for the due performance of the agreement. That is why the provisions of such an agreement, as the Court has already stated in its judgment of 30 April 1974 in case 181/73 Haegeman (1974) ECR 449, form an integral part of the Community legal system.

14. It follows from the Community nature of such provisions that their effect in the Community may not be allowed to vary according to whether their application is in practice the responsibility of the Community institutions or of the Member States and, in the latter case, according to the effects in the internal legal order of each Member State which the law of that state assigns to international agreements concluded by it. Therefore it is for the Court, within the framework of its jurisdiction in interpreting the provisions of agreements, to ensure their uniform application throughout the Community.

15. The governments which have submitted observations to the Court do not deny the Community nature of the provisions of agreements concluded by the Community. They contend, however, that the generally recognized criteria for determining the effects of provisions of a purely Community origin may not be applied to provisions of a free-trade agreement concluded by the Community with a non-member country.

16. In that respect the governments base their arguments in particular on the distribu-
    tion of powers in regard to the external relations of the Community, the principal
    of reciprocity governing the application of free-trade agreements, the institutional
    framework established by such agreements in order to settle differences between
    the contracting parties and safeguard clauses allowing the parties to derogate from
    the agreements.

17. It is true that the effects within the Community of provisions of an agreement con-
    cluded by the Community with a non-member country may not be determined
    without taking account of the international origin of the provisions in question. In
    conformity with the principles of public international law Community institutions
    which have power to negotiate and conclude an agreement with a non-member
    country are free to agree with that country what effect the provisions of the agree-
    ment are to have in the internal legal order of the contracting parties. Only if that
    question has not been settled by the agreement does it fall for decision by the
    courts having jurisdiction in the matter, and in particular by the Court of Justice
    within the framework of its jurisdiction under the Treaty, in the same manner as
    any question of interpretation relating to the application of the Agreement in the
    Community.

18. According to the general rules of international law there must be bona fide per-
    formance of every agreement. Although each contracting party is responsible for
    executing fully the commitments which it has undertaken it is nevertheless free
    to determine the legal means appropriate for attaining that end in its legal system
    unless the agreement, interpreted in the light of its subject-matter and purpose,
    itself specifies those means. Subject to that reservation the fact that the courts of
    one of the parties consider that certain of the stipulations in the agreement are
    of direct application whereas the courts of the other party do not recognize such
    direct application is not in itself such as to constitute a lack of reciprocity in the
    implementation of the Agreement.

19. As the governments have emphasized, the free-trade agreements provide for joint
    committees responsible for the administration of the agreements and for their
    proper implementation. To that end they may make recommendations and, in the
    cases expressly provided for by the agreement in question, take decisions.

20. The mere fact that the contracting parties have established a special institutional
    framework for consultations and negotiations inter se in relation to the implemen-
    tation of the Agreement is not in itself sufficient to exclude all judicial application
    of that agreement. The fact that a court of one of the parties applies to a specific
    case before it a provision of the Agreement involving an unconditional and precise
    obligation and therefore not requiring any prior intervention on the part of the
    Joint Committee does not adversely affect the powers that the Agreement confers
    on that committee.

21. As regards the safeguard clauses which enable the parties to derogate from certain
    provisions of the agreement it should be observed that they apply only in specific
    circumstances and as a general rule after consideration within the Joint Committee
    in the presence of both parties. Apart from specific situations which may involve
    their application, the existence of such clauses, which, moreover, do not affect the

provisions prohibiting tax discrimination, is not sufficient in itself to affect the direct applicability which may attach to certain stipulations in the Agreement.

22. It follows from all the foregoing considerations that neither the nature nor the structure of the agreement concluded with Portugal may prevent a trader from relying on the provisions of the said agreement before a court in the Community.

23. Nevertheless the question whether such a stipulation is unconditional and sufficiently precise to have direct effect must be considered in the context of the agreement of which it forms part. In order to reply to the question on the direct effect of the first paragraph of Article 21 of the Agreement between the Community and Portugal it is necessary to analyse the provision in the light of both the object and purpose of the Agreement and of its context.

24. The purpose of the Agreement is to create a system of free trade in which rules restricting commerce are eliminated in respect of virtually all trade in products originating in the territory of the parties, in particular by abolishing customs duties and charges having equivalent effect and eliminating quantitative restrictions and measures having equivalent effect.

25. Seen in that context the first paragraph of Article 21 of the Agreement seeks to prevent the liberalization of the trade in goods through the abolition of customs duties and charges having equivalent effect and quantitative restrictions and measures having equivalent effect from being rendered nugatory by fiscal practices of the contracting parties. That would be so if the product imported of one party were taxed more heavily than the similar domestic products which it encounters on the market of the other party.

26. It appears from the foregoing that the first paragraph of Article 21 of the Agreement imposes on the contracting parties an unconditional rule against discrimination in matters of taxation, which is dependent only on a finding that the products affected by a particular system of taxation are of like nature, and the limits of which are the direct consequence of the purpose of the Agreement. As such this provision may be applied by a court and thus produce direct effects throughout the Community.

27. The first part of the first question should therefore be answered to the effect that the first paragraph of Article 21 of the Agreement between the Community and Portugal is directly applicable and capable of conferring upon individual traders rights which the courts must protect.

Second part of the question

28. In the event of an answer in the affirmative to the part of the question concerning the direct effect of the provision at issue the Bundesfinanzhof asks further whether that provision contains a prohibit of discrimination analogous to that laid down in the first paragraph of Article 95 of the EEC Treaty.

29. In that respect it must be observed that although Article 21 of the Agreement and Article 95 of the EEC Treaty have the same object inasmuch as they aim at the elimination of tax discrimination, both provisions, which are moreover worded differently, must however be considered and interpreted in their own context.

30. As the Court has already stated in its judgment of 9 February 1982 in case 270/80 Polydor ((1982) ECR 329), the EEC Treaty and the Agreement on Free Trade

pursue different objectives. It follows that the interpretations given to Article 95 of the Treaty cannot be applied by way of simple analogy to the Agreement on Free Trade.

31. The second part of the question must therefore be answered to the effect that the first paragraph of Article 21 must be interpreted according to its terms and in the light of the objective which it pursues in the system of free trade established by the Agreement.

Third part of the question

32. Finally the Bundesfinanzhof raises the question whether the rule against tax discrimination contained in article 21 of the Agreement also applies to the importation of port wines.

Article 2 of the agreement provides that it applies to products originating in the Community or in Portugal:

'(i) which fall within chapters 25 to 99 of the Brussels nomenclature, excluding the products listed in annex i;

(ii) which are specified in Protocols nos 2 and 8, with due regard to the arrangements provided for in those protocols.'

33. Port wines are mentioned in article 4 of Protocol no 8 relating to the rules applicable to certain agricultural products. Article 4 provides that duties on imports into the Community of the products listed therein and originating in Portugal are to be reduced in the proportions and within the limits of the tariff quota indicated for each of them.

34. It is apparent from those provisions that the Agreement applies to port wines subject to certain limitations regarding the abolition of customs duties. On the other hand the arrangements laid down in the Protocol in no way affect the prohibition of tax discrimination contained in the first paragraph of Article 21 of the Agreement.

35. The last part of the first question must therefore be answered to the effect that the first paragraph of Article 21 of the Agreement between the Community and Portugal also applies to the importation of port wines.

Second question

36. In this question the Bundesfinanzhof seeks to obtain the criteria for interpretation which it needs in order to be able to decide whether the tax treatment to which the national authorities have subjected imported port wines is contrary to the first paragraph of Article 21 of the Agreement between the Community and Portugal. In order to answer that question it is necessary to compare the provision as it has been interpreted above with the facts as they appear in the order making the reference.

37. Question 2 (a) essentially asks whether the first paragraph of Article 21 of the Agreement allows the Federal Republic of Germany to apply to spirits added to port wines the tax on spirits at the full rate or whether that provision requires the member state to apply the reduced rate of tax which paragraph 79 (2) of the Branntweinmonopolgesetz provided for alcohol produced by fruit farm cooperative distilleries within the limits of their rights to distil.

38. The particulars in the order making reference do not show whether or not the alcohol added to the imported port wines was produced in conditions comparable to those on which the reduction in the spirits surcharge granted to fruit farm cooperative distilleries depended. On the other hand it is apparent from those particulars that the fruit farm cooperative distilleries referred to by the national law do not produce alcohol suitable for adding to liqueur wines.

39. It thus appears that there was no domestic alcohol on the market of the Federal Republic of Germany suitable for adding to wine to produce a liqueur wine which was similar to port wine and which could have qualified for the tax reduction provided for fruit farm cooperative distilleries.

40. In those circumstances the fact that the said reduction is not applied to port wines is not such as to have an adverse effect upon the liberalization of trade between the Community and Portugal referred to in the Agreement. Having regard to the object of the Agreement, the purely theoretical hypothesis that had the same product been manufactured in the Federal Republic of Germany in special conditions it would have been entitled to the tax reduction is not sufficient to establish an obligation to grant that reduction to the imported product.

41. Question 2 (a) must therefore be answered to the effect that there is no discrimination within the meaning of the first paragraph of Article 21 of the Agreement between the Community and Portugal where a Member State does not apply to products originating in Portugal a tax reduction provided for certain classes of producers or kinds of products if there is no like product on the market of the member state concerned which has in fact benefited from such reduction.

42. Question 2 (b) asks whether the first paragraph of Article 21 of the Agreement between the Community and Portugal must be interpreted as requiring the concept of like products to cover not only products 'directly' similar but also other products which are to be considered as 'equally similar'.

43. It is apparent from the order making the reference that the Bundesfinanzhof has put that question on the assumption that port wines may resemble not only other liqueur wines but also wines of a special kind of a high alcohol content resulting from natural fermentation which, in the Federal Republic of Germany, are not subject to any tax.

44. In that respect it must be emphasized that for the purposes of its application in the community the concept of similarity contained in the first paragraph of Article 21 of the Agreement between the Community and Portugal is one of Community law which must be interpreted uniformly and it is for the Court to ensure that this is the case.

45. In view of the purpose of that provision as described above products which differ inter se both as regards the method of their manufacture and their characteristics may not be regarded as like products within the meaning of the said provision. It follows that liqueur wines fortified with spirits on the one hand and wines resulting from natural fermentation on the other may not be regarded as like products within the meaning of the provision at issue.

46. Question 2 (b) must therefore be answered to the effect that products which differ inter se both as regards the method of their manufacture and their characteristics

may not be regarded as like products within the meaning of the first paragraph of Article 21 of the Agreement.

[...]

Operative part

On those grounds,

the Court,

in answer to the question referred to it by the Bundesfinanzhof by order of 24 March 1981 hereby rules:

1. The first paragraph of Article 21 of the Agreement between the Community and Portugal is directly applicable and capable of conferring on individual traders rights which the Courts must protect.

2. It must be interpreted according to its wording and in the light of the objective which it has in the context of the system of free trade established by the Agreement.

3. The provision also applies to the importation of port wines.

4. It must be interpreted as follows:

    (a) There is no discrimination within the meaning of the first paragraph of Article 21 of the Agreement between the Community and Portugal where a Member State does not apply to products originating in Portugal a tax reduction provided for certain classes of producers or kinds of products if there is no like product on the market of the Member State concerned which has in fact benefited from such reduction.

    (b) Products which differ both as regards the method of their manufacture and their characteristics may not be regarded as like products.

Judgment of the Court of 30 September 1987, Meryem Demirel v. Stadt Schwäbisch Gmünd, Case 12/86, European Court Reports 1987, p. 3719, paras. 4–25.

This case takes the *Haegeman* reasoning one step further. The Court was asked to interpret an association agreement that had been concluded as a mixed agreement. That fact might have put in doubt the jurisdiction of the Court to interpret an international agreement in the framework of a preliminary ruling procedure, insofar as the provisions to be interpreted were to fall within the Member States' competence. After having addressed that question and rejected the arguments advanced by Germany and the UK against its jurisdiction, the Court also discusses the question of direct effect (oddly enough referred to here as direct applicability) again.

4. The Verwaltungsgericht Stuttgart, to which application was made for annulment of the order that Mrs Demirel leave the country, referred the following questions to The Court of Justice:

    (1) Do Article 12 of the Association Agreement between The European Economic Community and Turkey and Article 36 of the Additional Protocol thereto, in conjunction with Article 7 of the Association Agreement, already lay down a

prohibition that under Community law is directly applicable in the Member States on the introduction of further restrictions on freedom of movement applicable to Turkish workers lawfully residing in a Member State in the form of a modification of an existing administrative practice?

(2) Is the expression 'freedom of movement' in the Association Agreement to be understood as giving Turkish workers residing in a Member State the right to bring children under the age of majority and spouses to live with them?

5. Reference is made to the report for the hearing for a fuller account of the facts in the main proceedings, the provisions of German legislation, the Agreement and the Protocol thereto, the course of the procedure and the observations submitted under Article 20 of the Protocol on the Statute of the Court of Justice of the EEC, which are mentioned or discussed hereinafter only in so far as is necessary for the reasoning of the Court.

Jurisdiction of the Court

6. Since, in their written observations, the government of the Federal Republic of Germany and the United Kingdom call in question the jurisdiction of the Court to interpret the provisions of the Agreement and the Protocol regarding the freedom of movement for workers, it is appropriate to consider the issue of the Court's jurisdiction before ruling on the questions submitted by the national court.

7. It should first be pointed out that, as the Court held in its judgment of 30 April 1974 in case 181/73 Haegeman v Belgium ((1974)) ECR 449, an agreement concluded by the Council under Articles 228 and 238 of the Treaty is, as far as the Community is concerned, an act of one of the institutions of the Community within the meaning of Article 177(1)(b), and, as from its entry into force, the provisions of such an agreement form an integral part of the Community legal system; within the framework of that system the Court has jurisdiction to give preliminary rulings concerning the interpretation of such an agreement.

8. However, the German government and the United Kingdom take the view that, in the case of 'mixed' agreements such as the agreement and the protocol at issue here, the Court's interpretative jurisdiction does not extend to provisions whereby Member States have entered into commitments with regard to Turkey in the exercise of their own powers which is the case of the provisions on freedom of movement for workers.

9. In that connection it is sufficient to state that that is precisely not the case in this instance. Since the agreement in question is an association agreement creating special, privileged links with a non-member country which must, at least to a certain extent, take part in the Community system, Article 238 must necessarily empower the Community to guarantee commitments towards non-member countries in all the fields covered by the Treaty. Since freedom of movement for workers is, by virtue of Article 48 et seq. of the EEC Treaty, one of the fields covered by that treaty, it follows that commitments regarding freedom of movement fall within the powers conferred on the Community by Article 238. Thus the question whether the Court has jurisdiction to rule on the interpretation of a provision in a mixed agreement containing a commitment which only the Member States could enter into in the sphere of their own powers does not arise.

10. Furthermore, the jurisdiction of the Court cannot be called in question by virtue of the fact that in the field of freedom of movement for workers, as Community law now stands, it is for the Member States to lay down the rules which are necessary to give effect in their territory to the provisions of the Agreement or the decisions to be adopted by the Association Council.

11. As the Court held in its judgment of 26 October 1982 in case 104/81 Hauptzollamt Mainz v Kupferberg ((1982)) ECR 3641, in ensuring respect for commitments arising from an agreement concluded by the Community institutions the Member States fulfil, within the Community system, an obligation in relation to the Community, which has assumed responsibility for the due performance of the agreement.

12. Consequently, the Court does have jurisdiction to interpret the provisions on freedom of movement for workers contained in the Agreement and the Protocol.

The questions referred to the Court

13. The Verwaltungsgericht's first question seeks essentially to establish whether Article 12 of the Agreement and Article 36 of the Protocol, read in conjunction with Article 7 of the Agreement, constitute rules of Community law which are directly applicable in the internal legal order of the Member States.

14. A provision in an agreement concluded by the Community with non-member countries must be regarded as being directly applicable when, regard being had to its wording and the purpose and nature of the agreement itself, the provision contains a clear and precise obligation which is not subject, in its implementation or effects, to the adoption of any subsequent measure.

15. According to Articles 2 to 5 thereof, the Agreement provides for a preparatory stage to enable Turkey to strengthen its economy with aid from the Community, a transitional stage for the progressive establishment of a customs union and for the alignment of economic policies, and a final stage based on the customs union and entailing closer coordination of economic policies.

16. In structure and content, the Agreement is characterized by the fact that, in general, it sets out the aims of the association and lays down guidelines for the attainment of those aims without itself establishing the detailed rules for doing so. Only in respect of certain specific matters are detailed rules laid down by the protocols annexed to the Agreement, later replaced by the Additional Protocol.

17. In order to achieve the aims set out in the Agreement, Article 22 confers decision-making powers on the Council of Association which consists of members of the governments of the Member States and members of the Council and Commission, on the one hand, and members of the Turkish government, on the other.

18. Title II of the Agreement, which deals with the implementation of the transitional stage, includes two chapters on the customs union and agriculture, together with a third chapter containing other economic provisions, of which Article 12 on the freedom of movement for workers forms part.

19. Article 12 of the Agreement provides that the contracting parties agree to be guided by Articles 48, 49 and 50 of the Treaty establishing the Community for the purpose of progressively securing freedom of movement for workers between them.

20. Article 36 of the Protocol provides that freedom of movement shall be secured by progressive stages in accordance with the principles set out in Article 12 of the Agreement between the end of the 12th and the 22nd year after the entry into force of that agreement, and that the Council of Association is to decide on the rules necessary to that end.

21. Article 36 of the Protocol gives the Council of Association exclusive powers to lay down detailed rules for the progressive attainment of freedom of movement for workers in accordance with political and economic considerations arising in particular out of the progressive establishment of the customs union and the alignment of economic policies, pursuant to such arrangements as the Council of Association may deem necessary.

22. The only decision which the Council of Association adopted on the matter was Decision no 1/80 of 19 September 1980 which, with regard to Turkish workers who are already duly integrated in the labour force of a Member State, prohibits any further restrictions on the conditions governing access to employment. In the sphere of family reunification, on the other hand, no decision of that kind was adopted.

23. Examination of Article 12 of the Agreement and Article 36 of the Protocol therefore reveals that they essentially serve to set out a programme and are not sufficiently precise and unconditional to be capable of governing directly the movement of workers.

24. Accordingly, it is not possible to infer from Article 7 of the Agreement a prohibition on the introduction of further restrictions on family reunification. Article 7, which forms part of Title I of the Agreement dealing with the principles of the association, provides in very general terms that the contracting parties are to take all appropriate measures, whether general or particular, to ensure fulfilment of the obligations arising from the Agreement and that they are to refrain from any measures liable to jeopardize the attainment of the objectives of the Agreement. That provision does no more than impose on the contracting parties a general obligation to cooperate in order to achieve the aims of the Agreement and it cannot directly confer on individuals rights which are not already vested in them by other provisions of the Agreement.

25. Consequently, the answer to be given to the first question is that Article 12 of the Agreement and Article 36 of the Protocol, read in conjunction with Article 7 of the Agreement, do not constitute rules of Community law which are directly applicable in the internal legal order of the Member States.

Judgment of the Court of 9 October 2001, Netherlands v. Parliament and Council, Case C-377/98, European Court Reports 2001, p. I-7079, paras. 50–68.

This is an action for annulment by the Netherlands against the Directive on the legal protection of biotechnological inventions. There were numerous pleas for annulment advanced by the Netherlands, but the fourth one is of special interest.

It argued that the directive breached a number of treaty obligations, if not of the Community, then in any case of the Netherlands. This claim is ultimately rejected by the Court, but the interest of the case resides primarily in how this is done and how the Court deals with the question of direct effect. Here, the CJEU appeared to dissociate direct effect from the possibility for the Court to oversee compliance by the Union with international agreements that are binding upon it.[1] The case can be read in conjunction with *Germany v Council (bananas)*, Case C-280/93, European Court Reports 1994, p. I-04973.

The fourth plea

50. The applicant submits that the obligations created by the Directive for Member States are incompatible with those resulting from their international undertakings, even though, according to Article 1(2) of the Directive, it does not affect obligations under international agreements. In particular, the Directive breaches the Agreement on Trade-Related Aspects of Intellectual Property Rights (hereinafter 'TRIPs'), as set out in Annex 1 C to the Agreement establishing the World Trade Organisation (hereinafter 'the WTO Agreement'), approved on behalf of the European Community, as regards matters within its competence, by Council Decision 94/800/EC of 22 December 1994 (OJ 1994 L 336, p. 1), the Agreement on Technical Barriers to Trade (hereinafter 'the TBT Agreement'), the EPC and the Convention on Biological Diversity signed on 5 June 1992 in Rio de Janeiro (hereinafter 'the CBD'), approved by the European Community by Council Decision 93/626/EEC of 25 October 1993 (OJ 1993 L 309, p. 1).

51. As their main argument, the Parliament and Council submit that the EPC does not create obligations for the Community, which is not a party to it. As regards the other three international legal instruments cited, the Council submits that the legality of a Community instrument can be called in question on grounds of breach of international agreements to which the Community is a party only if the provisions of those agreements have direct effect. That is not so in the present case.

52. It is common ground that, as a rule, the lawfulness of a Community instrument does not depend on its conformity with an international agreement to which the Community is not a party, such as the EPC. Nor can its lawfulness be assessed in the light of instruments of international law which, like the WTO agreement and the TRIPS and TBT agreements which are part of it, are not in principle, having regard to their nature and structure, among the rules in the light of which the Court is to review the lawfulness of measures adopted by the Community institutions (Case C-149/96 *Portugal* v *Council* [1999] ECR I-8395, paragraph 47).

53. However, such an exclusion cannot be applied to the CBD, which, unlike the WTO agreement, is not strictly based on reciprocal and mutually advantageous arrangements (see *Portugal* v *Council*, cited above, paragraphs 42 to 46).

---

[1] In *IATA and ELFAA*, the ECJ arguably went even further, by limiting its analysis to a simple confirmation. Case C-344/04, *IATA and ELFAA* [2006] ECR I-403, para. 39.

54. Even if, as the Council maintains, the CBD contains provisions which do not have direct effect, in the sense that they do not create rights which individuals can rely on directly before the courts, that fact does not preclude review by the courts of compliance with the obligations incumbent on the Community as a party to that agreement (Case C-162/96 *Racke* [1998] ECR I-3655, paragraphs 45, 47 and 51).

55. Moreover, and in any event, this plea should be understood as being directed, not so much at a direct breach by the Community of its international obligations, as at an obligation imposed on the Member States by the Directive to breach their own obligations under international law, while the Directive itself claims not to affect those obligations.

56. For that reason at least, the plea is admissible.

57. The applicant argues essentially, first, that Article 27(3)(b) of the TRIPS Agreement allows Member States not to grant a patent for plants and animals other than micro-organisms, whereas the Directive does not allow Member States that possibility.

58. In that regard, suffice it to note that, while the Directive does deprive the Member States of the choice which the TRIPS Agreement offers the parties to that agreement as regards the patentability of plants and animals, the option taken in Article 4 of the Directive is in itself compatible with the Agreement, which, moreover, does not prevent certain party States adopting a common position with a view to its application. The joint selection of an option offered by an international instrument to which the Member States are parties is an act that falls within the approximation of laws provided for by Article 100a of the Treaty.

59. Second, it is claimed that the Directive contains technical regulations within the meaning of the TBT Agreement which should have been notified to the secretariat of the World Trade Organisation.

60. It is, however, established that the Directive does not in any event contain any technical regulations within the meaning of the TBT Agreement, such a regulation being defined in Annex I to the WTO Agreement as a document which lays down product characteristics or their related processes and production methods. It is therefore not necessary to rule on the extent to which the legal protection of biotechnological inventions might fall within the scope of the TBT Agreement.

61. The applicant submits, thirdly, that Article 6(1) of the Directive, which rules out the patentability of inventions 'whose commercial exploitation would be contrary to *ordre public* or morality', is incompatible with Article 53 of the EPC, which excludes from patentability 'inventions the publication or exploitation of which would be contrary to *ordre public* or morality'. The difference in the terms used, it is argued, has an effect contrary to Article 1(2) of the Directive on the obligations which the EPC imposes on the Member States.

62. However, the applicant in no way indicates in what respect the slightly different wording used by the Directive on that point, inspired by the wording of Article 27(3) of the TRIPS Agreement, requires Member States to breach their obligations under the EPC in order to comply with their obligations under the Directive. In the absence of specific examples to the contrary, it seems reasonable to suppose that a breach of *ordre public* and morality as regards a specific invention could be

equally well established by reference to its publication, exploitation or commercial exploitation.

63. Fourthly and finally, the applicant and, to a greater extent, the Norwegian Government intervening in its support submit that the very purpose of the Directive, which is to make biotechnological inventions patentable in all the Member States, runs counter to the principle of equitable sharing of the benefits arising out of the utilisation of genetic resources, which is one of the objectives of the CBD.

64. However, the risks described by the applicant and that intervener are expressed in hypothetical terms and are not derived directly from the provisions of the Directive but, at the very most, from the use which might be made of them.

65. It cannot be assumed, in the absence of evidence, which is lacking in this case, that the mere protection of biotechnological inventions by patent would result, as is argued, in depriving developing countries of the ability to monitor their biological resources and to make use of their traditional knowledge, any more than it would result in promoting single-crop farming or in discouraging national and international efforts to preserve biodiversity.

66. Moreover, while Article 1 of the CBD states that its objective is the fair and equitable sharing of the benefits arising out of the utilisation of genetic resources, including by appropriate access to genetic resources and by appropriate transfer of relevant technologies, it specifies that this must be done taking into account all rights over those resources and technologies. There is no provision of the CBD which requires that the conditions for the grant of a patent for biotechnological inventions should include the consideration of the interests of the country from which the genetic resource originates or the existence of measures for transferring technology.

67. Finally, as regards the possibility that the Directive might represent an obstacle in the context of the international cooperation necessary to achieve the objectives of the CBD, it should be borne in mind that, under Article 1(2) of the Directive, the Member States are required to apply it in accordance with the obligations they have undertaken as regards *inter alia* biological diversity.

68. It follows from the foregoing that the fourth plea must be rejected.

Judgment of the Court (Grand Chamber) of 12 April 2005, Igor Simutenkov v. Ministerio de Educacion e Cultura, Case C-265/03, European Court Reports 2005, p. I-2579, paras. 1 and 15–41.

Mr Simutenkov was a Russian professional football player playing for Deportivo Tenerife in the Spanish second division. He was confronted with a national rule that limited the number of foreigners on any one team in the Spanish professional football league. He invoked a provision of non-discrimination for reasons of nationality contained in the EC-Russia Partnership Agreement of 1994. This case is of particular interest because it follows rather closely the scheme of analysis of the old *Kupferberg* case outlined above, in that the Court first discusses the question of direct effect of the non-discrimination clause in the EC–Russia Partnership Agreement and, only after having replied to that question in the affirmative, goes on to discuss the scope of that provision within the context of such a Partnership Agreement. In doing so, the Court refers to a large body of case law on both questions and thus achieves an almost pedagogical effect. It is also worth noting that the Court's affirmation of the clarity of the wording of Article 23(1) of the Partnership Agreement in paragraph 22 of the judgment appears to have been based on the English language version of the agreement. By contrast, the Spanish language version was markedly less clear.[2]

1. The reference for a preliminary ruling concerns the interpretation of Article 23(1) of the Agreement on partnership and cooperation establishing a partnership between the European Communities and their Member States, of one part, and the Russian Federation, of the other part, signed in Corfu on 24 June 1994 and approved on behalf of the Communities by Decision 97/800/ECSC, EC, Euratom: Council and Commission Decision of 30 October 1997 (OJ 1997 L 327, p. 1) ('the Communities–Russia Partnership Agreement').

[...]

The question referred for preliminary ruling

15. By its question the national court asks whether Article 23(1) of the Communities–Russia Partnership Agreement is to be construed as precluding the application to a professional sportsman of Russian nationality, who is lawfully employed by a club established in a Member State, of a rule drawn up by a sports federation of that State which provides that clubs may field in competitions at national level only a limited number of players from countries which are not parties to the EEA Agreement.

16. Mr Simutenkov and the Commission of the European Communities take the view that Article 23(1) of the Communities–Russia Partnership Agreement precludes a rule such as that laid down by the agreement of 28 May 1999.

17. The RFEF, by contrast, invokes in support of its position the words '[s]ubject to the laws, conditions and procedures applicable in each Member State', which feature at the beginning of Article 23(1). It infers from this proviso that the competence which legislation confers on it to issue licences to football players and the sports regulations which it has adopted must be applied in a manner which takes priority over the principle of non-discrimination laid down in that provision. It also submits that the issue of a licence and the rules relating thereto form part of the organisation of competitions and do not concern working conditions.

18. The Spanish Government adopts the views expressed by the RFEF and submits in particular that, under the national rules and the case-law which interprets them, a federation licence is not a working condition but rather an administrative permit which serves as an authorisation to take part in sporting competitions.

19. In order to provide a useful reply to the question posed, it is necessary, first of all, to examine whether Article 23(1) of the Communities–Russia Partnership

---

[2] On the question of how to interpret the different language versions, see the Opinion of Advocate General Stix-Hackl, points 14–27.

Agreement can be relied on by an individual before the courts of a Member State and, second, if the answer is affirmative, to determine the scope of the principle of non-discrimination which that provision lays down.

The direct effect of Article 23(1) of the Communities–Russia Partnership Agreement

20. It must be pointed out that, as this question concerning the effect of the provisions of the Communities–Russia Partnership Agreement within the legal systems of the parties to that Agreement ('the parties') has not been resolved therein, it is for the Court to resolve that question in the same way as any other question of interpretation concerning the application of agreements within the Community (judgment in Case C-149/96 *Portugal* v *Council* [1999] ECR I-8395, paragraph 34).

21. In this regard, according to well-established case-law, a provision in an agreement concluded by the Communities with a non-member country must be regarded as being directly applicable when, regard being had to its wording and to the purpose and nature of the agreement, the provision contains a clear and precise obligation which is not subject, in its implementation or effects, to the adoption of any subsequent measure (judgments in Case C-63/99 *Gloszczuk* [2001] ECR I-6369, paragraph 30, and in Case C-171/01 *Wählergruppe Gemeinsam* [2003] ECR I-4301, paragraph 54).

22. It follows from the wording of Article 23(1) of the Communities–Russia Partnership Agreement that that provision lays down, in clear, precise and unconditional terms, a prohibition precluding any Member State from discriminating, on grounds of nationality, against Russian workers, vis-à-vis their own nationals, so far as their conditions of employment, remuneration and dismissal are concerned. Workers who are entitled to the benefit of that provision are those who hold Russian nationality and who are lawfully employed in the territory of a Member State.

23. Such a rule of equal treatment lays down a precise obligation as to results and, by its nature, can be relied on by an individual before a national court as a basis for requesting that court to disapply discriminatory provisions without any further implementing measures being required to that end (judgments in Case C-162/00 *Pokrzeptowicz-Meyer* [2002] ECR I-1049, paragraph 22, and in *Wählergruppe Gemeinsam*, cited above, paragraph 58).

24. That interpretation cannot be brought into question by the words '[s]ubject to the laws, conditions and procedures applicable in each Member State', which feature at the beginning of Article 23(1) of the Communities–Russia Partnership Agreement, or by Article 48 of that Agreement. Those provisions cannot be construed as allowing the Member States to subject application of the principle of non-discrimination set out in Article 23(1) of that agreement to discretionary limitations, which would have the effect of rendering that provision meaningless and thus depriving it of any practical effect (*Pokrzeptowicz-Meyer*, cited above, paragraphs 23 and 24, and Case C-438/00 *Deutscher Handballbund* [2003] ECR I-4135, paragraph 29).

25. Nor does Article 27 of the Communities–Russia Partnership Agreement preclude Article 23(1) thereof from having direct effect. The fact that Article 27 provides that Article 23 is to be implemented on the basis of recommendations by the Cooperation Council does not make the applicability of Article 23, in its implementation or

effects, subject to the adoption of any subsequent measure. The role which Article 27 confers on that council is to facilitate compliance with the prohibition of discrimination but cannot be regarded as limiting the immediate application of that prohibition (see, in that regard, Case C-18/90 *Kziber* [1991] ECR I-199, paragraph 19, and Case C-262/96 *Sürül* [1999] ECR I-2685, paragraph 66).

26. The finding that the principle of non-discrimination set out in Article 23(1) of the Communities–Russia Partnership Agreement is directly effective is not, moreover, gainsaid by its purpose and nature.

27. Article 1 states that the purpose of the Agreement is to establish a partnership between the parties with a view to promoting, inter alia, the development between them of close political relations, trade and harmonious economic relations, political and economic freedoms, and the achievement of gradual integration between the Russian Federation and a wider area of cooperation in Europe.

28. The fact that the Agreement is thus limited to establishing a partnership between the parties, without providing for an association or future accession of the Russian Federation to the Communities, is not such as to prevent certain of its provisions from having direct effect. It is clear from the Court's case-law that when an agreement establishes cooperation between the parties, some of the provisions of that agreement may, under the conditions set out in paragraph 21 of the present judgment, directly govern the legal position of individuals (*Kziber*, cited above, paragraph 21, Case C-113/97 *Babahenini* [1998] ECR I-183, paragraph 17, and Case C-162/96 *Racke* [1998] ECR I-3655, paragraphs 34 to 36).

29. In the light of all of the foregoing, it must be held that Article 23(1) of the Communities–Russia Partnership Agreement has direct effect, with the result that individuals to whom that provision applies are entitled to rely on it before the courts of the Member States.

The scope of the principle of non-discrimination set out in Article 23(1) of the Communities–Russia Partnership Agreement

30. The question which has been referred by the national court is similar to that referred to the Court in the case which led to the above judgment in *Deutscher Handballbund*. In that judgment the Court ruled that the first indent of Article 38(1) of the Europe Agreement establishing an association between the European Communities and their Member States, of the one part, and the Slovak Republic, of the other part, signed in Luxembourg on 4 October 1993 and approved on behalf of the Communities by Decision 94/909/ECSC, EEC, Euratom of the Council and the Commission of 19 December 1994 (OJ 1994 L 359, p. 1) ('the Communities–Slovakia Association Agreement') had to be construed as precluding the application to a professional sportsman of Slovak nationality, who was lawfully employed by a club established in a Member State, of a rule drawn up by a sports federation in that State under which clubs were authorised to field, during league or cup matches, only a limited number of players from non-member countries that are not parties to the EEA Agreement.

31. The first indent of Article 38(1) of the Communities–Slovakia Association Agreement was worded as follows:

'Subject to the conditions and modalities applicable in each Member State:
– treatment accorded to workers of Slovak Republic nationality legally employed
in the territory of a Member State shall be free from any discrimination based
on nationality, as regards working conditions, remuneration or dismissal, as compared to its own nationals'.

32. The Court ruled, inter alia, that a rule which limits the number of professional
players, nationals of the non-member country in question, who might be fielded in
national competitions did relate to working conditions within the meaning of the
first indent of Article 38(1) of the Communities–Slovakia Association Agreement
inasmuch as it directly affected participation in league and cup matches of a Slovak
professional player who was already lawfully employed in the host Member State
(*Deutscher Handballbund*, cited above, paragraphs 44 to 46).

33. The Court also ruled that the interpretation of Article 48(2) of the EC Treaty (now,
after amendment, Article 39(2) EC) which it handed down in its judgment in Case
C-415/93 *Bosman* [1995] ECR I-4921 to the effect that the prohibition of discrimination on grounds of nationality applies to rules laid down by sporting associations
which determine the conditions under which professional sportsmen can engage
in gainful employment and precludes a limitation, based on nationality, on the
number of players who may be fielded at the same time, could be transposed to the
first indent of Article 38(1) of the Communities–Slovakia Association Agreement
(*Deutscher Handballbund*, paragraphs 31 to 37 and 48 to 51).

34. The wording of Article 23(1) of the Communities–Russia Partnership Agreement is
very similar to that of the first indent of Article 38(1) of the Communities–Slovakia
Association Agreement. The only significant difference between the respective
wording of those two provisions is in the use of the terms 'the Community and
its Member States shall ensure that the treatment accorded to Russian nationals…shall be free from any discrimination based on nationality' and 'treatment
accorded to workers of Slovak Republic nationality…shall be free from any discrimination based on nationality'. In view of the finding in paragraphs 22 and 23
of this judgment that the wording of Article 23(1) of the Communities–Russia
Partnership Agreement lays down, in clear, precise and unconditional terms, a
prohibition of discrimination on grounds of nationality, the difference in drafting highlighted above is not a bar to the transposition, to Article 23(1) of the
Communities–Russia Partnership Agreement, of the interpretation upheld by the
Court in *Deutscher Handballbund*.

35. Admittedly, unlike the Communities–Slovakia Association Agreement, the
Communities–Russia Partnership Agreement is not intended to establish an association with a view to the gradual integration of that non-member country into the
European Communities but is designed rather to bring about 'the gradual integration between Russia and a wider area of cooperation in Europe'.

36. However, it does not in any way follow from the context or purpose of that
Partnership Agreement that it intended to give to the prohibition of 'discrimination based on nationality, as regards working conditions…as compared to [the
Member State's] own nationals' any meaning other than that which follows from
the ordinary sense of those words. Consequently, in a manner similar to the first

indent of Article 38(1) of the Communities–Slovakia Association Agreement, Article 23(1) of the Communities–Russia Partnership Agreement establishes, for the benefit of Russian workers lawfully employed in the territory of a Member State, a right to equal treatment in working conditions of the same scope as that which, in similar terms, nationals of Member States are recognised as having under the EC Treaty, which precludes any limitation based on nationality, such as that in issue in the main proceedings, as the Court established in similar circumstances in the above judgments in *Bosman* and *Deutscher Handballbund*.

37. Furthermore, in the judgments in *Bosman* and *Deutscher Handballbund*, the Court held that a rule such as that in issue in the main proceedings related to working conditions (*Deutscher Handballbund*, paragraphs 44 to 46). The fact that Article 23(1) of the Communities–Russia Partnership Agreement applies only in regard to working conditions, remuneration or dismissal, and thus does not extend to rules concerning access to employment, is accordingly irrelevant.

38. In addition, the limitation based on nationality does not relate to specific matches between teams representing their respective countries but applies to official matches between clubs and thus to the essence of the activity performed by professional players. As the Court has also ruled, such a limitation cannot be justified on sporting grounds (*Bosman*, paragraphs 128 to 137; *Deutscher Handballbund*, paragraphs 54 to 56).

39. Moreover, no other argument has been put forward in the observations submitted to the Court that is capable of providing objective justification for the difference in treatment between, on the one hand, professional players who are nationals of a Member State or of a State which is a party to the EEA Agreement and, on the other, professional players who are Russian nationals.

40. Finally, as has been stated in paragraph 24 of the present judgment, the words '[s]ubject to the laws, conditions and procedures applicable in each Member State', which feature at the beginning of Article 23(1) of the Communities–Russia Partnership Agreement, and Article 48 of that Agreement cannot be construed as allowing Member States to subject the application of the principle of non-discrimination set out in the former of those two provisions to discretionary limitations, inasmuch as such an interpretation would have the effect of rendering that provision meaningless and thus depriving it of any practical effect.

41. In the light of the foregoing, the answer to the question referred must be that Article 23(1) of the Communities–Russia Partnership Agreement is to be construed as precluding the application to a professional sportsman of Russian nationality, who is lawfully employed by a club established in a Member State, of a rule drawn up by a sports federation of that State which provides that clubs may field in competitions organised at national level only a limited number of players from countries which are not parties to the EEA Agreement.

[…]

On those grounds, the Court (Grand Chamber) rules:

Article 23(1) of the Agreement on partnership and cooperation establishing a partnership between the European Communities and their Member States, of one part, and the Russian Federation, of the other part, signed in Corfu on 24 June

1994 and approved on behalf of the Communities by Decision 97/800/ECSC, EC, Euratom: Council and Commission Decision of 30 October 1997, must be construed as precluding the application to a professional sportsman of Russian nationality, who is lawfully employed by a club established in a Member State, of a rule drawn up by a sports federation of that State which provides that clubs may field in competitions organised at national level only a limited number of players from countries which are not parties to the Agreement on the European Economic Area.

Judgment of the Court (First Chamber) of 19 February 2009, Mehmet Soysal and Ibrahim Savatli v. Bundesrepublik Deutschland, Case C-228/06, European Court Reports 2009, p. I-1031, para. 59.

The *Soysal and Savatli* case concerned proceedings brought by Soysal and Savatli, Turkish nationals, against Germany in respect of the requirement for Turkish lorry drivers to obtain visas in order to provide services consisting in the international transport of goods by road. The Court reiterated that international agreements to which the Union is a party may have an effect on EU law through a principle of interpretation in conformity with international agreements.

59. In this respect, it is sufficient to recall that the primacy of international agreements concluded by the Community over provisions of secondary Community legislation means that such provisions must, so far as is possible, be interpreted in a manner that is consistent with those agreements (see Case C-61/94 *Commission v Germany* [1996] ECR I-3989, paragraph 52).

Judgment of the Court (Grand Chamber) of 21 December 2011, Air Transport Association of America and Others v. Secretary of State for Energy and Climate Change, Case C-366/10, not yet reported (ATAA case), paras. 50–55.

Since *Intertanko*,[3] it would appear that the Court does not start its analysis from the assumption that international agreements have direct effect unless clear indications exist to the contrary. In the present case, the Air Transport Association of America (ATA), American Airlines (AA), Continental Airlines (Continental) and United Air Lines (UAL), all of whose headquarters are in the US, contested the measures transposing in the UK Directive 2008/101 of the European Parliament and of the Council of 19 November 2008. This Directive amended Directive 2003/87/EC so as to include aviation activities in the scheme for greenhouse gas emission allowance trading, the EU Emissions Trading Scheme (ETS), within the Union. They contended that, in adopting the directive, the EU infringed a number of principles of customary

---

[3] See Chapter 13.

international law and various international agreements. According to them, the directive infringes, first, the Chicago Convention, the Kyoto Protocol, and the Open Skies Agreement, in particular because it imposes a form of tax on fuel consumption, and second, certain principles of customary international law in that it seeks to apply the allowance trading scheme beyond the EU's territorial jurisdiction. The High Court of Justice of England and Wales (Queen's Bench Division, Administrative Court) asked the CJEU whether the directive is valid in the light of those rules of international law.

50. It should also be pointed out that, by virtue of Article 216(2) TFEU, where international agreements are concluded by the European Union they are binding upon its institutions and, consequently, they prevail over acts of the European Union (see, to this effect, Case C-61/94 *Commission v Germany* [1996] ECR I-3989, paragraph 52; Case C-311/04 *Algemene Scheeps Agentuur Dordrecht* [2006] ECR I-609, paragraph 25; Case C-308/06 *Intertanko and Others* [2008] ECR I-4057, paragraph 42; and Joined Cases C-402/05 P and C-415/05 P *Kadi and Al Barakaat International Foundation v Council and Commission* [2008] ECR I-6351, paragraph 307).

51. It follows that the validity of an act of the European Union may be affected by the fact that it is incompatible with such rules of international law. Where such invalidity is pleaded before a national court, the Court of Justice ascertains, as is requested of it by the referring court's first question, whether certain conditions are satisfied in the case before it, in order to determine whether, pursuant to Article 267 TFEU, the validity of the act of European Union law concerned may be assessed in the light of the rules of international law relied upon (see, to this effect, *Intertanko and Others*, paragraph 43).

52. First, the European Union must be bound by those rules (see Joined Cases 21/72 to 24/72 *International Fruit Company and Others* [1972] ECR 1219, paragraph 7, and *Intertanko and Others*, paragraph 44).

53. Second, the Court can examine the validity of an act of European Union law in the light of an international treaty only where the nature and the broad logic of the latter do not preclude this (see Joined Cases C-120/06 P and C-121/06 P *FIAMM and Others v Council and Commission* [2008] ECR I-6513, paragraph 110).

54. Finally, where the nature and the broad logic of the treaty in question permit the validity of the act of European Union law to be reviewed in the light of the provisions of that treaty, it is also necessary that the provisions of that treaty which are relied upon for the purpose of examining the validity of the act of European Union law appear, as regards their content, to be unconditional and sufficiently precise (see *IATA and ELFAA*, paragraph 39, and *Intertanko and Others*, paragraph 45).

55. Such a condition [is] fulfilled where the provision relied upon contains a clear and precise obligation which is not subject, in its implementation or effects, to the adoption of any subsequent measure (see Case 12/86 *Demirel* [1987] ECR 3719, paragraph 14; Case C-213/03 *Pêcheurs de l'étang de Berre* [2004] ECR I-7357,

paragraph 39; and Case C-240/09 *Lesoochranárske zoskupenie* [2011] ECR I-0000, paragraph 44 and the case-law cited).

Judgment of the Court (Third Chamber) of 15 July 2010, Alexander Hengartner and Rudolf Gasser v. Landesregierung Vorarlberg, Case C-70/09, European Court Reports 2010, p. I-7233, paras. 41–43.

Further, it must also be borne in mind that the fact that provisions of an international agreement to which the Union is a party resemble Treaty provisions is not sufficient to warrant a simple transposition of the interpretation provided by the Court of the relevant Treaty provisions to the provisions of the international agreement at issue.

41. Moreover, the Court has observed that the Swiss Confederation did not join the internal market of the Community, the aim of which is the removal of all obstacles to create an area of total freedom of movement analogous to that provided by a national market, which includes inter alia the freedom to provide services and the freedom of establishment (see Case C-351/08 *Grimme* [2009] ECR I-0000, paragraph 27).

42. The Court has also stated that, in those circumstances, the interpretation given to the provisions of European Union law concerning the internal market cannot be automatically applied by analogy to the interpretation of the Agreement, unless there are express provisions to that effect laid down by the Agreement itself (see Case C-541/08 *Fokus Invest* [2010] ECR I-0000, paragraph 28).

43. Having regard to the above considerations, the answer to the question is that the provisions of the Agreement do not preclude a national of one of the contracting parties from being subjected in the territory of the other contracting party, as a recipient of services, to different treatment from that reserved to persons whose principal residence is in that territory, citizens of the Union, and persons who are equated to those citizens under European Union law, with respect to the charging of a tax payable for the provision of services such as the making available of a right to hunt.

12.1.2 Mixed agreements

Many of the international agreements concluded by the Union are so-called mixed agreements, which are concluded by both the EU and the Member States together.[4] A mixed agreement is, as Advocate General Sharpston remarked, 'a creature of pragmatic forces—a means of resolving the problems posed by the need for international agreements in a multi-layered system'.[5] Nevertheless, such agreements also form an

---

[4] See Chapter 4.

[5] Opinion of Advocate General Sharpston in Case C-240/09 *Lesoochranárske zoskupenie* [2011] ECR I-1255, point 56.

integral part of Union law, and the Court of Justice has jurisdiction to determine which parts of the agreement fall within the scope of EU law. For that to be the case, the Court must establish whether the EU has exercised its powers and adopted provisions in the field covered by the provision of the international agreement it is asked to interpret.

Judgment of the Court (Grand Chamber) of 8 March 2011, Lesoochranárske zoskupenie VLK v. Ministerstvo životného prostredia Slovenskej republiky, Case C-240/09, European Court Reports 2011, p. I-1255, paras. 29–43.

This case concerned the interpretation of Article 9(3) of the Convention on access to information, public participation in decision-making and access to justice in environmental matters approved on behalf of the European Community by Council Decision 2005/370/EC of 17 February 2005 ('the Aarhus Convention'). The reference for a preliminary ruling was made in proceedings between Lesoochranáske zoskupenie VLK, an association established in accordance with Slovak law whose objective is the protection of the environment, and the Ministerstvo životného prostredia Slovenskej republiky (Ministry of the Environment of the Slovak Republic), concerning the association's request to be a 'party' to the administrative proceedings relating to the grant of derogations to the system of protection for species such as the brown bear, access to protected countryside areas, or the use of chemical substances in such areas.

29. A preliminary point to be made is that Article 300(7) EC provides that '[a]greements concluded under the conditions set out in this Article shall be binding on the institutions of the Community and on Member States'.

30. The Aarhus Convention was signed by the Community and subsequently approved by Decision 2005/370. Therefore, according to settled case-law, the provisions of that convention now form an integral part of the legal order of the European Union (see, by analogy, Case C-344/04 *IATA and ELFAA* [2006] ECR I-403, paragraph 36, and Case C-459/03 *Commission* v *Ireland* [2006] ECR I-4635, paragraph 82). Within the framework of that legal order the Court therefore has jurisdiction to give preliminary rulings concerning the interpretation of such an agreement (see, inter alia, Case 181/73 *Haegeman* [1974] ECR 449, paragraphs 4 to 6, and Case 12/86 *Demirel* [1987] ECR 3719, paragraph 7).

31. Since the Aarhus Convention was concluded by the Community and all the Member States on the basis of joint competence, it follows that where a case is brought before the Court in accordance with the provisions of the EC Treaty, in particular Article 234 EC thereof, the Court has jurisdiction to define the obligations which the Community has assumed and those which remain the sole responsibility of the Member States in order to interpret the Aarhus Convention (see, by analogy, Joined Cases C-300/98 and C-392/98 *Dior and Others* [2000] ECR I-11307, paragraph 33, and Case C-431/05 *Merck Genéricos—Produtos Farmacêuticos* [2007] ECR I-7001, paragraph 33).

32. Next, it must be determined whether, in the field covered by Article 9(3) of the Aarhus Convention, the European Union has exercised its powers and adopted provisions to implement the obligations which derive from it. If that were not the case, the obligations deriving from Article 9(3) of the Aarhus Convention would continue to be covered by the national law of the Member States. In those circumstances, it would be for the courts of those Member States to determine, on the basis of national law, whether individuals could rely directly on the rules of that international agreement relevant to that field or whether the courts must apply those rules of their own motion. In that case, EU law does not require or forbid the legal order of a Member State to accord to individuals the right to rely directly on a rule laid down in the Aarhus Convention or to oblige the courts to apply that rule of their own motion (see, by analogy, *Dior and Others*, paragraph 48 and *MerckGenéricos—Produtos Farmacêuticos*, paragraph 34).

33. However, if it were to be held that the European Union has exercised its powers and adopted provisions in the field covered by Article 9(3) of the Aarhus Convention, EU law would apply and it would be for the Court of Justice to determine whether the provision of the international agreement in question has direct effect.

34. Therefore, it is appropriate to examine whether, in the particular field into which Article 9(3) of the Aarhus Convention falls, the European Union has exercised its powers and adopted provisions to implement obligations deriving from it (see, by analogy, *MerckGenéricos—Produtos Farmacêuticos*, paragraph 39).

35. In that connection, it must be observed first of all, that, in the field of environmental protection, the European Union has explicit external competence pursuant to Article 175 EC, read in conjunction with Article 174(2) EC (see, *Commission v Ireland*, paragraphs 94 and 95).

36. Furthermore, the Court has held that a specific issue which has not yet been the subject of EU legislation is part of EU law, where that issue is regulated in agreements concluded by the European Union and the Member State and it concerns a field in large measure covered by it (see, by analogy, Case C-239/03 *Commission v France* [2004] ECR I-9325, paragraphs 29 to 31).

37. In the present case, the dispute in the main proceedings concerns whether an environmental protection association may be a 'party' to administrative proceedings concerning, in particular, the grant of derogations to the system of protection for species such as the brown bear. That species is mentioned in Annex IV(a) to the Habitats Directive, so that, under Article 12 thereof, it is subject to a system of strict protection from which derogations may be granted only under the conditions laid down in Article 16 of that directive.

38. It follows that the dispute in the main proceedings falls within the scope of EU law.

39. It is true that, in its declaration of competence made in accordance with Article 19(5) of the Aarhus Convention and annexed to Decision 2005/370, the Community stated, in particular, that 'the legal instruments in force do not cover fully the implementation of the obligations resulting from Article 9(3) of the Convention as they relate to administrative and judicial procedures to challenge acts and omissions by private persons and public authorities other than the institutions of the

European Community as covered by Article 2(2)(d) of the Convention, and that, consequently, its Member States are responsible for the performance of these obligations at the time of approval of the Convention by the European Community and will remain so unless and until the Community, in the exercise of its powers under the EC Treaty, adopts provisions of Community law covering the implementation of those obligations'.

40. However, it cannot be inferred that the dispute in the main proceedings does not fall within the scope of EU law because, as stated in paragraph 36 of this judgment, a specific issue which has not yet been subject to EU legislation may fall within the scope of EU law if it relates to a field covered in large measure by it.

41. In that connection, it is irrelevant that Regulation No 1367/2006, which is intended to implement the provisions of Article 9(3) of the Aarhus Convention, only concerns the institutions of the European Union and cannot be regarded as the adoption by the European Union of provisions implementing the obligations which derive from Article 9(3) of the Aarhus Convention with respect to national administrative or judicial proceedings.

42. Where a provision can apply both to situations falling within the scope of national law and to situations falling within the scope of EU law, it is clearly in the interest of the latter that, in order to forestall future differences of interpretation, that provision should be interpreted uniformly, whatever the circumstances in which it is to apply (see, in particular, Case C-130/95 *Giloy* [1997] ECR I-4291, paragraph 28, and Case C-53/96 *Hermès* [1998] ECR I-3603, paragraph 32).

43. It follows that the Court has jurisdiction to interpret the provisions of Article 9(3) of the Aarhus Convention and, in particular, to give a ruling on whether or not they have direct effect.

Judgment of the Court of 16 June 1998, Hermès International (a partnership limited by shares) v. FHT Marketing Choice BV, Case C-53/96, European Court Reports 1998, p. I-3603, para. 28.

In *Hermès*, the Court also emphasized that even with respect to provisions of the agreement falling within the Member States' competences, the latter are under a duty to interpret provisions of Member State law in conformity with the international agreement in question.

28. It is true that the measures envisaged by Article 99 and the relevant procedural rules are those provided for by the domestic law of the Member State concerned for the purposes of the national trade mark. However, since the Community is a party to the TRIPs Agreement and since that agreement applies to the Community trade mark, the courts referred to in Article 99 of Regulation No 40/94, when called upon to apply national rules with a view to ordering provisional measures for the protection of rights arising under a Community trade mark, are required to do so, as far as possible, in the light of the wording and purpose of Article 50 of the TRIPs

Agreement (see, by analogy, Case C-286/90 *Poulsen and Diva Navigation* [1992] ECR I-6019, paragraph 9, and Case C-61/94 *Commission v Germany* [1996] ECR I-3989, paragraph 52).

Judgment of the Court (Second Chamber) of 7 October 2004, Commission of the European Communities v. French Republic, Case C-239/03, European Court Reports 2004, p. I-9325 (Étang de Berre), paras. 1 and 13–31.

This case looks at the powers of the Court in respect of mixed agreements through the lens of an infringement procedure brought by the Commission against France. The Commission alleged that France had breached the obligations resulting from the Convention for the Protection of the Mediterranean Sea against Pollution and its Protocol by discharging large amounts of sweet water and alluvial deposits from the river Durance into the Étang de Berre. That Convention is a mixed agreement. While Community internal law does not as yet contain detailed rules on sea pollution from effluents from the land, the Court found that it had jurisdiction. It also found that the Convention and the Protocol created rights and obligations in a field covered 'in large measure' by Community law.

1. By its application, the Commission of the European Communities requests the Court to declare that:
   – by failing to take all appropriate measures to prevent, abate and combat heavy and prolonged pollution of the Étang de Berre, and
   – by failing to take due account of the requirements of Annex III to the Protocol for the protection of the Mediterranean Sea against pollution from land-based sources, signed at Athens on 17 May 1980 and approved on behalf of the European Economic Community by Council Decision 83/101/EEC of 28 February 1983 (OJ 1983 L 67, p. 1; 'the Protocol'), by amending the authorisation for the discharge of substances covered by Annex II to the Protocol following the conclusion of the latter,
   the French Republic has failed to fulfil its obligations under Articles 4(1) and 8 of the Convention for the protection of the Mediterranean Sea against pollution, signed at Barcelona on 16 February 1976 and approved on behalf of the European Economic Community by Council Decision 77/585/EEC of 25 July 1977 (OJ 1977 L 240, p. 1; 'the Convention'), under Article 6(1) and (3) of the Protocol and under Article 300(7) EC.

   [...]

13. The Étang de Berre is a saltwater marsh of 15 000 hectares which communicates directly with the Mediterranean Sea through the Caronte Canal. The volume of water in the Étang de Berre is 900 000 000 m³.

14. The Commission received a complaint concerning damage to the aquatic environment of the Étang de Berre, principally as a result of fresh water from the Durance being artificially discharged into the Étang de Berre whenever the turbines of the

hydroelectric power station at Saint-Chamas run by Electricité de France ('EDF') were in operation.

15. EDF developed and operates the Saint-Chamas fall under:

– Law No 55-6 of 5 January 1955 relating to development of the Durance (JORF of 6 January 1955 and corrigendum at JORF of 20 February 1955), Article 1 of which declared as being in the public interest the construction of works for regulating the flow of the Durance, for use of the waters in irrigation and for the production of electric energy, a diversion being established between the Durance's confluence with the Verdon and the Étang de Berre;

– the Decree of 28 September 1959 granting the EDF (national service) the right to develop and operate the Serre-Ponçon fall and reservoir, on the Durance, and falls to be established on the diversion of the Durance, between its confluence with the Verdon and the Étang de Berre (JORF of 7 October 1959);

– an agreement between EDF and the Minister for Infrastructure dated 19 August 1966, clause 9 of which provides:

'Electricité de France will take all appropriate measures to stop discharges into the marsh once the solids content exceeds 5 grams per litre, except where, in the event of an incident on the electricity network, that step proves exceptionally unacceptable';

– the Decree of 6 April 1972 approving the agreement and the special conditions for the Salon and Saint-Chamas falls, on the Durance (departments of Bouches-du-Rhône, Vaucluse and Gard) (JORF of 18 April 1972; 'the 1972 Decree'). Clause 17 of those conditions imposes the obligation to comply with the requirements of the agreement of 19 August 1966 that relate to discharges into the Étang de Berre;

– the operating instructions relating to the 'transfer into the Durance of waters from the diversion, in connection with the reduction of liquid and solid inputs into the Étang de Berre' ('the operating instructions'), approved on 22 April 1997 by the Regional Department for Industry, Research and the Environment.

16. Point 2 of the operating instructions sets the objectives for reducing water and alluvium inputs in the following terms:

'Water inputs

– limit on inputs per annum: 2 100 hm^3

– limit on inputs from 1 May to 30 September: 400 hm^3

Alluvium inputs

– limit on inputs per annum: 200 000 tonnes

– limit of 2 g/1 for suspended matter

Compliance with the quotas

In the event of difficulty in complying with these quotas, EDF must inform the Étang de Berre Recovery Taskforce which will decide on the action to be taken.'

17. According to the case-file, EDF's Durance facilities not only serve to generate electricity at a regional level but also contribute to the security of electricity generation by providing a maximum output capacity that is immediately available to deal with incidents on the network.

18. After taking the view that the French Republic had failed to take all appropriate measures to prevent, abate and combat heavy and prolonged pollution of the Étang

de Berre or had failed to take due account of the provisions of Annex III to the Protocol by amending the authorisation for the discharge of substances covered by Annex II to the Protocol and, as a consequence, had failed to fulfil its obligations under Articles 4(1) and 8 of the Convention, Article 6(1) and (3) of the Protocol and Article 300(7) EC, on 10 May 1999 the Commission served a letter of formal notice on the French Government in order to enable it to submit its observations.

19. Since the Commission was not persuaded by the arguments set out by the French Republic in its letter of 5 October 1999, the Commission sent it a reasoned opinion reiterating the terms of the letter of formal notice and calling on it to take the measures necessary in order to comply with the reasoned opinion within a period of two months from notification thereof.

20. By letter of 31 October 2000 the French Government submitted to the Commission a dossier in response to the reasoned opinion.

21. Since the Commission considered that the dossier did not enable it to abandon its complaints set out in the reasoned opinion, it brought the present action.

The Court's jurisdiction

22. The French Government submits that the Court lacks jurisdiction to adjudicate on the action on the ground that the obligations which the French authorities are alleged to have infringed do not fall within the scope of Community law. It states that no Community directive regulates discharges of fresh water and alluvia into a saltwater marsh, so that the provisions of the Convention and the Protocol that cover such discharges do not fall within Community competence.

23. Since Treaty infringement proceedings can relate only to a failure to comply with obligations arising from Community law, it must be examined, before deciding if there has been a substantive infringement, whether the obligations owed by France which are the subject-matter of the action fall within the scope of Community law.

24. The Convention and the Protocol were concluded by the Community and its Member States under shared competence.

25. In accordance with case-law, mixed agreements concluded by the Community, its Member States and non-member countries have the same status in the Community legal order as purely Community agreements in so far as the provisions fall within the scope of Community competence (see, to that effect, Case 12/86 *Demirel* [1987] ECR 3719, paragraph 9, and Case C-13/00 *Commission* v *Ireland* [2002] ECR I-2943, paragraph 14).

26. From this the Court has inferred that, in ensuring compliance with commitments arising from an agreement concluded by the Community institutions, the Member States fulfil, within the Community system, an obligation in relation to the Community, which has assumed responsibility for the due performance of the agreement (*Demirel*, cited above, paragraph 11, and *Commission* v *Ireland*, cited above, paragraph 15).

27. In the present case, the provisions of the Convention and the Protocol without doubt cover a field which falls in large measure within Community competence.

28. Environmental protection, which is the subject-matter of the Convention and the Protocol, is in very large measure regulated by Community legislation, including

with regard to the protection of waters against pollution (see, in particular, Council Directive 91/271/EEC of 21 May 1991 concerning urban waste-water treatment (OJ 1991 L 135, p. 40), Council Directive 91/676/EEC of 12 December 1991 concerning the protection of waters against pollution caused by nitrates from agricultural sources (OJ 1991 L 375, p. 1) and Directive 2000/60/EC of the European Parliament and of the Council of 23 October 2000 establishing a framework for Community action in the field of water policy (OJ 2000 L 327, p. 1)).

29. Since the Convention and the Protocol thus create rights and obligations in a field covered in large measure by Community legislation, there is a Community interest in compliance by both the Community and its Member States with the commitments entered into under those instruments.

30. The fact that discharges of fresh water and alluvia into the marine environment, which are at issue in the present action, have not yet been the subject of Community legislation is not capable of calling that finding into question.

31. It follows from the foregoing that the application of Articles 4(1) and 8 of the Convention and Article 6(1) and (3) of the Protocol to discharges of fresh water and alluvia into a saltwater marsh, those discharges not having been the subject of specific Community legislation, falls within the Community framework since those articles are in mixed agreements concluded by the Community and its Member States and concern a field in large measure covered by Community law. The Court therefore has jurisdiction to assess a Member State's compliance with those articles in proceedings brought before it under Article 226 EC.

[…]

Judgment of the Court (Grand Chamber) of 16 November 2004, Anheuser-Busch Inc. v. Budějovický Budvar, národní podnik, Case C-245/02, European court Reports 2004, p. I-10989, paras. 41–43.

In general, the Court tends to take a wide view of its jurisdiction over provisions of mixed agreements in that regard. An example of that approach is the *Anheuser-Busch* case, which concerned the interpretation of Articles 2(1), 16(1), and 70 of the Agreement on Trade-Related Aspects of Intellectual Property Rights ('the TRIPs Agreement'), as set out in Annex 1 C to the Agreement establishing the World Trade Organization ('the WTO Agreement'). The reference was made in the proceedings between the breweries Anheuser-Busch, Inc., established in Saint Louis, Missouri (US), and Budějovický Budvar, národní podnik, established in Česke Budějovice (Czech Republic), concerning the labelling used by Budvar to market its beer in Finland, which, according to Anheuser-Busch, infringes the trademarks Budweiser, Bud, Bud Light and Budweiser King of Beers owned by it in that Member State.

41. It is apparent from its case-law that the Court has jurisdiction to interpret a provision of the TRIPs Agreement for the purpose of responding to the needs of the judicial authorities of the Member States where they are called upon to apply their

national rules with a view to ordering measures for the protection of rights created by Community legislation which fall within the scope of that agreement (see, to that effect, *Dior*, cited above, paragraphs 35 and 40 and the case-law cited there).

42. Since the Community is a party to the TRIPs Agreement, it is indeed under an obligation to interpret its trade-mark legislation, as far as possible, in the light of the wording and purpose of that agreement (see, with respect to a situation falling within the scope of both a provision of the TRIPs Agreement and Directive 89/104, Case C-49/02 *Heidelberger Bauchemie* [2004] ECR I-0000, paragraph 20).

43. The Court therefore has jurisdiction to interpret Article 16(1) of the TRIPs Agreement, which is the subject of the second and third questions referred for a preliminary ruling.

Judgment of the Court (Sixth Chamber) of 15 May 2003, Doris Salzmann, Case C-300/01, European court Reports 2003, p. I-4899, paras. 65–71.

In *Salzmann*, the Court made clear that its jurisdiction does not extend to the application of a mixed agreement between the third states party to the agreement *inter se*. There, the *Landesgericht Feldkirch* (Regional Court, Feldkirch) referred for a preliminary ruling three questions on the interpretation of what was then Article 73b of the EC Treaty (at the time of judgment Article 56 EC and now Article 63 TFEU) and point 1(e) of Annex XII to the Agreement on the European Economic Area of 2 May 1992 (the EEA Agreement). Those questions were raised in the course of an appeal brought by Ms Salzmann against the refusal of registration in the land register of the contract of sale of an unbuilt plot of land at Fußach in the Land of Vorarlberg (Austria).

65. In that regard, it must be recalled that the Court has, in principle, jurisdiction under Article 234 EC to give a preliminary ruling on the interpretation of the EEA Agreement where such a question is raised before a court or tribunal of a Member State of the European Union (*Andersson and Wåkerås-Andersson*, paragraph 27).

66. However, that jurisdiction to interpret the EEA Agreement under Article 234 EC applies solely with regard to the Communities. The Court therefore has no jurisdiction to rule on the interpretation of that agreement as regards its application in the EFTA States (*Andersson and Wåkerås-Andersson*, paragraph 28).

67. Nor has such jurisdiction has been conferred on the Court of Justice in the context of the EEA Agreement. Under Article 108(2) of that Agreement and Article 34 of the Agreement between the EFTA States on the establishment of a Surveillance Authority and a Court of Justice (OJ 1994 L 344, p. 1), the EFTA Court has jurisdiction to rule on the interpretation of the EEA Agreement applicable in the States of EFTA. There is no provision in the EEA Agreement for parallel jurisdiction to be exercised by the Court of Justice (*Andersson and Wåkerås-Andersson*, paragraph 29).

68. The fact that the EFTA State in question subsequently became a Member State of the European Union, so that the question emanates from a court or tribunal of one of the Member States, cannot have the effect of conferring on the Court

of Justice jurisdiction to interpret the EEA Agreement as regards its application to situations which do not come within the Community legal order (*Andersson and Wåkerås-Andersson*, paragraph 30).

69. The jurisdiction of the Court of Justice covers the interpretation of Community law, of which the EEA Agreement forms an integral part, as regards its application in the new Member States with effect from the date of their accession (*Andersson and Wåkerås-Andersson*, paragraph 31).

70. In this case, the Court has been asked to interpret the concept of 'existing legislation' within the meaning of point 1(e) of Annex XII to the EEA Agreement, for the purposes, for the national court, of determining whether or not the VGVG adopted on 23 September 1993 is more restrictive than the VGVG 1977 and whether, in 1993, the EEA Agreement precluded that amendment of legislation. The Court would thus be led to rule on the effects of the EEA Agreement, within the national legal system of which the referring court forms part, during the period prior to the accession of the Republic of Austria to the European Union, that is to say, in a situation which does not come within the Community legal order.

71. Accordingly, the Court has no jurisdiction to answer the third question submitted.

12.1.3 The status of decisions of institutions set up by international agreements concluded by the EU

Judgment of the Court of 14 November 1989, Hellenic Republic v. Commission of the European Communities, Case 30/88, European Court Reports 1989, p. 3711, paras. 12–13.

International agreements to which the Union is a party quite often provide for certain institutions to be established. The Court of Justice has held that legally binding decisions taken by such bodies have in principle the same status as the international agreement itself. The Court did so first as regards decisions taken by the EEC–Turkey Association Council.

12. It must be pointed out first of all that as the Court has consistently held (see, most recently, the judgment of 30 September 1987 in Case 12/86 *Demirel* v *Stadt Schwaebish Gmuend* ((1987)) ECR 3719, paragraph 7), the provisions of an agreement concluded by the Council under Articles 228 and 238 of the Treaty form, as from the entry into force of the agreement, an integral part of the Community legal system.

13. For the attainment of the objectives laid down by the EEC–Turkey Association Agreement and in the circumstances provided for by that agreement, Article 22 thereof confers a power of decision on the Association Council. With regard to Decision No 2/80, the Court has already held in its judgment of 27 September 1988 in Case 204/86 *Hellenic Republic v Council* ((1988)) ECR 5323, paragraph 20 that, by providing for cooperation with regard to '... the implementation of the

aid…made available to Turkey', the Association Council placed that aid within the institutional framework of the Association. Since it is directly connected with the Association Agreement, Decision No 2/80 forms, from its entry into force, an integral part of the Community legal system.

Judgment of the Court of 20 September 1990, S.Z. Sevince v. Staatssecretaris van Justitie, Case C-192/89, European court Reports 1990, p. I-3461, paras. 7–15.

The *Sevince* case concerned three questions referred by the *Raad van State* (Netherlands Court of Last Instance in Administrative Matters) on the interpretation of certain provisions of Decisions Nos 2/76 of 20 December 1976 and 1/80 of 19 September 1980 of the EEC–Turkey Association Council. The questions were raised in proceedings brought by Mr S.Z. Sevince, a Turkish national, against the *Staatssecretaris van Justitie* (State Secretary of Justice) concerning the latter's refusal to grant him a permit allowing him to reside in the Netherlands. The Court of Justice held that the fact that decisions taken by the Association Council form an integral part of the EU legal order also means that it has jurisdiction to interpret them, and that such decisions are capable of having direct effect on the basis of the same conditions as the international agreement pursuant to which they are taken.

The first question

7. The national court's first question is essentially whether an interpretation of Decisions Nos 2/76 and 1/80 may be given under Article 177 of the of the EEC Treaty.

8. By way of a preliminary observation, it should be borne in mind that, as the Court has consistently held, the provisions of an agreement concluded by the Council under Articles 228 and 238 of the EEC Treaty form an integral part of the Community legal system as from the entry into force of that agreement (see judgments in Case 12/86 *Demirel* [1987] ECR 3719, paragraph 7 and in Case 30/88 *Greece* v *Commission* [1989] ECR 3711, paragraph 12).

9. The Court has also held that, since they are directly connected with the Agreement to which they give effect, the decisions of the Council of Association, in the same way as the Agreement itself, form an integral part, as from their entry into force, of the Community legal system (see judgment in Case 30/88 *Greece* v *Commission*, *supra*, paragraph 13).

10. Since the Court has jurisdiction to give preliminary rulings on the Agreement, in so far as it is an act adopted by one of the institutions of the Community (see judgment in Case 181/73 *Haegeman* [1974] ECR 449), it also has jurisdiction to give rulings on the interpretation of the decisions adopted by the authority established by the Agreement and entrusted with responsibility for its implementation.

11. That finding is reinforced by the fact that the function of Article 177 of the EEC Treaty is to ensure the uniform application throughout the Community of all provisions forming part of the Community legal system and to ensure that the interpretation thereof does not vary according to the interpretation accorded to them by the

various Member States (see judgments in Case 104/81 *Kupferberg* [1982] ECR 3641 and in Joined Cases 267 to 269/81 *SPI and SAMI* [1983] ECR 801).

12. It must therefore be stated in reply to the first question submitted by the Raad van State that the interpretation of Decisions Nos 2/76 and 1/80 falls within the scope of Article 177 of the EEC Treaty.

The second question

13. The second question submitted by the Raad van State is whether Articles 2(1)(b) and 7 of Decision No 2/76 and Articles 6(1) and 13 of Decision No 1/80 have direct effect in the territory of the Member States.

14. In order to be recognized as having direct effect, the provisions of a decision of the Council of Association must satisfy the same conditions as those applicable to the provisions of the Agreement itself.

15. In Demirel, *supra*, the Court held that a provision in an agreement concluded by the Community with non-member countries must be regarded as being directly applicable when, regard being had to its wording and the purpose and nature of the agreement itself, the provision contains a clear and precise obligation which is not subject, in its implementation or effects, to the adoption of any subsequent measure (paragraph 14). The same criteria apply in determining whether the provisions of a decision of the Council of Association can have direct effect.

Opinion of the Court of 14 December 1991, Draft agreement between the Community, on the one hand, and the countries of the European Free Trade Association, on the other, relating to the creation of the European Economic Area, Opinion 1/91, European Court Reports 1991, p. I-6079, paras. 37–40.

In Opinion 1/91, the Court confirmed that not only decisions of an Association Council become an integral part of the EU legal order, but in principle any decision taken by an institution set up through an international agreement concluded by the Union, including decisions taken by a court set up by such an international agreement. The contentious issue was, however, whether the system of courts set up by the EEA Agreement was compatible with Community law. The Court concluded that it was not (see also Chapter 2, p. 62).

37. As for the second point, it must be observed in limine that international agreements concluded by means of the procedure set out in Article 228 of the Treaty are binding on the institutions of the Community and its Member States and that, as the Court of Justice has consistently held, the provisions of such agreements and the measures adopted by institutions set up by such agreements become an integral part of the Community legal order when they enter into force.

38. In this connection, it must be pointed out that the agreement is an act of one of the institutions of the Community within the meaning of indent (b) of the first paragraph of Article 177 of the EEC Treaty and that therefore the Court has jurisdiction to give preliminary rulings on its interpretation. It also has jurisdiction to rule on the agreement in the event that Member States of the Community fail to fulfil their obligations under the agreement.

39. Where, however, an international agreement provides for its own system of courts, including a court with jurisdiction to settle disputes between the Contracting Parties to the agreement, and, as a result, to interpret its provisions, the decisions of that court will be binding on the Community institutions, including the Court of Justice. Those decisions will also be binding in the event that the Court of Justice is called upon to rule, by way of preliminary ruling or in a direct action, on the interpretation of the international agreement, in so far as that agreement is an integral part of the Community legal order.

40. An international agreement providing for such a system of courts is in principle compatible with Community law. The Community's competence in the field of international relations and its capacity to conclude international agreements necessarily entails the power to submit to the decisions of a court which is created or designated by such an agreement as regards the interpretation and application of its provisions.

12.2 The status of WTO law within the EU legal order

The Council of Ministers gave an indication of what it intended the status of the WTO within the EU legal order to be in the preamble to the decision concluding the WTO Agreement, included here. However, the question remains whether that settles once and for all the debate as to the effect of WTO law within the Union legal order? That is patently not the case. The content of recital 11 is nowhere reflected in the decision as enacted and the preamble to a Union act has no binding legal force.[6] Therefore, in the absence of an explicit determination by the parties, the effect of treaties within the Union legal order is for the Court of Justice to determine and not for an institution which forms part of one of the parties to the agreement, and even less in a non-binding recital to the internal act concluding the agreement. Recital 11 is therefore merely an indication as to the intention of one of the parties to the WTO Agreements and as such at most a supplementary means of interpretation within the sense of Article 32 of the Vienna Convention on the Law of Treaties. Advocate General Tesauro already argued in his Opinion in *Hermès* that as there is no provision agreed upon by all the contracting parties that excludes direct effect, the recital in question could not be held to be susceptible of preventing the Court from coming to a different conclusion.[7]

---

[6] See Case C-7/11 *Caronna*, not yet reported, para. 40 and the case law cited there.

[7] Opinion of Advocate General Tesauro in Case C-53/96 *Hermès International v FHT Marketing Choice BV* [1998] ECR I-3603, point 24. Bourgeois has argued that recital 11 reflects the view traditionally held by most governments of the Member States that trade policy, as part of foreign policy, is the preserve of governments and that interference by courts is to be avoided in order to pursue fully the possibilities of resolving disputes by negotiation. If EU courts enforce WTO law, the political institutions would have their hands tied behind their backs. However, Bourgeois argues that this argument has become less persuasive as the flexibility of the GATT gave way to a determination by the WTO DSB of who is legally right or wrong, with the only flexibility left being that with regard remedies: J.H.J. Bourgeois, The European Court of Justice and the WTO: Problems and Challenges, *The EU, the WTO and the NAFTA: Towards a Common Law of International Trade* (J.H.H. Weiler (ed.), Oxford: Oxford University Press, 2000), 114–15.

Council Decision 94/800/EC of 22 December 1994 concerning the conclusion on behalf of the European Community, as regards matters within its competence, of the agreements reached in the Uruguay Round multilateral negotiations (1986–1994), Official Journal L 336, 23.12.1994, pp. 1–2.

THE COUNCIL OF THE EUROPEAN UNION,

[…]

Whereas the multilateral trade negotiations opened under the GATT, pursuant to the Declaration by Ministers adopted at Punta del Este on 20 September 1986, have led to the Final Act embodying the results of the Uruguay Round of multilateral trade negotiations;

[…]

Whereas, by its nature, the Agreement establishing the World Trade Organization, including the Annexes thereto, is not susceptible to being directly invoked in Community or Member State courts,

[…]

Judgment of the Court of 12 December 1972, International Fruit Company NV and others v. Produktschap voor Groenten en Fruit, Joined Cases 21-24/72, European Court Reports 1972, p. 1219, paras. 19–28.

The *International Fruit* case concerned the compatibility of certain regulations of the Commission with Article XI of the General Agreement on Tariffs and Trade (GATT). There, the Court confirmed that the task to determine the effect of GATT/WTO law within the EU legal order fell squarely within the jurisdiction of the Court, and determined that the obligations under the GATT did not meet the conditions for direct effect. The statement in paragraph 28 of this judgment, where the Court concludes that the validity of secondary Union legislation cannot be affected by a provision of the General Agreement, must be taken quite literally, as the settled case law of the Court of Justice right up until today demonstrates.

19. It is also necessary to examine whether the provisions of the General Agreement confer rights on citizens of the Community on which they can rely before the courts in contesting the validity of a Community measure.

20. For this purpose, the spirit, the general scheme and the terms of the General Agreement must be considered.

21. This agreement which, according to its preamble, is based on the principle of negotiations undertaken on the basis of 'reciprocal and mutually advantageous arrangements' is characterized by the great flexibility of its provisions, in particular those conferring the possibility of derogation, the measures to be taken when confronted with exceptional difficulties and the settlement of conflicts between the contracting parties.

22. Consequently, according to the first paragraph of Article XXII 'Each contracting party shall accord sympathetic consideration to, and shall afford adequate

opportunity for consultation regarding, such representations as may be made by any other contracting party with respect to . . . all matters affecting the operation of this Agreement'.

23. According to the second paragraph of the same article, 'the contracting parties'— this name designating 'the contracting parties acting jointly' as is stated in the first paragraph of Article XXV—'may consult with one or more contracting parties on any question to which a satisfactory solution cannot be found through the consultations provided under paragraph (1)'.

24. If any contracting party should consider 'that any benefit accruing to it directly or indirectly under this Agreement is being nullified or impaired or that the attainment of any objective of the Agreement is being impeded as a result of', *inter alia*, 'the failure of another contracting party to carry out its obligations under this Agreement', Article XXIII lays down in detail the measures which the parties concerned, or the contracting parties acting jointly, may or must take in regard to such a situation.

25. Those measures include, for the settlement of conflicts, written recommendations or proposals which are to be 'given sympathetic consideration', investigations possibly followed by recommendations, consultations between or decisions of the contracting parties, including that of authorizing certain contracting parties to suspend the application to any others of any obligations or concessions under the General Agreement and, finally, in the event of such suspension, the power of the party concerned to withdraw from that agreement.

26. Finally, where by reason of an obligation assumed under the General Agreement or of a concession relating to a benefit, some producers suffer or are threatened with serious damage, Article XIX gives a contracting party power unilaterally to suspend the obligation and to withdraw or modify the concession, either after consulting the contracting parties jointly and failing agreement between the contracting parties concerned, or even, if the matter is urgent and on a temporary basis, without prior consultation.

27. Those factors are sufficient to show that, when examined in such a context, Article XI of the General Agreement is not capable of conferring on citizens of the Community rights which they can invoke before the courts.

28. Accordingly, the validity of Regulations Nos 459/70, 565/70 and 686/70 of the Commission cannot be affected by Article XI of the General Agreement.

Judgment of the Court of 5 October 1994, Federal Republic of Germany v. Council of the European Union, Case C-280/93, European Court Report 1994, p. I-4973, paras. 108–110.

Germany brought an action for a declaration that Title IV and Article 21(2) of Council Regulation (EEC) No 404/93 of 13 February 1993 on the common organization of the market in bananas were void. However, the Court following its case law again found that the validity of a Union legal act cannot as a rule be affected by the GATT, including if the latter is invoked by a Member State.

108. [The Court] has noted that where, by reason of an obligation assumed under GATT or of a concession relating to a preference, some producers suffer or are threatened with serious damage, Article XIX gives a contracting party power unilaterally to suspend the obligation and to withdraw or modify the concession, either after consulting the contracting parties jointly and failing agreement between the contracting parties concerned, or even, if the matter is urgent and on a temporary basis, without prior consultation (see Joined Cases 21 to 24/72 *International Fruit Company* v *Produktschap voor Groenten en Fruit* [1972] ECR 1219, paragraphs 21, 25 and 26; Case 9/73 *Schlueter* v *Hauptzollamt Loerrach* [1973] ECR 1135, paragraph 29; Case 266/81 *SIOT* v *Ministero delle Finanze* [1983] ECR 731, paragraph 28; and Joined Cases 267 to 269/91 *Amministrazione delle Finanze dello Stato* v *SPI and SAMI* [1983] ECR 801, paragraph 23).

109. Those features of GATT, from which the Court concluded that an individual within the Community cannot invoke it in a court to challenge the lawfulness of a Community act, also preclude the Court from taking provisions of GATT into consideration to assess the lawfulness of a regulation in an action brought by a Member State under the first paragraph of Article 173 of the Treaty.

110. The special features noted above show that the GATT rules are not unconditional and that an obligation to recognize them as rules of international law which are directly applicable in the domestic legal systems of the contracting parties cannot be based on the spirit, general scheme or terms of GATT.

Judgment of the Court of 23 November 1999, Portuguese Republic v. Council of the European Union, Case C-149/96, European Court Reports 1999, p. I-8395, paras. 36–48.

After the Marrakech Agreement had established the WTO and had introduced an elaborate system of dispute settlement, many predicted that the Court of Justice of the EU would accept the direct effect of WTO law within the EU legal order. However, in an action brought by Portugal for the annulment of Council Decision 96/386/EC of 26 February 1996 concerning the conclusion of Memoranda of Understanding between the European Community and the Islamic Republic of Pakistan and between the European Community and the Republic of India on arrangements in the area of market access for textile products, the Court maintained its pre-Marrakech stance. It referred *inter alia* to the need not to deprive the legislative or executive organs of the contracting parties from reaching negotiated solutions to disagreements and, controversially, to the fact that other contracting parties did not grant WTO law any direct effect, thereby introducing a political reciprocity argument.

36. While it is true that the WTO agreements, as the Portuguese Government observes, differ significantly from the provisions of GATT 1947, in particular by reason of the strengthening of the system of safeguards and the mechanism for resolving disputes, the system resulting from those agreements nevertheless accords considerable importance to negotiation between the parties.

37. Although the main purpose of the mechanism for resolving disputes is in prin-ciple, according to Article 3(7) of the Understanding on Rules and Procedures Governing the Settlement of Disputes (Annex 2 to the WTO), to secure the with-drawal of the measures in question if they are found to be inconsistent with the WTO rules, that understanding provides that where the immediate withdrawal of the measures is impracticable compensation may be granted on an interim basis pending the withdrawal of the inconsistent measure.

38. According to Article 22(1) of that Understanding, compensation is a temporary measure available in the event that the recommendations and rulings of the dis-pute settlement body provided for in Article 2(1) of that Understanding are not implemented within a reasonable period of time, and Article 22(1) shows a prefer-ence for full implementation of a recommendation to bring a measure into confor-mity with the WTO agreements in question.

39. However, Article 22(2) provides that if the member concerned fails to fulfil its obligation to implement the said recommendations and rulings within a rea-sonable period of time, it is, if so requested, and on the expiry of a reasonable period at the latest, to enter into negotiations with any party having invoked the dispute settlement procedures, with a view to finding mutually acceptable compensation.

40. Consequently, to require the judicial organs to refrain from applying the rules of domestic law which are inconsistent with the WTO agreements would have the consequence of depriving the legislative or executive organs of the contracting parties of the possibility afforded by Article 22 of that memorandum of entering into negotiated arrangements even on a temporary basis.

41. It follows that the WTO agreements, interpreted in the light of their subject-matter and purpose, do not determine the appropriate legal means of ensuring that they are applied in good faith in the legal order of the contracting parties.

42. As regards, more particularly, the application of the WTO agreements in the Community legal order, it must be noted that, according to its preamble, the agreement establishing the WTO, including the annexes, is still founded, like GATT 1947, on the principle of negotiations with a view to 'entering into reciprocal and mutually advantageous arrangements' and is thus distin-guished, from the viewpoint of the Community, from the agreements con-cluded between the Community and non-member countries which introduce a certain asymmetry of obligations, or create special relations of integration with the Community, such as the agreement which the Court was required to interpret in Kupferberg.

43. It is common ground, moreover, that some of the contracting parties, which are among the most important commercial partners of the Community, have con-cluded from the subject-matter and purpose of the WTO agreements that they are not among the rules applicable by their judicial organs when reviewing the legality of their rules of domestic law.

44. Admittedly, the fact that the courts of one of the parties consider that some of the provisions of the agreement concluded by the Community are of direct application whereas the courts of the other party do not recognise such direct application is

not in itself such as to constitute a lack of reciprocity in the implementation of the agreement (Kupferberg, paragraph 18).

45. However, the lack of reciprocity in that regard on the part of the Community's trading partners, in relation to the WTO agreements which are based on 'reciprocal and mutually advantageous arrangements' and which must ipso facto be distinguished from agreements concluded by the Community, referred to in paragraph 42 of the present judgment, may lead to disuniform application of the WTO rules.

46. To accept that the role of ensuring that Community law complies with those rules devolves directly on the Community judicature would deprive the legislative or executive organs of the Community of the scope for manoeuvre enjoyed by their counterparts in the Community's trading partners.

47. It follows from all those considerations that, having regard to their nature and structure, the WTO agreements are not in principle among the rules in the light of which the Court is to review the legality of measures adopted by the Community institutions.

48. That interpretation corresponds, moreover, to what is stated in the final recital in the preamble to Decision 94/800, according to which 'by its nature, the Agreement establishing the World Trade Organisation, including the Annexes thereto, is not susceptible to being directly invoked in Community or Member State courts'.

Judgment of the Court of 22 June 1989, Fédération de l'industrie de l'huilerie de la CEE (Fediol) v. Commission of the European Communities, Case 70/87, European Court Reports 1989, p. 1781, paras. 18–22.

> Nevertheless, the Court in principle accepts two exceptions to the impossibility of reviewing EU acts on the basis of GATT/WTO law, the so-called *Fediol* and *Nakajima* exceptions, after the judgments in which they were first recognized. In *Fediol*, a case brought by the EEC Seed Crushers' and Oil Processors' Federation (Fediol) seeking the annulment of the Commission's Decision rejecting the applicant's complaint requesting the Commission to initiate a procedure to examine certain commercial practices of Argentina regarding the export of soya cake to the Community, the Court held that it would review an EU act on the basis of GATT/WTO law if the act in question explicitly refers to the relevant GATT/WTO rules.

18. The Commission further maintains that when, as in this case, its decision deals with the interpretation of GATT provisions, the complainant cannot be permitted to put forward submissions calling that interpretation in question, because the interpretation which the Commission, pursuant to Regulation No 2641/84, places on the term 'illicit commercial practice' and on the rules of international law, in particular those of GATT, is subject to review by the Court only in so far as the disregard or misapplication of those rules amounts to an infringement of the

provisions of Community law which vest rights in individuals, directly and specifi-cally; however, the GATT rules themselves are not sufficiently precise to give rise to such rights on the part of individuals.

19. It should be recalled that the Court has certainly held, on several occasions, that various GATT provisions were not capable of conferring on citizens of the Community rights which they can invoke before the courts (judgments of 12 December 1972 in Joined Cases 21 to 24/72 *International Fruit Company* ((1972)) ECR 1219; 24 October 1973 in Case 9/73 *Schlueter* ((1973)) ECR 1135; 16 March 1983 in Case 266/81 *SIOT* ((1983)) ECR 731; and 16 March 1983 in Joined Cases 267 to 269/81 *SPI and SAMI* ((1983)) ECR 801). Nevertheless, it cannot be inferred from those judgments that citizens may not, in proceedings before the Court, rely on the provisions of GATT in order to obtain a ruling on whether con-duct criticized in a complaint lodged under Article 3 of Regulation No 2641/84 constitutes an illicit commercial practice within the meaning of that regulation. The GATT provisions form part of the rules of international law to which Article 2(1) of that regulation refers, as is borne out by the second and fourth recitals in its preamble, read together.

20. It is also appropriate to note that the Court did indeed hold in the above-mentioned judgments of 12 December 1972 *International Fruit Company*, 24 October 1973 *Schlueter* and 16 March 1983 *SPI and SAMI*, that a particular feature of GATT is the broad flexibility of its provisions, especially those con-cerning deviations from general rules, measures which may be taken in cases of exceptional difficulty, and the settling of differences between the contracting parties. That view does not, however, prevent the Court from interpreting and applying the rules of GATT with reference to a given case, in order to establish whether certain specific commercial practices should be considered incom-patible with those rules. The GATT provisions have an independent meaning which, for the purposes of their application in specific cases, is to be deter-mined by way of interpretation.

21. Lastly, the fact that Article XXIII of GATT provides a special procedure for the settlement of disputes between contracting parties is not such as to preclude its interpretation by the Court. As the Court held in the judgment of 26 October 1982 in Case 104/81 *Kupferberg* (1982) ECR 3641, in the context of the joint committees which are set up by free-trade agreements and given responsibility for the administration and proper implementation of those agreements, the mere fact that the contracting parties have established a special institutional frame-work for consultations and negotiations inter se in relation to the implementation of the agreement is not in itself sufficient to exclude all judicial application of that agreement.

22. It follows that, since Regulation No 2641/84 entitles the economic agents con-cerned to rely on the GATT provisions in the complaint which they lodge with the Commission in order to establish the illicit nature of the commercial prac-tices which they consider to have harmed them, those same economic agents are entitled to request the Court to exercise its powers of review over the legality of the Commission's decision applying those provisions.

Judgment of the Court of 7 May 1991, Nakajima All Precision Co. Ltd v. Council of the European Communities, Case C-69/89, European Court Reports 1991, p. I-2069, paras. 26–32.

The *Nakajima* exception, named after a case concerning a manufacturer of typewriters and printers, producing four models of bottom-of-the-range serial-impact dot-matrix printers, which opposed certain anti-dumping measures, pertains to the situation in which an EU act was adopted in order to comply with the international obligations of the Union under the WTO.

2. The plea that the new basic regulation is unlawful for being in breach of the Anti-Dumping Code

26. Nakajima submits in this regard that Article 2(3)(b)(ii) of the new basic regulation cannot be applied in the present case because it is at variance with a number of the provisions in the Anti-Dumping Code. In particular, the applicant argues that Article 2(3)(b)(ii) is incompatible with Article 2(4) and (6) of the Anti-Dumping Code.

27. The Council takes the view that, as is the case with the General Agreement, the Anti-Dumping Code does not confer on individuals rights which may be relied on before the Court and that the provisions of that Code are not directly applicable within the Community. From this the Council concludes that Nakajima cannot place in question the validity of the new basic regulation on the ground that it may be in breach of certain provisions in the Anti-Dumping Code.

28. It should, however, be pointed out that Nakajima is not relying on the direct effect of those provisions in the present case. In making this plea in law, the applicant is in fact questioning, in an incidental manner under Article 184 of the Treaty, the applicability of the new basic regulation by invoking one of the grounds for review of legality referred to in Article 173 of the Treaty, namely that of infringement of the Treaty or of any rule of law relating to its application.

29. It ought to be noted in this regard that, in its judgment in Joined Cases 21 to 24/72 *International Fruit Company NV and Others* v *Produktschap voor Groenten en Fruit* [1972] ECR 1219, the Court ruled (at paragraph 18) that the provisions of the General Agreement had the effect of binding the Community. The same conclusion must be reached in the case of the Anti-Dumping Code, which was adopted for the purpose of implementing Article VI of the General Agreement and the recitals in the preamble to which specify that it is designed to 'interpret the provisions of…the General Agreement' and to 'elaborate rules for their application in order to provide greater uniformity and certainty in their implementation'.

30. According to the second and third recitals in the preamble to the new basic regulation, it was adopted in accordance with existing international obligations, in particular those arising from Article VI of the General Agreement and from the Anti-Dumping Code.

31. It follows that the new basic regulation, which the applicant has called in question, was adopted in order to comply with the international obligations of the

Community, which, as the Court has consistently held, is therefore under an obligation to ensure compliance with the General Agreement and its implementing measures (see the judgments in Case 104/81 *Hauptzollamt Mainz* v *Kupferberg* [1982] ECR 3641, at paragraph 11, and in Case 266/81 *SIOT* v *Ministero delle Finanze and Others* [1983] ECR 731, at paragraph 28).

32. In those circumstances, it is necessary to examine whether the Council went beyond the legal framework thus laid down, as Nakajima claims, and whether, by adopting the disputed provision, it acted in breach of Article 2(4) and (6) of the Anti-Dumping Code.

Judgment of the Court (Grand Chamber) of 1 March 2005, Léon Van Parys NV v. Belgisch Interventie- en Restitutiebureau (BIRB), Case C-377/02, European Court Reports 2005, p. I-1465, paras. 37–54.

The Court tends to interpret the existing exceptions rather strictly. In particular, the fact that the Union adopts a measure specifically to comply with a decision of the Dispute Settlement Body of the WTO (DSB) is not sufficient to qualify for the *Nakajima* exception. The Court made that quite clear in *Van Parys*, a case concerning a reference for a preliminary ruling made in proceedings between Léon Van Parys NV and the *Belgisch Interventie- en Restitutiebureau* (the Belgian Intervention and Refund Board), concerning the latter's refusal to issue the former with import licences for certain quantities of bananas originating in Ecuador and Panama. The Court concluded that an operator, in circumstances such as those at issue in the main proceedings, could not plead before a court of a Member State that Community legislation was incompatible with certain WTO rules, even if the DSB had stated that that legislation was incompatible with those rules.

37. By its first, third and fourth questions, the referring court essentially asks the Court to assess the validity of Regulations No 404/93, 2362/98, 2806/98, 102/1999 and 608/1999 in the light of Articles I and XIII of GATT 1994.

38. Before making that assessment, it is necessary to answer the question whether the WTO agreements give Community nationals a right to rely on those agreements in legal proceedings challenging the validity of Community legislation where the DSB has held that both that legislation and subsequent legislation adopted by the Community in order, inter alia, to comply with the relevant WTO rules are incompatible with those rules.

39. It is settled case-law in that regard that, given their nature and structure, the WTO agreements are not in principle among the rules in the light of which the Court is to review the legality of measures adopted by the Community institutions (Case C-149/96 *Portugal* v *Council* [1999] ECR I-8395, paragraph 47; order of 2 May 2001 in Case C-307/99 *OGT Fruchthandelsgesellschaft* [2001] ECR I-3159, paragraph 24; Joined Cases C-27/00 and C-122/00 *Omega Air and Others* [2002] ECR I-2569, paragraph 93; Case C-76/00 P *Petrotub and Republica* v *Council* [2003]

ECR I-79, paragraph 53 and Case C-93/02 P *Biret International* v *Council* [2003] ECR I-10497, paragraph 52).

40. It is only where the Community has intended to implement a particular obligation assumed in the context of the WTO, or where the Community measure refers expressly to the precise provisions of the WTO agreements, that it is for the Court to review the legality of the Community measure in question in the light of the WTO rules (see, as regards GATT 1947, Case 70/87 *Fediol* v *Commission* [1989] ECR 1781, paragraphs 19 to 22, and Case C-69/89 *Nakajima* v *Council* [1991] ECR I-2069, paragraph 31, and, as regards the WTO agreements, *Portugal* v *Council*, paragraph 49, and *Biret International* v *Council*, paragraph 53).

41. In the present case, by undertaking after the adoption of the decision of the DSB of 25 September 1997 to comply with the WTO rules and, in particular, with Articles I(1) and XIII of GATT 1994, the Community did not intend to assume a particular obligation in the context of the WTO, capable of justifying an exception to the impossibility of relying on WTO rules before the Community Courts and enabling the Community Courts to exercise judicial review of the relevant Community provisions in the light of those rules.

42. First, it should be noted that even where there is a decision of the DSB holding that the measures adopted by a member are incompatible with the WTO rules, as the Court has already held, the WTO dispute settlement system nevertheless accords considerable importance to negotiation between the parties (*Portugal* v *Council*, paragraphs 36 to 40).

43. Thus, although, in the absence of a resolution mutually agreed between the parties and compatible with the agreements in question, the main purpose of the dispute settlement system is in principle, according to Article 3(7) of the understanding, to secure the withdrawal of the measures in question if they are found to be inconsistent with the WTO rules, that provision provides, however, that where the immediate withdrawal of the measures is impracticable, compensation may be granted or the application of concessions or the enforcement of other obligations may be suspended on an interim basis pending the withdrawal of the inconsistent measure (see, to that effect, *Portugal* v *Council*, paragraph 37).

44. It is true that, according to Articles 3(7) and 22(1) of the understanding, compensation and the suspension of concessions or other obligations are temporary measures available in the event that the recommendations and rulings of the DSB are not implemented within a reasonable period of time, the latter of those provisions showing a preference for full implementation of a recommendation to bring a measure into conformity with the WTO agreements in question (*Portugal* v *Council*, paragraph 38).

45. However, Article 22(2) provides that, if the Member concerned fails to enforce those recommendations and decisions within a reasonable period, if so requested, and within a reasonable period of time, it is to enter into negotiations with any party having invoked the dispute settlement procedures with a view to agreeing compensation. If no satisfactory compensation has been agreed within 20 days after the expiry of the reasonable period, the complainant may request

authorisation from the DSB to suspend, in respect of that member, the application of concessions or other obligations under the WTO agreements.

46. Furthermore, Article 22(8) of the understanding provides that the dispute remains on the agenda of the DSB, pursuant to Article 21(6) of the understanding, until it is resolved, that is until the measure found to be inconsistent has been 'removed' or the parties reach a 'mutually satisfactory solution'.

47. Where there is no agreement as to the compatibility of the measures taken to comply with the DSB's recommendations and decisions, Article 21(5) of the understanding provides that the dispute shall be decided 'through recourse to these dispute settlement procedures', including an attempt by the parties to reach a negotiated solution.

48. In those circumstances, to require courts to refrain from applying rules of domestic law which are inconsistent with the WTO agreements would have the consequence of depriving the legislative or executive organs of the contracting parties of the possibility afforded by Article 22 of that memorandum of reaching a negotiated settlement, even on a temporary basis (*Portugal v Commission*, paragraph 40).

49. In the dispute in the main proceedings, it is apparent from the file that:
    – after declaring to the DSB its intention to comply with the DSB's decision of 25 September 1997, the Community amended its system for imports of bananas upon the expiry of the period allocated to it for that purpose;
    – as a result of the challenge by the Republic of Ecuador to the compatibility with the WTO rules of the new system of trade with third States arising from Regulation No 1637/98, the matter was referred to an ad hoc panel pursuant to Article 21(5) of the understanding and that panel held in a report adopted by the DSB on 6 May 1999 that that system continued to infringe Articles I(1) and XIII of GATT 1994;
    – in particular, the United States of America was authorised, in 1999, pursuant to Article 22(2) of the understanding and following an arbitration procedure, to suspend concessions to the Community up to a certain level;
    – the Community system was the subject of further amendments introduced by Regulation No 216/2001, applicable with effect from 1 April 2001 pursuant to the second paragraph of Article 2;
    – agreements were negotiated with the United States of America on 11 April 2001 and with the Republic of Ecuador on 30 April 2001, with a view to bringing the Community legislation into conformity with the WTO rules.

50. Such an outcome, by which the Community sought to reconcile its obligations under the WTO agreements with those in respect of the ACP States, and with the requirements inherent in the implementation of the common agricultural policy, could be compromised if the Community Courts were entitled to judicially review the lawfulness of the Community measures in question in light of the WTO rules upon the expiry of the time-limit, in January 1999, granted by the DSB within which to implement its decision of 25 September 1997.

51. The expiry of that time-limit does not imply that the Community had exhausted the possibilities under the understanding of finding a solution to the dispute between it and the other parties. In those circumstances, to require the Community Courts, merely on the basis that that time-limit has expired, to review the lawfulness of the

Community measures concerned in the light of the WTO rules, could have the effect of undermining the Community's position in its attempt to reach a mutually acceptable solution to the dispute in conformity with those rules.

52. It follows from the foregoing considerations that Regulation No 1637/98 and the regulations in issue in the main proceedings adopted to apply it, cannot be interpreted as measures intended to ensure the enforcement within the Community legal order of a particular obligation assumed in the context of the WTO. Neither do those measures expressly refer to specific provisions of the WTO agreements.

53. Second, as the Court held in paragraphs 43 and 44 of its judgment in *Portugal* v *Council*, to accept that the Community Courts have the direct responsibility for ensuring that Community law complies with the WTO rules would deprive the Community's legislative or executive bodies of the discretion which the equivalent bodies of the Community's commercial partners enjoy. It is not in dispute that some of the contracting parties, which are amongst the most important commercial partners of the Community, have concluded from the subject-matter and purpose of the WTO agreements that they are not among the rules applicable by their courts when reviewing the legality of their rules of domestic law. Such lack of reciprocity, if admitted, would risk introducing an anomaly in the application of the WTO rules.

54. It follows from all of the foregoing that an operator, in circumstances such as those in the main proceedings, cannot plead before a court of a Member State that Community legislation is incompatible with certain WTO rules, even if the DSB has stated that that legislation is incompatible with those rules.

Judgment of the Court (Second Chamber) of 27 September 2007, Ikea Wholesale Ltd v. Commissioners of Customs & Excise, Case C-351/04, European Court Reports 2007, p. I-7723, paras. 29–69.

In *Ikea Wholesale*, a case concerning a reference for a preliminary ruling made in the course of proceedings arising from the refusal of the UK Commissioners of Customs & Excise to reimburse anti-dumping duties on imports of cotton-type bed linen from Pakistan and India paid by Ikea Wholesale Ltd, the Court held that the fact that an EU act provides for the amendment of Union rules on the basis of a DSB report is not sufficient to qualify for the *Fediol* exception. Nevertheless, the Court of Justice followed the approach of the WTO DSB, without explicitly mentioning the fact that it did.[8]

29. It must be recalled, as a preliminary point that, according to settled case-law, given their nature and structure, the WTO agreements are not in principle among the rules in the light of which the Court is to review the legality of measures adopted by the Community institutions (Case C-93/02 P *Biret International* v *Council* [2003] ECR I-10497, paragraph 52, and Case C-377/02 *Van Parys* [2005] ECR I-1465, paragraph 39 and the case-law cited).

---

[8] See further below the judgments in *FTS International BV* and *Digitalnet OOD*.

30. It is only where the Community has intended to implement a particular obligation assumed in the context of the WTO, or where the Community measure refers
expressly to the precise provisions of the WTO agreements, that it is for the Court
to review the legality of the Community measure in question in the light of the
WTO rules (Case C-149/96 *Portugal* v *Council* [1999] ECR I-8395, paragraph 49;
Biret International v *Council*, paragraph 53; and *Van Parys*, paragraph 40 and the
case-law cited).

31. In accordance with Article 1 of Regulation No 1515/2001, the Council may, following a report adopted by the DSB, and depending on the circumstances, repeal
or amend the disputed measure or adopt any other special measures which are
deemed to be appropriate in the circumstances.

32. Regulation No 1515/2001 applies, according to its Article 4, to reports adopted
after 1 January 2001 by the DSB. In the present case, the DSB adopted the report of
the Appellate Body on 12 March 2001 together with that of the Panel as amended
by the Appellate Body's report.

33. Pursuant to Article 3 of Regulation No 1515/2001, any measures adopted pursuant
to that regulation are to take effect from the date of their entry into force and may
not serve as basis for the reimbursement of the duties collected prior to that date,
unless otherwise provided for. Recital (6) in the preamble to the regulation provides in that connection that the recommendations in reports adopted by the DSB
only have prospective effect. Therefore, 'any measures taken under [Regulation No
1515/2001] will take effect from the date of their entry into force, unless otherwise
specified, and . . . do not provide any basis for the reimbursement of the duties collected prior to that date'.

34. In this case, having regard to the provisions of Regulation No 1515/2001 and to the
DSB's recommendations, the Council first of all adopted Regulation No 1644/2001
on 7 August 2001. Next, on 28 January 2002, it adopted Regulation No 160/2002,
and finally, on 22 April 2002, Regulation No 696/2002 confirming the definitive
anti-dumping duty imposed by Regulation No 2398/97, as amended and suspended by Regulation No 1644/2001.

35. It follows from all of the foregoing that, in circumstances such as those in the main
proceedings, the legality of Regulation No 2398/97 cannot be reviewed in the light
of the Anti-dumping Agreement, as subsequently interpreted by the DSB's recommendations, since it is clear from the subsequent regulations that the Community, by
excluding repayment of rights paid under Regulation No 2398/97, did not in any way
intend to give effect to a specific obligation assumed in the context of the WTO.

The validity of Regulation No 2398/97 in the light of the basic regulation

36. The national court is also unsure as to the validity of Regulation No 2398/97 in the
light of the basic regulation. It asks, essentially, whether the Commission committed a manifest error of assessment in determining the normal 'constructed' value
of the goods concerned, the dumping margin, and the existence of injury caused
to the Community industry.

37. The applicant in the main proceedings relies on Article 2(6) of the basic regulation,
relating to the determination of the normal value of a product, Article 2(11) of

the basic regulation relating to determination of the dumping margin, and Article 3(5) of that regulation relating to determination of injury caused to a Community industry.

38. In that connection, Ikea submits that, as the DSB's interpretations of the articles of the Anti-Dumping Agreement in its decisions confirm the fact that the methods used by the relevant Community institutions to determine the dumping margin and injury are incorrect, those methods are also contrary to the basic regulation.

39. The Commission and the Council consider, by contrast, that Regulation No 2398/97 remains valid from the Community-law stand point. The Commission, supported by the Council, takes the view that the provisions of Regulation No 2398/97, disputed in the light of the basic regulation, constitute practices in force for many years which have not up to now been declared invalid by the Community Courts.

40. It must be recalled in that connection that, as the Advocate General observed in point 102 of his Opinion, in the sphere of the common commercial policy and, most particularly, in the realm of measures to protect trade, the Community institutions enjoy a broad discretion by reason of the complexity of the economic, political and legal situations which they have to examine (see, to that effect, Case 191/82 *Fediol* v *Commission* [1983] ECR 2913, paragraph 26, and Case 255/84 *Nachi Fujikoshi* v *Council* [1987] ECR 1861, paragraph 21).

41. Furthermore, it is settled case-law that the choice between the different methods of calculating the dumping margin, such as those set out in Article 2(11) of the basic regulation, together with the assessment of the normal value of a product or the determination of the existence of harm require an appraisal of complex economic situations and the judicial review of such an appraisal must therefore be limited to verifying whether relevant procedural rules have been complied with, whether the facts on which the contested choice is based have been accurately stated, and whether there has been a manifest error in the appraisal of those facts or a misuse of powers (see, to that effect, Case 240/84 *NTN Toyo Bearing and Others* v *Council* [1987] ECR 1809, paragraph 19; Case C-156/87 *Gestetner Holdings* v *Council and Commission* [1990] ECR I-781, paragraph 63; and Case C-150/94 *United Kingdom* v *Council* [1998] ECR I-7235, paragraph 54).

42. It is thus necessary to examine whether the Community institutions have committed a manifest error of assessment with regard to Community law in determining the normal 'constructed' value of the product concerned, the dumping margin and the existence of injury caused to the Community industry.

The calculation of the normal 'constructed' value of the product concerned

43. The normal value is calculated for all types of goods exported to the Community by all companies, in accordance with Article 2(3) of the basic regulation. The normal value is determined by adding to the production costs of the types of goods exported by each company a reasonable amount corresponding to selling, general and administrative costs and to profits.

44. As regards the imports from India, since only one company had representative global domestic sales and profitable domestic sales represented less than 80% but

more than 10% of total domestic sales, those sales were regarded as having been made in the course of normal trade. Therefore, the amounts corresponding to selling, administration and general costs and profits which were used in order to determine the normal value for all of the companies under investigation, correspond to the costs incurred and the profits made by each respective company, in accordance with Article 2(6) of the basic regulation. The same finding was made in regard to imports from Pakistan.

45. With regard to the use of the profit margin of only one company, Regulation No 2398/97 states, in recital (18) in its preamble, that the investigation was restricted to a sample of exporting producers in accordance with Article 17 of the basic regulation, and that the vast majority of the cooperating Indian companies are export-oriented companies with no domestic sales of the like product. The Commission selected for that sample five Indian exporting producers, two of which had declared at the time of the selection that they had made domestic sales of the like product.

46. However, recital (23) in the preamble to the provisional regulation states that the investigation revealed that only one of those exporting producers had made representative domestic sales of the like product during the investigation period. Moreover, the reference in Article 2(6)(a) of the basic regulation to a weighted average amount for profits determined for other exporters or producers does not rule out such amount being determined by reference to a weighted average of transactions and/or product types of a single exporter or producer.

47. In that connection, as the Advocate General stated in points 132 to 142 of his Opinion, the Council had not committed a manifest error of assessment in taking the view, when determining the amounts corresponding to selling, administrative and other general costs and to profits, that Article 2(6)(a) of the basic regulation may be applied where the information available concerns a single producer and permits the exclusion of information relating to sales which were not made in the normal course of trade.

48. First, the use in Article 2(6)(a) of the basic regulation of the plural in the expression 'other exporters or producers' does not exclude from consideration data from a single enterprise which, as one of the undertakings subject to investigation, engaged, on the domestic market of the State of origin, in representative sales of the like product during the investigation period. Second, the fact of excluding from the assessment of the profit margin the sales of other exporters or producers which were not made in the normal course of trade constitutes an appropriate method of constructing the normal value, in accordance with the principle established in Articles 1(2) and 2(1) of the basic regulation, according to which the normal value must in principle be based on data relating to sales made in the ordinary course of trade.

49. It follows that the Council did not commit a manifest error of assessment in calculating the normal 'constructed' value of the product concerned.

Determination of the dumping margin

50. As regards the final determination of the dumping margin, the national court seeks to ascertain whether the practice of 'zeroing' used in establishing the overall dumping margins, as it was applied in the anti-dumping investigation at issue in the main proceedings, is compatible with Article 2(11) of the basic regulation.

51. It must be recalled, as a preliminary point, that the errors supposedly committed in the calculation of selling, administrative and other costs and profits, and the practice of 'zeroing', concern the determination of the dumping margins. However, the unlawfulness of an adjustment made in the course of the determination as to whether dumping has taken place affects the legality of the imposition of an anti-dumping duty only in so far as the anti-dumping duty imposed exceeds the duty which would be applicable were it not for that adjustment.

52. Under Article 2(12) of the basic regulation the dumping margin is the amount by which the normal value exceeds the export price. That margin is thus determined by the authorities responsible for the investigation, in accordance with Article 2(10), which make a fair comparison between the normal value of the like product and the export price to the Community.

53. In the main proceedings, it is not disputed that the dumping margin was calculated by comparing the average normal 'constructed' weighted value by types of product type with a weighted average of prices by product type. Therefore, the institutions concerned first identified a number of different models of the product under investigation. For each of those they calculated a weighted average normal value and an average weighted export price and then compared them for each model. Since for some models the normal value was higher than the export price, dumping was established. However, for other models, as the normal value was lower than the export price, a negative dumping margin was established.

54. In order to calculate the overall amount of dumping for the product subject to the investigation, those institutions then added up the dumping amounts for all the models in respect of which dumping had been established. By contrast, those institutions treated all the negative dumping margins as zero. The total dumping amount was then expressed as a percentage of the cumulative value of all the export transactions of all the models, irrespective of whether they had or had not been the subject of dumping.

55. In that connection, it must be observed that the wording of Article 2 of the basic regulation makes no reference to the practice of 'zeroing'. To the contrary, that regulation expressly requires the Community institutions to make a fair comparison between the export price and the normal value, in accordance with the provisions of Article 2(10) and (11).

56. Article 2(11) of the basic regulation states that the weighted average normal value is to be compared with 'a weighted average of prices of all export transactions to the Community'. In this case, in making that comparison, the use of the practice of 'zeroing' negative dumping margins was in fact made by modifying the price of the export transactions. Therefore, by using that method the Council did not calculate the overall dumping margin by basing its calculation on comparisons which fully reflect all the comparable export prices and, therefore, in calculating the margin in that way, it committed a manifest error of assessment with regard to Community law.

57. It follows that the Community institutions acted in a manner incompatible with Article 2(11) of the basic regulation by applying, in the calculation of the dumping margin for the product under investigation, the practice of 'zeroing' to negative dumping margins for each of the relevant product types.

The determination of the existence of injury

58. The national court asks the Court to determine the validity of Regulation No 2398/97 insofar as, for the purposes of the examination of injury, that regulation failed to evaluate all the relevant injury factors having a bearing on the state of the Community industry and erred in determining the injury to the Community industry by relying on evidence obtained from companies outside the Community industry, contrary to Article 3(5) of the basic regulation.

59. It must be recalled that, under Article 1(1) of the basic regulation, an anti-dumping duty may be applied to a product which is the subject of dumping only if its release for free circulation in the Community causes injury, the term 'injury' being taken to mean, in accordance with Article 3(1), material injury to the Community industry, a threat of material injury to the Community industry or material retardation of the establishment of such an industry.

60. It must be held in that connection that, according to the recital (34) in the preamble to Regulation No 2398/97, the 35 complainant companies represent a major proportion of total Community production within the meaning of Article 5(4) of the basic regulation and that they therefore constitute the Community industry within the meaning of Article 4(1) of the basic regulation. However, it is clear from recital (41) in the preamble to Regulation No 2398/97 that the assessment of injury to the Community industry covered data relating to the Community as a whole and was not analysed solely at the level of the Community industry, as defined in Article 4(1).

61. With regard to the question whether the Community authorities committed a manifest error of assessment by failing to evaluate all the relevant injury factors having a bearing on the state of the Community industry, as set out in Article 3(5) of the basic regulation, it must be stated that that provision gives those authorities discretion in the examination and evaluation of the various items of evidence.

62. As the Advocate General observed in points 193 and 194 of his Opinion, that provision merely requires an evaluation of the 'relevant economic factors and indices having a bearing on the state of the [Community industry]' and it is clear from the wording of the last sentence of Article 3(5) of the basic regulation that the list of economic factors and indices 'is not exhaustive'.

63. Therefore, it must be held that, in evaluating, for the purpose of the examination of the impact of the dumped imports, only the relevant factors having a bearing on the state of the Community industry, the Community institutions did not exceed the margin of assessment which they are acknowledged to have in the evaluation of complex economic situations. Furthermore, in a fresh evaluation carried out under Regulation No 1644/2001, the errors allegedly committed in the evaluation of injury had no impact on the determination of the existence of injury to the Community industry.

64. In those circumstances, it must be held that the Community institutions did not commit a manifest error of assessment in the evaluation of the existence and extent of that injury.

65. In the light of the foregoing considerations, the answer to the first question must be that Article 1 of Regulation No 2398/97 is invalid in so far as the Council applied,

for the purpose of determining the dumping margin for the product subject to the investigation, the practice of 'zeroing' negative dumping margins for each of the product types concerned.

66. Therefore it is appropriate, without there being any need to answer the other questions relating to the validity of subsequent regulations, to examine the fifth question, which concerns the consequences to be drawn from the finding of invalidity of Article 1 of Regulation No 2398/97, regarding the right of the importer involved in the main proceedings to repayment of anti-dumping duties which it paid under that regulation.

67. It is for the national authorities to draw the consequences, in their legal system, of a declaration of invalidity made in the context of an assessment of validity in a reference for a preliminary ruling (Case 23/75 *Rey Soda* [1975] ECR 1279, paragraph 51), which has the consequence that anti-dumping duties, paid under Regulation No 2398/97 are not legally owed within the meaning of Article 236(1) of Regulation No 2913/92 and should, in principle, be repaid by the customs authorities in accordance with that provision, provided that the conditions to which such repayment is subject, including that set out in Article 236(2), are satisfied, this being a matter for the national court to verify.

68. Next, it must be observed that the national courts alone have jurisdiction to entertain actions for recovery of amounts unduly received by a national body on the basis of Community legislation declared subsequently to be invalid (see, to that effect, Case 20/88 *Roquette* v *Commission* [1989] ECR 1553, paragraph 14, and Case C-282/90 *Vreugdenhil* v *Commission* [1992] ECR I-1937, paragraph 12).

69. In those circumstances, the answer to the fifth question must be that an importer, such as that at issue in the main proceedings, which has brought an action before a national court against the decisions by which the collection of anti-dumping duties is claimed from it under Regulation No 2398/97, declared invalid by this judgment, is, in principle, entitled to rely on that invalidity in the dispute in the main proceedings in order to obtain repayment of those duties in accordance with Article 236(1) of Regulation No 2913/92.

Judgment of the Court (Grand Chamber) of 9 September 2008, Fabbrica italiana accumulatori motocarri Montecchio SpA (FIAMM) and Fabbrica italiana accumulatori motocarri Montecchio Technologies LLC (C-120/06 P), Giorgio Fedon & Figli SpA and Fedon America, Inc. (C-121/06 P) v. Council of the European Union and Commission of the European Communities, Joined Cases C-120/06 P and C-121/06 P, European Court Reports 2008, p. I-6513, paras. 106–133.

In an appeal against judgments of the Court of First Instance (CFI) dismissing the actions brought by FIAMM and Fedon seeking compensation for the damage allegedly suffered by them on account of the increased customs duty which the Dispute Settlement Body of the World Trade Organization authorized the US to levy on imports of their products, following a finding by the DSB that the Community regime governing the import of bananas was incompatible with the agreements and understandings annexed to the Agreement establishing the WTO, the Court held that the fact that the scope for negotiations within the WTO is severely limited by the operation of the WTO Dispute Settlement Body does not change anything fundamental to its analysis. In particular, the failure to implement a DSB finding as to the breach of WTO law by the Union does not entail the non-contractual liability of the Union.

106. The Court has consistently interpreted the second paragraph of Article 288 EC as meaning that the non-contractual liability of the Community and the exercise of the right to compensation for damage suffered depend on the satisfaction of a number of conditions, relating to the unlawfulness of the conduct of which the institutions are accused, the fact of damage and the existence of a causal link between that conduct and the damage complained of (see, inter alia, Case 26/81 *Oleifici Mediterranei v EEC* [1982] ECR 3057, paragraph 16, and Case C-146/91 *KYDEP v Council and Commission* [1994] ECR I-4199, paragraph 19).

107. Here, the applicants essentially contended in support of their claim for compensation before the Court of First Instance that the Community institutions acted unlawfully, and therefore wrongfully, in failing to bring the Community legislation into conformity with the WTO agreements within the reasonable period of time that the Community was allowed for that purpose after a decision of the DSB had found that legislation to be incompatible with the WTO agreements.

108. It is to be observed in that regard that the effects within the Community of provisions of an agreement concluded by the Community with non-member States may not be determined without taking account of the international origin of the provisions in question. In conformity with the principles of public international law, Community institutions which have power to negotiate and conclude such an agreement are free to agree with the non-member States concerned what effect the provisions of the agreement are to have in the internal legal order of the contracting parties. If that question has not been expressly dealt with in the agreement, it is the courts having jurisdiction in the matter and in particular the Court of Justice within the framework of its jurisdiction under the EC Treaty that have the task of deciding it, in the same manner as any other question of interpretation relating to the application of the agreement in question in the Community (see, in particular, Case 104/81 *Kupferberg* [1982] ECR 3641, paragraph 17, and *Portugal v Council*, paragraph 34), on the basis in particular of the agreement's spirit, general scheme or terms (see, to this effect, Case C-280/93 *Germany v Council* [1994] ECR I-4973, paragraph 110).

109. Therefore, specifically, it falls to the Court to determine, on the basis in particular of the abovementioned criteria, whether the provisions of an international agreement confer on persons subject to Community law the right to rely on that agreement in legal proceedings in order to contest the validity of a Community measure (see, with regard to the GATT 1947, Joined Cases 21/72 to 24/72 *International Fruit Company and Others* [1972] ECR 1219, paragraph 19).

110. As is apparent from its case-law, the Court considers that it can examine the validity of secondary Community legislation in the light of an international treaty only where the nature and the broad logic of the latter do not preclude this and, in addition, the treaty's provisions appear, as regards their content, to be unconditional and sufficiently precise (see, in particular, Case C-308/06 *Intertanko and Others* [2008] ECR I-0000, paragraph 45 and the case-law cited).

111. As regards, more specifically, the WTO agreements, it is settled case-law that, given their nature and structure, those agreements are not in principle among the rules in the light of which the Court is to review the legality of measures adopted by the Community institutions (see, in particular, *Portugal* v *Council*, paragraph 47; *Biret International* v *Council*, paragraph 52; and *Van Parys*, paragraph 39).

112. It is only where the Community has intended to implement a particular obligation assumed in the context of the WTO, or where the Community measure refers expressly to the precise provisions of the WTO agreements, that it is for the Court to review the legality of the Community measure in question in the light of the WTO rules (see *Biret International* v *Council*, paragraph 53, and *Van Parys*, paragraph 40 and the case-law cited).

113. The Court has already held that the common organisation of the market in bananas, as introduced by Regulation No 404/93 and subsequently amended, is not designed to ensure the implementation in the Community legal order of a particular obligation assumed in the context of the GATT and does not refer expressly to specific provisions of the GATT either (order in *OGT Fruchthandelsgesellschaft*, paragraph 28).

114. As regards, in particular, Regulation No 1637/98 and the regulations adopted to implement it, the Court stated in *Van Parys*, paragraph 52, that they do not expressly refer to specific provisions of the WTO agreements.

115. The Court also held in that judgment that, by undertaking after the adoption of the DSB's decision of 25 September 1997 to comply with the WTO rules and, in particular, with Articles I(1) and XIII of the GATT 1994, the Community did not intend to assume a particular obligation in the context of the WTO, capable of justifying an exception to the principle that WTO rules cannot be relied upon before the Community courts and enabling the Community courts to review the legality of Regulation No 1637/98 and the regulations adopted to implement it in the light of those rules (see, to this effect, *Van Parys*, paragraphs 41 and 52).

116. It should be remembered that the decisive factor here is that the resolution of disputes concerning WTO law is based, in part, on negotiations between the contracting parties. Withdrawal of unlawful measures is admittedly the solution recommended by WTO law, but other solutions are also authorised (Omega Air and Others, paragraph 89).

117. The Court thus held in *Van Parys*, paragraph 51, that the expiry of the period granted by the DSB for implementation of its decision of 25 September 1997 does not imply that the Community had exhausted the possibilities under the DSU of finding a solution to the dispute between it and the other parties. In those circumstances, to require the Community courts, merely on the basis that that period has expired, to review the legality of the Community measures concerned in the

light of the WTO rules could have the effect of undermining the Community's position in its attempt to reach a mutually acceptable solution to the dispute in conformity with those rules.

118. Referring in particular to the memorandum of understanding concluded with the United States of America on 11 April 2001, the Court observed more specifically that such an outcome, by which the Community sought to reconcile its obligations under the WTO agreements with those in respect of the ACP States, and with the requirements inherent in the implementation of the common agricultural policy, could have been compromised if the Community courts had been entitled to review the legality of the Community measures in question in the light of the WTO rules upon the expiry of the reasonable period of time granted by the DSB (see, to this effect, *Van Parys*, paragraphs 49 and 50).

119. The Court also pointed out that to accept that the Community courts have the direct responsibility for ensuring that Community law complies with the WTO rules would effectively deprive the Community's legislative or executive organs of the scope for manoeuvre enjoyed by their counterparts in the Community's trading partners. It is not in dispute that some of the contracting parties, including the Community's most important trading partners, have concluded from the subject-matter and purpose of the WTO agreements that they are not among the rules applicable by their courts when reviewing the legality of their rules of domestic law. Such lack of reciprocity, if accepted, would risk introducing an imbalance in the application of the WTO rules (*Van Parys*, paragraph 53).

120. As is apparent from the Court's case-law, there is also no reason to draw a distinction in these various respects according to whether the legality of the Community action is to be reviewed in annulment proceedings or for the purpose of deciding an action for compensation (see to this effect, with regard to the period preceding the expiry of the reasonable period of time allowed for implementing a decision of the DSB, Biret International v Council, paragraph 62).

121. First, as the Court has pointed out, the prospect of actions for damages is liable to hinder exercise of the powers of the legislative authority whenever it has occasion to adopt, in the public interest, legislative measures which may adversely affect the interests of individuals (Joined Cases 83/76, 94/76, 4/77, 15/77 and 40/77 Bayerische HNL Vermehrungsbetriebe and Others v Council and Commission [1978] ECR 1209, paragraph 5, and Joined Cases C-46/93 and C-48/93 Brasserie du pêcheur and Factortame [1996] ECR I-1029, paragraph 45).

122. Second, any determination by the Community courts that a Community measure is unlawful, even when not made in the exercise of their jurisdiction under Article 230 EC to annul measures, is inherently liable to have repercussions on the conduct required of the institution that adopted the measure in question.

123. Thus, in particular, it is settled case-law that when the Court rules, in proceedings under Article 234 EC, that a measure adopted by a Community authority is invalid, its decision has the legal effect of requiring the competent Community institutions to take the necessary measures to remedy that illegality, as the obligation laid down in Article 233 EC in the case of a judgment annulling a measure applies in such a situation by analogy (see, in particular, the order of

8 November 2007 in Case C-421/06 *Fratelli Martini and Cargill*, paragraph 52 and the case-law cited).

124. There is nothing to suggest that the position should be different in the case of a judgment delivered in an action for compensation in which it is found that a measure adopted by the Community or a failure by it to act is unlawful. As the Advocate General has observed in point 49 of his Opinion, any determination by the Community courts that a measure is unlawful, even when made in an action for compensation, has the force of res judicata and accordingly compels the institution concerned to take the necessary measures to remedy that illegality.

125. The distinction which the appellants seek to draw between the 'direct effect' of the WTO rules imposing substantive obligations and the 'direct effect' of a decision of the DSB, asserting that it should be open to individuals to have the legality of the conduct of the Community institutions reviewed by the Community courts in the light of the DSB decision itself if such a review is not possible in the light of the WTO rules which that decision has found to have been infringed, calls for the following comments.

126. Even though the Court has not yet been required to rule expressly on such a distinction, it nevertheless necessarily follows from its case-law mentioned above that there is no basis for the distinction.

127. In holding that the WTO rules which have been found by a decision of the DSB to have been infringed cannot, notwithstanding the expiry of the period of time laid down for implementing that decision, be relied upon before the Community courts for the purpose of having the legality of the conduct of the Community institutions reviewed by the Community courts in the light of those rules, the Court has necessarily excluded such a review in the light of the DSB decision itself.

128. A DSB decision, which has no object other than to rule on whether a WTO member's conduct is consistent with the obligations entered into by it within the context of the WTO, cannot in principle be fundamentally distinguished from the substantive rules which convey such obligations and by reference to which such a review is carried out, at least when it is a question of determining whether or not an infringement of those rules or that decision can be relied upon before the Community courts for the purpose of reviewing the legality of the conduct of the Community institutions.

129. A recommendation or a ruling of the DSB finding that the substantive rules contained in the WTO agreements have not been complied with is, whatever the precise legal effect attaching to such a recommendation or ruling, no more capable than those rules of conferring upon individuals a right to rely thereon before the Community courts for the purpose of having the legality of the conduct of the Community institutions reviewed.

130. First, as is apparent from paragraphs 113 to 124 of the present judgment, the considerations linked to the nature of the WTO agreements and to the reciprocity and flexibility characterising them continue to obtain after such a ruling or recommendation has been adopted and after the reasonable period of time allowed for its implementation has expired. The Community institutions continue in particular to have an element of discretion and scope for negotiation vis-à-vis their

trading partners with a view to the adoption of measures intended to respond to the ruling or recommendation, and such leeway must be preserved.

131. Second, as is apparent from Article 3(2) of the DSU, recommendations and rulings of the DSB cannot add to or diminish the rights and obligations provided in the agreements concerned. It follows in particular that a decision of the DSB finding an infringement of such an obligation cannot have the effect of requiring a party to the WTO agreements to accord individuals a right which they do not hold by virtue of those agreements in the absence of such a decision.

132. It should, in particular, be recalled in this regard that the Court has already held in relation to the provisions of the GATT 1994, which have been found by the DSB to have been infringed in the present case, that those provisions are not such as to create rights upon which individuals may rely directly before the courts by virtue of Community law (see, to this effect, the order in *OGT Fruchthandelsgesellschaft*, paragraphs 25 and 26).

133. It follows from all of the foregoing considerations that the Court of First Instance rightly decided that, notwithstanding the expiry of the period of time allowed for implementing a decision of the DSB, the Community courts could not, in the circumstances of the case in point, review the legality of the conduct of the Community institutions in the light of WTO rules.

Judgment of the Court (Third Chamber) of 14 June 2012, Compagnie internationale pour la vente à distance (CIVAD) SA v. Receveur des douanes de Roubaix and Others, Case C-533/10, not yet reported, paras. 36–44.

In a reference made in proceedings between Compagnie internationale pour la vente à distance (CIVAD) SA and the Receveur des douanes de Roubaix (Collector of Customs, Roubaix), the Directeur régional des douanes et droits indirects de Lille (Regional Director of Customs and Indirect Taxes, Lille) and the Administration des douanes (Customs Administration) concerning a request for repayment of anti-dumping duties which CIVAD had wrongly paid in respect of imports of cotton-type bed linen originating in Pakistan, the Court held that since it alone has jurisdiction to declare an act of the EU invalid, the fact that the DSB has found an anti-dumping regulation not to be in accordance with WTO law, does not affect the presumption that such a regulation is lawful under Union law.

36. By its second question, the referring court asks whether the third subparagraph of Article 236(2) of the Customs Code must be interpreted as requiring national authorities to repay, on their own initiative, anti-dumping duties collected pursuant to a regulation subsequently declared by the DSB to be not in accordance with the Agreement on Implementation of Article VI of the General Agreement on Tariffs and Trade 1994 (OJ 1994 L 336, p. 103) ('the anti-dumping agreement') set out in Annex 1A of the Agreement establishing the World Trade Organisation (WTO), signed in Marrakech on 15 April 1994 and approved by Council Decision 94/800/

EC of 22 December 1994 concerning the conclusion on behalf of the European Community, as regards matters within its competence, of the agreements reached in the Uruguay Round multilateral negotiations (1986–1994) (OJ 1994 L 336, p. 1).

37. It should be recalled first that, in accordance with the third subparagraph of Article 236(2) of the Customs Code, customs authorities are to repay and remit import and export duties on their own initiative where they themselves discover, within the three-year period following the date on which the amount of those duties was communicated to the debtor, that the amount was not legally owed within the meaning of Article 236(1) of that code.

38. A finding by the DSB that an anti-dumping regulation is not in accordance with the anti-dumping agreement is not a factor allowing import duties to be repaid pursuant to Article 236(1) and (2) of the Customs Code.

39. The acts of the European Union institutions, bodies, offices and agencies are presumed to be lawful, which implies that they produce legal effects until such time as they are withdrawn, annulled in an action for annulment or declared invalid following a reference for a preliminary ruling or a plea of illegality (Case C-475/01 *Commission* v *Greece* [2004] ECR I-8923, paragraph 18, and Case C-199/06 *CELF and Ministre de la Culture et de la Communication* [2008] ECR I-469, paragraph 60).

40. Since the Court of Justice alone has jurisdiction to declare an act, such as an anti-dumping regulation, of the European Union invalid and the purpose of that jurisdiction is to ensure legal certainty through the uniform application of EU law (see Joined Cases C-188/10 and C-189/10 *Melki and Abdeli* [2010] ECR I-5667, paragraph 54 and the case-law cited), the fact that the DSB has found that an anti-dumping regulation is not in accordance with the anti-dumping agreement does not affect the presumption that such a regulation is lawful.

41. Therefore, in the absence of a declaration of invalidity, amendment or repeal by the competent European Union institutions, Regulation No 2398/97 remained binding in its entirety and directly applicable in all Member States, even after the DSB's finding.

42. In that regard, it should be recalled that, in accordance with Articles 1 and 3 of Regulation No 1515/2001, whenever the DSB adopts a report concerning a measure taken by the European Union in anti-dumping or anti-subsidy matters, the Council may, as it considers appropriate, either repeal or amend the measure, or adopt any other special measures deemed to be appropriate and that, unless otherwise provided for, any measures thereby adopted by the Council take effect from the date of their entry into force and cannot serve as basis for the reimbursement of the duties collected prior to that date.

43. It follows that, since Regulation No 2398/97 was not declared invalid by the Court, until 27 September 2007, the date when the judgment in Ikea Wholesale was delivered and since it had not yet been repealed or amended by Regulation No 160/2002—irrespective of the DSB's findings on whether Regulation No 2398/97 was in accordance with the anti-dumping agreement—that regulation was presumed to be lawful, so that the national customs authorities could not consider, before that date, that duties imposed pursuant to that regulation were not legally

owed within the meaning of Article 236(1) of the Customs Code. Nor, in those circumstances, were they able before that date to repay anti-dumping duties paid under Regulation No 2398/97 on their own initiative on the basis of the third subparagraph of Article 236(2) of the Customs Code.

44. In those circumstances, the answer to the second question is that the third subparagraph of Article 236(2) of the Customs Code must be interpreted as not allowing national customs authorities to repay, on their own initiative, anti-dumping duties collected pursuant to a European Union regulation, on the basis of a finding by the DSB that that regulation was not in accordance with the anti-dumping agreement.

Judgment of the Court (Grand Chamber) of 11 September 2007, Merck Genéricos—Produtos Farmacêuticos Lda v. Merck & Co. Inc. and Merck Sharp & Dohme Lda, Case C-431/05, European Court Reports 2007, p. I-7001, paras. 1 and 28–48.

This case concerned a question referred by the Portuguese Supreme Court to the Court of Justice and pertained to the length of patent protection for a pharmaceutical preparation against hypertension that was produced as a generic medicine by Merck Genericos and as a much more expensive patented medicine by Merck & Co. Both companies derive from the German Merck concern that after World War II was split up between a German company and a separate US company. The Court found that the lack of direct effect of WTO law does not affect its jurisdiction to interpret WTO law as such and to interpret EU law in keeping with WTO law, nor does it diminish the duty of the national court to apply national law as far as possible in conformity with WTO law. However, the CJEU did not have jurisdiction to interpret the provision at hand.

1. The question referred for a preliminary ruling concerns the interpretation of Article 33 of the Agreement on Trade-Related Aspects of Intellectual Property Rights ('the TRIPs Agreement'), constituting Annex 1C to the Agreement establishing the World Trade Organisation ('the WTO'), signed at Marrakesh on 15 April 1994 and approved by Council Decision 94/800/EC concerning the conclusion on behalf of the European Community, as regards matters within its competence, of the agreements reached in the Uruguay Round multilateral negotiations (1986–1994) (OJ 1994 L 336, p. 1, 'the WTO Agreement').

[...]

28. The Supremo Tribunal de Justiça accordingly decided to stay proceedings and to refer the following questions to the Court for a preliminary ruling:
'1. Does the Court of Justice have jurisdiction to interpret Article 33 of the TRIPs Agreement?
2. If the first question is answered in the affirmative, must national courts apply that article, on their own initiative or at the request of one of the parties, in proceedings pending before them?'

Concerning the questions referred for a preliminary ruling

29. By its two questions, which may be examined together, the referring court asks, in substance, whether it is contrary to Community law for Article 33 of the TRIPs Agreement to be applied directly by a national court in proceedings before it.

30. A preliminary point to be made is that article 300(7) EC provides that 'agreements concluded under the conditions set out in this article shall be binding on the institutions of the Community and on Member States'.

31. The WTO Agreement, of which the TRIPs Agreement forms part, has been signed by the Community and subsequently approved by Decision 94/800. Therefore, according to settled case-law, the provisions of that convention now form an integral part of the Community legal order (see, inter alia, Case C-344/04 *IATA and ELFAA* [2006] ECR I-403, paragraph 36, and Case C-459/03 *Commission v Ireland* ECR I-4635, paragraph 82). Within the framework of that legal order the Court has jurisdiction to give preliminary rulings concerning the interpretation of that agreement (see, inter alia, Case 181/73 *Haegeman v Belgium* [1974] ECR 449, paragraphs 4 to 6, and Case 12/86 *Demirel* [1987] ECR 3719, paragraph 7).

32. The WTO Agreement was concluded by the Community and all its Member States on the basis of joint competence and, as the Court has earlier remarked in *Hermès*, paragraph 24, without any allocation between them of their respective obligations towards the other contracting parties.

33. It follows that, the TRIPs Agreement having been concluded by the Community and its Member States by virtue of joint competence, the Court, hearing a case brought before it in accordance with the provisions of the EC Treaty, in particular Article 234 EC, has jurisdiction to define the obligations which the Community has thereby assumed and, for that purpose, to interpret the provisions of the TRIPs Agreement (see, to that effect, *Dior and Others*, paragraph 33).

34. In addition, as the Court has previously held, when the field is one in which the Community has not yet legislated and which consequently falls within the competence of the Member States, the protection of intellectual property rights and measures taken for that purpose by the judicial authorities do not fall within the scope of Community law, so that the latter neither requires nor forbids the legal order of a Member State to accord to individuals the right to rely directly on a rule laid down in the TRIPs Agreement or to oblige the courts to apply that rule of their own motion (*Dior and Others*, paragraph 48).

35. On the other hand, if it should be found that there are Community rules in the sphere in question, Community law will apply, which will mean that it is necessary, as far as may be possible, to supply an interpretation in keeping with the TRIPs Agreement (see, to that effect, *Dior and Others*, paragraph 47), although no direct effect may be given to the provision of that agreement at issue (*Dior and Others*, paragraph 44).

36. In order to answer the question which of the two hypotheses set out in the two paragraphs above is concerned, in relation to the relevant sphere covering the provision of the TRIPs Agreement at issue in the main proceedings, it is necessary to examine the matter of the sharing of competence between the Community and its Member States.

37. That last question calls for a uniform reply at Community level that the Court alone is capable of supplying.

38. There is, therefore, some Community interest in considering the Court as having jurisdiction to interpret Article 33 of the TRIPs Agreement in order to ascertain, as the national court has asked it to, whether it is contrary to Community law for that provision to be given direct effect.

39. Having regard to the principles noted in paragraphs 34 and 35 above, it is now appropriate to examine whether, in the particular sphere into which Article 33 of the TRIPs Agreement falls, that is to say, that of patents, there is any Community legislation.

40. As Community law now stands, there is none.

41. Indeed, of the Community acts cited by the national court, only Directive 98/44 concerns the field of patents itself. However, it is only a specific isolated case in that field which is regulated by the directive, namely, the patentability of biotechnological inventions which is, moreover, quite distinct from the object of Article 33 of the TRIPs Agreement.

42. Regulation No 2100/94 sets up a system for the Community protection of plant varieties which, as the Advocate General has observed in point 48 of his Opinion, cannot be placed on the same footing as the system of patents, as the Commission of the European Communities has acknowledged. Thus, Article 19 of that regulation provides for a term of protection of 25 years, even of 30 years, from the grant of protection.

43. Lastly, with regard to Regulation No 1768/92, to which may be added Regulation (EC) No 1610/96 of the European Parliament and of the Council of 23 July 1996 concerning the creation of a supplementary protection certificate for plant protection products (OJ 1996 L 198, p. 30), it is to be borne in mind that the purpose of that certificate is to compensate for the long period which, for the products concerned, elapses between the filing of a patent application and the granting of authorisation to place the products on the market by providing, in certain circumstances, for a supplementary period of patent protection (see, so far as Regulation No 1768/92 is concerned, Joined Cases C-207/03 and C-252/03 *Novartis and Others* [2005] ECR I-3209, paragraph 2).

44. The supplementary certificate does not affect the domestic, and therefore perhaps different, extent of the protection conferred by the patent or, more specifically, the term as such of the patent, which is still governed by the domestic law under which it was obtained.

45. That is made clear by Article 5 of those two regulations, which states that 'the certificate shall confer the same rights as conferred by the basic patent and shall be subject to the same limitations and the same obligations', and by Article 13(1) of those regulations, which provides that '[t]he certificate shall take effect at the end of the lawful term of the basic patent'.

46. The fact is that the Community has not yet exercised its powers in the sphere of patents or that, at the very least, at internal level, that exercise has not to date been of sufficient importance to lead to the conclusion that, as matters now stand, that sphere falls within the scope of Community law.

47. Having regard to the principle recalled in paragraph 34 above, it must be concluded that, since Article 33 of the TRIPs Agreement forms part of a sphere in which, at this point in the development of Community law, the Member States remain principally competent, they may choose whether or not to give direct effect to that provision.

48. In those circumstances, the reply to be given to the questions referred must be that, as Community legislation in the sphere of patents now stands, it is not contrary to Community law for Article 33 of the TRIPs Agreement to be directly applied by a national court subject to the conditions provided for by national law.

Judgment of the Court (Third Chamber) of 18 July 2007, FTS International BV v. Belastingdienst—Douane West, Case C-310/06, European Court Reports 2007, p. I-6749, paras. 15, 19–25.

Despite the principled view of the Court of Justice denying direct effect to WTO law, the Court does seem to attempt to achieve results that diverge as little as possible from WTO law obligations through 'WTO conform' interpretations, such as in *Ikea Wholesale* (see pp. 975–81). In *FTS International*, the Court declared invalid a Commission regulation concerning the classification of boneless chicken cuts, frozen and salted in the Combined Nomenclature, because the Commission had exceeded the powers granted to it in the basic Regulation. The Court's interpretation was consistent with a WTO Appellate Body condemnation of that interpretation.

15. On 27 September 2005, the Dispute Settlement Body of the World Trade Organisation (WTO) found that frozen boneless chicken cuts with a salt content of 1.2 to 3% by weight should be classified under heading 0210 of the CN. In response to that recommendation, the Commission adopted Regulation (EC) No 949/2006 of 27 June 2006 amending Annex I to Regulation No 2658/87 (OJ 2006 L 174, p. 3). Regulation No 949/2006, which entered into force on that date, repealed Regulation No 1223/2002 and replaced additional note 7 to chapter 2 of Section I of Part Two of the CN with the following provisions:
'For the purposes of subheadings 0210 11 to 0210 93, the terms "meat and edible meat offal, salted, in brine", mean meat and edible meat offal deeply and homogeneously impregnated with salt in all parts and having a total salt content by weight of 1.2% or more, provided that it is the salting which ensures the long-term preservation. For the purposes of subheading 0210 99 the terms "meat and edible meat offal, salted, in brine" mean meat and edible meat offal deeply and homogeneously impregnated with salt in all parts and having a total salt content by weight of 1.2% or more.'
[...]

19. FTS claims that Regulation No 1223/2002 is invalid and maintains, in particular, that it is inconsistent with additional note 7 to chapter 2 of Section I of Part Two of the CN and also with the Explanatory Notes to headings 0207 and 0210 of the HS,

according to which meat which has been salted is covered by heading 0210, as was held by the Dispute Settlement Body of the WTO.

20. The Netherlands Government, the Italian Government and the Commission submit on the contrary that Regulation No 1223/2002 is valid. They maintain, in essence, that heading 0207 of the CN covers boneless chicken cuts, frozen and deeply and homogeneously impregnated with salt in all parts, which have a salt content by weight of 1.2 to 1.9%. The Commission adds that the inconsistency of Regulation No 1223/2002 with the WTO's rules has no effect on the validity of that regulation under Community law, in so far as those rules have no direct effect, and refers, in that regard, to Case C-149/96 *Portugal* v *Council* [1999] ECR I-8395 and Case C-377/02 *Van Parys* [2005] ECR I-1465.

21. At the outset it must be recalled that, according to settled case-law, the Council has conferred upon the Commission, acting in cooperation with the customs experts of the Member States, a broad discretion to define the subject-matter of tariff headings falling to be considered for the classification of particular goods. However, the Commission's power to adopt the measures mentioned in Article 9(1)(a), (b), (d) and (e) of Regulation No 2658/87 does not authorise it to alter the subject-matter of the tariff headings which have been defined on the basis of the HS established by the Convention whose scope the Community has undertaken, under Article 3 thereof, not to modify (see Case C-267/94 *France* v *Commission* [1995] ECR I-4845, paragraphs 19 and 20, and Case C-15/05 *Kawasaki Motors Europe* [2006] ECR I-3657, paragraph 35).

22. It must therefore be considered whether the Commission, by adopting Regulation No 1223/2002, amended heading 0210 of the CN, thus exceeding the limits of the powers which are conferred on it by Article 9 of Regulation No 2658/87.

23. Additional note 7 to chapter 2 of Section I of Part Two of the CN, in the version applicable at the time of the facts in the main proceedings, restricted itself to providing that for the purposes of subheading 0210 the terms 'meat and edible meat offal, salted' mean 'meat and edible meat offal deeply and homogeneously impregnated with salt in all parts and having a total salt content by weight of 1.2% or more'. Under that provision, boneless chicken cuts, frozen, impregnated with salt in all parts and with a salt content of at least 1.2% are thus covered by heading 0210.

24. By classifying goods whose salt content was between 1.2% and 1.9% under subheading 0207 14 10, Regulation No 1223/2002, in consequence, raised the threshold for the salt content of goods covered by heading 0210 beyond 1.9%, with the result that goods whose salt content was between 1.2% and 1.9%, which had until then been covered by heading 0210, were excluded from that heading and classified under subheading 0207 14 10, with a resulting increase in duty.

25. By thus classifying chicken meat with a salt content by weight of between 1.2% and 1.9% under subheading 0207 14 10, the Commission restricted the scope of heading 0210 and therefore exceeded the powers which are conferred on it under Article 9 of Regulation No 2658/87. Consequently, Regulation No 1223/2002 must be declared invalid.

Judgment of the Court (Sixth Chamber) of 22 November 2012, Digitalnet OOD and Others v. Nachalnik na Mitnicheski punkt—Varna Zapad pri Mitnitsa Varna, Joined Cases C-320/11, C-330/11, C-382/11, and C-383/11, not yet reported, paras. 25–48.

In this case, the Court adopted a wider interpretation of the term 'modem' in the Combined Nomenclature than the one provided by the relevant Explanatory Notes of 7 May 2008. In doing so, the Court relied explicitly on the fact that, as the Commission had pointed out, in the context of disputes WT/DS375/R, WT/DS376/R, and WT/DS377/R between the EU and a number of States, the WTO panel had given a broader definition to the term 'modem' than that set out in those Explanatory Notes.[9]

25. By these questions, which it is appropriate to examine together, the referring court seeks to ascertain how the CN must be interpreted, and, more specifically, which goods may be classified under CN subheading 8528 71 13. That court seeks to establish, inter alia, what the terms 'modem' and 'access to the internet' cover within the meaning of that subheading and within the meaning of the Explanatory Notes of 7 May 2008. The referring court is also uncertain whether the type of modem used is relevant for the purpose of tariff classification or whether it suffices that the modem makes internet access possible.

26. The general rules for the interpretation of the CN state that classification of goods is to be determined first according to the terms of the headings and section or chapter notes, and that the titles of sections, chapters and sub-chapters are provided for ease of reference only.

27. In that regard, it should be borne in mind that, according to settled case-law, in the interests of legal certainty and for ease of verification, the decisive criterion for the classification of goods for customs purposes is in general to be sought in their objective characteristics and properties as defined in the wording of the relevant heading of the CN and the notes to the sections or chapters (see, inter alia, Case C-339/98 *Peacock* [2000] ECR I-8947, paragraph 9; Case C-495/03 *Intermodal Transports* [2005] ECR I-8151, paragraph 47; Case C-376/07 *Kamino International Logistics* [2009] ECR I-1167, paragraph 31; and Joined Cases C-288/09 and C-289/09 *British Sky Broadcasting Group and Pace* [2011] ECR I-0000, paragraph 60).

28. It is apparent from an examination of the CN that subheading 8528 71 13 covers apparatus for television, not designed to incorporate a video display or screen, with a microprocessor incorporating a modem for gaining access to the internet, and having a function of interactive information exchange, capable of receiving television signals (*British Sky Broadcasting Group and Pace*, paragraph 67).

---

[9] See also Case T-274/02 *Ritek and Prodisc Technology v Council* [2006] ECR II-4305, where the Court of First Instance referred extensively to the report of the Appellate Body of the World Trade Organization (WTO) of 1 March 2001 (WT/DS141/AB/R) ('the *Bed linen report*') delivered in Case WTS/DS141 *European Communities—anti-dumping duties on cotton-type bed linen from India* ('Bed linen').

29. It should be noted that the expressions 'video reception' and 'television reception' refer to two identical concepts (*British Sky Broadcasting Group and Pace*, paragraph 68).

30. In order to be classified under CN subheading 8528 71 13, apparatus must be able, first, to receive television signals, and, second, to incorporate a modem for gaining access to the internet and having a function of interactive information exchange. Any apparatus which does not have one or other of those characteristics must be classified under CN subheading 8528 71 19, in accordance with general rule 3(c) for the interpretation of the CN.

31. It is not disputed that the apparatus at issue in the main proceedings is appropriate for the purpose of receiving television signals. By contrast, the applicants in the main proceedings, on the one hand, and the Director of customs, Varna, on the other, are in disagreement as to whether that apparatus incorporates a modem for internet access which allows an interactive information exchange.

32. The CN does not define the concept of 'modem' or that of 'access to the internet'. However, the Explanatory Notes of 7 May 2008, in force at the time of the imports at issue in the main proceedings, provide details as to the type of apparatus which may be considered to be modems, within the meaning of subheading 8528 71 13, and as to the characteristics which that apparatus must have in order to be regarded as allowing internet access and interactive information exchange.

33. According to the Court's case-law, the Explanatory Notes to the CN drawn up by the Commission may be an important aid to the interpretation of the scope of the various headings but do not have legally binding force (see, inter alia, Case C-35/93 *Develop Dr Eisbein* [1994] ECR I-2655, paragraph 21; Case C-400/05 *B.A.S. Trucks* [2007] ECR I-311, paragraph 28; and *British Sky Broadcasting Group and Pace*, paragraph 63).

34. The content of the Explanatory Notes to the CN must accordingly be consistent with the provisions of the CN and may not alter their scope (see, inter alia, *Kamino International Logistics*, paragraph 48, and *British Sky Broadcasting Group and Pace*, paragraph 64).

35. Accordingly, where it is apparent that they are contrary to the wording of the headings of the CN and the section or chapter notes, the Explanatory Notes to the CN must be disregarded (see, to that effect, Case C-229/06 *Sunshine Deutschland Handelsgesellschaft* [2007] ECR I-3251, paragraph 31; *Kamino International Logistics*, paragraphs 49 and 50; and *British Sky Broadcasting Group and Pace*, paragraph 65).

36. In that regard, it must be noted that, in its written observations and during the hearing, the Commission submitted that the Explanatory Notes of 7 May 2008 adopted an unduly narrow interpretation of the term 'modem' within the meaning of CN subheading 8528 71 13. It states, inter alia, that in the context of disputes WT/DS375/R, WT/DS376/R and WT/DS377/R between the European Union and a number of States, the WTO panel gave a broader definition to the term 'modem' than that set out in the Explanatory Notes of 7 May 2008. That institution takes the view, consequently, that those notes are contrary to the wording of the CN headings and must therefore be disregarded for the purposes of the interpretation requested by the referring court.

37. In order to provide an answer to the referring court, it is necessary to examine what is covered by the term 'modem for gaining access to the internet', within the meaning of CN subheading 8528 71 13, and to determine whether, as the Commission maintains, the definition which is given to that term in the Explanatory Notes of 7 May 2008 is overly restrictive.

38. It is settled case-law that the meaning and scope of terms for which European Union law provides no definition must be determined by considering their usual meaning in everyday language, while also taking into account the context in which they occur and the purposes of the rules of which they form part (see to that effect, inter alia, Case C-336/03 *easyCar* [2005] ECR I-1947, paragraph 21 and the case-law cited; and judgment of 5 March 2009 in Case C-556/07 *Commission v France*, paragraph 50).

39. According to equally settled case-law, even though the provisions of an agreement such as the ITA are not such as to create rights upon which individuals may rely directly before the courts under European Union law, where the European Union has legislated in the field in question, the primacy of international agreements concluded by the European Union over provisions of secondary Community legislation means that such provisions must, so far as is possible, be interpreted in a manner that is consistent with those agreements (*British Sky Broadcasting Group and Pace*, paragraph 83 and the case-law cited).

40. A modem, in the usual meaning of that word, is used to transfer, between computers, digital data via a support operating on an analogue basis, that is to say, in particular, a telephone line. The modem modulates the digital data into analogue data and, conversely, it demodulates the analogue data to convert them into digital data.

41. Moreover, it is apparent from point 7.880 of the report of the WTO panel, referred to in paragraph 36 of the present judgment, that 'the plain meaning of the term "modem" can include devices other than those that convert a digital signal to analogue for purposes of information transfer over a telephone line'. At point 7.878 of the same report, the panel notes that 'the term "modem" has been used in referring to other devices that provided modulation and demodulation over different mediums and also potentially without digital-to-analogue signal conversion' and that 'the term "modem" is used to refer to "cable modems" as well, which are in several ways technologically distinct from telephone line-based modems, in terms of the medium used, frequency range and other parameters'.

42. As regards the term 'for gaining access to the internet, and having a function of interactive information exchange' the WTO panel stated, at point 7.884 of its report, that it informs the nature of the 'communication function' referred to in the wording of CN subheading 8528 71 13. Therefore it is the functionality of the apparatus that is central to the definition. The incorporation of a modem in the apparatus fulfils the purpose of gaining internet access.

43. In that regard, it should be recalled that the intended use of a product may constitute an objective criterion for classification if it is inherent to the product, and that inherent character must be capable of being assessed on the basis of the product's objective characteristics and properties (see, inter alia, Case C-309/98 *Holz Geenen*

[2000] ECR I-1975, paragraph 15; Case C-183/06 *RUMA* [2007] ECR I-1559, paragraph 36; and *British Sky Broadcasting Group and Pace*, paragraph 76).

44. The Explanatory Notes of 7 May 2008 give a definition of a modem within the meaning of subheading 8528 71 13 and state that 'modems modulate and demodulate outgoing as well as incoming data signals' and that '[d]evices performing a similar function to that of a modem but which do not modulate and demodulate signals are not considered to be modems. Examples of such apparatus are ISDN-, WLAN- or Ethernet devices. An indication of the presence of such a device is an RJ 45 connector.'

45. It appears, therefore, that, by excluding from the concept of a 'modem' devices which fulfil similar functions to a modem because of technical considerations, whereas only the objective of the capacity for gaining access to the internet is relevant for the purpose of classification, the Explanatory Notes of 7 May 2008 regarding subheading 8528 71 13 have restricted the meaning of that term. Those notes therefore contradict the CN on that point and must be disregarded.

46. It follows from all of the foregoing considerations that, for the purposes of the meaning of CN subheading 8528 71 13, a 'modem for gaining access to the internet' is a device which is capable of accessing the internet and of ensuring interactivity or an exchange of information in both directions. It is solely the capacity to gain access to the internet, and not the technique used to achieve this, that is relevant for the purposes of classification.

47. Moreover, in order to be classified under CN subheading 8528 71 13, the apparatus must be capable of accessing the internet solely by means of the modem which is incorporated in it. Access to the internet, therefore, must not require the intervention of any another apparatus or mechanism.

48. It follows from all of the foregoing that the answer to the questions is that the CN must be interpreted as meaning that, for the purposes of classification of goods under subheading 8528 71 13, a modem for gaining access to the internet is a device which, alone and without the intervention of any other apparatus or mechanism, is able to access the internet and to ensure interactivity and an exchange of information in both directions. It is solely the capacity to gain access to the internet, and not the technique used to achieve this, that is relevant for the purposes of classification under that subheading.

12.3 The status of UN law within the EU legal order

From the perspective of the UN Charter, its relationship with other treaties is quite straightforward: the UN Charter takes precedence.

Charter of the United Nations
Article 103

In the event of a conflict between the obligations of the Members of the United Nations under the present Charter and their obligations under any other international agreement, their obligations under the present Charter shall prevail.

The United Nations features prominently in the constituent Treaties of the EU. In particular, the Treaties contain an obligation for the Union to respect the principles of the UN Charter.

Treaty on European Union
Article 3
[...]

5. In its relations with the wider world, the Union shall uphold and promote its values and interests and contribute to the protection of its citizens. It shall contribute to peace, security, the sustainable development of the Earth, solidarity and mutual respect among peoples, free and fair trade, eradication of poverty and the protection of human rights, in particular the rights of the child, as well as to the strict observance and the development of international law, including respect for the principles of the United Nations Charter.

[...]

Article 21

1. The Union's action on the international scene shall be guided by the principles which have inspired its own creation, development and enlargement, and which it seeks to advance in the wider world: democracy, the rule of law, the universality and indivisibility of human rights and fundamental freedoms, respect for human dignity, the principles of equality and solidarity, and respect for the principles of the United Nations Charter and international law.

The Union shall seek to develop relations and build partnerships with third countries, and international, regional or global organisations which share the principles referred to in the first subparagraph. It shall promote multilateral solutions to common problems, in particular in the framework of the United Nations

2. The Union shall define and pursue common policies and actions, and shall work for a high degree of cooperation in all fields of international relations, in order to:

[...]

(c) preserve peace, prevent conflicts and strengthen international security, in accordance with the purposes and principles of the United Nations Charter, with the principles of the Helsinki Final Act and with the aims of the Charter of Paris, including those relating to external borders;

[...]

Judgment of the Court of 30 July 1996, Bosphorus Hava Yollari Turizm ve Ticaret AS v. Minister for Transport, Energy and Communications and others, Case C-84/95, European Court Reports 1996, p. I-3953, paras. 11–15.

The *Bosphorus* case, concerning a question on the interpretation of Article 8 of Council Regulation (EEC) No. 990/93 of 26 April 1993 concerning trade between the EEC and the

Federal Republic of Yugoslavia (Serbia and Montenegro), arose in proceedings between Bosphorus Hava Yollari Turizm ve Ticaret AS and the Minister for Transport, Energy and Communications, Ireland and the Attorney General. Bosphorus Airways was a Turkish company operating principally as an air charterer and travel organizer. It leased for a period of four years two aircraft owned by the Yugoslav national airline JAT. The agreement, known as a 'dry lease', provided for the leasing of the aircraft only and excluded cabin and flight crew, who were provided by Bosphorus Airways. The latter company thus had complete control of the day-to-day management of the aircraft for that period. In that context, the Court of Justice held that if an EU act intends to implement a UN obligation, the act ought to be interpreted in the light of the UN rule in question.

11. As the Court has stated in its case-law, in interpreting a provision of Community law it is necessary to consider its wording, its context and its aims (Case 337/82 *St. Nikolaus Brennerei* v *Hauptzollamt Krefeld* [1984] ECR 1051, paragraph 10; Case C-83/94 *Leifer and Others* [1995] ECR I-3231, paragraph 22).

12. Nothing in the wording of the first paragraph of Article 8 of Regulation No 990/93 suggests that it is based on a distinction between ownership of an aircraft on the one hand and its day-to-day operation and control on the other. Nor is it anywhere stated in that provision that it is not applicable to an aircraft owned by a person or undertaking based in or operating from the Federal Republic of Yugoslavia if that person or undertaking does not have day-to-day operation and control of the aircraft.

13. As to context and aims, it should be noted that by Regulation No 990/93 the Council gave effect to the decision of the Community and its Member States, meeting within the framework of political cooperation, to have recourse to a Community instrument to implement in the Community certain aspects of the sanctions taken against the Federal Republic of Yugoslavia by the Security Council of the United Nations, which, on the basis of Chapter VII of the Charter of the United Nations, adopted Resolutions 713 (1991), 752 (1992) and 787 (1992) and strengthened those sanctions by Resolution 820 (1993).

14. To determine the scope of the first paragraph of Article 8 of Regulation No 990/93, account must therefore also be taken of the text and the aim of those resolutions, in particular Paragraph 24 of Resolution 820 (1993), which provides that 'all States shall impound all vessels, freight vehicles, rolling stock and aircraft in their territories in which a majority or controlling interest is held by a person or undertaking in or operating from the Federal Republic of Yugoslavia (Serbia and Montenegro)'.

15. Thus the wording of Paragraph 24 of Resolution 820 (1993) confirms that the first paragraph of Article 8 of Regulation No 990/93 is to apply to any aircraft which is the property of a person or undertaking based in or operating from the Federal Republic of Yugoslavia, and that it is not necessary for that person or undertaking also to have actual control of the aircraft. The word 'interest' in Paragraph 24 cannot, on any view, exclude ownership as a determining criterion for impounding. Moreover, that word is used in that paragraph in conjunction with the word 'majority', which clearly implies the concept of ownership.

Judgment of the Court of First Instance (Second Chamber, extended composition) of 21 September 2005, Yassin Abdullah Kadi v. Council of the European Union and Commission of the European Communities, T-315/01, European Court Reports 2005, p. II-3649, paras. 181–231.

> However, the relationship between obligations under the UN Charter and the constituent Treaties of the EU was prominently the subject of the *Kadi* litigation, which concerned the implementation by the EU of sanctions taken by the UN Security Council against an individual suspected of terrorist acts. The Court of First Instance held that EU acts implementing binding obligations under Chapter VII of the UN Charter could not be reviewed by it, except for their compliance with *Jus cogens*.

Concerning the relationship between the international legal order under the United Nations and the domestic or Community legal order

181. From the standpoint of international law, the obligations of the Member States of the United Nations under the Charter of the United Nations clearly prevail over every other obligation of domestic law or of international treaty law including, for those of them that are members of the Council of Europe, their obligations under the ECHR and, for those that are also members of the Community, their obligations under the EC Treaty.

182. As regards, first, the relationship between the Charter of the United Nations and the domestic law of the Member States of the United Nations, that rule of primacy is derived from the principles of customary international law. Under Article 27 of the Vienna Convention on the Law of Treaties of 23 May 1969, which consolidates those principles (and Article 5 of which provides that it is to apply to 'any treaty which is the constituent instrument of an international organisation and to any treaty adopted within an international organisation'), a party may not invoke the provisions of its internal law as justification for its failure to perform a treaty.

183. As regards, second, the relationship between the Charter of the United Nations and international treaty law, that rule of primacy is expressly laid down in Article 103 of the Charter which provides that, '[i]n the event of a conflict between the obligations of the Members of the United Nations under the present Charter and their obligations under any other international agreement, their obligations under the present Charter shall prevail'. In accordance with Article 30 of the Vienna Convention on the Law of Treaties, and contrary to the rules usually applicable to successive treaties, that rule holds good in respect of Treaties made earlier as well as later than the Charter of the United Nations. According to the International Court of Justice, all regional, bilateral, and even multilateral, arrangements that the parties may have made must be made always subject to the provisions of Article 103 of the Charter of the United Nations (judgment of 26 November 1984, delivered in the case concerning military and paramilitary activities in and against Nicaragua (*Nicaragua* v *United States of America*), ICJ Reports, 1984, p. 392, paragraph 107).

184. That primacy extends to decisions contained in a resolution of the Security Council, in accordance with Article 25 of the Charter of the United Nations, under which the Members of the United Nations agree to accept and carry out the decisions of the Security Council. According to the International Court of Justice, in accordance with Article 103 of the Charter, the obligations of the Parties in that respect prevail over their obligations under any other international agreement (Order of 14 April 1992 (provisional measures), Questions of Interpretation and Application of the 1971 Montreal Convention arising from the Aerial Incident at Lockerbie (*Libyan Arab Jamahiriya* v *United States of America*), ICJ Reports, 1992, p. 16, paragraph 42, and Order of 14 April 1992 (provisional measures), Questions of Interpretation and Application of the 1971 Montreal Convention arising from the Aerial Incident at Lockerbie (*Libyan Arab Jamahiriya* v *United Kingdom*), ICJ Reports, 1992, p. 113, paragraph 39).

185. With more particular regard to the relations between the obligations of the Member States of the Community by virtue of the Charter of the United Nations and their obligations under Community law, it may be added that, in accordance with the first paragraph of Article 307 EC, 'The rights and obligations arising from agreements concluded before 1 January 1958 or, for acceding States, before the date of their accession, between one or more Member States on the one hand, and one or more third countries on the other, shall not be affected by the provisions of this Treaty.'

186. According to the Court of Justice's settled case-law, the purpose of that provision is to make it clear, in accordance with the principles of international law, that application of the EC Treaty does not affect the duty of the Member State concerned to respect the rights of third countries under a prior agreement and to perform its obligations thereunder (Case C-324/93 *Evans Medical and Macfarlan Smith* [1995] ECR I-563, paragraph 27; Case 10/61 *Commission* v *Italy* [1962] ECR 1; Case C-158/91 *Levy* [1993] ECR I-4287, and Case C-124/95 *Centro-Com* [1997] ECR I-81, paragraph 56).

187. Now, five of the six signatory States to the Treaty establishing the European Economic Community, signed at Rome on 25 March 1957, were already members of the United Nations on 1 January 1958. While it is true that the Federal Republic of Germany was not formally admitted as a member of the UN until 18 September 1973, its duty to perform its obligations under the Charter of the United Nations also predates 1 January 1958, as is apparent from the Final Act of the Conference held in London from 28 September to 3 October 1954 (known as 'The Conference of the Nine Powers') and the Paris Agreements signed on 23 October 1954. Furthermore, all the States that subsequently acceded to the Community were members of the United Nations before accession.

188. What is more, Article 224 of the Treaty establishing the European Economic Community (now Article 297 EC) was specifically introduced into the Treaty in order to observe the rule of primacy defined above. Under that provision, 'Member States shall consult each other with a view to taking together the steps needed to prevent the functioning of the common market being affected by measures which a Member State may be called upon to take...in order to carry out obligations it has accepted for the purpose of maintaining peace and international security'.

189. Resolutions adopted by the Security Council under Chapter VII of the Charter of the United Nations are thus binding on all the Member States of the Community which must therefore, in that capacity, take all measures necessary to ensure that those resolutions are put into effect (Opinions of Advocate General Jacobs in Case C-84/95 *Bosphorus* [1996] ECR I-3953, at I-3956, paragraph 2, and Case C-177/95 *Ebony Maritime and Loten Navigation* [1997] ECR I-1111, at I-1115, paragraph 27).

190. It also follows from the foregoing that, pursuant both to the rules of general international law and to the specific provisions of the Treaty, Member States may, and indeed must, leave unapplied any provision of Community law, whether a provision of primary law or a general principle of that law, that raises any impediment to the proper performance of their obligations under the Charter of the United Nations.

191. Thus, in Centro-Com, cited in paragraph 186 above, the Court of Justice specifically held that national measures contrary to the common commercial policy provided for in Article 113 of the EC Treaty could be justified under Article 234 of the EC Treaty (now, after amendment, Article 307 EC) if they were necessary to ensure that the Member State concerned performed its obligations under the Charter of the United Nations and a resolution of the Security Council.

192. However, it follows from the case-law (*Dorsch Consult v Council and Commission*, paragraph 158 above, paragraph 74) that, unlike its Member States, the Community as such is not directly bound by the Charter of the United Nations and that it is not therefore required, as an obligation of general public international law, to accept and carry out the decisions of the Security Council in accordance with Article 25 of that Charter. The reason is that the Community is not a member of the United Nations, or an addressee of the resolutions of the Security Council, or the successor to the rights and obligations of the Member States for the purposes of public international law.

193. Nevertheless, the Community must be considered to be bound by the obligations under the Charter of the United Nations in the same way as its Member States, by virtue of the Treaty establishing it.

194. In that regard, it is not in dispute that at the time when they concluded the Treaty establishing the European Economic Community the Member States were bound by their obligations under the Charter of the United Nations.

195. By concluding a treaty between them they could not transfer to the Community more powers than they possessed or withdraw from their obligations to third countries under that Charter (see, by analogy, Joined Cases 21/72 to 24/72 *International Fruit Company and Others ('International Fruit')* [1972] ECR 1219, paragraph 11).

196. On the contrary, their desire to fulfil their obligations under that Charter follows from the very provisions of the Treaty establishing the European Economic Community and is made clear in particular by Article 224 and the first paragraph of Article 234 (see, by analogy, *International Fruit*, paragraphs 12 and 13, and the Opinion of Advocate General Mayras in those cases, ECR 1231, at page 1237).

197. Although that latter provision makes mention only of the obligations of the Member States, it implies a duty on the part of the institutions of the Community not to impede the performance of the obligations of Member States which stem from that Charter (Case 812/79 *Burgoa* [1980] ECR 2787, paragraph 9).

198. It is also to be observed that, in so far as the powers necessary for the performance of the Member States' obligations under the Charter of the United Nations have been transferred to the Community, the Member States have undertaken, pursuant to public international law, to ensure that the Community itself should exercise those powers to that end.

199. In this context it is to be borne in mind, first, that in accordance with Article 48(2) of the Charter of the United Nations, the decisions of the Security Council 'shall be carried out by the Members of the United Nations directly and through their action in the appropriate international agencies of which they are members' and, second, that according to the case-law (*Poulsen and Diva Navigation*, paragraph 158 above, paragraph 9, and *Racke*, paragraph 158 above, paragraph 45, and Case 41/74 *Van Duyn* [1974] ECR 1337, paragraph 22), the Community must respect international law in the exercise of its powers and, consequently, Community law must be interpreted, and its scope limited, in the light of the relevant rules of international law.

200. By conferring those powers on the Community, the Member States demonstrated their will to bind it by the obligations entered into by them under the Charter of the United Nations (see, by analogy, *International Fruit*, paragraph 15).

201. Since the entry into force of the Treaty establishing the European Economic Community, the transfer of powers which has occurred in the relations between Member States and the Community has been put into concrete form in different ways within the framework of the performance of their obligations under the Charter of the United Nations (see, by analogy, *International Fruit*, paragraph 16).

202. Thus it is, in particular, that Article 228a of the EC Treaty (now Article 301 EC) was added to the Treaty by the Treaty on European Union in order to provide a specific basis for the economic sanctions that the Community, which has exclusive competence in the sphere of the common commercial policy, may need to impose in respect of third countries for political reasons defined by its Member States in connection with the CFSP, most commonly pursuant to a resolution of the Security Council requiring the adoption of such sanctions.

203. It therefore appears that, in so far as under the EC Treaty the Community has assumed powers previously exercised by Member States in the area governed by the Charter of the United Nations, the provisions of that Charter have the effect of binding the Community (see, by analogy, on the question whether the Community is bound by the General Agreement on Tariffs and Trade (GATT) of 1947, *International Fruit*, paragraph 18; see also, in that it recognises that the Community exercises circumscribed powers when giving effect to a trade embargo imposed by a resolution of the Security Council, *Dorsch Consult* v *Council and Commission*, paragraph 158 above, paragraph 74).

204. Following that reasoning, it must be held, first, that the Community may not infringe the obligations imposed on its Member States by the Charter of the

United Nations or impede their performance and, second, that in the exercise of its powers it is bound, by the very Treaty by which it was established, to adopt all the measures necessary to enable its Member States to fulfil those obligations.

205. In this instance, the Council found in Common Position 2002/402, adopted pursuant to the provisions of Title V of the Treaty on European Union, that action by the Community within the confines of the powers conferred on it by the EC Treaty was necessary in order to put into effect certain restrictive measures against Usama bin Laden, members of the Al-Qaeda network and the Taliban and other associated individuals, groups, undertakings and entities, in accordance with Security Council Resolutions 1267 (1999), 1333 (2000) and 1390 (2002).

206. The Community put those measures into effect by adopting the contested regulation. As has been held at paragraph 135 above, it was competent to adopt that act on the basis of Articles 60 EC, 301 EC and 308 EC.

207. It must therefore be held that the arguments put forward by the institutions, as summarised in paragraph 153 above, are valid, subject to this reservation that it is not under general international law, as those parties would have it, but by virtue of the EC Treaty itself, that the Community was required to give effect to the Security Council resolutions concerned, within the sphere of its powers.

208. On the other hand, the applicant's arguments based on the view that the Community legal order is a legal order independent of the United Nations, governed by its own rules of law, must be rejected.

Concerning the scope of the review of legality that the Court must carry out

209. As a preliminary point, it is to be borne in mind that the European Community is based on the rule of law, inasmuch as neither its Member States nor its institutions can avoid review of the question whether their acts are in conformity with the basic constitutional charter, the Treaty, which established a complete system of legal remedies and procedures designed to enable the Court of Justice to review the legality of acts of the institutions (Case 294/83 *Les Verts v Parliament* [1986] ECR 1339, paragraph 23; Case 314/85 *Foto-Frost* [1987] ECR 4199, paragraph 16; Case C-314/91 *Weber v Parliament* [1993] ECR I-1093, paragraph 8; Joined Cases T-222/99, T-327/99 and T-329/99 *Martinez and Others v Parliament* [2001] ECR II-2823, paragraph 48; see also Opinion 1/91 of the Court of Justice of 14 December 1991, ECR I-6079, paragraph 21).

210. As the Court has repeatedly held (*Johnston*, paragraph 146 above, paragraph 18; Case C-97/91 *Oleificio Borelli v Commission* [1992] ECR I-6313, paragraph 14, Case C-1/99 *Kofisa Italia* [2001] ECR I-207, paragraph 46; Case C-424/99 *Commission v Austria* [2001] ECR I-9285, paragraph 45, and Case C-50/00 P *Unión de Pequeños Agricultores v Council* [2002] ECR I-6677, paragraph 39), 'judicial control...reflects a general principle of law which underlies the constitutional traditions common to the Member States...and which is also laid down in Articles 6 and 13 of the [ECHR]'.

211. In the case in point, that principle finds expression in the right, conferred on the applicant by the fourth paragraph of Article 230 EC, to submit the lawfulness of the contested regulation to the Court of First Instance, provided that the act is of

direct and individual concern to him, and to rely in support of his action on any plea alleging lack of competence, infringement of an essential procedural requirement, infringement of the EC Treaty or of any rule of law relating to its application, or misuse of powers.

212. The question that arises in this instance is, however, whether there exist any structural limits, imposed by general international law or by the EC Treaty itself, on the judicial review which it falls to the Court of First Instance to carry out with regard to that regulation.

213. It must be recalled that the contested regulation, adopted in the light of Common Position 2002/402, constitutes the implementation at Community level of the obligation placed on the Member States of the Community, as Members of the United Nations, to give effect, if appropriate by means of a Community act, to the sanctions against Usama bin Laden, members of the Al-Qaeda network and the Taliban and other associated individuals, groups, undertakings and entities, which have been decided and later strengthened by several resolutions of the Security Council adopted under Chapter VII of the Charter of the United Nations. The recitals of the preamble to that regulation refer expressly to Resolutions 1267 (1999), 1333 (2000) and 1390 (2002).

214. In that situation, as the institutions have rightly claimed, they acted under circumscribed powers, with the result that they had no autonomous discretion. In particular, they could neither directly alter the content of the resolutions at issue nor set up any mechanism capable of giving rise to such alteration.

215. Any review of the internal lawfulness of the contested regulation, especially having regard to the provisions or general principles of Community law relating to the protection of fundamental rights, would therefore imply that the Court is to consider, indirectly, the lawfulness of those resolutions. In that hypothetical situation, in fact, the origin of the illegality alleged by the applicant would have to be sought, not in the adoption of the contested regulation but in the resolutions of the Security Council which imposed the sanctions (see, by analogy, *Dorsch Consult* v *Council and Commission*, paragraph 158 above, paragraph 74).

216. In particular, if the Court were to annul the contested regulation, as the applicant claims it should, although that regulation seems to be imposed by international law, on the ground that that act infringes his fundamental rights which are protected by the Community legal order, such annulment would indirectly mean that the resolutions of the Security Council concerned themselves infringe those fundamental rights. In other words, the applicant asks the Court to declare by implication that the provision of international law at issue infringes the fundamental rights of individuals, as protected by the Community legal order.

217. The institutions and the United Kingdom ask the Court as a matter of principle to decline all jurisdiction to undertake such indirect review of the lawfulness of those resolutions which, as rules of international law binding on the Member States of the Community, are mandatory for the Court as they are for all the Community institutions. Those parties are of the view, essentially, that the Court's review ought to be confined, on the one hand, to ascertaining whether

the rules on formal and procedural requirements and jurisdiction imposed in this case on the Community institutions were observed and, on the other hand, to ascertaining whether the Community measures at issue were appropriate and proportionate in relation to the resolutions of the Security Council which they put into effect.

218. It must be recognised that such a limitation of jurisdiction is necessary as a corollary to the principles identified above, in the Court's examination of the relationship between the international legal order under the United Nations and the Community legal order.

219. As has already been explained, the resolutions of the Security Council at issue were adopted under Chapter VII of the Charter of the United Nations. In these circumstances, determining what constitutes a threat to international peace and security and the measures required to maintain or re-establish them is the responsibility of the Security Council alone and, as such, escapes the jurisdiction of national or Community authorities and courts, subject only to the inherent right of individual or collective self-defence mentioned in Article 51 of the Charter.

220. Where, acting pursuant to Chapter VII of the Charter of the United Nations, the Security Council, through its Sanctions Committee, decides that the funds of certain individuals or entities must be frozen, its decision is binding on the members of the United Nations, in accordance with Article 48 of the Charter.

221. In light of the considerations set out in paragraphs 193 to 204 above, the claim that the Court of First Instance has jurisdiction to review indirectly the lawfulness of such a decision according to the standard of protection of fundamental rights as recognised by the Community legal order, cannot be justified either on the basis of international law or on the basis of Community law.

222. First, such jurisdiction would be incompatible with the undertakings of the Member States under the Charter of the United Nations, especially Articles 25, 48 and 103 thereof, and also with Article 27 of the Vienna Convention on the Law of Treaties.

223. Second, such jurisdiction would be contrary to provisions both of the EC Treaty, especially Articles 5 EC, 10 EC, 297 EC and the first paragraph of Article 307 EC, and of the Treaty on European Union, in particular Article 5 EU, in accordance with which the Community judicature is to exercise its powers on the conditions and for the purposes provided for by the provisions of the EC Treaty and the Treaty on European Union. It would, what is more, be incompatible with the principle that the Community's powers and, therefore, those of the Court of First Instance, must be exercised in compliance with international law (*Poulsen and Diva Navigation*, paragraph 158 above, paragraph 9, and *Racke*, paragraph 158 above, paragraph 45).

224. It has to be added that, with particular regard to Article 307 EC and to Article 103 of the Charter of the United Nations, reference to infringements either of fundamental rights as protected by the Community legal order or of the principles of that legal order cannot affect the validity of a Security Council measure or its effect in the territory of the Community (see, by analogy, Case 11/70 Internationale

Handelsgesellschaft [1970] ECR 1125, paragraph 3; Case 234/85 *Keller* [1986] ECR 2897, paragraph 7, and Joined Cases 97/87 to 99/87 *Dow Chemical Ibérica and Others* v *Commission* [1989] ECR 3165, paragraph 38).

225. It must therefore be considered that the resolutions of the Security Council at issue fall, in principle, outside the ambit of the Court's judicial review and that the Court has no authority to call in question, even indirectly, their lawfulness in the light of Community law. On the contrary, the Court is bound, so far as possible, to interpret and apply that law in a manner compatible with the obligations of the Member States under the Charter of the United Nations.

226. None the less, the Court is empowered to check, indirectly, the lawfulness of the resolutions of the Security Council in question with regard to jus cogens, understood as a body of higher rules of public international law binding on all subjects of international law, including the bodies of the United Nations, and from which no derogation is possible.

227. In this connection, it must be noted that the Vienna Convention on the Law of Treaties, which consolidates the customary international law and Article 5 of which provides that it is to apply 'to any treaty which is the constituent instrument of an international organisation and to any treaty adopted within an international organisation', provides in Article 53 for a treaty to be void if it conflicts with a peremptory norm of general international law (jus cogens), defined as 'a norm accepted and recognised by the international community of States as a whole as a norm from which no derogation is permitted and which can be modified only by a subsequent norm of general international law having the same character'. Similarly, Article 64 of the Vienna Convention provides that: 'If a new peremptory norm of general international law emerges, any existing treaty which is in conflict with that norm becomes void and terminates'.

228. Furthermore, the Charter of the United Nations itself presupposes the existence of mandatory principles of international law, in particular, the protection of the fundamental rights of the human person. In the preamble to the Charter, the peoples of the United Nations declared themselves determined to 'reaffirm faith in fundamental human rights, in the dignity and worth of the human person'. In addition, it is apparent from Chapter I of the Charter, headed 'Purposes and Principles', that one of the purposes of the United Nations is to encourage respect for human rights and for fundamental freedoms.

229. Those principles are binding on the Members of the United Nations as well as on its bodies. Thus, under Article 24(2) of the Charter of the United Nations, the Security Council, in discharging its duties under its primary responsibility for the maintenance of international peace and security, is to act 'in accordance with the Purposes and Principles of the United Nations'. The Security Council's powers of sanction in the exercise of that responsibility must therefore be wielded in compliance with international law, particularly with the purposes and principles of the United Nations.

230. International law thus permits the inference that there exists one limit to the principle that resolutions of the Security Council have binding effect: namely, that they must observe the fundamental peremptory provisions of jus cogens. If

they fail to do so, however improbable that may be, they would bind neither the Member States of the United Nations nor, in consequence, the Community.

231. The indirect judicial review carried out by the Court in connection with an action for annulment of a Community act adopted, where no discretion whatsoever may be exercised, with a view to putting into effect a resolution of the Security Council may therefore, highly exceptionally, extend to determining whether the superior rules of international law falling within the ambit of jus cogens have been observed, in particular, the mandatory provisions concerning the universal protection of human rights, from which neither the Member States nor the bodies of the United Nations may derogate because they constitute 'intransgressible principles of international customary law' (Advisory Opinion of the International Court of Justice of 8 July 1996, The Legality of the Threat or Use of Nuclear Weapons, Reports 1996, p. 226, paragraph 79; see also, to that effect, Advocate General Jacobs's Opinion in *Bosphorus*, paragraph 189 above, paragraph 65).

Judgment of the Court (Grand Chamber) of 3 September 2008, Yassin Abdullah Kadi and Al Barakaat International Foundation v. Council of the European Union and Commission of the European Communities, Joined Cases C-402/05 P and C-415/05 P, European Court Reports 2008, p. I-6351, paras. 280–327.

On appeal, the Court of Justice overturned the Court of First Instance's judgment, taking the view that the respect for the UN Charter does not reach so far as to affect the protection of fundamental rights within the EU legal order. Thus, the primacy of international agreements has one clear limitation: it does not extend to primary Union law, including general principles of EU law.

280. The Court will now consider the heads of claim in which the appellants complain that the Court of First Instance, in essence, held that it followed from the principles governing the relationship between the international legal order under the United Nations and the Community legal order that the contested regulation, since it is designed to give effect to a resolution adopted by the Security Council under Chapter VII of the Charter of the United Nations affording no latitude in that respect, could not be subject to judicial review of its internal lawfulness, save with regard to its compatibility with the norms of jus cogens, and therefore to that extent enjoyed immunity from jurisdiction.

281. In this connection it is to be borne in mind that the Community is based on the rule of law, inasmuch as neither its Member States nor its institutions can avoid review of the conformity of their acts with the basic constitutional charter, the EC Treaty, which established a complete system of legal remedies and procedures designed to enable the Court of Justice to review the legality of acts of the institutions (Case 294/83 *Les Verts* v *Parliament* [1986] ECR 1339, paragraph 23).

282. It is also to be recalled that an international agreement cannot affect the allocation of powers fixed by the Treaties or, consequently, the autonomy of the Community

legal system, observance of which is ensured by the Court by virtue of the exclusive jurisdiction conferred on it by Article 220 EC, jurisdiction that the Court has, moreover, already held to form part of the very foundations of the Community (see, to that effect, Opinion 1/91 [1991] ECR I-6079, paragraphs 35 and 71, and Case C-459/03 *Commission v Ireland* [2006] ECR I-4635, paragraph 123 and case-law cited).

283. In addition, according to settled case-law, fundamental rights form an integral part of the general principles of law whose observance the Court ensures. For that purpose, the Court draws inspiration from the constitutional traditions common to the Member States and from the guidelines supplied by international instruments for the protection of human rights on which the Member States have collaborated or to which they are signatories. In that regard, the ECHR has special significance (see, inter alia, Case C-305/05 *Ordre des barreaux francophones et germanophone and Others* [2007] ECR I-5305, paragraph 29 and case-law cited).

284. It is also clear from the case-law that respect for human rights is a condition of the lawfulness of Community acts (Opinion 2/94, paragraph 34) and that measures incompatible with respect for human rights are not acceptable in the Community (Case C-112/00 *Schmidberger* [2003] ECR I-5659, paragraph 73 and case-law cited).

285. It follows from all those considerations that the obligations imposed by an international agreement cannot have the effect of prejudicing the constitutional principles of the EC Treaty, which include the principle that all Community acts must respect fundamental rights, that respect constituting a condition of their lawfulness which it is for the Court to review in the framework of the complete system of legal remedies established by the Treaty.

286. In this regard it must be emphasised that, in circumstances such as those of these cases, the review of lawfulness thus to be ensured by the Community judicature applies to the Community act intended to give effect to the international agreement at issue, and not to the latter as such.

287. With more particular regard to a Community act which, like the contested regulation, is intended to give effect to a resolution adopted by the Security Council under Chapter VII of the Charter of the United Nations, it is not, therefore, for the Community judicature, under the exclusive jurisdiction provided for by Article 220 EC, to review the lawfulness of such a resolution adopted by an international body, even if that review were to be limited to examination of the compatibility of that resolution with jus cogens.

288. However, any judgment given by the Community judicature deciding that a Community measure intended to give effect to such a resolution is contrary to a higher rule of law in the Community legal order would not entail any challenge to the primacy of that resolution in international law.

289. The Court has thus previously annulled a decision of the Council approving an international agreement after considering the internal lawfulness of the decision in the light of the agreement in question and finding a breach of a general principle of Community law, in that instance the general principle of non-discrimination (Case C-122/95 *Germany v Council* [1998] ECR I-973).

290. It must therefore be considered whether, as the Court of First Instance held, as a result of the principles governing the relationship between the international legal order under the United Nations and the Community legal order, any judicial review of the internal lawfulness of the contested regulation in the light of fundamental freedoms is in principle excluded, notwithstanding the fact that, as is clear from the decisions referred to in paragraphs 281 to 284 above, such review is a constitutional guarantee forming part of the very foundations of the Community.

291. In this respect it is first to be borne in mind that the European Community must respect international law in the exercise of its powers (*Poulsen and Diva Navigation*, paragraph 9, and *Racke*, paragraph 45), the Court having in addition stated, in the same paragraph of the first of those judgments, that a measure adopted by virtue of those powers must be interpreted, and its scope limited, in the light of the relevant rules of international law.

292. Moreover, the Court has held that the powers of the Community provided for by Articles 177 EC to 181 EC in the sphere of cooperation and development must be exercised in observance of the undertakings given in the context of the United Nations and other international organisations (Case C-91/05 *Commission v Council* [2008] ECR I-0000, paragraph 65 and case-law cited).

293. Observance of the undertakings given in the context of the United Nations is required just as much in the sphere of the maintenance of international peace and security when the Community gives effect, by means of the adoption of Community measures taken on the basis of Articles 60 EC and 301 EC, to resolutions adopted by the Security Council under Chapter VII of the Charter of the United Nations.

294. In the exercise of that latter power it is necessary for the Community to attach special importance to the fact that, in accordance with Article 24 of the Charter of the United Nations, the adoption by the Security Council of resolutions under Chapter VII of the Charter constitutes the exercise of the primary responsibility with which that international body is invested for the maintenance of peace and security at the global level, a responsibility which, under Chapter VII, includes the power to determine what and who poses a threat to international peace and security and to take the measures necessary to maintain or restore them.

295. Next, it is to be noted that the powers provided for in Articles 60 EC and 301 EC may be exercised only in pursuance of the adoption of a common position or joint action by virtue of the provisions of the EC Treaty relating to the CFSP which provides for action by the Community.

296. Although, because of the adoption of such an act, the Community is bound to take, under the EC Treaty, the measures necessitated by that act, that obligation means, when the object is to implement a resolution of the Security Council adopted under Chapter VII of the Charter of the United Nations, that in drawing up those measures the Community is to take due account of the terms and objectives of the resolution concerned and of the relevant obligations under the Charter of the United Nations relating to such implementation.

297. Furthermore, the Court has previously held that, for the purposes of the interpretation of the contested regulation, account must also be taken of the wording and purpose of Resolution 1390 (2002) which that regulation, according to the fourth recital in the preamble thereto, is designed to implement (*Möllendorf and Möllendorf-Niehuus*, paragraph 54 and case-law cited).

298. It must however be noted that the Charter of the United Nations does not impose the choice of a particular model for the implementation of resolutions adopted by the Security Council under Chapter VII of the Charter, since they are to be given effect in accordance with the procedure applicable in that respect in the domestic legal order of each Member of the United Nations. The Charter of the United Nations leaves the Members of the United Nations a free choice among the various possible models for transposition of those resolutions into their domestic legal order.

299. It follows from all those considerations that it is not a consequence of the principles governing the international legal order under the United Nations that any judicial review of the internal lawfulness of the contested regulation in the light of fundamental freedoms is excluded by virtue of the fact that that measure is intended to give effect to a resolution of the Security Council adopted under Chapter VII of the Charter of the United Nations.

300. What is more, such immunity from jurisdiction for a Community measure like the contested regulation, as a corollary of the principle of the primacy at the level of international law of obligations under the Charter of the United Nations, especially those relating to the implementation of resolutions of the Security Council adopted under Chapter VII of the Charter, cannot find a basis in the EC Treaty.

301. Admittedly, the Court has previously recognised that Article 234 of the EC Treaty (now, after amendment, Article 307 EC) could, if the conditions for application have been satisfied, allow derogations even from primary law, for example from Article 113 of the EC Treaty on the common commercial policy (see, to that effect, *Centro-Com*, paragraphs 56 to 61).

302. It is true also that Article 297 EC implicitly permits obstacles to the operation of the common market when they are caused by measures taken by a Member State to carry out the international obligations it has accepted for the purpose of maintaining international peace and security.

303. Those provisions cannot, however, be understood to authorise any derogation from the principles of liberty, democracy and respect for human rights and fundamental freedoms enshrined in Article 6(1) EU as a foundation of the Union.

304. Article 307 EC may in no circumstances permit any challenge to the principles that form part of the very foundations of the Community legal order, one of which is the protection of fundamental rights, including the review by the Community judicature of the lawfulness of Community measures as regards their consistency with those fundamental rights.

305. Nor can an immunity from jurisdiction for the contested regulation with regard to the review of its compatibility with fundamental rights, arising from the

alleged absolute primacy of the resolutions of the Security Council to which that measure is designed to give effect, find any basis in the place that obligations under the Charter of the United Nations would occupy in the hierarchy of norms within the Community legal order if those obligations were to be classified in that hierarchy.

306. Article 300(7) EC provides that agreements concluded under the conditions set out in that article are to be binding on the institutions of the Community and on Member States.

307. Thus, by virtue of that provision, supposing it to be applicable to the Charter of the United Nations, the latter would have primacy over acts of secondary Community law (see, to that effect, Case C-308/06 *Intertanko and Others* [2008] ECR I-0000, paragraph 42 and case-law cited).

308. That primacy at the level of Community law would not, however, extend to primary law, in particular to the general principles of which fundamental rights form part.

309. That interpretation is supported by Article 300(6) EC, which provides that an international agreement may not enter into force if the Court has delivered an adverse opinion on its compatibility with the EC Treaty, unless the latter has previously been amended.

310. It has however been maintained before the Court, in particular at the hearing, that the Community judicature ought, like the European Court of Human Rights, which in several recent decisions has declined jurisdiction to review the compatibility of certain measures taken in the implementing of resolutions adopted by the Security Council under Chapter VII of the Charter of the United Nations, to refrain from reviewing the lawfulness of the contested regulation in the light of fundamental freedoms, because that regulation is also intended to give effect to such resolutions.

311. In this respect, it is to be found that, as the European Court of Human Rights itself has noted, there exists a fundamental difference between the nature of the measures concerned by those decisions, with regard to which that court declined jurisdiction to carry out a review of consistency with the ECHR, and the nature of other measures with regard to which its jurisdiction would seem to be unquestionable (see *Behrami and Behrami* v *France* and *Saramati* v *France*, Germany and Norway of 2 May 2007, not yet published in the Reports of Judgments and Decisions, §151).

312. While, in certain cases before it the European Court of Human Rights has declined jurisdiction ratione personae, those cases involved actions directly attributable to the United Nations as an organisation of universal jurisdiction fulfilling its imperative collective security objective, in particular actions of a subsidiary organ of the UN created under Chapter VII of the Charter of the United Nations or actions falling within the exercise of powers lawfully delegated by the Security Council pursuant to that chapter, and not actions ascribable to the respondent States before that court, those actions not, moreover, having taken place in the territory of those States and not resulting from any decision of the authorities of those States.

313. By contrast, in paragraph 151 of *Behrami and Behrami v France* and *Saramati v France, Germany and Norway,* the European Court of Human Rights stated that in the case leading to its judgment in *Bosphorus Hava Yolları Turizm ve Ticaret Anonim Şirketi v Ireland*, concerning a seizure measure carried out by the authorities of the respondent State on its territory following a decision by one of its ministers, it had recognised its competence, notably ratione personae, vis-à-vis the respondent State, despite the fact that the source of the contested measure was a Community regulation taken, in its turn, pursuant to a resolution of the Security Council.

314. In the instant case it must be declared that the contested regulation cannot be considered to be an act directly attributable to the United Nations as an action of one of its subsidiary organs created under Chapter VII of the Charter of the United Nations or an action falling within the exercise of powers lawfully delegated by the Security Council pursuant to that chapter.

315. In addition and in any event, the question of the Court's jurisdiction to rule on the lawfulness of the contested regulation has arisen in fundamentally different circumstances.

316. As noted above in paragraphs 281 to 284, the review by the Court of the validity of any Community measure in the light of fundamental rights must be considered to be the expression, in a community based on the rule of law, of a constitutional guarantee stemming from the EC Treaty as an autonomous legal system which is not to be prejudiced by an international agreement.

317. The question of the Court's jurisdiction arises in the context of the internal and autonomous legal order of the Community, within whose ambit the contested regulation falls and in which the Court has jurisdiction to review the validity of Community measures in the light of fundamental rights.

318. It has in addition been maintained that, having regard to the deference required of the Community institutions vis-à-vis the institutions of the United Nations, the Court must forgo the exercise of any review of the lawfulness of the contested regulation in the light of fundamental rights, even if such review were possible, given that, under the system of sanctions set up by the United Nations, having particular regard to the re-examination procedure which has recently been significantly improved by various resolutions of the Security Council, fundamental rights are adequately protected.

319. According to the Commission, so long as under that system of sanctions the individuals or entities concerned have an acceptable opportunity to be heard through a mechanism of administrative review forming part of the United Nations legal system, the Court must not intervene in any way whatsoever.

320. In this connection it may be observed, first of all, that if in fact, as a result of the Security Council's adoption of various resolutions, amendments have been made to the system of restrictive measures set up by the United Nations with regard both to entry in the summary list and to removal from it [see, in particular, Resolutions 1730 (2006) of 19 December 2006, and 1735 (2006) of 22 December 2006], those amendments were made after the contested regulation had been

adopted so that, in principle, they cannot be taken into consideration in these appeals.

321. In any event, the existence, within that United Nations system, of the re-examination procedure before the Sanctions Committee, even having regard to the amendments recently made to it, cannot give rise to generalised immunity from jurisdiction within the internal legal order of the Community.

322. Indeed, such immunity, constituting a significant derogation from the scheme of judicial protection of fundamental rights laid down by the EC Treaty, appears unjustified, for clearly that re-examination procedure does not offer the guarantees of judicial protection.

323. In that regard, although it is now open to any person or entity to approach the Sanctions Committee directly, submitting a request to be removed from the summary list at what is called the 'focal' point, the fact remains that the procedure before that Committee is still in essence diplomatic and intergovernmental, the persons or entities concerned having no real opportunity of asserting their rights and that committee taking its decisions by consensus, each of its members having a right of veto.

324. The Guidelines of the Sanctions Committee, as last amended on 12 February 2007, make it plain that an applicant submitting a request for removal from the list may in no way assert his rights himself during the procedure before the Sanctions Committee or be represented for that purpose, the Government of his State of residence or of citizenship alone having the right to submit observations on that request.

325. Moreover, those Guidelines do not require the Sanctions Committee to communicate to the applicant the reasons and evidence justifying his appearance in the summary list or to give him access, even restricted, to that information. Last, if that Committee rejects the request for removal from the list, it is under no obligation to give reasons.

326. It follows from the foregoing that the Community judicature must, in accordance with the powers conferred on it by the EC Treaty, ensure the review, in principle the full review, of the lawfulness of all Community acts in the light of the fundamental rights forming an integral part of the general principles of Community law, including review of Community measures which, like the contested regulation, are designed to give effect to the resolutions adopted by the Security Council under Chapter VII of the Charter of the United Nations.

327. The Court of First Instance erred in law, therefore, when it held, in paragraphs 212 to 231 of Kadi and 263 to 282 of Yusuf and Al Barakaat, that it followed from the principles governing the relationship between the international legal order under the United Nations and the Community legal order that the contested regulation, since it is designed to give effect to a resolution adopted by the Security Council under Chapter VII of the Charter of the United Nations affording no latitude in that respect, must enjoy immunity from jurisdiction so far as concerns its internal lawfulness save with regard to its compatibility with the norms of jus cogens.

Judgment of the General Court (Seventh Chamber) of 30 September 2010, Yassin Abdullah Kadi v. European Commission, Case T-85/09, European Court Reports 2010, p. II-5177, paras. 112–151.[10]

In the second *Kadi* case, the General Court followed the Court of Justice's approach, holding that its task was to ensure 'in principle the full review' of the lawfulness of the contested EU act in the light of fundamental rights, without affording it any immunity from jurisdiction on the ground that it gives effect to resolutions adopted by the Security Council under Chapter VII of the UN Charter. Preceding this, the Court of First Instance made a thinly veiled criticism of the Court of Justice's judgment in the first *Kadi* case.

112. It should be made clear at the outset that, in the context of the present proceedings, the General Court is not bound under Article 61 of the Statute of the Court of Justice by the points of law decided by the Court of Justice in its judgment in Kadi.

113. The institutions and intervening governments have, moreover, forcefully reiterated in these proceedings the concerns—already expressed by them in the case culminating in the judgment of the Court of Justice in Kadi—regarding the risk that the system of sanctions put in place by the United Nations in the context of the fight against international terrorism would be disrupted if judicial review of the kind advocated by the applicant in the light of the judgment of the Court of Justice in Kadi were instituted at national or regional level.

114. It is true that, once it is accepted that the Security Council has inherent competence to adopt sanctions targeted at individuals rather than at States or their governments (smart sanctions), such judicial review is liable to encroach on the Security Council's prerogatives, in particular with regard to determining who or what constitutes a threat to international peace or security, to finding that such a threat exists and to determining the measures necessary to put an end to it.

115. More fundamentally, certain doubts may have been voiced in legal circles as to whether the judgment of the Court of Justice in Kadi is wholly consistent with, on the one hand, international law and, more particularly, Articles 25 and 103 of the Charter of the United Nations and, on the other hand, the EC and EU Treaties, and more particularly Article 177(3) EC, Articles 297 EC and 307 EC, Article 11(1) EU and Article 19(2) EU (see, also Article 3(5) TEU and Article 21(1) and (2) TEU, as well as declaration No 13 of the Conference of the Representatives of the Governments of the Member States concerning the common foreign and security policy annexed to the Treaty of Lisbon, which stresses that 'the [EU] and its Member States will remain bound by the provisions of the Charter of the United Nations and, in particular, by the primary responsibility

---

[10] The appeals to the judgment are currently pending before the Court of Justice as Joined Cases C-584/10 P, C-593/10 P and C-595/10 P *European Commission, Council of the European Union, and United Kingdom of Great Britain and Northern Ireland v Yassin Abdullah Kadi.* In his Opinion of 19 March 2013, Advocate General Bot proposed that the Court should set aside the judgment of the General Court and dismiss the action brought by Mr Yassin Abdullah Kadi.

of the Security council and of its members for the maintenance of international peace and security'.

116. In that regard, it has in particular been asserted that, even though the Court of Justice stated, at paragraph 287 of Kadi, that it was not for the Community judicature, under the exclusive jurisdiction provided for by Article 220 EC, to review the legality of a resolution adopted by the Security Council under Chapter VII of the Charter of the United Nations, the fact remains that a review of the legality of a Community act which merely implements, at Community level, a resolution affording no latitude in that respect necessarily amounts to a review, in the light of the rules and principles of the Community legal order, of the legality of the resolution thereby implemented.

117. It has, moreover, been observed that, at paragraphs 320 to 325 of Kadi, the Court of Justice in any event carried out a review of the conformity of the system of sanctions set up by the United Nations with the system of judicial protection of fundamental rights laid down by the EC Treaty and did so in response to the Commission's argument that those fundamental rights were now sufficiently protected in the framework of the system of sanctions, in view in particular of the improvement in the re-examination procedure which afforded the individuals and entities concerned an acceptable opportunity to be heard by the Sanctions Committee. In particular, the Court of Justice held, at paragraphs 322 and 323 of its judgment, that the re-examination procedure 'clearly... [did] not offer the guarantees of judicial protection' and that the individuals or entities concerned 'had no real opportunity of asserting their rights'.

118. Likewise, although the Court of Justice asserted, at paragraph 288 of its judgment in Kadi, that any judgment of the Community judicature holding a Community measure intended to give effect to such a resolution to be contrary to a higher rule of law in the Community legal order would not entail any challenge to the primacy of that resolution in international law, it has been pointed out that the necessary consequence of such a judgment—by virtue of which the Community measure in question is annulled—would be to render that primacy ineffective in the Community legal order.

119. Accordingly, while the Court of Justice normally views relations between Community law and international law in the light of Article 307 EC (see, in that regard, Case C-124/95 *Centro-Com* [1997] ECR I-81, paragraphs 56 to 61, in which the Court held that Article 234 of the EC Treaty (subsequently, after amendment, Article 307 EC) may allow derogations even from primary law—in that instance Article 133 EC), it held in Kadi that Article 307 EC does not apply when at issue are 'the principles of liberty, democracy and respect for human rights and fundamental freedoms enshrined in Article 6(1) EU as a foundation of the Union' (paragraph 303) or, in other words, 'the principles that form part of the very foundations of the Community legal order, one of which is the protection of fundamental rights' (paragraph 304). So far as those principles are concerned, the Court of Justice thus seems to have regarded the constitutional framework created by the EC Treaty as a wholly autonomous legal order, not subject to the higher rules of international law—in this case the law deriving from the Charter of the United Nations.

120. Finally, as the Charter of the United Nations is an agreement between States and was, moreover, adopted before the adoption of the Treaty establishing the European Economic Community, signed at Rome on 25 March 1957, the likening by the Court of Justice, at paragraphs 306 to 309 of its judgment in Kadi, of that charter to an international agreement concluded between the Community and one or more States or international organisations, within the meaning of Article 300 EC, in support of the conclusion that 'primacy [of the charter] at the level of Community law [does] not, however, extend to primary law' (paragraph 308), has given rise to a number of questions.

121. The General Court acknowledges that those criticisms are not entirely without foundation. However, with regard to their relevance, it takes the view that, in circumstances such as those of the present case—which concerns a measure adopted by the Commission to replace an earlier measure annulled by the Court of Justice in an appeal against the judgment of this Court dismissing an action for annulment of the earlier measure—the appellate principle itself and the hierarchical judicial structure which is its corollary generally advise against the General Court revisiting points of law which have been decided by the Court of Justice. That is a fortiori the case when, as here, the Court of Justice was sitting in Grand Chamber formation and clearly intended to deliver a judgment establishing certain principles. Accordingly, if an answer is to be given to the questions raised by the institutions, Member States and interested legal quarters following the judgment of the Court of Justice in Kadi, it is for the Court of Justice itself to provide that answer in the context of future cases before it.

122. It should be observed, as an ancillary point, that, although some higher national courts have adopted a rather similar approach to that taken by this Court in its judgment in Kadi (see, to that effect, the decision of the Tribunal fédéral de Lausanne (Switzerland) of 14 November 2007 in Case 1A.45/2007 *Youssef Mustapha Nada* v *Secrétariat d'État pour l'Économie* and the judgment of the House of Lords (United Kingdom) in *Al-Jedda* v *Secretary of State for Defence* [2007] UKHL 58, which is currently the subject of an action pending before the European Court of Human Rights (Case No 227021/08 *Al-Jedda* v *United Kingdom*), others have tended to follow the approach taken by the Court of Justice, holding the Sanctions Committee's system of designation to be incompatible with the fundamental right to effective review before an independent and impartial court (see, to that effect, the judgment of the Federal Court of Canada of 4 June 2009 in *Abdelrazik* v *Canada (Minister of Foreign Affairs)* 2009 FC 580, cited at paragraph 69 of the UK Supreme Court judgment in *Ahmed and Others*).

123. If the intensity and extent of judicial review were limited in the way advocated by the Commission and the intervening governments (see paragraphs 86 to 101 above) and by the Council (see paragraphs 102 to 111 above), there would be no effective judicial review of the kind required by the Court of Justice in *Kadi* but rather a simulacrum thereof. That would amount, in fact, to following the same approach as that taken by this Court in its own judgment in *Kadi*, which was held by the Court of Justice on appeal to be vitiated by an error of law. The General Court considers that in principle it falls not to it but to the Court of Justice to

reverse precedent in that way, if it were to consider this to be justified in light, in particular, of the serious difficulties to which the institutions and intervening governments have referred.

124. It is true, as the Commission and the Council point out, that the Court of Justice recalled in *Kadi* that the Community must respect international law in the exercise of its powers (paragraph 291), that observance of the undertakings given in the context of the United Nations is required in the sphere of the maintenance of international peace and security when the Community gives effect, by means of the adoption of Community measures taken on the basis of Articles 60 EC and 301 EC, to resolutions adopted by the Security Council under Chapter VII of the Charter of the United Nations (paragraph 293), that in the exercise of that latter power it is necessary for the Community to attach special importance to the fact that, in accordance with Article 24 of the Charter of the United Nations, the adoption by the Security Council of such resolutions constitutes the exercise of the primary responsibility with which that international body is invested for the maintenance of peace and security at the global level, a responsibility which, under Chapter VII, includes the power to determine what and who poses a threat to international peace and security and to take the measures necessary to maintain or restore them (paragraph 294), and that, in drawing up measures implementing a resolution of the Security Council under Chapter VII of the Charter of the United Nations, the Community must take due account of the terms and objectives of the resolution concerned and of the relevant obligations under the Charter of the United Nations relating to such implementation (paragraph 296).

125. The fact remains that the Court of Justice also stated, in *Kadi*, that the implementation of resolutions adopted by the Security Council under Chapter VII of the Charter of the United Nations must be undertaken in accordance with the procedure applicable in that respect in the domestic legal order of each Member of the United Nations (paragraph 298), that it is not a consequence of the principles governing the international legal order under the United Nations that any judicial review of the internal lawfulness of a Community measure such as the contested regulation in the light of fundamental freedoms is excluded by virtue of the fact that that measure is intended to give effect to such a resolution (paragraph 299), that such immunity from jurisdiction for such a measure cannot find a basis in the EC Treaty (paragraph 300), that the review, by the Court of Justice, of the validity of any Community measure in the light of fundamental rights must be considered to be the expression, in a community based on the rule of law, of a constitutional guarantee stemming from the EC Treaty as an autonomous legal system which is not to be prejudiced by an 'international agreement' (paragraph 316), and that accordingly 'the Community judicature must, in accordance with the powers conferred on it by the EC Treaty, ensure the review, in principle the full review, of the lawfulness of all Community acts in the light of the fundamental rights forming an integral part of the general principles of Community law, including review of Community measures which...are designed to give effect to the resolutions adopted by the Security Council under Chapter VII of the Charter of the United Nations' (paragraph 326).

126. The General Court therefore concludes that, in circumstances such as those of this case, its task is to ensure—as the Court of Justice held at paragraphs 326 and 327 of *Kadi*—'in principle the full review' of the lawfulness of the contested regulation in the light of fundamental rights, without affording the regulation any immunity from jurisdiction on the ground that it gives effect to resolutions adopted by the Security Council under Chapter VII of the Charter of the United Nations.

127. That must remain the case, at the very least, so long as the re-examination procedure operated by the Sanctions Committee clearly fails to offer guarantees of effective judicial protection, as the Court of Justice considered to be the case at paragraph 322 of *Kadi* (see also, to that effect, point 54 of the Opinion of Advocate General Poiares Maduro in that case).

128. The considerations in this respect, set out by the Court of Justice at paragraphs 323 to 325 of *Kadi*, in particular with regard to the focal point, remain fundamentally valid today, even if account is taken of the 'Office of the Ombudsperson', the creation of which was decided in principle by Resolution 1904 (2009) and which has very recently been set up. In essence, the Security Council has still not deemed it appropriate to establish an independent and impartial body responsible for hearing and determining, as regards matters of law and fact, actions against individual decisions taken by the Sanctions Committee. Furthermore, neither the focal point mechanism nor the Office of the Ombudsperson affects the principle that removal of a person from the Sanctions Committee's list requires consensus within the committee. Moreover, the evidence which may be disclosed to the person concerned continues to be a matter entirely at the discretion of the State which proposed that he be included on the Sanctions Committee's list and there is no mechanism to ensure that sufficient information be made available to the person concerned in order to allow him to defend himself effectively (he need not even be informed of the identity of the State which has requested his inclusion on the Sanctions Committee's list). For those reasons at least, the creation of the focal point and the Office of the Ombudsperson cannot be equated with the provision of an effective judicial procedure for review of decisions of the Sanctions Committee (see also, in that regard, the observations made at paragraphs 77, 78, 149, 181, 182 and 239 of the UK Supreme Court judgment in *Ahmed and Others* and the considerations expressed in Point III of the Ninth Report of the Monitoring Committee).

129. In those circumstances, the review carried out by the Community judicature of Community measures to freeze funds can be regarded as effective only if it concerns, indirectly, the substantive assessments of the Sanctions Committee itself and the evidence underlying them (see also, to that effect, the UK Supreme Court judgment in *Ahmed and Others*, paragraph 81).

130. With regard, more specifically, to the extent and intensity of the review which it is for this Court to carry out, the Commission submits that in *Kadi* the Court of Justice did not make a determination on that question (see paragraph 91 above). In the same vein, the Council maintains that the Court of Justice did not consider that question and did not provide the slightest guidance in that regard (see paragraphs 102 and 108 above).

131. That argument is clearly wrong.

132. First, the Court of Justice stated at the end of a lengthy passage of reasoning that the review of legality in question had to be 'in principle the full review' and had to be carried out 'in accordance with the powers conferred on [the Community judicature] by the EC Treaty' (judgment of the Court of Justice in *Kadi*, paragraph 326) and, what is more, expressly rejected the General Court's proposition that the measure at issue had to be afforded 'immunity from jurisdiction' on the ground that it merely gave effect to resolutions adopted by the Security Council under Chapter VII of the Charter of the United Nations (judgment of the Court of Justice in *Kadi*, paragraph 327). In so doing, the Court of Justice in fact gave a perfectly clear indication of what the scope and intensity of that review had to be.

133. Second, the Court of Justice concluded, at paragraph 336 of *Kadi*, that it had to be possible to apply that review to the lawfulness of the grounds on which the contested Community measure was founded. It is clear from the case-law cited at paragraph 336 in support of that conclusion (see, in particular, Joined Cases C-189/02 P, C-202/02 P, C-205/02 P to C-208/02 P and C-213/02 P *Dansk Rørindustri and Others* v *Commission* [2005] ECR I-5425, paragraph 462) that the review of the lawfulness of the grounds extends, inter alia, to ascertaining whether the contested act is well founded and whether it is vitiated by any defect.

134. Third, the Court of Justice pointed out, at paragraphs 342 to 344 of *Kadi*, that although overriding considerations relating to safety or the conduct of the international relations of the Community and of its Member States may militate against the communication of certain matters to the persons concerned, that does not mean, with regard to respect for the principle of effective judicial protection, that restrictive measures such as those imposed by the contested regulation escape all review by the Community judicature once it has been claimed that the act laying them down concerns national security and terrorism. In such a case, it is the task of the Community judicature to apply, in the course of the judicial review it carries out, techniques which accommodate, on the one hand, legitimate security concerns about the nature and sources of information taken into account in the adoption of the act concerned and, on the other, the need to accord the individual a sufficient measure of procedural justice.

135. It is obvious from those passages of the judgment of the Court of Justice in *Kadi* and from the reference made there to the judgment of the European Court of Human Rights in *Chahal* v *United Kingdom* of 15 November 1996, Reports of Judgments and Decisions 1996-V, § 131, that the Court of Justice intended that its review, 'in principle [a] full review', should extend not only to the apparent merits of the contested measure but also to the evidence and information on which the findings made in the measure are based.

136. The Monitoring Team understood it in that way, since point 19 of its Ninth Report states that in its judgment in *Kadi* the Court of Justice held that the procedures used by the European Union to implement sanctions had infringed the fundamental rights of the persons concerned 'by failing to communicate the evidence justifying the restrictive measures imposed upon them and thus precluding their right to defend themselves against them'.

137. Moreover, the Court of Justice has recently confirmed, in a case concerning implementation of the sanctions laid down by Regulation No 2580/2001, that the possibility of 'an adequate review by the courts' of the substantive legality of a Community freezing measure, 'particularly as regards the verification of the facts and the evidence and information relied upon in support of the measure', is indispensable if a fair balance between the requirements of the fight against international terrorism, on the one hand, and the protection of fundamental liberties and rights, on the other, is to be ensured (Case C-550/09 E and F [2010] ECR I-0000, paragraph 57).

138. Fourth, it should be noted that a considerable part of the reasoning elaborated by the Court of Justice in *Kadi* in its consideration of the applicant's pleas alleging infringement of his rights of defence and of the right to effective judicial review, draws on the reasoning of this Court elaborated in its consideration of the equivalent pleas raised by the applicant in *OMPI*. Thus, in particular, paragraphs 336, 340, 342, 343, 344, 345, 346, 348, 349, 351 and 352 of the judgment of the Court of Justice in *Kadi* at the very least reproduce the substance of the corresponding paragraphs 129, 128, 133, 156, 158, 160, 161, 162, 165, 166 and 173 of *OMPI*. The conclusion must therefore be that, by taking on the essential content of the General Court's reasoning in *OMPI*, with regard to the alleged infringements of the rights of the defence and the right to an effective judicial review, the Court of Justice approved and endorsed the standard and intensity of the review as carried out by the General Court in *OMPI*.

139. As regards the extent and intensity of the judicial review appropriate in the present case, it is therefore necessary to apply to this case the principles set out by the General Court in OMPI and in its subsequent decisions in the cases referred to at paragraph 82 above concerning the implementation of the measures referred to at paragraphs 32 to 35 above.

140. In that regard, it should be recalled that, at paragraph 153 of *OMPI*, the General Court held that the judicial review of the lawfulness of a Community decision to freeze funds is that provided for in the second paragraph of Article 230 EC, under which the Community judicature has jurisdiction in actions for annulment brought on grounds of lack of competence, infringement of an essential procedural requirement, infringement of the EC Treaty or of any rule of law relating to its application or misuse of powers.

141. At paragraph 159 of *OMPI*, paragraph 137 of *PMOI I*, paragraph 55 of *PMOI II* and paragraph 97 of the judgment in Case T-341/07 *Sison v Council* [2009] ECR II-0000, the General Court recognised that the competent Community institution had broad discretion as to what matters to take into consideration for the purpose of adopting economic and financial sanctions on the basis of Articles 60 EC, 301 EC and 308 EC, consistent with a common position adopted on the basis of the CFSP. This discretion concerns, in particular, the assessment of the considerations of appropriateness on which such decisions are based.

142. However, although the General Court acknowledges that the competent Community institution possesses some latitude in that sphere, that does not mean that the Court is not to review the interpretation made by that institution of

the relevant facts (see *PMOI I*, paragraph 138, *PMOI II*, paragraph 55, and *Sison* v *Council*, paragraph 98). The Community judicature must not only establish whether the evidence relied on is factually accurate, reliable and consistent, but must also ascertain whether that evidence contains all the relevant information to be taken into account in order to assess the situation and whether it is capable of substantiating the conclusions drawn from it. However, when conducting such a review, it is not its task to substitute its own assessment of what is appropriate for that of the competent Community institution (see, by analogy, Case C-525/04 P *Spain* v *Lenzing* [2007] ECR I-9947, paragraph 57 and the case-law cited).

143. At paragraph 154 of *OMPI* (see also *PMOI II*, paragraph 74), the General Court also held that the judicial review of the lawfulness of a Community decision to freeze funds extends to the assessment of the facts and circumstances relied on as justifying it, and to the evidence and information on which that assessment is based, as the Council had expressly recognised in its written pleadings in Case T-306/01 *Yusuf and Al Barakaat International Foundation* v *Council and Commission* [2005] ECR II-3533 (see paragraph 225 of that judgment). The General Court must also ensure that the rights of the defence are observed and that the requirement of a statement of reasons is satisfied and also, where applicable, that any overriding considerations relied on exceptionally by the competent Community institution in order to justify disregarding those rights are well founded.

144. At paragraph 155 of *OMPI* (and see also *PMOI II*, paragraph 75) the General Court stated that, in the current context, that review is all the more essential because it constitutes the only procedural safeguard ensuring that a fair balance is struck between the need to combat international terrorism and the protection of fundamental rights. Since the restrictions imposed by the competent Community institution on the rights of defence of the parties concerned must be offset by a strict judicial review which is independent and impartial (see, to that effect, Case C-341/04 *Eurofood IFSC* [2006] ECR I-3813, paragraph 66), the Community judicature must be able to review the lawfulness and merits of Community measures to freeze funds without its being possible to raise objections that the evidence and information used by the competent Community institution is secret or confidential.

145. In that regard, the General Court further stated, at paragraph 73 of *PMOI II*, that the Council is not entitled to base its decision to freeze funds on information or material in the file communicated by a Member State, if the said Member State is not willing to authorise its communication to the Community judicature whose task is to review the lawfulness of that decision. At paragraph 76 of *PMOI II*, the Court stated that the refusal of the Council and the French authorities to communicate, even to the Court alone, certain information on which the measure contested in that action was based, had the consequence that the Court was unable to review the lawfulness of the contested decision. At paragraph 78 of *PMOI II*, the Court concluded that, in those circumstances, the applicant's right to effective judicial protection had been infringed.

146. The General Court also noted in that regard, at paragraph 156 of *OMPI*, that, although the European Court of Human Rights recognises that the use of

confidential information may be necessary when national security is at stake, that does not mean, in that court's view, that national authorities are free from any review by the national courts simply because they state that the case concerns national security and terrorism (see the judgment of the European Court of Human Rights in *Chahal* v *United Kingdom*, § 131, and case-law cited, and its judgment in *Öcalan* v *Turkey* of 12 March 2003, No 46221/99, not published in the Reports of Judgments and Decisions, § 106 and case-law cited).

147. The General Court added, at paragraph 158 of *OMPI*, that it was not necessary for it to rule, in the action before it, on the separate question as to whether the applicant and/or its lawyers could be provided with the evidence and information alleged to be confidential, or whether they had to be provided only to the Court, in accordance with a procedure which remained to be defined so as to safeguard the public interests at issue whilst affording the party concerned a sufficient degree of judicial protection.

148. Those considerations, well established in the case-law resulting from *OMPI*, should be supplemented by certain considerations based on the nature and effects of fund-freezing measures such as those at issue here, viewed from a temporal perspective.

149. Such measures are particularly draconian for those who are subject to them. All the applicant's funds and other assets have been indefinitely frozen for nearly 10 years now and he cannot gain access to them without first obtaining an exemption from the Sanctions Committee. At paragraph 358 of its judgment in *Kadi*, the Court of Justice had already noted that the measure freezing his funds entailed a restriction of the exercise of the applicant's right to property that had to be classified as considerable, having regard to the general application of the measure and the fact that it had been applied to him since 20 October 2001. In *Ahmed and Others* (paragraphs 60 and 192), the UK Supreme Court took the view that it was no exaggeration to say that persons designated in this way are effectively 'prisoners' of the State: their freedom of movement is severely restricted without access to their funds and the effect of the freeze on both them and their families can be devastating.

150. It might even be asked whether—given that now nearly 10 years have passed since the applicant's funds were originally frozen—it is not now time to call into question the finding of this Court, at paragraph 248 of its judgment in *Kadi*, and reiterated in substance by the Court of Justice at paragraph 358 of its own judgment in *Kadi*, according to which the freezing of funds is a temporary precautionary measure which, unlike confiscation, does not affect the very substance of the right of the persons concerned to property in their financial assets but only the use thereof. The same is true of the statement of the Security Council, repeated on a number of occasions, in particular in Resolution 1822 (2008), that the measures in question 'are preventative in nature and are not reliant upon criminal standards set out under national law'. In the scale of a human life, 10 years in fact represent a substantial period of time and the question of the classification of the measures in question as preventative or punitive, protective or confiscatory, civil or criminal seems now to be an open one (see also, in that connection, the Ninth Report of the

Monitoring Team, paragraph 34). That is also the opinion of the United Nations High Commissioner for Human Rights who, in a report to the General Assembly of the United Nations of 2 September 2009, entitled 'Report...on the protection of human rights and fundamental freedoms while countering terrorism' (document A/HRC/12/22, point 42), makes the following statement:

'Because individual listings are currently open-ended in duration, they may result in a temporary freeze of assets becoming permanent which, in turn, may amount to criminal punishment due to the severity of the sanction. This threatens to go well beyond the purpose of the United Nations to combat the terrorist threat posed by an individual case. In addition, there is no uniformity in relation to evidentiary standards and procedures. This poses serious human rights issues, as all punitive decisions should be either judicial or subject to judicial review.'

151. Although a discussion of this question is outside the scope of these proceedings as it is defined by the pleas set out in the application, the General Court considers that, once there is acceptance of the premiss, laid down by the judgment of the Court of Justice in *Kadi*, that freezing measures such as those at issue in this instance enjoy no immunity from jurisdiction merely because they are intended to give effect to resolutions adopted by the Security Council under Chapter VII of the Charter of the United Nations, the principle of a full and rigorous judicial review of such measures is all the more justified given that such measures have a marked and long-lasting effect on the fundamental rights of the persons concerned.

12.4 General international law

Judgment of the Court of 24 November 1992, Anklagemyndigheden v. Peter Michael Poulsen and Diva Navigation Corp, Case C-286/90, European Court Reports 1992, p. I-6019, paras. 9–10.

Poulsen concerned criminal proceedings brought by the *Anklagemyndigheden* (Danish Public Prosecutor) against Peter Michael Poulsen and Diva Navigation Corp, who were being prosecuted on a charge that the crew of the vessel 'Onkel Sam', of which Mr Poulsen is the master and Diva Navigation the owner, had retained, transported, and stored on board salmon caught in the North Atlantic in contravention of Council Regulation (EEC) No. 3094/86 of 7 October 1986, laying down certain technical measures for the conservation of fishery resources. The Court held that it was settled case law that the Union must respect international law in the exercise of its competences. This includes respect for the principles of customary international law.

9. As a preliminary point, it must be observed, first, that the European Community must respect international law in the exercise of its powers and that, consequently, Article 6 abovementioned must be interpreted, and its scope limited, in the light of the relevant rules of the international law of the sea.

10. In this connexion, account must be taken of the Geneva Conventions of 29 April 1958 on the Territorial Sea and the Contiguous Zone (United Nations Treaty Series,

vol. 516, p. 205), on the High Seas (United Nations Treaty Series, vol. 450, p. 11) and on Fishing and Conservation of the Living Resources of the High Seas (United Nations Treaty Series, vol. 559, p. 285), in so far as they codify general rules recognized by international custom, and also of the United Nations Convention of 10 December 1982 on the Law of the Sea (Third Conference of the United Nations on the Law of the Sea Official Documents, vol. XVII, 1984, Document A/Conf. 62/122 and corrections, hereinafter 'the United Nations Convention on the Law of the Sea'). It has not entered into force, but many of its provisions are considered to express the current state of customary international maritime law (see judgments of the International Court of Justice in the Delimitation of the Maritime Boundary in the Gulf of Maine Region Case, *Canada* v *United States of America*, ICJ [1984], p. 294, paragraph 94; Continental Shelf Case, *Libyan Arab Jamahiriya* v *Malta*, ICJ [1985], p. 30, paragraph 27; Military and Paramilitary Activity in and against Nicaragua Case, *Nicaragua* v *United States of America*, substantive issues, ICJ [1986], p. 111–112, paragraphs 212 and 214).

Judgment of the of First Instance (Fourth Chamber) of 22 January 1997, Opel Austria GmbH v. Council of the European Union, Case T-115/94, European Court Reports 1997, p. I-39, paras. 90–125.

In *Opel Austria*, a case concerning an action seeking the annulment of Council Regulation (EC) No. 3697/93 of 20 December 1993 withdrawing tariff concessions in accordance with Article 23(2) and Article 27(3)(a) of the Free Trade Agreement between the Community and Austria (General Motors Austria), the Court of First Instance relied extensively on the principle of good faith in international law as codified in Article 18 of the 1969 Vienna Convention on the Law of Treaties.

90. The Court holds in this connection, first, that the principle of good faith is a rule of customary international law whose existence is recognized by the International Court of Justice (see the judgment of 25 May 1926, German interests in Polish Upper Silesia, CPJI, Series A, No 7, pp. 30 and 39) and is therefore binding on the Community.

91. That principle has been codified by Article 18 of the first Vienna Convention, which provides as follows:
   'A State is obliged to refrain from acts which would defeat the object and purpose of a treaty when:
   (a) it has signed the treaty or has exchanged instruments constituting the treaty subject to ratification, acceptance or approval, until it shall have made its intention clear not to become a party to the treaty; or
   (b) it has expressed its consent to be bound by the treaty, pending the entry into force of the treaty and provided that such entry into force is not unduly delayed.'

92. In this case, the Council adopted the contested regulation on 20 December 1993, that is to say, seven days after the Communities, as the last Contracting Parties, had approved the EEA Agreement and deposited their instruments of approval

(see paragraph 23 of this judgment). Accordingly, as from 13 December 1993 the Communities were aware of the date on which the EEA Agreement would enter into force. According to Article 129(3) of the EEA Agreement (as replaced by Article 6 of the Adjustment Protocol) and Articles 1(1) and 22(3) of the Adjustment Protocol, the EEA Agreement was to enter into force on the first day of the month following the last deposit of ratification or approval.

93. Secondly, the principle of good faith is the corollary in public international law of the principle of protection of legitimate expectations which, according to the case-law, forms part of the Community legal order (see Case 112/77 *Töpfer* v *Commission* [1978] ECR 1019, paragraph 19). Any economic operator to whom an institution has given justified hopes may rely on the principle of protection of legitimate expectations (see, inter alia, Joined Cases T-466/93, T-469/93, T-473/93, T-474/93 and T-477/93 *O'Dwyer and Others* v *Council* [1995] ECR II-2071, paragraph 48).

94. In a situation where the Communities have deposited their instruments of approval of an international agreement and the date of entry into force of that agreement is known, traders may rely on the principle of protection of legitimate expectations in order to challenge the adoption by the institutions, during the period preceding the entry into force of that agreement, of any measure contrary to the provisions of that agreement which will have direct effect on them after it has entered into force.

95. Consequently, the applicant is entitled to require a review of the legality of the contested regulation in the light of the provisions of the EEA Agreement which have direct effect after its entry into force.

96. However, before considering the various arguments raised by the applicant in that regard, it must first be established whether and to what extent the provisions of the EEA Agreement take the place of the provisions of the FTA and whether the EEA Agreement is applicable to the products at issue in this case.

97. The FTA, which was applicable at the material time and was the basis on which the contested regulation was adopted, was not abrogated or suspended when the EEA Agreement entered into force. According to Article 120 of the EEA Agreement, however, the application of the provisions of that Agreement prevail over provisions of the FTA 'to the extent that the same subject-matter is governed' by the EEA Agreement. The provisions of the EEA Agreement concerned in this case govern the same subject-matter as the relevant articles of the FTA. Article 10 of the EEA Agreement governs the same subject-matter as Articles 3 and 6 of the FTA, namely customs duties on imports and charges having equivalent effect. Article 61 of the EEA Agreement, relating to State aids, is more specific than, and its scope as wide as, Article 23(1)(iii) of the FTA; it is almost identical to Article 92 of the EC Treaty. Moreover, the specific provisions applicable to State aid within the Community are taken up in Annex XV to the EEA Agreement. As for the procedures provided for in Article 27(2) and (3)(a) of the FTA, it should be noted that, pursuant to Article 108 of the EEA Agreement, the EFTA States are to establish an EFTA Surveillance Authority and an EFTA Court. Those two institutions are accorded, particularly in the fields of competition and State aid, powers

and procedures analogous to those existing in the Community in the same fields. The allocation of competence and cooperation between the EFTA Surveillance Authority and the Commission in the field of State aid are governed by Article 62 of the EEA Agreement. Consequently, following the entry into force of the EEA Agreement, the application of those provisions of the Agreement prevails over that of the relevant provisions of the FTA.

98. In that context, without ruling on the compatibility of the aid granted by the Republic of Austria with the FTA or the EEA Agreement, the Court notes that the Council complied with the procedure provided for in the State-aid provisions of the FTA before it adopted the contested regulation. However, as appears from the previous paragraph, after the EEA Agreement entered into force the application of the State-aid provisions of that Agreement prevailed over the application of the corresponding provisions of the FTA. In that regard, the EEA Agreement contains its own rules and procedures allowing the Contracting Parties to abolish State aid which is incompatible with the functioning of the Agreement.

99. As to the question whether the Agreement is applicable to the products referred to in the contested regulation, it is not disputed that those products originated in Contracting Parties of the EEA Agreement and that they fall within Chapters 25 to 97 of the Harmonized Commodity Description and Coding System. Consequently, by virtue of Article 8(2) and (3)(a) of the EEA Agreement, that agreement is applicable to those products with effect from its entry into force.

100. Secondly, it is necessary to consider whether Article 10 of the EEA Agreement is capable of having direct effect following the entry into force of that agreement.

101. As appears from Article 228(7) of the EC Treaty, international agreements concluded by the Community in conformity with the Treaty are binding on the institutions and the Member States. It is settled case-law that the provisions of such an agreement form an integral part of the Community legal order once the agreement has entered into force (see *Haegeman*, cited above, paragraph 5). It is also settled case-law that the provisions of such an agreement may have direct effect if they are unconditional and sufficiently precise (see, for example, Case 87/75 *Bresciani* [1976] ECR 129, paragraph 25, and Case 104/81 *Hauptzollamt Mainz* v *Kupferberg* [1982] ECR 3641, paragraph 23).

102. In that regard, the Court observes that nothing in the case-file suggests that the EEA Agreement, which was concluded by the Community on the basis of Article 238 of the EC Treaty, was not concluded in conformity with the Treaty. It follows that since the Agreement entered into force on 1 January 1994 the provisions of the Agreement form an integral part of the Community legal order. It should also be borne in mind that the first sentence of Article 10 of the EEA Agreement provides that customs duties on imports and exports and any charges having equivalent effect are prohibited between the Contracting Parties. The second sentence of that article provides that, without prejudice to the arrangements set out in Protocol 5, customs duties of a fiscal nature are likewise prohibited. Article 10 thus lays down an unconditional and precise rule, subject to a single exception which is itself unconditional and precise. It follows

that ever since the EEA Agreement entered into force Article 10 has had direct effect.

103. Thirdly, it is necessary to decide whether, by reintroducing a duty of 4.9%, the contested regulation infringed Article 10 of the EEA Agreement.

104. Article 6 of the EEA Agreement provides:

'Without prejudice to future developments of case-law, the provisions of this Agreement, in so far as they are identical in substance to corresponding rules of the Treaty establishing the European Economic Community and the Treaty establishing the European Coal and Steel Community and to acts adopted in application of these two Treaties, shall, in their implementation and application, be interpreted in conformity with the relevant rulings of the Court of Justice of the European Communities given prior to the date of signature of this Agreement.'

105. The Council contends that, notwithstanding that provision, Article 10 of the EEA Agreement should not be interpreted in the same way as the corresponding provisions of the EC Treaty, because there are major differences between the EC Treaty and the EEA Agreement (see paragraph 62 of this judgment).

106. That argument cannot be accepted. It is clear from the case-law that in order to determine whether the interpretation of a provision contained in the EC Treaty must be extended to an identical provision contained in an agreement such as the EEA Agreement, that provision should be analysed in the light of both the purpose and the objective of the Agreement and in its context (see Case 270/80 *Polydor v Harlequin* [1982] ECR 329, paragraph 8, and C-163/90 *Administration des Douanes et Droits Indirects v Legros and Others* [1992] ECR I-4625, paragraph 23). According to Article 1(1) of the EEA Agreement, the aim of that agreement is to promote a continuous and balanced strengthening of trade and economic relations between the Contracting Parties with equal conditions of competition, and the respect of the same rules, with a view to creating a homogeneous European Economic Area. To that end, the Contracting Parties decided to eliminate virtually all trade barriers, in conformity with the provisions of the GATT on the establishment of free-trade areas.

107. In that context, the EEA Agreement involves a high degree of integration, with objectives which exceed those of a mere free-trade agreement. Thus, as is clear from Article 1(2), the EEA involves, inter alia, the free movement of goods, persons, services and capital and the setting up of a system ensuring that competition is not distorted and that the rules relating thereto are equally respected. The rules applicable to relations between the Contracting Parties in the fields covered by the Agreement essentially correspond to the parallel provisions of the EC and ECSC Treaties and the measures adopted in pursuance of those treaties. The EEA Agreement also aims to extend to the EEA future Community law in the fields covered by the Agreement as it is created, develops or changes and a decision-making procedure is provided to that end. The Agreement further provides that the EFTA States are to set up a surveillance authority, the EFTA Surveillance Authority, with equivalent powers and similar functions to those of the Commission, and a court of justice, the EFTA Court. Article 109 of the EEA

Agreement provides that, on the one hand, the EFTA Surveillance Authority and, on the other, the Commission acting in conformity with the EC Treaty, the ECSC Treaty and the Agreement, are to monitor the fulfilment of the obligations under the EEA Agreement. According to Article 108(2) of the EEA Agreement and the Agreement between the EFTA States of 2 May 1992 on the establishment of a Surveillance Authority and a Court of Justice (OJ 1994 L 344, p. 1; hereinafter 'the EFTA Surveillance Agreement'), the EFTA Court has jurisdiction similar to that of the Court of Justice and the Court of First Instance.

108. Thus, by establishing an EFTA Surveillance Authority and an EFTA Court with powers and jurisdiction similar to those of the Commission and the Court of Justice, a two-pillar system has been created in which the EFTA Surveillance Authority and the EFTA Court monitor the application of the Agreement on the part of the EFTA States, while the Commission, the Court of Justice and the Court of First Instance do so on the part of the Community. That system is reinforced by a large number of factors intended to make sure that it is homogeneous. They include, in addition to the similarity between the terms of the various provisions of the Agreement and the EC and ECSC Treaties, the fourth and 15th recitals in the preamble to the Agreement and Article 6 thereof, as well as, inter alia, Article 3 of the EFTA Surveillance Agreement. In particular, by virtue of the fourth recital in the preamble to the Agreement, the Contracting Parties' objective is '[to establish] a dynamic and homogeneous European Economic Area, based on common rules and equal conditions of competition and providing for the adequate means of enforcement including at the judicial level, and achieved on the basis of equality and reciprocity and of an overall balance of benefits, rights and obligations for the Contracting Parties'. The 15th recital in the preamble— added by the Contracting Parties after the Court of Justice had held in Opinion 1/91, cited above, that the judicial system in the first version of the Agreement, providing for a Court of Justice of the European Economic Area, was incompatible with the EEC Treaty—stipulates further that 'in full deference to the independence of the courts, the objective of the Contracting Parties is to arrive at, and maintain, a uniform interpretation and application of this Agreement and those provisions of Community legislation which are substantially reproduced in this Agreement and to arrive at an equal treatment of individuals and economic operators as regards the four freedoms and the conditions of competition'. As recalled in paragraph 104 of this judgment, Article 6 of the EEA Agreement provides that the provisions of the EEA Agreement which are identical in substance to the Community rules are to be interpreted in conformity with the rulings of the Court of Justice and of the Court of First Instance given prior to the date of signature of the Agreement. Finally, it is clear from Article 3(2) of the EFTA Surveillance Agreement that, when interpreting and applying the EEA Agreement, the EFTA Surveillance Authority and the EFTA Court are to pay due account to the principles laid down by the relevant rulings by the Court of Justice and the Court of First Instance given after the date of signature of the EEA Agreement (see the judgments of the EFTA Court in Restamark, cited above, paragraphs 24, 33 and 34, and in *Scottish Salmon Growers Association*

v *EFTA Surveillance Authority*, E-2/94, Report of the EFTA Court, 1 January 1994—30 June 1995, p. 59, paragraphs 11 and 13).

109. Contrary to the Council's contention, the significance in regard to the interpretation and application of the Agreement of the Contracting Parties' objective of establishing a dynamic and homogeneous EEA has not been diminished by the Court of Justice in Opinion 1/91, cited above. When the Court held that the divergences existing between the aims and context of the Agreement, on the one hand, and the aims and context of Community law on the other, stood in the way of the achievement of the objective of homogeneity in the interpretation and application of the law in the EEA, it was considering the judicial system contemplated by the EEA Agreement for the purposes of ascertaining whether that system might jeopardize the autonomy of the Community legal order in pursuing its own objectives; and not a specific case in which it is necessary to determine whether a provision of the EEA Agreement identical in substance to a provision of Community law must be interpreted in conformity with the rulings of the Court of Justice and the Court of First Instance.

110. It follows from those findings that Article 6 of the EEA Agreement must be interpreted as meaning that where a provision of the EEA Agreement is identical in substance to corresponding rules of the EC and ECSC Treaties and to the acts adopted in application of those two treaties it must be interpreted in conformity with the relevant rulings of the Court of Justice and of the Court of First Instance given prior to the date of signature of the EEA Agreement.

111. The Court further finds that Article 10 of the EEA Agreement is identical in substance to Articles 12, 13, 16 and 17 of the EC Treaty which, with effect from the end of the transitional period, prohibit customs duties on imports or exports and any charges having equivalent effect between the Member States. Consequently, by virtue of Article 6 of the EEA Agreement, Article 10 must be interpreted in conformity with the relevant rulings of the Court of Justice and the Court of First Instance prior to the date of signature of the Agreement.

112. In this regard it is necessary, first, to reject the Commission's argument to the effect that, since it appears from Article 10 of the EEA Agreement that customs duties of a fiscal nature are not regarded as necessarily covered by the notion of customs duties on imports and exports and charges having equivalent effect, that article and the corresponding provisions of the EC Treaty are not identical in substance. Suffice it to say that the EC Treaty contains a corresponding provision, namely Article 17 of the Treaty, which makes it clear that the prohibitions set out in Article 9 of the Treaty are to apply even if the customs duties are of a fiscal nature, and is intended to prevent circumvention of the prohibition on customs duties on imports and exports and any charges having equivalent effect (see *Sociaal Fonds voor de Diamantarbeiders* v *Brachfeld*, cited above, paragraph 7/10).

113. Secondly, contrary to the Commission's submission, the interpretation of Article 10 of the EEA Agreement proposed by the applicant does not make it impossible to apply Article 64 of the EEA Agreement. In the field of State aid, Article 64 authorizes the competent authority of the Contracting Party affected by a

distortion of competition to adopt measures, subject to certain conditions, in order to offset the effects of the distortion. Since it constitutes an exception to the other provisions of the EEA Agreement, Article 64 may therefore be applied notwithstanding the other provisions of the Agreement. However, before measures are adopted, the procedure provided for in Article 64 of the EEA Agreement must have been carried out and the conditions which it lays down must have been complied with.

114. Thirdly, the various safeguard clauses in the EEA Agreement allowing the Contracting Parties to derogate from its provisions may be used only in particular circumstances and, as a general rule, following consideration of the arguments for and against in the EEA Joint Committee. Outside the specific situations which may give rise to their application, those clauses have no impact on the objective pursued by Article 10 in the context of the EEA Agreement or, consequently, on the interpretation to be given to that article. That conclusion is confirmed in particular by the fact that until the Treaty on European Union entered into force, Article 115 of the EEC Treaty allowed the Member States themselves to take the necessary measures in case of urgency during the transitional period and that, as the applicant has correctly observed, in *Sociaal Fonds voor de Diamantarbeiders v Brachfeld* the Court of Justice specifically declared pecuniary charges levied during the transitional period unlawful.

115. Fourthly, the Commission's argument that Article 26 of the EEA Agreement would be unnecessary if Article 10 had to be interpreted in conformity with the rulings of the Court of Justice must also be rejected. Article 26 of the EEA Agreement provides that anti-dumping measures, countervailing duties and measures against illicit commercial practices attributable to third countries are not to be applied in relations between the Contracting Parties unless otherwise specified in the EEA Agreement. The first paragraph of Protocol 13 states that the application of Article 26 is limited to the areas covered by the provisions of the Agreement in which the acquis communautaire is fully integrated into the Agreement. It follows from the second paragraph of that protocol that Article 26 does not apply in situations where one Contracting Party introduces measures directed at third countries that are intended to avoid circumvention of anti-dumping measures, countervailing duties or measures against illicit commercial practices attributable to third countries.

116. Article 26, in conjunction with Protocol 13 of the Agreement, must therefore be interpreted as governing situations in which anti-dumping measures, countervailing duties or measures against illicit commercial practices attributable to third countries may be introduced by the Contracting Parties as between themselves, notwithstanding the other provisions of the EEA Agreement. Moreover, Article 26 applies not only to measures adopted in the form of duties but also to any other measures, no matter what form they take, including undertakings accepted by Commission decisions in dumping cases. Consequently, Article 26 of the EEA Agreement has its own justification, which is independent of that of Article 10 of the EEA Agreement.

117. In any event, the contested regulation was not adopted in order to prevent circumvention of anti-dumping measures, countervailing duties or illicit commercial

practices attributable to third countries. What is more, the field of State aid comes under Articles 61 to 64 of the EEA Agreement. Furthermore, the whole of the acquis communautaire in this field, in particular the Community Framework on State Aid to the Motor Vehicle Industry (89/C 123/03; OJ 1989 C 123, p. 3) has been integrated into the Agreement. Consequently, such measures cannot be authorized under Article 26 of the EEA Agreement either and it is unnecessary to make a determination as to whether the measures established by the contested regulation must be regarded as countervailing duties.

118. It should be noted for completeness' sake that, in regard to free-trade agreements with the EFTA countries, whose subject-matter is much more limited than that of the EEA Agreement, the Court of Justice held in *Legros and Others*, cited above (paragraph 26), which was concerned with Article 6 of the Agreement between the Community and the Kingdom of Sweden [Council Regulation (EEC) No 2838/72 of 19 December 1972 concluding an Agreement between the European Economic Community and the Kingdom of Sweden (OJ 1972 L 300, p. 96)], relating to charges having equivalent effect, that, in the context of the objective of eliminating trade barriers, the elimination of customs duties on imports was of prime importance, as was the elimination of charges having equivalent effect, which, according to the case-law of the Court of Justice, are closely linked to customs charges stricto sensu (see, in particular, Joined Cases 37/73 and 38/73 *Sociaal Fonds voor de Diamantarbeiders* v *Indiamex* [1973] ECR 1609, paragraphs 12 and 13, and Case C-260/90 *Leplat* [1992] ECR I-643, paragraph 15). The Court of Justice concluded that the free-trade agreement would be deprived of much of its effectiveness if the term 'charge having equivalent effect' contained in Article 6 of the Agreement were to be interpreted as having more limited scope than the same term appearing in the EEC Treaty.

119. In view of all these factors, it is accordingly necessary to consider whether, following the entry into force of the EEA Agreement, the contested regulation is contrary to Article 10 of that agreement when interpreted, pursuant to Article 6, in conformity with the relevant rulings of the Court of Justice and the Court of First Instance prior to the date of signature of the EEA Agreement.

120. In that regard it is necessary to reject the Council's argument that the measure introduced by the contested regulation does not constitute a duty but a sui generis safeguard measure which, as such, does not come under Article 10 of the EEA Agreement. The very title of the contested regulation refers to 'withdrawing tariff concessions'. Furthermore, Article 1 of the regulation provides that 'a 4.9% duty is hereby reintroduced for F-15 car gearboxes produced by General Motors Austria' and the 23rd recital in its preamble refers to 'the introduction of duties at a level equal to the level of customs duties which would have prevailed if the [FTA] had not entered into force'. Finally, at the hearing, the Council's representative accepted, in replying to a question put by the Court, that the characterization of the measure is of little significance, since, whether it be characterized as an anti-dumping duty, a countervailing duty, the withdrawal of a tariff concession, the introduction of a duty or a sui generis safeguard measure, its effect is identical.

121. In addition, it is settled case-law that 'any pecuniary charge, however small and whatever its designation and mode of application, which is imposed unilaterally on domestic or foreign goods by reason of the fact that they cross a frontier, and which is not a customs duty in the strict sense, constitutes a charge having equivalent effect within the meaning of Articles 9 and 12 of the Treaty, even if it is not imposed for the benefit of the State, is not discriminatory or protective in effect or if the product on which the charge is imposed is not in competition with any domestic product' (*Sociaal Fonds voor de Diamantarbeiders* v *Brachfeld*, paragraph 15/18).

122. The measure introduced by the contested regulation constitutes a pecuniary charge imposed unilaterally by the Community on F-15 gearboxes by reason of the fact that they cross a frontier. Consequently, it must be held that the measure constitutes, at the very least, a charge having equivalent effect within the meaning of Article 10 of the EEA Agreement and it is unnecessary to determine whether it must be regarded as a customs duty on imports in the strict sense. It is therefore clear that, following the entry into force of the EEA Agreement, the contested regulation was contrary to that article.

123. It follows that, by adopting the contested regulation in the period preceding the entry into force of the EEA Agreement after the Communities had deposited their instruments of approval, the Council infringed the applicant's legitimate expectations.

124. According to the case-law, moreover, Community legislation must be certain and its application foreseeable by individuals. The principle of legal certainty requires that every measure of the institutions having legal effects must be clear and precise and must be brought to the notice of the person concerned in such a way that he can ascertain exactly the time at which the measure comes into being and starts to have legal effects. That requirement of legal certainty must be observed all the more strictly in the case of a measure liable to have financial consequences in order that those concerned may know precisely the extent of the obligations which it imposes on them (see Case 169/80 *Administration des Douanes* v *Gondrand Frères and Garancini* [1981] ECR 1931, paragraph 17; Case 70/83 *Kloppenburg* v *Finanzamt Leer* [1984] ECR 1075, paragraph 11; Case 325/85 *Ireland* v *Commission* [1987] ECR 5041, paragraph 18; Joined Cases T-18/89 and T-24/89 *Tagaras* v *Court of Justice* [1991] ECR II-53, paragraph 40).

125. By adopting the contested regulation on 20 December 1993 when it knew with certainty that the EEA Agreement would enter into force on 1 January 1994, the Council knowingly created a situation in which, with effect from January 1994, two contradictory rules of law would co-exist, namely the contested regulation, which is directly applicable in the national legal systems and re-establishes a 4.9% import duty on F-15 gearboxes produced by the applicant; and Article 10 of the EEA Agreement, which has direct effect and prohibits customs duties on imports and any charges having equivalent effect. Consequently, the contested regulation cannot be regarded as Community legislation which is certain and its operation/application cannot be regarded as foreseeable by those subject to it. It follows that the Council also infringed the principle of legal certainty.

Judgment of the Court (Fourth Chamber) of 25 February 2010, Firma Brita GmbH v. Hauptzollamt Hamburg-Hafen, Case C-386/08, European Court Reports 2010, p. I-1289, paras. 40-4.

The Court of Justice now regularly refers to the 1969 Vienna Convention as a codification of the principles of general international law governing the law of treaties. It did so, for example, in *Brita*, a case concerning the interpretation of the EC–Israel Association Agreement in the context of a customs dispute between Brita GmbH and the Hauptzollamt Hamburg-Hafen (the main customs office of the port of Hamburg) concerning the refusal of the Hauptzollamt to grant Brita preferential treatment with regard to the importation of products manufactured in the West Bank.

40. The international law of treaties was consolidated, essentially, in the Vienna Convention. Under Article 1 thereof, the Vienna Convention applies to treaties between States. However, under Article 3(b) of the Vienna Convention, the fact that the Vienna Convention does not apply to international agreements concluded between States and other subjects of international law is not to affect the application to them of any of the rules set forth in that convention to which they would be subject under international law independently of the convention.

41. It follows that the rules laid down in the Vienna Convention apply to an agreement concluded between a State and an international organisation, such as the EC–Israel Association Agreement, in so far as the rules are an expression of general international customary law. Consequently, the EC–Israel Association Agreement must be interpreted in accordance with those rules.

42. In addition, the Court has held that, even though the Vienna Convention does not bind either the Community or all its Member States, a series of provisions in that convention reflect the rules of customary international law which, as such, are binding upon the Community institutions and form part of the Community legal order (see, to that effect, *Racke*, paragraphs 24, 45 and 46; see, also, as regards the reference to the Vienna Convention for the purposes of the interpretation of association agreements concluded by the European Communities, Case C-416/96 *El-Yassini* [1999] ECR I-1209, paragraph 47, and Case C-268/99 *Jany and Others* [2001] ECR I-8615, paragraph 35 and the case-law cited).

43. Pursuant to Article 31 of the Vienna Convention, a treaty is to be interpreted in good faith in accordance with the ordinary meaning to be given to the terms of the treaty in their context and in the light of its object and purpose. In that respect, account is to be taken, together with the context, of any relevant rules of international law applicable in the relations between the parties.

44. Among the relevant rules that may be relied on in the context of the relations between the parties to the EC–Israel Association Agreement is the general international law principle of the relative effect of treaties, according to which treaties do not impose any obligations, or confer any rights, on third States ('pacta tertiis nec nocent nec prosunt'). That principle of general international law finds particular expression in Article 34 of the Vienna Convention, under which a treaty does not create either obligations or rights for a third State without its consent.

Judgment of the Court (Grand Chamber) of 21 December 2011, Air Transport Association of America and Others v. Secretary of State for Energy and Climate Change, Case C-366/10, not yet reported (ATAA case), paras. 101–110.

Since the entry into force of the Treaty of Lisbon, the Court of Justice's analysis of the status of customary international law has to start from Article 3(5) TEU.

The Court derived from that provision the obligation for the EU to observe international law in its entirety when it adopts an act, including customary international law, which is binding upon the EU institutions. The CJEU proposed to perform a two-stage analysis: first, do the principles mentioned by the referring court actually form part of international law; and second, can they be relied upon by individuals to call into question the validity of the measure at issue? The Court relied on the case law of the International Court of Justice and the Permanent Court of International Justice, as well as on a number of international agreements, as a basis for determining the status in international law of the principles at issue. The CJEU held that principles of customary international law it had recognized as such could be relied upon by an individual for the purpose of the Court's examination of the validity of an EU act subject to two conditions: first, in so far as those principles are capable of calling into question the competence of the EU to adopt that act; and second, in so far as the act in question is liable to affect rights which the individual derives from EU law or to create obligations under EU law in this regard. It is important to note that these conditions differ from those applicable to international agreements outlined above.

101. Under Article 3(5) TEU, the European Union is to contribute to the strict observance and the development of international law. Consequently, when it adopts an act, it is bound to observe international law in its entirety, including customary international law, which is binding upon the institutions of the European Union (see, to this effect, Case C-286/90 *Poulsen and Diva Navigation* [1992] ECR I-6019, paragraphs 9 and 10, and Case C-162/96 *Racke* [1998] ECR I-3655, paragraphs 45 and 46).

102. Thus, it should be examined first whether the principles to which the referring court makes reference are recognised as forming part of customary international law. If they are, it should, secondly, then be determined whether and to what extent they may be relied upon by individuals to call into question the validity of an act of the European Union, such as Directive 2008/101, in a situation such as that in the main proceedings.

a) Recognition of the principles of customary international law relied upon

103. The referring court mentions a principle that each State has complete and exclusive sovereignty over its airspace and another principle that no State may validly purport to subject any part of the high seas to its sovereignty. It also mentions the principle of freedom to fly over the high seas.

104. These three principles are regarded as embodying the current state of customary international maritime and air law and, moreover, they have been respectively codified in Article 1 of the Chicago Convention (see, on the recognition of such

a principle, the judgment of the International Court of Justice of 27 June 1986 in *Military and Paramilitary Activities in and against Nicaragua (Nicaragua v United States of America), I.C.J. Reports 1986*, p. 392, paragraph 212), in Article 2 of the Geneva Convention of 29 April 1958 on the High Seas (*United Nations Treaty Series*, Vol. 450, p. 11) (see also, on the recognition of this principle, the judgment of the Permanent Court of International Justice of 7 September 1927 in *the Case of the S.S. 'Lotus'*, PCIJ 1927, Series A, No 10, p. 25) and in the third sentence of Article 87(1) of the United Nations Convention on the Law of the Sea, signed in Montego Bay on 10 December 1982, which entered into force on 16 November 1994 and was concluded and approved on behalf of the European Community by Council Decision 98/392/EC of 23 March 1998 (OJ 1998 L 179, p. 1).

105. Nor has the existence of those principles of international law been contested by the Member States, the institutions of the European Union, the Republic of Iceland or the Kingdom of Norway in their written observations or at the hearing.

106. As regards the fourth principle set out by the referring court, namely the principle that aircraft overflying the high seas are subject to the exclusive jurisdiction of the State in which they are registered, it must be found by contrast that, apart from the fact that the United Kingdom Government and, to a certain extent, the German Government dispute the existence of such a principle, insufficient evidence exists to establish that the principle of customary international law, recognised as such, that a vessel on the high seas is in principle governed only by the law of its flag (see *Poulsen and Diva Navigation*, paragraph 22) would apply by analogy to aircraft overflying the high seas.

b) Whether and under what circumstances the principles at issue may be relied upon

107. The principles of customary international law mentioned in paragraph 103 of the present judgment may be relied upon by an individual for the purpose of the Court's examination of the validity of an act of the European Union in so far as, first, those principles are capable of calling into question the competence of the European Union to adopt that act (see Joined Cases 89/85, 104/85, 114/85, 116/85, 117/85 and 125/85 to 129/85 *Ahlström Osakeyhtiö and Others v Commission* [1988] ECR 5193, paragraphs 14 to 18, and Case C-405/92 *Mondiet* [1993] ECR I-6133, paragraphs 11 to 16) and, second, the act in question is liable to affect rights which the individual derives from European Union law or to create obligations under European Union law in his regard.

108. In the main proceedings, those principles of customary international law are relied upon, in essence, in order for the Court to determine whether the European Union had competence, in the light thereof, to adopt Directive 2008/101 in that it extends the application of Directive 2003/87 to aircraft operators of third States whose flights which arrive at and depart from an aerodrome situated in the territory of a Member State of the European Union are carried out in part over the high seas and over the third States' territory.

109. Therefore, even though the principles at issue appear only to have the effect of creating obligations between States, it is nevertheless possible, in circumstances such as those of the case which has been brought before the referring court, in which Directive 2008/101 is liable to create obligations under European Union

law as regards the claimants in the main proceedings, that the latter may rely on those principles and that the Court may thus examine the validity of Directive 2008/101 in the light of such principles.

110. However, since a principle of customary international law does not have the same degree of precision as a provision of an international agreement, judicial review must necessarily be limited to the question whether, in adopting the act in question, the institutions of the European Union made manifest errors of assessment concerning the conditions for applying those principles (see, to this effect, *Racke*, paragraph 52).

Judgment of the Court (Grand Chamber) of 16 October 2012, Hungary v. Slovakia, Case C-364/10, not yet reported, paras. 40–52.

This case concerned an action for infringement brought by Hungary against Slovakia for violating Article 21 TFEU and Directive 2004/38/EC by not allowing the Hungarian President to make a planned visit to Slovakia in August 2009. Slovakia contended that EU law did not apply to the dispute, since the planned visit of the President of Hungary to Slovakia was going to be in his official capacity as Head of State. Starting from the principle that EU law must be interpreted in the light of relevant rules of international law, the Court found that the status of Head of State has a specific character, resulting from the fact that it is governed by international law. With the exception of Article 1 of the New York Convention of 14 December 1973 on the Prevention and Punishment of Crimes against Internationally Protected Persons, including Diplomatic Agents, the Court did not elaborate further on the rules of international law to which it was referring. It concluded that the fact that a Union citizen performs the duties of a Head of State is such as to justify a limitation, based on international law, on the exercise of the right of free movement conferred on that person by Article 21 TFEU.

40. In order to rule on the first head of complaint, it should be stated from the outset that citizenship of the Union is intended to be the fundamental status of nationals of the Member States (see, inter alia, Case C-184/99 *Grzelczyk* [2001] ECR I-6193, paragraph 31; Case C-135/08 *Rottmann* [2010] ECR I-1449, paragraph 43; and Case C-256/11 *Dereci and Others* [2011] ECR I-0000, paragraph 62).

41. To that end, Article 20 TFEU confers the status of citizen of the Union on every person holding the nationality of a Member State (see, inter alia, Case C-224/98 *D'Hoop* [2002] ECR I-6191, paragraph 27; Case C-148/02 *Garcia Avello* [2003] ECR I-11613, paragraph 21; and Case C-34/09 *Ruiz Zambrano* [2011] ECR I-0000, paragraph 40).

42. It follows that, since Mr Sólyom is of Hungarian nationality, he unquestionably enjoys that status.

43. It is true, first, that, in accordance with Article 21 TFEU, citizenship of the Union confers on each Union citizen a primary and individual right to move and reside freely within the territory of the Member States, subject to the limitations and restrictions laid down by the Treaties and the measures adopted for their

implementation (Case C-162/09 *Lassal* [2010] ECR I-9217, paragraph 29, and Case C-434/09 *McCarthy* [2011] ECR I-0000, paragraph 27).

44. Second, it is necessary to note that EU law must be interpreted in the light of the relevant rules of international law, since international law is part of the European Union legal order and is binding on the institutions (see, to that effect, *Racke*, paragraphs 45 and 46, and Joined Cases C-402/05 P and C-415/05 P *Kadi and Al Barakaat International Foundation* v *Council and Commission* [2008] ECR I-6351, paragraph 291).

45. In the present case, it is therefore necessary to establish whether, as the Slovak Republic claims, the fact that Mr Sólyom, while a Union citizen, was carrying out, at the material time, the duties of the Hungarian Head of State is liable to constitute a limitation, on the basis of international law, on the application of the right of free movement conferred on him by Article 21 TFEU.

46. To that end, it should be noted that, on the basis of customary rules of general international law and those of multilateral agreements, the Head of State enjoys a particular status in international relations which entails, inter alia, privileges and immunities.

47. In particular, Article 1 of the New York Convention of 14 December 1973 on the Prevention and Punishment of Crimes against Internationally Protected Persons, including Diplomatic Agents, states, inter alia, that every Head of State, while on the territory of a foreign State, enjoys that protection.

48. Thus, the presence of a Head of State on the territory of another State imposes on that latter State the obligation to guarantee the protection of the person who carries out that duty, irrespective of the capacity in which his stay is effected.

49. The status of Head of State therefore has a specific character, resulting from the fact that it is governed by international law, with the consequence that the conduct of such a person internationally, such as that person's presence in another State, comes under that law, in particular the law governing diplomatic relations.

50. Such a specific character is capable of distinguishing the person who enjoys that status from all other Union citizens, with the result that that person's access to the territory of another Member State is not governed by the same conditions as those applicable to other citizens.

51. Accordingly, the fact that a Union citizen performs the duties of a Head of State is such as to justify a limitation, based on international law, on the exercise of the right of free movement conferred on that person by Article 21 TFEU.

52. In the light of all of the foregoing, it must be held that, in the circumstances of the present case, neither Article 21 TFEU nor, *a fortiori*, Directive 2004/38 obliged the Slovak Republic to guarantee access to its territory to the President of Hungary and that, therefore, the first head of complaint must be rejected as unfounded.

Select Bibliography

Bourgeois, J., Effects of International Agreements on European Community Law: Are the Dice Cast?, *Michigan Law Review*, 1984, 1250–73.

—— and Lynskey, O., The Extent to Which the EC Legislature Takes Account of WTO Obligations: Jousting Lessons from the European Parliament, *Law and Practice of EU*

External Relations (A. Dashwood and M. Maresceau (eds), Cambridge: Cambridge University Press, 2008), 202–23.

Cheyne, I., International Instruments as a Source of Community Law, *The General Law of EC External Relations* (A. Dashwood and C. Hillion (eds), London: Sweet & Maxwell, 2000), 254–75.

Dani, M., Remedying European Legal Pluralism: The FIAMM and Fedon Litigation and the Judicial Protection of International Trade Bystanders, *European Journal of International Law*, vol. 21(2), 2010, 303–40.

De Baere, G., European Integration and the Rule of Law in Foreign Policy, *Philosophical Foundations of European Union Law* (J. Dickson and P. Eleftheriadis (eds), Oxford: Oxford University Press, 2012), 354–83.

—— and Ryngaert, C., The ECJ's Judgment in *Air Transport Association of America* and the International Legal Context of the EU's Climate Change Policy, 18 *EFA Rev*, forthcoming.

de Búrca, G., The EU, the European Court of Justice and the International Legal Order after Kadi, *Harvard International Law Journal*, 2009, 1–49.

Eeckhout, P., EC Law and UN Security Council Resolutions—In Search of the Right Fit', *Law and Practice of EU External Relations* (A. Dashwood and M. Maresceau (eds), Cambridge: Cambridge University Press, 2008), 104–28.

——, *EU External Relations Law* (2nd edn, Oxford: Oxford University Press, 2011), 323–436.

Halberstam, D. and Stein, E., The United Nations, the European Union, and the King of Sweden: Economic Sanctions and Individual Rights in a Plural World Order, *Common Market Law Review*, 2009, 13–72.

Higgins, R., The ICJ, the ECJ and the Integrity of International Law, *The International and Comparative Law Quarterly*, 2003, 1–20.

Jacobs, F., Direct Effect and Interpretation of International Agreements in the Recent Case Law of the European Court of Justice, *Law and Practice of EU External Relations* (A. Dashwood and M. Maresceau (eds), Cambridge: Cambridge University Press, 2008), 13–33.

Kaddous, C., Effects of International Agreements in the EU Legal Order, *EU Foreign Relations Law: Constitutional Fundamentals* (M. Cremona and B. de Witte (eds), Oxford and Portland, OR: Hart Publishing, 2008), 291–313.

Klabbers, J., *Treaty Conflict and the European Union* (Cambridge: Cambridge University Press, 2009), 113–226.

Koskenniemi, M. (ed.), *International Law Aspects of the European Union* (The Hague, London, and Boston: Kluwer Law International, 1998).

Koutrakos, P., *EU International Relations Law* (Oxford and Portland, OR: Hart Publishing, 2006), 217–49; 301–28.

Kuijper, P.J. and Bronckers, M., WTO Law in the European Court of Justice, *Common Market Law Review*, 2005, 1313–55.

Lenaerts, K. and De Smijter, E., The European Union as an Actor under International Law, *YEL*, vol. 19, 1999–2000, 95–138.

Lickova, M., European Exceptionalism in International Law, *European Journal of International Law*, vol. 19(3), 2008, 463–90.

Mendez, M., The Legal Effect of Community Agreements: Maximalist Treaty Enforcement and Judicial Avoidance Techniques, *European Journal of International Law*, vol. 21(1), 2010, 83–104.

Rosas, A., The Status in EU Law of International Agreements Concluded by EU Member States, *Fordham International Law Journal*, vol. 35(5), 2011, 1304–45.

Tridimas, T. and Gutiérrez-Fons, J., EU Law, International Law and Economic Sanctions against Terrorism: The Judiciary in Distress?, *Fordham International Law Journal*, 2009, 660–730.

Verwey, D., *The European Community, the European Union and the International Law of Treaties* (The Hague: T.M.C. Asser Press, 2004).

Wouters, J. and De Man, P., International Association of Independent Tanker Owners (Intertanko), International Association of Dry Cargo Shipowners (Intercargo), Greek Shipping Co-operation Committee, Lloyd's Register and International Salvage Union v Secretary of State for Transport, *American Journal of International Law*, vol. 103(3), 2009, 555–60.

——, Nollkaemper, A., and de Wet, E. (eds), *The Europeanisation of International Law: The Status of International Law in the EU and its Member States* (The Hague: T.M.C. Asser Press, 2008).

13

International Agreements of the Member States

13.1 Prior agreements of the Member States with third countries

Article 351 TFEU (former Article 307 EC and previously Article 234 EEC) deals with the fate of an international agreement that a Member State has concluded with one or more third countries prior to the establishment of the EU or, for acceding states, before the date of their accession. According to Article 351(1) TFEU, such prior agreements shall not be affected by the provisions of the Treaties. This paragraph reflects Article 34 of the 1969 *Vienna Convention on the Law of Treaties* according to which a treaty—here the TEU and the TFEU—cannot create rights and obligations for third states which are not party to it. Accordingly, the Court has no jurisdiction under Article 267 TFEU 'to give a ruling on the interpretation of provisions of international law which bind Member States outside the framework of' EU law.[1] This was also the finding of the Court in *Peralta*, the relevant excerpt of which is included here.

Furthermore, the prior agreement between a Member State and a third country continues to be valid and applicable under international law irrespective of possible incompatibilities between it and the EU Treaties. It follows that national legislation which implements a Member State's obligation under an 'old' agreement cannot be held to be incompatible with Union law. This was the Court's judgment in the leading case, *Minne*.

Judgment of the Court of 14 July 1994, Criminal proceedings against Matteo Peralta, Case C-379/92, European Court Reports 1994, p. I-3453, paras. 15–17.

The case concerned a reference for a preliminary ruling in criminal proceedings before an Italian court, pertaining to criminal sanctions imposed on an Italian national for discharging harmful substances other than hydrocarbons into the sea. Of interest here are the findings of the Court with regard to the Marpol Convention. Finding that this Convention had not become part of Community law, the Court declined its jurisdiction to rule on the question of the compatibility of Italian law with the provisions of Marpol.

---

[1] Case 130/73, *Vandeweghe and Others v. Berufsgenossenschaft für die chemische Industrie* [1973] ECR 1329, para. 2.

Observance of international conventions on the discharge of harmful substances into the sea

15. From the papers in the case it appears that, although its order for reference does not state a question in these terms, the national court is asking this Court about the compatibility of the Italian legislation with the International Convention for the Prevention of Pollution from Ships, called 'the Marpol Convention' (United Nations Treaty Series, Volume 1341, No 22484). It appears to consider that this Convention produces effects in the Community legal order.

16. In so far as the Italian court raises the question of the compatibility of the Italian legislation with the Marpol Convention, it is sufficient to find that the Community is not a party to that convention. Moreover, it does not appear that the Community has assumed, under the EEC Treaty, the powers previously exercised by the Member States in the field to which that convention applies, nor, consequently, that its provisions have the effect of binding the Community (see the judgment in Joined Cases 21/72 to 24/72 *International Fruit Company and Others* v *Produktschap voor Groenten en Fruit* [1972] ECR 1219, paragraph 18).

17. Whether a national provision adopted by a Member State is compatible with a convention such as the Marpol Convention is not therefore a matter on which the Court may rule.

Judgment of the Court (Sixth Chamber) of 3 February 1994, National Office of Employment v. Minne, Case C-13/93, European Court Reports 1994, p. I-371, paras. 1–5 and 17–19.

In this reference for a preliminary ruling the Court was asked whether Belgian legislation, which contained different exceptions from the prohibition of night work for men and women, was compatible with the principle of non-discrimination under Article 5 of Directive 76/207/EEC. The Court observed that such differences might be derived from the ILO Convention No. 89 concerning Night Work of Women Employed in Industry. That Convention was ratified by Belgium in 1952 and denounced with effect for February 1993, that is after the material time in which the case arose. The Court accepted the hypothesis that implementation of the ILO Convention could justify a breach of Article 5 of Directive 76/207/EEC, as follows.

1. By judgment of 8 January 1993, which was received at the Court on 15 January 1993, the Cour du Travail de Liège referred to the Court for a preliminary ruling under Article 177 of the EEC Treaty a question on the interpretation of Article 5 of Council Directive 76/207/EEC of 9 February 1976 on the implementation of the principle of equal treatment for men and women as regards access to employment, vocational training and promotion, and working conditions (Official Journal 1976 L 39, p. 40) ('the directive').

2. That question arose in proceedings between Mrs Minne and the Belgian Office National de l'Emploi (National Employment Office) ('the ONEM') concerning the granting of unemployment benefit.

3. From 15 July 1986 to 31 March 1990, Mrs Minne, who was living in Belgium, worked in the hotel and catering industry at Capellen (Luxembourg), where she was required to work nights. She ceased working when she moved to live in the Province of Liège (Belgium), where she applied for unemployment benefit from 2 April 1990.

4. The ONEM refused to grant her that benefit on the ground that she had declared that she was no longer prepared to work at night for family reasons.

5. The Tribunal du Travail (Labour Court), Verviers, before which the matter was brought at first instance, took the view that the decision by the ONEM was unjustified on the ground that Belgian legislation prohibited women in the hotel and catering industry from working between midnight and 6 a.m.

[...]

17. Since the German Government has contended that the denunciation of Convention No 89 became effective only in February 1993 and therefore after the material time in this case, it should be pointed out that the Court, in its judgment of 2 August 1993 in Case C-158/91 *Ministère Public and Direction du Travail et de l' Emploi* v *Levy* (not yet published in the ECR), held that national courts are under a duty to ensure that Article 5 of the directive is fully complied with by leaving unapplied any contrary provision of national legislation, unless the application of such a provision is necessary in order to ensure the performance by the Member State concerned, pursuant to the first paragraph of Article 234 of the EEC Treaty, of obligations arising from agreements concluded with non-member countries before the entry into force of that Treaty.

18. However, it falls to the national court, and not to the Court of Justice in the context of a preliminary ruling, to ascertain, with a view to determining the extent to which those obligations constitute an obstacle to the application of Article 5 of the directive, what are the obligations thus imposed on the Member State concerned by an earlier international agreement and whether the national provisions in question are designed to implement those obligations.

19. In the light of the foregoing, the answer to the question referred to the Court must be that Article 5 of Directive 76/207 precludes a Member State which prohibits night-work for both men and women from maintaining divergent systems of derogations which differ primarily in respect of the procedure for the adoption of derogations and of the duration of the night-work authorized, if such a difference is not justified by the need to ensure the protection of women, particularly with regard to pregnancy and maternity. Article 5 of the directive cannot apply to the extent to which those national provisions were adopted in order to ensure the performance by the Member State of obligations arising under an international agreement concluded with non-member countries before the entry into force of the EEC Treaty.

Judgment of the Court (Grand Chamber) of 3 September 2008, Yassin Abdullah Kadi and Al Barakaat International Foundation v. Council of the European Union, Joined Cases C-402/05 P and C-415/05 P, European Court Reports 2008, p. I-6351.

Prior agreements of Member States do, however, not enjoy unfettered primacy over EU law. In *Kadi*, the Court of First Instance (CFI) had argued that Member States had undertaken under the UN Charter a binding obligation to respect the primacy of UN law, including UN Security Council resolutions. By virtue of Article 351(1) TFEU, such obligations had to be honoured, thereby preventing European Courts from reviewing the legality of EU regulations that implemented UN sanctions. The Court disagreed (see Chapter 12, pp. 99–1023, Case T-315/01 *Kadi v. Council and Commission* [2005] ECR II-3649, paras 185–8 and Joined Cases C-402/05 P and C-415/05 P *Kadi and Al Barakaat International Foundation v. Council and Commission* [2008] ECR I-6351, paras 300–4). It follows that Article 351(1) TFEU has to be read in context. While it allows Member States to honour obligations under prior international agreements in disregard of 'ordinary' Union law, the same cannot be said for the core essence of the Union's legal order. Today, these 'untouchable' principles are reflected in Article 2 TEU on the Union's values.

Importantly, the Treaty does not only set such a 'negative' limit, but also puts on Member States a 'positive' duty to remove incompatibilities between prior international commitments and ordinary EU law under Article 351(2) first sentence TFEU. They should hence renegotiate and adjust the relevant agreement or, where the third state does not accept a satisfactory solution, withdraw from the agreement in line with the provisions on denunciation contained in the agreement at issue. The Court has underlined the extent of this duty in *Commission v. Belgium*.

Judgment of the Court (Grand Chamber) of 14 September 1999, Commission of the European Communities v. Kingdom of Belgium, Case C-170/98, European Court Reports 1999, p. I-5493, paras. 1 and 41–43.

In this case, the Commission asked for a declaration from the Court that in having failed to renegotiate an agreement with Zaire containing a cargo-sharing clause, Belgium failed to fulfil its obligations under Regulation 4055/86. The Court found indeed that Belgium was in violation of its relevant obligations.

1. By application lodged at the Court Registry on 8 May 1998, the Commission of the European Communities brought an action under Article 169 of the EC Treaty (now Article 226 EC) for a declaration that, by failing either to adjust the agreement with the Republic of Zaire (now the Democratic Republic of the Congo) in such a way as to provide for fair, free and non-discriminatory access by Community nationals to the cargo shares due to Belgium or to denounce that agreement, the Kingdom of Belgium had failed to fulfil its obligations under Council Regulation (EEC) No 4055/86 of 22 December 1986 applying the principle of freedom to provide services

to maritime transport between Member States and between Member States and third countries (OJ 1986 L 378, p. 1), in particular Articles 3 and 4(1) thereof.

[...]

41. The position of the Belgian Government is essentially that it does not contest the existence of the obligation to amend the provisions at issue, but submits that political developments in the Congo made it impossible to arrange negotiations. It undertakes to finalise the adjustment of the Agreement once the political situation in the Congo so permits.

42. The existence of a difficult political situation in a third State which is a contracting party, as in the present case, cannot justify a failure to fulfil obligations. If a Member State encounters difficulties which make it impossible to adjust an agreement, it must denounce the agreement.

43. Accordingly, by failing either to adjust the Belgium–Zaire Agreement in such a way as to provide for fair, free and non-discriminatory access by Community nationals to the cargo shares due to Belgium or to denounce that agreement, the Kingdom of Belgium has failed to fulfil its obligations under Regulation No 4055/86, in particular Articles 3 and 4(1) thereof.

Judgment of the Court (Grand Chamber) of 3 March 2009, Commission of the European Communities v. Republic of Austria, Case C-205/06, European Court Reports 2009, p. I-1301, paras. 1–3 and 16–45.

The duty of renegotiation, adjustment, or termination may at times put Member States into a difficult political situation vis-à-vis the third country concerned. The treaty therefore calls upon all Member States to assist each other to this end and to adopt a common attitude where necessary (Article 351(2) second sentence TFEU). In particular, where Member States have concluded similar treaties with the same third country, a common approach is warranted. The Court has also asked the Commission to lend its assistance to this exercise in the three cases relating to Member States' bilateral investment treaties with third states, being aware that the renegotiation between Finland,[2] Sweden[3] and Austria with, for example China or Russia, would not be an easy task. The Court also specified further the extent of incompatibilities between EU law and Member States' agreements with third states concluded prior to the Member States accession. It accepted that even a conflict between the two, which has not yet materialized but may in the future occur, is sufficient for the Member States to be under a duty to renegotiate, adjust, or terminate such a treaty. The international law mechanisms (renegotiation, suspension, or denunciation of the treaty) that exist in order to resolve the conflict once it exists, were deemed insufficient by the Court to guarantee the effective implementation of measures taken by the Union. The relevant paragraphs of the judgment against Austria read as follows.

---

[2] Case C-118/07, *Commission of the European Communities v. Republic of Finland* [2009] ECR I-10889.
[3] Case C-249/06, *Commission of the European Communities v. Kingdom of Sweden* [2009] ECR I-1335.

1. By its application, the Commission of the European Communities requests the Court to declare that, by not having taken appropriate steps to eliminate incompatibilities concerning the provisions on transfer of capital contained in the investment agreements entered into with the Republic of Korea, the Republic of Cape Verde, the People's Republic of China, Malaysia, the Russian Federation and the Republic of Turkey, the Republic of Austria has failed to fulfil its obligations under the second paragraph of Article 307 EC.

Legal framework

2. Prior to its accession to the European Union, the Republic of Austria entered into bilateral investment agreements with the People's Republic of China (this agreement entered into force on 11 October 1986 (BGBl. 537/1986)), Malaysia (this agreement entered into force on 1 January 1987 (BGBl. 601/1986)), the Russian Federation (this agreement entered into force on 1 September 1991 (BGBl. 387/1991), initially concluded with the former Union of Soviet Socialist Republics and made applicable between the Republic of Austria and the Russian Federation pursuant to an exchange of letters (BGBl. 257/1994)), the Republic of Korea (this agreement entered into force on 1 November 1991 (BGBl. 523/1991)), the Republic of Turkey (this agreement entered into force on 1 January 1992 (BGBl. 612/1991)) and the Republic of Cape Verde (this agreement entered into force on 1 April 1993 (BGBl. 83/1993)).

3. Each of those agreements contains a clause under which each party guarantees to the investors of the other party, without undue delay, the free transfer, in freely convertible currency, of payments connected with an investment.

[...]

Arguments of the parties

16. The Commission takes the view that the absence, in the agreements at issue, of any provision expressly reserving for the Republic of Austria the possibility of applying measures which may, where appropriate, be decided upon by the Council on the basis of Articles 57 EC, 59 EC and 60 EC is liable to make it more difficult, or even impossible, for that Member State to comply with its Community obligations and that, by not taking appropriate steps to remove such an incompatibility, that Member State has failed to fulfil its obligations under the second paragraph of Article 307 EC.

17. The Commission claims that, were the Council to adopt restrictions on movements of capital and on payments, the period of time required for the denunciation or renegotiation of the agreements at issue would have the consequence that the Republic of Austria would be obliged, in the intervening period, under international law, to continue to apply the agreements in question, including their respective transfer clauses, in accordance, moreover, with the first paragraph of Article 307 EC. As a result, the measures adopted by the Council would not be uniformly applied within the Community.

18. The Republic of Austria considers that, in the absence of restrictions on movements of capital and on payments decided upon by the Council, it is free to regulate the

movement of capital with third countries on the basis of Article 56 EC. It contends that, so long as no restriction has been decided upon by the Council, the question of the compatibility of the agreements at issue with a provision of the Treaty which has not been the subject of any application does not arise.

19. The Federal Republic of Germany, the Republic of Lithuania, the Republic of Hungary and the Republic of Finland concur with the arguments put forward by the Republic of Austria and take the view that the investment agreements in question are not incompatible with existing Community measures on free movement of capital, as those measures do not affect such agreements. According to those Member States, the failure to fulfil obligations relied on by the Commission is purely hypothetical in nature.

20. Those Member States contend that the objective of an action for failure to fulfil obligations under Article 226 EC is not to review situations in which the alleged failure is hypothetical, but to remedy actual failures by Member States to fulfil their obligations.

21. The Federal Republic of Germany and the Republic of Hungary point out that a potential future incompatibility with secondary Community legislation on the part of an agreement entered into with a third country does not fall within the scope of application of Article 307 EC and can, if at all, be confirmed only if the Council actually exercises its competence within the area covered by that article.

22. The Republic of Finland points out that the Commission has failed to prove the existence of the alleged failure to fulfil obligations and cannot, according to the case-law of the Court, act on the basis of assumptions.

23. The Republic of Lithuania adds that the objective of the second paragraph of Article 307 EC is not to ensure formal compliance with Community law on the part of the provisions of international agreements entered into by the Member States, but to ensure effective application of the provisions of Community law, in particular where the Member States have, prior to the respective dates of their accession, concluded international agreements with third countries on the same matters.

Findings of the Court

24. The various investment agreements at issue concluded by the Republic of Austria contain equivalent provisions which guarantee the free transfer, without undue delay and in freely convertible currency, of payments connected with an investment.

25. In particular, the following matters are thus guaranteed: the free transfer of funds in order to create, manage or extend an investment; the freedom to repatriate the income from that investment; and the freedom to transfer the funds necessary to repay loans and the funds arising from the liquidation or assignment of that investment.

26. Those agreements are to that extent consistent with the wording of Article 56(1) EC, according to which '…all restrictions on the movement of capital between Member States and between Member States and third countries shall be prohibited', and of Article 56(2) EC, under which 'all restrictions on payments between

Member States and between Member States and third countries shall be prohibited', and are in line with the objective pursued by that article.

27. It is true that the Treaty provisions to which the present action by the Commission refers grant the Council the power to restrict, in certain circumstances, the movement of capital and payments between Member States and third countries, including the movements covered by the transfer clauses here at issue.

28. The provisions in question, contained in Articles 57(2) EC, 59 EC and 60(1) EC, introduce, with a view to protecting the general Community interest and enabling the Community to comply, as appropriate, with its international obligations and with those of the Member States, exceptions to the principle of free movement of capital and payments between Member States and between Member States and third countries.

29. Article 57(2) EC allows the Council, acting by qualified majority on a proposal from the Commission, to adopt certain measures restricting the movement of capital to or from third countries involving, inter alia, direct investment. Where those measures constitute a 'step back' in Community law as regards the liberalisation of the movement of capital to or from third countries, unanimity is required.

30. Article 59 EC authorises the Council, on a proposal from the Commission and after consulting the European Central Bank, to take safeguard measures where movements of capital to or from third countries 'cause, or threaten to cause, serious difficulties for the operation of economic and monetary union', provided that they are strictly necessary and that they relate to a period 'not exceeding six months'.

31. Article 60(1) EC allows the Council, on a proposal from the Commission, in order to implement a common position or a joint action in the area of the common foreign and security policy, to take 'necessary urgent measures' on the movement of capital and on payments. Such action could, for example, be required in order to give effect to a resolution of the Security Council of the United Nations Organisation.

32. It is common ground that the agreements at issue do not contain any provision reserving such possibilities for the Community to restrict movements of funds connected with investments. It is therefore necessary to examine whether the Republic of Austria was, for that reason, under an obligation to take the appropriate steps to which the second paragraph of Article 307 EC refers.

33. Under the first paragraph of Article 307 EC, the rights and obligations arising from an agreement concluded before the date of accession of a Member State between it and a third country are not affected by the provisions of the Treaty. The purpose of that provision is to make it clear, in accordance with the principles of international law, that application of the Treaty is not to affect the duty of the Member State concerned to respect the rights of third countries under a prior agreement and to perform its obligations thereunder (see Case 812/79 *Burgoa* [1980] ECR 2787, paragraph 8; Case C-84/98 *Commission* v *Portugal* [2000] ECR I-5215, paragraph 53; and Case C-216/01 *Budějovický Budvar* [2003] ECR I-13617, paragraphs 144 and 145).

34. The second paragraph of Article 307 EC obliges the Member States to take all appropriate steps to eliminate incompatibilities with Community law which have

been established in agreements concluded prior to their accession. Under that provision, the Member States are required, where necessary, to assist each other to that end and, where appropriate, to adopt a common attitude.

35. The provisions of Articles 57(2) EC, 59 EC and 60(1) EC confer on the Council the power to restrict, in certain specific circumstances, movements of capital and payments between Member States and third countries.

36. In order to ensure the effectiveness of those provisions, measures restricting the free movement of capital must be capable, where adopted by the Council, of being applied immediately with regard to the States to which they relate, which may include some of the States which have signed one of the agreements at issue with the Republic of Austria.

37. Accordingly, those powers of the Council, which consist in the unilateral adoption of restrictive measures with regard to third countries on a matter which is identical to or connected with that covered by an earlier agreement concluded between a Member State and a third country, reveal an incompatibility with that agreement where, first, the agreement does not contain a provision allowing the Member State concerned to exercise its rights and to fulfil its obligations as a member of the Community and, second, there is also no international-law mechanism which makes that possible.

38. Contrary to what is contended by the Republic of Austria, the measures put forward by it and which, in its view, are such as to enable it to fulfil its Community obligations do not appear to guarantee that this will be the case.

39. In the first place, the periods of time necessarily involved in any international negotiations which would be required in order to reopen discussion of the agreements at issue are inherently incompatible with the practical effectiveness of those measures.

40. In the second place, the possibility of relying on other mechanisms offered by international law, such as suspension of the agreement, or even denunciation of the agreements at issue or of some of their provisions, is too uncertain in its effects to guarantee that the measures adopted by the Council could be applied effectively.

41. Moreover, as it pointed out again at the hearing, the Republic of Austria intends to introduce, in the investment agreements under negotiation or when the existing agreements are renewed, a clause which would reserve certain powers to regional organisations and would, therefore, make it possible to apply any measures restricting movements of capital and payments which might be adopted by the Council.

42. While acknowledging that such a clause should, in principle, as the Commission admitted at the hearing, be considered capable of removing the established incompatibility, it is common ground that, in the cases referred to by the Commission, the Republic of Austria has not taken any steps, within the period prescribed by the Commission in its reasoned opinion, with regard to the third countries concerned, designed to eliminate the risk of conflict with measures liable to be adopted by the Council under Articles 57(2) EC, 59 EC and 60(1) EC which may arise from the application of the investment agreements concluded with those third countries.

43. It must be added that, as follows from the judgment delivered today in Case C-249/06 *Commission v Sweden* [2009] ECR I-0000, the incompatibilities with

the Treaty to which the investment agreements with third countries give rise and which militate against the application of the restrictions on movement of capital and on payments which the Council may adopt under Articles 57(2) EC, 59 EC and 60(1) EC are not limited to the Member State which is the defendant in the present case.

44. It must therefore be stated that, in accordance with the second paragraph of Article 307 EC, where necessary, the Member States must assist each other with a view to eliminating the incompatibilities established and must adopt, where appropriate, a common attitude. In the context of its duty, under Article 211 EC, to ensure that the provisions of the Treaty are applied, it is for the Commission to take any steps which may facilitate mutual assistance between the Member States concerned and their adoption of a common attitude.

45. It follows from the foregoing that, by not having taken appropriate steps to eliminate incompatibilities concerning the provisions on transfer of capital contained in the investment agreements entered into with the Republic of Korea, the Republic of Cape Verde, the People's Republic of China, Malaysia, the Russian Federation and the Republic of Turkey, the Republic of Austria has failed to fulfil its obligations under the second paragraph of Article 307 EC.

Finally, the duty of renegotiation, adjustment or termination may also arise in situations where Member States have concluded certain agreements with a third country during their EU membership, but the Union has only become exclusively competent for the subject matter at a later stage by virtue of the ERTA effect.[4] However, as the Member States have lost their competence to conclude treaties in the area, they are also not competent to renegotiate their own agreements. In return, the Commission may face a substantial workload adjusting a large number of Member States' agreements, some of them probably of little practical significance. To overcome such practical problems, the Union may decide to adopt specific legislation organizing the renegotiation of Member States agreements in order to bring them into line with Union law.

Regulation (EC) No 847/2004 of the European Parliament and of the Council of 29 April 2004 on the negotiation and implementation of air service agreements between Member States and third countries, Official Journal L 157, 30.4.2004, pp. 7–17.

THE EUROPEAN PARLIAMENT AND THE COUNCIL OF THE
EUROPEAN UNION,
Having regard to the Treaty establishing the European Community, and in particular Article 80(2) thereof,
Having regard to the proposal from the Commission,

---

[4] On the ERTA-effect, see Chapter 1.

Having regard to the Opinion of the European Economic and Social Committee,
Acting in accordance with the procedure laid down in Article 251 of the Treaty,

Whereas:

(1) International aviation relations between Member States and third countries have been traditionally governed by bilateral air service agreements between Member States and third countries, their Annexes and other related bilateral or multilateral arrangements.

(2) Following the judgments of the Court of Justice of the European Communities in cases C-466/98, C-467/98, C-468/98, C-469/98, C-471/98, C-472/98, C-475/98 and C-476/98, the Community has exclusive competence with respect to various aspects of such agreements.

(3) The Court has also clarified the right of Community air carriers to benefit from the right of establishment within the Community, including the right to non-discriminatory market access.

(4) Where it is apparent that the subject-matter of an agreement falls partly within the competence of the Community and partly within that of its Member States, it is essential to ensure close cooperation between the Member States and the Community institutions, both in the process of negotiation and conclusion and in the fulfilment of the commitments entered into. That obligation to cooperate flows from the requirement of unity in the international representation of the Community. The Community institutions and the Member States should take all necessary steps to ensure the best possible cooperation in that regard.

(5) The cooperation procedure between Member States and the Commission established by this Regulation should be without prejudice to the division of competencies between the Community and Member States, in accordance with Community law as interpreted by the Court of Justice.

(6) All existing bilateral agreements between Member States and third countries that contain provisions contrary to Community law should be amended or replaced by new agreements that are wholly compatible with Community law.

(7) Without prejudice to the Treaty, and in particular Article 300 thereof, Member States may wish to make amendments to existing agreements and make provision to manage their implementation until such time as an agreement concluded by the Community enters into force.

(8) It is essential to ensure that a Member State conducting negotiations takes account of Community law, broader Community interests and ongoing Community negotiations.

(9) If a Member State wishes to involve air carriers in the process of negotiation, all air carriers with an establishment in the territory of the Member State concerned should be treated equally.

(10) Establishment on the territory of a Member State implies the effective and real exercise of air transport activity through stable arrangements; the legal form of such an establishment, whether a branch or a subsidiary with a legal personality, should not be the determining factor in this respect. When an undertaking is established on the territory of several Member States, as defined by the Treaty, it should ensure, in order to

avoid any circumvention of national law, that each of the establishments fulfils the obligations which may, in accordance with Community law, be imposed by the national law applicable to its activities.

(11) In order to ensure that the rights of Community air carriers are not unduly restricted, no new arrangements that reduce the number of Community air carriers which may be designated to provide air services in a given market should be introduced in bilateral air service agreements.

(12) Member States should establish non-discriminatory and transparent procedures for the distribution of traffic rights between Community air carriers. In applying those procedures Member States should have due regard to the need to preserve continuity of air services.

(13) The measures necessary for the implementation of this Regulation should be adopted in accordance with Council Decision 1999/468/EC of 28 June 1999 laying down the procedures for the exercise of implementing powers conferred on the Commission.

(14) Any Member State may invoke the confidentiality of the provisions of bilateral agreements it has negotiated and request the Commission not to share the information with other Member States.

(15) Arrangements for greater cooperation over the use of Gibraltar airport were agreed in London on 2 December 1987 by the Kingdom of Spain and the United Kingdom in a joint declaration by the Ministers of Foreign Affairs of the two countries. Such arrangements have yet to enter into operation.

(16) Since the objectives of this Regulation, namely the coordination of negotiations with third countries with a view to concluding air service agreements, the necessity to guarantee a harmonised approach in the implementation and application of those agreements and the verification of their compliance with Community law, cannot be sufficiently achieved by the Member States and can therefore, by reason of the Community-wide scope of this Regulation, be better achieved at Community level, the Community may adopt measures in accordance with the principle of subsidiarity, as set out in article 5 of the Treaty. In accordance with the principle of proportionality, as set out in that article, this Regulation does not go beyond what is necessary in order to achieve those objectives,

HAVE ADOPTED THIS REGULATION:

Article 1

Notification to the Commission

1. A Member State may, without prejudice to the respective competencies of the Community and its Member States, enter into negotiations with a third country concerning a new air service agreement or the modification of an existing air service agreement, its Annexes or any other related bilateral or multilateral arrangement, the subject matter of which falls partly within the competence of the Community, provided that:

– any relevant standard clauses, developed and laid down jointly between Member States and the Commission, are included in such negotiations; and

– the notification procedure set out in paragraphs 2, 3 and 4 is complied with.

Where appropriate, the Commission shall be invited to participate as an observer in any such negotiations.

2. Where a Member State intends to enter into such negotiations it shall notify the Commission of its intentions in writing. This notification shall include a copy of the existing agreement, if available, other relevant documentation and an indication of the provisions to be addressed in the negotiations, the objectives of the negotiations and any other relevant information. The Commission shall make the notification and, on request, the accompanying documentation, available to other Member States, subject to the requirements of confidentiality.

The information shall be transmitted at least one calendar month before formal negotiations are scheduled to commence with the third country concerned. If, due to exceptional circumstances, formal negotiations are scheduled at less than one month's notice, the Member State shall transmit the information as soon as possible.

3. Member States may make comments to the Member State which has notified its intention to enter into negotiations in accordance with paragraph 2. That Member State shall take such comments into account as far as possible in the course of the negotiations.

4. If, within 15 working days of receipt of the notification referred to in paragraph 2, the Commission concludes that the negotiations are likely to:

– undermine the objectives of Community negotiations underway with the third country concerned, and/or

– lead to an agreement which is incompatible with Community law it shall inform the Member State accordingly.

Article 2

Consultation of stakeholders and participation in negotiations

Insofar as air carriers and other interested parties are to be involved in the negotiations referred to in Article 1, Member States shall treat equally all Community air carriers with an establishment on their respective territories to which the Treaty applies.

Article 3

Prohibition on introducing more restrictive arrangements

A Member State shall not enter into any new arrangement with a third country, which reduces the number of Community air carriers which may, in accordance with existing arrangements, be designated to provide services between its territory and that country, neither in respect of the entire air transport market between the two parties nor on the basis of specific city pairs.

Article 4

Conclusion of agreements

1. Upon signature of an agreement, the Member State concerned shall notify the Commission of the outcome of the negotiations together with any relevant documentation.

2. Where the negotiations have resulted in an agreement which incorporates the relevant standard clauses referred to in Article 1(1), the Member State shall be authorised to conclude the agreement.

3. Where the negotiations have resulted in an agreement which does not incorporate the relevant standard clauses referred to in Article 1(1), the Member State shall be authorised, in accordance with the procedure referred to in Article 7(2), to conclude the agreement, provided that this does not harm the object and purpose of the Community common transport policy. The Member State may provisionally apply the agreement pending the outcome of this procedure.

4. Notwithstanding paragraphs 2 and 3, if the Commission is actively negotiating with the same third country on the basis of a country-specific mandate or on the basis of Council Decision 2004/.../EC of... authorising the Commission to open negotiations with third countries on the replacement of certain provisions in existing bilateral agreements with a Community agreement, the Member State concerned may be authorised, in accordance with the procedure referred to in Article 7(2), to apply provisionally and/or conclude the agreement.

Article 5

Distribution of traffic rights

Where a Member State concludes an agreement, or amendments to an agreement or its Annexes, that provide for limitations on the use of traffic rights or the number of Community air carriers eligible to be designated to take advantage of traffic rights, that Member State shall ensure a distribution of traffic rights among eligible Community air carriers on the basis of a non-discriminatory and transparent procedure.

Article 6

Publication of procedures

Member States shall inform the Commission without delay of the procedures that they shall apply for the purposes of Article 5 and, where appropriate, Article 2. For information purposes, the Commission shall ensure that these procedures are published in the Official Journal of the European Union within eight weeks of their receipt. Any new procedures and subsequent changes to existing procedures shall be communicated to the Commission at least eight weeks before they enter into force, so that the Commission can ensure their publication in the Official Journal of the European Union within that eight-week period.

Article 7

Committee procedure

1. The Commission shall be assisted by the committee established under Article 11 of Council Regulation (EEC) No 2408/92 of 23 July 1992 on access for Community air carriers to intra-Community air routes.

2. Where reference is made to this paragraph, Articles 3 and 7 of Decision 1999/468/EC shall apply, having regard to the provisions of Article 8 thereof.

3. The Committee shall adopt its rules of procedure.

Article 8

Confidentiality

In notifying the Commission of negotiations and their outcome as envisaged in Articles 1 and 4, Member States shall clearly inform the Commission if any information therein is to be considered confidential and whether it can be shared with other Member States.

The Commission and Member States shall ensure that any information identified as confidential is treated according to Article 4(1)(a) of Regulation (EC) No 1049/2001 of the European Parliament and of the Council of 30 May 2001 regarding public access to European Parliament, Council and Commission documents.

Article 9

Gibraltar

1. The application of this Regulation to the airport of Gibraltar is understood to be without prejudice to the respective legal positions of the Kingdom of Spain and the United Kingdom with regard to the dispute over sovereignty over the territory in which the airport is situated.

2. Application of this Regulation to Gibraltar airport shall be suspended until the arrangements included in the Joint Declaration made by the Foreign Ministers of the Kingdom of Spain and the United Kingdom on 2 December 1987 enter into operation. The Governments of Spain and the United Kingdom will inform the Council of such date of entry into operation.

Article 10

Entry into force

This Regulation shall enter into force on the thirtieth day following its publication in the Official Journal of the European Union.

This Regulation shall be binding in its entirety and directly applicable in all Member States.

13.2 New agreements between Member States and third countries

The EU Treaties do not contain any specific provision addressing agreements between third countries and Member States concluded while being an EU member. The reason for that silence is that these are subject to the general principles of Union law. This means that Member States may not conclude agreements in areas for which the Union has acquired exclusive external competence. In areas, where the Member States have retained their national competence, they may exercise their treaty-making power only in line with substantive Union law.

It follows from the first principle that the conclusion of a new agreement with a third country in an area of exclusive Union competence is internationally valid but in breach of Union law. Accordingly, the Commission may bring an infringement case before the CJEU against the Member State in question in order to force it to withdraw from such agreement. Exceptionally, however, it may also be in the interest of the Union that Member States conclude agreements in areas of Union competence. In particular, where it is important to be part of an international law-making treaty, but the latter does not allow accession of the Union as such, the Union might wish to authorize Member States to become party to such a treaty in the interest of the Union. The authorization is normally contained in a formal Council decision upon proposal from the Commission.

Council Decision 2004/246/EC of 2 March 2004 authorising the Member States to sign, ratify or accede to, in the interest of the European Community, the Protocol 2003 to the International Convention on the Establishment of an International Fund for Compensation for Oil Pollution Damage, 1992, and authorising Austria and Luxemburg, in the interest of the European Community, to accede to the underlying instruments, Official Journal L 78, 16.3.2004, pp. 22–3.

THE COUNCIL OF THE EUROPEAN UNION,
Having regard to the Treaty establishing the European Community, and in particular Article 61(c), in conjunction with Article 300(2), first subparagraph, and Article 300(3), second subparagraph, thereof,
Having regard to the proposal from the Commission,
Having regard to the assent of the European Parliament,

Whereas:
(1) The Protocol to the International Convention on the Establishment of an International Fund for Compensation for Oil Pollution Damage, 1992, (hereinafter the Supplementary Fund Protocol), is aimed at ensuring adequate, prompt, and effective compensation of persons who suffer damage caused by oil spills caused by tankers. By significantly raising the limits of compensation available in the present international system, the Supplementary Fund Protocol addresses one of the most significant shortcomings in the international regulation of oil pollution liability.
(2) Articles 7 and 8 of the Supplementary Fund Protocol affect Community legislation on jurisdiction and the recognition and enforcement of judgments, as laid down in Council Regulation (EC) No 44/2001 of 22 December 2000 on jurisdiction and the recognition and enforcement of judgments in civil and commercial matters.
(3) The Community has exclusive competence in relation to Articles 7 and 8 of the Protocol, insofar as those articles affect the rules laid down in Regulation (EC) No 44/2001. The Member States retain their competence for matters covered by the Protocol which do not affect Community law.
(4) Pursuant to the Supplementary Fund Protocol, only sovereign States may be party to it; it is not therefore possible for the Community to ratify or accede to the Protocol, nor is there a prospect that it will be able to do so in the near future.
(5) The Council should therefore, exceptionally, authorise the Member States to sign and conclude the Supplementary Fund Protocol in the interest of the Community, under the conditions set out in this Decision.
(6) The United Kingdom and Ireland are bound by Regulation (EC) No 44/2001 and are therefore taking part in the adoption and application of this Decision.
(7) In accordance with Articles 1 and 2 of the Protocol on the position of Denmark annexed to the Treaty on European Union and to the Treaty establishing the European Community, Denmark is not taking part in the adoption of this Decision, and is not bound by it or subject to its application.

(8) Only Contracting Parties to the underlying instruments may become Contracting Parties to the Supplementary Fund Protocol. Austria and Luxembourg are not currently parties to the underlying instruments. Since the underlying instruments contain provisions affecting Regulation (EC) No 44/2001, Austria and Luxembourg should also be authorised to accede to these instruments.

(9) Member States, with the exception of Austria and Luxembourg, should sign or ratify the Protocol, as far as possible before the end of June 2004. The choice of either signing and subsequently ratifying the Protocol, or signing it without reservation as to ratification, acceptance or approval, is left to the Member States.

(10) The situation of Austria and Luxembourg is different in that they cannot become Contracting Parties to the Supplementary Fund Protocol until they have acceded to the underlying instruments. For this reason, Austria and Luxembourg should therefore accede to the underlying instruments and to the Supplementary Fund Protocol, as far as possible by 31 December 2005,

HAS ADOPTED THIS DECISION:

Article 1

1. The Member States are hereby authorised to sign, ratify or accede to, in the interest of the European Community, the Protocol of 2003 to the International Convention on the Establishment of an International Fund for Compensation for Oil Pollution Damage, 1992, (the Supplementary Fund Protocol) subject to the conditions set out in the following articles.

2. In addition, Austria and Luxembourg are authorised to accede to the underlying instruments.

3. The text of the Supplementary Fund Protocol is attached in Annex I to this Decision. The text of the underlying instruments is attached in Annexes II and III to this Decision.

4. In this Decision, the term 'underlying instruments' shall mean the Protocol of 1992 to amend the International Convention on Civil Liability for Oil Pollution Damage, 1969 and the Protocol of 1992 to amend the International Convention on the Establishment of an International Fund for Compensation for Oil Pollution Damage, 1971.

5. In this Decision, 'Member State' means all the Member States with the exception of Denmark.

Article 2

1. Member States shall take the necessary steps to express their consent to be bound pursuant to Article 19(2) thereof by the Supplementary Fund Protocol within a reasonable time and, if possible, before 30 June 2004, with the exception of Austria and Luxembourg, which express their consent to be bound by the Protocol under the conditions laid down in paragraph 3 of this article.

2. Member States shall exchange information with the Commission within the Council, by 30 April 2004, on the date on which they expect their internal procedures to be completed.

3. Austria and Luxembourg shall take the necessary steps to express their consent to be bound by the underlying instruments and the Supplementary Fund Protocol, as far as possible, by 31 December 2005.

Article 3

When signing, ratifying or acceding to the instruments referred to in Article 1, Member States shall inform the Secretary-General of the International Maritime Organisation in writing that such signature, ratification or accession has taken place in accordance with this Decision.

Article 4

Member States shall, at the earliest opportunity, use their best endeavours to ensure that the Supplementary Fund Protocol, and the underlying instruments, are amended in order to allow the Community to become a Contracting Party to them.

Article 5

This Decision is addressed to the Member States in accordance with the Treaty establishing the European Community.

Judgment of the Court of 5 November 2002, Commission of the European Communities v. Kingdom of Belgium, Case C-471/98, European Court Reports 2002, p. I-9681, paras. 134–142.

> The second principle, namely that Member State agreements for which national competence still exists must comply with substantive Union law, was made clear by the Court in the *Open Skies* cases.[5] In those cases, it accepted that the so-called 'ownership and control' clause in an air-service agreement with the US did not fall within exclusive Union competence, but violated the freedom of establishment under Article 49 TFEU (then Article 52 TEC and later Article 43 TEC). The findings of the Court in this regard from one of those cases, the *Commission v. Belgium* case, are included here.

134. As regards the question whether the Kingdom of Belgium has infringed Article 52 of the Treaty, it should be borne in mind that, under that article, freedom of establishment includes the right to take up and pursue activities as self-employed persons and to set up and manage undertakings, in particular companies or firms within the meaning of the second paragraph of Article 58 of the EC Treaty (now the second paragraph of Article 48 EC) under the conditions laid down for its own nationals by the legislation of the Member State in which establishment is effected.

135. Articles 52 and 58 of the Treaty thus guarantee nationals of Member States of the Community who have exercised their freedom of establishment and companies or

---

[5] Cases C-466/98, C-467/98, C-468/98, C-469/98, C-471/98, C-472/98, C-475/98, C-476/98, *Commission v. the United Kingdom, Denmark, Sweden, Finland, Belgium, Luxembourg, Austria and Germany* [2002] ECR I-9427.

firms which are assimilated to them the same treatment in the host Member State as that accorded to nationals of that Member State (see Case C-307/97 *Saint-Gobain* v *Finanzamt Aachen-Innenstadt* [1999] ECR I-6161, paragraph 35), both as regards access to an occupational activity on first establishment and as regards the exercise of that activity by the person established in the host Member State.

136. The Court has thus held that the principle of national treatment requires a Member State which is a party to a bilateral international treaty with a non-member country for the avoidance of double taxation to grant to permanent establishments of companies resident in another Member State the advantages provided for by that treaty on the same conditions as those which apply to companies resident in the Member State that is party to the treaty (see *Saint-Gobain*, paragraph 59, and judgment of 15 January 2002 in Case C-55/00 *Gottardo* v *INPS* [2002] ECR I-413, paragraph 32).

137. In this case, the clause on the ownership and control of airlines does, amongst other things, permit the United States of America to withdraw, suspend or limit the operating licences or technical authorisations of an airline designated by the Kingdom of Belgium but of which a substantial part of the ownership and effective control is not vested in that Member State or Belgian nationals.

138. There can be no doubt that airlines established in the Kingdom of Belgium of which a substantial part of the ownership and effective control is vested either in a Member State other than the Kingdom of Belgium or in nationals of such a Member State ('Community airlines') are capable of being affected by that clause.

139. By contrast, the formulation of that clause shows that the United States of America is in principle under an obligation to grant the appropriate operating licences and required technical authorisations to airlines of which a substantial part of the ownership and effective control is vested in the Kingdom of Belgium or Belgian nationals ('Belgian airlines').

140. It follows that Community airlines may always be excluded from the benefit of the air transport agreement between the Kingdom of Belgium and the United States of America, while that benefit is assured to Belgian airlines. Consequently, Community airlines suffer discrimination which prevents them from benefiting from the treatment which the host Member State, namely the Kingdom of Belgium, accords to its own nationals.

141. Contrary to what the Kingdom of Belgium maintains, the direct source of that discrimination is not the possible conduct of the United States of America but the clause on the ownership and control of airlines, which specifically acknowledges the right of the United States of America to act in that way.

142. It follows that the clause on the ownership and control of airlines is contrary to Article 52 of the Treaty.

13.3 Agreements between Member States

The general principle of supremacy also governs the relationship of Union law and bilateral agreements concluded between the Member States. In that respect, it is irrelevant whether the agreement had been concluded prior to EU membership or not. While the starting point is thus rather easy to handle, the situation is more complicated as to the possible effect of EU supremacy for the application of the bilateral Member State agreement. It appears that four different scenarios need to be distinguished.

Judgment of the Court of 27 February 1962, Commission of the European Economic Community v. Italian Republic, Case 10/61, European Court Reports, pp. 10–11.

First, there can be an outright incompatibility between an *inter se* Member State agreement and the EU Treaties, with the consequence that the former remains valid, but cannot be applied to justify a breach of the latter. Accordingly, the Court held in *Commission v. Italy* that the GATT continues to apply for the treaty relations of a Member State with third countries by virtue of Article 351(1) TFEU (then Article 234 EEC), but that the EC Treaty prevails over obligations between Member States under the GATT.

[...]

'In fact, in matters governed by the EEC Treaty, that treaty takes precedence over agreements concluded between member states before its entry into force, including agreements made within the framework of GATT.

[...]

As a result of Article 234, different tariffs are applied to member States and third countries, even though they are parties to the same Geneva Agreement of 1956. This is the normal effect of the Treaty establishing the EEC. The manner in which member States proceed to reduce customs duties amongst themselves cannot be criticized by third countries since this abolition of customs duties is accomplished according to the provisions of the treaty and does not interfere with the rights held by third countries under agreements still in force.'

Similarly, international agreements between certain Member States on the designation of goods[6] or public morality[7] may not impede the free circulation of goods; and Council of Europe Conventions binding on the Member States cannot be invoked to limit the free circulation of workers under Union law.[8] Union law also prevails over provisions of the 1971 Berne Convention on the protection of literary and artistic works.[9] In

---

[6] Case C-286/86, *Minstère de la Public v. Deserbais* [1998] ECR I-4907, para. 18.

[7] Case 121/85, *Conegate v. HM Customs and Excise* [1986] ECR 1007, para. 25.

[8] Case C-473/93, *Commission v. Luxemburg* [1996] ECR I-3207, para. 40; Case C-147/03, *Commission v. Austria*, [2005] ECR I-5969, para. 73.

[9] Cases C-241/91 P and C-242/91 P, *RTE and ITP v. Commission* [1995] ECR I-743, paras. 84 and 86; Case C-28/04 *Tod's SpA et Tod's France SARL ./. Heyrau SA* [2005] ECR I-5781, paras 33–7.

the same vein, rules on the jurisdiction, recognition, and enforcement of judgments in civil and commercial matters set by an international convention cannot compromise the relevant Union principles.[10]

Judgment of the Court of 9 November 1995, Jean-Louis Thévenon and Stadt Speyer – Sozialamt v. Landesversicherungsanstalt Rheinland-Pfalz, Case C-475/93, European Court Reports 1995, p. I-3813, paras. 12–28.

Second, there can be situations where Union law has replaced a prior bilateral agreement between Member States. The Court's approach to that situation was developed with respect to the relationship between the Union's system for the social insurance of workers under Regulation 1408/71 and bilateral social security agreements between Member States.[11] The choice of words by the Court in these cases ('replacement') suggests that those social security agreements were implicitly abrogated by the Member States when concluding the EU Treaty. In *Thévenon*, the Court had to decide whether the system of calculating pension rights had to be calculated in line with a 1950 Franco-German Convention or in accordance with Community Regulation 1408/71. The Court said the following.

12. It must be observed in limine that, according to Article 9 of the Franco-German convention, French or German employees who have been successively or alternately affiliated in the two countries to one or more invalidity insurance schemes are to be credited, for the purposes of calculating the level of invalidity pension, with the insurance periods completed under all such schemes.

13. Article 6 of Regulation No 1408/71, which reproduces in this respect Article 5 of Regulation No 3 of the Council on social security for migrant workers (Journal Officiel 1958, 30, p. 561), provides that, subject to the provisions of Articles 7, 8 and 46(4), Regulation No 1408/71 is to replace, as regards persons and matters which it covers, the provisions of any social security convention binding two or more Member States. The Franco-German convention is not included amongst the conventions expressly reserved.

14. Regulation No 1408/71 does not provide that contribution periods completed in one or more other Member States are to be added, for the purposes of increasing the amount of the pension, to the contribution periods completed in the Member State in which the pension is applied for. According to that regulation, the periods of insurance completed in different Member States are to be aggregated only for the purposes of the acquisition, retention and recovery of pension rights.

---

[10] Case C-533/08, *TNT Express Nederland BV v. AXA Versicherung AG* [2010] ECR I-4107, paras 49–56.
[11] Case 82/72, *Walder* [1973] ECR 599, paras 5–6; Case C-227/89, *Roenfeldt* [1991] ECR I-323, para. 14; Case C-475/93, *Thévenon v. Landesversicherungsanstalt Rheinland-Pfalz* [1995] ECR I-3813, para. 15.

15. Next, the Court stressed in the judgment in Case 82/72 Walder [1973] ECR 599, paragraphs 6 and 7, relating to the interpretation of Articles 5 and 6 of Regulation No 3 and Articles 6 and 7 of Regulation No 1408/71, that it is clear from those provisions that the replacement by the Community regulations of the provisions of social security conventions concluded between Member States is mandatory in nature and does not allow of exceptions, save for the cases expressly stipulated by the regulations, even where the social security conventions are more advantageous to the persons covered by them than the Community regulations.

16. The plaintiffs in the main action argue, however, that Mr Thévenon's pension has to be calculated in accordance with the provisions of the Franco-German convention, since the Court held on similar facts in Roenfeldt that, in the case of migrant workers, bilateral social security conventions must continue to apply, even after the entry into force of Regulation No 1408/71, where an insured person is thereby placed in a more favourable position.

17. That argument cannot be accepted.

18. It is appropriate, first, briefly to recall the factual and legal circumstances of the Roenfeldt case, relating to the application of the provisions of a social security convention between the Kingdom of Denmark and the Federal Republic of Germany, which for the most part were similar to those at issue in this case.

19. Mr Roenfeldt, a German national, had worked initially in Germany from 1941 to 1957 and then in Denmark until 1971, during which periods he had paid contributions to the German and Danish social insurance schemes respectively. From 1971 onwards he worked in Germany and was accordingly subject to compulsory insurance there.

20. When he was about to reach the age of 63, Mr Roenfeldt took steps to obtain early retirement, as is permitted under German legislation. However, he was unable to do so because, according to the Federal Insurance Office for Salaried Employees, contributions paid in Denmark could not be taken into account for the calculation of pension rights in Germany until the applicant had reached the general statutory age-limit under Danish law, namely 67 years.

21. Mr Roenfeldt brought proceedings to annul that decision, arguing that, irrespective of the retirement age laid down by Danish legislation, the contribution periods completed in Denmark had to be taken into account in calculating the German pension. In support of that argument he cited the social insurance convention concluded between the Federal Republic of Germany and the Kingdom of Denmark.

22. At the time of Mr Roenfeldt' s return to Germany, the Kingdom of Denmark had not yet joined the European Communities and the convention between the two countries was still in force, having not yet been replaced by Regulation No 1408/71.

23. The Court found in its judgment, first, that the German-Danish convention had been replaced with effect from 1 April 1973 by the rules of Community law contained in Regulation No 1408/71 (paragraph 14) and that the question was therefore whether, and how, Community law required account to be taken of insurance periods completed in Denmark before Regulation No 1408/71 entered into force

in that country following its accession to the Communities, for the purpose of granting a retirement pension in some other Member State (paragraph 15).

24. In replying to that question, the Court ruled that Articles 48 and 51 of the Treaty preclude the loss of social security advantages for the workers concerned which would result from the inapplicability, following the entry into force of Regulation No 1408/71, of conventions operating between two or more Member States and incorporated in their national law.

25. However, as argued by the governments and institutions which have submitted observations, that principle cannot apply in factual and legal circumstances such as those obtaining in this case.

26. A worker such as Mr Thévenon, who did not exercise his right to freedom of movement until after the entry into force of Regulation No 1408/71, that is to say, after the Franco-German convention had already been replaced by the regulation as regards persons and matters covered by it, cannot claim to have suffered the loss of social security advantages which he would have enjoyed under the Franco-German convention.

27. Consequently, the particular circumstances which prompted the Court in Roenfeldt to allow the exception to the rule laid down by Article 6 of Regulation No 1408/71 are not present in a case such as that which is the subject of the main proceedings.

28. Accordingly, it should be stated in reply to the question from the national court that Articles 48(2) and 51 of the Treaty must be interpreted as meaning that they do not preclude the replacement by Regulation No 1408/71, pursuant to Article 6 thereof, of a convention binding two Member States exclusively where, prior to the entry into force of Regulation No 1408/71, an insured person completed insurance periods in only one of the signatory States, even where the application of the bilateral social security convention would have placed that insured person in a more favourable position.

Judgment of the Court of 27 September 1988, Annunziata Matteucci v. Communauté française of Belgium and Commissariat général aux relations internationales of the Communauté française of Belgium, Case C-235/87, European Court Reports 1988, p. 5589, paras. 17–23.

Third, and conversely, there may be situations where a bilateral agreement between Member States confers rights to nationals of those two EU Member States only. However, the application of Union law would then not lead to the non-application of the agreement, but to the extension of the right under the agreement to other EU nationals by virtue of the Union principle of non-discrimination. This point was made by the Court in *Matteucci*, where the question at issue was whether Belgium would be prevented from including Italian nationals for scholarships funded by the German government according to a Belgian–German bilateral Convention in the field of culture.

17. The CGRI (i.e. the Belgian administration) points out that in this case the scholarships are not awarded by the Belgian authorities but by the authorities of the Federal Republic of Germany on the basis of a list of candidates which the CGRI draws up. To impose obligations on the host Member State (in this case, Belgium) would therefore be otiose, in so far as the authorities of the country where the training is given (in this case, Germany) are in any event bound by the provisions of the bilateral agreement, under which only nationals of the two countries are eligible for scholarships, and Miss Matteucci is not a national of either country.

18. That argument was challenged by the Italian Government. It considers that the authorities of the country where the training is given cannot refuse to respect the choice made by the authorities of the host country where the latter have opted, pursuant to Article 7 of Regulation No 1612/68, for a Community worker who is not a national of the host country. Since Article 7 of Regulation No 1612/68 requires the host Member State to grant the same social advantages to Community workers as to its own nationals, another Member State may not prevent the host Member State from fulfilling the obligations imposed on it by Community law.

19. The Italian Government's argument must be accepted. Article 5 of the Treaty provides that the Member States must take all appropriate measures, whether general or particular, to ensure fulfilment of the obligations arising out of the Treaty. If, therefore, the application of a provision of Community law is liable to be impeded by a measure adopted pursuant to the implementation of a bilateral agreement, even where the agreement falls outside the field of application of the Treaty, every Member State is under a duty to facilitate the application of the provision and, to that end, to assist every other Member State which is under an obligation under Community law.

20. The French Government further submitted that the bilateral agreement in question was concluded before the entry into force of the EEC Treaty and that Member States are not bound to amend such an agreement pursuant to Article 234 of the Treaty, since its field of application falls outside the Community's jurisdiction.

21. It must be observed in that connection that Article 234 of the Treaty relates to agreements concluded between one or more Member States on the one hand, and one or more third countries on the other; therefore it is not concerned with agreements concluded solely between Member States.

22. Moreover, the Court has consistently held (see in particular the judgment of 27 February 1962 in Case 10/61 *Commission* v *Italy* ((1962)) ECR 1) that, in matters governed by the EEC Treaty, that Treaty takes precedence over agreements concluded between Member States before its entry into force.

23. The answer to the question put by the national court must therefore be that Article 7 of Regulation No 1612/68 must be interpreted as meaning that it does not allow the authorities of a Member State to refuse to award a scholarship to study in another Member State to a worker residing and pursuing an activity as an employed person in the territory of the first Member State but having the nationality of a third Member State on the ground that the worker does not have the nationality of the Member State of residence. A bilateral agreement which reserves the scholarships in question for nationals of the two Member States which are the

parties to the agreement cannot prevent the application of the principle of equality of treatment between national and Community workers established in the territory of one of those two Member States.

Judgment of the Court (Grand Chamber) of 12 December 2006, Test Claimants in Class IV of the ACT Group Litigation v. Commissioners of Inland Revenue, Case C-374/04 European Court Reports 2006, p. I-11673, paras. 1–2, 75–94.

Fourth, in the specific area of taxation, where bilateral agreements between Member States had been expressly authorised by Article 293 second indent TEC (abolished by the Treaty of Lisbon), there is a need to decide on a case-by-case basis whether a privilege under a double taxation agreement must be extended by virtue of Union law to other EU nationals or not.[12] In *Test Claimants*, the Court adopted the narrow approach with the following reasoning.

1. This reference for a preliminary ruling concerns the interpretation of Articles 43 EC, 56 EC, 57 EC and 58 EC.
2. The reference has been made in proceedings between groups of companies and the Commissioners of Inland Revenue relating to the refusal by the latter to grant a tax credit to non-resident companies in those groups for dividends paid to them by resident companies.

[...]

75. By Question 1(b) to (d), the national court essentially asks whether Articles 43 EC and 56 EC preclude a Member State from applying Double Taxation Conventions (DTCs) concluded with other Member States in terms of which, on a payment of dividends by a resident company, companies receiving those dividends which reside in some Member States are not entitled to a tax credit, while companies receiving such dividends which reside in certain other Member States are granted a partial tax credit.
76. In that context, the national court also asks whether it is permissible for a Member State to apply a provision of a DTC, known as a 'limitation of benefits' provision, pursuant to which it does not grant a tax credit to a company resident in the other contracting Member State if that company is controlled by a company resident in a third State with which the first Member State has concluded a DTC which, when dividends are paid, makes no provision for a tax credit for a company which is resident in a third country and receives the dividends and whether it is relevant in that regard that the non-resident company to which the dividends are paid is controlled by a company resident in a Member State or a non-member country.

---

[12] The Court answered in the affirmative in Case C-307/97, *Compagnie de Saint-Gobain Zweigniederlassung Deutschland v. Finanzamt Aachen-Innenstadt* [1999] ECR I-6161, para. 59, but refused such an extension in Case C-376/03, *D v. Inspecteur van de Belastingdienst/Particulieren/Ondernemingen buitenland te Heerlen*, [2005] ECR I-5821, paras 49–63.

77. For the reasons set out in paragraphs 37 to 40 of this judgment, it is appropriate to consider the national measures at issue in the main proceedings both from the point of view of freedom of establishment and that of free movement of capital.

78. According to the claimants in the main proceedings, it is contrary to the freedoms of movement for a Member State to confer a tax advantage on nationals of a Member State while refusing it to nationals of another Member State. Under reference to paragraph 26 of the judgment in *Commission v France*, they contend that the grant of such an advantage cannot be made dependent on the existence of reciprocal advantages granted by the other contracting Member State.

79. The claimants in the main proceedings argue that the extension of advantages conferred by a DTC concluded with a particular Member State to natural or legal persons covered by another DTC would not affect the system of bilateral tax conventions. It is necessary to distinguish between, on the one hand, the right of Member States to allocate their taxing powers in order to avoid the same income being taxed more than once in a number of Member States and, on the other, the exercise by Member States of their taxing powers thus allocated. While a difference in treatment would be justified if it were to reflect differences between tax conventions as regards the allocation of taxing powers, in order, in particular, to reflect variations between the tax systems of the Member States concerned, a Member State cannot, in order to avoid or mitigate economic double taxation, exercise its powers in a selective and arbitrary manner.

80. Conversely, the United Kingdom Government, the German Government, the French Government, Ireland, the Italian Government and the Netherlands Government, together with the Commission, contest the argument that a Member State cannot protect a resident of another Member State against economic double taxation unless it grants the same protection to residents of all Member States. Were that proposition to be accepted, the equilibrium and reciprocity underlying the existing DTCs would be undermined, taxpayers would be able more easily to avoid the provisions of DTCs intended to combat tax avoidance and the legal certainty of taxpayers would be affected accordingly.

81. It should be pointed out in that regard that, in the absence of unifying or harmonising measures at Community level for the elimination of double taxation, the Member States retain competence for determining the criteria for taxation on income with a view to eliminating double taxation by means, inter alia, of international agreements. In those circumstances, the Member States remain at liberty to determine the connecting factors for the allocation of fiscal jurisdiction by means of bilateral agreements (see *Gilly*, paragraphs 24 and 30; *Saint-Gobain ZN*, paragraph 57; *D.*, paragraph 52; and *Bouanich*, paragraph 49).

82. The claimants in the main proceedings object to the difference in treatment imposed on companies that are not resident in the United Kingdom by reason of the fact that the DTCs concluded by that Member State with certain other Member States provide a tax credit for companies resident in those Member States while the DTCs concluded by the United Kingdom with other Member States do not so provide.

83. In order to determine whether such a difference in treatment is discriminatory, it is necessary to consider whether, as regards the measures at issue, the non-resident companies concerned are in an objectively comparable situation.

84. As the Court noted in paragraph 54 of *D.*, the scope of a bilateral tax convention is limited to the natural or legal persons referred to in it.

85. In order to avoid distributed profits being taxed both by the Member State in which the distributing company is resident and by that of the company receiving them, each of the DTCs concluded by the United Kingdom provides for an allocation of taxing powers between that Member State and the other contracting State. While some of those DTCs do not provide for dividends received by a non-resident company from a company resident in the United Kingdom to be subject to tax in that Member State, other DTCs do provide for such a liability to tax. It is in the latter case that the DTCs provide, each according to its separate conditions, for the grant of a tax credit to a non-resident company to which dividends are paid.

86. As the United Kingdom Government, supported in that regard by most of the other Governments which submitted observations to the Court, observes, the terms under which the DTCs provide for a tax credit for non-resident companies which receive dividends from a resident company vary depending not only on the particular characteristics of the national tax regimes concerned, but also on when the DTCs were negotiated and the extent of the issues on which the Member States concerned managed to reach agreement.

87. The situations in which the United Kingdom grants a tax credit to companies resident in the other contracting State which receive dividends from a United Kingdom-resident company are those in which the United Kingdom also retains the right to tax the companies on those dividends. The rate of tax which the United Kingdom may charge in such cases varies according to the circumstances and, in particular according to whether the DTC provides for a full or a partial tax credit. There is thus a direct link between the entitlement to a tax credit and the rate of tax laid down under such a DTC (see, to that effect, Case C-58/01 *Océ Van der Grinten* [2003] ECR I-9809, paragraph 87).

88. Thus, the grant of a tax credit to a non-resident company receiving dividends from a resident company, as provided for under a number of DTCs concluded by the United Kingdom, cannot be regarded as a benefit separable from the remainder of those DTCs, but is an integral part of them and contributes to their overall balance (see, to that effect, *D.*, paragraph 62).

89. The same applies to the provisions of the DTCs which make the grant of such a tax credit subject to the condition that the non-resident company is not owned, directly or indirectly, by a company resident in a Member State or a non-member country with which the United Kingdom has concluded a DTC which does not provide for such a tax credit.

90. Even where such provisions extend to the situation of a company which is not resident in one of the contracting Member States, they apply only to persons resident in one of those Member States and, by contributing to the overall balance of the DTCs in question, are an integral part of them.

91. The fact that those reciprocal rights and obligations apply only to persons resident in one of the two contracting Member States is an inherent consequence of bilateral double taxation conventions. It follows, as regards the taxation of dividends paid by a company resident in the United Kingdom, that a company resident in a Member State which has concluded a DTC with the United Kingdom which does not provide for such a tax credit is not in the same situation as a company resident in a Member State which has concluded a DTC which does provide for one (see, to that effect, *D.*, paragraph 61).

92. It follows that the Treaty provisions on freedom of establishment do not preclude a situation in which the entitlement to a tax credit laid down in a DTC concluded by a Member State with another Member State for companies resident in the second State which receive dividends from a company resident in the first State does not extend to companies resident in a third Member State with which the first State has concluded a DTC which does not provide for such an entitlement.

93. Since such a situation does not discriminate against non-resident companies receiving dividends from a resident company, the conclusion drawn in the preceding paragraph also applies to the Treaty provisions relating to free movement of capital.

94. In view of the foregoing, the answer to Question 1(b) to (d) must be that Articles 43 EC and 56 EC do not preclude a situation in which a Member State does not extend the entitlement to a tax credit provided for in a DTC concluded with another Member State for companies resident in the second State which receive dividends from a company resident in the first State to companies resident in a third Member State with which it has concluded a DTC which does not provide for such an entitlement for companies resident in that third State.

[...]

13.4 The significance of Member State agreements for the EU

Judgment of the Court of 12 December 1972, International Fruit Company NV and others v. Produktschap voor Groenten en Fruit, Joined Cases 21-24/72, European Court Reports 1972, p. 1219, paras. 10–18.

According to Article 216(2) TFEU (previously Article 300(7) EC), the Union is only bound by agreements to which it has become itself a party. An exceptional situation arose, however, with respect to the GATT 1947. Prior to having been accepted as a founding member of the WTO in 1994, the then Community became bound to this text via the fact that all Member States had accepted the GATT 1947 in their own name, but transferred exclusive competence in this field to the Community. As this 'succession' by the Community to the Member States had been accepted by the other contracting parties to the GATT in Geneva practice, the question came up whether

secondary acts adopted by the institutions could be challenged as being incompatible with the GATT, although the Community had never formally expressed consent to
be bound. When asked to judge upon the compatibility of certain import restrictions
for apples contained in Regulations 459/70, 565/70 and 686/70, the ECJ found the
following in *International Fruit Company*:

10. It is clear that at the time when they concluded the treaty establishing the European
    Economic Community the Member States were bound by the obligations of the
    general agreement.
11. By concluding a treaty between them they could not withdraw from their obliga-
    tions to third countries.
12. On the contrary, their desire to observe the undertakings of the General Agreement
    follows as much from the very provisions of the EEC Treaty s from the declarations
    mad by member States on the presentation of the treaty to the Contracting Parties
    of the General Agreement in accordance with the obligation under Article XXIV
    thereof.
13. That intention was made clear in particular by Article 110 of the EEC Treaty,
    which seeks the adherence of the Community to the same aims as those sought by
    the General Agreement, as well as by the first paragraph of Article 234 which pro-
    vides that the rights and obligations arising from agreements concluded before
    the entry into force of the treaty, and in particular multilateral agreements con-
    cluded with the participation of Member States, are not affected by the provisions
    of the treaty.
14. The Community has assumed the functions in the tariff and trade policy, progres-
    sively during the transitional period and in their entirety on the expiry of that
    period, by virtue of Articles 111 and 113 of the Treaty.
15. By conferring those powers on the Community, the Member States showed their
    wish to bind it by the obligations entered into under the General Agreement.
16. Since the entry into force of the EEC Treaty and more particularly, since the setting
    up of the common external tariff, the transfer of powers which has occurred in the
    relations between member States and the Community has been put into concrete
    form in different ways within the framework of the General Agreement and has
    been recognized by the other contracting parties.
17. In particular, since that time, the Community, acting through its own institutions,
    has appeared as a partner in the tariff negotiations and as a party to the agree-
    ments of all types concluded within the framework of the General Agreement,
    in accordance with the provisions of Article 114 of the EEC Treaty which pro-
    vides that the tariff and trade agreements 'shall be concluded...on behalf of the
    Community'.
18. It therefore appears that, in so far as under the EEC Treaty the Community has
    assumed the powers previously exercised by member States in the area governed
    by the General Agreement, the provisions of that agreement have the effect of
    binding the Community.

Judgment of the Court of 16 March 1983, Amministrazione delle Finanze dello Stato v. Società Petrolifera Italiana SpA (SPI) and SpA Michelin Italiana (SAMI), Joined Cases 267 to 269/81, European Court Reports 1983, p. 801, paras. 12–20.

If substitution has taken place, the Court of Justice also has jurisdiction to ensure the uniform application of the agreement. Accordingly, the Court affirmed early on the possibility to interpret the GATT and its legal effects on the entire Community.

Consequences of the substitution of the Community for the Member States in relation to commitments under GATT (Question (A))

12. The Corte Suprema di Cassazione refers first to the case-law of the Court of Justice on the substitution of the Community for the Member States in relation to the fulfilment of the commitments under GATT and on the Court's jurisdiction under Article 177 of the Treaty to interpret the provisions of agreements binding the Community (in that regard it mentions in particular the judgments of 12 December 1972 in Joined Cases 21 to 24/72, *International Fruit Company* v *Produktschap voor Groenten en Fruit*, [1972] ECR 1219, of 24 October 1973 in Case 9/73, *Schlüters Hauptzollamt Lörrach* [1973] ECR 1135, of 30 April 1974 in Case 181/73, *Haegeman v Belgian State*, [1974] ECR 449, and 11 November 1975 in Case 38/75, 827 *Nederlandse Spoorwegen v Inspecteur der Invoerrechten en Accijnzen*, [1975] ECR 1439). It then raises the question whether the relevant provisions of GATT and of the Tariff Protocols concluded by the Community are covered by the jurisdiction to give preliminary rulings conferred upon the Court by Article 177, even where the national court is requested to apply them with reference to relations between individuals for purposes other than that of determining whether a Community measure is valid.

13. In addition, the Corte Suprema di Cassazione asks from what date and within what limits that substitution took place, regard being had to the fact that the Community negotiated tariff concessions and made bindings within the framework of GATT before 1 July 1968, the date of the introduction of the Common Customs Tariff.

14. As the Court had occasion to stress in the judgments cited, it is important that the provisions of GATT should, like the provisions of all other agreements binding the Community, receive uniform application throughout the Community. Any difference in the interpretation and application of provisions binding the Community as regards non-member countries would not only jeopardize the unity of the commercial policy, which according to Article 113 of the Treaty must be based on uniform principles, but also create distortions in trade within the Community, as a result of differences in the manner in which the agreements in force between the Community and non-member countries were applied in the various Member States.

15. It follows that the jurisdiction conferred upon the Court in order to ensure the uniform interpretation of Community law must include a determination of the scope and effect of the rules of GATT within the Community and also of the effect of the

tariff protocols concluded in the framework of GATT. In that regard it does not matter whether the national court is required to assess the validity of Community measures or the compatibility of national legislative provisions with the commitments binding the Community.

16. Because both the facts relating to these cases and the measures adopted by the Community evidencing its participation in the system of GATT were spread over some time, special problems arise in relation to the application ratione temporis of the principles established above.

17. In that connexion it should be pointed out first, as the Court stated in its judgment of 12 December 1972 in the *International Fruit* case, cited above, that the substitution of the Community for the Member States in relation to commitments under GATT took place on 1 July 1968, following the introduction of the Common Customs Tariff. It was at that time that the Community, in advance of the time fixed for the end of the transitional period, assumed its full powers in relation to the sphere covered by GATT.

18. On the other hand, in relation to the matters governed by the Tariff Protocols, including the concessions and bindings agreed in the framework of Schedule XL (EEC) which forms an integral part of those protocols, the effect of the conclusion of those agreements was, by virtue of Article 228 of the Treaty, to bind the Member States in the same way as the Community itself. For the reasons stated above, and subject to the considerations set out below concerning the internal effect of the protocols, it is in any event important that they should be interpreted and applied in the same way throughout the Community.

19. The answer to be given to the question submitted is therefore that, since as regards the fulfilment of the commitments laid down in GATT the Community has been substituted for the Member States with effect from 1 July 1968, the date on which the Common Customs Tariff was brought into force, the provisions of GATT have since that date been amongst those which the Court of Justice has jurisdiction, by virtue of Article 177 of the EEC Treaty, to interpret by way of a preliminary ruling, regardless of the purpose of such interpretation. With regard to the period prior to that date, such interpretation is a matter exclusively for the courts of the Member States.

20. The Tariff Protocols of 16 July 1962 and 30 June 1967 are acts of the institutions of the Community within the meaning of subparagraph (b) of the first paragraph of Article 177 of the Treaty and as such fall within the jurisdiction to give preliminary rulings conferred upon the Court of Justice.

Outside the area of the common commercial policy, the Union has, however, not become bound by agreements that all the Member States have concluded. For example, despite the fact that the European Convention on Human Rights is a source for the general principles of Union law, it is not binding on the Union. Accordingly, individual applications against the Union before the European Court of Human Rights are inadmissible, until the Union formally accedes to the Convention, as foreseen under Articles 6(2) TEU and 218(6)(a)(ii) TFEU.

Judgment of the Court (Grand Chamber) of 3 June 2008, The Queen, on the application of International Association of Independent Tanker Owners (Intertanko) and Others v. Secretary of State for Transport, Case C-308/06, European Court Reports 2008, p. I-4057, paras. 42–54.

Falling short of binding the Union, certain agreements concluded by all Member States, may nevertheless be relevant for the interpretation of Union law. In *Intertanko*, the Court was asked whether the strict liability regime for environmental damage occurring on the high sea under Directive 2005/35/EC[13] was compatible with UNCLOS (to which the Community became a party) and Marpol 73/78 (to which it did not). The Court's response is included below. In finding that the Union was not bound by Marpol, it distinguished between it and GATT as far as the question of functional succession is concerned. The Court pointed out that the EU had not succeeded in the obligations of its Member States in Marpol since it had not obtained exclusive competence in the fields covered by this convention (paragraph 47). It also made clear that the mere fact that a Union act aims to achieve certain results provided for by an international agreement is not sufficient to make it binding on the Union. However, the Court concluded that Marpol should be taken into account in the interpretation of internal EU legislation (paragraph 52). As to UNCLOS, to which the EU is a party, it found that it was not directly applicable in the domestic legal order. Still, the Court did not explain anywhere in its judgment whether and how it took account of the provisions of Marpol 73/78 when interpreting the EU directive at hand.

42. It is clear from Article 300(7) EC that the Community institutions are bound by agreements concluded by the Community and, consequently, that those agreements have primacy over secondary Community legislation (see, to this effect, Case C-61/94 *Commission* v *Germany* [1996] ECR I-3989, paragraph 52, and Case C-311/04 *Algemene Scheeps Agentuur Dordrecht* [2006] ECR I-609, paragraph 25).

43. It follows that the validity of a measure of secondary Community legislation may be affected by the fact that it is incompatible with such rules of international law. Where that invalidity is pleaded before a national court, the Court of Justice thus reviews, pursuant to Article 234 EC, the validity of the Community measure concerned in the light of all the rules of international law, subject to two conditions.

44. First, the Community must be bound by those rules (see Joined Cases 21/72 to 24/72 *International Fruit Company and Others* [1972] ECR 1219, paragraph 7).

45. Second, the Court can examine the validity of Community legislation in the light of an international treaty only where the nature and the broad logic of the latter do not preclude this and, in addition, the treaty's provisions appear, as regards their content, to be unconditional and sufficiently precise (see to this effect, in particular, Case C-344/04 IATA and ELFAA [2006] ECR I-403, paragraph 39).

---

[13] OJ L 255, 30.9.2005, pp. 11–21; corrigenda at OJ L 33, 4.2.2006, p. 87, and OJ L 105, 13.4.2006, p. 65.

46. It must therefore be examined whether Marpol 73/78 and UNCLOS meet those conditions.

47. First, with regard to Marpol 73/78, it is to be observed at the outset that the Community is not a party to this Convention.

48. Furthermore, as the Court has already held, it does not appear that the Community has assumed, under the EC Treaty, the powers previously exercised by the Member States in the field to which Marpol 73/78 applies, nor that, consequently, its provisions have the effect of binding the Community (Case C-379/92 *Peralta* [1994] ECR I-3453, paragraph 16). In this regard, Marpol 73/78 can therefore be distinguished from GATT 1947 within the framework of which the Community progressively assumed powers previously exercised by the Member States, with the consequence that it became bound by the obligations flowing from that agreement (see to this effect, in particular, *International Fruit Company and Others*, paragraphs 10 to 18). Accordingly, this case-law relating to GATT 1947 cannot be applied to Marpol 73/78.

49. It is true that all the Member States of the Community are parties to Marpol 73/78. Nevertheless, in the absence of a full transfer of the powers previously exercised by the Member States to the Community, the latter cannot, simply because all those States are parties to Marpol 73/78, be bound by the rules set out therein, which it has not itself approved.

50. Since the Community is not bound by Marpol 73/78, the mere fact that Directive 2005/35 has the objective of incorporating certain rules set out in that Convention into Community law is likewise not sufficient for it to be incumbent upon the Court to review the directive's legality in the light of the Convention.

51. Admittedly, as is clear from settled case-law, the powers of the Community must be exercised in observance of international law, including provisions of international agreements in so far as they codify customary rules of general international law (see, to this effect, Case C-286/90 *Poulsen and Diva Navigation* [1992] ECR I-6019, paragraphs 9 and 10; Case C-405/92 *Mondiet* [1993] ECR I-6133, paragraphs 13 to 15; and Case C-162/96 *Racke* [1998] ECR I-3655, paragraph 45). None the less, it does not appear that Regulations 9 and 11(b) of Annex I to Marpol 73/78 and Regulations 5 and 6(b) of Annex II to that Convention are the expression of customary rules of general international law.

52. In those circumstances, it is clear that the validity of Directive 2005/35 cannot be assessed in the light of Marpol 73/78, even though it binds the Member States. The latter fact is, however, liable to have consequences for the interpretation of, first, UNCLOS and, second, the provisions of secondary law which fall within the field of application of Marpol 73/78. *In view of the customary principle of good faith, which forms part of general international law, and of Article 10 EC, it is incumbent upon the Court to interpret those provisions taking account of Marpol 73/78.*[14]

53. Second, UNCLOS was signed by the Community and approved by Decision 98/392, thereby binding the Community, and the provisions of that Convention

---

[14] Emphasis added.

accordingly form an integral part of the Community legal order (see Case C-459/03 *Commission* v *Ireland* [2006] ECR I-4635, paragraph 82).

54. It must therefore be determined whether the nature and the broad logic of UNCLOS, as disclosed in particular by its aim, preamble and terms, preclude examination of the validity of Community measures in the light of its provisions.

Judgment of the Court (Grand Chamber) of 21 December 2011, Air Transport Association of America and Others v. Secretary of State for Energy and Climate Change, Case C-366/10, not yet reported (ATAA case), paras. 1 and 60–72.

The Court was asked in this reference for a preliminary ruling to decide whether different sources of international law can be relied upon to determine the legality of EU legislation. One of those was the Chicago Convention, to which the EU is not a party contrary to all its Member States. The Court carried out a careful analysis of the scope of EU legislation in the field and concluded that no 'functional succession' had taken place so far. Accordingly, the Convention could not serve as a yardstick to invalidate EU secondary law.

1. This reference for a preliminary ruling concerns, first, the circumstances in which principles of customary international law and provisions of international treaties may be relied upon in the context of a reference for a preliminary ruling on the validity of a measure and, secondly, the validity, in the light of international treaty law and customary international law, of Directive 2008/101/EC of the European Parliament and of the Council of 19 November 2008 amending Directive 2003/87/EC so as to include aviation activities in the scheme for greenhouse gas emission allowance trading within the Community (OJ 2009 L 8, p. 3).

[...]

60. As has been stated in paragraph 3 of the present judgment, it is undisputed that the European Union is not a party to the Chicago Convention while, on the other hand, all of its Member States are contracting parties.

61. Although the first paragraph of Article 351 TFEU implies a duty on the part of the institutions of the European Union not to impede the performance of the obligations of Member States which stem from an agreement prior to 1 January 1958, such as the Chicago Convention, it is, however, to be noted that that duty of the institutions is designed to permit the Member States concerned to perform their obligations under a prior agreement and does not bind the European Union as regards the third States party to that agreement (see, to this effect, Case 812/79 *Burgoa* [1980] ECR 2787, paragraphs 8 and 9).

62. Consequently, in the main proceedings, it is only if and in so far as, pursuant to the EU and FEU Treaties, the European Union has assumed the powers previously exercised by its Member States in the field, as set out in paragraphs 57 to 59 of the present judgment, to which that international convention applies that

the convention's provisions would have the effect of binding the European Union (see, to this effect, *International Fruit Company and Others*, paragraph 18; Case C 379/92 *Peralta* [1994] ECR I-3453, paragraph 16; and Case C-301/08 *Bogiatzi* [2009] ECR I-10185, paragraph 25).

63. Indeed, in order for the European Union to be capable of being bound, it must have assumed, and thus had transferred to it, all the powers previously exercised by the Member States that fall within the convention in question (see, to this effect, *Intertanko and Others*, paragraph 49, and *Bogiatzi*, paragraph 33). Therefore, the fact that one or more acts of European Union law may have the object or effect of incorporating into European Union law certain provisions that are set out in an international agreement which the European Union has not itself approved is not sufficient for it to be incumbent upon the Court to review the legality of the act or acts of European Union law in the light of that agreement (see, to this effect, *Intertanko and Others*, paragraph 50).

64. As the Swedish Government has essentially pointed out in its written observations, both Article 80(2) EC and Article 100(2) TFEU provide that the European Union is able to adopt appropriate provisions concerning air transport.

65. Certain matters falling within the Chicago Convention have been covered by legislation adopted at European Union level, in particular on the basis of Article 80(2) EC. As regards air transport, as the Court has already had occasion to point out in Case C-382/08 *Neukirchinger* [2011] ECR I-0000, paragraph 23, that is true, for example, of Regulation (EC) No 1592/2002 of the European Parliament and of the Council of 15 July 2002 on common rules in the field of civil aviation and establishing a European Aviation Safety Agency (OJ 2002 L 240, p. 1) and of Council Regulation (EEC) No 3922/91 of 16 December 1991 on the harmonisation of technical requirements and administrative procedures in the field of civil aviation (OJ 1991 L 373, p. 4), as amended by Regulation (EC) No 1900/2006 of the European Parliament and of the Council of 20 December 2006 (OJ 2006 L 377, p. 176).

66. The European Union legislature has likewise adopted Directive 2006/93/EC of the European Parliament and of the Council of 12 December 2006 on the regulation of the operation of aeroplanes covered by Part II, Chapter 3, Volume 1 of Annex 16 to the Convention on International Civil Aviation, second edition (1988) (OJ 2006 L 374, p. 1).

67. As regards the issue of taxation of the fuel load, the Council has also adopted Directive 2003/96/EC of 27 October 2003 restructuring the Community framework for the taxation of energy products and electricity (OJ 2003 L 283, p. 51) which, in Article 14(1)(b), lays down a tax exemption for energy products supplied for use as fuel for the purpose of air navigation other than in private pleasure-flying, in order that, as is apparent from recital 23 in the preamble to that directive, the European Union complies in particular with certain international obligations, including those connected with the tax exemptions on energy products intended for civil aviation which are granted to airlines on the basis of the Chicago Convention and of international bilateral air service agreements concluded by the European Union and/or the Member States with certain third States (see Case C-79/10 *Systeme Helmholz* [2011] ECR I-0000, paragraphs 24 and 25).

68. It should, moreover, be pointed out that, by the adoption of Council Decision 2011/530/EU of 31 March 2011 on the signing, on behalf of the Union, and provisional application of a Memorandum of Cooperation between the European Union and the International Civil Aviation Organisation providing a framework for enhanced cooperation (OJ 2011 L 232, p. 1), the European Union has sought to develop a framework for cooperation as regards security audits and inspections in the light of the standards set out in Annex 17 to the Chicago Convention.

69. Nevertheless, whilst it is true that the European Union has in addition acquired certain exclusive powers to agree with third States commitments falling within the field of application of the European Union legislation on international air transport and, consequently, of the Chicago Convention (see, to this effect, Case C-476/98 *Commission v Germany* [2002] ECR I-9855, paragraph 124), that does not mean that it has exclusive competence in the entire field of international civil aviation as covered by that convention.

70. As the French and Swedish Governments have pointed out, the Member States have retained powers falling within the field of the Chicago Convention, such as those relating to the award of traffic rights, to the setting of airport charges and to the determination of prohibited areas in their territory which may not be flown over.

71. Consequently, it must be concluded that, since the powers previously exercised by the Member States in the field of application of the Chicago Convention have not to date been assumed in their entirety by the European Union, the latter is not bound by that convention.

72. It follows that in the context of the present reference for a preliminary ruling the Court cannot examine the validity of Directive 2008/101 in the light of the Chicago Convention as such.

ATAA case, Opinion of Advocate General Kokott, of 6 October 2011, points 163–171.

Interestingly, the Court did not repeat its *Intertanko* finding that EU secondary law could nevertheless be interpreted in light of the Chicago Convention. However, Advocate-General Kokott, in her Opinion of 6 October 2011, carried out this analysis.

163. As already stated in the context of the first question, the European Union is not bound by the Chicago Convention; therefore that convention cannot serve as a benchmark against which the validity of EU acts can be reviewed. However, as all of the EU Member States are Parties to the Chicago Convention, it must nevertheless be taken into account when interpreting provisions of secondary EU law. Consequently, Directive 2008/101 (or Directive 2003/87 as amended by Directive 2008/101) is to be interpreted as far as possible consistently with the Chicago Convention.

164. It is, however, apparent from a review of the provisions of the Chicago Convention mentioned by the referring court that there is no conflict with Directive 2008/101 in any event.

165. First, as far as Article 1 of the Chicago Convention is concerned, this merely gives expression to the principle of the sovereignty of States and air sovereignty in particular. As already stated above in relation to customary international law, Directive 2008/101 does not contain any extraterritorial provisions and does not infringe the sovereign rights of third countries. This reasoning can readily be transposed to Article 1 of the Chicago Convention.

166. It should be noted with regard to Article 11 of the Chicago Convention that the very wording of the provisions contained therein shows that they relate only to the admission to and departure from the territory of the Contracting States of aircraft engaged in international air navigation and to the operation and navigation of such aircraft while within the territory of the Contracting States. This is also confirmed by the overall context of Article 11: the provision forms part of Chapter II of the Chicago Convention, which is dedicated to flight over territory of Contracting States. No inference can be drawn from Article 11 of the Chicago Convention as to whether an emissions trading scheme applied by one Contracting State is to be permitted to take account of parts of flights that take place outside the territory of that State.

167. The only substantive requirement laid down by Article 11 of the Chicago Convention in relation to the laws and regulations of Contracting States concerning the admission, departure and operation of aircraft is the prohibition of discrimination against aircraft on grounds of their nationality: the laws and regulations concerned are to 'be applied to the aircraft of all contracting States without distinction as to nationality'. None of the parties involved in the present case has cast any doubt on the fact that the EU emissions trading scheme satisfies that requirement.

168. Nor can it be inferred from the last half-sentence in Article 11 of the Chicago Convention that it would be prohibited for a Contracting State to take account, within the framework of its emissions trading scheme, of parts of flights taking place outside that State's territory. That clause merely states that the laws and regulations of a Contracting State '[are to] be complied with upon entering or departing from or while within the territory of that State'. It is this and only this— compliance with rules upon entering or departing—that the European Union demands of airlines in the context of its emissions trading scheme. The EU emissions trading scheme does not contain rules that would have to be observed during parts of flights that take place outside the territory of the European Union.

169. Finally, as far as Article 12 of the Chicago Convention is concerned, this deals with rules of the air. However, no such rules of the air are to be found in Directive 2003/87 as amended by Directive 2008/101, whether for the territory of the European Union, for the airspace above third countries, or over the high seas, which are specifically mentioned in the third sentence of Article 12 of the Convention. In particular, as already mentioned, the EU emissions trading scheme does not require airlines and the aircraft operated by them to adhere to

any particular flight path, specific speed limits, or limits on fuel consumption and exhaust gases.

170. Nor does the reference made by the claimants in the main proceedings to Annex 2 to the Chicago Convention, in which certain rules of the air are laid down, form an appropriate basis for their argument. There is admittedly a provision in section 3.1.4 on 'dropping or spraying' from aircraft in flight. However, the EU emissions trading scheme is in no way comparable to a rule on the dropping or spraying of substances; after all, it does not contain any rules or limits on the emission of greenhouse gases from the engines of individual aircraft when flying to and from aerodromes in the European Union.

171. Since there is therefore no risk of any conflict with Articles 1, 11 or 12 of the Chicago Convention, there is no reason to interpret and apply Directive 2008/101 restrictively in the light of the Chicago Convention. In particular, it is not appropriate, having regard to that convention, to restrict the scope of application of the EU emissions trading scheme to parts of flights that take place within the territory of the European Union.

Judgment of the Court (Grand Chamber) of 24 June 2008, Commune de Mesquer v. Total France SA and Total International Ltd, Case C-188/07, European Court Reports 2008, p. I-4501, paras. 85–86.

Nevertheless, an agreement to which all Member States have acceded upon authorization in the interest of the Union (see example above, pp. 1056-8) may be significant when applying and interpreting secondary law. Whereas the Court already accepted the principle, it was not yet called upon to apply it. We are therefore left for the time being with the following finding in *Commune de Mesquer v. Total*, where the question arose whether a Community directive may apply to the accidental disposal of oil on the high sea to the detriment of two international conventions in the area, which claim to be exclusive on the matter.

85. Moreover, contrary to the arguments put forward by the Total companies at the hearing, the Community is not bound by the Liability Convention or the Fund Convention. In the first place, the Community has not acceded to those international instruments and, in the second place, it cannot be regarded as having taken the place of its Member States, if only because not all of them are parties to those conventions (see, by analogy, Case C-379/92 *Peralta* [1994] ECR I-3453, paragraph 16, and Case C-308/06 *Intertanko and Others* [2008] ECR I-0000, paragraph 47), or as being indirectly bound by those conventions as a result of Article 235 of the United Nations Convention on the Law of the Sea, signed at Montego Bay on 10 December 1982, which entered into force on 16 November 1994 and was approved by Council Decision 98/392/EC of 23 March 1998 (OJ 1998 L 179, p. 1), paragraph 3 of which confines itself, as the French Government pointed out

at the hearing, to establishing a general obligation of cooperation between the parties to the convention.

86. Furthermore, as regards Decision 2004/246 authorising the Member States to sign, ratify or accede to, in the interest of the Community, the Protocol of 2003 to the Fund Convention, it suffices to state that that decision and the Protocol of 1993 cannot apply to the facts at issue in the main proceedings.

13.5 International agreements mentioned in the Treaty to which the EU has not become a party

Judgment of the Court (Grand Chamber) of 9 November 2010, B and D, Joined Cases C-57/09 and C-101/09, European Court Reports 2010, p. I-10979, paras. 76–78.

A final *cas de figure* are international agreements mentioned in the Treaty to which the EU has not become a party. This is the case for the 1951 Geneva Convention on the Status of Refugees. The Magna Carta of international refugee law is not open to the EU's formal accession, but EU primary and secondary law refer to it. Article 78(1) second sentence TFEU states that the Union's immigration policy 'must be in accordance with' the Geneva Convention, and it is also reflected in the preamble of Council Directive 2004/83/EC of 29 April 2004 on minimum standards for the qualification and status of third country nationals or stateless persons as refugees or as persons who otherwise need international protection and the content of the protection granted (OJ L 304, 30.9.2004, pp. 12–23). Against that background, the Court of Justice has on numerous occasions affirmed the binding nature of the Geneva Convention for the Union as a matter of Union law, despite the fact that it has not become a party to it under international law. It did so, for example, in *B and D*, joined cases concerning Turkish nationals of Kurdish origin. The proceedings concerned the rejection by the German Federal Office for Migration and Refugees of B's application for asylum and recognition of refugee status, and its revocation of D's refugee status and right of asylum.

76. One of the legal bases for Directive 2004/83 was point (1)(c) of the first paragraph of Article 63 EC, under which the Council was required to adopt measures on asylum, in accordance with the 1951 Geneva Convention and other relevant treaties, within the area of minimum standards with respect to 'the qualification of nationals of third countries as refugees'.

77. Recitals 3, 16 and 17 to Directive 2004/83 state that the 1951 Geneva Convention constitutes the cornerstone of the international legal regime for the protection of refugees and that the provisions of the directive for determining who qualifies for refugee status and the content of that status were adopted to guide the competent authorities of the Member States in the application of that convention on the basis of common concepts and criteria (*Salahadin Abdulla and Others*, paragraph 52, and Case C 31/09 *Bolbol* [2010] ECR I 0000, paragraph 37).

78. Directive 2004/83 must for that reason be interpreted in the light of its general scheme and purpose, and in a manner consistent with the 1951 Geneva Convention and the other relevant treaties referred to in point (1) of the first paragraph of Article 63 EC, now Article 78(1) TFEU. As is apparent from recital 10 to that directive, Directive 2004/83 must also be interpreted in a manner consistent with the fundamental rights and the principles recognised, in particular, by the Charter of Fundamental Rights of the European Union (*Salahadin Abdulla and Others*, paragraphs 53 and 54, and *Bolbol*, paragraph 38).

Select Bibliography

Cremona, M., Member States as Trustees of the Community Interest: Participating in International Agreements on Behalf of the European Community, EUI Working Paper LAW 2009/17.

Klabbers, J., *Treaty Conflict and the European Union* (Cambridge: Cambridge University Press, 2008).

Index

Page numbers suffixed with *tab* refer to information in tables.